OrganizationalBehaviour

Concepts, Controversies, Applications   Sixth Canadian Edition

OrganizationalBehaviour

Concepts, Controversies, Applications   Sixth Canadian Edition

Nancy Langton
University of British Columbia

Stephen P. Robbins
San Diego State University

Timothy A. Judge
University of Notre Dame

With contributions by

Katherine Breward, Ph.D.
University of Winnipeg

Toronto

Vice-President, Editorial Director: Gary Bennett
Editor-in-Chief: Nicole Lukach
Acquisitions Editor: Nick Durie
Marketing Manager: Jenna Wulff
Developmental Editor: Lise Dupont
Project Manager: Lesley Deugo
Production Editor: Claudia Forgas
Copy Editor: Claudia Forgas
Proofreaders: Marcia Gallego, Kelli Howey
Compositor: Hermia Chung
Photo Researcher/Permissions Editor: Monika Schurmann
Manufacturing Manager: Susan Johnson
Art Director: Julia Hall
Cover and Interior Designer: Anthony Leung
Cover Image: Credit: Vasily Kandinsky
Several Circles (Einige Kreise), January-February 1926
Oil on canvas
55 1/4 x 55 3/8 inches (140.3 x 140.7 cm)
Solomon R. Guggenheim Museum, New York
Solomon R. Guggenheim Founding Collection, By Gift
41.283

Library and Archives Canada Cataloguing in Publication

Langton, Nancy
    Organizational behaviour: concepts, controversies, applications / Nancy Langton, Stephen P. Robbins, Timothy A. Judge.—6th Canadian ed.

Includes bibliographical references and index.
ISBN 978-0-13-231031-4

1. Organizational behavior—Textbooks. 2. Management—Textbooks. I. Robbins, Stephen P., 1943– II. Judge, Tim III. Title.

HD58.7.L35 2013   658   C2011-906493-6

ISBN: 978-0-13-231031-4

BRIEF CONTENTS

CONTENTS

CHAPTER 9   Conflict and Negotiation   322

PART 4 Sharing the Organizational Vision 362

CHAPTER 10 Organizational Culture 362

OB AT WORK

CHAPTER 11 Leadership 394

PREFACE

Welcome to the sixth Canadian edition of *Organizational Behaviour*. Since its arrival in Canada, *Organizational Behaviour* has enjoyed widespread acclaim across the country for its rich Canadian content and has quickly established itself as the leading textbook in the field.

Organizational Behaviour, Sixth Canadian Edition, is truly a Canadian product. While it draws upon the strongest aspects of its American cousin, it expresses its own vision and voice. It provides the context for understanding organizational behaviour (OB) in the Canadian workplace and highlights the many Canadian contributions to the field. Indeed, it goes a step further than most OB textbooks prepared for the Canadian marketplace.

Specifically, it asks, in many instances:

- How does this theory apply in the Canadian workplace of today?

- What are the implications of the theory for managers and employees working in the twenty-first century?

- What are the implications of the theory for everyday life? OB, after all, is not something that applies only in the workplace.

This textbook is sensitive to important Canadian issues. Subject matter reflects the broad multicultural flavour of Canada, and also highlights the roles of women and visible minorities. Examples reflect the broad range of organizations in Canada: large, small, public and private sector, unionized and non-unionized.

Organizational Behaviour continues to be a vibrant and relevant text because it is a product of the Canadian classroom. It is used in Canada by the first author and her colleagues. Thus, there is a "front-line" approach to considering revisions. We also solicit considerable feedback from OB instructors and students throughout the country. While we have kept the features of the previous edition that adopters continue to say they like, there is also a great deal that is new.

Our Pedagogical Approach in Writing the Textbook

- *Relevance.* The text reminds both teacher and student alike that we have entered the twenty-first century and must contend with a new paradigm of work that is more globally focused and competitive, relies more heavily on part-time and contract jobs, and places a higher premium on entrepreneurial skills, either within the traditional workplace structure, as an individual seeking out an alternative job, or as the creator of your own new business.

  From its beginning, this textbook was the first to emphasize that OB is for everyone, from the bottom-rung employee to the CEO, as well as to anyone who has to interact with others to accomplish a task. We continue to emphasize this theme. We remind readers of the material's relevance beyond a "9-to-5" job by concluding each chapter with a summary that outlines the implications not only for the workplace, but also for individuals in their daily lives. We also include the feature **OB in the Street**, which further emphasizes how OB applies outside the workplace.

- *Writing style.* Clarity and readability are the hallmarks of this text. Our reviewers find the text "conversational," "interesting," "student-friendly," and "very clear and understandable." Students say they really like the informal style and personal examples.

- *Examples, examples, examples.* From our teaching experience, we know that students may not remember a concept, but they will remember an example. This textbook is packed full of recent real-world examples drawn from a variety of organizations: business and not-for-profit, large and small, and local and international. We also use examples taken from the world at large, to illustrate the broader applicability of OB material.

- *Comprehensive literature coverage.* This textbook is regularly singled out for its comprehensive and up-to-date coverage of OB from both academic journals as well as business periodicals.

- *Skill-building emphasis.* Each chapter's **OB at Work** section is full of exercises to help students make the connections between theories and real-world applications. Exercises at the end of each chapter reinforce critical thinking, behavioural analysis, and team building.

Highlights of the Sixth Edition

The sixth edition was conceived as a "break out" revision, designed to evolve with today's students. A concerted effort has been made to update every dimension of the book—from the new interior design, through the new chapter-opening vignettes, to the new "Blog It" exercises in the margins, the new boxed features, and the new "Global Implications" sections. Also included are more relevant examples, updated theory coverage, and a continued emphasis on providing the latest research findings. Based on reviews from numerous instructors and students across Canada, we have found that many potential users want chapters that have the right balance of theory, research, and application material, while being relevant to student learning. To accomplish this, we have:

- Continued to highlight the importance of Learning Outcomes as a "road map" leading to focused reading and increased learning comprehension. Learning Outcomes appear initially as an enumerated list on the chapter-opening page and then the numbered outcomes appear throughout the chapter again in the margins to direct readers to the section where the Learning Outcome is addressed. Finally, the numbered outcomes guide each chapter's summary.

- Continued to feature thoroughly updated chapter-opening vignettes as well as the subsequent references back to the vignettes that appear throughout the chapter, usually at the start of major sections.

- Added a new "Big Idea/Lessons Learned" feature that appears at the beginning and end of each chapter. These new resources are designed to work hand-in-hand. At the beginning of the chapter, a "Big Idea" item appears in the margin which is meant to give readers a big picture view of the topic at hand. Then, at the end of the chapter a "lessons learned" appears in the margin to recap the key takeaways for the chapter.

- Incorporated new "Blog It" resources in the margins that allow students to share their feedback on chapter topics. This feature provides a venue for students to tell their own stories relating to OB and to communicate with other students reactions to chapter-specific topics and scenarios. The URL provided in the margin allows students to blog 24/7.

- Continued to integrate a series of relevant and helpful questions throughout the chapters (look for questions that are set on top of a bubble design) to encourage students to think about how OB applies to their everyday lives and engage students in their reading of the material. These questions first appear as bullet lists in the right corner of chapter opener, under the heading "OB Is for Everyone," and then appear throughout each chapter.

- Updated the boxed features throughout the text, including new **OB in Action, OB in the Street, OB in the Workplace, Focus on Research, Focus on Ethics,** and **Focus on Diversity** boxes. This edition marks the most extensive overhaul of this content ever.

- Addressed and highlighted how OB principles vary across cultures in new **Global Implications** sections. Chapters now conclude with references to the cultural differences that exist within and between countries. Until recently, most OB research was conducted in Western countries. That is changing, however, and compared with even a few years ago, we are now in a much better position to answer the question "How does what we know about OB vary based on culture?" Some OB principles vary little across cultures, while others vary a great deal.

- Continued to include the popular **OB for You** feature at the end of each chapter, to highlight the relevance of the chapter to one's everyday life.

- Highlighted the key **Learning About Yourself Exercises** that are available to students, both at the start of the chapters and throughout the chapters themselves. Some of these exercises appear right in the chapter, while more can be found and completed on MyOBLab at **www.pearsoned.ca/ myoblab**.

- Built in barcodes at the end of each chapter, which allow students to download free a "ScanLife" application to their smartphones. With this app, students interact with Pearson Canada's "Study on the Go" online content, including popular study tools such as Glossary Flashcards, Audio Summaries, and Quizzes, which can be accessed any time of day.

- Reflected the ever-changing world of organizational behaviour through a series of new case incidents that tie in with videos as well as new comprehensive cases (see the **Additional Cases** section at the end of the textbook).

- Continued to include our **OB on the Edge** feature, which highlights what's new and hot in OB. OB on the Edge is unique to the Canadian edition, and is a distinct feature that does not appear in any other organizational behaviour textbook in the market. The feature provides an opportunity to explore challenging issues, and encourages students to read more about these hot topics. In this edition, we cover four topics in this innovative feature: *Stress; Trust; The Toxic Workplace;* and *Spirituality in the Workplace.*

Chapter-by-Chapter Highlights: What's New

The sixth edition is a "break out" revision, which means that we made a concerted effort to thoroughly update each and every aspect of the book. Taken together, the changes we made render this text the leader in the market and the undisputed pioneer vis-à-vis meaningful application of OB concepts and theories. Each chapter offers new examples, new cutting-edge research, improved discussions of current issues, and a wide variety of application material. The key *changes* are listed below.

Chapter 1: What Is Organizational Behaviour?

- Kicked off the chapter with a new *Opening Vignette* that introduces Yellow House Events (Toronto, Ontario) and describes some of the organizational-behaviour-related challenges its founder faced

- Expanded the discussion of the importance of interpersonal skills

- Updated the section titled *Today's Challenges in the Canadian Workplace*, which-investigates the workplace issues faced by the manager and employees of Yellow House Events

- Incorporated a new *OB in the Workplace* box, which discusses the effects of employee empowerment (see "Habaàero's Employees Help Set Policies")

- Addressed the importance of customer service

- Described the need for managers and employees to stimulate innovation and change

- Expanded the section on developing effective employees to address absenteeism and turnover

- Updated the section called "Responding to Globalization"

- Added a new section titled "OB: Making Sense of Behaviour in Organizations," which continues the analysis of the Yellow House Events founder's organizational and managerial decisions

- Established a new *Ethical Dilemma Exercise* about misrepresentation and withholding information in business ("Lying in Business")

- Offered a suggested book list on the topic of leadership in *Point/Counterpoint*

- Included new *Case Incident* on the subject of using metrics to manage employees (see "Data Will Set You Free")

- Revised the following glossary definitions: job satisfaction, workplace diversity, ethical dilemmas and ethical choices, absenteeism, turnover

Chapter 2: Perception, Personality, and Emotions

- Revised the *Opening Vignette*, which describes some of the perceptions about Walmart Canada and ties into the subject of the chapter (how our perceptions, personalities, emotions, and experiences affect our behaviour)

- Added a new figure to illustrate how individuals typically overestimate their own good behaviours and underestimate the good behaviour of others (see Exhibit 2-3: "Percentage of Individuals Rating Themselves Above Average on Each Attribute")

- Updated the *Focus on Diversity* box to discuss what types of questions employers can ask about a person's mental health history (see "Law Society's Questions About Mental Health Challenged")

- Significantly strengthened the section that discusses why perception and judgment matter in organizational contexts (i.e., during employment interviews, when discussing performance expectations, and during performance evaluations)

- Expanded the description of the Big Five Personality Model

- Discussed narcissism and how it affects organizational behaviour

- Expanded the section on the differences among affect, emotions, and mood

- Added a new *OB in the Street* box, which discusses how perceived emotions can affect relationships (see "How Perception Causes Fights in Relationships")

- Described new research on surface acting and displaying fake emotions

- Updated the section on emotions and the need for emotional intelligence (EI) in the workplace

- Incorporated a new *Global Implications* section, which examines global attitudinal differences toward perception, attribution, personality, and emotions

- Presented a new *Case Incident*, which examines negative emotions in the workplace (see "The Upside of Anger?")

- Included a new *Case Incident*, which discusses the pros and cons of agreeableness (see "The Nice Trap?")

- Revised the following glossary definitions: Big Five Model, affect

Chapter 3: Values, Attitudes, and Diversity in the Workplace

- Set the stage for the chapter by including a new *Opening Vignette* about casino operator SaskGaming (Saskatchewan). The vignette explores the relationship between organizational values and attitudes and the impact of those aspects on workplace diversity

- Added a new *OB in the Street* box which discusses whether lapses in ethics outside of work should affect a person's day job (see "Stanley Cup Rioting Leads to Employee Firing")

- Incorporated a new *OB in the Workplace* box on diversity and values in the nonprofit sector (see "The Nonprofit Sector Looks to Diversify Its Workforce")

- Updated the section on generational differences

- Highlighted, in tabular format, some of the cultural differences between Canadian and American young adults

- Significantly expanded the section on francophone and anglophone management styles and values

- Described the differences between general and specific attitudes

- Revised the content on job satisfaction, its causes, and how it is affected by absenteeism and turnover

- Updated the section on employee engagement to examine job involvement and psychological empowerment in the workplace

- Created a new section that describes effective diversity programs

- Incorporated a new table that describes leading companies' diversity initiatives (see Exhibit 3-5: "Practices used by 45 of Canada's Most Welcoming Places to Work")

- Added a new *OB in the Street* box that addresses diversity in corporate boards (see "Adding Diversity to Boards of Directors")

- Established a new *Global Implications* section, which examines the global approaches to job satisfaction and diversity management

- Offered a new *Case Incident* that discusses job satisfaction as a state of mind (see "Thinking Your Way to a Better Job")

- New/updated glossary definitions: value system, collectivism, core self-evaluation, job involvement, psychological empowerment, biographical characteristics, ability, protected groups

OB on the Edge: Stress at Work

- Provided new research findings on the effects of stress on job performance

- Featured statistics describing stress levels by province and gender (see "Stressed Quite a Lot, 2010 [Percent]")

- Incorporated new research on the physiological symptoms of stress

- Expanded the section on "role stress" and physical and mental wellness programs

- Updated the box offering tips for how to reduce stress in the workplace (see "Toward Less Stressful Work")

Chapter 4: Theories of Motivation

- Included a new *Opening Vignette* that discusses the success of figure skater Patrick Chan and explores the sources that motivate him to continue skating and participating in competitions

- Added new *Focus on Research* box that examines how internal dialogue affects motivation (see "Talking to Yourself Can Be a Powerful Self-Motivator")

- Incorporated a new figure exploring Maslow's Hierarchy of Needs as applied to the workplace (see Exhibit 4-1: "Maslow's Hierarchy of Needs Applied to the Workplace")

- Revised and expanded the section on McClelland's theory of needs

- Created a new section on the importance of providing performance feedback, including tips on how to do so effectively (see "OB in Action: Giving More Effective Feedback")

- Introduced a new *OB in the Workplace* box that examines the benefits of results-only work environments (see "Results-Only Work Environments")

- Updated the *Research Findings* section that discusses the effects of goal setting

- Revised the *Research Findings* section on inequitable pay

- Strengthened the discussion of organizational and procedural justice

- Explored the subject of self-determination theory in the section that discusses cognitive evaluation theory

- Presented new research findings on extrinsic vs. intrinsic rewards

- Created new *Global Implications* section that discusses the cross-cultural transferability of motivation theories

- Updated the *Point/Counterpoint* feature on the subject of failure (see "Failure Motivates/Failure Demotivates")

- Revised the following glossary definitions: lower-order needs, self-actualization, higher-order needs, goal-setting theory, self-efficacy, self-determination theory

Chapter 5: Motivation in Action

- Introduced the Whole Foods chain in the *Opening Vignette* and explored its management and rewards programs

- Included new research findings on whether salary is an important motivator

- Featured a new table that explores what Boomers and Gen Y value (see Exhibit 5-1: "What Boomers and Generation Y Value as Much as Compensation")

- Provided new research findings and updated examples of various pay structures

- Presented new information on organizational-based incentives

- Established a new *OB in the Workplace* box that looks at how far some teachers will go to improve test scores (see "Bonuses Lead to Cheating")

- Created a new *OB in the Workplace* box that examines how some operations can be criticized for being *too* efficient (see "Starbucks Aims for Better Coffee")

- Added a new *Focus on Research* box that discusses the impact autonomy can have on productivity (see "Autonomy and Productivity")

- Synthesized new research findings on job enrichment and how management can contribute to it

- Presented a new *Research Findings* section investigating whether telework can increase employee motivation

- Included a new section describing the impact that social and physical contexts can have on motivation and job satisfaction

- Incorporated new material on the types of employee involvement programs and how they relate to motivational theories

- Investigated the cross-cultural differences in motivational approaches in the new *Global Implications* section

- Addressed the impact that praise and compliments have on motivation in the new *Point/Counterpoint* feature (see "Praise Motivates!/Praise Is Highly Overrated")

- Revised the following glossary definitions: job design, job characteristics model (JCM), telework, employee involvement, participative management, representative participation

Chapter 6: Groups and Teamwork

- Introduced Cirque du Soleil (Montreal, Quebec) and its recipe for successful teamwork in the new *Opening Vignette*

- Updated the *Focus on Research* box which explores whether virtual teams can develop strong trust (see "If I Can't See You, Can I Trust You?")

- Added a new *Focus on Research* box that looks at how teams adapt to competitive and cooperative reward systems (see "The Impact of Rewards on Team Functioning")

- Updated the discussion of how diversity affects performance
- Revised the section dealing with why process is important to team effectiveness
- Discussed worldwide research regarding the use of teamwork, self-managed teams, culturally diverse teams, and group cohesiveness in the new *Global Implications* section
- Included new facts and findings in the *Point/Counterpoint* feature (see "Sports Teams Are Good Models for Workplace Teams/Sports Teams Are Not the Model for All Teams")
- Explored how Toyota integrates teamwork as one of its core values in the new *Case Incident* (see "Toyota's Team Culture")
- Described IBM's unique approach to multicultural, multinational teamwork in the new *Case Incident* (see "IBM's Multicultural Multinational Teams")
- Added the following new glossary definition: mental models

OB on the Edge: Trust

- Examined the relationship between lack of trust and why employees quit their jobs
- Updated the definition of trust and the description of how it functions in relationships
- Added a new box offering tips on how to increase the level of trust within an organization (see "Increasing Organizational Candour")
- Revised the section on distrust to include new research findings and to introduce the concept of "tempered trust"
- Incorporated a new boxed feature examining how to trust wisely and well (see "The Rules for Trusting Wisely")

Chapter 7: Communication

- Opened the chapter with a new story that explores the communication plan developed by the Toronto Leaside Girls Hockey Association to win more ice time for practice
- Added a new *Focus on Research* box that summarizes the importance of communication when the economy is faltering (see "Communicating in Bad Times")
- Presented a new *OB in the Workplace* box that describes how the selection of an inappropriate communication channel can have disastrous effects (see "Some Emails Should Be Left Unsent")
- Expanded the section on barriers to effective communication to discuss emotions, language, silence, and nonverbal communication
- Suggested methods of dealing with rumours in the new *OB in Action* box (see "Reducing Rumours")
- Described the time-consuming nature of email and offered strategies for keeping the volume of email under control
- Explored how new technologies like social networking, blogs, and Twitter affect the workplace

- Included a new *OB in the Workplace* box which describes how one RCMP officer was disciplined for his Facebook posts (see "An RCMP Officer's Facebook Posts Land Him in Trouble")

- Discussed the challenges of information overload, the difficulties of using technologies that render you "always on call," and the importance of information security

- Introduced a new *OB in Action* box which outlines a code of conduct for social networking within the workplace (see "Social Networking Responsibly")

- Created a new *Global Implications* section which examines the impact of cross-cultural factors on communication

- Explored the non-work related use of company computers and the Internet in the new *Ethical Dilemma Exercise* (see "Defining the Boundaries of Technology")

- Included a new *Case Incident* which emphasizes the limitations of email communication in certain situations (see "Dianna Abdala")

- Added the following glossary definitions: formal channels, informal channels, and blog

Chapter 8: Power and Politics

- Introduced a new *Opening Vignette* that explores a Tim Hortons franchise that brought a class-action lawsuit against the company, arguing abuse of power by senior management

- Updated the definition of power to include new research findings relating to our perceptions of those in positions of power

- Included a new *Focus on Research* box which discusses the desire for power vs. the desire for control (see "Power: It's All About Control")

- Added a new *Focus on Research* box which examines how holding positions of power can affect the behaviour of those who hold it (see "The Cookie Experiment")

- Revised the section on workplace harassment to include new research findings about workplace bullying and sexual harassment

- Created a new *Global Implications* section which examines the effect of culture on empowerment, perceptions of politics, and preferred influence tactics

- Established a new *Case Incident* that discusses the changing attitudes toward dress codes and the impact of dress on image management (see "Dressing for Success")

- Established a new *Case Incident* that examines the use of persuasion in the workplace (see "The Persuasion Imperative")

- Added the following new glossary definition: dependency

Chapter 9: Conflict and Negotiation

- Featured a new *Opening Vignette* dealing with the dispute (and subsequent conflict resolution) between Pacific National Exhibition (PNE) and CUPE 1004, which, for the first time, took place during the PNE's annual fair

- Addressed how to minimize the negative effects of workplace conflict in the new section titled "Resolution-Focused View of Conflict"

- Presented new examples of conflict management strategies

- Updated the section on third-party conflict resolution to describe the role of a consultant

- Expanded the *Research Findings* section on the effects of conflict

- Added a new example of distributive bargaining to introduce the concept of a fixed pie

- Explored the effectiveness of various bid strategies when participating in eBay auctions in an *OB in the Street* box (see "How Anchor Value Can Reap Higher Returns on eBay")

- Featured a new section that examines the role of individual differences (like personality, mood/emotions, and gender) on negotiations

- Discussed how conflict is handled in different cultures, whether differences exist in negotiating styles across cultures, and how the display of emotions affect negotiations in different cultures in a new *Global Implications* section

- Presented a new *Case Incident* on the use of mediation to settle employment disputes (see "Mediation: Master Solution to Employment Disputes?")

- Added the following new glossary definitions: consultant, fixed pie

OB on the Edge: The Toxic Workplace

- Introduced a new *Opening Vignette* which tells the story of one person's poor workplace behaviour (in this case, that of a BC Lions football player) and how the situation was handled by the manager (the team coach)

- Added a new section on workplace bullying

- Presented two new *Fact Boxes*: one lists the possible negative effects associated with the experience of rudeness in the workplace, and the other presents statistics revealing the frequency of some inappropriate management behaviours

- Featured a new box that lists the behaviours commonly associated with poor managers (see "Do You Have a Bad Boss?")

- Included a box with tips for how to deal with a toxic manager (see "How to Deal with a Toxic Boss")

- Included a box that lists the typical characteristics of a toxic organization (see "What Does a Toxic Organization Look Like?")

Chapter 10: Organizational Culture

- Updated the *Opening Vignette* which discusses the strong organizational culture created by the co-founders of the successful Boston Pizza franchise

- Clarified the definition of organizational culture and listed the seven primary characteristics that capture the essence of an organization's culture

- Strengthened the visual representation of the "layers" of culture (see Exhibit 10-2: "Layers of Culture")

- Expanded the "function of culture" section to address the difficulties associated with establishing a strong culture in a decentralized organization

- Discussed how an organization's culture creates a climate (shared perceptions of environment) that affects an individual's job satisfaction, involvement, commitment, and motivation

- Added a new *OB in the Workplace* box to address what can happen when employees do not buy into their organization's culture (see "Making Culture Work")

- Described the differences between "strong" and "weak" organizational cultures

- Strengthened the section relating to the importance of "stories" to establishing organizational culture

- Provided a more effective example of the influence of the employee selection process on sustaining workplace culture

- Included a new *OB in the Workplace* box that describes how Apple maintains a culture of secrecy (see "Apple's Culture of Secrecy")

- Revised the section that explains the stages of socialization

- Summarized new research findings on how to establish a positive ethical organizational culture

- Integrated a new *Global Implications* section that discusses how organizational culture is affected by the global context in which it is situated

- Explored the concept of the "5S" principles and how they are incorporated into organizational culture in the new *Case Incident* (see "Is a 5S Culture for You?")

- Added the following glossary definitions: organizational climate, core values, material symbols

Chapter 11: Leadership

- Introduced a new *Opening Vignette* that discusses Lieutenant Colonel Maryse Carmichael, who was recently appointed the first female Commanding Officer (CO) of Canada's Snowbirds, and explores the factors that affect one's ability to lead and inspire others

- Revised the section on trait theories to include new research findings and additional information on emotional intelligence

- Updated the discussion of the Ohio State Studies and the Michigan Studies

- Discussed how to apply the Fiedler contingency model to the workplace

- Updated the discussion of Hersey and Blanchard's Situational Leadership®

- Integrated new research findings on the path-goal theory

- Expanded the discussion of leadership substitutes and neutralizers

- Included a new definition of charisma and new research on charismatic leadership

- Listed the key characteristics of charismatic leaders (see Exhibit 11-5: "Key Characteristics of Charismatic Leaders")

- Updated the *Research Findings* section devoted to transformational leadership to address the strengths and weaknesses of this leadership approach

- Expanded the discussion of the effectiveness of formal and informal mentoring

- Investigated new research on the similarities and differences between women's and men's leadership styles

- Created a new *Global Implications* section which discusses research on leadership practices in Brazil, France, Egypt, and China

- Questioned whether the ends justify a leader's ethically ambiguous means in a new *Ethical Dilemma Exercise* (see "Do the Ends Justify the Means?")

- Revised the following glossary definitions: trait theories of leadership, identification-based trust

Chapter 12: Decision Making, Creativity, and Ethics

- Introduced a new *Opening Vignette* exploring the value-based business decisions of the founders of Kicking Horse Coffee, a fair trade coffee company

- Revised the explanations of "bounded rationality" and "satisficing" as applied to decision making

- Included a new *OB in the Street* box that explores whether intuition can help you win at chess (see "Intuition Comes to the Chess Board")

- Addressed the topic of risk aversion and its implications on decision making

- Added a new *OB in the Street* box to exemplify the implications of groupthink among market analysts (see "Groupthink among Analysts")

- Introduced new research on the links between creativity and mood

- Described in an *OB in the Workplace* box the Canadian army's written code of ethics, which underscores the need for ethical behaviour in warfare (see "Ethics and the Army")

- Included new research findings explaining how Canadians, and Canadian executives, feel about the subject of corporate social responsibility

- Incorporated a new *Global Implications* section that reviews global differences in decision making and ethics

- Presented a new *Point/Counterpoint* section that weighs action against inaction (see "When in Doubt, Do!/Wait! Not so Fast")

- Examined whether having multiple people involved in a decision is always advantageous in a new *Case Incident* called "If Two Heads Are Better Than One, Are Four Even Better?"

- New glossary definition: risk aversion

OB on the Edge: Spirituality in the Workplace

- Updated the discussion of the difference between spirituality and religion

- Included new research about the impact of spiritual activity on peoples' lives

Chapter 13: Organizational Structure

- Introduced a new *Opening Vignette* dealing with T4G (Toronto), a Canadian technical services company with a unique organizational structure

- Incorporated a new Learning Objective ("What are the behavioural implications of different organizational designs?")

- Included new examples of customer departmentalization

- Described changing attitudes toward organizational design and the chain of command

- Included new material on centralization and decentralization

- Presented new material on the pros and cons of bureaucracy and the matrix structure

- Updated the section on virtual organizations

- Created a new section on lean organizations and strategies for handling organizational downsizing

- Revised the section on why organizational structures differ, including new material on strategy and environment

- Added a new section on organizational designs and how they affect employee behaviour

- Reviewed the cultural influences on organizational structure, employee structure preferences, and boundaryless organizations in the new *Global Implications* section

- Featured a new *Point/Counterpoint* section on mergers (see "Mergers Are Bad for the Employee/Mergers Keep the Company Alive")

- New glossary definitions: authority, unity of command

Chapter 14: Organizational Change

- Introduced a new *Opening Vignette* dedicated to Sears Canada and the unique and many-faceted challenges it faces as tough American competitors like Target and J. Crew enter the Canadian marketplace

- Included new material on forces for change

- Updated discussions of resistance to change, and how it is overcome

- Added a new *OB in the Workplace* box that explores how the National Research Council dealt with a major change (see "The NRC Changes Its Research Focus to Market Drivers")

- Incorporated a new *OB in Action* box on how to speed up the pace of change (see "How to Speed Up the Pace of Change")

- Created a new section on how to create an organizational culture that embraces change

- Discussed how learning organizations address fragmentation, competition, and reactiveness

- Addressed culture-bound change issues in the new *Global Implications* section

- Featured a new *Case Incident* which discusses whether Toyota is truly an innovative company ("Innovation [and Continuity] at Toyota")

Pedagogical Features

The pedagogical features of *Organizational Behaviour: Concepts, Controversies, Applications,* Sixth Canadian Edition, are designed to complement and reinforce the textual material. This textbook offers the most complete assortment of pedagogy available in any OB book on the market.

- The text is developed in a "story-line" format that emphasizes how the topics fit together. Each chapter opens with a list of learning outcomes related to a main example that threads through the chapter. The opening vignette is carried throughout the chapter to help students apply a real life example to the concepts they are learning. The learning outcome questions appear in the margin of the text, to indicate where they are addressed. The opening questions are repeated and answered at the end of each chapter to summarize the chapter content.

- **OB Is for Everyone** in the chapter-opener highlights the integrated questions that students will encounter throughout each chapter (in the form of bubble notes). Right from the start, these questions encourage students to think about how OB applies to everyday lives.

- From the outset, students are introduced to the key self-assessments that they will be engaged in within each chapter.

- NEW! A "Big Idea/Lessons Learned" feature appears at the beginning and end of each chapter. These new resources are designed to work hand-in-hand. At the beginning of the chapter, a "Big Idea" item appears in the margin which is meant to give readers a big picture view of the topic at hand. Then, at the end of the chapter a "lessons learned" appears in the margin to recap the key take-aways from the chapter.

- NEW! A "Blog It" feature encourages students to share their feedback on chapter topics. The idea is to provide a venue for students to tell their own stories relating to OB and to communicate with other students their reactions to chapter-specific topics and scenarios. The URL provided in the margin allows students to blog 24/7.

- Exclusive to the Canadian edition, **OB in the Street**, **OB in the Workplace**, **Focus on Ethics**, **Focus on Diversity**, and **Focus on Research** help students see the links between theoretical material and applications.

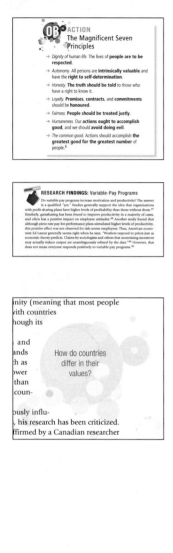

- **OB in Action** features provide tips for using the concepts of OB in everyday life, such as Managing Virtual Teams, Choosing Strategies to Deal with Conflicts, Social Networking Responsibly, and Reducing Biases and Errors in Decision Making.

- To help instructors and students readily spot significant discussions of research findings, we have included a research icon to indicate where these discussions appear. This helps emphasize the strong research foundation that underlies OB.

- Continue to integrate a series of relevant and helpful questions throughout the chapters (look for questions that are set on top of a bubble design) to encourage students to think about how OB applies to their everyday lives and engage students in their reading of the material. These questions first appear as a bullet list in the chapter opener, under the heading OB Is for Everyone, and then appear throughout each chapter as bubble notes.

- NEW! The **Global Implications** section addresses and highlights how OB principles vary across cultures. Chapters now conclude with references to the cultural differences that exist within and between countries. Until recently, most OB research was conducted in Western countries. That is changing, however, and compared with even a few years ago, we are now in a much better position to answer the question "How does what we know about OB vary based on culture?" Some OB principles vary little across cultures, while others vary a great deal.

- **Summary and Implications** provides responses to the outcomes-based questions at the beginning of each chapter, while the **Snapshot Summary** provides a study tool that helps students to see the overall connections among concepts presented within each chapter.

- Each chapter concludes with **OB at Work**, a set of resources designed to help students apply the lessons of the chapter. Included in **OB at Work** are the following features:

  - **For Review** and **For Critical Thinking** provide thought-provoking questions to review the chapter and consider ways to apply the material presented.

  - **OB for You** outlines how OB can be used by individuals in their daily lives.

- **Point/Counterpoint** promotes debate on contentious OB issues. This feature presents more focused arguments.

- **Learning About Yourself, Breakout Group, Working with Others**, and **Ethical Dilemma** exercises are valuable application exercises for the classroom. The many new exercises included here are ones that we have found particularly stimulating in our own classrooms. Our students say they like these exercises *and* they learn from them. Additional exercises can be found on MyOBLab at **www.pearsoned.ca/myoblab**.

- **Case Incidents** (two per chapter) deal with real-world scenarios and require students to exercise their decision-making skills. Each case enables an instructor to quickly generate class discussion on a key theme within the chapter.

- **From Concepts to Skills** provides a wide range of applications for students. The section begins with a practical set of tips on topics such as reading emotions, setting goals, and solving problems creatively, which demonstrate real-world applications of OB theories. These tips are followed by the features *Practising Skills* and *Reinforcing Skills*. *Practising Skills* presents an additional case or group activity to apply the chapter's learning outcomes. *Reinforcing Skills* asks students to talk about the material they have learned with others, or to apply it to their own personal experiences.

- NEW! **Study on the Go.** At the end of each chapter, you will find a unique QR code providing access to Study on the Go, an unprecedented mobile integration between text and online content. Students link to Pearson's unique Study on the Go content directly from their smartphones, allowing them to study whenever and wherever they wish! Go to one of the sites below to see how you can download an app to your smartphone for free. Once the app is installed, your phone will scan the code and link to a website containing Pearson's Study on the Go content, including the popular study tools Glossary Flashcards, Audio Summaries, and Quizzes, which can be accessed anytime.

ScanLife http://getscanlife.com/

NeoReader http://get.neoreader.com/

QuickMark http://www.quickmark.com.tw/

- Exclusive to the Canadian edition, **OB on the Edge** (following each part) takes a close look at some of the hottest topics in the field: work-related stress, trust, behavioural pathologies that can make an organization "toxic," and spirituality in the workplace. Since this is a stand-alone feature, these topics can be introduced at the instructor's discretion.

- Our reviewers have asked for more cases, and more comprehensive and integrated cases. To address this request, we include 10 new cases, featuring a variety of challenges and Canadian companies and organizations. All of these cases require students to apply material from a variety of chapters.

Supplements

We have created an outstanding supplements package for *Organizational Behaviour*, Sixth Canadian Edition. In particular, we have provided access to MyOBLab, an online study tool for students and an online homework and assessment tool for faculty. An access code to MyOBLab at **www.pearsoned.ca/myoblab** is included with this textbook. MyOBLab provides students with an assortment of tools to help enrich and expedite learning. It lets students assess their understanding through auto-graded tests and assignments, develop a personalized study plan to address areas of weakness, and practise a variety of learning tools to master organizational behaviour principles. Some of these tools are described below:

- *Auto-Graded Tests and Assignments.* MyOBLab comes with two sample tests per chapter. Students can work through these diagnostic tests to identify areas they have not fully understood. These sample tests generate a personalized study plan. Instructors can also assign these sample tests or create assignments, quizzes, or tests using a mix of publisher-supplied content and their own custom exercises.

- *Personalized Study Plan.* In MyOBLab, students are treated as individuals with specific learning needs. Students have limited study time so it is important for them to study as effectively as possible. A personalized study plan is generated from each student's results on sample tests and instructor assignments. Students can clearly see the topics they have mastered—and, more importantly, the concepts they need to work on.

- *PowerPoint Slides.* This tool provides students with highlights and visuals of key concepts.

- *Glossary Flashcards.* This study aid is useful for students' review of key concepts.

- *eBook+.* Students can study without leaving the online environment. They can access the eText online, including animated text figures prepared by Cathy Heyland (Selkirk College).

- *Self-Assessment Library.* The Self-Assessment Library helps students create a skills portfolio. It is an interactive library containing behavioural questionnaires that help students discover things about themselves, their attitudes, and their personal strengths and weaknesses. Learning more about themselves gives students interesting insights into how they might behave in an organizational setting and motivates them to learn more about OB theories and practices that they can apply today and in the future.

- *HR Implications.* This feature spotlights those facets of each chapter topic that are relevant to human resource management.

- *Research Navigator.* Research navigator helps students quickly and efficiently make the most of their research time by providing four exclusive databases of reliable source content including the EBSCO Academic Journal and Abstract Database, New York Times Search by Subject Archive, "Best of the Web" Link Library, and Financial Times Article Archive and Company Financials.

The following materials are available for instructors:

- *Instructor's Resource Manual with Video Guide.* The Instructor's Resource Manual includes learning objectives, chapter outlines and synopses, annotated lecture outlines, teaching guides for in-text exercises, a summary and analysis of **Point/Counterpoint** features, and answers to questions found under **OB at Work**'s *For Review* and *For Critical Thinking* sections, **Case Incidents**, and **Video Case Incidents**. There are additional cases, exercises, and teaching materials as well.

- *Pearson TestGen.* The Pearson TestGen contains over 1800 items in TestGen format, including multiple choice, true/false, and discussion questions that relate not only to the body of the text but to **From Concepts to Skills**, **Point/Counterpoint**, and case materials. For each question we have provided the correct answer, a reference to the relevant section of the text, a difficulty rating, and a classification (recall/applied). TestGen software enables instructors to view and edit the existing questions, add questions, generate tests, and distribute the tests in a variety of formats. Powerful search and sort functions make it easy to locate questions and arrange them in any order desired. TestGen also enables instructors to administer tests on a local area network, have the tests graded electronically and have the results prepared in electronic or printed reports. TestGen is compatible with Windows and Macintosh operating systems, and can be downloaded from the TestGen website located at **www.pearsoned.com/testgen**. Contact your local sales representative for details and access.

- *Electronic Transparencies in PowerPoint.* This package includes nearly 700 slides of content and exhibits from the text for electronic presentation.

- *Pearson Canada Video Library.* Pearson Canada has developed an exciting video package consisting of segments from CBC programs and from Prentice Hall's *Organizational Behavior*, 13th edition Video Library. These segments show students issues of organizational behaviour as they affect real individuals and companies. Teaching notes are provided in the Instructor's Resource Manual with Video Guide. The videos are available in DVD (0-13-231031-7) format.

- *Image Gallery.* This package provides instructors with images to enhance their teaching.

Most of these instructor supplements are available for download from a password-protected section of Pearson Canada's online catalogue **(vig.pearsoned.ca)**. Navigate to your textbook's catalogue page to view a list of those supplements that are available. See your local sales representative for details and access.

- *Innovative Solutions Team.* Pearson's Innovative Solutions Team works with faculty and campus course designers to ensure that Pearson technology products, assessment tools, and online course materials are tailored to meet your specific needs. This highly qualified team is dedicated to helping schools take full advantage of a wide range of educational technology, by assisting in the integration of a variety of instructional materials and media formats.

Acknowledgments

A number of people worked hard to give this sixth Canadian edition of *Organizational Behaviour* a new look.

I received incredible support for this project from a variety of people at Pearson Canada. Nick Durie, Acquisitions Editor, Lise Dupont, Senior Developmental Editor, and Lesley Deugo, Project Manager, worked hard to keep this project on track. Anthony Leung, Senior Designer, was responsible for the beautiful interior and cover design. Steve O'Hearn, President of Higher Education, and Gary Bennett, Vice President, Editorial Director of Higher Education, are extremely supportive on the management side of Pearson Canada. This kind of support makes it much easier for an author to get work done and meet dreams and goals. Monika Schurmann was very helpful in doing the photo research and made some incredible finds in her search for photos to highlight OB concepts. There are a variety of other people at Pearson who also had a hand in making sure that the manuscript would be transformed into this book and then delivered to you. To all of them I extend my thanks for jobs well done. The Pearson sales team is an exceptional group, and I know they will do everything possible to make this book successful. I continue to appreciate and value their support and interaction.

Claudia Forgas was the Production Editor and Copyeditor for the project and continues to amaze for how well she makes sure everything is in place and written clearly. Claudia provided a wealth of support, great ideas, and goodwill throughout the production process. Turning the manuscript into the textbook you hold in your hands could not have happened without her inspired leadership. I am grateful for the opportunity to work with her again. Marcia Gallego, as the proofreader, was extremely diligent about checking for consistency throughout the text. Both performed a number of helpful fact-checking activities. Their keen eyes helped to make these pages as clean as they are.

I also want to acknowledge my divisional secretary, Nancy Tang, who helps keep me on track in a variety of ways. I could not ask for a better, more dedicated, or more cheerful assistant. She really helps keep things together.

In our continuing effort to improve the textbook, we conducted many reviews to elicit feedback. Many thanks to several students from the Northern Alberta Institute of Technology (NAIT) who a provided us with suggestions for improving the textbook. The students are Barb Kosak, Prudence Musinguzi, Andres Sarrate, and Robert Tucci. Student input helps keep the material fresh and alive.

Finally, I want to acknowledge the many reviewers of this textbook for their detailed, helpful comments. I appreciate the time and care that they put into their reviewing. The reviewers include Ian Anderson (Algonquin College), Julia Dotson (Confederation College), Patricia Fitzgerald (St. Mary's University), Judith Hunter (Sheridan Institute of Technology and Advanced Learning), Martha Reavley (University of Windsor), and Yanelia Yabar (Red Deer College).

ABOUT THE AUTHORS

Nancy Langton received her Ph.D. from Stanford University. Since completing her graduate studies, Dr. Langton has taught at the University of Oklahoma and the University of British Columbia. Currently a member of the Organizational Behaviour and Human Resources division in the Sauder School of Business, UBC, she teaches at the undergraduate, MBA and Ph.D. level and conducts executive programs on attracting and retaining employees, time management, family business issues, as well as women and management issues. Dr. Langton has received several major three-year research grants from the Social Sciences and Humanities Research Council of Canada, and her research interests have focused on human resource issues in the workplace, including pay equity, gender equity, and leadership and communication styles. She is currently conducting longitudinal research with entrepreneurs in the Greater Vancouver Region, trying to understand the relationship between their human resource practices and the success of their businesses. Her articles on these and other topics have appeared in such journals as *Administrative Science Quarterly*, *American Sociological Review*, *Sociological Quarterly*, *Journal of Management Education*, and *Gender, Work and Organizations*. She has won Best Paper commendations from both the Academy of Management and the Administrative Sciences Association of Canada.

Dr. Langton routinely wins high marks from her students for teaching. She has been nominated many times for the Commerce Undergraduate Society Awards, and has won several honourable mention plaques. She has also won the Sauder School of Business's most prestigious award for teaching innovation, The Talking Stick. The award was given for Dr. Langton's redesign of the undergraduate organizational behaviour course as well as the many activities that were a spin-off of these efforts. She was also part of the UBC MBA Core design team that won the Alan Blizzard award, a national award that recognizes innovation in teaching.

In Dr. Langton's "other life," she engages in the artistry of quiltmaking, and one day hopes to win first prize at *Visions*, the juried show for quilts as works of art. When she is not designing quilts, she is either reading novels recommended by her book club colleagues, or studying cookbooks for new ideas. All of her friends would say that she makes from scratch the best pizza in all of Vancouver, and one has even offered to supply venture capital to open a pizza parlour.

Stephen P. Robbins

Education

Ph.D., University of Arizona

Professional Experience

Academic Positions: Professor, San Diego State University, Southern Illinois University at Edwardsville, University of Baltimore, Concordia University in Montreal, and University of Nebraska at Omaha.

Research: Research interests have focused on conflict, power, and politics in organizations, behavioural decision making, and the development of effective interpersonal skills.

Books Published: World's best-selling author of textbooks in both management and organizational behaviour. His books have sold more than 5 million copies, have been translated into 20 languages, and editions have been adapted for Canada, Australia, South Africa, and India, such as these:

- *Essentials of Organizational Behavior*, 10th ed. (Prentice Hall, 2010)
- *Management*, 10th ed. with Mary Coulter (Prentice Hall, 2009)
- *Human Resource Management*, 10th ed., with David DeCenzo (Wiley, 2010)
- Prentice Hall's Self-Assessment Library 3.4 (Prentice Hall, 2010)
- *Fundamentals of Management*, 7th ed., with David DeCenzo and Mary Coulter (Prentice Hall, 2011)
- *Supervision Today!* 6th ed., with David DeCenzo (Prentice Hall, 2010)
- *Training in Interpersonal Skills*, 5th ed., with Phillip Hunsaker (Prentice Hall, 2009)
- *Managing Today!* 2nd ed. (Prentice Hall, 2000)
- *Organization Theory*, 3rd ed. (Prentice Hall, 1990)
- *The Truth About Managing People*, 2nd ed. (Financial Times/Prentice Hall, 2008)
- *Decide and Conquer: Make Winning Decisions and Take Control of Your Life* (Financial Times/Prentice Hall, 2004).

Other Interests

In his "other life," Dr. Robbins actively participates in masters' track competition. Since turning 50 in 1993, he has won 18 national championships and 12 world titles. He is the current world record holder at 100 metres (12.37 seconds) and 200 metres (25.20 seconds) for men 65 and over.

Timothy A. Judge

Education

Ph.D., University of Illinois at Urbana-Champaign

Professional Experience

Academic Positions: Visiting Franklin D. Schurz Professor of Management, Mendoza College of Business, University of Notre Dame; Matherly-McKethan Eminent Scholar in Management, Warrington College of Business Administration, University of Florida; Stanley M. Howe Professor in Leadership, Henry B. Tippie College of Business, University of Iowa; Associate Professor (with tenure), Department of Human Resource Studies, School of Industrial and Labor Relations, Cornell University; Lecturer, Charles University, Czech Republic, and Comenius University, Slovakia; Instructor, Industrial/Organizational Psychology, Department of Psychology, University of Illinois at Urbana-Champaign.

Research: Dr. Judge's primary research interests are in (1) personality, moods, and emotions, (2) job attitudes, (3) leadership and influence behaviours, and (4) careers (person-organization fit, career success). Dr. Judge has published more than 120 articles in these and other major topics in journals such as *Journal of Organizational Behavior, Personnel Psychology, Academy of Management Journal, Journal of Applied Psychology, European Journal of Personality,* and *European Journal of Work and Organizational Psychology.*

Fellowship: Dr. Judge is a fellow of the American Psychological Association, the Academy of Management, the Society for Industrial and Organizational Psychology, and the American Psychological Society.

Awards: In 1995, Dr. Judge received the Ernest J. McCormick Award for Distinguished Early Career Contributions from the Society for Industrial and Organizational Psychology. In 2001, he received the Larry L. Cummings Award for mid-career contributions from the Organizational Behavior Division of the Academy of Management. In 2007, he received the Professional Practice Award from the Institute of Industrial and Labor Relations, University of Illinois.

Books Published: H. G. Heneman III and T. A. Judge, *Staffing Organizations*, 6th ed. (Madison, WI: Mendota House/Irwin, 2009).

Other Interests

Although he cannot keep up (literally!) with Dr. Robbins' accomplishments on the track, Dr. Judge enjoys golf, cooking and baking, literature (he's a particular fan of Thomas Hardy, and is a member of the Thomas Hardy Society), and keeping up with his three children, who range in age from 20 to 6.

CHAPTER 1

What Is Organizational Behaviour?

PART 1

UNDERSTANDING

THE WORKPLACE

How can people skills help you run a successful business?

LEARNING OUTCOMES

1. What is organizational behaviour?

2. What challenges do managers and employees face in today's workplace?

3. Isn't organizational behaviour common sense? Or just like psychology?

Grail Noble runs Toronto-based Yellow House Events, an event-management business she started in 2003.[1] For the first several years she worked independently, but in 2006, she wanted to expand. However, she was cautious. So, she kept her home office and hired an intern, who had studied event planning.

Initially, one Yellow House client worried that the intern was too young (although she was 23 and had a post-graduate degree) to run high-level events. Instead the intern proved herself and impressed the client. That intern quickly became a full-time employee and, several promotions later, is now the company's director of operations. Noble found the work ethic of her Generation Y employee inspirational, which led her to secure cool office digs (critical for this generation) and hire more young staff members. She now employs six Gen Ys, all of whom have a post-graduate degree.

Noble had to learn how to best work with her Gen-Y staff, for whom the line between work and personal life is often blurred. They will work late into the night, but want to be able to "update their Facebook status at any hour of the workday." They also create more of a party atmosphere in the workplace, something Noble has had to get used to, and are definitely more particular about *what* they work on and *who* they work with. Still, she thinks these challenges are worth it. She built her business by "harnessing the energy of Generation Y." Together they have helped Yellow House post 1200 percent growth over five years, placing the company 41st on the 2011 *PROFIT* magazine list of the top-200-fastest-growing companies in Canada.

The challenges that managers such as Noble face illustrate several concepts you will find as you study the field of organizational behaviour. Let's take a look, then, at what organizational behaviour is.

THE BIG IDEA

OB helps managers and employees make sense of the workplace, and also applies to work in groups of all kinds.

OB IS FOR EVERYONE

- Why do some people do well in organizational settings while others have difficulty?

- Do you know what a "typical" organization looks like?

- Does job satisfaction really make a difference?

- Are you ready to take on more responsibility at work?

- What people-related challenges have you noticed in the workplace?

- Why should you care about understanding other people?

Defining Organizational Behaviour

 1   What is organizational behaviour?

Organizational behaviour (often abbreviated as OB) is a field of study that looks at the impact that individuals, groups, and structure have on behaviour within organizations for the purpose of applying such knowledge toward improving an organization's effectiveness. Because the organizations studied are often business organizations, OB is frequently applied to topics such as jobs, absenteeism, turnover, productivity, motivation, working in groups, and job satisfaction. Although debate exists about their relative importance, OB also examines the core topics of motivation, leader behaviour and power, interpersonal communication, group structure and processes, learning, attitude development and perception, change processes, conflict, work design, and work stress.[2]

Why do some people do well in organizational settings while others have difficulty?

Much of OB is relevant beyond the workplace. The study of OB can cast light on the interactions among family members, students working as a team on a class project, the voluntary group that comes together to do something about reviving the downtown area, the parents who sit on the board of their children's daycare centre, or even the members of a lunchtime pickup basketball team.

What Do We Mean by Organization?

An **organization** is a consciously coordinated social unit, composed of a group of people, that functions on a relatively continuous basis to achieve a common goal or set of goals. Manufacturing and service firms are organizations, and so are schools, hospitals, churches, military units, retail stores, police departments, volunteer organizations, start-ups, and local, provincial, and federal government agencies. Thus, when we say "organization" throughout this textbook, we are referring not only to large manufacturing firms but also to small mom-and-pop stores, as well as to the variety of other forms of organization that exist. Businesses that employ no more than 100 people made up 98 percent of the employers in Canada in 2009, and employed 39 percent of

organizational behaviour A field of study that investigates the impact of individuals, groups, and structure on behaviour within organizations; its purpose is to apply such knowledge toward improving an organization's effectiveness.

organization A consciously coordinated social unit, composed of a group of people, that functions on a relatively continuous basis to achieve a common goal or set of goals.

David and Penny Chapman understand the importance of organizational behaviour and treating employees well. When Markdale, Ontario-based Chapman's Ice Cream factory burned down in September 2009, many employees feared that they had lost their jobs. However, the owners quickly put together plans with senior managers on rebuilding the factory and keeping ice cream production going by working with other nearby ice cream producers. Not one employee lost a paycheque, though many had to be bussed to jobs at other locations or put up in hotels.

the workforce. Less than 1 percent of employers have more than 500 employees, and they employ 46 percent of the workforce. Most of these large organizations are in the public sector.[3]

The examples in this textbook present various organizations so that you can gain a better understanding of the many types of organizations that exist. Though you might not have considered this before, the college or university you attend is every bit as much a "real" organization as is lululemon athletica or Air Canada or the Vancouver Canucks. A small for-profit organization that hires unskilled workers to renovate and build in the inner city of Winnipeg is as much a real organization as is London, Ontario-based EllisDon, one of North America's largest construction companies. Therefore, the theories we cover should be considered in light of the variety of organizations you may encounter. We try to point out instances where the theory may be less applicable (or especially applicable) to a particular type of organization. For the most part, however, you should expect that the discussions in this textbook apply across the broad spectrum of organizations. Throughout, we highlight applications to a variety of organizations in our feature *OB in the Workplace*.

Do you know what a "typical" organization looks like?

OB Is for Everyone

It might seem natural to think that the study of OB is for leaders and managers of organizations. However, many organizations also have informal leadership opportunities. In organizations in which employees are asked to share in a greater number of decision-making processes rather than simply follow orders, the roles of managers and employees are becoming blurred.[4] For instance, employees in some retail operations are asked to make decisions about when to accept returned items, rather than defer the decision to the manager.

OB is not just for managers and employees. Entrepreneurs and self-employed individuals may not act as managers, but they certainly interact with other individuals and organizations as part of their work. OB applies equally well to all situations in which you interact with others: on the basketball court, at the grocery store, in school, or in church. In fact, OB is relevant anywhere that people come together and share experiences, work on goals, or meet to solve problems. To help you understand these broader connections, you will find a feature called *OB in the Street* throughout the textbook.

The Importance of Interpersonal Skills

Until the late 1980s, business school curricula emphasized the technical aspects of management, focusing on economics, accounting, finance, and quantitative techniques. Course work in human behaviour and people skills received minimal attention. Over the past three decades, however, business school faculty have come to realize the role that understanding human behaviour plays in determining organizational effectiveness, and required courses on people skills have been added to many curricula. Employers are looking for people skills as well. In a 2009 survey of Canadian chief financial officers, 34 percent said that a job applicant's people skills were more important than industry experience and software proficiency. Five years earlier, only 1 percent cared about interpersonal skills.[5]

Organizations that invest in the development of employees' interpersonal skills are more likely to attract and keep high-performers. Regardless of labour market conditions, outstanding employees are always in short supply.[6] Companies known as good places to work—such as Toronto-based Royal Bank of Canada, Fredericton-based NB Power, Halifax-based IMP Group, Winnipeg-based Ceridian, Regina-based SaskTel, Calgary-based Agrium, and Vancouver-based Ledcor[7]—have been found to generate superior financial performance.[8] A recent survey of hundreds of workplaces, and over 200 000 respondents, showed that the social relationships among co-workers and supervisors were strongly related to overall job satisfaction. Positive social relationships also were associated with lower stress at work and lower intentions to quit.[9] So, having managers with good interpersonal skills is likely to make the workplace more pleasant, which in turn makes it easier to hire and keep qualified people. Creating a pleasant workplace appears to make good economic sense, particularly because wages and benefits are not the main reasons people like their jobs or stay with an employer.[10]

Succeeding in the workplace takes good people skills. This textbook has been written to help managers and employees develop those people skills. To learn more about the kinds of people skills needed in the workplace, see the *Working with Others Exercise* on page 28. To find out about the strengths and weaknesses in your people skills, see the *Learning About Yourself Exercise* on page 27.

SELF-ASSESSMENT LIBRARY

LEARNING ABOUT YOURSELF

1. The Competing Values Framework: Identifying Your Interpersonal Skills
(page 27)

Today's Challenges in the Canadian Workplace

2 What challenges do managers and employees face in today's workplace?

Shortly after Grail Noble of Yellow House Events hired her first Gen-Y full-time employee, she realized that she needed to know more about the work habits of this younger generation.[11] She worked carefully with her early hires to learn about their work preferences. What she found was that Gen Ys like to be empowered, and they want to work in entrepreneurial cultures. She opened her financial records to the employees, so that they could really understand the business. "I think business owners who try to shield employees from both good and bad news are making a mistake," she says.

That openness helped Noble when times got tough. During late 2008 and all of 2009, companies stopped holding events because of the recession. Yellow House's revenue fell by 50 percent. She asked her staff a simple question: "What are we going to do to overcome this?"

Noble is committed to being a good employer, surrounded by a good team. Will keeping them involved with the numbers be enough? What factors affect good teamwork? How can Noble motivate her employees to perform well in their jobs?

OB considers that organizations are made up of individuals, groups, and the entire organizational structure. Each of these units represents a different level within an organization, moving from the smallest unit, the individual, to the largest, the entire organization. Each level contributes to the variety of activities that occur in today's workplace. Exhibit 1-1 presents the three levels of analysis we consider in this textbook, and shows that as we move from the individual level to the organization systems level, we deepen our understanding of behaviour in organizations. The three basic levels are like building blocks: Each level is constructed upon the previous level. Group concepts are built on the foundation we lay out on individual behaviour. We then overlay structural constraints on the individual and group in order to arrive at OB.

EXHIBIT 1-1 Basic OB Model

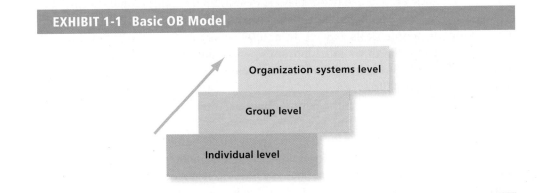

When we look at the different levels in an organization, we recognize that each has challenges that can affect how the levels above and/or below might operate. We consider the challenges at the individual, group, and organizational levels.

Challenges at the Individual Level

At the individual level, managers and employees need to learn how to work with people who may be different from themselves on a variety of dimensions, including personality, perception, values, and attitudes. Individuals also have different levels of job satisfaction and motivation, and these affect how managers manage employees. Perhaps the greatest issue facing individuals (and organizations) is how to behave ethically in the face of competing demands from different stakeholders.

Individual Differences

People enter groups and organizations with certain characteristics that influence their behaviour, the more obvious of these being personality characteristics, perception, values, and attitudes. These characteristics are essentially intact when an individual joins an organization, and for the most part, there is little that those in the organization can do to alter them. Yet they have a very real impact on behaviour. In this light, we look at perception, personality, values, and attitudes, and their impact on individual behaviour in Chapters 2 and 3.

Job Satisfaction

Employees are increasingly demanding **job satisfaction**, a positive feeling about your job resulting from an evaluation of its characteristics. As we discuss in Chapter 3, overall job satisfaction in the Canadian workplace is somewhat low.[12] The belief that satisfied employees are more productive than dissatisfied employees has been a basic assumption among managers for years, though only now has research begun to support it.[13] Ample evidence shows employees who are more satisfied and treated fairly are more willing to engage in the above-and-beyond organizational citizenship

Microsoft Canada was named Canada's Best Workplace (large employers) in 2011. HR director Carolyn Buccongello, referring to the 2011 annual company-wide survey, said that 95 percent of Microsoft Canada employees reported that they are proud to work there. Results like this indicate strong job satisfaction. Pictured here are president Eric Gales (far right) and several employees volunteering at a local food bank. The company empowers employees to spend up to 40 hours of work time per year contributing to their communities.[14]

job satisfaction A positive feeling about one's job resulting from an evaluation of its characteristics.

behaviour we've said is so vital in the contemporary business environment.[15] Researchers with strong humanistic values argue that satisfaction is a legitimate objective of an organization. They believe that organizations should be responsible for providing employees with jobs that are challenging and intrinsically rewarding.

Job satisfaction is also of concern because it is negatively related to absenteeism and turnover, which cost organizations considerable amounts of money annually.

Does job satisfaction really make a difference?

Motivation

A recent survey of Canadian employees found that only 24 percent agreed that to a great extent they received recognition for work well done.[16] To address this concern, Chapter 4 discusses the importance of rewards in motivating employees, while Chapter 5 describes specific rewards that can be used in the workplace. You may find the discussion of motivation and rewards particularly interesting in *Case Incident—How a UPS Manager Cut Turnover* on page 29, where a manager faces the challenge of motivating different types of employees to reduce turnover.

Empowerment

At the same time that managers are being held responsible for employee satisfaction and happiness, they are also being asked to share more of their power with employees. If you read any popular business periodical nowadays, you will find that managers are referred to as *coaches, advisers, sponsors,* or *facilitators,* rather than *bosses.*[17] In many organizations, employees have become *associates* or *teammates.*[18] The roles of managers and employees have become blurred as the responsibilities of employees have grown. Decision making is being pushed down to the operating level, where employees solve work-related problems and are being given the freedom to make choices about schedules and procedures.

Are you ready to take on more responsibility at work?

What's going on is that managers are empowering employees. **Empowerment** means managers are giving employees more responsibility for what they do. In the process, managers are learning how to give up control, and employees are learning how to take responsibility for their work and make appropriate decisions. The roles for both managers and employees are changing, often without much guidance on how to perform the new functions. *OB in the Workplace* looks at how Habañero empowers its employees.

OB in the WORKPLACE
Habañero's Employees Help Set Policies

What do empowered employees do? Steven Fitzgerald, president of Vancouver-based IT firm Habañero Consulting Group, believes in empowering his employees.[19] Employees share human resource duties by mentoring each other, encouraging career development, and making sure everyone understands their jobs.

Fitzgerald knows that an "all work and no play" ethic is not a good way to define the business. As a result, he gives his employees autonomy, telling them they will be "judged on the quality of their work—not the number of hours they put in." Habañero allows telecommuting and flextime, and does not track sick days.

empowerment Giving employees responsibility for what they do.

In 2006, Habañero started to grow too quickly, and some of the new hires did not fit into the company culture. Employees complained about the new hires. Together, Fitzgerald and his employees put together a new recruiting process. Now, up to 12 employees interview job candidates, explaining the culture and what the job is like. This new interview process has led to employees who better fit with the organization, and a turnover rate of 1.5 percent in 2010.

More recently, Fitzgerald's employees noted that Habañero's invoicing model, which was based on a target number of billable hours per month, contradicted the company's commitment to work-life balance. The employees worked with management to develop a new model of project-based billing that was more consistent with a truly flexible workplace, while still maintaining profitability. Fitzgerald is pleased with how empowerment has worked for Habañero. He says that knowing what employees want and acting on that knowledge can help you "attract people who are engaged for the right reasons."

Throughout this textbook, you will find references to empowerment. We discuss it in terms of power in Chapter 8, and how leaders contribute to empowerment in Chapter 11.

Behaving Ethically

In an organizational world characterized by cutbacks, expectations of increasing productivity, and tough competition, it's not surprising that many employees feel pressured to cut corners, break rules, and engage in other forms of questionable practices. Increasingly they face **ethical dilemmas** and **ethical choices**, in which they are required to identify right and wrong conduct. Should they "blow the whistle" if they uncover illegal activities taking place in their company? Do they follow orders with which they don't personally agree? Should they give an inflated performance evaluation to an employee they like, knowing that such an evaluation could save that employee's job? Do they allow themselves to "play politics" to advance their careers?

Ethics starts at the individual level. **Ethics** is the study of moral values or principles that guide our behaviour and inform us whether actions are right or wrong. Ethical principles help us "do the right thing," such as not padding expense reports, or not phoning in sick to attend the opening of *Harry Potter and the Deathly Hallows—Part 2*.

As we show in Chapter 12, the study of ethics does not come with black and white answers. This chapter's *Ethical Dilemma Exercise* on page 29 asks you to consider whether it is ever appropriate to lie in a business situation. As you may conclude when doing that exercise, many factors need to be considered in determining the ethical thing to do. Those individuals who strive hard to create their own set of ethical values will more often do the right thing. Companies that promote a strong ethical mission, encourage employees to behave with integrity, and provide strong ethical leadership can influence employee decisions to behave ethically.[20]

Throughout this textbook, you will find references to ethical and unethical behaviour. The *Focus on Ethics* feature will provide you with thought-provoking illustrations of how ethics is treated in various organizations.

Challenges at the Group Level

The behaviour of people in a group is more than the sum total of all the individuals acting in their own way. People's behaviour when they are in a group differs from their behaviour when they are alone. Therefore, the next step in developing an understanding of OB is the study of group behaviour.

Chapter 6 lays the foundation for an understanding of the dynamics of group and team behaviour. That chapter discusses how individuals are influenced by the patterns

ethical dilemmas and **ethical choices** Situations in which individuals are required to define right and wrong conduct.

ethics The study of moral values or principles that guide our behaviour and inform us whether actions are right or wrong.

of behaviour they are expected to exhibit, what the team considers to be acceptable standards of behaviour, and how to make teams more effective.

Chapters 7, 8, and 9 examine some of the more complex issues of interaction, including communication, power and politics, and conflict and negotiation. These chapters give you an opportunity to think about how communication processes sometimes become complicated because of office politicking and interpersonal and group conflict.

Few people work entirely alone, and some organizations make widespread use of teams. Therefore, most individuals interact with others during the workday. This can lead to a need for greater interpersonal skills. The workplace is also made up of people from a variety of different backgrounds. Thus, learning how to work with people from different cultures has become more important. We discuss some of the challenges that occur at the group level below.

> What people-related challenges have you noticed in the workplace?

Working with Others

Much of the success in any job involves developing good interpersonal, or "people," skills. In fact, The Conference Board of Canada identified the skills that form the foundation for a high-quality workforce in today's workplace, including the ability to communicate, think, and solve problems, learn continuously, and work with others. The ability to demonstrate positive attitudes and behaviours and take responsibility for one's actions are also key skills.[21] Because many people will work in small and medium-sized firms in the future, Human Resources and Skills Development Canada has noted that additional important skills are team building and priority management.[22]

In Canada's increasingly competitive and demanding workplace, neither managers nor employees can succeed on their technical skills alone. To learn more about

Bombardier Aerospace is a Quebec-based world leader in aircraft manufacturing and was named one of Canada's best diversity employers in 2011 by the *Globe and Mail*. Elisabeth Bussé, director of leadership development and talent management, says, "Increasing diversity is a business strategy: We want our employees to be representative of the community in which we do business." Bombardier was selected for a number of initiatives, including "Women in Leadership." Companies are judged on their diversity and inclusiveness programs for five major employee groups: women; members of visible minorities; people with disabilities; Aboriginal peoples; and lesbian, gay, bisexual, and transgendered/transsexual people.[23]

the interpersonal skills needed in today's workplace, read *From Concepts to Skills* on pages 31–34.

Workforce Diversity

The ability to adapt to many different people is one of the most important and broad-based challenges facing organizations. The term we use to describe this challenge is *workforce diversity*. **Workforce diversity** acknowledges a workforce of women and men; a variety of racial and ethnic groups; individuals with a variety of physical or psychological abilities; and people who differ in age and sexual orientation. We discuss workforce diversity issues in Chapter 3.

One of the challenges in Canadian workplaces is the mix of generations—members of the Elder, Baby Boomer, Generation X, Generation Y, and Millennial groups work side by side. Due to their very different life experiences, they bring to the workplace different values and different expectations.

We used to assume that people in organizations who differed from the stereotypical employee would somehow simply fit in. We now recognize that employees don't set aside their cultural values and lifestyle preferences when they go to work. The challenge for organizations, therefore, is to accommodate diverse groups of people by addressing their different lifestyles, family needs, and work styles.[24] However, what motivates one person may not motivate another. One person may like a straightforward and open style of communication that another finds uncomfortable and threatening. To work effectively with different people, you will need to understand their culture and how it has shaped them, and learn to adapt your interaction style.

> Why should you care about understanding other people?

The *Focus on Diversity* feature found throughout this textbook highlights diversity issues that arise in organizations. Our first example looks at ways that Regina-based SGI values the diversity of its employees.

FOCUS ON DIVERSITY

SGI: Top Diversity Employer

How does an organization accommodate its diverse employees? Regina-based Saskatchewan Government Insurance (SGI) must have some clue.[25] The company was named one of Canada's top diversity employers in 2011. Its workforce demonstrates SGI's commitment to diversity: 10 percent of employees are Aboriginal, 5 percent are visible minorities, and 7.5 percent have a disability.

SGI has developed a number of programs to support its workforce. The Aboriginal Advisory Network provides an opportunity for First Nation employees to talk about their own issues and also get career counselling. As the company's website notes, the purpose of the network is "to increase the understanding and appreciation of Aboriginal culture and issues."

The company also hosts a diversity celebration each year with "performances from different cultural groups—from Greek traditional dancing to First Nation dancing." This helps employees learn about each other's heritages.

For its 2009 brokers' calendar, SGI encouraged Canadian artists to submit works of art that reflect the different cultural perspectives found in Canada. Such works might reflect, for instance, "an ethnic glimpse of Oktoberfest in Kitchener, a powwow in Saskatoon."

SGI strives to have a workforce that is as diverse as its customers—a goal the company finds makes good business sense.

workforce diversity The mix of people in organizations in terms of gender, race, ethnicity, disability, sexual orientation, age, and demographic characteristics such as education and socio-economic status.

Challenges at the Organizational Level

OB becomes more complex when we move to the organizational level of analysis. Just as groups are not just the sum of individuals, organizations are not the sum of individuals and groups. There are many more interacting factors that place constraints on individual and group behaviour. In Chapter 10, we look at organizational culture, which is generally considered the glue that holds organizations together. In Chapter 11, we consider how leadership and management affect employee behaviour. In Chapter 12, we discuss decision making and creativity, and then look at the issues of ethics and corporate social responsibility.

The design of an organization has a big impact on how effective an organization is, and we discuss organizational design in Chapter 13. If the organization is not effective, change may be in order, a topic we consider in Chapter 14. As we have noted already, and as will become clear throughout this textbook, change has become a key issue for organizations.

Canadian businesses face many challenges today. The structure of the workplace is changing. The need to develop effective, committed employees is critical. Meanwhile, Canadian businesses face greater competition because of the global economy. Many companies have expanded their operations overseas, which means they have to learn how to manage people from different cultures.

Improving Customer Service

American Express recently turned Joan Weinbel's worst nightmare into a non-event. It was 10:00 p.m. Joan was home, packing for a week-long trip, when she suddenly realized she had left her AmEx Gold card at a restaurant 50 kilometres away earlier in the evening. She had a flight to catch at 7:30 the next morning, and she wanted her card for the trip. She called American Express. The phone was quickly answered by a courteous and helpful AmEx customer service representative who told Ms Weinbel not to worry. He asked her a few questions and told her "Help is on the way." To say Joan was flabbergasted when her doorbell rang at 11:45 p.m. is an understatement—it was less than two hours after her call. At the door was a courier with a new card. How the company was able to produce the card and get it to her so quickly still puzzles Joan, but she said the experience made her a customer for life.

Today, the majority of employees in developed countries work in service jobs, including 78 percent in Canada.[26] In the United States, 80 percent work in service industries. In Australia, the United Kingdom, Germany, and Japan, the percentages are 73, 69, 68, and 65, respectively. Service jobs include technical support representatives, fast-food counter workers, sales clerks, waiters and waitresses, nurses, automobile repair technicians, consultants, credit representatives, financial planners, and flight attendants. The common characteristic of these jobs is substantial interaction with an organization's customers.

Many an organization has failed because its employees failed to please customers. Management needs to create a customer-responsive culture. OB can provide considerable guidance in helping managers create such cultures—in which employees are friendly and courteous, accessible, knowledgeable, prompt in responding to customer needs, and willing to do what's necessary to please the customer.[27]

Stimulating Innovation and Change

Today's successful organizations must foster innovation and master the art of change, or they will become candidates for extinction, like Eatons and Canadian Airlines. Victory will go to the organizations that maintain their flexibility, continually improve their quality, and beat their competition to the marketplace with a constant stream of innovative products and services. Domino's single-handedly brought on the demise

Richard Branson, CEO of Virgin Group, thinks that "the customer is only right sometimes" more accurately reflects how customers should be treated. Instead, he believes that by recognizing the value of employees, who are the ambassadors of the organization, they will give great customer service.

of small pizza parlours whose managers thought they could continue doing what they had been doing for years. Domino's started out simply in 1965, and continually innovated as the pizza market became more demanding. In 2010, it overhauled the crust, the sauce, and the toppings because Domino's had come in last in pizza taste tests. Amazon.ca is putting a lot of independent bookstores out of business as it proves you can successfully sell books (and most anything else) from a website. After years of lacklustre performance, Boeing realized it needed to change its business model. The result was its 787 Dreamliner and a return to being the world's largest airplane manufacturer.

An organization's employees can be the impetus for innovation and change, or they can be a major stumbling block. The challenge for managers is to stimulate their employees' creativity and tolerance for change. The field of OB provides a wealth of ideas and techniques to aid in realizing these goals.

The Use of Temporary (Contingent) Employees

One of the more comprehensive changes taking place in organizations is the addition of temporary, or contingent, employees. Downsizing has eliminated millions of "permanent" jobs, and the number of openings for nonpermanent workers has increased. In 2009, temporary work was responsible for 12.5 percent of paid employment, down from its peak of 13.2 percent in 2005.[28] Eighteen percent of employees were working part-time in June 2011.[29] These include part-timers, on-call workers, short-term hires, temps, day labourers, independent contractors, and leased workers.

Some contingent employees prefer the freedom of a temporary status that permits them to attend school, care for their children, or have the flexibility to travel or pursue other interests. For instance, 35 percent of those working part-time in June 2011 were between the ages of 15 and 24.[30] But many others would prefer to have full-time work if it were available. Because contingent employees lack the security and stability that permanent employees have, they don't always identify with the organization or display the commitment of other employees. Temporary workers typically lack pension plans and have few or no extended health care benefits, such as dental care, prescription plans, and vision care. They are also paid less. For instance, in 2009, temporary employees earned 14 percent less and seasonal and casual employees earned 34 percent less than those who held permanent jobs.[31] Organizations face the challenge of motivating employees who do not feel as connected to the organization as do full-time employees.

Improving Quality and Productivity

Increased competition is forcing managers to reduce costs and, at the same time, improve the quality of the products and services their organization offers, as well as productivity.

An organization or group is productive if it achieves its goals by transferring inputs (employee labour, materials used to produce goods) to outputs (finished goods or services) at the lowest cost. **Productivity** implies a concern for both **effectiveness** and **efficiency**. A hospital is *effective* when it successfully meets the needs of its clientele. It is efficient when it can do so at a low cost. If a hospital manages to achieve higher output from its present staff—by reducing the average number of days a patient is confined to a bed, or by increasing the number of staff-patient contacts per day—we say that the hospital has gained productive *efficiency*. Similarly, a student team is effective when it puts together a group project that gets a high mark. It is efficient when all the members manage their time appropriately and are not at each other's throats. Popular measures of organizational efficiency include return on investment, profit per dollar of sales, and output per hour of labour.

As you study OB, you will begin to understand those factors that influence the effectiveness and efficiency of individuals, groups, and the overall organization.

productivity A performance measure including effectiveness and efficiency.

effectiveness The achievement of goals.

efficiency The ratio of effective work output to the input required to produce the work.

When service organizations assess their effectiveness, they must include customer needs and requirements. Why? Because a clear chain of cause and effect runs from employee attitudes and behaviour to customer attitudes and behaviour to a service organization's productivity.[32] Sears has carefully documented this chain.[33] The company's management found that a 5 percent improvement in employee attitudes leads to a 1.3 percent increase in customer satisfaction, which in turn translates into a 0.5 percent improvement in revenue growth. By training employees to improve the employee-customer interaction, Sears was able to improve customer satisfaction by 4 percent over a 12-month period, generating an estimated $200 million in additional revenues.

Developing Effective Employees

Absenteeism, the failure to report to work, is a huge cost and disruption to employers. About 8 percent of full-time employees in Canada miss work in any given week for personal reasons (including own illness or disability or family responsibilities). This number is up from 6.3 percent in 2000. The average employee missed 8 days of work in 2000, compared with 9.1 days in 2010, which means that about 100 million work days were lost in 2010 due to absenteeism.[34] In the federal public sector, the numbers are even higher: employees averaged 12.1 days off in 2000–1, which rose to an average of 16.9 days in 2008–9.[35]

It's obviously difficult for an organization to operate smoothly and attain its objectives if employees fail to report to their jobs. The workflow is disrupted, and important decisions may be delayed, thus impacting an organization's effectiveness and efficiency.

Turnover is voluntary or involuntary permanent withdrawal from an organization. A high rate of turnover of employees increases recruiting, selection, and training costs. Moreover, a high rate of turnover of knowledgeable and experienced personnel can disrupt the efficient running of an organization. Turnover can create an opportunity to replace an underperforming individual with someone who has higher skills or motivation, open up increased opportunities for promotions, and bring new and fresh ideas to the organization.[36] However, turnover often costs the organization people it does not want to lose. So when turnover is excessive, or when it involves valuable performers, it can be a disruptive factor that hinders the organization's effectiveness. This chapter's *Case Incident—"Data Will Set You Free"* on page 30 explores some of the ways companies use data to manage turnover.

One of the major challenges facing organizations today is how to engage employees effectively so that they are committed to the organization and are not engaging in absenteeism and turnover. We use the term **organizational citizenship behaviour (OCB)** to describe discretionary behaviour that is not part of an employee's formal job requirements, but that nevertheless promotes the effective functioning of the organization.[37] Recent research has also looked at expanding the work on OCB to team behaviour.[38]

Successful organizations need employees who will engage in "good citizenship" behaviours, providing performance that is beyond expectations, such as making constructive statements about their work group and the organization, helping others on their team, volunteering for extra job activities, avoiding unnecessary conflicts, showing care for organizational property, respecting the spirit as well as the letter of rules and regulations, and gracefully tolerating the occasional work-related impositions and nuisances.

Toronto-based BBDO Canada, one of the country's leading creative agencies, encourages an entrepreneurial spirit as a way of inspiring organizational citizenship behaviour. The agency's chairman and CEO, Gerry Frascione, notes that a team leader on the Campbell Soup account overheard a Campbell's representative musing about a program that would launch Campbell Soup ads when the temperature dipped. "Instead of waiting to get approvals, she acted very entrepreneurially and took it

absenteeism The failure to report to work.

turnover Voluntary or involuntary permanent withdrawal from an organization.

organizational citizenship behaviour (OCB) Discretionary behaviour that is not part of an employee's formal job requirements, but that nevertheless promotes the effective functioning of the organization.

upon herself and made the whole thing happen in one week," says Frascione. "She went back to the client, analyzed the situation, fleshed out the opportunity, came up with an integrated communication plan, came up with a budget, and it was all done within five days."[39]

Organizations want and need employees who will do those things that are not in any job description. And the evidence indicates that organizations that have such employees outperform those that don't.[40] As a result, OB is concerned with organizational citizenship behaviour.

Helping Employees with Work-Life Balance

Employees are increasingly complaining that the line between work and nonwork time has become blurred, creating personal conflicts and stress.[41] At the same time, however, today's workplace presents opportunities for workers to create and structure their roles.

How do work-life conflicts come about? First, the creation of global organizations means the world never sleeps. At any time on any day, thousands of General Electric employees are working somewhere. The need to consult with colleagues or customers 8 or 10 time zones away means that many employees of global firms are "on call" 24 hours a day. Second, communication technology allows employees to do their work at home, in their cars, or on the ski slopes at Whistler—but it also means many feel like they never really get away from the office. Third, organizations are asking employees to be available in off-work hours via cellphones and email.

Employees are increasingly recognizing that work affects personal lives, and they are not happy about it. Recent studies suggest that employees want jobs that give them flexibility in their work schedules so they can better manage work-life conflicts.[42] In fact, balancing work and life demands now surpasses job security as an employee priority.[43] The next generation of employees is likely to show similar concerns.[44] Most college and university students say that attaining a balance between personal life and work is a primary career goal; they want "a life" as well as a job. Organizations that don't help their people achieve work-life balance will find it increasingly difficult to attract and retain the most capable and motivated employees.

Creating a Positive Work Environment

Although competitive pressures on most organizations are stronger than ever, some organizations are trying to realize a competitive advantage by encouraging a positive work environment. For example, Jeff Immelt and Jim McNerney, both disciples of Jack Welch (former CEO of GE), have tried to maintain high performance expectations (a characteristic of GE's culture) while also encouraging a positive work environment in their organizations (GE and Boeing, respectively). "In this time of turmoil and cynicism about business, you need to be passionate, positive leaders," Immelt recently told his top managers.[45]

A real growth area in OB research has been **positive organizational scholarship** (also called *positive organizational behaviour*), which studies how organizations develop human strengths, foster vitality and resilience, and unlock potential. Researchers in this area argue that too much of OB research and management practice has been targeted toward identifying what is wrong with organizations and their employees. In response, they try to study what is *good* about organizations.[46] Some key independent variables in positive OB research are engagement, hope, optimism, and resilience in the face of strain.

Positive organizational scholars have studied a concept called "reflected best-self"— asking employees to think about situations in which they were at their "personal best" to understand how to exploit their strengths. The idea is that we all have things at which we are unusually good, yet too often we focus on addressing our limitations and too rarely think about how to exploit our strengths.[47]

positive organizational scholarship An area of OB research that concerns how organizations develop human strength, foster vitality and resilience, and unlock potential.

Dallas, Texas-based Pizza Hut has responded to globalization by expanding its restaurants and delivery services worldwide. The company considers mainland China to be the primary market for new restaurant development because of the country's enormous growth potential. Currently, Pizza Hut is the number one casual dining brand in mainland China, with 531 Pizza Hut Casual Dining restaurants in over 130 cities and an additional 120 Pizza Hut Home Service delivery units.[48]

Although positive organizational scholarship does not deny the negative (such as critical feedback), it does challenge researchers to look at OB through a new lens and pushes organizations to think about how to use their employees' strengths rather than dwell on their limitations.

Responding to Globalization

In recent years, businesses in Canada have faced tough competition from those in the United States, Europe, Japan, and China, as well as from other businesses within our borders. To survive, they have had to reduce costs, increase productivity, and improve quality. A number of Canadian companies have found it necessary to merge in order to survive. For instance, Rona, the Boucherville, Quebec-based home improvement store, bought out Lansing, Revy, and Revelstoke in recent years to defend its turf against the Atlanta, Georgia-based Home Depot, with the result that in 2011, it was still holding its own against chief rivals Home Depot and Lowes.[49]

Some employers have outsourced jobs to other countries where labour costs are lower to remain profitable. For instance, Toronto-based Dell Canada's technical service lines are handled by technicians working in India. Toronto-based Wall & Associates, a full-service chartered accounting and management consulting firm, outsources document management to Uganda. Employees in Uganda are willing to work for $1 an hour to sort and record receipts. While these wages might seem low, on average, Ugandans make only $1 a day.

Twenty or 30 years ago, national borders protected most firms from foreign competitive pressures. This is no longer the case. Trading blocs such as the North American Free Trade Agreement (NAFTA) and the European Union (EU) have significantly reduced tariffs and barriers to trade, and North America and Europe no longer have a monopoly on highly skilled labour. The Internet has also enabled companies to become more globally connected, by opening up international sales and by increasing the opportunities to carry on business. Even small firms can bid on projects in different countries and compete with larger firms via the Internet.

As multinational corporations develop operations worldwide, as companies develop joint ventures with foreign partners, and as employees increasingly pursue job opportunities across national borders, managers and employees must become capable of working with people from different cultures. The changing and global competitive environment means that not only individuals but also organizations have to become increasingly flexible, by learning new skills, new ways of thinking, and new ways of doing business.

OB: Making Sense of Behaviour in Organizations

As Grail Noble encouraged her employees to act more like owners of Yellow House Events, it meant that she had to listen to feedback that she did not necessarily like.[50] In one case, the employees complained about one of her largest clients. They found it demotivating to manage the client's events, because of the way the client interacted with them. Noble listened to her employees, reviewed the email exchanges employees and the client had written, and reflected on her own experiences with the client. She decided to fire the client after Yellow House finished the work they had already committed to doing. "That was a very tough decision," she acknowledges. "But my people are my brand and product. At that point, the money wasn't worth their unhappiness." What can Noble learn from organizational behaviour to do an even better job of managing her employees?

3 Isn't organizational behaviour common sense? Or just like psychology?

We have thus far considered how OB can be applied in the workplace. In this next section, we consider the discipline of OB, looking first at the fields of study that have contributed to it. We then discuss the fact that OB is a scientific discipline, with careful research that is conducted to test and evaluate theories.

The Building Blocks of OB

OB emerged as a distinct field in the 1940s in the United States[51] as an applied behavioural science that builds upon contributions from a number of behavioural disciplines, mainly psychology, social psychology, sociology, and anthropology. Psychology's contributions have been mainly at the individual, or micro, level of analysis, while the other three disciplines have contributed to our understanding of macro concepts, such as group processes and organization. Exhibit 1-2 presents an overview of the major contributions to the study of OB.

Psychology

Psychology seeks to measure, explain, and sometimes change the behaviour of humans and other animals. Those who have contributed and continue to add to the knowledge of OB are learning theorists, personality theorists, counselling psychologists, and, most important, industrial and organizational psychologists.

Early industrial and organizational psychologists studied the problems of fatigue, boredom, and other working conditions that could impede efficient work performance. More recently, their contributions have been expanded to include learning, perception, personality, emotions, training, leadership effectiveness, needs and motivational forces, job satisfaction, decision-making processes, performance appraisals, attitude measurement, employee selection techniques, job design, and work stress.

Social Psychology

Social psychology, generally considered a branch of psychology, blends concepts from both psychology and sociology to focus on people's influence on one another. One major study area is *change*—how to implement it and how to reduce barriers to its acceptance. Social psychologists also contribute to measuring, understanding, and

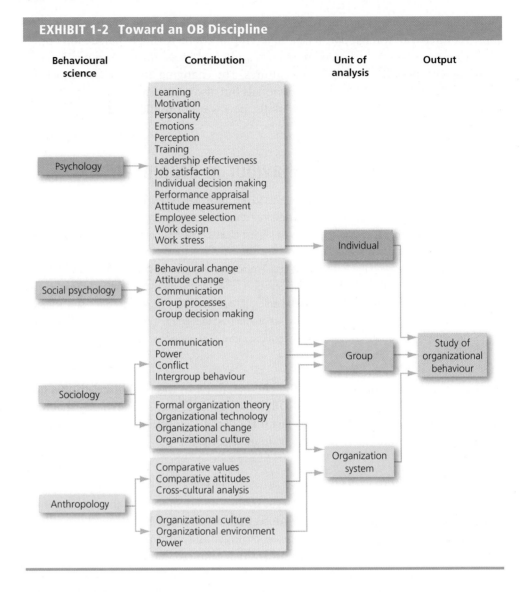

EXHIBIT 1-2 Toward an OB Discipline

changing attitudes; identifying communication patterns; and building trust. Finally, they have made important contributions to our study of group behaviour, power, and conflict.

Sociology

While psychology focuses on the individual, sociology studies people in relation to their social environment or culture. Sociologists have contributed to OB through their study of group behaviour in organizations, particularly formal and complex organizations. Perhaps most important, sociologists have studied organizational culture, formal organizational theory and structure, organizational technology, communication, power, and conflict.

Anthropology

Anthropology is the study of societies to learn about human beings and their activities. Anthropologists' work on cultures and environments has helped us understand differences in fundamental values, attitudes, and behaviour between people in different countries and within different organizations. Much of our current understanding of organizational culture, organizational environments, and differences among national cultures is the result of the work of anthropologists or those using their methodologies.

The Rigour of OB

Whether you want to respond to the challenges of the Canadian workplace, manage well, or guarantee satisfying and rewarding employment for yourself, it pays to understand organizational behaviour. OB provides a systematic approach to the study of behaviour in organizations. Underlying this systematic approach is the belief that behaviour is not random. It stems from and is directed toward some end that the individual believes, rightly or wrongly, is in his or her best interest. OB is even being adopted by other disciplines, as *OB in the Street* shows.

OB in the STREET
Is OB Just for the Workplace?

Can finance learn anything from OB?   It may surprise you to learn that, increasingly, other business disciplines are employing OB concepts.[52] Marketing has the closest overlap with OB. Trying to predict consumer behaviour is not that different from trying to predict employee behaviour. Both require an understanding of the dynamics and underlying causes of human behaviour, and there is a lot of correspondence between the disciplines.

What is perhaps more surprising is the degree to which the so-called hard disciplines are making use of soft OB concepts. Behavioural finance, behavioural accounting, and behavioural economics (also called *economic psychology*) all have grown in importance and interest in the past several years.

On reflection, the use of OB by these disciplines should not be so surprising. Your common sense will tell you that humans are not perfectly rational creatures, and in many cases, our actions don't conform to a rational model of behaviour. Although some elements of irrationality are incorporated into economic thought, finance, accounting, and economics, researchers find it increasingly useful to draw from OB concepts.

For example, investors have a tendency to place more weight on private information (information that only they, or a limited group of people, know) than on public information, even when there is reason to believe that the public information is more accurate. To understand this phenomenon, finance researchers use OB concepts. In addition, behavioural accounting research might study how feedback influences auditors' behaviour, or the functional and dysfunctional implications of earnings warnings on investor behaviour.

The point is that while you take separate courses in various business disciplines, the lines between them are increasingly being blurred as researchers draw from common disciplines to explain behaviour. We think that this is a good thing because it more accurately matches the way managers actually work, think, and behave.

OB Looks at Consistencies

Certainly there are differences among individuals. Placed in similar situations, all people don't act exactly alike. However, there are certain fundamental consistencies underlying the behaviour of most individuals that can be identified and then modified to reflect individual differences.

These fundamental consistencies are very important because they allow predictability. When you get into your car, you make some definite and usually highly accurate predictions about how other people will behave. In North America, for instance, you predict that other drivers will stop at stop signs and red lights, drive on the right side of the road, pass on your left, and not cross the solid double line on mountain roads. Your predictions about the behaviour of people behind the wheels of their cars are almost always correct. Obviously, the rules of driving make predictions about driving behaviour fairly easy.

What may be less obvious is that there are rules (written and unwritten) in almost every setting. Therefore, it can be argued that it's possible to predict behaviour (undoubtedly, not always with 100 percent accuracy) in supermarkets, classrooms, doctors' offices, elevators, and in most structured situations. For instance, do you turn around and face the doors when you get into an elevator? Almost everyone does. Is there a sign inside the elevator that tells you to do this? Probably not! Just as we make predictions about drivers, where there are definite rules of the road, we can make predictions about the behaviour of people in elevators, where there are few written rules. This example supports a major point of this textbook: Behaviour is generally predictable, and the *systematic study* of behaviour is a means to making reasonably accurate predictions.

OB Looks Beyond Common Sense

Each of us is a student of behaviour. Whether or not you have explicitly thought about it before, you have been "reading" people almost all your life, watching their actions and trying to interpret what you see and predict what people might do under different conditions. Unfortunately, the casual or common sense approach to reading others can often lead to erroneous predictions. However, you can improve your predictive ability by supplementing intuition with a more systematic approach.

The systematic approach used in this textbook uncovers important facts and relationships and provides a base from which to make more accurate predictions of behaviour. Underlying this systematic approach is the belief that behaviour is not random. Rather, we can identify certain fundamental consistencies underlying the behaviour of all individuals and modify them to reflect individual differences.

These fundamental consistencies are very important. Why? Because they allow predictability. Behaviour is generally predictable, and the *systematic study* of behaviour is a means to making reasonably accurate predictions. When we use the phrase **systematic study**, we mean looking at relationships, attempting to attribute causes and effects, and basing our conclusions on scientific evidence—that is, on data gathered under controlled conditions and measured and interpreted in a reasonably rigorous manner. Exhibit 1-3 illustrates the common methods researchers use to study topics in OB.

Evidence-based management (EBM) complements systematic study by basing managerial decisions on the best available scientific evidence. We would want doctors to make decisions about patient care based on the latest available evidence, and EBM argues that managers should do the same, becoming more scientific in how they think about management problems. For example, a manager might pose a managerial question, search for the best available evidence, and apply the relevant information to the question or case at hand. You might think it's difficult to argue against this (what manager would say that decisions should not be based on evidence?), but the vast majority of management decisions are still made "on the fly," with little or systematic study of available evidence.[53]

Systematic study and EBM add to **intuition**, or those "gut feelings" about what makes others (and ourselves) "tick." Of course, the things you have come to believe in an unsystematic way are not necessarily incorrect. Jack Welch (former CEO of GE) noted, "The trick, of course, is to know when to go with your gut." If we make all decisions with intuition or gut instinct, we are likely working with incomplete information—like making an investment decision with only half the data.

Relying on intuition is made worse because we tend to overestimate the accuracy of what we think we know. In a recent survey, 86 percent of managers thought their organization was treating their employees well, but only 55 percent of employees thought so.[54] Surveys of human resource managers have also shown many managers hold "common sense" opinions regarding effective management that have been flatly refuted by empirical evidence.

systematic study Looking at relationships, attempting to attribute causes and effects, and drawing conclusions based on scientific evidence.

evidence-based management (EBM) Basing managerial decisions on the best available scientific evidence.

intuition A gut feeling not necessarily supported by research.

EXHIBIT 1-3 Research Methods in OB

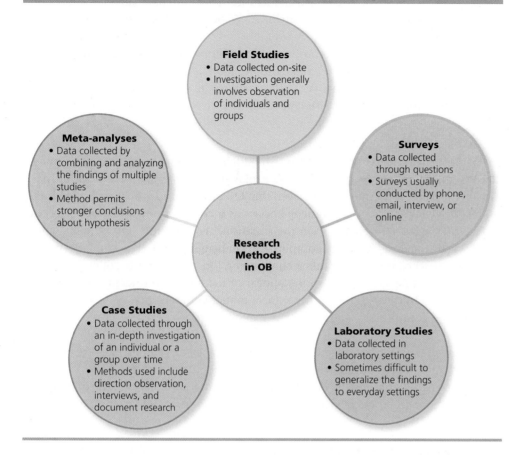

Field Studies
- Data collected on-site
- Investigation generally involves observation of individuals and groups

Meta-analyses
- Data collected by combining and analyzing the findings of multiple studies
- Method permits stronger conclusions about hypothesis

Surveys
- Data collected through questions
- Surveys usually conducted by phone, email, interview, or online

Research Methods in OB

Case Studies
- Data collected through an in-depth investigation of an individual or a group over time
- Methods used include direction observation, interviews, and document research

Laboratory Studies
- Data collected in laboratory settings
- Sometimes difficult to generalize the findings to everyday settings

We find a similar problem in looking to the business and popular media for management wisdom. The business press tends to be dominated by fads. As a writer for the *New Yorker* put it, "Every few years, new companies succeed, and they are scrutinized for the underlying truths they might reveal. But often there is no underlying truth; the companies just happened to be in the right place at the right time."[55] Although we try to avoid it, we might also fall into this trap. It's not that the business press stories are all wrong; it's that without a systematic approach, it's hard to know the truth.

We are not advising that you throw your intuition, or all the business press, out the window. Nor are we arguing that research is always right. Researchers make mistakes, too. What we are advising is to use evidence as much as possible to inform your intuition and experience. That is the promise of OB.

Throughout this textbook, the *Focus on Research* feature will highlight some of the careful studies that form the building blocks of OB. We have also marked major research findings in every chapter with an icon (shown in the margin at right) so that you can easily see what the research says about various concepts we cover.

FOCUS ON RESEARCH

If understanding behaviour were simply common sense, we would not observe many of the problems that occur in the workplace, because managers and employees would know how to behave. Unfortunately, as you will see from examples throughout the textbook, many individuals and managers exhibit less than desirable behaviour in the workplace. With a stronger grounding in OB, you might be able to avoid some of these mistakes. This chapter's *Point/Counterpoint* on page 26 looks at how systematic OB is.

OB Has Few Absolutes

There are few, if any, simple and universal principles that explain OB. In contrast, the physical sciences—chemistry, astronomy, physics—have laws that are consistent and apply in a wide range of situations. They allow scientists to generalize about the pull of gravity or to confidently send astronauts into space to repair satellites. But as one noted behavioural researcher aptly concluded, "God gave all the easy problems to the physicists."

Social scientists study human problems—and human beings are complex. Because people are not alike, our ability to make simple, accurate, and sweeping generalizations is limited. Two people often act very differently in the same situation, and the same person's behaviour changes in different situations.

OB Takes a Contingency Approach

Just because people can behave differently at different times does not mean, of course, that we cannot offer reasonably accurate explanations of human behaviour or make valid predictions. It does mean, however, that OB must consider behaviour within the context in which it occurs—a strategy known as a **contingency approach**. In other words, OB's answers "depend upon the situation." For example, OB scholars would avoid stating that everyone likes complex and challenging work (the general concept). Why? Because not everyone wants a challenging job. A job that is appealing to one person may not be to another, so the appeal of the job is contingent on the person who holds it. OB theories mirror the subject matter with which they deal. People are complex and complicated, and so too must be the theories developed to explain their actions.

Consistent with the contingency approach, *Point/Counterpoint* debates are provided in each chapter. These debates are included to highlight the fact that within OB there are disagreements. Through the *Point/Counterpoint* format, you will gain the opportunity to explore different points of view, discover how diverse perspectives complement and

---

EXHIBIT 1-4

"I'm a social scientist, Michael. That means I can't explain electricity or anything like that, but if you ever want to know about people I'm your man."

Source: Drawing by Handelsman in *The New Yorker*, Copyright © 1986 by the New Yorker Magazine. Reprinted by permission.

contingency approach An approach taken by OB that considers behaviour within the context in which it occurs.

EXHIBIT 1-5 The Fundamentals of OB

- OB considers the multiple levels in an organization: individual, group, and organizational.
- OB is built from the wisdom and research of multiple disciplines, including psychology, sociology, social psychology, and anthropology.
- OB takes a systematic approach to the study of organizational phenomena. It is research-based.
- OB takes a contingency approach to the consideration of organizational phenomena. Recommendations depend on the situation.

oppose each other, and gain insight into some of the debates currently taking place within the OB field.

So in Chapter 5 you will find the argument that praise motivates, followed by the argument that there is little evidence to support the claim that praise is an important motivator. Similarly, in other chapters you will read both sides of debates on such controversial issues as whether leaders can be successful in any environment and whether keeping secrets is desirable. These arguments are meant to demonstrate that OB is a lively field and, like many disciplines, has disagreements over specific findings, methods, and theories. Some of the *Point/Counterpoint* arguments are more charged than others, but each makes some valid points that you should find thought-provoking. The key is to be able to decipher under what conditions each argument may be right or wrong.

OB in Summary

We have discussed the meaning of OB throughout this chapter, and revealed different aspects of what OB covers. The essential points of OB that you should keep in mind as you study this topic are illustrated in Exhibit 1-5.

LESSONS LEARNED

- OB is for everyone.
- OB draws upon a rigorous multidisciplinary research base.

Summary and Implications

1 What is organizational behaviour? Organizational behaviour (OB) is a field of study that investigates the impact that individuals, groups, and structure have on behaviour within an organization. It uses that knowledge to make organizations work more effectively. Specifically, OB focuses on how to improve productivity, reduce both absenteeism and turnover, and increase employee job satisfaction. OB also helps us understand how people can work together more effectively in the workplace.

OB recognizes differences, helps us see the value of workforce diversity, and calls attention to practices that may need to be changed when managing and working in different countries. It can help improve quality and employee productivity by showing managers how to empower their people, as well as how to design and implement change programs. It offers specific insights to improve people skills.

2 What challenges do managers and employees face in today's workplace? OB considers three levels of analysis—the individual, the group, and the organization—which, combined, help us understand behaviour in organizations. Each level has different challenges.

At the individual level, we encounter employees who have different characteristics, and thus we consider how to better understand and make the most of these differences. Because employees have become more cynical about their employers,

SNAPSHOT SUMMARY

1. **Defining Organizational Behaviour**
   What Do We Mean by Organization?
   OB Is for Everyone
   The Importance of Interpersonal Skills
2. **Today's Challenges in the Canadian Workplace**
   Challenges at the Individual Level
   Challenges at the Group Level
   Challenges at the Organizational Level

job satisfaction and motivation have become important issues in today's organizations. Employees are also confronted with the trend toward an empowered workplace. Perhaps the greatest challenge individuals (and organizations) face is how to behave ethically.

At the group level, individuals are increasingly expected to work in teams, which means that they need to do so more effectively. Employees are expected to have good interpersonal skills. The workplace is now made up of people from many different backgrounds, which requires that we have a greater ability to understand those different from ourselves.

At the organizational level, Canadian businesses face many challenges today. They must continuously improve not only productivity but also the quality of their products and services. They must also embrace change in order to remain innovative. They must develop effective employees who are committed to the organization, while recognizing that employees increasingly are demanding a balance between personal life and work. Some organizations are trying to realize a competitive advantage by encouraging a positive work environment. Canadian businesses also face ongoing competition from US businesses, as well as growing competition from the global marketplace. Organizations also have to learn how to be more sensitive to cultural differences, not only because Canada is a multicultural country, but also because competitive companies often develop global alliances or set up plants in foreign countries, where being aware of other cultures becomes a key to success.

3 **Isn't organizational behaviour common sense? Or just like psychology?** OB is built on contributions from a number of behavioural disciplines, including psychology, sociology, social psychology, and anthropology. We all hold generalizations about the behaviour of people. Some of our generalizations may provide valid insights into human behaviour, but many are wrong. If understanding behaviour were simply common sense, we would see fewer problems in the workplace, because managers and employees would know how to behave. OB provides a more systematic approach to improving predictions of behaviour than would be made from common sense alone.

for Review

1. Define organizational behaviour.

2. What is an organization? Is the family unit an organization? Explain.

3. "Behaviour is generally predictable, so there is no need to formally study OB." Do you agree or disagree with this statement? Why?

4. What are some of the challenges and opportunities that managers face in today's workplace?

5. What are the three levels of analysis in our OB model? Are they related? If so, how?

6. Why is job satisfaction an important consideration for OB?

7. What are effectiveness and efficiency, and how are they related to OB?

8. What does it mean to say OB takes a contingency approach in its analysis of behaviour?

for Critical Thinking

1. "OB is for everyone." Build an argument to support this statement.

2. Why do you think the subject of OB might be criticized as being "only common sense," when we would rarely hear such a criticism of a course in physics or statistics? Do you think this criticism of OB is fair?

3. On a scale of 1 to 10 measuring the sophistication of a scientific discipline in predicting phenomena, mathematical physics would probably be a 10. Where do you think OB would fall on the scale? Why?

4. Can empowerment lead to greater job satisfaction?

for You

■ As you journey through this course in OB, bear in mind that the processes we describe are as relevant to you as an individual as they are to organizations, managers, and employees.

■ When you work together with student teams, join a student organization, or volunteer time to a community group, know that your ability to get along with others has an effect on your interactions with the other people in the group and the achievement of the group's goals.

■ If you are aware of how your perceptions and personality affect your interactions with others, you can be more careful in forming your initial impression of others.

■ By knowing how to motivate others who are working with you, how to communicate effectively, and when to negotiate and compromise, you can get along in a variety of situations that are not necessarily work-related.

OB at work

POINT ⬇

COUNTERPOINT ⬇

Find the Quick Fix to OB Issues

Walk into your nearest major bookstore. You will undoubtedly find a large section of books devoted to management and managing human behaviour. A close look at the titles will reveal that there is certainly no shortage of popular books on topics related to OB. To illustrate the point, consider the following book titles that are currently available on the topic of leadership:

- *Killing Cockroaches: And Other Scattered Musings on Leadership* (B&H Publishing, 2009)
- *Leadership Lessons from a Chef: Finding Time to Be Great* (Wiley, 2008)
- *Leadership 101 for White Men: How to Work Successfully with Black Colleagues and Customers* (Morgan James, 2008)
- *High Altitude Leadership: What the World's Most Forbidding Peaks Teach Us About Success* (Jossey-Bass, 2008)
- *A Pirate Captain's Guide to Leadership* (Lighthouse, 2008)
- *The Verbal Judo Way of Leadership* (Looseleaf, 2007)
- *If Harry Potter Ran General Electric: Leadership Wisdom from the World of Wizards* (Currency/Doubleday, 2006)
- *The Leadership Secrets of Santa Claus* (Performance Systems, 2004)
- *Leadership Wisdom from the Monk Who Sold His Ferrari* (Hay House, 2003)

Organizations are always looking for leaders; and managers and manager-wannabes are continually looking for ways to improve their leadership skills. Publishers respond to this demand by offering hundreds of titles that claim to provide insights into the subject of leadership. Books like these can provide people with the secrets to leadership that others know about. Moreover, isn't it better to learn about management and leadership from people in the trenches, as opposed to the latest esoteric musings from the "Ivory Tower"? Many of the most important insights we gain from life are not necessarily the product of careful empirical research studies.

Beware of the Quick Fix!

We all want to find quick and simple solutions to our complex problems. But here is the bad news: For problems related to OB, quick and simple solutions are often wrong because they fail to consider the diversity among organizations, situations, and individuals. As Einstein said, "Everything should be made as simple as possible, but not simpler."

When it comes to understanding people at work, there are plenty of simplistic ideas and books promoted by consultants. Consider three recent bestsellers. *Our Iceberg Is Melting* looks at change through the eyes of a penguin. *Who Moved My Cheese?* is a fable about two mice that is meant to convey the benefits of accepting change. And *Whale Done!* proposes that managers can learn a lot about motivating people from techniques used by whale trainers at Sea World in San Diego. Are the "insights" from these books generalizable to people working in hundreds of different countries, in a thousand different organizations, and doing a million different jobs? It's very unlikely.

Popular books on OB often have cute titles and are fun to read, but they can make the job of managing people seem much simpler than it is. Some are based on the author's opinions rather than substantive research.

OB is a complex subject. Few, if any, simple statements about human behaviour are generalizable to all people in all situations. Should you really try to apply leadership insights you got from a book about Geronimo or Tony Soprano to managing software engineers in the twenty-first century?

Most of the offerings available at your local bookstore tend to be overly simplistic solutions. To the degree that people buy these books and enthusiastically expect them to provide the secrets to effective management, they do a disservice to themselves and those they are trying to manage.

LEARNING ABOUT **YOURSELF** EXERCISE

The Competing Values Framework: Identifying Your Interpersonal Skills

From the list below, identify what you believe to be your strongest skills, and then identify those in which you think your performance is weak. You should identify about 4 strong skills and 4 weak skills.

1. Taking initiative
2. Goal setting
3. Delegating effectively
4. Personal productivity and motivation
5. Motivating others
6. Time and stress management
7. Planning
8. Organizing
9. Controlling
10. Receiving and organizing information
11. Evaluating routine information
12. Responding to routine information
13. Understanding yourself and others
14. Interpersonal communication
15. Developing subordinates
16. Team building
17. Participative decision making
18. Conflict management
19. Living with change
20. Creative thinking
21. Managing change
22. Building and maintaining a power base
23. Negotiating agreement and commitment
24. Negotiating and selling ideas

Scoring Key:

These skills are based on the Competing Values Framework (pages 31–33), and they appear in detail in Exhibit 1-7 on page 32. Below, you will see how the individual skills relate to various managerial roles. Using the skills you determined to be strongest, identify which roles you feel especially prepared for right now. Then, using the skills you determined to be weakest, identify areas in which you might want to gain more skills. You should also use this information to determine whether you are currently more internally or externally focused, or oriented more toward flexibility or control.

Director: 1, 2, 3
Producer: 4, 5, 6
Coordinator: 7, 8, 9
Monitor: 10, 11, 12

Mentor: 13, 14, 15
Facilitator: 16, 17, 18
Innovator: 19, 20, 21
Broker: 22, 23, 24

After reviewing how your strengths and weaknesses relate to the skills that today's managers and leaders need, as illustrated in Exhibit 1-7, you should consider whether you need to develop a broader range of skills.

Source: Created based on material from R. E. Quinn, S. R. Faerman, M. P. Thompson, and M. R. McGrath, *Becoming a Master Manager: A Competency Framework* (New York: Wiley, 1990), Chapter 1.

OB at work

| SELF-ASSESSMENT LIBRARY | LEARNING ABOUT YOURSELF |

More Learning About Yourself Exercises

An additional self-assessment relevant to this chapter appears on MyOBLab (**www.pearsoned.ca/myoblab**).

IV.G.1 How Much Do I Know About OB?

When you complete the additional assessments, consider the following:

1. Am I surprised about my score?

2. Would my friends evaluate me similarly?

BREAKOUT **GROUP** EXERCISES

Form small groups to discuss the following topics, as assigned by your instructor.

1. Consider a group situation in which you have worked. To what extent did the group rely on the technical skills of the group members vs. their interpersonal skills? Which skills seemed most important in helping the group function well?

2. Identify some examples of "worst jobs." What conditions of these jobs made them unpleasant? To what extent were these conditions related to behaviours of individuals?

3. Develop a list of "organizational puzzles," that is, behaviour you have observed in organizations that seemed to make little sense. As the term progresses, see if you can begin to explain these puzzles, using your knowledge of OB.

WORKING WITH **OTHERS** EXERCISE

Interpersonal Skills in the Workplace

This exercise asks you to consider the skills outlined in the Competing Values Framework on pages 31–33 to develop an understanding of managerial expertise. Steps 1–4 can be completed in 15–20 minutes.

1. Using the skills listed in the Learning About Yourself Exercise, identify the 4 skills that you think all managers should have.

2. Identify the 4 skills that you think are least important for managers to have.

3. In groups of 5–7, reach a consensus on the most-needed and least-needed skills identified in steps 1 and 2.

4. Using Exhibit 1-7, determine whether your "ideal" managers would have trouble managing in some dimensions of organizational demands.

5. Your instructor will lead a general discussion of your results.

Lying in Business

Do you think it's ever okay to lie?[56] If you were negotiating for the release of hostages, most people would probably agree that if lying would lead to the hostages' safety, it's okay. What about in business, where the stakes are rarely life or death? Business executives such as Martha Stewart have gone to jail for lying (submitting a false statement to federal investigators). Is misrepresentation or omitting factors okay as long as there is no outright lie?

Consider the negotiation process. A good negotiator never shows all his cards, right? And so omitting certain information is just part of the process. Well, it may surprise you to learn that the law will hold you liable for omitting information if partial disclosure is misleading or if one side has superior information not accessible to the other.

In one case (*Jordan v. Duff and Phelps*), a company (Duff and Phelps) withheld information from an employee

(Jordan) about the impending sale of the company. The problem: Jordan was leaving the organization and therefore sold his shares in the company. Ten days later, when the sale of the company became public, those shares became worth much more. Jordan sued his former employer on the grounds that it should have disclosed this information to him. Duff and Phelps countered that it had never lied to Jordan. The US Court of Appeals argued that in such situations, one party cannot take "opportunistic advantage" of the other. In the eyes of the law, sometimes omitting relevant facts can be as bad as lying.

In a business context, is it ever okay to lie? When? Do you think it's fair to fire an employee who lies, no matter what the nature of the lie? Is withholding information for your own advantage the same as lying? Why or why not?

How a UPS Manager Cut Turnover

When Jennifer Shroeger was promoted to district manager for UPS's operation in Buffalo, New York, she faced a serious problem: Turnover was out of control.[57] Part-time employees—who load, unload, and sort packages and who account for half of Buffalo's workforce—were leaving at the rate of 50 percent a year. Cutting this turnover rate became her highest priority.

UPS relies heavily on part-time employees, some of whom eventually become full-time employees. Most of UPS's current executives began as part-timers while attending university, then moved into full-time positions. UPS has always treated its part-timers well, giving them high pay, flexible work hours, full benefits, and substantial financial aid to go back to school, but these pluses did not seem to be enough to keep employees at UPS in Buffalo.

Shroeger developed a comprehensive plan to reduce turnover. It focused on improving hiring, communication, the workplace, and supervisory training.

Shroeger began by modifying the hiring process to screen out people who essentially wanted full-time jobs. She reasoned that unfulfilled expectations were frustrating

the hires whose preferences were for full-time work. Given that it typically took new part-timers six years to work up to a full-time job, it made sense to try to identify people who actually preferred part-time work.

Next, Shroeger analyzed the large database of information that UPS had on her district's employees. The data led her to the conclusion that she had five distinct groups working for her—differentiated by age and stages in their careers. And these groups had different needs and interests. In response, Shroeger modified the communication style and motivation techniques she used with each employee to reflect the group to which he or she belonged. For instance, Shroeger found that college students are most interested in building skills that they can apply later in their careers. As long as these employees saw that they were learning new skills, they were content to keep working at UPS. So Shroeger began offering them Saturday sessions for career-planning discussions.

To further help new employees adjust, she turned some of her best shift supervisors into trainers who provided specific guidance during new hires' first week. Finally,

CASE INCIDENTS (Continued)

Shroeger expanded training so supervisors had the skills to handle increased empowerment. Because she recognized that her supervisors—most of whom were part-timers themselves—were the ones best equipped to understand the needs of part-time employees, supervisors were taught how to assess difficult management situations, how to communicate in different ways, and how to identify the needs of different people. Supervisors learned to demonstrate interest in their employees as individuals. For instance, they were taught to inquire about employees' hobbies, where they went to school, and the like. Four years later, the attrition rate in Shroeger's district had dropped from 50 percent to 6 percent.

Questions

1. In dollars-and-cents terms, why did Jennifer Shroeger want to reduce turnover?

2. What are the implications from this case for motivating part-time employees?

3. What are the implications from this case for managing in future years when there may be a severe labour shortage?

4. Is it unethical to teach supervisors "to demonstrate interest in their employees as individuals"? Explain.

5. What facts in this case support the argument that OB should be approached from a contingency perspective?

"Data Will Set You Free"

Ford CEO Alan Mulally is known for starting meetings by saying "Data will set you free" and for trying to change Ford's culture to one based on increased accountability, more information sharing, and hard metrics.[58] "You can't manage a secret," he is also fond of saying. It's not yet clear whether Mulally's approach explains why Ford weathered the recession in better shape than its US rivals GM and Chrysler. However, Mulally's approach is a departure for Ford, which was notorious for its self-contained fiefdoms where little information was shared. Some companies have found that managing people according to hard metrics has paid off. Consider Freescale Semiconductor, a computer chip manufacturer based in Austin, Texas.

Freescale has discovered that in order to have the right people at the right time to do the right job, it needs an extensive and elaborate set of metrics to manage 24 000 employees in 30 countries. Of particular concern to Freescale is retention. "There's no greater cost than human capital, especially in the technology industry," says Jignasha Patel, Freescale's director of global talent sourcing and inclusion. "When you've got a tenured employee that decides to walk out the door, it's not just one person leaving, it's that person's knowledge and network and skills."

To manage talent and prevent turnover, Freescale holds line managers accountable for recruiting, hiring, and retaining employees. To do that, managers project their talent needs into the future and reconcile those with projected availabilities. Patel provides line managers with census data that help them make their projections, but ultimately the responsibility is theirs. "What we have done is taken all of our inclusion data, all our metrics, and we've moved the accountability over to the business unit," Patel says.

Patel also provides Freescale managers with benchmark data so they can compare their effectiveness with that of other units. The benchmark data include the number of people hired, turnovers, and promotions—and breakdowns by demographic categories. "There's [a return on investment] for everything we do," says Patel.

Questions

1. Why do you think Freescale focuses on metrics? Why don't more organizations follow its approach?

2. As a manager, would you want to be accountable for the acquisition and retention of employees you supervise? Why or why not?

3. In general, what do you think are the advantages and limitations of such metrics?

4. Freescale focused on metrics for the acquisition and retention of employees. Do you think metrics can be applied to other areas of management, such as employee attitudes, employee performance, or skill development? How might those metrics be measured and managed?

FROM CONCEPTS TO SKILLS

Developing Interpersonal Skills

We note in this chapter that having a broad range of interpersonal skills to draw on makes us more effective organizational participants. So what kinds of interpersonal skills does an individual need in today's workplace? Robert Quinn, Kim Cameron, and their colleagues have developed a model known as the "Competing Values Framework" that can help us identify some of the most useful skills.[59] They note that the range of issues organizations face can be divided along two dimensions: an internal-external and a flexibility-control focus. This idea is illustrated in Exhibit 1-6. The internal-external dimension refers to the extent that organizations focus on one of two directions: either inwardly, toward employee needs and concerns and/or production processes and internal systems; or outwardly, toward such factors as the marketplace, government regulations, and the changing social, environmental, and technological conditions of the future. The flexibility-control dimension refers to the competing demands of organizations to stay focused on doing what has been done in the past vs. being more flexible in orientation and outlook.

Because organizations face the competing demands shown in Exhibit 1-6, it becomes obvious that managers and employees need a

---

EXHIBIT 1-6 Competing Values Framework

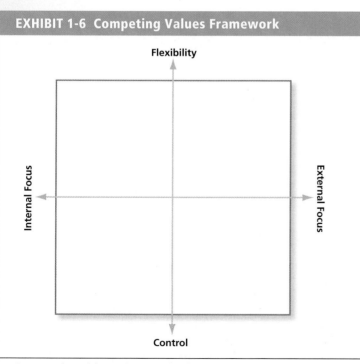

Source: Adapted from *Diagnosing and Changing Organizational Culture: Based on the Competing Values Framework* by K. Cameron and R. E. Quinn. Copyright © 2006, Jossey-Bass. Reproduced with permission of John Wiley & Sons, Inc.

variety of skills to help them function within the various quadrants at different points in time. For instance, the skills needed to operate an efficient assembly-line process are not the same as those needed to scan the external environment or to create opportunities in anticipation of changes in the environment. Quinn and his colleagues use the term *master manager* to indicate that successful managers learn and apply skills that will help them manage across the range of organizational demands; at some times moving toward flexibility, at others moving toward control, sometimes being more internally focused, sometimes being more externally driven.[60]

As organizations increasingly cut their layers, reducing the number of managers while also relying more on the use of teams in the workplace, the skills of the master manager apply as well to the employee. In other words, considering the Competing Values Framework, we can see that both managers and individual employees need to learn new skills and new ways of interpreting their organizational contexts. Continuing to use traditional skills and practices that worked in the past is not an option. The growth in self-employment also indicates a need to develop more interpersonal skills, particularly for anyone who goes on to build a business that involves hiring and managing employees.

Exhibit 1-7 outlines the many skills required of today's manager. It gives you an indication of the complex roles that managers and employees fill in the changing workplace. The skills are organized in terms of four major roles: maintaining flexibility, maintaining control, maintaining an external focus, and maintaining an internal focus. The *Learning About Yourself Exercise* on page 27 helps you identify your own strengths and weak-

EXHIBIT 1-7 Skills for Mastery in the New Workplace

Source: *Beyond Rational Management: Mastering the Paradoxes and Competing Demands of High Performance* by Robert E. Quinn. Copyright © 1991, Jossey-Bass. Reproduced with permission of John Wiley & Sons, Inc.

nesses in these skill areas so that you can have a better sense of how close you are to becoming a successful manager. For instance, on the flexibility side, organizations want to inspire their employees toward high-performance behaviour. Such behaviour includes looking ahead to the future and imagining possible new directions for the organization. To do these things, employees need to think and act like mentors and facilitators. It is also important to have the skills of innovators and brokers. On the control side, organizations need to set clear goals about productivity expectations, and they have to develop and implement systems to carry out the production process. To be effective on the production side, employees need to have the skills of monitors, coordinators, directors, and producers. The *Working with Others Exercise* on page 28 helps you better understand how closely your views on the ideal skills of managers and leaders match the skills needed to be successful in the broad range of activities that managers and leaders encounter.

At this point, you may wonder whether it is possible for people to learn all of the skills necessary to become a master manager. More important, you may wonder whether we can change our individual style, say from more controlling to more flexible. Here is what Peggy Kent, chair, former president, and CEO of Century Mining Corporation (a mid-tier Canadian gold producer), said about how her managerial style changed from controlling to more flexible over time: "I started out being very dictatorial. Everybody in head office reported to me. I had to learn to trust other executives so we could work out problems together."[61] So, while it is probably true that each of us has a preferred style of operating, it is also the case that we can develop new skills if that is something we choose to do.

Practising Skills

As the father of two young children, Marshall Rogers thought that serving on the board of Marysville Daycare would be a good way to stay in touch with those who cared for his children during the day.[62] But he never dreamed that he would become involved in union-management negotiations with daycare-centre employees.

Late one Sunday evening, in his ninth month as president of the daycare centre, Rogers received a phone call from Grace Ng, a union representative of the Provincial Government Employees' Union (PGEU). Ng informed Rogers that the daycare employees would be unionized the following week. Rogers was stunned to hear this news. Early the next morning, he had to present his new marketing plan to senior management at Techtronix Industries, where he was vice-president of marketing. Somehow he made it through the meeting, wondering why he had not been aware of the employees' unhappiness, and how this action would affect his children.

Following his presentation, Rogers received documentation from the Labour Relations Board indicating that the daycare employees had been working to unionize themselves for more than a year. Rogers immediately contacted Xavier Breslin, the board's vice-president, and together they determined that no one on the board had been aware that the daycare workers were unhappy, let alone prepared to join a union.

Hoping that there was some sort of misunderstanding, Rogers called Emma Reynaud, the Marysville supervisor. Reynaud attended most board meetings, but had never mentioned the union-organizing drive. Yet Reynaud now told Rogers that she had actively encouraged the other daycare employees to consider joining the PGEU because the board had not been interested in the employees' concerns, had not increased their wages sufficiently over the past two years, and had not maintained communication channels between the board and the employees.

All of the board members had full-time jobs elsewhere, and many were upper- and middle-level managers in their own companies. They were used to dealing with unhappy employees in their own workplaces, although none had experienced a union-organizing drive. Like Rogers, they had chosen to serve on the board of Marysville to stay informed about the day-to-day events of the centre. They had not really thought of themselves as the centre's employer, although, as board members, they represented all the parents of children enrolled at Marysville. Their main tasks on the daycare-centre board had been setting fees for the children and wages for the daycare employees. The board members usually saw the staff members several times a week, when they picked up their children, yet the unhappiness represented by the union-organizing drive was surprising to all of them. When they met at an emergency board meeting that evening, they tried to evaluate what had gone wrong at Marysville.

Questions

1. If you were either a board member or a parent, how would you know that the employees taking care of your children were unhappy with their jobs?

2. What might you do if you learned about their unhappiness?

3. What might Rogers have done differently as president of the board?

4. In what ways does this case illustrate that knowledge of OB can be applied beyond your own workplace?

Reinforcing Skills

1. Talk to several managers you know and ask them what skills they think are most important in today's workplace. Ask them to specifically consider the use of teams in their workplace, and what skills their team members most need to have but are least likely to have. How might you use this information to develop greater interpersonal skills?

2. Talk to several managers you know and ask them what skills they have found to be most important in doing their jobs. Why did they find these skills most important? What advice would they give a would-be manager about skills worth developing?

CHAPTER 2

Perception, Personality, and Emotions

Can a company win best employer in Canada awards and also be regarded as the worst employer in Canada?

LEARNING OUTCOMES

1. What is perception?
2. What is personality and how does it affect behaviour?
3. Can emotions help or get in the way when we are dealing with others?

almart Canada.[1] Just the thought of the retailer being in Canada upsets some people. There was strong resistance when Walmart first announced it was coming to Canada in 1994, and a belief that the retailer would somehow destroy the fabric of Canadian society. Eighteen years after its arrival, Mississauga, Ontario-based Walmart Canada serves more than 1 million Canadians each day, employs more than 85 000 Canadians in 325 stores across Canada, and is Canada's third-largest employer. The company was ranked as one of Canada's best employers on the Hewitt Associates survey of Canada's Best Employers five times between 2001 and 2007. It has also appeared on KPMG's list of Canada's 25 Most Admired Corporate Cultures, most recently in 2009. It was one of Workplace Institute's winners in 2011 for Best Employers Award for 50-Plus Canadians, which it's won several times previously. In presenting the award, Workplace Institute noted, "Wal-Mart has exceptional hiring and recognition programs and a workplace culture that supports diversity." With all of these positive statements about Walmart Canada, customers are not necessarily convinced of Walmart's greatness. When asked in a 2011 survey how likely they would be to change their shopping habits once Target opens stores in Canada, 57 percent of Walmart shoppers indicated a willingness to shop at Target. Less than 20 percent of Canadian Tire, Shoppers Drug Mart, and Costco customers indicated a willingness to shop at Target. How can the perception of the company be so negative for some individuals?

All of our behaviour is somewhat shaped by our perceptions, personalities, emotions, and experiences. In this chapter, we consider the role that perception plays in affecting the way we see the world and the people around us. We also consider how personality characteristics affect our attitudes toward people and situations. We then consider how emotions shape many of our work-related behaviours.

THE BIG IDEA

Individual differences can have a large impact on how groups and organizations function.

OB IS FOR EVERYONE

- What causes people to have different perceptions of the same situation?

- Can people be mistaken in their perceptions?

- Whom do you tend to blame when someone makes a mistake? Ever wonder why?

- Have you ever misjudged a person? Do you know why?

- Can perception really affect outcomes?

- Are people born with their personalities?

- Do you think it is better to be a Type A or a Type B personality?

- Ever wonder why the grocery clerk is always smiling?

SELF-ASSESSMENT LIBRARY
LEARNING ABOUT YOURSELF

- Gender Role Perceptions
- Machiavellianism
- Narcissism
- Self-Monitoring
- Risk-Taking
- Personality Type
- Feelings
- Emotional Intelligence

Perception

① What is perception?

BLOG IT

Should you hide your emotions?
Is it possible to effectively hide
emotions while working with others?
Should this be a requirement in
the workplace, or should people be
allowed to show emotions freely?

www.obstudentjournals.blogspot.com

Perception is the process by which individuals organize and interpret their impressions to give meaning to their environment. However, what we perceive can be substantially different from objective reality. We often disagree about what is real. As we have seen, Walmart Canada has won many awards, but not every Canadian respects the retailer.

Why is perception important in the study of organizational behaviour (OB)? Simply because people's behaviour is based on their perception of what reality is, not on reality itself. *The world as it is perceived is the world that is behaviourally important.* A 2010 study of political behaviour suggests that once individuals hold particular perceptions, it can be quite difficult to change their minds, even if they are shown contrary evidence.[2]

Factors Influencing Perception

How do we explain that individuals may look at the same thing, yet perceive it differently, and both be right? A number of factors operate to shape and sometimes distort perception. These factors can reside in the *perceiver*; in the object, or *target*, being perceived; or in the context of the *situation* in which the perception is made. Exhibit 2-1 summarizes the factors that influence perception. This chapter's *Working with Others Exercise* on page 76 will help you understand how your perceptions affect your evaluation of others.

What causes people to have different perceptions of the same situation?

The Perceiver

When you ("the perceiver") look at a target and attempt to interpret what you see, that interpretation is heavily influenced by your personal characteristics. Characteristics that affect perception include your attitudes, personality, motives, interests, past experiences, and expectations. For instance, if you expect police officers to be authoritative, young people to be lazy, or individuals holding public office to be corrupt, you may perceive them as such, regardless of their actual traits. A 2010 study found that one's perceptions of others reveals a lot about the person themselves.[3] People with positive perceptions

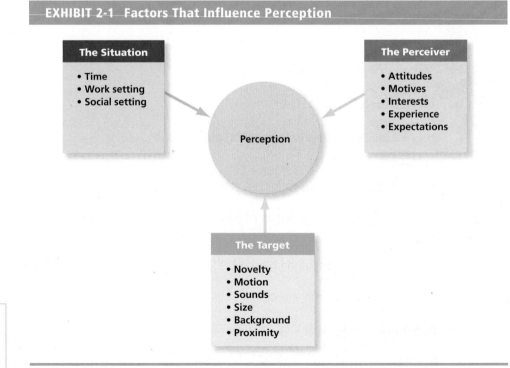

EXHIBIT 2-1 Factors That Influence Perception

The Situation
- Time
- Work setting
- Social setting

The Perceiver
- Attitudes
- Motives
- Interests
- Experience
- Expectations

Perception

The Target
- Novelty
- Motion
- Sounds
- Size
- Background
- Proximity

perception The process by which individuals organize and interpret their impressions in order to give meaning to their environment.

of others tended to describe themselves (and be described by others) as "enthusiastic, happy, kind-hearted, courteous, emotionally stable and capable." Negative perceptions of others were related to increased narcissism and antisocial behaviour.

The Target

A target's characteristics also affect what we perceive. Loud people are more likely to be noticed in a group than are quiet ones. So too are extremely attractive or unattractive individuals. Novelty, motion, sounds, size, and other characteristics of a target shape the way we see it.

Because we don't look at targets in isolation, the relationship of a target to its background influences perception. For instance, we often perceive women, First Nations, Asians, or members of any other group that has clearly distinguishable characteristics as alike in other, unrelated ways as well.

The Situation

The situation or context is also important. The time at which we see an object or event can influence attention, as can location, light, heat, or any number of situational factors. For example, at a nightclub on Saturday night, you may not notice a young guest "dressed to the nines." Yet that same person so attired for your Monday morning management class would certainly catch your attention (and that of the rest of the class). Neither the perceiver nor the target changed between Saturday night and Monday morning, but the situation is different.

Perceptual Errors

Perceiving and interpreting why others do what they do takes time. As a result, we develop techniques to make this task more manageable. These techniques are frequently valuable—they allow us to make accurate perceptions rapidly and provide valid data for making predictions. However, they are not foolproof. They can and do get us into trouble. Some of the errors that distort the perception process are attribution theory, selective perception, halo effect, contrast effects, projection, and stereotyping.

Can people be mistaken in their perceptions?

Attribution Theory

Attribution theory tries to explain the ways we judge people differently, depending on the meaning we attribute to a given behaviour.[4] Basically, the theory suggests that when we observe what seems like atypical behaviour by an individual, we try to make sense of it. We consider whether the individual is responsible for the behaviour (the cause is internal), or whether something outside the individual caused the behaviour (the cause is external). *Internally* caused behaviour is believed to be under the personal control of the individual. *Externally* caused behaviour is believed to result from outside causes; we see the person as having been forced into the behaviour by the situation. For example, if a student is late for class, the instructor might attribute his lateness to partying into the wee hours of the morning and then oversleeping. This would be an internal attribution. But if the instructor assumes a major automobile accident tied up traffic on the student's regular route to school, that is making an external attribution. In trying to determine whether behaviour is internally or externally caused, we rely on three rules about the behaviour: (1) distinctiveness, (2) consensus, and (3) consistency. Let's discuss each of these in turn.

Whom do you tend to blame when someone makes a mistake? Ever wonder why?

attribution theory The theory that when we observe what seems like atypical behaviour by an individual, we attempt to determine whether it is internally or externally caused.

Distinctiveness   **Distinctiveness** refers to whether an individual acts similarly across a variety of situations. Is the student who arrives late for class today also the one who is always goofing off in team meetings, and not answering urgent emails? What we want to know is whether this behaviour is unusual. If it is, we are likely to give it an external attribution. If it's not, we will probably judge the behaviour to be internal.

Consensus   If everyone who is faced with a similar situation responds in the same way, we can say the behaviour shows **consensus**. The tardy student's behaviour would meet this criterion if all students who took the same route to school were also late. From an attribution perspective, if consensus is high, you would probably give an external attribution to the student's tardiness. But if other students who took the same route made it to class on time, you would attribute the cause of lateness for the student in question to an internal cause.

Consistency   Finally, an observer looks for **consistency** in a person's actions. Does the person respond the same way over time? If a student is usually on time for class, being 10 minutes late will be perceived differently from the student who is late almost every class. The more consistent the behaviour, the more we are inclined to attribute it to internal causes.

Exhibit 2-2 summarizes the key elements in attribution theory. It illustrates, for instance, how to evaluate an employee's behaviour on a new task. To do this, you might note that employee Kim Randolph generally performs at about the same level on other related tasks as she does on her current task (low distinctiveness). You see that other employees frequently perform differently—better or worse— than Kim does on that current task (low consensus). Finally, if Kim's performance on this current task is consistent over time (high consistency), you or anyone else who is judging Kim's work is likely to hold her primarily responsible for her task performance (internal attribution).

> Have you ever misjudged a person? Do you know why?

How Attributions Get Distorted   One of the more interesting findings from attribution theory is that there are errors or biases that distort attributions. When we judge the behaviour of other people, we tend to underestimate the influence of external factors

distinctiveness A behavioural rule that considers whether an individual acts similarly across a variety of situations.

consensus A behavioural rule that considers if everyone faced with a similar situation responds in the same way.

consistency A behavioural rule that considers whether the individual has been acting in the same way over time.

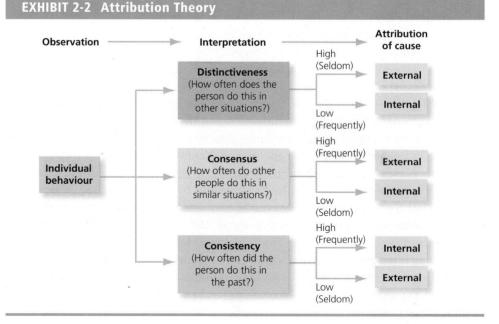

EXHIBIT 2-2 Attribution Theory

EXHIBIT 2-3 Percentage of Individuals Rating Themselves Above Average on Each Attribute

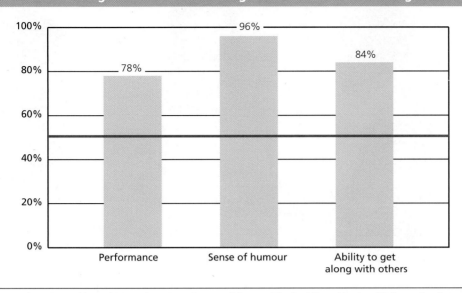

Source: Based on C. Merkle and M. Weber, *True Overconfidence—The Inability of Rational Information Processing to Account for Overconfidence* (March 2009). Available at SSRN: http://ssrn.com/abstract=1373675

and overestimate the influence of internal, or personal, factors.[5] This **fundamental attribution error** can explain why a sales manager attributes the poor performance of his or her sales agents to laziness rather than acknowledging the impact of the innovative product line introduced by a competitor. A 2011 study suggests this same error occurs when we judge leaders to be charismatic, based on limited information.[6] For instance, Steve Jobs, CEO of Apple, gave spellbinding presentations that led him to be considered a charismatic visionary. What the audience does not see is "the ten hours of practice Jobs [committed] to every ten minute pitch," which might make him look less charismatic.[7]

We use **self-serving bias** when we judge ourselves, however. This means that when we are successful, we are more likely to believe it was because of internal factors, such as ability or effort. When we fail, however, we blame external factors, such as luck. In general, people tend to believe that their own behaviour is more positive than the behaviour of those around them. Research suggests, however, that individuals tend to overestimate their own good behaviour, and underestimate the good behaviour of others.[8] Exhibit 2-3 illustrates this point.

Selective Perception

Because it's impossible for us to see everything, any characteristic that makes a person, object, or event stand out will increase the probability that it will be perceived. This tendency explains why you are more likely to notice cars that look like your own. It also explains why some people may be reprimanded by their manager for doing something that goes unnoticed when other employees do it. Since we cannot observe everything going on about us, we engage in **selective perception**.

But how does selectivity work as a shortcut in judging other people? Since we cannot take in all that we observe, we take in bits and pieces. But we do not choose randomly; rather, we select according to our interests, background, experience, and attitudes. Selective perception allows us to speed-read others, but not without the risk of coming to an inaccurate conclusion. Because we see what we want to see, we can draw unwarranted conclusions from an ambiguous situation. Selective perception led the Law Society of BC to discriminate against lawyers who suffer from a mental illness, as *Focus on Diversity* shows.

fundamental attribution error The tendency to underestimate the influence of external factors and overestimate the influence of internal factors when making judgments about the behaviour of others.

self-serving bias The tendency for individuals to attribute their own successes to internal factors while putting the blame for failures on external factors.

selective perception People's selective interpretation of what they see based on their interests, background, experience, and attitudes.

The behaviours that both women and men engage in can affect the perceptions that others have about their ability to become senior managers. A 2010 study found that assertiveness and independence were top qualities to exhibit, and individuals who did not do so were deemed less suited to be CEOs.[9] Those judging the suitability were engaging in selective perception.

FOCUS ON DIVERSITY

Law Society's Question About Mental Health Challenged

Should employees be required to reveal that they have a mental illness? In July 2011, the BC Human Rights Tribunal ruled that the Law Society of BC had discriminated against a lawyer with a mental disability.[10] The lawyer, Peter Mokua Gichuru, was awarded almost $100 000 by the tribunal.

Gichuru's problems started when he began applying for work as an articling student and had to fill out a law society admission program form with the following question: "Have you ever been treated for schizophrenia, paranoia, or a mood disorder described as a major affective illness, bipolar mood disorder, or manic depressive illness?" He answered "yes."

Gichuru had been suffering from bouts of depression for almost five years and was on antidepressants when he was faced with the law society's question. He felt that his articles were delayed because he answered truthfully about his mental health. He also felt that his difficulties in keeping his articling positions and finding others were a result of his answer to the question.

In making its determination, the tribunal found that the law society, while acting in good faith, went beyond what was necessary to determine the fitness of someone to practise law. The law society changed the question related to mental health history on the admission form as a result of Gichuru's appeal. It now reads:

> Based upon your personal history, your current circumstances or any professional opinion or advice you have received, do you have any existing condition that is reasonably likely to impair your ability to function as a lawyer or articled student? If the answer is "yes" to the question above, please provide a general description of the impairment.

Those who answer "yes" to this new question are followed on a case-by-case basis, but the information is kept confidential and is not disclosed to potential employers. While Gichuru still has some concerns about the use of the information, he testified that it "is a dramatic improvement . . . and that on its face it does not discriminate between so-called physical and mental illnesses."

Halo Effect

When we draw a general impression of an individual on the basis of a single characteristic, such as intelligence, likeability, or appearance, a **halo effect** operates.[11] If you are a critic of Prime Minister Stephen Harper, try listing 10 things you admire about him. If you are an admirer, try listing 10 things you dislike about him. No matter which group describes you, odds are that you will not find this an easy exercise! That is the halo effect: Our general views contaminate our specific ones.

The reality of the halo effect was confirmed in a classic study. Subjects were given a list of traits and asked to evaluate the person to whom those traits applied.[12] When traits such as intelligent, skillful, practical, industrious, determined, and warm were used, the person was judged to be wise, humorous, popular, and imaginative. When cold was substituted for warm, a completely different set of perceptions was obtained, though otherwise the list was identical. Clearly, the subjects were allowing a single trait to influence their overall impression of the person being judged.

Contrast Effects

There is an old saying among entertainers: "Never follow an act that has children or animals in it." Why? Audiences love children and animals so much that you will look bad in comparison.

This example demonstrates how **contrast effects** can distort perceptions. We don't evaluate a person in isolation. Our reaction to one person is often influenced by other people we have recently encountered.

In a series of job interviews, for instance, interviewers can make distortions in any given candidate's evaluation as a result of his or her place in the interview schedule. The candidate is likely to receive a more favourable evaluation if preceded by mediocre applicants, and a less favourable evaluation if preceded by strong applicants.

Projection

It's easy to judge others if we assume that they are similar to us. For instance, if you want challenge and responsibility in your job, you assume that others want the same. Or you are honest and trustworthy, so you take it for granted that other people are

Aboriginal hip-hop artists, led by Winnipeg's Most (pictured here), have created a coalition against the negative stereotyping of Indigenous rappers by the mainstream media. This initiative is an opportunity for Indigenous hip hop to define itself in a sustainable and healthy manner for the future. Aboriginal musician Jarrett Martineau says that hip hop is popular with Aboriginal youth because it deals with oppression and dispossession and because First Nations culture has a strong tradition of storytelling.[13]

halo effect Drawing a general impression of an individual on the basis of a single characteristic.

contrast effects The concept that our reaction to one person is often influenced by other people we have recently encountered.

equally reliable. This tendency to attribute our own characteristics to other people is called **projection**.

People who engage in projection tend to perceive others according to what they themselves are like, rather than perceiving others as they really are. Because they always judge people as being similar to themselves, when they observe someone who is actually like them, their perceptions are naturally correct. But when they observe others who are not like them, their perceptions are not as accurate. Managers who engage in projection compromise their ability to respond to individual differences. They tend to see people as more homogeneous than they really are.

Stereotyping

When we judge someone on the basis of our perception of the group to which he or she belongs, we are using the shortcut called **stereotyping**.

We rely on generalizations every day because they help us make decisions quickly. They are a means of simplifying a complex world. It's less difficult to deal with an unmanageable number of stimuli if we use **heuristics** (judgment shortcuts in decision making) or stereotypes. For example, it does make sense to assume that Tre, the new employee from accounting, is going to know something about budgeting, or that Allie from finance will be able to help you figure out a forecasting problem. The problem occurs, of course, when we generalize inaccurately or too much. In organizations, we frequently hear comments that represent stereotypes based on gender, age, race, religion, ethnicity, and even weight:[14] "Women will not relocate for a promotion," "men are not interested in child care," "older workers cannot learn new skills," "Asian immigrants are hard-working and conscientious," "overweight people lack discipline." Stereotypes can be so deeply ingrained and powerful that they influence life-and-death decisions. One study showed that, controlling for a wide array of factors (such as aggravating or mitigating circumstances), the degree to which black defendants in murder trials looked "stereotypically black" essentially doubled their odds of receiving a death sentence if convicted.[15]

One of the problems of stereotypes is that they *are* widespread and often useful generalizations, despite the fact that they may not contain a shred of truth when applied

projection Attributing one's own characteristics to other people.

stereotyping Judging someone on the basis of one's perception of the group to which that person belongs.

heuristics Judgment shortcuts in decision making.

Muslim women in Canada often experience discrimination in being hired, or how their co-workers treat them, when they wear a hijab. Some co-workers of nurse practitioner Sharon Hoosein, shown here, were surprised that she returned to work following her maternity leave. They assumed that because of her religion she would be expected to stay at home to raise children rather than work.

to a particular person or situation. So we constantly have to check ourselves to make sure we are not unfairly or inaccurately applying a stereotype in our evaluations and decisions. Stereotypes are an example of the warning, "The more useful, the more danger from misuse." Stereotypes can lead to strong negative reactions, such as prejudice, which we describe below.

Prejudice   **Prejudice** is an unfounded dislike of a person or group based on their belonging to a particular stereotyped group. For instance, an individual may dislike people of a particular religion, or state that they do not want to work with someone of a particular ethnicity. Prejudice can lead to negative consequences in the workplace and, in particular, to discrimination. For instance, an individual of a particular ethnic group might be passed over for a management position because of the belief that employees might not see that person as a good manager. In another instance, an individual in his 50s who is looking for work but cannot find a job may be discriminated against because of the belief that younger workers are more appealing than older workers. Prejudice generally starts with stereotypes and then has negative emotional content added. Prejudice is harmful to the person who is the target of the behaviour. A 2011 study by researchers from the University of Toronto found that Asian women are more likely to take racism than sexism personally and were more negatively affected by racism.[16]

Why Do Perception and Judgment Matter?

People in organizations are always judging one another. Managers must appraise their employees' performances. We evaluate how much effort our co-workers are putting into their jobs. When a new person joins a work team, the other members immediately "size her up." Individuals even make judgments about people's virtues based on whether they exercise, as a recent study by McMaster University professor Kathleen Martin Ginis showed.[17] In many cases, judgments have important consequences for the organization. A 2010 study found that in organizations that did not seem to value innovation, employees who wanted to see change were often afraid to speak out, due to fear of negative perceptions from co-workers who valued the status quo.[18] Another 2010 study found that positive employee perceptions of an organization have a positive impact on retention, customer loyalty, and financial outcomes.[19] A 2011 study noted that individuals who misperceive how well they have done on a task (positively or negatively) tended to prepare less and to perform poorly in subsequent tasks.[20]

Can perception really affect outcomes?

Let's briefly look at a few of the most obvious applications of judgment shortcuts in the workplace: employment interviews, performance expectations, and performance evaluations.

Employment Interviews

It's fair to say that few people are hired without undergoing an interview. But interviewers make perceptual judgments that are often inaccurate[21] and draw early impressions that quickly become entrenched. Research shows we form impressions of others within a tenth of a second, based on our first glance.[22] If these first impressions are negative, they tend to be more heavily weighted in the interview than if that same information came out later.[23] Most interviewers' decisions change very little after the first four or five minutes of an interview. As a result, information that comes out early in the interview carries greater weight than information that comes out later, and a "good applicant" is probably characterized more by the absence of unfavourable characteristics than by the presence of favourable ones. This chapter's *Ethical Dilemma Exercise* on page 77 illustrates how the perception of people with tattoos affects hiring practices.

prejudice An unfounded dislike of a person or group based on their belonging to a particular stereotyped group.

Performance Expectations

People attempt to validate their perceptions of reality even when they are faulty.[24] The terms **self-fulfilling prophecy** and *Pygmalion effect* describe how an individual's behaviour is determined by others' expectations. If a manager expects big things from her people, they are not likely to let her down. Similarly, if she expects only minimal performance, they will likely meet those low expectations. Expectations become reality. The self-fulfilling prophecy has been found to affect the performance of students, soldiers, and even accountants.[25]

Performance Evaluations

Performance evaluations very much depend on the perceptual process.[26] An employee's future is closely tied to the appraisal—promotion, pay raises, and continuation of employment are among the most obvious outcomes. Although the appraisal can be objective (for example, a salesperson is appraised on how many dollars of sales he generates in his territory), many jobs are evaluated in subjective terms. Subjective evaluations, though often necessary, are problematic because all the errors we have discussed thus far—selective perception, contrast effects, halo effect, and so on—affect them. Ironically, sometimes performance ratings say as much about the evaluator as they do about the employee!

As you can see, perception plays a large role in how people are evaluated. Personality, which we review next, is another major factor affecting how people relate to and evaluate one another in the workplace.

Personality

2 What is personality and how does it affect behaviour?

Walmart faced great outrage from Canadians when it first entered Canada in 1994.[27] Target will arrive in Canada in 2013, taking over more than 130 Zellers locations. Walmart and Target have different personalities. "Target stocks its shelves with low-cost bedspreads, shower curtains, and clothes with bright colors and funky designs. Walmart is for the necessities: cheap Cheerios, laundry detergent, bulk meat, paper plates."

The image of Target is fun, while Walmart's image is frugal. In other words, they have different personalities.

Organizational personalities can be interesting, but even more interesting is the impact of individual personalities on organizational behaviour. Why are some people quiet and passive, while others are loud and aggressive? Are certain personality types better adapted for certain job types? Before we can answer these questions, we need to address a more basic one: What is personality?

What Is Personality?

When we talk of personality, we don't mean that a person has charm, a positive attitude toward life, a smiling face, or is a finalist for "Happiest and Friendliest." When psychologists talk of personality, they mean a dynamic concept describing the growth and development of a person's whole psychological system.

Gordon Allport produced the most frequently used definition of *personality* more than 70 years ago. He said personality is "the dynamic organization within the individual of those psychophysical systems that determine his unique adjustments to his environment."[28] For our purposes, you should think of **personality** as the stable patterns of behaviour and consistent internal states that determine how an individual reacts to and interacts with others. It's most often described in terms of measurable traits that a person exhibits.

self-fulfilling prophecy A concept that proposes a person will behave in ways consistent with how he or she is perceived by others.

personality The stable patterns of behaviour and consistent internal states that determine how an individual reacts to and interacts with others.

Measuring Personality

The most important reason managers need to know how to measure personality is that research has shown that personality tests are useful in hiring decisions. Scores on personality tests help managers forecast who is the best fit for a job.[29] Some managers use personality tests to better understand and more effectively manage the people who work for them. The most common means of measuring personality is through self-report surveys, with which individuals evaluate themselves on a series of factors, such as "I worry a lot about the future." Though self-report measures work well when well constructed, one weakness of these measures is that the respondent might lie or practise impression management—that is, the person could "fake it" on the test to create a good impression. Evidence shows that when people know that their personality scores are going to be used for hiring decisions, they rate themselves as about half a standard deviation more conscientious and emotionally stable than if they are taking the test just to learn more about themselves.[30] Another problem is accuracy. A perfectly good candidate could have just been in a bad mood when the survey was taken.

Observer ratings provide an independent assessment of personality. Here, a co-worker or another observer does the rating (sometimes with the subject's knowledge and sometimes without). Though the results of self-reports and observer ratings are strongly correlated, research suggests that observer ratings are a better predictor of success on the job.[31] However, each can tell us something unique about an individual's behaviour in the workplace.

Personality Determinants

An early argument in personality research centred on whether an individual's personality was predetermined at birth or the result of the individual's interaction with his or her environment. Clearly, there is no simple answer. Personality appears to be a result of both influences. In addition, today we recognize a third factor—the situation. Thus, an adult's personality is now generally considered to be made up of both hereditary and environmental factors, moderated by situational conditions.

Heredity

Heredity refers to those factors that were determined at conception. Physical stature, facial attractiveness, gender, temperament, muscle composition and reflexes, energy level, and biological rhythms are characteristics that are generally considered to be either completely or substantially influenced by your parents' biological, physiological, and inherent psychological makeup. The heredity approach argues that the ultimate explanation of an individual's personality is a person's genes.

Are people born with their personalities?

If heredity played little or no part in determining personality, you would expect to find few similarities between identical twins who were separated at birth and raised separately. But researchers who looked at more than 100 sets of separated twins found a lot in common.[32] For almost every behavioural trait, a significant part of the variation between the twins turned out to be associated with genetic factors. For instance, one set of twins, who had been separated for 39 years and raised 70 kilometres apart, were found to drive the same model and colour car, chain-smoke the same brand of cigarette, own dogs with the same name, and regularly vacation within three blocks of each other in a beach community 2000 kilometres away.

Researchers have found that genetics can explain about 50 percent of the personality differences and more than 30 percent of the variation in occupational and leisure interests found in individuals. In other words, blood-related siblings are likely to

EXHIBIT 2-4

Source: Peanuts, reprinted by permission of Universal Uclick.

have more similar personalities, occupations, and leisure interests than unrelated people.

Does personality change over one's lifetime? Most research in this area suggests that while some aspects of our personalities do change over time, the rank orderings do not change very much. For example, people's scores on measures of conscientiousness tend to increase as they get older. However, there are still strong individual differences in conscientiousness, and despite the fact that most of us become more responsible over time, people tend to change by about the same amount, so that the rank order stays roughly the same.[33] For instance, if you are more conscientious than your sibling now, that is likely to be true in 20 years, even though you both should become more conscientious over time. Consistent with the notion that the teenage years are periods of great exploration and change, research has shown that personality is more changeable in adolescence and more stable among adults.[34]

Personality Traits

The early work in the structure of personality revolved around attempts to identify and label enduring characteristics that describe an individual's behaviour. Popular characteristics include shy, aggressive, submissive, lazy, ambitious, loyal, and timid. Those characteristics, when they are exhibited in a large number of situations, are called **personality traits**.[35] The more consistent the characteristic and the more frequently it occurs in diverse situations, the more important that trait is in describing the individual.

A number of early research efforts tried to identify the *primary* traits that govern behaviour.[36] However, for the most part, they resulted in long lists of traits that were difficult to generalize from and provided little practical guidance to organizational decision makers. Two exceptions are the Myers-Briggs Type Indicator and the Big Five Personality Model, the dominant frameworks for identifying and classifying traits.

Keep in mind that each of us reacts differently to personality traits. This is partially a function of how we perceive those traits. In Exhibit 2-4, you will note that Lucy tells Linus a few things about his personality.

The Myers-Briggs Type Indicator

The **Myers-Briggs Type Indicator (MBTI)** is the most widely used personality-assessment instrument in the world.[37] It's a 100-question personality test that asks people how they usually feel or act in particular situations. On the basis of their answers, individuals are classified as extraverted or introverted (E or I), sensing or intuitive (S or N), thinking or feeling (T or F), and judging or perceiving (J or P). These terms are defined as follows:

- *Extraverted/introverted.* Extraverted individuals are outgoing, sociable, and assertive. Introverts are quiet and shy. E/I measures where we direct our energy when dealing with people and things.

personality traits Enduring characteristics that describe an individual's behaviour.

Myers-Briggs Type Indicator (MBTI) A personality test that taps four characteristics and classifies people into 1 of 16 personality types.

- *Sensing/intuitive.* Sensing types are practical and prefer routine and order. They focus on details. Intuitives rely on unconscious processes and look at the "big picture." This dimension looks at how we process information.

- *Thinking/feeling.* Thinking types use reason and logic to handle problems. Feeling types rely on their personal values and emotions.

- *Judging/perceiving.* Judging types want control and prefer their world to be ordered and structured. Perceiving types are flexible and spontaneous.

These classifications together describe 16 personality types. To illustrate, let's look at three examples:

- *INTJs are visionaries.* They usually have original minds and great drive for their own ideas and purposes. They are skeptical, critical, independent, determined, and often stubborn.

- *ESTJs are organizers.* They are realistic, logical, analytical, decisive, and have a natural head for business or mechanics. They like to organize and run activities.

- *ENTPs are conceptualizers.* They are innovative, individualistic, versatile, and attracted to entrepreneurial ideas. They tend to be resourceful in solving challenging problems, but may neglect routine assignments.

A book profiling 13 contemporary business people who created super-successful firms including Apple Computer, FedEx, Honda Motor, Microsoft, and Sony found that all are intuitive thinkers (NTs).[38] This result is particularly interesting because intuitive thinkers represent only about 5 percent of the population.

The MBTI is widely used by organizations including Apple Computer, AT&T, Citigroup, GE, 3M, many hospitals and educational institutions, and even the US Armed Forces. In spite of its popularity, the evidence is mixed as to whether the MBTI is a valid measure of personality—with most of the evidence suggesting that it is not.[39] One problem is that it forces a person into either one type or another (that is, you are either introverted or extraverted). There is no in-between, though people can be both extraverted and introverted to some degree. The best we can say is that the MBTI can be a valuable tool for increasing self-awareness and providing career guidance. But because results tend to be unrelated to job performance, managers probably should not use it as a selection test for job candidates.

The Big Five Personality Model

The MBTI may lack valid supporting evidence, but that cannot be said for the **Big Five Personality Model**. An impressive body of research supports the notion that five basic personality dimensions underlie all others and encompass most of the significant variation in human personality.[40] The Big Five personality factors are as follows:

- **Extraversion**. This dimension captures a person's comfort level with relationships. Extraverts tend to be gregarious, assertive, and sociable. Introverts tend to be reserved, timid, and quiet.

- **Agreeableness**. This dimension refers to a person's propensity to defer to others. Highly agreeable people are cooperative, warm, and trusting. People who score low on agreeableness are cold, disagreeable, and antagonistic.

- **Conscientiousness**. This dimension is a measure of reliability. A highly conscientious person is responsible, organized, dependable, and persistent. Those who score low on this dimension are easily distracted, disorganized, and unreliable.

- **Emotional stability**. This dimension—often labelled by its converse, *neuroticism*—taps into a person's ability to withstand stress. People with

Big Five Personality Model A personality assessment model that taps five basic dimensions.

extraversion A personality factor that describes the degree to which a person is sociable, talkative, and assertive.

agreeableness A personality factor that describes the degree to which a person is good-natured, cooperative, and trusting.

conscientiousness A personality factor that describes the degree to which a person is responsible, dependable, persistent, and achievement-oriented.

emotional stability A personality dimension that characterizes someone as calm, self-confident, secure (positive) vs. nervous, depressed, and insecure (negative).

EXHIBIT 2-5 Big Five Personality Factors

Low   **Extraversion**   **High**

Reserved	Gregarious
Timid	Assertive
Quiet	Sociable

Agreeableness

Cold	Cooperative
Disagreeable	Warm
Antagonistic	Empathetic
	Trusting

Conscientiousness

Easily distracted	Responsible
Disorganized	Organized
Unreliable	Dependable
	Persistent

Emotional Stability

Hostile	Calm
Anxious	Self-confident
Depressed	Secure
Insecure	

Openness to Experience

Unimaginative	Creative
Inflexible	Flexible
Literal-minded	Curious
Dull	Artistic

positive emotional stability tend to be calm, self-confident, and secure. Those with high negative scores tend to be nervous, anxious, depressed, and insecure.

- **Openness to experience**. The final dimension addresses a person's range of interests and fascination with novelty. Extremely open people are creative, curious, and artistically sensitive. Those at the other end of the openness category are conventional and find comfort in the familiar.

Researchers at the University of Toronto have recently created a "fake proof" personality test to measure the Big Five factors.[41] Professor Jordan Peterson, one of the researchers, noted that it is common for people to try to "make themselves look better than they actually are on these questionnaires. . . . This sort of faking can distort the predictive validity of these tests, with significant negative economic consequences. We wanted to develop a measure that could predict real-world performance even in the absence of completely honest responding."[42]

Exhibit 2-5 shows the characteristics for the high and low dimensions of each Big Five personality factor.

RESEARCH FINDINGS: The Big Five

Research on the Big Five has found a relationship between the personality dimensions and job performance.[43] As the authors of the most-cited review put it, "The preponderance of evidence shows that individuals who are dependable, reliable, careful, thorough, able to plan, organized, hardworking, persistent, and achievement-oriented tend to have higher job performance in most if not all occupations."[44] In addition, employees who score higher in conscientiousness develop higher

openness to experience A personality factor that describes the degree to which a person is imaginative, artistically sensitive, and curious.

levels of job knowledge, probably because highly conscientious people learn more (a review of 138 studies revealed conscientiousness was rather strongly related to grade point average).[45] Higher levels of job knowledge then contribute to higher levels of job performance.[46]

Although conscientiousness is the Big Five trait most consistently related to job performance, the other traits are related to aspects of performance in some situations. All five traits also have other implications for work and for life. Let's look at the implications of these traits, one at a time. (Exhibit 2-6 summarizes the discussion.)

Emotional stability. People who score high on emotional stability are happier than those who score low. Of the Big Five traits, emotional stability is most strongly related to life satisfaction, job satisfaction, and low stress levels. This is probably true because high scorers are more likely to be positive and optimistic in their thinking and experience fewer negative emotions. People low on emotional stability are hyper-vigilant (looking for problems or impending signs of danger), and are especially vulnerable to the physical and psychological effects of stress.

Extraversion. Extraverts tend to be happier in their jobs and in their lives as a whole. They experience more positive emotions than do introverts, and they more freely express these feelings. They also tend to perform better in jobs that require significant interpersonal interaction, perhaps because they have more social skills—they usually have more friends and spend more time in social situations than introverts. Finally, extraversion is a relatively strong predictor of leadership emergence in groups; extraverts are more socially dominant, "take charge" sorts of people, and they are generally more assertive than introverts.[47] One downside of extraversion is that extraverts are more impulsive than introverts; they are more likely to be absent from work and engage in risky behaviour such as unprotected sex, drinking, and other impulsive or sensation-

EXHIBIT 2-6 How the Big Five Traits Influence OB

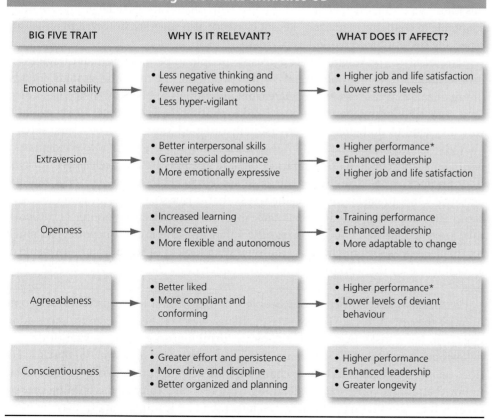

BIG FIVE TRAIT	WHY IS IT RELEVANT?	WHAT DOES IT AFFECT?
Emotional stability	• Less negative thinking and fewer negative emotions • Less hyper-vigilant	• Higher job and life satisfaction • Lower stress levels
Extraversion	• Better interpersonal skills • Greater social dominance • More emotionally expressive	• Higher performance* • Enhanced leadership • Higher job and life satisfaction
Openness	• Increased learning • More creative • More flexible and autonomous	• Training performance • Enhanced leadership • More adaptable to change
Agreeableness	• Better liked • More compliant and conforming	• Higher performance* • Lower levels of deviant behaviour
Conscientiousness	• Greater effort and persistence • More drive and discipline • Better organized and planning	• Higher performance • Enhanced leadership • Greater longevity

*In jobs requiring significant teamwork or frequent interpersonal interactions.

Indra Nooyi, CEO and chair of PepsiCo, scores high on all personality dimensions of the Big Five Model. She is described as sociable, agreeable, conscientious, emotionally stable, and open to experiences. These personality traits have contributed to Nooyi's high job performance and career success at PepsiCo and are the reason she landed the CEO position.

seeking acts.[48] One study also found that extraverts were more likely to lie during job interviews than introverts.[49]

Openness to experience. Individuals who score high on openness to experience are more creative in science and in art than those who score low. Because creativity is important to leadership, open people are more likely to be effective leaders. They also are more comfortable with ambiguity and change than are those who score lower on this trait. As a result, open people cope better with organizational change and are more adaptable in changing contexts.[50] Recent evidence also suggests, however, that they are especially susceptible to workplace accidents.[51]

Agreeableness. You might expect agreeable people to be happier than disagreeable people, and they are, but only slightly. When people choose romantic partners, friends, or organizational team members, agreeable individuals are usually their first choice. Thus, agreeable individuals are better liked than disagreeable people, which explains why they tend to do better in interpersonally oriented jobs such as customer service. They also are more compliant and rule abiding and less likely to get into accidents as a result. Agreeable children do better in school and as adults are less likely to get involved in drugs or excessive drinking.[52] They also are less likely to engage in organizational deviance. One downside of agreeableness is that it is associated with lower levels of career success (especially earnings). Agreeable individuals may be poorer negotiators; they are so concerned with pleasing others that they often don't negotiate as much for themselves as they might.[53] For an interesting look at the upside and downside of agreeableness in the workplace, read this chapter's *Case Incident—The Nice Trap?* on page 79.

Conscientiousness. Conscientious people live longer than less conscientious people because they tend to take better care of themselves (eat better, exercise more) and engage in fewer risky behaviours (smoking, drinking/drugs, risky sexual or driving behaviour).[54] Still, probably because they are so organized and structured, conscientious people don't adapt as well to changing contexts. They are generally performance-oriented and have more trouble learning complex skills early in the training process because their focus is on performing well rather than on learning. Finally, they are often less creative than less conscientious people, especially artistically.[55]

It is unusual for two people to share the CEO role, but Ronnen Harary (left) and Anton Rabie (right), co-CEOs of Toronto-based toy company Spin Master (pictured with executive vice-president Ben Varadi), like the arrangement. Rabie is an extrovert, while Harary is an introvert. The childhood friends feel their personalities complement each other, making an ideal management team.

Other Personality Attributes Influencing OB

Although the Big Five traits have proven highly relevant to OB, they don't exhaust the range of traits that can describe someone's personality. Now we will look at other, more specific attributes that are powerful predictors of behaviour in organizations. The first relates to one's core self-evaluation. The others are Machiavellianism, narcissism, self-monitoring, propensity for risk-taking, and Type A and B and proactive personalities. We shall briefly introduce these attributes and summarize what we know about their ability to explain and predict employee behaviour.

If you want to know more about your own personality attributes, this chapter's *Learning About Yourself Exercises* on pages 70–75 present you with a variety of personality measures to explore.

Core Self-Evaluation

People who have positive **core self-evaluations** like themselves and see themselves as effective, capable, and in control of their environment. Those with negative core self-evaluations tend to dislike themselves, question their capabilities, and view themselves as powerless over their environment.[56]

People with positive core self-evaluations perform better than others because they set more ambitious goals, are more committed to their goals, and persist longer at attempting to reach these goals. For example, one study of life-insurance agents found that core self-evaluations were critical predictors of performance. In life-insurance sales, 90 percent of sales calls end in rejection, so an agent has to believe in him- or herself to persist. In fact, this study showed that the majority of successful salespersons had positive core self-evaluations.[57] Such people also provide better customer service, are more popular co-workers, and have careers that both begin on better footing and ascend more rapidly over time.[58]

You might wonder whether someone can be too positive. What happens when someone thinks he is capable, but he is actually incompetent? One study of *Fortune* 500 CEOs, for example, showed that many are overconfident, and their perceived infallibility often causes them to make bad decisions.[59] While many people are overconfident, just as many people sell themselves short and are less happy and effective than they

core self-evaluation The degree to which an individual likes or dislikes himself or herself, whether the person sees himself or herself as capable and effective, and whether the person feels in control of his or her environment or powerless over the environment.

could be because of lack of confidence. If we decide we cannot do something, for example, we won't try, and not doing it only reinforces our self-doubts.

Machiavellianism

The personality characteristic of **Machiavellianism** (Mach) is named after Niccolò Machiavelli, who wrote in the sixteenth century on how to gain and use power. An individual high in Machiavellianism is pragmatic, maintains emotional distance, and believes that ends can justify means. "If it works, use it" is consistent with a high-Mach perspective.

A considerable amount of research has related high- and low-Mach personalities to certain behavioural outcomes.[60] High Machs manipulate more, win more, are persuaded less, and persuade others more than do low Machs.[61] They like their jobs less, are more stressed by their work, and engage in more deviant work behaviours.[62] Yet high-Mach outcomes are moderated by situational factors. It has been found that high Machs do better (1) when they interact face to face with others rather than indirectly; (2) when the situation has a minimum number of rules and regulations, thus allowing room for improvising; and (3) when emotional involvement with details irrelevant to winning distracts low Machs.[63]

Should we conclude that high Machs make good employees? That answer depends on the type of job and whether you consider ethical implications in evaluating performance. In jobs that require bargaining skills (such as labour negotiation) or that offer substantial rewards for winning (as in commissioned sales), high Machs will be productive. But if the ends cannot justify the means, if there are absolute standards of behaviour, or if the three situational factors noted in the preceding paragraph are not in evidence, our ability to predict a high Mach's performance will be severely limited.

If you are interested in determining your level of Machiavellianism, you might want to complete *Learning About Yourself Exercise #1* on page 70.

SELF-ASSESSMENT LIBRARY

LEARNING ABOUT YOURSELF

1. How Machiavellian Are You?
   (page 70)

Narcissism

Hans likes to be the centre of attention. He likes to look at himself in the mirror a lot. He has extravagant dreams and seems to consider himself a person of many talents. Hans is a narcissist. The term is from the Greek myth of Narcissus, the story of a man so vain and proud that he fell in love with his own image. In psychology, **narcissism** describes a person who has a grandiose sense of self-importance, requires excessive admiration, has a sense of entitlement, and is arrogant.[64] Are today's youth narcissistic? Despite claims to that effect, the evidence is unclear. High school seniors in 2006 were more likely than in 1975 to agree they would be "very good" spouses (56 percent of 2006 seniors, compared with 37 percent in 1975), parents (54 percent of 2006 seniors, 36 percent in 1975), and workers (65 percent of 2006 seniors, 49 percent in 1975). On the other hand, scores on the Narcissistic Personality Inventory—the most common measure of narcissism—have not increased since 1982.[65]

Whether it is increasing or not, narcissism can have pretty toxic consequences. A 2011 study found that narcissists were more likely to cheat on exams than others, in part because they did not feel guilty doing so.[66] A study found that while narcissists thought they were *better* leaders than their colleagues, their supervisors actually rated them as *worse*. For example, an Oracle executive described that company's CEO, Larry Ellison, as follows: "The difference between God and Larry is that God does not believe he is Larry."[67] Because narcissists often want to gain the admiration of others and receive affirmation of their superiority, they tend to "talk down" to those who threaten them, treating others as if they were inferior. Narcissists also tend to be selfish and exploitive, and they often carry the attitude that others exist for their benefit.[68] Studies indicate that narcissists are rated by their bosses as less effective at their jobs than others,

Machiavellianism The degree to which an individual is pragmatic, maintains emotional distance, and believes that ends can justify means.

narcissism The tendency to be arrogant, have a grandiose sense of self-importance, require excessive admiration, and have a sense of entitlement.

particularly when it comes to helping other people.[69] Despite these negative outcomes, one 2011 study found that having two or more narcissists on a team can lead to more creativity.[70] Because narcissists want admiration from their peers, they will attempt to outdo one another, raising the competitiveness within the team.

Self-Monitoring

Self-monitoring refers to an individual's ability to adjust his or her behaviour to external, situational factors.[71] Individuals high in self-monitoring show considerable adaptability in adjusting their behaviour to external situational factors. They are highly sensitive to external cues and can behave differently in different situations. High self-monitors are capable of presenting striking contradictions between their public personae and their private selves. Low self-monitors cannot disguise themselves in the same way. They tend to display their true dispositions and attitudes in every situation. There is high behavioural consistency between who they are and what they do.

Research suggests that high self-monitors tend to pay closer attention to the behaviour of others and are more capable of conforming than are low self-monitors.[72] High self-monitoring managers tend to be more mobile in their careers and receive more promotions (both internal and cross-organizational) and are more likely to occupy central positions in an organization.[73] High self-monitors also receive better performance ratings, are more likely to emerge as leaders, and show less commitment to their organizations.[74]

If you are interested in determining whether you are a high or low self-monitor, you might want to complete *Learning About Yourself Exercise #2* on page 71.

Risk-Taking

People differ in their willingness to take chances, a quality that affects how much time and information managers require before they make a decision. In one study, 79 managers worked on simulated exercises that required them to make hiring decisions.[75] High **risk-taking** managers made more rapid decisions and used less information in making their choices than did the low risk-taking managers. Interestingly, the decision accuracy was the same for both groups.

Although previous studies have shown managers in large organizations to be more risk averse than are growth-oriented entrepreneurs who actively manage small businesses, recent findings suggest that managers in large organizations may actually be more willing to take risks than entrepreneurs.[76] The work population as a whole also differs in risk propensity.[77] It makes sense to recognize these differences and even to consider aligning risk-taking propensity with specific job demands. A high risk-taking propensity may lead to more effective performance for a stock trader in a brokerage firm because that type of job demands rapid decision making. On the other hand, a willingness to take risks might prove a major obstacle to an accountant who performs auditing activities. The latter job might be better filled by someone with a low risk-taking propensity. If you are interested in determining where you stand on risk-taking, you might want to complete *Learning About Yourself Exercise #3* on page 72.

Type A and Type B Personalities

Do you know people who are excessively competitive and always seem to be chronically pushed for time? If you do, it's a good bet that those people have a Type A personality. A person with a **Type A personality** is "aggressively involved in a chronic, incessant struggle to achieve more and more in less and less time, and, if required to do so, against the opposing efforts of other things or other persons."[78] In North American culture, such characteristics tend to be highly prized and positively associated with ambition and the successful acquisition of material goods.

SELF-ASSESSMENT LIBRARY

LEARNING ABOUT YOURSELF

2. Are You a High Self-Monitor?
(page 71)

SELF-ASSESSMENT LIBRARY

LEARNING ABOUT YOURSELF

3. Are You a Risk-Taker?
(page 72)

self-monitoring A personality trait that measures an individual's ability to adjust behaviour to external, situational factors.

risk-taking A personality willingness to take chances or risks.

Type A personality A personality with aggressive involvement in a chronic, incessant struggle to achieve more and more in less and less time and, if necessary, against the opposing efforts of other things or other people.

Type As tend to have the following characteristics:

- Are always moving, walking, and eating rapidly
- Feel impatient with the rate at which most events take place
- Strive to think or do two or more things at once
- Cannot cope with leisure time
- Are obsessed with numbers, measuring their success in terms of how many or how much of everything they acquire

Do you think it is better to be a Type A or a Type B personality?

A person with a **Type B personality** is exactly the opposite of a Type A, "rarely harried by the desire to obtain a wildly increasing number of things or participate in an endless growing series of events in an ever-decreasing amount of time."[79]

Type Bs tend to have the following characteristics:

- Never suffer from a sense of time urgency, with its accompanying impatience
- Feel no need to display or discuss either their achievements or accomplishments unless such exposure is demanded by the situation
- Play for fun and relaxation, rather than to exhibit their superiority at any cost
- Can relax without guilt

Type As operate under moderate to high levels of stress. They subject themselves to more or less continuous time pressure, creating a life of deadlines. These characteristics result in some rather specific behavioural outcomes. Type As are fast workers because they emphasize quantity over quality. In managerial positions, Type As demonstrate their competitiveness by working long hours and, not infrequently, making poor decisions because they make them too fast.

Stressed Type As are also rarely creative. Because of their concern with quantity and speed, they rely on past experiences when faced with problems. They will not take the time that is necessary to develop unique solutions to new problems. They rarely vary in their responses to specific challenges in their environment. As a result, their behaviour is easier to predict than that of Type Bs.

Are Type As or Type Bs more successful in organizations? Type As do better than Type Bs in job interviews because they are more likely to be judged as having desirable traits such as high drive, competence, aggressiveness, and success motivation.[80] Despite the hard work of Type As, Type Bs are the ones who appear to make it to the top. Great salespeople are usually Type As; senior executives are usually Type Bs. Why? The answer lies in the tendency of Type As to trade off quality of effort for quantity. Promotions in corporate and professional organizations "usually go to those who are wise rather than to those who are merely hasty, to those who are tactful rather than to those who are hostile, and to those who are creative rather than to those who are merely agile in competitive strife."[81]

If you are interested in determining whether you have a Type A or Type B personality, you might want to complete *Learning About Yourself Exercise #4* on page 74.

Proactive Personality

Did you ever notice that some people actively take the initiative to improve their current circumstances or create new ones? These are people with a proactive personality.[82] People with a **proactive personality** identify opportunities, show initiative, take action, and persevere until meaningful change occurs. They create positive change in their environment, regardless or even in spite of constraints or obstacles.[83] Not surprisingly, proactives have many behaviours that organizations desire. They are

SELF-ASSESSMENT LIBRARY

LEARNING ABOUT YOURSELF

4. Are You a Type A?
   (page 74)

Type B personality A personality that is described as easy-going, relaxed, and patient.

proactive personality A person who identifies opportunities, shows initiative, takes action, and perseveres until meaningful change occurs.

more likely to be seen as leaders and more likely to act as change agents within the organization.[84]

Other actions of proactives can be positive or negative, depending on the organization and the situation. Proactives are more likely to challenge the status quo or voice their displeasure when situations are not to their liking.[85] If an organization requires people with entrepreneurial initiative, proactives make good candidates; however, they are also more likely to leave an organization to start their own business.[86] As individuals, proactives are more likely to achieve career success.[87] They select, create, and influence work situations in their favour. Proactives are more likely to seek out job and organizational information, develop contacts in high places, engage in career planning, and demonstrate persistence in the face of career obstacles.

Emotions

Despite the fact that Walmart Canada has won numerous "Best Employer" and "Best Culture" awards, which are based partly on responses of employees, not all Walmart employees agree with those findings.[88] Comments from Walmart employees at RateMyEmployer.ca show a range of emotions from "love it" to "hate it." Over the past 10 years, at least 20 different groups of Walmart employees across the country have tried to unionize. A recent drive in Trail, BC, told fellow employees that unionizing would be "making Walmart an even BETTER place to work." Obviously there are strong feelings about the employer. Could emotions affect how individual employees perceive Walmart?

3 Can emotions help or get in the way when we are dealing with others?

Each of us has a range of personality characteristics, but we also bring with us a range of emotions. Given the obvious role that emotions play in our everyday life, it might surprise you to learn that, until very recently, the topic of emotions was given little or no attention within the field of OB.[89] Why? We offer two possible explanations.

First is the *myth of rationality*.[90] Until very recently, the protocol of the work world kept a damper on emotions. A well-run organization did not allow employees to express frustration, fear, anger, love, hate, joy, grief, or similar feelings thought to be the antithesis of rationality. Though researchers and managers knew emotions were an inseparable part of everyday life, they tried to create organizations that were emotion-free. Of course, that was not possible.

The second explanation is that many believed emotions of any kind were disruptive.[91] Researchers looked at strong negative emotions—especially anger—that interfered with an employee's ability to work effectively. They rarely viewed emotions as constructive or contributing to enhanced performance.

Certainly some emotions, particularly when exhibited at the wrong time, can reduce employee performance. But employees do bring their emotions to work every day, and no study of OB would be complete without considering their role in workplace behaviour.

What Are Emotions and Moods?

Let's look at three terms that are closely intertwined: *affect, emotions,* and *moods.* **Affect** is a generic term that covers a broad range of feelings people experience, including both emotions and moods.[92] **Emotions** are intense feelings that are directed at someone or something.[93] **Moods** are feelings that are less intense than emotions and that lack a contextual stimulus.[94]

Most experts believe emotions are more fleeting than moods.[95] For example, if someone is rude to you, you would likely feel angry. That intense feeling probably comes and goes fairly quickly, maybe even in a matter of seconds. When you are in a bad mood, though, you can feel bad for several hours.

affect A broad range of feelings that people experience.

emotions Intense feelings that are directed at someone or something.

moods Feelings that tend to be less intense than emotions and that lack a contextual stimulus.

Emotions are reactions to a person (seeing a friend at work may make you feel glad) or an event (dealing with a rude client may make you feel angry). You show your emotions when you are "happy about something, angry at someone, afraid of something."[96] Moods, in contrast, are not usually directed at a person or an event. But emotions can turn into moods when you lose focus on the event or object that started the feeling. And, by the same token, good or bad moods can make you more emotional in response to an event. So when a colleague criticizes how you spoke to a client, you might show emotion (anger) toward a specific object (your colleague). But as the specific emotion starts to go away, you might just feel generally dispirited. You cannot attribute this feeling to any single event; you are just not your normal self. You might then overreact to other events. This affect state describes a mood. Exhibit 2-7 shows the relationships among affect, emotions, and mood.

First, as the exhibit shows, *affect* is a broad term that encompasses emotions and moods. Second, there are differences between emotions and moods. Some of these differences—that emotions are more likely to be caused by a specific event, and emotions are more fleeting than moods—we just discussed. Other differences are subtler. For example, unlike moods, emotions like anger and disgust tend to be more clearly revealed by facial expressions. Also, some researchers speculate that emotions may be more action oriented—they may lead us to some immediate action—while moods may be more cognitive, meaning they may cause us to think or brood for a while.[97]

Finally, the exhibit shows that emotions and moods are closely connected and can influence each other. Getting your dream job may generate the emotion of joy, which can put you in a good mood for several days. Similarly, if you are in a good or bad mood, it might make you experience a more intense positive or negative emotion than otherwise. In a bad mood, you might blow up in response to a co-worker's comment that would normally have generated only a mild reaction.

Affect, emotions, and moods are separable in theory; in practice the distinction isn't always crystal clear. In some areas, researchers have studied mostly moods, in other areas mainly emotions. So, when we review the OB topics on emotions and moods, you may see more information on emotions in one area and on moods in another. This is simply the state of the research. *OB in the Street* discusses how our perception of emotions can affect our romantic relationships.

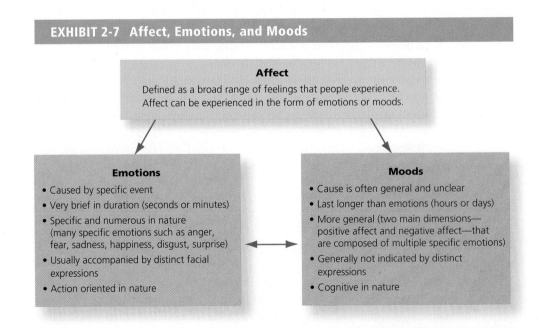

EXHIBIT 2-7 Affect, Emotions, and Moods

Affect
Defined as a broad range of feelings that people experience.
Affect can be experienced in the form of emotions or moods.

Emotions
- Caused by specific event
- Very brief in duration (seconds or minutes)
- Specific and numerous in nature (many specific emotions such as anger, fear, sadness, happiness, disgust, surprise)
- Usually accompanied by distinct facial expressions
- Action oriented in nature

Moods
- Cause is often general and unclear
- Last longer than emotions (hours or days)
- More general (two main dimensions—positive affect and negative affect—that are composed of multiple specific emotions)
- Generally not indicated by distinct expressions
- Cognitive in nature

OB in the STREET

How Perception Causes Fights in Relationships

What happens if you think your partner is neglecting you? A 2011 study found that how people perceive the emotions of their romantic partner during a conflict affected their overall view of and reactions to the conflict.[98] The researchers studied the arguments that 105 university students had during an eight-week period. They looked at two types of emotions: "hard" (asserting power) and "soft" (expressing vulnerability). They also looked at two types of perceptions: "perceived threat" (perception that the partner is being hostile, critical, blaming, or controlling) and "perceived neglect" (perception that the partner does not seem committed to or invested in the relationship).

The researchers found that when a person sees his or her partner react with hard emotion, that person perceives a threat to control, power, and status in the relationship. When a person sees his or her partner show little emotion, or less soft emotion than desired, that person perceives partner neglect. The perceived threat and neglect increase the person's own hard and soft emotions.

One of the study's co-authors explained the results as follows: "[W]hat you perceive your partner to be feeling influences different types of thoughts, feelings and reactions in yourself, whether what you perceive is actually correct. . . . If a person perceives the other as angry, they will perceive a threat so they will respond with a hard emotion like anger or blame. Likewise, if a person is perceived to be sad or vulnerable, they will perceive a neglect and will respond [with] either flat or soft [emotions]."[99]

Choosing Emotions: Emotional Labour

If you have ever had a job working in retail sales or waiting on tables in a restaurant, you know the importance of projecting a friendly demeanour and smiling. Even though there were days when you did not feel cheerful, you knew management expected you to be upbeat when dealing with customers. So you faked it. Every employee expends physical and mental labour by putting body and mind into the job. But jobs also require **emotional labour**, an employee's expression of organizationally desired emotions during interpersonal transactions at work.[100]

> Ever wonder why the grocery clerk is always smiling?

The concept of emotional labour emerged from studies of service jobs. Airlines expect their flight attendants, for instance, to be cheerful; we expect funeral directors to be sad; and we expect doctors to be emotionally neutral. But really, emotional labour is relevant to almost every job. Your managers expect you, for example, to be courteous, not hostile, in interactions with co-workers. The true challenge arises when employees have to project one emotion while simultaneously feeling another.[101] This difference is **emotional dissonance**, and it can take a heavy toll on employees. Bottled-up feelings of frustration, anger, and resentment can eventually lead to emotional exhaustion and burnout.[102] It is because of emotional labour's increasing importance in effective job performance that an understanding of emotion has gained heightened relevance within the field of OB.

Emotional labour creates dilemmas for employees. There are people with whom you have to work that you just don't like. Maybe you consider their personality abrasive. Maybe you know they have said negative things about you behind your back. Regardless, your job requires you to interact with these people on a regular basis. So you are forced to pretend to be friendly.

emotional labour When an employee expresses organizationally desired emotions during interpersonal interactions.

emotional dissonance Inconsistencies between the emotions people feel and the emotions they show.

It can help you, on the job especially, if you separate emotions into *felt* or *displayed* emotions.[103] **Felt emotions** are an individual's actual emotions. In contrast, **displayed emotions** are those that the organization requires employees to show and considers appropriate in a given job. They are not natural; they are learned. "The ritual look of delight on the face of the first runner-up as the [winner] is announced is a product of the display rule that losers should mask their sadness with an expression of joy for the winner."[104] Similarly, most of us know that we are expected to act sad at funerals, regardless of whether we consider the person's death to be a loss, and to pretend to be happy at weddings, even if we don't feel like celebrating.[105]

Effective managers have learned to be serious when giving an employee a negative performance evaluation and to hide their anger when they have been passed over for promotion. A salesperson who has not learned to smile and appear friendly, regardless of his true feelings at the moment, is not typically going to last long on most sales jobs. How we *experience* an emotion is not always the same as how we *show* it.[106]

Displaying fake emotions requires us to suppress real ones. **Surface acting** is hiding one's inner feelings and hiding emotional expressions in response to display rules. For example, when an employee smiles at a customer even when he does not feel like it, he is surface acting. **Deep acting** is trying to modify one's true inner feelings based on display rules. A health care provider trying to genuinely feel more empathy for her patients is deep acting.[107] Surface acting deals with one's *displayed* emotions, and deep acting deals with one's *felt* emotions. Research shows that surface acting is more stressful to employees than deep acting because it entails faking one's true emotions.[108] Displaying emotions we don't really feel is exhausting, so it is important to give employees who engage in surface displays a chance to relax and recharge. A study that looked at how cheerleading instructors spent their breaks from teaching found those who used their breaks to rest and relax were more effective instructors after their breaks.[109] Instructors who did chores during their breaks were only about as effective after their break as they were before. Though much of the research on emotional labour shows negative consequences for those displaying false positive emotions, a 2011 study suggests that as people age, engaging in positive emotions and attitudes, even when the circumstances warrant otherwise, actually enhances emotional well-being.[110] For further discussion on the costs and benefits of emotional display rules in organizations, read this chapter's *Point/Counterpoint* on page 69 and *Case Incident—The Upside of Anger?* on page 78.

Why Should We Care About Emotions in the Workplace?

Research is increasingly showing that emotions are actually critical to rational thinking.[111] We must have the ability to experience emotions to be rational. Why? Because our emotions provide important information about how we understand the world around us. Would we really want a manager to make a decision about firing an employee without regarding either his or the employee's emotions? The key to good decision making is to employ both thinking *and* feeling in our decisions.

There are other reasons to be concerned about understanding emotions in the workplace.[112] People who know their own emotions and are good at reading others' emotions may be more effective in their jobs. That, in essence, is the theme underlying contemporary research on emotional intelligence. The entire workplace can be affected by positive or negative workplace emotions, another issue we consider below. Finally, we consider affective events theory, which has increased our understanding of emotions at work.

Emotional Intelligence

Diane Marshall is an office manager. Her awareness of her own and others' emotions is almost zero. She is moody and unable to generate much enthusiasm or interest in her employees. She does not understand why employees get upset with her. She often

felt emotions An individual's actual emotions.

displayed emotions Emotions that are organizationally required and considered appropriate in a given job.

surface acting Hiding one's inner feelings to display what is expected.

deep acting Trying to modify one's true inner feelings to match what is expected.

overreacts to problems and chooses the most ineffectual responses to emotional situations.[113] Diane Marshall has low emotional intelligence. **Emotional intelligence (EI)** is a person's ability to (1) be self-aware (to recognize one's own emotions when one experiences them), (2) detect emotions in others, and (3) manage emotional cues and information. People who know their own emotions and are good at reading emotional cues—for instance, knowing why they are angry and how to express themselves without violating norms—are most likely to be effective.[114] One simulation study showed that students who were good at identifying and distinguishing among their feelings were able to make more profitable investment decisions.[115]

The most recent study on EI (2011) reviewed and analyzed most of the previous studies on EI and concluded that EI is strongly and positively correlated with job performance—emotionally intelligent people are better workers.[116] Another illuminating study looked at the successes and failures of 11 American presidents—from Franklin Roosevelt to Bill Clinton. They were evaluated on six qualities—communication, organization, political skill, vision, cognitive style, and emotional intelligence. It was found that the key quality that differentiated the successful (such as Roosevelt, Kennedy, and Reagan) from the unsuccessful (such as Johnson, Carter, and Nixon) was EI.[117] Some researchers argue that EI is particularly important for leaders.[118]

EI has been a controversial concept in OB. It has supporters and detractors. In the following sections, we review the arguments for and against the effectiveness of EI in OB. If you are interested in determining your EI, you might want to complete *Learning About Yourself Exercise #5* on page 75. This chapter's *From Concepts to Skills* on pages 80–81 gives you some insight into reading the emotions of others.

The Case for EI

The arguments in favour of EI include its intuitive appeal, the fact that EI predicts criteria that matter, and the idea that EI is biologically based.

Intuitive Appeal   There is a lot of intuitive appeal to the EI concept. Almost everyone would agree that it is good to possess street smarts and social intelligence. People who can detect emotions in others, control their own emotions, and handle social interactions well will have a powerful leg up in the business world, so the thinking goes.[119] As just one example, partners in a multinational consulting firm who scored above the median on an EI measure delivered $1.2 million more in business than did the other partners.[120]

EI Predicts Criteria That Matter   More and more evidence suggests that a high level of EI means a person will perform well on the job. One study found that EI predicted the performance of employees in a cigarette factory in China.[121] Another study found that being able to recognize emotions in others' facial expressions and to emotionally "eavesdrop" (that is, pick up subtle signals about people's emotions) predicted peer ratings of how valuable those people were to their organization.[122] Finally, a review of 59 studies indicated that, overall, EI correlated moderately with job performance.[123]

EI Is Biologically Based   One study has shown that people with damage to the part of the brain that governs emotional processing (lesions in an area of the prefrontal cortex) score significantly lower than others on EI tests. Even though these brain-damaged people scored no lower on standard measures of intelligence than people without similar brain damage, they were still impaired in normal decision making. But they scored significantly lower on EI tests and were impaired in normal decision making, as demonstrated by their poor performance in a card game with monetary rewards. This study suggests that EI is neurologically based in a way that is unrelated to standard measures of intelligence.[124] There is also evidence EI is genetically influenced, further supporting the idea that it measures a real underlying biological factor.[125]

SELF-ASSESSMENT LIBRARY

LEARNING ABOUT YOURSELF

5. What's Your EI at Work?
(page 75)

emotional intelligence (EI) An assortment of noncognitive skills, capabilities, and competencies that influence a person's ability to succeed in coping with environmental demands and pressures.

The Case Against EI

For all its supporters, EI has just as many critics. Its critics say that EI is vague and impossible to measure, and they question its validity.

EI Is Too Vague a Concept   To many researchers, it's not clear what EI is. Is it a form of intelligence? Most of us would not think that being self-aware or self-motivated or having empathy is a matter of intellect. Moreover, different researchers often focus on different skills, making it difficult to get a definition of EI. One researcher may study self-discipline, another empathy, another self-awareness. As one reviewer noted, "The concept of EI has now become so broad and the components so variegated that . . . it is no longer even an intelligible concept."[126]

EI Cannot Be Measured   Many critics have raised questions about measuring EI. Because EI is a form of intelligence, they argue, there must be right and wrong answers about it on tests. Some tests do have right and wrong answers, although the validity of some questions is doubtful. One measure asks you to associate particular feelings with specific colours, as if purple always makes us feel cool and not warm. Other measures are self-reported, meaning that there is no right or wrong answer. For example, an EI test question might ask you to respond to the statement "I'm good at 'reading' other people," and have no right or wrong answers. The measures of EI are diverse, and researchers have not subjected them to as much rigorous study as they have measures of personality and general intelligence.[127]

The Validity of EI Is Suspect   Some critics argue that because EI is so closely related to intelligence and personality, once you control for these factors, EI has nothing unique to offer. There is some foundation to this argument. EI appears to be highly correlated with measures of personality, especially emotional stability.[128] If this is true, then the evidence for a biological component to EI is not valid, and biological markers such as brain activity and heritability are attributable to other well known and much more researched psychological variables. But there has not been enough research on whether EI adds insight beyond measures of personality and general intelligence in predicting job performance. Still, EI is wildly popular among consulting firms and in the popular press. One company's promotional materials for an EI measure claimed, "EI accounts for more than 85 percent of star performance in top leaders."[129] To say the least, it's difficult to validate this statement with the research literature.

Weighing the arguments for and against EI, it's still too early to tell whether the concept is useful. It *is* clear, though, that the concept is here to stay.

Negative Workplace Emotions

Negative emotions can lead to a number of deviant workplace behaviours. Anyone who has spent much time in an organization realizes that people often engage in voluntary actions that violate established norms and threaten the organization, its members, or both. These actions are called **employee deviance**.[130] Deviant actions fall into categories such as production (leaving early, intentionally working slowly); property (stealing, sabotage); political (gossiping, blaming co-workers); and personal aggression (sexual harassment, verbal abuse).[131]

Many of these deviant behaviours can be traced to negative emotions. For instance, envy is an emotion that occurs when you resent someone for having something you don't, and strongly desire—such as a better work assignment, larger office, or higher salary.[132] It can lead to malicious deviant behaviours, such as hostility, "backstabbing," and other forms of political behaviour that negatively distort others' successes and positively distort your own accomplishments.[133] Angry people look for other people to blame for their bad mood, interpret other people's behaviour as hostile, and have

employee deviance Voluntary actions that violate established norms and threaten the organization, its members, or both.

trouble considering others' points of view.[134] It's not hard to see how these thought processes, too, can lead directly to verbal or physical aggression. Evidence suggests that people who feel negative emotions, particularly those who feel angry or hostile, are more likely than others to engage in deviant behaviour at work.[135]

Managing emotions in the workplace becomes important both to ward off negative behaviour and to encourage positive behaviour in those around us. *Focus on Research* looks at the issue of "catching" moods from others. You may be surprised to learn the extent to which your mood can affect the mood of others. Once aggression starts, it's likely that other people will become angry and aggressive, so the stage is set for a serious escalation of negative behaviour.

FOCUS ON RESEARCH

Moods Affect the Success of Groups

Can you catch moods from those around you? A study of 70 work groups sought to discover whether moods could be spread throughout the group.[136] There were four to eight members in each group. While performing tasks, each group was observed by two people, who tried to judge the mood of the group from posture, facial expression, and vocal expression of group members. To assess the accuracy of the observations, group members filled out questionnaires that asked about their typical behaviour with members of their group, and their mood at the time of the observation.

The researchers found that members of groups do seem to adopt similar moods when the moods are "high-energy" (for example, cheerful enthusiasm, hostile irritability) rather than when they are "low-energy" (for example, serene warmth, depressed sluggishness). The entire group felt unpleasant moods the most strongly. Those who observed the work groups were able to accurately identify many of the moods the groups experienced, just by watching postures and the facial and vocal expressions of group members. The researchers also found that facial and postural cues were more likely to signal the mood of the group than vocal cues. They suggested that group members may feel it's inappropriate to express their moods verbally in some work settings, so that facial gestures become the more likely avenue of mood expression.

Affective Events Theory

Understanding emotions at work has been significantly helped by a model called **affective events theory (AET)**.[137] AET demonstrates that employees react emotionally to things that happen to them at work, and that this emotional reaction influences their job performance and satisfaction.

Exhibit 2-8 summarizes AET. The theory begins by recognizing that emotions are a response to an event in the work environment. The work environment includes everything surrounding the job—characteristics of the job, such as the variety of tasks and degree of autonomy, job demands, and requirements for expressing emotional labour. This environment creates work events that can be hassles, uplifting events, or both. Examples of hassles are colleagues who refuse to carry their share of work, conflicting directions by different managers, and excessive time pressures. Uplifting events include meeting a goal, getting support from a colleague, and receiving recognition for an accomplishment.[138]

These work events trigger positive or negative emotional reactions, to which employees' personalities and moods predispose them to respond with greater or lesser intensity. People who score low on emotional stability are more likely to react strongly to negative events. In addition, a person's emotional response to a given event can change

affective events theory (AET) The theory that employees react emotionally to things that happen to them at work and that this emotional reaction influences their job performance and satisfaction.

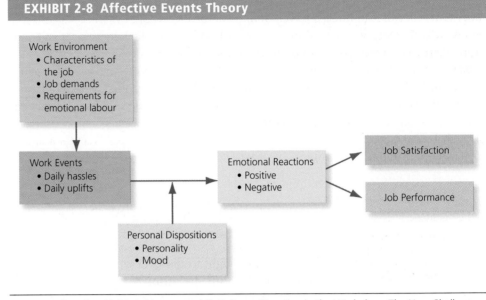

EXHIBIT 2-8 Affective Events Theory

Source: Based on N. M. Ashkanasy and C. S. Daus, "Emotion in the Workplace: The New Challenge for Managers," *Academy of Management Executive*, February 2002, p. 77.

depending on his or her mood. Finally, emotions influence a number of job performance and satisfaction variables, such as organizational citizenship behaviour (OCB), organizational commitment, intentions to quit, level of effort, and workplace deviance. Tests of affective events theory suggest the following:[139]

- An emotional episode is actually a series of emotional experiences, precipitated by a single event and containing elements of both emotions and mood cycles.

- Current emotions influence job satisfaction at any given time, along with the history of emotions surrounding the event.

- Because moods and emotions fluctuate over time, their effect on performance also fluctuates.

- Emotion-driven behaviours are typically short in duration and of high variability.

- Because emotions, even positive ones, tend to be incompatible with behaviours required to do a job, they typically have a negative influence on job performance.

An example might help better explain AET.[140] You work as an aeronautical engineer for Bombardier. Because of the downturn in the demand for commercial jets, you have just learned that the company is considering laying off several thousand employees. This could include you. This event is likely to elicit a negative emotional reaction: You are fearful that you might lose your job and primary source of income. Also, because you are prone to worry a lot and obsess about problems, your feelings of insecurity are increased. This event also puts into place a series of subevents that create an episode: You talk with your boss and he assures you that your job is safe; you hear rumours that your department is high on the list to be eliminated; you run into a former colleague who was laid off six months ago and still has not found work. These, in turn, create emotional ups and downs. One day, you are feeling more upbeat and sure that you will survive the cuts. The next day, you might be depressed and anxious, convinced that your department will be eliminated. These swings in your emotions take your attention away from your work and result in reduced job performance and satisfaction. Finally, your response is magnified because this is the fourth large layoff that Bombardier has initiated in the past three years.

In summary, AET offers two important messages.[141] First, emotions provide valuable insights into how workplace hassles and uplifting events influence employee performance and satisfaction. Second, employees and managers should not ignore emotions or the events that cause them, even when they appear minor, because they accumulate.

GLOBAL IMPLICATIONS

In considering potential global differences in this chapter's concepts, let's consider the four areas that have attracted the most research: (1) perception, (2) attributions, (3) personality, and (4) emotions.

Perception

Several studies have examined how people observe the world around them.[142] In one study, researchers showed East Asians and US subjects a photo with a focal object (like a train) with a busy background and tracked their eye movements. They found that the US subjects were more likely to look at the focal object, whereas the East Asian subjects were more likely to look at the background. Thus, the East Asians appeared to focus more on the context or environment than on the most important object in it. As one of the researchers concluded, "If people are seeing different things, it may be because they are looking differently at the world."[143]

Perceptual differences across cultures have been found to be rooted in the brain's architecture. Using a functional Magnetic Resonance Imaging (fMRI) device to scan subjects' brains, one researcher found that when Singaporeans were shown pictures where either the foreground or background was varied, their brains were less attuned to new foreground images and more attuned to new background images than those of US subjects.[144] This finding suggests that perception is not universal, and that the cultural tendency to focus on either an object/person or a context is part of the "hard wiring" of our brains.

Finally, culture affects what we remember as well. When asked to remember events, US subjects recall more about personal details and their own personal characteristics, whereas Asians recall more about personal relationships and group activities.[145]

As a set, these studies provide striking evidence that Eastern and Western cultures differ in one of the deepest aspects of organizational behaviour: how we see the world around us.

Attributions

The evidence on cultural differences in perception is mixed, but most studies suggest that there *are* differences across cultures in the attributions people make.[146]

Asians overall are less likely to make the fundamental attribution error. The Japanese in particular are less likely to attribute a person's behaviour to internal factors than external or situational forces. A study also found Korean managers less likely to use the self-serving bias—they tended to accept responsibility for group failure "because I was not a capable leader" instead of attributing failure to group members.[147] On the other hand, Asian managers are more likely to lay blame on institutions or whole organizations, whereas Western observers are more likely to believe individual managers should be the focus of blame or praise.[148] That probably explains why US newspapers prominently report the names of individual executives when firms do poorly, whereas Asian media provide more coverage of how the firm as a whole has failed. This tendency to make group-based attributions also explains why individuals from Asian cultures are more likely to make group-based stereotypes.[149] Attribution theory was developed largely based on experiments with US and Western European workers. But these studies suggest caution in making attribution theory predictions in non-Western societies, especially in countries with strong collectivistic traditions.

These differences in attribution tendencies don't mean that the basic concepts of attribution and blame completely differ across cultures, though. Recent studies suggest that Chinese managers assess blame for mistakes using the same distinctiveness, consensus, and consistency cues Western managers use.[150] Chinese managers also become angry and punish those who are deemed responsible for failure, a reaction shown in many studies of Western managers. This finding means that the basic process of attribution applies across cultures but that it takes more evidence for Asian managers to conclude someone else should be blamed.

Personality

The five personality factors identified in the Big Five model appear in almost all cross-cultural studies.[151] These studies have included a wide variety of diverse cultures—such as China, Israel, Germany, Japan, Spain, Nigeria, Norway, Pakistan, and the United States. Differences tend to be in the emphasis on particular dimensions and whether countries are predominantly individualist or collectivist. For example, Chinese managers use the dimension of conscientiousness more often and agreeableness less often than do US managers. The Big Five appear to predict behaviour more accurately in individualistic cultures than collectivistic cultures.[152] However, there is a surprisingly high amount of agreement that the Big Five variables are useful predictors, especially among individuals from developed countries. A comprehensive review of studies covering people from what was then the 15-nation European Community found conscientiousness to be a valid predictor of performance across jobs and occupational groups.[153] US studies have reached the same conclusion.

Emotions

People vary in the degree to which they experience emotions. In China, for example, people report experiencing fewer positive and negative emotions than people in other cultures, and the emotions they experience are less intense than what other cultures report. Compared with mainland Chinese, Taiwanese are more like Canadian employees in their experience of emotions: On average, Taiwanese report more positive and fewer negative emotions than their Chinese counterparts.[154] In general, people in most cultures appear to experience certain positive and negative emotions, but the frequency of their experience and their intensity varies to some degree.[155]

In general, people from all over the world interpret negative and positive emotions the same way. We all view negative emotions, such as hate, terror, and rage, as dangerous and destructive. And we all desire positive emotions, such as joy, love, and happiness. However, some cultures value certain emotions more than others. For example, Americans value enthusiasm, while the Chinese consider negative emotions to be more useful and constructive. In general, pride is seen as a positive emotion in Western, individualistic cultures such as the United States, but Eastern cultures such as China and Japan tend to view pride as undesirable.[156]

The norms for the expression of emotions vary by culture as well. For example, some fundamentalist Muslims see smiling as a sign of sexual attraction, so women have learned not to smile at men so as not to be misinterpreted.[157] And research has shown that in collectivistic countries, people are more likely to believe that the emotional displays of another have something to do with their own relationship with the person expressing the emotion, while people in individualistic cultures don't think that another's emotional expressions are directed at them. Evidence indicates that in Canada a bias exists against expressing emotions, especially intense negative emotions. French retail clerks, in contrast, are infamous for being surly toward customers (a report from the French government itself confirmed this). Reports also indicate that serious German shoppers have been turned off by Walmart's friendly greeters and helpful personnel.[158]

Summary and Implications

1 **What is perception?** Perception is the process by which individuals organize and interpret their impressions to give meaning to their environment. A number of factors operate to shape and sometimes distort perception. The perceiver's attitudes, motives, interests, past experiences, and expectations all shape the way he or she sees an event. The target's characteristics also affect what is perceived; novelty, motion, sounds, size, and other characteristics of the target shape the way it is seen. The situation, or context, in which something or someone is perceived is also important.

2 **What is personality and how does it affect behaviour?** Personality is the stable patterns of behaviour and consistent internal states that determine how an individual reacts to and interacts with others. A review of the personality literature offers general guidelines that can lead to effective job performance. As such, it can improve hiring, transfer, and promotion decisions. Personality attributes give us a framework for predicting behaviour. Personality affects how people react to others, and the types of jobs that they may desire. For example, individuals who are shy, introverted, and uncomfortable in social situations would probably make poor salespeople. Individuals who are submissive and conforming might not be effective as advertising "idea" people. Be aware, though, that measuring personality is not an exact science, and as you no doubt learned from the discussion of attribution theory, it's easy to attribute personality characteristics in error.

3 **Can emotions help or get in the way when we are dealing with others?** Emotions are intense feelings that are directed at someone or something. Positive emotions can be motivating for everyone in the workplace. Negative emotions may make it difficult to get along with others. Can managers control the emotions of their colleagues and employees? No. Emotions are a natural part of an individual's makeup. At the same time, managers err if they ignore the emotional elements in OB and assess individual behaviour as if it were completely rational. Managers who understand the role of emotions will significantly improve their ability to explain and predict individual behaviour.

Do emotions affect job performance? Yes. Emotions, especially negative ones, can hinder performance. That is probably why organizations, for the most part, try to remove emotions from the workplace. But emotions can also enhance performance. How? Two ways.[159] First, emotions can increase arousal levels, thus acting as motivators to higher performance. Second, the concept of emotional labour recognizes that feelings can be part of a job's required behaviour. So, for instance, the ability to effectively manage emotions in leadership and sales positions may be critical to success in those positions. Research also indicates the importance of emotional intelligence, the assortment of noncognitive skills, capabilities, and competencies that influence a person's ability to succeed in coping with environmental demands and pressures.

OB at Work

for Review

1. Define *perception*.

2. What is attribution theory? What are its implications for explaining behaviour in organizations?

3. What is stereotyping? Give an example of how stereotyping can create perceptual distortion.

4. Give some positive results of using shortcuts when judging others.

5. Describe the factors in the Big Five Personality Model. Which factor shows the greatest value in predicting behaviour? Why does it?

6. What behavioural predictions might you make if you knew that an employee had (a) a negative core self-evaluation? (b) a low Mach score? (c) low self-monitoring? (d) a Type A personality?

7. To what extent do people's personalities affect how they are perceived?

8. What is emotional labour and why is it important to understanding OB?

9. What is emotional intelligence and why is it important?

10. Explain affective events theory. What are its implications for managing emotions?

for Critical Thinking

1. How might the differences in experience of students and instructors affect their perceptions of classroom behaviour (for example, students' written work and class comments)?

2. An employee does an unsatisfactory job on an assigned project. Explain the attribution process that this person's manager will use to form judgments about this employee's job performance.

3. One day your boss comes in and he is nervous, edgy, and argumentative. The next day he is calm and relaxed. Does this behaviour suggest that personality traits are not consistent from day to day?

4. What, if anything, can managers do to manage employees' emotions? Are there ethical implications in any of these actions? If so, what?

5. Give some examples of situations where expressing emotions might enhance job performance.

for You

- The discussion of perception might get you thinking about how you view the world. When we perceive someone as a troublemaker, for instance, this may be only a perception, and not a real characteristic of that person. It is always good to question your perceptions, just to be sure that you are not reading something into a situation that is not there.

- One important thing to consider when looking for a job is whether your personality will fit the organization to which you are applying. For instance, let's say that you are considering working for a highly structured company. If you, by nature, are much less formal, then that company may not be a good fit for you.

- Sometimes personalities get in the way when working in groups. You may want to see if you can figure out ways to get personality differences to work in favour of group goals.

- Emotions need not always be suppressed when working with others. While emotions can sometimes hinder performance, positive emotions can motivate you and those around you.

Display Rules Make Good Business Sense

Organizations today realize that good customer service means good business. After all, who wants to end a shopping trip at the grocery store with a surly cashier? Research clearly shows that organizations that provide good customer service have higher profits than those with poor customer service.[160] An integral part of customer-service training is to set forth display rules to teach employees to interact with customers in a friendly, helpful, professional way—and evidence indicates that such rules work: Having display rules increases the odds that employees will display the emotions expected of them.[161]

As one Starbucks manager says, "What makes Starbucks different is our passion for what we do. We're trying to provide a great experience for people, with a great product. That's what we all care about."[162] Starbucks may have good coffee, but a big part of the company's growth has been the customer experience. For instance, the cashiers are friendly and will get to know you by name if you are a repeat customer.

Asking employees to act friendly is good for them, too. Research shows that employees of organizations that require them to display positive emotions actually feel better as a result.[163] And if someone feels that being asked to smile is bad for him, that person does not belong in the service industry in the first place.

Display Rules Do Not Make Sense

Organizations have no business trying to regulate the emotions of their employees. Companies should not be "the thought police" and force employees to feel and act in ways that serve only organizational needs. Service employees should be professional and courteous, yes, but many companies expect them to take abuse and refrain from defending themselves. That's wrong. As philosopher Jean Paul Sartre wrote, we have a responsibility to be authentic—true to ourselves—and within reasonable limits, organizations have no right to ask us to be otherwise.

Service industries have no business teaching their employees to be smiling punching bags. Most customers might even prefer that employees be themselves. Employees should not be openly nasty or hostile, of course, but who appreciates a fake smile? Think about trying on an outfit in a store and the clerk automatically says it looks "absolutely wonderful" when you know it does not and you sense that the clerk is lying. Most customers would rather talk with a "real" person than someone enslaved to an organization's display rules. Furthermore, if an employee does not feel like slapping on an artificial smile, then it's only going to create friction between her and her employer.[164]

Finally, research shows that forcing display rules on employees takes a heavy emotional toll.[165] It's unnatural to expect someone to smile all the time or to passively take abuse from customers, clients, or fellow employees. Organizations can improve their employees' psychological health by encouraging them to be themselves, within reasonable limits.

LEARNING ABOUT **YOURSELF** EXERCISE #1

How Machiavellian Are You?

For each statement, circle the number that most closely resembles your attitude.

Statement	Disagree			Agree	
	A Lot	A Little	Neutral	A Little	A Lot
1. The best way to handle people is to tell them what they want to hear.	1	2	3	4	5
2. When you ask someone to do something for you, it is best to give the real reason for wanting it rather than giving reasons that might carry more weight.	1	2	3	4	5
3. Anyone who completely trusts anyone else is asking for trouble.	1	2	3	4	5
4. It is hard to get ahead without cutting corners here and there.	1	2	3	4	5
5. It is safest to assume that all people have a vicious streak, and it will come out when they are given a chance.	1	2	3	4	5
6. One should take action only when it is morally right.	1	2	3	4	5
7. Most people are basically good and kind.	1	2	3	4	5
8. There is no excuse for lying to someone else.	1	2	3	4	5
9. Most people more easily forget the death of their father than the loss of their property.	1	2	3	4	5
10. Generally speaking, people won't work hard unless they're forced to do so.	1	2	3	4	5

Scoring Key:

To obtain your Mach score, add the number you have checked on questions 1, 3, 4, 5, 9, and 10. For the other 4 questions (2, 6, 7, and 8), reverse the numbers you have checked: 5 becomes 1, 4 is 2, 2 is 4, and 1 is 5. Total your 10 numbers to find your score. The higher your score, the more Machiavellian you are. Among a random sample of American adults, the national average was 25.

Source: R. Christie and F. L. Geis, *Studies in Machiavellianism* (New York: Academic Press, 1970). Reprinted by permission.

Are You a High Self-Monitor?

Indicate the degree to which you think the following statements are true or false by circling the appropriate number. For example, if a statement is always true, circle the 5 next to that statement.

5 = **Certainly, always true**

4 = **Generally true**

3 = **Somewhat true, but with exceptions**

2 = **Somewhat false, but with exceptions**

1 = **Generally false**

0 = **Certainly, always false**

1.	In social situations, I have the ability to alter my behaviour if I feel that something else is called for.	0	1	2	3	4	5
2.	I am often able to read people's true emotions correctly through their eyes.	0	1	2	3	4	5
3.	I have the ability to control the way I come across to people, depending on the impression I wish to give them.	0	1	2	3	4	5
4.	In conversations, I am sensitive to even the slightest change in the facial expression of the person I'm conversing with.	0	1	2	3	4	5
5.	My powers of intuition are quite good when it comes to understanding others' emotions and motives.	0	1	2	3	4	5
6.	I can usually tell when others consider a joke in bad taste, even though they may laugh convincingly.	0	1	2	3	4	5
7.	When I feel that the image I am portraying isn't working, I can readily change it to something that does.	0	1	2	3	4	5
8.	I can usually tell when I've said something inappropriate by reading the listener's eyes.	0	1	2	3	4	5
9.	I have trouble changing my behaviour to suit different people and different situations.	0	1	2	3	4	5
10.	I have found that I can adjust my behaviour to meet the requirements of any situation I find myself in.	0	1	2	3	4	5
11.	If someone is lying to me, I usually know it at once from that person's manner of expression.	0	1	2	3	4	5
12.	Even when it might be to my advantage, I have difficulty putting up a good front.	0	1	2	3	4	5
13.	Once I know what the situation calls for, it is easy for me to regulate my actions accordingly.	0	1	2	3	4	5

Scoring Key:

To obtain your score, add up the numbers circled, except reverse scores for questions 9 and 12. On those, a circled 5 becomes a 0, 4 becomes 1, and so forth. High self-monitors are defined as those with scores of 53 or higher.

Source: R. D. Lennox and R. N. Wolfe, "Revision of the Self-Monitoring Scale," *Journal of Personality and Social Psychology*, June 1984, p. 1361. Copyright © 1984 by the American Psychological Association. Reprinted by permission.

OB at work

Are You a Risk-Taker?

For each of the following situations, indicate the minimum odds of success you would demand before recommending that one alternative be chosen over another. Try to place yourself in the position of the adviser to the central person in each of the situations.

1. Mr. B, a 45-year-old accountant, has recently been informed by his physician that he has developed a severe heart ailment. The disease will be sufficiently serious to force Mr. B to change many of his strongest life habits—reducing his workload, drastically changing his diet, giving up favourite leisure-time pursuits. The physician suggests that a delicate medical operation could be attempted. If successful, the operation would completely relieve the heart condition. But its success cannot be assured, and, in fact, the operation might prove fatal.

   Imagine that you are advising Mr. B. Listed below are several probabilities or odds that the operation will prove successful. Check the *lowest probability* that you would consider acceptable for the operation to be performed.

   _____ Mr. B should not have the operation, no matter what the probabilities.

   _____ The chances are 9 in 10 that the operation will be a success.

   _____ The chances are 7 in 10 that the operation will be a success.

   _____ The chances are 5 in 10 that the operation will be a success.

   _____ The chances are 3 in 10 that the operation will be a success.

   _____ The chances are 1 in 10 that the operation will be a success.

2. Mr. D is the captain of University X's varsity football team. University X is playing its traditional rival, University Y, in the final game of the season. The game is in its final seconds, and Mr. D's team, University X, is behind in the score. University X has time to make one more play. Mr. D, the captain, must decide on a strategy. Would it be best to try a play that would be almost certain to work and try to settle for a tie score? Or, on the other hand, should he try a more complicated and risky play that would bring victory if it succeeded or defeat if it failed?

   Imagine that you are advising Mr. D. Listed below are several probabilities or odds that the risky play will work. Check the *lowest probability* that you would consider acceptable for the risky play to be attempted.

   _____ Mr. D should not attempt the risky play, no matter what the probabilities.

   _____ The chances are 9 in 10 that the risky play will work.

   _____ The chances are 7 in 10 that the risky play will work.

   _____ The chances are 5 in 10 that the risky play will work.

   _____ The chances are 3 in 10 that the risky play will work.

   _____ The chances are 1 in 10 that the risky play will work.

3. Ms. K is a successful businesswoman who has participated in a number of civic activities of considerable value to the community. Ms. K has been approached by the leaders of her political party as a possible candidate in the next provincial election. Ms. K's party is a minority party in the district, though the party has won occasional elections in the past. Ms. K would like to hold political office, but to do so would involve a serious financial sacrifice, since the party has insufficient campaign funds. She would also have to endure the attacks of her political opponents in a hot campaign.

LEARNING ABOUT **YOURSELF** EXERCISE #3 (Continued)

Imagine that you are advising Ms. K. Listed below are several probabilities or odds of Ms. K's winning the election in her district. Check the *lowest probability* that you would consider acceptable to make it worthwhile for Ms. K to run for political office.

_____ Ms. K should not run for political office, no matter what the probabilities.

_____ The chances are 9 in 10 that Ms. K will win the election.

_____ The chances are 7 in 10 that Ms. K will win the election.

_____ The chances are 5 in 10 that Ms. K will win the election.

_____ The chances are 3 in 10 that Ms. K will win the election.

_____ The chances are 1 in 10 that Ms. K will win the election.

4. Ms. L, a 30-year-old research physicist, has been given a 5-year appointment by a major university laboratory. As she contemplates the next 5 years, she realizes that she might work on a difficult long-term problem. If a solution to the problem could be found, it would resolve basic scientific issues in the field and bring high scientific honours. If no solution were found, however, Ms. L would have little to show for her 5 years in the laboratory, and it would be hard for her to get a good job afterward. On the other hand, she could, as most of her professional associates are doing, work on a series of short-term problems for which solutions would be easier to find. Those solutions, though, would be of lesser scientific importance.

Imagine that you are advising Ms. L. Listed below are several probabilities or odds that a solution will be found to the difficult long-term problem that Ms. L has in mind. Check the *lowest probability* that you would consider acceptable to make it worthwhile for Ms. L to work on the more difficult long-term problem.

_____ Ms. L should not choose the long-term, difficult problem, no matter what the probabilities.

_____ The chances are 9 in 10 that Ms. L will solve the long-term problem.

_____ The chances are 7 in 10 that Ms. L will solve the long-term problem.

_____ The chances are 5 in 10 that Ms. L will solve the long-term problem.

_____ The chances are 3 in 10 that Ms. L will solve the long-term problem.

_____ The chances are 1 in 10 that Ms. L will solve the long-term problem.

Scoring Key:

These situations were based on a longer questionnaire. Your results are an indication of your general orientation toward risk rather than a precise measure. To calculate your risk-taking score, add up the chances you were willing to take and divide by 4. (For any of the situations in which you would not take the risk, regardless of the probabilities, give yourself a 10.) The lower your number, the more risk-taking you are.

Source: Adapted from N. Kogan and M. A. Wallach, *Risk Taking: A Study in Cognition and Personality* (New York: Holt, Rinehart and Winston, 1964), pp. 256–261. Reprinted with permission of Wadsworth, a division of Thompson Learning: www.thompsonrights.com. Fax 800-730-2215.

LEARNING ABOUT **YOURSELF** EXERCISE #4

Are You a Type A?

Circle the number on the scale below that best characterizes your behaviour for each trait.

1. Casual about appointments	1	2	3	4	5	6	7	8	Never late
2. Not competitive	1	2	3	4	5	6	7	8	Very competitive
3. Never feel rushed	1	2	3	4	5	6	7	8	Always feel rushed
4. Take things one at a time	1	2	3	4	5	6	7	8	Try to do many things at once
5. Slow doing things	1	2	3	4	5	6	7	8	Fast (eating, walking, etc.)
6. Express feelings	1	2	3	4	5	6	7	8	"Sit on" feelings
7. Many interests	1	2	3	4	5	6	7	8	Few interests outside work

Scoring Key:

Total your score on the 7 questions. Now multiply the total by 3. A total of 120 or more indicates that you are a hard-core Type A. Scores below 90 indicate that you are a hard-core Type B. The following gives you more specifics:

Points	Personality type
120 or more	A1
106–119	A
100–105	A2
90–99	B1
Less than 90	B

Source: Adapted from *Journal of Chronic Diseases*, Vol. 22, Issue 2, June 1969. R. W. Bortner, "Short Rating Scale as a Potential Measure of Pattern A Behavior," pp. 87–91. Copyright © 1969. With permission from Elsevier.

What's Your EI at Work?

Evaluating the following 25 statements will allow you to rate your social skills and self-awareness, the components of emotional intelligence (EI).

EI, the social equivalent of IQ, is complex, in no small part because it depends on some pretty slippery variables—including your innate compatibility, or lack thereof, with the people who happen to be your co-workers. But if you want to get a rough idea of how your EI stacks up, this quiz will help.

As honestly as you can, estimate how you rate in the eyes of peers, bosses, and subordinates on each of the following traits, on a scale of 1–4, with 4 representing strong agreement, and 1 representing strong disagreement.

_____ I usually stay composed, positive, and unflappable even in trying moments.

_____ I can think clearly and stay focused on the task at hand under pressure.

_____ I am able to admit my own mistakes.

_____ I usually or always meet commitments and keep promises.

_____ I hold myself accountable for meeting my goals.

_____ I'm organized and careful in my work.

_____ I regularly seek out fresh ideas from a wide variety of sources.

_____ I'm good at generating new ideas.

_____ I can smoothly handle multiple demands and changing priorities.

_____ I'm result-oriented, with a strong drive to meet my objectives.

_____ I like to set challenging goals and take calculated risks to reach them.

_____ I'm always trying to learn how to improve my performance, including asking advice from people younger than I am.

_____ I readily make sacrifices to meet an important organizational goal.

_____ The company's mission is something I understand and can identify with.

_____ The values of my team—or of our division or department, or the company—influence my decisions and clarify the choices I make.

_____ I actively seek out opportunities to further the overall goals of the organization and enlist others to help me.

_____ I pursue goals beyond what's required or expected of me in my current job.

_____ Obstacles and setbacks may delay me a little, but they don't stop me.

_____ Cutting through red tape and bending outdated rules are sometimes necessary.

_____ I seek fresh perspectives, even if that means trying something totally new.

_____ My impulses or distressing emotions don't often get the best of me at work.

_____ I can change tactics quickly when circumstances change.

_____ Pursuing new information is my best bet for cutting down on uncertainty and finding ways to do things better.

_____ I usually don't attribute setbacks to a personal flaw (mine or someone else's).

_____ I operate from an expectation of success rather than a fear of failure.

Scoring Key:

Total your score. A score below 70 indicates very low EI. EI is not unimprovable. Says Dan Goleman, author of _Working with Emotional Intelligence_, "Emotional intelligence can be learned, and in fact we are each building it, in varying degrees, throughout life. It's sometimes called maturity. EI is nothing more or less than a collection of tools that we can sharpen to help ensure our own survival."

Source: A. Fisher, "Success Secret: A High Emotional IQ," _Fortune_, October 26, 1998, p. 298. Reprinted with the permission of Time Warner Inc. Quiz copyright Daniel Goleman.

SELF-ASSESSMENT LIBRARY   LEARNING ABOUT YOURSELF

More Learning About Yourself Exercises

Additional self-assessments relevant to this chapter appear on MyOBLab (**www.pearsoned.ca/myoblab**).

IV.C.2. What Are My Gender Role Perceptions?
IV.A.1. Am I a Narcissist?
IV.D.1. How Are You Feeling Right Now?
I.E.1. What's My Emotional Intelligence Score?

When you complete the additional assessments, consider the following:

1. Am I surprised about my score?
2. Would my friends evaluate me similarly?

BREAKOUT **GROUP** EXERCISES

Form small groups to discuss the following topics, as assigned by your instructor. Each person in the group should first identify 3–5 key personal values.

1. Think back to your perception of this course and your instructor on the first day of class. What factors might have affected your perceptions of what the rest of the term would be like?

2. Describe a situation where your perception turned out to be wrong. What perceptual errors did you make that might have caused this to happen?

3. Compare your scores on the Learning About Yourself Exercises at the end of the chapter. What conclusions could you draw about your group based on these scores?

WORKING WITH **OTHERS** EXERCISE

Evaluating Your Stereotypes

1. Your instructor will choose 4 volunteers willing to reveal an interesting true-life background fact about themselves. Examples of such background facts are as follows:
   - I can perform various dances, including polka, rumba, bossa nova, and salsa.
   - I am the youngest of 4 children and I attended Catholic high school.
   - Neither of my parents attended school beyond grade 8.
   - My mother is a homemaker and my father is an author.

2. The instructor will put the 4 facts on the board without revealing to which person each belongs, and the 4 students will remain in the front of the room for the first part of the group discussion below.

3. Students in the class should silently decide which person belongs to which fact.

4. Students should break into groups of about 5 or 6 and try to reach a consensus about which person belongs to which fact. Meanwhile, the 4 students can serve as observers to group discussions, listening in on rationales for how students decide to link the facts with the individuals.

5. After 15 minutes of group discussion, several groups will be asked to present their consensus to the class, with justifications.

6. The classroom discussion will focus on perceptions, assumptions, and stereotyping that led to the decisions made.

7. At the end of the discussion, the instructor will reveal which student belongs to each fact.

ETHICAL **DILEMMA** EXERCISE

Hiring Based on Body Art

When Christine Giacomoni applied for a job at the Sherwood Park (Alberta) location of the Real Canadian Superstore, she was wearing a nose stud.[166] She got the job. Six months later, however, she was told that she could no longer wear her small nose stud at work. The company had just recently decided to apply their policy for front-line workers about no nose studs to employees like Giacomoni, who worked in the deli.

The United Food and Commercial Workers (UFCW), Giacomoni's union, grieved this action for her. The complaint ended up in front of a labour arbitrator. The union argued that this company was out of touch with reality. The company argued that nose studs offended customers. They hired Ipsos Reid to survey shoppers, and the results of the poll indicated that "a significant portion" of shoppers would stop shopping at a store that allowed employee facial piercings.

Ultimately, a judge ruled against Real Canadian Superstore's policy. Meanwhile, Giacomoni left to take a job at TELUS, in part because of the store's policy against her piercing. TELUS does not mind that she has a nose stud.

Many employees are aware that tattoos and body piercings can hurt one's chances of being hired. Consider Russell Parrish, 29, who lives near Orlando, Florida, and has dozens of tattoos on his arms, hands, torso, and neck. In searching for a job, Parrish walked into 100 businesses, and in 60 cases, he was refused an application. "I want a career," Parrish says. "I want the same shot as everybody else."

Employers are mixed in their reactions to employees with tattoos or piercings. At Vancouver-based White Spot restaurants, employees cannot have visible tattoos (or pink or blue hair). They are allowed a small, simple nose stud. BC's Starbucks shops don't allow any pierced tongues or visible tattoos. Staff may not wear more than two reasonably sized earrings per ear. At Victoria-based Arq Salons, nearly everyone has a tattoo. "We work in an artistic field," manager Yasmin Morris explains, then adds that staff cannot wear jeans. "We don't want people to look too casual."

A survey of employers revealed that 58 percent indicated that they would be less likely to hire someone with visible tattoos or body piercings. The career centre at the University of Calgary's Haskayne School of Business advises students to "start out understated" when it comes to piercing. "We coach our students to be conservative, and if they do have any facial piercings, we suggest they remove them for the first interview until they find out what the culture's like in the organization," centre director Voula Cocolakis said. "We don't want them to be taken out of the 'yes' pile because of a facial piercing. We want them to interview and compete in the job market based on their qualifications."

In-house policies toward tattoos vary because, legally, employers can do as they wish. As long as the rule is applied equally to everyone (it would not be permissible to allow tattoos on men but not on women, for example), policies against tattoos are perfectly legal. Though not hiring people with tattoos is discrimination, it is not a form of discrimination that is covered by the Canadian Human Rights Act.

Thirty-six percent of those aged 18 to 25, and 40 percent of those aged 26 to 40, have at least one tattoo, whereas only 15 percent of those over 40 do, according to a fall 2006 survey by the Pew Research Center. One study in *American Demographics* suggested that 57 percent of senior citizens viewed visible tattoos as "freakish."

How does the matter of perception explain why some employers ban tattoos, while others don't mind them? Is it fair for employers to reject applicants who have tattoos? Is it fair to require employees, if hired, to conceal their tattoos? Should it be illegal to allow tattoos to be a factor at all in the hiring process?

CASE INCIDENTS

The Upside of Anger?

A researcher doing a case study on emotions in organizations interviewed Laura, a 22-year-old customer-service representative in Australia. The following is a summary of the interview (with some paraphrasing of the interviewer questions):[167]

INTERVIEWER: How would you describe your workplace?

LAURA: Very cold, unproductive, [a] very, umm, cold environment, atmosphere.

INTERVIEWER: What kinds of emotions are prevalent in your organization?

LAURA: Anger, hatred toward other people, other staff members.

INTERVIEWER: So it seems that managers keep employees in line using fear tactics?

LAURA: Yeah. [The general manager's] favourite saying is, "Nobody's indispensable." So, it's like, "I can't do that because I'll get sacked!"

INTERVIEWER: How do you survive in this situation?

LAURA: You have to cater your emotions to the sort of situation, the specific situation . . . because it's just such a hostile environment, this is sort of the only way you can survive.

INTERVIEWER: Are there emotions you have to hide?

LAURA: Managers don't like you to show your emotions . . . They don't like to show that there is anything wrong or anything emotional in the working environment.

INTERVIEWER: Why do you go along?

LAURA: I feel I have to put on an act because . . . to show your true emotions, especially toward my managers [Laura names two of her senior managers], it would be hatred sometimes. So, you just can't afford to do that because it's your job and you need the money.

INTERVIEWER: Do you ever rebel against this system?

LAURA: You sort of put on a happy face just so you can annoy [the managers]. I find that they don't like people being happy, so you just annoy them by being happy. So, yeah. It just makes you laugh. You just "put it on" just because you know it annoys [management]. It's pretty vindictive and manipulative, but you just need to do that.

INTERVIEWER: Do you ever find that this gets to you?

LAURA: I did care in the beginning, and I think it just got me into more trouble. So now I just tell myself, "I don't care." If you tell yourself something for long enough, eventually you believe it. Yeah, so now I just go "Oh well."

INTERVIEWER: Do you intend to keep working here?

LAURA: It's a means to an end now. So every time I go [to work] and every week I just go, "Well, one week down, one week less until I go away." But if I knew that I didn't have this goal, I don't know if I could handle it, or if I would even be there now.

INTERVIEWER: Is there an upside to working here?

LAURA: I'm so much better at telling people off now than I ever used to be. I can put people in place in about three sentences. Like, instead of, before I would walk away from it. But now I just stand there and fight. . . . I don't know if that's a good thing or a bad thing.

Questions

1. Do you think Laura is justified in her responses to her organization's culture? Why or why not?

2. Do you think Laura's strategic use and display of emotions serve to protect her?

3. Assuming that Laura's description is accurate, how would *you* react to the organization's culture?

4. Research shows that acts of co-workers (37 percent) and management (22 percent) cause more negative emotions for employees than do acts of customers (7 percent). What can Laura's company do to change its emotional climate?

The Nice Trap?

In these pages we have already noted that one downside of agreeableness is that agreeable people tend to have lower levels of career success.[168] Though agreeableness does not appear to be related to job performance, agreeable people do earn less money. Though we are not sure why this is so, it may be that agreeable individuals are less aggressive in negotiating starting salaries and pay raises for themselves.

Yet there is clear evidence that agreeableness is something employers value. Recent books argue in favour of the "power of nice"[169] and "the kindness revolution."[170] Articles in the business press have argued that the sensitive, agreeable CEO—as manifested in CEOs such as GE's Jeff Immelt and Boeing's Jim McNerney—signals a shift in business culture.[171] In many circles, individuals desiring success in their careers are exhorted to be "complimentary," "kind," and "good."[172]

Take the example of 500-employee Lindblad Expeditions. It emphasizes agreeableness in its hiring decisions. The VP of HR commented, "You can teach people any technical skill, but you can't teach them how to be a kindhearted, generous-minded person with an open spirit."

So, while employers want agreeable employees, agreeable employees are not better job performers, and they are *less* successful in their careers. One might explain this apparent contradiction by noting that employers value agreeable employees for other reasons: They are more pleasant to be around, and they may help others in ways that are not reflected in their job performance. While the former point seems fair enough—agreeable people are better liked—it's not clear that agreeable individuals actually help people more. A review of the organizational citizenship literature revealed a pretty weak correlation between an employee's agreeableness and how much he or she helped others.

Moreover, a recent study of CEOs and CEO candidates revealed that this contradiction applies to organizational leaders as well. Using ratings made of candidates from an executive search firm, the researchers studied the personalities and abilities of 316 CEO candidates for companies involved in buyout and venture capital transactions. They found that what gets a CEO candidate hired is not what makes him or her effective. Specifically, CEO candidates who were rated high on "nice" traits, such as respecting others, developing others, and teamwork, were more likely to be hired. However, these same characteristics—especially teamwork and respecting others for venture capital CEOs—made the organizations that the CEOs led less successful.

Questions

1. Do you think there is a contradiction between what employers want in employees (agreeableness) and what kinds of employees (those who are not agreeable) actually perform best? Why or why not?

2. Often, the effects of personality depend on the situation. Can you think of some job situations in which agreeableness is an important virtue? And in which it is harmful?

3. In research we conducted, we found that the negative effects of agreeableness on earnings is stronger for men than for women (that is, being agreeable hurt men's earnings more than women's). Why do you think this might be the case?

FROM CONCEPTS TO SKILLS

Reading Emotions

Understanding another person's felt emotions is very difficult. But we can learn to read others' displayed emotions.[173] We do this by focusing on verbal, nonverbal, and paralanguage cues.

The easiest way to find out what someone is feeling is to ask them. Saying something as simple as "Are you okay? What's the problem?" can often provide you with the information to assess an individual's emotional state. But relying on a verbal response has two drawbacks. First, almost all of us conceal our emotions to some extent for privacy and to reflect social expectations. So we might be unwilling to share our true feelings. Second, even if we want to verbally convey our feelings, we may be unable to do so. As we noted earlier, some people have difficulty understanding their own emotions and, hence, are unable to express them verbally. So, at best, verbal responses provide only partial information.

Let's say you are talking with a co-worker. Does the fact that his back is rigid, his teeth clenched, and his facial muscles tight tell you something about his emotional state? It probably should. Facial expressions, gestures, body movements, and physical distance are nonverbal cues that can provide additional insights into what a person is feeling. The facial expressions shown in Exhibit 2-9, for instance, are a window into a person's feelings. Notice the difference in facial features: the height of the cheeks, the raising or lowering of the brow, the turn of the mouth, the positioning of the lips, and the configuration of muscles around the eyes. Even something as subtle as the distance someone chooses to position him- or herself from you can convey how much intimacy, aggressiveness, repugnance, or withdrawal that person feels.

EXHIBIT 2-9   Facial Expressions and Emotions

Each picture portrays a different emotion. Try to identify them before looking at the answers.

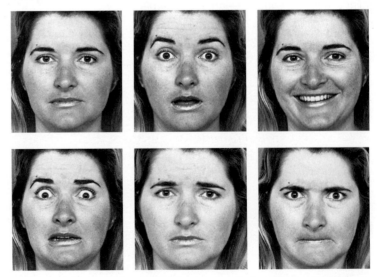

Top, left to right: neutral, surprise, happiness. Bottom: fear, sadness, anger.

Source: Paul Ekman, PhD/Paul Ekman Group, LLC.

OB at work

When you speak with someone, you may notice a sharp change in the tone of her voice and the speed at which she speaks. You are tapping into the third source of information on a person's emotions—paralanguage. This is communication that goes beyond the specific spoken words. It includes pitch, amplitude, rate, and voice quality of speech. Paralanguage reminds us that people convey their feelings not only in what they say, but also in how they say it.

Practising Skills

Part A. Form groups of 2. Each person is to spend a couple of minutes thinking of a time in the past when he or she was emotional about something. Examples might include being upset with a parent, sibling, or friend; being excited or disappointed about an academic or athletic achievement; being angry with someone over an insult or slight; being disgusted by something someone has said or done; or being happy because of something good that happened. Do not share this event with the other person in your group.

Part B. Now you will conduct 2 role plays. Each will be an interview. In the first, 1 person will play the interviewer and the other will play the job applicant. The job is for a summer management internship with a large retail chain. Each role play will last no longer than 10 minutes. The interviewer is to conduct a normal job interview, except you are to continually rethink the emotional episode you envisioned in part A. Try hard to convey this emotion while, at the same time, being professional in interviewing the job applicant.

Part C. Now reverse positions for the second role play. The interviewer becomes the job applicant and vice versa. The new interviewer will conduct a normal job interview, except that he or she will continually rethink the emotional episode chosen in part A.

Part D. Spend 10 minutes analyzing the interview, with specific attention focused on these questions: What emotion(s) do you think the other person was conveying? What cues did you pick up? How accurate were you in reading those cues?

Reinforcing Skills

1. Watch the actors in an emotion-laden film, such as *Death of a Salesman* or *12 Angry Men,* for clues to the emotions they are exhibiting. Try to determine the various emotions projected and explain how you arrived at your conclusion.

2. Spend a day specifically looking for emotional cues in the people with whom you interact. Did paying attention to emotional cues improve communication?

Values, Attitudes, and Diversity in the Workplace

At SaskGaming, diversity is valued and respected. How does this affect the company's workplace?

LEARNING OUTCOMES

1. What are values?
2. How can we understand values across cultures?
3. Are there unique Canadian values?
4. What are attitudes and why are they important?
5. How do we respond to diversity in the workplace?

Regina-based SaskGaming, which operates two casinos (Casino Regina and Casino Moose Jaw), faces an interesting perception problem.[1] Not everyone thinks that gambling is okay, and a number of studies show the negative impact of gambling. Still, gambling is legal, and SaskGaming is committed to being a good employer. In fact, it was named one of Canada's Top 100 Employers in both 2008 and 2009, one of Saskatchewan's Top 10 Employers for the third year in a row in 2009, and one of Canada's Best Diversity Employers in 2010.

SaskGaming lists its four organizational values on its website: respect, integrity, passion, and innovation. These values operate under the company's mandate: to "offer casino entertainment in a socially responsible manner, generating quality employment, economic benefit to the community and profit for Saskatchewan people in partnership with First Nations."

Generally, we expect that an organization's values, like those of an individual, will be reflected in corresponding behaviour and attitudes. If a company stated that it valued gambling in a socially responsible manner, and yet no behaviour followed from that statement, we would question whether that value was really so important to the company. However, in SaskGaming's case, the company backs up its value statements with concrete policies and actions to show support for its values. Does having strong values make for a better workplace?

In this chapter, we look more carefully at how values influence behaviour, and consider the relationship between values and attitudes. We then consider two specific issues that arise from our discussion of values and attitudes: job satisfaction and workforce diversity.

THE BIG IDEA

Values affect our behaviours and attitudes, and can have a big impact on how people with different backgrounds get along in the workplace.

OB IS FOR EVERYONE

- How do countries differ in their values?
- Are Gen-Ys really different from their elders?
- What can you learn about OB from Aboriginal culture?
- What would you need to know to set up a business in Asia?

Values

1   What are values?

BLOG IT

What leads to job satisfaction?
Describe a job that you had and
indicate the factors that determined
how satisfied you were with that job.

www.obstudentjournals.blogspot.com

Is capital punishment right or wrong? How about racial or gender quotas in hiring—are
they right or wrong? If a person likes power, is that good or bad? The answers to these
questions are value-laden. Some might argue, for example, that capital punishment is
right because it is an appropriate response to crimes such as murder. However, others
might argue just as strongly that no government has the right to take anyone's life.

Values represent basic convictions that "a specific mode of conduct or end-state of
existence is personally or socially preferable to an opposite or converse mode of conduct or end-state of existence."[2] They contain a judgmental element in that they carry
an individual's ideas as to what is right, good, or desirable. Values have both content
and intensity attributes. The content attribute says a mode of conduct or end-state of
existence is *important*. The intensity attribute specifies *how important* it is. When we rank
an individual's values in terms of their intensity, we obtain that person's **value system**.
All of us have a hierarchy of values that forms our value system, and these influence
our attitudes and behaviour.[3]

Values tend to be relatively stable and enduring.[4] Most of our values are formed in
our early years—with input from parents, teachers, friends, and others. As children, we
were told that certain behaviours or outcomes are always desirable or always undesirable. There were few grey areas. It is this absolute or "black-or-white" learning of values
that more or less ensures their stability and endurance.

Below we examine two frameworks for understanding values: Milton Rokeach's
terminal and instrumental values, and Kent Hodgson's general moral principles.

Rokeach Value Survey

Milton Rokeach created the Rokeach Value Survey (RVS), which consists of two sets of
values, each containing 18 individual value items.[5] One set, called **terminal values**,
refers to desirable end-states of existence. These are the goals that individuals would
like to achieve during their lifetime. They include

- A comfortable life (a prosperous life)
- An exciting life (a stimulating, active life)
- A sense of accomplishment (lasting contribution)
- Equality (brotherhood, equal opportunity for all)
- Inner harmony (freedom from inner conflict)
- Happiness (contentedness)[6]

The other set, called **instrumental values**, refers to preferable ways of behaving, or means for achieving the terminal
values. They include

- Ambitious (hard-working, aspiring)
- Broad-minded (open-minded)
- Capable (competent, effective)
- Courageous (standing up for your beliefs)
- Imaginative (daring, creative)
- Honest (sincere, truthful)[7]

Several studies confirm that RVS values vary among groups.[9]
People in the same occupations or categories (corporate managers, union members, parents, students) tend to hold similar

values Basic convictions that a
specific mode of conduct or end-state
of existence is personally or socially
preferable to an opposite or converse
mode of conduct or end-state of
existence.

value system A hierarchy based on
a ranking of an individual's values in
terms of their intensity.

terminal values Goals that
individuals would like to achieve
during their lifetime.

instrumental values Preferable
ways of behaving.

OB in ACTION

The Magnificent Seven Principles

→ *Dignity of human life.* The lives of **people are to be
respected**.

→ *Autonomy.* All persons are **intrinsically valuable** and
have the **right to self-determination**.

→ *Honesty.* **The truth should be told** to those who
have a right to know it.

→ *Loyalty.* **Promises**, **contracts**, and **commitments**
should be **honoured**.

→ *Fairness.* **People should be treated justly**.

→ *Humaneness.* Our **actions ought to accomplish
good**, and we should **avoid doing evil**.

→ *The common good.* Actions should accomplish **the
greatest good for the greatest number** of
people.[8]

EXHIBIT 3-1	Value Ranking of Executives, Union Members, and Activists (Top Five Only)				
EXECUTIVES		**UNION MEMBERS**		**ACTIVISTS**	
Terminal	Instrumental	Terminal	Instrumental	Terminal	Instrumental
1. Self-respect	1. Honest	1. Family security	1. Responsible	1. Equality	1. Honest
2. Family security	2. Responsible	2. Freedom	2. Honest	2. A world of peace	2. Helpful
3. Freedom	3. Capable	3. Happiness	3. Courageous	3. Family security	3. Courageous
4. A sense of accomplishment	4. Ambitious	4. Self-respect	4. Independent	4. Self-respect	4. Responsible
5. Happiness	5. Independent	5. Mature love	5. Capable	5. Freedom	5. Capable

Source: Based on W. C. Frederick and J. Weber, "The Values of Corporate Managers and Their Critics: An Empirical Description and Normative Implications," in *Business Ethics: Research Issues and Empirical Studies,* ed. W. C. Frederick and L. E. Preston (Greenwich, CT: JAI Press, 1990), pp. 123–144.

values. One study compared corporate executives, members of the steelworkers' union, and members of a community activist group. Although there was a good deal of overlap among the three groups,[10] there were also some very significant differences (see Exhibit 3-1). The activists ranked "equality" as their most important terminal value; executives and union members ranked this value 12 and 13, respectively. Activists ranked "helpful" as their second-highest instrumental value. The other two groups both ranked it 14. Because executives, union members, and activists all have a vested interest in what corporations do, these differences can create serious conflicts when these groups have to reach agreement on the organization's economic and social policies.[11]

Hodgson's General Moral Principles

Ethics is the study of moral values or principles that guide our behaviour and inform us whether actions are right or wrong. Thus, ethical values are related to moral judgments about right and wrong.

In recent years, there has been concern that individuals are not grounded in moral values. It is believed that this lack of moral roots has resulted in a number of business scandals, such as those at WorldCom, Enron, Hollinger International, and even in the sponsorship scandal of the Canadian government. We discuss the issue of ethics further in Chapter 12.

Management consultant Kent Hodgson has identified seven general moral principles that individuals should follow when making decisions about behaviour. He calls these "the Magnificent Seven" and suggests that they are universal values that managers should use to make *principled, appropriate,* and *defensible* decisions.[12] They are presented in *OB in Action—The Magnificent Seven Principles.* With these principles in mind, *OB in the Street* considers whether management was right to fire employees who participated in the Stanley Cup riots in Vancouver.

OB in the STREET
Stanley Cup Rioting Leads to Employee Firing

Should an ethical lapse in your nightlife affect your day job? After the Vancouver Canucks lost in Game 7 of the Stanley Cup finals, riots broke out throughout Vancouver's downtown core.[13] Many of the rioters were young men and women in their teens and early 20s. Many Vancouverites were appalled at the rioting, the looting, the fires, and the attacks on police and firefighters.

ethics The study of moral values or principles that guide our behaviour and inform us whether actions are right or wrong.

Many of the rioters boasted about their behaviour on Facebook, and even posted pictures of their activities. Others were shown in videos taken at the scene and then posted to YouTube and other social media sites. As perpetrators were identified, law-abiding citizens started calling for justice—customers and clients complained to companies where some of these individuals were employed.

One young woman, a part-time receptionist at a downtown Vancouver Toyota dealership, lost her job because she was seen gleefully stealing clothing in a video clip taken at the scene. One young man, who apparently did not engage in the riots, provided status updates on Facebook live from the scene; his comments applauding the riots included "awesome" and "vancouver needed remodeling anyway. . . ." He was fired. His employer, Delta, BC-based RiteTech, was listed on his Facebook page and received more than 100 emails and 20 phone calls complaining about the 21-year-old's postings.

Employees did these activities outside their work time and may not have expected their employers to respond so harshly. Managers, on the other hand, found that the rioters' actions could negatively affect their business and harm other employees, and may have considered their actions to be in the best interest of the common good.

Assessing Cultural Values

2 How can we understand values across cultures?

> SaskGaming's decision to value diversity in its workplace reflects a dominant value of Canada as a multicultural country.[14] The approach to diversity is very different in the United States, which considers itself a melting pot with respect to different cultures. SaskGaming has other values that guide employees. These include respect, integrity, passion, and innovation. What do we know about the values of other countries? What values make Canada unique?

In Chapter 1, we noted that managers have to become capable of working with people from different cultures. Thus, it is important to understand how values differ across cultures.

Hofstede's Framework for Assessing Cultures

One of the most widely referenced approaches for analyzing variations among cultures was done in the late 1970s by Geert Hofstede.[15] He surveyed more than 116 000 IBM employees in 40 countries about their work-related values, and found that managers and employees vary on 5 value dimensions of national culture:

power distance A national culture attribute that describes the extent to which a society accepts that power in institutions and organizations is distributed unequally.

- *Power distance.* **Power distance** describes the degree to which people in a country accept that power in institutions and organizations is distributed unequally. A high rating on power distance means that large inequalities of power and wealth exist and are tolerated in the culture, as in a class or caste system that discourages upward mobility. A low power distance rating characterizes societies that stress equality and opportunity.

individualism A national culture attribute that describes the degree to which people prefer to act as individuals rather than as members of groups.

collectivism A national culture attribute that describes a tight social framework in which people expect others in groups of which they are a part to look after them and protect them.

- *Individualism vs. collectivism.* **Individualism** is the degree to which people prefer to act as individuals rather than as members of groups and believe in individual rights above all else. **Collectivism** emphasizes a tight social framework in which people expect others in groups of which they are a part to look after them and protect them.

masculinity A national culture attribute that describes the extent to which the culture favours traditional masculine work roles of achievement, power, and control. Societal values are characterized by assertiveness and materialism.

femininity A national culture attribute that sees little differentiation between male and female roles; women are treated as the equals of men in all respects.

- *Masculinity vs. femininity.* Hofstede's construct of **masculinity** is the degree to which the culture favours traditional masculine roles, such as achievement, power, and control, as opposed to viewing men and women as equals. A high masculinity rating indicates the culture has separate roles for men and women, with men dominating the society. A high **femininity** rating means the culture sees little differentiation between male and female roles and treats women as the equals of men in all respects.

- *Uncertainty avoidance.* The degree to which people in a country prefer structured over unstructured situations defines their uncertainty avoidance. In cultures that score high on uncertainty avoidance, people have an increased level of anxiety about uncertainty and ambiguity, and use laws and controls to reduce uncertainty. Cultures low on **uncertainty avoidance** are more accepting of ambiguity and are less rule-oriented, take more risks, and more readily accept change.

- *Long-term vs. short-term orientation.* This newest addition to Hofstede's typology measures a society's long-term devotion to traditional values. People in a culture with **long-term orientation** look to the future and value thrift, persistence, and tradition. In a culture with **short-term orientation**, people value the here and now; they accept change more readily and don't see commitments as impediments to change.

How do different countries score on Hofstede's dimensions? Exhibit 3-2 shows the ratings for the countries for which data are available. For example, power distance is higher in Malaysia and Slovak Republic than in any other countries. Canada is tied with the Netherlands as one of the top five individualistic countries in the world, falling just behind the United States, Australia, and Great Britain. Canada also tends to be short term in orientation and is low in power distance (people in Canada tend not to accept built-in class differences among people). Canada is also relatively low on uncertainty avoidance, meaning that most adults are relatively tolerant of uncertainty and ambiguity. Canada scores relatively high on masculinity (meaning that most people emphasize traditional gender roles) in comparison with countries such as Denmark, Finland, Norway, and Sweden, although its score is lower than that of the United States.

You will notice regional differences. Western and Northern nations such as Canada and the Netherlands tend to be more individualistic. Poorer countries such as Mexico and the Philippines tend to be higher on power distance. South American nations tend to be higher than other countries on uncertainty avoidance, and Asian countries tend to have a long-term orientation.

How do countries differ in their values?

Hofstede's cultural dimensions have been enormously influential on OB researchers and managers. Nevertheless, his research has been criticized. First, although Hofstede's work was updated and reaffirmed by a Canadian researcher at the Chinese University of Hong Kong (Michael Bond), who conducted research on values in 22 countries on 5 continents,[16] the original work is more than 30 years old and was based on a single company (IBM). A lot has happened in the world scene since then. Some of the most obvious changes include the fall of the Soviet Union, the transformation of Central and Eastern Europe, the end of apartheid in South Africa, the spread of Islam throughout the world today, and the rise of China as a global power. Second, few researchers have read the details of Hofstede's methodology closely and are therefore unaware of the many decisions and judgment calls he had to make (for example, reducing the number of cultural values to just five). Some results are unexpected. For example, Japan, which is often considered a highly collectivistic nation, is considered only average on collectivism under Hofstede's dimensions.[17] Despite these concerns, many of which Hofstede refutes,[18] he has been one of the most widely cited social scientists ever, and his framework has left a lasting mark on OB.

The GLOBE Framework for Assessing Cultures

Begun in 1993, the Global Leadership and Organizational Behavior Effectiveness (GLOBE) research program is an ongoing cross-cultural investigation of leadership and

uncertainty avoidance A national culture attribute that describes the extent to which a society feels threatened by uncertain and ambiguous situations and tries to avoid them.

long-term orientation A national culture attribute that emphasizes the future, thrift, and persistence.

short-term orientation A national culture attribute that emphasizes the past and present, respect for tradition, and fulfillment of social obligations.

Exhibit 3-2 Hofstede's Cultural Values by Nation

Country	Power Distance Index	Individualism Index	Masculinity Index	Uncertainty Avoidance Index	Long-Term Orientation Index
Argentina	49	46	56	86	20
Australia	36	90	61	51	21
Austria	11	55	79	70	60
Belgium	65	75	54	94	82
Brazil	69	38	49	76	44
Canada	39	80	52	48	36
Canada French	54	73	45	60	na
Chile	63	23	28	86	31
China	80	20	66	30	87
Colombia	67	13	64	80	13
Costa Rica	35	15	21	86	na
Czech Republic	57	58	57	74	70
Denmark	18	74	16	23	35
Ecuador	78	8	63	67	na
El Salvador	66	19	40	94	20
Finland	33	63	26	59	38
France	68	71	43	86	63
Germany	35	67	66	65	83
Great Britain	35	89	66	35	51
Greece	60	35	57	112	45
Guatemala	95	6	37	101	na
Hong Kong	68	25	57	29	61
India	77	48	56	40	51
Indonesia	78	14	46	48	62
Iran	58	41	43	59	14
Ireland	28	70	68	35	24
Israel	13	54	47	81	38
Italy	50	76	70	75	61
Jamaica	45	39	68	13	na
Japan	54	46	95	92	88
Korea (South)	60	18	39	85	100
Malaysia	104	26	50	36	41
Mexico	81	30	69	82	24
Netherlands	38	80	14	53	67
New Zealand	22	79	58	49	33
Norway	31	69	8	50	35
Pakistan	55	14	50	70	50
Panama	95	11	44	86	na
Peru	64	16	42	87	25
Philippines	94	32	64	44	27
Poland	68	60	64	93	38
Portugal	63	27	31	104	28
Singapore	74	20	48	8	72
Slovak Republic	104	52	110	51	77
South Africa (white)	49	65	83	49	na
Spain	57	51	42	86	48
Sweden	31	71	5	29	53
Switzerland	34	68	70	58	74
Taiwan	58	17	45	69	93
Thailand	64	20	34	64	32
Turkey	66	37	45	85	46
United States	40	91	62	46	26
Uruguay	61	36	38	100	26
Venezuela	81	12	73	76	16
Vietnam	70	20	40	30	57

Scores range from 0 = extremely low on dimension to 100 = extremely high.

Source: Geert Hofstede, Gert Jan Hofstede, Michael Minkov, *Cultures and Organizations, Software of the Mind*, Third Revised Edition, McGrawHill 2010, ISBN 0-07-166418-1. By permission by the author.

national culture. Using data from 825 organizations in 62 countries, the GLOBE team identified nine dimensions on which national cultures differ.[19] Some—such as power distance, individualism/collectivism, uncertainty avoidance, gender differentiation (similar to masculinity vs. femininity), and future orientation (similar to long-term vs. short-term orientation)—resemble the Hofstede dimensions. The main difference is that the GLOBE framework added dimensions, such as humane orientation (the degree to which a society rewards individuals for being altruistic, generous, and kind to others) and performance orientation (the degree to which a society encourages and rewards group members for performance improvement and excellence).

Which framework is better? That is hard to say, and each has its adherents. We give more emphasis to Hofstede's dimensions here because they have stood the test of time and the GLOBE study confirmed them. However, researchers continue to debate the differences between these frameworks, and future studies may, in time, favour the more nuanced perspective of the GLOBE study.[20]

In this chapter's *Working with Others Exercise* on page 116, you have the opportunity to compare the cultural values of two countries and determine how differences might affect group behaviour. The *Ethical Dilemma Exercise* on page 117 asks you to consider when something is a gift and when it is a bribe. Different cultures take different approaches to this question.

Values in the Canadian Workplace

Studies have shown that when individual values align with organizational values, the results are positive. Individuals who have an accurate understanding of the job requirements and the organization's values adjust better to their jobs, and have greater levels of satisfaction and organizational commitment.[21] In addition, shared values between the employee and the organization lead to more positive work attitudes,[22] lower turnover,[23] and greater productivity.[24]

3 Are there unique Canadian values?

Individual and organizational values do not always align. Moreover, within organizations, individuals can have very different values. Two major factors lead to a potential clash of values in the Canadian workplace: generational differences and cultural differences. *OB in the Workplace* considers the difficulties the nonprofit sector has had in retaining younger people and minorities.

OB in the WORKPLACE
The Nonprofit Sector Looks to Diversify Its Workforce

How can the nonprofit sector attract and keep younger and diverse employees? Ottawa-based HR Council for the Nonprofit Sector (HR Council) wants to change the face of the nonprofit sector, which, far from being diverse, is dominated by Caucasians (89 percent of employees) and Baby Boomers (39 percent of employees are 45 or older).[25] As the Baby Boomers retire from the nonprofit sector, efforts are underway to increase the number of younger and diverse employees in the sector's labour force.

Avnish Mehta joined the board of directors of the HR Council to get involved in its diversity project. "I'm a visible minority, but I'm a born-and-raised Calgarian . . . and I thought I would be able to bring a little bit of a different flair to the way that things are being built," says Mehta. "My goal is to be able to lend the voice of young people in this sector, to show there are people who are motivated," he adds.

As a member of the HR Council's diversity project, Mehta is trying to find ways to recruit more diverse employees. The project found that first-year turnover rates for new immigrants and visible minorities were higher than for other groups.

Tanara Pickard, a project manager for the HR Council, said that part of the problem for immigrants and minorities relates to "cultural differences in workplace etiquette." As well, there is the question of values. "What we were finding is that because the not-for-profit sector is so values-driven, rather than focused on cost and the bottom line, they're looking for people to have a good fit within their organization," Pickard says.

Mehta suggests that nonprofits may need to consider changing their organizational structure to be more inclusive. "Maybe some of the [organizational] structures that we've relied on for such a long time are maybe not the best ones for motivating us [minorities] to stick around."

Let's look at the findings and implications of generational and cultural differences in Canada.

Generational Differences

Research suggests that generational differences exist in the workplace among the Baby Boomers (born between the mid-1940s and the mid-1960s), the Generation Xers (born between the mid-1960s and the late 1970s), and the Generation Ys (born between 1979 through 1994).[26] Gen-Xers are squeezed in the workplace between the much larger Baby Boomer and Gen-Y groups. With Generation Y starting to climb the ladder in organizations, while Boomers are continuing to hold on to their jobs rather than retire, the impact of having these two large generations—one younger and one older—in the workplace is gaining attention. Bear in mind that our discussion of these generations presents broad generalizations, and you should certainly avoid stereotyping individuals on the basis of these generalizations. There are individual differences in values. For instance, there is no law that says a Baby Boomer cannot think like someone from Generation Y. Despite these limitations, values do change over generations.[27] We can

Robert Dutton, president and CEO of Boucherville, Quebec-based Rona, started working at the company under a grandfather, and then later found himself working with fellow Baby Boomers. Recently he has realized that Generation Y is starting to make up a larger portion of Rona's dealers, and finds that it has changed his life to "have the chance to work with young people—to share ideas with them, their thoughts, their vision for the future."[28] Dutton started the group Young Rona Business Leaders to help develop the talent that will be the future of Rona.

gain some useful insights from analyzing values this way to understand how others might view things differently from ourselves, even when they are exposed to the same situation. In this chapter's *Learning About Yourself Exercise* on page 115, you have the opportunity to examine some of the things that you value.

SELF-ASSESSMENT LIBRARY

LEARNING ABOUT YOURSELF

1. What Do You Value?
(page 115)

Baby Boomers

Baby Boomers (called *Boomers* for short) are a large cohort born after World War II, when veterans returned to their families and times were good. Boomers entered the workforce from the mid-1960s through the mid-1980s. They brought with them a large measure of the "hippie ethic" and distrust of authority. But they placed a great deal of emphasis on achievement and material success. They work hard and want to enjoy the fruits of their labours. They are pragmatists who believe ends can justify means. Boomers see the organizations that employ them merely as vehicles for their careers. Terminal values such as a sense of accomplishment and social recognition rank high with them.

Generation X

The lives of Gen-Xers (Generation Xers) have been shaped by globalization, two-career parents, MTV, AIDS, and computers. They value flexibility, life options, and the achievement of job satisfaction. Family and relationships are very important to this cohort. Gen-Xers are skeptical, particularly of authority. They also enjoy team-oriented work. In search of balance in their lives, Gen-Xers are less willing to make personal sacrifices for the sake of their employer than previous generations were. On the Rokeach Value Survey, they rate high on true friendship, happiness, and pleasure.

Generation Y

The most recent entrants to the workforce, *Generation Y* (also called *Millennials, Netters, Nexters,* and *Generation Nexters*), grew up during prosperous times. They have high

When Sean Durfy, CEO of Calgary-based WestJet, announced in March 2011 that he was stepping down from the position, he said it was for "family reasons." While that has often been code for "being let go," in Durfy's case it was more likely the truth. His wife had been ill for four years, and the couple has young children. Instead, there was talk that Durfy's announcement was the start of what might be expected from other Generation X-ers, who "work to live rather than live to work." Baby Boomers were expected to sacrifice one's family to climb the corporate ladder. But this may no longer be true of younger generations.

expectations and seek meaning in their work. Gen-Ys have life goals more oriented toward becoming rich (81 percent) and famous (51 percent) than do Generation Xers (62 percent and 29 percent, respectively), but they also see themselves as socially responsible. Gen-Ys are at ease with diversity and are the first generation to take technology for granted. More than other generations, they tend to be questioning, electronically networked, and entrepreneurial. At the same time, some have described Gen-Ys as entitled and needy. They grew up with parents who watched (and praised) their every move. One employer said, "This is the most high-maintenance workforce in the history of the world. The good news is they're also going to be the most high-performing."[29] Bruce Tulgan, author of *Not Everyone Gets a Trophy: How to Manage Generation Y*, suggests that managers need to give Gen-Ys extra direction, encouragement, and feedback to keep them focused and loyal.[30]

Are Gen-Ys really different from their elders?

The Generations Meet in the Workplace

An understanding that individuals' values differ but tend to reflect the societal values of the period in which they grew up can be a valuable aid in explaining and predicting behaviour. Baby Boomers currently dominate the workplace, but their years of being in charge are limited. In 2013, half of them will be at least 55 and 18 percent will be over 60.[31] Recent research suggests that Baby Boomers and Generation Y have a significant amount in common in their views toward the workplace, and that this might have profound effects on the organization of the workplace in the future.[32] Members of these two generations, much more than those from Generation X, want more flexible workplaces, more opportunity for time off to explore themselves, and more work-life balance. Generation Y will certainly change the face of the workplace in significant ways. Its members have mastered a communication and information system that many of their parents have yet to understand. In Chapter 5, we discuss further motivational differences between the Baby Boomers and Gen-Ys.

Cultural Differences

Canada is a multicultural country. One in five Canadians is an immigrant, according to the 2006 Census (the 2011 Census was still being conducted at the time of writing).[33] In 2006, 46 percent of Metropolitan Toronto's population, 40 percent of Vancouver's population, and 21 percent of Montreal's population were made up of immigrants.[34] The 2006 Census found that 20.1 percent of Canada's population spoke neither of the country's two official languages as their first language. In Vancouver and Toronto, this rate was 41 percent and 44 percent, respectively, so considerably more than one-third of the population of those two cities does not speak either English or French as a first language.[35] Of those who speak other languages, 16 percent speak Chinese (mainly Mandarin or Cantonese). The other dominant languages in Canada are Italian (in fourth place), followed by German, Punjabi, and Spanish.[36] These figures indicate the very different cultures that are part of the Canadian fabric of life.

Though we live in a multicultural society, there are some tensions among people from different races and ethnic groups. For instance, a Statistics Canada survey on ethnic diversity found that while most Canadians (93 percent) say they have never or rarely experienced unfair treatment because of ethnic or cultural characteristics, 20 percent of visible minorities reported having been unfairly treated sometimes or often.[37] Canadians often define themselves as "not Americans" and point out differences in the values of the two countries. Ipsos Reid recently conducted a national survey of Americans and Canadians, ages 18 to 34, and found a number of differences between the two countries' young adults. Both groups rated health care, education, and

EXHIBIT 3-3 Differences between Canadian and American Young Adults, 18 to 34		
	Canada	**United States**
Text messages per week (sent and received)	78.7	129.6
Online social media	Facebook: 81% had a profile MySpace: 23% had registered a profile	Facebook: 57% had registered a profile MySpace: 54% had registered a profile
Married	25%	39%
Domestic partnerships	18%	7%
Own a home	35%	45%
Employed on a full- or part-time basis or self-employed	62%	64%
Some post-secondary education	76%	68%
Actively participate in a recycling program	88%	72%
Use public transportation once a week or more often	33%	20%
Favourite sport	NHL hockey (58%)	NFL football (57%)

Source: Based on Ipsos Reid, *A Check-up on the Habits and Values of North America's Young Adults (Part 1)* (Calgary: Ipsos Reid, 2009), http://www.ipsos-na.com/news-polls/pressrelease.aspx?id=4532

employment as their top concerns. "When we compare the lifestyles of young adults in the United States and Canada, one could describe the Americans as more 'traditional' and more 'domestic' in their values and focus, whereas Canadians are more of the 'free-spirit' type," said Samantha McAra, senior research manager with Ipsos Reid.[38] Exhibit 3-3 shows some of the other differences between Canadian and American young adults.

In his book *Fire and Ice*, Michael Adams finds that there is a growing dissimilarity between Canadian and American values. The two groups differ in 41 of the 56 values that Adams examined. For 24 values the gap has actually widened between 1992 and 2000, indicating that Canadians' social values are growing more distinct from those of Americans.[39] Adams suggests that the September 11 attacks have had an impact on the American personality. He finds Americans are more accepting of patriarchy and hierarchy these days, and he concludes that it is "the supposedly bold, individualistic Americans who are the nodding conformists, and the supposedly shy, deferential and law-abiding Canadians who are most likely to assert their personal autonomy and political agency."[40]

In what follows, we identify a number of cultural values that influence workplace behaviour in Canada. Be aware that these are generalizations, and it would be a mistake to assume that everyone coming from the same cultural background acts similarly. Rather, these overviews are meant to encourage you to think about cultural differences and similarities so that you can better understand people's behaviour.

Francophone and Anglophone Values

Quebec is generally seen as culturally, linguistically, politically, and legally distinct from the rest of Canada.[41] French, not English, is the dominant language in Quebec, and Roman Catholicism, not Protestantism, is the dominant religion. Unlike the rest of Canada, where the law is based on English common law principles, Quebec's legal system is based on the French civil code. From time to time, Quebec separatists threaten that the province will leave Canada. Thus, it will be of interest to managers and employees in Canadian firms to be aware of some of the potential cultural differences when managing in francophone environments compared with anglophone environments.

A number of studies have shown that English-speaking Canadians and French-speaking Canadians have distinctive value priorities. In general, Canadian anglophone managers are seen to be more individualistic than Canadian francophone managers,[42] although more recent research finds greater similarity between anglophone and francophone middle managers in terms of their individualistic-collectivistic orientation.[43] Francophones have also been shown to be more concerned about the interpersonal aspects of the workplace than task competence.[44] They have also been found to be more committed to their work organizations.[45] Earlier studies suggested that anglophones took more risks,[46] but more recent studies have found that this point has become less true and that French-speaking Canadians had the highest values for "reducing or avoiding ambiguity and uncertainty at work."[47]

Canadian anglophone business people have been found to use a more cooperative negotiating style when dealing with one another, compared with Canadian francophone business people.[48] However, Canadian francophones are more likely than Canadian anglophones to use a more cooperative approach during cross-cultural negotiations.[49] Other studies indicate that anglophone managers tend to value autonomy and intrinsic job values, such as achievement, and thus are more achievement-oriented, while francophone managers tend to value affiliation and extrinsic job values, such as technical supervision.[50] A recent study conducted at the University of Ottawa and Laval University suggests that some of the differences reported in previous research may be decreasing.[51] Another study suggests that anglophones and francophones are not very different personality-wise.[52] Yet another study indicates that French Canadians have become more like English Canadians in valuing autonomy and self-fulfillment.[53] These studies are consistent with a recent study that suggests there are few differences between francophones and anglophones.[54]

Professor Carolyn Egri of the business school at Simon Fraser University led a cross-cultural study that found that Canadian anglophone and francophone managers tend to use somewhat different influence styles.[55] Specifically, Canadian anglophone managers are significantly more likely to use behaviours that are beneficial to the organization than Canadian francophone managers. Canadian francophone managers are more likely to focus on their own needs more than the organization's and use destructive/legal (what the authors term "get out of my way or get trampled") and destructive/illegal (what the authors term "burn, pillage and plunder") behaviour dimensions than Canadian anglophone managers. The study also examined the influence styles of American and Mexican managers and found that Mexican managers scored significantly higher than Canadian francophone managers on the use of destructive behaviours, with American managers' use of these behaviours more similar to Canadian anglophones. The results of this study suggest that Canadian francophone managers might serve as a bridge between Mexican managers at one end and American and Canadian anglophone managers on the other, as the francophone style is sometimes a blend of the other groups. The study's authors concluded that Canadian francophones would do well in "joint ventures, business negotiations, and other organizational interactions that involve members of more divergent cultural groups. For example, a national Canadian firm may find it strategically advantageous to utilize Canadian-Francophones in negotiating business contracts with Mexican firms."[56]

Despite some cultural and lifestyle value differences, both francophone and anglophone managers today would have been exposed to more of the same types of organizational theories during their training in post-secondary school, which might also influence their outlooks as managers. Thus we would not expect to find large differences in the way that firms in francophone Canada are managed, compared with those in the rest of Canada. Throughout the textbook, you will find examples of Quebec-based businesses that support this conclusion.

Aboriginal Values

Entrepreneurial activity among Canada's Aboriginal peoples has been increasing at the same time that there are more partnerships and alliances between Aboriginal and non-Aboriginal businesses. Because of these business interactions, it is important to examine the types of differences we might observe in how each culture manages its businesses. For instance, sustainability is an important value in Aboriginal logging companies. Chilanko Forks, BC-based Tsi Del Del, a logging company, received the 2011 Aboriginal Forest Products Business Leadership Award because of the substantial amount of revenues the company put into education.[57] For every cubic metre harvested, the Alexis Creek First Nations–owned company puts 50 cents into a post-secondary educational fund. The fund is used to train the next generation of loggers. Andrew Gage, vice-president of the Forest Products Association of Canada, says that it's a wise investment for the company. "You are not going to find a group of people that are more committed to sustainable harvesting. They share those values that our industry has been trying to get to for the last decade or so."[58]

What can you learn about OB from Aboriginal culture?

"Aboriginal values are usually perceived (by non-Aboriginals) as an impediment to economic development and organizational effectiveness."[59] These values include reluctance to compete, a time orientation different from the Western one, and an emphasis on consensus decision making.[60] Aboriginal people do not necessarily agree that these values are business impediments, however.

Specifically, although Canadian businesses and government have historically assumed that "non-Native people must teach Native people how to run their own organizations," the First Nations of Canada are not convinced.[61] They believe that traditional culture, values, and languages do not have to be compromised in the building of a self-sustaining economy. Moreover, they believe that their cultural values may actually be a positive force in conducting business.[62]

In recent years, Canadian businesses facing Native land claims have met some difficulties in trying to accommodate demands for appropriate land usage. In some cases, accommodation can mean less logging or mining by businesses until land claims are worked out. Cliff Hickey and David Natcher, two anthropologists from the University of Alberta, collaborated with the Little Red River Cree Nation in northern Alberta to develop a new model for forestry operations on First Nations land and achieve better communication between businesses and Native leaders.[63] The anthropologists sought to balance the Native community's traditional lifestyle with the economic concerns of forestry operations. *OB in Action—Ground Rules for Developing Business Partnerships with Aboriginal People* outlines several of Hickey and Natcher's recommended ground rules, which they say could be used in oil and gas developments as well. Johnson Sewepegaham, chief of the Little Red River Cree, said his community would use these recommendations to resolve difficulties on treaty lands for which Vernon, BC-based Tolko Industries and Vancouver-based Ainsworth jointly hold

OB in ACTION

Ground Rules for Developing Business Partnerships with Aboriginal People

→ Modify management operations to **reduce negative impact on wildlife species**.

→ Modify operations to **ensure community access** to lands and resources.

→ **Protect** all those **areas identified by community members** as having biological, cultural, and historical significance.

→ **Recognize and protect Aboriginal and treaty rights** to hunting, fishing, trapping, and gathering activities.

→ **Increase** forest-based **economic opportunities** for community members.

→ **Focus feedback** on **performance**, not personalities.

→ **Increase** the **involvement of community members** in decision making.[64]

forest tenure. The two companies presented their general development plan to the Cree in fall 2008.[65] In 2009, the Cree were effective in persuading Tolko to revise its tree harvesting activities in a way that recognizes and respects the First Nations' ecological and cultural needs.[66]

Lindsay Redpath of Athabasca University has noted that Aboriginal cultures are more collectivist in orientation than are non-Aboriginal cultures in Canada and the United States.[67] Aboriginal organizations are much more likely to reflect and advance the goals of the community. There is also a greater sense of family within the workplace, with greater affiliation and loyalty. Power distance in Aboriginal cultures is smaller than in non-Aboriginal cultures of Canada and the United States, and there is an emphasis on consensual decision making. Aboriginal cultures are lower on uncertainty avoidance than non-Aboriginal cultures in Canada and the United States. Aboriginal organizations and cultures tend to have fewer rules and regulations. Each of these differences suggests that businesses created by Aboriginal people will differ from non-Aboriginal businesses, and both research and anecdotal evidence support this conjecture.[68] For instance, Richard Prokopanko, director of government relations for Vancouver-based Alcan, says that shifting from handling issues in a generally legalistic, contract-oriented manner to valuing more dialogue and collaboration has helped ease some of the tension that had built up over 48 years between Alcan and First Nations people.[69]

Asian Values

The largest visible minority group in Canada are the Chinese. Over 1 million Chinese live in Canada, representing 26 percent of the country's visible minority population.[70] The Chinese in this country are a diverse group; they come from different countries, speak different languages, and practise different religions. The Chinese are only one part of the entire East and Southeast Asian population that influences Canadian society. It's predicted that by 2017 almost one-half of all visible minorities in Canada will come from two groups, South Asian and Chinese, and that these groups will be represented in almost equal numbers.[71] As well, many Canadian organizations, particularly those in British Columbia, conduct significant business with Asian firms. Asian cultures differ from Canadian culture on many of the GLOBE dimensions discussed earlier. For instance, Asian cultures tend to exhibit greater power distance and greater collectivism. These differences in values can affect individual interactions.

What would you need to know to set up a business in Asia?

Professor Rosalie Tung of Simon Fraser University and her student Irene Yeung examined the importance of *guanxi* (personal connections with the appropriate authorities or individuals) for a sample of North American, European, and Hong Kong firms doing business with companies in mainland China.[72] They suggest that their findings are also relevant in understanding how to develop relationships with firms from Japan, South Korea, and Hong Kong.

"*Guanxi* refers to the establishment of a connection between two independent individuals to enable a bilateral flow of personal or social transactions. Both parties must derive benefits from the transaction to ensure the continuation of such a relationship."[73] *Guanxi* relations are based on reciprocation, unlike Western networked relationships, which may be characterized more by self-interest. *Guanxi* relationships are meant to be long-term and enduring, in contrast with the immediate gains sometimes expected in Western relationships. *Guanxi* also relies less on institutional law, and more on personal power and authority, than do Western relationships. Finally, *guanxi* relations are governed more by the notion of shame (that is, external pressures on performance), while Western relations often rely on guilt (that is, internal pressures on performance) to maintain agreements. *Guanxi* is seen as extremely important for business success in China—more than such factors as the right location, price, or strategy, or product differentiation and quality. For Western firms wanting to do business with Asian firms, an understanding of *guanxi* and an effort to build relationships are important strategic advantages.

Our discussion about differences in cross-cultural values should suggest to you that understanding other cultures matters. When Canadian firms develop operations across Canada, south of the border, or overseas, employees need to understand other cultures to work more effectively and get along with others.

Attitudes

Despite recognition over the years as a good employer, the employees at SaskGaming's Casino Regina went on strike for almost two months in June and July 2010.[74] The employees had been without a collective agreement since May 2009.

Fran Mohr, spokesperson for the Public Service Alliance of Canada (PSAC), which represents the striking employees, was relieved to see the strike end. "We are happy it's finally over. I feel like a lot of weight has been lifted off my shoulders," said Mohr. "It's a big thing having 400 people walking a picket line day after day. It's a really good feeling to be going back. It feels like we've been gone a long time."

Though the casino had to run much shorter hours, public attitude seemed to favour the employees during the course of the strike. Those on the picket line received frequent donations of food and money. Mohr, a cashier at the casino, said the public understood why the employees went on strike. "We love what we do and no one wants to go on strike, but at some point you have to stand up for yourself. We have our families to consider and I think our clientele really respects that." The attitudes of the striking employees toward their employer were considerably negative before the strike began and became stronger as the strike progressed. So how do employees' attitudes get formed, and can they really be changed?

4 What are attitudes and why are they important?

Attitudes are evaluative statements—either positive or negative—about objects, people, or events. They reflect how we feel about something. When I say, "I like my job," I am expressing my attitude about work.

Specific attitudes tend to predict specific behaviours, whereas general attitudes tend to predict general behaviours. For instance, asking an employee about her intention to stay with an organization for the next six months is likely to better predict turnover for that person than asking her how satisfied she is with her job. On the other hand, overall job satisfaction would better predict a general behaviour, such as whether the employee is engaged in her work or motivated to contribute to her organization.[75]

In organizations, attitudes are important because they affect job behaviour.[76] Employees may believe, for example, that supervisors, auditors, managers, and time-and-motion engineers are all conspiring to make them work harder for the same or less money. This may then lead to a negative attitude toward management when an employee is asked to stay late for help on a special project.

Employees may also be negatively affected by the attitudes of their co-workers or clients. *From Concepts to Skills* on page 119 looks at whether it's possible to change someone's attitude, and how that might happen in the workplace.

A person can have thousands of attitudes, but OB focuses our attention on a limited number of work-related attitudes.[77] Below we consider four important attitudes that affect organizational performance: job satisfaction, organizational commitment, job involvement, and employee engagement.

attitudes Positive or negative feelings about objects, people, or events.

Job Satisfaction

Our definition of **job satisfaction**—a positive feeling about a job resulting from an evaluation of its characteristics—is clearly broad.[78] A survey conducted by Mercer in 2011 found that Canadians are not all that satisfied: 36 percent said they were thinking about leaving their employers and another 20 percent were ambivalent about staying or going.[79]

What Causes Job Satisfaction?

Think about the best job you have ever had. What made it so? Chances are you liked the work you did and the people with whom you worked. Interesting jobs that provide training, variety, independence, and control satisfy most employees.[80] There is also a strong correspondence between how well people enjoy the social context of their workplace and how satisfied they are overall. Interdependence, feedback, social support, and interaction with co-workers outside the workplace are strongly related to job satisfaction even after accounting for characteristics of the work itself.[81]

You have probably noticed that pay comes up often when people discuss job satisfaction. For people who are poor (for example, living below the poverty line) or who live in poor countries, pay does correlate with job satisfaction and overall happiness. But once an individual reaches a level of comfortable living (in Canada, that occurs at about $40 000 a year, depending on the region and family size), the relationship between pay and job satisfaction virtually disappears. People who earn $80 000 are, on average, no happier with their jobs than those who earn close to $40,000.[82] High-paying jobs have average satisfaction levels no higher than those that pay much less. One researcher even found no significant difference when he compared the overall well-being of the richest people on the *Forbes* 400 list with that of Maasai herders in East Africa.[83] *Case Incident—Thinking Your Way to a Better Job* on page 118 considers the effect state of mind has on a person's job satisfaction.

Money does motivate people, as we will discover in Chapter 4. But what motivates us is not necessarily the same as what makes us happy. A recent poll found that entering first-year university students rated becoming "very well off financially" first on a list of 19 goals, ahead of choices such as helping others, raising a family, or becoming

When asked "On a scale of 1 (not at all) to 7 (completely) how satisfied are you with your life?" *Forbes* magazine's "richest Americans" averaged 5.8 and an East African Maasai tribe, who engage in traditional herding and lead nomadic lives, averaged 5.7. The results of this study suggest that money does not buy life satisfaction.[84]

job satisfaction A positive feeling about a job resulting from an evaluation of its characteristics.

proficient in an academic pursuit. Maybe your goal isn't to be happy. But if it is, money is probably not going to do much to get you there.[85]

Job satisfaction is not just about job conditions. Personality also plays a role. Research has shown that people who have positive **core self-evaluations**—who believe in their inner worth and basic competence—are more satisfied with their jobs than those with negative core self-evaluations. Not only do they see their work as fulfilling and challenging, they are more likely to gravitate toward challenging jobs in the first place. Those with negative core self-evaluations set less ambitious goals and are more likely to give up when confronting difficulties. Thus, they are more likely to be stuck in boring, repetitive jobs than those with positive core self-evaluations.[86]

So what are the consequences of job satisfaction? We examine this question below.

Job Satisfaction and Productivity

The idea that "happy workers are productive workers" developed in the 1930s and 1940s, largely as a result of the Hawthorne studies at Western Electric. Based on those conclusions, managers focused on working conditions and the work environment to make employees happier. Then, in the 1980s, an influential review of the research suggested that the relationship between job satisfaction and job performance was not particularly high. The authors of that review even labelled it "illusory."[87]

More recently, a review of more than 300 studies corrected some errors in that earlier review and found the correlation between job satisfaction and job performance is moderately strong, even across international contexts. This conclusion also appears to be generalizable across international contexts. The correlation is higher for complex jobs that provide employees with more discretion to act on their attitudes.[88] A review of 16 studies that assessed job performance and satisfaction over time also linked job satisfaction to job performance[89] and suggested the relationship mostly works one way: Satisfaction was a likely cause of better performance, but higher performance was not a cause of higher job satisfaction.

We cannot be entirely sure, however, whether satisfaction causes productivity or productivity causes satisfaction.[90] In other words, if you do a good job, you intrinsically feel good about it. In addition, your higher productivity should increase your recognition, your pay level, and your likelihood of promotion. Cumulatively, these rewards, in turn, increase your level of satisfaction with the job. Most likely, satisfaction can lead to high levels of performance for some people, while for others, high performance is satisfying. *Point/Counterpoint* on page 114 further explores the debate on whether job satisfaction is created by the situation or by an individual's characteristics.

As we move from the individual to the organization level, we also find support for the satisfaction-performance relationship.[91] When we gather satisfaction and productivity data for the organization as a whole, we find organizations with more satisfied employees tend to be more effective than organizations with less satisfied employees.

Job Satisfaction and Organizational Citizenship Behaviour

In Chapter 1, we defined **organizational citizenship behaviour (OCB)** as discretionary behaviour that is not part of an employee's formal job requirements and is not usually rewarded, but that nevertheless promotes the effective functioning of the organization.[92] Individuals who are high in OCB will go beyond their usual job duties, providing performance that is beyond expectations. Examples of such behaviour include helping colleagues with their workloads, taking only limited breaks, and alerting others to work-related problems.[93] More recently OCB has been associated with the following workplace behaviours: "altruism, conscientiousness, loyalty, civic virtue, voice, functional participation, sportsmanship, courtesy, and advocacy participation." [94] Organizational citizenship is important, as it can help the organization function more efficiently and more effectively.[95]

core self-evaluation Bottom-line conclusions individuals have about their capabilities, competence, and worth as a person.

organizational citizenship behaviour (OCB) Discretionary behaviour that is not part of an employee's formal job requirements, but that nevertheless promotes the effective functioning of the organization.

Service organizations know that whether customers are satisfied and loyal depends on how front-line employees deal with customers. Singapore Airlines has earned a reputation among world travellers for outstanding customer service. The airline's "putting people first" philosophy applies to both its employees and customers. In recruiting flight attendants, the airline selects people who are warm, hospitable, and happy to serve others. Through extensive training, Singapore Airlines moulds recruits into attendants focused on complete customer satisfaction.

It seems logical to assume that job satisfaction should be a major determinant of an employee's OCB.[96] Satisfied employees would seem more likely to talk positively about an organization, help others, and go beyond the normal expectations in their jobs.[97] They might go beyond the call of duty because they want to reciprocate their positive experiences. Consistent with this thinking, evidence suggests job satisfaction is moderately correlated with OCBs; people who are more satisfied with their jobs are more likely to engage in OCBs.[98] Why? Fairness perceptions help explain the relationship.[99] Those who feel their co-workers support them are more likely to engage in helpful behaviours, whereas those who have antagonistic relationships with co-workers are less likely to do so.[100]

Job Satisfaction and Customer Satisfaction

As we noted in Chapter 1, employees in service jobs often interact with customers. Since service organization managers should be concerned with pleasing customers, it is reasonable to ask: Is employee satisfaction related to positive customer outcomes? For front-line employees who have regular contact with customers, the answer is yes. Satisfied employees increase customer satisfaction and loyalty.[101]

Why? In service organizations, customer retention and defection are highly dependent on how front-line employees deal with customers. Satisfied employees are more likely to be friendly, upbeat, and responsive—which customers appreciate. Because satisfied employees are less prone to turnover, customers are more likely to encounter familiar faces and receive experienced service. These qualities build customer satisfaction and loyalty. In addition, the relationship seems to apply in reverse: Dissatisfied customers can increase an employee's job dissatisfaction. Employees who interact with rude, thoughtless, or unreasonably demanding customers report lower job satisfaction.[102]

Job Satisfaction and Absenteeism and Turnover
We find a consistent negative relationship between satisfaction and absenteeism, but it is moderate to weak.[103] While it

certainly makes sense that dissatisfied employees are more likely to miss work, other factors affect the relationship. Organizations that provide liberal sick leave benefits are encouraging all their employees—including those who are highly satisfied—to take days off. You can find work satisfying yet still want to enjoy a three-day weekend if those days come free with no penalties. When numerous alternative jobs are available, dissatisfied employees have high absence rates, but when there are few they have the same (low) rate of absence as satisfied employees.[104]

The relationship between job satisfaction and turnover is stronger than between satisfaction and absenteeism.[105] The satisfaction-turnover relationship also is affected by alternative job prospects. If an employee is presented with an unsolicited job offer, job dissatisfaction is less predictive of turnover because the employee is more likely leaving because of "pull" (the lure of the other job) than "push" (the unattractiveness of the current job). Similarly, job dissatisfaction is more likely to translate into turnover when employment opportunities are plentiful because employees perceive it is easy to move. Finally, when employees have high "human capital" (high education, high ability), job dissatisfaction is more likely to translate into turnover because they have, or perceive, many available alternatives.[106]

How Employees Can Express Dissatisfaction

Job dissatisfaction and antagonistic relationships with co-workers predict a variety of behaviours organizations find undesirable, including unionization attempts, substance abuse, stealing at work, undue socializing, and tardiness. Researchers argue that these behaviours are indicators of a broader syndrome called *deviant behaviour in the workplace* (or *employee withdrawal*).[107] If employees don't like their work environment, they will respond somehow, though it is not always easy to forecast exactly *how*. One worker might quit. Another might use work time to surf the Internet or take work supplies home for personal use. In short, workers who don't like their jobs "get even" in various ways—and because those ways can be quite creative, controlling only one behaviour, such as with an absence control policy, leaves the root cause untouched. To effectively control the undesirable consequences of job dissatisfaction, employers should attack the source of the problem—the dissatisfaction—rather than try to control the different responses.

Exhibit 3-4 presents a model—the exit-voice-loyalty-neglect framework—that can be used to examine individual responses to job dissatisfaction along two dimensions: whether they are constructive or destructive and whether they are active or passive. Four types of behaviour result:[108]

- **Exit**. Actively attempting to leave the organization, including looking for a new position as well as resigning. This is a destructive action from the point of view of the organization.

- **Voice**. Actively and constructively attempting to improve conditions, including suggesting improvements, discussing problems with superiors, and some forms of union activity.

- **Loyalty**. Passively but optimistically waiting for conditions to improve, including speaking up for the organization in the face of external criticism and trusting the organization and its management to "do the right thing."

- **Neglect**. Passively allowing conditions to worsen, including chronic absenteeism or lateness, reduced effort, and increased error rate. This is a destructive action from the point of view of the organization.

Exit and neglect behaviours reflect employee choices of lowered productivity, absenteeism, and turnover in the face of dissatisfaction. But this model also presents

exit Dissatisfaction expressed by actively attempting to leave the organization.

voice Dissatisfaction expressed by actively and constructively attempting to improve conditions.

loyalty Dissatisfaction expressed by passively waiting for conditions to improve.

neglect Dissatisfaction expressed by passively allowing conditions to worsen.

EXHIBIT 3-4 Responses to Job Dissatisfaction

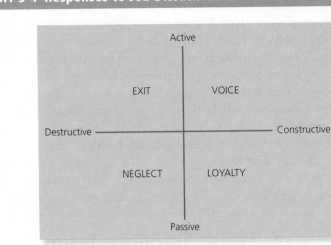

Source: "When Bureaucrats Get the Blues: Responses to Dissatisfaction Among Federal Employees" by Caryl Rusbult, David Lowery. *Journal of Applied Social Psychology 15*, no. 1, p. 83. Copyright © 1985, John Wiley and Sons.

constructive behaviours such as voice and loyalty that allow individuals to tolerate unpleasant situations or to work toward satisfactory working conditions. It helps us understand situations, such as those we sometimes find among unionized workers, where low job satisfaction is coupled with low turnover.[109] Union members often express dissatisfaction through the grievance procedure or through formal contract negotiations. These voice mechanisms allow them to continue in their jobs while convincing themselves that they are acting to improve the situation.

Managers Often "Don't Get It"

Given the evidence we have just reviewed, it should come as no surprise that job satisfaction can affect the bottom line. One study by a management consulting firm separated large organizations into high morale (where more than 70 percent of employees expressed overall job satisfaction) and medium or low morale (fewer than 70 percent). The stock prices of companies in the high morale group grew 19.4 percent, compared with 10 percent for the medium or low morale group. Despite these results, many managers are unconcerned about employee job satisfaction. Still others overestimate how satisfied employees are with their jobs, so they don't think there's a problem when there is. In one study of 262 large employers, 86 percent of senior managers believed their organization treated its employees well, but only 55 percent of the employees agreed. Another study found 55 percent of managers thought morale was good in their organization, compared with only 38 percent of employees.[110] Managers first need to care about job satisfaction, and then they need to measure it rather than just assume that everything is going well.

Organizational Commitment

organizational commitment The degree to which an employee identifies with a particular organization and its goals, and wishes to maintain membership in the organization.

In **organizational commitment** an employee identifies with a particular organization and its goals, and wishes to remain a member.[111]

Professor John Meyer at the University of Western Ontario and his colleagues have identified and developed measures for three types of commitment:[112]

affective commitment An individual's emotional attachment to and identification with an organization, and a belief in its values.

- **Affective commitment**. An individual's emotional attachment to an organization and a belief in its values. For example, a PetSmart employee may be affectively committed to the company because of its involvement with animals.

- **Normative commitment**. The obligation an individual feels to stay with an organization for moral or ethical reasons. An employee spearheading a new initiative may remain with an employer because she feels she would "leave the employer in the lurch" if she left.

- **Continuance commitment**. An individual's perceived economic value of remaining with an organization. An employee may be committed to an employer because she is paid well and feels it would hurt her family to quit.

A positive relationship appears to exist between organizational commitment and job productivity, but it is a modest one.[113] A review of 27 studies suggested that the relationship between commitment and performance is strongest for new employees, and considerably weaker for more experienced employees.[114] The research evidence demonstrates negative relationships between organizational commitment and both absenteeism and turnover.[115]

Different forms of commitment have different effects on behaviour. One study found managerial affective commitment more strongly related to organizational performance than was continuance commitment.[116] Another study showed that continuance commitment was related to a lower intention to quit but an increased tendency to be absent and lower job performance. These results make sense in that continuance commitment really isn't a commitment at all. Rather than an allegiance (affective commitment) or an obligation (normative commitment) to an employer, a continuance commitment describes an employee "tethered" to an employer simply because there isn't anything better available.[117]

How can companies increase organizational commitment? Research on a number of companies known for employees with high organizational commitment identified five reasons why employees commit themselves:[118]

- They are proud of [the company's] aspirations, accomplishments, and legacy; they share its values.

A major focus of Nissan Motor Company's Diversity Development Office in Japan is helping female employees develop their careers. Nissan provides women such as the assembly-line workers shown here with one-on-one counselling services of career advisers and training programs to develop applicable skills. Women can also visit Nissan's corporate intranet to read interviews with "role models," women who have made substantial contributions to the company. Nissan believes that hiring more women and supporting their careers will contribute to the company's competitive edge.

normative commitment The obligation an individual feels to stay with an organization.

continuance commitment An individual's calculation to stay with an organization based on the perceived costs of leaving the organization.

- They know what each person is expected to do, how performance is measured, and why it matters.

- They are in control of their own destinies; they savour the high-risk, high-reward work environment.

- They are recognized mostly for the quality of their individual performance.

- They have fun and enjoy the supportive and highly interactive environment.

These findings suggest a variety of ways for organizations to increase the commitment of employees. Earlier in the chapter, we discussed the role of satisfaction on organizational citizenship behaviour (OCB). We should also note that when individuals have high organizational commitment, they are likely to engage in more OCB.

Job Involvement

Related to job satisfaction is **job involvement**,[119] which measures the degree to which people identify psychologically with their job and consider their perceived performance level important to self-worth.[120] Employees with a high level of job involvement strongly identify with and really care about the kind of work they do. Another closely related concept is **psychological empowerment**, employees' beliefs in the degree to which they influence their work environment, their competence, the meaningfulness of their job, and their perceived autonomy.[121] High levels of both job involvement and psychological empowerment are positively related to organizational citizenship and job performance.[122] High job involvement is also related to reduced absences and lower resignation rates.[123]

Employee Engagement

A new concept that comes out of the work on job involvement is **employee engagement**, an individual's involvement with, satisfaction with, and enthusiasm for the work he or she does. For example, we might ask employees about the availability of resources and the opportunities to learn new skills, whether they feel their work is important and meaningful, and whether their interactions with co-workers and supervisors are rewarding.[124] Highly engaged employees have a passion for their work and feel a deep connection to their company; disengaged employees have essentially "checked out"—putting time but not energy or attention into their work.[125] Calgary-based Vista Projects, an engineering procurement and construction management firm, consults with its employees for engagement ideas. Doing so has resulted in educational initiatives, opportunities for company ownership, and time off for religious holidays.[126] To encourage engagement, the president of Charlottetown, PEI-based Holland College visits the college's 13 sites routinely to give employees an opportunity to raise concerns.

A study of nearly 8000 business units in 36 companies found that those whose employees had high average levels of engagement had higher levels of customer satisfaction, were more productive, had higher profits, and had lower levels of turnover and accidents than at other companies.[127] Toronto-based Molson Coors Canada found that engaged employees were five times less likely to have safety incidents, and when one did occur, it was much less serious, and less costly for the engaged employee than for a disengaged one ($63 per incident vs. $392).

Such promising findings have earned employee engagement a following in many business organizations and management consulting firms. However, the concept is relatively new and still generates active debate about its usefulness. One review of the literature concluded that the meaning of the term is ambiguous for both practitioners and academics,[128] while another reviewer called engagement "an umbrella term for whatever one wants it to be."[129] Still, a 2011 study that draws from the best current

job involvement The degree to which a person identifies with a job, actively participates in it, and considers performance important to self-worth.

psychological empowerment Employees' belief in the degree to which they affect their work environment, their competence, the meaningfulness of their job, and their perceived autonomy in their work.

employee engagement An individual's involvement with, satisfaction with, and enthusiasm for the work he or she does.

research to create a model of work engagement suggests that there is a lot of promise to this concept.[130]

Organizations will likely continue using employee engagement, and it will remain a subject of research. The ambiguity surrounding it arises from its newness and may also, ironically, reflect its popularity. Engagement is a very general concept, perhaps broad enough to capture the intersection of the other variables we have discussed. In other words, it may be what these attitudes have in common.

Managing Diversity in the Workplace

Managers at SaskGaming consider managing diversity part of their contribution to supporting the future of Saskatchewan.[131] The 1000 employees working in two casinos—Casino Regina and Casino Moose Jaw—represent considerable diversity: 42.5 percent are of Aboriginal descent, 5.8 percent are persons with disabilities, and 11.5 percent are visible minorities. The company provides quality employment, helping young people develop skills and leadership abilities. SaskGaming's training program is also intended to "provide a foundation for our employees to assume leadership roles within their communities." The company invests in the communities where employees live and work as well. In 2010, it contributed $750 000 and considerable volunteer hours to community organizations and events. Why does managing diversity well make a difference?

5 How do we respond to diversity in the workplace?

Organizations increasingly face diversity concerns as workplaces become more heterogeneous. **Biographical characteristics** such as age, gender, race, disability, and length of service are some of the most obvious ways employees differ. Others include length of service (tenure), religion, sexual orientation, and gender identity. There is also diversity in **ability**, an individual's current capacity to perform the various tasks in a job. Earlier in the chapter, we discussed cultural and generational differences and their implications in the Canadian workplace.

Many organizations have attempted to incorporate workforce diversity initiatives into their workplaces to improve relations among co-workers. For example, Dell Canada is one of a number of companies in Canada that have developed diversity policies for their workplace. Dell Canada's policy states the following:

> *Diversity, inclusiveness and respect for all Dell employees form the basis of Dell's Winning Culture and are essential to Dell's success. Dell values each individual's distinct contribution and leverages our collective strengths to ensure that Dell remains the technology solutions company of choice for customers around the world.*[132]

Dell's statement on diversity is typical of statements found in company annual reports and employee information packets to signal corporate values to those who interact with the company. Some corporations choose to signal the value of diversity because they think it is an important strategic goal. Other organizations recognize that the purchasing power of diverse groups is substantial.

When companies design and then publicize statements about the importance of diversity, they are essentially producing value statements. The hope, of course, is that the statements will influence the behaviour of members of the organization, particularly since preference for people who are ethnically like ourselves may be ingrained in us at an early age. In a study published in 2011, researchers from Concordia University and the University of Montreal found that Asian Canadian and French Canadian preschoolers preferred to interact with kids of their own ethnic group.[133]

There is little research showing that values can be changed successfully.[134] Because values tend to be relatively stable, workplaces try to address diversity issues through education aimed at changing attitudes.

biographical characteristics Personal characteristics—such as age, gender, race, and length of tenure—that are objective and easily obtained from personnel records. These characteristics are representative of surface-level diversity.

ability An individual's capacity to perform the various tasks in a job.

Effective Diversity Programs

Joan Vogelesang, CEO of Montreal-based animation software company Toon Boom, says that Canadian companies do not make use of the diversity in employees they have. She thinks Canadian companies need to look beyond imperfect English and cultural customs when hiring. She practises what she preaches: Most of her executive team are first-generation immigrants. Her employees speak 20 languages among them. "Two of our staff members speak Japanese. You can hardly do business in Japan if you don't speak it," she says.[135]

Vogelesang's description of diversity as a competitive advantage speaks to the need for effective diversity programs that have three distinct components. First, they should teach people about the legal framework for equal employment opportunity and encourage fair treatment of all people, regardless of their demographic characteristics. Second, they should teach people how a diverse workforce will be better able to serve a diverse market of customers and clients. Third, they should foster personal development practices that bring out the skills and abilities of all workers, acknowledging how differences in perspective can be a valuable way to improve performance for everyone.[136] A 2011 study by researchers at the University of Toronto Scarborough found that focusing on the positive benefits of diversity, rather than telling people what they should and should not do, was more likely to reduce people's prejudices toward other groups.[137]

Much concern about diversity has to do with fair treatment.[138] Most negative reactions to employment discrimination are based on the idea that discriminatory treatment is unfair. Regardless of race or gender, people are generally in favour of diversity-oriented programs if they believe the policies ensure everyone has a fair opportunity to show their skills and abilities.

A major study of the consequences of diversity programs came to what might seem a surprising conclusion.[139] Organizations that provided diversity training were not consistently more likely to have women and minorities in upper management positions than organizations that did not. On closer examination, though, these results are not surprising. Experts have long known that one-shot training sessions without strategies to

Joan Vogelesang, CEO of Montreal-based animation software company Toon Boom, says that Canadian companies do not make use of the diversity in employees they have. She thinks Canadian companies need to look beyond imperfect English and cultural customs when hiring. She practises what she preaches: Most of her executive team are first-generation immigrants. Her employees speak 20 languages among them. She is pictured with Francisco Del Cueto, CTO (left), and Steven Chu, COO (right).

encourage effective diversity management back on the job are not likely to be very effective. Some diversity programs, such as those of Toronto-based Corus Entertainment, Ottawa-based Health Canada, Regina-based Information Services Corporation, and Brampton, Ontario-based Loblaw Companies, are truly effective in improving representation in management. They include strategies to measure the representation of women and minorities in managerial positions, and they hold managers accountable for achieving more demographically diverse management teams.

Organizational leaders should examine their workforce to determine whether the **protected groups** covered by Canada's Employment Equity Act (women, people with disabilities, Aboriginal people, and visible minorities) have been underutilized. If groups of employees are not proportionally represented in top management, managers should look for any hidden barriers to advancement. They can often improve recruiting practices, make selection systems more transparent, and provide training for those employees who have not had adequate exposure to necessary work-related experiences in the past. Exhibit 3-5 presents examples of what some of the leading companies are doing as part of their diversity initiatives.[140]

Management should also clearly communicate the company's diversity policies and their rationale to employees so they can understand how and why certain practices are followed. Communications should focus as much as possible on qualifications and job performance; emphasizing that certain groups need more assistance could well backfire.

protected groups The four groups designated by the Employment Equity Act as the beneficiaries of employment equity (women, people with disabilities, Aboriginal people, and visible minorities).

EXHIBIT 3-5 Practices Used by 45 of Canada's Most Welcoming Places to Work

Company (Location)	Industry	Number of Employees	Diversity Activities
Bell Aliant Regional Communications (Halifax)	Wired telecommunications carriers	7460	Created a diversity team that represents women, Aboriginal people, visible minorities, people with disabilities, new Canadians, LGBT, and francophone employees
Cameco Corp. (Saskatoon)	Mining	2800	Partners with the Mining Industry Human Resources Council and Women in Mining to study employment barriers women face in the mining industry
Bombardier Aerospace (Dorval)	Aircraft manufacturing	16 659	Launched a network for female employees in 2008 and is developing a recruitment strategy to attract and retain women
Ontario Public Service (Toronto)	Government support	64 725	Provides a "quiet room" to meet employees' diverse religious and spiritual needs
City of Vancouver	Government	6901	Provides diversity training workshops to new employees. Translated training materials into various languages
Newalta Corp. (Calgary)	Recycling and industrial waste management	1669	Created an online diversity area with e-learning modules and newsletters to keep employees up-to-date on best practices

Source: Based on MediaCorp Canada, "Canada's Best Diversity Employers, 2011," *Canada's Top 100 Employers*, February 2011, http://www.canadastop100.com/diversity/

To ensure the top-level management team represents the diversity of its workforce and client base, Safeway implemented the Retail Leadership Development (RLD) program, a formal career development program. This program is open to all employees, so it is inclusive, but women and underrepresented racial or ethnic groups are particularly encouraged to participate. Interested individuals take tests to determine whether they have management potential. Safeway managers are charged with providing promising RLD participants with additional training and development opportunities to ensure they have the skills needed for advancement, and are given performance bonuses if they meet concrete diversity goals. The RLD program has increased the number of white women store managers by 31 percent since its inception, and the number of women-of-colour store managers by 92 percent.[141] *OB in the Street* looks at what corporate boards in Canada can do to recruit more diverse members.

OB in the **STREET**
Adding Diversity to Boards of Directors

Why should corporate boards pay more attention to diversity? The Canadian Board Diversity Council together with KPMG published a study in 2011 of the boards of 450 of the *Financial Post* 500 companies.[142] The study found that women held 15 percent of board seats on the FP500 companies; visible minorities 5.3 percent; persons with disabilities 2.9 percent; and Aboriginal people (including First Nations, Inuit, and Métis) 8 percent. With the exception of Aboriginal representation, the numbers were far fewer than the representation of these categories in society at large. Pamela Jeffery, founder and president of the council, called the results "disappointing."

Does the lack of diversity hurt the bottom line? Accounting firm Ernst & Young finds that the lack of diversity on boards can make it difficult for companies to innovate. Directors who sat on FP500 boards that had more women, people of colour, or Aboriginal diversity believed that the boards made better decisions because the diversity led to better discussions with more perspectives. Board members expressed some frustration about finding new directors and reported that "their own networks are almost exclusively made up of white men."

The council does not favour using quotas to change the situation. Instead, it recommends that with the large wave of retirements from boards expected in the next several years, FP500 boards use rigorous, transparent recruiting processes "to replace one of every three retiring directors with a director of a diverse background."

Just because the company's managers may value diversity, this does not mean that all employees will share that value. Consequently, even if they are required to attend diversity training, employees may exhibit negative attitudes toward individuals because of their gender or ethnicity. Additionally, what attitudes are appropriately displayed outside of the workplace may be questioned by some employers, as you will discover in *Case Incident—You Can't Do That* on page 117. Finally, the workplace is not the only place where people's attitudes toward racial diversity gets displayed, underscoring that the responsibility for education about reacting to diversity goes beyond employers. In September 2011, at an exhibition game between the Philadelphia Flyers and the Detroit Red Wings played in London, Ontario, someone from the audience threw a banana at Flyers' player Wayne Simmonds, one of the few black players in the NHL. Retired Montreal Canadiens forward Georges Laraque, when asked to comment on the incident, noted that "throughout [my] career, [I] had to endure the 'N' word a number of times."[143]

Cultural Intelligence

Are some individuals better than others at dealing with people from different cultures? Management professors Christopher Earley of the London School of Business and Elaine Mosakowski of the University of Colorado at Boulder have recently introduced the idea of **cultural intelligence**, or CQ, to suggest that people vary in how they deal with other cultures. This term is defined as "the seemingly natural ability to interpret someone's unfamiliar and ambiguous gestures in just the way that person's compatriots and colleagues would, even to mirror them."[144]

Earley and Mosakowski suggest that CQ "picks up where emotional intelligence leaves off." Those with CQ try to figure out whether a person's behaviour is representative of all members of a group or just that person. Thus, for example, a person with high CQ who encounters two German engineers would be able to determine which of the engineers' conduct is explained by the fact of being an engineer, by being German, and by behaviour that is simply particular to the individual. A 2010 study found that CQ is particularly helpful to expatriates on international assignment because the ability to be confident about and interested in being in new cultural environments makes it easier to adjust to the demands of foreign assignments.[145]

RESEARCH FINDINGS: Cultural Intelligence

According to the researchers, "cultural intelligence resides in the body [the physical] and the heart [the emotional/motivational], as well as the head [the cognitive]." Individuals who have high *cognitive* CQ look for clues to help them identify a culture's shared understandings. Specifically, an individual does this by looking for consistencies in behaviours across a variety of people from the same cultural background. Individuals with high *physical* CQ learn the customs and gestures of those from other cultures and therefore act more like them. This increases understanding, trust, and openness between people of different cultures. One study found that job candidates who used some of the mannerisms of recruiters who had different cultural backgrounds from themselves were more likely to receive job offers than those who did not do so.[146] Those with high *emotional/motivational* CQ believe that they are capable of understanding people from other cultures, and will keep trying to do so, even if they are faced with difficulties in doing so.

Based on their research, Earley and Mosakowski have discovered that most managers fall into the following cultural intelligence profiles:

- *Provincial*. They work best with people of similar background, but have difficulties working with those from different backgrounds.

- *Analyst*. They analyze a foreign culture's rules and expectations to figure out how to interact with others.

- *Natural*. They use intuition rather than systematic study to understand those from other cultural backgrounds.

- *Ambassador*. They communicate convincingly that they fit in, even if they do not know much about the foreign culture.

- *Mimic*. They control actions and behaviours to match others, even if they do not understand the significance of the cultural cues observed.

- *Chameleon*. They have high levels of all three CQ components. They could be mistaken as being from the foreign culture. According to research, only about 5 percent of managers fit this profile.

Exhibit 3-6 can help you assess your own CQ.

cultural intelligence The ability to understand someone's unfamiliar and ambiguous gestures in the same way as would people from that person's culture.

EXHIBIT 3-6 Measuring Your Cultural Intelligence

Rate the extent to which you agree with each statement, using the following scale:

1 = strongly disagree
2 = disagree
3 = neutral
4 = agree
5 = strongly agree

_____ Before I interact with people from a new culture, I ask myself what I hope to achieve.

_____ If I encounter something unexpected while working in a new culture, I use this experience to figure out new ways to approach other cultures in the future.

_____ I plan how I'm going to relate to people from a different culture before I meet them.

_____ When I come into a new cultural situation, I can immediately sense whether something is going well or something is wrong.

Total _____ ÷ 4 = **Cognitive CQ**

_____ It's easy for me to change my body language (for example, eye contact or posture) to suit people from a different culture.

_____ I can alter my expression when a cultural encounter requires it.

_____ I modify my speech style (for example, accent or tone) to suit people from a different culture.

_____ I easily change the way I act when a cross-cultural encounter seems to require it.

Total _____ ÷ 4 = **Physical CQ**

_____ I have confidence that I can deal well with people from a different culture.

_____ I am certain that I can befriend people whose cultural backgrounds are different from mine.

_____ I can adapt to the lifestyle of a different culture with relative ease.

_____ I am confident that I can deal with a cultural situation that is unfamiliar.

Total _____ ÷ 4 = **Emotional/motivational CQ**

Interpretation: Generally, an average of less than 3 would indicate an area calling for improvement, while an average of greater than 4.5 reflects a true CQ strength.

Source: P. C. Earley and E. Mosakowski, "Cultural Intelligence," *Harvard Business Review* 82, no. 10 (October 2004), pp. 139–146. Reprinted by permission of *Harvard Business Review*.

GLOBAL IMPLICATIONS _____

Although a number of topics were covered in this chapter, we review only three in terms of their application beyond Canada and the United States. First, we consider whether job satisfaction is simply a US concept. Second, we examine whether employees in Western cultures are more satisfied with their jobs than people from other cultures. Finally, we look at international differences in how diversity is managed.

Is Job Satisfaction a US Concept?

Most of the research on job satisfaction has been conducted in the United States. So, is job satisfaction a US concept? The evidence strongly suggests it is *not*; people in other cultures can and do form judgments of job satisfaction. Moreover, similar factors seem to cause, and result from, job satisfaction across cultures: We noted earlier that pay is positively, but relatively weakly, related to job satisfaction. This relationship appears to hold in other industrialized nations as well.

Are Employees in Western Cultures More Satisfied with Their Jobs?

Although job satisfaction appears relevant across cultures, that does not mean there are no cultural differences in job satisfaction. Evidence suggests that employees in Western cultures have higher levels of job satisfaction than those in Eastern cultures.[147] Do employees in Western cultures have better jobs? Or are they simply more positive (and less self-critical)? Although both factors are probably at play, evidence suggests that people in Eastern cultures find negative emotions less disagreeable than do people in Western cultures, who tend to emphasize positive emotions and individual happiness.[148] That may be why employees in Western cultures such as the United States and Scandinavia are more likely to have higher levels of satisfaction.

Does organizational commitment vary cross-nationally? A recent study explored this question and compared the organizational commitment of Chinese employees with that of Canadian and South Korean employees.[149] Although results revealed that the three types of commitment—normative, affective, and continuance—are present in all three cultures, they differ in importance. In addition, the study found that Canadians and South Koreans are closer to each other in values than either is with the Chinese. Normative commitment (an obligation to remain with an organization for moral or ethical reasons) and affective commitment (an emotional attachment to the organization and belief in its values) were highest among Chinese employees. Continuance commitment (the perceived economic value of remaining with an organization) was *lower* among Chinese employees than among Canadian, British, and South Korean employees.

Is Diversity Managed Differently across Cultures?

Besides the mere presence of diversity in international work settings, there are international differences in how diversity is managed. Each country has its own legal framework for dealing with diversity, and these frameworks are a powerful reflection of the diversity-related concerns of each country. Many countries require specific targets and quotas for achieving employment equity goals, whereas the legal framework in Canada specifically forbids their use. The types of demographic differences considered important for diversity management also vary across countries. For example, in India the nondiscrimination framework includes quotas and set-aside programs for individuals from lower castes.[150] A case study of the multinational Finnish company TRANSCO found that it was possible to develop a consistent global philosophy for diversity management. However, differences in legal and cultural factors across nations forced TRANSCO to develop unique policies to match the cultural and legal frameworks of each country in which it operated.[151]

LESSONS LEARNED

- Values represent basic convictions about what is important, right, and good.
- Attitudes tend to predict behaviours.
- Job satisfaction leads to better performance.

Summary and Implications

1 What are values? Values guide how we make decisions about and evaluations of behaviours and events. They represent our basic convictions about what is important, right, and good for an individual. Although they do not have a direct impact on behaviour, values strongly influence a person's attitudes. So knowledge of an individual's values can provide insight into his or her attitudes.

2 How can we understand values across cultures? Geert Hofstede found that managers and employees vary on five value dimensions of national culture. These include power distance, individualism vs. collectivism, masculinity vs. femininity, uncertainty avoidance, and long-term vs. short-term orientation. His insights were expanded by the GLOBE research program, an ongoing cross-cultural investigation of leadership and national culture.

3 Are there unique Canadian values? Recent research suggests that Canadian values tend to be affected by generational and cultural differences. The three dominant age groups of adults in the Canadian workplace are the Baby Boomers (born between the mid-1940s and mid-1960s), the Generation Xers (born between the mid-1960s and the late 1970s), and the Generation Ys (born between 1979 through 1994). Canada is a multicultural country, and there are a number of groups that contribute to its diverse values, such as Aboriginal people, French Canadians, and various immigrant groups. Canadian values differ from American values and those of its other trading partners in a variety of ways.

4 What are attitudes and why are they important? *Attitudes* are positive or negative feelings about objects, people, or events. Attitudes affect the way people respond to situations. When I say, "I like my job," I am expressing my attitude to work and I am likely to be more committed in my behaviour than if my attitude was one of not liking my job. A person can have thousands of attitudes, but OB focuses our attention on a limited number of job-related attitudes. These job-related attitudes tap positive or negative evaluations that employees hold about aspects of their work environment. Most of the research in OB has been concerned with four attitudes: job satisfaction, organizational commitment, job involvement, and employee engagement.

5 How do we respond to diversity in the workplace? Many organizations have attempted to incorporate workforce diversity initiatives into their workplaces to improve relations among co-workers. Organizations have introduced diversity training programs to improve cultural awareness. Recent research suggests that individuals who score high on cultural intelligence have an easier time dealing with people from other cultures.

OB at Work

for Review

for Critical Thinking

for You

for Review

1. How does ethics relate to values?

2. Describe the five value dimensions of national culture proposed by Geert Hofstede.

3. How might differences in generational values affect the workplace?

4. Compare Aboriginal and non-Aboriginal values.

5. What might explain low levels of employee job satisfaction in recent years?

6. Are satisfied employees productive employees? Explain your answer.

7. Contrast exit, voice, loyalty, and neglect as employee responses to job satisfaction.

8. What is the relationship between job satisfaction and organizational commitment? Job satisfaction and employee engagement? Which is the stronger relationship?

9. How can managers get employees to more readily accept working with colleagues who are different from themselves?

10. What is cultural intelligence? How do its three dimensions relate to understanding people from other cultures?

for Critical Thinking

1. "Thirty-five years ago, young employees we hired were ambitious, conscientious, hard-working, and honest. Today's young workers don't have the same values." Do you agree or disagree with this manager's comments? Support your position.

2. Do you think there might be any relationship between the possession of certain personal values and successful career progression in organizations such as the Toronto Stock Exchange, the Canadian Union of Postal Workers (CUPW), and the City of Regina's police department? Discuss.

3. "Managers should do everything they can to enhance the job satisfaction of their employees." Do you agree or disagree? Support your position.

4. "Organizations should do everything they can to encourage organizational citizenship behaviour." Do you agree or disagree? Support your position.

5. When employees are asked whether they would again choose the same work or whether they would want their children to follow in their footsteps, fewer than half typically answer "yes." What, if anything, do you think this implies about employee job satisfaction?

for You

- You will encounter many people who have values different from yours in the classroom and in various kinds of activities in which you participate, as well as in the workplace. You should try to understand value differences, and to figure out ways to work positively with people who are different from you.

- We indicated that a moderate number of Canadians are very satisfied with their jobs, and we mentioned the sources of some of the satisfactions. We also identified some of the reasons people are dissatisfied with their jobs. This information may help you understand your own feelings about whether you are satisfied with your job.

- You may be able to use some of the information on attitudes to think about how to better work with people from different cultures. An understanding of how cultures differ may provide insight when you observe people doing things differently from the way you do them.

POINT

Managers Create Job Satisfaction

A review of the evidence has identified four factors conducive to high levels of employee job satisfaction: mentally challenging work, equitable rewards, supportive working conditions, and supportive colleagues.[152] Management is able to control each of these factors.

Mentally challenging work. Generally, people prefer jobs that give them opportunities to use their skills and abilities and offer a variety of tasks, freedom, and feedback on how well they are doing. These characteristics make work mentally challenging.

Equitable rewards. Employees want pay systems that they perceive as just, unambiguous, and in line with their expectations. When they see pay as fair—based on job demands, individual skill level, and community pay standards—satisfaction is likely to result.

Supportive working conditions. Employees want their work environments to be safe and personally comfortable and to facilitate their doing a good job. Most prefer working relatively close to home, in clean and up-to-date facilities with adequate tools and equipment.

Supportive colleagues. People get more out of work than merely money or tangible achievements. Work also fills the need for social interaction. Not surprisingly, therefore, friendly and supportive co-workers lead to increased job satisfaction. The boss's behaviour is also a major factor; employee satisfaction is increased when the immediate supervisor is understanding and friendly, offers praise for good performance, listens to employees' opinions, and shows a personal interest in employees.

COUNTERPOINT

Satisfaction Is Individually Determined

The notion that managers and organizations can control the level of employee job satisfaction is inherently attractive. It fits nicely with the view that managers directly influence organizational processes and outcomes. Unfortunately, a growing body of evidence challenges this idea. The most recent findings indicate that job satisfaction is largely genetically determined.[153]

Whether people are happy is essentially determined by gene structure. Approximately 50 to 80 percent of people's differences in happiness, or subjective well-being, has been found to be attributable to their different genes. Identical twins, for example, tend to have very similar careers, report similar levels of job satisfaction, and change jobs at similar rates.

Analysis of satisfaction data for a selected sample of individuals over a 50-year period found that individual results were stable over time, even when subjects changed employers and occupations. This and other research suggests that an individual's disposition toward life—positive or negative—is established by his or her genetic makeup, holds over time, and influences disposition toward work.

Given these findings, most managers can do little to influence employee satisfaction. Despite their manipulating job characteristics, working conditions, and rewards, people will inevitably return to their own "set point." A bonus may temporarily increase the satisfaction level of a negatively disposed employee, but it is unlikely to sustain it. Sooner or later, a dissatisfied employee will find new fault with the job.

The only place managers will have any significant influence is in the selection process. If managers want satisfied employees, they need to screen out negative people who derive little satisfaction from their jobs, irrespective of work conditions.

LEARNING ABOUT **YOURSELF** EXERCISE

What Do You Value?

There are 16 items in the list below. Rate how important each one is to you on a scale of 0 (not important) to 100 (very important). Write a number between 0 and 100 on the line to the left of each item.

Not Important				Somewhat Important					Very Important	
0	10	20	30	40	50	60	70	80	90	100

_____ **1.** An enjoyable, satisfying job.

_____ **2.** A high-paying job.

_____ **3.** A good marriage.

_____ **4.** Meeting new people; social events.

_____ **5.** Involvement in community activities.

_____ **6.** My religion.

_____ **7.** Exercising, playing sports.

_____ **8.** Intellectual development.

_____ **9.** A career with challenging opportunities.

_____ **10.** Nice cars, clothes, home, and so on.

_____ **11.** Spending time with family.

_____ **12.** Having several close friends.

_____ **13.** Volunteer work for nonprofit organizations, such as the Canadian Cancer Society.

_____ **14.** Meditation, quiet time to think, pray, and so on.

_____ **15.** A healthy, balanced diet.

_____ **16.** Educational reading, television, self-improvement programs, and so on.

Scoring Key:

Transfer the numbers for each of the 16 items to the appropriate column; then add up the 2 numbers in each column.

	Professional	Financial	Family	Social
	1. _____	2. _____	3. _____	4. _____
	9. _____	10. _____	11. _____	12. _____
Totals	_____	_____	_____	_____
	Community	Spiritual	Physical	Intellectual
	5. _____	6. _____	7. _____	8. _____
	13. _____	14. _____	15. _____	16. _____
Totals	_____	_____	_____	_____

The higher the total in any value dimension, the higher the importance you place on that value set. The closer the numbers are in all 8 dimensions, the more well rounded you are.

Source: R. N. Lussier, *Human Relations in Organizations: A Skill Building Approach*, 2nd ed. (Homewood, IL: Richard D. Irwin, 1993). Reprinted by permission of the McGraw-Hill Companies, Inc.

OB at work

More Learning About Yourself Exercises

Additional self-assessments relevant to this chapter appear on MyOBLab (**www.pearsoned.ca/myoblab**).

IV.C.1 What's My Attitude toward Older People?

I.B.3 How Satisfied Am I with My Job?

IV.B.1 Am I Engaged?

I.E.1 What's My Emotional Intelligence Score?

When you complete the additional assessments, consider the following:

1. Am I surprised about my score?
2. Would my friends evaluate me similarly?

BREAKOUT **GROUP** EXERCISES

Form small groups to discuss the following topics, as assigned by your instructor. Each person in the group should first identify 3 to 5 key personal values.

1. Identify the extent to which values overlap in your group.

2. Try to uncover with your group members the source of some of your key values (for example, parents, peer group, teachers, church).

3. What kind of workplace would be most suitable for the values that you hold most closely?

WORKING WITH **OTHERS** EXERCISE

Understanding Cultural Values

Objective	To compare the cultural values of two countries, and determine how differences might affect group behaviour.
Time	Approximately 30 minutes.

Procedure

1. Break into groups of 5 or 6.

2. Pretend that you are a group of students working on a project. Half of you are from Canada and hold typically "Canadian" cultural values; the other half are from the country assigned and hold that country's cultural values.

3. Consider the values of power distance, individualism, and uncertainty avoidance, and discuss the differences between Canadian cultural values and the values of the country assigned to you.

4. Answer the following questions:

   What challenges might you expect in working together?

   What steps could be taken to work together more effectively?

ETHICAL **DILEMMA** EXERCISE

Is It a Bribe or a Gift?

The Corruption of Foreign Public Officials Act prohibits Canadian firms from making payments to foreign government officials with the aim of gaining or maintaining business.[154] But payments are acceptable if they don't violate local laws. For instance, payments to officers working for foreign corporations are legal. Many countries don't have such legal guidelines.

Bribery is a common way of doing business in many underdeveloped countries. Government jobs there often don't pay very well, so it's tempting for officials to supplement their income with bribes. In addition, in many countries, the penalties for demanding and receiving bribes are few or nonexistent.

You are a Canadian who works for a large European multinational computer manufacturer. You are currently working to sell a $5-million system to a government agency in Nigeria. The Nigerian official who heads up the team that will decide who gets this contract has asked you for a payment of $20 000. He said this payment will not guarantee you get the order, but without it he could not be very encouraging. Your company's policy is very flexible on the issue of "gifts" to facilitate sales. Your boss says that it's okay to pay the $20 000, but only if you can be relatively assured of the order.

You are not sure what you should do. The Nigerian official has told you specifically that any payment to him is not to be mentioned to anyone else on the Nigerian team. You know for certain that three other companies are also negotiating, but it's unconfirmed that two of those companies have turned down the payment request.

What would you do?

CASE INCIDENTS

You Can't Do That

Paul Fromm is a high school teacher employed in one of the most ethnically diverse school districts in Canada.[155] He is an excellent teacher, and receives high ratings from his students.

During weekends and summer holidays, when he is not working, he participates in conferences held by white supremacists and anti-Semitic groups. For instance, he attended a conference at which swastikas were waving, and individuals gave Nazi salutes. Fromm also attended a celebration of Adolf Hitler's birthday.

Though it is known that Fromm attends these conferences, he has never expressed racist views in the classroom or discriminated against any student. "I am here to teach English, not to make a political statement.

This is my job, that's what I do. And I do it very well," he says.

The school board and some of the teachers are upset with Fromm's behaviour. They feel that what he does, even though outside of work time, is not consistent with the school board's values of encouraging multicultural diversity. Some suggest he should be fired.

Questions

1. What, if anything, should the school board do in this instance?

2. Should Fromm consider not going to further conferences of this sort?

Thinking Your Way to a Better Job

You have probably been dissatisfied with a job at one time or another in your life.[156] When faced with a dissatisfying job, researchers and job holders alike usually think in terms of job satisfaction: Ask for more pay, take control over your work, change your schedule, minimize contact with a toxic co-worker, or even change jobs. While each of these remedies may be appropriate in certain situations, increasingly researchers are uncovering an interesting truth about job satisfaction: it is as much a state of mind as a function of job conditions.

Here, we are not talking about the dispositional source of job satisfaction. It's true that some people have trouble finding any job satisfying, whereas others cannot be brought down by even the most onerous of jobs. However, by state of mind, we mean changeable, easily implemented ways of thinking that can affect your job satisfaction. Lest you think we have gone the way of self-help gurus Deepak Chopra and Wayne Dyer, think again. There is some solid, albeit fairly preliminary, evidence supporting the view that our views of our job and life can be significantly impacted by changing the way we think.

One main area where this "state of mind" research might help you change the way you think about your job (or life) is in gratitude. Researchers have found that when people are asked to make short lists of things for which they are grateful, they report being happier, and the increased happiness seems to last well beyond the moments when people made the list.

Indeed, gratitude may explain why, when the economy is in bad shape, people actually become more satisfied with their jobs. One survey revealed that, from 2007 to 2008, when the economy slid into recession, the percentage of people reporting that they were "very satisfied" with their jobs increased to a whopping 38 percent (from 28 percent to 38 percent). When we see other people suffering, particularly those we see as similar to ourselves, it often leads us to realize that, as bad as things may seem, they can always be worse. As *Wall Street Journal* columnist Jeffrey Zaslow wrote, "People who still have jobs are finding reasons to be appreciative."

Questions

1. So, right now, make a short list of things about your job and life for which you are grateful. Now, after having done that, do you feel more positively about your job and your life?

2. Now try doing this every day for a week. Do you think this exercise might make a difference in how you feel about your job and your life?

FROM CONCEPTS TO SKILLS

Changing Attitudes

Can you change unfavourable employee attitudes? Sometimes! It depends on who you are, the strength of the employee's attitude, the magnitude of the change, and the technique you choose to try to change the attitude.

People are most likely to respond to changes suggested by someone who is liked, credible, and convincing. If people like you, they are more apt to identify and adopt your message. Credibility implies trust, expertise, and objectivity. So you are more likely to change someone's attitude if that person views you as believable, knowledgeable about what you are saying, and unbiased in your presentation. Finally, successful attitude change is enhanced when you present your arguments clearly and persuasively.

It's easier to change a person's attitude if he or she is not strongly committed to it. Conversely, the stronger the belief in the attitude, the harder it is to change it. Also, attitudes that have been expressed publicly are more difficult to change because doing so requires admitting having made a mistake.

It's also easier to change attitudes when the change required is not very significant. To get a person to accept a new attitude that varies greatly from his or her current position requires more effort. It may also threaten other deeply held attitudes.

Practising Skills

All attitude-change techniques are not equally effective across situations. Oral persuasion techniques are most effective when you use a positive, tactful tone; present strong evidence to support your position; tailor your argument to the listener; use logic; and support your evidence by appealing to the person's fears, frustrations, and other emotions. But people are more likely to embrace change when they can experience it. The use of training sessions where employees share and personalize experiences, and practise new behaviours, can be a powerful stimulant for change. Consistent with self-perception theory, changes in behaviour can lead to changes in attitudes.

Form groups of 2. Person A is to choose any topic that he or she feels strongly about and state his or her position on the topic in 30 words or less. Person B's task will be to try to change Person A's attitude on this topic. Person B will have 10 minutes to make his or her case. When the time is up, the roles are reversed. Person B picks the topic and Person A has 10 minutes to try to change Person B's attitude.

Potential topics (you can choose either side of a topic) include the following: politics; the economy; world events; social practices; or specific management issues, such as that organizations should require all employees to undergo regular drug testing, there is no such thing as organizational loyalty any more, the customer is always right, and layoffs are an indication of management failures.

Questions

1. Were you successful at changing the other person's attitude? Why or why not?

2. Was the other person successful at changing your attitude? Why or why not?

3. What conclusions can you draw about changing the attitudes of yourself and others?

Reinforcing Skills

1. Try to convince a friend or relative to go with you to see a movie or play that you know he or she does not want to see.

2. Try to convince a friend or relative to try a different brand of toothpaste.

OB on the EDGE

Stress @Work

Long-haul truck driving is not an easy job. Drivers face heavy traffic, demanding schedules, challenges accessing healthy food, and fatigue. Surrey, BC-based Coastal Pacific Xpress (CPx) looks after its drivers and, for this, won an Award of Excellence from the British Columbia Medical Association in June 2011.[1] The award specifically noted CPx's "Focus on Fitness Friday," where drivers and staff get healthy meals and snacks, and are encouraged to exercise by walking. All employees have free access to pedometers, and CPx donates $2 to charity for every 1000 steps recorded on its pedometers on Focus on Fitness Fridays.

Employees are also encouraged to track their heart rate, Body Mass Index, weight, oxygen saturation levels, and other vital signs using on-site LifeClinic kiosks. Laurie Forbes, vice-president of administration, notes that "healthy drivers cope better with stress, have less downtime due to illness, are better-rested and safer drivers."

Being sensitive to workplace stress is putting increased responsibilities on managers. When Janie Toivanen was diagnosed with severe depression, she approached her employer, Vancouver-based Electronic Arts (EA) Canada, to request indefinite stress leave.[2] Instead, just days later, she was fired. After working there for six years, she "felt like she had been thrown away." Toivanen thought EA cared about its employees, and could not believe it would not do anything to help her as she struggled to overcome her illness. She subsequently filed a complaint with the BC Human Rights Tribunal and was awarded, among other things, $20 000 for injury to her dignity, feelings, and self-respect and $19 744 in severance pay.

Are We Overstressed?

Stress appears to be a major factor in the lives of many Canadians. A 2010 survey conducted by Statistics Canada found that Canadians experience a great deal of stress, with those from Quebec topping the list.[3] The survey also found that women were more stressed than men. The inset *Stressed Quite a Lot, 2010* reports the findings.

The impact of stress on the Canadian economy is huge, costing an estimated $33 billion a year in lost productivity, and considerably more than that in medical costs. To address these costs, Prime Minister Stephen Harper announced the creation of the Mental Health Commission of Canada in 2007. At the launch of the commission, Harper noted that mental health disorders are "now the fastest-growing category of disability insurance claims in Canada."[4]

Shannon Wagner, a clinical psychologist and a specialist in workplace stress research at the University of Northern British Columbia, notes that changes in the nature of jobs may be increasing the levels of stress in the workplace. While many jobs are not as physically demanding, they are often more mentally demanding. "A lot of people now are identifying techno-stress and the 24/7 workday, which we didn't have even 10 or 15 years ago, this feeling of being constantly plugged in, of checking email 500 times a day."[5]

An additional problem is that employees are increasingly asked to donate labour to their employers, according to Professor Linda Duxbury of Carleton University's Sprott School of Business and Professor Chris Higgins of the Richard Ivey School of Business at the University of Western Ontario. Their survey of 31 571 Canadians found that in the previous

month half of them had worked an extra 2.5 days of unpaid overtime, and more than half had donated 3.5 days of working at home to catch up.[6] Canadians are frequently reporting that they want more balance in their work and family lives.[7]

Jobs and Stress Levels

How do jobs rate in terms of stress? The inset *The Most and Least Stressful Jobs* on page 124 shows how selected occupations ranked in an evaluation of 250 jobs. Among the criteria used in the rankings were overtime, quotas, deadlines, competitiveness, physical demands, environmental conditions, hazards encountered, initiative required, stamina required, win-lose situations, and working in the public eye.

Stress is not something that can be ignored in the workplace. A recent poll by Ipsos Reid found that 66 percent of the CEOs surveyed said that "stress, burnout or other physical and mental health issues" have a negative effect on productivity.[8] A study conducted in 15 developed countries found that individuals who report that they are stressed in their jobs are 25 percent more likely to quit and 25 percent more likely to miss days of work.[9] Canadian, French, and Swedish employees reported the highest stress levels. In Canada, 41 percent of employees noted that they "often" or "always" experience stress at work, while only 31 percent of employees in Denmark and Switzerland reported stress levels this high. "In the wake of years of fiscal downsizing, workers across all sectors are working harder and longer than ever while trying to balance family responsibilities," said Scott Morris, former head of the Vancouver-based consulting firm Priority Management Systems.[10] Daniel Ondrack, a professor at the Rotman School of Management at the

Stressed Quite a Lot, 2010 (Percent)

	Males	Females
Canada	22.0	24.9
Newfoundland and Labrador	16.6	14.6
Prince Edward Island	12.4*	14.3
Nova Scotia	17.0	21.1
New Brunswick	18.6	21.9
Quebec	24.0	29.5
Ontario	22.2	25.1
Manitoba	17.7	23.3
Saskatchewan	19.1	19.5
Alberta	21.2	23.1
British Columbia	23.0	22.6
Yukon	15.7	20.4
Northwest Territories	14.9	19.0*
Nunavut	18.7*	17.7*

*Use with caution.

Note: Population aged 15 and older who reported experiencing quite a lot or extreme stress most days of their lives.

Source: From "Perceived life stress, quite a lot, by sex, by province and territory," Statistics Canada's Summary Tables, http://www40.statcan.ca/l01/cst01/health107b-eng.htm, July 14, 2011

University of Toronto, notes that "one of the major reasons for absenteeism is the logistical problems workers face in just getting to work, including transporting children to school and finding daycare. Single parents, especially female, have to juggle all the daycare and family responsibilities, and that makes it extremely difficult for people to keep up with work demands."[11]

What Is Stress?

Stress is a dynamic condition in which an individual is confronted with an opportunity, demand, or resource related to what the individual desires and for which the outcome is perceived to be both uncertain and important.[12] This is a complicated definition. Let's look at its components more closely.

Stress is not necessarily bad in and of itself. Although stress is typically discussed in a negative context, it also has a positive value.[13] Consider, for example, the superior performance that an athlete or stage performer gives in "clutch" situations. Such individuals often use stress positively to rise to the occasion and perform at or near their maximum. Similarly, many professionals see the pressures of heavy workloads and deadlines as positive challenges that enhance the quality of their work and the satisfaction they get from their job. In short, some stress can be good, and some can be bad.

Recently, researchers have argued that *challenge stressors*—or stressors associated with workload, pressure to complete tasks, and time urgency—operate quite differently from *hindrance stressors*—or stressors that keep you from reaching your goals (red tape, office politics, confusion over job responsibilities). Although research has just started to accumulate, early evidence suggests that challenge stressors produce less strain than hindrance stressors.[14] Role ambiguity, role con-

The Most and Least Stressful Jobs

How do jobs rate in terms of stress? According to *Health* magazine, the top 10 most and least stressful jobs are as follows.[15]

Ten Most Stressful Jobs
1. Inner-city high school teacher
2. Police officer
3. Miner
4. Air traffic controller
5. Medical intern
6. Stockbroker
7. Journalist
8. Customer-service/complaint worker
9. Secretary
10. Waiter

Ten Least Stressful Jobs
1. Forester
2. Bookbinder
3. Telephone line worker
4. Toolmaker
5. Millwright
6. Repairperson
7. Civil engineer
8. Therapist
9. Natural scientist
10. Sales representative

flict, role overload, job insecurity, environmental uncertainty, and situational constraints were all consistently negatively related to job performance.[16] Evidence also suggests that challenge stress improves job performance in a supportive work environment, whereas hindrance stress reduces job performance in all work environments.[17] It appears that employees who have a stronger affective commitment to their organization can transfer psychological stress into greater focus and higher sales performance, whereas employees with low levels of commitment perform worse under stress.[18]

More typically, stress is associated with *demands* and *resources*. Demands are responsibilities, pressures, obligations, and even uncertainties that individuals face in the workplace. Resources are things within an individual's control that can be used to resolve the demands. For example, when you take a test, you feel stress because you confront opportunities and performance pressures. To the extent that you can apply resources to the demands on you—such as being prepared for the exam—you will feel less stress.

Under the demands-resources perspective, having resources to cope with stress is just as important in offsetting it as demands are in increasing it.[19]

Causes of Stress

The workplace provides a variety of stressors:[20]

- *Environmental factors.* Uncertainty is the biggest reason people have trouble coping with organizational changes.[21] Two types of environmental uncertainty are economic and technological. Changes in the business cycle create *economic uncertainties*. When the economy is contracting, for example, people become increasingly anxious about their job security. Because new innovations can make an employee's skills and experience obsolete in a very short time, computers, robotics, automation, and similar forms of *technological change* are a threat to many people and cause them stress.

- *Organizational factors.* There is no shortage of factors within an organization that can cause

stress. Pressures to avoid errors or complete tasks in a limited time, work overload, a demanding and insensitive boss, and unpleasant co-workers are a few examples. We have categorized these factors around task, role, and interpersonal demands.[22]

- *Task demands* relate to a person's job. They include the design of the individual's job (autonomy, task variety, degree of automation), working conditions, and the physical work layout. Assembly lines can put pressure on people when they perceive the line's speed to be excessive. Working in an overcrowded room or in a visible location where noise and interruptions are constant can increase anxiety and stress.[23] As customer service grows ever more important, emotional labour becomes a source of stress.[24] Do you think you could put on a happy face when you are having a bad day?

- *Role demands* relate to pressures placed on a person as a function of the particular role he or she plays in the organization.

- *Interpersonal demands* are pressures created by other employees. Lack of social support from colleagues and poor interpersonal relationships can cause stress, especially among employees with a high social need. A rapidly growing body of research has also shown that negative co-worker and supervisor behaviours, including fights, bullying, incivility, racial harassment, and sexual harassment, are especially strongly related to stress at work.[25]

- *Personal factors.* The typical individual works about 40 to 50 hours a week. But the experiences and

problems that people encounter in the other 120-plus nonwork hours can spill over to the job. Our final category, then, encompasses factors in the employee's personal life: family issues, personal economic problems, and personality characteristics.

- National surveys consistently show that people hold *family* and personal relationships dear. Marital difficulties, the breaking off of a relationship, caring for elderly parents, and discipline troubles with children create stress employees often cannot leave at the front door when they arrive at work.[26]

- Regardless of income level—people who make $100 000 per year seem to have as much trouble handling their finances as those who earn $20 000—some people are poor money managers or have wants that exceed their earning capacity. The *economic* problems of overextended financial resources create stress and take attention away from work.

- Studies in three diverse organizations found that participants who reported stress symptoms before beginning a job accounted for most of the variance in stress symptoms reported nine months later.[27] The researchers concluded that some people may have an inherent tendency to accentuate negative aspects of the world in general. If this is true, then stress symptoms expressed on the job may actually originate in the person's *personality*.

When we review stressors individually, it's easy to overlook that stress is an additive phenomenon—it builds up.[28] Each new and persistent stressor

adds to an individual's stress level. A single stressor may seem relatively unimportant in and of itself, but if it is added to an already high level of stress, it can be "the straw that breaks the camel's back."

Consequences of Stress

Stress manifests itself in a number of ways, such as high blood pressure, ulcers, irritability, difficulty in making routine decisions, loss of appetite, accident proneness, and the like. These symptoms can be placed under three general categories: physiological, psychological, and behavioural symptoms.[30]

- *Physiological symptoms.* Most early research concerned with stress was

directed at physiological symptoms because most researchers in this area were specialists in the health and medical sciences. Their work led to the conclusion that stress could create changes in metabolism, increase heart and breathing rates, increase blood pressure, cause headaches, and induce heart attacks. Because symptoms are complex and difficult to measure objectively, researchers concluded there were few, if any, consistent relationships.[31] More recently, some evidence suggests stress may have harmful physiological effects. One study linked stressful job demands to increased susceptibility to upper respiratory illnesses and poor immune system functioning, especially for individuals with low self-efficacy.[32] Furthermore, stress hits workers at all ages, and it is not unusual for employees in their 20s, 30s, and 40s to suffer long-term disabilities, claiming illnesses that are either psychiatric (such as depression) or more difficult to diagnose (such as chronic fatigue syndrome or fibromyalgia, a musculoskeletal discomfort). The increase in disability claims may be the result of downsizing taking its toll on the psyches of those in the workforce.[33]

- *Psychological symptoms.* Job dissatisfaction is "the simplest and most obvious psychological effect" of stress.[34] But stress also shows itself in other psychological states—for instance, tension, anxiety, irritability, boredom, and procrastination.

   The evidence indicates that when people are placed in jobs that make multiple and conflicting demands or in which there is a lack of clarity as to the person's duties, authority, and responsibilities, both stress and dissatisfaction increase.[35] Similarly, the less control people

have over the pace of their work, the greater the stress and dissatisfaction. Although more research is needed to clarify the relationship, jobs providing a low level of variety, significance, autonomy, feedback, and identity create stress and reduce satisfaction and involvement in the job.[36]

- *Behavioural symptoms.* Behaviourally related stress symptoms include changes in productivity, absence, and turnover, as well as changes in eating habits, increased smoking or consumption of alcohol, rapid speech, fidgeting, and sleep disorders. More recently, stress has been linked to aggression and violence in the workplace.

Why Do Individuals Differ in Their Experience of Stress?

Some people thrive on stressful situations, while others are overwhelmed by them. What differentiates people in terms of their ability to handle stress? What individual difference variables moderate the relationship between *potential* stressors and *experienced* stress? At least four variables—perception, job experience, social support, and personality—are relevant.

- *Perception.* Individuals react in response to their *perception* of reality rather than to reality itself. Perception, therefore, moderates the relationship between a potential stress condition and an employee's reaction to it. Layoffs may cause one person to fear losing his job, while another sees an opportunity to get a large severance allowance and start her own business.[37] So stress potential does not lie in objective conditions; instead it lies

in an employee's interpretation of those conditions.

- *Job experience.* Experience on the job tends to be negatively related to work stress. Two explanations have been offered.[38] First is selective withdrawal. Voluntary turnover is more probable among people who experience more stress. Therefore, people who remain with the organization longer are those with more stress-resistant traits or those who are more resistant to the stress characteristics of their organization. Second, people eventually develop coping mechanisms to deal with stress. Because this takes time, senior members of the organization are more likely to be fully adapted and should experience less stress.

- *Social support.* Collegial relationships with co-workers or supervisors can buffer the impact of stress.[39] Social support helps ease the negative effects of even high-strain jobs. Outside the job, involvement with family, friends, and community can provide the support if it is missing at work.

- *Personality.* Personality affects not only the degree to which people experience stress but also how they cope with it. Perhaps the most widely studied personality trait in stress is *Type A personality*, discussed in Chapter 2. Type A—particularly that aspect that manifests itself in hostility and anger—is associated with increased levels of stress and risk for heart disease.[40] People who are quick to anger, maintain a persistently hostile outlook, and project a cynical mistrust of others are at increased risk of experiencing stress in situations. Stressed Type As recover from stressful situations slower than Type B personalities, which suggests Type A individuals

tend to have higher rates of death associated with hypertension, coronary heart disease, and coronary artery disease.[41]

How Do We Manage Stress?

Below we discuss ways that individuals can manage stress, and what programs organizations use to help employees manage stress.

Individual Approaches

An employee can take personal responsibility for reducing his or her stress level. Individual strategies that have proven effective include time management techniques, physical exercise, relaxation techniques, and a close social support network.

- *Time management.* Many people manage their time poorly. The well-organized employee, like the well-organized student, can often accomplish twice as much as the person who is poorly organized. So understanding and using basic time management principles can help individuals cope better with tensions created by job demands.[42] A few of the more well-known time management principles are (1) making daily lists of activities to be accomplished; (2) prioritizing activities by importance and urgency; (3) scheduling activities according to the priorities set; and (4) knowing your daily productivity cycle and handling the most demanding parts of your job during the high part of your cycle, when you are most alert and productive.[43]

- *Physical activity.* Physicians have recommended noncompetitive physical exercise, such as aerobics, walking, jogging, swimming, and riding a bicycle as a way to deal with excessive stress levels. These forms of physical exercise increase heart capacity, lower at-rest heart rate, provide a mental diversion from work pressures, and slow the physical and mental effects of aging.[44]

- *Relaxation techniques.* Individuals can teach themselves to reduce tension through relaxation techniques such as meditation, hypnosis, and biofeedback. The objective is to reach a state of deep relaxation, in which you feel somewhat detached from the immediate environment and from body sensations.[45] Deep relaxation for 15 or 20 minutes a day releases tension and provides a pronounced sense of peacefulness, as well as significant changes in heart rate, blood pressure, and other physiological factors.

- *Building social supports.* Having friends, family, or colleagues to talk to provides an outlet when stress levels become excessive. Expanding your social support network provides you with someone to listen to your problems and to offer a more objective perspective on the situation.

The inset *Tips for Reducing Stress* offers additional ideas for managing stress.

Organizational Approaches

Employees who work at Montreal-based Ericsson Canada, a global telecommunications supplier, have access to a comprehensive wellness program. They can engage in activities that address their intellectual, emotional, social, physical, and spiritual well-being. "The program has really evolved over the years," says Louise Leonhardt, manager of human resources. "We've found it helps people balance their life, just like the on-site daycare does."

Employees who work at Toronto-based BCS Group, a publishing, advertising, and public relations agency, receive biweekly shiatsu massages, paid for by the company. The company spends about $700 a month for the massages, equivalent to the amount it used to spend providing coffee to the employees. "It's in my company's best interest to have my employees be healthy," says Caroline Tapp-McDougall, BCS Group publisher.[47]

Most firms that have introduced wellness programs have found significant benefits. Health Canada reports that businesses get back $3.39 for each corporate dollar they invest in wellness initiatives. For individuals with three to five risk factors (such as

---

Tips for Reducing Stress

- At least two or three times a week, spend time with supportive friends or family.
- Ask for support when you are under pressure. This is a sign of health, not weakness.
- If you have spiritual or religious beliefs, increase or maintain your involvement.
- Use a variety of methods to reduce stress. Consider exercise, nutrition, hobbies, positive thinking, and relaxation techniques such as meditation or yoga.[46]

high cholesterol, being overweight, or smoking) the return was $2.04 for each dollar spent.[48] The savings come about because there is less turnover, greater productivity, and reduced medical claims.[49] While many Canadian businesses report having wellness initiatives, only 24 percent have "fully implemented wellness strategies" (which includes multi-year goals and an evaluation of results), according to a 2010 survey.[50]

So what can organizations do to reduce employee stress? In general, strategies to reduce stress include improved processes for choosing employees, placement of employees in appropriate jobs, realistic goal setting, designing jobs with employee needs and skills in mind, increased employee involvement, improved organizational communication, offering employee sabbaticals, and, as mentioned, establishment of corporate wellness programs.

Certain jobs are more stressful than others, but individuals also differ in their response to stress situations. We know, for example, that individuals with little experience or an external locus of control tend to be more prone to stress. Selection and placement decisions should take these facts into consideration. Although management should not restrict hiring to only experienced individuals with an internal locus of control, such individuals may adapt better to high-stress jobs and perform those jobs more effectively.

Individuals perform better when they have specific and challenging goals and receive feedback on how well they are progressing toward them.[51] Goals can reduce stress as well as provide motivation.[52] Specific goals that are perceived as attainable clarify performance expectations. Additionally, goal feedback reduces uncertainties as to actual job performance. The result is

Toward Less Stressful Work

- Avoid high-stress jobs—such as stockbroker, customer service/ complaint worker, police officer, waiter, medical intern, secretary, and air traffic controller—unless you are confident in your ability to handle stress.

- If you do experience stress at work, try to find a job that has plenty of control (so you can decide how to perform your work) and supportive co-workers.

- Lack of money is the top stressor reported by people under age 30, so pursue a career that pays you well but does not have a high degree of stress.[53]

less employee frustration, role ambiguity, and stress.

Redesigning jobs to give employees more responsibility, more meaningful work, more autonomy, and increased feedback can reduce stress because these factors give the employee greater control over work activities and lessen dependence on others. Of course, not all employees want jobs with increased responsibility. The right design for employees with a low need for growth might be less responsibility and increased specialization. If individuals prefer structure and routine, more structured jobs should also reduce uncertainties and stress levels.

Role stress is detrimental to a large extent because employees feel uncertain about goals, expectations, how they will be evaluated, and the like. By giving these employees a voice in the decisions that directly affect their job performance, management can increase employee control and reduce role stress. So managers should consider *increasing employee involvement* in decision making.[54]

Increasing formal organizational communication with employees reduces uncertainty by lessening role ambiguity and role conflict. Given the

importance that perceptions play in moderating the stress-response relationship, management can also use effective communication as a means to shape employee perceptions. Remember that what employees categorize as demands, threats, or opportunities are merely interpretations, and those interpretations can be affected by the symbols and actions communicated by management.

Some employees need an occasional escape from the frenetic pace of their work. In recent years, companies such as Charles Schwab, DuPont, L.L.Bean, Nike, and 3Com have begun to provide extended voluntary leaves.[55] These *sabbaticals*—ranging in length from a few weeks to several months—allow employees to travel, relax, or pursue personal projects that consume time beyond normal vacation weeks. Proponents say that these sabbaticals can revive and rejuvenate workers who might be headed for burnout.

Our final suggestion is to offer organizationally supported wellness programs. These typically provide workshops to help people quit smoking, control alcohol use, lose weight, eat better, and develop a regular

exercise program; they focus on the employee's total physical and mental condition.[56] A study of 36 programs designed to reduce stress (including wellness programs) showed that interventions to help employees reframe stressful situations and use active coping strategies led to an appreciable reduction in stress levels.[57] Most wellness programs assume that employees need to take personal responsibility for their physical and mental health and that the organization is merely a means to that end. The inset *Toward Less Stressful Work* offers additional ideas.

FACEOFF

When organizations provide on-site daycare facilities, they are filling a needed role in parents' lives, and making it easier for parents to attend to their job demands rather than worry about child-care arrangements.

When employees expect organizations to provide child care, they are shifting their responsibilities to their employers, rather than keeping their family needs and concerns private. Moreover, it is unfair to offer child-care benefits when not all employees have children.

RESEARCH EXERCISES

1. Look for data on stress levels in other countries. How do these data compare with the Canadian data presented above? Are the sources of stress the same in different countries? What might you conclude about how stress affects people in different cultures?

2. Find out what three Canadian organizations in three different industries have done to help employees manage stress. Are there common themes in these programs? Did you find any unusual programs? To what extent are these programs tailored to the needs of the employees in those industries?

YOUR PERSPECTIVE

1. Think of all the technical avenues enabling employees to be connected 24/7 to the workplace: email, texting, company web pages. A generation ago, most employees could go home after a day at work and not be "on call." What are the positive benefits of this change? What are the down-

sides? As an employee facing the demand to "stay connected" to your workplace, how would you try to maintain a balance in your life?

2. How much responsibility should individuals take for managing their own stress? To what extent should organizations become involved in the personal lives of their employees when trying to help them manage stress? What are the pros and cons for whether employees or organizations take responsibility for managing stress?

WANT TO KNOW MORE?

If you are wondering how stressed you are, go to **www.heartandstroke. ca** and click on "Health Information," "Heart Disease," and then "Other Resources for Heart Disease" to take a stress test. The site also offers tips on reducing stress.

Theories of Motivation

Figure skater Patrick Chan set three world records at the 2011 World Figure Skating Championships. How did motivation influence his impressive performance?

LEARNING OUTCOMES

1 What is motivation?

2 How do needs motivate people?

3 Are there other ways to motivate people?

4 Do equity and fairness matter?

5 What role does reinforcement play in motivation?

6 What are the ethics behind motivation theories?

atrick Chan, currently Canada's number one male figure skater, is motivated.[1] After placing a disappointing fifth in the Vancouver 2010 Winter Olympics, despite skating a personal best in the free skate program, he had to make a decision. Chan had to either introduce the very challenging quadruple jump (the hallmark of elite skaters such as Kurt Browning) into his routines or continue to hope that a quadruple was not necessary for champion skaters.

Chan took the loss in the Olympics with grace. "I think after overcoming the Olympics and not doing your best, that's the biggest challenge and that's the Mount Everest of athletes. I think now I can go to Worlds in March [2010] and say, you know, this is a walk in the park."

In preparing for the World Figure Skating Championships, Chan had to consider the impact of figure skating's judging system. At one time, the perfect score was 6.0, although it was not quite clear how that score was achieved. Under the new system introduced in 2004, every element—"from jumps to spins to the step sequences in between—[has] an assigned value." Judges then add or subtract points based on how well the skater executes each element.

Chan won a gold medal at the 2010 Grand Prix Finals in Beijing. Then at the 2011 Moscow Worlds, he not only won gold but also set three world records in doing so. At the end of 2011, Chan had won his second consecutive gold in the Grand Prix Finals held in Quebec City. By January 2012, he had won his fifth national title. So what made Chan's loss at the Olympics motivational rather than make him want to quit skating completely?

In this chapter, we examine the subjects of motivation and rewards. We look at what motivation is, and how needs can be used to motivate individuals. We also present theories of motivation, and then consider the roles that fairness, reinforcement, and ethics play in motivation.

THE BIG IDEA

Successfully motivating individuals requires identifying their needs and making it possible for them to achieve their needs.

OB IS FOR EVERYONE

- Are managers manipulating employees when they link rewards to productivity? Is this ethical?

- Why do some managers do a better job of motivating people than others?

- How important is fairness to you?

- What can you do if you think your salary is unfair?

SELF-ASSESSMENT LIBRARY

LEARNING ABOUT YOURSELF

- Motivation
- Goals
- Self-Confidence
- Disciplining Others

What Is Motivation?

We define **motivation** as the process that accounts for an individual's intensity, direction, and persistence of effort toward reaching a goal.[2]

The three key elements in our definition are intensity, direction, and persistence. *Intensity* describes how hard a person tries. This is the element most of us focus on when we talk about motivation. However, high intensity is unlikely to lead to favourable job-performance outcomes unless the effort is channelled in a *direction* that is beneficial. Therefore, we consider the quality of effort as well as its intensity. Finally, the effort requires *persistence*. This measures how long a person can maintain effort. Motivated individuals stay with a task long enough to achieve their goal.

Many people incorrectly view motivation as a personal trait—something some people have and others don't. Along these lines, Douglas McGregor proposed two distinct views of human beings. **Theory X**, which is basically negative, suggests that employees dislike work, will attempt to avoid it, and must be coerced, controlled, or threatened with punishment to achieve goals. **Theory Y**, which is basically positive, suggests that employees like work, are creative, seek responsibility, and will exercise self-direction and self-control if they are committed to the objectives.[3]

Our knowledge of motivation tells us that neither theory alone fully accounts for employee behaviour. What we know is that motivation is the result of the interaction of the individual and the situation. Certainly, individuals differ in their basic motivational drive. But the same employee who is quickly bored when pulling the lever on a drill press may enthusiastically pull a slot machine lever in Casino Windsor for hours on end. You may read the latest bestseller at one sitting, yet find it difficult to concentrate on a textbook for more than 20 minutes. It's not necessarily you—it's the situation. So as we analyze the concept of motivation, keep in mind that the level of motivation varies both *among* individuals and *within* individuals at different times.

You should also realize that what motivates people will also vary among individuals and situations. Motivation theorists talk about **intrinsic motivators** and **extrinsic motivators**. Extrinsic motivators come from outside the person and include such things as pay, bonuses, and other tangible rewards. Intrinsic motivators come from a person's internal desire to do something, due to such things as interest, challenge, and personal satisfaction. Individuals are intrinsically motivated when they genuinely care about their work, look for better ways to do it, and are energized and fulfilled by doing it well.[4] The rewards the individual gets from intrinsic motivation come from the work itself rather than from external factors such as increases in pay or compliments from the boss.

Are individuals primarily intrinsically or extrinsically motivated? Theory X suggests that people are almost exclusively driven by extrinsic motivators. However, Theory Y suggests that people are more intrinsically motivated. This view is consistent with that of Alfie Kohn, author of *Punished by Rewards*, who suggests that it's only necessary to provide the right environment, and people will be motivated.[5] We discuss his ideas further in Chapter 5.

Intrinsic and extrinsic motivation may reflect the situation, however, rather than individual personalities. For example, suppose your mother has asked you or your brother to take her to a meeting an hour away. You may be willing to drive her, without any thought of compensation, because it will make you feel good to do something for her. That is intrinsic motivation. But if you have a love-hate relationship with your brother, you may insist that he buy you lunch for helping out. Lunch would then be an extrinsic motivator—something that came from outside yourself and motivated you to do the task. Later in the chapter, we review the evidence regarding the significance of extrinsic vs. intrinsic rewards, and also examine how to increase intrinsic motivation. Meanwhile, you might consider whether you can motivate yourself through self-talk, an idea considered in *Focus on Research*.

motivation The intensity, direction, and persistence of effort a person shows in reaching a goal.

Theory X The assumption that employees dislike work, will attempt to avoid it, and must be coerced, controlled, or threatened with punishment to achieve goals.

Theory Y The assumption that employees like work, are creative, seek responsibility, and will exercise self-direction and self-control if they are committed to the objectives.

intrinsic motivators A person's internal desire to do something, due to such things as interest, challenge, and personal satisfaction.

extrinsic motivators Motivation that comes from outside the person and includes such things as pay, bonuses, and other tangible rewards.

Talking to Yourself Can Be a Powerful Self-Motivator

How does internal dialogue affect our motivation? In the children's book *The Little Engine That Could*, the title character says, "I think I can, I think I can," motivating himself to do the job through positive self-talk. In a 2010 study, researchers examined whether this type of talk is the best way to motivate one's self, or whether it is better to ask "Can I do this?"[6]

Subjects were asked to spend one minute either "wondering whether they would complete a task or telling themselves they would." Then they were asked to complete some puzzles. Subjects who asked themselves whether they would complete the task were more successful than those who said they would. Several similar studies were conducted, and the results of each of them indicate that intrinsic motivation increased when subjects asked themselves a question about performance.

These findings suggest that asking yourself whether you will go to the gym three times next week will be more effective than telling yourself that you will go to the gym three times next week. One of the authors of the study summarized the results as follows: "The popular idea is that self-affirmations enhance people's ability to meet their goals. It seems, however, that when it comes to performing a specific behaviour, asking questions is a more promising way of achieving your objectives."[7]

Needs Theories of Motivation

Theories of motivation generally fall into two categories: needs theories and process theories. *Needs theories* describe the types of needs that must be met to motivate individuals. *Process theories* help us understand the actual ways in which we and others can be motivated. There are a variety of needs theories, including Maslow's hierarchy of needs, Alderfer's ERG theory, Herzberg's motivation-hygiene theory (sometimes called the *two-factor theory*), and McClelland's theory of needs. We briefly review these to illustrate the basic properties of needs theories.

Needs theories are widely criticized for not standing up to scientific review. However, you should know them because (1) they represent a foundation from which contemporary theories have grown, and (2) practising managers still regularly use these theories and their terminology in explaining employee motivation.

2 How do needs motivate people?

Maslow's Hierarchy of Needs Theory

It's probably safe to say that the most well-known theory of motivation is Abraham Maslow's **hierarchy of needs theory**.[8] Maslow hypothesized that within every human being there exists a hierarchy of five needs:

- *Physiological.* Includes hunger, thirst, shelter, sex, and other bodily needs.

- *Safety.* Includes security and protection from physical and emotional harm.

- *Social.* Includes affection, belongingness, acceptance, and friendship.

- *Esteem.* Includes internal esteem factors such as self-respect, autonomy, and achievement; and external esteem factors such as status, recognition, and attention.

- *Self-actualization.* Includes growth, achieving one's potential, and self-fulfillment. This is the drive to become what one is capable of becoming.

Although no need is ever fully met, a substantially satisfied need no longer motivates. Thus, as each of these needs becomes substantially satisfied, the next need becomes

hierarchy of needs theory A hierarchy of five needs—physiological, safety, social, esteem, and self-actualization—in which, as each need is substantially satisfied, the next need becomes dominant.

Source: How Great Companies Get Their Mojo From Maslow by Chip Conley and Tony Hsieh. Copyright © 2007, Jossey-Bass. Reprinted with permission of John Wiley & Sons, Inc.

dominant. This is what Maslow means by moving up the steps of the hierarchy. So if you want to motivate someone, according to Maslow, you need to understand what level of the hierarchy that person is currently on and focus on satisfying the needs at or above that level. Exhibit 4-1 identifies Maslow's hierarchy of needs on the left, and then illustrates how these needs are applied in the workplace.[9]

Maslow separated the five needs into higher and lower orders. Physiological and safety needs were **lower-order needs**, and social, esteem, and **self-actualization** were **higher-order needs**. The differentiation between the two orders was made on the premise that higher-order needs are satisfied internally (within the person), whereas lower-order needs are mainly satisfied externally (by such things as pay, union contracts, and tenure).

Maslow's needs theory continues to receive wide recognition, particularly among practising managers. It is intuitively logical and easy to understand, even though there is little research supporting the theory. Maslow himself provided no empirical evidence, and there is little evidence that need structures are organized along the dimensions proposed by Maslow, that unsatisfied needs motivate, or that a satisfied need activates movement to a new need level.[10] One 2011 study differs in its findings, however. Using data from 123 countries, the study found that Maslow's needs are universally related to individual happiness, but that the order of need fulfillment had little bearing on life satisfaction and enjoyment. Lower-order needs were related to positive life evaluation, while higher-order needs were linked to enjoying life. The researchers concluded that the findings overall supported Maslow's theory.[11]

ERG Theory

Clayton Alderfer reworked Maslow's hierarchy of needs to align it more closely with the empirical research. His revised need hierarchy is called **ERG theory**.[12]

Alderfer argued that there are three groups of core needs—*existence* (similar to Maslow's physiological and safety needs), *relatedness* (similar to Maslow's social needs), and *growth* (similar to Maslow's esteem needs and self-actualization). Unlike Maslow, Alderfer did not assume that these needs existed in a rigid hierarchy. An individual could focus on all three need categories simultaneously. Despite these differences, empirical research has not been any more supportive of ERG theory than it has of Maslow's theory.[13]

Motivation-Hygiene Theory

Psychologist Frederick Herzberg proposed the **motivation-hygiene theory** (also called the *two-factor theory*).[14] Believing that an individual's relationship to work is basic and that attitude toward this work can very well determine success or failure, Herzberg investigated the question, "What do people want from their jobs?" He asked people to

lower-order needs Needs that are satisfied externally, such as physiological and safety needs.

self-actualization The drive to become what a person is capable of becoming.

higher-order needs Needs that are satisfied internally, such as social, esteem, and self-actualization needs.

ERG theory A theory that posits three groups of core needs: existence, relatedness, and growth.

motivation-hygiene theory A theory that relates intrinsic factors to job satisfaction and associates extrinsic factors with dissatisfaction. Also called the *two-factor theory*.

EXHIBIT 4-2 Comparison of Satisfiers and Dissatisfiers

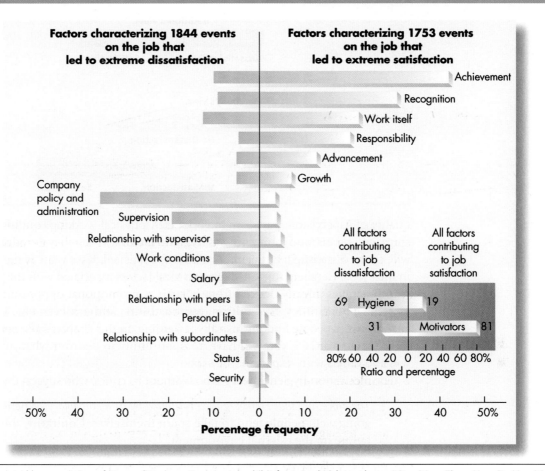

describe, in detail, situations in which they felt exceptionally good or bad about their jobs. He then tabulated and categorized the response. Exhibit 4-2 illustrates factors affecting job attitudes, as reported in 12 investigations conducted by Herzberg.

Herzberg concluded that the replies people gave when they felt good about their jobs significantly differed from when they felt bad. As shown in Exhibit 4-2, intrinsic factors, such as achievement, recognition, the work itself, responsibility, advancement, and growth, seem to be related to job satisfaction. Respondents who felt good about their work tended to attribute these characteristics to themselves. On the other hand, dissatisfied respondents tended to cite extrinsic factors, such as company policy and administration, supervision, interpersonal relations, and work conditions.

According to Herzberg, the data suggest that the opposite of satisfaction is not dissatisfaction, as was traditionally believed. Removing dissatisfying characteristics from a job does not necessarily make the job satisfying. As illustrated in Exhibit 4-3, Herzberg proposes that his findings indicate the existence of a dual continuum: the opposite of "Satisfaction" is "No Satisfaction," and the opposite of "Dissatisfaction" is "No Dissatisfaction."

Herzberg explained that the factors leading to job satisfaction (motivators) are separate and distinct from those that lead to job dissatisfaction (hygiene factors). Therefore, managers who seek to eliminate factors that create job dissatisfaction may bring about peace but not necessarily motivation. They will be placating rather than motivating their employees. As a result, Herzberg characterized conditions such as

EXHIBIT 4-3 Contrasting Views of Satisfaction and Dissatisfaction

quality of supervision, pay, company policies, physical working conditions, relationships with others, and job security as **hygiene factors**. When they are adequate, people will not be dissatisfied; but neither will they be satisfied. If we want to motivate people in their jobs, Herzberg suggested emphasizing factors associated with the work itself or with outcomes directly derived from it, such as promotional opportunities, personal growth opportunities, recognition, responsibility, and achievement. These are the characteristics people find intrinsically rewarding. In this chapter's *Working with Others Exercise* on page 165, you will have an opportunity to discover what motivates both you and others with respect to one's job.

The motivation-hygiene theory is not without its critics, who suggest the following:[15]

- *The procedure that Herzberg used is limited by its methodology.* When things are going well, people tend to take credit themselves. Contrarily, they blame failure on the external environment.

- *The reliability of Herzberg's methodology is questionable.* Raters have to make interpretations, so they may contaminate the findings by interpreting one response in one manner while treating a similar response differently.

- *No overall measure of satisfaction was used.* A person may dislike part of their job, yet still think the job is acceptable overall.

- *Herzberg assumed that a relationship exists between satisfaction and productivity.* But the research methodology he used looked only at satisfaction, not at productivity. To make such research relevant, one must assume a strong relationship between satisfaction and productivity.[16]

Regardless of these criticisms, Herzberg's theory has been widely read, and few managers are unfamiliar with his recommendations.

McClelland's Theory of Needs

You have one beanbag, and five targets are set up in front of you. Each target is farther away than the last and thus more difficult to hit. Target A is a cinch. It sits almost within arm's reach. If you hit it, you get $2. Target B is a bit farther out, but about 80 percent of the people who try can hit it. It pays $4. Target C pays $8, and about half the people who try can hit it. Very few people can hit Target D, but the payoff is $16 for those who do. Finally, Target E pays $32, but it's almost impossible to achieve. Which target would you try for? If you selected C, you are likely to be a high achiever. Why? Read on.

McClelland's theory of needs was developed by David McClelland and his associates.[17] The theory focuses on three needs, defined as follows:

- **Need for achievement (nAch).** The drive to excel, to achieve in relation to a set of standards, to strive to succeed.

- **Need for power (nPow)**. The need to make others behave in a way that they would not have behaved otherwise.

- **Need for affiliation (nAff)**. The desire for friendly and close interpersonal relationships.

Anne Sweeney, co-chair of Disney Media Networks and president of Disney/ABC Television Group, is a high achiever. Sweeney's Disney/ABC Television Group was the first media company to feature television content on new platforms, such as the iPod and iPad. More recently, she was instrumental in Disney's becoming an equity partner in Hulu.com. Sweeney's unofficial motto is "create what's next."

Of the three needs, McClelland and subsequent researchers focused most of their attention on nAch. High achievers perform best when they perceive their probability of success as 0.5—that is, a 50–50 chance of success.[18] They dislike gambling with high odds because they get no achievement satisfaction from success that comes by pure chance. Similarly, they dislike low odds (high probability of success) because then there is no challenge to their skills. They like to set goals that require stretching themselves a little.

Relying on an extensive amount of research, we can make some reasonably well-supported predictions of the relationship between achievement need and job performance. Although less research has been done on power and affiliation needs, findings are consistent there, too. First, when jobs have a high degree of personal responsibility, feedback, and an intermediate degree of risk, high achievers are strongly motivated. They are successful in entrepreneurial activities such as running their own businesses, for example, and managing self-contained units within large organizations.[19] Second, a high need to achieve does not necessarily make someone a good manager, especially in large organizations. People with a high achievement need are interested in how well they do personally and not in influencing others to do well. High-nAch salespeople do not necessarily make good sales managers, and the good general manager in a large organization does not typically have a high need to achieve.[20] Third, needs for affiliation and power tend to be closely related to managerial success. The best managers are high in their need for power and low in their need for affiliation.[21] In fact, a high power motive may be a requirement for managerial effectiveness.[22]

McClelland's theory has had the best research support of the different needs theories. Unfortunately, it has less practical effect than the others. Because McClelland argued that the three needs are subconscious—meaning we may be high on them but not know it—measuring them is not easy. In the most common approach, a trained expert presents pictures to individuals, asks them to tell a story about each, and then scores their responses in terms of the three needs. However, the process is time consuming and expensive, and few organizations have been willing to invest time and resources in measuring McClelland's concept.

Summarizing Needs Theories

The needs theories we have just reviewed all propose a similar idea: Individuals have needs that, when unsatisfied, will result in motivation. For instance, if you have a need to be praised, you may work harder at your task in order to receive recognition from your manager or other co-workers. Similarly, if you need money and you are asked to do something (within reason) that offers money as a reward, you will be motivated to complete that task.

Where needs theories differ is in the types of needs they consider and whether they propose a hierarchy of needs (where some needs have to be satisfied before others) or simply a list of needs. Exhibit 4-4 illustrates the relationship among the four needs theories that we discussed, and Exhibit 4-5 indicates whether the theory proposes a hierarchy of needs, and the contribution of and empirical support for each theory.

need for power (nPow) The need to make others behave in a way that they would not have behaved otherwise.

need for affiliation (nAff) The desire for friendly and close interpersonal relationships.

EXHIBIT 4-4 Relationship of Various Needs Theories

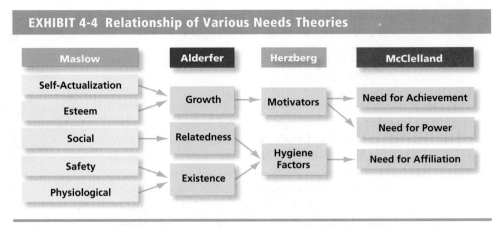

What can we conclude from needs theories? We can safely say that individuals do have needs, and that they can be highly motivated to achieve those needs. The types of needs, and their importance, vary by individual, and probably vary over time for the same individual as well. When rewarding individuals, you should consider their specific needs. Obviously, in a workplace, it would be difficult to design a reward structure that

EXHIBIT 4-5 Summarizing the Various Needs Theories

Theory	Maslow	Alderfer	Herzberg	McClelland
Is there a hierarchy of needs?	The theory argues that lower-order needs must be satisfied before one progresses to higher-order needs.	More than one need can be important at the same time. If a higher-order need is not being met, the desire to satisfy a lower-level need increases.	Hygiene factors must be met if a person is not to be dissatisfied. They will not lead to satisfaction, however. Motivators lead to satisfaction.	People vary in the types of needs they have. Their motivation and how well they perform in a work situation are related to whether they have a need for achievement, power, or affiliation.
What is the theory's impact/ contribution?	The theory enjoys wide recognition among practising managers. Most managers are familiar with it.	The theory is seen as a more valid version of the need hierarchy. It tells us that achievers will be motivated by jobs that offer personal responsibility, feedback, and moderate risks.	The popularity of giving employees greater responsibility for planning and controlling their work can be attributed to this theory (see, for instance, the job characteristics model in Chapter 5). It shows that more than one need may operate at the same time.	The theory tells us that high-need achievers do not necessarily make good managers, since high achievers are more interested in how they do personally.
What empirical support/criticisms exist?	Research has not validated the hierarchical nature of needs. However, a 2011 study found that the needs are universally related to individual happiness.	It ignores situational variables.	It is not really a theory of motivation: It assumes a link between satisfaction and productivity that was not measured or demonstrated.	It has mixed empirical support, but the theory is consistent with our knowledge of individual differences among people. Good empirical support exists on needs achievement in particular.

could completely take into account the specific needs of every employee. To better understand what might motivate you in the workplace, look at this chapter's *Learning About Yourself Exercise* on page 164.

Process Theories of Motivation

> After finishing fifth at the Vancouver 2010 Winter Olympics, Patrick Chan had to work on improving his performance.[23] A year later, Chan placed first at the 2011 World Figure Skating Championships in Moscow (which included a quadruple jump), winning his first World Title, and breaking records in doing so. His short program score broke the record previously held by former Olympic champion Evgeni Plushenko. His total score beat the former record of Japan's Daisuke Takahashi (who won the bronze medal in the 2010 Olympics) by more than 16 points.
>
> What motivated Chan's dramatic improvement in the year between the Olympics and the World Figure Skating Championships? Chan acknowledges that the disappointing experience at the Olympics made him "push himself and improve in order to capture the world's top spot." But winning his first World Title does not make Chan feel at ease about his next competition. He knows he has to keep practising to improve. "It's funny but I didn't feel totally satisfied with my free [skate] in Moscow. I felt that I wasn't as connected to the Phantom [of the Opera] as I am to this new program which gives me goose bumps when I skate it."
>
> Chan is motivated by a mix of intrinsic and extrinsic motivation. Like any talented athlete, he wants to be number one. But he also gets joy out of skating well. What makes someone like Patrick Chan show up at the skating rink, day after day, practising his routines?

Process theories go beyond individual needs and focus on the broader picture of how one motivates one's self and others. Process theories include expectancy theory, goal-setting theory (and its application, management by objectives), and self-efficacy theory.

Expectancy Theory

Currently, one of the most widely accepted explanations of motivation is Victor Vroom's **expectancy theory**.[24]

From a practical perspective, expectancy theory says that employees will be motivated to exert a high level of effort when they believe the following:

- That the effort will lead to good performance

- That good performance will lead to organizational rewards, such as a bonus, a salary increase, or a promotion

- That the rewards will satisfy employees' personal goals

The theory focuses on the three relationships (expectancy, instrumentality, and valence) illustrated in Exhibit 4-6 and described in the following pages. This exhibit also provides an example of how you might apply the theory.

Effort-Performance Relationship

The effort-performance relationship is commonly called **expectancy**. It answers the question: *If I give a maximum effort, will it be recognized in my performance appraisal?* For many employees, the answer is "no." Why? Their skill level may be deficient, which means that no matter how hard they try, they are not likely to be high performers. The organization's performance appraisal system may be designed to assess nonperformance factors such as loyalty, initiative, or courage, which means more effort will not necessarily result in a higher evaluation. Another possibility is that employees, rightly or wrongly, think the boss does not like them. As a result, they expect to get a poor appraisal, regardless of level of effort. These examples suggest one possible source of low motivation is employees' belief that, no matter how hard they work, the likelihood

SELF-ASSESSMENT LIBRARY

Learning About Yourself

1. What Motivates You?
(page 164)

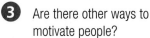 Are there other ways to motivate people?

expectancy theory The theory that individuals act based on their evaluation of whether their effort will lead to good performance, whether good performance will be followed by a given outcome, and whether that outcome is attractive.

expectancy The belief that effort is related to performance.

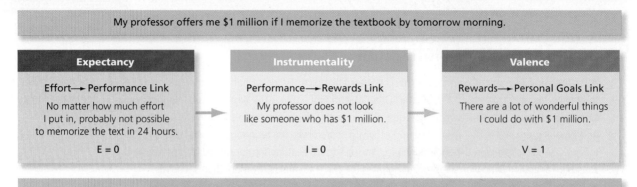

EXHIBIT 4-6 How Does Expectancy Theory Work?

My professor offers me $1 million if I memorize the textbook by tomorrow morning.

Expectancy	Instrumentality	Valence
Effort → Performance Link	Performance → Rewards Link	Rewards → Personal Goals Link
No matter how much effort I put in, probably not possible to memorize the text in 24 hours.	My professor does not look like someone who has $1 million.	There are a lot of wonderful things I could do with $1 million.
E = 0	I = 0	V = 1

Conclusion: Though I value the reward, I will not be motivated to do this task.

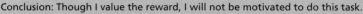

Using employee performance software, convenience-store retailer 7-Eleven measures the efforts of store managers and employees at its 8800 North American stores. The company ties employee compensation to performance outcomes based on 7-Eleven's five fundamental strategic initiatives—product assortment, value, quality, service, and cleanliness—as well as meeting goals set for new products. Many other companies reward simply on sales, which does not capture the full range of value-added services that employees provide.

of getting a good performance appraisal is low. Expectancy can be expressed as a probability, and ranges from 0 to 1.

The *Point/Counterpoint* discussion on page 163 further examines whether failure motivates or demotivates.

Performance-Rewards Relationship

The performance-rewards relationship is commonly called **instrumentality**. It answers the question: *If I get a good performance appraisal, will it lead to organizational rewards?* Many organizations reward a lot of things besides performance. When pay is based on factors such as having seniority, being cooperative, or "kissing up" to the boss, employees are likely to see the performance–rewards relationship as weak and demotivating. Instrumentality ranges from –1 to +1. A negative instrumentality indicates that high performance reduces the chances of getting the desired outcome. An instrumentality of 0 indicates that there is no relationship between performance and receiving the desired outcome.

Are managers manipulating employees when they link rewards to productivity? Is this ethical?

instrumentality The belief that performance is related to rewards.

Golfers such as Hamilton, Ontario's Alena Sharp, who won the 25th Canadian Women's PGA Championship in September 2011, illustrate the effectiveness of the expectancy theory of motivation, where rewards are tied to effort and outcome. Players on the LPGA tour are paid strictly according to their performance, unlike members of professional sports teams. Sharp's first LPGA Tour victory came in 2004. As Sharp has put more effort into her play, she has been increasing her earnings. In 2010, she earned $163 000 compared to $97 000 in 2006.[25]

Rewards-Personal Goals Relationship

The rewards-personal goals relationship is commonly called **valence**. It answers the question: *If I'm rewarded, are the rewards attractive to me?* The employee works hard in the hope of getting a promotion but gets a pay raise instead. Or the employee wants a more interesting and challenging job but receives only a few words of praise. Or the employee puts in extra effort to be relocated to the Paris office but instead is transferred to Singapore. It's important to tailor rewards to individual employee needs. Unfortunately, many managers are limited in the rewards they can distribute, which makes it difficult to personalize rewards. Moreover, some managers incorrectly assume that all employees want the same thing. They overlook the motivational effects of differentiating rewards. In either case, employee motivation may be lower because the specific need the employee has is not being met through the reward structure. Valence ranges from –1 (very undesirable reward) to +1 (very desirable reward).

> Why do some managers do a better job of motivating people than others?

Vancouver-based Radical Entertainment, creator of such digital entertainment as *Prototype* and *Crash of the Titans,* makes sure the company meets the needs of its employees, because it does not want to lose them to the United States.[26] The company employs a "Radical fun guru" whose job is to make the workplace so much fun no one wants to leave. The company provides free food all day, including catered lunches a few times a week, and there is a log cabin on-site, fitted out with big screens, DVDs, and gaming equipment, where employees can take time out to recharge during their long workdays. Radical Entertainment offers these benefits to meet the needs of its young employees, who find greater motivation from being part of a cool workplace than having a bigger pension plan.

Expectancy Theory in the Workplace

Does expectancy theory work? Although it has its critics,[27] most of the research evidence supports the theory.[28] Research in cross-cultural settings has also indicated support for expectancy theory.[29]

valence The value or importance an individual places on a reward.

EXHIBIT 4-7 Steps to Increasing Motivation, Using Expectancy Theory

Improving Expectancy	Improving Instrumentality	Improving Valence
Improve the ability of the individual to perform.	Increase the individual's belief that performance will lead to reward.	Make sure that the reward is meaningful to the individual.
• Make sure employees have skills for the task. • Provide training. • Assign reasonable tasks and goals.	• Observe and recognize performance. • Deliver rewards as promised. • Indicate to employees how previous good performance led to greater rewards.	• Ask employees what rewards they value. • Give rewards that are valued.

Exhibit 4-7 gives some suggestions for what a manager can do to increase the motivation of employees, using insights from expectancy theory. To appreciate how expectancy theory might apply in the workplace, see this chapter's *Case Incident—Wage Reduction Proposal* on page 167 for an example of what happens when expected rewards are withdrawn.

The Importance of Providing Performance Feedback

For employees to understand the relationship between rewards and performance, as well as considering whether rewards are equitable, they need to be given performance feedback. Many managers, however, find providing performance feedback to employees so unpleasant[30] they have to be pressured by organizational policies and controls to do so.[31] Why the reluctance to give performance feedback? There seem to be at least three reasons.

First, managers are often uncomfortable discussing performance weaknesses directly with employees. Even though almost every employee could stand to improve in some areas, managers fear a confrontation when presenting negative feedback.

Second, employees become defensive when their weaknesses are pointed out. Some employees challenge the evaluation by criticizing the manager or redirecting blame to someone else. A survey of 151 area managers, for instance, found that 98 percent encountered some type of aggression after giving employees negative appraisals.[32]

Finally, employees tend to have an inflated assessment of their own performance. By definition, half of all employees must be below-average performers, but the average employee estimates his or her own performance level at around the 75th percentile.[33] So even when managers are providing good news, employees are likely to perceive it as not good enough.

An effective review—one in which the employee perceives the appraisal as fair, the manager as sincere, and the climate as constructive—can result in the employee's leaving the interview in an upbeat mood, informed about the performance areas needing improvement, and determined to correct the deficiencies.[34] In addition, the performance review should be more like a counselling activity than a judgment process, allowing the review to evolve out of the employee's own self-evaluation. For more tips on performance feedback, see *OB in Action—Giving More Effective Feedback*.

Goal-Setting Theory

You have heard the phrase a number of times: "Just do your best. That's all anyone can ask for." But what does "do your best" mean? Do we ever know if we have achieved that vague

OB in ACTION
Giving More Effective Feedback

Managers can use the following tips to give more effective feedback:

→ Relate feedback to existing performance **goals** and clear **expectations**.

→ Give **specific** feedback tied to observable behaviour or measurable results.

→ Channel feedback toward **key result areas**.

→ Give feedback as **soon** as possible.

→ Give positive feedback for **improvement**, not just final results.

→ Focus feedback on **performance**, not personalities.

→ Base feedback on **accurate** and **credible** information.[35]

goal? Might you have done better in your high school English class if your parents had said, "You should strive for 75 percent or higher on all your work in English" instead of "do your best"?

The research on **goal setting theory** by Edwin Locke and his colleague, professor Gary Latham at the University of Toronto, shows that intentions to work toward a **goal** are a major source of work motivation.[36] Goals tell an employee what needs to be done and how much effort will need to be expended.[37]

Goal-setting theory has an impressive base of research support.[38] But as a manager, how do you make it operational? That is often left up to the individual manager or leader. Some managers explicitly set aggressive performance targets—what General Electric called "stretch goals." For example, some CEOs, such as Procter & Gamble's A. G. Laffey and SAP's Hasso Plattner, are known for the demanding performance goals they set. The problem with leaving it up to the individual manager is that, in many cases, managers don't set goals. A recent survey revealed that when asked whether their job had clearly defined goals, only a minority of employees agreed.[39]

Hasso Plattner, co-founder of the German software firm SAP, motivates employees by setting stretch goals. Plattner set a shockingly optimistic goal of 15 percent annual growth for SAP's software licence revenues. Employees responded by achieving an even higher growth rate of 18 percent. Plattner set another stretch goal by announcing a bonus plan that would pay $381 million to hundreds of managers and key employees if they could double the company's market capitalization, from a starting point of $57 billion, by the end of 2010. For Plattner, setting stretch goals is a way to inject entrepreneurial energy into the 40-year-old company.

A more systematic way to utilize goal setting is with a **management by objectives (MBO)** program.[40] In MBO, managers and employees jointly set performance goals that are tangible, verifiable, and measurable; progress on goals is periodically reviewed, and rewards are allocated on the basis of this progress.

A relatively new way of using goal setting in the workplace is by creating a Results-Only Work Environment (ROWE). In this type of environment, employees focus only on achieving results and manage their time accordingly, as this *OB in the Workplace* describes.

OB in the WORKPLACE
Results-Only Work Environments

Can a focus only on results change the federal government? Peter Hadwen, an Ottawa-based consultant, is trying to change the face of the federal government.[41] He thinks employees would be more productive if government departments were turned into Results-Only Work Environments (ROWEs). Employees would not be working to the clock, worrying about meetings, or being in the office at all. Employees could organize their time any way they wish, as long as they achieve the work results expected of them.

Though Hadwen has consulted for such government bureaucracies as Transport Canada, the Department of Fisheries and Oceans, and the Treasury Board Secretariat for a number of years, selling their managers on ROWE is not easy. "There's always a bit of skepticism regarding the ability to measure results," he says. "But with enough effort and discussion, we can get past that. Especially when dealing with organizations that are transaction focused, and which have a defined process and manner of doing things."

Best Buy, Netflix, and IBM have all turned to ROWE to make their workplaces happier and more efficient. The idea was created by two former employees of Best Buy, Cali

goal-setting theory A theory that says that specific and difficult goals, with feedback, lead to higher performance.

goal What an individual is trying to accomplish.

management by objectives (MBO) An approach to goal setting in which specific measurable goals are jointly set by managers and employees; progress on goals is periodically reviewed, and rewards are allocated on the basis of this progress.

Ressler and Jody Thompson, who wrote the book *Why Work Sucks and How to Fix It* to describe ROWE. The system makes employees more accountable, and leads to greater work-life balance. "People have a feeling that they are less beholden to a clock than they are to a work result on their own time. As such, it leads to less stress and a better morale," Hadwen says.

Though the federal government has been slow to implement ROWE, Waterloo, Ontario-based 46 MKS, which produces life-cycle management software, has picked up on the idea of ROWE to evaluate its employees. Because the organization operates globally (97 percent of its revenue comes from outside Canada), everyone is encouraged to work when, where, and how they want to, including odd hours, as long as they get the job done.

ROWE is effective because it encourages intrinsic motivation. Employees working under ROWE have more autonomy, they work on things that really matter, and they feel that the work they do actually makes a difference.[42]

How Does Goal Setting Motivate?

According to Locke, goal setting motivates in four ways (see Exhibit 4-8):[43]

- *Goals direct attention.* Goals indicate where individuals should direct their efforts when they are choosing among things to do. For instance, recognizing that an important assignment is due in a few days, goal setting may encourage you to say no when friends invite you to a movie this evening.

- *Goals regulate effort.* Goals suggest how much effort an individual should put into a given task. For instance, if earning a high mark in accounting is more important to you than earning a high mark in organizational behaviour, you will likely put more effort into studying accounting.

- *Goals increase persistence.* Persistence represents the effort spent on a task over time. When people keep goals in mind, they will work hard on them, even in the face of obstacles.

- *Goals encourage the development of strategies and action plans.* Once goals are set, individuals can develop plans for achieving those goals. For instance, a goal to become more fit may include plans to join a gym, work out with friends, and change eating habits.

In order for goals to be effective, they should be "SMART." SMART stands for

- Specific: Individuals know exactly what is to be achieved.

- Measurable: The goals proposed can be tracked and reviewed.

- Attainable: The goals, even if difficult, are reasonable and achievable.

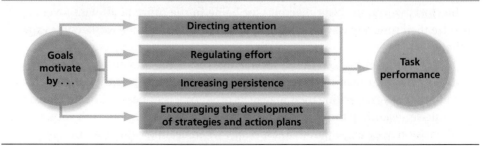

EXHIBIT 4-8 Locke's Model of Goal Setting

Source: Adapted from E. A. Locke and G. P. Latham, *A Theory of Goal Setting and Task Performance* (Englewood Cliffs, NJ: Prentice Hall, 1980). Reprinted by permission of Edwin A. Locke.

- Results-oriented: The goals should support the vision of the organization.

- Time-bound: The goals are to be achieved within a stated time.

From Concepts to Skills on pages 168–169 presents additional ideas on how to effectively engage in goal setting.

RESEARCH FINDINGS: The Effects of Goal Setting

Locke and his colleagues have spent considerable time studying the effects of goal setting in various situations. The evidence strongly supports the value of goals. More to the point, we can say the following:

- *Specific goals increase performance, under certain conditions.* In early research, specific goals were linked to better performance.[44] However, other research indicates that specific goals can lead to poorer performance in complex tasks. Employees may be too goal-focused on complex tasks, and therefore not consider alternative and better solutions to such tasks.[45]

- *Difficult goals, when accepted, result in higher performance than do easy goals.* Research clearly shows that goal difficulty leads to positive performance for the following reasons.[46] First, challenging goals get our attention and thus tend to help us focus. Second, difficult goals energize us because we have to work harder to attain them. Third, when goals are difficult, people persist in trying to attain them. Finally, difficult goals lead us to discover strategies that help us perform the job or task more effectively. If we have to struggle to solve a difficult problem, we often think of a better way to go about it. However, this relationship does not hold when employees view the goals as impossible, rather than just difficult.[47]

- *Feedback leads to higher performance.* Feedback allows individuals to know how they are doing, relative to their goals.[48] Feedback encourages individuals to adjust their direction, effort, and action plans if they are falling short of their goals. Self-generated feedback—with which employees are able to monitor their own progress—has been shown to be a more powerful motivator than externally generated feedback.[49]

- *Goals are equally effective whether participatively set, assigned, or self-set.* Research indicates that how goals are set is not clearly related to performance.[50] In some cases, participatively set goals yielded superior performance; in others, individuals performed best when assigned goals by their boss. But a major advantage of participation may be that it increases acceptance of the goal as a desirable one toward which to work.[51] Commitment is important. If participation isn't used, then the individual assigning the goal needs to clearly explain its purpose and importance.[52]

- *Goal commitment affects whether goals are achieved.* Goal-setting theory assumes that an individual is committed to the goal and is determined not to lower or abandon it. In terms of behaviour, the individual (1) believes he or she can achieve the goal and (2) wants to achieve it.[53] Goal commitment is most likely to occur when goals are made public, when the individual has an internal locus of control (see Chapter 12), and when the goals are self-set rather than assigned.[54] Goal-setting theory does not work equally well on all tasks. The evidence suggests that goals seem to have a more substantial effect on performance when tasks are simple rather than complex, well learned rather than novel, and independent rather than interdependent.[55] On interdependent tasks, group goals are preferable.

Although goal setting has positive outcomes, some goals may be *too* effective.[56] When learning something is important, goals related to performance may cause people to become too focused on outcomes and ignore changing conditions. In this case, a goal to learn and generate alternative solutions will be more effective than a goal to perform. Some authors have also argued that goals can lead employees to be too focused on a single standard to the exclusion of all others. Consider the narrow focus on short-term stock prices in many businesses—so much attention to this one standard for performance may have led organizations to ignore long-term success, and even to engage in such unethical behaviour as accounting fraud or excessively risky investments. Of course it is possible for organizations to establish goals for ethical performance. Despite differences of opinion, most researchers do agree that goals are powerful in shaping behaviour. Managers should make sure they are actually aligned with the company's objectives.

Goal-setting theory is consistent with expectancy theory. The goals can be considered the effort-performance link—in other words, the goals determine what must be done. Feedback can be considered the performance-reward relationship, where the individual's efforts are recognized. Finally, the implication of goal setting is that the achievement of the goals will result in intrinsic satisfaction (and may of course be linked to external rewards).

Self-Efficacy Theory

Self-efficacy refers to an individual's belief that he or she is capable of performing a task.[57] The higher your self-efficacy, the more confidence you have in your ability to succeed in a task. So, in difficult situations, people with low self-efficacy are more likely to lessen their effort or give up altogether, while those with high self-efficacy will try harder to master the challenge.[58] In addition, individuals high in self-efficacy seem to respond to negative feedback with increased effort and motivation, while those low in self-efficacy are likely to lessen their effort when given negative feedback.[59] How can managers help their employees achieve high levels of self-efficacy? By bringing together goal-setting theory and self-efficacy theory (also known as *social cognitive theory* or *social learning theory*).

Goal-setting theory and self-efficacy theory don't compete with one another; rather, they complement each other. As Exhibit 4-9 shows, when a manager sets difficult goals for employees, this leads employees to have a higher level of self-efficacy, and also leads them to set higher goals for their own performance. Why? Research has shown that setting difficult goals for people communicates your confidence in them. For example, imagine that your boss sets a higher goal for you than for your co-workers. How would you interpret this? As long as you did not feel you were being picked on, you would probably think, "Well, I guess my boss thinks I'm capable of performing better than others." This sets in motion a psychological process in which you are more confident in yourself (higher self-efficacy) and you set higher personal goals, causing you to perform better both in the workplace and outside it.

The researcher who developed self-efficacy theory, Albert Bandura, argues that there are four ways self-efficacy can be increased:[60]

- *Enactive mastery.* Gaining relevant experience with the task or job. If you have been able to do the job successfully in the past, then you are more confident that you will be able to do it in the future.

- *Vicarious modelling.* Becoming more confident because you see someone else doing the task. For example, if your friend loses weight, then it increases your confidence that you can lose weight, too. Vicarious modelling is most effective when you see yourself as similar to the person you are observing.

self-efficacy An individual's belief that he or she is capable of performing a task.

EXHIBIT 4-9 Joint Effects of Goals and Self-Efficacy on Performance

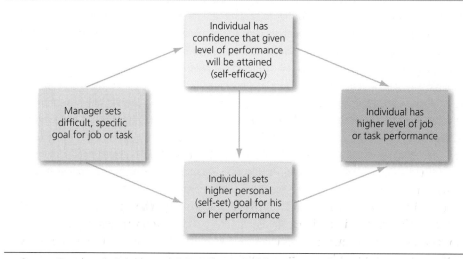

Source: Based on E. A. Locke and G. P. Latham, "Building a Practically Useful Theory of Goal Setting and Task Motivation: A 35-Year Odyssey," *American Psychologist*, September 2002, pp. 705–717.

- *Verbal persuasion.* Becoming more confident because someone convinces you that you have the skills necessary to be successful. Motivational speakers use this tactic a lot.

- *Arousal.* An energized state, which drives a person to complete a task. The person gets "psyched up" and performs better. But if the task is something that requires a steady, lower-key perspective (say, carefully editing a manuscript), arousal may in fact hurt performance.

What are the OB implications of self-efficacy theory? Well, it's a matter of applying Bandura's sources of self-efficacy to the work setting. Training programs often make use of enactive mastery by having people practise and build their skills. In fact, one of the reasons training works is because it increases self-efficacy.[61]

The best way for a manager to use verbal persuasion is through the *Pygmalion effect* or the *Galatea effect.* The Pygmalion effect is a form of a self-fulfilling prophecy in which believing something can make it true (also see Chapter 2). The Pygmalion effect increases self-efficacy by communicating to an individual's teacher or supervisor that the person is of high ability. In some studies, teachers were told their students had very high IQ scores, when in fact they had a range of IQs—some high, some low, and some in between. Consistent with the Pygmalion effect, the teachers spent more time with the students they *thought* were smart, gave them more challenging assignments, and expected more of them—all of which led to higher student self-efficacy and better student grades.[62] This has also been used in the workplace.[63] The Galatea effect occurs when high performance expectations are communicated directly to an employee. Sailors who were told, in a convincing manner, that they would not get seasick in fact were much less likely to get seasick.[64]

Note that intelligence and personality are absent from Bandura's list. Much research shows that intelligence and personality (especially conscientiousness and emotional stability) can increase self-efficacy.[65] Those individual traits are so strongly related to self-efficacy (people who are intelligent, conscientious, and emotionally stable are much more likely to have high self-efficacy than those who score low on these characteristics) that some researchers would argue that self-efficacy does not exist.[66] They believe it is simply a by-product in a smart person with a confident personality. Although Bandura strongly disagrees with this conclusion, more research is needed.

Responses to the Reward System

4 Do equity and fairness matter?

After the new judging system for figure skating and ice dancing was put into place in 2004, Skate Canada immediately had analysts review how points would be allocated for figure skating, and Canadian skaters were instructed on how to make best use of the system.[67]

"We were fortunate with how well-educated our federation made us about the system," said Jeff Buttle, who won a silver medal for Canada at the 2005 World Figure Skating Championships in Moscow after finishing 15th under the old system in 2003. "We sat down right from the beginning of that first season and talked about what we needed to be focusing on to maximize our scores."

Still, the new system was not without controversy. While it allows gifted "total" skaters—like Jeff Buttle, Patrick Chan, and Joannie Rochette—to earn high scores on overall skating skills rather than focusing on jumps, the scoring is still somewhat subjective. This subjectivity causes frustration for the skaters. At the 2009 World Championships in Los Angeles, the Canadian team was surprised when Brian Joubert of France beat Patrick Chan, who is well regarded for "footwork, transitions and overall skating skills." As Buttle pointed out, "Joubert may be a better jumper in the sense that he can do the quad, but people who don't even watch skating could easily see the difference in quality between Patrick and Brian." Outcomes like this can make the system seem unfair, with individuals giving the best performances not getting the highest marks. When individuals encounter unfairness in rewards systems, how do they respond?

To a large extent, motivation theories are about rewards. The theories suggest that individuals have needs and will exert effort in order to have those needs met. The needs theories specifically identify those needs. Goal-setting and expectancy theories portray processes by which individuals act and then receive desirable rewards (intrinsic or extrinsic) for their behaviour.

Three additional process theories ask us to consider how individuals respond to rewards. Equity theory suggests that individuals evaluate and interpret rewards. Fair process goes one step further, suggesting that employees are sensitive to a variety of fairness issues in the workplace that extend beyond the reward system but also affect employee motivation. Cognitive evaluation theory examines how individuals respond to the introduction of extrinsic rewards for intrinsically satisfying activities.

Equity Theory

Jane Pearson graduated from university last year with a degree in accounting. After interviews with a number of organizations on campus, she accepted an articling position with one of the nation's largest public accounting firms and was assigned to the company's Edmonton office. Jane was very pleased with the offer she received: challenging work with a prestigious firm, an excellent opportunity to gain valuable experience, and the highest salary any accounting major at her university was offered last year—$5500 a month. But Jane was the top student in her class; she was ambitious and articulate, and fully expected to receive a commensurate salary.

Twelve months have passed since Jane joined her employer. The work has proved to be as challenging and satisfying as she had hoped. Her employer is extremely pleased with her performance; in fact, she recently received a $300-a-month raise. However, Jane's motivational level has dropped dramatically in the past few weeks. Why? Her employer has just hired a new graduate from Jane's university, who lacks the one-year experience Jane has gained, for $5850 a month—$50 more than Jane now makes! It would be an understatement to describe Jane as irate. Jane is even talking about looking for another job.

How important is fairness to you?

EXHIBIT 4-10 Equity Theory

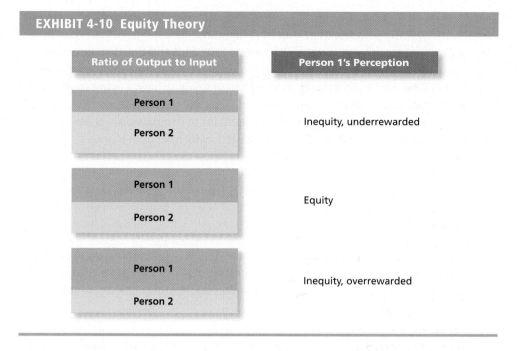

Ratio of Output to Input	Person 1's Perception
Person 1 / Person 2	Inequity, underrewarded
Person 1 / Person 2	Equity
Person 1 / Person 2	Inequity, overrewarded

Jane's situation illustrates the role that equity plays in motivation. We perceive what we get from a job situation (outcomes such as salary levels, raises, recognition, challenging assignments, working conditions) in relation to what we put into it (inputs such as effort, experience, education, competence, creativity), and then we compare our outcome-input ratio with that of relevant others. (This idea is illustrated in Exhibit 4-10.) If we perceive our ratio to be equal to that of the relevant others with whom we compare ourselves, a state of equity is said to exist. We perceive our situation as fair and justice prevails. When we see the ratio as unequal, we experience equity tension. When we see ourselves as underrewarded, the tension creates anger; when we see ourselves as overrewarded, it creates guilt. J. Stacy Adams has proposed that this negative state of tension provides the motivation to do something to correct it.[68]

To Whom Do We Compare Ourselves?

The referent that an employee selects when making comparisons adds to the complexity of **equity theory**.[69] There are four referent comparisons that an employee can use:

- *Self-inside.* An employee's experiences in a different position inside his or her current organization.

- *Self-outside.* An employee's experiences in a situation or position outside his or her current organization.

- *Other-inside.* Another individual or group of individuals inside the employee's organization.

- *Other-outside.* Another individual or group of individuals outside the employee's organization.

Employees might compare themselves with friends, neighbours, co-workers, colleagues in other organizations, or compare their present job with previous jobs they have had. Which referent an employee chooses will be influenced by the information the employee holds about referents, as well as by the attractiveness of the referent. Four moderating variables are gender, length of tenure, level in the organization, and amount of education or professionalism.[70]

equity theory A theory that says that individuals compare their job inputs and outcomes with those of others and then respond to eliminate any inequities.

Gender Research shows that both men and women prefer same-sex comparisons. Women are typically paid less than men in comparable jobs and have lower pay expectations than men for the same work.[71] For instance, in 2005 full-time female employees earned, on average, 70.5 cents for every dollar earned by full-time male employees.[72] So a woman who uses another woman as a referent tends to have a lower comparative standard for pay than a woman who uses a man as the referent. If women are to be paid equally to men in comparable jobs, the standard of comparison—as used by both employees and employers—needs to be expanded to include both sexes.

Length of Tenure Employees with short tenure in their current organizations tend to have little information about others inside the organization, so they rely on their own personal experiences. Employees with long tenure rely more heavily on co-workers for comparison.

Level in the Organization and Amount of Education Upper-level employees, those in the professional ranks, and those with more education tend to have better information about people in other organizations and will make more other-outside comparisons.

What Happens When We Feel Treated Inequitably?

Based on equity theory, employees who perceive an inequity will make one of six choices.[73]

- *Change their inputs* (exert less effort if underpaid, or more if overpaid; for example, Patrick Chan decided to practise even harder to place first in subsequent competitions).

> What can you do if you think your salary is unfair?

- *Change their outcomes* (individuals paid on a piece-rate basis can increase their pay by producing a higher quantity of units of lower quality).

- *Adjust perceptions of self* ("I used to think I worked at a moderate pace, but now I realize I work a lot harder than everyone else.")

- *Adjust perceptions of others* ("Mike's job isn't as desirable as I thought.")

- *Choose a different referent* ("I may not make as much as my brother-in-law, but I'm doing a lot better than my Dad did when he was my age.")

- *Leave the field* (quit the job).

RESEARCH FINDINGS: Inequitable Pay

Some of these propositions have been supported, but others have not.[74] First, inequities created by overpayment do not seem to have a very significant impact on behaviour in most work situations. Apparently, people have a great deal more tolerance of overpayment inequities than of underpayment inequities or are better able to rationalize them. It's pretty damaging to a theory when half the equation (how people respond to overreward) falls apart. Second, not all people are equity sensitive.[75] A small part of the working population actually prefers outcome-input ratios less than the referent comparisons. Predictions from equity theory are not likely to be very accurate with these "benevolent types."

Note too that while most research on equity theory has focused on pay, employees seem to look for equity in the distribution of other organizational rewards. High-status job titles and large and lavishly furnished offices may function as outcomes for some employees in their equity equation.[76]

Fair Process and Treatment

Recent research has expanded the meaning of equity, or fairness.[77] Historically, equity theory focused on **distributive justice**, or the perceived fairness of the *amount* and *allocation* of rewards among individuals. But, increasingly, equity is thought of from the standpoint of **organizational justice**, or the overall larger perception of what is fair in the workplace. Employees perceive their organizations as just when they believe the outcomes they have received and the way they received them are fair.[78] One key element of organizational justice is an individual's *perception* of justice. In other words, fairness or equity can be subjective, residing in our perception. What one person sees as unfair, another may see as perfectly appropriate. In general, people have an egocentric, or self-serving, bias. They see allocations or procedure favouring themselves as fair.[79] In a recent poll, 61 percent of respondents said they are paying their fair share of taxes, but an almost equal number (54 percent) felt the system as a whole is unfair, saying some people skirt it.[80]

Beyond its focus on perceptions of fairness, the other key element of organizational justice is the view that justice is multidimensional. How much we get paid relative to what we think we should be paid (distributive justice) is obviously important. But, according to researchers, *how* we get paid is just as important. Thus, people also care about **procedural justice**—the perceived fairness of the *process* used to determine the distribution of rewards.[81] Two key elements of procedural justice are process control and explanations. *Process control* is the opportunity to present your point of view about desired outcomes to decision makers. *Explanations* are clear reasons management gives for the outcome. Thus, for employees to see a process as fair, they need to feel they have some control over the outcome and that they were given an adequate explanation about why the outcome occurred. It's also important that a manager is *consistent* (across people and over time), is *unbiased*, makes decisions based on *accurate information*, and is *open to appeals*.[82] Exhibit 4-11 shows a model of organizational justice.

EXHIBIT 4-11 Model of Organizational Justice

Distributive Justice

Definition: perceived fairness of outcome
Example: I got the pay raise I deserved.

Procedural Justice

Definition: perceived fairness of process used to determine outcome

Example: I had input into the process used to give raises and was given a good explanation of why I received the raise I did.

Interactional Justice

Definition: perceived degree to which one is treated with dignity and respect

Example: When telling me about my raise, my supervisor was very nice and complimentary.

Organizational Justice

Definition: overall perception of what is fair in the workplace

Example: I think this is a fair place to work.

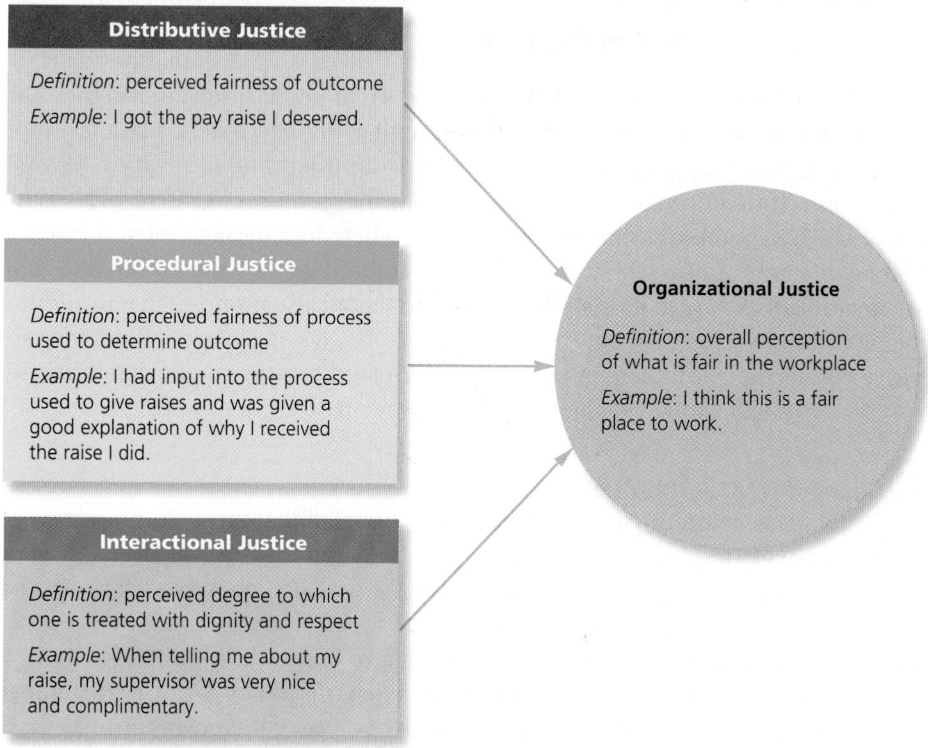

distributive justice The perceived fairness of the amount and allocation of rewards among individuals.

organizational justice An overall perception of what is fair in the workplace, composed of distributive, procedural, and interactional justice.

procedural justice The perceived fairness of the process used to determine the distribution of rewards.

A recent addition to research on organizational justice is **interactional justice**, an individual's perception of the degree to which she is treated with dignity, concern, and respect. When people are treated in an unjust manner (at least in their own eyes), they respond by retaliating (for example, badmouthing a supervisor).[83] Because people intimately connect interactional justice or injustice to the person who communicates the information (usually one's supervisor), we would expect perceptions of injustice to be more closely related to one's supervisor. Generally, that is what the evidence suggests.[84]

Of these three forms of organizational justice, distributive justice is most strongly related to organizational commitment satisfaction with outcomes such as pay. Procedural justice relates most strongly to job satisfaction, employee trust, withdrawal from the organization, job performance, and organizational citizenship behaviour. There is less evidence on how interactional justice affects employee behaviour.[85]

Managers can help foster employees' perceptions of fairness. First, they should realize that employees are especially sensitive to unfairness in procedures when bad news has to be communicated (that is, when distributive justice is low). Thus, it's especially important to openly share information about how allocation decisions are made, follow consistent and unbiased procedures, and engage in similar practices to increase the perception of procedural justice. Second, when addressing perceived injustices, managers need to focus their actions on the source of the problem. Professor Daniel Skarlicki of the Sauder School of Business at the University of British Columbia has found that it is when unfavourable outcomes are combined with unfair procedures or poor interpersonal treatment that resentment and retaliation (for example, theft, badmouthing, and sabotage) are most likely.[86] *Case Incident—Bullying Bosses* on page 166 describes what could happen to the motivation and behaviour of employees who have bullies for bosses.

Self-Determination Theory

"It's strange," said Marcia. "I started work at the Humane Society as a volunteer. I put in fifteen hours a week helping people adopt pets. And I loved coming to work. Then, three months ago, they hired me full-time at eleven dollars an hour. I'm doing the same work I did before. But I'm not finding it near as much fun."

Does Marcia's reaction seem counterintuitive? There is an explanation for it. It's called **self-determination theory**, which proposes that people prefer to feel they have control over their actions, so anything that makes a previously enjoyed task feel more like an obligation than a freely chosen activity will undermine motivation.[87] Much research on self-determination theory in OB has focused on **cognitive evaluation theory**, which hypothesizes that extrinsic rewards will reduce intrinsic interest in a task. When people are paid for work, it feels less like something they *want* to do and more like something they *have* to do. Self-determination theory also proposes that in addition to being driven by a need for autonomy, people seek ways to achieve competence and positive connections to others. A large number of studies support self-determination theory.[88] As we will show, its major implications relate to work rewards.

Extrinsic vs. Intrinsic Rewards

Historically, motivation theorists have generally assumed that intrinsic motivators are independent of extrinsic motivators. That is, the stimulation of one would not affect the other. But cognitive evaluation theory suggests otherwise. It argues that when extrinsic rewards are used by organizations as payoffs for superior performance, the intrinsic rewards, which are derived from individuals doing what they like, are reduced.

When organizations use extrinsic rewards as payoffs for superior performance, employees feel less like they are doing a good job because of their own intrinsic desire to excel and more like they are doing a good job because that is what the organization

interactional justice The perceived quality of the interpersonal treatment received from a manager.

self-determination theory A theory of motivation that is concerned with the beneficial effects of intrinsic motivation and the harmful effects of extrinsic motivation.

cognitive evaluation theory Offering extrinsic rewards (for example, pay) for work effort that was previously rewarding intrinsically will tend to decrease the overall level of a person's motivation.

wants. Eliminating extrinsic rewards can also shift from an external to an internal explanation of an individual's perception of why she works on a task. If you are reading a novel a week because your contemporary literature instructor requires you to, you can attribute your reading behaviour to an external source. If you stop reading novels the moment the course ends, this is more evidence that your behaviour was due to an external source. However, if you find yourself continuing to read a novel a week when the course ends, your natural inclination is to say, "I must enjoy reading novels, because I'm still reading one a week!"

Recent studies examining how extrinsic rewards increased motivation for some creative tasks suggests we might need to place cognitive evaluation theory's predictions in a broader context.[89] Goal setting is more effective in improving motivation, for instance, when we provide rewards for achieving the goals. The original authors of self-determination theory acknowledge that extrinsic rewards such as verbal praise and feedback about competence can improve even intrinsic motivation under specific circumstances. Deadlines and specific work standards do, too, if people believe they are in control of their behaviour.[90] This is consistent with the central theme of self-determination theory: rewards and deadlines diminish motivation if people see them as coercive.

What does self-determination theory suggest for providing rewards? Consider two situations. If a senior sales representative really enjoys selling and making the deal, a commission indicates she has been doing a good job at this valued task. The reward will increase her sense of competence by providing feedback that could improve intrinsic motivation. On the other hand, if a computer programmer values writing code because she likes to solve problems, a reward for working to an externally imposed standard she does not accept could feel coercive, and her intrinsic motivation would suffer. She would be less interested in the task and might reduce her effort.

A recent outgrowth of cognitive evaluation research is **self-concordance**, which considers how strongly people's reasons for pursuing goals are consistent with their interests and core values.[91] If individuals pursue goals because of an intrinsic interest, they are more likely to attain their goals, and are happy even if they do not attain them. Why? Because the process of striving toward them is fun. In contrast, people who pursue goals for extrinsic reasons (money, status, or other benefits) are less likely to attain their goals and are less happy even when they do achieve them. Why? Because the goals are less meaningful to them.[92] OB research suggests that people who pursue work goals for intrinsic reasons are more satisfied with their jobs, feel like they fit into their organizations better, and may perform better.[93]

Of course, organizations cannot simply ignore financial rewards. When people feel they are being treated unfairly in the workplace, pay often becomes a focal point of their concerns. If tasks are dull or unpleasant, extrinsic rewards will probably increase intrinsic motivation.[94] Even when a job is inherently interesting, there still exists a powerful norm for extrinsic payment.[95] But creating fun, challenging, and empowered workplaces may do more for motivation and performance than focusing simply on the compensation system.

Increasing Intrinsic Motivation

Our discussion of motivation theories and our discussion of how to apply motivation theories in the workplace has focused heavily on improving extrinsic motivation. Professor Kenneth Thomas of the Naval Postgraduate School in Monterey, California, developed a model of intrinsic motivation that draws from the job characteristics model (see Chapter 5) and cognitive evaluation theory.[96] He identified four key rewards that increase an individual's intrinsic motivation:

- *Sense of choice.* The opportunity to select what one will do and perform the way one thinks best. Individuals can use their own judgment to carry out the task.

self-concordance The degree to which a person's reasons for pursuing a goal is consistent with the person's interests and core values.

EXHIBIT 4-12 Building Blocks for Intrinsic Rewards

Leading for Choice	Leading for Competence
• **Delegated authority** • **Trust in workers** • **Security (no punishment) for honest mistakes** • **A clear purpose** • **Information**	• **Knowledge** • **Positive feedback** • **Skill recognition** • **Challenge** • **High, noncomparative standards**
Leading for Meaningfulness	Leading for Progress
• **A noncynical climate** • **Clearly identified passions** • **An exciting vision** • **Relevant task purposes** • **Whole tasks**	• **A collaborative climate** • **Milestones** • **Celebrations** • **Access to customers** • **Measurement of improvement**

Source: Reprinted with permission of the publisher. From *Intrinsic Motivation at Work: Building Energy and Commitment.* Copyright © K. Thomas. 1997. Berrett-Koehler Publishers Inc., San Francisco, CA. All rights reserved. www.bkconnection.com.

- *Sense of competence.* The feeling of accomplishment for doing a good job. Individuals are more likely to feel a sense of accomplishment when they carry out challenging tasks.

- *Sense of meaningfulness.* The opportunity to pursue worthwhile tasks. Individuals feel good about what they are doing and believe that what they are doing matters.

- *Sense of progress.* The feeling of accomplishment that one is making progress on a task, and that it is moving forward. Individuals feel that they are spending their time wisely in doing their jobs.

Thomas also identified four sets of behaviours managers can use to build intrinsic rewards for their employees:

- *Leading for choice.* Empowering employees and delegating tasks.

- *Leading for competence.* Supporting and coaching employees.

- *Leading for meaningfulness.* Inspiring employees and modelling desired behaviours.

- *Leading for progress.* Monitoring and rewarding employees.

Exhibit 4-12 describes what managers can do to increase the likelihood that intrinsic rewards are motivational.

Motivating through Reinforcement

5 What role does reinforcement play in motivation?

Patrick Chan did not win a medal in the Vancouver 2010 Winter Olympics.[97] Though he performed a personal best in the free skate program, it was not enough. Some wondered whether he should have mastered a quadruple and put the jump into his program. Although he practised quadruple jumps in the run-up to the Olympics, several weeks before the start of the games, he decided not to risk it. "My decision is pretty certain now that I don't want to make any changes and risk putting the quad in the most important competition of probably my life," he said. "We kind of went the way of sticking with two triple Axels and a good solid program."

Though he might have been playing it too safe, American Evan Lysacek (who won the gold medal) did not have any quads in his program. Russian Evgeni Plushenko (who won the silver medal) successfully performed the quad in his free skate, but was bitter about his scores. He said his jumps were the hardest that any of the male finalists attempted and added: "You need to skate, you need to spin, you need to skate, yes, but figure skating is not only skating, you need to jump, hard jumps like quad." He also said that without a quad, men's figure skating was merely "dancing." He vowed to perfect a double quad for his next competition to regain his position at number one.

This threat may have been enough to motivate Chan to add quadruple jumps to his repertoire. When he won the 2011 Moscow World Figure Skating Championships, he landed two quadruple jumps at the start of his program. When asked whether quad jumps were really necessary to compete at the highest level, Chan responded, "No doubt it does make a difference and there is also the respect you get for having one." Chan intends to ride the momentum coming out of the World Championships by defending his title in 2012, and then going back to the Olympics in 2014. Meanwhile, he will add a new quad salchow to his program. So how does reinforcement work, and does it motivate?

The motivation theories we have covered to this point emphasize how people's needs and thought processes can be used to motivate them. As a behaviourist, B. F. Skinner found it "pointless to explain behaviour in terms of unobservable inner states such as needs, drives, attitudes, or thought processes."[98]

Skinner's view of motivation is much simpler. He suggested that people learn how to behave to get something they want or to avoid something they don't want.[99] This idea is known as **operant conditioning**, which means behaviour is influenced by the reinforcement or lack of reinforcement brought about by the consequences of the behaviour.

Skinner argued that creating pleasing consequences to follow specific forms of behaviour would increase the frequency of that behaviour. People will most likely engage in desired behaviours if they are positively reinforced for doing so. Rewards are most effective if they immediately follow the desired behaviour. In addition, behaviour that is not rewarded, or is punished, is less likely to be repeated.

You see illustrations of operant conditioning everywhere. For example, any situation where reinforcements are contingent on some action on your part involves the use of operant conditioning. Your instructor says that if you want a high grade in the course, you must supply correct answers on the test. A commissioned salesperson who wants to earn a high income must generate high sales in her territory. Of course, the linkage can also work to teach the individual to engage in behaviours that work against the best interests of the organization. Assume that your boss tells you that if you will work overtime during the next three-week busy season, you will be compensated for it at the next performance appraisal. However, when performance appraisal time comes, you find that you are given no positive reinforcement for your overtime work. The next time your manager asks you to work overtime, you will probably decline! Your behaviour can be explained by operant conditioning: If a behaviour fails to be positively reinforced, the probability that the behaviour will be repeated declines.

Methods of Shaping Behaviour

There are four ways in which to shape behaviour: through positive reinforcement, negative reinforcement, punishment, and extinction.

Following a response with something pleasant is called *positive reinforcement*. Following a response with the termination or withdrawal of something unpleasant is called *negative reinforcement*. *Punishment* is causing an unpleasant condition in an attempt to eliminate an undesirable behaviour. Eliminating any reinforcement that is maintaining a behaviour is called *extinction*. Exhibit 4-13 presents examples of each type

operant conditioning A type of conditioning in which desired voluntary behaviour leads to a reward or prevents a punishment.

EXHIBIT 4-13 Types of Reinforcement	
Reinforcement Type	**Example**
Positive reinforcement	A manager praises an employee for a job well done.
Negative reinforcement	An instructor asks a question and a student looks through her lecture notes to avoid being called on. She has learned that looking busily through her notes prevents the instructor from calling on her.
Punishment	A manager gives an employee a two-day suspension from work without pay for showing up drunk.
Extinction	An instructor ignores students who raise their hands to ask questions. Hand-raising becomes extinct.

of reinforcement. Negative reinforcement should not be confused with punishment: Negative reinforcement strengthens a behaviour because it takes away an unpleasant situation.

Schedules of Reinforcement

While consequences have an effect on behaviour, the timing of those consequences or reinforcements is also important. The two major types of reinforcement schedules are *continuous* and *intermittent*. A **continuous reinforcement** schedule reinforces the desired behaviour each and every time it is demonstrated. Take, for example, the case of someone who has historically had trouble arriving at work on time. Every time he is not tardy, his manager might compliment him on his desirable behaviour. In an intermittent schedule, on the other hand, not every instance of the desirable behaviour is reinforced, but reinforcement is given often enough to make the behaviour worth repeating. Evidence indicates that the intermittent, or varied, form of reinforcement tends to promote more resistance to extinction than does the continuous form.[100]

An **intermittent reinforcement** schedule can be of a ratio or interval type. Ratio schedules depend on how many responses the subject makes. The individual is reinforced after giving a certain number of specific types of behaviour. Interval schedules depend on how much time has passed since the previous reinforcement. With interval schedules, the individual is reinforced on the first appropriate behaviour after a particular time has elapsed. A reinforcement can also be classified as fixed or variable. When these factors are combined, four types of intermittent schedules of reinforcement result: **fixed-interval schedule**, **variable-interval schedule**, **fixed-ratio schedule**, and **variable-ratio schedule**.

Exhibit 4-14 summarizes the five schedules of reinforcement and their effects on behaviour.

Reinforcement in the Workplace

Managers want employees to behave in ways that most benefit the organization. Therefore, they look for ways to reinforce positive behaviour and extinguish negative behaviour. Consider the situation in which an employee's behaviour is significantly different from that sought by management. If management rewarded the individual only when he or she showed desirable responses, there might be very little reinforcement taking place. Instead, managers can reinforce each successive step that moves the individual closer to the desired response. If an employee who usually turns in his work two days late succeeds in turning in his work only one day late, managers can reinforce that improvement. Reinforcement would increase as responses more closely approximated the desired behaviour.

continuous reinforcement A desired behaviour is reinforced each and every time it is demonstrated.

intermittent reinforcement A desired behaviour is reinforced often enough to make the behaviour worth repeating, but not every time it is demonstrated.

fixed-interval schedule The reward is given at fixed time intervals.

variable-interval schedule The reward is given at variable time intervals.

fixed-ratio schedule The reward is given at fixed amounts of output.

variable-ratio schedule The reward is given at variable amounts of output.

EXHIBIT 4-14	Schedules of Reinforcement		
Reinforcement Schedule	**Nature of Reinforcement**	**Effect on Behaviour**	**Example**
Continuous	Reward given after each desired behaviour	Fast learning of new behaviour but rapid extinction	Compliments
Fixed-interval	Reward given at fixed time intervals	Average and irregular performance with rapid extinction	Weekly paycheques
Variable-interval	Reward given at variable time intervals	Moderately high and stable performance with slow extinction	Pop quizzes
Fixed-ratio	Reward given at fixed amounts of output	High and stable performance attained quickly but also with rapid extinction	Piece-rate pay
Variable-ratio	Reward given at variable amounts of output	Very high performance with slow extinction	Commissioned sales

While variable-ratio and variable-interval reinforcement schedules produce the best results for improving behaviour, most work organizations rely on fixed-interval (weekly or monthly) pay or fixed-ratio (piece-rate) pay. In the next chapter, we will discuss the idea of variable pay, as well as reactions to it. We will also look at how rewards in general are used in the workplace.

Motivation for Whom?

A current debate among organizational behaviour scholars is, Who benefits from the theories of motivation?[101] Some argue that motivation theories are only intended to help managers get more productivity out of employees, and are little concerned with employees beyond improvements in productivity. Thus, needs theories, process theories, and theories concerned with fairness could be interpreted not as ways to help employees get what they want or need, but rather as means to help managers get what they want from employees. In his review of "meaningful work" literature, professor Christopher Michaelson of the Wharton School at the University of Pennsylvania finds that researchers propose that organizations have a moral obligation to provide employees with "free choice to enter, honest communication, fair and respectful treatment, intellectual challenge, considerable independence to determine work methods, democratic participation in decision making, moral development, due process and justice, nonpaternalism, and fair compensation."[102]

6 What are the ethics behind motivation theories?

Michaelson suggests that scholars concerned with meaningful work should focus on the conditions of the workplace and improving those conditions. He also suggests that researchers have a moral obligation to make workplaces better for employees. While productivity may be a by-product of better work conditions, the important thing is for employers to treat employees well, and to consider the needs of employees as an end in itself. By contrast, he argues, mainstream motivation theory does not consider the moral obligation of employers to their employees, but it does consider ways to ensure employees are more productive.

While this debate is not easily resolved, and may well guide the elaboration of motivation theories in years to come, it does inspire a provocative analysis of why employers provide the workplace conditions they do. To further provoke your thoughts on this matter, the *Ethical Dilemma Exercise* on page 166 asks you to consider whether motivation is just manipulation.

Putting It All Together

While it's always dangerous to synthesize a large number of complex ideas into a few simple guidelines, the following suggestions summarize the essence of what we know about motivating employees in organizations:

- *Recognize individual differences.* Employees have different needs and should not be treated alike. Managers should spend the time necessary to understand what is important to each employee and then align goals, level of involvement, and rewards with individual needs.

- *Use goals and feedback.* Employees should have challenging, specific goals, as well as feedback on how well they are doing in pursuit of those goals.

- *Allow employees to participate in decisions that affect them.* Employees can contribute to a number of decisions that affect them: setting work goals, choosing their own benefits packages, solving productivity and quality problems, and the like. This can increase employee productivity, commitment to work goals, motivation, and job satisfaction.

- *When giving rewards, be sure that they reward desired performance.* Rewards should be linked to the type of performance expected. It is important that employees perceive a clear linkage. How closely rewards are actually correlated to performance criteria is less important than the perception of this relationship. If individuals perceive this relationship to be low, the results will be low performance, a decrease in job satisfaction, and an increase in turnover and absenteeism.

- *Check the system for equity.* Employees should be able to perceive rewards as equating with the inputs they bring to the job. At a simplistic level, this means that experience, skills, abilities, effort, and other obvious inputs should explain differences in performance and, hence, pay, job assignments, and other obvious rewards.

GLOBAL IMPLICATIONS

Most current motivation theories were developed in the United States and Canada.[103] Goal-setting and expectancy theories emphasize goal accomplishment as well as rational and individual thought—characteristics consistent with Canadian and American culture. Let's look at several motivation theories and consider their cross-cultural transferability.

Needs Theories

Maslow's needs theory says people start at the physiological level and progress up the hierarchy to safety, social, esteem, and self-actualization needs. This hierarchy, if it applies at all, aligns with Canadian and US culture. In Japan, Greece, and Mexico, where uncertainty-avoidance characteristics are strong, security needs would be on top of the hierarchy. Countries that score high on nurturing characteristics—Denmark, Sweden, Norway, the Netherlands, and Finland—would have social needs on top.[104] Group work will motivate employees more when the country's culture scores high on the nurturing criterion.

The view that a high achievement need acts as an internal motivator presupposes two cultural characteristics—willingness to accept a moderate degree of risk (which excludes countries with strong uncertainty avoidance characteristics) and concern with performance (which applies to countries with strong achievement characteristics). This combination is found in Anglo-American countries such as the United States, Canada, and Great Britain[105] and much less so in Chile and Portugal.

Goal Setting

Setting specific, difficult, individual goals may have different effects in different cultures. Most goal-setting research has been done in the United States and Canada, where individual achievement and performance are most highly valued. To date, research has not shown that group-based goals are more effective in collectivistic than in individualistic cultures. There is evidence that in collectivistic and high-power-distance cultures, achievable moderate goals can be more highly motivating than difficult ones.[106] Finally, assigned goals appear to generate greater goal commitment in high rather than low power-distance cultures.[107] Much more research is needed to assess how goal constructs might differ across cultures.

Equity Theory

Equity theory has gained a strong following in Canada and the United States because the reward systems assume that employees are highly sensitive to equity in reward allocations. In Canada and the United States, equity is meant to closely tie pay to performance. However, in collectivistic cultures, especially the former socialist countries of Central and Eastern Europe, employees expect rewards to reflect their individual needs as well as their performance.[108] Consistent with a legacy of communism and centrally planned economies, employees exhibited an entitlement attitude—that is, they expected outcomes to be *greater* than their inputs.[109] These findings suggest that Canadian-style pay practices may need modification, especially in Russia and former communist countries, to be perceived as fair by employees.

Intrinsic and Extrinsic Motivation

A recent study found interesting differences in managers' perceptions of employee motivation.[110] The study examined managers from three distinct cultural regions: North America, Asia, and Latin America. The results of the study revealed that North American managers perceive their employees as being motivated more by extrinsic factors (for example, pay) than intrinsic factors (for example, doing meaningful work). Asian managers perceive their employees as being motivated by both extrinsic and intrinsic factors, while Latin American managers perceive their employees as being motivated by intrinsic factors.

Even more interesting, these differences affected evaluations of employee performance. As expected, Asian managers focused on both types of motivation when evaluating their employees' performance, and Latin American managers focused on intrinsic motivation. Oddly, North American managers, though believing that employees are motivated primarily by extrinsic factors, actually focused more on intrinsic factors when evaluating employee performance. Why the paradox? One explanation is that North Americans value uniqueness, so any deviation from the norm—such as being perceived as being unusually high in intrinsic motivation—is rewarded.

Latin American managers' focus on intrinsic motivation when evaluating employees may be related to a cultural norm termed *simpatía*, a tradition that compels employees to display their internal feelings. Consequently, Latin American managers are more sensitized to these displays and can more easily notice their employees' intrinsic motivation.

Cross-Cultural Consistencies

Don't assume that there are *no* cross-cultural consistencies. The desire for interesting work seems important to almost all employees, regardless of their national culture. In a study of 7 countries, employees in Belgium, Britain, Israel, and the United States ranked work number 1 among 11 work goals, and employees in Japan, the Netherlands, and Germany ranked it either second or third.[111] In a study comparing job-preference outcomes among graduate students in the United States, Canada, Australia, and Singapore,

LESSONS LEARNED

- Recognize individual differences.
- Goals and feedback help motivate individuals.
- Rewards signal what is important to the employer (or leader).

growth, achievement, and responsibility had identical rankings as the top three.[112] Meta-analytic evidence shows that individuals in both individualistic and collectivistic cultures prefer an equitable distribution of rewards (the most effective employees get paid the most) over an equal division (everyone gets paid the same regardless of performance).[113] Across nations, the same basic principles of procedural justice are respected, and employees around the world prefer rewards based on performance and skills over rewards based on seniority.[114]

Summary and Implications

1 **What is motivation?** *Motivation* is the process that accounts for an individual's intensity, direction, and persistence of effort toward reaching a goal. *Intensity* is concerned with how hard a person tries. This is the element most of us focus on when we talk about motivation. However, high intensity is unlikely to lead to good job performance unless the effort is channelled in a useful *direction*. Finally, the effort requires *persistence*.

2 **How do needs motivate people?** All needs theories of motivation, including Maslow's hierarchy of needs, Alderfer's ERG theory, Herzberg's motivation-hygiene theory (sometimes called the *two-factor theory*), and McClelland's theory of needs, propose a similar idea: Individuals have needs that, when unsatisfied, will result in motivation. Needs theories suggest that motivation will be high to the degree that the rewards individuals receive for high performance satisfy their dominant needs.

3 **Are there other ways to motivate people?** Process theories focus on the broader picture of how someone can set about motivating another individual. Process theories include expectancy theory, goal-setting theory (and its application, management by objectives), and self-efficacy theory. Expectancy theory says that an employee will be motivated to exert a high level of effort when he or she believes (1) that effort will lead to good performance; (2) that good performance will lead to organizational rewards, such as a bonus, a salary increase, or a promotion; and (3) that the rewards will satisfy his or her personal goals. Goal-setting theory suggests that intentions to work toward a goal are a major source of work motivation. That is, goals tell an employee what needs to be done and how much effort will need to be expended. Specific goals increase performance; difficult goals, when accepted, result in higher performance than do easy goals; and feedback leads to higher performance than does nonfeedback. Achieving goals can be affected by one's self-efficacy, which refers to an individual's belief that he or she is capable of performing a task. The higher one's self-efficacy, the more confidence a person has about succeeding in a task.

4 **Do equity and fairness matter?** Individuals look for fairness in the reward system. Rewards should be perceived by employees as related to the inputs they bring to the job. Simply stated, employees expect that experience, skills, abilities, effort, and other job inputs should explain differences in performance and, hence, pay, job assignments, and other obvious rewards.

5 **What role does reinforcement play in motivation?** B. F. Skinner suggested that behaviour is influenced by whether or not it is reinforced. Managers might consider how their actions toward employees reinforce (or do not reinforce) employee behaviour. For example, when an employee goes above and beyond the call of duty, but that action is not recognized (or reinforced), that employee may be reluctant to exert great effort at a later time. Skinner also noted that schedules of reinforcement affect behaviour. For instance, individuals are less likely to perform well when their behaviour is continuously reinforced than when it is randomly reinforced.

6 **What are the ethics behind motivation theories?** A current debate among OB scholars is about who benefits from the theories of motivation. Some argue that motivation theories are only intended to help managers get more productivity out of employees, and are little concerned with employees beyond improvements in productivity. The theories can thus be interpreted as a means to help managers get what they want from employees. Although this debate is certainly controversial, motivation theories can also be applied in nonwork settings, and can just as easily help individuals figure out how to motivate themselves.

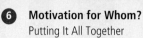

SNAPSHOT SUMMARY

6 **Motivation for Whom?**
Putting It All Together

for Review

1. Define *motivation*. What are the key elements of motivation?

2. What are the implications of Theories X and Y for motivation practices?

3. Does motivation come from within a person, or is it a result of the situation? Explain.

4. Compare and contrast Maslow's hierarchy of needs theory with Herzberg's motivation-hygiene (two-factor) theory.

5. Explain the difference between hygiene factors and motivators in Herzberg's motivation-hygiene (two-factor) theory.

6. Identify the variables in expectancy theory.

7. What is the role of self-efficacy in goal setting?

8. Contrast distributive and procedural justice. What implications might they have for designing pay systems in different countries?

9. Explain cognitive evaluation theory. What does it assume about the effects of intrinsic and extrinsic rewards on behaviour?

10. Describe the four types of intermittent reinforcers.

for Critical Thinking

1. Identify three activities you really enjoy (for example, playing tennis, reading a novel, going shopping). Next, identify three activities you really dislike (for example, visiting the dentist, cleaning the house, following a low-fat diet). Using the expectancy model, analyze each of your answers to assess why some activities stimulate your effort while others don't.

2. Expectancy theory argues that for people to be motivated, they have to value the rewards that they will receive for their effort. This suggests the need for recognizing individual differences. Does this view contradict the principles of equity theory? Discuss.

3. To what extent will you be motivated to study under the following circumstances:
   a. The instructor gives only one test—a final examination at the end of the course.
   b. The instructor gives four exams during the term, all of which are announced on the first day of class.
   c. The student's grade is based on the results of numerous exams, none of which are announced by the instructor ahead of time.

4. "The cognitive evaluation theory is contradictory to reinforcement and expectancy theories." Do you agree or disagree? Explain.

5. Analyze the application of Maslow's and Herzberg's theories to an African or Caribbean nation where more than a quarter of the population is unemployed.

for You

- Don't think of motivation as something that should be done for you. Think about motivating others and yourself as well. How can you motivate yourself? After finishing a particularly long and dry chapter in a text, you could take a snack break. Or you might buy yourself a new CD once that major accounting assignment is finished.

- Be aware of the kinds of things that motivate you, so you can choose jobs and activities that suit you best.

- When working in a group, keep in mind that you and the other members can think of ways to make sure everyone feels motivated throughout the project.

POINT

COUNTERPOINT

Failure Motivates

Failure Demotivates

Many of the best lessons we learn in life come from our failures. Consider Chris Gardner.[115] In 1982, Gardner was homeless, raising a 20-month-old son in San Francisco, and peddling medical devices few wanted to buy. Unable to afford both housing and child care, Gardner boarded himself and his son where he could—even in the bathroom at the Bay Area Rapid Transit office. A happy ending was nowhere in sight.

After seeing a stockbroker drive a red Ferrari, Gardner resolved that he would be a stockbroker, too. He looked up the offices of Dean Witter, then one of the largest US investment banking firms (it later merged with Morgan Stanley). Gardner was able to line up an interview for a spot in the firm's internship program.

The night before his interview, Gardner was taken to jail for a backlog of parking tickets he could not afford to pay. Unshaven and dishevelled, in yesterday's clothes, he explained his situation in the interview, and Dean Witter took a chance on him. Gardner remembered advice his mother had given him: "You can only depend on yourself. The cavalry ain't coming."

At Dean Witter, Gardner made 200 calls a day. "Every time I picked up the phone," he said, "I knew I was getting closer to digging myself out of the hole." Gardner made it at Dean Witter, became a top earner at Bear Stearns, and now runs his own brokerage firm in Chicago. His story became a bestselling book and a major motion picture (*The Pursuit of Happyness*) starring Will Smith, which Gardner helped produce. A table in his office is piled high with letters from people inspired by his story. On occasion, he will call one of the letter writers. He says, "I find myself saying over and over 'Baby steps count.'"

Not only does failure bring perspective to people such as Gardner, it provides important feedback on how to improve. The important thing is to learn from failure and to persist. As Gardner told students in his commencement address at the University of California in 2009, "You can draw inspiration from others, but what happens when there ain't nobody else there? You have to be there for yourself."

Do people learn from failure? One of the decision-making errors people make is escalation of commitment: They persist in a failed venture because they think persistence is a virtue or because their ego is involved, even when logic suggests they should move on. One research study found that managers often illogically persist in launching new products, even when the evidence becomes clear that the product is going nowhere. As the authors note, "It sometimes takes more courage to kill a product that's going nowhere than to sustain it." Learning from failure is a nice ideal, but most people are too defensive to do that. Failure is helpful only if the person benefits from it, and that is a big assumption. Many times people don't recover, or they would have been more successful if not for the failure.

Evidence shows that when people fail they often rationalize their failures to preserve their self-esteem, and thus don't learn at all. Although the example of Chris Gardner is interesting, it does not prove that his success comes from learning from his failures. When we fail or experience painful episodes, we often wish to explain the past—by rationalizing that the failure and painful experiences were key to our success. These rationalizations may not be correct, but we engage in them to preserve our fragile self-esteem and to make sense of what is often simply bad luck. We need to believe in ourselves to motivate ourselves, and because failing undermines that self-belief, we have to do what we can to recover our self-confidence.[116]

Although it makes a nice story that failure is actually good, as one songwriter wrote, "The world is not a song." Failure hurts, and to either protect ourselves or recover from the pain, we often do not learn from failure—we rationalize it away.

What Motivates You?

Circle the number that most closely agrees with how you feel. Consider your answers in the context of your current job or a past work experience.

	Strongly Disagree			Strongly Agree	
1. I try very hard to improve on my past performance at work.	1	2	3	4	5
2. I enjoy competition and winning.	1	2	3	4	5
3. I often find myself talking to those around me about nonwork matters.	1	2	3	4	5
4. I enjoy a difficult challenge.	1	2	3	4	5
5. I enjoy being in charge.	1	2	3	4	5
6. I want to be liked by others.	1	2	3	4	5
7. I want to know how I am progressing as I complete tasks.	1	2	3	4	5
8. I confront people who do things I disagree with.	1	2	3	4	5
9. I tend to build close relationships with co-workers.	1	2	3	4	5
10. I enjoy setting and achieving realistic goals.	1	2	3	4	5
11. I enjoy influencing other people to get my way.	1	2	3	4	5
12. I enjoy belonging to groups and organizations.	1	2	3	4	5
13. I enjoy the satisfaction of completing a difficult task.	1	2	3	4	5
14. I often work to gain more control over the events around me.	1	2	3	4	5
15. I enjoy working with others more than working alone.	1	2	3	4	5

Scoring Key:

To determine your dominant needs—and what motivates you—place the number 1 through 5 that represents your score for each statement next to the number for that statement.

Achievement	Power	Affiliation
1._____	2._____	3._____
4._____	5._____	6._____
7._____	8._____	9._____
10._____	11._____	12._____
13._____	14._____	15._____
Totals:_____	_____	_____

Add up the total of each column. The sum of the numbers in each column will be between 5 and 25 points. The column with the highest score tells you your dominant need.

Source: Based on R. Steers and D. Braunstein, "A Behaviorally Based Measure of Manifest Needs in Work Settings," *Journal of Vocational Behavior*, October 1976, p. 254; and R. N. Lussier, *Human Relations in Organizations: A Skill Building Approach* (Homewood, IL: Richard D. Irwin, 1990), p. 120.

SELF-ASSESSMENT LIBRARY	LEARNING ABOUT YOURSELF

More Learning About Yourself Exercises

Additional self-assessments relevant to this chapter appear on MyOBLab (**www.pearsoned.ca/myoblab**).

I.C.5 What Are My Course Performance Goals?

IV.A.3 How Confident Am I in My Abilities to Succeed?

II.B.5 How Good Am I at Disciplining Others?

When you complete the additional assessments, consider the following:

1. Am I surprised about my score?

2. Would my friends evaluate me similarly?

BREAKOUT **GROUP** EXERCISES

Form small groups to discuss the following topics, as assigned by your instructor:

1. One of the members of your team continually arrives late for meetings and does not turn drafts of assignments in on time. Choose one of the available theories and indicate how the theory explains the member's current behaviour and how the theory could be used to motivate the group member to perform more responsibly.

2. You are unhappy with the performance of one of your instructors and would like to encourage the instructor to present more lively classes. Choose one of the available theories and indicate how the theory explains the instructor's current behaviour. How could you as a student use the theory to motivate the instructor to present more lively classes?

3. Harvard University recently changed its grading policy to recommend to instructors that the average course mark should be a B. This was the result of a study showing that more than 50 percent of students were receiving an A or A– for coursework. Harvard students are often referred to as "the best and the brightest," and they pay over $36 000 (US) per academic year for their education, so they expect high grades. Discuss the impact of this change in policy on the motivation of Harvard students to study harder.

WORKING WITH OTHERS EXERCISE

Positive Reinforcement vs. Punishment

This 10-step exercise takes approximately 20 minutes.[117]

Exercise Overview (Steps 1–4)

1. Two volunteers are selected to receive reinforcement or punishment from the class while performing a particular task. The volunteers leave the room.

2. The instructor identifies an object for the student volunteers to locate when they return to the room. (The object should be unobstructed but clearly visible to the class. Examples that have worked well include a small triangular piece of paper that was left behind when a notice was torn off a classroom bulletin board, a smudge on the chalkboard, and a chip in the plaster of a classroom wall.)

3. The instructor specifies the actions that will be in effect when the volunteers return to the room. For punishment, students should hiss or boo when the first volunteer is moving away from the object. For positive reinforcement, they should cheer and applaud when the second volunteer is getting closer to the object.

4. The instructor should assign a student to keep a record of the time it takes each of the volunteers to locate the object.

Volunteer 1 (Steps 5 and 6)

5. Volunteer 1 is brought back into the room and is told, "Your task is to locate and touch a particular object in the room, and the class has agreed to help you. You cannot use words or ask questions. Begin."

6. Volunteer 1 continues to look for the object until it is found, while the class engages in the punishing behaviour.

Volunteer 2 (Steps 7 and 8)

7. Volunteer 2 is brought back into the room and is told, "Your task is to locate and touch a particular object in the room, and the class has agreed to help you. You cannot use words or ask questions. Begin."

8. Volunteer 2 continues to look for the object until it is found, while the class assists by giving positive reinforcement.

Class Review (Steps 9 and 10)

9. The timekeeper will present the results on how long it took each volunteer to find the object.

10. The class will discuss the following: What was the difference in behaviour of the two volunteers? What are the implications of this exercise for shaping behaviour in organizations?

ETHICAL **DILEMMA** EXERCISE

Is Motivation Manipulation?

Managers are interested in the subject of motivation because they are concerned with learning how to get the most effort from their employees. Is this ethical? For example, when managers link rewards to productivity, aren't they manipulating employees?

"To manipulate" is defined as "(1) to handle, manage, or use, especially with skill, in some process of treatment or performance; (2) to manage or influence by artful skill; (3) to adapt or change to suit one's purpose or advantage." Aren't one or more of these definitions compatible with the notion of managers skillfully seeking to influence employee productivity for the benefit of the manager and the organization?

Do managers have the right to seek control over their employees? Does anyone, for that matter, have the right to control others? Does control imply manipulation? And if so, is there anything wrong with managers manipulating employees through goal setting or other motivational techniques?

CASE INCIDENTS

Bullying Bosses

"It got to where I was twitching, literally, on the way into work," states Carrie Clark, a 52-year-old retired teacher and administrator.[118] After enduring 10 months of repeated insults and mistreatment from her supervisor, she finally quit her job. "I had to take care of my health."

Although many individuals recall bullies from their elementary school days, some are realizing that bullies can exist in the workplace as well. And these bullies do not just pick on the weakest in the group; rather, any subordinate in their path may fall prey to their torment, according to Dr. Gary Namie, director of the Workplace Bullying and Trauma Institute. Dr. Namie further says workplace bullies are not limited to men—women are at least as likely to be bullies. However, gender discrepancies are found in victims of bullying, as women are more likely to be targets.

What motivates a boss to be a bully? Dr. Harvey Hornstein, a retired professor from Teachers College at Columbia University, suggests that supervisors may use bullying as a means to subdue a subordinate who poses a threat to the supervisor's status. In addition, supervisors may bully individuals to vent frustrations. Many times, however, the sheer desire to wield power may be the primary reason for bullying.

What is the impact of bullying on employee motivation and behaviour? Surprisingly, even though victims of workplace bullies may feel less motivated to go to work every day, it does not appear that they discontinue performing their required job duties. However, it does appear that victims of bullies are less motivated to perform extra-role or citizenship behaviours. Helping others, speaking positively about the organization, and going beyond the call of duty are behaviours that are reduced as a result of bullying. According to Dr. Bennett Tepper of the University of North Carolina, fear may be the reason that many employees continue to perform their job duties. And not all individuals reduce their citizenship behaviours. Some continue to engage in extra-role behaviours to make themselves look better than their colleagues.

What should you do if your boss is bullying you? Don't necessarily expect help from co-workers. As Emelise Aleandri, an actress and producer from New York who left her job after being bullied, stated, "Some people were afraid to do anything. But others didn't mind what was happening at all, because they wanted my job." Moreover, according to Dr. Michelle Duffy of the University of Kentucky, co-workers often blame victims of bullying in order to resolve their guilt. "They do this by wondering whether maybe the person deserved the treatment, that he or she has been annoying, or lazy, they did something to earn it," states Dr. Duffy. One example of an employee who observed this phenomenon first-hand

is Sherry Hamby, who was frequently verbally abused by her boss and then eventually fired. She stated, "This was a man who insulted me, who insulted my family, who would lay into me while everyone else in the office just sat there and let it happen. The people in my office eventually started blaming me."

What can a bullied employee do? Dr. Hornstein suggests that employees try to ignore the insults and respond only to the substance of the bully's gripe. "Stick with the substance, not the process, and often it won't escalate," he states. Of course, that is easier said than done.

Questions

1. What aspects of motivation might workplace bullying reduce? For example, are there likely to be effects on an employee's self-efficacy? If so, what might those effects be?

2. If you were a victim of workplace bullying, what steps would you take to try to reduce its occurrence? What strategies would be most effective? What strategies might be ineffective? What would you do if one of your colleagues were a victim of an abusive supervisor?

3. What factors do you believe contribute to workplace bullying? Are bullies a product of the situation, or do they have flawed personalities? What situations and what personality factors might contribute to the presence of bullies?

Wage Reduction Proposal

The following proposal was made to employees of Montreal-based Quebecor's Vidéotron cable division:[119]

> Employees are asked to increase the number of hours worked per week to 40 from 35, while receiving the same pay as working the shorter work week. In addition, they are asked to accept less paid holiday time.

> Quebecor spokesman Luc Lavoie justified the request made to the employees by saying, "They have the richest work contract in the country, including eight weeks of holiday and high absenteeism."

> The company made it clear that if this proposal were not accepted, it would sell its cable television and Internet installation and repair operations to Entourage Technology Solutions.

The employees, members of Canadian Union of Public Employees (CUPE) Local 2815, were reluctant to agree to these conditions. If they accepted, 300 to 400 employees were likely to be laid off, and the company could still consider outsourcing the work later.

Questions

1. Analyze this proposal in terms of motivation concepts.

2. As an employee, how would you respond if you received this proposal?

3. If you were the executive vice-president of the company, and a number of your non-unionized employees asked you for a holiday cash gift, would you have responded differently? Why or why not?

FROM CONCEPTS TO SKILLS

Setting Goals

You can be more effective at setting goals if you use the following eight suggestions:[120]

1. *Identify your key tasks.* Goal setting begins by defining what it is that you want to accomplish.

2. *Establish specific and challenging goals for each key task.* Identify the level of performance expected. Specify the target toward which you will work.

3. *Specify the deadlines for each goal.* Putting deadlines on each goal reduces ambiguity. Deadlines, however, should not be set arbitrarily. Rather, they need to be realistic, given the tasks to be completed.

4. *Allow the employee to participate actively.* When employees participate in goal setting, they are more likely to accept the goals. However, it must be sincere participation. That is, employees must perceive that you are truly seeking their input, not just going through the motions.

5. *Prioritize goals.* When you have more than one goal, it's important for you to rank the goals in order of importance. The purpose of prioritizing is to encourage you to take action and expend effort on each goal in proportion to its importance.

6. *Rate goals for difficulty and importance.* Goal setting should not encourage people to choose easy goals. Instead, goals should be rated for their difficulty and importance. When goals are rated, individuals can be given credit for trying difficult goals, even if they don't fully achieve them.

7. *Build in feedback mechanisms to assess goal progress.* Feedback lets you know whether your level of effort is sufficient to attain the goal. Feedback should be frequent and recurring.

8. *Link rewards to goal attainment.* Linking rewards to the achievement of goals will help motivate you.

Practising Skills

You worked your way through college while holding down a part-time job bagging groceries at the Food Town supermarket chain. You liked working in the food industry, and when you graduated, you accepted a position with Food Town as a management trainee. Three years have passed, and you have gained experience in the grocery store industry and in operating a large supermarket. About a year ago, you received a promotion to store manager at one of the chain's locations. One of the things you have liked about Food Town is that it gives store managers a great deal of autonomy in running their stores. The company provides very general guidelines to its managers. Top management is concerned with the bottom line; for the most part, how you get there is up to you. Now that you are finally a store manager, you want to establish an MBO-type program in your store. You like the idea that everyone should have clear goals to work toward and then be evaluated against those goals.

Your store employs 70 people, although except for the managers, most work only 20 to 30 hours per week. You have 6 people reporting to you: an assistant manager; a weekend manager; and grocery, produce, meat, and bakery managers. The only highly skilled jobs belong to the butchers, who have strict training and regulatory guidelines. Other less-skilled jobs include cashier, shelf stocker, maintenance worker, and grocery bagger.

Specifically describe how you would go about setting goals in your new position. Include examples of goals for the jobs of butcher, cashier, and bakery manager.

1. Set personal and academic goals you want to achieve by the end of this term. Prioritize and rate them for difficulty.

2. Where do you want to be in five years? Do you have specific five-year goals? Establish three goals you want to achieve in five years. Make sure these goals are specific, challenging, and measurable.

Reinforcing Skills

CHAPTER 5

Motivation in Action

Will employees find a grocery retailer's offer of discounts for being healthy motivating or a type of interference with their lifestyle?

LEARNING OUTCOMES

1. Is money an important motivator?
2. What does an effective reward system look like?
3. How can jobs be designed to increase motivation?
4. How do employees become more involved in the workplace?
5. Can we simplify how we think about motivation?

John Mackey, the CEO of Austin, Texas-based Whole Foods, a fast-growing upscale grocery retailer with stores in Vancouver, West Vancouver, Toronto, Oakville, London (England), and cities across the United States recently implemented an incentive program to help his employees engage in healthier living. By meeting certain health requirements, employees can earn up to an extra 10 percent discount on the store's products (in addition to the 20 percent discount they already receive).[1]

To be eligible to participate in the program, employees must be non-smokers with a body mass index (BMI) below 30. Eligible participants are screened for their cholesterol count, blood pressure, and BMI, and awarded a discount from 2 percent to 10 percent, based on the measurements. The bonuses are awarded as follows: Bronze (2 percent), Silver (5 percent), Gold (7 percent), and Platinum (10 percent). To earn Bronze level, an employee must have a blood pressure of 140/90, total cholesterol count of 195 or less, and a BMI of 30 or less. Platinum level demands blood pressure of 110/70, total cholesterol count below 150, and a BMI of less than 24.

The thinking behind Mackey's program is that incentives might help his employees achieve new fitness levels. The program was widely criticized when it was announced. Rosemary Bennett, senior communications officer for the Ontario Human Rights Commission, says that even though the program is voluntary, weight issues are sometimes treated as a disability. "If it's an incentive program, it should be for an incentive people can do things about. Human rights are about accommodation and equality and providing as level a playing field as you possibly can, and the way you do that is to look at the individual circumstances." Does it make sense for Mackey to motivate his employees this way?

In this chapter, we focus on how to apply motivation concepts. We review a number of reward programs and consider whether rewards are overrated. We also discuss how to create more motivating jobs and workplaces, both of which have been shown to be alternatives to rewards in motivating individuals.

OB IS FOR EVERYONE

- What is the impact of unions on pay for performance?
- Ever wonder why employees do some strange things?
- Are rewards overrated?
- When might job redesign be most appropriate?
- How can flexible workplaces increase motivation?
- Do employers really like flexible arrangements?
- Would you find telework motivating?

From Theory to Practice: The Role of Money

1 Is money an important motivator?

BLOG IT

Does money motivate you?

Would you take a 15% pay cut to get

- High-quality colleagues?
- Opportunities for promotion?
- Access to new experiences and challenges?

www.obstudentjournals.blogspot.com

The most commonly used reward in organizations is money. As one author notes, "Money is probably the most emotionally meaningful object in contemporary life: only food and sex are its close competitors as common carriers of such strong and diverse feelings, significance, and strivings."[2] A 2010 survey of Canadian employees found that overall, 46 percent believe they are underpaid. More employees in Quebec think they are underpaid (54 percent) than those in Ontario (38 percent). The survey's results are similar to a 2011 poll conducted in the United States, in which 45 percent felt they were underpaid.[3]

The motivation theories we have presented only give us vague ideas of how money relates to individual motivation. For instance, Theory X suggests that individuals need to be extrinsically motivated. Money is certainly one such extrinsic motivator. According to Maslow's hierarchy of needs, individuals' basic needs must be met, including food, shelter, and safety. Generally, money can be used to satisfy those needs. Herzberg's motivation-hygiene theory, on the other hand, suggests that money (and other extrinsic motivators) are necessary but not sufficient conditions for individuals to be motivated. Process theories are relatively silent about the role of money specifically, indicating more how rewards motivate, without specifying particular types of rewards. Expectancy theory does note that individuals need to value the reward, or it won't be very motivational.

Despite the importance of money in attracting and retaining employees, and rewarding and recognizing them, not enough research has been done on this topic.[4] With respect to job satisfaction, one 2010 study found that pay level was only moderately correlated, and concluded that a person could be satisfied with his or her pay level, and still not have job satisfaction.[5] A 2011 study concluded that "money leads to autonomy but it does not add to well-being or happiness."[6] Supporting this idea, recent research suggests that money is not the sole motivator for Generation Y and Baby Boomer employees. Both generations find having "a great team, challenging assignments, a range of new experiences, and explicit performance evaluation and recognition" as important as money.[7] Exhibit 5-1 illustrates the key differences and similarities of what the two generations value in addition to money.

A number of studies suggest that there are personality traits and demographic factors that correlate with an individual's attitude toward money.[8] People who highly value money score higher on "attributes like sensation seeking, competitiveness, materialism, and control." People who desire money score higher on self-esteem, need for achievement, and Type A personality measures. Men seem to value money more than women, who value recognition for doing a good job more.[9]

EXHIBIT 5-1 **What Baby Boomers and Generation Y Value as Much as Compensation**

Baby Boomers	Generation Y
High-quality colleagues	High-quality colleagues
An intellectually stimulating workplace	Flexible work arrangements
Autonomy regarding work tasks	Prospects for advancement
Flexible work arrangements	Recognition from one's company or boss
Access to new experiences and challenges	A steady rate of advancement and promotion
Giving back to the world through work	Access to new experiences and challenges
Recognition from one's company or boss	

Source: S. A. Hewlett, L. Sherbin, and K. Sumberg, "How Gen Y & Boomers Will Reshape Your Agenda," *Harvard Business Review*, July/August 2009, p. 76.

What these findings suggest is that when organizations develop reward programs, they need to consider very carefully the importance to the individual of the specific rewards offered. The *Ethical Dilemma Exercise* on page 206 gives you an intriguing look at the amount of money needed to motivate some Canadian CEOs.

Creating Effective Reward Systems

2 What does an effective reward system look like?

At Whole Foods, departments are organized around teams because the retailer is determined not to have an "us vs. them" mindset in the workplace.[10] The team is responsible for managing the department and is given a set of guidelines for doing so. Teams have decision-making responsibility in a number of areas, including recruiting. In order to make sure that individuals function together as a team, bonus payments are based on team performance. Sales and margin figures for all departments are available for employees to inspect at any time.

Whole Foods fosters team spirit through various incentives, including the following:[11]

- self-directed teams that meet regularly to discuss issues, solve problems, and appreciate each other's contributions
- gainsharing and other team member incentive programs
- stock options and stock purchase plan
- commitment to make jobs more fun by combining work and play and through friendly competition to improve the stores.

To encourage a shared collective vision, Whole Foods also has a salary cap "that limits the maximum cash compensation (wages plus profit incentive bonuses) paid to any Team Member in the calendar year to 19 times the company-wide annual average salary of all full-time Team Members."[12]

All of these actions signal to employees that they are valued as important contributors to the company's success. What else can a company do to make sure its employees feel valued?

As we saw in Chapter 3, pay is not a primary factor driving job satisfaction. However, it does motivate people, and companies often underestimate the importance of pay in keeping top talent. A recent study found that although only 45 percent of employers thought that pay was a key factor in losing top talent, 71 percent of top performers indicated that it was a main reason.[13]

Given that pay is so important, we need to understand what to pay employees and how to pay them. To do that, management must make some strategic decisions. Will the organization lead, match, or lag the market in pay? How will individual contributions be recognized? In this section, we consider four major strategic rewards decisions that need to be made: (1) what to pay employees (which is decided by establishing a pay structure); (2) how to pay individual employees (which is decided through variable-pay plans and skill-based pay plans); (3) what benefits to offer, especially whether to offer employees choice in benefits (flexible benefits); and (4) how to construct employee recognition programs.

What to Pay: Establishing a Pay Structure

When organizations set pay rates, they balance *internal equity*—the worth of the job to the organization (usually established through a technical process called *job evaluation*)—and *external equity*—the external competitiveness of an organization's pay relative to pay elsewhere in its industry (usually established through pay surveys). Obviously, the best pay system pays the job what it is worth (internal equity) while also paying competitively relative to the labour market.

Pay is often the highest single operating cost for an organization, and it's a strategic decision with clear trade-offs. Paying above the market results in better-qualified, more highly motivated employees who will stay with the organization longer. Paying below the market results in higher turnover as people are lured to better-paying jobs.

Companies often underestimate the importance of pay in keeping top talent. A recent study found that competitive pay led to more satisfied customers as well as employees with higher morale and increased productivity.[14]

How to Pay: Rewarding Individuals through Variable-Pay Programs

"Why should I put any extra effort into this job?" asks a frustrated grade 4 teacher. "I can excel or I can do the bare minimum. It makes no difference. I get paid the same. Why do anything above the minimum to get by?" Similar comments have been voiced by schoolteachers (and some other unionized employees) for decades because pay increases are tied to seniority.

A number of organizations—business firms as well as school districts and other government agencies—are moving away from paying people based solely on credentials or length of service and toward using variable-pay programs. Piece-rate wages, merit-based pay, bonuses, gainsharing, profit-sharing plans, stock options, and employee stock ownership plans are all forms of **variable-pay programs**, which base a portion of an employee's pay on some individual, group, and/or organizational measure of performance. Earnings therefore fluctuate up and down with the measure of performance,[15] as Jason Easton, corporate communications manager at Toronto-based GM Canada, explains: "In any given year the variable pay can actually be zero, below the target or above the target, depending on how the company has performed."[16]

Burnaby, BC-based TELUS and Hamilton, Ontario-based ArcelorMittal Dofasco are just a couple of examples of companies that use variable pay with rank-and-file employees. About 10 to 15 percent of the base pay of ArcelorMittal Dofasco's blue-collar workers is subject to variable compensation, while more than half of the CEO's compensation is based on variable pay.[17] GM Canada gave performance-based bonuses to its salaried employees in 2011, generating discontent among union employees who had no such provision in their collective agreement.[18]

Variable-pay plans have long been used to compensate salespeople and executives. Recently they have begun to be applied to other employees. A recent international survey by Hewitt Associates of large organizations in 46 countries found that more than 80 percent offered variable pay in 2010. In Canada, 9.6 percent of the payroll, on average, goes to variable pay.[19]

The fluctuation in variable pay is what makes these programs attractive to management. It turns part of an organization's fixed labour costs into a variable cost, thus reducing expenses when performance declines. When the economy falters, companies with variable pay are able to reduce their labour costs much faster than others.[20] When pay is tied to performance, the employee's earnings recognize contribution rather than become a form of entitlement. Low performers find, over time, that their pay stagnates, while high performers enjoy pay increases commensurate with their contributions.

Despite some reservations by employees, management professor Maria Rotundo of the Rotman School of Management at the University of Toronto noted that merit pay can work. "It all hinges on fair measures" during the performance appraisal. Managers need to explain why people get different amounts of money, or people "get angry, jealous and disenchanted."[21]

Individual-Based Incentives

There are four major forms of individual-based variable-pay programs: piece-rate wages, merit-based pay, bonuses, and skill-based pay.

Piece-Rate Wages The **piece-rate pay plan** has long been popular as a means for compensating production employees by paying a fixed sum for each unit of production completed. A pure piece-rate plan provides no base salary and pays the employee only for what he or she produces. People who work at baseball parks selling peanuts and soft

variable-pay programs A reward program in which a portion of an employee's pay is based on some individual and/or organizational measure of performance.

piece-rate pay plan An individual-based incentive plan in which employees are paid a fixed sum for each unit of production completed.

drinks frequently are paid this way. At a rate of 25 cents for every bag of peanuts sold, they make $50 if they sell 200 bags during a game, and $10 if they sell only 40 bags. The Vancouver Canucks' four best players were well paid for the 2011–2012 season: The Sedin twins were paid $6.1 million, Roberto Luongo was paid $5.3 million, and Ryan Kesler earned $5 million, regardless of how many games they helped their team win.[22] Would it be better to pay each of them a fixed amount for each win? It seems unlikely they would accept such a deal, and it may cause unanticipated consequences as well (such as cheating). So, although incentives are motivating and relevant for some jobs, it is unrealistic to think they can constitute the only piece of some employees' pay.

Merit-Based Pay   **Merit-based pay plans** pay for individual performance based on performance appraisal ratings. Most large organizations have merit-based pay plans, especially for salaried employees. IBM Canada's merit pay plan, for example, provides increases to employees' base salary based on their annual performance evaluation. Since the 1990s, when the economy stumbled badly, an increasing number of Japanese companies have abandoned seniority-based pay in favour of merit-based pay. Koichi Yanashita of Takeda Chemical Industries commented, "The merit-based salary system is an important means to achieve goals set by the company's top management, not just a way to change wages."[23]

The thinking behind merit pay is that people who are high performers should be given bigger raises. For merit pay to be effective, however, individuals need to perceive a strong relationship between their performance and the rewards they receive.[24] Unfortunately, the evidence suggests that this is not the case.[25]

Despite the intuitive appeal of paying for performance, merit-based pay plans have several limitations. One is that they are typically based on an annual performance appraisal and thus are only as valid as the performance ratings. Another limitation is that the pay raise pool fluctuates based on economic or other conditions that have little to do with an individual employee's performance. One year, a colleague at a top university who performed very well in teaching and research was given a pay raise of $300. Why? Because the budget for pay raises was very small. Yet that is hardly pay for performance. Unions typically resist merit-based pay plans and prefer seniority-based pay, where all employees get the same raises.

Finally, merit pay systems may result in gender and racial discrimination in pay. A 2010 study found that when organizations have merit-based cultures, managers tend to favour male employees over female employees, with men getting larger monetary rewards. The researchers conclude that there may be "unrecognized risks behind certain organizational efforts used to reward merit."[26]

Bonuses   An annual **bonus** is a significant component of total compensation for many jobs.[27] Bonuses reward employees for recent performance rather than historical performance and are one-time rewards rather than ongoing entitlements. They are used by such companies as Ontario Hydro Energy, the Bank of Montreal, and Molson Coors Brewing Company. The incentive effects of performance bonuses should be higher because, rather than paying for performance that may have occurred years ago (and was rolled into their base pay), bonuses reward only recent performance. Moreover, when times are bad, firms can cut bonuses to reduce compensation costs. Steel company Nucor, for example, guarantees its employees only about $10 per hour, but bonuses can be substantial. In 2006, the average Nucor employee made roughly $91 000. When the recession hit, bonuses were cut dramatically: In 2009, total pay had dropped 40 percent.[28]

Bonuses are not free from organizational politics (which we discuss in Chapter 8), and they can sometimes result in negative behaviour, when employees engage in negative behaviours to ensure they will receive bonuses. *Focus on Ethics* raises the

merit-based pay plan An individual-based incentive plan based on performance appraisal ratings.

bonus An individual-based incentive plan that rewards employees for recent performance rather than historical performance.

possibility that part of the US financial crisis that began in September 2008 was due to the way bonuses were awarded to executives.

FOCUS ON ETHICS

Huge Bonuses, Disastrous Results for the United States

Did bonuses help fuel a financial meltdown? During a two-week period in September 2008, the American economy almost looked to be in free fall.[29] The US government bought up the assets of mortgage insurers Freddie Mac and Fannie May. Global financial services firm Merrill Lynch, founded in 1914, agreed to be bought by Bank of America for very little money. Global financial services firm Lehman Brothers, founded in 1850, went into bankruptcy. Morgan Stanley was in merger discussions. Major American insurance corporation AIG received an $85-billion bailout from the US government. Independent investment banks Goldman Sachs, founded in 1869, and Morgan Stanley, founded in 1935, announced that they would become bank holding companies. Investment banks issue and sell securities and provide advice on mergers and acquisitions. By becoming bank holding companies, the two companies are now subjected to greater regulation than they were previously.

There is no simple answer to why all of these corporations faced collapse or near collapse all at once, but the role that bonuses played in the financial meltdown has been raised. The trigger for the economic crisis was the collapse of many subprime mortgages during 2007 and 2008. In the preceding years, numerous Americans had been given mortgages for homes, even though they had no down payments, and sometimes did not even have jobs. The loan payments were low at the beginning, but eventually many of those given subprime mortgages started to default on their loans.

Why would someone give out a loan to an individual who did not have a job or did not provide clear evidence of earnings? The banking industry rewarded mortgage brokers for making loans, giving out bonus payments based on the size of loans. The loans were then bundled together to make new financial instruments. These resulted in commissions and bonuses for those packaging the instruments. Several Wall Street CEOs who lost their jobs because of the fallout from subprime loans earned "tens of millions in bonuses during the heady days of 2005 and 2006."

The collapse of so many financial institutions at once suggests that rewarding individuals based on financial measures can cause problems.

Skill-Based Pay **Skill-based pay** (also called competency-based or knowledge-based pay) is an alternative to job-based pay and bases pay levels on the basis of how many skills employees have or how many jobs they can do.[30] Frito-Lay Corporation ties its compensation for front-line operations managers to developing their skills in leadership, workforce development, and functional excellence. For employers, the lure of skill-based pay plans is that they increase the flexibility of the workforce: Filling staffing needs is easier when employee skills are interchangeable. Skill-based pay also facilitates communication across the organization because people gain a better understanding of each other's jobs.

What about the downside? People can "top out"—that is, they can learn all the skills the program calls for them to learn. This can frustrate employees after they have been challenged by an environment of learning, growth, and continual pay raises. Finally, skill-based plans don't address level of performance. They deal only with whether someone can perform the skill. *OB in the Street* examines the question of whether athletic scholarships should be given for athletic skills, with little regard for academic merit.

skill-based pay An individual-based incentive plan that sets pay levels on the basis of how many skills employees have or how many jobs they can do.

OB in the STREET
Scholarships for Jocks: Skills or Smarts?

Should university athletes be awarded money just for their athletic abilities? Jack Drover, athletic director at Mount Allison University in Sackville, New Brunswick, thinks not.[31] He objects to student-athlete awards that are often offered because of what coaches and teams need, rather than what the individual student needs.

Many university presidents react negatively to schools using financial rewards to recruit athletes. Some high school athletes can get full-tuition scholarships to university, even though they have not achieved high marks in school. While not every university finds this problematic, some feel awarding scholarships that don't recognize academic achievement or financial need is "an affront to the values of higher education."

Schools across the country interpret the rules for scholarships differently, which may affect the quality of school sports teams. Universities in Ontario (which rarely give scholarships to first-year students) have had particular difficulty competing with schools across the country. For example, since 1995, only three football teams in Ontario have won the Vanier Cup: the Ottawa Gee Gees (2000), the Wilfrid Laurier Golden Hawks (2005), and the Queen's Golden Gaels (2009); the University of Ottawa is one of the few schools in the province that gives many athletic scholarships. In contrast, the Saint Mary's Huskies of Halifax, Nova Scotia, has been in the Vanier Cup final five times since 1999, winning twice. Rivals claim that a reason for the team's success is its "plentiful" athletic scholarships.

Some members of Canadian Interuniversity Sport (CIS) suggest that schools should be allowed to make their own decisions, including giving "full ride" scholarships, which would cover more than just tuition. With this model, CIS members would have to face a cap on how much money could be awarded for scholarships, and the money could be allocated across many athletes, or a few stars. However, CIS members could not decide on this approach to scholarships, and "tuition only" scholarships remain in place.

Group-Based Incentives

There is one major form of group-based pay-for-performance program: gainsharing.

Gainsharing **Gainsharing** is a formula-based group incentive plan that uses improvements in group productivity from one period to another to determine the total amount of money to be shared.[32] For instance, if last month a company produced 1000 items using 10 000 person hours, and this month production of the same number of items was produced with only 9000 person hours, the company experiences a savings of 1000 person hours, at the average cost per hour to hire a person. Productivity savings can be divided between the company and employees in any number of ways, but 50-50 is fairly typical. Approximately 45 percent of *Fortune* 1000 firms have implemented gainsharing plans.[33]

Gainsharing differs from profit sharing, discussed below, in that it ties rewards to productivity gains rather than profits. Employees in a gainsharing plan can receive incentive awards even when the organization is not profitable. Because the benefits accrue to groups of employees, high-performing employees pressure weaker performers to work harder, improving performance for the group as a whole.[34] Delta, BC-based Avcorp Industries, and governments, such as Ontario's Town of Ajax and Kingston Township, have introduced gainsharing. It has been found to improve productivity in a majority of cases, and often has a positive impact on employee attitudes.[35]

gainsharing A group-based incentive plan in which improvements in group productivity determine the total amount of money to be shared.

Organizational-Based Incentives

There are two major forms of organizational-based pay-for-performance programs: profit-sharing and stock option plans, which include employee stock ownership plans.

Profit-Sharing Plans A **profit-sharing plan** is an organization-wide plan in which the employer shares profits with employees based on a predetermined formula. The plan can distribute direct cash outlays or stock options. Though senior executives are most likely to be rewarded through profit-sharing plans, employees at any level can be recipients. Burlington, Ontario-based O.C. Tanner Canada pays all of its employees' bonuses based on profits, twice a year.

Profit-sharing plans do not necessarily focus employees on the future, because employees and managers look for ways to cut costs today, without considering longer-term organizational needs. They also tend to ignore factors such as customer service and employee development, which may not be seen as having a direct link to profits. Employees can see inconsistent rewards with such a plan. Gregg Saretsky, WestJet's president and CEO, worries about the flatness of the company's stock price compared with how it soared after the company's initial public offering in 1999. With 84 percent owning shares, most of WestJet employees' compensation is affected by stock prices. However, pay is not the only motivator at WestJet. "You have to have fun and feel you can make a contribution and drive a difference. WestJetters have that in spades," says Saretsky.[36] Vancouver-based 1-800-GOT-JUNK? made no payment in 2007 when the company used its profits to invest in international expansion. Tania Hall, senior PR manager, acknowledged that the lack of a reward cheque could "test employee staying power. This is an opportunity to grow and be part of shaping the future, and you're either in or not."[37]

Three Canadian studies by Professor Richard J. Long of the University of Saskatchewan's College of Commerce show that a profit-sharing plan is most effective in workplaces where there is more involvement by employees, more teamwork, and a managerial philosophy that encourages participation.[38] Employees working under profit-sharing plans have a greater feeling of psychological ownership.[39]

Employee Stock Ownership Plans and Stock Options An **employee stock ownership plan (ESOP)**[40] is a company-established benefit plan in which employees acquire stock as part of their benefits. Stock options give employees the right to buy stocks in the company at a later date for a guaranteed price. In either case, the idea is that employees will be more likely to think about the consequences of their behaviour on the bottom line if they own part of the company.

Canadian companies lag far behind the United States in the use of ESOPs because Canada's tax environment is less conducive to such plans. Nevertheless, Edmonton-based PCL Constructors has been owned by its employees since 1977, with 80 percent of employees owning shares. Ross Grieve, the company's president and CEO, says that ownership "elevates [the employees'] commitment to the organization."[41] Toronto-based I Love Rewards and Edmonton-based Cybertech are other examples of companies that have employee stock ownership plans.

profit-sharing plan An organization-wide incentive plan in which the employer shares profits with employees based on a predetermined formula.

employee stock ownership plan (ESOP) A company-established benefit plan in which employees acquire stock as part of their benefits.

RESEARCH FINDINGS: ESOPs

The research on ESOPs indicates that while they increase employee satisfaction,[42] their impact on performance is less clear. A study by the Toronto Stock Exchange found positive results for public companies with ESOPs:[43]

- Five-year profit growth was 123 percent higher.
- Net profit margin was 95 percent higher.

- Productivity, measured by revenue per employee, was 24 percent higher.
- Return on average total equity was 92.3 percent higher.
- Return on capital was 65.5 percent higher.

ESOPs have the potential to increase employee job satisfaction and work motivation. For this potential to be realized, employees need to psychologically experience ownership.[44] In addition to their financial stake in the company, they need to be kept regularly informed on the status of the business, and have the opportunity to exercise influence over it to achieve significant improvements in the organization's performance.[45] ESOPs for top management can reduce unethical behaviour. CEOs are more likely to manipulate firm earnings reports to make themselves look good in the short run when they don't have an ownership share, even though this manipulation will eventually lead to lower stock prices. However, when CEOs own a large value of stock, they report earnings accurately because they don't want the negative consequences of declining stock prices.[46]

RESEARCH FINDINGS: Variable-Pay Programs

Do variable-pay programs increase motivation and productivity? The answer is a qualified "yes." Studies generally support the idea that organizations with profit-sharing plans have higher levels of profitability than those without them.[47] Similarly, gainsharing has been found to improve productivity in a majority of cases, and often has a positive impact on employee attitudes.[48] Another study found that although piece-rate pay-for-performance plans stimulated higher levels of productivity, this positive effect was not observed for risk-averse employees. Thus, American economist Ed Lazear generally seems right when he says, "Workers respond to prices just as economic theory predicts. Claims by sociologists and others that monetizing incentives may actually reduce output are unambiguously refuted by the data."[49] However, that does not mean everyone responds positively to variable-pay programs.[50]

Teamwork, unions, public sector employees, and ethical considerations present distinct challenges to pay-for-performance programs.

Teamwork Incentive pay, especially when it is awarded to individuals, can have a negative effect on group cohesiveness and productivity, and in some cases it may not offer significant benefits to a company.[51] For example, Montreal-based National Bank of Canada offered a $5 employee bonus for every time employees referred clients for loans, mutual funds, or other bank products. But the bonus so upset employees that the plan was abandoned after just three months.[52] Tellers complained that the bonus caused colleagues to compete against one another. Meanwhile, the bank could not determine whether the referrals actually generated new business.

If an organization wants a group of individuals to function as a "team" (which we define in Chapter 6), emphasis needs to be on team-based rewards, rather than individual rewards. We will discuss the nature of team-based rewards in Chapter 6.

Unions In Canada, there are considerably more unionized workplaces than there are in the United States. Consequently, the unionized context must be considered when motivation theories and practices are examined. Unionized employees are typically paid on the basis of seniority and job categories, with very little range within a category, and few opportunities to receive performance-based pay.

Moreover, organized labour is, in general, cool to the idea of pay for performance. Prem Benimadhu, an analyst at The Conference Board of Canada, notes, "Canadian unions have been very allergic to variable compensation."[53] Andrew Jackson, senior economist for the Canadian Labour Congress in Ottawa, adds that "it hurts co-operation in the workplace. It can lead to competition between workers, speeding up the pace of work. It's a bad thing if it creates a stressful work environment where older workers can't keep up."[54] Union members are also concerned that factors out of their control might affect whether bonuses are awarded. *OB in the Workplace* illustrates one union's view of rewards that recognize performance.

What is the impact of unions on pay for performance?

OB in the WORKPLACE
No Toronto Hydro Jackets for Union Members

Why would unions oppose rewards for their members? Toronto Hydro discovered that rewarding its unionized employees for a job well done can be a tricky business.[55] A ruling by an arbitrator brought in to settle a dispute between Toronto Hydro and the Canadian Union of Public Employees (CUPE) Local 1 stopped the practice of free lunches, dinners, and such rewards as tickets to events, pen and pencil sets, extra breaks, cellphones, and Toronto Hydro jackets.

Bruno Silano, the local's president, argued that it is demoralizing for employees of some departments to get extra rewards, while other employees do not. Robert Herman, the arbitrator, agreed, stating, "the rewards, bestowed at the discretion of management, violated the union's right as exclusive bargaining agent on behalf of its members."

The arbitrator's ruling does not apply to other companies operating with collective agreements, unless the union specifically objects to extra rewards for its members. Toronto labour lawyer Stewart Saxe noted that most unions go along with company reward plans "for obvious political reasons." Toronto Hydro still gives the forbidden perks to non-union employees.

Public Sector Employees There are special challenges in pay-for-performance programs for public sector employees (those who work for local, provincial, or federal governments). Because public sector work is often of a service nature, it can be hard to measure productivity in the same way manufacturing or retail firms do. One might be able to count how many children an employee places in foster homes, but this might not really address the quality of those placements. Therefore, it becomes more difficult to make a meaningful link between rewards and productivity.

Because pay-for-performance programs can be difficult to administer in the public sector, several researchers have suggested that goal-setting theory be used to improve performance in public sector organizations instead.[56] More recently, another researcher found that goal difficulty and goal specificity, as well as the belief that the goal could be achieved, significantly improved motivation of public sector employees.[57] Because many public sector employees are also unionized, the challenges faced in motivating unionized employees also apply to government employees.

Ethical Considerations Organizations need to consider the ethical implications of their performance-based plans. The recent collapse of financial institutions in the United States provides one example of employees manipulating performance results to increase their bonuses. Walmart has been accused by a number of employees of demanding that they work many unpaid hours.[58] According to company policy, Walmart's store managers are told to keep payroll costs below fixed targets and not to allow employees to work overtime. Yet they are reprimanded and face possible demotion or dismissal if they miss their targets. When store managers pressure employees to do work without recording the hours on time sheets, they are simply following practices to ensure that they will be rewarded for performance by their superiors.

Flexible Benefits: Developing a Benefits Package

Alain Bourdeau and Yasmin Murphy have very different needs in terms of employee benefits. Alain is married and has three young children and a wife who is at home full time. Yasmin, too, is married, but her husband has a high-paying job with the federal government, and they have no children. Alain is concerned about having a good dental plan and enough life insurance to support his family in case it's needed. In contrast, Yasmin's husband already has her dental needs covered on his plan, and life insurance is a low priority for both Yasmin and her husband. Yasmin is more interested in extra vacation time and long-term financial benefits such as a tax-deferred savings plan.

A standardized benefits package for all employees at an organization would be unlikely to satisfactorily meet the needs of both Alain and Yasmin. Some organizations, therefore, cover both sets of needs by offering flexible benefits.

Consistent with expectancy theory's thesis that organizational rewards should be linked to each individual employee's personal goals, **flexible benefits** individualize rewards by allowing each employee to choose the compensation package that best satisfies his or her current needs. It replaces the traditional "one-benefit-plan-fits-all" programs designed for a male with a wife and two children at home that dominated organizations for more than 50 years.[59] The average organization provides fringe benefits worth approximately 40 percent of an employee's salary. Flexible benefits can be uniquely tailored to accommodate differences in employee needs based on age, marital status, spouse's benefit status, number and age of dependants, and the like.

The three most popular types of benefits plans are modular plans, core-plus plans, and flexible spending accounts.[60] *Modular plans* are predesigned packages of benefits, with each module put together to meet the needs of a specific group of employees. A module designed for single employees with no dependants might include only essential benefits. Another, designed for single parents, might have additional life insurance, disability insurance, and expanded health coverage. *Core-plus plans* consist of a core of essential benefits and a menu-like selection of other benefit options from which employees can select. Typically, each employee is given "benefit credits," which allow the "purchase" of additional benefits that uniquely meet his or her needs. *Flexible spending accounts* allow employees to set aside pretax dollars up to the dollar amount offered in the plan to pay for particular benefits, such as eye care and dental premiums. Flexible spending accounts can increase employee take-home pay because employees don't pay taxes on the dollars they spend out of these accounts.

Intrinsic Rewards: Employee Recognition Programs

A few years ago, 1500 employees were surveyed in a variety of work settings to find out what they considered to be the most powerful workplace motivator. Their response? Recognition, recognition, and more recognition![61]

Expectancy theory tells us that a key component of motivation is the link between performance and rewards (that is, having your behaviour recognized). Employee recognition programs cover a wide spectrum of activities. They range from a spontaneous and private "thank you" on up to widely publicized formal programs in which specific types of behaviour are encouraged and the procedures for attaining recognition are clearly identified.[62] Some research suggests financial incentives may be more motivating in the short term, but in the long run it's nonfinancial incentives that are motivating.[63]

Toronto-based software developer RL Solutions developed a formal program for employees to recognize co-workers who go above and beyond in working with clients or in other aspects of their work. Those recognized by their co-workers receive cash and/ or other rewards. Employees are also recognized with bonuses when they refer good job

flexible benefits A benefits plan that allows each employee to put together a benefits package individually tailored to his or her own needs and situation.

candidates to the company.[64] Brian Scudamore, CEO of Vancouver-based 1-800-GOT-JUNK? understands the importance of showing employees that they are appreciated. "I believe that the best way to engage someone is with heartfelt thanks. We have created a culture of peer recognition, and 'thank yous' have become contagious. Whether it's a card, kudos at the huddle or basic one-on-one thanks, gratitude goes a long way toward building team engagement, loyalty and, of course, happiness."[65] Scudamore says that actions like these keep the company growing, and employees having fun.

A recent survey of Canadian firms found that 34 percent of companies recognize individual or group achievements with cash or merchandise.[66] Other ways of recognizing performance include sending employees personal thank-you notes or emails for good performance, putting employees on prestigious committees, sending employees for training, and giving an employee an assistant for a day to help clear backlogs. Recognition and praise, however, need to be meaningful, as *Case Incident—Thanks for Nothing* on page 207 illustrates.[67] For a longer discussion of whether praise really motivates, see *Point/Counterpoint* on page 202.

Beware the Signals That Are Sent by Rewards

Perhaps more often than we would like, organizations engage in what has been called "the folly of rewarding A, while hoping for B"[68]; in other words, hoping employees will engage in one type of behaviour, while managers reward for another type. Expectancy theory suggests that individuals will generally perform in ways that raise the probability of receiving the rewards offered. Exhibit 5-2 provides examples of common management reward follies. By focusing on test scores (easy to measure) rather than learning (harder to measure), administrators in the Atlanta, Georgia, school district encouraged teachers to change students' answers on tests, as *OB in the Workplace* shows.

Ever wonder why employees do some strange things?

OB in the WORKPLACE
Bonuses Lead to Cheating

How far will teachers go to comply with the law? The United States' No Child Left Behind Act expects school districts to adhere to strict standards regarding test scores and failure rates for children. Schools that do not comply with the standards receive less funding.

A number of teachers in the Atlanta public school district faced serious allegations in summer 2011, after investigators uncovered the "largest-ever cheating scandal" in the United States.[69] A total of 178 teachers were named in the investigators' report, and 82 confessed to test cheating.

For the previous several years, teachers were belittled or told that "Walmart was hiring" if their students' scores were low, and some were fired. For some, the pressure to perform became too much. At one school, teachers gathered together to change the answers on the tests before the tests were scanned and scored, apparently with the approval of administrators. Trying to explain this kind of behaviour, one teacher said, "It is not that the teachers are bad people and want to do it. It is that they are scared."

While teachers feared for their jobs, the schools were receiving thousands of dollars from the federal government because of improved test scores. The former superintendent of the Atlanta school district, Beverly Hall, received bonuses of tens of thousands of dollars because of the higher test scores in the district. In other words, the federal government, by linking bonuses to improved test scores, may have helped create the cheating scandal, particularly in an underfunded school district.

EXHIBIT 5-2 Management Reward Follies	
We hope for . . .	**But we reward . . .**
Teamwork and collaboration	The best team members
Innovative thinking and risk-taking	Proven methods and not making mistakes
Development of people skills	Technical achievements and accomplishments
Employee involvement and empowerment	Tight control over operations and resources
High achievement	Another year's effort
Long-term growth; environmental responsibility	Quarterly earnings
Commitment to total quality	Shipping on schedule, even with defects
Candour; surfacing bad news early	Reporting good news, whether it's true or not; agreeing with the manager, whether or not (s)he's right

Sources: Constructed from S. Kerr, "On the Folly of Rewarding A, While Hoping for B," *Academy of Management Executive* 9, no. 1 (1995), pp. 7–14; and "More on the Folly," *Academy of Management Executive* 9, no. 1 (1995), pp. 15–16. Copyright © Academy of Management, 1990.

Research suggests that there are three major obstacles to ending these follies:[70]

1. *Individuals are unable to break out of old ways of thinking about reward and recognition practices.* Management often emphasizes quantifiable behaviours to the exclusion of nonquantifiable behaviours; management is sometimes reluctant to change the existing performance system; and employees sometimes have an entitlement mentality (they don't want change because they are comfortable with the current system for rewards).

2. *Organizations often don't look at the big picture of their performance system.* Consequently, rewards are allocated at subunit levels, with the result that units often compete against each other.

3. *Both management and shareholders often focus on short-term results.* They don't reward employees for longer-range planning.

Organizations would do well to ensure that they do not send the wrong message when offering rewards. When organizations outline an organizational objective of "team performance," for example, but reward each employee according to individual productivity, this does not send a message that teams are valued. When a retailer tells commissioned employees that they are responsible for monitoring and replacing stock, those employees will nevertheless concentrate on making sales. Employees motivated by the promise of rewards will do those things that earn them the rewards they value.

Gordon Nixon, president and CEO of the Royal Bank of Canada, highlights changes RBC made to be sure it was rewarding the right things: "We constantly reinforce the values of the organization and ensure it is living up to those values by the way we respect people, the way we compensate and promote people, the way we recognize [them]. We changed our review process to ensure there is alignment with respect to values and culture—that there is alignment between our values and how people are recognized and rewarded."[71]

Can We Eliminate Rewards?

Alfie Kohn, in his book *Punished by Rewards*, argues that "the desire to do something, much less to do it well, simply cannot be imposed; in this sense, it is a mistake to talk about motivating other people. All we can do is set up certain conditions that will maximize the probability

Are rewards overrated?

of their developing an interest in what they are doing and remove the conditions that function as constraints."[72]

Based on his research and consulting experience, Kohn proposes a number of actions that organizations can take to create a more supportive, motivating work environment.

Abolish Incentive Pay   Pay employees generously and fairly so they don't feel exploited. They will be more able to focus on the goals of the organization, rather than have their paycheque as their main goal.

Re-evaluate Evaluation   Instead of making performance appraisals look and feel like a punitive effort—who gets raises, who gets promoted, who is told they are performing poorly—structure the performance evaluation system more like a two-way conversation to trade ideas and questions. The discussion of performance should not be tied to compensation. "Providing feedback that employees can use to do a better job ought never to be confused or combined with controlling them by offering (or withholding) rewards."[73]

Create the Conditions for Authentic Motivation   A noted economist summarized the evidence about pay for productivity as follows: "Changing the way workers are *treated* may boost productivity more than changing the way they are *paid*."[74] There is some consensus about what the conditions for authentic motivation might be: helping employees rather than putting them under surveillance; listening to employee concerns and thinking about problems from their viewpoint; and providing plenty of feedback so they know what they have done right and what they need to improve.[75]

Encourage Collaboration   People are more likely to perform better in well-functioning groups where they can get feedback and learn from one another.[76] Therefore, it's important to provide the necessary supports to create well-functioning teams.

Enhance Content   People are generally the most motivated when their jobs give them an opportunity to learn new skills, provide variety in the tasks that are performed, and enable them to demonstrate competence. Some of this can be fostered by carefully matching people to their jobs, and by giving them the opportunity to try new jobs. It's also possible to increase the meaningfulness of many jobs, as we discuss later in this chapter.

But what about jobs that don't seem inherently interesting? One psychologist suggests that in cases where the jobs are fundamentally unappealing, the manager might acknowledge frankly that the task is not fun, give a meaningful rationale for why it must be done, and then give people as much choice as possible in how the task is completed.[77] One sociologist studying a group of garbage collectors in San Francisco discovered that they were quite satisfied with their work because of the way it was organized: Relationships among the crew were important, tasks and routes were varied to provide interest, and each worker owned a share of the company, and thus felt "pride of ownership."[78]

Provide Choice   "We are most likely to become enthusiastic about what we are doing—and do it well—when we are free to make decisions about the way we carry out a task."[79] Extrinsic rewards (and punishments) remove choice, because they focus us on rewards, rather than on tasks or goals. Research suggests that burnout, dissatisfaction, absenteeism, stress, and coronary heart disease are related to situations where individuals did not have enough control over their work situations.[80] By *choice* we do not mean lack of management, but rather, involving people in the decisions that are to be made. A number of studies indicate that participative management, when it includes full participation by everyone, is successful.[81]

It would be difficult for many organizations to implement these ideas immediately and expect that they would work. Managers would need to relinquish control and take on the job of coach. Employees would need to believe that their participation and input mattered. Nevertheless, these actions, when implemented, can lead to quite a different workplace than what we often see. Moreover, Kohn suggests that sometimes it's not the type or amount of rewards that makes a difference as much as whether the work itself is intrinsically interesting.

Below we examine how to create more motivating jobs and workplaces in order to make work itself more intrinsically rewarding for employees. You might consider whether Starbucks is moving in the right direction to create an intrinsically motivating workplace after you read *OB in the Workplace*.

OB in the WORKPLACE
Starbucks Aims for Better Coffee

Can management make operations too efficient? Starbucks recently revised coffee-making procedures after complaints from customers suggested that the chain's coffee was too mechanized.[82] In a bid to bring back the perception of better coffee at its stores, Starbucks told its baristas to focus on making no more than two drinks at a time, rather than multiple drinks at once.

Starbucks studied how baristas make coffee, trying to get the routine down to the least amount of time possible in order to "eliminate wasteful activity and speed up service." For instance, beans are no longer stored below the counter because it wastes time to bend over to scoop beans.

Baristas were also told to steam just enough milk for one drink at a time, not a whole pitcher to be used for several drinks. The corporation envisions a more efficient operation, but employees fear longer lines. They also do not think the new rules make sense: "While I'm blending a frappuccino, it doesn't make sense to stand there and wait for the blender to finish running, because I could be making an iced tea at the same time," barista Tyler Swain says.

Starbucks says that the baristas just need to get comfortable with the new method, and all will be well. If a customer does need to wait longer, baristas should simply let the customer know. While the operation may be more efficient, employees complain about the lack of autonomy they have in preparing orders.

Motivating by Job Redesign

Research in **job design** suggests that the way the elements in a job are organized can act to increase or decrease effort. This research also offers detailed insights into just what those elements are. We will first review the job characteristics model and then discuss some ways jobs can be redesigned. Finally, we will explore some alternative work arrangements.

The Job Characteristics Model

Developed by OB researchers J. Richard Hackman from Harvard University and Greg Oldham from the University of Illinois, the **job characteristics model (JCM)** says we can describe any job in terms of five core job dimensions:[83]

- **Skill variety**. The degree to which the job requires a variety of different activities so the employee can use a number of different skills and talents.

3 How can jobs be designed to increase motivation?

job design The way the elements in a job are organized.

job characteristics model (JCM) A model that proposes that any job can be described in terms of five core job dimensions: skill variety, task identity, task significance, autonomy, and feedback.

skill variety The degree to which the job requires a variety of different activities.

EXHIBIT 5-3 Examples of High and Low Job Characteristics	
Skill Variety	
High variety	The owner-operator of a garage who does electrical repair, rebuilds engines, does body work, and interacts with customers
Low variety	A body shop worker who sprays paint eight hours a day
Task Identity	
High identity	A cabinet maker who designs a piece of furniture, selects the wood, builds the object, and finishes it to perfection
Low identity	A worker in a furniture factory who operates a lathe solely to make table legs
Task Significance	
High significance	Nursing the sick in a hospital intensive care unit
Low significance	Sweeping hospital floors
Autonomy	
High autonomy	A telephone installer who schedules his or her own work for the day, makes visits without supervision, and decides on the most effective techniques for a particular installation
Low autonomy	A telephone operator who must handle calls as they come according to a routine, highly specified procedure
Feedback	
High feedback	An electronics factory worker who assembles a radio and then tests it to determine if it operates properly
Low feedback	An electronics factory worker who assembles a radio and then routes it to a quality control inspector who tests it for proper operation and makes needed adjustments

Source: G. Johns, *Organizational Behavior: Understanding and Managing Life at Work*, 4th ed. Copyright © 1997. Adapted by permission of Pearson Education, Inc., Upper Saddle River, NJ.

- **Task identity**. The degree to which the job requires completion of a whole and identifiable piece of work.

- **Task significance**. The degree to which the job has an impact on the lives or work of other people.

- **Autonomy**. The degree to which the job provides substantial freedom, independence, and discretion to the individual in scheduling the work and determining the procedures to be used in carrying it out.

- **Feedback**. The degree to which carrying out the work activities required by the job results in the individual obtaining direct and clear information about the effectiveness of his or her performance.

Jobs can be rated as high or low on these dimensions. Examples of jobs with high and low ratings appear in Exhibit 5-3.

Exhibit 5-4 presents the job characteristics model. Note how the first three dimensions—skill variety, task identity, and task significance—combine to create meaningful work the incumbent will view as important, valuable, and worthwhile. Note, too, that jobs with high autonomy give incumbents a feeling of personal responsibility for the results and that, if a job provides feedback, employees will know how effectively they are performing. From a motivational standpoint, the JCM proposes that individuals

task identity The degree to which the job requires completion of a whole and identifiable piece of work.

task significance The degree to which the job has a substantial impact on the lives or work of other people.

autonomy The degree to which the job provides substantial freedom, independence, and discretion to the individual in scheduling the work and determining the procedures to be used in carrying it out.

feedback The degree to which carrying out the work activities required by the job results in the individual obtaining direct and clear information about the effectiveness of his or her performance.

EXHIBIT 5-4 The Job Characteristics Model

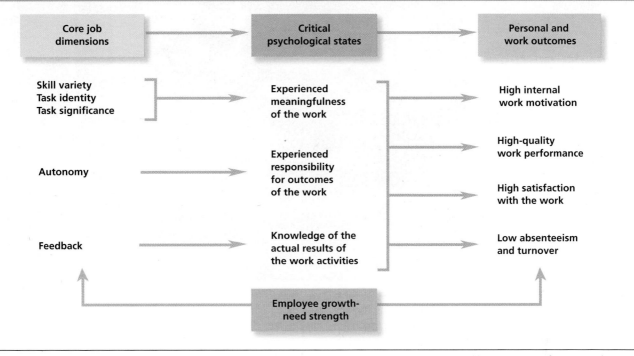

Source: J. RICHARD HACKMAN & GREG R. OLDHAM, WORK REDESIGN, 1st Edition, © 1980. Reprinted by permission of Pearson Education, Inc., Upper Saddle River, NJ.

obtain internal rewards when they learn (knowledge of results) that they personally (experienced responsibility) have performed well on a task they care about (experienced meaningfulness).[84] The more these three psychological states are present, the greater will be employees' motivation, performance, and satisfaction, and the lower their absenteeism and likelihood of leaving. As Exhibit 5-4 shows, individuals with a high growth need are more likely to experience the critical psychological states when their jobs are enriched—and respond to them more positively—than are their counterparts with low growth need. Autonomy does not mean the same for every person, as *Focus on Research* shows.

FOCUS ON RESEARCH   ## Autonomy and Productivity

Can autonomy really make a difference? Research published in 2011 by Professors Marylène Gagné and Devasheesh Bhave of Concordia's John Molson School of Business found that every culture values autonomy, and that the perception of autonomy has a positive impact on employees.[85] "However, managers can't simply export North American methods of granting autonomy anywhere and expect them to work. Even in Canada, approaches to giving workers more autonomy need to be constantly rethought as the country becomes more multicultural," says Gagné.

The researchers found that how autonomy is applied makes a difference in how it is perceived. In some cultures, too much freedom in the workplace can be viewed as management disorganization. However, if employees feel they have some control over their activities, they generally show more commitment and productivity, particularly when the work is complex or demands creativity.

Working on a fish-processing line requires being comfortable with job specialization. One person cuts off heads, another guts the fish, a third removes the scales. Each person performs the same task repetitively as fish move down the line. Such jobs are low on skill variety, task identity, task significance, autonomy, and feedback.

A survey of college and university students highlights the underlying theme of the JCM. When the students were asked about what was most important to them as they thought about their careers, their top four answers were as follows:

- Having idealistic and committed co-workers (very important to 68 percent of the respondents)

- Doing work that helps others (very important to 65 percent)

- Doing work that requires creativity (very important to 47 percent)

- Having a lot of responsibility (very important to 39 percent)[86]

Salary and prestige ranked lower in importance than these four job characteristics.

Motivating Potential Score

We can combine the core dimensions into a single predictive index, called the **motivating potential score (MPS)**, which is calculated as follows:

$$\text{Motivating Potential Score (MPS)} = \left[\frac{\text{Skill variety} + \text{Task identity} + \text{Task significance}}{3} \right] \times \text{Autonomy} \times \text{Feedback}$$

To be high on motivating potential, jobs must be high on at least one of the three factors that lead to experienced meaningfulness and high on both autonomy and feedback. If jobs score high on motivating potential, the model predicts motivation, performance, and satisfaction will improve and absence and turnover will be reduced.

The first part of the *Working with Others Exercise* on page 205 provides an opportunity for you to apply the JCM to a job of your choice. You will also calculate the job's MPS. In the second part of the *Working with Others Exercise*, you can redesign the job to show how you might increase its motivating potential. *From Concepts to Skills* on pages 208–209 provides specific guidelines on the kinds of changes that can help increase the motivating potential of jobs.

---

motivating potential score (MPS)
A predictive index suggesting the motivation potential in a job.

RESEARCH FINDINGS

RESEARCH FINDINGS: JCM

Most evidence supports the JCM concept that the presence of a set of job characteristics—variety, identity, significance, autonomy, and feedback—generates higher and more satisfying job performance and reduces absenteeism and turnover costs.[87] However, we can better calculate motivating potential by simply adding the characteristics rather than using the formula.[88] On the critical issue of productivity, the evidence is inconclusive.[89] In some situations, job enrichment increases productivity; in others, it decreases productivity. However, even when productivity goes down, there does seem to be consistently more conscientious use of resources and a higher quality of product or service.

While many employees want challenging, interesting, and complex work, some people prosper in simple, routinized work.[90] The variable that seems to best explain who prefers a challenging job is the strength of an individual's higher-order needs.[91] Individuals with high growth needs are more responsive to challenging work. Many employees meet their higher-order needs *off* the job. There are 168 hours in a week, and work rarely consumes more than 30 percent of them. That leaves considerable opportunity, even for individuals with strong growth needs, to find higher-order need satisfaction outside the workplace.

When might job redesign be most appropriate?

Job Redesign in the Canadian Context: The Role of Unions

Labour unions have been largely resistant to participating in discussions with management over job redesign issues. Redesigns often result in loss of jobs, and labour unions try to prevent job loss. Union head offices, however, can sometimes be at odds with their membership over the acceptance of job redesign. Some members value the opportunity for skill development and more interesting work.

Some of the larger unions have been more open to discussions about job redesign. For instance, the Communications, Energy and Paperworkers Union of Canada (CEP) asserted that unions should be involved in the decisions and share in the benefits of work redesign.[92] The CEP believes that basic wages, negotiated through a collective agreement, must remain the primary form of compensation, although the union is open to other forms of compensation as long as they do not detract from basic wages determined through collective bargaining.

While managers may regard job redesign as more difficult under a collective agreement, the reality is that for change to be effective in the workplace, management must gain employees' acceptance of the plan whether or not they are unionized.

How Can Jobs Be Redesigned?

Let's look at some of the ways to put JCM into practice to make jobs more motivating.

Job Rotation

If employees suffer from overroutinization, one alternative is **job rotation**, or the periodic shifting of an employee from one task to another with similar skill requirements at the same organizational level (what many call *cross-training*). When an activity is no longer challenging, the employee is rotated to another job at the same level that has similar skill requirements.[93]

At McDonald's, this approach is used as a way to make sure that the new employees learn all of the tasks associated with making, packaging, and serving hamburgers and other items. At Singapore Airlines, a ticket agent may take on the duties of a baggage

job rotation The periodic shifting of an employee from one task to another.

handler. Extensive job rotation is one of the reasons Singapore Airlines is rated one of the best airlines in the world and a highly desirable place to work.

A Statistics Canada survey found that about 19 percent of firms with 10 or more employees engaged in job rotation.[94] Employees in technical trades and clerical and administrative positions were more likely to rotate jobs than managerial and professional employees.

The strengths of job rotation are that it reduces boredom, increases motivation, and helps employees better understand how their work contributes to the organization. An indirect benefit is that employees with a wider range of skills give management more flexibility in scheduling work, adapting to changes, and filling vacancies.[95]

However, job rotation has drawbacks. Training costs are increased, and productivity is reduced by moving an employee into a new position just when efficiency at the prior job is creating organizational economies. Job rotation also creates disruptions when members of the work group have to adjust to the new employee. The manager may also have to spend more time answering questions and monitoring the work of the recently rotated employee.

Job Enrichment

Job enrichment expands jobs by increasing the degree to which the employee controls the planning, execution, and evaluation of the work. An enriched job organizes tasks to allow the employee to do a complete activity, increases the employee's freedom and independence, increases responsibility, and provides feedback so individuals can assess and correct their own performance.[96] To find out whether an enriched job matches your own work preferences, see the *Learning About Yourself Exercise* on page 203. *From Concepts to Skills* on pages 208–209 provides specific guidelines on the kinds of changes that can help enrich jobs.

Some newer versions of job enrichment concentrate more specifically on improving the meaningfulness of work. One significant method is to relate employee experiences to customer outcomes, simply by providing employees with stories from customers who benefited from the company's products or services. Researchers recently found that when university fundraisers briefly interacted with the undergraduates who would receive the scholarships they raised, they persisted 42 percent longer, and raised nearly twice as much money, as those who did not interact with potential recipients.[97] Another method for improving the meaningfulness of work is providing employees with mutual assistance programs.[98] Employees who can help one another directly through their work come to see themselves, and the organizations for which they work, in more positive, pro-social terms. This, in turn, can increase employee affective commitment.

The evidence on job enrichment shows it reduces absenteeism and turnover costs and increases satisfaction, but not all job enrichment programs are equally effective.[99] A review of 83 organizational interventions designed to improve performance management showed that frequent, specific feedback related to solving problems was linked to consistently higher performance, but infrequent feedback that focused more on past problems than future solutions was much less effective.[100] Some recent evidence suggests job enrichment works best when it compensates for poor feedback and reward systems.[101] One recent study showed employees with a higher preference for challenging work experienced larger reductions in stress following job redesign than individuals who did not prefer challenging work.[102]

Alternative Work Arrangements

Beyond redesigning work itself and including employees in decisions, another approach to motivation is to alter work arrangements. Below we consider how flextime, job sharing, and telework might address one of Kohn's ideas for

SELF-ASSESSMENT LIBRARY

LEARNING ABOUT YOURSELF

1. Is an Enriched Job for You?
   (page 203)

job enrichment The vertical expansion of jobs, which increases the degree to which the employee controls the planning, execution, and evaluation of the work.

How can flexible workplaces increase motivation?

increasing motivation that we discussed above: creating better work environments for people. These arrangements are likely to be especially important for a diverse workforce of dual-earner couples, single parents, and employees caring for a sick or aging relative. *Case Incident—Working at Bob's in Rio* on page 208 asks you to look at various possibilities for making the work setting better for employees.

Do employers really like flexible arrangements?

Flextime

Flextime is short for "flexible work time." Employees must work a specific number of hours a week, but they are free to vary the hours of work within certain limits. As shown in Exhibit 5-5, each day consists of a common core, usually six hours, with a flexibility band surrounding it. The core may be 9 a.m. to 3 p.m., with the office actually opening at 6 a.m. and closing at 6 p.m. All employees are required to be at their jobs during the common core period, but they may accumulate their other two hours before and/or after the core time. Some flextime programs allow extra hours to be accumulated and turned into a free day off each month.

Flextime has become an extremely popular scheduling option, although in Canada women are less likely than men to have flexible work schedules.[103] More managers

---

EXHIBIT 5-5 Examples of Flextime Schedules

Schedule 1

Percent Time:	100% = 40 hours per week
Core Hours:	9:00 a.m.–5:00 p.m., Monday through Friday (1 hour lunch)
Work Start Time:	Between 8:00 a.m. and 9:00 a.m.
Work End Time:	Between 5:00 p.m. and 6:00 p.m.

Schedule 2

Percent Time:	100% = 40 hours per week
Work Hours:	8:00 a.m.–6:30 p.m., Monday through Thursday (1/2 hour lunch)
	Friday off
Work Start Time:	8:00 a.m.
Work End Time:	6:30 p.m.

Schedule 3

Percent Time:	90% = 36 hours per week
Work Hours:	8:30 a.m.–5:00 p.m., Monday through Thursday (1/2 hour lunch)
	8:00 a.m.–Noon Friday (no lunch)
Work Start Time:	8:30 a.m. (Monday–Thursday); 8:00 a.m. (Friday)
Work End Time:	5:00 p.m. (Monday–Thursday); Noon (Friday)

Schedule 4

Percent Time:	80% = 32 hours per week
Work Hours:	8:00 a.m.–6:00 p.m., Monday through Wednesday (1/2 hour lunch)
	8:00 a.m.–11:30 a.m. Thursday (no lunch)
	Friday off
Work Start Time:	Between 8:00 a.m. and 9:00 a.m.
Work End Time:	Between 5:00 p.m. and 6:00 p.m.

---

flextime An arrangement where employees work during a common core period each day but can form their total workday from a flexible set of hours outside the core.

(42.4 percent) enjoy the freedom of flextime than do manufacturing employees (23.3 percent).[104]

Most of the performance evidence stacks up favourably. Flextime tends to reduce absenteeism and frequently improves employee productivity and satisfaction,[105] probably for several reasons. Employees can schedule their work hours to align with personal demands, reducing tardiness and absences, and they can work when they are most productive. Other research on the impact of flextime on the Canadian workplace has found that employees have positive attitudes and view it as their most preferred option.[106] Managers are in favour,[107] and women with flextime suffer less stress.[108]

Flextime can help employees balance work and family lives, as happens at Goodfish Lake, Alberta-based Goodfish Lake Development Corporation (GFLDC). GFLDC is an Aboriginal business that provides dry-cleaning, clothing manufacturing and repair, protective clothing rentals, and bakery services to Fort McMurray. Many of the company's employees are women who have husbands that work full time in Fort McMurray. This can make it difficult for GFLDC's female employees to care for their children, so the company created flexible schedules to help employees balance work and home life.[109] A 2010 study by University of Toronto researchers found that flextime can lead to longer hours of work overall and more multi-tasking. These in turn lead to greater work-life conflict and stress.[110] So the management of flextime is an important issue for employees.

Flextime's other major drawback is that it is not applicable to every job. It works well with clerical tasks where an employee's interaction with people outside his or her department is limited. It is not a viable option for receptionists, salespeople in retail stores, or similar jobs where people must be at their workstations at fixed times that suit the needs of customers and clients.

job sharing The practice of having two or more people split a 40-hour-a-week job.

In response to the recession of 2008, the Canadian government included a job-sharing incentive as an alternative to layoffs. Over 165 000 Canadian employees benefited from the program, which allowed employees to draw employment insurance benefits to compensate them for their reduced wages. Calgary-based Standen's, run by president and CEO Mel Svendsen (in forefront), makes heat-treated alloy steel parts and was able to get through the recession without laying off a single member of the team, in part by using this program. While most of the stimulus funding support ended on March 31, 2011, the job-sharing support was extended into 2011.[116]

Job Sharing

Job sharing allows two or more people to split a 40-hour-a-week job. While popular in Europe, it is not a common arrangement in Canada. In 2007, about 14 percent of Canadian employers offered this arrangement.[111] Reasons it is not more widely adopted are likely the difficulty of finding compatible partners to share a job and the historically negative perceptions of individuals not completely committed to their job and employer.[112]

Job sharing allows the organization to draw upon the talents of more than one individual in a given job. A bank manager who oversees two job sharers describes it as an opportunity to get two heads, but "pay for one."[113] It also opens up the opportunity to acquire skilled employees—for instance, women with young children, retirees, and others desiring flexibility—who might not be available on a full-time basis.[114] Many Japanese firms are increasingly considering job sharing—but for a very different reason.[27] Because Japanese executives are extremely reluctant to fire people, job sharing is seen as a potentially humanitarian means of avoiding layoffs due to overstaffing.[115]

From the employee's perspective, job sharing increases flexibility and can increase motivation and satisfaction for those for whom a 40-hour-a-week job is just not practical. But the major drawback from management's perspective is finding compatible pairs of employees who can successfully coordinate the demands of one job. "Job sharing must be well planned, and needs clear job descriptions," says Julianna Cantwell, HR consultant with Edmonton-based Juna Consulting.[117]

Job sharing can be a creative solution to some organizational problems. For example, Nunavut has had great difficulty finding doctors willing to commit to serving the territory for more than short periods of time.[118] Dr. Sandy MacDonald, director of Medical Affairs and Telehealth for Nunavut, allows doctors to work for three months at a time. "In the past, the government was trying to get some of them to sign up for two or three years, and most people don't want to do that initially, or they would leave positions unfilled because someone would only come for two or three weeks or a month," he says. Meanwhile, doctors working in Nunavut were overworked because there were not enough doctors on call. MacDonald's approach has changed that—now more doctors are available because of the job-sharing solution.

Telework

Telework refers to employees working anywhere away from the office that they have access to smartphones, tablets, and other mobile computing devices.[119] (A closely related term—*the virtual office*—is increasingly being used to describe employees who work out of their home on a relatively permanent basis.)

More than 1 billion people worldwide worked remotely at the end of 2010, and it is forecast that more than one-third of all workers will be mobile by 2013.[121] About 40 percent of Canadian companies offered telework in 2008, up from 25 percent in 2007.[122] Bob Fortier, president of the Canadian Telework Association, estimates that between 1.5 million and 2 million individuals worked remotely in Canada in 2011, compared with 100 000 in the late 1980s.[123] At Cisco's downtown Toronto office, there are 200 desks for 500 employees. "Everyone else works remotely and just comes in occasionally for meetings," said Jeff Seifert, chief technology officer for Cisco's Canadian division. An internal survey in 2009 of Cisco employees found increased productivity and satisfaction due to the teleworking. It also saved the company $277 million in a year.[124] Longueuil, Quebec-based SICO Paints, Manitoba Hydro, and the Saskatchewan Government are other examples of workplaces that encourage telework.

What kinds of jobs lend themselves to telework? There are three categories: routine information-handling tasks, mobile activities, and professional and other knowledge-related tasks.[125] Writers, attorneys, analysts, and employees who spend the majority of their time on computers or the phone—telemarketers, customer-service representatives, reservation agents, and product-support specialists—are natural candidates for telework.

Bob Fortier, president of the Canadian Telework Association, says, "Mobile work is here to stay." He says that telework has many benefits: It helps attract employees who are looking for flexible work, reduces turnover, and reduces carbon emissions. However, some managers worry about supervising employees who work off-site. "In an ideal situation, teleworkers work from home or on the road a set number of hours a week, but come into the office to work and interact with managers for the rest of the time. This gives them a healthy balance," says Fortier.[120]

Would you find telework motivating?

telework An arrangement where employees do their work outside the office anywhere they have access to smartphones, tablets, and other mobile computing devices.

As teleworkers, they can access information on their computer screens at home as easily as on the company screen in any office.

RESEARCH FINDINGS: Telework

A recent Ipsos Reid study found that 42 percent of employees reported that they would be more likely to stay with their current employer, or enticed to take a new job, if the employer offered the opportunity to telework.[126] Other researchers looking at teleworking in Canada have found that it results in increased productivity,[127] decreased stress,[128] and better service to customers and clients.[129] Teleworking has been found to reduce turnover[130] and decrease absenteeism.[131] Further potential pluses for management include a larger labour pool from which to select and reduced office-space costs. A positive relationship exists between teleworking and supervisor performance ratings.[132]

The major downside for management is less direct supervision of employees. In addition, in today's team-focused workplace, teleworking may make it more difficult for management to coordinate teamwork.[133] From the employee's standpoint, teleworking offers a considerable increase in flexibility—but not without costs. For employees with a high social need, teleworking can increase feelings of isolation and reduce job satisfaction. And all teleworkers are vulnerable to the "out of sight, out of mind" effect.[134] Employees who are not at their desks, who miss meetings, and who don't share in day-to-day informal workplace interactions may be at a disadvantage when it comes to raises and promotions. Finally, a 2011 study by University of Toronto researchers found greater psychological stress for women than men when employees were contacted frequently at home by supervisors, co-workers, or clients. The researchers concluded that women may face greater difficulties balancing work and home life while working at home.[135]

The Social and Physical Context of Work

The job characteristics model shows most employees are more motivated and satisfied when their intrinsic work tasks are engaging. However, having the most interesting workplace characteristics in the world may not always lead to satisfaction if you feel isolated from your co-workers, and having good social relationships can make even the most boring and onerous tasks more fulfilling. Research demonstrates that social aspects and work context are as important as other job design features.[136] Policies such as job rotation, employee empowerment, and employee participation have positive effects on productivity, at least partially because they encourage more communication and a positive social environment.

Some social characteristics that improve job performance include interdependence, social support, and interactions with other people outside work. Social interactions are strongly related to positive moods and give employees more opportunities to clarify their work role and how well they are performing. Social support gives employees greater opportunities to obtain assistance with their work. Constructive social relationships can bring about a positive feedback loop as employees assist one another in a "virtuous circle."

The work context is also likely to affect employee satisfaction. Work that is hot, loud, and dangerous is less satisfying than work conducted in climate-controlled, relatively quiet, and safe environments. This is probably why most people would rather work in a coffee shop than a metalworking foundry. Physical demands make people physically uncomfortable, which is likely to show up in lower levels of job satisfaction.

To assess why an employee is not performing to her best level, look at the work environment to see whether it's supportive. Does the employee have adequate tools, equipment, materials, and supplies? Does the employee have favourable working conditions, helpful co-workers, supportive work rules and procedures, sufficient information to make job-related decisions, adequate time to do a good job, and the like? If not, performance will suffer.

Employee Involvement

Those who work at Whole Foods demonstrate high employee involvement.[137] Employees have the freedom to make decisions, including helping each other, figuring out how to manage breaks, and solving customer problems. To make this level of involvement work well, employees are given training and development opportunities, feedback, and targets.

One particularly effective practice that encourages employee involvement is the annual visits employees make to other store branches. Comparable teams from different stores are encouraged to learn from one another and give feedback, which encourages healthy rivalry and cross-fertilization of ideas. What other ways can companies encourage employee involvement?

4 How do employees become more involved in the workplace?

What is **employee involvement**? It's a participative process that uses employees' input to increase their commitment to the organization's success. The logic is that if we engage employees in decisions that affect them and increase their autonomy and control over their work lives, they will become more motivated, more committed to the organization, more productive, and more satisfied with their jobs.[138]

Examples of Employee Involvement Programs

Let's look at two major forms of employee involvement—participative management and representative participation—in more detail.

Participative Management

The distinct characteristic common to all **participative management** programs is joint decision making, in which subordinates share a significant degree of decision-making power with their immediate superiors. Participative management has, at times, been promoted as the solution for poor morale and low productivity. But for it to work, the issues in which employees are engaged must be relevant to their interests so they will be motivated, employees must have the competence and knowledge to make a useful contribution, and trust and confidence must exist among all parties.[139]

Dozens of studies have been conducted on the participation-performance relationship. The findings, however, are mixed.[140] Organizations that institute participative management do have higher stock returns, lower turnover rates, and higher estimated labour productivity, although these effects are typically not large.[141] A careful review of the research at the individual level shows participation typically has only a modest influence on variables such as employee productivity, motivation, and job satisfaction. Of course, this does not mean participative management cannot be beneficial under the right conditions. What it says, however, is that it is not a sure means for improving employee performance.

Representative Participation

Almost every country in western Europe requires companies to practise **representative participation**, called "the most widely legislated form of employee involvement around the world."[142] Its goal is to redistribute power within an organization, putting labour on a more equal footing with the interests of management and stockholders by letting employees be represented by a small group of employees who actually participate.

The two most common forms are works councils and board representatives.[143] Works councils are groups of nominated or elected employees who must be consulted when management makes decisions about employees. Board representatives are

employee involvement A participative process that uses the input of employees and is intended to increase employee commitment to an organization's success.

participative management A process in which subordinates share a significant degree of decision-making power with their immediate superiors.

representative participation A system in which employees participate in organizational decision making through a small group of representative employees.

employees who sit on a company's board of directors and represent the interests of the firm's employees.

The influence of representative participation on working employees seems to be minimal.[144] Works councils are dominated by management and have little impact on employees or the organization. While participation might increase the motivation and satisfaction of employee representatives, there is little evidence this effect trickles down to the operating employees they represent. Overall, "the greatest value of representative participation is symbolic. If one is interested in changing employee attitudes or in improving organizational performance, representative participation would be a poor choice."[145]

Linking Employee Involvement Programs and Motivation Theories

Employee involvement draws on a number of the motivation theories we discussed in Chapter 4. Theory Y is consistent with participative management and Theory X with the more traditional autocratic style of managing people. In terms of Herzberg's two-factor theory, employee involvement programs could provide intrinsic motivation by increasing opportunities for growth, responsibility, and involvement in the work itself. The opportunity to make and implement decisions—and then see them work out—can help satisfy an employee's needs for responsibility, achievement, recognition, growth, and enhanced self-esteem. And extensive employee involvement programs clearly have the potential to increase employee intrinsic motivation in work tasks.

Motivation: Putting It All Together

5 Can we simplify how we think about motivation?

In Chapter 4, we reviewed basic theories of motivation, considering such factors as how needs affect motivation, the importance of linking performance to rewards, and the need for fair process. In this chapter, we considered various ways to pay and recognize people, and looked at job design and creating more flexible workplaces. Three Harvard University professors recently completed two studies that suggest a way to put all of these ideas together to understand (1) what motivates people and (2) how to use this knowledge to make sure that organizational processes motivate.[146]

According to the study authors, research suggests that four basic emotional drives (needs) guide individuals.[147] These are the drive to acquire; the drive to bond; the drive to comprehend; and the drive to defend. People want to acquire any number of scarce goods, both tangible and intangible (such as social status). They want to bond with other individuals and groups. They want to understand the world around them. As well, they want to protect against external threats to themselves and others, and want to ensure justice occurs.

Understanding these different drives makes it possible to motivate individuals more effectively. As the study authors point out, "each drive is best met by a distinct organizational lever." The drive to acquire is met through organizational rewards. The drive to bond can be met by "creat[ing] a culture that promotes teamwork, collaboration, openness, and friendship." The drive to comprehend is best met through job design and creating jobs that are "meaningful, interesting, and challenging." The drive to defend can be accomplished through an organization's performance management and resource allocation processes; this includes fair and transparent processes for managing performance and adequate resources to do one's job. Exhibit 5-6 indicates concrete ways that organizational characteristics can address individual drives.

EXHIBIT 5-6 How to Fulfill the Drives That Motivate Employees

DRIVE	PRIMARY LEVER	ACTIONS
1 Acquire	Reward System	• Sharply differentiate good performers from average and poor performers • Tie rewards clearly to performance • Pay as well as your competitors
2 Bond	Culture	• Foster mutual reliance and friendship among co-workers • Value collaboration and teamwork • Encourage sharing of best practices
3 Comprehend	Job Design	• Design jobs that have distinct and important roles in the organization • Design jobs that are meaningful and foster a sense of contribution to the organization
4 Defend	Performance Management and Resource Allocation Processes	• Increase the transparency of all processes • Emphasize their fairness • Build trust by being just and transparent in granting rewards, assignments, and other forms of recognition

Source: N. Nohria, B. Groysberg, and L.-E. Lee, "Employee Motivation: A Powerful New Model," *Harvard Business Review* 86, no. 7–8 (July–August 2008), p. 82. Reprinted by permission of *Harvard Business Review*.

GLOBAL IMPLICATIONS

Do the motivational approaches we have discussed vary by culture? Because we have covered some very different approaches in this chapter, let's break down our analysis by approach. Not every approach has been studied by cross-cultural researchers, so we consider cross-cultural differences in (1) variable pay, (2) flexible benefits, (3) job characteristics and job enrichment, (4) telework, and (5) employee involvement.

Variable Pay

You would probably think individual pay systems (such as merit pay or pay-for-performance) work better in individualistic cultures such as the United States than in collectivistic cultures such as China or Venezuela. Similarly, you would probably hypothesize that group-based rewards such as gainsharing or profit sharing work better in collectivistic cultures than in individualistic cultures. Unfortunately, there isn't much research on the issue. One recent study did suggest, though, that beliefs about the fairness of a group incentive plan were more predictive of pay satisfaction for employees in the United States than for employees in Hong Kong. One interpretation of these findings is that US employees are more critical in appraising a group pay plan, and therefore it's more critical that the plan be communicated clearly and administered fairly.[148]

Flexible Benefits

Today, almost all major corporations in the United States offer flexible benefits. They are becoming the norm in other countries, too. A recent survey of 136 Canadian organizations found that 93 percent have adopted or will adopt flexible benefits in the near

GLOBE/Hofstede Cultural Dimension	Reward Preference	Examples
High uncertainty avoidance	Certainty in compensation systems: • Seniority-based pay • Skill-based pay	Greece, Portugal, Japan
Individualism	Compensation based on individual performance: • Pay for performance • Individual incentives • Stock options	Australia, United Kingdom, United States
Humane orientation (Hofstede's masculinity vs. femininity dimension)	Social benefits and programs: • Flexible benefits • Workplace child-care programs • Career-break schemes • Maternity leave programs	Sweden, Norway, the Netherlands

EXHIBIT 5-7 Reward Preferences in Different Countries

Source: Based on R. S. Schuler and N. Rogovsky, "Understanding Compensation Practice Variations across Firms: The Impact of National Culture," *Journal of International Business Studies* 29, no. 1 (First Quarter 1998), pp. 159–177. Reprinted by permission of Palgrave/Macmillan.

term.[149] And a similar survey of 307 firms in the United Kingdom found that while only 16 percent have flexible benefits programs in place, another 60 percent are either in the process of implementing them or are seriously considering it.[150]

In Exhibit 5-7, we show the link between a country's rating on GLOBE/Hofstede cultural dimensions, which we discussed in Chapter 3, and its preferences for particular types of rewards. Countries that put a high value on uncertainty avoidance prefer pay based on objective measures, such as skill or seniority, because the outcomes are more certain. Countries that put a high value on individualism place more emphasis on an individual's responsibility for performance that leads to rewards. Countries that put a high value on humane orientation offer social benefits and programs that provide work-family balance, such as child care, maternity leave, and sabbaticals.[151] Managers who receive overseas assignments should consider a country's cultural orientation when designing and implementing reward practices.

Job Characteristics and Job Enrichment

A few studies have tested the job characteristics model in different cultures, but the results are not very consistent.[152] One study suggested that when employees are "other oriented" (concerned with the welfare of others at work), the relationship between intrinsic job characteristics and job satisfaction is weaker. The fact that the job characteristics model is relatively individualistic (considering the relationship between the employee and his or her work) suggests job enrichment strategies may not have the same effects in collectivistic cultures as in individualistic cultures (such as the United States).[153] However, another study suggested the degree to which jobs had intrinsic job characteristics predicted job satisfaction and job involvement equally well for US, Japanese, and Hungarian employees.[154]

Telework

Does the degree to which employees telework vary by nation? Does its effectiveness depend on culture? First, one study suggests that telework is more common in the United States than in all the European Union (EU) nations except the Netherlands. In the study, 24.6 percent of US employees engaged in teleworking, compared with only

13.0 percent of EU employees. Of the EU countries, the Netherlands had the highest rate of teleworking (26.4 percent); the lowest rates were in Spain (4.9 percent) and Portugal (3.4 percent). What about the rest of the world? Unfortunately, there are few data comparing teleworking rates in other parts of the world. Similarly, we don't really know whether teleworking works better in the United States than in other countries. However, the same study that compared telework rates between the United States and the EU determined that employees in Europe appeared to have the same level of interest in telework: regardless of country, interest is higher among employees than among employers.[155]

Employee Involvement

Employee involvement programs differ among countries.[156] A study comparing the acceptance of employee involvement programs in four countries, including the United States and India, confirmed the importance of modifying practices to reflect national culture.[157] Specifically, while US employees readily accepted these programs, managers in India who tried to empower their employees through employee involvement programs were rated low by those employees. These reactions are consistent with India's high power-distance culture, which accepts and expects differences in authority. Similarly, Chinese employees who were very accepting of traditional Chinese values showed few benefits from participative decision making, but employees who were less traditional were more satisfied and had higher performance ratings under participative management.[158] This study illustrates the substantial differences in how management practices are perceived by individuals within as well as between countries.

Summary and Implications

❶ Is money an important motivator? The most commonly used reward in organizations is money. Despite the importance of money in attracting and retaining employees, and rewarding and recognizing them, little attention has been given to individual differences in people's feelings about money.[159] Some studies indicate that money is not employees' top priority. A number of studies suggest that there are personality traits and demographic factors that correlate with an individual's attitude toward money.[160] People who value money highly score higher on "attributes like sensation seeking, competitiveness, materialism, and control." People who desire money score higher on self-esteem, need for achievement, and Type A personality measures. Men seem to value money more than women do.

❷ What does an effective reward system look like? In general, an effective reward system links pay to performance, which is consistent with expectancy theory predictions. In variable-pay or pay-for-performance programs, companies operate reward programs at three levels: individual (piece-rate wages, merit-based pay, bonuses, and skill-based pay), group (gainsharing), and organizational (profit-sharing plans, stock options, and employee stock ownership plans). Under variable-pay programs, individuals should perceive a strong relationship between their performance and the rewards they receive, and thus be more motivated. Research in Canada, which looked at both unionized and non-unionized workplaces, found that variable-pay programs result in "increased productivity, a safer work environment, a better understanding of the business by employees, and little risk of employees losing base pay."[161] Other effective rewards are flexible benefits plans that meet the diverse needs of a workforce and recognition programs that acknowledge individual efforts in concrete ways, such as thank-you notes, employee-of-the-month programs, and public acknowledgments.

LESSONS LEARNED

- Money is not a motivator for all individuals.
- Effective reward systems link pay to performance.
- Jobs characterized by variety, autonomy, and feedback are more motivating.

SNAPSHOT SUMMARY

❶ From Theory to Practice: The Role of Money

❷ Creating Effective Reward Systems
What to Pay: Establishing a Pay Structure
How to Pay: Rewarding Individuals through Variable-Pay Programs
Flexible Benefits: Developing a Benefits Package
Intrinsic Rewards: Employee Recognition Programs
Beware the Signals That Are Sent by Rewards
Can We Eliminate Rewards?

3 **How can jobs be designed to increase motivation?** An understanding of work design can help managers design jobs that affect employee motivation positively. Managers can add more variety to jobs through job rotation and enlargement. They can also enrich jobs, and increase autonomy, following the job characteristics model. The model looks at a job's skill variety, task identity, task significance, autonomy, and feedback. It tells us that jobs in which people have control over key elements in their work score higher in motivating potential than jobs in which people don't have such control. Jobs that offer autonomy, feedback, and similar complex task characteristics tend to be more motivating for employees.

4 **How do employees become more involved in the workplace?** The major forms of employee involvement are participative management and representative participation. In participative management programs, subordinates share a significant degree of decision-making power with their immediate superiors. Representative participation is a system in which employees participate in organizational decision making through a small group of representative employees. Employee involvement programs can increase employee intrinsic motivation in work tasks.

5 **Can we simplify how we think about motivation?** We have covered a lot of material in Chapters 4 and 5 in trying to understand how best to motivate. Recent research suggests that organizational processes should meet the four basic emotional drives of individuals: to acquire, bond, comprehend, and defend. In doing so, a greater level of motivation can be achieved.

for **Review**

1. What role, if any, does money play in employee recognition and job redesign?

2. What are the pros and cons of variable-pay programs from an employee's viewpoint? From management's viewpoint?

3. What is the difference between gainsharing and profit sharing?

4. What is an ESOP? How might it positively influence employee motivation?

5. Why is employee recognition an important reward?

6. What can firms do to create more motivating work environments for their employees?

7. Describe three jobs that score high on the JCM. Describe three jobs that score low.

8. What are the advantages of flextime from an employee's perspective? From management's perspective?

9. What are the advantages of job sharing from an employee's perspective? From management's perspective?

10. From an employee's perspective, what are the pros and cons of telework?

for **Critical Thinking**

1. "Employee recognition may be motivational for the moment, but it doesn't have any staying power. Why? Because employees can't take recognition to Roots or The Bay!" Do you agree or disagree? Discuss.

2. "Performance cannot be measured, so any effort to link pay with performance is a fantasy. Differences in performance are often caused by the system, which means the organization ends up rewarding the circumstances. It's the same thing as rewarding the weather forecaster for a pleasant day." Do you agree or disagree with this statement? Support your position.

3. "Job redesign is a way of exploiting employees by increasing their responsibilities." Comment on this statement, and explain whether you agree with it or not.

4. What can management do to improve employees' perceptions that their jobs are interesting and challenging?

5. Individuals vary in their emotional drives (or needs). How can we use that information to motivate employees?

for **You**

■ Because the people you interact with appreciate recognition, consider including a brief note on a nice card to show thanks for a job well done. Or you might send a basket of flowers. Sometimes just sending a pleasant, thankful email is enough to make a person feel valued. All of these things are easy enough to do, and appreciated greatly by the recipient.

■ If you are working on a team or in a volunteer organization, try to find ways to motivate co-workers using the job characteristics model. For instance, make sure that everyone has some tasks over which they have autonomy, and make sure people get feedback on their work.

■ When you are working on a team project, think about whether everyone on the team should get the same reward, or whether rewards should be allocated according to performance. Individual-based performance rewards may decrease team cohesiveness if individuals do not cooperate with one another.

POINT

Praise Motivates!

Some of the most memorable, and meaningful, words we have ever heard have probably been words of praise.[162] Genuine compliments mean a lot to people—and can go a long way toward inspiring the best performance. Numerous research studies show that students who receive praise from their teachers are more motivated, and often this motivation lasts well after the praise is given. Too often we assume that simple words mean little, but most of us yearn for genuine praise from people in a position to evaluate us.

Companies are starting to learn this lesson. Walt Disney, Lands' End, and Hallmark have worked to use praise as a work reward to motivate employees. A recent research study of two retail stores suggested managers who praise their employees get higher performance out of them.

Praise is important even to long-term relationships. The Gottman Institute, a relationship research and training firm in Seattle, says its research suggests the happiest marriages are those in which couples make five times as many positive statements to and about each other as negative ones.

Finally, a recent neuropsychology study found that praise activated the same part of the human brain as material rewards, which points to another benefit to praise: It may be just as motivating as money and, best of all, it's free.

COUNTERPOINT

Praise Is Highly Overrated

Sure, in theory it's nice to receive compliments, but in practice praise has some real pitfalls. First, a lot of praise is not genuine, and false praise breeds narcissism. Researcher Jean Twenge says scores on narcissism have risen steadily since 1982, and lavishing praise may be the culprit. If told we are wonderful time after time, we start to believe it even when we are not.

Second, praise is paradoxical—if we tell everyone they are special, soon it means nothing to those who do achieve something terrific. In the animated film *The Incredibles*, a superhero's mom tells her son "Everyone's special!" His reply: "Which is another way of saying no one is."

Third, praise can be manipulative. A study of hairdressers found those who complimented their customers earned significantly higher tips. So praise often means the "praiser" wants something from the "praisee."

Fourth, some of the most motivating people are difficult to please. Think of Jack Welch, former CEO of GE, or A. G. Lafley, ex-CEO of Procter & Gamble. They are known for being difficult to please, which means most people will work harder to meet their expectations. When you dish out kudos for an employee who merely shows up, you have sent a message that simply showing up is enough.

Often what people really need is a gentle kick in the pants. As Steve Smolinsky of the Wharton School at the University of Pennsylvania says, "You have to tell students, 'It's not as good as you can do. . . . You can do better.'"

One management consultant says, "People want to know how they're doing. Don't sugarcoat it. Just give them the damn data."

LEARNING ABOUT **YOURSELF** EXERCISE

Is an Enriched Job for You?

People differ in what they like and dislike in their jobs. Listed below are 12 pairs of jobs. For each pair, indicate which job you would prefer. Assume that everything else about the jobs is the same—pay attention only to the characteristics actually listed for each pair of jobs. If you would prefer the job in Column A, indicate how much you prefer it by putting a checkmark in a blank to the left of the Neutral point. If you prefer the job in Column B, check 1 of the blanks to the right of Neutral. Check the Neutral blank only if you find the 2 jobs equally attractive or unattractive. Try to use the Neutral blank rarely.

Column A

Column B

1. A job that offers little or no challenge.

   Strongly prefer A — Neutral — Strongly prefer B

   A job that requires you to be completely isolated from co-workers.

2. A job that pays well.

   Strongly prefer A — Neutral — Strongly prefer B

   A job that allows considerable opportunity to be creative and innovative.

3. A job that often requires you to make important decisions.

   Strongly prefer A — Neutral — Strongly prefer B

   A job in which there are many pleasant people to work with.

4. A job with little security in a somewhat unstable organization.

   Strongly prefer A — Neutral — Strongly prefer B

   A job in which you have little or no opportunity to participate in decisions that affect your work.

5. A job in which greater responsibility is given to those who do the best work.

   Strongly prefer A — Neutral — Strongly prefer B

   A job in which greater responsibility is given to loyal employees who have the most seniority.

6. A job with a manager who sometimes is highly critical.

   Strongly prefer A — Neutral — Strongly prefer B

   A job that does not require you to use much of your talent.

7. A very routine job.

   Strongly prefer A — Neutral — Strongly prefer B

   A job in which your co-workers are not very friendly.

8. A job with a manager who respects you and treats you fairly.

   Strongly prefer A — Neutral — Strongly prefer B

   A job that provides constant opportunities for you to learn new and interesting things.

9. A job that gives you a real chance to develop yourself personally.

   Strongly prefer A — Neutral — Strongly prefer B

   A job with excellent vacation and fringe benefits.

10. A job in which there is a real chance you could be laid off.

    Strongly prefer A — Neutral — Strongly prefer B

    A job with very little chance to do challenging work.

11. A job with little freedom and independence to do your work in the way you think best.

    Strongly prefer A — Neutral — Strongly prefer B

    A job with poor working conditions.

12. A job with very satisfying teamwork.

    Strongly prefer A — Neutral — Strongly prefer B

    A job that allows you to use your skills and abilities to the fullest extent.

OB at work

LEARNING ABOUT **YOURSELF** EXERCISE (Continued)

Scoring Key:

This questionnaire taps the degree to which you have a strong vs. weak desire to obtain growth satisfaction from your work. Each item on the questionnaire yields a score from 1 to 7 (that is, "Strongly prefer A" is scored 1; "Neutral" is scored 4; and "Strongly prefer B" is scored 7). To obtain your individual growth-need strength score, average the 12 items as follows:

Numbers 1, 2, 7, 8, 11, 12 (direct scoring, where "Strongly prefer A" is scored 1)

Numbers 3, 4, 5, 6, 9, 10 (reverse scoring, where "Strongly prefer B" is scored 1)

Average scores for typical respondents are close to the midpoint of 4. Research indicates that if you score high on this measure, you will respond positively to an enriched job. Conversely, if you score low, you will tend not to find enriched jobs satisfying or motivating.

You can use this questionnaire to identify areas where you can improve your interview skills. If you scored 3 or less on any statement, you should consider what you can do to improve that score.

Source: J. R. Hackman and G. R. Oldham, *Work Redesign* (Reading, MA: Addison-Wesley, 1980). Reprinted with permission.

SELF-ASSESSMENT LIBRARY   LEARNING ABOUT YOURSELF

More Learning About Yourself Exercises

An additional self-assessment relevant to this chapter appears on MyOBLab (**www.pearsoned.ca/myoblab**).

I.C.8 What's My Job's Motivating Potential?

When you complete the additional assessment, consider the following:

1. Am I surprised about my score?

2. Would my friends evaluate me similarly?

BREAKOUT **GROUP** EXERCISES

Form small groups to discuss the following topics, as assigned by your instructor:

1. How might the job of student be redesigned to make it more motivating?

2. What is your ideal job? To what extent does it match up with the elements of the JCM?

3. Would you prefer working from home or working at the office? Why?

Analyzing and Redesigning Jobs

Break into groups of 5 to 7 members each.[163] Each student should describe the worst job he or she has ever had. Use any criteria you want to select 1 of these jobs for analysis by the group.

Members of the group will analyze the job selected by determining how well it scores on the job characteristics model. Use the following scale for your analysis of each job dimension:

> **7 = Very high**
>
> **6 = High**
>
> **5 = Somewhat high**
>
> **4 = Moderate**
>
> **3 = Somewhat low**
>
> **2 = Low**
>
> **1 = Very low**

The following sample questions can guide the group in its analysis of the job in question:

- *Skill variety.* Describe the different identifiable skills required to do this job. What is the nature of the oral, written, and/or quantitative skills needed? Physical skills? Does the job holder get the opportunity to use all of his or her skills?

- *Task identity.* What is the product that the job holder creates? Is he or she involved in its production from beginning to end? If not, is he or she involved in a particular phase of its production from beginning to end?

- *Task significance.* How important is the product? How important is the job holder's role in producing it? How important is the job holder's contribution to the people he or she works with? If the job holder's job were eliminated, how inferior would the product be?

- *Autonomy.* How much independence does the job holder have? Does he or she have to follow a strict schedule? How closely is he or she supervised?

- *Feedback.* Does the job holder get regular feedback from his or her manager? From peers? From his or her staff? From customers? How about intrinsic performance feedback when doing the job?

Using the formula found on page 188, calculate the job's motivating potential score. Discuss whether you think this score accurately reflects your perceptions of the motivating potential of these professions.

Using the suggestions offered in the chapter for redesigning jobs, describe specific actions that management could take to increase this job's motivating potential.

Calculate the costs to management of redesigning the job in question. Do the benefits exceed the costs?

Conclude the exercise by having a representative of each group share his or her group's analysis and redesign suggestions with the entire class. Possible topics for class discussion might include similarities in the jobs chosen, problems in rating job dimensions, and the cost-benefit assessment of design changes.

ETHICAL **DILEMMA** EXERCISE

Are CEOs Paid Too Much?

Critics have described the astronomical pay packages given to Canadian and American CEOs as "rampant greed."[164] In 2010, the average total compensation (salary, bonus, share units, stock options, etc.) of Canada's 100 best-paid CEOs was $6 million, an increase of 13 percent over 2009.[165] This was more than 135 times what the average full-time Canadian employee earned in 2010 ($44 365.88).[166]

How do you explain such large pay packages for CEOs? Some say this represents a classic economic response to a situation in which the demand is great for high-quality top-executive talent, and the supply is low. Other arguments in favour of paying executives millions a year are the need to compensate people for the tremendous responsibilities and stress that go with such jobs; the motivating potential that seven- and eight-figure annual incomes provide to senior executives and those who might aspire to be; and the influence of senior executives on the company's bottom line.

Critics of executive pay practices in Canada and the United States argue that CEOs choose board members whom they can count on to support ever-increasing pay for top management. If board members fail to "play along," they risk losing their positions, their fees, and the prestige and power inherent in board membership.

In addition, it is not clear that executive compensation is tied to firm performance. For instance, KPMG found in one survey that for 40 percent of the respondents, there was no correlation between the size of the bonus and how poorly or well the company fared. Consider the data in Exhibit 5-8, which illustrates the disconnect that can sometimes happen between CEO compensation and firm performance. *National Post Business* writers calculate a "Bang for the Buck" formula that can be used to determine which CEOs were overpaid (or underpaid), based on their company's performance between 2006 and 2009.

Is high compensation of CEOs a problem? If so, does the blame for the problem lie with CEOs or with the shareholders and boards that knowingly allow the practice? Are Canadian and American CEOs greedy? Are these CEOs acting unethically? Should their pay reflect more closely some multiple of their employees' wages? What do you think?

EXHIBIT 5-8 2009 Compensation of Canada's "Most Overpaid" CEOs*

CEO(s)	Was Paid (3-Year Avg.)	Should Have Been Paid	Amount Overpaid
1. James Balsillie and Michael Lazaridis, Research In Motion, Waterloo, Ontario	$141 594 333	$16 991 320	$124 603 013
2. William Doyle, Potash Corp. of Saskatchewan Inc., Saskatoon, Saskatchewan	$65 391 333	$4 577 393	$60 813 940
3. Marcel Coutu, Canadian Oil Sands Trust, Calgary, Alberta	$22 853 333	$4 570 667	$18 282 666
4. Edward Sampson, Niko Resources Ltd., Calgary, Alberta	$17 218 667	$860 933	$16 357 734
5. A.Regent, Peter Munk, and G. Wilkins, Barrick Gold Corp., Toronto, Ontario	$19 823 333	$4 955 833	$14 867 500

National Post Business calculated a "Bang for the Buck" formula to derive the amount overpaid, taking into account CEO performance variables.
Source: Based on information in "CEO Scorecard," http://www.financialpost.com/executive/ceo/scorecard/index.html; and "Guide to Using the CEO Scorecard," *Financial Post Magazine*, November 2, 2009.

Thanks for Nothing

Although it may seem fairly obvious that receiving praise and recognition from one's company is a motivating experience, sadly, many companies are failing miserably when it comes to saying thanks to their employees.[167] According to Curt Coffman, global practice leader at Gallup, 71 percent of US employees are "disengaged," essentially meaning that they could not care less about their organization. Coffman states, "We're operating at one-quarter of the capacity in terms of managing human capital. It's alarming." Employee recognition programs, which became more popular as the US economy shifted from industrial to knowledge-based, can be an effective way to motivate employees and make them feel valued. In many cases, however, recognition programs are doing "more harm than good," according to Coffman.

Take Ko, a 50-year-old former employee of a dot-com in California. Her company proudly instituted a rewards program designed to motivate employees. What were the rewards for a job well done? Employees would receive a badge that read "U Done Good" and, each year, would receive a T-shirt as a means of annual recognition. Once an employee received 10 "U Done Good" badges, he or she could trade them in for something bigger and better— a paperweight. Ko states that she would have preferred a raise. "It was patronizing. There wasn't any deep thought involved in any of this." To make matters worse, she says, the badges were handed out arbitrarily and were not tied to performance. And what about those T-shirts? Ko states that the company instilled a strict dress code, so employees could not even wear the shirts if they wanted to. Needless to say, the employee recognition program seemed like an empty gesture rather than a motivator.

Even programs that provide employees with more expensive rewards can backfire, especially if the rewards are given insincerely. Eric Lange, an employee of a trucking company, recalls a time when one of the company's vice-presidents achieved a major financial goal for the company. The vice-president, who worked in an office next to Lange, received a Cadillac Seville as his company car and a new Rolex wristwatch that cost the company $10 000. Both were lavish gifts, but the way they were distributed left a sour taste in the vice-president's mouth. He entered his office to find the Rolex in a cheap cardboard box sitting on his desk, along with a brief letter explaining that he would be receiving a tax form in order to pay taxes on the watch. Lange states of the vice-president, "He came into my office, which was right next door, and said, 'Can you believe this?'" A mere two months later, the vice-president pawned the watch. Lange explains, "It had absolutely no meaning for him."

Such experiences resonate with employees who may find more value in a sincere pat on the back than in gifts from management that either are meaningless or are not conveyed with respect or sincerity. However, sincere pats on the back may be hard to come by. A Gallup poll found that 61 percent of employees stated that they have not received a sincere "thank you" from management in the past year. Findings such as these are troubling, as verbal rewards are not only inexpensive for companies to hand out but also quick and easy to distribute. Of course, verbal rewards do need to be paired sometimes with tangible benefits that employees value—after all, money talks. In addition, when praising employees for a job well done, managers need to ensure that the praise is given in conjunction with the specific accomplishment. In this way, employees may not only feel valued by their organization, but will also know what actions to take to be rewarded in the future.

Questions

1. If praising employees for doing a good job seems to be a fairly easy and obvious motivational tool, why do you think companies and managers don't often do it?

2. As a manager, what steps would you take to motivate your employees after observing them perform well?

3. Are there any downsides to giving employees too much verbal praise? What might these downsides be, and how could you alleviate them as a manager?

4. As a manager, how would you ensure that recognition given to employees is distributed fairly and justly?

Working at Bob's in Rio

Bob's is one of the largest fast-food chains in Latin America.[168] It's a McDonald's clone, with headquarters in Rio de Janeiro and more than half of its 225 outlets located in Brazil. What's it like to work at Bob's? A day at an outlet in a mall in São Paulo provides some insights.

The most notable characteristic of this fast-food restaurant is the youth of the 12 employees. Silvana, who supervises the training of new hires, has had two promotions in her four years on the job. Yet she is only 21 years old. Levy, the short-order cook, is 20 and has been doing his job for a year. Elisangela is 21 and has been a Bob's employee for two years. The restaurant's manager, who has seven years at Bob's, is 23. Simone is one of the oldest employees at 25.

Bob's employees have another commonality besides their youth. They are all from a humble social background. Middle-class kids want to avoid working in fast-food places.

The jobs at Bob's have a highly structured routine. For instance, if you are working the grill, you need to know that a Big Bob gets two slices of beef, 11 grams of lettuce, and 7 grams of sliced onions on a sesame seed bun; a Bob's Burger is also two slices of beef with special sauce but only a slice of tomato on a plain bun; and a

Franburgao gets a chicken breast, tomato, and curry sauce on a sesame seed bun. If you are working the french-fryer, you need to check the temperature of the oil, make sure it's 174 degrees Celsius, put one package of fries into the bin, push it down slowly into the oil until you hear the click, wait for the machine to bring it back up, shake the bin three times, and pour the fries into the steel container.

Employees seem generally content with their jobs. In spite of having to wear a silly red tie, a blue and red baseball cap, and an apron that says Bob's, these people are glad to have a job in a country where as many as one in five is unemployed. Standard employees earn 500 reals (less than $450 Cdn. a month). The manager's salary is around 1300 reals a month.

Questions

1. Describe an entry-level job at Bob's in JCM terms.

2. What type of employee do you think would fit well at Bob's?

3. Could jobs at Bob's be enriched to make employees more productive?

4. Could flextime work at Bob's? Explain.

FROM CONCEPTS TO SKILLS

Designing Enriched Jobs

How does management enrich an employee's job? The following suggestions, based on the JCM, specify the types of changes in jobs that are most likely to lead to improving their motivating potential (also see Exhibit 5-9).[169]

1. *Combine tasks.* Managers should seek to take existing and fractionalized tasks and put them back together to form a new and larger module of work. This increases skill variety and task identity.

2. *Create natural work units.* The creation of natural work units means that the tasks an employee does form an identifiable and meaningful whole. This increases employee "ownership" of the work and improves the likelihood that employees will view their work as meaningful and important rather than as irrelevant and boring.

3. *Establish client relationships.* The client is the user of the product or service that the employee works on (and may be an "internal customer" as well as someone outside the organization). Wherever possible, managers should try to establish direct relationships between employees and their clients. This increases skill variety, autonomy, and feedback for the employee.

4. *Expand jobs vertically.* Vertical expansion gives employees responsibilities and control that were formerly reserved for management. It seeks to partially close the gap between the "doing" and the "controlling" aspects of the job, and it increases employee autonomy.

5. *Open feedback channels.* By increasing feedback, employees not only learn how well they are performing their jobs, but also whether their

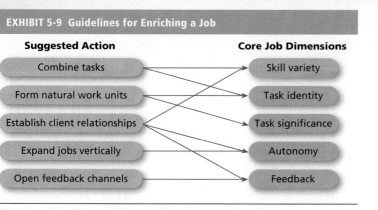

EXHIBIT 5-9 Guidelines for Enriching a Job

Suggested Action	Core Job Dimensions
Combine tasks	Skill variety
Form natural work units	Task identity
Establish client relationships	Task significance
Expand jobs vertically	Autonomy
Open feedback channels	Feedback

Source: J. R. Hackman and J. L. Suttle (eds.), *Improving Life at Work* (Goodyear Pub Co., 1977), p. 138.

performance is improving, deteriorating, or remaining at a constant level. Ideally, this feedback about performance should be received directly as the employee does the job, rather than from management on an occasional basis. For instance, at many restaurants you can find feedback cards on the table to indicate the quality of service received during the meal.

Practising Skills

You own and manage Sunrise Deliveries, a small freight transportation company that makes local deliveries of products for your customers. You have a total of nine employees—an administrative assistant, two warehouse personnel, and six delivery drivers.

The drivers' job is pretty straightforward. Each morning they come in at 7:30 a.m., pick up their daily schedule, and then drive off in their preloaded trucks to make their stops. They occasionally will also pick up packages and return them to the Sunrise warehouse, where they will be unloaded and redirected by the warehouse workers.

You have become very concerned with the high turnover among your drivers. Of your current six drivers, three have been working for you less than two months and only one's tenure exceeds six months. This is frustrating because you are paying your drivers more than many of the larger delivery companies like UPS and FedEx. This turnover is getting expensive because you are constantly having to spend time finding and training replacements. It's also hard to develop a quality customer-service program when customers constantly see new faces. When you have asked departing drivers why they are quitting, common complaints include: "There's no room for advancement," "The job is boring," and "All we do is drive." What should you do to solve this problem?

Reinforcing Skills

1. Think of the worst job you have ever had. Analyze the job according to the five dimensions identified in the JCM. Redesign the job to make it more satisfying and motivating.

2. Spend one to three hours at various times observing employees in your college dining hall. What actions would you recommend to make these jobs more motivating?

6

Groups and Teamwork

How can a team come together and rehearse a new performance in just a few short months?

LEARNING OUTCOMES

1. What are teams and groups?

2. How does one become a team player?

3. Do teams go through stages while they work?

4. How do we create effective teams?

5. Are teams always the answer?

Quebec-based Cirque du Soleil is recognized worldwide for the many creative shows it has produced since its start in 1984.[1] The company has 5000 employees, with 2000 of them located at its headquarters in Montreal. Its employees represent "more than 50 nationalities and speak 25 different languages," which could present challenges in developing a spirit of teamwork.

Teamwork, however, is what Cirque du Soleil does best. According to Lyn Heward, the company's director of creation, "no matter what your product is . . . your results lie in having a passionate strong team of people. People are the driving force. I think because the Cirque's product is the sum total of people, it's a little more evident." Heward notes the importance of building trust so that everyone can work together interdependently. Guy Laliberté, the founder and majority owner of Cirque, emphasizes that the whole is much bigger than the sum of the parts, as each individual employee is "but a quarter note in a grand symphony."

Cirque assesses 60 to 70 new candidates a year, trying to find individuals who will add to the many talented employees on board. Candidates are evaluated on a number of dimensions, but team skills are important. Specifically, recruiters evaluate whether individuals can effectively work in teams to solve problems and whether they generously share ideas with others.

For teams to excel, a number of conditions need to be met. Effective teams need wise leadership, a variety of resources, and a way to solve problems. Team members need to be dedicated, and they need to build trust. In this chapter, we examine when it's best to have a team, how to create effective teams, and how to deal with diversity on teams.

THE BIG IDEA

Effective teams do not simply happen. They require attention to process, team composition, and rewards.

OB IS FOR EVERYONE

- Ever wonder what causes flurries of activity in groups?
- Should individuals be paid for their "teamwork" or their individual performance?
- Why do some teams seem to get along better than others?
- Why don't some team members pull their weight?

SELF-ASSESSMENT LIBRARY
LEARNING ABOUT YOURSELF

- Building and Leading a Team
- Team Efficacy

1 What are teams and groups?

BLOG IT

Are you a good team player?
What is the biggest challenge you have faced working on a team? What caused the challenge, and describe what you did or would have done to resolve the matter.
www.obstudentjournals.blogspot.com

Teams vs. Groups: What's the Difference?

There is some debate whether groups and teams are really separate concepts or whether the two terms can be used interchangeably. We think that there is a subtle difference between the terms. A **group** is two or more people with a common relationship. Thus a group could be co-workers, or people meeting for lunch or standing at the bus stop. Unlike teams, groups do not necessarily engage in collective work that requires inter-dependent effort.

A **team** is "a small number of people with complementary skills who are committed to a common purpose, performance goals, and approach for which they hold themselves mutually accountable."[2] Groups become teams when they meet the following conditions:[3]

- Team members share *leadership*.
- Both individuals and the team as a whole share *accountability* for the work of the team.
- The team develops its own *purpose* or *mission*.
- The team works on *problem-solving* continuously, rather than just at scheduled meeting times.
- The team's measure of *effectiveness* is the team's outcomes and goals, not individual outcomes and goals.

Thus, while not all groups are teams, all teams can be considered groups. Much of what we discuss in this chapter applies equally well to both. We will offer some suggestions on creating effective teams later in the chapter.

Why Have Teams Become So Popular?

How do we explain the current popularity of teams? As organizations have restructured themselves to compete more effectively and efficiently, they have turned to teams as a better way to use employee talents. Management has found that teams are more flexible and responsive to changing events than are traditional departments or other forms of permanent groupings. Teams have the capability to quickly assemble, deploy, refocus, and disband. Teams also can be more motivational. Recall from the job characteristics model in Chapter 5 that having greater task identity is one way of increasing motivation. Teams allow for greater task identity, with team members working on tasks together.

Research suggests that teams typically outperform individuals when the tasks being done require multiple skills, judgment, and experience.[4] However, teams are not necessarily appropriate in every situation. Are teams truly effective? What conditions affect their potential? How do members work together? These are some of the questions we will answer in this chapter.

Types of Teams

Teams can be classified based on their objective. The four most common kinds of teams you are likely to find in an organization are

- Problem-solving (or process-improvement) teams
- Self-managed (or self-directed) teams
- Cross-functional (or project) teams
- Virtual teams

The types of relationships that members within each team have to one another are shown in Exhibit 6-1.

group Two or more people with a common relationship.

team A small number of people who work closely together toward a common objective and are accountable to one another.

EXHIBIT 6-1 Four Types of Teams

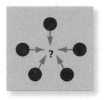

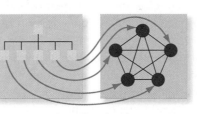

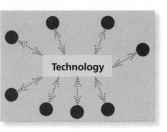

Problem-solving	Self-managed	Cross-functional	Virtual

Problem-Solving Teams

A **problem-solving (or process-improvement) team** is typically made up of 5 to 12 employees from the same department who meet for a few hours each week to discuss ways of improving quality, efficiency, and the work environment.[5] Such teams can also be planning teams, task forces, or committees that are organized to get tasks done. During meetings, members share ideas or offer suggestions on how to improve work processes and methods. Rarely, however, are these teams given the authority to unilaterally implement any of their suggested actions. Montreal-based Clairol Canada is an exception. When a Clairol employee identifies a problem, he or she has the authority to call together an ad hoc group to investigate, and then define and implement solutions. Clairol presents GOC (Group Operating Committee) Awards to teams for their efforts.

Self-Managed Teams

Problem-solving teams were on the right track, but they did not go far enough in involving employees in work-related decisions and processes. This led to experiments with truly autonomous teams that could not only solve problems but also implement solutions and assume responsibility for outcomes.

A **self-managed (or self-directed) team** is typically made up of 10 to 15 employees. The employees perform highly related or interdependent jobs and take on many

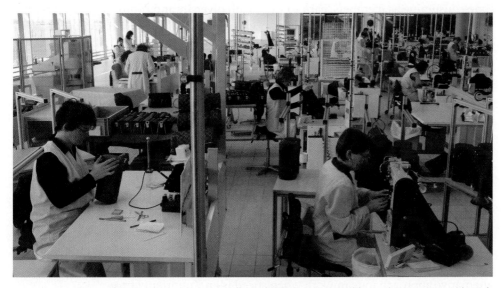

At the Louis Vuitton factory in Ducey, France, all employees work in problem-solving teams, with each team focusing on one product at a time. Team members are encouraged to suggest improvements in manufacturing work methods and processes as well as product quality. When a team was asked to make a test run on a prototype of a new handbag, team members discovered that decorative studs were causing the bag's zipper to bunch up. The team alerted managers, who had technicians move the studs away from the zipper, which solved the problem.

problem-solving (or process-improvement) team A group of 5 to 12 employees from the same department who meet for a few hours each week to discuss ways of improving quality, efficiency, and the work environment.

self-managed (or self-directed) team A group of 10 to 15 employees who take on many of the responsibilities of their former managers.

of the responsibilities of their former managers.[6] Typically, this includes planning and scheduling of work, assigning tasks to members, making operating decisions, taking action on problems, and working with suppliers and customers. Fully self-managed teams even select their own members and leader and have the members evaluate one another's performance. Supervisory positions can take on decreased importance and may even be eliminated.

Research on the effectiveness of self-managed work teams has not been uniformly positive.[7] When disputes arise, members stop cooperating and power struggles ensue, which leads to lower group performance.[8] Moreover, although individuals on these teams do tend to report higher levels of job satisfaction compared with other individuals, they also sometimes have higher absenteeism and turnover rates.

Cross-Functional Teams

As vice-president, operations and special projects for Mississauga, Ontario-based Walmart Canada, Don Swann used a **cross-functional (or project) team** to develop Walmart's Supercentre format for Canada. The team has representatives from all parts of retail business, "including store design, replenishment, systems, merchandising, marketing, operations, HR and finance." He created the cross-functional team because he knew that "we couldn't take a Supercentre from the U.S. and 'drop' it into the Canadian market. We needed to create a Supercentre that was uniquely Canadian."[9]

Cross-functional teams are made up of employees from about the same hierarchical level, but from different work areas, who come together to accomplish a task.[10] For instance, if a business school wanted to design a new integrated curriculum in business for undergraduates, it might bring together a group of faculty members, each of whom represents one discipline (for example, finance, accounting, marketing, and organizational behaviour) to work together to design the new program. Each individual would be expected to contribute knowledge of his or her field, and ways to package together the knowledge in a more integrated fashion.

Cross-functional teams are an effective means for allowing people from diverse areas within an organization (or even between organizations) to exchange information, develop new ideas, solve problems, and coordinate complex projects. Of course, cross-functional teams are not easy to manage.[11] Their early stages of development are often time-consuming as members learn to work with diversity and complexity. It takes time to build trust and teamwork, especially among people from different backgrounds, with different experiences and perspectives.

Skunkworks Skunkworks are cross-functional teams that develop spontaneously to create new products or work on complex problems. Such teams are typically found in the high-tech sector, and are generally sheltered from other organizational members. This gives the team the ability to work on new ideas in isolation, without being watched over by organization members, during creative stages. Skunkworks are thus able to ignore the structure and bureaucratic rules of the organization while they work.

The first skunkworks team appeared in the 1940s, at Lockheed Aerospace Corporation.[12] The team was to create a jet fighter as fast as possible, and avoid bureaucratic delays. In just 43 days, the team of 23 engineers and a group of support personnel put together the first American fighter to fly at more than 800 kilometres an hour.

Not all skunkworks projects are as successful. Many companies, including IBM and Xerox, have had mixed results in using them. Still, skunkworks do offer companies an alternative approach to teamwork when speed is an important factor.

Virtual Teams

Problem-solving, self-managed, and cross-functional teams do their work face to face. **Virtual teams** use computer technology to tie together physically dispersed members

cross-functional (or project) team A group of employees at about the same hierarchical level, but from different work areas, who come together to accomplish a task.

virtual team A team that uses computer technology to tie together physically dispersed members in order to achieve a common goal.

Queen's School of Business started an innovative executive MBA program in 2011 that relies on a virtual team of students. While there are three residential sessions during the program, most courses are taught in virtual boardroom sessions with students participating from home. "The program offers the same real-time connectivity and interactivity as our boardroom learning centres, but offers more accessibility to a top-ranked program to participants who wouldn't otherwise have the time or be able to physically be in a boardroom location on weekends," said Gloria Saccon, director of the executive MBA program.[13]

in order to achieve a common goal.[14] They allow people to collaborate online—using communication links such as wide-area networks, video conferencing, and email—whether they are only a room away or continents apart. Virtual teams are so pervasive, and technology has advanced so far, that it's probably a bit of a misnomer to call these teams "virtual." Nearly all teams today do at least some of their work remotely.

Despite their ubiquity, virtual teams face special challenges. They may suffer because there is less social rapport and less direct interaction among members. They are not able to duplicate the normal give-and-take of face-to-face discussion. Especially when members have not personally met, virtual teams tend to be more task oriented and exchange less social-emotional information than face-to-face teams. Not surprisingly, virtual team members report less satisfaction with the group interaction process than do face-to-face teams. An additional concern about virtual teams is whether members are able to build the same kind of trust that face-to-face teams build. *Focus on Research* explores the trust issue.

FOCUS ON RESEARCH

If I Can't See You, Can I Trust You?

Can team members build trust if they never meet face to face? A study examining how virtual teams work on projects indicates that virtual team members can develop close interaction and trust.[15] These qualities simply evolve differently than in face-to-face groups.

In face-to-face groups, trust comes from direct interaction, over time. In virtual teams, trust is either established at the outset or it generally does not develop. The researchers found that initial electronic messages set the tone for how interactions occurred throughout the project.

In one team, for instance, when the appointed leader sent an introductory message that had a distrustful tone, the team suffered low morale and poor performance throughout the project. The researchers suggest that virtual teams should start with an electronic "courtship," where members provide some personal information. Then the teams should assign clear roles to members, helping members identify with one another.

Finally, the researchers emphasized the importance of a positive outlook. They noted that teams that had the best attitude (eagerness, enthusiasm, and intense action orientation in messages) did considerably better than teams that had one or more pessimists among them.

For virtual teams to be effective, management should ensure that (1) trust is established among team members (one inflammatory remark in a team member email can severely undermine team trust); (2) team progress is monitored closely (so the team does not lose sight of its goals and no team member "disappears"); and (3) the efforts and products of the virtual team are publicized throughout the organization (so the team does not become invisible).[16] For even more tips, see *OB in Action—Managing Virtual Teams*.

OB in ACTION
Managing Virtual Teams

Establishing trust and commitment, encouraging communication, and assessing team members pose tremendous challenges for virtual team managers. Here are a few tips to make the process easier:

→ Establish **regular times** for group interaction.

→ Set up **firm rules** for communication.

→ Use **visual forms of communication** where possible.

→ **Copy the style of face-to-face teams**. For example, allow time for informal chitchat and socializing, and celebrate achievements.

→ **Give and receive feedback** and offer assistance on a regular basis. Be persistent with people who are not communicating with you or one another.

→ Agree on **standard technology** so all team members can work together easily.

→ Consider using **360-degree feedback** to better understand and evaluate team members.

→ Provide a **virtual meeting room** via an intranet, website, or bulletin board.

→ Note which employees **effectively use email** to build team rapport.

→ **Smooth the way for the next assignment** if membership on the team, or the team itself, is not permanent.

→ **Be available** to employees, but don't wait for them to seek you out.

→ Encourage **informal, off-line conversation** between team members.[17]

From Individual to Team Member

2 How does one become a team player?

Ellie Syracopoulos is the manager of Cirque du Soleil's graphic communications team.[18] Her team works behind the scenes to create promotional materials that make Cirque du Soleil's "charm jump out from the page." To achieve the high-quality production she expects, Syracopoulos emphasizes a work environment that encourages creativity. She finds that "open communication, flexibility and gratitude" form the building blocks for that environment.

She insists that when her team is working, they must be focused on each other and the job at hand, and not be confronted with external distractions. Her basic instructions to her team are as follows:

- "Turn off email notifications
- Turn down your phone ringer
- Do not bring your cell phone to a meeting
- Block off time each day to focus on hot projects, and stick to it!"

How can individual team members actually become a team?

For either a group or a team to function, individuals have to achieve some balance between their own needs and the needs of the group. When individuals come together to form groups and teams, they bring with them their personalities and all their previous experiences. They also bring their tendencies to act in different ways at different times, depending on the effects that different situations and different people have on them.

One way to think of these differences is in terms of possible pressures that individual group members put on one another through roles, norms, and status expectations. As we consider the process of how individuals learn to work in groups and teams, we will use the terms interchangeably. Many of the processes that each go through are the same, with the major difference being that teams within the workplace are often set up on a nonpermanent basis, in order to accomplish projects.

Roles

Shakespeare said, "All the world's a stage, and all the men and women merely players." Using the same metaphor, all group members are actors, each playing a **role**. By this term, we mean a set of expected behaviour patterns of a person in a given position in a social unit. The understanding of role behaviour would be dramatically simplified if each of us chose one role and "played it out" regularly and consistently. Unfortunately, we are required to play a number of diverse roles, both on and off our jobs.

As we will see, one of the tasks in understanding behaviour is grasping the role that a person is currently playing. For example, on the job a person might have the roles of electrical engineer, member of middle management, and primary company spokesperson in the community. Off the job, there are still more roles: spouse, parent, church member, food bank volunteer, and coach of the softball team. Many of these roles are compatible; some create conflicts. For instance, how does one's religious involvement influence managerial decisions regarding meeting with clients on the Sabbath? We address role conflict below.

Role Conflict

Most roles are governed by **role expectations**, that is, how others believe a person should act in a given situation. When an individual is confronted by conflicting role expectations, the result is role conflict. **Role conflict** exists when an individual finds that complying with one role requirement may make it more difficult to comply with another.[19] At the extreme, it can include situations in which two or more role expectations are mutually contradictory!

All of us have faced and will continue to face role conflicts. The critical issue, from our standpoint, is how conflicts imposed by different expectations within the organization affect behaviour. Certainly, they increase internal tension and frustration. There are a number of behavioural responses individuals may engage in. They may, for example, give a formalized bureaucratic response. The conflict is then resolved by relying on the rules, regulations, and procedures that govern organizational activities.

For example, an employee faced with the conflicting requirements imposed by the corporate controller's office and his own plant manager decides in favour of his immediate boss—the plant manager. Other behavioural responses may include withdrawal, stalling, negotiation, or redefining the facts or the situation to make them appear congruent.

Role Ambiguity

Role ambiguity exists when a person is unclear about the expectations of his or her role. In teams, role ambiguity can lead to confusion, stress, and even bad feelings. For instance, suppose two group members each think that the other one is responsible for preparing the first draft of a report. At the next group meeting, neither brings a draft report, and both are annoyed that the other person did not do the work.

role A set of expected behaviours of a person in a given position in a social unit.

role expectations How others believe a person should act in a given situation.

role conflict A situation in which an individual finds that complying with one role requirement may make it more difficult to comply with another.

role ambiguity A person is unclear about his or her role.

OB in ACTION

Creating a Team Charter

When you form a new team, you may want to develop a team charter, so that everyone agrees on the basic norms for group performance. Consider including answers to the following in your charter:

→ What are team members' **names and contact information** (e.g., phone, email)?

→ How will **communication** among team members take place (e.g., phone, email)?

→ What will the **team ground rules** be (e.g., where and when to meet, attendance expectations, workload expectations)?

→ How will **decisions** be made (e.g., consensus, majority vote, leader rules)?

→ What **potential conflicts** may arise in the team? Among team members?

→ How will **conflicts be resolved** by the group?[23]

Groups benefit when individuals know their roles. Roles within groups and teams should be balanced. Edgar Schein suggests that **role overload** occurs when what is expected of a person "far exceeds what he or she is able to do."[20] **Role underload** occurs when too little is expected of someone, and that person feels that he or she is not contributing to the group.

Norms

Have you ever noticed that golfers don't speak while their partners are putting on the green, or that employees don't criticize their bosses in public? Why? The answer is "norms!"

Norms are acceptable standards of behaviour within a group that are shared by the group's members. All groups have established norms that tell members what they ought and ought not to do under certain circumstances. When agreed to and accepted by the group, norms act as a means of influencing the behaviour of group members, with a minimum of external controls. Norms differ among groups, communities, and societies, but all of these entities have norms.[21]

Formalized norms are written up in organizational manuals that set out rules and procedures for employees to follow. But, by far, most norms in organizations are informal. You don't need someone to tell you that throwing paper airplanes or engaging in prolonged gossip sessions at the water cooler is an unacceptable behaviour when the "big boss from Toronto" is touring the office. Similarly, we all know that when we are in an employment interview discussing what we did not like about our previous job, there are certain things we should not talk about (such as difficulty in getting along with co-workers or our manager). There are other things it's appropriate to talk about (inadequate opportunities for advancement, or unimportant and meaningless work).

Norms can cover virtually any aspect of group behaviour.[22] Some of the most common norms have to do with issues such as

- *Performance.* How hard to work, the level of output, what kind of quality, levels of tardiness

- *Appearance.* Dress codes, when to look busy, when to "goof off," how to show loyalty

- *Social arrangement.* With whom to eat lunch, whether to form friendships on and off the job

- *Allocation of resources.* Pay, assignments, allocation of tools and equipment

OB in Action—Creating a Team Charter presents a way for teams to develop norms when the team first forms.

The "How" and "Why" of Norms

How do norms develop? Why are they enforced? A review of the research allows us to answer these questions.[24]

Norms typically develop gradually as group members learn what behaviours are necessary for the team to function effectively. Of course, critical events in the group might short-circuit the process and quickly prompt new norms. Most norms develop in one or more of the following four ways:

- *Explicit statements made by a group member.* Often, instructions from the group's supervisor or a powerful member establish norms. The team leader might

role overload Too much is expected of someone.

role underload Too little is expected of someone, and that person feels that he or she is not contributing to the group.

norms Acceptable standards of behaviour within a group that are shared by the group's members.

specifically say that no personal phone calls are allowed during working hours or that coffee breaks must be no longer than 10 minutes.

- *Critical events in the group's history.* These set important precedents. A bystander is injured while standing too close to a machine and, from that point on, members of the work group regularly monitor one another to ensure that no one other than the operator gets within two metres of any machine.

- *Primacy.* The first behavioural pattern that emerges in a group frequently sets team expectations. Groups of students who are friends often choose seats near one another on the first day of class and become upset if an outsider takes "their" seats in a later class.

- *Carry-over behaviours from past situations.* Group members bring expectations with them from other groups to which they have belonged. Thus, work groups typically prefer to add new members who are similar to current ones in background and experience. This is likely to increase the probability that the expectations they bring are consistent with those already held by the group.

Groups don't establish or enforce norms for every conceivable situation, however. The norms that the groups will enforce tend to be those that are important to them.[25] What makes a norm important?

- *It facilitates the group's survival.* Groups don't like to fail, so they seek to enforce any norm that increases their chances for success. This means that groups try to protect themselves from interference from other groups or individuals.

- *It increases the predictability of group members' behaviours.* Norms that increase predictability enable group members to anticipate one another's actions and to prepare appropriate responses.

- *It reduces embarrassing interpersonal problems for group members.* Norms are important if they ensure the satisfaction of their members and prevent as much interpersonal discomfort as possible.

- *It allows members to express the central values of the group and clarify what is distinctive about the group's identity.* Norms that encourage expression of the group's values and distinctive identity help solidify and maintain the group.

Conformity

As a group member, you desire acceptance by the group. Because of your desire for acceptance, you are susceptible to conforming to the group's norms. Considerable evidence shows that the group can place strong pressures on individual members to change their attitudes and behaviours to conform to the group's standard.[26]

The impact that group pressures for **conformity** can have on an individual member's judgment and attitudes was demonstrated in the now classic studies of noted social psychologist Solomon Asch.[27] Asch found that subjects gave answers that they knew were wrong, but that were consistent with the replies of other group members, about 35 percent of the time. The results suggest that group norms can pressure us toward conformity. We desire to be one of the group and avoid being visibly different.

Research by University of British Columbia professor Sandra Robinson and colleague Anne O'Leary-Kelly indicates that conformity may explain why some work groups are more prone to antisocial behaviour than others.[28] Individuals working with others who exhibited antisocial behaviour at work were more likely to engage in antisocial behaviour themselves. Of course, not all conformity leads to negative behaviour. Other research has indicated that work groups can have more positive influences, leading to more prosocial behaviour in the workplace.[29]

conformity Adjusting one's behaviour to align with the norms of the group.

Overall, research continues to indicate that conformity to norms is a powerful force in groups and teams.

Stages of Group and Team Development

3 Do teams go through stages while they work?

As Cirque du Soleil's creative team and cast prepared for the October 2011 opening of *Michael Jackson: The Immortal World Tour*, they faced a number of questions. Would the show capture the magic of Michael Jackson? What was the show's writer and director, Jamie King, going to be like? Who would fill some of the key roles in the show? What would it be like to produce a show unlike any other that Cirque had done in the past? Could the team all work well together? To build a successful team that produces a high-quality, creative performance, Cirque's cast members had to go through several stages. So what stages do teams go through as they develop?

When people get together for the first time with the purpose of achieving some objective, they discover that acting as a team is not something simple, easy, or genetically programmed. Working in a group or team is often difficult, particularly in the initial stages, when people don't necessarily know one another. As time passes, groups and teams go through various stages of development, although the stages are not necessarily exactly the same for each group or team. In this section, we discuss two models of group development. The five-stage model describes the standardized sequence of stages groups pass through. The punctuated-equilibrium model describes the pattern of development specific to temporary groups with deadlines. These models can be applied equally to groups and teams.

The Five-Stage Model

From the mid-1960s, it was believed that groups passed through a standard sequence of five stages.[30] As shown in Exhibit 6-2, these five stages have been labelled *forming, storming, norming, performing,* and *adjourning.* Although we now know that not all groups pass through these stages in a linear fashion, the five-stage model of group development can still help in addressing any anxieties you might have about working in groups and teams. The model shows how individuals move from being independent to working interdependently with group members.

- *Stage I: Forming.* Think about the first time you met with a new team. Do you remember how some people seemed silent and others felt confused about the task you were to accomplish? Those feelings arise during the first stage of group development, known as **forming**. Forming is characterized by a great deal of uncertainty about the team's purpose, structure, and leadership. Members are "testing the waters" to determine what types of behaviour are acceptable. This stage is complete when members have begun to think of themselves as part of a team.

- *Stage II: Storming.* Do you remember how some people in your team just did not seem to get along, and sometimes power struggles even emerged? These reactions are typical of the **storming** stage, which is one of intragroup conflict. Members accept the existence of the team, but resist the constraints that the team imposes on individuality. Furthermore, there is conflict over who will control the team. When this stage is complete, a relatively clear hierarchy of leadership will emerge within the team.

  Some teams never really emerge from the storming stage, or they move back and forth through storming and the other stages. A team that remains forever planted in the storming stage may have less ability to complete the task because of all the interpersonal problems.

forming The first stage in group development, characterized by much uncertainty.

storming The second stage in group development, characterized by intragroup conflict.

EXHIBIT 6-2 Stages of Group Development and Accompanying Issues

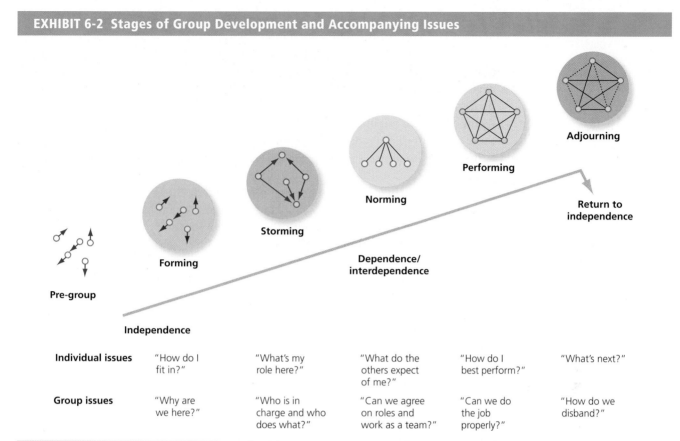

	Forming	Storming	Norming	Performing	Adjourning
Individual issues	"How do I fit in?"	"What's my role here?"	"What do the others expect of me?"	"How do I best perform?"	"What's next?"
Group issues	"Why are we here?"	"Who is in charge and who does what?"	"Can we agree on roles and work as a team?"	"Can we do the job properly?"	"How do we disband?"

- *Stage III: Norming.* Many teams resolve the interpersonal conflict and reach the third stage, in which close relationships develop and the team demonstrates cohesiveness. There is now a strong sense of team identity and camaraderie. This **norming** stage is complete when the team structure solidifies, and the team has assimilated a common set of expectations of what defines correct member behaviour.

- *Stage IV: Performing.* Next, and you may have noticed this in some of your own team interactions, some teams just seem to come together well and start to do their work. This fourth stage, when significant task progress is being made, is called **performing**. The structure at this point is fully functional and accepted. Team energy has moved from getting to know and understand one another to performing the task at hand.

- *Stage V: Adjourning.* For permanent work groups and teams, performing is the last stage in their development. However, for temporary committees, teams, task forces, and similar groups that have a limited task to perform, there is an **adjourning** stage. In this stage, the group prepares for its disbandment. High task performance is no longer the group's top priority. Instead, attention is directed toward wrapping up activities. Group members' responses vary at this stage. Some members are upbeat, basking in the group's accomplishments. Others may be depressed over the loss of camaraderie and friendships gained during the work group's life.

  For some teams, the end of one project may mean the beginning of another. In this case, a team has to transform itself in order to get on with a new project that may need a different focus and different skills, and may need to take on new members. Thus the adjourning stage may lead to renewal of the team to get the next project started.

norming The third stage in group development, characterized by close relationships and cohesiveness.

performing The fourth stage in group development, when the group is fully functional.

adjourning The final stage in group development for temporary groups, where attention is directed toward wrapping up activities rather than task performance.

Putting the Five-Stage Model into Perspective

Many interpreters of the five-stage model have assumed that a group becomes more effective as it progresses through the first four stages. This assumption may be generally true, but what makes a group effective is more complex than this model acknowledges.[31] Under some conditions, high levels of conflict are conducive to high group performance, as long as the conflict is directed toward the task and not toward group members. So we might expect to find situations where groups in Stage II outperform those in Stages III or IV. Similarly, groups do not always proceed clearly from one stage to the next. Sometimes, in fact, several stages go on simultaneously, as when groups are storming and performing at the same time. Teams even occasionally go backwards to previous stages. Therefore, you should not assume that all groups follow the five-stage process precisely, or that Stage IV is always the most preferable.

The five-stage model also ignores organizational context.[32] For instance, a study of a cockpit crew in an airliner found that, within 10 minutes, three strangers assigned to fly together for the first time had become a high-performing team. How could a team come together so quickly? The answer lies in the strong organizational context surrounding the tasks of the cockpit crew. This context provided the rules, task definitions, information, and resources needed for the team to perform. They did not need to develop plans, assign roles, determine and allocate resources, resolve conflicts, and set norms the way the five-stage model predicts.

The Punctuated-Equilibrium Model

Temporary groups with deadlines don't seem to follow the previous model. Studies indicate that temporary groups with deadlines have their own unique sequence of action (or inaction):[33]

- The first meeting sets the group's direction.

- The first phase of group activity is one of inertia.

- A transition takes place at the end of the first phase, which occurs exactly when the group has used up half its allotted time.

- The transition initiates major changes.

- A second phase of inertia follows the transition.

- The group's last meeting is characterized by markedly accelerated activity.

This pattern is called the punctuated-equilibrium model, developed by Professor Connie Gersick, a Visiting Scholar at the Yale University School of Management, and is shown in Exhibit 6-3.[34] It is important for you to understand these shifts in group behaviour, if for no other reason than when you are in a group that is not working well or one that has gotten off to a slow start, you can start to think of ways to help the group move to a more productive phase.

Ever wonder what causes flurries of activity in groups?

Phase 1

As both a team member and possibly a team leader, it's important that you recognize that the first meeting sets the team's direction. A framework of behavioural patterns and assumptions through which the team will approach its project emerges in this first meeting. These lasting patterns can appear as early as the first few seconds of the team's life.

Once set, the team's direction becomes "written in stone" and is unlikely to be re-examined throughout the first half of the team's life. This is a period of inertia—that is, the team tends to stand still or become locked into a fixed course of action. Even if it

EXHIBIT 6-3 The Punctuated-Equilibrium Model

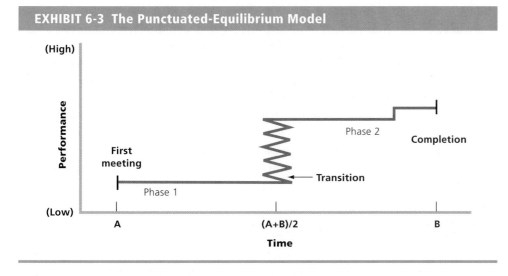

gains new insights that challenge initial patterns and assumptions, the team is incapable of acting on these new insights in Phase 1. You may recognize that in some teams, during the early period of trying to get things accomplished, no one really did his or her assigned tasks. You may also recognize this phase as one where everyone carries out the tasks, but not in a very coordinated fashion. Thus, the team is performing at a relatively low state. This does not necessarily mean that it is doing nothing at all, however.

Phase 2

At some point, the team moves out of the inertia stage and recognizes that work needs to get completed. One of the more interesting discoveries made in these studies was that each team experienced its transition at the same point in its calendar—precisely halfway between its first meeting and its official deadline.[35] The similarity occurred despite the fact that some teams spent as little as an hour on their project, while others spent six months. It was as if the teams universally experienced a midlife crisis at this point. The midpoint appears to work like an alarm clock, heightening members' awareness that their time is limited and that they need to "get moving." When you work on your next team project, you might want to examine when your team starts to "get moving."

This transition ends Phase 1 and is characterized by a concentrated burst of changes, dropping of old patterns, and adoption of new perspectives. The transition sets a revised direction for Phase 2, which is a new equilibrium or period of inertia. In this phase, the team executes plans created during the transition period. The team's last meeting is characterized by a final burst of activity to finish its work. There have been a number of studies that support the basic premise of punctuated equilibrium, though not all of them found that the transition in the team occurred exactly at the midpoint.[36]

Applying the Punctuated-Equilibrium Model

We can use this model to describe typical experiences of student teams created for doing group term projects. At the first meeting, a basic timetable is established. Members size up one another. They agree they have nine weeks to do their project. The instructor's requirements are discussed and debated. From that point, the group meets regularly to carry out its activities. About four or five weeks into the project, however, problems are confronted. Criticism begins to be taken seriously. Discussion becomes more open. The group reassesses where it has been and aggressively moves to make necessary changes. If the right changes are made, the next four or five weeks find the group developing a first-rate project. The group's last meeting, which will probably occur just before the project is due, lasts longer than the others. In it, all final issues are discussed and details resolved.

In summary, the punctuated-equilibrium model characterizes deadline-oriented teams as exhibiting long periods of inertia, interspersed with brief revolutionary changes triggered primarily by their members' awareness of time and deadlines. To use the terminology of the five-stage model, the team begins by combining the *forming* and *norming* stages, then goes through a period of *low performing*, followed by *storming*, then a period of *high performing*, and, finally, *adjourning*.

Several researchers have suggested that the five-stage and punctuated-equilibrium models are at odds with each other.[37] However, it makes more sense to view the models as complementary: The five-stage model considers the interpersonal process of the group, while the punctuated-equilibrium model considers the time challenges that the group faces.[38]

Creating Effective Teams

4 How do we create effective teams?

Cirque du Soleil has a multicultural workforce, with employees representing over 60 different cultures.[39] The company recognizes that it can use this diversity to its advantage by developing and sharing the cultural assets the employees bring to the workplace. Lyn Heward, the company's director of creation, notes that Cirque can draw on "Brazilian percussion and capoeira, Australian didgeridoo, Ukrainian and African dancing, Wushu, Peking Opera and Kung Fu" through the cultural backgrounds of its employees. Diversity can make it harder to be cohesive when teams first develop. Thus, Cirque holds training "boot camps," where new recruits are pushed to their limits. The goal, according to stage director Franco Dragone, is to "turn athletes into artists and form a cohesive team of brothers." What other factors might contribute to the effectiveness of the Cirque du Soleil performers?

When we consider team effectiveness, we refer to such objective measures as the team's productivity, managers' ratings of the team's performance, and aggregate measures of member satisfaction. Some of the considerations necessary to create effective teams are outlined next. However, we are also interested in team process. Exhibit 6-4 lists the characteristics of an effective team.

There is no shortage of efforts that try to identify the factors that lead to team effectiveness.[40] However, studies have taken what was once a "veritable laundry list of characteristics"[41] and organized them into a relatively focused model with four general categories summarized in Exhibit 6-5:[42]

- Resources and other contextual influences that make teams effective

- Team composition

- Work design

- Team process (those things that go on in the team that influence how effective the team is)

Keep in mind two caveats as you review the issues that lead to effective teams:

- First, teams differ in form and structure. Since the model we present attempts to generalize across all varieties of teams, you need to be careful not to rigidly apply the model's predictions to all teams.[44] The model should be used as a guide, not as an inflexible prescription.

OB in ACTION

Harming Your Team

- → **Refuse to share** issues and concerns. Team members refuse to share information and engage in silence, avoidance, and meetings behind closed doors where not all members are included.

- → **Depend** too much **on the leader**. Members rely too much on the leader and do not carry out their responsibilities.

- → **Fail to follow through** on decisions. Teams do not take action after decision making, showing that the needs of the team have low priority, or that members are not committed to the decisions that were made.

- → **Hide conflict**. Team members do not reveal that they have a difference of opinion, and this causes tension.

- → **Fail at conflict resolution**. Infighting, put-downs, and attempts to hurt other members damage the team.

- → **Form subgroups**. The team breaks up into smaller groups that put their needs ahead of the team as a whole.[43]

EXHIBIT 6-4 Characteristics of an Effective Team	
1. **Clear purpose**	The vision, mission, goal, or task of the team has been defined and is now accepted by everyone. There is an action plan.
2. **Informality**	The climate tends to be informal, comfortable, and relaxed. There are no obvious tensions or signs of boredom.
3. **Participation**	There is much discussion, and everyone is encouraged to participate.
4. **Listening**	The members use effective listening techniques such as questioning, paraphrasing, and summarizing to get out ideas.
5. **Civilized disagreement**	There is disagreement, but the team is comfortable with this and shows no signs of avoiding, smoothing over, or suppressing conflict.
6. **Consensus decisions**	For important decisions, the goal is substantial but not necessarily unanimous agreement through open discussion of everyone's ideas, avoidance of formal voting, or easy compromises.
7. **Open communication**	Team members feel free to express their feelings on the tasks as well as on the group's operation. There are few hidden agendas. Communication takes place outside of meetings.
8. **Clear rules and work assignments**	There are clear expectations about the roles played by each team member. When action is taken, clear assignments are made, accepted, and carried out. Work is distributed among team members.
9. **Shared leadership**	While the team has a formal leader, leadership functions shift from time to time depending on the circumstances, the needs of the group, and the skills of the members. The formal leader models the appropriate behaviour and helps establish positive norms.
10. **External relations**	The team spends time developing key outside relationships, mobilizing resources, and building credibility with important players in other parts of the organization.
11. **Style diversity**	The team has a broad spectrum of team-player types including members who emphasize attention to task, goal setting, focus on process, and questions about how the team is functioning.
12. **Self-assessment**	Periodically, the team stops to examine how well it is functioning and what may be interfering with its effectiveness.

Source: G. M. Parker, *Team Players and Teamwork: The New Competitive Business Strategy* (San Francisco: Jossey-Bass, 1990), Table 2, p. 33. Copyright © 1990 by Jossey-Bass Inc., Publishers. Reprinted by permission of John Wiley & Sons, Inc.

- Second, the model assumes that it's already been determined that teamwork is preferable over individual work. Creating "effective" teams in situations where individuals can do the job better is equivalent to solving the wrong problem perfectly.

OB in Action—Harming Your Team presents activities that can make a team ineffective. You might want to evaluate your own team experience against this checklist to give you some idea of how well your team is functioning, or to understand what might be causing problems for your team. Then consider the factors that lead to more effective teams below. For an applied look at the process of building an effective team, see the *Working with Others Exercise* on page 245, which asks you to build a paper tower with teammates and then analyze how the team performed. Also, read this chapter's *Point/ Counterpoint* on page 242 for a debate on whether sports teams are good models for developing effective teams in the workplace.

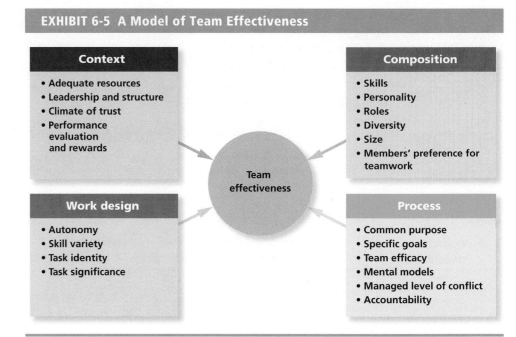

EXHIBIT 6-5 A Model of Team Effectiveness

Context
- Adequate resources
- Leadership and structure
- Climate of trust
- Performance evaluation and rewards

Composition
- Skills
- Personality
- Roles
- Diversity
- Size
- Members' preference for teamwork

Work design
- Autonomy
- Skill variety
- Task identity
- Task significance

Process
- Common purpose
- Specific goals
- Team efficacy
- Mental models
- Managed level of conflict
- Accountability

Team effectiveness

Context

Teams can require a great deal of maintenance to function properly. They need management support, as well as an organizational structure that supports teamwork. The four contextual factors that appear to be most significantly related to team performance are the presence of adequate resources, effective leadership, a climate of trust, and a performance evaluation and reward system that reflects team contributions.

Adequate Resources

All work teams rely on resources outside the team to sustain them. A scarcity of resources directly reduces the ability of a team to perform its job effectively. As one set of researchers concluded, after looking at 13 factors potentially related to team performance, "perhaps one of the most important characteristics of an effective work group is the support the group receives from the organization."[45] This support includes technology, adequate staffing, administrative assistance, encouragement, and timely information.

Teams must receive the necessary support from management and the larger organization if they are going to succeed in achieving their goals.

Leadership and Structure

Leadership plays a crucial role in the development and success of teams.

Professor Richard Hackman of Harvard University, who is the leading expert on teams, suggests that the role of team leader involves the following:[46]

- Creating a real team rather than a team in name only

- Setting a clear and meaningful direction for the team's work

- Making sure that the team structure will support working effectively

- Ensuring that the team operates within a supportive organizational context

- Providing expert coaching

Kerry Molinaro, President of Burlington, Ontario-based IKEA Canada, believes that teams are the best way to bring employees together. IKEA's leadership style is informal, and the company values people who are humble and trustworthy. These qualities also make them good team members.

There are some practical problems that must be resolved when a team first starts working together. Team members must agree on who is to do what, and ensure that all members contribute equally in sharing the workload. The team also needs to determine how schedules will be set, what skills need to be developed, how the team will resolve conflicts, and how the team will make and modify decisions. Agreeing on the specifics of work and how they fit together to integrate individual skills requires team leadership and structure. This leadership, incidentally, can be provided by management or by the team members themselves. Although you might think there is no role for leaders in self-managed teams, that could not be further from the truth. It is true that, in self-managed teams, team members absorb many of the duties typically assumed by managers. However, a manager's job becomes managing *outside* (rather than inside) the team.

Leadership is especially important in **multi-team systems**—where different teams need to coordinate their efforts to produce a desired outcome. In such systems, leaders need to empower teams by delegating responsibility to them, and they need to play the role of facilitator, making sure the teams are coordinating their efforts so that they work together rather than against one another.[47] The *Learning About Yourself Exercise* on page 243 will help you evaluate how suited you are to building and leading a team.

Recent research suggests that women may make better team leaders than men, as *Focus on Research* shows.

FOCUS ON RESEARCH

A Leader's Gender Can Affect Team Performance

Do men's and women's approaches to team leadership lead to different outcomes? "The more women participating equally in a project, the better the outcome," suggests Professor Jennifer Berdahl of the Rotman School of Management at the University of Toronto.[48] Berdahl's research looked at 169 students enrolled in her organizational behaviour courses. She found that all of the teams started out with one person taking a leadership role. However, if the groups were predominantly male, the same person stayed in charge the entire time. In predominantly female teams, women shared leadership roles, and were more egalitarian in how they worked. Male-led teams, whether they were predominantly male groups or mixed-gender groups, received poorer grades on their projects than teams where women shared leadership roles.

Berdahl gives this advice to students: "In a creative project team, it's really important to ensure there is equal opportunity for participation."

A leader, of course, is not always needed. For instance, the evidence indicates that self-managed teams often perform better than teams with formally appointed leaders.[49] Leaders can also obstruct high performance when they interfere with self-managed teams.[50] On self-managed teams, team members absorb many of the duties typically assumed by managers.

Climate of Trust

Members of effective teams trust one another. For team members to achieve a climate of trust, they must feel that the team is capable of getting the task done, and they must believe that "the team will not harm the individual or his or her interests."[51] Interpersonal trust among team members facilitates cooperation, reduces the need to monitor one another's behaviour, and bonds members around the belief that others on the team won't take advantage of them. Team members are more likely to take risks and expose vulnerabilities when they believe they can trust others on their team. *OB in Action—Building Trust* shows the dimensions that underlie the concept of trust.

multi-team systems Systems in which different teams need to coordinate their efforts to produce a desired outcome.

OB in ACTION
Building Trust

The following actions, in order of importance, help build one's trustworthiness.

→ **Integrity**—built through **honesty** and **truthfulness**.

→ **Competence**—demonstrated by technical and interpersonal **knowledge** and **skills**.

→ **Consistency**—shown by **reliability**, **predictability**, and **good judgment** in handling situations.

→ **Loyalty**—one's willingness to **protect** and **stand up** for another person.

→ **Openness**—one's willingness to **share ideas** and **information** freely.[52]

Team members must also trust their leaders.[53] Trust in leadership is important in that it allows the team to be willing to accept and commit to their leader's goals and decisions. Management at Mississauga, Ontario-based Flynn Canada invests in employees to help them become good team players. The company also helps employees build trust in one another so that they can learn to work effectively. Employees are encouraged to take pride in their work and successful outcomes. They are also encouraged to be open with one another. "Personally, what attracted me to Flynn is that it's got scale and horsepower but it has a heart and soul; it's not just another corporate entity. We are authentic in our interactions with each other. What you see is what you get," says Gerard Montocchio, vice-president of human resources."[54]

Performance Evaluation and Rewards

How do you get team members to be both individually and jointly accountable? The traditional individually oriented evaluation must be modified to reflect team performance.[55]

Individual performance evaluations, fixed hourly wages, individual incentives, and the like are not consistent with the development of high-performance teams. So in addition to evaluating and rewarding employees for their individual contributions, management should consider group-based appraisals, profit sharing, gainsharing, small-group incentives, and other system modifications that will reinforce team effort and commitment. Managers need to carefully consider the balance between paying on the basis of group performance[56] and the level of trust among team members. Recent research found that when team members did not trust their colleagues' ability, honesty, and dependability, they preferred individual-based rewards rather than team-based rewards. Even when trust improved over time from working together, there was still a preference for individual-based rewards, suggesting that "teams must have a very high level of trust for members to truly embrace group-based pay."[57]

One additional consideration when deciding whether and how to reward team members is the effect of pay dispersion on team performance. Research by Nancy Langton, your Vancouver-based author, shows that when there is a large discrepancy in wages among group members, collaboration is lowered.[58] A study of baseball player salaries also found that teams where players were paid more similarly often outperformed teams with highly paid "stars" and lowly paid "scrubs."[59] How teams are structured and rewarded is the topic of *Focus on Research*.

> Should individuals be paid for their "teamwork" or their individual performance?

FOCUS ON RESEARCH

The Impact of Rewards on Team Functioning

Can competitive teams learn to cooperate? Researchers at Michigan State University composed 80 four-person teams from undergraduate business students.[60] In a command-and-control computer simulation developed for the US Department of Defense, each team's mission was to monitor a geographic area, keep unfriendly forces from moving in, and support friendly forces. Team members played on networked computers, and performance was measured by both speed (how quickly they identified targets and friendly forces) and accuracy (the number of friendly fire errors and missed opportunities).

Teams were rewarded either cooperatively (in which case team members shared rewards equally) or competitively (in which case team members were rewarded based on their individual contributions). After playing a few rounds, the reward structures were switched so that the cooperatively rewarded teams were given competitive rewards and the competitively rewarded teams were now cooperatively rewarded.

The researchers found the initially cooperatively rewarded teams easily adapted to the competitive reward conditions and learned to excel. However, the formerly competitively rewarded teams could not adapt to cooperative rewards. It seems teams that start out being cooperative can learn to be competitive, but competitive teams find it much harder to learn to cooperate.

In a follow-up study, researchers found the same results: cooperative teams more easily adapted to competitive conditions than competitive teams did to cooperative conditions. However, they also found competitive teams could adapt to cooperative conditions when given freedom to allocate their roles (as opposed to having the roles assigned). That freedom may lead to intrateam cooperation, and thus the process of structuring team roles helps the formerly competitive team learn to be cooperative.

Composition

This category includes variables that relate to how teams should be staffed. In this section, we will address the skills, personality, and roles of team members, the diversity and size of the team, and members' preference for teamwork.

Skills

To perform effectively, a team requires three different types of skills:

1. It needs people with *technical expertise*.

2. It needs people with the *problem-solving* and *decision-making skills* to be able to identify problems, generate alternatives, evaluate those alternatives, and make competent choices.

3. It needs people with good listening, feedback, conflict resolution, and other *interpersonal skills*.[61]

No team can achieve its performance potential without developing all three types of skills. The right mix is crucial. Too much of one at the expense of others will result in lower team performance. But teams don't need to have all the complementary skills in place at the beginning. It's not uncommon for one or more members to take responsibility to learn the skills in which the group is deficient, thereby allowing the team to reach its full potential. Exhibit 6-6 identifies some important teamwork skills that help teams function well.

Personality

Teams have different needs, and people should be selected for the team on the basis of their personalities and preferences, as well as the team's needs for diversity and specific roles. We demonstrated in Chapter 2 that personality has a significant influence on individual employee behaviour. This can also be extended to team behaviour.

Many of the dimensions identified in the Big Five Personality Model have been shown to be relevant to team effectiveness. A recent review of the literature suggests that three

Why do some teams seem to get along better than others?

EXHIBIT 6-6	Teamwork Skills
Orients team to problem-solving situation	Assists the team in arriving at a common understanding of the situation or problem. Determines the important elements of a problem situation. Seeks out relevant data related to the situation or problem.
Organizes and manages team performance	Helps team establish specific, challenging, and accepted team goals. Monitors, evaluates, and provides feedback on team performance. Identifies alternative strategies or reallocates resources to address feedback on team performance.
Promotes a positive team environment	Assists in creating and reinforcing norms of tolerance, respect, and excellence. Recognizes and praises other team members' efforts. Helps and supports other team members. Models desirable team member behaviour.
Facilitates and manages task conflict	Encourages desirable and discourages undesirable team conflict. Recognizes the type and source of conflict confronting the team and implements an appropriate resolution strategy. Employs "win-win" negotiation strategies to resolve team conflicts.
Appropriately promotes perspective	Defends stated preferences, argues for a particular point of view, and withstands pressure to change position for another that is not supported by logical or knowledge-based arguments. Changes or modifies position if a defensible argument is made by another team member. Projects courtesy and friendliness to others while arguing position.

Source: G. Chen, L. M. Donahue, and R. J. Klimoski, "Training Undergraduates to Work in Organizational Teams," *Academy of Management Learning & Education* 3, no. 1 (March 2004), p. 40. Copyright © Academy of Management, 2002.

of the Big Five traits are especially important for team performance.[62] Specifically, teams that rate higher on mean levels of conscientiousness and openness to experience tend to perform better. Moreover, a 2011 study found that the level of team member agreeableness also matters: Teams did worse when they had one or more highly disagreeable members.[63] Perhaps one bad apple *can* spoil the whole bunch!

Research has also provided us with a good idea about why these personality traits are important to teams. Conscientious people are valuable in teams because they are good at backing up other team members, and they are also good at sensing when that support is truly needed. Open team members communicate better with one another and throw out more ideas, which leads teams composed of open people to be more creative and innovative.[64]

Even if an organization does a really good job of selecting individuals for team roles, most likely they will find there are not enough, say, conscientious people to go around. Suppose an organization needs to create 20 teams of 4 people each and has 40 highly conscientious people and 40 who score low on conscientiousness. Would the organization be better off (a) putting all the conscientious people together (forming 10 teams with the highly conscientious people and 10 teams of members low on conscientiousness) or (b) "seeding" each team with 2 people who scored high and 2 who scored low on conscientiousness?

Perhaps surprisingly, the evidence tends to suggest that option (a) is the best choice; performance across the teams will be higher if the organization forms 10 highly conscientious teams and 10 teams low in conscientiousness. "This may be because, in such teams, members who are highly conscientious not only must perform their own tasks but also must perform or re-do the tasks of low-conscientious members. It may also be because such diversity leads to feelings of contribution inequity."[65]

Roles

Teams have different needs, and members should be selected to ensure all the various roles are filled. A study of 778 major league baseball teams over a 21-year period highlights the importance of assigning roles appropriately.[66] As you might expect, teams with more experienced and skilled members performed better. However, the experience and skill of those in core roles who handle more of the workflow of the team, and who are central to all work processes (in this case, pitchers and catchers), were especially vital. In other words, put your most able, experienced, and conscientious workers in the most central roles in a team.

Within almost any group, two sets of role relationships need to be considered: task-oriented roles and maintenance roles. **Task-oriented roles** are performed by group members to ensure that the tasks of the group are accomplished. These roles include initiators, information seekers, information providers, elaborators, summarizers, and consensus makers. **Maintenance roles** are carried out to ensure that group members maintain good relations. These roles include harmonizers, compromisers, gatekeepers, and encouragers.

Effective teams maintain some balance between task orientation and maintenance of relations. Exhibit 6-7 identifies a number of task-oriented and maintenance behaviours in the key roles that you might find in a team.

On many teams, there are individuals who will be flexible enough to play multiple roles and/or complete one another's tasks. This is an obvious plus to a team because it greatly improves its adaptability and makes it less reliant on any single member.[67] Selecting members who themselves value flexibility, and then cross-training them to be able to do one another's jobs, should lead to higher team performance over time.

Diversity

Group diversity refers to the presence of a heterogeneous mix of individuals within a group.[68] Individuals can be different not only in functional characteristics (jobs, positions, or work experiences) but also in demographic or cultural characteristics (age, race, sex, and citizenship). Many of us hold the optimistic view that diversity should be a good thing—diverse teams should benefit from differing perspectives and do better. Two meta-analytic reviews of the research literature show, however, that demographic diversity is essentially unrelated to team performance overall.[69] One qualifier is that gender and ethnic diversity have more negative effects in occupations dominated by white or male employees, but in more demographically balanced occupations, diversity is less of a problem. Diversity in function and expertise are positively related to group performance, but these effects are quite small and depend on the situation.

One of the pervasive challenges with teams is that while diversity may have real potential benefits, a team is deeply focused on commonly held information. But to realize their creative potential, diverse teams need to focus not on their similarities but on their differences. Some evidence suggests that when team members believe others have more expertise, they will work to support those members, leading to higher levels of effectiveness.[70] The key is for members of diverse teams to communicate what they uniquely know and also what they don't know. Proper leadership can also improve the performance of diverse teams. When leaders provide an inspirational common goal for members with varying types of education and knowledge, teams are very creative. When leaders don't provide such goals, diverse teams fail to take advantage of their unique skills and are actually *less* creative than teams with homogeneous skills.

Size

Generally speaking, the most effective teams have five to nine members. And experts suggest using the smallest number of people who can do the task. Unfortunately, there is a pervasive tendency for managers to err on the side of making teams too large. While a minimum of four or five may be necessary to develop diversity of views and skills, managers seem to seriously underestimate how coordination problems can dramatically increase as team members are added. When teams have excess members, cohesiveness and mutual accountability decline, social loafing increases, and more and more people

task-oriented roles Roles performed by group members to ensure that the tasks of the group are accomplished.

maintenance roles Roles performed by group members to maintain good relations within the group.

group diversity The presence of a heterogeneous mix of individuals within a group.

EXHIBIT 6-7 Roles Required for Effective Team Functioning			
	Function	**Description**	**Example**
Roles that build task accomplishment	*Initiating*	Stating the goal or problem, making proposals about how to work on it, setting time limits.	"Let's set up an agenda for discussing each of the problems we have to consider."
	Seeking information and opinions	Asking group members for specific factual information related to the task or problem, or for their opinions about it.	"What do you think would be the best approach to this, Jack?"
	Providing information and opinions	Sharing information or opinions related to the task or problems.	"I worked on a similar problem last year and found..."
	Clarifying	Helping one another understand ideas and suggestions that come up in the group.	"What you mean, Sue, is that we could . . . ?"
	Elaborating	Building on one another's ideas and suggestions.	"Building on Don's idea, I think we could . . ."
	Summarizing	Reviewing the points covered by the group and the different ideas stated so that decisions can be based on full information.	Appointing a recorder to take notes on a blackboard.
	Consensus taking	Providing periodic testing on whether the group is nearing a decision or needs to continue discussion.	"Is the group ready to decide about this?"
Roles that build and maintain a team	*Harmonizing*	Mediating conflict among other members, reconciling disagreements, relieving tensions.	"Don, I don't think you and Sue really see the question that differently."
	Compromising	Admitting error at times of group conflict.	"Well, I'd be willing to change if you provided some help on . . ."
	Gatekeeping	Making sure all members have a chance to express their ideas and feelings and preventing members from being interrupted.	"Sue, we haven't heard from you on this issue."
	Encouraging	Helping a group member make his or her point. Establishing a climate of acceptance in the group.	"I think what you started to say is important, Jack. Please continue."

Source: From Ancona / Kochan / Scully / Van Maanen. Managing for the Future, 1E. © 1996 South-Western, a part of Cengage Learning, Inc. Reproduced by permission. www.cengage.com/permissions

do less talking compared with others. So in designing effective teams, managers should try to keep the number of members to less than 10. If a work unit is larger and you want a team effort, consider breaking the unit into subteams.[71] Uneven numbers in teams may help provide a mechanism to break ties and resolve conflicts, while an even number of team members may foster the need to create more consensus.

Size and Social Loafing   One of the most important findings related to the size of a team has been labelled **social loafing**. Social loafing is the tendency for individuals

social loafing The tendency for individuals to expend less effort when working collectively than when working individually.

Employees in Taigu County, China, are collecting harvest grapes for the production of red wine. In collectivist societies such as China, employees perform better in a group than when working alone and they are less likely to engage in social loafing. Unlike individualistic cultures such as the United States, where people are dominated by self-interest, the Chinese are motivated by in-group goals.

to expend less effort when working collectively than when working individually.[72] It directly challenges the logic that the productivity of the team as a whole should at least equal the sum of the productivity of each individual in that team. Research looking at teams working on a rope-pulling task showed, the larger the team, the less individual effort expended.[73] One person pulling on a rope alone exerted an average of 63 kilograms of force. In groups of three, per-person force dropped to 53 kilograms. And in groups of eight, it fell to only 31 kilograms per person. Other research supports these findings.[74] More may be better in the sense that the total productivity of a group of four is greater than that of one or two people, but the individual productivity of each group member declines.

What causes this social loafing effect? It may be due to a belief that others in the team are not carrying their fair share. If you view others as lazy or inept, you can re-establish equity by reducing your effort. Another explanation is the dispersion of responsibility. Because the results of the team cannot be attributed to any single person, the relationship between an individual's input and the team's output is clouded. In such situations, individuals may be tempted to become "free riders" and coast on the team's efforts. In other words, there will be a reduction in efficiency when individuals believe that their contribution cannot be measured. To reduce social loafing, teams should not be larger than necessary, and individuals should be held accountable for their actions. You might also consider the ideas presented on dealing with shirkers in this chapter's *Ethical Dilemma Exercise* on page 245.

> Why don't some team members pull their weight?

Members' Preference for Teamwork

Not every employee is a team player. Given the option, many employees will "select themselves out" of team participation. When people who would prefer to work alone are required to team up, there is a direct threat to the team's morale.[75] This suggests that, when selecting team members, individual preferences should be considered, as well as abilities, personalities, and skills. High-performing teams are likely to be composed of people who prefer working as part of a team. *Case Incident—Toyota's Team Culture* on page 246 discusses how the auto manufacturer hires employees who are more likely to be good team members.

Work Design

Effective teams need to work together and take collective responsibility to complete significant tasks. They must be more than a "team-in-name-only."[76] The work design category includes variables such as freedom and autonomy, the opportunity to utilize different skills and talents, the ability to complete a whole and identifiable task or product, and the participation in a task or project that has a substantial impact on others. The evidence indicates that these characteristics enhance member motivation and increase team effectiveness.[77] These work design characteristics motivate teams because they increase members' sense of responsibility and ownership over the work, and because they make the work more interesting to perform.[78] These recommendations are consistent with the job characteristics model we presented in Chapter 5.

Process

Process variables make up the final component of team effectiveness. The process category includes member commitment to a common purpose, establishment of specific goals, team efficacy, shared mental models, a managed level of conflict, and a system of accountability. These will be especially important in larger teams, and in teams that are highly interdependent.[79]

Why are processes important to team effectiveness? We learned from social loafing that 1 + 1 + 1 does not necessarily add up to 3. When each member's contribution is not clearly visible, individuals tend to decrease their effort. Social loafing, in other words, illustrates a process loss from using teams. But teams should create outputs greater than the sum of their inputs, as when a diverse group develops creative alternatives. Exhibit 6-8 illustrates how group processes can have an impact on a group's actual effectiveness.[80] Scientists often work in teams because they can draw on the diverse skills of various individuals to produce more meaningful research than could be generated by all the researchers working independently—that is, they produce positive synergy, and their process gains exceed their process losses.

Common Purpose

Effective teams begin by analyzing the team's mission, developing goals to achieve that mission, and creating

At the Olympic Village for the 2010 Winter Games in Vancouver, teams were housed in apartment buildings. In short order, teams put up their country's flags on balconies in a display of team spirit. The Australian team, however, also put up their boxing Kangaroo flag. The International Olympic Committee asked them to take it down because the flag is a commercial trademark, but the team refused, as they viewed it as their good luck charm. Many Canadians in Vancouver sided with the Australians, and the Australians' iconic flag did not come down.

EXHIBIT 6-8 Effects of Group Processes

Potential group effectiveness + Process gains − Process losses = Actual group effectiveness

A study of 23 National Basketball Association teams found that "shared experience"—tenure on the team and time on court—tended to improve turnover and boost win-loss performance significantly. Why do you think teams that stay together longer tend to play better?

strategies for achieving the goals. Teams that establish a clear sense of what needs to be done and how consistently perform better.[81] Members of successful teams put a tremendous amount of time and effort into discussing, shaping, and agreeing upon a purpose that belongs to them both collectively and individually. This common purpose, when accepted by the team, becomes the equivalent of what celestial navigation is to a ship captain—it provides direction and guidance under any and all conditions. Like a ship following the wrong course, teams that don't have good planning skills are doomed; perfectly executing the wrong plan is a lost cause.[82] Effective teams also show **reflexivity**, meaning that they reflect on and adjust their master plan when necessary. A team has to have a good plan, but it also has to be willing and able to adapt when conditions call for it.[83]

Specific Goals

Successful teams translate their common purpose into specific, measurable, and realistic performance goals. Just as we demonstrated in Chapter 4, how goals lead individuals to higher performance, goals also energize teams. These specific goals facilitate clear communication. They also help teams maintain their focus on achieving results.

Consistent with the research on individual goals, team goals should be challenging. Difficult goals have been found to raise team performance on those criteria for which they are set. So, for instance, goals for quantity tend to raise quantity, goals for speed tend to raise speed, goals for accuracy tend to raise accuracy, and so on.[84]

Team Efficacy

Effective teams have confidence in themselves. They believe they can succeed. We call this team *efficacy*.[85] Teams that have been successful raise their beliefs about future success, which, in turn, motivates them to work harder.

One of the factors that helps teams build their efficacy is **cohesiveness**—the degree to which members are attracted to one another and are motivated to stay on the team.[86] Though teams differ in their cohesiveness, it is important because it has been found to be related to the team's productivity.[87]

reflexivity A team characteristic of reflecting on and adjusting the master plan when necessary.

cohesiveness The degree to which team members are attracted to one another and are motivated to stay on the team.

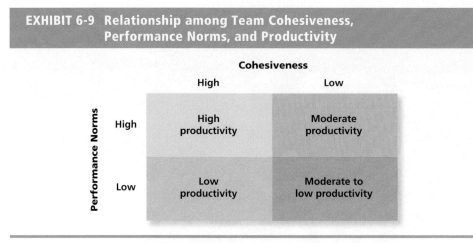

EXHIBIT 6-9 Relationship among Team Cohesiveness, Performance Norms, and Productivity

OB in ACTION
Increasing Group Cohesiveness

To increase socio-emotional cohesiveness:

→ Keep the group relatively **small**.

→ Strive for a **favourable public image** to increase the status and prestige of belonging.

→ Encourage **interaction** and **cooperation**.

→ Emphasize members' **common characteristics** and interests.

→ **Point out environmental threats** (e.g., competitors' achievements) to rally the group.

To increase instrumental cohesiveness:

→ Regularly update and **clarify the group's goal(s)**.

→ Give every group member a **vital "piece of the action."**

→ Channel each group member's special talents toward the **common goal(s)**.

→ **Recognize** and equitably reinforce **every member's contributions**.

→ Frequently remind group members they **need one another** to get the job done.[88]

Studies consistently show that the relationship of cohesiveness and productivity depends on the performance-related norms established by the group.[89] If performance-related norms are high (for example, high output, quality work, cooperation with individuals outside the group), a cohesive group will be more productive than a less cohesive group. If cohesiveness is high and performance norms are low, productivity will be low. If cohesiveness is low and performance norms are high, productivity increases—but less than in the high cohesiveness–high norms situation. Where cohesiveness and performance-related norms are both low, productivity will tend to fall into the low-to-moderate range. These conclusions are summarized in Exhibit 6-9.

Most studies of cohesiveness focus on socio-emotional cohesiveness, the "sense of togetherness that develops when individuals derive emotional satisfaction from group participation."[90] There is also instrumental cohesiveness: the "sense of togetherness that develops when group members are mutually dependent on one another because they believe they could not achieve the group's goal by acting separately." Teams need to achieve a balance of these two types of cohesiveness to function well. *OB in Action—Increasing Group Cohesiveness* indicates how to increase both socio-emotional and instrumental cohesiveness.

What, if anything, can management do to increase team efficacy? Two possible options are helping the team to achieve small successes and skill training. Small successes build team confidence. As a team develops an increasingly stronger performance record, it also increases the collective belief that future efforts will lead to success. In addition, managers should consider providing training to improve members' technical and interpersonal skills. The greater the abilities of team members, the greater the likelihood that the team will develop confidence and the capability to deliver on that confidence.

Mental Models

Effective teams have accurate and common **mental models**—knowledge and beliefs (a "psychological map") about how the work gets done. If team members have the wrong mental models, which is particularly likely to happen with teams under acute stress, their performance suffers.[91] For example, in the Iraq war, many military leaders

mental models Team members' knowledge and beliefs about how the work gets done by the team.

said they underestimated the power of the insurgency and the infighting among Iraqi religious sects. The similarity of team members' mental models matters, too. If team members have different ideas about how to do things, the teams will fight over how to do things rather than focus on what needs to be done.[92]

Managed Level of Conflict

Conflict on a team is not necessarily bad. Though relationship conflicts—those based on interpersonal incompatibilities, tension, and animosity toward others—are almost always dysfunctional, teams that are completely void of conflict are likely to be less effective, with the members becoming withdrawn and only superficially harmonious.[93] On teams performing nonroutine activities, disagreements among members about task content (called *task conflicts*) stimulate discussion, promote critical assessment of problems and options, and can lead to better team decisions. The way conflicts are resolved can also make the difference between effective and ineffective teams. Effective teams resolved conflicts by explicitly discussing the issues, whereas ineffective teams had conflicts focused more on personalities and the way things were said.[94]

Kathleen Eisenhardt of the Stanford Graduate School of Business and her colleagues studied top management teams in technology-based companies to understand how they manage conflict.[96] Their research identified six tactics that helped teams successfully manage the interpersonal conflict that can accompany group interactions. These are presented in *OB in Action—Reducing Team Conflict*. By handling the interpersonal conflict well, these groups were able to achieve their goals without letting conflict get in the way.

Groups need mechanisms by which they can manage the conflict, however.[97] From the research reported above, we could conclude that sharing information and goals, and striving to be open and get along, are helpful strategies for negotiating our way through the maze of conflict. A sense of humour, and a willingness to understand the points of others without insisting that everyone agree on all points, are also important. Group members should try to focus on the issues, rather than on personalities, and strive to achieve fairness and equity in the group process.

Accountability

Successful teams make members individually and jointly accountable for the team's purpose, goals, and approach.[98] They clearly define what they are individually responsible for and what they are jointly responsible for. This reduces the ability for individuals to engage in social loafing. *From Concepts to Skills* on pages 248–249 discusses how to conduct effective team meetings.

Beware! Teams Aren't Always the Answer

Despite considerable success in the use of teams, they are not necessarily appropriate in all situations, as Exhibit 6-10 suggests. Teamwork takes more time and often more resources than individual work. Teams have increased communication demands, conflicts to be managed, and meetings to be run. So the benefits of using teams have to exceed the costs, and that is not always the case.[99] A study done by Statistics Canada found that the introduction of teamwork lowered turnover in the service industries, for both high- and low-skilled employees. However, manufacturing companies experienced higher turnover if they introduced teamwork and formal teamwork training, compared with not doing so (15.8 percent vs. 10.7 percent).[100]

OB in ACTION
Reducing Team Conflict

→ Work with **more, rather than less, information,** and debate on the basis of facts.

→ Develop **multiple alternatives** to enrich the level of debate.

→ Develop commonly agreed-upon **goals**.

→ Use **humour** when making tough decisions.

→ Maintain a **balanced power** structure.

→ Resolve issues **without forcing consensus**.[95]

 Are teams always the answer?

EXHIBIT 6-10

Source: Dlibert, reprinted by permission of Universal Uclick.

How do you know if the work of your group would be better done in teams? It's been suggested that three tests be applied to see if a team fits the situation:[101]

- *Can the work be done better by more than one person?* Simple tasks that don't require diverse input are probably better left to individuals.

- *Does the work create a common purpose or set of goals for the people in the group that is more than the sum of individual goals?* For instance, the service departments of many new-car dealers have introduced teams that link customer service personnel, mechanics, parts specialists, and sales representatives. Such teams can better manage collective responsibility for ensuring that customers' needs are properly met.

- *Are the members of the group interdependent?* Teams make sense where there is interdependence between tasks—where the success of the whole depends on the success of each one, *and* the success of each one depends on the success of the others. Soccer, for instance, is an obvious *team* sport because of the interdependence of the players. Swim teams, by contrast, except for relays, rely heavily on individual performance to win a meet. They are groups of individuals performing individually, whose total performance is merely the aggregate summation of their individual performances.

GLOBAL IMPLICATIONS

Research on global considerations in the use of teams is just beginning, but four areas are particularly worth mentioning: the extent of teamwork, self-managed teams, team cultural diversity, and group cohesiveness.

Extent of Teamwork

One study comparing US workers to Canadian and Asian workers revealed that 51 percent of workers in Asian-Pacific countries and 48 percent of Canadian employees report high levels of teamwork. But only 32 percent of US employees say their organization has a high level of teamwork.[102] Thus, Canadians engage in a great deal more teamwork than do Americans.

Self-Managed Teams

Evidence suggests self-managed teams have not fared well in Mexico, largely due to that culture's low tolerance of ambiguity and uncertainty and employees' strong respect for hierarchical authority.[103] Thus, in countries relatively high in power distance—where roles of leaders and followers are clearly delineated—a team may need to be structured so leadership roles are spelled out and power relationships identified.

Team Cultural Diversity and Team Performance

How do teams composed of members from different countries perform? The evidence indicates that the cultural diversity of team members interferes with team processes, at least in the short term.[104] However, cultural diversity does seem to be an asset for tasks that call for a variety of viewpoints. But culturally heterogeneous team members have more difficulty learning to work with one another and solving problems. The good news is while newly formed culturally diverse teams underperform newly formed culturally homogeneous teams, the differences disappear after about three months.[105] Fortunately, some team performance–enhancing strategies seem to work well in many cultures. One study found that teams in the European Union made up of members from collectivistic and individualistic countries benefited equally from group goals.[106] Read about IBM's use of multicultural project teams in *Case Incident—IBM's Multicultural Multinational Teams* on page 247.

Group Cohesiveness

Researchers studied teams from an international bank with branches in the United States (an individualistic culture) and in Hong Kong (a collectivistic culture) to determine the factors that affected group cohesiveness.[107] Teams were entirely composed of individuals from the branch country. The results showed that, regardless of what culture the teams were from, giving teams difficult tasks and more freedom to accomplish those tasks created a more tight-knit group. Consequently, team performance was enhanced.

However, the teams differed in the extent to which increases in task complexity and autonomy resulted in greater group cohesiveness. Teams in individualistic cultures responded more strongly than did teams in collectivistic cultures, became more united and committed, and, as a result, received higher performance ratings from their supervisors than did teams from collectivistic cultures.

These findings suggest that individuals from collectivistic cultures already have a strong predisposition to work together as a group, so there is less need for increased cohesiveness. However, managers in individualistic cultures may need to work harder to increase team cohesiveness. One way to do this is to give teams more challenging assignments and provide them with more independence.

Summary and Implications

1 **What are teams and groups?** Groups and teams differ. The outputs of groups are simply the sum of individual efforts. A team, because of the close collaboration among members, produces output that is greater than the sum of individual efforts. Teams have become an essential part of the way business is being done these days. In fact, it is more surprising to find an organization that *does not* use teams. Teams can be classified based on their objective. The four most common forms of teams you are likely to find in an organization are problem-solving (or process-improvement) teams; self-managed (or self-directed) teams; cross-functional (or project) teams; and virtual teams. A problem-solving team meets for a few hours each week to discuss ways of improving quality, efficiency, and the work environment. A self-managed team consists of members who take on many responsibilities of their former managers and direct themselves. A cross-functional team consists of employees from about the same hierarchical level, but from different work areas, who come together to accomplish a task. A virtual team uses computer technology to tie together physically dispersed members in order to achieve a common goal.

2 **How does one become a team player?** In order for either a group or a team to function, individuals have to achieve some balance between their own needs and the needs of the group. Individuals on the team need to understand their roles, and then work together to create a set of group norms.

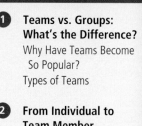

SNAPSHOT SUMMARY

1 Teams vs. Groups: What's the Difference?
Why Have Teams Become So Popular?
Types of Teams

2 From Individual to Team Member
Roles
Norms

3 **Do teams go through stages while they work?** Two different models illustrate how teams develop. The first, the five-stage model, describes the standardized sequence of stages groups pass through: forming, storming, norming, performing, and adjourning. Through these stages, group members learn how to settle conflicts and develop norms, which enable them to perform. The second, the punctuated-equilibrium model, describes the pattern of development specific to temporary groups with deadlines. In this model, the group shows two great periods of activity, first midway through the project, after which it performs at a higher level than it did previously. The second peak in activity takes place right before the project comes due.

4 **How do we create effective teams?** For teams to be effective, careful consideration must be given to resources, the team's composition, work design, and process variables. The four contextual factors that appear to be most significantly related to team performance are the presence of adequate resources, effective leadership and structure, a climate of trust, and a performance evaluation and reward system that reflects team contributions. Effective teams are neither too large nor too small—typically they range in size from 5 to 12 people. They have members who fill role demands, are flexible, and who prefer to be part of a group. Teams will be more effective if members have freedom and opportunity to do their tasks and believe that the task will have a substantial impact on others. Finally, effective teams also have members committed to a common purpose and specific team goals.

5 **Are teams always the answer?** Teams are not necessarily appropriate in every situation. How do you know if the work of your group would be better done in teams? It's been suggested that three tests be applied to see if a team fits the situation: (1) Can the work be done better by more than one person? (2) Does the work create a common purpose or set of goals for the people in the group that is more than the sum of individual goals? and (3) Are the members of the group interdependent? This third test asks whether the success of the whole depends on the success of each one *and* the success of each one depends on the success of the others.

for Review

1. Contrast self-managed and cross-functional teams.

2. Contrast virtual and face-to-face teams.

3. How do norms develop in a team?

4. Describe the five-stage model of group development.

5. Describe the punctuated-equilibrium model of group development.

6. What are the characteristics of an effective team?

7. What is the difference between task-oriented roles and maintenance roles?

8. Contrast the pros and cons of having diverse teams.

9. What are the effects of team size on performance?

10. How can a team minimize social loafing?

for Critical Thinking

1. Identify five roles you play. What behaviours do they require? Are any of these roles in conflict? If so, in what way? How do you resolve these conflicts?

2. How could you use the punctuated-equilibrium model to better understand team behaviour?

3. Have you experienced social loafing as a team member? What did you do to prevent this problem?

4. Would you prefer to work alone or as part of a team? Why? How do you think your answer compares with that of others in your class?

5. What effect, if any, do you think workforce diversity has on a team's performance and satisfaction?

for You

■ Because the people you interact with appreciate recognition, consider including a brief note on a nice card to show thanks for a job well done. Or you might send a basket of flowers. Sometimes just sending a pleasant, thankful email is enough to make a person feel valued. All of these things are easy enough to do, and appreciated greatly by the recipient.

■ Know that you will be asked to work on teams and groups both during your undergraduate years and later on in life, so understanding how teams work is an important skill to have.

■ Think about the roles that you play on teams. Teams need task-oriented people to get the job done, but they also need maintenance-oriented people who help keep people working together and feeling committed to the team.

■ Help your team set specific, measurable, realistic goals, as this leads to more successful outcomes.

OB at work

Sports Teams Are Good Models for Workplace Teams

Studies from hockey, football, soccer, basketball, and baseball have found a number of elements that successful sports teams have that can be extrapolated to successful work teams:[108]

Goals foster team cohesion. A study of basketball teams found that while those that set team goals and those that did not had similar levels of cohesion when the season began, those with goals were more cohesive at the end of the season.

Successful teams score early wins. Early successes build teammates' faith in themselves and their capacity as a team. For instance, research on hockey teams of relatively equal ability found that 72 percent of the time the team that was ahead at the end of the first period went on to win the game. So managers should give teams early tasks that are simple, as well as "easy wins."

Successful teams avoid losing streaks. A couple of failures can lead to a downward spiral if a team becomes demoralized and believes it is helpless to end its losing streak. Managers need to instill confidence in team members that they can turn setbacks around.

Practice makes perfect. Successful sports teams execute on game day but learn from their mistakes in practice. A wise manager carves out time for work teams to experiment and learn.

Successful teams use halftime breaks. The best coaches in basketball and football use halftime during a game to reassess what is working and what is not. Managers of work teams should similarly build in assessments at around the halfway point in a team project to evaluate how the team can improve.

Being slightly behind can be motivating. A recent study of 6572 NCAA basketball games revealed that the team slightly behind at halftime won more games than it lost. Teams that are slightly ahead may suffer from "victory disease" by relaxing and trying not to lose, whereas those slightly behind may be more motivated.

Winning teams have a stable membership. Studies of professional basketball teams have found that the more stable a team's membership, the more likely the team is to win. The more time teammates have together, the more able they are to anticipate one another's moves and the clearer they are about one another's roles.

Sports Teams Are Not the Model for All Teams

There are flaws in using sports as a model for developing effective work teams. Here are five caveats:

All sport teams are not alike. In baseball, for instance, there is little interaction among teammates. Rarely are more than two or three players directly involved in a play. The performance of the team is largely the sum of the performance of the individual players. Basketball has much more interdependence among players: Team members are densely clustered and must switch from offence to defence at a moment's notice. The performance of the team is more than the sum of its individual players. So when using sports teams as a model for work teams, be sure you are making the correct comparison.

Work teams are more varied and complex. In an athletic league, the design of the task, the design of the team, and the team's context vary relatively little from team to team. But these variables can differ greatly between work teams. As a result, coaching plays a much more significant part in a sports team's performance than a work team's. Performance of work teams is a function of getting the teams' structural and design variables right. Managers of work teams should focus more on getting the team set up for success than on coaching.

A lot of employees cannot relate to sports metaphors. Not everyone on work teams is conversant with sports. And members from different cultures may not know the sports metaphors you are using. Moreover, different cultures view the team metaphor differently. In Latin America, the work team is considered a family. "Families are involved in all parts of your life, and are expected to celebrate with you socially. Your involvement in your sports team is more limited. Less caretaking, more competitive."[109]

Work team outcomes are not easily defined in terms of wins and losses. Sports teams typically measure success in terms of wins and losses. Success is rarely as clear or black and white for work teams.

Sports team metaphors oversimplify. Sports team metaphors simplify a complicated world. While such shortcuts hold an intuitive appeal, we also have to recognize that rather than expanding our minds to the full range of possibilities, sports metaphors reduce and simplify—not something to recommend to the enlightened manager.

LEARNING ABOUT **YOURSELF** EXERCISE

How Good Am I at Building and Leading a Team?

Use the following rating scale to respond to the 18 questions on building and leading an effective team.

Strongly Disagree 1	Disagree 2	Slightly Disagree 3	Slightly Agree 4	Agree 5	Strongly Agree 6

1. I am knowledgeable about the different stages of development that teams can go through in their life cycles.   1 2 3 4 5 6

2. When a team forms, I make certain that all team members are introduced to one another at the outset.   1 2 3 4 5 6

3. When the team first comes together, I provide directions, answer team members' questions, and clarify goals, expectations, and procedures.   1 2 3 4 5 6

4. I help team members establish a foundation of trust among one another and between themselves and me.   1 2 3 4 5 6

5. I ensure that standards of excellence, not mediocrity or mere acceptability, characterize the team's work.   1 2 3 4 5 6

6. I provide a great deal of feedback to team members regarding their performance.   1 2 3 4 5 6

7. I encourage team members to balance individual autonomy with interdependence among other team members.   1 2 3 4 5 6

8. I help team members become at least as committed to the success of the team as to their own personal success.   1 2 3 4 5 6

9. I help team members learn to play roles that assist the team in accomplishing its tasks, as well as building strong interpersonal relationships.   1 2 3 4 5 6

10. I articulate a clear, exciting, passionate vision of what the team can achieve.   1 2 3 4 5 6

11. I help team members become committed to the team vision.   1 2 3 4 5 6

12. I encourage a win-win philosophy in the team; that is, when one member wins, every member wins.   1 2 3 4 5 6

13. I help the team avoid making the group's survival more important than accomplishing its goal.   1 2 3 4 5 6

14. I use formal process-management procedures to help the group become faster, more efficient, and more productive, and to prevent errors.   1 2 3 4 5 6

15. I encourage team members to represent the team's vision, goals, and accomplishments to outsiders.   1 2 3 4 5 6

16. I diagnose and capitalize on the team's core competence.   1 2 3 4 5 6

17. I encourage the team to achieve dramatic breakthrough innovations, as well as small continuous improvements.   1 2 3 4 5 6

18. I help the team work toward preventing mistakes, not just correcting them after the fact.   1 2 3 4 5 6

LEARNING ABOUT **YOURSELF** EXERCISE (Continued)

Scoring Key:

This instrument assesses team development behaviours in five areas: diagnosing team development (items 1, 16); managing the forming stage (items 2–4); managing the storming stage (items 10–12, 14, 15); managing the norming stage (items 6–9, 13); and managing the performing stage (items 5, 17, 18). Add up your score. Your total score will range between 18 and 108.

Based on a norm group of 500 business students, the following can help estimate where you are relative to others:

95 or above = You're in the top quartile of being able to build and lead a team

72–94 = You're in the second quartile

60–71 = You're in the third quartile

Below 60 = You're in the bottom quartile

Source: Adapted from D. A. Whetten and K. S. Cameron, *Developing Management Skills,* 3rd ed. © 1995, pp. 534–535. Adapted by permission of Pearson Education, Inc. Upper Saddle River, NJ.

SELF-ASSESSMENT LIBRARY LEARNING ABOUT YOURSELF

More Learning About Yourself Exercises

An additional self-assessment relevant to this chapter appears on MyOBLab (**www.pearsoned.ca/myoblab**).

IV.E.2 What Is My Team Efficacy?

When you complete the additional assessment, consider the following:

1. Am I surprised about my score?

2. Would my friends evaluate me similarly?

BREAKOUT **GROUP** EXERCISES

Form small groups to discuss the following topics, as assigned by your instructor:

1. One of the members of your team continually arrives late for meetings and does not turn drafts of assignments in on time. In general, this group member is engaging in social loafing. What can the members of your group do to reduce social loafing?

2. Consider a team with which you have worked. Was there more emphasis on task-oriented or maintenance-oriented roles? What impact did this have on the group's performance?

3. Identify 4 or 5 norms that a team could put into place near the beginning of its life that might help the team function better over time.

The Paper Tower Exercise

Step 1 Each group will receive 20 index cards, 12 paper clips, and 2 marking pens. Groups have 10 minutes to plan a paper tower that will be judged on the basis of 3 criteria: height, stability, and beauty. No physical work (building) is allowed during this planning period.

Step 2 Each group has 15 minutes for the actual construction of the paper tower.

Step 3 Each tower will be identified by a number assigned by your instructor. Each student is to individually examine all the paper towers. Your group is then to come to a consensus as to which tower is the winner (5 minutes). A spokesperson from your group should report its decision and the criteria the group used in reaching it.

Step 4 In your small groups, discuss the following questions (your instructor may choose to have you discuss only a subset of these questions):

    a. What percentage of the plan did each member of your group contribute, on average?

    b. Did your group have a leader? Why or why not?

    c. How did the group generally respond to the ideas that were expressed during the planning period?

    d. To what extent did your group follow the five-stage model of group development?

    e. List specific behaviours exhibited during the planning and building sessions that you felt were helpful to the group. Explain why you found them to be helpful.

    f. List specific behaviours exhibited during the planning and building sessions that you felt were dysfunctional to the group. Explain why you found them dysfunctional.

Source: This exercise is based on *The Paper Tower Exercise: Experiencing Leadership and Group Dynamics*, by Phillip L. Hunsaker and Johanna S. Hunsaker, unpublished manuscript. A brief description is included in "Exchange," *Organizational Behavior Teaching Journal* 4, no. 2 (1979), p. 49. Reprinted by permission of the authors. The materials list was suggested by Professor Sally Maitlis, Sauder School of Business, University of British Columbia.

Dealing with Shirkers

We have noted that one of the most common problems in groups is social loafing, which means group members contribute less than if they were working on their own. We might call such individuals "shirkers"—those who are contributing far less than other group members.

Most of us have experienced social loafing, or shirking, in groups. And we may even admit to times when we shirked ourselves. We discussed earlier in the chapter some ways of discouraging social loafing, such as limiting group size, holding individuals responsible for their contributions, and setting group goals. While these tactics may be effective, in our experience, many students simply work around shirkers. "We just did it ourselves—it was easier that way," says one group member.

Consider the following questions for dealing with shirking in groups:

1. If group members end up "working around" shirkers, do you think this information should be communicated to the instructor so that this individual's contribution to the project is judged more fairly? If so, does the group have an ethical responsibility to communicate this to the shirking group member? If not, isn't the shirking group member unfairly reaping the rewards of a "free ride"?

2. Do you think confronting the shirking group member is justified? Does this depend on the skills of the shirker (whether he or she is capable of doing good-quality work)?

3. Social loafing has been found to be higher in Western, more individualistic nations than in other countries. Do you think this means we should tolerate shirking on the part of North American workers to a greater degree than if it occurred with someone from Asia?

CASE INCIDENTS

Toyota's Team Culture

Many companies proudly promote their team culture. At Toyota, the promotion seems sincere.[110]

Teamwork is one of Toyota's core values, along with trust, continuous improvement, long-term thinking, standardization, innovation, and problem solving. The firm's value statement says the following: "To ensure the success of our company, each team member has the responsibility to work together, and communicate honestly, share ideas, and ensure team member understanding."

So how does Toyota's culture reflect its emphasis on teamwork?

First, although individualism is a prominent value in Western culture, it is deemphasized at Toyota. In its place is an emphasis on systems, in which people and products are seen as intertwined value streams and people are trained to be problem solvers so as to make the product system leaner and better.

Second, before hiring, Toyota tests candidates to ensure they are not only competent and technically skilled but also oriented toward teamwork—able to trust their team, be comfortable solving problems collaboratively, and motivated to achieve collective outcomes.

Third, and not surprisingly, Toyota structures its work around teams. Every Toyota employee knows the adage "All of us are smarter than any of us." Teams are used not only in the production process but also at every level and in every function: in sales and marketing, in finance, in engineering, in design, and at the executive level.

Fourth, Toyota considers the team to be the power centre of the organization. The leader serves the team, not the other way around. When asked whether he would feature himself in advertisements the way other automakers had (most famously, "Dr. Z," Daimler's CEO Dieter Zetsche), Toyota USA's CEO, Yuki Funo, said, "No. We want to show everybody in the company. The heroes. Not one single person."

Questions

1. Do you think Toyota has succeeded because of its team-oriented culture, or do you think it would have succeeded without it?

2. Do you think you would be comfortable working in Toyota's culture? Why or why not?

3. In response to the recession and the firm's first-ever quarterly loss, Toyota's managers accepted a 10 percent pay cut in 2009 to avoid employee layoffs. Do you think such a response is a good means of promoting camaraderie? What are the risks in such a plan?

4. Recently, DCH Group, a company comprised of 33 auto dealerships, decided to adapt Toyota's culture to its own, particularly its emphasis on teamwork. DCH's CEO, Susan Scarola, said, "Trying to bring it down to day-to-day operations is tough. It was not something that everybody immediately embraced, even at the senior level." Do you think the culture will work in what is typically the dog-eat-dog world of auto dealerships? Why or why not?

IBM's Multicultural Multinational Teams

Historically, IBM was one of the most tradition-bound companies on the planet.[111] It was famous for its written and unwritten rules—such as its no-layoff policy, its focus on individual promotions and achievement, the expectation of lifetime service at the company, and its requirement of suits and white shirts at work.

How times have changed.

IBM has clients in 170 countries and now does two-thirds of its business outside the United States. As a result, it has overturned virtually all aspects of its old culture. One relatively new focus is in the teamwork area. While IBM, like almost all large organizations, uses work teams extensively, the way it does so is unique.

To instill in its managers an appreciation of local culture, and as a means of opening up emerging markets, IBM sends hundreds of its employees to month-long volunteer project teams in regions of the world where most big companies don't do business. Al Chakra, a software development manager located in Raleigh, North Carolina, was sent to join GreenForest, a furniture manufacturing team in Timisoara, Romania. With Chakra were IBM employees from five other countries. Together, the team helped GreenForest become more computer savvy to help its business. In return for the IBM team's assistance, GreenForest was charged . . . well . . . nothing.

This is hardly pure altruism at work. IBM calculates these multicultural, multinational teams are good investments for several reasons. First, they help lay the groundwork for opening up business in emerging economies, many of which might be expected to enjoy greater future growth than mature markets. Stanley Litow, the IBM VP who oversees the program, also thinks it helps IBMers develop multicultural team skills and an appreciation of local markets. He notes, "We want to build a lead-ership cadre that learns about these places and also learns to exchange their diverse backgrounds and skills." Among the countries where IBM has sent its multicultural teams are Turkey, Tanzania, Vietnam, Ghana, and the Philippines.

As for Chakra, he was thrilled to be selected for the team. "I felt like I won the lottery," he said. He advised GreenForest on how to become a paperless company in three years and recommended computer systems to boost productivity and increase exports to Western Europe.

Another team member, Bronwyn Grantham, an Australian who works at IBM in London, advised GreenForest about sales strategies. Describing her team experience, Grantham said, "I've never worked so closely with a team of IBMers from such a wide range of competencies."

Questions

1. If you calculate the person-hours devoted to IBM's team projects, they amount to more than 180 000 hours of management time each year. Do you think this is a wise investment of IBM's human resources? Why or why not?

2. Why do you think IBM's culture changed from formal, stable, and individualistic to informal, impermanent, and team oriented?

3. Would you like to work on one of IBM's multicultural, multinational project teams? Why or why not?

4. Multicultural project teams often face problems with communication, expectations, and values. How do you think some of these challenges can be overcome?

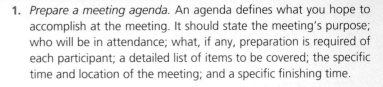

FROM CONCEPTS TO SKILLS

Conducting a Team Meeting

Team meetings have a reputation for inefficiency. For instance, noted Canadian-born economist John Kenneth Galbraith has said, "Meetings are indispensable when you don't want to do anything."

When you are responsible for conducting a meeting, what can you do to make it more efficient and effective? Follow these 12 steps:[112]

1. *Prepare a meeting agenda.* An agenda defines what you hope to accomplish at the meeting. It should state the meeting's purpose; who will be in attendance; what, if any, preparation is required of each participant; a detailed list of items to be covered; the specific time and location of the meeting; and a specific finishing time.

2. *Distribute the agenda in advance.* Participants should have the agenda sufficiently in advance so they can adequately prepare for the meeting.

3. *Consult with participants before the meeting.* An unprepared participant cannot contribute to his or her full potential. It is your responsibility to ensure that members are prepared, so check with them ahead of time.

4. *Get participants to go over the agenda.* The first thing to do at the meeting is to have participants review the agenda, make any changes, then approve the final agenda.

5. *Establish specific time parameters.* Meetings should begin on time and have a specific time for completion. It is your responsibility to specify these time parameters and to hold to them.

6. *Maintain focused discussion.* It is your responsibility to give direction to the discussion; to keep it focused on the issues; and to minimize interruptions, disruptions, and irrelevant comments.

7. *Encourage and support participation of all members.* To maximize the effectiveness of problem-oriented meetings, each participant must be encouraged to contribute. Quiet or reserved personalities need to be drawn out so their ideas can be heard.

8. *Maintain a balanced style.* The effective group leader pushes when necessary and is passive when need be.

9. *Encourage the clash of ideas.* You need to encourage different points of view, critical thinking, and constructive disagreement.

10. *Discourage the clash of personalities.* An effective meeting is characterized by the critical assessment of ideas, not attacks on people. When running a meeting, you must quickly intercede to stop personal attacks or other forms of verbal insult.

11. *Be an effective listener.* You need to listen with intensity, empathy, and objectivity, and do whatever is necessary to get the full intended meaning from each participant's comments.

12. *Bring proper closure.* You should close a meeting by summarizing the group's accomplishments. Clarify what actions, if any, need to follow the meeting, and allocate follow-up assignments. If any decisions are made, you also need to determine who will be responsible for communicating and implementing them.

Practising Skills

Jameel Saumur is the leader of a five-member project team that has been assigned the task of moving his engineering firm into the booming area of high-speed intercity rail construction. Saumur and his team members have been researching the field, identifying specific business opportunities, negotiating alliances with equipment vendors, and evaluating high-speed rail experts and consultants from around the world. Throughout the process, Tonya Eckler, a highly qualified and respected engineer, has challenged a number of things Saumur said during team meetings and in the workplace. For example, at a meeting two weeks ago, Saumur presented the team with a list of 10 possible high-speed rail projects and started evaluating the company's ability to compete for them. Eckler contradicted virtually all of Saumur's comments, questioned his statistics, and was quite pessimistic about the possibility of getting contracts on these projects. After this latest display of displeasure, two other group members, Bryan Worth and Maggie Ames, are complaining that Eckler's actions are damaging the team's effectiveness. Eckler was originally assigned to the team for her unique expertise and insight. If you had to advise this team, what suggestions would you make to get the team on the right track to achieve its fullest potential?

Reinforcing Skills

1. Interview three managers at different organizations. Ask them about their experiences in managing teams. Have each describe teams that they thought were effective and why they succeeded. Have each also describe teams that they thought were ineffective and the reasons that might have caused this.

2. Contrast a team you have been in where members trusted each other with another team you have been in where members lacked trust in one another. How did the conditions in each team develop? What were the consequences in terms of interaction patterns and performance?

OB on the EDGE

Trust

Joseph Reaume opened Sunnyside Garage (today known as Reaume Chevrolet Buick GMC) in Windsor in 1931, never dreaming how far the company would go.[1] Today, Steve and Rick Reaume carry on the legacy of their great-grandfather, running one of the oldest General Motors dealerships in Canada.

Steve Reaume, dealer principal, attributes the success of the business to the trust they have built in the community. "Our customers have always come first with us," he says. "They are the reason we have been in business for over 80 years."

The brothers are from the fourth generation, and there are fifth-generation family members in the business as well. Jenn Reaume-Natyshak, assistant financing and leasing manager/sales, is Steve's daughter. She says, "I'm very proud and committed to 'The Tradition of Trust' banner we display. As part of the 5th generation, I promise to always live up to that tradition." Jenn's twin brother, Jeff, is a general sales manager, and younger brother Craig is general parts and service manager at the business. All three have recently become shareholders as Steve has begun to put his exit strategy plan in place.

Trust also plays a part in how the Reaumes treat their employees. Says Dan Nedin, parts manager, "A dealership built on honesty was the reason I started my career with the Reaume family. It's resulted in loyalty of employees . . . and customers."

Trust, or lack of trust, is an increasingly important leadership issue in today's organizations.[2] Trust is fragile. It takes a long time to build, can be easily destroyed, and is hard to regain.[3]

A survey of Canadian employees concluded that three out of four Canadians do not trust the people they work for.[4] According to a recent survey by Edmonton-based David Aplin Recruiting, the most common reason employees quit jobs is lack of trust in senior leaders. The next most important reasons given were "insufficient pay, unhealthy or undesirable culture, [and] lack of honesty/integrity/ethics." Managers and human resources professionals don't know there's a trust deficit in the workplace and think employees are leaving for insufficient pay, likely because employees "aren't going to cite lack of trust as their reason for leaving. It would be experienced by many as burning a bridge on the way out the door," Aplin says.[5] The inset *Why Integrity Is Questioned by Employees* on page 252 shows some of the issues that cause employees to wonder about the integrity of their managers.

What Is Trust?

Trust is a psychological state that exists when you agree to make yourself vulnerable to another because you have positive expectations about how things are going to turn out.[6] Trust is a history-dependent process based on relevant but limited samples of experience.[7] It takes time to form, building incrementally and accumulating. Most of us find it hard, if not impossible, to trust someone immediately if we don't know anything about them. At the extreme, in the case of total ignorance, we can gamble, but we cannot trust.[8] But as we get to know someone and the relationship matures, we gain confidence in our ability to form a positive expectation.

There is inherent risk and vulnerability in any trusting relationship. Trust involves making oneself vulnerable, as when, for example, we disclose intimate information or rely on another's promises.[9] By its very nature, trust provides the opportunity for disappointment or to be taken advantage of.[10] But trust is not taking risk per se; rather, it is a willingness to take risk.[11] So when I trust someone, I expect that he or she will not take advantage of me. This willingness to take risks is common to all trust situations.[12]

What Determines Trust?

What are the key dimensions of trust? Research has identified five important criteria: integrity, competence, consistency, loyalty, and openness.[13] These dimensions of trust are presented in the illustration on the right and listed in their order of importance in determining one's trustworthiness.

- *Integrity.* Honesty and truthfulness. Of all five dimensions, integrity seems to be most critical when someone assesses another's trustworthiness.[14] For instance, when 570 white-collar employees were recently given a list of 28 attributes related to leadership, honesty was rated the most important by far.[15] Integrity also means having consistency between what you do and say.

- *Competence.* Technical and interpersonal knowledge and skills. Does the person know what he or she is talking about? You are unlikely to listen to or depend upon someone whose abilities you don't respect. You need to believe that the person has the skills and abilities to carry out what he or she promises to do.

- *Consistency.* Reliability, predictability, and good judgment in handling situations. "Inconsistencies between words and action decrease trust."[16] This dimension is particularly relevant for managers. "Nothing is noticed more quickly . . . than a discrepancy between what executives preach and what they expect their associates to practice."[17]

- *Loyalty.* Willingness to protect and save face for another person. Trust requires that you can depend on someone not to act opportunistically.

- *Openness.* Willingness to share ideas and information freely. Can you rely on the person to give you the full truth?

In addition to these factors, a review of the findings for the effects of leadership on building trust indicates that several characteristics of leadership are most likely to build trust. Leaders who engage in procedural justice (ensuring fair procedures and outcomes) and interactional justice (treating people fairly when procedures are carried out), and who encourage participative decision making and use a transformational leadership style, are most successful at building trust.[18]

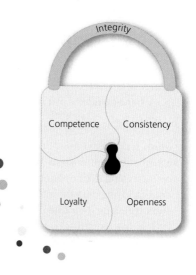

Why Integrity Is Questioned by Employees

Employees are often distrustful of a manager's integrity for the following reasons:

- *Sticky labels.* It is easy for a manager to get branded a "liar," but difficult to build a reputation as a person who is totally trustworthy. Generally people require far more evidence of positive behaviour than of negative behaviour.

- *Competing stakeholders.* Managers often send different messages to different stakeholders. So they might tell employees that "customers always come first," and yet the staff interpret downsizing as sending the opposite message. Meanwhile, shareholders believe that cuts to staff can increase profitability, and the value of their shares.

- *Shifting policies.* When new managers take the place of old ones, employees can sometimes see changes in behaviour as being inconsistent with the previous management's message. This can cause employees to become cynical.

- *Changing fashions.* Employees often become cynical when managers try out new fads in management techniques. New ways of managing can send a message to employees that management does not really know how to manage.

- *Unclear priorities.* When managers are uncertain about the priorities of the company or their job, this uncertainty can appear to employees to be a lack of integrity.

- *Blind spots.* Sometimes managers are not aware of their own integrity problems. This happens when what a manager says does not match up with what he or she does. For instance, managers might say that employees should be empowered, but then not give up some of their own power so that this happens.[19]

Basic Principles of Trust

Research offers a few principles that help us better understand how trust and mistrust are created:[20]

- *Mistrust drives out trust.* People who are trusting demonstrate their trust by increasing their openness to others, disclosing relevant information, and expressing their true intentions. People who mistrust conceal information and act opportunistically to take advantage of others. A few mistrusting people can poison an entire organization.

- *Trust begets trust.* Exhibiting trust in others tends to encourage reciprocity.

- *Trust can be regained (sometimes).* Once it is violated, trust can be regained, but only in certain situations.[21] When an individual's trust in another is broken because the other party failed to do what was expected of him, it can be restored when the individual observes a consistent pattern of trustworthy behaviours by the transgressor. However, when the same untrustworthy behaviour occurs with deception, trust never fully recovers, even when the person deceived is given apologies, promises, or a consistent pattern of trustworthy actions.[22]

- *Mistrusting groups self-destruct.* The corollary to the previous principle is that when group members mistrust one another, they repel and separate. They pursue their own interests rather than the group's. Members of mistrusting groups tend to be suspicious of one another, are constantly on guard against exploitation, and restrict communication with others in the group.

- *Trust increases cohesion.* Trust holds people together.[23] If one person needs help or falters, that person knows that the others will be there to fill in.

- *Mistrust generally reduces productivity.* Mistrust focuses attention on the differences in members' interests, making it difficult for people to visualize common goals. People respond by concealing information and secretly pursuing their own interests. When employees encounter problems, they avoid calling on others, fearing that those others will take advantage of them. A climate of mistrust tends to stimulate dysfunctional forms of conflict and make cooperation difficult.

What Can Leaders Do to Increase Trust?

Professors Linda Duxbury of the Carleton University School of

Business and Christopher Higgins of the University of Western Ontario's Richard Ivey School of Business found that employees who work in environments characterized by trust and respect report less stress and greater productivity than those who work in environments where trust is lacking.[25] To improve the climate of trust in an organization, it is important to build social capital and build team trust.

Building Social Capital

Maintaining integrity in organizations is a way of building social capital among members of the organization. Scholars use the term *social capital* to refer to strong relationships within organizations that help organizations function smoothly.[26] Social capital is built on trust, and allows deals to move faster, teams to be more pro-

ductive, and people to perform more creatively.[27]

Some companies seem better able to build social capital than others. The inset *Increasing Organizational Candour* indicates ways that organizations can increase the level of trust available internally.

Building Team Trust

Professor Kurt Dirks of Washington University in St. Louis studied the effect of trust in one's coach on team performance during basketball season for 30 teams in Division I and Division III of the NCAA (National Collegiate Athletic Association).[28] His findings show that basketball players' trust in their coach improves team performance. The two teams with the highest level of trust in their coach had outstanding records for the season he studied. The team with the lowest

level of trust won only 10 percent of its games, and the coach was fired at the end of the season.

As these results indicate, team leaders have a significant impact on a team's trust climate. The following points summarize ways to build team trust:[30]

- *Demonstrate that you are working for others' interests, as well as your own.* All of us are concerned with our own self-interest, but if others see you using them, your job, or the organization for your personal goals to the exclusion of your team's, department's, and organization's interests, your credibility will be undermined.

- *Be a team player.* Support your work team both through words and actions. Defend the team and team members when they are attacked by outsiders. Doing so will demonstrate your loyalty to your work group.

- *Practise openness.* Mistrust comes as much from what people don't know as from what they do know. Openness leads to confidence and trust. So keep people informed, explain your decisions, be candid about problems, and fully disclose relevant information.

- *Be fair.* Before making decisions or taking actions, consider how others will perceive them in terms of objectivity and fairness. Give credit where it's due, be objective and impartial in performance evaluations, and pay attention to equity perceptions in reward distributions.

- *Speak your feelings.* Managers and leaders who convey only hard facts come across as cold and distant. By sharing your feelings, you will encourage others to view you as real and human. They will know who you are, and their respect for you will increase.

- *Show consistency in the basic values that guide your decision making.* Mistrust comes from not knowing what to expect. Take the time to think about your values and beliefs. Then let them consistently guide your decisions. When you know your central purpose, your actions will follow accordingly, and you will project a consistency that earns trust.

- *Maintain confidences.* You trust those you can confide in and rely on. So

if people tell you something in confidence, they need to feel assured that you won't discuss it with others or betray that confidence. If people perceive you as someone who "leaks" personal confidences, or someone who cannot be depended upon, you won't be perceived as trustworthy.

- *Demonstrate competence.* Develop the admiration and respect of others by demonstrating technical and professional ability and good business sense. Pay particular attention to developing and displaying your communication, team-building, and other interpersonal skills.

- *Work on continuous improvement.* Teams should approach their own development as part of a search for continuous improvement.

High-performance teams are characterized by high mutual trust among members. That is, members believe in the integrity, character, and ability of one another. Since trust begets trust and distrust begets distrust, maintaining trust requires careful attention by leaders and team members.[31] High trust can have a downside, though, if it inspires team members to not pay attention to one another's work. Team members with high trust may not monitor each other, and if the low monitoring is accompanied by high individual autonomy, the team can perform poorly.[32]

Does Distrust Ever Pay Off?

A 2010 study by Rotman School of Management professors Nancy Carter and Mark Weber found that people who are more trusting are better able to detect lies in other people.[33] However, Professor Roderick Kramer of the Graduate School of Business at Stanford University suggests that always being completely trusting may not be a desirable strategy. Instead, he offers "tempered trust," which means to trust wisely and well as a better way for individuals to act. His views are quite contrary to most management literature, which discusses the benefits of trust. Essentially, Kramer argues that distrust can be beneficial.[34]

Kramer believes that we are hard-wired to trust: "trust is our default position; we trust routinely, reflexively, and somewhat mindlessly, across a broad range of social situations."[35] Many times this trust serves us well, but sometimes it lets us down. Witness the many people who were taken in by the charms of stockbroker Bernie Madoff, and lost millions of dollars because of their trust in him.

So what does Kramer suggest we do? Start with some *prudent paranoia.* "Prudent paranoia is a form of constructive suspicion regarding the intentions and actions of people and organizations."[36] Kramer argues that such paranoia can be an early warning signal during difficult times. For instance, during times of mergers and

The Rules for Trusting Wisely

- *Know yourself.* If you tend to trust the wrong people too quickly, learn to interpret the cues better. If you have difficulty building trusting relationships, learn how to do this.[37]

- *Start small.* Start with small acts of trust, and see if they are reciprocated.

- *Write an escape clause.* Have a plan for how the relationship will end, so that people can trust more fully and with more commitment.

- *Send strong signals.* Signal trustworthiness more clearly and retaliate strongly when your trust is abused.

- *Recognize the other person's dilemma.* The other person is also trying to figure out whether you can be trusted. Reassure that person about whether or how much he or she should trust you.

- *Look at roles as well as people.* A person's role or position can provide some guarantee of his or her expertise and motivation.

- *Remain vigilant and always question.* Do not just engage in due diligence initially. Keep your due diligence up-to-date.

YOUR PERSPECTIVE

1. Why might corporations be willing to neglect the importance of trust and instead engage in behaviours such as those that could lead to corporate scandals?

2. What steps can organizations take to make sure that they are seen as trustworthy by the rest of society?

WANT TO KNOW MORE?

If you would like to read more on this topic, see R. F. Hurley, "The Decision to Trust," *Harvard Business Review*, September 2006, pp. 55–62; S. A. Joni, "The Geography of Trust," *Harvard Business Review*, March 2004, pp. 82–88; R. M. Kramer, "Rethinking Trust," *Harvard Business Review*, June 2009, p. 71; and J. O'Toole and W. Bennis, "What's Needed Next: A Culture of Candor," *Harvard Business Review*, June 2009, pp. 54–61.

acquisitions, employees are naturally distrustful of other departments, and wonder whether they will lose their jobs. Managers may watch out to see who may be threatening their power base. Those with high emotional intelligence are most likely to practise prudent paranoia; after all, one of the signs of emotional intelligence is paying attention to one's environment and responding accordingly.

The inset *The Rules for Trusting Wisely* presents some of Kramer's tips for starting on "a lifelong process of learning how to trust wisely and well."[38]

RESEARCH EXERCISES

1. Look for data on the extent to which companies in other countries are trusted by the citizens of those countries. How does this compare with the extent to which Canadians trust companies? Can you draw any inferences about what leads to greater or less trust of corporations?

2. Identify three Canadian organizations that are trying to improve their image to be more trustworthy. What effect is this having on the organizations' bottom lines?

CHAPTER

7

Communication

PART 3

INTERACTING

EFFECTIVELY

How can a nonprofit organization better use communication to convince its community to invest more in girls' hockey?

LEARNING OUTCOMES

1. How does communication work?

2. What are the barriers to communication?

3. How does communication flow in organizations?

4. How is information managed?

Ted Reeve Arena, one of 48 community arenas owned by the city of Toronto, is run by a volunteer board that decides how to allocate ice time to hockey leagues in the community.[1] Players and coaches from the Toronto Leaside Girls Hockey Association (TLGHA) felt they received limited access to the arena, especially compared with some other leagues. This was costing the Association an average of $200 000 in fees to rent ice time elsewhere. In the fall of 2009, TLGHA decided to fight back and launched an extensive communication campaign to let the community know about its concerns. The main goal was to force the city of Toronto to enforce its ice allocation policy at all publicly owned arenas.

In developing its communication campaign, the TLGHA carefully considered its target audience: the city's then mayor David Miller; members of Toronto city council; the TLGHA players and their families and fans; and the news media. The intent was to communicate effectively with these different groups to gain their support.

In this chapter, we explore the foundations of communication. By learning how to communicate effectively with others, we can improve our relationships with those around us, and work more effectively on teams.

OB IS FOR EVERYONE

- Does body language really make a difference?
- How can you communicate better when you are stressed out?
- Ever notice that communicating via email can lead to misunderstandings?
- How can you improve cross-cultural communication?

How does communication work?

The Communication Process

Individuals spend nearly 70 percent of their waking hours communicating—writing, reading, speaking, listening—which means that they have many opportunities in which to engage in poor communication. Communication is an important consideration for organizations and individuals alike. Communication is a foundation for many things that happen among groups and within the workplace—from motivating, to providing information, to controlling behaviour, to expressing emotion. Good communication skills are very important to your career success. A recent study of recruiters found that they rated communication skills as *the* most important characteristic of an ideal job candidate.[2]

No group can exist without **communication**, which is the *transfer* and *understanding* of a message between two or more people. Communication can be thought of as a process, or flow, as shown in Exhibit 7-1. The *sender* initiates a message by encoding a thought. The *message* is the actual physical product of the sender's *encoding*. When we speak, the speech is the message. When we write, the writing is the message. When we gesture, the movements of our arms and the expressions on our faces are the message. The *channel* is the medium through which the message travels. The sender selects it, determining whether to use a formal or informal channel. **Formal channels** are established by the organization and transmit messages related to the professional activities of members. They traditionally follow the authority chain within the organization. Other forms of messages, such as personal or social, follow **informal channels**, which are spontaneous and emerge as a response to individual choices.[3] The *receiver* is the person(s) to whom the message is directed, who must first translate the symbols into understandable form. This step is the *decoding* of the message. *Noise* represents communication barriers that distort the clarity of the message, such as perceptual problems, information overload, semantic difficulties, or cultural differences. The final link in the communication process is a feedback loop. *Feedback* is the check on how successful we have been in transferring our messages as originally intended. It determines whether understanding has been achieved.

The model indicates that communication is both an interactive and iterative process. The sender has to keep in mind the receiver (or audience), and in finalizing the communication may decide to revisit decisions about the message, the encoding, and/or the feedback.

Choosing a Channel

Why do people choose one **channel** of communication over another; for instance, a phone call instead of a face-to-face talk? One answer might be anxiety! An estimated 5 to 20 percent of the population[4] suffers from debilitating **communication apprehension**, or anxiety, which is undue tension and anxiety about oral communication, written communication, or both. We all know people who dread speaking in front of a group, but some people may find it extremely difficult to talk with others face to face

communication The transfer and understanding of a message between two or more people.

formal channels Communication channels established by an organization to transmit messages related to the professional activities of members.

informal channels Communication channels that are created spontaneously and that emerge as responses to individual choices.

channel The medium through which a message travels.

communication apprehension Undue tension and anxiety about oral communication, written communication, or both.

EXHIBIT 7-1 The Communication Process Model

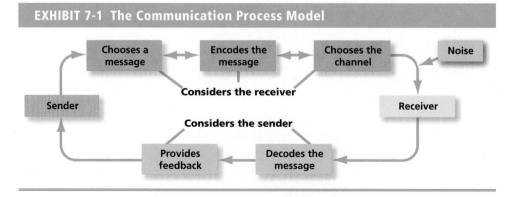

EXHIBIT 7-2 Information Richness of Communication Channels

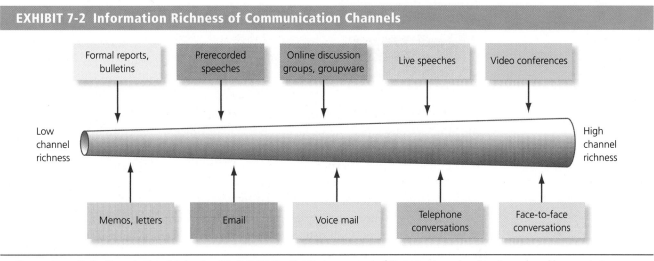

Source: From Daft. *Organizational Behavior*, 1E. © 2001 South-Western, a part of Cengage Learning, Inc. Reproduced by permission. www.cengage.com/permissions.

or become extremely anxious when they have to use the telephone. As a result, they may rely on memos, letters, or email to convey messages when a phone call would not only be faster but also more appropriate.

But what about the 80 to 95 percent of the population who don't suffer from this problem? Is there any general insight we might be able to provide regarding choice of communication channel? The answer is a qualified "yes." A model of media richness has been developed to explain channel selection among managers.[5]

Research has found that channels differ in their capacity to convey information. Some are rich in that they have the ability to (1) handle multiple cues simultaneously, (2) facilitate rapid feedback, and (3) be very personal. Others are lean in that they score low on these three factors. As Exhibit 7-2 illustrates, face-to-face conversation scores highest in terms of **channel richness** because it provides for the maximum amount of information to be transmitted during a communication episode. That is, it offers multiple information cues (words, postures, facial expressions, gestures, intonations), immediate feedback (both verbal and nonverbal), and the personal touch of "being there." Mississauga, Ontario-based Phonak Canada, a manufacturer of advanced hearing systems, holds monthly town-hall meetings for all staff. The firm shares information, introduces new employees, and recognizes notable achievements. It provides an opportunity to make sure that everyone in the company is on the same page.[6] *Focus on Research* explains why face-to-face meetings are so important.

FOCUS ON RESEARCH   ## Communicating in Bad Times

Can communication really make a difference during bad economic times? A 2011 study found that when economic times are bad, it is particularly important for management to create an atmosphere of trust.[7] They can do this by communicating directly with employees—bulletin boards, intranets, newsletters, and email can all be effective. However, face-to-face communication is the most important way of communicating.

Impersonal written media such as formal reports and bulletins rate lowest in richness. Two students were suspended from class for choosing YouTube, a very rich channel, to distribute their message. Their actions also raised concerns about privacy in the classroom, as *Focus on Ethics* reveals.

channel richness The amount of information that can be transmitted during a communication episode.

 YouTube's Darker Side

Is it okay for students to post a teacher's outburst on YouTube? Two grade 9 students from École Secondaire Mont-Bleu in Gatineau, Quebec, were suspended from school after teachers discovered a video the students had posted on YouTube.[8] One of the students provoked the teacher during class time while the other secretly taped the scene for about 50 minutes with a compact digital camera.

The students, who have academic problems, were in a special-education class. The teacher had 33 years of experience, and specialized in teaching students with learning disabilities. After the incident, the teacher went on sick leave, and his union said, "He is so embarrassed that he may never return to class."

There was no apparent explanation for why the students decided to provoke and then film the teacher. Other students have said that "the teacher was good at helping them improve their grades."

"I think students are just trying to embarrass the teachers they don't like," school board president Jocelyn Blondin said. "In the future, students will have to keep their cellphones in their pockets and use them outside of class," she predicted shortly after the incident.

Teachers and school boards are trying to determine strategies for handling these kinds of events in classrooms. The Gatineau school no longer allows personal electronic devices in the classroom. In Ontario, changes to the Safe Schools Act made in 2007 state that students who engage in online bullying are to be suspended from classes.

The choice of one channel over another depends on whether the message is routine or nonroutine. Routine messages tend to be straightforward and have a minimum of ambiguity. Nonroutine messages are likely to be complicated and have the potential for misunderstanding. Individuals can communicate routine messages efficiently through channels that are lower in richness. However, they communicate nonroutine messages more effectively by selecting rich channels. Evidence indicates that high-performing managers tend to be more media sensitive than low-performing managers.[9] That is, they are better able to match appropriate media richness with the ambiguity involved in the communication. Rob Sobey, president of the Dartmouth, Nova Scotia-based Lawtons Drugs chain, knows that memos do not help in a crisis when staff morale needs boost-

According to Rob Sobey, president of Lawtons Drugs, a memo never motivates. It can thank and compliment, but in a true crisis, you need to hold a town hall meeting to communicate seminal information. Use of a rich communication channel to communicate a nonroutine message is more likely to be successful.

ing. "A memo never motivates. A memo can thank and compliment, but you need the town hall meeting [in a true crisis]. You have to put yourself out there in the flesh."[10]

One study found that managers preferred delivering bad news (layoffs, promotion denials, and negative feedback) via email, and that the messages were delivered more accurately this way. However, sending negative information through email is generally not recommended. One of the co-authors of the study noted that "offering negative comments face-to-face is often taken as a sign that the news is important and the deliverer cares about the recipient."[11] It appears that a CEO's use of a channel relatively low in richness (email) to convey a nonroutine and complex message did a lot of harm to his company, as this *OB in the Workplace* shows.

OB in the WORKPLACE
Some Emails Should Be Left Unsent

Is email the best way to communicate sensitive messages? Neal L. Patterson, CEO at medical software maker Cerner Corp., likes email.[12] Maybe too much so. Upset with his staff's work ethic, he sent a seething email to his firm's 400 managers. Here are some of its highlights:

> Hell will freeze over before this CEO implements ANOTHER EMPLOYEE benefit in this Culture. . . . We are getting less than 40 hours of work from a large number of our Kansas City-based employees. The parking lot is sparsely used at 8 a.m.; likewise at 5 p.m. As managers—you either do not know what your EMPLOYEES are doing; or YOU do not CARE. . . . You have a problem and you will fix it or I will replace you. . . . What you are doing, as managers, with this company makes me SICK.

Patterson's email suggested managers schedule meetings at 7:00 a.m., 6:00 p.m., and Saturday mornings; promised a staff reduction of 5 percent and the institution of a time-clock system; and announced his intention to charge unapproved absences to employees' vacation time.

Within hours, copies of the email had made their way onto a Yahoo! website. And within 3 days, Cerner's stock price had plummeted 22 percent. Although we can wonder whether such harsh criticism should be communicated at all, one thing is clear: Patterson erred by selecting the wrong channel for his message. Such an emotional and sensitive message might have been better received in a face-to-face meeting.

The media richness model is consistent with organizational trends and practices of the past decade. It is not just coincidence that more and more senior managers use meetings to facilitate communication and regularly leave the isolated sanctuary of their executive offices to manage by walking around. These executives are relying on richer channels of communication to transmit the more ambiguous messages they need to convey. The past decade has been characterized by organizations closing facilities, imposing large layoffs, restructuring, merging, consolidating, and introducing new products and services at an accelerated pace—all nonroutine messages high in ambiguity and requiring the use of channels that can convey a large amount of information. It is not surprising, therefore, to see the most effective managers expanding their use of rich channels.

Barriers to Effective Communication

When the Toronto Leaside Girls Hockey Association (TLGHA) decided to launch its campaign to get more ice time, it faced significant challenges.[13] There were sexist attitudes toward girls' and women's hockey to overcome. As Ward 30 councillor Paula Fletcher noted, the anti-female

2 What are the barriers to communication?

attitudes were "left over from the past" and "need[ed] to change. It's just shocking that in this day and age, girls' hockey is being treated so poorly."

Because of such difficulties, the communication team for TLGHA had to consider the best way to deliver the message of change. Approaching the volunteer-run boards of the arenas did appear to be a good strategy, as the problem was a city-wide issue. Therefore, the association threatened to launch a human-rights complaint against the city in a letter sent to the mayor. Are there other things the communication team might have considered to make sure everyone was ready to listen to their concerns?

A number of factors have been identified as barriers to communication. This section presents the most prominent ones.

Filtering

Filtering occurs when a sender manipulates information so that the receiver will view it more favourably. For example, when a manager tells a senior executive what the manager feels the executive wants to hear, the manager is filtering information. The more vertical levels in the organization's hierarchy, the more opportunities there are for filtering. But some filtering will occur wherever there are status differences. Factors such as fear of conveying bad news and the desire to please the boss often lead employees to tell their superiors what they think they want to hear, thus distorting upward communications.

Selective Perception

Receivers in the communication process selectively see and hear based on their needs, motivations, experience, background, and other personal characteristics. Receivers also project their interests and expectations into communications as they decode them. For example, the employment interviewer who believes that young people are more interested in spending time on leisure and social activities than working extra hours to further their careers is likely to be influenced by that stereotype when interviewing young job applicants. As we discussed in Chapter 2, we don't see reality; rather, we interpret what we see and call it "reality." One 2011 study found that people perceived that they communicated better with people with whom they were close (friends and partners) than with strangers. However, in ambiguous conversations, it turned out that their ability to communicate with close friends was no better than their ability to communicate with strangers.[14]

Defensiveness

When people feel that they are being threatened, they tend to react in ways that reduce their ability to achieve mutual understanding. That is, they become defensive—engaging in behaviours such as verbally attacking others, making sarcastic remarks, being overly judgmental, and questioning others' motives. So when individuals interpret another's message as threatening, they often respond in ways that hinder effective communication.

Emotions

You may interpret the same message differently when you are angry or distraught than when you are happy. Extreme emotions such as jubilation or depression are most likely to hinder effective communication. In such instances, we are most prone to disregard our rational and objective thinking processes and substitute emotional judgments.

Information Overload

Individuals have a finite capacity for processing data. When the information we have to work with exceeds our ability to process it, the result is **information overload**. With emails, phone calls, faxes, meetings, and the need to keep current in one's field, more

filtering A sender's manipulation of information so that it will be seen more favourably by the receiver.

information overload The state of having more information than one can process.

and more employees are saying that they are suffering from too much information. The information can be distracting as well. A recent study of employees who have tracking software on their computers found that they clicked on their email program more than 50 times in the course of a day, and used instant messaging 77 times. The study also found that, on average, employees visited 40 websites during the workday.[15]

What happens when individuals have more information than they can sort out and use? They tend to select out, ignore, pass over, or forget information. Or they may put off further processing until the overload situation is over. Regardless, the result is lost information and less effective communication.

Language

Even when we are communicating in the same language, words mean different things to different people. Age and context are two of the biggest factors that influence such differences.

When Michael Schiller, a business consultant, was talking with his 15-year-old daughter about where she was going with her friends, he told her, "You need to recognize your ARAs and measure against them." Schiller said that in response, his daughter "looked at him like he was from outer space." (For the record, *ARA* stands for accountability, responsibility, and authority.) Those new to corporate lingo may find acronyms such as *ARA*, words such as *skeds* (schedules), and phrases such as *bake your noodle* (provide a service) bewildering, in the same way parents may be mystified by teen slang.[16]

In short, our use of language is far from uniform. If we knew how each of us modified the language, we could minimize communication difficulties, but we usually don't know. Senders tend to assume that the words and terms they use mean the same to the receiver as to them.

Silence

It's easy to ignore silence or lack of communication, precisely because it is defined by the absence of information. However, research suggests silence and withholding communication are both common and problematic.[17] One survey found over 85 percent of managers reported remaining silent about at least one issue of significant concern.[18] Employee silence means managers lack information about ongoing operational

Call-centre operators at Convergys Corp. in New Delhi, India, speak English in serving their customers from North America and the United Kingdom. But even though the operators and customers speak a common language, communication barriers exist because of differences in the countries' cultures and language accents. To overcome these barriers, the operators receive training in North American and British pop culture so they can make small talk and are taught to speak with Western accents so they can be more easily understood by the calling clients.

problems. Moreover, silence regarding discrimination, harassment, corruption, and misconduct means top management cannot take action to eliminate this behaviour. Finally, employees who are silent about important issues may also experience psychological stress.

A study looking at the human factors that caused airline accidents found that pilots who had "take charge" attitudes with their crews were more likely to make wrong decisions than pilots who were more inclusive and consulted with their crews before deciding what to do.[19] It was the communication style of the pilot that affected the crew's behaviour. Crew members were not willing to intervene, even when they had necessary information, when they regularly worked under "decisive" pilots. That kind of silence can be fatal. In his book *Outliers*, Malcolm Gladwell noted, "The kinds of errors that cause plane crashes are invariably errors of teamwork and communication. One pilot knows something important and somehow doesn't tell the other pilot."

Silence is less likely where minority opinions are treated with respect, work group identification is high, and high procedural justice prevails.[20] Practically, this means managers must make sure they behave in a supportive manner when employees voice divergent opinions or express concerns, and they must take these concerns under advisement. One act of ignoring or belittling an employee for expressing concerns may well lead the employee to withhold important information in the future.

Professors Craig Pinder of the Peter B. Gustavson School of Business at the University of Victoria and Karen Harlos of the Desautels Faculty of Management at McGill University have noted that silence generally has often been thought to represent *inaction* or *nonbehaviour*, much as we saw with the airline pilots. But silence is not necessarily inaction, nor a failure to communicate. Silence can, in fact, be a powerful form of communication.[21] It can mean someone is thinking or contemplating a response to a question. It can mean a person is anxious and fearful of speaking. It can signal agreement, dissent, frustration, or anger.

Failing to pay close attention to the silent portion of a conversation can result in missing a vital part of the message. Astute communicators watch for gaps, pauses, and hesitations. They hear and interpret silence. They treat pauses, for instance, as analogous to a flashing yellow light at an intersection—they pay attention to what comes next. Is the person thinking, deciding how to frame an answer? Is the person suffering from communication apprehension? Sometimes the real message in a communication is buried in the silence.

The *Learning About Yourself Exercise* on page 282 will help you determine whether you are a good listener. Effective listening skills are discussed in *From Concepts to Skills* on pages 286–287.

Nonverbal Communication

Every time we deliver a verbal message, we also impart a nonverbal message.[22] Sometimes the nonverbal component may stand alone. Anyone who has ever paid a visit to a singles bar or a nightclub is aware that communication need not be verbal to convey a message. A glance, a stare, a smile, a frown, a provocative body movement—they all convey meaning. This example illustrates that no discussion of communication would be complete without a discussion of **nonverbal communication**. This type of communication includes body movements, facial expressions, and the physical distance between the sender and receiver.

It has been argued that every body movement has a meaning and that no movement is accidental.[23] Through body language, we can say such things as, "Help me, I'm confused," or "Leave me alone, I'm really angry." Rarely do we send our messages consciously. We act out our state of being with nonverbal body language, even if we are

Does body language really make a difference?

SELF-ASSESSMENT LIBRARY

LEARNING ABOUT YOURSELF

1. Listening Self-Inventory
(page 282)

nonverbal communication
Messages conveyed through body movements, facial expressions, and the physical distance between the sender and receiver.

not aware of doing so. We lift one eyebrow for disbelief. We rub our noses for puzzlement. We clasp our arms to isolate ourselves or to protect ourselves. We shrug our shoulders for indifference, wink one eye for intimacy, tap our fingers for impatience, slap our forehead for forgetfulness.[24]

The two most important messages that body language conveys are (1) the extent to which an individual likes another and is interested in his or her views and (2) the relative perceived status between a sender and receiver.[25] For instance, we are more likely to position ourselves closer to people we like and to touch them more often. Similarly, if you feel that you are of higher status than another, you are more likely to display body movements—such as crossed legs or a slouched seated position—that reflect a casual and relaxed manner.[26]

While we may disagree with the specific meaning of certain movements (and different cultures may interpret specific body movements differently), body language adds to and often complicates verbal communication. For instance, if you read the transcript of a meeting, you do not grasp the impact of what was said in the same way you would if you had been there or had seen the meeting on video. Why? There is no record of nonverbal communication. The *intonations*, or emphasis, given to words or phrases is missing.

The *facial expression* of a person also conveys meaning. A snarling face says something different from a smile. Facial expressions, along with intonations, can show arrogance, aggressiveness, fear, shyness, and other characteristics that would never be communicated if you read a transcript of the meeting.

The way individuals space themselves in terms of *physical distance*, commonly called **proxemics**, also has meaning. What is considered proper spacing is largely dependent on cultural norms. For instance, studies have shown that those from "contact" cultures (for example, Arabs, Latin Americans, southern Europeans) are more comfortable with body closeness and touch than those from "noncontact" cultures (for example, Asians, North Americans, northern Europeans).[27] These differences can lead to confusion. If someone stands closer to you than expected according to your cultural norms, you may interpret the action as an expression of aggressiveness or sexual interest. However, if the person stands farther away than you expect, you might think he or she is displeased with you or uninterested. Someone whose cultural norms differ from yours might be very surprised by your interpretation.

It's important for the receiver to be alert to these nonverbal aspects of communication. You should look for nonverbal cues, as well as listen to the literal meaning of a sender's words. In particular, you should be aware of contradictions between the messages. The manager may say that she is free to talk to you about that raise you have been seeking, but you may see nonverbal signals (such as looking at her watch) that suggest this is not the time to discuss the subject. It's not uncommon for people to express one emotion verbally and another nonverbally. These contradictions often suggest that actions speak louder (and more accurately) than words. The *Working with Others Exercise* on page 283 will help you see the value of nonverbal communication in interpersonal relations.

We should also monitor body language with some care. For instance, while it is often thought that people who cross their arms in front of their chest are showing resistance to a message, individuals might also do this if they are feeling cold, regardless of their reaction to a message.

Stress

One of the most difficult times to communicate properly is when one is under stress. One consultant has identified several tips for communicating under stress. These tips are also appropriate for encouraging less stressful communication.[28]

How can you communicate better when you are stressed out?

proxemics The study of physical space in interpersonal relationships.

- *Speak clearly.* Be direct about what you want to say, and avoid hiding behind words. For instance, as difficult as it might be to say, "You did not receive the position," the listener is better able to process the information when it is spoken that directly.

- *Be aware of the nonverbal part of communicating.* Tone, facial expression, and body language send signals that may or may not be consistent with your message. In a stressful situation, it is best to speak in a neutral manner.

- *Think carefully about how you state things.* In many situations, it is better to be restrained so that you do not offend your listener. For instance, when you threaten someone if they do not do exactly what you want ("I insist on speaking to your manager this minute"), you simply escalate the situation. It is better to state what you want calmly, so that you can be heard accurately.

Case Incident—Jeremy W. Caputo Has Communication Problems on page 285 indicates what happens when a person does not communicate effectively.

Organizational Communication

3 How does communication flow in organizations?

How an organization communicates with its constituents plays an important role in whether the constituents actually hear the message.[29] Writing a letter to the mayor threatening a human rights complaint was certainly provocative. But this was not the only communication the Toronto Leaside Girls Hockey Association (TLGHA) launched. The association set other communication targets: reach 10 million people through the media (including a feature in the *Toronto Star*), get 900 Facebook fans, and get 2000 signatures on a petition.

The tactics the association used included the association president sending emails to parents to explain the plan of action; developing a Facebook fan page ("Fairness for Girls' Hockey in Toronto"); and conducting interviews on radio and television, and with the major local newspapers. TLGHA also created an online petition, which was ranked among "the top five most popular petitions on ipetitions.com." The association updated its Facebook page daily and included a "petition quote of the day."

What was the result of all of this attention to communication? When Toronto city council finally debated the issue, it was long and rancorous. The seven-hour debate took place over four days. Then-mayor David Miller sided with TLGHA, saying that the girls did not get enough ice time. The volunteer boards of the eight arenas were "ordered to allocate their ice equitably." So what can organizations do to make communication more effective?

In this section, we explore ways that communication occurs in organizations, including the direction of communication, formal small-group networks, the grapevine, and electronic communications.

Direction of Communication

Communication can flow downward, upward, and/or laterally in organizations.[30] We will explore each of these directional flows and their implications.

Downward

Communication that flows from one level of a group or organization to a lower level is downward communication. When we think of managers communicating with employees, the downward pattern is the one we usually have in mind. Group leaders and managers use this approach to assign goals, provide job instructions, inform employees of policies and procedures, identify problems that need attention, and offer feedback about performance.

When engaging in downward communication, managers must explain the reasons *why* a decision was made. One study found that employees were twice as likely to be committed to changes when the reasons behind them were fully explained. Although this may seem like common sense, many managers feel they are too busy to explain things, or that explanations will "open up a big can of worms." Evidence clearly indicates, though, that explanations increase employee commitment and support of decisions.[31] Toronto-based RL Solutions, a health care software developer, shares all of its performance and financial information with employees, so that everyone feels that they are in the loop.[32]

Upward

Upward communication flows to a higher level in the group or organization. It's used to provide feedback to higher-ups, inform them of progress toward goals, and relay current problems. Upward communication keeps managers aware of how employees feel about their jobs, co-workers, and the organization in general. Managers also rely on upward communication for ideas on how things can be improved. Port Coquitlam, BC-based Benefits by Design, a benefits administration agency, encourages an open-door policy so that staff members can take their concerns to their managers as soon as possible.[33]

Given that job responsibilities of most managers and supervisors have expanded, upward communication is increasingly difficult because managers are overwhelmed and easily distracted. As well, sometimes managers subtly (or not so subtly) discourage employees from speaking up.[34] To engage in effective upward communication, try to reduce distractions (meet in a conference room if you can, rather than your boss's office or cubicle), communicate in headlines, not paragraphs (your job is to get your boss's attention, not to engage in a meandering discussion), support your headlines with actionable items (what you believe should happen), and prepare an agenda to make sure you use your boss's attention well.[35]

In general, few Canadian firms rely on upward communication. In their study of 375 Canadian organizations, David Saunders, dean of Queen's School of Business, and Joanne Leck, associate dean (research) at the University of Ottawa School of Management, found that unionized organizations were more likely to use upward communication.[36] The form of upward communication most used was grievance procedures.

Lateral

When communication occurs among members of the same work group, among members of work groups at the same level, among managers at the same level, or among any horizontally equivalent employees, we describe it as lateral (or horizontal) communication.

Horizontal communication is often necessary to save time and to ease coordination. In some cases, lateral relationships are formally sanctioned. Often, they are informally created to short-circuit the vertical hierarchy and speed up action. So lateral communication can, from management's perspective, be good or bad. Because strict adherence to the formal vertical structure for all communications can slow the efficient and accurate transfer of information, lateral communication can be beneficial. In such cases, it occurs with the knowledge and support of managers. But it can create dysfunctional conflicts when the formal vertical channels are breached, when members go above or around their managers to get things done, or when employers find out that actions have been taken or decisions made without their knowledge.

Small-Group Networks

Communication networks define the channels by which information flows. These channels are one of two varieties—either formal or informal. **Formal networks** are typically vertical, follow the authority chain, and are limited to task-related communications. Exhibit 7-3 illustrates three common formal small-group networks: *chain*,

communication networks
Channels by which information flows.

formal networks Task-related communications that follow the authority chain.

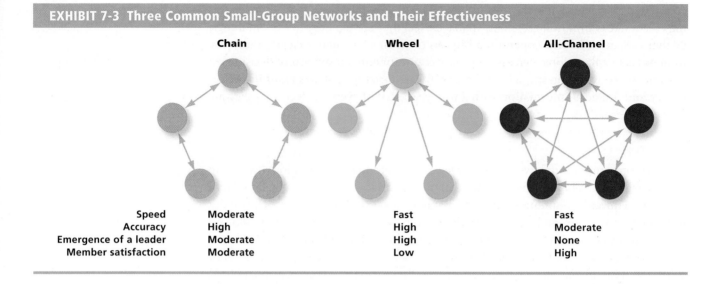

EXHIBIT 7-3 Three Common Small-Group Networks and Their Effectiveness

	Chain	Wheel	All-Channel
Speed	Moderate	Fast	Fast
Accuracy	High	High	Moderate
Emergence of a leader	Moderate	High	None
Member satisfaction	Moderate	Low	High

wheel, and *all-channel*. The chain network rigidly follows the formal chain of command. The wheel network relies on the leader to act as the central conduit for all the group's communication. The all-channel network permits all group members to communicate actively with one another. As Exhibit 7-3 illustrates, the effectiveness of each network depends on the dependent variable you are concerned about. For instance, the structure of the wheel network facilitates the emergence of a leader, the all-channel network is best if high member satisfaction is most important, and the chain network is best if accuracy is most important. Thus, we conclude that no single network is appropriate for all occasions.

The Grapevine

The most common **informal network** in the organization is the **grapevine**. Research has found that 75 percent of employees hear about matters first through rumours on the grapevine.[37] A recent study shows that grapevine or word-of-mouth information from peers about a company has important effects on whether job applicants join an organization.[38] Thus it is an important source of information for many employees.

The grapevine has three main characteristics.[39] First, it is not controlled by management. Second, most employees perceive it as more believable and reliable than formal communiqués issued by top management. Finally, it is largely used to serve the interests of the people within it.

Is the information that flows along the grapevine accurate? The evidence indicates that about 75 percent of what is carried is accurate.[40] But what conditions foster an active grapevine? What gets the rumour mill rolling?

It is frequently assumed that rumours start because they make titillating gossip. Research indicates that rumours emerge as a response to situations that are important to us, where there is ambiguity, and under conditions that arouse anxiety.[41] The secrecy and competition that typically prevail in large organizations around such issues as the appointment of new senior managers, the relocation of offices, and the realignment of work assignments create conditions that encourage and sustain rumours on the grapevine. A rumour will persist either until the wants and expectations creating the uncertainty underlying the rumour are fulfilled or until the anxiety is reduced. This chapter's *Point/Counterpoint* on page 281 examines different perspectives on keeping secrets.

What can we conclude from this discussion? Certainly the grapevine is an important part of any group's or organization's communication network and well worth understanding.[42] It gives managers a feel for the morale of their organization, identifies issues

informal networks Communications that flow along social and relational lines.

grapevine The organization's most common informal network.

employees consider important, and helps tap into employee anxieties. The grapevine also serves employees' needs: Small talk creates a sense of closeness and friendship among those who share information, although research suggests it often does so at the expense of those in the "out" group.[43] Managers can reduce the negative consequences of rumours by explaining decisions and openly discussing worst-case possibilities.[44] *OB in Action—Reducing Rumours* gives some tips for reducing the negative consequences of rumours.

Electronic Communications

An indispensable—and in about 71 percent of cases, the primary—medium of communication in today's organizations is electronic. Electronic communications—which include email, instant messaging, text messaging, social networking sites, and blogs—make it possible for you to work, even if you are away from your workstation.

Email

Email's growth has been spectacular, and its use is now so pervasive that it's hard to imagine life without it. As a communication tool, email has a long list of benefits. Email messages can be quickly written, edited, and stored. They can be distributed to one person or thousands with a click of a mouse. They can be read, in their entirety, at the convenience of the recipient. And the cost of sending formal email messages to employees is a fraction of the cost of printing, duplicating, and distributing a comparable letter or brochure.[46]

Email, of course, is not without drawbacks. Email has added considerably to the number of hours worked per week, according to a study by Christina Cavanagh, professor of management communications at the Richard Ivey School of Business, University of Western Ontario.[47] One researcher suggests that knowledge workers devote about

> Ever notice that communicating via email can lead to misunderstandings?

OB in ACTION
Reducing Rumours

→ **Provide information**: Rumours tend to thrive in the absence of formal communication.

→ **Explain actions** and **decisions** that seem problematic.

→ **Do not shoot** the **messenger**: Respond to rumours calmly and rationally.

→ **Maintain open** communication **channels**: Encourage people to talk about their concerns and ideas.[45]

Toronto-based Upverter was started by three friends (left to right) Zak Homuth, Stephen Hamer, and Michael Woodworth (shown here at the Maker Faire, an event that showcases grassroots innovation). The three, all trained as electrical engineers, wanted to create a network for online collaboration for hardware designers. They launched a "crowd-sourced library of parts and design tools," and the company took off quickly after they demonstrated the service at DemoFall 2011 in Santa Clara, California.

28 percent of their day to email.[48] While the increase in the volume of email seems to have slowed, up just 9 percent between 2006 and 2007 (compared with 26 percent between 2005 and 2006), the volume of junk mail shows no let-up.[49] Canadians divert 42 percent of their email directly to "junk mail" folders, according to an Ipsos Reid study. Over one-third of the survey respondents said they had trouble handling all of their email, and only 43 percent thought that email increased efficiency at work.

The following are some of the most significant limitations of email and what organizations should do to reduce or eliminate these problems:

- *Misinterpreting the message.* It's true that we often misinterpret verbal messages, but the potential for misinterpretation with email is even greater. One research team found that we can accurately decode an email's intent and tone only 50 percent of the time, yet most of us vastly overestimate our ability to send and interpret clear messages. If you are sending an important message, make sure you reread it for clarity. Moreover, if you are upset about the presumed tone of someone else's message, keep in mind that you may be misinterpreting it.[50]

- *Communicating negative messages.* When companies have negative information to communicate, managers need to think carefully. Email may not be the best way to communicate the message. When RadioShack decided to lay off 400 employees, it was widely criticized for doing it via email. Employees need to be careful communicating negative messages via email, too. Justen Deal, 22, wrote an email critical of some strategic decisions made by his employer, pharmaceutical giant Kaiser Permanente. In the email, he criticized the "misleadership" of Kaiser CEO George Halvorson and questioned the financing of several information technology projects. Within hours, Deal's computer was seized; he was later fired.[51]

- *Time-consuming nature of email.* An estimated 6 trillion emails are sent every year, of which approximately 60 percent, or 36 trillion, are nonspam messages,[52] and someone has to answer all those nonspam messages! A survey of Canadian managers revealed 58 percent spent 2 to 4 hours per day reading and responding to emails. The average worker checks his or her email 50 times a day. Some people, such as venture capitalist and Dallas Mavericks owner Mark Cuban, receive more than 1000 messages a day (Cuban says 10 percent are of the "I want" variety). Although you probably don't receive *that* many, most of us have trouble keeping up with all email, especially as we advance in our career. Experts suggest the following strategies:

  - *Do not check email in the morning.* Take care of important tasks before getting ensnared in emails. Otherwise, you may never get to those tasks.
  - *Check email in batches.* Don't check email continually throughout the day. Some experts suggest twice a day. "You wouldn't want to do a new load of laundry every time you have a dirty pair of socks," says one expert.
  - *Unsubscribe.* Stop newsletters and other subscriptions you don't really need.
  - *Stop sending email.* The best way to receive lots of email is to send lots of email, so send less. Shorter emails garner shorter responses. "A well-written message can and should be as concise as possible," says one expert.
  - *Declare email bankruptcy.* Some people, like recording artist Moby and venture capitalist Fred Wilson, become so overwhelmed by email they declare "email bankruptcy." They wipe out their entire inbox and start over.

    Although some of these steps may not work for you, keep in mind that email can be less productive than it seems: We often seem busy but get less accomplished through email than we might think.[53]

- *Email emotions.* We tend to think of email as a sort of sterile, faceless form of communication. Some researchers say the lack of visual and vocal cues means emotionally positive messages, such as those including praise, will be seen as more emotionally neutral than the sender intended.[54] But, as you no doubt know, emails are often highly emotional. One CEO said, "I've seen people not talk to each other, turf wars break out and people quit their jobs as a result of emails." Email tends to make senders feel free to write things they would never be comfortable saying in person. Facial expressions tend to temper our emotional expressions, but in email, there is no other face to look at, and so many of us fire away. An increasingly common way of communicating emotions in email is with emoticons (see Exhibit 7-4). For example, Yahoo!'s email software allows users to pick from 75 graphical emoticons. Although emoticons used to be considered for personal use only, adults are increasingly using them in business emails. Still, some see them as too informal for business use.

  If you find yourself angry or upset as you write an email, save it as a draft, and look at it again once you are on a more even keel. When others send flaming messages, remain calm and try not to respond in kind. And, as hard as it might sometimes be, try to see the flaming message from the other party's point of view. That in itself may calm your nerves.[55] *Case Incident—Dianna Abdala* on page 284 considers the limitations of communicating by email.

- *Privacy concerns.* There are two privacy issues with email. First, you need to be aware that your emails may be, and often are, monitored. Also, you cannot always trust that the recipient of your email will keep it confidential. For these reasons, you should not write anything you would not want made public. Second, you need to exercise caution in forwarding email from your company's email account to a personal, or "public" (for example, Gmail, Yahoo!, MSN), email account. These accounts often are not as secure as corporate accounts, so when you forward a company email to them, you may be violating your organization's policy or unintentionally disclosing confidential data. Many employers hire vendors to sift through emails, using software to catch not only the obvious keywords ("insider trading") but also the vague ("that thing we talked about") or guilt ridden ("regret"). One survey found that nearly 40 percent of companies have employees whose only job is to read other employees' email. You are being watched—so be careful what you email![56]

Focus on Ethics illustrates that employees cannot assume that their email is private.

EXHIBIT 7-4 Showing Emotions in Email

Email need not be emotion-free. Over the years, email users have developed a way of displaying text, as well as a set of symbols (emoticons) for expressing emotions. For instance, the use of all caps (as in THIS PROJECT NEEDS YOUR IMMEDIATE ATTENTION!) is the email equivalent of shouting. The following highlights some emoticons:

:)	Smile	:-e	Disappointed
\<g\>	Grin	:-@	Scream
:(	Frown	:-0	Yell
;)	Wink	:-D	Shock or surprise
:-[	Really sad face	:'(	Crying

FOCUS ON ETHICS ## Your Email Can Get You Fired

Should your email be safe from your manager's eyes? A recent poll conducted by Environics found that 35 percent of Canadians say they have sent emails from their work-based email address that they worry could come back to hurt them.[57] Even so, about the same percentage of employees believe their employers probably check on email accounts, and 52 percent think their employer has the right to do so. Moreover, 30 percent of Canadians know someone who has been disciplined because of an email sent at work.

While a City of Toronto employee was merely disciplined after sending "inappropriate" pictures using a city computer, Fred Jones (not his real name) was fired from a Canadian company for forwarding dirty jokes to his clients. Until this incident, Jones had been a high-performing employee who sold network computers for his company. Jones thought that he was only sending the jokes to clients who liked them, and assumed that the clients would tell him if they did not want to receive the jokes. Instead, a client complained to the company about receiving the dirty jokes. After an investigation, the company fired Jones. Jones is still puzzled about being fired. He views his email as private; to him, sending jokes is the same as telling them at the water cooler.

Jones was not aware that under current law, employee information, including email, is not necessarily private. Most federal employees, provincial public sector employees, and employees working for federally regulated industries are covered by the federal Privacy Act and Access to Information Act, in place since 1985. Many private sector employees are not covered by privacy legislation, however.

Ann Cavoukian, Information and Privacy Commissioner of Ontario, notes that "employees deserve to be treated like adults and companies should limit surveillance to rare instances, such as when there is suspicion of criminal activity or harassment."[58] She suggests that employers use respect and courtesy when dealing with employees' email, and she likens email to office phone calls, which generally are not monitored by the employer. It is clearly important, in any event, that employees be aware of their company's policy on email. The *Ethical Dilemma Exercise* on page 284 asks you to consider the boundaries of the non–work-related use of computers by employees.

Instant Messaging and Text Messaging

Instant messaging (IM) and text messaging (TM), which have been popular among teens for more than a decade, are now rapidly moving into business.[59]

The growth of IM and TM has been spectacular. In 2002, Canadians sent 174 million text messages, while the estimate for 2011 is 72.6 billion, a staggering increase.[60] More people use IM than email as their primary communication tool at work.[61]

IM and TM represent fast and inexpensive means for managers to stay in touch with employees and for employees to stay in touch with one another. In an increasing number of cases, this is not just a luxury, it is a business imperative.

Despite the advantages of IM and TM, email is still probably a better device for conveying long messages that need to be saved. IM is preferable for one- or two-line messages that would just clutter up an email inbox. On the downside, some IM/TM users find the technology intrusive and distracting. Its continual presence can make it hard for employees to concentrate and stay focused. For example, a survey of managers revealed that in 86 percent of meetings, at least some participants checked TM, and another survey revealed 20 percent of managers report having been reprimanded for using wireless devices during meetings.[62] Finally, because instant messages can be intercepted easily, many organizations are concerned about the security of IM/TM.[63]

One other point: It's important to not let the informality of text messaging ("omg! r u serious? brb") spill over into business emails. Many prefer to keep business communication relatively formal. A survey of employers revealed that 58 percent rate grammar, spelling, and punctuation as "very important" in email messages.[64] By making sure your professional communications are, well, professional, you will show yourself to be mature and serious. Avoid jargon and slang, use formal titles, use formal email addresses for yourself (lose that partygirl@yahoo.com address), and take care to make your message concise and well written. That does not mean, of course, that you have to give up TM or IM; you just need to maintain the boundaries between how you communicate with your friends and how you communicate professionally.

Social Networking

Nowhere has communication been more transformed than in social networking. You are doubtless familiar with and perhaps a user of social networking platforms such as Facebook. LinkedIn, XING, and ZoomInfo are all professional websites that allow users to set up lists of contacts and do everything from casually "pinging" them with updates to hosting chat rooms for all or some of the users' contacts. Some companies, such as IBM, have their own social networks. IBM is selling its BluePages tool to companies and individual users. Microsoft is doing the same thing with its SharePoint tool.

To get the most out of social networks and avoid irritating your contacts, use them for high-value items only—not as an everyday or even every-week tool. Remember that a prospective employer might check your Facebook entry. Some entrepreneurs have developed software that mines such websites for companies (or individuals) that want to check up on a job applicant (or potential date). So keep in mind that what you post may be read by people other than your intended contacts.[65] Employees have been disciplined for Facebook postings, as this *OB in the Workplace* shows.

OB in the WORKPLACE

An RCMP Officer's Facebook Posts Land Him in Trouble

What was he thinking? A 26-year-old RCMP officer based in Nanaimo, BC, ended up under investigation for comments he posted on Facebook, including "Night shift and St. Paddy's Day, can't wait to drop kick all the drunk idiots" and "Bar watch shift tonight, I'm gonna catch me a ginger."[66] The officer, who has not been named, thought he was just joking among friends. He also blamed it on the stress of his job. "I've got a stressful job and the way I deal with it is I use humour. It's obviously pretty stupid to post that stuff on there. I didn't intend it to go out in the public."

The BC RCMP detachments received social media guidelines in the weeks before the officer's Facebook account came under scrutiny.

RCMP E Division senior media relations officer Rob Vermeulen noted, "You're accountable on and off duty. If there's a lesson we can already learn, for police officers and everyone else, there's no reasonable expectation of privacy of stuff we post to the Internet."

Blogs

Peter Aceto, CEO of Toronto-based ING Direct Canada, is a big fan of the **blog (web log)**, a website about a single person or company that is usually updated daily. He encourages his employees to have blogs and has one himself (http://blog.ingdirect. ca/author/paceto/). Aceto allows readers to post comments and rate his blog entries.

Obviously, Aceto is not the only fan of blogs. Experts estimate that more than 112 million blogs and more than 350 million blog entries are now read daily. While

blog (web log) A website where entries are written, and generally displayed in reverse chronological order, about news, events, and personal diary entries.

most blogs are written by individuals, many organizations and organizational leaders have blogs that speak for the organization.

OB in the Street considers employers' responses to blogging.

OB in the STREET

When a Personal Blog Becomes a Workplace Issue

Should blog entries about work be a concern for employers?   Andrew McDonald landed an internship with the television channel Comedy Central, and on his first day at work, he started a blog.[67] His supervisors asked him to change various things about the blog, essentially removing all specific references to Comedy Central. Kelly Kreth was fired from her job as a marketing director for blogging about her co-workers. So was Jessa Werner, who later said, "I came to the realization that I probably shouldn't have been blogging about work."

Although some companies have policies in place governing the content of blogs, many don't. Many bloggers think their personal blogs are outside their employer's purview, and 39 percent of individual bloggers say they have posted comments that could be construed as harmful to their company's reputation.

If someone else in a company happens to read a blog entry, there is nothing to keep him or her from sharing that information with others, and the employee could be dismissed as a result. Some companies may not fire an employee over any blog entry short of one that broke the law. But most organizations are unlikely to be so forgiving of any blog entry that might cast a negative light on them. In short, if you are going to have a personal blog, maintain a strict work-personal "firewall."

As a variant of blogs (which are generally either personal or company-owned), Twitter is a service that allows users to post "micro-blog" entries about any topic, including work. Many organizational leaders send Twitter messages ("tweets"), but they can come from any employee about any work topic, leaving organizations with less control over the communication of important or sensitive information. While many CEOs worry about the use of Twitter, Peter Aceto posts to Twitter at least five times a day. One of his tweets in November 2010 informed his 3785 Twitter followers that his daughter had just scored her first goal. Aceto uses social media because "I felt my personal involvement in being transparent would be important for our brand."[68] A 2010 study found that only 8 percent of CEOs at the world's largest companies have Twitter accounts, while 64 percent have no social media presence at all.[69]

Managing Information

4 How is information managed?

We all have more information at our disposal than ever. It brings us many benefits, but also three important challenges: information overload, being always on call, and information security. We consider each in turn.

Dealing with Information Overload

Do you find yourself bombarded with information—from email, blogs, Internet surfing, IMs, cellphones, and television? You are not alone. Basex, a company that looks at worker efficiency, found the largest part of an average employee's day—43 percent—is spent on matters that are neither important nor urgent, such as responding to non-crucial emails and surfing the web. (In fairness to email, Basex also found 25 percent of an employee's time was spent composing and responding to important email.[70])

Semiconductor manufacturer Intel designed an 8-month experiment to see how limiting information overload might aid productivity. One group of employees was told to limit both digital and in-person contact for 4 hours on Tuesdays, while another group followed its usual routine. The first group was more productive, and 75 percent of its members suggested the program be expanded.[71] "It's huge. We were expecting less," remarked Nathan Zeldes, an Intel engineer who led the experiments. "When people are uninterrupted they can sit back and design chips and really think."[72]

Some of the biggest technology companies, including Microsoft, Intel, Google, and IBM, are banding together to study the issue more systematically. As one of the team members, IBM's John Tang, noted, "There's a competitive advantage to figuring out how to address this problem."[73]

We have already reviewed some ways of reducing the time sunk into emails. More generally, as the Intel study shows, it may make sense to connect to technology less frequently, to, in the words of one article, "avoid letting the drumbeat of digital missives constantly shake up and reorder to-do lists." Lynaia Lutes, an account supervisor for a small Texas company, was able to think much more strategically by taking a break from digital information each day. In the past, she said, "I basically completed an assignment" but didn't approach it strategically. By creating such breaks for yourself, you may be better able to prioritize and think about the big picture and, thereby, be more effective.[75]

OB in ACTION

Social Networking Responsibly

→ **Don't write** anything you would be **uncomfortable** having your employer read.

→ Keep in mind that **what you publish** could be public for a **long time**.

→ If you are writing about your company, **be transparent about your role** in the organization.

→ **Get approval** from the organization before posting **private** or internal **conversations**.

→ **Be up-front** about correcting errors and updating previous posts.[74]

Being Always on Call

As information technology and immediate communication have become a more prevalent component of modern organizational life, more employees find they are never able to get offline. The addictive potential of constant communication is so great that some harried managers jokingly refer to their BlackBerrys as "Crackberries."[76] Some business travellers were disappointed when airlines began offering wireless Internet connections in flight because they could no longer use their time in flight as a rare opportunity to relax without a constant barrage of organizational communications. The negative impacts of these communication devices can spill over into employees' personal lives as well. Both employees and their spouses relate the use of electronic communication technologies outside of work to higher levels of work-life conflict.[77] Employees must balance the need for constant communication with their own personal need for breaks from work, or they risk burnout from being on call 24 hours a day.

Information Security

Security is a huge concern for nearly all organizations with private or proprietary information about clients, customers, and employees. A Merrill Lynch survey of 50 executives found 52 percent rated leaks of company information as their number one information security concern, topping viruses and hackers. In response, most companies actively monitor employee Internet use and email records, and some even use video surveillance and record phone conversations. Necessary though they may be, such practices may seem invasive to employees. An organization can buttress employee concerns by involving them in the creation of information-security policies and giving them some control over how their personal information is used.[78]

To help you find a balance between your desire to network and to behave ethically toward the company in which you are employed, *OB in Action—Social Networking Responsibly* summarizes rules established by IBM.

GLOBAL IMPLICATIONS

Effective communication is difficult under the best of conditions. Cross-cultural factors clearly create the potential for increased communication problems.

Cultural Barriers to Communication

Researchers have identified four specific problems related to language difficulties in cross-cultural communication.[79] First, there are *barriers caused by semantics*. As we have noted previously, words mean different things to different people. This is particularly true for people from different national cultures. Some words, for instance, don't translate between cultures. Understanding the word *sisu* will help you communicate with people from Finland, but this word does not have an exact translation in English. It means something akin to "guts" or "dogged persistence." Similarly, the new capitalists in Russia may have difficulty communicating with their English-speaking counterparts because English terms such as *efficiency*, *free market*, and *regulation* cannot be directly translated into Russian.

Second, there are *barriers caused by word connotations*. Words imply different things in different languages. The Japanese word *hai* translates as "yes," but its connotation may be "yes, I'm listening," rather than "yes, I agree." Western executives may be hampered in their negotiations if they don't understand this connotation.

Third are *barriers caused by tone differences*. In some cultures, language is formal; in others, it's informal. In some cultures, the tone changes depending on the context: People speak differently at home, in social situations, and at work. Using a personal, informal style in a situation where a more formal style is expected can be embarrassing and offensive.

Fourth are *differences in tolerance for conflict and methods for resolving conflicts*. Individuals from individualist cultures tend to be more comfortable with direct conflicts and will make the source of their disagreements overt. Collectivists are more likely to acknowledge conflict only implicitly and avoid emotionally charged disputes. They may attribute conflicts to the situation more than to the individuals and therefore may not require explicit apologies to repair relationships, whereas individualists prefer explicit statements accepting responsibility for conflicts and public apologies to restore relationships.

Cultural Context

Cultures tend to differ in the degree to which context influences the meaning individuals take from communication.[80] In **high-context cultures** like China, Vietnam, and Saudi Arabia, people rely heavily on nonverbal and subtle situational cues when communicating with others. What is not said may be more significant than what is said. A person's official status, place in society, and reputation carry considerable weight in communications. In contrast, people from Europe and North America reflect their **low-context cultures**. They rely essentially on words to convey meaning. Body language or formal titles are secondary to spoken and written words (see Exhibit 7-5).

What do these contextual differences mean in terms of communication? Actually, quite a lot! Communication in high-context cultures implies considerably more trust by both parties.

What may appear, to an outsider, as a casual and insignificant conversation is important because it reflects the desire to build a relationship and create trust. Oral agreements imply strong commitments in high-context cultures. Also, who you are—your age, seniority, rank in the organization—are highly valued and heavily influence your credibility. But in low-context cultures, enforceable contracts will tend to be in writing,

high-context cultures Cultures that rely heavily on nonverbal and subtle situational cues in communication.

low-context cultures Cultures that rely heavily on words to convey meaning in communication.

Globalization has changed the way Toyota Motor Corporation provides employees with the information they need for decision making. In the past, Toyota transferred employee knowledge on the job from generation to generation through "tacit understanding," a common communication method used in the conformist and subdued Japanese culture. Today, however, as a global organization, Toyota transfers knowledge of its production methods to overseas employees by bringing them to its training centre in Japan, shown here, to teach them production methods by using how-to manuals, practice drills, and lectures.

EXHIBIT 7-5 High- vs. Low-Context Cultures

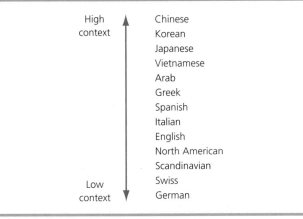

precisely worded, and highly legalistic. Similarly, low-context cultures value directness. Managers are expected to be explicit and precise in conveying intended meaning. It's quite different in high-context cultures, where managers tend to "make suggestions" rather than give orders.

A Cultural Guide

When communicating with people from a different culture, what can you do to reduce misperceptions, misinterpretations, and misevaluations? Following these four rules can be helpful:[81]

> How can you improve cross-cultural communication?

- *Assume differences until similarity is proven.* Most of us assume that others are more similar to us than they actually are. But people from different countries often are very different from us. So you are

Ottawa-based Donna Cona made history when it designed and installed the computer network for the government of Nunavut. Two-thirds of the firm's software engineers are Aboriginal. Peter Baril, Nunavut's director of information technology operations, notes: "Donna Cona's quiet and knowledgeable approach was perhaps the most important skill brought to our project. No other style could have worked in this predominantly Aboriginal environment."

far less likely to make an error if you assume that others are different from you, rather than assuming similarity until difference is proven.

- *Emphasize description rather than interpretation or evaluation.* Interpreting or evaluating what someone has said or done, in contrast with describing, is based more on the observer's culture and background than on the observed situation. As a result, delay judgment until you have had sufficient time to observe and interpret the situation from the differing perspectives of all the cultures involved.

- *Practise empathy.* Before sending a message, put yourself in the recipient's shoes. What are his or her values, experiences, and frames of reference? What do you know about his or her education, upbringing, and background that can give you added insight? Try to see the other person as he or she really is.

- *Treat your interpretations as a working hypothesis.* Once you have developed an explanation for a new situation, or think you empathize with someone from a foreign culture, treat your interpretation as a hypothesis that needs further testing rather than as a certainty. Carefully assess the feedback provided by recipients to see if it confirms your hypothesis. For important decisions or communiqués, you can also check with other foreign and home-country colleagues to ensure that your interpretations are on target.

LESSONS LEARNED

- Just because something is said, it does not mean that it was heard.
- Communication is rarely "objective." Both the sender's and receiver's reality affects the framing and understanding of the message.
- Information overload is a serious problem for most individuals.

SNAPSHOT SUMMARY

 The Communication Process
Choosing a Channel

Summary and Implications

1 **How does communication work?** Findings in the chapter suggest that the goal of perfect communication is unattainable. Yet there is evidence that demonstrates a positive relationship between effective communication (which includes factors such as perceived trust, perceived accuracy, desire for interaction, top-management receptiveness, and upward information requirements) and employee productivity.[82] Therefore, choosing the correct channel, being an effective listener, and using feedback well may make for more effective communication.

2 **What are the barriers to communication?**   Human beings will always be subject to errors in communication because of factors including filtering, selective perception, defensiveness, emotions, information overload, language, and stress. What is said may not be what is heard. Whatever the sender's expectations, the decoded message in the mind of the receiver represents the receiver's reality. This "reality" will determine the individual's reactions, including performance, motivation, and degree of satisfaction in the workplace. Nonverbal cues help provide a clearer picture of what someone is trying to say. Silence can be an important communication clue, and failing to pay attention to silence can result in missing some or all of a message. Good communicators hear and interpret silence.

3 **How does communication flow in organizations?**   Communication can flow down, upward, and laterally, and by formal and informal channels in organizations. We noted that there are three common formal small-group networks: *chain*, *wheel*, and *all-channel*. The most common informal network in the organization is the *grapevine*. Greater use of informal channels will increase communication flow, reduce uncertainty, and improve group performance and satisfaction. We also noted that email, although pervasive, is causing more stress and can be misused, so it is not always the most effective means of communication. Instant messaging, text messaging, and social networking have found their way into the workplace with mixed results.

4 **How is information managed?**   Dealing with information overload is a challenge many employees face. Reducing the amount of time spent on emails, social networking, text messaging, and instant messaging by connecting to technology less frequently is one way of minimizing interruptions and being able to stay productive. Employees must also balance the need for constant communication with their own personal need for breaks from work, or they risk burnout. Information security is a top concern for nearly all organizations, and most have safeguards in place, including monitoring of employee technology use, to avoid leaks of company information.

OB at Work

OB at work

for Review

1. Describe the communication process and identify its key components. Give an example of how this process operates with both oral and written messages.

2. Contrast encoding and decoding.

3. What does the expression "sometimes the real message in a communication is buried in the silence" mean?

4. What is nonverbal communication? Does it aid or hinder verbal communication?

5. Identify three common formal small-group networks and give the advantages of each.

6. What conditions stimulate the emergence of rumours?

7. What are the advantages and disadvantages of email? Of instant messaging?

8. What are the key challenges in managing information?

9. List four specific problems related to language difficulties in cross-cultural communication.

10. Contrast high- and low-context cultures. What do the differences mean for communication?

for Critical Thinking

1. "Ineffective communication is the fault of the sender." Do you agree or disagree? Discuss.

2. What can you do to improve the likelihood that your message will be received and understood as you intended?

3. How might managers use the grapevine for their benefit?

4. Using the concept of channel richness, give examples of messages best conveyed by email, in face-to-face communication, and on the company bulletin board.

5. "Most people are poor listeners." Do you agree or disagree? Defend your position.

for You

- If you are having difficulty communicating with someone, you might consider that both you and the other person are contributing something to that breakdown. This tends to be true even if you are inclined to believe that the other person is the party more responsible for the breakdown.

- Often, either selective perception or defensiveness gets in the way of communication. As you work in your groups on student projects, try to observe communication flows more critically to help you understand ways that communication can be improved and dysfunctional conflict avoided.

POINT

Keeping Secrets Means Keeping One's Word

We are better off keeping more things to ourselves.[83] Workplace gossip is out of control, and very often, we cannot trust people with secrets. Tell a friend never, ever to tell something to someone else, and you have aroused in them an irresistible desire to share the "juicy news" with others. A good rule of thumb is that if you are sure a confidante has told no one else, that probably means he or she has told only three other people. You might think this is a paranoid reaction, but research suggests that so-called confidantes rarely keep secrets, even when they swear they will.

Keeping our own secrets is normal, and most children learn to do it at an early age. People survive by protecting themselves, and when someone is keeping a secret, that person usually has a good reason for doing so.

Even when we feel like confiding in someone else, it's prudent to keep confidential information to ourselves. Research shows that few of us are able to keep secrets, and that if we fear certain negative consequences of telling our secrets (for example, our confidante will think less of us or will tell others), those fears don't stop us from blabbing and are often justified.

Organizational secrets are all the more important to keep quiet. Organizations are rumour mills, and we can permanently damage our careers and the organizations for which we work by disclosing confidential information. Improper disclosure of organizational proprietary information is a huge cost and concern for organizations. A recent poll of managers revealed that 84 percent of employees think it's very common for employees to engage in office gossip, while 63 percent of managers think it has a negative effect on the workplace.

COUNTERPOINT

Keeping Secrets Can Be Unhealthy

The problem with keeping secrets is that they are expensive to maintain.

One social psychologist found that when people are instructed not to disclose certain information, it becomes more distracting and difficult for them to do so. In fact, the more people are instructed to keep something to themselves, the more they see the secret in everything they do. "We don't realize that in keeping it secret we've created an obsession in a jar," he says. So keeping things hidden takes a toll on our psyche—it (usually unnecessarily) adds to the mental burdens we carry with us.

Another psychologist has found that these costs are real. This researcher found that young people who experienced a traumatic experience often had more health problems later in life. As he researched the topic further, he found out why. Generally, these people conceal the event from others. He even did an experiment that showed that when people who have experienced traumatic events shared them, they later had fewer health problems than people who had not shared them. There isn't one identifiable reason why sharing these traumatic events seems to help people, but the result has been found repeatedly.

There is another positive effect of gossip: The threat of it helps people behave. One study revealed that in a "dictator game," concern about gossip led individuals to share resources more equally. So for our own well-being and that of others, we are better off sharing than keeping secrets.[84]

LEARNING ABOUT **YOURSELF** EXERCISE

Listening Self-Inventory

Go through this 15-item questionnaire twice. The first time, mark yes or no next to each question. Mark as truthfully as you can in light of your behaviour in recent meetings or gatherings you attended. The second time, mark a plus (+) next to your answer if you are satisfied with that answer, or a minus (–) next to the answer if you wish you could have answered that question differently.

	Yes	No	+ or –
1. I frequently attempt to listen to several conversations at the same time.	_____	_____	_____
2. I like people to give me only the facts and then let me make my own interpretations.	_____	_____	_____
3. I sometimes pretend to pay attention to people.	_____	_____	_____
4. I consider myself a good judge of nonverbal communications.	_____	_____	_____
5. I usually know what another person is going to say before he or she says it.	_____	_____	_____
6. I usually end conversations that don't interest me by diverting my attention from the speaker.	_____	_____	_____
7. I frequently nod, frown, or whatever to let the speaker know how I feel about what he or she is saying.	_____	_____	_____
8. I usually respond immediately when someone has finished talking.	_____	_____	_____
9. I evaluate what is being said while it is being said.	_____	_____	_____
10. I usually formulate a response while the other person is still talking.	_____	_____	_____
11. The speaker's delivery style frequently keeps me from listening to content.	_____	_____	_____
12. I usually ask people to clarify what they have said rather than guess at the meaning.	_____	_____	_____
13. I make a concerted effort to understand other people's point of view.	_____	_____	_____
14. I frequently hear what I expect to hear rather than what is said.	_____	_____	_____
15. Most people feel that I have understood their point of view when we disagree.	_____	_____	_____

Scoring Key:

The correct answers to the 15 questions, based on listening theory, are as follows: (1) No; (2) No; (3) No; (4) Yes; (5) No; (6) No; (7) No; (8) No; (9) No; (10) No; (11) No; (12) Yes; (13) Yes; (14) No; (15) Yes. To determine your score, add up the number of incorrect answers, multiply by 7, and subtract that total from 105. If you scored between 91 and 105, you have good listening habits. Scores of 77 to 90 suggest significant room for improvement. Scores below 76 indicate that you are a poor listener and need to work hard on improving this skill.

Source: E. C. Glenn and E. A. Pood, "Listening Self-Inventory," *Supervisory Management*, January 1989, pp. 12–15. Reprinted by permission.

SELF-ASSESSMENT LIBRARY | LEARNING ABOUT YOURSELF

More Learning About Yourself Exercises

Additional self-assessments relevant to this chapter appear on MyOBLab (**www.pearsoned.ca/myoblab**).

II.A.1 What's My Face-to-Face Communication Style?

IV.E.3 Am I a Gossip?

When you complete the additional assessments, consider the following:

1. Am I surprised about my score?

2. Would my friends evaluate me similarly?

BREAKOUT **GROUP** EXERCISES

Form small groups to discuss the following topics, as assigned by your instructor:

1. What differences have you observed in the ways that men and women communicate?

2. How do you know when a person is listening to you? When someone is ignoring you?

3. Describe a situation in which you ignored someone. What impact did it have on that person's subsequent communication behaviours?

WORKING WITH OTHERS EXERCISE

An Absence of Nonverbal Communication

This exercise will help you see the value of nonverbal communication in interpersonal relations.

1. The class is to divide into pairs (Party A and Party B).

2. Party A is to select a topic from the following list:

   a. Managing in the Middle East is significantly different from managing in North America.

   b. Bureaucracies are frustrating to work in.

   c. An employer has a responsibility to provide every employee with an interesting and challenging job.

   d. Everyone should register to vote.

   e. Organizations should require all employees to undergo regular drug testing.

   f. Individuals who have majored in business or economics make better employees than those who have majored in history or English.

   g. The place where you get your college or university degree is more important in determining career success than what you learn while you're there.

   h. Effective managers often have to lie as part of their job.

   i. It's unethical for a manager to purposely distort communications to get a favourable outcome.

3. Party B is to choose his or her position on this topic (for example, arguing *against* the view that "employers have a responsibility to provide every employee with an interesting and challenging job"). Party A now must automatically take the opposite position.

4. The 2 parties have 10 minutes in which to debate their topic. The catch is that individuals can only communicate verbally. They may *not* use gestures, facial movements, body movements, or any other nonverbal communication. It may help for both parties to maintain an expressionless look and to sit on their hands to remind them of these restrictions.

5. After the debate is over, the class should discuss the following:

   a. How effective was communication during these debates?

   b. What barriers to communication existed?

   c. What purposes does nonverbal communication serve?

   d. Relate the lessons learned in this exercise to problems that might occur when communicating on the telephone or through email.

ETHICAL **DILEMMA** EXERCISE

Defining the Boundaries of Technology

You work for a company that has no specific policies regarding non–work-related uses of computers and the Internet. It also has no electronic monitoring devices to determine what employees are doing on their computers. Are any of the following actions unethical? Explain your position on each.

1. Using the company's email system for personal reasons during the workday

2. Playing computer games during the workday

3. Using your office computer for personal use (to check sports sites, to shop online) during the workday

4. Looking for a mate on an Internet dating service during the workday

5. Visiting "adult" websites on your office computer during the workday

6. Using your employer's portable communication device (for example, a BlackBerry) for personal use

7. Conducting any of the preceding activities at work but before or after normal work hours

8. For telecommuters working from home, using a computer and Internet access line paid for by your employer to visit online shopping or dating-service sites during normal working hours

---

CASE INCIDENTS

Dianna Abdala

Consider the case of Dianna Abdala.[85] In 2005, Abdala was a recent graduate of Suffolk University's law school. She passed the bar exam and was offered a job at a law firm started by William Korman, a former state prosecutor.

The following is a summary of their email communications:

————Original Message————

From: Dianna Abdala
Sent: Friday, February 03, 2006 9:23 p.m.
To: William A. Korman
Subject: Thank you

Dear Attorney Korman,

At this time, I am writing to inform you that I will not be accepting your offer. After careful consideration, I have come to the conclusion that the pay you are offering would neither fulfill me nor support the lifestyle I am liv-

ing in light of the work I would be doing for you. I have decided instead to work for myself, and reap 100 percent of the benefits that I sew [sic].

Thank you for the interviews.

Dianna L. Abdala, Esq.

————Original Message————

From: William A. Korman
To: Dianna Abdala
Sent: Monday, February 06, 2006 12:15 p.m.
Subject: RE: Thank you

Dianna- -

Given that you had two interviews, were offered and accepted the job (indeed, you had a definite start date), I am surprised that you chose an e-mail and a 9:30 p.m. voice-mail message to convey this information to me. It

smacks of immaturity and is quite unprofessional. Indeed, I did rely upon your acceptance by ordering stationary [*sic*] and business cards with your name, reformatting a computer, and setting up both internal and external e-mails for you here at the office. While I do not quarrel with your reasoning, I am extremely disappointed in the way this played out. I sincerely wish you the best of luck in your future endeavors.
Will Korman

————Original Message————

From: Dianna Abdala
Sent: Monday, February 06, 2006 4:01 p.m.
To: William A. Korman
Subject: Re: Thank you

A real lawyer would have put the contract into writing and not exercised any such reliance until he did so.
Again, thank you.

————Original Message————

From: William A. Korman
To: Dianna Abdala
Sent: Monday, February 06, 2006 4:18 p.m.
Subject: RE: Thank you

Thank you for the refresher course on contracts. This is not a bar exam question. You need to realize that this is a very small legal community, especially the criminal defense bar. Do you really want to start pissing off more experienced lawyers at this early stage of your career?

————Original Message————

From: Dianna Abdala
To: William A. Korman
Sent: Monday, February 06, 2006 4:28 p.m.
Subject: Re: Thank you
bla bla bla

After this e-mail exchange, Korman forwarded the correspondence to several colleagues, and it quickly spread.

Questions

1. With whom do you side here—Abdala or Korman?
2. What mistakes do you think each party made?
3. Do you think this exchange will damage Abdala's career? Korman's firm?
4. What does this exchange tell you about the limitations of email?

Jeremy W. Caputo Has Communication Problems

Jeremy W. Caputo has only four employees at his public relations firm, Message Out.[86] But he seems to have done a pretty good job of alienating them.

According to his employees, Caputo, 47, is a brilliant guy who has a lot to learn in terms of being a better communicator. His communication style appears to be a regular source of conflict in his firm. Caputo admits he has a problem. "I'm probably not as verbally reinforcing [as I could be] when someone is doing a good job. I'm a very self-confident person. I don't need to be told I'm doing a good job—but there are people who do."

Caputo's employees had no problem listing off things that he does that bother them. He does not meet deadlines; he does a poor job of communicating with clients (which often puts the employees in an uncomfortable position); he does not listen fully to employee ideas before dismissing them; his voice tone is frequently condescending; and he is often quick to criticize employees and is stingy with praise.

Questions

1. A lot of bosses are accused of being "poor communicators." Why do you think this is?
2. What does this case suggest regarding the relationship between reinforcement theory (see Chapter 4, pages 154–156) and communication?
3. What, specifically, do you think Caputo needs to do to improve his communication skills?
4. Assuming that Caputo wants to improve, how would you suggest he go about learning to be a better communicator?

FROM CONCEPTS TO SKILLS

Effective Listening

Too many people take listening skills for granted.[87] They confuse hearing with listening.

What's the difference? Hearing is merely picking up sound vibrations. Listening is making sense out of what we hear. That is, listening requires paying attention, interpreting, and remembering sound stimuli.

The average person normally speaks at a rate of 125 to 200 words per minute. However, the average listener can comprehend up to 400 words per minute. This leaves a lot of time for idle mind-wandering while listening. For most people, it also means they have acquired a number of bad listening habits to fill in the "idle time."

The following eight behaviours are associated with effective listening skills. If you want to improve your listening skills, look to these behaviours as guides:

1. *Make eye contact.* How do you feel when somebody doesn't look at you when you are speaking? If you are like most people, you are likely to interpret this behaviour as aloofness or lack of interest. We may listen with our ears, but others tend to judge whether we are really listening by looking at our eyes.

2. *Exhibit affirmative head nods and appropriate facial expressions.* The effective listener shows interest in what is being said. How? Through nonverbal signals. Affirmative head nods and appropriate facial expressions, when added to good eye contact, convey to the speaker that you are listening.

3. *Avoid distracting actions or gestures.* The other side of showing interest is avoiding actions that suggest your mind is somewhere else. When listening, don't look at your watch, shuffle papers, play with your pencil, or engage in similar distractions. They make the speaker feel that you are bored or uninterested. Maybe more important, they indicate that you are not fully attentive and may be missing part of the message that the speaker wants to convey.

4. *Ask questions.* The critical listener analyzes what he or she hears and asks questions. This behaviour provides clarification, ensures understanding, and assures the speaker that you are listening.

5. *Paraphrase.* Paraphrasing means restating what the speaker has said in your own words. The effective listener uses phrases such as "What I hear you saying is . . ." or "Do you mean . . . ?" Why rephrase what has already been said? Two reasons! First, it's an excellent control device to check on whether you are listening carefully. You cannot paraphrase accurately if your mind is wandering or if you are thinking about what you are going to say next. Second, it's a control for accuracy. By rephrasing what the speaker has said in your own words and feeding it back to the speaker, you verify the accuracy of your understanding.

6. *Avoid interrupting the speaker.* Let the speaker complete his or her thought before you try to respond. Don't try to second-guess where the speaker's thoughts are going. When the speaker is finished, you will know!

7. *Don't overtalk.* Most of us would rather voice our own ideas than listen to what someone else says. Too many of us listen only because it's the price we have to pay to get people to let us talk. While talking may be more fun and silence may be uncomfortable, you cannot talk and listen at the same time. The good listener recognizes this fact and does not overtalk.

8. *Make smooth transitions between the roles of speaker and listener.* When you are a student sitting in a lecture hall, you find it relatively easy to get into an effective listening frame of mind. Why? Because communication is essentially one-way: The teacher talks and you listen. But the teacher-student dyad is not typical. In most work situations, you are continually shifting back and forth between the

roles of speaker and listener. The effective listener, therefore, makes transitions smoothly from speaker to listener and back to speaker. From a listening perspective, this means concentrating on what a speaker has to say and practising not thinking about what you are going to say as soon as you get an opportunity.

Practising Skills

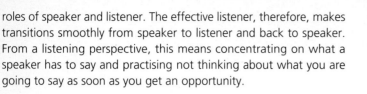

Form groups of 2. This exercise is a debate. Person A can choose any contemporary issue. Some examples include business ethics, the value of unions, stiffer grading policies, same-sex marriage, money as a motivator. Person B then selects a position on this issue. Person A must automatically take the counter-position. The debate is to proceed for 8 to 10 minutes, with only one catch. Before each person speaks, he or she must first summarize, in his or her own words and without notes, what the other has said. If the summary does not satisfy the speaker, it must be corrected until it does. What impact do the summaries have on the quality of the debate?

Reinforcing Skills

1. In another class—preferably one with a lecture format—practise active listening. Ask questions, paraphrase, exhibit affirming nonverbal behaviours. Then ask yourself: Was this harder for me than a normal lecture? Did it affect my note taking? Did I ask more questions? Did it improve my understanding of the lecture's content? What was the instructor's response?

2. Spend an entire day fighting your urge to talk. Listen as carefully as you can to everyone you talk to, and respond as appropriately as possible to understand, not to make your own point. What, if anything, did you learn from this exercise?

Power and Politics

What brought a former senior vice-president to file a class action suit against Tim Hortons? Power and politics tell much of the story.

LEARNING OUTCOMES

1 What is power?

2 How does one get power?

3 How does dependency affect power?

4 What tactics can be used to increase power?

5 What does it mean to be empowered?

6 How are power and harassment related?

7 Why do people engage in politics?

Arch and Anne Jollymore are not happy with Tim Hortons' senior management.[1] The couple, who own several Tim Hortons franchises, brought a class action lawsuit against the company that was heard in August 2011. They argued that the company's management forced changes in the production of donuts and other baked goods that enriched management and shareholders at the expense of the franchise owners.

One of the key complaints is the move to using "flash frozen" baked goods in the coffee shops in 2002. Before then, each Tim Hortons store had its own baker, who made all the baked goods from scratch, and baked them on the premises. The move has made donut production more expensive.

The franchise owners who signed on to the lawsuit complain bitterly about what they see as the company's abuse of power. An email sent to Roland Walton, head of Tim Hortons' Canadian operations, shortly after the lawsuit was launched, explained the power differential between management and franchisees: "[T]he feeling is that [the company's] attitude is 'We're still the best game in town, if you don't like it or aren't happy, there is a waiting list to get stores.'"

A major theme throughout this chapter is that power and politics are a natural process in any group or organization. Although you might have heard the saying "Power corrupts, and absolute power corrupts absolutely," power is not always bad.

Understanding how to use power and politics effectively makes organizational life more manageable, because it can help you gain the support you need to do your job effectively.

THE BIG IDEA

Power is not necessarily a zero-sum game. Sharing power may in fact increase everyone's power.

OB IS FOR EVERYONE

- Have you ever wondered how you might increase your power?
- What do you need to be truly empowered?
- Why do some people seem to engage in politics more than others?
- In what situations does impression management work best?

SELF-ASSESSMENT LIBRARY

LEARNING ABOUT YOURSELF

- Workplace Politics
- Political Skills

1 What is power?

BLOG IT

Do you think power is good or bad?
Give some personal examples of how you have seen power used positively and negatively.
www.obstudentjournals.blogspot.com

A Definition of Power

Power refers to a capacity that A has to influence the behaviour of B, so that B acts in accordance with A's wishes.[2] This definition implies that there is a *potential* for power if someone is dependent on another. But one can have power and not impose it.

Probably the most important aspect of power is that it is a function of **dependency**. The more that B depends on A, the more power A has in the relationship. Dependence, in turn, is based on the alternatives that B perceives and the importance that B places on the alternative(s) that A controls. A person can have power over you only if he or she controls something you desire. If you are attending college or university on funds totally provided by your parents, you probably recognize the power that your parents hold over you. You are dependent on them for financial support. But once you are out of school, have a job, and are making a good income, your parents' power is reduced significantly. Who among us, though, has not known or heard of the rich relative who is able to control a large number of family members merely through the implicit or explicit threat of "writing them out of the will"?

Within larger organizations, the information technology (IT) group often has considerable power, because everyone, right up to the CEO, is dependent on this group to keep computers and networks running. Since few people have the technical expertise to do so, IT personnel end up being viewed as irreplaceable. This gives them a lot of power within the organization.

Power makes people uncomfortable.[3] People who have power deny it, people who want it try not to look like they are seeking it, and those who are good at getting it are secretive about how they do so.[4] Commenting on a recent study, one researcher noted, "A person's sense of power is an extremely pervasive feeling in everyday life."[5]

Part of the discomfort about power may have to do with how people perceive those in power. A 2011 study found that people who behave rudely—putting their feet up on a chair, ordering a meal brusquely—were believed by those watching this behaviour to be more likely to "get to make decisions" and able to "get people to listen to what [they] say" than people who behave politely. The researchers concluded that "norm violators are perceived as having the capacity to act as they please."[6] As a result, they seem more powerful. A 2010 study found that people who have power judged others much more negatively for speeding, dodging taxes, and keeping a stolen bike than if they engaged in this behaviour themselves. The researchers found that those who had legitimate power were even more likely to indulge in moral hypocrisy than those who did not feel personally entitled to their power.[7]

Power should not be considered a bad thing, however. "Power, if used appropriately, should actually be a positive influence in your organization," says Professor Patricia Bradshaw of the Schulich School of Business at York University. "Having more power doesn't necessarily turn you into a Machiavellian monster. It can help your team and your organization achieve its goals and increase its potential."[8]

A major theme of this chapter is that power and political behaviour are natural processes in any group or organization. By learning how power works in organizations, you will be better able to use your knowledge to become a more effective manager. *Focus on Research* provides insight into the dynamics of power, choice, and personal control.

power A capacity that A has to influence the behaviour of B, so that B acts in accordance with A's wishes.

dependency B's relationship to A when A possesses something that B requires.

FOCUS ON RESEARCH

Power: It's All About Control

Why is choice less important when you have a sense of personal power? A 2011 study examining how people think about power suggests that the desire for power is directly related to control.[9] In one of the experiments that was part of the study, subjects were asked to think about their feelings about being in the role of a boss or an employee, after reading a description of the role. Subjects in the employee role read about being in a powerless situation, while those in the boss role read about being in a powerful situation. Afterward, subjects were asked to choose whether to "buy eyeglasses or ice cream from a store that had three options or a store that had fifteen options." Subjects in the powerless employee situation chose the scenario with more options, even if it meant driving farther or waiting longer.

In other words, people who have power do not feel the need for as much choice, and people who lack power demand to have more choice. This research suggests that "power satisfies the thirst for choice and choice quenches the desire for power because each replenishes a sense of control."

"People instinctively prefer high to low power positions," says M. Ena Inesi, one of the researchers, of London Business School. For those in low power positions, "it feels good when you have choice, and it doesn't feel good when choice is taken away."

Bases of Power

Where does power come from? What is it that gives an individual or a group influence over others? The answer to these questions was developed by social scientists John French and Bertrand Raven, who first presented a five-category classification scheme of sources or bases of power: coercive, reward, legitimate, expert, and referent.[10] They subsequently added one new dimension, information power, to that schema (see Exhibit 8-1).[11]

2 How does one get power?

Coercive Power

Coercive power is defined by French and Raven as dependent on fear of the negative results that might occur if one fails to comply. It rests on the application, or the threat of the application, of physical sanctions such as the infliction of pain, the generation of frustration through restriction of movement, or the controlling by force of basic physiological or safety needs.

EXHIBIT 8-1 Measuring Bases of Power

Does a person have one or more of the six bases of power? These descriptions help identify the person's power base.

Power Base	Statement
Coercive	The person can make things difficult for people, and you want to avoid getting him or her angry.
Reward	The person is able to give special benefits or rewards to people, and you find it advantageous to trade favours with him or her.
Legitimate	The person has the right, considering his or her position and your job responsibilities, to expect you to comply with legitimate requests.
Expert	The person has the experience and knowledge to earn your respect, and you defer to his or her judgment in some matters.
Referent	You like the person and enjoy doing things for him or her.
Information	The person has data or knowledge that you need.

Source: Adapted from G. Yukl and C. M. Falbe, "Importance of Different Power Sources in Downward and Lateral Relations," *Journal of Applied Psychology*, June 1991, p. 417.

coercive power Power that is based on fear.

In India, Naina Lal Kidwai is a powerful woman in the banking industry. She derives her power as managing director and vice chairman of HSBC Securities and Capital Markets, a group within the Hongkong and Shanghai Banking Corporation. Kidwai's formal power is based on her position at the bank.

At the organizational level, A has coercive power over B if A can dismiss, suspend, or demote B, assuming that B values his or her job. Similarly, if A can assign B work activities that B finds unpleasant or treat B in a manner that B finds embarrassing, A possesses coercive power over B.

Reward Power

The opposite of coercive power is **reward power**. People will go along with the wishes or directives of another if doing so produces positive benefits; therefore, someone who can distribute rewards that others view as valuable will have power over those others. These rewards can be either financial—such as controlling pay rates, raises, and bonuses—or nonfinancial, including offering recognition, promotions, interesting work assignments, friendly colleagues, and preferred work shifts or sales territories.[12]

Legitimate Power

In formal groups and organizations, probably the most frequent access to one or more of the bases of power is through a person's structural position. This is called **legitimate power**. It represents the power a person receives as a result of his or her position in the formal hierarchy of an organization.

Legitimate power is broader than the power to coerce and reward. Specifically, it includes acceptance by members of an organization of the authority of a position. We associate power so closely with the concept of hierarchy that just drawing longer lines in an organization chart leads people to infer that the leaders are especially powerful, and when a powerful executive is described, people tend to put the person at a higher position when drawing an organization chart.[13] When school principals, bank presidents, or generals speak (assuming that their directives are viewed to be within the authority of their positions), teachers, tellers, and privates listen and usually comply. You will note in Exhibit 8-2 that one of the men in the meeting identifies himself as the rule maker, which means that he has legitimate power. The Milgram experiment, discussed in *Focus on Research*, looks at the extremes individuals sometimes go to in order to comply with authority figures.

reward power Power that achieves compliance based on the ability to distribute rewards that others view as valuable.

legitimate power Power that a person receives as a result of his or her position in the formal hierarchy of an organization.

FOCUS ON RESEARCH

A Shocking Experiment

Would you shock someone if you were told to do so? A classic experiment conducted by Stanley Milgram studied the extent to which people are willing to obey those in authority.[14] Subjects were recruited for an experiment that asked them to administer electric shocks to a "student" who was supposed to learn a list of words. The experiments were conducted at Yale University, and subjects were assured by the experimenter, who was dressed in a white lab coat, that punishment was an effective way to learn. The subjects were placed in front of an instrument panel that indicated the shocks could go from 15 volts to 450 volts. With each wrong answer, subjects were to administer the next-highest shock level. After the shocks reached a middle level, the "student" started to cry out in pain. The experimenter would instruct the subject to continue administering shocks. What the experimenter was trying to find out was the level at which subjects would stop administering the electric shock. No subject stopped before 300 volts, and 65 percent of the subjects continued to the end of the experiment, even though, at the upper levels, the instrument panel was

EXHIBIT 8-2

"I was just going to say 'Well, I don't make the rules.' But, of course, I do make the rules."

Source: © Leo Cullum/ The New Yorker Collection/ www.cartoonbank.com

marked "Danger XXX." It should be noted that subjects were not actually administering shocks, and that the "student" was actually a confederate and was simply acting as if in pain. However, the subjects believed that they were administering electric shocks. This experiment suggests that many people will obey those who appear to have legitimate authority, even in questionable circumstances.

Expert Power

Expert power is influence based on expertise, special skills, or knowledge. Expertise has become one of the most powerful sources of influence as the world has become more technologically oriented. While it is generally acknowledged that physicians have expertise and hence expert power—most of us follow the advice that our doctor gives us—you should also recognize that computer specialists, tax accountants, economists, and other specialists can have power as a result of their expertise. Young people may find they have increased power in the workplace these days because of their technical knowledge and expertise that Baby Boomer managers may not have.

Referent Power

Referent power develops out of admiration of another and a desire to be like that person. Sometimes teachers and coaches have referent power because of our admiration of them. Referent power explains why celebrities are paid millions of dollars to endorse products in commercials. Mississauga, Ontario-based Alexis Life Sciences uses endorsements from Don Cherry of *Hockey Night in Canada* and popular athletes such as Alexandre Bilodeau, Clara Hughes, and Joannie Rochette to convince people to buy COLD-FX, its cold and flu product. Similarly, Nike Canada uses sports celebrities, such as Montreal Canadiens defenceman P. K. Subban, to promote its products.

expert power Influence based on special skills or knowledge.

referent power Influence based on possession by an individual of desirable resources or personal traits.

Information Power

Information power comes from access to and control over information. People in an organization who have data or knowledge that others need can make those others dependent on them. Managers, for instance, because of their access to privileged sales, cost, salary, profit, and similar data, can use this information to control and shape subordinates' behaviour. Similarly, departments that possess information that is critical to a company's performance in times of high uncertainty—for example, the legal department when a firm faces a major lawsuit or the human resource department during critical labour negotiations—will gain increased power in their organization until those uncertainties are resolved. Withholding information can result in poor-quality performance by those who need the information.[15]

The *Working with Others Exercise* on page 316 gives you the opportunity to explore the effectiveness of different bases of power in changing someone's behaviour.

Evaluating the Bases of Power

Generally, people will respond in one of three ways when faced with those who use the bases of power described above:

- *Commitment.* The person is enthusiastic about the request, and shows initiative and persistence in carrying it out.

- *Compliance.* The person goes along with the request grudgingly, puts in minimal effort, and takes little initiative in carrying out the request.

- *Resistance.* The person is opposed to the request and tries to avoid it with such tactics as refusing, stalling, or arguing about it.[16]

A review of the research on the effectiveness of these forms of power finds that they differ in their impact on a person's performance.[17] Exhibit 8-3 summarizes some of this research. Coercive power leads to resistance from individuals, decreased satisfaction, and increased mistrust. Reward power results in compliance if the rewards are consistent with what individuals want as rewards, something the *Ethical Dilemma Exercise* on page 317 shows clearly. Legitimate power also results in compliance, but it does

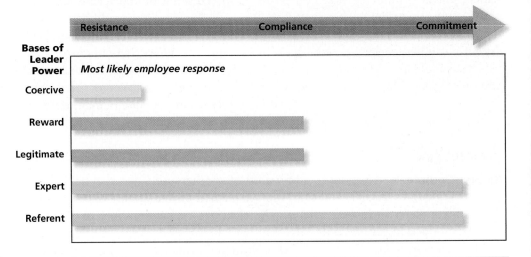

EXHIBIT 8-3 Continuum of Responses to Power

Resistance — Compliance — Commitment

Bases of Leader Power

Most likely employee response

- Coercive
- Reward
- Legitimate
- Expert
- Referent

Source: R. M. Steers and J. S. Black, *Organizational Behavior*, 5th ed. (New York: HarperCollins, 1994), p. 487. Reprinted by permission of Pearson Education Inc., Upper Saddle River, New Jersey.

information power Power that comes from access to and control over information.

not generally result in increased commitment. In other words, legitimate power does not inspire individuals to act beyond the basic level. Expert and referent powers are the most likely to lead to commitment from individuals. Ironically, the least effective bases of power for improving commitment—coercive, reward, and legitimate—are the ones most often used by managers, perhaps because they are the easiest to introduce.[18] Research shows that deadline pressure increases group members' reliance on individuals with expert and information power.[19]

Dependency: The Key to Power

Franchisees are at the heart of Tim Hortons' business model.[20] To acquire a store, an owner pays a start-up fee of nearly a half-million dollars. Owners buy all of their supplies from the company (which ensures that products taste the same throughout the country). They also pay a percentage of yearly sales to cover "rent, royalties and advertising." Franchisees have very limited autonomy in running their franchise. For example, when the company introduced its "Always Fresh" baking system, franchisees had no choice but to buy the pre-baked products sold by Maidstone Bakeries in Brantford, Ontario. The purchased donuts cost more than the donuts baked in-store. There was no other supplier, and thus no real way to force the company to lower its charges for supplies. What factors might lead one entity (a person or an organization) to have greater power over another?

3 How does dependency affect power?

In this section, we show how an understanding of dependency is central to furthering your understanding of power itself.

The General Dependency Postulate

Let's begin with a general postulate: *The greater B's dependency on A, the greater the power A has over B.* When you possess anything that others require but that you alone control, you make them dependent upon you and, therefore, you gain power over them.[21] Another way to frame dependency is to think about a relationship in terms of "who needs whom?" The person who has most need is the one most dependent on the relationship.[22]

Dependency is inversely proportional to the alternative sources of supply. If something is plentiful, possession of it will not increase your power. If everyone is intelligent, intelligence gives no special advantage. Similarly, in the circles of the super rich, money does not result in power. But if you can create a monopoly by controlling information, prestige, or anything that others crave, they become dependent on you. Alternatively, the more options you have, the less power you place in the hands of others. This explains, for example, why most organizations develop multiple suppliers rather than give their business to only one.

What Creates Dependency?

Dependency is increased when the resource you control is important, scarce, and cannot be substituted.[23]

Importance

If nobody wants what you have, there is no dependency. To create dependency, the thing(s) you control must be perceived

Because Xerox Corporation has staked its future on development and innovation, Sophie Vanderbroek is in a position of power at Xerox. As the company's chief technology officer, she manages Xerox's 4000 scientists and engineers at the company's global research centres. The group's mission is "to pioneer high-impact technologies that enable us to lead in our core markets and to create future markets for Xerox." Xerox depends on Vanderbroek to make that mission a reality.

as important. In some organizations, people who control the budget have a great deal of importance. In other organizations, those who possess the knowledge to keep technology working smoothly are viewed as important. What is important is situational. It varies among organizations and undoubtedly also varies over time within any given organization.

> Have you ever wondered how you might increase your power?

Scarcity

As noted previously, if something is plentiful, possession of it will not increase your power. A resource must be perceived as scarce to create dependency.

Scarcity can help explain how low-ranking employees gain power if they have important knowledge not available to high-ranking employees. Possession of a scarce resource—in this case, important knowledge—makes those who don't have it dependent on those who do. Thus, an individual might refuse to show others how to do a job or might refuse to share information, thereby increasing his or her importance.

The scarcity-dependency relationship can further be seen in the power of occupational categories. For example, college and university administrators have no problem finding English instructors to staff classes. There are more individuals who have degrees enabling them to work as English instructors than there are positions available in Canada. The market for corporate finance professors, by contrast, is extremely tight, with the demand high and the supply limited. The result is that the bargaining power of finance faculty allows them to negotiate higher salaries, lighter teaching loads, and other benefits.

Nonsubstitutability

The fewer substitutes there are for a resource, the more power comes from control over that resource. During his tenure as CEO, the common belief at Apple Computer, for example, was that Steve Jobs was not replaceable. His passing in October 2011 means that Apple now has to contend with replacing the company's charismatic figurehead. The unanswered question at the time of his death was whether Apple could continue to be innovative and edgy without Jobs at the helm. In another example, when a union goes on strike and management is not permitted to replace the striking employees, the union has considerable control over the organization's ability to carry out its tasks.

People are often able to ask for special rewards (higher pay or better assignments) because they have skills that others do not.

Influence Tactics

4 What tactics can be used to increase power?

Tim Hortons' management used a number of influence tactics to persuade its franchisees to adopt the "Always Fresh" baking system in their stores.[24] Management started with a taste test at the 2000 annual convention, an inspirational appeal that convinced some of the franchisees that the taste was much better. Management then used rational persuasion to convince owners that the increased cost was worth the gain in convenience. Under the in-house baking system, franchise owners were paying about 5 to 9 cents to make one donut. According to some franchisees, they were told that the new process would result in donuts that cost about 11.5 cents to produce. "We all knew that that was more than we were paying to bake in-house, but we all felt the same," Ottawa franchisee Greg Gilson said. "The convenience of it would be worth the offset of the three to four cents." Thus, management further influenced the decisions of the franchisees by emphasizing convenience. However, when the final cost turned out to be about 18 cents per donut, head office used its legitimate power to require the owners to buy the "flash frozen" donuts from Maidstone Bakeries. So how and why do influence tactics work?

How do individuals translate their bases of power into specific, desired actions? Research indicates that people use common tactics to influence outcomes.[25] One study identified the nine influence tactics managers and employees use to increase their power:[26]

1. *Rational persuasion.* Using facts and data to make a logical or rational presentation of ideas.

2. *Inspirational appeals.* Appealing to values, ideals, and goals when making a request.

3. *Consultation.* Getting others involved to support one's objectives.

4. *Ingratiation.* Using flattery, creating goodwill, and being friendly prior to making a request.

5. *Personal appeals.* Appealing to loyalty and friendship when asking for something.

6. *Exchange.* Offering favours or benefits in exchange for support.

7. *Coalitions.* Getting the support of other people to provide backing when making a request.

8. *Pressure.* Using demands, threats, and reminders to get someone to do something.

9. *Legitimacy.* Claiming the authority or right to make a request, or showing that it supports organizational goals or policies.

Some tactics are more effective than others. Rational persuasion, inspirational appeals, and consultation tend to be the most effective, especially when the audience is highly interested in the outcomes of a decision process. Pressure tends to frequently backfire and is typically the least effective of the nine tactics.[27] You can also increase your chance of success by using more than one type of tactic at the same time or sequentially, as long as your choices are compatible.[28] For instance, using both ingratiation and legitimacy can lessen the negative reactions that might come from appearing to "dictate" outcomes, but only when the audience does not really care about the outcomes of a decision process or the policy is routine.[29]

The effectiveness of some influence tactics depends on the direction of influence.[30] Studies have found that rational persuasion is the only tactic that is effective across organizational levels. Inspirational appeals work best as a downward-influencing tactic with subordinates. When pressure works, it's generally only to achieve downward influence. The use of personal appeals and coalitions is most effective with lateral influence attempts. In addition to the direction of influence, a number of other factors have been found to affect which tactics work best. These include the sequencing of tactics, a person's skill in using the tactic, and the culture of the organization.

You are more likely to be effective if you begin with "softer" tactics that rely on personal power such as personal and inspirational appeals, rational persuasion, and consultation. If these fail, you can move to "harder" tactics (which emphasize formal power and involve greater costs and risks), such as exchange, coalitions, and pressure.[31] Interestingly, it has been found that using a single soft tactic is more effective than using a single hard tactic, and that combining two soft tactics or a soft tactic and rational persuasion is more effective than any single tactic or a combination of hard tactics.[32] The effectiveness of tactics depends on the audience.[33] People especially likely to comply with soft power tactics tend to be more reflective, are intrinsically motivated, have high self-esteem, and have greater desire for control. People especially likely to comply with hard power tactics are more action oriented and extrinsically motivated and are more focused on getting along with others than with getting their own way.

People differ in their **political skill**, or the ability to influence others in such a way as to enhance their own objectives. Those who are politically skilled are more effective in their use of influence tactics, regardless of the tactics they are using. Political skill also appears to be more effective when the stakes are high—such as when the individual is accountable for important organizational outcomes. Finally, the politically skilled are able to exert their influence without others detecting it, which is a key element in being effective (it's damaging to be labelled political).[34]

Finally, we know that cultures within organizations differ markedly—for example, some are warm, relaxed, and supportive; others are formal and conservative. The organizational culture in which a person works, therefore, will have a bearing on defining which tactics are considered appropriate. Some cultures encourage the use of participation and consultation, some encourage reason, and still others rely on pressure. People who fit the culture of the organization tend to obtain more influence.[35] Specifically, extraverts tend to be more influential in team-oriented organizations, and highly conscientious people are more influential in organizations that value working alone on technical tasks. Part of the reason people who fit the culture are influential is that they are able to perform especially well in the domains deemed most important for success. In other words, they are influential because they are competent. So the organization itself will influence which subset of influence tactics is viewed as acceptable for use. The kinds of tactics used have also changed over time, as *Case Incident—The Persuasion Imperative* on page 319 shows.

Empowerment: Giving Power to Employees

5 What does it mean to be empowered?

Thus far, our discussion has implied—to some extent, at least—that power is something that is more likely to reside in the hands of managers, to be used as part of their interaction with employees. However, in today's workplace, there is a movement toward sharing more power with employees by putting them in teams and also by making them

WestJet has an empowerment culture. As Sean Durfy, WestJet's former president and CEO, notes: "If you empower people to do the right things, then they will. If you align the interests of the people with the interests of the company, it's very powerful. That's what we do." WestJet's empowerment culture is admired by others as well. In 2011, the company was named one of "Canada's Most Admired Corporate Cultures for Western Canada" by Waterstone Human Capital. Two years earlier, WestJet was named to Waterstone Human Capital's Inaugural Hall of Fame after having placed on its "Canada's 10 Most Admired Corporate Cultures" list four times in a row, including three times in a row at number one.

political skill The ability to influence others in such a way as to enhance one's objectives.

responsible for some of the decisions regarding their jobs. For instance, at Vancouver-based iQmetrix Software Development, employees are part of a results-only workplace, where they are encouraged to make their own decisions.[36] Organizational specialists refer to this increasing responsibility as *empowerment*.

Definition of Empowerment

The definition of *empowerment* that we use here refers to the freedom and the ability of employees to make decisions and commitments.[37] Unfortunately, neither managers nor researchers agree on the definition of empowerment. One study found that executives were split about 50-50 in their definition.[38] One group of executives "believed that empowerment was about delegating decision making within a set of clear boundaries." Empowerment would start at the top, specific goals and tasks would be assigned, responsibility would be delegated, and people would be held accountable for their results. The other group believed that empowerment was "a process of risk-taking and personal growth." This type of empowerment starts at the bottom, with considering the employees' needs, showing them what empowered behaviour looks like, building teams, encouraging risk-taking, and demonstrating trust in employees' ability to perform.

One difficulty with empowerment is that managers often give lip service to the idea,[39] with organizations telling employees that they have decision-making responsibility, but not giving them the authority to carry out their decisions. This leads to a great deal of cynicism in many workplaces, particularly when "empowered" employees are micromanaged. For an employee to be fully empowered, he or she needs access to the information required to make decisions; rewards for acting in appropriate, responsible ways; and the authority to make the necessary decisions. Empowerment means that employees understand how their job fits into the organization and are able to make decisions regarding job action guided by the organization's purpose and mission.

Not every employee appreciates being empowered, however. One study found that sometimes empowerment can make employees ill if they are put in charge at work but lack the confidence to handle their responsibilities.[40]

At Vancouver-based Great Little Box Company (GLBC), which designs and manufactures corrugated containers, employees are given the freedom to do whatever they feel is necessary and appropriate to make customers happy. If a customer is dissatisfied with the product, the employee can say, "OK, I'll bring this product back and return it for you," without having to get prior authorization.

EXHIBIT 8-4 Characteristics of Empowered People

Robert E. Quinn and Gretchen M. Spreitzer, in their research on the characteristics of empowered people (through both in-depth interviews and survey analysis), found four characteristics that most empowered people have in common:

- Empowered people have a sense of *self-determination* (this means that they are free to choose how to do their work; they are not micromanaged).

- Empowered people have a sense of *meaning* (they feel that their work is important to them; they care about what they are doing).

- Empowered people have a sense of *competence* (this means that they are confident about their ability to do their work well; they know they can perform).

- Empowered people have a sense of *impact* (this means that people believe they can have influence on their work unit; others listen to their ideas).

Source: Reprinted from R. E. Quinn and G. M. Spreitzer, "The Road to Empowerment: Seven Questions Every Leader Should Consider," *Organizational Dynamics*, Autumn 1997, p. 41, with permission from Elsevier.

When employees are empowered, it means that they are expected to act, at least in a small way, as owners of the company, rather than just employees. Ownership is not necessary in the financial sense, but in terms of identifying with the goals and mission of the organization. For employees to be empowered, however, and have an ownership mentality, four conditions need to be met, according to Professor Dan Ondrack at the Rotman School of Management at the University of Toronto:[41]

> What do you need to be truly empowered?

- There must be a clear definition of the values and mission of the company.

- The company must help employees acquire the relevant skills.

- Employees need to be supported in their decision making, and not criticized when they try to do something extraordinary.

- Employees need to be recognized for their efforts.

Exhibit 8-4 outlines what two researchers discovered in studying the characteristics of empowered people.

The Abuse of Power

6 How are power and harassment related?

Studies indicate that when someone is in a position of power, he or she may be more willing to exert that power.[42] *Focus on Research* shows how this idea played out in one particular study.

FOCUS ON RESEARCH

The Cookie Experiment

Who eats the fourth cookie? In a study known as the "cookie experiment," three psychologists instructed teams of three students to write a short paper during a meeting.[43] Two of the team members (the "subordinates") were to do the actual writing, and the third team member (the "boss") was assigned to evaluate the work and determine the pay the two writers would receive. Part way through the meeting, experimenters brought in a plate of five cookies. As expected, no one ate the fifth cookie (rules of etiquette suggest that one should not eat the last item on a plate).

The researchers were interested, then, in who ate the fourth cookie, given that it was extra. "Bosses" were far more likely to take the fourth cookie than "subordinates," and were much more likely to chew with their mouths open and scatter crumbs widely, signs that their power enabled them to act in less-inhibited ways.

The authors concluded that people with power behave very differently than those without it. Powerful people are generally less inhibited and sometimes act in counter-normative ways. Powerless people "are more likely to feel negative moods and emotions, to attend to punishment and threat, to make more careful, controlled judgments about others' intentions, attitudes, and actions, and to inhibit their own behaviors and act contingently upon others."

Below we examine ways in which power can be unacceptably exhibited at work.

Harassment in the Workplace

People who engage in harassment in the workplace are typically abusing their power position. The manager-employee relationship best characterizes an unequal power relationship, where position power gives the manager the capacity to reward and coerce. Managers give employees their assignments, evaluate their performance, make recommendations for salary adjustments and promotions, and even decide whether employees retain their job. These decisions give a manager power. Since employees want favourable performance reviews, salary increases, and the like, it's clear that managers control the resources that most employees consider important and scarce.

Although co-workers do not have position power, they can have influence and use it to harass peers. In fact, although co-workers appear to engage in somewhat less severe forms of harassment than do managers, co-workers are the most frequent perpetrators of harassment, particularly sexual harassment, in organizations. How do co-workers exercise power? Most often they provide or withhold information, cooperation, and support.

Some categories of harassment have long been illegal in Canada, including those based on race, religion, and national origin, as well as sexual harassment. Unfortunately, some types of harassment that occur in the workplace are not deemed illegal, even if they create problems for employees and managers. We focus here on two types of harassment that have received considerable attention in the press: workplace bullying and sexual harassment.

Workplace Bullying

Many of us are aware, anecdotally if not personally, of managers who harass employees, demanding overtime without pay or excessive work performance. Further, some of the recent stories of workplace violence have reportedly been the result of an employee feeling intimidated at work. In research conducted in the private and public sector in southern Saskatchewan, Céleste Brotheridge, a professor at the Université du Québec à Montréal, found that bullying was rather prevalent in the workplace. Forty percent of the respondents noted that they had experienced one or more forms of bullying weekly in the past six months. Ten percent experienced bullying at a much greater level: five or more incidents a week. Brotheridge notes that bullying has a negative effect on the workplace: "Given bullying's deleterious effects on employee health, it is reason for concern."[44]

There is no clear definition of workplace bullying, and Marilyn Noble, a Fredericton-based adult educator, remarks that in some instances there can be a fine line between managing and bullying. However, recent research suggests that bosses who feel inadequate or overwhelmed are more likely to bully.[45] As one of the study's co-authors explained: "The combination of having a high-power role and fearing that one is not up to the task . . . causes power holders to lash out."[46]

The effects of bullying can be devastating. Professors Sandy Hershcovis of the University of Manitoba and Julian Barling of Queen's University found that the consequences of bullying were more harmful to its victims than those who suffered sexual harassment. Bullied employees more often quit their jobs, were less satisfied with their jobs, and had more difficult relationships with their supervisors.[47]

Quebec introduced the first anti-bullying labour legislation in North America on June 1, 2004. The legislation defines psychological harassment as "any vexatious behaviour in the form of repeated and hostile or unwanted conduct, verbal comments, actions or gestures that affect an employee's dignity or psychological or physical integrity and that results in a harmful work environment for the employee."[48] Under the Quebec law, bullying allegations will be sent to mediation, where the accuser and the accused will work with an independent third party to try to resolve the problem. If mediation fails, employers who have allowed psychological harassment can be fined up to $10 000 and ordered to pay financial damages to the victim.

Sexual Harassment

Sexual harassment is wrong. It can also be costly to employers. Just ask executives at Walmart, the World Bank, and the United Nations.[49] The Supreme Court of Canada defines **sexual harassment** as unwelcome behaviour of a sexual nature in the workplace that negatively affects the work environment or leads to adverse job-related consequences for the employee.[50] Despite the legal framework for defining sexual harassment, there continues to be disagreement as to what *specifically* constitutes sexual harassment. Sexual harassment includes unwanted physical touching, recurring requests for dates when it is made clear the person is not interested, and coercive threats that a person will lose her or his job if she or he refuses a sexual proposition. The problems of interpreting sexual harassment often surface around some of its more subtle forms— unwanted looks or comments, off-colour jokes, sexual artifacts such as nude calendars in the workplace, sexual innuendo, or misinterpretations of where the line between "being friendly" ends and "harassment" begins. Most studies confirm that the concept of power is central to understanding sexual harassment.[51] It's about an individual controlling or threatening another individual. This seems to be true whether the harassment comes from a manager, a co-worker, or an employee.

Because of power inequities, sexual harassment by a manager typically creates great difficulty for an employee being harassed. If there are no witnesses, it's the manager's word against the employee's word. Are there others whom this manager has harassed, and if so, will they come forward? Because of the manager's control over resources, many of those who are harassed are afraid of speaking out for fear of retaliation by the manager.

Workplaces are not the only place where sexual harassment occurs. While nonconsensual sex between professors and students is rape and subject to criminal charges, it's harder to evaluate apparently consensual relationships that occur outside the classroom. There is some argument over whether truly consensual sex is ever possible between students and professors. In an effort to underscore the power discrepancy and potential for abuse of it by professors, in 2009 Yale University implemented a policy forbidding romantic relationships between professors and undergraduate students.[52] Deputy Provost Charles Long explained the university's decision: "I think we have a responsibility to protect students from behavior that is damaging to them and to the objectives for their being here." Most universities have been unwilling to adopt such an extreme stance, and it's not clear that in Canada such a policy would stand up in the courts. Carleton University does not prohibit relationships between individuals in authority and those who are not, but does include the following statement in its sexual harassment policy: "No individual in a position of authority is permitted to grade or supervise the performance of any student, or evaluate an employee or a

sexual harassment Unwelcome behaviour of a sexual nature in the workplace that negatively affects the work environment or leads to adverse job-related consequences for the employee.

colleague, with whom they are sexually involved or have been within the past five years."[53]

One recent study found that nearly two-thirds of university students experience some type of sexual harassment, but most of these incidents go unreported.[54] However, much of this harassment comes from student-on-student incidents. Matt Abbott, a student at the University of New Brunswick, says that "certain aspects of sexual violence are almost normal within the dating culture in campus communities." A University of British Columbia student, Anoushka Ratnarajah, notes that "'the line' with respect to sexual harassment and the issue of consent are still fuzzy for many students."[55]

A recent review of the literature shows the damage caused by sexual harassment. As you would expect, individuals who are sexually harassed report more negative job attitudes (such as lower job satisfaction, diminished organizational commitment) as a result. This review also revealed that sexual harassment undermines the victims' mental and physical health. However, sexual harassment also negatively affects the group in which the victim works, lowering its level of productivity. The authors of this study conclude that sexual harassment "is significantly and substantively associated with a host of harms."[56]

We have seen how sexual harassment can wreak havoc on an organization, not to mention on the victims themselves. But it can be avoided. A manager's role in preventing sexual harassment is critical. Some ways managers can protect themselves and their employees from sexual harassment are as follows:

- Make sure an active policy defines what constitutes sexual harassment, informs employees that they can be fired for sexually harassing another employee, and establishes procedures for how complaints can be made.

- Assure employees that they will not encounter retaliation if they issue a complaint.

- Investigate every complaint and include the legal and human resource departments.

- Make sure that offenders are disciplined or terminated.

- Set up in-house seminars to raise employee awareness about the issues surrounding sexual harassment.

Politics: Power in Action

7 Why do people engage in politics?

Archibald Jollymore was a senior executive at Tim Hortons before he retired and became the owner of a franchise in Burlington, Ontario.[57] His cousin is Ron Joyce, co-founder of Tim Hortons. Joyce sold the company to Wendy's in 1995 and regrets doing so. There is speculation that Joyce is the financial backer behind the lawsuit, although neither Joyce nor Jollymore confirms this. Joyce does not like the direction the company has taken under his successor, Paul D. House, and is vocal in his complaints about the executive team. With respect to the "Always Fresh" donuts, Joyce said publicly, "This is not a philosophy that I would have embraced if I still owned the company." Thus, politics, rather than money, may be part of the reason behind the lawsuit.

The lawsuit has also pitted franchise operators against one another. Some claim that they lost money with the "Always Fresh" baking system, while others suggest that it was "a welcome transition." Some franchisees even launched a website to encourage others to stand up against the lawsuit. "How comfortable are you sharing your profitability with the media?" the website asks. "Do we want the press reporting about the Tim Hortons' brand in a negative way?" In other words, the franchise owners are forming coalitions to either foster or hinder the lawsuit, depending on their perspective on the matter. Why is politics so prevalent in organizations? Is it merely a fact of life?

When people get together in groups, power will be exerted. People want to carve out a niche from which to exert influence, to earn awards, and to advance their careers.[58] When employees in organizations convert their power into action, we describe them as being engaged in politics. Those with good political skills have the ability to use their bases of power effectively.[59] In this section, we look at political behaviour, the types of political activity people use to try to influence others, and impression management. Political skills are not confined to adults, of course. Even young children are quite adept at waging careful, deliberate campaigns to wear their parents down, so that they can get things that they want.

Definition of Political Behaviour

There has been no shortage of definitions for organizational politics. One clever definition of politics comes from Tom Jakobek, Toronto's former budget chief, who said, "In politics, you may have to go from A to C to D to E to F to G and then to B."[60]

For our purposes, we will define **political behaviour** in organizations as those activities that are outside one's formal role, and that influence, or attempt to influence, the distribution of advantages and disadvantages within the organization.[61]

This definition encompasses key elements from what most people mean when they talk about organizational politics. Political behaviour is outside one's specified job requirements. The behaviour requires some attempt to use one's bases of power. Our definition also encompasses efforts to influence the goals, criteria, or processes used for decision making when we state that politics is concerned with "the distribution of advantages and disadvantages within the organization." Our definition is broad enough to include such varied political behaviours as withholding key information from decision makers, joining a coalition, whistle-blowing, spreading rumours, leaking confidential information about organizational activities to the media, exchanging favours with others in the organization for mutual benefit, and lobbying on behalf of or against a particular individual or decision alternative. Exhibit 8-5 provides a quick measure to help you assess how political your workplace is.

Now that you have learned a bit about political behaviour, you may want to assess your own political behaviour in the *Learning About Yourself Exercise* on page 315.

Political behaviour is not confined to just individual hopes and goals. Politics might also be used to achieve organizational goals. For instance, if a CEO wants to change the way employees are paid, say from salaries to commissions, this change might not be a popular choice for employees. While it might make good organizational sense to make this change (perhaps the CEO believes doing so will increase productivity), simply imposing the change through the use of power ("go along with this or you are fired") might not be very popular. Instead, the CEO may try to pitch the reasons for the change to sympathetic managers and employees, trying to get them to understand the necessity for the change. Burnaby, BC-based TELUS used a direct approach with its employees after four-and-a-half years of unsuccessful bargaining with union leaders. Management became frustrated with the impasse and explained their wage and benefit offer directly to employees in the hopes of getting the employees to side with management rather than their union leaders. The union was outraged by this behaviour, and it took several more months for union members and management to finally complete a new collective agreement in fall 2005.

The Reality of Politics

Why, you may wonder, must politics exist? Isn't it possible for an organization to be politics-free? It's *possible*, but most unlikely. Organizations are made up of individuals and groups with different values, goals, and interests.[62] This sets up the potential for conflict over resources. Organizational members sometimes disagree about the alloca-

SELF-ASSESSMENT LIBRARY

LEARNING ABOUT YOURSELF

1. How Political Are You?
   (page 315)

political behaviour Those activities that influence, or attempt to influence, the distribution of advantages and disadvantages within the organization.

EXHIBIT 8-5 A Quick Measure of How Political Your Workplace Is

How political is your workplace? Answer the 12 questions using the following scale:

SD = Strongly disagree
D = Disagree
U = Uncertain
A = Agree
SA = Strongly agree

1. Managers often use the selection system to hire only people who can help them in their future. _____

2. The rules and policies concerning promotion and pay are fair; it's how managers carry out the policies that is unfair and self-serving. _____

3. The performance ratings people receive from their managers reflect more of the managers' "own agenda" than the actual performance of the employee. _____

4. Although a lot of what my manager does around here appears to be directed at helping employees, it's actually intended to protect my manager. _____

5. There are cliques or "in-groups" that hinder effectiveness around here. _____

6. My co-workers help themselves, not others. _____

7. I have seen people deliberately distort information requested by others for purposes of personal gain, either by withholding it or by selectively reporting it. _____

8. If co-workers offer to lend some assistance, it is because they expect to get something out of it. _____

9. Favouritism rather than merit determines who gets ahead around here. _____

10. You can usually get what you want around here if you know the right person to ask. _____

11. Overall, the rules and policies concerning promotion and pay are specific and well-defined. _____

12. Pay and promotion policies are generally clearly communicated in this organization. _____

This questionnaire taps the three salient dimensions that have been found to be related to perceptions of politics: manager behaviour; co-worker behaviour; and organizational policies and practices. To calculate your score for items 1–10, give yourself 1 point for Strongly disagree; 2 points for Disagree; and so forth (through 5 points for Strongly agree). For items 11 and 12, reverse the score (that is, 1 point for Strongly agree, etc.). Sum up the total: The higher the total score, the greater the degree of perceived organizational politics.

Source: G. R. Ferris, D. D. Frink, D. P. S. Bhawuk, J. Zhou, and D. C. Gilmore, "Reactions of Diverse Groups to Politics in the Workplace," *Journal of Management* 22, no. 1 (1996), pp. 32–33. Reprinted by permission of SAGE Publications.

tion of resources such as departmental budgets, space allocations, project responsibilities, and salary adjustments.

Resources in organizations are also limited, which often turns potential conflict into real conflict. If resources were abundant, all the constituencies within the organization could satisfy their goals. Because they are limited, not everyone's interests can be provided for. Furthermore, whether true or not, gains by one individual or group are often *perceived* as being at the expense of others within the organization. These forces create a competition among members for the organization's limited resources.

Maybe the most important factor behind politics within organizations is the realization that most of the "facts" that are used to allocate the limited resources are open to interpretation. What, for instance, is *good* performance? What is an *adequate* improvement? What constitutes an *unsatisfactory* job? It's in this large and ambiguous middle

When American figure skater Johnny Weir's low scores were announced at the men's 2010 Olympic Figure Skating finals, almost the entire crowd booed the judges in the Vancouver stadium. Some thought that the judges were engaging in politics to send a message to him that his style of artistic skating was not "masculine" enough for the sport.

ground of organizational life—where the facts *don't* speak for themselves—that politics flourish.

Finally, because most decisions must be made in a climate of ambiguity—where facts are rarely fully objective, and thus are open to interpretation—people within organizations will use whatever influence they can to spin the facts to support their goals and interests. That, of course, creates the activities we call *politicking*. For more about how one engages in politicking, see *From Concepts to Skill*s on pages 320–321.

Therefore, to answer the earlier question about whether it is possible for an organization to be politics-free, we can say "yes"—but only if all the members of that organization hold the same goals and interests, organizational resources are not scarce, and performance outcomes are completely clear and objective. However, that does not describe the organizational world that most of us live in.

RESEARCH FINDINGS: Politicking

Our earlier discussion focused on the favourable outcomes for individuals who successfully engage in politicking. But for most people—who have modest political skills or are unwilling to play the politics game—outcomes tend to be predominantly negative.[63] There is, for instance, very strong evidence indicating that perceptions of organizational politics are negatively related to job satisfaction.[64] The perception of politics also tends to increase job anxiety and stress. This seems to be because of the perception that, by not engaging in politics, a person may be losing ground to others who are active politickers, or, conversely, because of the additional pressures individuals feel because of having entered into and competing in the political arena.[65] Not surprisingly, when politicking becomes too much to handle, it can lead employees to quit.[66] Finally, there is preliminary evidence suggesting that politics leads to self-reported declines in employee performance.[67] Perceived organizational politics appears to have a demotivating effect on individuals, and thus leads to decreased performance levels.

Types of Political Activity

Within organizations, we can find a variety of political activities in which people engage. These include the following:[68]

- *Attacking or blaming others.* Used when trying to avoid responsibility for failure.

- *Using information.* Withholding or distorting information, particularly to hide negative information.

- *Managing impressions.* Bringing positive attention to oneself or taking credit for positive accomplishments of others.

- *Building support for ideas.* Making sure that others will support one's ideas before they are presented.

- *Praising others.* Making important people feel good.

- *Building coalitions.* Joining with other people to create a powerful group.

- *Associating with influential people.* Building support networks.

- *Creating obligations.* Doing favours for others so they will owe you favours later.

Individuals will use these political activities for different purposes. Some of these activities (such as attacking or blaming others) are more likely to be used to defend one's position, while other activities (such as building support for ideas and managing impressions) are meant to enhance one's image.

Impression Management

The process by which individuals attempt to control the impression others form of them is called **impression management**.[69] Being perceived positively by others should have benefits for people in organizations. It might, for instance, help them initially to get the jobs they want in an organization and, once hired, to get favourable evaluations, superior salary increases, and more rapid promotions. In a political context, it might help bring more advantages their way. *Case Incident—Dressing for Success* on page 318 looks at impression management through the company dress code.

Why do some people seem to engage in politics more than others?

Impression management does not imply that the impressions people convey are necessarily false (although, of course, they sometimes are).[70] Some activities may be done with great sincerity. For instance, you may *actually* believe that ads contribute little to sales in your region or that you are the key to the tripling of your division's sales. However, if the image claimed is false, you may be discredited.[71] The impression manager must be cautious not to be perceived as insincere or manipulative.[72] This chapter's *Point/Counterpoint* on page 314 considers the ethics of managing impressions.

RESEARCH FINDINGS:
Impression Management Techniques

Most of the studies undertaken to test the effectiveness of impression management techniques have related it to two criteria: interview success and performance evaluations. Let's consider each of these.

The evidence indicates that most job applicants use impression management techniques in interviews[73] and that, when impression management behaviour is used, it

impression management The process by which individuals attempt to control the impression others form of them.

works.[74] In one study, for instance, interviewers felt that applicants for a position as a customer-service representative who used impression management techniques performed better in the interview, and they seemed somewhat more inclined to hire these people.[75] Moreover, when the researchers considered applicants' credentials, they concluded that it was the impression management techniques alone that influenced the interviewers. That is, it did not seem to matter if applicants were well or poorly qualified. If they used impression management techniques, they did better in the interview.

In what situations does impression management work best?

Research indicates that some impression management techniques work better than others in an interview. Researchers have compared applicants who used techniques that focused on promoting one's accomplishments (called *self-promotion*) to applicants who used techniques that focused on complimenting the interviewer and finding areas of agreement (referred to as *ingratiation*). In general, applicants appear to use self-promotion more than ingratiation.[76] What is more, self-promotion tactics may be more important to interviewing success. Applicants who work to create an appearance of competence by enhancing their accomplishments, taking credit for successes, and explaining away failures do better in interviews. These effects reach beyond the interview: Applicants who use more self-promotion tactics also seem to get more follow-up job-site visits, even after adjusting for grade-point average, gender, and job type. Ingratiation also works well in interviews, meaning that applicants who compliment the interviewer, agree with his or her opinions, and emphasize areas of fit do better than those who don't.[77]

In terms of performance ratings, the picture is quite different. Ingratiation is positively related to performance ratings, meaning that those who ingratiate with their supervisors get higher performance evaluations. However, self-promotion appears to backfire: Those who self-promote actually seem to receive *lower* performance evaluations.[78] There is an important qualifier to this general result. It appears that individuals high in political skill are able to translate impression management into higher performance appraisals, whereas those lower in political skill are more likely to be hurt by their attempts at impression management.[79]

What explains these results? If you think about them, they make sense. Ingratiating always works because everyone—both interviewers and supervisors—likes to be treated nicely. However, self-promotion may work only in interviews and backfire on the job because, whereas the interviewer has little idea whether you are blowing smoke about your accomplishments, the supervisor knows because it's his or her job to observe you. Thus, if you are going to self-promote, remember that what works in an interview will not always work once you are on the job.

Making Office Politics Work

One thing to be aware of is that extreme office politics can have a negative effect on employees. Researchers have found that organizational politics is associated with less organizational commitment,[80] lower job satisfaction,[81] and decreased job performance.[82] Individuals who experience greater organizational politics are more likely to report higher levels of job anxiety,[83] and they are more likely to consider leaving the organization.[84]

Is there an effective way to engage in office politics that is less likely to be disruptive or negative? We discuss different negotiation strategies in Chapter 9, including a *win-lose* strategy, which means if I win, you lose, and a *win-win* strategy, which means creating situations where both of us can win. *Fast Company*, a business magazine, identifies several rules that may help improve the climate of the organization while negotiating through the office politics maze:[85]

General Electric wants its managers to share their power with employees. GE is breaking down autocratic barriers between labour and management that "cramp people, inhibit creativity, waste time, restrict visions, smother dreams, and above all, slow things down." GE expects managers to behave more democratically by fostering teamwork and rewarding employees who suggest ideas for improvement. This photo illustrates GE's move toward democracy, as a manager and an employee at the company's plant in Louisville, Kentucky, work together to improve the plant's profitability.

- *Nobody wins unless everybody wins.* The most successful proposals look for ways to acknowledge, if not include, the interests of others. This requires building support for your ideas across the organization. "Real political skill isn't about campaign tactics," says Lou Di Natale, a veteran political consultant at the University of Massachusetts. "It's about pulling people toward your ideas and then pushing those ideas through to other people." When ideas are packaged to look like they are best for the organization as a whole and will help others, it is harder for others to counteract your proposal.

- *Don't just ask for opinions—change them.* It's helpful to find out what people think and then, if necessary, set out to change their opinions so that they can see what you want to do. It's also important to seek out the opinions of those you don't know well, or who are less likely to agree with you. Gathering together people who always support you is often not enough to build an effective coalition.

- *Everyone expects to be paid back.* In organizations, as in life, we develop personal relationships with those around us. It's those personal relationships that affect much of the behaviour in organizations. By building good relationships with colleagues, supporting them in their endeavours, and showing appreciation for what they accomplish, you are building a foundation of support for your own ideas.

- *Success can create opposition.* As part of the office politics, success can be viewed as a *win-lose* strategy, which we identified above. Some people may feel that your success comes at their expense. So, for instance, your higher profile may mean that a project of theirs will be received less favourably. You have to be prepared to deal with this opposition.

GLOBAL **IMPLICATIONS** _____

Although culture might enter any of the topics we have covered to this point, three questions are particularly important: (1) Does culture influence views on empowerment? (2) Does culture influence perceptions of politics? And (3) Does culture affect the influence tactics people prefer to use?

Views on Empowerment

Four US researchers investigated the effects of empowerment on employees of a multinational firm by looking at four of the company's comparable plants: one in the Midwestern United States, one in central Mexico, one in west-central India, and one in the south of Poland.[86] These four locations were chosen because they differed on power distance and individualism (concepts we discussed in Chapter 3). India and Mexico are considered high in power distance, and the United States is considered the lowest in power distance. Mexico and India are high in collectivity, the United States is highly individualistic, and Poland is moderately individualistic.

The findings showed that Indian employees gave their supervisors low ratings when empowerment was high, while employees in the other three countries rated their supervisors favourably when empowerment was high. In both the United States and Mexico, empowerment had no effect on satisfaction with co-workers. However, satisfaction with co-workers was higher when employees were empowered in Poland. In India, empowerment led to lower satisfaction with co-workers.

Similar findings in a study comparing empowerment in the United States, Brazil, and Argentina suggest that in hierarchical societies, empowerment may need to be introduced with care.[87] Employees in those countries may be more used to working in teams, but they also expect their manager to be the person with all the answers. Professor Marylène Gagné of Concordia's John Molson School of Business, who has studied empowerment cross-culturally,[88] notes that "in some cultures, bosses can't ask the opinion of subordinates, because it makes them appear weak. So managers in these environments have to find other ways to make people feel autonomous. There is no simple recipe."[89]

Perceptions of Politics

We have already noted that (based on research conducted mostly in the United States) when people see their work environment as political, the effect on their overall work attitudes and behaviours is usually negative. When employees of two agencies in a recent study in Nigeria viewed their work environments as political, they reported higher levels of job distress and were less likely to help their co-workers. Thus, although developing countries such as Nigeria are perhaps more ambiguous and more political environments in which to work, the negative consequences appear to be the same as in the United States.[90]

Preference for Influence Tactics

Evidence indicates that people in different countries tend to prefer different influence tactics.[91] A study comparing managers in the United States and China found that US managers prefer rational appeal, whereas Chinese managers prefer coalition tactics.[92] These differences tend to be consistent with the values in these two countries. Reason is consistent with the US preference for direct confrontation and the use of rational persuasion to influence others and resolve differences. Similarly, coalition tactics are consistent with the Chinese preference for using indirect approaches for difficult or controversial requests. Research also has shown that individuals in Western, individualistic cultures tend to engage in more self-enhancement (such as self-promotion) behaviours than individuals in Eastern, more collectivistic cultures.[93]

A study of Swedish, German, Czech, Polish, and Finnish managers found that Swedish managers saw mere differences in opinion as conflicts, so they adopted a conflict-avoidant strategy that emphasized more passive forms of persuasion.[94] German managers, on the other hand, saw disagreement as a useful opportunity to gain new knowledge and fostered some rational discussion as an influence technique. Finnish managers preferred discussion-oriented influence tactics as well. Czech and Polish managers believed managers were under pressure to halt conflicts quickly when they arose, since conflict resolution is time consuming. Therefore, the Czech and Polish managers switched to more autocratic, power-oriented influence styles.

Are the same influence tactics equally effective across a country? Though researchers usually compare two very different cultures, it is also important to examine differences within a given culture, because those differences can sometimes be greater than differences between cultures. China is a big country with different cultures and traditions. A recent study of mainland Chinese, Taiwanese, and Hong Kong managers explored how the three cultural subgroups differ according to the influence tactics they prefer to use.[95] Though managers from all three places believe that rational persuasion and exchange are the most effective influence tactics, managers in Taiwan tend to use inspirational appeals and ingratiation more than managers from either mainland China or Hong Kong. The study also found that managers from Hong Kong rate pressure as more effective in influencing others than do managers in Taiwan or mainland China. Such differences have implications for business relationships. For example, Taiwanese or mainland Chinese managers may be taken aback by the use of pressure tactics by a Hong Kong manager. Likewise, managers from Hong Kong may not be persuaded by managers from Taiwan, who tend to use ingratiating tactics. Such differences in influence tactics may make business dealings difficult. Companies should address these issues, perhaps making their managers aware of the differences within cultures.

> **LESSONS LEARNED**
> - Effective leaders use expert and/or referent power.
> - To maximize your power, increase others' dependence on you.
> - Politics is inevitable; managing politics well is a skill.

Summary and Implications

1 **What is power?**   Power refers to a capacity that A has to influence the behaviour of B, so that B acts in accordance with A's wishes.

2 **How does one get power?**   There are six bases or sources of power: coercive, reward, legitimate, expert, referent, and information. These forms of power differ in their ability to improve a person's performance. *Coercive power* tends to result in negative performance responses from individuals; it decreases satisfaction, increases mistrust, and creates fear. *Reward power* may improve performance, but it can also lead to unethical behaviour. *Legitimate power* does not have a negative effect, but does not generally stimulate employees to improve their attitudes or performance, and it does not generally result in increased commitment. Ironically, the least effective bases of power—coercive, legitimate, and reward—are the ones most likely to be used by managers, perhaps because they are the easiest to implement. By contrast, effective leaders use *expert* and/or *referent power*; these forms of power are not derived from the person's position. *Information power* comes from access to and control over information and can be used in both positive (sharing) and negative (withholding) ways in the organization.

3 **How does dependency affect power?**   To maximize your power, you will want to increase others' dependence on you. You can, for instance, increase your power in relation to your employer by developing knowledge or a skill that he or she needs and for which there is no ready substitute. However, you will not be alone in attempting to build your bases of power. Others, particularly employees and peers, will seek to make you dependent on them. The result is a continual struggle for power.

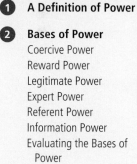

SNAPSHOT SUMMARY

1 **A Definition of Power**

2 **Bases of Power**
  Coercive Power
  Reward Power
  Legitimate Power
  Expert Power
  Referent Power
  Information Power
  Evaluating the Bases of Power

3 **Dependency: The Key to Power**
  The General Dependency Postulate
  What Creates Dependency?

4 **What tactics can be used to increase power?** One particular study identified nine tactics, or strategies, that managers and employees use to increase their power: rational persuasion, inspirational appeals, consultation, ingratiation, personal appeals, exchange, coalitions, pressure, and legitimacy.[96]

5 **What does it mean to be empowered?** *Empowerment* refers to the freedom and the ability of employees to make decisions and commitments. There is a lot of positive press on empowerment. However, much of the talk in organizations about empowerment does not result in employees being empowered. Some managers do not fully understand how to go about empowering their employees, and others find it difficult to share their power with employees. As well, some employees have little or no interest in being empowered, and empowerment is not something that works well in every culture.

6 **How are power and harassment related?** People who engage in harassment in the workplace are typically abusing their power position. Harassment can come in many forms, from gross abuse of power toward anyone of lower rank, to abuse of individuals because of their personal characteristics, such as race, religion, national origin, and gender.

7 **Why do people engage in politics?** People use politics to influence others to help them achieve their personal objectives. Whenever people get together in groups, power will be exerted. People also use impression management to influence people. Impression management is the process by which individuals attempt to control the impression others form of them. Though politics is a natural occurrence in organizations, when it is carried to an extreme it can damage relationships among individuals.

for Review

1. What is power? How do you get it?

2. Contrast the bases of power with influence tactics.

3. How might people respond to the different bases of power that someone might use?

4. Which of the six bases of power lie with the individual? Which are derived from the organization?

5. Define the general dependency postulate.

6. What creates dependency? Give an applied example.

7. Identify the range of empowerment that might be available to employees.

8. Define *sexual harassment*. Who is most likely to harass an employee: a boss, a co-worker, or a subordinate? Explain.

9. How are power and politics related?

10. Define *political behaviour*. Why is politics a fact of life in organizations?

for Critical Thinking

1. Based on the information presented in this chapter, what would you do, as a recent graduate entering a new job, to maximize your power and accelerate your career progress?

2. "Politics is not inherently bad. It is merely a way to get things accomplished within organizations." Do you agree or disagree? Defend your position.

3. You are a sales representative for an international software company. After four excellent years, sales in your territory are off 30 percent this year. Describe three impression management techniques you might use to convince your manager that your sales record is better than should be expected under the circumstances.

4. Which impression management techniques have you used? What ethical implications, if any, are there in using impression management?

5. "Sexual harassment should not be tolerated in the workplace." "Workplace romances are a natural occurrence in organizations." Are both of these statements true? Can they be reconciled?

for You

- Power and politics should not simply be viewed as a win-lose situation. Through power and politics, one builds coalitions to work together effectively. It's possible to make sure that everyone is included.

- There are a variety of ways to increase your power in an organization. As an example, you could acquire more knowledge about a situation and then use that information to negotiate a bonus with your employer. Even if you don't get the bonus, the knowledge may help you in other ways.

- To increase your power, consider how dependent others are on you. Dependency is affected by your importance and substitutability and by the scarcity of options. If you have needed skills that no one else has, you will have more power.

- Politics is a reality of most organizations. Being comfortable with politics is important. Politics is often about making deals with other people for mutual gain.

- Political skills can be developed. Remembering to take time to join in an office birthday celebration for someone is part of developing the skill of working with others effectively.

Managing Impressions Is Unethical

Managing impressions is wrong for both ethical and practical reasons.

First, managing impressions is just another name for lying. Don't we have a responsibility, both to ourselves and to others, to present ourselves as we really are? Australian philosopher Tony Coady wrote, "Dishonesty has always been perceived in our culture, and in all cultures but the most bizarre, as a central human vice." Immanuel Kant's categorical imperative asks us to consider the following: If you want to know whether telling a lie on a particular occasion is justifiable, you must try to imagine what would happen if everyone were to lie. Surely, you would agree that a world in which no one lies is preferable to one in which lying is common, because in such a world we could never trust anyone. Thus, we should try to present the truth as best we can. Impression management goes against this virtue.

Practically speaking, impression management generally backfires in the long run. Remember Sir Walter Scott's quote, "Oh what a tangled web we weave, when first we practise to deceive!" Once we start to distort the facts, where do we stop? Dr. Philip Baker, former dean of the Faculty of Medicine at the University of Alberta, wanted to give the 2011 graduating class a memorable speech at their graduation dinner. Unfortunately, he didn't write his own speech, but mostly reused a speech given by Dr. Atul Gawande at Stanford University in 2010.[97] When the truth came out, Baker had to resign as dean.

People are most satisfied with their jobs when their values match the culture of the organizations. If either side misrepresents itself in the interview process, then odds are, people will not fit in the organizations they choose. What is the benefit in this?

This does not imply that a person should not put his or her best foot forward. But that means exhibiting qualities that are good no matter the context—being friendly, being positive and self-confident, being qualified and competent, while still being honest.

There Is Nothing Wrong with Managing Impressions

Let's be real, here. Everybody fudges to some degree in the process of applying for a job. If you really told the interviewer what your greatest weakness or worst mistake was, you would never get hired. What if you answered, "I find it hard to get up in the morning and get to work"?

These sorts of "white lies" are expected and act as a kind of social lubricant. If we really knew what people were thinking, we would go crazy. Moreover, you can quote all the philosophy you want, but sometimes it's necessary to lie. You mean you would not lie to save the life of a family member? It's naive to think we can live in a world without lying.

Sometimes a bit of deception is necessary to get a job. I know a gay applicant who was rejected from a job he really wanted because he told the interviewer he had written two articles for gay magazines. What if he had told the interviewer a little lie? Would harm really have been done? At least he would have a job.

As another example, when an interviewer asks you what you earned on your previous job, that information will be used against you, to pay you a salary lower than you deserve. Is it wrong to boost your salary a bit? Or would it be better to disclose your actual salary and be taken advantage of?

The same goes for complimenting interviewers, agreeing with their opinions, and so forth. If an interviewer tells you, "We believe in community involvement," are you supposed to tell the interviewer you have never volunteered for anything?

Of course, you can go too far. We are not advocating that people totally fabricate their backgrounds. What we are talking about here is a reasonable amount of enhancement. If we can help ourselves without doing any real harm, then impression management is not the same as lying and actually is something we should teach others.

LEARNING ABOUT **YOURSELF** EXERCISE

How Political Are You?

To determine your political tendencies, please review the following statements. Check the answer that best represents your behaviour or belief, even if that particular behaviour or belief is not present all the time.

	True	False
1. You should make others feel important through an open appreciation of their ideas and work.	✓	
2. Because people tend to judge you when they first meet you, always try to make a good first impression.	✓	
3. Try to let others do most of the talking, be sympathetic to their problems, and resist telling people that they are totally wrong.		✓
4. Praise the good traits of the people you meet and always give people an opportunity to save face if they are wrong or make a mistake.	✓	
5. Spreading false rumours, planting misleading information, and backstabbing are necessary, if somewhat unpleasant, methods to deal with your enemies.		✓
6. Sometimes it is necessary to make promises that you know you will not or cannot keep.	✓	✓
7. It's important to get along with everybody, even with those who are generally recognized as windbags, abrasive, or constant complainers.	✓	
8. It's vital to do favours for others so that you can call in these IOUs at times when they will do you the most good.	✓	
9. Be willing to compromise, particularly on issues that are minor to you but major to others.	✓	
10. On controversial issues, it's important to delay or avoid your involvement if possible.	✓	

Scoring Key:

According to the author of this instrument, a complete organizational politician will answer "true" to all 10 questions. Organizational politicians with fundamental ethical standards will answer "false" to questions 5 and 6, which deal with deliberate lies and uncharitable behaviour. Individuals who regard manipulation, incomplete disclosure, and self-serving behaviour as unacceptable will answer "false" to all or almost all of the questions.

Source: J. F. Byrnes, "The Political Behavior Inventory." Reprinted by permission of Dr. Joseph F. Byrnes, Bentley College, Waltham, Massachusetts.

SELF-ASSESSMENT LIBRARY LEARNING ABOUT YOURSELF

More Learning About Yourself Exercises

Additional self-assessments relevant to this chapter appear on MyOBLab (**www.pearsoned.ca/myoblab**).

IV.F.1 Is My Workplace Political?
II.C.3 How Good Am I at Playing Politics?

When you complete the additional assessments, consider the following:

1. Am I surprised about my score?
2. Would my friends evaluate me similarly?

BREAKOUT **GROUP** EXERCISES

Form small groups to discuss the following topics, as assigned by your instructor:

1. Describe an incident where you tried to use political behaviour in order to get something you wanted. What influence tactics did you use?

2. In thinking about the incident described above, were your influence tactics effective? Why?

3. Describe an incident where you saw someone engaging in politics. What was your reaction to observing the political behaviour? Under what circumstances do you think political behaviour is appropriate?

WORKING WITH **OTHERS** EXERCISE

Understanding Bases of Power

Step 1:   Your instructor will divide the class into groups of about 5 or 6 (making sure there are at least 5 groups).[98] Each group will be assigned 1 of the following bases of power: (1) coercive, (2) reward, (3) legitimate, (4) expert, and (5) referent. Refer to your text for discussion of these terms.

Step 2:   Each group is to develop a role play that highlights the use of the power assigned. The role play should be developed using the following scenario:

> *You are the leader of a group that is trying to develop a website for a new client. One of your group members, who was assigned the task of researching and analyzing the websites of your client's competition, has twice failed to bring the analysis to scheduled meetings, even though the member knew the assignment was due. Consequently, your group is falling behind in getting the website developed. As leader of the group, you have decided to speak with this team member and to use your specific brand of power to influence the individual's behaviour.*

Step 3:   Each group should select 1 person to play the group leader and another to play the member who has not done the assignment. You have 10 minutes to prepare an influence plan.

Step 4:   Each group will conduct its role play. In the event of multiple groups assigned the same power base, 1 of the groups may be asked to volunteer. While you are watching the other groups' role plays, try to put yourself in the place of the person being influenced, to see whether that type of influence would cause you to change your behaviour.

Immediately after each role play, while the next one is being set up, you should pretend that you were the person being influenced, and then record your reaction using the questionnaire opposite. To do this, take out a sheet of paper and tear it into 5 (or 6) pieces. At the top of each piece of paper, write the type of influence that was used. Then write the letters A, B, C, and D in a column, and indicate which number on the scale (see opposite) reflects the influence attempt.

WORKING WITH **OTHERS** EXERCISE (CONTINUED)

Reaction to Influence Questionnaire

For each role play, think of yourself as being on the receiving end of the influence attempt described, and record your own reaction.

Type of power used _____

A. As a result of the influence attempt, I will . . .

| **definitely not comply** | 1 | 2 | 3 | 4 | 5 | **definitely comply** |

B. Any change that does come about will be . . .

| **temporary** | 1 | 2 | 3 | 4 | 5 | **long-lasting** |

C. My own personal reaction is . . .

| **resistant** | 1 | 2 | 3 | 4 | 5 | **accepting** |

D. As a result of this influence attempt, my relationship with my group leader will probably be . . .

| **worse** | 1 | 2 | 3 | 4 | 5 | **better** |

Step 5: For each influence type, 1 member of each group will take the pieces of paper from group members and calculate the average group score for each of the 4 questions. For efficiency, this should be done while the role plays are being conducted.

Step 6: Your instructor will collect the summaries from each group, and then lead a discussion based on these results.

Step 7: Discussion.

1. Which kind of influence is most likely to immediately result in the desired behaviour?

2. Which will have the most long-lasting effects?

3. What effect will using a particular base of power have on the ongoing relationship?

4. Which form of power will others find most acceptable? Least acceptable? Why?

5. Are there some situations where a particular type of influence strategy might be more effective than others?

ETHICAL **DILEMMA** EXERCISE

Swapping Personal Favours?

Jack Grubman was a powerful man on Wall Street.[99] As a star analyst of telecom companies for the Salomon Smith Barney unit of Citigroup, his recommendations carried a lot of weight with investors.

For years, Grubman had been negative on the stock of AT&T. But then he upgraded his opinion on the stock. Based on email evidence, it appears that Grubman's decision to upgrade AT&T was not based on the stock's fundamentals. There were other factors involved.

At the time, his boss at Citigroup, Sanford Weill, was in the midst of a power struggle with co-CEO John Reed to become the single head of the company. Meanwhile,

Salomon was looking for additional business to increase its revenues. Getting investment banking business fees from AT&T would be a big plus toward improving revenues. Salomon's efforts at getting that AT&T business would definitely be improved if Grubman would upgrade his opinion on the stock. Furthermore, Weill sought Grubman's upgrade to win favour with AT&T CEO Michael Armstrong, who sat on Citigroup's board. Weill wanted Armstrong's backing in his efforts to oust Reed.

Grubman had his own concerns. Although he was earning tens of millions a year in his job, he was a man of modest background. He was the son of a city worker. He wanted the best for his twin daughters, which included entry to an exclusive nursery school—a school that a year earlier had reportedly turned down Madonna's daughter. Weill made a call on Grubman's behalf to the school and pledged a $1-million donation from Citigroup.

At approximately the same time, Weill also asked Grubman to "take a fresh look" at his neutral rating on AT&T. Shortly after being asked to review his rating, Grubman turned positive, raised his rating, and AT&T awarded Salomon an investment-banking job worth nearly $45 million.

Did Sanford Weill do anything unethical? How about Jack Grubman? What do you think?

CASE INCIDENTS

Dressing for Success

Jennifer Cohen thought she had a good grip on her company's dress code. She was wrong.[100]

Cohen works for a marketing firm. Before a meeting, an older colleague pulled 24-year-old Cohen aside and told her that she was dressing inappropriately by wearing Bermuda shorts and sleeveless tops. Cohen was stunned by the rebuke. "Each generation seems to have a different idea of what is acceptable in the workplace," she said. "In this case, I was highly offended."

What offended Cohen even more was what came next: Cohen was not allowed to attend the meeting because her attire was deemed inappropriate.

Cohen's employer is not alone. Although many employers have "casual" days at work, the number of employers who are enforcing more formal dress codes has increased, according to a survey of employers by the Society for Human Resource Management. Heading into Summer 2011, Renfrew County, near Ottawa, updated its dress code to prevent government employees from wearing flip-flops.

Ironically, as more employers enforce more formal dress codes, other employers known for their formality are going the other way. IBM, which once had a dress code of business suits with white shirts, has thrown out dress codes altogether. IBM researcher Dan Gruhl typically goes to work at IBM's San Jose, California, office in flip-flops and shorts. "Having a relaxed environment encourages you to think more openly," he says. Although not going quite as far as IBM, other traditional employers, such as Ford, General Motors, and Procter & Gamble, have relaxed dress codes. At Toronto-based Google Canada, an even simpler code is in place: Employees must wear clothes.

Still, for every Google, there are more companies that have tightened the rules. Even the National Basketball Association (NBA) has adopted an off-court dress code for its players. As for Cohen, she still bristles at the dress code. "When you're comfortable, you don't worry," she says. "You focus on your work."

Questions

1. Do you think Cohen had a right to be offended? Why or why not?

2. In explaining why she was offended, Cohen argued, "People my age are taught to express themselves, and saying something negative about someone's fashion is saying something negative about them." Do you agree with Cohen?

3. Does an employer have an unfettered right to set a company's dress code? Why or why not?

4. How far would you go to conform to an organization's dress code? If your boss dressed in a relatively formal manner, would you feel compelled to dress in a like manner to manage impressions?

The Persuasion Imperative

There may have been a time when a boss gave orders and subordinates followed them.[101] If you have watched the television series *Mad Men*—based on Madison Avenue marketing executives in the 1960s—you have seen an image of deference to authority, respectful obedience to those higher up in the hierarchy, and a paternalistic relationship between boss and employee.

With time comes change. Organizations are no longer male dominated, as they were in the 1950s. Laws and policies are in place that better protect employees against the sometimes-capricious whims of supervisors.

Another sign of shifting cultural values is the way managers use their power. Commandments are out. Persuasion is in.

When IBM manager Kate Riley Tenant needed to reassign managers and engineers to form a database software team, she had to persuade IBM employees from all corners of the globe, none of whom directly reported to her. According to Tenant, it's a big change from when she started in the field 20 years ago. "You just decided things, and people went off and executed," she said. Now, "not everybody reports to you, and so there's much more negotiation and influence."

John Churchill, a manager with Gerdau Ameristeel Corporation, agrees. The question now, he says, is "How do I influence this group and gain credibility?"

At IBM, the challenge of persuading employees across reporting relationships has become so significant that the firm developed a two-hour online course to help managers persuade other employees to help with projects crucial to its business. IBM's tips for managers include the following:

- Build a shared vision
- Negotiate collaboratively
- Make trade-offs
- Build and maintain your network

Despite meeting initial resistance, after completing the training program, Tenant was able to persuade most IBM managers and engineers to join the team.

This does not mean authority has lost all its power. Robert Cialdini, a social psychologist who has studied persuasion for decades, lists authority as one of his keys to influence. Even more important may be the so-called bandwagon effect (or what Cialdini calls "social proof")—Cialdini and others have found that people are often deeply persuaded by observing what others are doing. From his research, no message more effectively got hotel guests to reuse their towels than citing statistics that others were reusing their towels.

So, if you are a manager who needs to persuade, present the vision behind the request and be collaborative, but it also would not hurt to tell those you are trying to persuade about others who have already agreed to your request.

Questions

1. Are the precepts of the IBM training program consistent with the concepts in this chapter? Why or why not?

2. Again based on the chapter, are there other keys to persuasion and influence that might be added to the IBM program?

3. If you had a manager who wanted you to do something against your initial inclination, which of IBM's elements would work best on you? Why?

4. Drawing from Chapter 3, do you think generational values explain the changing nature of the employer-employee relationship?

FROM CONCEPTS TO SKILLS

Politicking

Forget, for a moment, the ethics of politicking and any negative impressions you may have of people who engage in organizational politics.[102] If you wanted to be more politically adept in your organization, what could you do? The following eight suggestions are likely to improve your political effectiveness:

1. *Frame arguments in terms of organizational goals.* Effective politicking requires camouflaging your self-interest. No matter that your objective is self-serving; all the arguments you marshal in support of it must be framed in terms of the benefits that the organization will gain. People whose actions appear to blatantly further their own interests at the expense of the organization's are almost universally denounced, are likely to lose influence, and often suffer the ultimate penalty of being expelled from the organization.

2. *Develop the right image.* If you know your organization's culture, you understand what the organization wants and values from its employees—in terms of dress; associates to cultivate, and those to avoid; whether to appear risk-taking or risk-averse; the preferred leadership style; the importance placed on getting along well with others; and so forth. Then you are equipped to project the appropriate image. Because the assessment of your performance is not a fully objective process, both style and substance must be addressed.

3. *Gain control of organizational resources.* The control of organizational resources that are scarce and important is a source of power. Knowledge and expertise are particularly effective resources to control. They make you more valuable to the organization and, therefore, more likely to gain security, advancement, and a receptive audience for your ideas.

4. *Make yourself appear indispensable.* Because we are dealing with appearances rather than objective facts, you can enhance your power by appearing to be indispensable. That is, you don't have to really be indispensable as long as key people in the organization believe that you are. If the organization's prime decision makers believe there is no ready substitute for what you are giving the organization, they are likely to go to great lengths to ensure that your desires are satisfied.

5. *Be visible.* Because performance evaluation has a substantial subjective component, it's important that your manager and those in power in the organization be made aware of your contribution. If you are fortunate enough to have a job that brings your accomplishments to the attention of others, it may not be necessary to take direct measures to increase your visibility. But your job may require you to handle activities that are low in visibility, or your specific contribution may be indistinguishable because you are part of a team endeavour. In such cases, without appearing to be tooting your own horn, you will want to call attention to yourself by highlighting your successes in routine reports, having satisfied customers relay their appreciation to senior executives, being seen at social functions, being active in professional associations, developing powerful allies who speak positively about your accomplishments, and similar tactics. Of course, the skilled politician actively lobbies to get those projects that will increase his or her visibility.

6. *Develop powerful allies.* It helps to have powerful people in your camp. Cultivate contacts with potentially influential people above you, at your own level, and in the lower ranks. They can provide you

with important information that may not be available through normal channels. There will be times, too, when decisions will be made in favour of those with the greatest support. Having powerful allies can provide you with a coalition of support if and when you need it.

7. *Avoid "tainted" members.* In almost every organization, there are fringe members whose status is questionable. Their performance and/or loyalty is suspect. Keep your distance from such individuals. Given the reality that effectiveness has a large subjective component, your own effectiveness might be called into question if you are perceived as being too closely associated with tainted members.

8. *Support your manager.* Since he or she evaluates your performance, you will typically want to do whatever is necessary to have your manager on your side. You should make every effort to help your manager succeed, make her look good, and support her if she is under siege, and to spend the time to find out what criteria she will be using to assess your effectiveness. Do not undermine your manager, and do not speak negatively of her to others.

Practising Skills

You used to be the star marketing manager for Hilton Electronics Corporation. But for the past year, you have been outpaced again and again by Sean, a new manager in the design department who has been accomplishing everything expected of him and more. Meanwhile, your best efforts to do your job well have been sabotaged and undercut by Maria—your and Sean's manager. For example, before last year's international consumer electronics show, Maria moved $30 000 from your budget to Sean's. Despite your best efforts, your marketing team could not complete all the marketing materials normally developed to showcase all of your organization's new products at this important industry show. Also, Maria has chipped away at your staff and budget ever since. Although you have been able to meet most of your goals with less staff and budget, Maria has continued to slice away resources from your group. Just last week, she eliminated two positions in your team of eight marketing specialists to make room for a new designer and some extra equipment for Sean. Maria is clearly taking away your resources while giving Sean whatever he wants and more. You think it's time to do something, or soon you will not have any team or resources left. What do you need to do to make sure your division has the resources to survive and grow?

Reinforcing Skills

1. Keep a one-week journal of your behaviour, describing incidents when you tried to influence others around you. Assess each incident by asking: Were you successful at these attempts to influence them? Why or why not? What could you have done differently?

2. Outline a specific action plan, based on concepts in this module, that would improve your career progression in the organization in which you currently work or in which you would like to be employed.

Conflict and Negotiation

The Pacific National Exhibition and CUPE 1004 needed to negotiate a new collective bargaining agreement. What caused talks to break down and how might that have been avoided?

LEARNING OUTCOMES

1. What is conflict?

2. How can conflict be resolved?

3. What are the effects of conflict?

4. How does one negotiate effectively?

5. How do individual differences influence negotiations?

O n August 20, 2011, one day before the opening of the Vancouver-based Pacific National Exhibition's (PNE's) annual fair, talks between management and the union representing PNE's 4000 employees broke down.[1] PNE employees, including ride operators, maintenance personnel, administrators, games operators, ushers, and parking lot attendants, had been without a contract since the start of the year. It was the first time in 25 years that a contract agreement had not been reached prior to the opening of the fair.

The local chapter of CUPE (1004) was seeking more job security, cost of living wage increases totalling 7.5 percent over three years, and improved equity for their lowest paid employees, many of whom earned less than $10 per hour. Unionized employees rejected PNE's offer of a 3.75 percent raise over three years. They confirmed their position in a strike vote that took place in mid-September, in which 92 percent of employees supported a strike.

Despite the fact that the fair was over when the vote took place, a number of important upcoming events were scheduled at the PNE, including professional hockey and soccer games and a Pearl Jam concert. With staff on strike, those events were at risk of being cancelled. "If the new [contract agreement] talks broke down on Monday or Tuesday and everyone was annoyed . . . we could serve strike notice in time for the Giant's game on Friday" observed CUPE business agent Steve Varty after the mid-September vote.

In this chapter, we look at sources of conflict and strategies for resolving conflict, including negotiation.

THE BIG IDEA

Resolving conflicts and engaging in successful negotiations requires understanding your objectives and the objectives of the other party.

OB IS FOR EVERYONE

- Is conflict always bad?
- Can someone else be asked to help resolve a conflict?
- Should you try to win at any cost when you bargain?
- How does anxiety affect negotiating outcomes?
- Ever wonder if men and women negotiate differently?

Conflict Defined

1 What is conflict?

BLOG IT

Are you a reluctant or an enthusiastic negotiator?
Describe a situation where you had to negotiate for something you wanted. Did you have a good or bad outcome? What factors led to that outcome?
www.obstudentjournals.blogspot.com

Several common themes underlie most definitions of conflict.[2] Conflict must be *perceived* by the parties to it; if no one is aware of a conflict, then it is generally agreed that no conflict exists. Conflict also involves opposition or incompatibility, and some form of interaction between the parties.[3] These factors set the conditions that determine the beginning point of the conflict process. We can define **conflict**, then, as a process that begins when one party perceives that another party has negatively affected, or is about to negatively affect, something that the first party cares about.[4]

This definition is deliberately broad. It describes that point in any ongoing activity when an interaction "crosses over" to become an interparty conflict. It encompasses the wide range of conflicts that people experience in groups and organizations—incompatibility of goals, differences over interpretations of facts, disagreements based on behavioural expectations, and the like. Finally, our definition is flexible enough to cover the full range of conflict levels—from subtle forms of disagreement to overt and violent acts.

Conflict has positive sides and negative sides, which we will discuss further when we cover functional and dysfunctional conflict. For more on this debate, refer to the *Point/Counterpoint* discussion on page 347.

Functional vs. Dysfunctional Conflict

The general view on conflict is that not all conflict is bad.[5] Some conflicts support the goals of the group and improve its performance; these are **functional**, or constructive, forms of conflict. But there are conflicts that hinder group performance; these are **dysfunctional**, or destructive, forms of conflict. The criterion that differentiates functional from dysfunctional conflict is group performance. If a group is unable to achieve its goals because of conflict, then the conflict is dysfunctional.

Is conflict always bad?

Exhibit 9-1 provides a way of visualizing conflict behaviour. All conflicts exist somewhere along this continuum. At the lower part of the continuum, we have conflicts characterized by subtle, indirect, and highly controlled forms of tension. An illustration might be a student politely objecting to a point the instructor has just made in class.

conflict A process that begins when one party perceives that another party has negatively affected, or is about to negatively affect, something that the first party cares about.

functional conflict Conflict that supports the goals of the group and improves its performance.

dysfunctional conflict Conflict that hinders group performance.

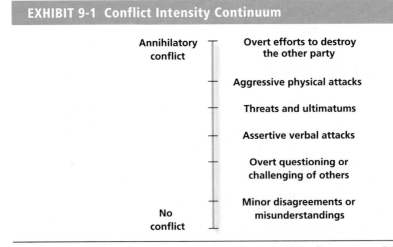

EXHIBIT 9-1 Conflict Intensity Continuum

Annihilatory conflict — Overt efforts to destroy the other party

— Aggressive physical attacks

— Threats and ultimatums

— Assertive verbal attacks

— Overt questioning or challenging of others

No conflict — Minor disagreements or misunderstandings

Sources: Based on S. P. Robbins, *Managing Organizational Conflict: A Nontraditional Approach* (Upper Saddle River, NJ: Prentice Hall, 1974), pp. 93–97; and F. Glasl, "The Process of Conflict Escalation and the Roles of Third Parties," in *Conflict Management and Industrial Relations*, ed. G. B. J. Bomers and R. Peterson (Boston: Kluwer-Nijhoff, 1982), pp. 119–140.

Conflict intensities escalate as they move upward along the continuum, until they become highly destructive. Strikes and lockouts, riots, and wars clearly fall in this upper range. For the most part, you should assume that conflicts that reach the upper ranges of the continuum are almost always dysfunctional. Functional conflicts are typically confined to the lower range of the continuum.

RESEARCH FINDINGS: Cognitive and Affective Conflict

Research on conflict has yet to clearly identify those situations where conflict is more likely to be constructive than destructive. However, there is growing evidence that the source of the conflict is a significant factor determining functionality.[6] **Cognitive conflict**, which is task-oriented and occurs because of differences in perspectives and judgments, can often result in identifying potential solutions to problems. Thus it would be regarded as functional conflict. **Affective conflict**, which is emotional and aimed at a person rather than an issue, tends to be dysfunctional conflict.

One study of 53 teams found that cognitive conflict, because it generates more alternatives, led to better decisions, more acceptance of the decisions, and ownership of the decisions. Teams experiencing affective conflict, where members had personality incompatibilities and disputes, had poorer decisions and lower levels of acceptance of the decisions.[7] It also appears that the friction and interpersonal hostilities inherent in affective conflicts increase personality clashes and decrease mutual understanding, which hinders the completion of organizational tasks. Unfortunately, managers spend a lot of effort resolving personality conflicts among staff members; one survey indicated this task consumes 18 percent of their time.[8]

Because conflict can involve our emotions in a variety of ways, it can also lead to stress. You may want to refer to *OB on the Edge—Stress at Work* on pages 122–129 to get some ideas on how to manage the stress that might arise from conflicts you experience.

Resolution-Focused View of Conflict

Researchers have begun to recognize some problems with encouraging conflict.[9] As we will see, there are some very specific cases in which conflict can be beneficial. However, workplace conflicts are not productive, they take time away from job tasks or interacting with customers, and hurt feelings and anger often linger after conflicts appear to be over. People seldom can wall off their feelings into neat categories of "task" or "relationship" disagreements, so task conflicts sometimes escalate into relationship conflicts.[10] Conflicts produce stress, which may lead people to become more close minded and adversarial.[11] Studies of conflict in laboratories also fail to take account of the reductions in trust and cooperation that occur even with relationship conflicts. Longer-term studies show that all conflicts reduce trust, respect, and cohesion in groups, which reduces their long-term viability.[12]

In light of these findings, researchers have started to focus more on managing the whole context in which conflicts occur, both before and after the behavioural stage of conflict occurs. A growing body of research suggests we can minimize the negative effects of conflict by focusing on preparing people for conflicts, developing resolution strategies, and facilitating open discussion.

Sources of Conflict

There are a number of conditions that can give rise to conflict. They *need not* lead directly to conflict, but at least one of these conditions is necessary if conflict is to surface. For simplicity's sake, these conditions (which we can also look at as causes or sources of conflict) have been condensed into three general categories: communication, structure, and personal variables.[13]

cognitive conflict Conflict that is task-oriented and related to differences in perspectives and judgments.

affective conflict Conflict that is emotional and aimed at a person rather than an issue.

A lack of functional conflict among General Motors management in the past decades resulted in concessions to union demands for general health benefits and pensions. Burdened by health costs that GM provided to more than 1 million employees, retirees, and dependants, the automaker was forced into bankruptcy and more mass layoffs even after it closed factories as part of its cost-cutting strategy. The Chevy Blazer SUV shown here was one of the last GM vehicles to roll off the assembly line at a plant in Linden, New Jersey. GM closed the plant after 68 years of operation, which marked the end of automobile manufacturing in a state where the industry once employed thousands of workers and helped fuel the state's economic engine.

Communication

As we saw in Chapter 7, communication can be a source of conflict through semantic difficulties, misunderstandings, and "noise" in the communication channels.[14]

A review of the research suggests that differing word connotations, jargon, insufficient exchange of information, and noise in the communication channel are all barriers to communication and potential antecedent conditions to conflict. Research has further demonstrated a surprising finding: The potential for conflict increases when either too little or too much communication takes place. Apparently, an increase in communication is functional up to a point, whereupon it is possible to overcommunicate, with a resultant increase in the potential for conflict.

Structure

Conflicts between two people can be structural in nature; that is, they can be the consequence of the requirements of the job or the workplace more than personality. For instance, it is not uncommon for the sales department to be in conflict with the production department, if sales perceives that products will be delivered late to customers. The term *structure* in this context includes variables such as size of the group, degree of specialization in the tasks assigned to group members, composition of the group, jurisdictional clarity, reward systems, leadership style, goal compatibility, and the degree of dependence between groups.

A review of structural variables that can lead to conflict in the workplace suggests the following:[15]

- *Size, specialization, and composition* of the group act as forces to stimulate conflict. The larger the group and the more specialized its activities, the greater the likelihood of conflict. The potential for conflict tends to be greatest where group members are younger and where turnover is high.

- *The greater the ambiguity* in precisely defining where responsibility for actions lies, the greater the potential for conflict to emerge. Such jurisdictional ambiguities increase intergroup fighting for control of resources and territory.

- *Reward systems* create conflict when one member's gain is at another's expense. Similarly, the performance evaluation process can create conflict when individuals feel that they are unfairly evaluated, or when managers and employees have differing ideas about the employees' job responsibilities.

- *Leadership style* can create conflict if managers tightly control and oversee the work of employees, allowing employees little discretion in how they carry out tasks.

- *The diversity of goals* among groups is a major source of conflict. When groups within an organization seek diverse ends, some of which are inherently at odds—such as when the sales team promises products that the development team has not yet finalized—opportunities for conflict increase.

- *If one group is dependent on another* (in contrast to the two being mutually independent), or if interdependence allows one group to gain at another's expense, opposing forces are stimulated.

Personal Variables

Have you ever met people to whom you take an immediate dislike? You disagree with most of their opinions. The sound of their voice, their smirk when they smile, and their personality annoy you. We have all met people like that. When you have to work with such individuals, there is often the potential for conflict.

Our last category of potential sources of conflict is personal variables, which include personality, emotions, and values. Personality does appear to play a role in the conflict process: Some people just tend to get in conflicts a lot. In particular, people high in the personality traits of disagreeableness, neuroticism, or self-monitoring are prone to tangle with other people more often, and to react poorly when conflicts occur.[16] Emotions can also cause conflict. An employee who shows up to work irate from her hectic morning commute may carry that anger with her to her 9:00 a.m. meeting. The problem? Her anger can annoy her colleagues, which can result in a tension-filled meeting.[17]

Conflict Resolution

Each side in the PNE dispute used the media to influence public opinion, and there were mutual accusations of bad faith bargaining, so some hard feelings were inevitable.[18] CUPE 1004 and the PNE recognized they could not solve the impasse alone. When talks resumed after the strike vote in September 2011, a mediator was called in to assist the process. What other approaches might the parties use to try to resolve a conflict?

2 How can conflict be resolved?

Conflict in the workplace can affect the effectiveness of individuals, teams, and the entire organization.[19] One study found that 20 percent of managers' time is spent managing conflict.[20]

Once conflict arises, what can be done to resolve it? The way a conflict is defined goes a long way toward establishing the sort of outcomes that might settle it. For instance, if I define our salary disagreement as a zero-sum or *win-lose situation*—that is, if you get the increase in pay you want, there will be just that amount less for me—I am going to be far less willing to look for mutual solutions than if I frame the conflict as a potential *win-win situation*. So individual attitudes toward a conflict are important, because attitudes typically define the set of possible settlements.

Conflict Management Strategies

Conflict researchers often use *dual concern theory* to describe people's conflict management strategies.[21] Dual concern theory considers how one's degree of *cooperativeness* (the degree to which one tries to satisfy the other person's concerns) and *assertiveness* (the degree to which one tries to satisfy one's own concerns) determine how a conflict is handled.[22] The five conflict-handling strategies identified by the theory are as follows:

- *Forcing.* Imposing one's will on the other party.

- *Problem solving.* Trying to reach an agreement that satisfies both one's own and the other party's aspirations as much as possible.

- *Avoiding.* Ignoring or minimizing the importance of the issues creating the conflict.

- *Yielding.* Accepting and incorporating the will of the other party.

- *Compromising.* Balancing concern for oneself with concern for the other party in order to reach a solution.

Forcing is a win-lose solution, as is yielding, while problem solving seeks a win-win solution. Avoiding conflict and pretending it does not exist, and compromising, so that neither person gets what they want, can yield lose-lose solutions. Exhibit 9-2 illustrates these five strategies, along with specific actions that one might take when using them.

EXHIBIT 9-2 Conflict-Handling Strategies and Accompanying Behaviours

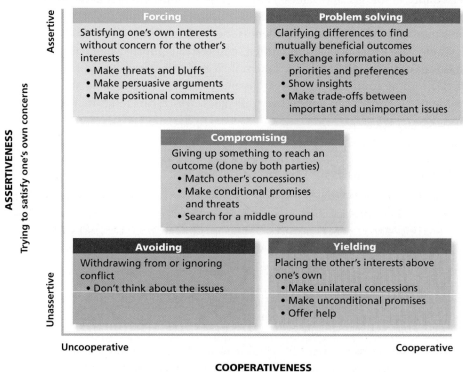

Sources: Based on K. W. Thomas, "Conflict and Negotiation Processes in Organizations," in *Handbook of Industrial and Organizational Psychology*, vol. 3, 2nd ed., ed. M. D. Dunnette and L. M. Hough (Palo Alto, CA: Consulting Psychologists Press, 1992), p. 668; C. K. W. De Dreu, A. Evers, B. Beersma, E. S. Kluwer, and A. Nauta, "A Theory-Based Measure of Conflict Management Strategies in the Workplace," *Journal of Organizational Behavior* 22, no. 6 (September 2001), pp. 645–668; and D. G. Pruitt and J. Rubin, *Social Conflict: Escalation, Stalemate and Settlement* (New York: Random House, 1986).

OB in ACTION
Choosing Strategies to Deal with Conflicts

Forcing

→ In **emergencies**

→ On **important** but unpopular **issues**

→ On **vital issues** when you know you are right

→ Against **people who take advantage** of noncompetitive behaviour

Problem solving

→ If both sets of concerns are **too important for compromise**

→ To **merge different perspectives**

→ To **gain commitment** through a consensus

→ To **mend a relationship**

Avoiding

→ When an issue is **trivial**

→ When your **concerns won't be met**

→ When potential **disruption outweighs the benefits** of resolution

→ To let people **cool down** and regain perspective

Yielding

→ When you find **you are wrong**

→ To show your **reasonableness**

→ When **issues are more important to others** than yourself

→ To **build social credits** for later issues

→ When **harmony and stability** are especially important

Compromising

→ When **goals are important but not worth more assertive approaches**

→ When opponents are committed to **mutually exclusive goals**

→ To achieve **temporary settlements** to complex issues

→ To arrive at **expedient solutions** under time pressure[23]

Choosing a particular strategy for resolving conflict depends on a variety of factors. Research shows that while people may choose among the strategies, they have an underlying disposition to handle conflicts in certain ways.[24] In addition, some situations call for particular strategies. For instance, when a small child insists on trying to run into the street, a parent may need a forcing strategy to restrain the child. Co-workers who are having a conflict over setting deadlines to complete a project on time may decide that problem solving is the best strategy to use.

This chapter's *Learning About Yourself Exercise* on page 348 gives you the opportunity to discover your preferred conflict-handling strategy. *OB in Action—Choosing Strategies to Deal with Conflicts* indicates the situations in which each strategy is best used.

SELF-ASSESSMENT LIBRARY

LEARNING ABOUT YOURSELF

1. What Is Your Primary Conflict-Handling Style?
   (page 348)

What Can Individuals Do to Manage Conflict?

There are a number of conflict resolution techniques that individuals can use to try to defuse conflict inside and outside of the workplace. These include the following:[25]

- *Problem solving.* Requesting a face-to-face meeting to identify the problem and resolve it through open discussion.

- *Developing overarching goals.* Creating a shared goal that requires both parties to work together, and motivates them to do so.

- *Smoothing.* Playing down differences while emphasizing common interests with the other party.

- *Compromising.* Agreeing with the other party that each will give up something of value to reach an accord.

- *Avoidance.* Withdrawing from or suppressing the conflict.

The choice of technique may depend on how serious the issue is to you, whether you take a win-win or a win-lose approach, and your preferred conflict management style.

When the conflict is specifically work-related, there are additional techniques that might be used:

- *Expansion of resources.* The scarcity of a resource—say, money, promotion opportunities, office space—can create conflict. Expansion of the resource can create a win-win solution.

- *Authoritative command.* Management can use its formal authority to resolve the conflict and then communicate its desires to the parties involved.

- *Altering the human variable.* Behavioural change techniques such as human relations training can alter attitudes and behaviours that cause conflict.

- *Altering the structural variables.* The formal organization structure and the interaction patterns of conflicting parties can be changed through job redesign, transfers, creation of coordinating positions, and the like.

Resolving Personality Conflicts

Personality conflicts are an everyday occurrence in the workplace. A 2011 study found that Canadian supervisors spend about 16 percent of their time handling disputes among employees.[26] A variety of factors lead to personality conflicts at work, including the following:[27]

- Misunderstandings based on age, race, or cultural differences

- Intolerance, prejudice, discrimination, or bigotry

- Perceived inequities

- Misunderstandings, rumours, or falsehoods about an individual or group

- Blaming for mistakes or mishaps (finger-pointing)

Personality conflicts can result in lowered productivity when people find it difficult to work together. The individuals experiencing the conflict may seek sympathy from other members of the work group, causing co-workers to take sides. The ideal solution would be for the two people having a conflict to work it out between themselves, without involving others, but this does not always happen. *OB in Action—Handling Personality Conflicts* suggests ways of dealing with personality conflicts in the workplace.

Resolving Intercultural Conflicts

While some personality conflicts may be stimulated by cultural differences, it's important to consider intercultural conflicts as a separate form of conflict. Canada is a multicultural society, and its organizations increasingly interact in a global environment, setting up alliances and joint ventures with partners from other parts of the world. Greater contact with people from other cultures can lead to greater understanding, but it can also lead to misunderstanding when individuals ignore the different perspectives that might result from cultural differences.

In Chapter 7, we discussed the idea that people from high- and low-context cultures have different expectations about how to interact with one another. In high-context cultures, communication is based on nonverbal and subtle situational

OB in ACTION
Handling Personality Conflicts

Tips for employees having a personality conflict

→ **Communicate directly** with the other person to resolve the perceived conflict (emphasize problem solving and common objectives, not personalities).

→ **Avoid dragging** co-workers into the conflict.

→ If dysfunctional conflict persists, **seek help** from direct supervisors or human resource specialists.

Tips for third-party observers of a personality conflict

→ **Do not take sides** in someone else's personality conflict.

→ **Suggest the parties work things out** themselves in a constructive and positive way.

→ If dysfunctional conflict persists, **refer the problem** to parties' direct supervisors.

Tips for managers whose employees are having a personality conflict

→ **Investigate and document** conflict.

→ If appropriate, **take corrective action** (e.g., feedback or behaviour shaping).

→ If necessary, **attempt informal dispute resolution**.

→ **Refer difficult conflicts** to human resource specialists or hired counsellors for formal resolution attempts and other interventions.[28]

EXHIBIT 9-3 Strategies for Dealing with Intercultural Conflict

Behaviour	Rank
Listening rather than talking	1
Being sensitive to others' needs	2 (tie)
Being cooperative rather than competitive	2 (tie)
Being an inclusive leader	4
Compromising rather than domineering	5
Trying to engage in rapport	6
Being compassionate and understanding	7
Emphasizing harmony by avoiding conflict	8
Nurturing people	9

Source: Adapted from R. L. Tung, "American Expatriates Abroad: From Neophytes to Cosmopolitans," *Journal of World Business* 33, no. 2 (Summer 1998), p. 136, Table 6. With permission from Elsevier.

cues. Status and one's place in society are also very important. Low-context cultures, such as those in North America, rely more on words and less on subtle situational cues. In low-context cultures, there is also less formality when communicating with people of different status. As a result of these differences, people from one cultural context may misinterpret the actions of those from another, which could produce conflict.

Professor Rosalie Tung of the Business School at Simon Fraser University studied 409 Canadian and American expatriates who were living in 51 different countries worldwide to determine the factors that made it easier (or harder) to adjust to living in a foreign culture.[29] As part of that study, she asked expatriates to identify the characteristics that they thought best facilitated interaction with the host country's nationals. The list, presented in Exhibit 9-3, provides some guidance for what behaviours individuals might try when dealing with conflict with someone from another culture. The list is ordered from the attribute ranked most important to least important.

RESEARCH FINDINGS: Cultural Views on Conflict

Across cultures, people have different ideas about the appropriateness and effects of conflict. For instance, Mexicans expect conflict to be kept private, while Americans expect conflict to be dealt with directly and openly.[30] We suggest in Exhibit 9-4 that there is an optimal level of conflict in the workplace to maximize productivity, but this is decidedly a North American viewpoint. Many Asian cultures believe that conflict almost always has a negative effect on the work unit.[31]

Collectivistic cultures value harmony among members more than individualistic cultures do. Consistent with this idea, research shows that those from Asian cultures show a preference for conflict avoidance, compared with Americans and Britons.[32] Research also shows that Chinese and East Asian managers prefer compromising as a strategy,[33] even though from a North American perspective, this might be viewed as suboptimal. Compromise may be viewed as a way of saving face, so that each party gets to preserve pride and dignity.[34]

Studies show that North Americans prefer a problem-solving approach to conflicts, because this presents both parties with a win-win solution.[35] Win-win solutions are less likely to be achieved in Asian cultures, however. East Asian managers tend to ignore conflict rather than make it public,[36] and more often than not, Japanese managers tend to choose nonconfrontational styles.[37] Chinese managers prefer compromising and

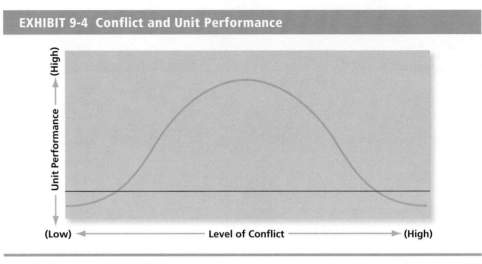

EXHIBIT 9-4 Conflict and Unit Performance

avoiding to manage conflict.[38] These preferences make it difficult to negotiate a win-win solution. In general, Westerners are more comfortable with competition, which may explain why research finds that Westerners are more likely to choose forcing as a strategy than are Asians.[39]

Taken together, these research findings suggest the importance of being aware of cultural differences with respect to conflict. Using one's own culture's conflict resolution strategies may result in even greater conflict.[40] Some individuals and some cultures prefer harmonious relations over asserting themselves, and may not react well to the confrontational dynamics more common among North Americans. Similarly, North Americans expect that negotiations may lead to a legal contract, whereas Asian cultures rely less on legal contracts and more on relational contracts.

Third-Party Conflict Resolution

Occasionally, individuals or group representatives reach a stalemate and are unable to resolve their differences. In such cases, they may turn to alternative dispute resolution (ADR), where a third party helps both sides find a solution outside a courtroom. There are four basic third-party roles: mediator, arbitrator, conciliator, and consultant.[41]

Can someone else be asked to help resolve a conflict?

Mediator

A **mediator** is a neutral third party who facilitates a negotiated solution by using reasoning and persuasion, suggesting alternatives, and the like. Mediators can be much more aggressive in proposing solutions than conciliators. Mediators are widely used in labour-management negotiations and in civil court disputes. British Columbia's Motor Vehicle Branch uses mediation to help settle accident claims. In Ontario, all disputes between companies and employees now go to mediation within 100 days. Pilot projects found that more than 60 percent of the disputes were partly or fully resolved within 60 days after the start of the mediation session.[42]

The overall effectiveness of mediated negotiations is fairly impressive. The settlement rate is approximately 60 percent, with satisfaction with the mediator at about 75 percent. But the situation is the key to whether mediation will succeed; the conflicting parties must be motivated to bargain and resolve their conflict. Additionally, conflict intensity cannot be too high; mediation is most effective under moderate levels of conflict. Finally, perceptions of the mediator are important; to be effective, the mediator must be perceived as neutral and noncoercive.

mediator A neutral third party who facilitates a negotiated solution by using reasoning, persuasion, and suggestions for alternatives.

Case Incident—Mediation: Master Solution to Employment Disputes? on page 352 looks at situations in which mediation has succeeded and failed.

Arbitrator

An **arbitrator** is a third party with the authority to dictate an agreement. Arbitration can be voluntary (requested by the parties) or compulsory (forced on the parties by law or contract).

The big advantage of arbitration over mediation is that it always results in a settlement. Whether or not there is a negative side depends on how "heavy-handed" the arbitrator appears. If one party is left feeling overwhelmingly defeated, that party is certain to be dissatisfied and unlikely to accept the arbitrator's decision graciously. Therefore, the conflict may resurface at a later time.

Conciliator

A **conciliator** is a trusted third party who provides an informal communication link between the negotiator and the opponent. Conciliation is used extensively in international, labour, family, and community disputes. In practice, conciliators typically act as more than mere communication conduits. They also engage in fact-finding, interpreting messages, and persuading disputants to develop agreements.

In Canada, the first step in trying to resolve a labour relations dispute can be to bring in a conciliation officer when agreement cannot be reached. This may be a good faith effort to resolve the dispute. Sometimes, however, it is used so that the union can reach a legal strike position or management can engage in a lockout. Provinces vary somewhat in how they set out the ability to engage in a strike after going through a conciliation process. For instance, in Nova Scotia, once the conciliation officer files a report that the dispute cannot be resolved through conciliation, there is a 14-day waiting period before either party can give 48 hours' notice of either a strike or a lockout.[43]

Consultant

A **consultant** is a skilled and impartial third party who attempts to facilitate problem solving through communication and analysis, aided by a knowledge of conflict management. Unlike other third parties, the consultant does not try to settle the issues but rather works to improve relationships between the conflicting parties so they can reach a settlement themselves. Instead of putting forward specific solutions, the consultant tries to help the parties learn to understand and work with each other. This approach has a longer-term focus: to build new and positive perceptions and attitudes between the conflicting parties.

Conflict Outcomes

 What are the effects of conflict?

> One of the unfortunate side effects of the dispute between PNE and CUPE 1004 was a loss of mutual trust, especially since it was the first time an agreement was not reached prior to the start of the fair. This conflict deepened the existing divide between unionized employees and management, with strong potential for negative impact on employees' work values. Is there a way to minimize these negative outcomes when conflict becomes inevitable? How could the situation have been handled differently to reduce the impact on employee attitudes once the issue is resolved?

As Exhibit 9-4 on page 332 demonstrates, conflict can be functional and improve group performance, or it can be dysfunctional and hinder group performance. As well, we see there is an optimal level of conflict that results in the highest level of unit performance.

arbitrator A third party to a negotiation who has the authority to dictate an agreement.

conciliator A trusted third party who provides an informal communication link between the negotiator and the opponent.

consultant An impartial third party, skilled in conflict management, who attempts to facilitate creative problem solving through communication and analysis.

Conflict is constructive when it improves the quality of decisions, stimulates creativity and innovation, encourages interest and curiosity among group members, provides the medium through which problems can be aired and tensions released, and fosters an environment of self-evaluation and change. The evidence suggests that conflict can improve the quality of decision making by allowing all points to be weighed in important decisions, particularly the ones that are unusual or held by a minority.[44] Conflict can prevent groupthink (discussed in Chapter 12). It does not allow the group passively to "rubber-stamp" decisions that may be based on weak assumptions, inadequate consideration of relevant alternatives, or other problems. Conflict challenges the status quo and therefore supports the creation of new ideas, promotes reassessment of group goals and activities, and increases the probability that the group will respond to change. An open discussion focused on higher-order goals can make these functional outcomes more likely. Groups that are extremely polarized do not manage their underlying disagreements effectively and tend to accept suboptimal solutions, or they tend to avoid making decisions altogether rather than working out the conflict.[45]

Dean Tjosvold of Lingnan University in Hong Kong suggests three desired outcomes for conflict:[46]

- *Agreement.* Equitable and fair agreements are the best outcome. If agreement means that one party feels exploited or defeated, this will likely lead to further conflict later.

- *Stronger relationships.* When conflict is resolved positively, this can lead to better relationships and greater trust. If the parties trust each other, they are more likely to keep the agreements they make.

- *Learning.* Handling conflict successfully teaches one how to do it better next time. It gives an opportunity to practise the skills one has learned about handling conflict.

Below we examine what research tells us about the constructive effects of conflict.

RESEARCH FINDINGS:
The Constructive Effects of Conflict

Research studies in diverse settings confirm that conflict can be functional and improve productivity. For instance, studies demonstrate that groups composed of members with different interests tend to produce higher-quality solutions to a variety of problems than do homogeneous groups.[47] Team members with greater differences in work styles and experience also tend to share more information with one another.[48] One study found that high-conflict groups improved their decision-making ability 73 percent more than groups characterized by low-conflict conditions.[49] An investigation of 22 teams of systems analysts found that the more incompatible team members were, the more likely they were to be more productive.[50] Research and development scientists have been found to be most productive when a certain amount of intellectual conflict exists.[51]

The above research findings suggest that conflict within a group can lead to strength rather than weakness. However, factors such as personality, social support, and communication moderate how well groups can deal with internal conflict. At an individual level, both a person's personality (agreeableness) and his or her level of social support influence that person's response to conflict. Agreeable employees and those with lower levels of social support respond to conflict more negatively.[52]

Open communication is important to resolving conflict. Group members who discuss differences of opinion openly and are prepared to manage conflict when it arises resolve conflicts successfully.[53] Group members with cooperative conflict styles and a strong underlying identification to the overall group goals are more effective than those with a more competitive style.[54] Managers need to emphasize shared interests in resolving conflicts, so group members who disagree with one another don't become too entrenched in their points of view and start to take the conflicts personally.

Unfortunately, not all conflict results in positive outcomes. A substantial body of literature documents how dysfunctional conflict can reduce group effectiveness.[55] Among the more undesirable outcomes are stopping communication, reducing group cohesiveness, and subordinating group goals due to infighting among members. At the extreme, conflict can bring group functioning to a halt and potentially threaten the group's survival.

Negotiation

The dispute between PNE and CUPE 1004 was resolved on September 23, 2011, when over 80 percent of unionized employees accepted a negotiated deal that included raises of 1.5 percent a year over three years and improved contracting and scheduling regulations.[56] It was a very different story four years earlier when CUPE 1004 used a mediator to assist with strike negotiations with the City of Vancouver. The city's outdoor employees had been on strike for 82 days when they voted on whether to accept a mediator's recommendations to resolve the dispute. Two-thirds of the membership needed to accept the deal for it to go through. The outdoor employees rejected the mediator's recommendations, largely due to perceived unfairness. "There's just no way that our members can accept returning to work with less than what other civic workers have negotiated in this round of bargaining," said Mike Jackson, CUPE 1004 president. "After almost three months on strike, it is an insult to be offered less than other civic workers in the region. . . . We're also baffled at why CUPE 15 got the same Olympic agreement that we had tabled to the mediator and we got an inferior agreement," stated Jackson. Why did these two negotiations end so differently? How do perceptions of fairness influence the negotiation process?

4 How does one negotiate effectively?

Earlier in the chapter, we reviewed a number of conflict resolution strategies. One well-developed strategy is to negotiate a resolution. Negotiation permeates the interactions of almost everyone in groups and organizations: Labour bargains with management; managers negotiate with employees, peers, and senior management; salespeople negotiate with customers; purchasing agents negotiate with suppliers; employees agree to cover for one another for a few minutes in exchange for some past or future benefit. In today's loosely structured organizations, in which members work with colleagues over whom they have no direct authority and with whom they may not even share a common boss, negotiation skills become critical for teams to work together effectively.

We define **negotiation** as a process in which two or more parties try to agree on the exchange rate for goods or services they are trading.[57] Note that we use the terms *negotiation* and *bargaining* interchangeably.

Within a negotiation, be aware that individuals have issues, positions, and interests. *Issues* are items that are specifically placed on the bargaining table for discussion. *Positions* are the individual's stand on the issues. For instance, salary may be an issue for discussion. The salary you hope to receive is your position. Finally, *interests* are the underlying concerns that are affected by the negotiation resolution. For instance, the reason that you might want a six-figure salary is that you are trying to buy

negotiation A process in which two or more parties exchange goods or services and try to agree on the exchange rate for them.

Negotiation skills are critical in the buyer-seller relationship. At this open-air cheese market in Alkmaar, Netherlands, two purchasing agents for food buyers taste a sample of Edam cheese before they negotiate prices with the seller of the cheese.

a house in Vancouver, and that is your only hope of being able to make mortgage payments.

Negotiators who recognize the underlying interests of themselves and the other party may have more flexibility in achieving a resolution. For instance, in the example just given, an employer who offers you a mortgage at a lower rate than the bank does, or who provides you with an interest-free loan that can be used against the mortgage, may be able to address your underlying interests without actually meeting your salary position. You may be satisfied with this alternative, if you understand what your interest is.

Interest-based bargaining enabled the Information Services Corporation (ISC) to sign a mutually beneficial three-year contract with the Saskatchewan Government and General Employees' Union (SGEU) Local 2214 in May 2010, after nine days of bargaining. The agreement provided for wage and pension increases plus greater dental plan benefits for employees and efficiencies in recruitment and leave for the government.[58] ISC union chairperson Barb Wright called the result "a true testament to the interest-based bargaining process."[59]

Below we discuss bargaining strategies and how to negotiate.

Bargaining Strategies

There are two general approaches to negotiation—*distributive bargaining* and *integrative bargaining*.[60] These are compared in Exhibit 9-5.

Distributive Bargaining

Distributive bargaining is a negotiating strategy that operates under zero-sum (win-lose) conditions. That is, any gain I make is at your expense, and vice versa. You see a used car advertised for sale online. It appears to be just what you have been looking to buy. You go out to see the car. It's great, and you want it. The owner tells you the asking price. You don't want to pay that much. The two of you then negotiate over the price. Every dollar you can get the seller to cut from the car's price is a dollar you save, and every dollar more the seller can get from you comes at your expense. So the essence of distributive bargaining is negotiating over who

Should you try to win at any cost when you bargain?

distributive bargaining Negotiation that seeks to divide up a fixed amount of resources; a win-lose solution.

EXHIBIT 9-5 Distributive vs. Integrative Bargaining

Bargaining Characteristic	Distributive Bargaining	Integrative Bargaining
Available resources	Fixed amount of resources to be divided	Variable amount of resources to be divided
Primary motivations	I win, you lose	I win, you win
Primary interests	Opposed to each other	Convergent or congruent with each other
Focus of relationships	Short-term	Long-term

Source: Based on R. J. Lewicki and J. A. Litterer, *Negotiation* (Homewood, IL: Irwin, 1985), p. 280.

gets what share of a fixed pie. By **fixed pie**, we mean a set amount of goods or services to be divided up. When the pie is fixed, or parties believe it is, they tend to bargain distributively.

A party engaged in distributive bargaining focuses on trying to get the opponent to agree to a specific target point, or to get as close to it as possible. Examples of this tactic are persuading your opponent of the impossibility of reaching his or her target point and the advisability of accepting a settlement near yours; arguing that your target is fair, while your opponent's is not; and attempting to get your opponent to feel emotionally generous toward you and thus accept an outcome close to your target point.

When engaged in distributive bargaining, one of the best things you can do is to make the first offer, and to make it an aggressive one. Research consistently shows that the best negotiators are those who make the first offer, and whose initial offer has very favourable terms. Why is this so? One reason is that making the first offer shows power; research shows that individuals in power are much more likely to make initial offers, speak first at meetings, and thereby gain the advantage. Another reason is the anchoring bias (the tendency for people to fixate on initial information). Once that anchoring point is set, people fail to adequately adjust it based on subsequent information. A savvy negotiator sets an anchor with the initial offer, and scores of negotiation studies show that such anchors greatly favour the person who sets it.[61]

For example, say you have a job offer, and your prospective employer asks you what sort of starting salary you would be looking for. You have just been given a great gift—you have a chance to set the anchor, meaning that you should ask for the highest salary that you think the employer could reasonably offer. For most of us, asking for a million dollars is only going to make us look ridiculous, which is why we suggest being on the high end of what you think is *reasonable*. Too often, we err on the side of caution, being afraid of scaring off the employer, and thus settle for too little. It *is* possible to scare off an employer, and it's true that employers do not like candidates to be overly aggressive in salary negotiations, but liking is not the same as respect or doing what it takes to hire or retain someone.[62] What happens much more often is that we ask for less than what we could have gotten.

OB in the Street shows that in the context of eBay auctions, however, sellers who start with a low price on an item can end up getting a higher selling price.

OB in the STREET

A Low Anchor Value Can Reap Higher Returns on eBay

Should a seller use a high or a low starting bid in an eBay auction? In their analysis of auction results on eBay, a group of researchers found that *lower* starting bids gener-

> **fixed pie** The belief that there is only a set amount of goods or services to be divvied up between the parties.

ated higher final prices.[63] As just one example, Nikon digital cameras with ridiculously low starting bids (one penny) sold for an average of $312, whereas those with higher starting prices went for an average of $204.

What explains such a counterintuitive result? The researchers found that low starting bids attract more bidders, and this increased traffic generates more competing bidders, so in the end the price is higher. Although this may seem irrational, negotiation and bidding behaviour are not always rational, and as you have probably experienced first-hand, once you start bidding for something, you want to win, forgetting that for many auctions the one with the highest bid is often the loser (the so-called winner's curse).

If you are thinking of participating in an auction, consider the following two points. First, some buyers think sealed-bid auctions—where bidders submit a single bid in a concealed fashion—present an opportunity to get a "steal" because a price war cannot develop among bidders. However, evidence routinely indicates that sealed-bid auctions are bad for the winning bidder (and thus good for the seller) because the winning bid is higher than would otherwise be the case. Second, buyers sometimes think jumping bids—placing a bid higher than the auctioneer is asking—is a smart strategy because it drives away competing bidders early in the game. Again, this is a myth. Evidence indicates bid jumping is good at causing other bidders to follow suit, thus increasing the value of the winning bid.

Another distributive bargaining tactic is revealing a deadline. Negotiators who reveal deadlines speed concessions from their negotiating counterparts, making them reconsider their position. And even though negotiators don't *think* this tactic works, in reality, negotiators who reveal deadlines do better.[64]

Integrative Bargaining

In contrast to distributive bargaining, **integrative bargaining** operates under the assumption that there exists one or more settlements that can create a win-win solution. In terms of intraorganizational behaviour, all things being equal, integrative bargaining is preferable to distributive bargaining. Why? Because the former builds long-term relationships and makes working together in the future easier. It bonds negotiators and allows both sides to leave the bargaining table feeling that they have achieved a victory. For instance, in union-management negotiations, both sides might sit down to figure out other ways to reduce costs within an organization, so that it is possible to have greater wage increases. Distributive bargaining, on the other hand, leaves one party a loser. It tends to build animosities and deepen divisions when people must work together on an ongoing basis.

Research shows that over repeated bargaining episodes, when the "losing" party feels positive about the negotiation outcome, the party is much more likely to bargain cooperatively in subsequent negotiations. This points to the important advantage of integrative negotiations: Even when you "win," you want your opponent to feel positively about the negotiation.[65]

Why, then, don't we see more integrative bargaining in organizations? The answer lies in the conditions necessary for this type of negotiation to succeed. These include parties who are open with information and candid about their concerns, sensitivity by both parties to the other's needs, the ability to trust one another, and a willingness by both parties to maintain flexibility.[66] Because these conditions often don't exist in organizations, it isn't surprising that negotiations often take on a win-at-any-cost dynamic.

There are ways to achieve more integrative outcomes. Individuals who bargain in teams reach more integrative agreements than those who bargain individually. This happens because more ideas are generated when more people are at the bargaining table. So try bargaining in teams.[67] Another way to achieve higher joint-gain settlements is to put more issues on the table. The more negotiable issues that are introduced into

integrative bargaining Negotiation that seeks one or more settlements that can create a win-win solution.

a negotiation, the more opportunity there is for "logrolling," where issues are traded because of differences in preferences. This approach creates better outcomes for each side than if each issue were negotiated individually.[68]

Finally, you should realize that compromise may be your worst enemy in negotiating a win-win agreement. This is because compromising reduces the pressure to bargain integratively. After all, if you or your opponent caves in easily, it does not require anyone to be creative to reach a settlement. Thus, people end up settling for less than they could have obtained if they had been forced to consider the other party's interests, trade off issues, and be creative.[69] Think of the classic example where two sisters are arguing over who gets an orange. Unknown to them, one sister wants the orange to drink the juice, whereas the other sister wants the orange peel to bake a cake. If one sister simply gives in and gives the other sister the orange, then they will not be forced to explore their reasons for wanting the orange, and thus they will never find the win-win solution: They could each have the orange because they want different parts of it! A poor compromise may sometimes be the result of negotiation anxiety. A 2011 study found that negotiators who feel anxious "expect lower outcomes, make lower first offers, respond more quickly to offers, exit bargaining situations earlier, and ultimately obtain worse outcomes." If self-efficacy is high, this will moderate some of the harmful effects of anxiety.[70] So it is important to feel prepared, and do what you can to reduce anxiety before negotiating a deal.

How does anxiety affect negotiating outcomes?

How to Negotiate

Exhibit 9-6 provides a simplified model of the negotiation process. It views negotiation as made up of five steps: (1) developing a strategy; (2) defining ground rules; (3) clarification and justification; (4) bargaining and problem solving; and (5) closure and implementation.

Developing a Strategy

Before you start negotiating, you need to do your homework. What is the nature of the conflict? What is the history leading up to this negotiation? Who is involved, and what are their perceptions of the conflict? What do you want from the negotiation? What are *your* goals? It often helps to put your goals in writing and develop a range of outcomes—from "most hopeful" to "minimally acceptable"—to keep your attention focused.

You also want to prepare an assessment of what you think are the other party's goals.[71] What are they likely to ask for? How entrenched are they likely to be in their position? What intangible or hidden interests may be important to them? On what terms might they be willing to settle? When you can anticipate your opponent's position, you are better equipped to counter arguments with the facts and figures that support your position. You might also be able to anticipate better negotiating options for yourself, as *Case Incident—David Out-Negotiating Goliath: Apotex and Bristol-Myers Squibb* on page 351 shows. You want to be sure, however, that the information that you consider regarding your opponent is relevant to the negotiation. A 2011 study found that too much of the wrong kind of information can make for worse bargaining outcomes. In some cases, the person with extraneous information stopped looking for mutually beneficial outcomes earlier than those who did not have this information.[72]

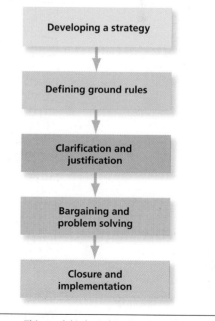

EXHIBIT 9-6 The Negotiation Process

Developing a strategy

↓

Defining ground rules

↓

Clarification and justification

↓

Bargaining and problem solving

↓

Closure and implementation

Source: This model is based on R. J. Lewicki, "Bargaining and Negotiation," *Exchange: The Organizational Behavior Teaching Journal* 6, no. 2 (1981), pp. 39–40.

EXHIBIT 9-7 Staking Out the Bargaining Zone

In determining goals, parties are well advised to consider their "target and resistance" points, as well as their *best alternative to a negotiated agreement* (**BATNA**).[73] The buyer and the seller are examples of two negotiators. Each has a *target point* that defines what he or she would like to achieve. Each also has a *resistance point*, which marks the lowest outcome that is acceptable—the point below which each would break off negotiations rather than accept a less favourable settlement. The area between these two points makes up each negotiator's aspiration range. As long as there is some overlap between the buyer's and seller's aspiration ranges, there exists a **bargaining zone** where each side's aspirations can be met. Referring to Exhibit 9-7, if the buyer's resistance point is $450, and the seller's resistance point is $500, then the two may not be able to reach agreement because there is no overlap in their aspiration ranges.

One's BATNA represents the alternative that an individual will face if negotiations fail. For instance, during the PNE and CUPE 1004 negotiations, for both the unionized employees and PNE management, the BATNA was the loss of revenue from sport and entertainment events and the fair of the following year. In the end, both sides must have concluded that it was preferable to get the conflict resolved.

As part of your strategy, you should determine not only your BATNA but also some estimate of the other side's as well.[74] If you go into your negotiation having a good idea of what the other party's BATNA is, even if you are not able to meet theirs, you might be able to get them to change it. Think carefully about what the other side is willing to give up. People who underestimate their opponent's willingness to give on key issues before the negotiation even starts end up with lower outcomes from a negotiation.[75]

You can practise your negotiating skills in the *Working with Others Exercise* on page 349.

Defining Ground Rules

Once you have done your planning and developed a strategy, you are ready to begin defining the ground rules and procedures with the other party over the negotiation itself. Who will do the negotiating? Where will it take place? What time constraints, if any, will apply? To what issues will negotiation be limited? Will there be a specific procedure to follow if an impasse is reached? During this phase, the parties will also exchange their initial proposals or demands. *From Concepts to Skills* on pages 353–354 directly addresses some of the actions you should take to improve the likelihood that you can achieve a good agreement.

Clarification and Justification

When initial positions have been exchanged, both you and the other party will explain, amplify, clarify, bolster, and justify your original demands. This part of the process need not be confrontational. Rather, it's an opportunity for educating and informing each other on the issues, why they are important, and how each arrived at their initial demands. This is the point at which you might want to provide the other party with

BATNA The *best alternative to a negotiated agreement*; the outcome an individual faces if negotiations fail.

bargaining zone The zone between each party's resistance point, assuming that there is overlap in this range.

any documentation that helps support your position. The *Ethical Dilemma Exercise* on page 350 considers whether it is ever appropriate to lie during negotiations.

Bargaining and Problem Solving

The essence of the negotiation process is the actual give and take in trying to hash out an agreement. A 2011 study found that those who used competing and collaborating (essentially a combination of the forcing and problem solving conflict resolution styles discussed earlier in the chapter) as part of their strategy to gain a higher starting salary were more successful (and received higher increases) than those who used compromising and accommodating strategies.[76] The study looked at the influence of individual differences and negotiation strategies on starting salary outcomes based on a sample of 149 newly hired employees in various industry settings. Results indicated that those who chose to negotiate increased their starting salaries by an average of $5000. Individuals who negotiated by using competing and collaborating strategies, characterized by an open discussion of one's positions, issues, and perspectives, further increased their salaries as compared with those who used compromising and accommodating strategies. Individual differences, including risk aversion and integrative attitudes, played a significant role in predicting whether individuals negotiated, and if so, what strategies they used.

OB in Action—Tips for Getting to Yes gives you further ideas on how to make negotiating work for you, based on the popular book *Getting to Yes*.[77]

> ## OB in ACTION
> ## Tips for Getting to Yes
>
> R. Fisher and W. Ury present four principles for win-win negotiations in their book *Getting to Yes*:[78]
>
> → **Separate** the **people from** the **problem.** Work on the issues at hand, rather than getting involved in personality issues between the parties.
>
> → Focus on **interests, not positions.** Try to identify what each person needs or wants, rather than coming up with an unmovable position.
>
> → Look for ways to achieve **mutual gains.** Rather than focusing on one "right" solution for your position, brainstorm for solutions that will satisfy the needs of both parties.
>
> → Use **objective criteria** to achieve a fair solution. Try to focus on fair standards, such as market value, expert opinion, norms, or laws to help guide decision making.

Closure and Implementation

The final step in the negotiation process is formalizing the agreement that has been worked out and developing procedures that are necessary for implementation and monitoring. For major negotiations—which would include everything from labour-management negotiations, to bargaining over lease terms, to buying real estate, to negotiating a job offer for a senior management position—this will require hammering out the specifics in a formal contract. For most cases, however, closure of the negotiation process is nothing more formal than a handshake.

Individual Differences in Negotiation Effectiveness

Are some people better negotiators than others? The answer is more complex than you might think. Three factors influence how effectively individuals negotiate: personality, mood/emotions, and gender.

⑤ How do individual differences influence negotiations?

Personality Traits in Negotiation

Can you predict an opponent's negotiating tactics if you know something about his or her personality? Because personality and negotiation outcomes are related but only weakly, the answer is, at best, "sort of." Negotiators who are agreeable or extraverted are not very successful in distributive bargaining. Why? Because extraverts are outgoing and friendly, they tend to share more information than they should. And agreeable people are more interested in finding ways to cooperate rather than to butt heads. These traits, while slightly helpful in integrative negotiations, are liabilities when interests are opposed. So the best distributive bargainer appears to be a disagreeable introvert—someone more interested in his or her own outcomes than in pleasing the other party and having a pleasant social exchange. People who are highly interested in having positive relationships with other people, and who are not very concerned about their own outcomes, are especially poor negotiators. These people tend to be very anxious about disagreements and plan to give in quickly to avoid unpleasant conflicts even before negotiations start.[79]

Research also suggests intelligence predicts negotiation effectiveness, but, as with personality, the effects are not especially strong.[80] In a sense, these weak links are good news because they mean you are not severely disadvantaged, even if you are an agreeable extravert, when it comes time to negotiate. We all can learn to be better negotiators. In fact, people who think so are more likely to do well in negotiations because they persist in their efforts even in the face of temporary setbacks.[81]

Moods/Emotions in Negotiation

Do moods and emotions influence negotiation? They do, but the way they do appears to depend on the type of negotiation.[82] In distributive negotiations, it appears that negotiators in a position of power or equal status who show anger negotiate better outcomes because their anger induces concessions from their opponents. This appears to hold true even when the negotiators are instructed to show anger despite not being truly angry. On the other hand, for those in a less powerful position, displaying anger leads to worse outcomes. So if you are a boss negotiating with a peer or a subordinate, displaying anger may help you, but if you are an employee negotiating with a boss, it might hurt you.

In integrative negotiations, in contrast, positive moods and emotions appear to lead to more integrative agreements (higher levels of joint gain).

Gender Differences in Negotiation

Do men and women negotiate differently? And does gender affect negotiation outcomes? The answer to the first question appears to be no.[83] The answer to the second is a qualified yes.[84]

> Ever wonder if men and women negotiate differently?

A popular stereotype is that women are more cooperative and pleasant in negotiations than are men. The evidence doesn't support this belief. However, men have been found to negotiate better outcomes than women, although the difference is relatively small. It's been postulated that men and women place divergent values on outcomes. "It is possible that a few hundred dollars more in salary or the corner office is less important to women than forming and maintaining an interpersonal relationship."[85]

The belief that women are "nicer" than men in negotiations is probably due to a confusion between gender and the lower degree of power women typically hold in most large organizations. Because women are expected to be "nice" and men "tough," research shows women are penalized when they initiate negotiations.[86] Moreover, when women and men actually do conform to these stereotypes—women act "nice" and men "tough"—it becomes a self-fulfilling prophecy, reinforcing the stereotypical gender differences between male and female negotiators.[87] Thus, one of the reasons negotiations favour men is that women are "damned if they do, damned if they don't." Negotiate tough, and they are penalized for violating a gender stereotype. Negotiate nice, and it only reinforces and lets others take advantage of the stereotype.

Evidence also suggests women's own attitudes and behaviours hurt them in negotiations. Managerial women demonstrate less confidence in anticipation of negotiating and are less satisfied with their performance afterward, even when their performance and the outcomes they achieve are similar to those for men.[88] Women are also less likely than men to see an ambiguous situation as an opportunity for negotiation. It appears that women may unduly penalize themselves by failing to engage in negotiations when such action would be in their best interests.

The outcomes of negotiations for women and men also seem to differ. One researcher found that when women negotiated to buy a car, the opening offer by the salesperson was higher than it was for men.[89] In a study of salary offers, researchers found that men were offered higher starting salaries in a negotiating process than were women.[90] While in each of these instances the opening offers were just that, offers to be negotiated, women also fared less well than men at the end of the negotiating process, even when they used the same negotiating tactics as men. A 2011 study found that during negotiations, particularly for salary, women may desire social approval, and thus bargain less assertively. The same women were much more assertive when bargaining on behalf of someone else.[91] A 2011 study by professor Linda Schweitzer of the Sprott School of Business, Carleton University, and three colleagues found that women tended to have lower expectations about salaries and promotions as they enter the workforce.[92]

The results of these studies may shed some light on the pay and promotion discrepancies between men and women, which we discuss in Chapter 11. If women expect and then negotiate even slightly lower starting salaries, then over time, with raises based on percentages of salaries, the gap between men's and women's salaries can grow quite substantially.

Respected for her intelligence, confident negotiating skills, and successful outcomes, Christine Lagarde is the managing director of the International Monetary Fund (IMF). Prior to that she was the minister for the economy, finance, and employment in France, where she used her negotiating skills to boost French exports by 10 percent. She is also known for her much earlier work as a labour and antitrust lawyer for the global law firm Baker & McKenzie, during which she negotiated with France's trade unions to change the country's labour laws, including ending the 35-hour limit on the workweek, to help boost the nation's sluggish economy.

GLOBAL IMPLICATIONS

Below we look at (1) how conflict is handled in different cultures, (2) whether there are differences in negotiating styles across cultures, and (3) how the display of emotions affects negotiations in different cultures.

Conflict Resolution and Culture

Research suggests that differences across countries in conflict resolution strategies may be based on collectivistic tendencies and motives.[93] Collectivistic cultures see people as deeply embedded in social situations, whereas individualistic cultures see people as autonomous. As a result, collectivists are more likely to seek to preserve relationships and promote the good of the group as a whole than individualists. To preserve peaceful relationships, collectivists will avoid direct expression of conflicts, preferring to use more indirect methods for resolving differences of opinion. Collectivists may also be more interested in demonstrations of concern and working through third parties to resolve disputes, whereas individualists will be more likely to confront differences of opinion directly and openly.

Some research supports this theory. Compared with collectivistic Japanese negotiators, individualistic US negotiators are more likely to see offers from their counterparts as unfair and reject them. Another study revealed that while US managers are more likely to use competing tactics when faced with a conflict, Chinese managers are more likely to use compromising and avoiding.[94] Interview data, however, suggest top management teams in Chinese high-technology firms prefer integration even more than compromising and avoiding.[95]

Cultural Differences in Negotiating Style

Negotiating styles vary across national cultures, as the following examples suggest:[96]

- *France.* The French like conflict. They frequently gain recognition and develop their reputations by thinking and acting against others. As a result, the French tend to take a long time in negotiating agreements, and they are not overly concerned about whether their opponents like or dislike them.[97]

- *China.* The Chinese draw out negotiations because they believe negotiations never end. Just when you think you have pinned down every detail and reached a final solution with a Chinese executive, that executive might smile and start the process all over again. The Chinese negotiate to develop a relationship and a commitment to work together rather than to tie up every loose end.[98]

- *Japan.* The Japanese also negotiate to develop relationships and a commitment to work together. One study compared US and Japanese negotiators and found that the Japanese negotiators tend to communicate indirectly and adapt their behaviours to the situation. A follow-up study showed that early offers by US negotiators led to the anchoring effect (see the "Distributive Negotiation" section), whereas early offers by Japanese negotiators led to more information sharing and better integrative outcomes.[99]

- *United States.* Americans are known around the world for their impatience and their desire to be liked. Astute negotiators from other countries often turn these characteristics to their advantage by dragging out negotiations and making friendship conditional on the final settlement.

The cultural context of a negotiation significantly influences the amount and type of preparation for bargaining, the relative emphasis on task vs. interpersonal relationships, the tactics used, and even the place where the negotiation should be conducted. Exhibit 9-8 identifies whether countries focus more on win-win or win-lose solutions. These findings are based on research on 300 negotiators in 12 countries. As you will note, 100 percent of Japanese negotiators said they focus on finding a win-win solution. By contrast, only 37 percent of Spanish negotiators said the same.[100]

Culture, Negotiations, and Emotions

As a rule, no one likes to face an angry counterpart in negotiations. However, East Asian negotiators may respond less favourably than people from other cultures.[101]

Two separate studies found that East Asian negotiators were less likely to accept offers from negotiators who displayed anger during negotiations. Another study explicitly compared how US and Chinese negotiators react to an angry counterpart. When confronted with an angry negotiator, Chinese negotiators increased their use of distributive negotiating tactics, whereas US negotiators decreased their use of these tactics.

LESSONS LEARNED

- A medium level of conflict often results in higher productivity than an absence of conflict.
- Negotiators should identify their BATNA (best alternative to negotiated agreement).
- In relationships with long-term consequences, it is best to use a win-win strategy in bargaining.

EXHIBIT 9-8 Negotiating Attitude: Win-Win or Win-Lose?

Country	Japan	China	Argentina	France	India	US	UK	Mexico	Germany	Nigeria	Brazil	Spain
Negotiator focuses on win-win solution (%)	100	82	81	80	78	71	59	50	55	47	44	37

Source: Based on J. W. Salacuse, "Ten Ways That Culture Affects Negotiating Style: Some Survey Results," *Negotiation Journal*, July 1998, pp. 221–240.

Why might East Asian and Chinese negotiators respond more negatively to angry negotiators? The authors of the research speculated that because their cultures emphasize respect and deference, they may be particularly likely to perceive angry behaviour as disrespectful, and thus deserving of uncooperative tactics in response.

Summary and Implications

1 What is conflict? Conflict occurs when one party perceives that another party's actions will have a negative effect on something the first party cares about. Many people automatically assume that all conflict is bad. However, conflict can be either functional (constructive) or dysfunctional (destructive) to the performance of a group or unit. An optimal level of conflict encourages communication, prevents stagnation, stimulates creativity, allows tensions to be released, and plants the seeds of change, yet not so much as to be disruptive or to deter activities. For simplicity's sake, the sources of conflict have been condensed into three general categories: communication, structure, and personal variables.

2 How can conflict be resolved? The way a conflict is defined goes a long way toward establishing the sort of outcomes that might settle it. One can work toward a *win-lose solution* or a *win-win solution*. Conflict management strategies are determined by the extent to which one wants to cooperate with another party, and the extent to which one asserts his or her own concerns. Occasionally, individuals or group representatives reach a stalemate and are unable to resolve their differences through direct negotiations. In such cases, they may turn to alternative dispute resolution (ADR), where a third party helps both sides find a solution. ADR typically involves a mediator, arbitrator, conciliator, or consultant.

3 What are the effects of conflict? Conflict can be functional and improve group performance, or it can be dysfunctional and hinder group performance. A substantial body of literature documents how dysfunctional conflict can reduce group effectiveness. Among the more undesirable consequences of conflict are stopping communication, reducing group cohesiveness, and subordinating group goals due to infighting between members. At the extreme, conflict can bring group functioning to a halt and potentially threaten the group's survival.

4 How does one negotiate effectively? *Negotiation* is a process in which two or more parties exchange goods or services and try to agree on the exchange rate for them. Negotiation is an ongoing activity in groups and organizations. Distributive bargaining can resolve disputes, but it often negatively affects one or more negotiators' satisfaction because it is focused on the short term and because it is confrontational. Integrative bargaining, by contrast, tends to provide outcomes that satisfy all parties and build lasting relationships.

5 How do individual differences influence negotiations? Three areas that affect negotiations are personality traits, moods and emotions, and gender differences. There are no strong links between personality and negotiating styles, suggesting we all can learn to be better negotiators. In distributive negotiations, those in powerful positions who use anger end up with better outcomes than those in lower status positions who use anger. In integrative negotiations, in contrast, positive moods and emotions appear to lead to more integrative agreements (higher levels of joint gain). The evidence suggests that men and women use relatively similar styles in negotiation, but have somewhat different success rates.

SNAPSHOT SUMMARY

1 Conflict Defined
Functional vs. Dysfunctional Conflict
Resolution-Focused View of Conflict
Sources of Conflict

2 Conflict Resolution
Conflict Management Strategies
What Can Individuals Do to Manage Conflict?
Resolving Personality Conflicts
Resolving Intercultural Conflicts
Third-Party Conflict Resolution

3 Conflict Outcomes

4 Negotiation
Bargaining Strategies
How to Negotiate

5 Individual Differences in Negotiation Effectiveness
Personality Traits in Negotiation
Moods/Emotions in Negotiation
Gender Differences in Negotiation

for Review

1. What are the advantages and disadvantages of conflict?

2. Under what conditions might conflict be beneficial to a group?

3. What is the difference between functional and dysfunctional conflict? What determines functionality?

4. What is dual concern theory?

5. What causes personality conflicts, and how can they be resolved?

6. What is the difference between a conciliator and a mediator?

7. What defines the bargaining zone in distributive bargaining?

8. Why isn't integrative bargaining more widely practised in organizations?

9. How can you improve your negotiating effectiveness?

10. How do men and women differ, if at all, in their approaches to negotiations?

for Critical Thinking

1. Do you think competition and conflict are different? Explain.

2. "Participation is an excellent method for identifying differences and resolving conflicts." Do you agree or disagree? Discuss.

3. From your own experience, describe a situation you were involved in where the conflict was dysfunctional. Describe another example, from your experience, where the conflict was functional. Now analyze how other parties in both conflicts might have interpreted the situation in terms of whether the conflicts were functional or dysfunctional.

4. Assume that one of your co-workers had to negotiate a contract with someone from China. What problems might he or she face? If the co-worker asked for advice, what suggestions would you give to help facilitate a settlement?

5. Michael Eisner, former CEO at the Walt Disney Corporation, wanted to stimulate conflict inside his firm. But he wanted to minimize conflict with outside parties—agents, contractors, unions, etcetera. What do Eisner's goals say about conflict levels, functional vs. dysfunctional conflict, and managing conflict?

for You

- It may seem easier, but avoiding conflict does not necessarily have a more positive outcome than working with someone to resolve the conflict.

- Trying to achieve a win-win solution in a conflict situation tends to lead to better relationships and greater trust.

- It's not always possible to resolve conflict on one's own. There are alternative dispute resolution options, including having someone help mediate the conflict.

- It's better to focus more on interests rather than positions when engaged in a negotiation. Doing so gives you the ability to arrive at more flexible solutions.

POINT

Conflict Is Good for an Organization

Let's briefly review how stimulating conflict can provide benefits to the organization:[102]

- *Conflict is a means by which to bring about radical change.* It's an effective device by which management can drastically change the existing power structure, current interaction patterns, and entrenched attitudes. If there is no conflict, it means the real problems are not being addressed.

- *Conflict facilitates group cohesiveness.* While conflict increases hostility between groups, external threats tend to cause a group to pull together as a unit. Conflict with another group brings together those within each group. Such intragroup cohesion is a critical resource that groups draw on in good and especially in bad times.

- *Conflict improves group and organizational effectiveness.* Groups or organizations devoid of conflict are likely to suffer from apathy, stagnation, groupthink, and other debilitating diseases. In fact, more organizations probably fail because they have *too little* conflict, not because they have too much. Stagnation is the biggest threat to organizations, but since it occurs slowly, its ill effects often go unnoticed until it's too late. Conflict can break complacency—though most of us don't like conflict, it often is the last best hope of saving an organization.

- *Conflict brings about a slightly higher, more constructive level of tension.* Constructive levels of tension enhance the chances of solving the conflicts in a way satisfactory to all parties concerned. When the level of tension is very low, the parties may not be sufficiently motivated to do something about a conflict.

COUNTERPOINT

All Conflicts Are Dysfunctional!

It may be true that conflict is an inherent part of any group or organization. It may not be possible to eliminate it completely. However, just because conflicts exist is no reason to glorify them. All conflicts are dysfunctional, and it is one of management's major responsibilities to keep conflict intensity as low as humanly possible. A few points will support this case:

- *The negative consequences from conflict can be devastating.* The list of negatives associated with conflict is awesome. The most obvious are increased turnover, decreased employee satisfaction, inefficiencies between work units, sabotage, labour grievances and strikes, and physical aggression. One study estimated that managing conflict at work costs the average employer nearly 450 days of management time a year.[103]

- *Effective managers build teamwork.* A good manager builds a coordinated team. Conflict works against such an objective. A successful work group is like a successful sports team: Members all know their roles and support their teammates. When a team works well, the whole becomes greater than the sum of the parts. Management creates teamwork by minimizing internal conflicts and facilitating internal coordination.

- *Competition is good for an organization, but not conflict.* Competition and conflict should not be confused with each other. *Conflict* is behaviour directed against another party, whereas *competition* is behaviour aimed at obtaining a goal without interference from another party. Competition is healthy; it's the source of organizational vitality. Conflict, on the other hand, is destructive.

- *Conflict is avoidable.* It may be true that conflict is inevitable when an organization is in a downward spiral, but the goal of good leadership and effective management is to avoid the spiral to begin with.

OB at work

What Is Your Primary Conflict-Handling Style?

Indicate how often you rely on each of the following tactics by circling the number you feel is most appropriate.

When I have a conflict at work, I do the following:

		Not at All				Very Much
1.	I give in to the wishes of the other party.	1	2	3	4	5
2.	I try to realize a middle-of-the-road solution.	1	2	3	4	5
3.	I push my own point of view.	1	2	3	4	5
4.	I examine issues until I find a solution that really satisfies me and the other party.	1	2	3	4	5
5.	I avoid a confrontation about our differences.	1	2	3	4	5
6.	I concur with the other party.	1	2	3	4	5
7.	I emphasize that we have to find a compromise solution.	1	2	3	4	5
8.	I search for gains.	1	2	3	4	5
9.	I stand for my own and the other party's goals and interests.	1	2	3	4	5
10.	I avoid differences of opinion as much as possible.	1	2	3	4	5
11.	I try to accommodate the other party.	1	2	3	4	5
12.	I insist we both give in a little.	1	2	3	4	5
13.	I fight for a good outcome for myself.	1	2	3	4	5
14.	I examine ideas from both sides to find a mutually optimal solution.	1	2	3	4	5
15.	I try to make differences loom less large.	1	2	3	4	5
16.	I adapt to the other party's goals and interests.	1	2	3	4	5
17.	I strive whenever possible toward a 50-50 compromise.	1	2	3	4	5
18.	I do everything to win.	1	2	3	4	5
19.	I work out a solution that serves my own, as well as the other party's, interests as well as possible.	1	2	3	4	5
20.	I try to avoid a confrontation with the other party.	1	2	3	4	5

Scoring Key:

To determine your primary conflict-handling strategy, place the number 1 through 5 that represents your score for each statement next to the number for that statement. Then total up the columns.

Yielding	Compromising	Forcing	Problem-solving	Avoiding
1. _____	2. _____	3. _____	4. _____	5. _____
6. _____	7. _____	8. _____	9. _____	10. _____
11. _____	12. _____	13. _____	14. _____	15. _____
16. _____	17. _____	18. _____	19. _____	20. _____
Totals _____	_____	_____	_____	_____

Your primary conflict-handling style is the category with the highest total. Your fallback intention is the category with the second-highest total.

Source: C. K. W. De Dreu, A. Evers, B. Beersma, E. S. Kluwer, and A. Nauta, "A Theory-Based Measure of Conflict Management Strategies in the Workplace," *Journal of Organizational Behavior* 22, no. 6 (September 2001), pp. 645–668. With permission.

SELF-ASSESSMENT LIBRARY LEARNING ABOUT YOURSELF

More Learning About Yourself Exercises

Additional self-assessments relevant to this chapter appear at MyOBLab (**www.pearsoned.ca/myoblab.com**).

II.C.5 What's My Preferred Conflict-Handling Style?
II.C.6 What's My Negotiating Style?

When you complete the additional assessments, consider the following:

1. Am I surprised about my score?

2. Would my friends evaluate me similarly?

BREAKOUT **GROUP** EXERCISES

Form small groups to discuss the following topics, as assigned by your instructor:

1. You and 2 other students carpool to school every day. The driver has recently taken to playing a new radio station quite loudly. You do not like the music, or the loudness. Using one of the conflict-handling strategies outlined in Exhibit 9-2 on page 328, indicate how you might go about resolving this conflict.

2. Using the example above, identify a number of BATNAs (*best* alternative *to a n*egotiated *a*greement) available to you, and then decide whether you should continue carpooling.

3. Which conflict-handling strategy is most consistent with how you deal with conflict? Is your strategy effective? Why or why not?

WORKING WITH **OTHERS** EXERCISE

A Negotiation Role Play

This role play is designed to help you develop your negotiating skills. The class is to break into pairs. One person will play the role of Terry, the department supervisor. The other person will play Dale, Terry's boss.

The Situation: Terry and Dale work for hockey-equipment manufacturer Bauer. Terry supervises a research laboratory. Dale is the manager of R & D. Terry and Dale are former skaters who have worked for Bauer for more than 6 years. Dale has been Terry's boss for 2 years.

One of Terry's employees has greatly impressed Terry. This employee is Lisa Roland. Lisa was hired 11 months ago. She is 24 years old and holds a master's degree in mechanical engineering. Her entry-level salary was $52 500 a year. She was told by Terry that, in accordance with corporation policy, she would receive an initial performance evaluation at 6 months and a comprehensive review after 1 year. Based on her performance record, Lisa was told she could expect a salary adjustment at the time of the 1-year review.

Terry's evaluation of Lisa after 6 months was very positive. Terry commented on the long hours Lisa was working, her cooperative spirit, the fact that others in the lab enjoyed working with her, and her immediate positive impact on the project she had been assigned. Now that Lisa's first anniversary is coming up, Terry has again reviewed Lisa's performance. Terry thinks Lisa may be the best new person the R & D group has ever hired. After only a year, Terry has ranked Lisa as the number 3 performer in a department of 11.

Salaries in the department vary greatly. Terry, for instance, has a basic salary of $93 800, plus eligibility for a bonus that might add another $7000 to $11 000 a year. The salary range of the 11 department members is $42 500 to $79 000. The lowest salary is a recent hire with a bachelor's degree in physics. The 2 people that Terry has rated above Lisa earn base salaries of $73 800 and $78 900. They are both 27 years old and have been at Bauer for 3 and 4 years, respectively. The median salary in Terry's department is $65 300.

Terry's Role: You want to give Lisa a big raise. While she is young, she has proven to be an excellent addition to the department. You don't want to lose her. More important, she knows in general what other people in the department are earning, and she thinks she is underpaid. The company typically gives 1-year raises of 5 percent, although 10 percent is not unusual and 20 to 30 percent increases have been approved on occasion. You would like to get Lisa as large an increase as Dale will approve.

Dale's Role: All your supervisors typically try to squeeze you for as much money as they can for their people. You understand this because you did the same thing when you were a supervisor, but your boss wants to keep a lid on costs. He wants you to keep raises for recent hires generally in the range of 5 to 8 percent. In fact, he has sent a memo to all managers and supervisors stating this objective. However, your boss is also very concerned with equity and paying people what they are worth. You feel assured that he will support any salary recommendation you make, as long as it can be justified. Your goal, consistent with cost reduction, is to keep salary increases as low as possible.

The Negotiation: Terry has a meeting scheduled with Dale to discuss Lisa's performance review and salary adjustment. Take a couple of minutes to think through the facts in this exercise and to prepare a strategy. Then you have up to 15 minutes to conduct your negotiation. When your negotiation is complete, the class will compare the various strategies used and the outcomes that resulted.

ETHICAL **DILEMMA** EXERCISE

Is It Unethical to Lie and Deceive during Negotiations?

The topic of lying as it relates to negotiation is important because, for many people, there is no such thing as lying when it comes to negotiating.[104]

It's been said that the whole notion of negotiation is built on ethical quicksand: To succeed, you must deceive. Is this true? Apparently a lot of people think so. For instance, one study found that 28 percent of negotiators lied about a common-interest issue during negotiations, while another study found that 100 percent of negotiators either failed to reveal a problem or actively lied about it during negotiations if they were not directly asked about the issue.

Is it possible for someone to maintain high ethical standards and, at the same time, deal with the daily need to negotiate with bosses, peers, staff, people from other organizations, friends, and even relatives?

We can probably agree that bald-faced lies during negotiation are wrong. At least most ethicists would prob-

ably agree. The universal dilemma surrounds the little lies—the omissions, evasions, and concealments that are often necessary to best an opponent.

During negotiations, when is a lie a lie? Is exaggerating benefits, downplaying negatives, ignoring flaws, or saying "I don't know" when in reality you do considered lying? Is declaring that "this is my final offer and nonnegotiable" (even when you are posturing) a lie? Is pretending to bend over backward to make meaningful concessions lying? Rather than being unethical practices, the use of these "lies" is considered by many as indicators that a negotiator is strong, smart, and savvy.

When are evasiveness and deception out of bounds? Is it naive to be completely honest and bare your soul during negotiations? Or are the rules of negotiations unique: Is any tactic that will improve your chance of winning acceptable?

CASE INCIDENTS

David Out-Negotiating Goliath: Apotex and Bristol-Myers Squibb

Peter Dolan survived many crises in his five-year tenure as CEO of drug giant Bristol-Myers Squibb.[105] There were a corporate accounting scandal, allegations of insider trading, FBI raids of his office, and a stock price that dropped 60 percent during his tenure. But in the end, what may have done Dolan in was his negotiation performance against the head of Apotex, a Canadian drug company founded by Dr. Barry Sherman.

At its peak, Plavix—a drug to prevent heart attacks—was Bristol-Myers's best-selling drug and accounted for a staggering one-third of its profits. So when Apotex developed a generic Plavix knockoff, Dolan sought to negotiate an agreement that would pay Apotex in exchange for a delayed launch of Apotex's generic competitor. Dolan sent one of his closest lieutenants, Andrew Bodnar, to negotiate with Sherman. Bodnar and Sherman developed a good rapport, and at several points in their negotiations asked their attorneys to leave them alone. At one key point in the negotiations, Bodnar flew to Toronto alone, without Bristol-Myers's attorneys, as a "gesture of goodwill. The thinking was that the negotiations would be more effective this way."

As Dolan, Bodnar, and Bristol-Myers became increasingly concerned with reaching an agreement with Sherman and Apotex, they developed a blind spot. Privately, Sherman was betting that the Federal Trade Commission (FTC) would not approve the noncompete agreement the two parties were negotiating, and his goal in the negotiation was to extract an agreement from Bristol-Myers that would position Apotex favourably should the FTC reject the deal. Indeed, he nonchalantly inserted a clause in the deal that would require Bristol-Myers to pay Apotex $60 million if the FTC rejected the deal. "I thought the FTC would turn it down, but I didn't let on that I did," Sherman said. "They seemed blind to it."

In the meantime, Apotex covertly began shipping its generic equivalent to the United States. Thus, Sherman also managed to launch the generic equivalent without Bristol-Myers even considering the possibility that he would do so while still engaged in negotiations. The company was only able to sell Apotex in the United States for three weeks before a federal judge stopped sales, but in that short period of time, about a six-month supply of the drug had entered the US market. This cost Bristol-Myers about $1 billion in lost sales.

"It looks like a much smaller generic private company completely outmaneuvered two of the giants of the pharmaceutical industry," said Gbola Amusa, European pharmaceutical analyst for Sanford C. Bernstein and Company.

"It's not clear how or why that happened. The reaction from [Bristol-Myers] investors and analysts has ranged from shock to outright anger." Within a few months, Dolan was out at Bristol-Myers. In 2008, Bodnar was indicted for negotiating the agreement with Apotex and not informing US federal regulators of all of its details. Sherman had no obligation to report the deal to US regulators, as Apotex is a Canadian company.

Questions

1. What principles of distributive negotiation did Sherman use to gain his advantage?

2. Do you think Sherman behaved ethically? Why or why not?

3. What does this incident tell you about the role of deception in negotiation?

Mediation: Master Solution to Employment Disputes?

We typically think of mediation as the province of marital counsellors and labour strife.[106] More organizations use mediation to resolve conflicts than you might think. In fact, in Canada, the United States, Great Britain, Ireland, and India, mediation is growing rapidly as a means to settle employment disputes. We introduced mediation in this chapter; let's look at some examples of when it has succeeded and when it has failed.

Where Mediation Has Worked

- Surviving passengers who were on the BC Ferries *Queen of the North,* which sank in March 2006, reluctantly agreed to a mediated settlement in 2010 that may get them only $500 for the trauma they suffered. The passengers and their lawyer agreed that it was time to put the incident behind them and move on.

- The Equal Employment Opportunity Commission (EEOC), the federal agency that oversees employment discrimination complaints in the United States, uses mediation extensively. Safeway, the third-largest US supermarket chain, uses the EEOC to mediate numerous employment disputes. Says Donna Gwin, Safeway's director of human resources, "Through mediation, we have had the opportunity to proactively resolve issues and avoid potential charges in the future. We have seen the number of charges filed with EEOC against us actually decline. We believe that our participating in mediation and listening to employees' concerns has contributed to that decline."

Where Mediation Has Not Worked

- In spring 2011, Nortel Networks Corp. announced that the mediation efforts between the company and some of its creditors to determine how to divide the remaining assets ended in failure, significantly delaying payment to creditors and other stakeholders.

- Former NHL player Steve Moore and Detroit Redwings player Todd Bertuzzi will meet in court in September 2012 because of a $38 million lawsuit filed by Moore for injuries faced after he was hit by Bertuzzi during a 2004 hockey game. The two were ordered to try to settle the lawsuit through mediation, but were unable to do so.

Questions

1. Drawing from the preceding examples, what factors do you think differentiate occasions when mediation was successful and when it failed?

2. One successful mediator, Boston's Paul Finn, argues that if the disputing parties are seeking justice, "It's best to go somewhere else." Why do you think he says that?

3. Do you think a mediator should find out *why* the parties want what they want? Why or why not?

4. The EEOC reports that whereas 85 percent of employees agree to mediate their charges, employers agree to mediate only 30 percent of the time. Why do you think this disparity exists?

FROM CONCEPTS TO SKILLS

Negotiating

Once you have taken the time to assess your own goals, to consider the other party's goals and interests, and to develop a strategy, you are ready to begin actual negotiations. The following five suggestions should improve your negotiating skills:[107]

1. *Begin with a positive overture.* Studies on negotiation show that concessions tend to be reciprocated and lead to agreements. As a result, begin bargaining with a positive overture—perhaps a small concession—and then reciprocate your opponent's concessions.

2. *Address problems, not personalities.* Concentrate on the negotiation issues, not on the personal characteristics of your opponent. When negotiations get tough, avoid the tendency to attack your opponent. It's your opponent's ideas or position that you disagree with, not him or her personally. Separate the people from the problem, and don't personalize differences.

3. *Pay little attention to initial offers.* Treat an initial offer as merely a point of departure. Everyone has to have an initial position. These initial offers tend to be extreme and idealistic. Treat them as such.

4. *Emphasize win-win solutions.* Inexperienced negotiators often assume that their gain must come at the expense of the other party. As noted with integrative bargaining, that need not be the case. There are often win-win solutions. But assuming a zero-sum game means missed opportunities for trade-offs that could benefit both sides. So if conditions are supportive, look for an integrative solution. Frame options in terms of your opponent's interests, and look for solutions that can allow your opponent, as well as yourself, to declare a victory.

5. *Create an open and trusting climate.* Skilled negotiators are better listeners, ask more questions, focus their arguments more directly, are less defensive, and have learned to avoid words and phrases that can irritate an opponent (for example, "generous offer," "fair price," "reasonable arrangement"). In other words, they are better at creating the open and trusting climate necessary for reaching an integrative settlement.

Practising Skills

As marketing director for Done Right, a regional home-repair chain, you have come up with a plan you believe has significant potential for future sales. Your plan involves a customer information service designed to help people make their homes more environmentally sensitive. Then, based on homeowners' assessments of their homes' environmental impact, your firm will be prepared to help them deal with problems or concerns they may uncover. You are really excited about the competitive potential of this new service. You envision pamphlets, in-store appearances by environmental experts, as well as contests for consumers and school kids. After several weeks of preparations, you make your pitch to your boss, Nick Castro. You point out how the market for environmentally sensitive products is growing and how this growing demand represents the perfect opportunity for Done Right. Nick seems impressed by your presentation, but he has expressed one major concern: He thinks your workload is already too heavy. He does not see how you are going to have enough time to start this new service and still be able to look after all of your other assigned marketing duties. You really want to start the new service. What strategy will you follow in your negotiation with Nick?

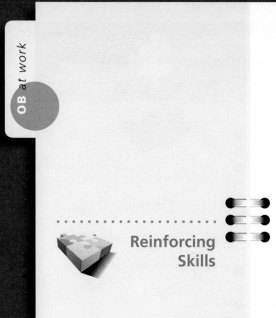

Reinforcing Skills

1. Negotiate with a team member or work colleague to handle a small section of work that you are not going to be able to get done in time for an important deadline.

2. The next time you purchase a relatively expensive item (such as an automobile, apartment lease, appliance, jewellery), attempt to negotiate a better price and gain some concessions such as an extended warranty, smaller down payment, maintenance services, or the like.

OB on the EDGE

The Toxic Workplace

It's not unusual to find employees acting badly in today's workplace, but it is sometimes unusual to find managers doing something about it. BC Lions coach Wally Buono fired team leader and quarterback Casey Printers on October 13, 2010. Two days earlier, in a game against the Winnipeg Blue Bombers, Printers had thrown down his helmet angrily when teammate O'Neill Wilson missed Printers' pass. The fumble led to a game-changing interception and touchdown by the Bombers. As the game ended, Printers lashed out at Wilson in front of live TV cameras, something his coach found highly inappropriate.

"What happened in the fourth quarter was an embarrassment to all of us," Buono said. "The BC Lions, as an organization, [doesn't] condone that type of behaviour. We've worked hard for many, many years to build the reputation of an organization that has dignity and has class and has discipline, and in the fourth quar-ter there was none of that."[1] Centre Angus Reid, one of Printers' teammates, explained why Buono's action made sense: "I think the real issue is when you have a guy that's paid to be your leader [Printers], and he's the one who ends up causing post-game problems—and I'm putting the performance aside—I think that's when you have to say, well, we can't have this guy as our leader anymore."[2]

What Is Happening in Our Workplaces?

Workplaces today are receiving highly critical reviews, being called everything from "uncivil" to "toxic."

Lynne Anderson and Christine Pearson, two management professors from St. Joseph's University and the University of North Carolina, respectively, note that "historians may view the dawn of the twenty-first century as a time of thoughtless acts and rudeness: We tailgate, even in the slow lane; we dial wrong numbers and then slam the receiver on the innocent respondent; we break appointments with nonchalance."[3] The workplace has often been seen as one of the places where civility still ruled, with co-workers treating one another with a mixture of formality and friendliness, distance and politeness. However, with downsizing, re-engineering, budget cuts, pressures for increased productivity, autocratic work environments, and the use of part-time employees, there has been an increase in "uncivil and aggressive workplace behaviours."[4]

What does civility in the workplace mean? A simple definition of workplace civility is behaviour "involving politeness and regard for others in the workplace, within workplace norms for respect."[5] Workplace incivility, then, "involves acting with disregard for others in the workplace, in violation of workplace norms for respect."[6] Of course, different workplaces will have different norms for what determines mutual respect. For instance, in most restaurants, if the staff were rude to you when you were there for dinner, you would be annoyed, and perhaps even complain to the manager. However, at The Elbow Room in downtown Vancouver, if customers complain they are in a hurry, manager Patrick Savoie might well say, "If you're in a hurry, you should have

gone to McDonald's."[7] Such a comeback is acceptable to the diners at The Elbow Room, because rudeness is its trademark.

Most work environments are not expected to be characterized by such rudeness. However, this has been changing in recent years. Robert Warren, a University of Manitoba marketing professor, notes that "simple courtesy has gone by the board."[8]

Instead, we see workplaces characterized by workplace bullying, "the repeated, health-harming mistreatment of one or more persons (the targets) by one or more perpetrators that takes one or more of the following forms: verbal abuse; offensive conduct/behaviours (including nonverbal) which are threatening, humiliating, or intimidating; and work interference—sabotage—which prevents work from getting done."[9]

What Do We Know About Workplace Bullying?

The WBI-Zogby survey is the largest scientific study of bullying in the United States. A recent large study on bullying found the following:[10]

- Most bullies are bosses (72 percent).
- 60 percent of bullies are men.
- 57 percent of targets are women.
- Bullying is four times more prevalent than illegal forms of harassment.
- 62 percent of employers ignore or worsen the problem.
- 45 percent of targets suffer stress-related health problems.
- 40 percent of bullied individuals never tell their employers.
- Only 3 percent of bullied people file lawsuits.

The evidence suggests that rudeness, bullying, and violence are all on

FACTBOX

What happens when employees experience rudeness in the workplace?

- "48% decreased their work effort,
- 47% decreased their time at work,
- 38% decreased their work quality,
- 66% said their performance declined,
- 80% lost work time worrying about the incident,
- 63% lost time avoiding the offender, and
- 78% said their commitment to the organization declined."[11]

the rise. The victims of these negative behaviours are not just the ones who suffer, however.[12] Witnesses to bullying also suffer.[13]

While rudeness is on the rise, professor André Roberge at Laval University suggests that some of the rudeness is generational. He finds that "young clerks often lack both knowledge and civility. Employers are having to train young people in simple manners because that is not being done at home."[14] Professor Warren backs this up: "One of the biggest complaints I hear from businesses when I go to talk about graduates is the lack of interpersonal skills."[15]

Workplace Violence

Recently, researchers have suggested that incivility may be the beginning

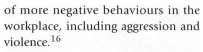

of more negative behaviours in the workplace, including aggression and violence.[16]

Dave Burns chose a deadly way to exhibit the anger he had stored up after being suspended from his job for inappropriate jokes and poor behaviour.[17] He shot and killed a parts manager and injured another employee on March 10, 2010, at the Great West Chrysler dealership in Edmonton, before turning the gun on himself. According to witnesses, Burns did not get along with the two men who were shot. "He wasn't interested in taking hostages," the witness tearfully said. "He never said a word. It wasn't a cry for help. This was about anger and vengeance, plain and simple."

Workplace violence, according to the International Labour Organization (ILO), includes

any incident in which a person is abused, threatened or assaulted in circumstances relating to [his or her] work. These behaviours would originate from customers or co-workers at any level of the organization. This definition would include all forms of harassment, bullying, intimidation, physical threats, assaults, robbery and other intrusive behaviour.[18]

No Canadian statistics on anger at work are available, although 53 percent of women and 47 percent of men reported experiencing workplace violence in 2004. About 17 percent of the incidents where violent victimization occurred happens in the workplace.[19] Studies show that anger pervades the US workplace. Between 1992 and 2006, there was an average of 800 workplace killings each year.[20] A 2000 Gallup poll conducted in the United States found that 25 percent of the working adults surveyed felt like screaming or shouting because of job stress, 14 percent had considered hitting a co-worker, and 10 percent worry about colleagues becoming violent. Almost half of American workers experienced yelling and verbal abuse on the job in 2008, and about 2.5 percent report that they have pushed, slapped, or hit someone at work.[21] Twenty employees are murdered each week in the United States.[22]

Canadian workplaces are not murder-free, however. Between 2001 and 2005, an average of 14 employees were killed each year while "on-the-job."[23] Most of these workplace incidents were carried out by male spouses and partners of female employees. Surprisingly, Canada scores higher than the United States on workplace violence. In an ILO study involving 130 000 workers in 32 countries, Argentina was ranked the most violent. Romania was second, France third, and Canada fourth. The United States placed ninth.[24]

Sixty-four percent of union representatives who were surveyed reported an increase in workplace aggression, based on their review of incident reports, grievance files, and other solid evidence.[25] To understand the seriousness of this situation, consider that one-quarter of Nova Scotia teachers surveyed reported that they faced physical violence at work during the 2009–2010 school year.[26]

What Causes Incivility (and Worse) in the Workplace?

If employers and employees are acting with less civility toward each other, what is causing this to happen?

Managers and employees often have different views of the employee's role in the organization. Jeffrey Pfeffer, a professor of organizational behaviour at the Graduate School of Business at Stanford University, notes that many companies don't really value their employees: "Most managers, if they're being honest with themselves, will admit it: When they look at their people, they see costs, they see salaries, they see benefits, they see overhead. Very few companies look at their people and see assets."[27]

Most employees, however, like to think that they are assets to their organization. The realization that they are simply costs and not valued members of an organization can cause frustration for employees.

In addition, "employers' excessive demands and top-down style of management are contributing to the rise of 'work rage,'" claims Gerry Smith, vice-president of organizational health and training at Toronto-based Shepell•fgi and author of *Work Rage*.[28] He cites demands coming from a variety of sources: "overtime, downsizing, rapid technological changes, company restructuring and difficulty balancing the demands of job and home."[29] Smith worries about the consequences of these demands: "If you push people too hard, set unrealistic expectations and cut back their benefits, they're going to strike back."[30]

Smith's work supports the findings of studies that report the most common cause of anger and bullying is the actions of supervisors or managers.[31] Other common causes of anger identified by the researchers include lack of productivity by co-workers and others; tight deadlines; heavy workload; interaction with the public; and bad treatment. The inset *Do You Have a Bad Boss?* describes some of the bad behaviour of bosses.

A 2011 study found that how managers deal with displays of anger at work can do much to defuse tensions. Co-workers want to see the manager take some responsibility for a fellow employee's anger, rather than disciplining the employee, if the manager or the working conditions are the source of the anger.[32]

Do You Have a Bad Boss?

You know you have a bad boss if he or she . . . (percent reporting bosses who did this)[33]

> . . . fails to keep promises (39%)

> . . . fails to give credit when due (37%)

> . . . gave you the "silent treatment" at least once in the past year (31%)

> . . . makes negative comments about you behind your back to other employees or managers (25%)

> . . . invades your personal privacy (24%)

> . . . blames others to cover up mistakes or to minimize their own embarrassment (23%)

FACTBOX

Percentage of employees who say their managers

- make inappropriate comments—74%

- show favouritism—70%

- are unwilling to follow due process—63%

- treat employees with disrespect—62%

- bully or intimidate—57%[34]

The Psychological Contract

Some researchers have looked at this frustration in terms of a breakdown of the psychological contract formed between employees and employers.

An employer and employee begin to develop psychological contracts as they are first introduced to each other in the hiring process.[35] These contracts continue over time as the employer and the employee come to understand each other's expectations about the amounts and quality of work to be performed and the types of rewards to be given. For instance, when an employee is continually asked to work late and/or be available at all hours through pagers and email, the employee may assume that doing so will result in greater rewards or faster promotion down the line. The employer may have had no such intention, and may even be thinking that the employee should be grateful simply to have a job. Later, when the employee does not get expected (though never promised) rewards, he or she is disappointed.

Sandra Robinson, an organizational behaviour professor at the Sauder School of Business at the University of British Columbia, and her colleagues have found that when a psychological contract is violated (perceptually or actually), the relationship between the employee and the employer is damaged. The result can be a loss of trust.[36] The breakdown in trust can cause employees to be less ready to accept decisions or obey rules.[37] The erosion of trust can also lead employees to take revenge on the employer. So they don't carry out their end of a task. Or they refuse to pass on messages. They engage in any number of subtle and not-so-subtle behaviours that affect the way work gets done—or prevents work from getting done.

Recent research on the psychological contract suggests that violations of implicit or explicit promises may not be necessary to affect employee intentions to stay with the organization and/or engage in citizenship behaviours. Professors Samantha Montes and David Zweig of the Rotman School of Management found that employees expect decent pay, developmental opportunities, and support (whether or not employers promise to deliver such); and when they don't receive those things, their behaviour toward the organization becomes negative.[38]

How to Deal with a Toxic Boss

- *Empathize, and don't take it personally.* It's difficult, but if you try to understand your boss's perspective, it may help you cope more effectively.

- *Draw a line.* When behaviour is inappropriate or abusive, stand up for yourself. At some point, no job is worth being harassed or abused.

- *Don't sabotage or be vindictive.* If you take revenge, you become part of the problem.

- *Be patient and take notes.* You may find it useful to have notes at your disposal should the boss shine the spotlight on you.[39]

The Toxic Organization

Pfeffer suggests that companies have become "toxic places to work."[40] He notes that companies, particularly in Silicon Valley, ask their employees to sign contracts on the first day of work indicating the employee's understanding that the company has the right to fire at will and for any reason. Some employers also ask their employees to choose between having a life and having a career. Pfeffer relates a joke people used to tell about Microsoft: "We offer flexible time—you can work any 18 hours you want."[41] This kind of attitude can be toxic to employees, though this does not imply that Microsoft is a toxic employer. The inset *How to Deal with a Toxic Boss* gives tips, should you find yourself in that situation.

What does it mean to be a toxic organization? The inset *What Does a Toxic Organization Look Like?* describes one. The late professor Peter Frost of the Sauder School of Business at the University of British Columbia noted that there will always be pain in organizations, but that sometimes it becomes so intense or prolonged that conditions within the organization begin to break down. In other words, the situation becomes toxic. This is not dissimilar to what the liver or kidneys do when toxins become too intense in a human body.[42]

What causes organizations to be toxic? Like Pfeffer, professors Frost and Robinson identify a number of factors. Downsizing and organizational change are two main factors, particularly in recent years. Sometimes organizations experience unexpected events—such as the sudden death of a key manager, an unwise move by senior management, strong competition from a start-up company—that lead to toxicity. Other organizations are toxic throughout their system due to policies and practices that create distress. Such factors

as unreasonable stretch goals or performance targets, or unrelenting internal competition, can create toxicity. There are also toxic managers who lead through insensitivity, vindictiveness, and failure to take responsibility, or they are control freaks or are unethical.

What Are the Effects of Incivility and Toxicity in the Workplace?

In general, researchers have found that the effects of workplace anger are sometimes subtle: a hostile work environment and the tendency to do only enough work to get by.[44]

Those who feel chronic anger in the workplace are more likely to report "feelings of betrayal by the organization, decreased feelings of loyalty, a decreased sense that respondent values and the organization's values are similar, a decreased sense that the employer treated the respondent with dignity and respect, and a decreased sense that employers had fulfilled promises made to respondents."[45] So do these feelings make a difference? Apparently so. Researchers have found that those who felt angry with their employers were less likely to put forth their best effort, more likely to be competitive toward other employees, and less likely to suggest "a quicker and

better way to do their job."[46] All of these actions tend to decrease the productivity possible in the workplace.

It's not just those who work for an organization who are affected by incivility and toxicity. Poor service, from indifference to rudeness to outright hostility, characterizes many transactions in Canadian businesses. "Across the country, better business bureaus, provincial government consumer-help agencies and media ombudsmen report a lengthening litany of complaints about contractors, car dealers, repair shops, moving companies, airlines and department stores."[47] This suggests that customers and clients may well be feeling the impact of internal workplace dynamics.

The Toxin Handler

Employees of toxic organizations suffer pain from their experiences in a toxic environment. In some organizations, mechanisms, often informal, are set up to deal with the results of toxicity.

Frost and Robinson identified a special role that some employees play in trying to relieve the toxicity within an organization: the toxin handler. This person tries to mitigate the pain by softening the blow of downsizing, or change, or the behaviour of the toxic leader. Essentially, the toxin handler helps others around him or her deal with the strains of the organiza-

---

What Does a Toxic Organization Look Like?

Toxic organizations have the following characteristics:[43]

- inability to achieve operation goals and commitments
- problem-solving processes driven by fear with few good decisions
- poor internal communication
- huge amounts of waste that result from poor decisions, and lots of rework
- interpersonal relationships driven by manipulative and self-centred agendas

tion by counselling, advising, shielding employees from the wrath of angry managers, reinterpreting the managers' messages to make them less harsh, etcetera.

So who takes on this role? Certainly no organization to date has a line on its organizational chart for "the toxin handler." Often the role emerges as part of an individual's position in an organization; for instance, a manager in the human resource department may take on this role. In many cases, however, handlers are pulled into the role "bit by bit—by their colleagues, who turn to them because they are trustworthy, calm, kind and nonjudgmental."[48]

Frost and Robinson, in profiling these individuals, suggest that toxin handlers are predisposed to say yes, have a high tolerance for pain, have a surplus of empathy, and when they notice people in pain, have a need to make the situation right. But these are not individuals who thrive simply on dealing with the emotional needs of others. Quoting one of the managers in their study, Frost and Robinson cite the full range of activities of most toxin handlers: "These people are usually relentless in their drive to accomplish organizational targets and rarely lose focus on business issues. Managing emotional pain is one of their means."[49]

The inset *How Toxin Handlers Alleviate Organizational Pain* identifies the many tasks that toxin handlers take on in an organization. Frost and Robinson suggest that these tasks will probably need to be handled forever,

FACEOFF

Manners are an over-romanticized concept. The big issue is not that employees need to be concerned about their manners. Rather, employers should be paying better wages.

The Golden Rule, "Do unto others as you would have others do unto you," should still have a role in today's workplace. Being nice pays off.

and they recommend that organizations take steps to actively support people performing this role.

RESEARCH EXERCISES

1. Look for data on violence and anger in the workplace in other countries. How do these data compare with the Canadian and American data presented here? What might you conclude about how violence and anger in the workplace are expressed in different cultures?

2. Identify three Canadian organizations that are trying to foster better and/or less toxic environments for their employees. What kind of effect is this having on the organizations' bottom lines?

YOUR PERSPECTIVE

1. Is it reasonable to suggest, as some researchers have, that young people today have not learned to be civil to others or do not place a high priority on doing so? Do you see this as one of the causes of incivility in the workplace?

2. What should be done about managers who create toxicity in the workplace while being rewarded because they achieve bottom-line results? Should bottom-line results justify their behaviour?

WANT TO KNOW MORE?

If you would like to read more on this topic, see Linnda Durré, *Surviving the Toxic Workplace* (New York: McGraw Hill, 2010); Peter Frost, *Toxic Emotions at Work* (Cambridge, MA: Harvard Business School Press, 2003); and K. Macklem, "The Toxic Workplace: A Poisoned Work Environment Can Wreak Havoc on a Company's Culture and Its Employees," *Macleans.ca*, January 31, 2005. You can find the latter article at www.macleans.ca/article.jsp?content=20050131_99562_99562.

How Toxin Handlers Alleviate Organizational Pain

- They listen empathetically.
- They suggest solutions.
- They work behind the scenes to prevent pain.

- They carry the confidences of others.
- They reframe difficult messages.[50]

CHAPTER

10

PART 4

SHARING THE

ORGANIZATIONAL VISION

Organizational Culture

How does a pizza franchise business ensure quality control across the country? Developing a strong culture is part of the answer.

LEARNING OUTCOMES

1 What is the purpose of organizational culture?

2 How do you read an organization's culture?

3 How do you create and maintain organizational culture?

4 Can organizational culture have a downside?

5 How do you change organizational culture?

When you walk into a Boston Pizza restaurant in BC, Ontario, or Quebec, you will find many similarities, but a few differences too.[1] The Quebec restaurants carry poutine, while the Ontario restaurants have a meatball sub on the menu and use a different type of pepperoni on the pizzas than those made in BC and Quebec.

Despite these menu differences, the similarity that binds the Richmond, BC-based Boston Pizza restaurants throughout Canada and the United States is the strong organizational culture created by the company's co-owners, Jim Treliving and George Melville. The two men believe that a strong culture makes for a strong organization, and they emphasize the importance of finding the right people, having good systems in place, training employees, and communicating effectively.

The emphasis on a strong culture seems to be paying off for Boston Pizza. It has been named one of Canada's 10 Most Admired Corporate Cultures, and its three-year average revenue growth far exceeded industry standards and the TSX 60 Composite index.

In this chapter, we show that every organization has a culture. We examine how that culture reveals itself and the impact it has on the attitudes and behaviours of members of that organization. An understanding of what makes up an organization's culture and how it is created, sustained, and learned enhances our ability to explain and predict the behaviour of people at work.

OB IS FOR EVERYONE

- What does organizational culture do?
- What kind of organizational culture would work best for you?
- Is culture the same as rules?

THE BIG IDEA

A strong organizational culture can guide individual decisions and help everyone work together toward the same goals.

SELF-ASSESSMENT LIBRARY
LEARNING ABOUT YOURSELF

- Organizational Cultural Fit
- Organization Commitment

What is the purpose of organizational culture?

 BLOG IT

Do you prefer strong or weak cultures?
What kind of culture would you prefer to work in? Why?
www.obstudentjournals.blogspot.com

SELF-ASSESSMENT LIBRARY

LEARNING ABOUT YOURSELF

1. What Kind of Organizational Culture Fits You Best?
(page 387)

What Is Organizational Culture?

When Henry Mintzberg, professor at McGill University and one of the world's leading management experts, was asked to compare organizational structure and corporate culture, he said, "Culture is the soul of the organization—the beliefs and values, and how they are manifested. I think of the structure as the skeleton, and as the flesh and blood. And culture is the soul that holds the thing together and gives it life force."[2]

Mintzberg's culture metaphor provides a clear image of how to think about culture. Culture provides stability to an organization and gives employees a clear understanding of "the way things are done around here." Culture sets the tone for how an organization operates and how individuals within the organization interact. Think of the different impressions you have when a receptionist tells you that "Ms. Dettweiler" will be available in a moment, while at another organization you are told that "Emma" will be with you as soon as she gets off the phone. It's clear that in one organization the rules are more formal than in the other.

As we discuss organizational culture, you may want to remember that organizations differ considerably in the cultures they adopt. Consider the different cultures of Calgary-based WestJet Airlines and Montreal-based Air Canada. WestJet is viewed as having a "young, spunky, can-do environment, where customers will have more fun."[3] Air Canada, by contrast, is considered less helpful and friendly. One analyst even suggested that Air Canada staff "tend to make their customers feel stressed" by their confrontational behaviour.[4] Our discussion of culture should help you understand how these differences across organizations occur.

As you start to think about different organizations where you might work, you will want to research their cultures. For instance, some organizations' cultures are admired more than others: Toronto-based Shoppers Drug Mart, Calgary-based WestJet Airlines, Vancouver-based Ledcor Group, and Toronto-based ING Direct are 4 of the 10 companies named "Most Admired Corporate Cultures" of 2011. An organization that expects employees to work 15 hours a day may not be where you would like to work. To help you think more about culture and its impact on you, you may want to complete the *Learning About Yourself Exercise* on page 387, which helps you assess whether you would be more comfortable in a formal, rule-oriented culture or a more informal, flexible culture.

Definition of *Organizational Culture*

Organizational culture refers to a system of shared meaning held by members that distinguishes the organization from other organizations.[5]

Seven primary characteristics capture the essence of an organization's culture:[6]

- *Innovation and risk-taking.* The degree to which employees are encouraged to be innovative and take risks.

- *Attention to detail.* The degree to which employees are expected to work with precision, analysis, and attention to detail.

- *Outcome orientation.* The degree to which management focuses on results, or outcomes, rather than on the techniques and processes used to achieve these outcomes.

- *People orientation.* The degree to which management decisions take into consideration the effect of outcomes on people within the organization.

- *Team orientation.* The degree to which work activities are organized around teams rather than individuals.

- *Aggressiveness.* The degree to which people are aggressive and competitive rather than easygoing and supportive.

organizational culture A system of shared meaning held by members that distinguishes the organization from other organizations.

- *Stability.* The degree to which organizational activities emphasize maintaining the status quo in contrast to growth.

Each of these characteristics exists on a continuum from low to high.

When individuals consider their organization in terms of these seven characteristics, they get a composite picture of the organization's culture. This picture becomes the basis for feelings of shared understanding that members have about the organization, how things are done in it, and the way members are supposed to behave. Exhibit 10-1 demonstrates how these characteristics can be mixed to create highly diverse organizations. To help you understand some of the characteristics of culture, you may want to look at the *Working with Others Exercise* on page 388, which asks you to rate your classroom culture.

Levels of Culture

Because organizational culture has multiple levels,[7] the metaphor of an iceberg has often been used to describe it.[8] However, a simmering volcano may better represent the layers of culture: beliefs, values, assumptions bubble below the surface, producing observable aspects of culture at the surface. Exhibit 10-2 reminds us that culture is very visible at the level of **artifacts**. These are what you see, hear, and feel when you encounter an organization's culture. You may notice, for instance, that employees in two offices have very different dress policies, or one office displays great works of art while another posts company mottos on the wall. These visible artifacts emerge from the organization's culture.

Exhibit 10-2 also shows us that beliefs, values, and assumptions, unlike artifacts, are not always readily observable. Instead, we rely on the visible artifacts (material symbols, special language used, rituals carried out, and stories told to others) to help us uncover the organization's beliefs, values, and assumptions. **Beliefs** are the understandings of how objects and ideas relate to each other. **Values** are the stable, long-lasting beliefs about what is important. For instance, Winnipeg-based Palliser Furniture, a manufacturer of leather- and fabric-upholstered furniture, promotes the following corporate

Vancouver-based Playland amusement park hires hundreds of young people each summer to run the rides, sell tickets, and manage the games booths. Managers want to make sure that new employees will fit into the "fun culture" of the environment. Instead of one-on-one interviews, applicants are put into teams where they solve puzzles together, while managers watch the group dynamics. Amy Nguyen (left) and Chloe Wong are two of the teens hired after they did well in the group interview.

EXHIBIT 10-1 Contrasting Organizational Cultures

Organization A	Organization B
• Managers must fully document all decisions.	• Management encourages and rewards risk-taking and change.
• Creative decisions, change, and risks are not encouraged.	• Employees are encouraged to "run with" ideas, and failures are treated as "learning experiences."
• Extensive rules and regulations exist for all employees.	• Employees have few rules and regulations to follow.
• Productivity is valued over employee morale.	• Productivity is balanced with treating its people right.
• Employees are encouraged to stay within their own department.	• Team members are encouraged to interact with people at all levels and functions.
• Individual effort is encouraged.	• Many rewards are team-based.

artifacts Aspects of an organization's culture that you see, hear, and feel.

beliefs The understandings of how objects and ideas relate to each other.

values The stable, long-lasting beliefs about what is important.

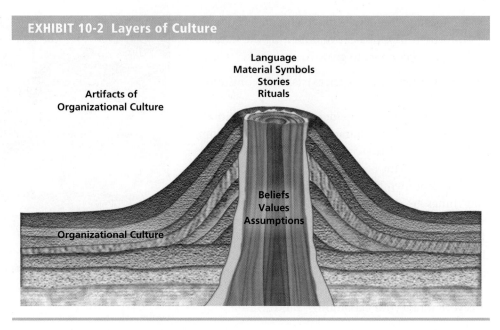

EXHIBIT 10-2 Layers of Culture

Language
Material Symbols
Stories
Rituals

Artifacts of
Organizational Culture

Beliefs
Values
Assumptions

Organizational Culture

values: "demonstrate integrity in all relationships; promote the dignity and value of each other; respect the environment; support our community; and strive for excellence in all we do."[9] **Assumptions** are the taken-for-granted notions of how something should be. When basic assumptions are held by the entire group, members will have difficulty conceiving of another way of doing things. For instance, in Canada, some students hold a basic assumption that universities should not consider costs when setting tuition, and should keep tuition low for greater access by students. Beliefs, values, and assumptions, if we can uncover them, help us understand why organizations do the things that we observe.

Culture's Functions

Culture performs a number of functions within an organization:

- It has a boundary-defining role because it creates distinction between one organization and others.

- It conveys a sense of identity to organization members.

- It helps create commitment to something larger than an individual's self-interest.

- It enhances stability; it is the social glue that helps hold the organization together by providing appropriate standards for what employees should say and do.

- It serves as a control mechanism that guides and shapes the attitudes and behaviour of employees, and helps them make sense of the organization.

This last function is of particular interest to us.[10] As the following quotation makes clear, culture defines the rules of the game:

> *Culture by definition is elusive, intangible, implicit, and taken for granted. But every organization develops a core set of assumptions, understandings, and implicit rules that govern day-to-day behaviour in the workplace. Until newcomers learn the rules, they are not accepted as full-fledged members of the organization. Transgressions of the rules on the part of high-level executives or front-line employees result in universal disapproval and powerful penalties. Conformity to the rules becomes the primary basis for reward and upward mobility.*[11]

assumptions The taken-for-granted notions of how something should be.

Today's trend toward decentralized organizations makes culture more important than ever, but ironically it also makes establishing a strong culture more difficult. When formal authority and control systems are reduced, culture's *shared meaning* points everyone in the same direction. However, employees organized in teams may show greater allegiance to their team and its values than to the values of the organization as a whole. In virtual organizations, the lack of frequent face-to-face contact makes establishing a common set of norms very difficult. Strong leadership that communicates frequently about common goals and priorities is especially important in innovative organizations.[12]

> What does organizational culture do?

Culture Creates Climate

If you have worked with someone whose positive attitude inspired you to do your best, or with a lacklustre team that drained your motivation, you have experienced the effects of climate. **Organizational climate** refers to the shared perceptions organizational members have about their organization and work environment.[13] This aspect of culture is like team spirit at the organizational level. When everyone has the same general feelings about what is important or how well things are working, the effect of these attitudes will be more than the sum of the individual parts. The same appears true for organizations. One meta-analysis found that across dozens of different samples, psychological climate was strongly related to individuals' level of job satisfaction, involvement, commitment, and motivation.[14] A positive overall workplace climate has been linked to higher customer satisfaction and financial performance as well.[15]

Dozens of dimensions of climate have been studied, including safety, justice, diversity, and customer service, to name a few.[16] A person who encounters a positive climate for performance will think about doing a good job more often and will believe others support his or her success. Someone who encounters a positive climate for diversity will feel more comfortable collaborating with co-workers regardless of their demographic background. Climate also influences the habits people adopt. If the climate for safety is positive, everyone wears safety gear and follows safety procedures even if individually they would not normally think very often about being safe. *OB in the Workplace* offers one example of an employee-first corporate culture.

OB in the WORKPLACE
Making Culture Work

What can a CEO do if employees don't buy into the company culture? Wadood Ibrahim, CEO of Winnipeg-based Protegra, believes in the importance of having a strong, employee-first corporate culture.[17] In fact, Protegra has been recognized for its corporate culture twice, placing first in the 2009 and 2011 "Best Small and Medium Employers in Canada" rankings conducted jointly by Queen's University Centre for Business Venturing and Aon Hewitt.

Protegra has an egalitarian culture at its core. Employees do not have corporate titles, and they are encouraged to participate in the employee share-ownership program.

After a period of growth in the early 2000s, the company's culture started to get muddied. The socialization process was not as strong as it should be, and communication about the company's values was lax. In order to make sure that everyone understood the company's culture, Ibrahim brought employees together to talk about what they saw as the company's core values. The common theme was respect, teamwork, and dependability. From his discussion with employees, Ibrahim codified the culture for

organizational climate The shared perceptions organizational members have about their organization and work environment.

his employees—"what Protegra was, what it aspired to be and how employees were expected to apply its values." This exercise led to 10 employees leaving, because they were not on board with the vision. Ibrahim saw this as a good thing: "We got alignment on values and vision," and the company has performed much better since.

In order to strengthen the company's culture further, in 2009 Ibrahim unveiled an internal website called "the Enduring Culture Machine." The site contains an in-depth explanation of Protegra's values and it's "meant to be a primer for new recruits, a communication tool for existing employees and a mechanism to protect and strengthen Protegra's culture over the long haul." Creativity and empowerment are still important, Ibrahim explains, "but [new staff] need to abide by basic company principles."

Do Organizations Have Uniform Cultures?

Organizational culture represents a common perception the organization's members hold. We should expect, therefore, that individuals with different backgrounds or at different levels in the organization will tend to describe its culture in similar terms.[18]

The fact that organizational culture has common properties does not mean that there cannot be subcultures within it. Most large organizations have a dominant culture and numerous sets of subcultures.[19] A **dominant culture** expresses the core values that are shared by a majority of the organization's members. When we talk about an organization's culture, we are referring to its dominant culture, which gives an organization its distinct personality.[20] **Subcultures** tend to develop in large organizations to reflect common problems, situations, or experiences faced by groups of members in the same department or location. The purchasing department can have a subculture that includes the **core values** of the dominant culture plus additional values unique to members of the purchasing department.

If organizations were composed only of numerous subcultures, organizational culture as an independent variable would be significantly less powerful. It is the "shared

dominant culture A system of shared meaning that expresses the core values shared by a majority of the organization's members.

subcultures Mini-cultures within an organization, typically defined by department designations and geographical separation.

core values The primary or dominant values that are accepted throughout the organization.

Organizational culture guides and shapes the attitudes of employees at New Zealand Air. One of the airline's guiding principles is to champion and promote New Zealand and its national heritage both within the country and overseas. In this photo, a cabin crew member dressed in traditional Maori clothing and a pilot touch noses to represent the sharing of a single breath following a ceremony for the airline's purchase of a Boeing airplane in Everett, Washington. This expression of representing their country with pride creates a strong bond among employees.

meaning" aspect of culture that makes it such a potent device for guiding and shaping behaviour. This is what allows us to say that Microsoft's culture values aggressiveness and risk-taking,[21] and then to use that information to better understand the behaviour of Microsoft executives and employees. But many organizations also have subcultures that can influence the behaviour of members.

Strong vs. Weak Cultures

It is possible to differentiate between strong and weak cultures.[22] If most employees (responding to management surveys) have the same opinions about the organization's mission and values, the culture is strong; if opinions vary widely, the culture is weak.

In a **strong culture**, the organization's core values are both intensely held and widely shared.[23] The more members who accept the core values and the greater their commitment to those values, the stronger the culture is. A strong culture will have a great influence on the behaviour of its members because the high degree of shared experiences and intensity create an internal climate of high behavioural control. American retailer Nordstrom has developed one of the strongest service cultures in the retailing industry. Nordstrom employees know what is expected of them, and these expectations go a long way in shaping their behaviour.

A strong culture builds cohesiveness, loyalty, and organizational commitment. These qualities, in turn, lessen employees' tendency to leave the organization.[24]

Reading an Organization's Culture

> Boston Pizza claims to be Canada's number one casual dining restaurant. It has reached that status by developing a strong organizational culture.[25] The company's reward structure is designed to encourage all employees to meet corporate targets. "We feel strongly that everyone should participate and everyone should be rewarded in company growth and success," says the company's president and CEO, Mark Pacinda.
>
> As part of its emphasis on building a strong culture, the company pays careful attention to its hiring strategy. The company also provides long-term incentives for employees to stay at Boston Pizza, so that there is a stable set of individuals in place to help socialize new employees into the culture.
>
> Co-owner George Melville recognizes that when hiring franchisees, business skills and money are not enough. Employees have to fit into the culture as well. He reports that they once hired a person who had money and superb business skills, but who "was basically a jerk." The senior management realized that they had to let him go after six months. "The idea that you can build a team around somebody who isn't a team builder is a mistake," says Melville. Why does culture have such a strong influence on people's behaviour?

2 How do you read an organization's culture?

As we noted in Exhibit 10-2, the artifacts of culture inform outsiders and employees about the underlying values and beliefs of the organization's culture. These artifacts, or physical manifestations of culture, include stories, rituals, material symbols, and language. The extent to which organizations have artifacts of their culture indicates whether they have strong or weak cultures. *From Concepts to Skills* on pages 392–393 offers additional ideas on how to "read" an organization's culture.

What kind of organizational culture would work best for you?

Stories

When Toronto-based Bank of Montreal (BMO) decided several years ago to become a leader in customer service in the banking industry, it needed a way of communicating this message to the bank's employees. The decision: "Every meeting starts with a customer

strong culture A culture in which the core values are intensely held and widely shared.

Legend has it that a woman who was a frequent flyer on Southwest Airlines complained constantly about the service, dispiriting the customer service department. Finally, the head of customer relations asked Herb Kelleher, the founder, what they should do. Kelleher's response to the customer was brief: "Dear Mrs. X, We will miss you. Love, Herb." Employees were thrilled to get this kind of support from their CEO.

story." No matter what kind of meeting is being held, one staff member has to tell a recent story about an interaction with a customer—ranging from feel-good stories to horror stories of something that went wrong for the customer. By focusing on customer stories, employees know they need to pay attention to interactions so that they can share the stories. Susan Brown, a senior VP with BMO, explains the importance of the story focus for the bank: "If you want to change culture, a great way to do it is the customer story. It's part of the evolution of developing a customer-centric culture."[26] Stories circulate through many organizations. They typically tell about the organization's founders, rule breaking, rags-to-riches successes, reductions in the workforce, relocation of employees, reactions to past mistakes, and organizational coping.[27] These stories anchor the present in the past and explain and legitimize current practices.[28]

Rituals

Rituals are repetitive sequences of activities that express and reinforce the key values of the organization; what goals are most important; and which people are important and which are expendable.[29]

One well-known corporate ritual is Walmart's company chant. Begun by the company's founder, Sam Walton, as a way to motivate and unite his workforce, "Gimme a W, gimme an A, gimme an L, give me an M, A, R, T!" has become a company ritual that bonds Walmart employees and reinforces Walton's belief in the importance of his employees to the company's success. Similar corporate chants are used by IBM, Ericsson, Novell, Deutsche Bank, and PricewaterhouseCoopers.[30]

Material Symbols

The layout of corporate headquarters, the types of cars given to top executives, and the presence or absence of corporate aircraft are a few examples of **material symbols**. Others include the size of offices, the elegance of furnishings, executive perks, and dress code.[31] In addition, corporate logos, signs, brochures, and advertisements reveal aspects of the organization's culture.[32] These material symbols convey to employees, customers, and clients who is important, the degree of egalitarianism top management desires, and the kinds of behaviour (for example, risk-taking, conservative, authoritar-

rituals Repetitive sequences of activities that express and reinforce the key values of the organization; what goals are most important; and which people are important and which are expendable.

material symbols What conveys to employees who is important, the degree of egalitarianism top management desires, and the kinds of behaviour that are appropriate.

At Walmart, culture is transmitted to employees through the daily ritual of the "Walmart cheer." The cheer is performed at both US and international stores. Employees are asked to do the cheer in every morning meeting. Shown here are employees of a Walmart store in Evergreen Park, Illinois, chanting the motivational cheer that helps preserve a small-family spirit and work environment within the world's largest retailer.

ian, participative, individualistic, social) that are appropriate. For instance, pictures of all Creo employees hang in the Burnaby, BC-based company's entrance lobby, which visibly conveys Creo's anti-hierarchical culture.

Companies differ in how much separation they make between their executives and employees. This plays out in how material benefits are distributed to executives. Some companies provide their top executives with chauffeur-driven limousines and, when they travel by air, unlimited use of the corporate jet. Other companies might pay for car and air transportation for top executives, only the car is a Chevrolet with no driver, and the jet seat is in the economy section of a commercial airliner. At Bolton, Ontario-based Husky Injection Molding Systems, a more egalitarian culture is favoured. Employees and management share the parking lot, dining room, and even washrooms. *Case Incident—Is a 5S Culture for You?* on page 390 indicates how some companies are using a methodology called 5S to introduce order into plant layouts.

Language

Many organizations and units within organizations use language to help identify with the culture, show their acceptance of it, and help preserve it. Baristas at Starbucks call drinks *short*, *tall*, or *grande*, not *small*, *medium*, or *large*, and they know the difference between a half-decaf double tall almond skinny mocha and an iced short schizo skinny hazelnut cappuccino with wings.[33] Students and employees at Grant MacEwan College are informed by the philosophy of the college's namesake. Dr. Grant MacEwan, historian, writer, politician, and environmentalist, was never a formal part of the management of the organization. However, many phrases from his writing and creed have found their way into formal college publications and calendars, as well as informal communications, including his most well known, "I have tried to leave things in the vineyard better than I found them."[34]

Over time, organizations often develop unique terms to describe equipment, offices, key staff, suppliers, customers, or products that relate to their business. New employees are frequently overwhelmed with acronyms and jargon that, after six months on the job, have become fully part of their language. Once assimilated, this terminology acts as a common denominator that unites members of a given culture or subculture.

Creating and Sustaining an Organization's Culture

3 How do you create and maintain organizational culture?

One of the challenges Boston Pizza co-owners Jim Treliving and George Melville face in managing the 325 restaurants and more than 16 000 employees across Canada is making sure that everyone is on the same page.[35] The individual restaurants in the chain are not owned by the company. Instead, franchisees invest a considerable amount of money in order to gain the right to own a Boston Pizza restaurant. Thus, there could be a conflict between what the co-founders want done, and what a franchisee feels is best for his or her investment.

Treliving and Melville try to prevent this conflict by carefully vetting franchise candidates. Potential franchisees are informed of the initial $60 000 fee and start-up costs that could run between $1.5 and $2.4 million. Despite the size of their investment, franchisees must demonstrate a "willingness to adhere to the Boston Pizza system." Franchisees are given a lot of help in starting out, however.

When Hank Van Poelgeest opened up the first Boston Pizza restaurant in St. John's, Newfoundland, in January 2006, he naturally worried. A lot of preparation had gone into the opening, which involved months of planning, and a careful choice of location, and a team of nine people had been sent from head office to help hire and train staff. The new staff did a dress rehearsal of the grand opening four times to make sure nothing went wrong.

The preparation was so thorough that the opening exceeded all expectations. "We wanted to use the first couple of weeks as a slow beginning," says Van Poelgeest, "but we've never had a slow beginning." What role does culture play in creating high-performing employees?

An organization's culture does not pop out of thin air, and once established, it rarely fades away. What forces influence the creation of a culture? What reinforces and sustains these forces once they are in place? Exhibit 10-3 summarizes how an organization's culture is established and sustained. We describe each part of this process next.

How a Culture Begins

An organization's current customs, traditions, and general way of doing things are largely due to what it has done before and how successful it was in doing it. This leads us to the ultimate source of an organization's culture: its founders.[36]

Is culture the same as rules?

Founders traditionally have a major impact on an organization's early culture. Free of previous customs or ideologies, they have a vision of what the organization should be. Because new organizations are typically small, it's possible for the founders to impose their vision on all organizational members. Jim Treliving, the co-owner of Boston Pizza, keeps his vision alive by stopping in at every Boston Pizza wherever he is travelling, shaking hands with the staff, and thanking them for their

EXHIBIT 10-3 How Organizational Cultures Form

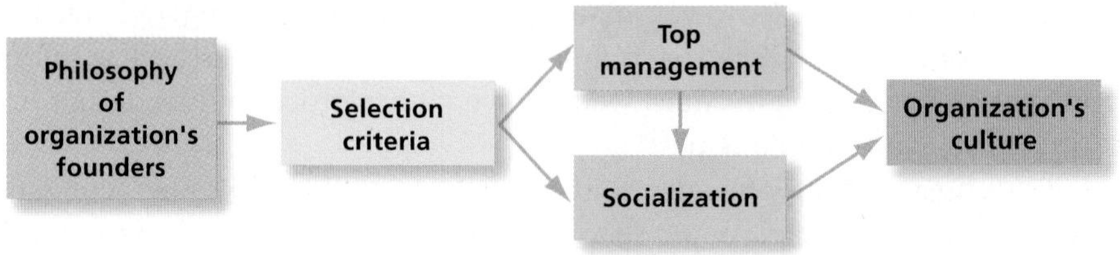

Philosophy of organization's founders → Selection criteria → Top management / Socialization → Organization's culture

hard work. According to Treliving, "you take people in as franchisees and they become part of your family."[37]

Culture creation occurs in three ways.[38] First, founders only hire and keep employees who think and feel the way they do. Second, they indoctrinate and socialize these employees to their way of thinking and feeling. Finally, the founders' own behaviour encourages employees to identify with the founders and thereby internalize those beliefs, values, and assumptions. When the organization succeeds, the founders' vision is viewed as a primary determinant of that success. At that point, the founders' personality becomes embedded in the culture of the organization.

The culture at Toronto-based PCL, the largest general contracting organization in Canada, is still strongly influenced by the vision of Ernest Poole, who founded the company in 1906. "Poole's rules," which include "Employ highest grade people obtainable" and "Encourage integrity, loyalty and efficiencies," still influence the way the company hires and trains its employees long after the founder's death.[39] Other contemporary examples of founders who have had an immeasurable impact on their organizations' cultures are Ted Rogers of Toronto-based Rogers Communications, Frank Stronach of Aurora, Ontario-based Magna International, and Richard Branson of UK-based Virgin Group.

Keeping a Culture Alive

Once a culture is in place, practices within the organization maintain it by giving employees a set of similar experiences.[40] The selection process, performance evaluation criteria, training and career development activities, and promotion procedures ensure that those hired fit in with the culture, reward those who support it, and penalize (and even expel) those who challenge it. Three forces play a particularly important part in sustaining a culture: *selection* practices, the actions of *top management*, and *socialization* methods. Let's take a closer look at each.

Selection

The explicit goal of the selection process is to identify and hire individuals who have the knowledge, skills, and abilities to perform successfully.

The final decision, because it is significantly influenced by the decision maker's judgment of how well the candidates will fit into the organization, identifies people whose values are essentially consistent with at least a good portion of the organization's values.[41]

Selection also provides information about the organization to applicants. Windsor, Ontario-based Windsor Family Credit Union makes job candidates go through a process that has as many as eight steps so that the organization and the employee can determine if they are a good fit for each other.[42] To signal to job candidates that dignity and respect are important parts of Kitchener, Ontario-based Mennonite Savings and Credit Union's culture, job candidates are provided with interview questions in advance. The credit union encourages two-way communication throughout the hiring process.[43] *OB in the Workplace* shows how another company's method of interviewing ensures that applicants are right for the job.

OB in the WORKPLACE
Playland's Interviews Are More Than Fun and Games

How does a company make sure an applicant is right for the job?   At Playland, Vancouver's largest amusement park, applicants for a summer job don't do one-on-one interviews with managers or the human resource department.[44] Instead, they are asked to deconstruct a JENGA tower with a group of nine other applicants and answer a variety of "interesting questions." When an applicant removes a block from the tower, they answer a question printed on it.

Amy Nguyen, a 15-year-old high school student applying for her first job, had the following question: "There's a customer who had to line up a long time for food and he was very upset by the time he got to the front of the line. What would you do?"

"I said I would apologize, look cute and tell him, 'Let me see if my manager can do anything for you,'" says Nguyen. This answer got her a second interview, and she eventually got the job.

Jennifer Buensuceso, a PNE gaming manager at Playland, thinks the new way of hiring is much better than when she faced a one-on-one question and answer format when she was hired. She says the new method helps managers learn about the applicant's "team-building and individuality. You get to see them think out of the box."

This format is also good for nervous teens and those whose first language is not English. Getting them to play relaxes them, and helps managers to see "who shows natural leadership skills, who's outgoing, who works well on a team and who's good at problem-solving."[45]

Careful hiring practices mean that those who perceive a conflict between their values and those of the organization can remove themselves from the applicant pool. Selection, therefore, becomes a two-way street: It allows the employer or applicant to avoid a mismatch and sustains organizational culture by selecting out those individuals who might attack or undermine the organization's core values.

Top Management

The actions of top management also have a major impact on the organization's culture.[46] Through words and behaviour, senior executives establish norms that filter through the organization about, for instance, whether risk-taking is desirable; how much freedom managers should give their employees; what is appropriate dress; and what actions will pay off in terms of pay raises, promotions, and other rewards. Apple's culture of secrecy stems from how private Steve Jobs was, as *OB in the Workplace* shows.

OB in the WORKPLACE
Apple's Culture of Secrecy

How did Steve Jobs influence Apple's organizational culture? When Steve Jobs, founder and figurehead of Apple Computer, took a leave of absence from the company in January 2011, few details were given about the reason for the leave.[47] This was the third secretive medical leave in seven years. At the time of his second leave, in January 2009, Jobs reportedly had a "hormonal imbalance" and needed some time off. Then word leaked that Jobs had received a liver transplant.

Jobs made two brief appearances for the company in March and June of 2011, appearing thin and gaunt. Shareholders knew that he had pancreatic cancer (that eventually leaked out), but concrete information about the CEO's health was not forthcoming.

Apple's culture of secrecy has not been limited to Jobs' health. The company is known for trying to keep all sorts of information secret, from product information to release dates. The company sometimes gives misleading information not only to reporters, but even to its employees to prevent premature leaks about product development. "I was at the iPod launch," said Edward Eigerman, a former systems engineer at Apple. "No one that I worked with saw that coming." How does the company maintain such a high level of secrecy? Mainly through its culture and norms. Employees sign nondisclosure agreements, and they are fired if it's determined they have leaked information to the press or other parties. "They make everyone super, super paranoid about security," said Mark Hamblin, a former Apple employee. "I have never seen anything else like it at another company."

Apple's culture of secrecy may be a reflection of Jobs' personality rather than simply a business strategy. Regis McKenna, a Silicon Valley marketing veteran who has advised Apple in the past, noted that "what most people don't understand is that Steve has always been very personal about his life. He has always kept things close to the vest since I've known him, and only confided in relatively few people." With the passing of Jobs, perhaps the company's culture of secrecy will change.

Socialization

No matter how effectively the organization recruits and selects new employees, they are not fully indoctrinated in the organization's culture and can disrupt beliefs and customs already in place. The process that helps new employees adapt to the prevailing culture is called **socialization**.[48] As a 2011 study suggests, socialization done well will develop a new employee's self-efficacy, hope, optimism, and resilience.[49]

New employees at the Japanese electronics company Sanyo are socialized through a particularly long training program. At their intensive five-month course, trainees eat and sleep together in company-subsidized dorms and are required to vacation together at company-owned resorts. They learn the Sanyo way of doing everything—from how to speak to managers to proper grooming and dress.[50] The company considers this program essential for transforming young employees, fresh out of school, into dedicated *kaisha senshi*, or corporate warriors.

Starbucks does not go to the extreme that Sanyo does, but it seeks the same outcome.[51] All new employees go through 24 hours of training. Classes cover everything necessary to transform new employees into brewing consultants. They learn the Starbucks philosophy, the company jargon, and even how to help customers make decisions about beans and grind, as well as about espresso machines. The result is employees who understand Starbucks' culture and who project an enthusiastic and knowledgeable image to customers.

Monique Leroux, chair of the board, president, and CEO of Desjardins Group, recently led an organizational restructuring at Desjardins. To help accomplish this goal, she established 10 multidisciplinary teams with equal numbers of women and men on each, sending a clear message about gender equality to the cooperative. Leroux is a mentor to many women, and among her many activities geared to supporting women in a traditionally male-dominated financial industry, Leroux has also helped Desjardins launch scholarships and internships for young women interested in finance. Desjardins was named one of Canada's 10 Most Admired Corporate Cultures in 2010.

socialization The process that adapts new employees to an organization's culture.

EXHIBIT 10-4

"I don't know how it started, either. All I know is that it's part of our corporate culture."

Source: © Mick Stevens/ The New Yorker Collection/ www.cartoonbank.com

An organization continues to socialize its employees throughout their career in the organization, which further contributes to sustaining the culture. (Sometimes, however, employees are not fully socialized. For instance, you will note in Exhibit 10-4 that employees had learned they were supposed to wear checkerboard caps to work, but clearly did not know why.) As part of its continual socialization process, the CEO of Windsor, Ontario-based Windsor Family Credit Union takes employees to breakfast quarterly to find out about their questions, concerns, and their work.[52] This provides an opportunity to make sure employees understand the overall goals of the organization.

We can think of socialization as a process composed of three stages: prearrival, encounter, and metamorphosis.[53] This process (illustrated in Exhibit 10-5) has an impact on the new employee's work productivity, commitment to the organization's objectives, and eventual decision to stay with the organization.

The Prearrival Stage   The **prearrival stage** explicitly recognizes that each individual arrives with a set of values, attitudes, and expectations about both the work to be done and the organization. One major purpose of a business school, for example, is to socialize business students to the attitudes and behaviours business firms want. Newcomers to high-profile organizations with a strong market position will make their own assumptions about what it must be like to work there.[54] What people know before they join the organization and how proactive their personality is are critical predictors of how well they adjust to a new culture.[55]

One way to capitalize on the importance of prehire characteristics is to use the selection process to inform prospective employees about the organization as a whole. We have also seen how the selection process ensures the inclusion of the "right type"—those who will fit in. "Indeed, the ability of the individual to present the appropriate face during the selection process determines his or her ability to move into the organization in the first place. Thus, success depends on the degree to which the aspiring member has correctly anticipated the expectations and desires of those in the organization in charge of selection."[56] For a detailed example of how an organization considers its hiring process as a way of maintaining corporate culture, read this chapter's *Case Incident—Wegmans Hires for Passion* on page 391.

The Encounter Stage   Upon entering the organization, the new employee begins the **encounter stage**, and confronts the possibility that expectations—of the job, co-workers,

prearrival stage The period of learning in the socialization process that occurs before a new employee joins the organization.

encounter stage The stage in the socialization process in which a new employee sees what the organization is really like and confronts the possibility that expectations and reality may diverge.

EXHIBIT 10-5 A Socialization Model

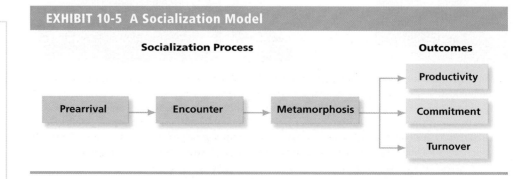

Socialization Process			Outcomes
Prearrival → Encounter → Metamorphosis			Productivity
			Commitment
			Turnover

In a study conducted by the US Reputation Institute and *Canadian Business* magazine in 2010, Tim Hortons was rated as the company with the best corporate reputation in Canada. Potential employees can learn a lot about the company's culture by observing its retail operations.[57]

boss, and the organization in general—may differ from reality. If the employee's expectations are fairly accurate, the encounter stage merely reaffirms earlier perceptions.

However, this is often not the case. At the extreme, new members may become totally disillusioned with the realities of their job and resign. Proper selection should significantly reduce the probability of that outcome, and so too should encouraging friendship ties in the organization—newcomers are more committed when friends and co-workers help them "learn the ropes."[58] A 2011 study by professor Alan Saks of the Rotman School of Business at the University of Toronto and professor Jamie Gruman of the School of Hospitality and Tourism Management at the University of Guelph demonstrates the benefits of orientation, training, and mentorship programs for new employees. These activities help employees adjust better because they make them feel happier, more confident that they will more likely fit with the organization, and therefore more engaged.[59]

The Metamorphosis Stage   Finally, to work out any problems discovered during the encounter stage, the new employee changes or goes through the **metamorphosis stage**. The options presented in Exhibit 10-6 are designed to bring about the desired metamorphosis. The more management relies on formal, collective, fixed, and serial socialization programs and emphasizes divestiture, the more likely that newcomers' differences and perspectives will be stripped away and replaced by standardized and predictable behaviours. These *institutional* practices are common in police departments, fire departments, and other organizations that value rule following and order. Programs that are informal, individual, random, variable, and disjunctive and emphasize investiture are more likely to give newcomers an innovative sense of their role and methods of working. Creative fields, such as research and development, advertising, and filmmaking, rely on these *individual* practices. Most research suggests high levels of institutional practices encourage person-organization fit and high levels of commitment, whereas individual practices produce more role innovation.[60]

We can say that metamorphosis and the entry socialization process is complete when

- The new employee has become comfortable with the organization and his or her job

- The new employee has internalized the norms of the organization and the work group, and understands and accepts these norms

- The new employee feels accepted by his or her peers as a trusted and valued individual, is self-confident that he or she has the competence to complete the job successfully, and understands the system—not only his or her own tasks but also the rules, procedures, and informally accepted practices

metamorphosis stage The stage in the socialization process in which a new employee adjusts to the values and norms of the job, work group, and organization.

New employees at Broad Air Conditioning in Changsha, China, are indoctrinated in the company's military-style culture by going through a 10-day training session of boot camp, where they are divided into platoons and live in barracks. Boot camp prepares new hires for the military formality that prevails at Broad, where employees begin their work week standing in formation during a flag-raising ceremony of two company flags and the flag of China. All employees live in dorms on the company campus and receive free food and lodging. To motivate its workers, Broad has scattered throughout the campus 43 life-size bronze statues of inspirational leaders from Confucius to Jack Welch, the former CEO of General Electric.

- The new employee understands how he or she will be evaluated and knows what criteria will be used to measure and appraise his or her work; he or she knows what is expected and what constitutes a job "well done"

As Exhibit 10-5 on page 376 shows, successful metamorphosis should have a positive impact on the new employee's productivity and commitment to the organization. It should reduce the tendency to leave the organization. This chapter's *Ethical Dilemma Exercise* on page 389 explores whether you would be comfortable working in an organization whose culture accepts snooping on its employees.

EXHIBIT 10-6 Entry Socialization Options

Formal vs. Informal The more a new employee is segregated from the ongoing work setting and differentiated in some way to make explicit his or her newcomer's role, the more formal socialization is. Specific orientation and training programs are examples. Informal socialization puts the new employee directly into his or her job, with little or no special attention.

Individual vs. Collective New members can be socialized individually. This describes how it's done in many professional offices. They can also be grouped together and processed through an identical set of experiences, as in military boot camp.

Fixed vs. Variable This refers to the time schedule in which newcomers make the transition from outsider to insider. A fixed schedule establishes standardized stages of transition. This characterizes rotational training programs. It also includes probationary periods, such as the 8- to 10-year "associate" status accounting and law firms use before deciding whether to name a candidate as a partner. Variable schedules give no advance notice of their transition timetable. Variable schedules describe the typical promotion system, where individuals are not advanced to the next stage until they are "ready."

Serial vs. Random Serial socialization is characterized by the use of role models who train and encourage the newcomer. Apprenticeship and mentoring programs are examples. In random socialization, role models are deliberately withheld. The new employee is left on his or her own to figure things out.

Investiture vs. Divestiture Investiture socialization assumes that the newcomer's qualities and qualifications are the necessary ingredients for job success, so these qualities and qualifications are confirmed and supported. Divestiture socialization tries to strip away certain characteristics of the recruit. Fraternity and sorority "pledges" go through divestiture socialization to shape them into the proper role.

Sources: Based on J. Van Maanen, "People Processing: Strategies of Organizational Socialization," *Organizational Dynamics,* Summer 1978, pp. 19–36; and E. H. Schein, "Organizational Culture," *American Psychologist,* February 1990, p. 116.

The Liabilities of Organizational Culture

Culture enhances organizational commitment and increases the consistency of employee behaviour.[61] These are clearly benefits to an organization. From an employee's standpoint, culture is valuable because it spells out how things are done and what is important. However, we should not ignore the potentially dysfunctional aspects of culture, especially of a strong culture, on an organization's effectiveness. Below, we consider culture's impact on change, diversity, and mergers and acquisitions.

 Can organizational culture have a downside?

Barrier to Change

Culture is a liability when the shared values are not in agreement with those that will further the organization's effectiveness. For example, when an organization's environment is undergoing rapid change, its entrenched culture may no longer be appropriate.[62] Consistency of behaviour, an asset in a stable environment, may then burden the organization and make it difficult to respond to changes. For many organizations with strong cultures, practices that led to previous successes can lead to failure when those practices no longer match up well with environmental needs.[63]

Barrier to Diversity

Hiring new employees who differ from the majority in race, gender, disability, or other characteristics creates a paradox:[64] Management demonstrates support for the differences that these employees bring to the workplace, but newcomers who wish to fit in must accept the organization's core cultural values. Because diverse behaviours and unique strengths are likely to diminish as people attempt to assimilate, strong cultures can become liabilities when they effectively eliminate these advantages.

By limiting the range of values and styles that are acceptable, strong cultures put considerable pressure on employees to conform. It's not a coincidence that employees at Disney theme parks appear to be almost universally attractive, clean, and wholesome-looking, with bright smiles. That is the image Walt Disney Company wants to project. It selects employees who will maintain that image. Once the theme-park employees are on the job, a strong culture—supported by formal rules and regulations—ensures that they will act in a relatively uniform and predictable way.

Organizations seek out and hire diverse individuals because of the new strengths these people bring to the workplace. Yet these diverse behaviours and strengths are likely to diminish in strong cultures as people try to fit in. Strong cultures, therefore, can be liabilities when they effectively eliminate the unique strengths that people of different backgrounds bring to the organization. Moreover, strong cultures can also be liabilities when they support institutional bias or become insensitive to people who are different.

Barrier to Mergers and Acquisitions

Historically, when management looked at merger or acquisition decisions, the key factors were related to financial advantages or product synergy. In recent years, cultural compatibility has become the primary concern.[65] All things being equal, whether the merger or acquisition actually works seems to have more to do with how well the two organizations' cultures match up.

Strategies for Merging Cultures

Organizations can use several strategies when considering how to merge the cultures of two organizations:[66]

- *Assimilation.* The entire new organization is determined to take on the culture of one of the merging organizations. This strategy works best when one of the organizations has a relatively weak culture. However, if a culture is simply imposed on an organization, it rarely works.

- *Separation.* The organizations remain separate and keep their individual cultures. This strategy works best when the organizations have little overlap in the industries in which they operate.

- *Integration.* A new culture is formed by merging parts of each of the organizations. This strategy works best when aspects of each organization's culture need to be improved.

Potential merger partners might do well to conduct a **bicultural audit** before concluding that a merger should occur. Through questionnaires, interviews, and/or focus groups, potential merger partners should examine differences in the "vision, values, structure, management practices and behaviours" of the merging parties.[67] This examination should indicate whether there are commonalities from which to build a successful merger, or differences that could cause extreme difficulties in merging the two organizations. If the decision after a bicultural audit is to merge, the management team should bridge any existing culture gaps by[68]

- Defining a structure that is appropriate for both organizations, along with a reorganization plan

- Identifying and implementing a management style that is appropriate for both organizations

- Reinforcing internal communication to make sure that employees are kept aware of changes that will occur

- Getting agreement on what will be considered in performance evaluations, including expected behaviours and performance criteria

Changing Organizational Culture

 How do you change organizational culture?

Boston Pizza co-owners Jim Treliving and George Melville did not actually found the company.[69] It was started in Edmonton in 1964 by Greek immigrant Gus Agioritis. Treliving was an RCMP officer who became excited about the Boston Pizza concept, and opened his first franchise restaurant in Penticton, BC. In 1973, Melville became Treliving's business partner, after being his accountant for four years. By 1983, the two men owned 16 of the Boston Pizza restaurants, and decided to buy the entire Western-Canada–based chain of 46 restaurants. They hoped to expand the chain across the country.

To achieve a successful expansion, Treliving and Melville recognized the importance of introducing a number of systems and operating standards that would apply to all of the restaurants. They developed the Three Pillar Success Strategy, "which emphasizes continually improving guest experience, franchise profitability and building the brand, to promote expansion." The strategy is continuously communicated to all members of the organization. As president Mark Pacinda says: "We make sure we're constantly communicating and being very consistent with our message, our goals and our objectives." Why have Treliving and Melville been so successful in creating an organizational culture that enabled a small franchise to expand across the country?

Trying to change the culture of an organization is quite difficult and requires that many aspects of the organization change at the same time, especially the reward structure. Culture is such a challenge to change because it often represents the established mindset of employees and managers.

John Kotter, professor of leadership at Harvard Business School, has created a detailed approach to implementing change, which we discuss in Chapter 14.[70] Efforts directed at changing organizational culture do not usually yield immediate or dramatic results. Cultural change is actually a lengthy process—measured in years, not months. But we can ask the question, "Can culture be changed?" And the answer is, "Yes!" This

bicultural audit An examination of the differences between two potential merger partners prior to a merger to determine whether the cultures will be able to work together.

chapter's *Point/Counterpoint* on page 386 outlines the conditions under which cultural change is most likely to occur.

Below we consider two particular kinds of changes organizations might want to make to their culture: creating an ethical culture and creating a positive organizational culture.

Creating an Ethical Culture

The organizational culture most likely to shape high ethical standards among its members is one that is high in risk tolerance, low to moderate in aggressiveness, and focuses on means, as well as outcomes.[71] This type of culture also takes a long-term perspective and balances the rights of multiple stakeholders, including the communities in which the business operates, its employees, and its stockholders. Managers are supported for taking risks and innovating, are discouraged from engaging in unbridled competition, and guided to pay attention not just to *what* goals are achieved but also to *how*.

If the culture is strong and supports high ethical standards, it should have a very powerful and positive influence on employee behaviour. Johnson & Johnson, for example, has a strong culture that has long stressed corporate obligations to customers, employees, the community, and shareholders, in that order. When poisoned Tylenol (a Johnson & Johnson product) was found on store shelves some years ago, company employees across the United States independently pulled the product from these stores before management had even issued a statement about the tampering. No one had to tell these individuals what was morally right; they knew what Johnson & Johnson would expect them to do.

What can management do to create a more ethical culture? Research suggests managers can have an effect on the ethical behaviour of employees by adhering to the following principles:[72]

- *Be a visible role model.* Employees will look to the actions of top management as a benchmark for appropriate behaviour. Senior managers who take the ethical high road provide a positive message for all employees.

- *Communicate ethical expectations.* Minimize ethical ambiguities by creating and disseminating an organizational code of ethics. It should state the organization's primary values and the ethical rules that employees are expected to follow.

- *Provide ethics training.* Set up seminars, workshops, and similar ethics training programs. Use these to reinforce the organization's standards of conduct, to clarify what practices are and are not permissible, and to address possible ethical dilemmas.

- *Visibly reward ethical acts and punish unethical ones.* Include in managers' performance appraisals a point-by-point evaluation of how their decisions measured against the organization's code of ethics. Review the means taken to achieve goals, as well as the ends themselves. Visibly reward those who act ethically. Just as importantly, conspicuously punish unethical acts.

- *Provide protective mechanisms.* Provide formal mechanisms so employees can discuss ethical dilemmas and report unethical behaviour without fear of reprimand. These might include ethics counsellors, ombudspersons, or ethics officers.

Setting a positive ethical climate has to start at the top of the organization.[73] A study of 195 managers demonstrated that when top management emphasizes strong ethical values, supervisors are more likely to practise ethical leadership. This positive ethical attitude transfers down to line employees, who show lower levels of deviant behaviour and higher levels of cooperation and assistance. The general ethical behaviour and attitudes of other members of the department matter too for shaping individual ethical behaviour. Finally, employees whose ethical values are similar to those of their department are more likely to be promoted, so we can think of ethical culture as flowing from the bottom up as well.[74]

Creating a Positive Organizational Culture

At first blush, creating a positive culture may sound hopelessly naive, or like a Dilbert-style conspiracy. The one thing that makes us believe this trend is here to stay is that there are signs that management practice and OB research are converging.

A **positive organizational culture** emphasizes building on employee strengths, rewards more often than it punishes, and emphasizes individual vitality and growth.[75] Let's consider each of these areas.

Building on Employee Strengths

A lot of OB, and management practice, considers how to fix employee problems. Although a positive organizational culture does not ignore problems, it emphasizes showing employees how they can capitalize on their strengths. As management guru Peter Drucker said, "Most [employees] do not know what their strengths are. When you ask them, they look at you with a blank stare, or they respond in terms of subject knowledge, which is the wrong answer." Do you know what your strengths are? Wouldn't it be better to be in an organizational culture that helped you discover those, and learn ways to make the most of them?

Larry Hammond used this approach—finding and exploiting employee strengths—when you would least expect it: during the darkest days of his business. Hammond is CEO of Auglaize Provico, an agribusiness company. The company was in the midst of its worst financial struggles and had to lay off one-quarter of its workforce. At that low point, Hammond decided to try a different approach. Rather than dwell on what was wrong, he took advantage of what was right. "If you really want to [excel], you have to know yourself—you have to know what you're good at, and you have to know what you're not so good at," says Hammond. With the help of Gallup consultant Barry Conchie, Auglaize Provico focused on discovering and using employee strengths and helped turn the company around. "You ask Larry [Hammond] what the difference is, and he'll say that it's individuals using their natural talents," says Conchie.[76]

Rewarding More Often Than Punishing

Although most organizations are sufficiently focused on extrinsic rewards like pay and promotions, they often forget about the power of smaller (and cheaper) rewards like praise. Part of creating a positive organizational culture is "catching employees doing something right." Another part is articulating praise. Many managers withhold praise either because they are afraid employees will coast, or because they think praise is not valued. Because employees generally don't ask for praise, managers usually don't realize the costs of failing to do it. Failing to praise can become a "silent killer" like escalating blood pressure.

Take the example of Elzbieta Górska-Kolodziejczyk, a plant manager for International Paper's facility in Kwidzyn, Poland. The job environment at the plant is bleak and difficult. Employees work in a windowless basement. Staffing is only roughly one-third of its prior level, while production has tripled. These challenges had done in the previous three managers. So when Górska-Kolodziejczyk took over, she knew she had her work cut out for her. Although she had many items on her list of ways to transform the organization, at the top of her list was recognition and praise. She initially found it difficult to give praise to those who were not used to it, especially men. "They were like cement at the beginning," she said. "Like cement." Over time, however, she found they valued and even reciprocated praise. One day a department supervisor pulled her over to tell her she was doing a good job. "This I do remember, yes," she said.[77]

positive organizational culture
A culture that emphasizes building on employee strengths, rewards more than punishes, and emphasizes individual vitality and growth.

Emphasizing Vitality and Growth

A positive organizational culture emphasizes not only organizational effectiveness, but individuals' growth as well. No organization will get the best out of employees who see themselves as mere tools or parts of the organization. A positive culture realizes the difference between a job and a career and supports not only what the employee does to contribute to organizational effectiveness, but also what the organization can do to make the employee more effective (personally and professionally).

Limits of Positive Culture

Is a positive culture the answer to all organizational problems? Though companies such as WestJet, GE, Xerox, Boeing, and 3M have embraced aspects of a positive organizational culture, it is a new enough area that there is some uncertainty about how and when it works best.

Not all cultures value being positive as much as Canadian and US cultures do, and, even within these countries, there surely are limits to how far we should go to preserve a positive culture. For example, Admiral, a British insurance company, has established a Ministry of Fun in its call centres to organize such events as poem writings, foosball, conker (a British game involving chestnuts) competitions, and fancy dress days. When does the pursuit of a positive culture start to seem coercive or even Orwellian? As one critic notes, "Promoting a social orthodoxy of positiveness focuses on a particular constellation of desirable states and traits but, in so doing, can stigmatize those who fail to fit the template."[78]

Our point is that there may be benefits to establishing a positive culture, but an organization also needs to be careful to be objective and not pursue it past the point of effectiveness.

GLOBAL **IMPLICATIONS**

We considered global cultural values (collectivism and individualism, power distance, and so on) in Chapter 3. Here, our focus is a bit narrower: How is organizational culture affected by a global context?

Organizational cultures often reflect national culture. The culture at AirAsia, a Malaysian-based airline, emphasizes informal dress so as not to create status differences. The carrier has lots of parties, participative management, and no private offices, reflecting Malaysia's relatively collectivistic culture. However, the culture of Air Canada does not reflect the same degree of informality. If Air Canada were to set up operations in Malaysia or merge with AirAsia, it would need to take these cultural differences into account. So when an organization opens up operations in another country, it ignores the local culture at its own risk.

Three times a week, employees at the Canadian unit of Japanese video game maker Tecmo Koei begin the day by standing next to their desks, facing their boss, and saying "Good morning" in unison. Employees then deliver short speeches on topics that range from corporate principles to 3D game engines. Tecmo Koei also has employees punch a time clock and asks women to serve tea to top executive guests. Although these practices are consistent with Tecmo Koei's culture, they do not fit Canadian culture very well. "It's kind of like school," says one Canadian employee.[79]

The management of ethical behaviour is one area where national culture can rub up against corporate culture.[80] Many strategies for improving ethical behaviour are based on the values and beliefs of the host country. Canadian managers tend to endorse the supremacy of anonymous market forces and implicitly or explicitly view profit maximization as a moral obligation for business organizations. This worldview sees bribery, nepotism, and favouring personal contacts as highly unethical. Any action that deviates from profit maximization may indicate that inappropriate or corrupt behaviour may be

LESSONS LEARNED

- Reward systems generally signal the parts of the organizational culture that are valued.
- Culture can have both positive and negative effects on organizations.
- Organizational culture can make change difficult, if not impossible.

occurring. In contrast, managers in developing economies are more likely to see ethical decisions as embedded in a social environment. That means doing special favours for family and friends is not only appropriate but may even be an ethical responsibility. Managers in many nations also view capitalism skeptically and believe the interests of employees should be put on a par with the interests of shareholders.

Summary and Implications

1 What is the purpose of organizational culture? *Organizational culture* is a system of shared meaning held by members that distinguishes the organization from other organizations. Culture provides stability to an organization and gives employees a clear understanding of "the way things are done around here." Culture performs a number of functions within an organization. First, it creates distinctions between one organization and others. Second, it conveys a sense of identity to organization members. Third, it helps create commitment to the organization. Fourth, it's the social glue that helps hold the organization together. Finally, it helps employees make sense of the organization. Organizations can have subcultures, with individual groups or teams creating their own cultures that may not completely reflect the overall organizational culture.

2 How do you read an organization's culture? Organizations differ in the extent to which they can be characterized as having strong or weak cultures. In a strong culture, the organization's core values are both intensely held and widely shared. In a weak culture, employees do not feel any great attachment to their organization or their co-workers. The artifacts of culture inform outsiders and employees about the underlying values and beliefs of the organization's culture. These artifacts—or aspects of an organization's culture that you see, hear, and feel—include stories, rituals, material symbols, and language, and can be used to help people read the organization's culture.

3 How do you create and maintain organizational culture? The original culture of an organization is derived from the philosophy of its founders. That philosophy then influences what types of employees are hired. The culture of the organization is then reinforced by top management, who signal what is acceptable behaviour and what is not. Employees are socialized into the culture, and will be more easily socialized to the extent that the employee's values match those of the organization.

4 Can organizational culture have a downside? Many of culture's functions are valuable for both the organization and the employee. Culture enhances organizational commitment and increases the consistency of employee behaviour. Culture also reduces ambiguity for employees by telling them what is important and how things are done. However, a strong culture can have negative effects. Culture can act as a barrier to change, it can make it difficult to create an inclusive environment, and it can hinder the success of mergers and acquisitions.

5 How do you change organizational culture? Changing organizational culture is not easy. It is not unusual for managers to try changing the structure, the technology, or the people, but this often is not enough. Because culture is the shared beliefs within the organizations, it influences all of the activities in which people engage. Thus, it's important to change the reward structure, and to work carefully to change employee beliefs, in order to get real culture change. Organizations may want to change their culture to an ethical culture or a positive organizational culture. An ethical culture signals that a company values an ethical climate and the ethical behaviour of its members. A positive organizational culture emphasizes employee strengths, rewards more often than it punishes, and emphasizes individuals' vitality and growth.

OB at Work

for Review

1. What are the levels of organizational culture?

2. Why do subcultures develop in an organization?

3. Can an employee survive in an organization if he or she rejects its core values? Explain.

4. How can an outsider assess an organization's culture?

5. How is language related to organizational culture?

6. What benefits can socialization provide for the organization? For the new employee?

7. How does a strong culture affect an organization's efforts to improve diversity?

8. Identify the steps a manager can take to implement cultural change in an organization.

9. What is a positive organizational culture?

for Critical Thinking

1. Is socialization brainwashing? Explain.

2. If management sought a culture characterized as innovative and autonomous, what might its socialization program look like?

3. Can you identify a set of characteristics that describe your college's or university's culture? Compare them with what several of your peers have noted. How closely do they agree?

4. "We should be opposed to the manipulation of individuals for organizational purposes, but a degree of social uniformity enables organizations to work better." Do you agree or disagree with this statement? What are its implications for organizational culture? Discuss.

5. Today's workforce is increasingly made up of part-time or contingent employees. Is organizational culture really important if the workforce is mostly temporary employees?

for You

- Increase your understanding of culture by looking for similarities and differences across groups and organizations. For instance, do you have two courses where the classroom environment differs considerably? What does this suggest about the underlying assumptions in teaching students? Similarly, compare customer service at two local coffee shops or sandwich shops. What does the employee behaviour suggest about each organization's culture?

- Carefully consider the culture of any organization at which you are thinking of being employed. You will feel more comfortable in cultures that share your values and expectations. You may find yourself reacting very negatively if an organization's culture (and values) does not match your own.

- Keep in mind that groups create mini-cultures of their own. When you work in a group on a student project, be aware of the values and norms that are being supported early on in the group's life. These will greatly influence the group's culture.

Organizational Culture Does Not Change

An organization's culture is made up of relatively stable characteristics. It develops over many years and is rooted in deeply held values to which employees are strongly committed. In addition, there are a number of forces continually operating to maintain a given culture. These would include written statements about the organization's mission and philosophy; the design of physical spaces and buildings; the dominant leadership style; hiring criteria; past promotion practices; entrenched rituals; popular stories about key people and events; the organization's historical performance evaluation criteria; and the organization's formal structure.

Selection and promotion policies are particularly important devices that work against cultural change. Employees chose the organization because they perceived their values to be a "good fit" with those of the organization. They become comfortable with that fit and will strongly resist efforts to disturb the equilibrium.

Those in control in organizations will also select senior managers who will continue the current culture. Even attempts to change a culture by going outside the organization to hire a new chief executive are unlikely to be effective. The evidence indicates that the culture is more likely to change the executive than the other way around. Why? It's too entrenched, and change becomes a potential threat to member self-interest.

We're not saying that culture can never be changed. In the unusual case when an organization confronts a survival-threatening crisis—a crisis that is universally acknowledged as a true life-or-death situation—members of the organization will be responsive to efforts at cultural change. However, anything less than a crisis is unlikely to be effective in bringing about cultural change.

How to Change an Organization's Culture

Changing an organization's culture is extremely difficult, but it *can* be done. The evidence suggests that cultural change is most likely to occur when most or all of the following conditions exist:

- *A dramatic crisis.* This is the shock that undermines the status quo and calls into question the relevance of the current culture. Examples of these crises might be a surprising financial setback, the loss of a major customer, or a dramatic technological breakthrough by a competitor.

- *Turnover in leadership.* New top leadership, which can provide an alternative set of key values, may be perceived as more capable of responding to the crisis. Top leadership definitely refers to the organization's chief executive, but also might need to include all senior management positions.

- *Young and small organization.* The younger the organization, the less entrenched its culture will be. It's also easier for management to communicate its new values when the organization is small.

- *Weak culture.* The more widely held a culture is, and the higher the agreement among members on its values, the more difficult it will be to change. Weak cultures are more open to change than strong ones.

LEARNING ABOUT **YOURSELF** EXERCISE

What Kind of Organizational Culture Fits You Best?

For each of the following statements, circle the level of agreement or disagreement that you personally feel:

SA	=	**Strongly Agree**
A	=	**Agree**
U	=	**Uncertain**
D	=	**Disagree**
SD	=	**Strongly disagree**

1. I like being part of a team and having my performance assessed in terms of my contribution to the team. SA A U D SD

2. No person's needs should be compromised in order for a department to achieve its goals. SA A U D SD

3. I like the thrill and excitement from taking risks. SA A U D SD

4. If a person's job performance is inadequate, it's irrelevant how much effort he or she made. SA A U D SD

5. I like things to be stable and predictable. SA A U D SD

6. I prefer managers who provide detailed and rational explanations for their decisions. SA A U D SD

7. I like to work where there isn't a great deal of pressure and where people are essentially easygoing. SA A U D SD

Scoring Key:

For items 1, 2, 3, 4, and 7, score as follows: Strongly agree = +2, Agree = +1, Uncertain = 0, Disagree = –1, Strongly disagree = –2.

For items 5 and 6, reverse the score (Strongly agree = –2, and so on). Add up your total. Your score will fall somewhere between +14 and –14.

What does your score mean? The lower your score, the more comfortable you will be in a formal, mechanistic, rule-oriented, and structured culture. This is often associated with large corporations and government agencies. Positive scores indicate a preference for informal, humanistic, flexible, and innovative cultures, which are more likely to be found in research units, advertising firms, high-tech companies, and small businesses.

SELF-ASSESSMENT LIBRARY   LEARNING ABOUT YOURSELF

More Learning About Yourself Exercises

An additional self-assessment relevant to this chapter appears on MyOBLab (**www.pearsoned.ca/myoblab**).

III.B.2   How Committed Am I to My Organization?

When you complete the additional assessment, consider the following:

1. Am I surprised about my score?

2. Would my friends evaluate me similarly?

BREAKOUT **GROUP** EXERCISES

Form small groups to discuss the following topics, as assigned by your instructor:

1. Choose 2 courses that you are taking this term, ideally in different faculties, and describe the culture of the classroom in each. What are the similarities and differences? What values about learning might you infer from your observations of culture?

2. Identify artifacts of culture in your current or previous workplace. From these artifacts, would you conclude that the organization had a strong or weak culture?

3. Have you or someone you know worked somewhere where the culture was strong? What was your reaction to that strong culture? Did you like that environment, or would you prefer to work where there is a weaker culture? Why?

WORKING WITH **OTHERS** EXERCISE

Rate Your Classroom Culture

Listed here are 14 statements. Using the 5-item scale (from Strongly Agree to Strongly Disagree), respond to each statement by circling the number that best represents your opinion.

	Strongly Agree	Agree	Neutral	Disagree	Strongly Disagree
1. I feel comfortable challenging statements made by my instructor.	5	4	3	2	1
2. My instructor heavily penalizes assignments that are not turned in on time.	1	2	3	4	5
3. My instructor believes that "it's final results that count."	1	2	3	4	5
4. My instructor is sensitive to my personal needs and problems.	5	4	3	2	1
5. A large portion of my grade depends on how well I work with others in the class.	5	4	3	2	1
6. I often feel nervous and tense when I come to class.	1	2	3	4	5
7. My instructor seems to prefer stability over change.	1	2	3	4	5
8. My instructor encourages me to develop new and different ideas.	5	4	3	2	1
9. My instructor has little tolerance for sloppy thinking.	1	2	3	4	5
10. My instructor is more concerned with how I came to a conclusion than with the conclusion itself.	5	4	3	2	1
11. My instructor treats all students alike.	1	2	3	4	5
12. My instructor frowns on class members helping each other with assignments.	1	2	3	4	5
13. Aggressive and competitive people have a distinct advantage in this class.	1	2	3	4	5
14. My instructor encourages me to see the world differently.	5	4	3	2	1

Scoring Key:

Calculate your total score by adding up the numbers you circled. Your score will fall between 14 and 70.

A high score (49 or above) describes an open, risk-taking, supportive, humanistic, team-oriented, easy-going, growth-oriented culture. A low score (35 or below) describes a closed, structured, task-oriented, individualistic, tense, and stability-oriented culture. Note that differences count, so a score of 60 is a more open culture than one that scores 50. Also, realize that one culture isn't preferable over another. The "right" culture depends on you and your preferences for a learning environment.

Form teams of 5 to 7 members each. Compare your scores. How closely do they align? Discuss and resolve any discrepancies. Based on your team's analysis, what type of student do you think would perform best in this class?

ETHICAL **DILEMMA** EXERCISE

Is There Room for Snooping in an Organization's Culture?

Although some of the spying Hewlett-Packard performed on some members of its board of directors appeared to violate California law, much of it was legal. Moreover, many companies spy on their employees—sometimes with and sometimes without their knowledge or consent. Organizations differ in their culture of surveillance. Some differences are due to the type of business. A US Department of Defense contractor has more reason—perhaps even an obligation—to spy on its employees than does an orange juice producer.

However, surveillance in most industries is on the upswing. There are several reasons for this, including the huge growth of two sectors with theft and security problems (services and information technology, respectively) and the increased availability of surveillance technology.

Consider the following surveillance actions and, for each action, decide whether it would never be ethical (mark *N*), would sometimes be ethical (mark *S*), or would always be ethical (mark *A*). For those you mark *S*, indicate what factors your judgment would depend on.

1. Sifting through an employee's trash for evidence of wrongdoing

2. Periodically reading email messages for disclosure of confidential information or inappropriate use

3. Conducting video surveillance of workspace

4. Monitoring websites visited by employees and determining the appropriateness and work-relatedness of those visited

5. Taping phone conversations

6. Posing as a job candidate, an investor, a customer, or a colleague (when the real purpose is to solicit information)

Would you be less likely to work for an employer that engaged in some of these methods? Why or why not? Do you think use of surveillance says something about an organization's culture?

CASE INCIDENTS

Is a 5S Culture for You?

Jay Scovie looked at his workspace.[81] He took pride in how nice and tidy he had made it look. As it turns out, his pride was misplaced. Sweeping visible clutter from your workspace by packing it into boxes hidden in a closet was not acceptable to his employer, Japanese manufacturer Kyocera. Scovie's habit drew the attention of Dan Brown, Kyocera's newly appointed inspector. "It became a topic of repeated conversation," Scovie said.

Why the obsession with order? Kyocera has joined a growing list of organizations that base their culture on 5S, a concept borrowed from lean manufacturing and based on five phases or principles:

1. **Sorting** *(Seiri).* Going through all tools, materials, and supplies so as to keep only what is essential.

2. **Straightening** *(Seiton).* Arranging tools, supplies, equipment, and parts in a manner that promotes maximum efficiency. For everything there should be a place, and everything should be in its place.

3. **Shining** *(Seiso).* Systematic cleaning to make the workplace and workspace as clean and neat as possible. At the end of the shift or workday, everything is left as it was when the workday started.

4. **Standardizing** *(Seiketsu).* Knowing exactly what your responsibilities are to keep the first three S's.

5. **Sustaining** *(Shitsuke).* Maintaining and reviewing standards, rigorous review, and inspection to ensure order does not slowly slip back into disorder or chaos.

Other companies are following Kyocera in making 5S an important part of their culture, including London, Ontario-based 3M Canada, Markham, Ontario-based Steelcase, and St. Thomas, Ontario-based Waltec. Lawn mower manufacturer Toro organizes printer output according to 5S principles, and Virginia Mason Hospital in Seattle uses 5S to coordinate office space and arrange the placement of medical equipment, such as stethoscopes. Paul Levy, president and CEO of Beth Israel Deaconess Medical Center in Boston, has used 5S to reduce errors and time lost searching for equipment.

At Kyocera, Brown exercises some discretion—he asked one employee to remove a hook on her door while allowing another to keep a whale figurine on her desk. "You have to figure out how to balance being too picky with upholding the purpose of the program," he said. While Brown was happy with Scovie's desk (if not the closet), he wanted to look inside. Scovie tried to redirect the conversation but relented when Brown pressed. Inside one of Scovie's desk drawers was a box full of CDs, small electronic devices, and items Kyocera no longer makes. "Obviously, we're at the sorting stage here," Scovie told Brown.

Questions

1. What would you see as the value in Kyocera using 5S?

2. What are some advantages and disadvantages of trying to impose a similar culture in Canadian companies?

3. What might your response be to having to engage in the 5S principles in your workplace?

Wegmans Hires for Passion

Typically, grocery stores are not thought of as great places to work.[82] Hours are anything but 9 to 5, and the pay is low compared with other occupations. The result is an industry that sees high annual turnover rates. However, employees at Wegmans, an American chain, view working for a grocer a bit differently. Instead of viewing their job as a temporary setback on the way to a more illustrious career, many employees at Wegmans view working for the grocer as their career. And given Wegmans' high profitability, it looks like the grocer will be around long enough to make such careers a reality for those who pursue them.

Why is Wegmans so effective? One reason is its culture. The chain began in 1930 when brothers John and Walter Wegman opened their first grocery store. One of its distinguishing features was a café that seated 300 customers. The store's immediate focus on fine foods quickly separated it from other grocers—a focus that is maintained by the company's employees, many of whom are hired based on their interest in food.

In 1950, Walter's son, Robert, became president and immediately added a generous number of employee benefits, such as profit sharing and medical coverage, completely paid for by the company. What was Robert's reason for offering such great benefits? "I was no different from them," he said, referring to the company's employees.

Now, Robert's son, Danny, is president of the company, and he has continued the Wegmans tradition of taking care of its employees. To date, Wegmans has paid for college and university scholarships for a number of its employees, both full time and part time. In addition to benefits, employees receive pay that is well above the market average. As a result, annual turnover at Wegmans for full-time employees is a mere 6 percent, compared with an industry average of 24 percent.

The culture that has developed at Wegmans is an important part of the company's success. Employees are proud to say they work at Wegmans. For example, Sara Goggins, a 19-year-old college student who works part time at Wegmans, recalls when Danny Wegman personally complimented her on a store display that she helped set up. "I love this place," she says. "If teaching doesn't work out, I would so totally work at Wegmans." And Kelly Schoeneck, a store manager, recounts that a few years ago, her supervisor asked her to analyze a frequent-shopper program that a competitor had recently adopted.

Though she assumed that her supervisor would take credit for her findings, Schoeneck's supervisor had her present her findings directly to Robert Wegman.

Maintaining a culture of driven, happy, and loyal employees who are eager to help one another is not easy. Wegmans carefully selects each employee, and growth is often slow and meticulous, with only two new stores opened each year. When a new store is opened, employees from existing stores are brought in to the new store to maintain the culture. The existing employees are then able to transmit their knowledge and the store's values to new employees.

Managers especially are ingrained in the Wegmans culture. More than half started working at Wegmans when they were teenagers. One observer says, "When you're a 16-year-old kid, the last thing you want to do is wear a geeky shirt and work for a supermarket. But at Wegmans, it's a badge of honor. You are not a geeky cashier. You are part of the social fabric."

Employees at Wegmans are not selected based on intellectual ability or experience alone. "Just about everybody in the store has some genuine interest in food," states Jeff Burris, a store supervisor. Those employees who do not express this interest may not fit in and are sometimes not hired.

Questions

1. Would you characterize Wegmans' culture as strong or weak? Why? How is the strength of the culture at Wegmans likely to affect its employees, particularly new hires?

2. Wegmans attempts to maintain its core cultural values by hiring individuals who are passionate about the food industry and by staffing new stores partly with existing employees. What are some advantages and disadvantages of trying to impose a similar culture throughout different areas of a company?

3. What is the primary source of Wegmans' culture, and what are some ways that it has been able to sustain itself?

4. How might stories and rituals play a role in maintaining Wegmans' corporate culture?

FROM CONCEPTS TO SKILLS

How to "Read" an Organization's Culture

The ability to read and assess an organization's culture can be a valuable skill.[83]

If you are looking for a job, you will want to choose an employer whose culture is compatible with your values and in which you will feel comfortable. If you can accurately assess a prospective employer's culture before you make your decision, you may be able to save yourself a lot of grief and reduce the likelihood of making a poor choice. Similarly, you will undoubtedly have business transactions with numerous organizations during your professional career. You will be trying to sell a product or service, negotiate a contract, or arrange a joint venture, or you may merely be seeking out which individual in an organization controls certain decisions. The ability to assess another organization's culture can be a definite plus in successfully completing these pursuits.

For the sake of simplicity, we will approach the problem of reading an organization's culture from the point of view of a job applicant. We will assume you are interviewing for a job. Here is a list of things you can do to help learn about a potential employer's culture:

- Observe the physical surroundings. Pay attention to signs, pictures, style of dress, length of hair, degree of openness between offices, and office furnishings and arrangements.
- With whom did you meet? Just the person who would be your immediate manager? Or potential colleagues, managers from other departments, or senior executives? Based on what they revealed, to what degree do people other than the immediate manager have input into the hiring decision?
- How would you characterize the style of the people you met? Formal? Casual? Serious? Jovial?
- Does the organization have formal rules and regulations printed in a human resource policy manual? If so, how detailed are these policies?
- Ask questions of the people you meet. The most valid and reliable information tends to come from asking the same questions of many people (to see how closely their responses align) and by talking with boundary spanners. *Boundary spanners* are employees whose work links them to the external environment and includes jobs such as human resource interviewer, salesperson, purchasing agent, labour negotiator, public relations specialist, and company lawyer.

Questions that will give you insights into organizational processes and practices might include the following:

- What is the background of the founders?
- What is the background of current senior managers? What are their functional specializations? Were they promoted from within or hired from outside?
- How does the organization integrate new employees? Is there an orientation program? Training? If so, could you describe these features?
- How does your manager define his or her job success? (Amount of profit? Serving customers? Meeting deadlines? Acquiring budget increases?)

- How would you define fairness in terms of reward allocations?
- Can you identify some people here who are on the "fast track"? What do you think has put them on the fast track?
- Can you identify someone who seems to be considered a deviant in the organization? How has the organization responded to this person?
- Can you describe a decision that someone made here that was well received?
- Can you describe a decision that did not work out well? What were the consequences for the decision maker?
- Could you describe a crisis or critical event that has occurred recently in the organization? How did top management respond? What was learned from this experience?

Practising Skills

After spending your first three years after college graduation as a freelance graphic designer, you are looking at pursuing a job as an account executive at a graphic design firm. You feel that the scope of assignments and potential for technical training far exceed what you would be able to do on your own, and you are looking to expand your skills and meet a brand-new set of challenges. However, you want to make sure you "fit" in to the organization where you are going to be spending more than eight hours every workday. What is the best way for you to find a place where you will be happy, and where your style and personality will be appreciated?

Reinforcing Skills

1. Do some comparisons of the atmosphere or feeling you get from various organizations. Because of the number and wide variety that you will find, it will probably be easiest for you to do this exercise using restaurants, retail stores, or banks. Based on the atmosphere that you observe, what type of organizational culture do you think these organizations might have? If you can, interview three employees at each organization for their descriptions of their organization's culture.

2. Think about changes (major and minor) that you have dealt with over the past year. Perhaps these changes involved other people and perhaps they were personal. Did you resist the change? Did others resist the change? How did you overcome your resistance or the resistance of others to the change?

Leadership

Lieutenant Colonel Maryse Carmichael leads Canada's Snowbirds, the country's top military aerobatic team. In her role, she faces many exciting challenges, including finding new ways to capture the hearts and minds of a nation. So what does it take to lead at an elite level?

LEARNING OUTCOMES

1. What is the difference between a manager and a leader?

2. Are there specific traits, behaviours, and situations that affect how one leads?

3. How does a leader lead with vision?

4. Are there leadership roles for nonmanagers?

5. What are some of the contemporary issues in leadership?

eadership in a team setting is something that Lieutenant Colonel Maryse Carmichael knows a lot about.[1] Since May 2010 she has been the Commanding Officer (CO) of the 431 Air Demonstration Squadron, better known as Canada's Snowbirds. Carmichael is responsible for 14 pilots and 71 ground employees, and she knows the importance of maintaining strong relationships with her staff. In fact, it was the military's desire to promote strong relationships that led to the creation of her position.

Previously, the squadron's CO had always been a Major and a flying member of the demonstration team. With so many staff on the ground, however, it became hard to manage personnel effectively while on the road. The Canadian Forces created a new CO role at the Lieutenant Colonel level, responsible for administration and command of the fleet, maintenance, and personnel. Carmichael's two decades of experience with the Canadian Air Force in a number of flying and non-flying roles made her a natural choice for the newly defined position. She entered the job having established the trust and respect of both pilots and ground personnel, since she had proven herself in both areas.

Carmichael believes that working with the Snowbirds provides an opportunity for leadership at two levels. "For me it is about looking at the overall operations of the entire squadron and the future of the squadron." But it is also about a broader kind of leadership. "We demonstrate to the Canadian public the skills, professionalism, and teamwork of the Canadian Forces." For Carmichael, it is not enough to inspire her own team; she seeks to inspire an entire nation.

In this chapter, we review leadership studies to determine what makes an effective leader. We consider factors that affect one's ability to lead and examine inspirational leadership and self-management. Finally, we discuss contemporary issues in leadership.

OB IS FOR EVERYONE

- Have you ever wondered if there was one *right* way to lead?
- Can anyone be a leader?
- How do you manage yourself?
- Do men and women lead differently?

Are Managers and Leaders the Same?

1 What is the difference between a manager and a leader?

BLOG IT

What is your leadership style?
What do you do to encourage others to join you in achieving a goal?
www.obstudentjournals.blogspot.com

Leadership and *management* are two terms that are often confused. What is the difference between them?

John Kotter of the Harvard Business School argues that "managers promote stability while leaders press for change and only organizations that embrace both sides of the contradiction can survive in turbulent times."[2]

McGill University professor Rabindra Kanungo notes there is a growing consensus emerging "among management scholars that the concept of 'leadership' must be distinguished from the concept of 'supervision/management.'"[3] Exhibit 11-1 illustrates Kanungo's distinctions between leadership and management. Leaders establish direction by developing a vision of the future; then they align people by communicating this vision and inspiring them to overcome hurdles. In other words, leaders need to develop followers. Managers implement the vision and strategy provided by leaders, coordinate and staff the organization, and handle day-to-day problems. Organizations need strong leadership *and* strong management for optimal effectiveness.

In our discussion of leadership, we will focus on two major tasks of those who lead in organizations: managing those around them to get the day-to-day tasks done, and inspiring others to do the extraordinary. It will become clear that successful leaders rely on a variety of interpersonal skills in order to encourage others to perform at their best. It will also become clear that, no matter the place in the hierarchy, from CEO to team leader, a variety of individuals can be called on to perform leadership roles.

Leadership as Supervision

2 Are there specific traits, behaviours, and situations that affect how one leads?

Lt.-Col. Maryse Carmichael served as a Snowbird pilot from early 2000 until late 2001, at which point she received a promotion to an Executive Officer role, followed by relocation to the air force base at Bagotville, Quebec.[4] She says that returning to the Snowbirds as Commanding Officer has given her a new perspective on leadership: "This time around it is really about the entire squadron, about leading the men and women of 431 Squadron to accomplish our mission every day. So it has a broader focus this time."

EXHIBIT 11-1 Distinguishing Leadership from Management

Management	Leadership
1. Engages in day-to-day caretaker activities: Maintains and allocates resources	Formulates long-term objectives for reforming the system: Plans strategy and tactics
2. Exhibits supervisory behaviour: Acts to make others maintain standard job behaviour	Exhibits leading behaviour: Acts to bring about change in others congruent with long-term objectives
3. Administers subsystems within organizations	Innovates for the entire organization
4. Asks how and when to engage in standard practice	Asks what and why to change standard practice
5. Acts within established culture of the organization	Creates vision and meaning for the organization
6. Uses transactional influence: Induces compliance in manifest behaviour using rewards, sanctions, and formal authority	Uses transformational influence: Induces change in values, attitudes, and behaviour using personal examples and expertise
7. Relies on control strategies to get things done by subordinates	Uses empowering strategies to make followers internalize values
8. Status quo supporter and stabilizer	Status quo challenger and change creator

Source: Copyright 1998, Canadian Psychological Association. Permission granted for use of material.

Her focus on the big picture makes sense in more ways than one. Military jobs are unique in that roles and responsibilities are highly formalized and defined in great detail, and the level of compliance with policies and procedures is extremely high. Penalties for non-compliance are also highly formalized and follow standardized procedures. This helps senior officers maintain a strong focus on strategic decision making rather than on acting as supervisors, since lower level employees have full information and very little ambiguity about managing their day-to-day tasks. So, what makes an effective leader?

In this section, we discuss theories of leadership that were developed before 1980. These early theories focused on the supervisory nature of leadership—that is, how individuals managed the day-to-day functioning of employees. The theories took different approaches in understanding how best to lead in a supervisory capacity. The three general types of theories that emerged were (1) trait theories, which propose leaders have a particular set of traits that makes them different from nonleaders; (2) behavioural theories, which propose that particular behaviours make for better leaders; and (3) contingency theories, which propose the situation has an effect on leaders. When you think about these theories, remember that although they have been considered "theories of leadership," they rely on an older understanding of what "leadership" means, and they don't convey Kanungo's distinction between leadership and supervision.

Trait Theories: Are Leaders Different from Others?

Have you ever wondered whether there is some fundamental personality difference that makes some people "born leaders"? **Trait theories of leadership** focus on personal qualities and characteristics. We recognize leaders like South Africa's Nelson Mandela, Virgin Group CEO Richard Branson, and Apple co-founder Steve Jobs as *charismatic*, *enthusiastic*, and *courageous*. Trait theory emerged in the hope that if it were possible to identify the traits of leaders, it would be easier to select people to fill leadership roles. Being able to select good leaders is important because not all people know how to be good leaders, as *Focus on Research* shows.

FOCUS ON RESEARCH

Bad Bosses Everywhere

Doesn't leadership come naturally? Although much is expected of leaders, what is surprising is how rarely they seem to meet the most basic definitions of effectiveness.[5] A recent study of 700 employees revealed that many believe their supervisors don't give credit when it's due, gossip about them behind their backs, and don't keep their word. The situation is so bad that for many employees, the study's lead author says, "They don't leave their company, they leave their boss."

Key findings of the study are as follows:

- 39 percent said their supervisor failed to keep promises.
- 37 percent said their supervisor failed to give credit when due.
- 31 percent said their supervisor gave them the "silent treatment" in the past year.
- 27 percent said their supervisor made negative comments about them to other employees or managers.
- 24 percent said their supervisor invaded their privacy.
- 23 percent said their supervisor blames others to cover up mistakes or minimize embarrassment.

Why do companies promote such people into leadership positions? One reason may be the Peter Principle. When people are promoted into one job (say, as a supervisor or

---

trait theories of leadership
Theories that consider personal qualities and characteristics that differentiate leaders from nonleaders.

coach) based on how well they did another (say, salesperson or player), that assumes that the skills of one role are the same as the other. The only time such people stop being promoted is when they reach their level of incompetence. Judging from the results of this study, that level of leadership incompetence is reached all too often.

A 2010 study found that lack of respect for a leader by employees—for instance, when employees feel that the leader is not the best person for the job—has a significant impact on whether employees will follow that leader. The researchers found that simply naming someone "the leader" did not by itself create effective leadership.[6]

Research efforts at isolating leadership traits resulted in a number of dead ends. For instance, a review in the late 1960s of 20 studies identified nearly 80 leadership traits, but only 5 of these traits were common to 4 or more of the investigations.[7] By the 1990s, after numerous studies and analyses, about the best thing that could be said was that most "leaders are not like other people," but the particular traits that were isolated varied a great deal from review to review.[8] It was a pretty confusing state of affairs.

A breakthrough, of sorts, came when researchers began organizing traits around the Big Five Personality Model (see Chapter 2).[9] Most of the dozens of traits in various leadership reviews fit under one of the Big Five (ambition and energy are part of extraversion, for instance), giving strong support to traits as predictors of leadership.

A comprehensive review of the leadership literature, when organized around the Big Five, found extraversion to be the most important trait of effective leaders[10] but more strongly related to leader emergence than to leader effectiveness. Sociable and dominant people are more likely to assert themselves in group situations, but leaders need to make sure they are not too assertive—one study found that leaders who scored very high on assertiveness were less effective than those who were moderately high.[11]

Unlike agreeableness and emotional stability, conscientiousness and openness to experience also showed strong and consistent relationships to leadership, though not quite as strong as extraversion. Overall, the trait approach does have something to offer. Leaders who like being around people and are able to assert themselves (extraverted), are disciplined and keep commitments they make (conscientious), and are creative and flexible (open) do have an advantage when it comes to leadership, suggesting that good leaders do have key traits in common.

One reason is that conscientiousness and extraversion are positively related to leaders' self-efficacy, which explained most of the variance in subordinates' ratings of leader performance.[12] People are more likely to follow someone who is confident that she is going in the right direction.

Another trait that may indicate effective leadership is emotional intelligence (EI), discussed in Chapter 2. Advocates of EI argue that without it, a person can have outstanding training, a highly analytical mind, a compelling vision, and an endless supply of terrific ideas but still not make a great leader. This may be especially true as individuals move up in an organization.[13] Why is EI so critical to effective leadership? A core component of EI is empathy. Empathetic leaders can sense others' needs, listen to what followers say (and don't say), and read the reactions of others. As one leader noted, "The caring part of empathy, especially for the people with whom you work, is what inspires people to stay with a leader when the going gets rough. The mere fact that someone cares is more often than not rewarded with loyalty."[14]

The link between EI and leadership effectiveness is still much less investigated than other traits. One reviewer noted, "Speculating about the practical utility of the EI construct might be premature. Despite such warnings, EI is being viewed as a panacea for many organizational malaises with recent suggestions that EI is essential for leadership effectiveness."[15] But until more rigorous evidence accumulates, we cannot be confident about the connection.

Based on the latest findings, we offer two conclusions. First, traits can predict leadership. Twenty years ago, the evidence suggested otherwise. But this was probably because of the lack of a valid framework for classifying and organizing traits. The Big Five seem to have rectified that. Second, traits do a better job at predicting the emergence of leaders and the appearance of leadership than in actually distinguishing between *effective* and *ineffective* leaders.[16] The fact that an individual exhibits the traits and others consider that person to be a leader does not necessarily mean that the leader is successful at getting his or her group to achieve its goals. This chapter's *Point/Counterpoint* on page 423 raises further issues on whether leaders are born or made. *Case Incident—The Kinder, Gentler Leader?* on page 427 looks at the trend toward leaders who have a sensitive and caring style. *Case Incident—Moving from Colleague to Supervisor* on page 426 helps you think about the challenges one faces when moving from being a co-worker to taking on leadership responsibilities.

Behavioural Theories: Do Leaders Behave in Particular Ways?

The failures of early trait studies led researchers in the late 1940s through the 1960s to go in a different direction. They wondered whether there was something unique in the way that effective leaders behave. Trait research provides a basis for *selecting* the right people for leadership. In contrast, behavioural theories implied we could *train* people to be leaders. Many argued that **behavioural theories of leadership** had advantages over trait theories.

The Ohio State Studies

The most comprehensive and replicated behavioural theories resulted from the Ohio State Studies in the late 1940s,[17] which sought to identify independent dimensions of leader behaviour. Beginning with more than a thousand dimensions, the studies narrowed the list to two that substantially accounted for most of the leadership behaviour described by employees. Researchers called these *initiating structure* and *consideration*. **Initiating structure** is the extent to which a leader is likely to define and structure his or her role and those of employees in order to attain goals; it includes behaviour that attempts to organize work, work relationships, and goals. A leader high in initiating structure is someone who "assigns group members to particular tasks," "expects workers to maintain definite standards of performance," and "emphasizes the meeting of deadlines."

Consideration is the extent to which a leader's job relationships are characterized by mutual trust, respect for employees' ideas, and regard for their feelings. A leader high in consideration helps employees with personal problems, is friendly and approachable, treats all employees as equals, and expresses appreciation and support. In a recent survey, when asked to indicate the factors that most motivated them at work, 66 percent of employees mentioned appreciation.[18]

The Michigan Studies

Leadership studies at the University of Michigan's Survey Research Center had similar objectives: to locate behavioural characteristics of leaders that appeared related to performance effectiveness.[19] The Michigan group also came up with two behavioural dimensions: the **employee-oriented leaders** emphasized interpersonal relations by taking a personal interest in the needs of employees and accepting individual differences among them; the **production-oriented leaders** emphasized the technical or task aspects of the job—focusing on accomplishing the group's task. These dimensions are closely related to the Ohio State dimensions. Employee-oriented leadership is similar to consideration, and production-oriented leadership is similar to initiating structure. In fact, most leadership researchers use the terms synonymously.[20]

At one time, the results of testing behavioural theories were thought to be disappointing. One 1992 review concluded, "Overall, the research based on a two-factor conceptualization of leadership behavior has added little to our knowledge about

behavioural theories of leadership Theories that propose that specific behaviours differentiate leaders from nonleaders.

initiating structure The extent to which a leader is likely to define and structure his or her role and the roles of employees in order to attain goals.

consideration The extent to which a leader is likely to have job relationships characterized by mutual trust, respect for employees' ideas, and regard for their feelings.

employee-oriented leader A leader who emphasizes interpersonal relations.

production-oriented leader A leader who emphasizes the technical or task aspects of the job.

Sally Jewell, CEO of Recreational Equipment (REI), is an employee-oriented leader. During her tenure as CEO, Jewell has turned a struggling company into one with record sales. But she credits REI's success to the work of employees, stating that she does not believe in "hero CEOs." Jewell respects each employee's contribution to the company and includes in her leadership people who are very different from herself. Described as a leader high in consideration, she listens to employees' ideas and empowers them in performing their jobs.

effective leadership."[21] However, a more recent review of 160 studies found the followers of leaders high in consideration were more satisfied with their jobs, were more motivated, and had more respect for their leader. Initiating structure was more strongly related to higher levels of group and organization productivity and more positive performance evaluations.

RESEARCH FINDINGS

RESEARCH FINDINGS:
Behavioural Theories of Leadership

While the results of the behavioural studies have been somewhat mixed,[22] a careful evaluation of the situations that leaders face provides some insights into when leaders should be production-oriented and when they should be people-oriented:[23]

- When subordinates experience a lot of pressure because of deadlines or unclear tasks, leaders who are people-oriented will increase employee satisfaction and performance.
- When the task is interesting or satisfying, there is less need for leaders to be people-oriented.
- When it's clear how to perform the task and what the goals are, leaders who are people-oriented will increase employee satisfaction, while those who are task-oriented will increase dissatisfaction.
- When people don't know what to do, or individuals don't have the knowledge or skills to do the job, it's more important for leaders to be production-oriented than people-oriented.

The followers of leaders who are high in people orientation are more satisfied with their jobs, more motivated, and also have more respect for their leaders. Leaders who are high in task orientation show higher levels of group and organizational productivity and receive more positive performance evaluations.

Contingency Theories: Does the Situation Matter?

Some leaders may have the right traits or display the right behaviours and still fail.[24] Moreover, many leaders who leave while their organizations are still successful—such as GE's Jack Welch or Procter & Gamble's A. G. Lafley—have their legacies clouded by events after their departure. As important as traits and behaviours are in identifying effective or ineffective leaders, they do not guarantee success. The context matters, too.

The relationship between leadership style and effectiveness suggests that there is no one right style, but that style *depends* upon the situation the leader faces. There has been no shortage of studies attempting to isolate critical situational factors that affect leadership effectiveness. The volume of studies is illustrated by the number of moderating variables that researchers have identified in their discussions of **situational, or contingency, theories**. These variables include the degree of structure in the task being performed; the quality of leader-member relations; the leader's position power; the clarity of the employee's role; group norms; information availability; employee acceptance of the leader's decisions; and employee maturity.[25]

We consider four situational theories below: the Fiedler contingency model, Hersey and Blanchard's Situational Leadership®, path-goal theory, and substitutes for leadership.

Have you ever wondered if there was one *right* way to lead?

situational, or contingency, theories Theories that propose leadership effectiveness is dependent on the situation.

Fiedler Contingency Model

The first comprehensive contingency model for leadership was developed by Fred Fiedler.[26] The **Fiedler contingency model** proposes that effective group performance depends on the proper match between the leader's style and the degree to which the situation gives the leader control.

Fiedler created the *least preferred co-worker (LPC)* questionnaire to determine whether individuals were primarily interested in good personal relations with co-workers, and thus *relationship-oriented*, or primarily interested in productivity, and thus *task-oriented*. Fiedler assumed that an individual's leadership style is fixed. Therefore, if a situation requires a task-oriented leader and the person in that leadership position is relationship-oriented, either the situation has to be modified or the leader must be removed and replaced for optimum effectiveness to be achieved.

After assessing an individual's basic leadership style through an LPC questionnaire, the next step is to match the leader with the situation. Fiedler identified three contingency dimensions that determine the situation a leader faces. That situation will then affect the leader's effectiveness:

- *Leader-member relations.* The degree of confidence, trust, and respect members have for their leader.

- *Task structure.* The degree to which job assignments are procedurized (that is, structured or unstructured).

- *Position power.* The degree of influence a leader has over power-based activities such as hiring, firing, discipline, promotions, and salary increases.

The next step is to evaluate the situation in terms of these three variables. Fiedler stated that the better the leader-member relations, the more highly structured the job, and the stronger the position power, the more control the leader has. A very favourable situation (in which the leader has a great deal of control) might include a payroll manager who is well respected and whose employees have confidence in her (good leader-member relations); activities to be done—such as wage computation, cheque writing, and report filing—that are specific and clear (high task structure); and provision of considerable freedom to reward and punish employees (strong position power). An unfavourable situation might be that of the disliked chairperson of a volunteer United Way fundraising team. In this job, the leader has very little control.

Fiedler suggested that task-oriented leaders perform best in situations of high and low control, while relationship-oriented leaders perform best in moderate control situations.[27] In a high control situation, a leader can "get away" with task orientation, because the relationships are good, and followers are easily influenced.[28] In a low control situation (which is characterized by poor relations, ill-defined task, and low influence), task orientation may be the only thing that makes it possible to get something done. In a moderate control situation, being relationship-oriented may smooth the way to getting things done.

How would you apply Fiedler's findings? You would match leaders with the type of situation—in terms of leader-member relations, task structure, and position power—for which they were best suited. Because Fiedler views an individual's leadership style as fixed, there are only two ways to improve leader effectiveness.

First, you can change the leader to fit the situation—as a baseball manager puts a right- or left-handed pitcher into the game depending on the hitter. If a group situation rates highly unfavourable but is currently led by a relationship-oriented manager, the group's performance could be improved under a manager who is task-oriented. The second alternative is to change the situation to fit the leader, by restructuring tasks or increasing or decreasing the leader's power to control factors such as salary increases, promotions, and disciplinary actions.

Fiedler's theory has been found to be more difficult to apply in the workplace than some of the other contingency theories we review.[29]

Fiedler contingency model A leadership theory that proposes that effective group performance depends on the proper match between the leader's style and the degree to which the situation gives the leader control.

Hersey and Blanchard's Situational Leadership®

Paul Hersey and Ken Blanchard's **Situational Leadership® (SL)**, which focuses on followers, has been incorporated into the leadership system of more than 700 of the *Fortune* 1000 companies, and more than a million managers a year from a wide variety of organizations are being taught its basic elements.[30]

SL says successful leadership is achieved by selecting the right leadership style contingent on the followers' *readiness,* or the extent to which they are willing and able to accomplish a specific task. A leader should choose one of four behaviours, depending on follower readiness. This idea is illustrated in Exhibit 11-2.

If followers are *unable* and *unwilling* to do a task, the leader needs to give clear and specific directions; if they are *unable* and *willing,* the leader needs to display high task orientation to compensate for followers' lack of ability and high relationship orientation to get them to "buy into" the leader's desires. If followers are *able* and *unwilling,* the leader needs to use a supportive and participative style; if they are both *able* and *willing,* the leader does not need to do much.

SL has intuitive appeal. It acknowledges the importance of followers and builds on the logic that leaders can compensate for their limited ability and motivation. Yet research efforts to test and support the theory have generally been disappointing.[31] Why? Possible explanations include internal ambiguities and inconsistencies in the model itself as well as problems with research methodology in tests. So despite its intuitive appeal and wide popularity, any endorsement must be cautious for now.

Path-Goal Theory

Developed by University of Toronto professor Martin Evans in the late 1960s and subsequently expanded upon by Robert House (formerly at the University of Toronto, but now at the Wharton School of Business at the University of Pennsylvania), **path-goal theory** extracts elements from the Ohio State leadership research on initiating structure and consideration and the expectancy theory of motivation.[32] It says that it's the leader's job to provide followers with the information, support, or other resources necessary to achieve their goals. (The term *path-goal* implies effective leaders clarify followers' paths to their work goals and make the journey easier by reducing roadblocks.)

Situational Leadership® (SL) A leadership theory that focuses on the readiness of followers.

path-goal theory A leadership theory that says it is the leader's job to assist followers in attaining their goals and to provide the necessary direction and/or support to ensure that their goals are compatible with the overall objectives of the group or organization.

EXHIBIT 11-2 Hersey and Blanchard's Situational Leadership®

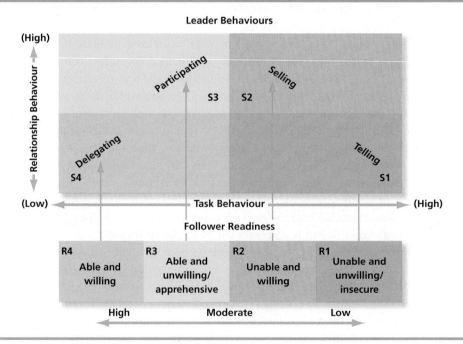

According to this theory, leaders should follow three guidelines to be effective:[33]

- *Determine the outcomes subordinates want.* These might include good pay, job security, interesting work, and autonomy to do one's job.

- *Reward individuals with their desired outcomes* when they perform well.

- *Let individuals know what they need to do to receive rewards* (that is, the path to the goal), remove any barriers that would prevent high performance, and express confidence that individuals have the ability to perform well.

Path-goal theory identifies four leadership behaviours that might be used in different situations to motivate individuals:

- The *directive leader* lets followers know what is expected of them, schedules work to be done, and gives specific guidance as to how to accomplish tasks. This closely parallels the Ohio State dimension of initiating structure. This behaviour is best used when individuals have difficulty doing tasks or the tasks are ambiguous. It would not be very helpful when used with individuals who are already highly motivated, have the skills and abilities to do the task, and understand the requirements of the task.

- The *supportive leader* is friendly and shows concern for the needs of followers. This is essentially synonymous with the Ohio State dimension of consideration. This behaviour is often recommended when individuals are under stress, or otherwise show that they need to be supported.

- The *participative leader* consults with followers and uses their suggestions before making a decision. This behaviour is most appropriate when individuals need to buy in to decisions.

- The *achievement-oriented leader* sets challenging goals and expects followers to perform at their highest level. This behaviour works well with individuals who like challenges and are highly motivated. It would be less effective with less capable individuals, or those who are highly stressed from overwork.

As Exhibit 11-3 illustrates, path-goal theory proposes two types of contingency variables that affect the leadership behaviour-outcome relationship: environmental

EXHIBIT 11-3 Path-Goal Theory

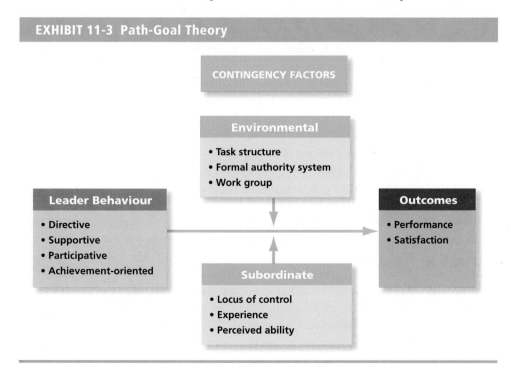

variables that are outside the control of the employee and variables that are part of the personal characteristics of the employee. The theory proposes that employee performance and satisfaction are likely to be positively influenced when the leader compensates for what is lacking in either the employee or the work setting. However, the leader who spends time explaining tasks when those tasks are already clear or when the employee has the ability and experience to handle them without interference is likely to be ineffective because the employee will see such directive behaviour as redundant or even insulting.

RESEARCH FINDINGS: Path-Goal Theory

Testing path-goal theory has not been easy. A review of the evidence suggests mixed support, which indicates "that either effective leadership does not rest in the removal of roadblocks and pitfalls to employee path instrumentalities as path-goal theories propose or that the nature of these hindrances is not in accord with the proposition of the theories."[34] Another review found the lack of support to be "shocking and disappointing."[35] Others argue that adequate tests of the theory have yet to be conducted.[36] Thus, the jury is out. Because path-goal theory is so complex to test, that may remain the case for some time.

One of the dangers of any theory of situational leadership is the assumption that the behaviour of the leader should adjust to meet followers' needs. It may be that leaders act on employees' perceived needs rather than their real needs. Recall from Chapter 2 that "perceptions are reality." A 2010 study found that "if managers view followers positively—that they are good citizens, industrious, enthusiastic—they will treat their employees positively. If they think of their employees negatively—that they are conforming, insubordinate and incompetent—they will treat them that way."[37] By extension, managers may not adopt the appropriate situational leadership behaviour if they have incorrect perceptions of their employees.

Substitutes for Leadership

The previous three theories argue that leaders are needed, but that leaders should consider the situation in determining which style of leadership to adopt. However, numerous studies collectively demonstrate that, in many situations, leaders' actions are irrelevant. Experience and training are among the *substitutes* that can replace the need for a leader's support or ability to create structure. Organizational characteristics such as explicit formalized goals, rigid rules and procedures, and cohesive work groups can also replace formal leadership, while indifference to organizational rewards can neutralize its effects. *Neutralizers* make it impossible for leader behaviour to make any difference to follower outcomes. These are shown in Exhibit 11-4.[38]

This observation should not be surprising. After all, we have introduced a number of variables—such as attitudes, personality, ability, and group norms—that affect employee performance and satisfaction. It's simplistic to think employees are guided to goal accomplishments solely by the actions of their leader. Leadership is simply another independent variable in our overall OB model.

There are many possible substitutes for and neutralizers of many different types of leader behaviours across many different situations. Moreover, sometimes the difference between substitutes and neutralizers is fuzzy. If I am working on a task that is intrinsically enjoyable, theory predicts that leadership will be less important because the task itself provides enough motivation. But does that mean intrinsically enjoyable tasks neutralize leadership effects, or substitute for them, or both? Another problem is that while substitutes for leadership (such as employee characteristics, the nature of the task, and so forth) matter to performance, that does not necessarily mean that leadership does not matter to performance.[39]

EXHIBIT 11-4 Substitutes and Neutralizers for Leadership

Characteristics of Individual	Effect on Leadership
Experience/training	Substitutes for task-oriented leadership
Professionalism	Substitutes for relationship-oriented and task-oriented leadership
Indifference to rewards	Neutralizes relationship-oriented and task-oriented leadership

Characteristics of Job	
Highly structured task	Substitutes for task-oriented leadership
Provides its own feedback	Substitutes for task-oriented leadership
Intrinsically satisfying	Substitutes for relationship-oriented leadership

Characteristics of Organization	
Explicit formalized goals	Substitutes for task-oriented leadership
Rigid rules and procedures	Substitutes for task-oriented leadership
Cohesive work groups	Substitutes for relationship-oriented and task-oriented leadership

Source: Based on S. Kerr and J. M. Jermier, "Substitutes for Leadership: Their Meaning and Measurement," *Organizational Behavior and Human Performance*, December 1978, p. 378.

Inspirational Leadership

Lt.-Col. Maryse Carmichael's leadership role extends out into the community, where the Snowbirds are a source of inspiration and wonder (not to mention an important tool used for recruitment purposes).[40] "If I can influence not only young girls but boys to follow their passion then that's great," Carmichael says. That is why she ensures that new candidates for pilot jobs are not screened solely on the basis on flying ability. "Teamwork is so important," she adds, noting that to a large degree teamwork is what defines the Snowbirds. But the desire and ability to engage with communities and do public relations work is critical too. After all, for many Canadians, the Snowbirds are the face of the military. "People often hear about Canadian Forces in Afghanistan but you rarely get to meet them. We get to meet Canadians on a daily basis." She vividly remembers her own first experience seeing the Snowbirds at a show in Beauport, Quebec, when she was five years old. "It's sometimes hard to quantify what we do," she says. "How can you explain that we motivate young people to dream?" What does it take to be an inspiring leader?

 3 How does a leader lead with vision?

The leadership theories we have discussed above ignore the importance of the leader as a communicator who inspires others to act beyond their immediate self-interests. In this section, we present two contemporary leadership theories with a common theme. They view leaders as individuals who inspire followers through their words, ideas, and behaviours. These theories are charismatic leadership and transformational leadership.

Charismatic Leadership

The following individuals are frequently cited as being charismatic leaders: Frank Stronach of Aurora, Ontario-based Magna International; Mogens Smed, CEO of Calgary-based DIRTT (Doing It Right This Time); Pierre Trudeau, the late prime minister; René Lévesque, the late Quebec premier; Lucien Bouchard, former Bloc Québécois leader; Michaëlle Jean, former Governor General; and Craig Kielburger, who founded Kids Can Free the Children as a teenager. So what do they have in common?

What Is Charismatic Leadership?

Max Weber, a sociologist, defined *charisma* (from the Greek for "gift") more than a century ago as "a certain quality of an individual personality, by virtue of which he or she is set apart from ordinary people and treated as endowed with supernatural, superhuman, or at least specifically exceptional powers or qualities. These are not accessible to the ordinary person and are regarded as of divine origin or as exemplary, and on the basis of them the individual concerned is treated as a leader."[41] Weber argued that charismatic leadership was one of several ideal types of authority.

The first researcher to consider charismatic leadership in terms of OB was Robert House. According to House's **charismatic leadership theory**, followers make attributions of heroic or extraordinary leadership abilities when they observe certain behaviours.[42] A number of studies have attempted to identify the characteristics of the charismatic leader and have documented four—they have a vision, they are willing to take personal risks to achieve that vision, they are sensitive to followers' needs, and they exhibit behaviours that are out of the ordinary (see Exhibit 11-5).[43]

How Charismatic Leaders Influence Followers

How do charismatic leaders actually influence followers? The evidence suggests a four-step process.[44] It begins by the leader articulating an appealing **vision**, a long-term strategy for how to attain a goal by linking the present with a better future for the organization. Desirable visions fit the times and circumstances and reflect the uniqueness of the organization. Steve Jobs championed the iPod, noting, "It's as Apple as anything Apple has ever done." People in the organization must also believe the vision is challenging yet attainable. The creation of the iPod achieved Apple's goal of offering groundbreaking and easy-to-use technology.

Second, a vision is incomplete without an accompanying **vision statement**, a formal articulation of an organization's vision or mission. Charismatic leaders may use vision statements to imprint on followers an overarching goal and purpose. They then communicate high performance expectations and express confidence that followers can attain them. This enhances follower self-esteem and self-confidence.

Next, through words and actions, the leader conveys a new set of values and sets an example for followers to imitate. One study of Israeli bank employees showed, for example, that charismatic leaders were more effective because their employees personally identified with them.[45] Charismatic leaders also set a tone of cooperation and mutual support. A study of 115 government employees found they had a stronger sense of personal belonging at work when they had charismatic leaders, increasing their willingness to engage in helping and compliance-oriented behaviour.[46]

---

charismatic leadership theory
A leadership theory that states that followers make attributions of heroic or extraordinary leadership abilities when they observe certain behaviours.

vision A long-term strategy for attaining a goal or goals.

vision statement A formal articulation of an organization's vision or mission.

EXHIBIT 11-5 Key Characteristics of Charismatic Leaders

1. *Vision and articulation*. Has a vision—expressed as an idealized goal—that proposes a future better than the status quo; and is able to clarify the importance of the vision in terms that are understandable to others.

2. *Personal risk*. Willing to take on high personal risk, incur high costs, and engage in self-sacrifice to achieve the vision.

3. *Sensitivity to followers' needs*. Perceptive of others' abilities and responsive to their needs and feelings.

4. *Unconventional behaviour*. Engages in behaviours that are perceived as novel and counter to norms.

Source: Based on J. A. Conger and R. N. Kanungo, *Charismatic Leadership in Organizations* (Thousand Oaks, CA: Sage, 1998), p. 94.

Finally, the charismatic leader engages in emotion-inducing and often unconventional behaviour to demonstrate courage and convictions about the vision. Followers "catch" the emotions their leader is conveying.[47]

What are examples of visions? The late Steve Jobs' vision of elegance in design influenced how all of Apple's products were built. Facebook founder and CEO Mark Zuckerberg's vision for his company is to have it be a one-stop place for everyone's communication needs, including text messaging.

RESEARCH FINDINGS: Charismatic Leadership

Research shows impressive correlations between charismatic leadership and high performance and satisfaction among followers.[48] People working for charismatic leaders are motivated to exert extra work effort and, because they like and respect their leader, express greater satisfaction. It also appears that organizations with charismatic CEOs are more profitable. And charismatic professors enjoy higher course evaluations.[49]

However, charisma may not always be generalizable; its effectiveness may depend on the situation. Charisma appears to be most successful when the follower's task has an ideological component or when the environment involves a high degree of stress and uncertainty.[50] Even in laboratory studies, when people are psychologically aroused, they are more likely to respond to charismatic leaders.[51] This may explain why charismatic leaders tend to surface in politics, religion, wartime, or a business firm that is in its infancy or facing a life-threatening crisis.

People are especially receptive to charismatic leadership when they sense a crisis, when they are under stress, or when they fear for their lives. More generally, some people's personalities are especially susceptible to charismatic leadership.[52] Consider self-esteem. If a person lacks self-esteem and questions his or her self-worth, that person is more likely to absorb a leader's direction rather than establish his or her own way of leading or thinking.

A 2010 study found that it is possible for a person to learn how to communicate charismatically, which would then lead that person to be perceived more as a leader. People

The creative vision of Steve Jobs, Apple's charismatic co-founder, was to make state-of-the-art technology that is easy for people to use. As Apple CEO, Jobs inspired, motivated, and led employees to develop products such as Macintosh computers, iPod music players, iPads, and iPhones. "The iPhone is like having your life in your pocket," said Jobs. In October 2011, Jobs passed away, and Apple employees and others paid tribute to him as the ultimate consumer-electronics visionary.

who are perceived to be charismatic show empathy, enthusiasm, and self-confidence; have good speaking and listening skills; and make eye contact.[53] To learn more about how to be charismatic yourself, see the *Working with Others Exercise* on page 425.

The Dark Side of Charismatic Leadership

When organizations are in need of great change, charismatic leaders are often able to inspire their followers to meet the challenges of change. Be aware that a charismatic leader may become a liability to an organization once the crisis is over and the need for dramatic change subsides.[54] Why? Because then the charismatic leader's overwhelming self-confidence can be a liability. He or she is unable to listen to others, becomes uncomfortable when challenged by aggressive employees, and begins to hold an unjustifiable belief in his or her "rightness" on issues. Some would argue that Stephane Dion's behaviour after the Liberal party lost 19 seats in the 2008 federal election, first refusing to step down, and then trying to form a coalition government shortly thereafter, would fit this description.

Many have argued that the financial scandals and large losses experienced by investors in North America, including the ponzi scheme created by Bernie Madoff and the near bankruptcy of the Caisse de dépôt et placement du Québec because of the "audacious investment strategies" of Henri-Paul Rousseau, point to some of the dangers of charismatic leadership.[55]

Charismatic leadership, by its very nature, silences criticism. Thus, employees follow the lead of their visionary CEOs unquestioningly. Professor David Leighton, of the Richard Ivey School of Business at the University of Western Ontario, notes that even boards of directors and auditors are reluctant to challenge these CEOs. He finds that Canada's "more balanced culture" is less likely to turn CEOs into heroes.[56]

A study of 29 companies that went from good to great (their cumulative stock returns were all at least three times better than the general stock market over 15 years) found that a key difference in successful charismatic leaders may be the *absence* of being ego-driven.[57] Although the leaders of these firms were fiercely ambitious and driven, their ambition was directed toward their company rather than themselves. They took responsibility for mistakes and poor results but gave credit for successes to other people. These individuals are called **level 5 leaders** because they have four basic leadership qualities—individual capability, team skills, managerial competence, and the ability to stimulate others to high performance—plus a fifth quality: a paradoxical blend of personal humility and professional will. Level 5 leaders channel their ego needs away from themselves and into the goal of building a great company while getting little notoriety in the business press.

Transformational Leadership

A stream of research has focused on differentiating transformational from transactional leaders.[58] The Ohio and Michigan State studies, the Fiedler contingency model, and path-goal theory describe **transactional leaders**—those who guide their followers toward established goals by clarifying role and task requirements. **Transformational leaders** inspire followers to transcend their self-interests for the good of the organization, and can have an extraordinary effect on their followers.[59] Andrea Jung at Avon, Richard Branson of the Virgin Group, and Jim McNerney of Boeing are all examples of transformational leaders. They pay attention to the concerns and developmental needs of individual followers; they change followers' awareness of issues by helping them to look at old problems in new ways; and they excite and inspire followers to put out extra effort to achieve group goals. Exhibit 11-6 briefly identifies and defines the characteristics that differentiate these two types of leaders.

Transactional and transformational leadership are not opposing approaches to getting things done.[60] They complement each other, though they are not equally

level 5 leaders Leaders who are fiercely ambitious and driven, but their ambition is directed toward their company rather than themselves.

transactional leaders Leaders who guide or motivate their followers in the direction of established goals by clarifying role and task requirements.

transformational leaders Leaders who inspire followers to transcend their own self-interests and who are capable of having a profound and extraordinary effect on followers.

EXHIBIT 11-6 Characteristics of Transactional and Transformational Leaders

Transactional Leader

Contingent reward: Contracts exchange of rewards for effort, promises rewards for good performance, recognizes accomplishments.

Management by exception (active): Watches and searches for deviations from rules and standards, takes corrective action.

Management by exception (passive): Intervenes only if standards are not met.

Laissez-faire: Abdicates responsibilities, avoids making decisions.

Transformational Leader

Idealized influence: Provides vision and sense of mission, instills pride, gains respect and trust.

Inspirational motivation: Communicates high expectations, uses symbols to focus efforts, expresses important purposes in simple ways.

Intellectual stimulation: Promotes intelligence, rationality, and careful problem solving.

Individualized consideration: Gives personal attention, treats each employee individually, coaches, advises.

Source: Reprinted from B. M. Bass, "From Transactional to Transformational Leadership: Learning to Share the Vision," *Organizational Dynamics,* Winter 1990, p. 22, with permission from Elsevier.

important. Transformational leadership *builds on* transactional leadership and produces levels of follower effort and performance that go beyond what transactional leadership alone can do. But the reverse is not true. So if you are a good transactional leader but do not have transformational qualities, you will likely only be a mediocre leader. The best leaders are transactional *and* transformational.

Full Range of Leadership Model

Exhibit 11-7 shows the full range of leadership model. Laissez-faire is the most passive and therefore the least effective of the leader behaviours.[61] Management by exception—active or passive—is slightly better than laissez-faire, but it's still considered ineffective. Management by exception leaders tend to be available only when there is a problem, which is often too late. Contingent reward leadership can be an effective style of leadership, but will not get employees to go above and beyond the call of duty.

Only with the four remaining leadership styles—all aspects of transformational leadership—are leaders able to motivate followers to perform above expectations and transcend their own self-interest for the sake of the organization. Individualized consideration, intellectual stimulation, inspirational motivation, and idealized influence all result in extra effort from employees, higher productivity, higher morale and satisfaction, higher organizational effectiveness, lower turnover, lower absenteeism, and greater organizational adaptability. Based on this model, leaders are generally most effective when they regularly use each of the four transformational behaviours.

How Transformational Leadership Works

Transformational leaders are more effective because they themselves are more creative and also because they encourage those who follow them to be creative, too.[62] In companies with transformational leaders, there is greater decentralization of responsibility, managers have more propensity to take risks, and compensation plans are geared toward long-term results, all of which facilitate corporate entrepreneurship.[63]

Companies with transformational leaders also show greater agreement among top managers about the organization's goals, which yields superior organizational performance.[64] Similar results, showing that transformational leaders improve performance by building consensus among group members, have been demonstrated in the Israeli military.[65] Transformational leaders are able to increase follower self-efficacy, giving the group a "can do" spirit.[66] Followers of transformational leaders are more likely to

EXHIBIT 11-7 Full Range of Leadership Model

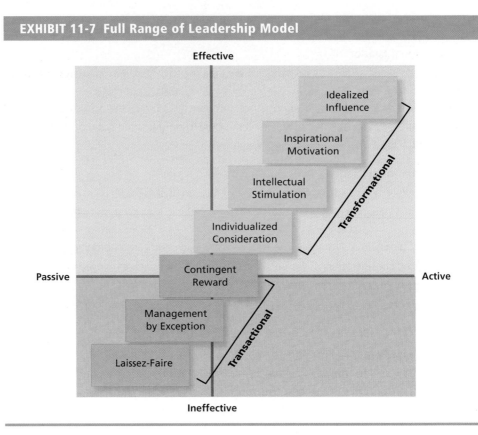

pursue ambitious goals, be familiar with and agree on the strategic goals of the organization, and believe that the goals they are pursuing are personally important.[67]

Research has shown that vision explains part of the effect of transformational leadership. One study found that vision was even more important than a charismatic (effusive, dynamic, lively) communication style in explaining the success of entrepreneurial firms.[68] Finally, transformational leadership also engenders commitment on the part of followers and instills in them a greater sense of trust in the leader.[69]

RESEARCH FINDINGS: Transformational Leadership

Transformational leadership has been impressively supported at various job levels and in disparate occupations (school principals, marine commanders, ministers, presidents of MBA associations, military cadets, union shop stewards, schoolteachers, sales reps). One recent study of R & D firms found that teams whose project leaders scored high on transformational leadership produced better-quality products as judged one year later and were more profitable five years later.[70] A review of 87 studies testing transformational leadership found that it was related to the motivation and satisfaction of followers and to the higher performance and perceived effectiveness of leaders.[71]

Transformational leadership is not equally effective in all situations, however. It has a greater impact on the bottom line in smaller, privately held firms than in more complicated organizations.[72] The personal nature of transformational leadership may be most effective when leaders can directly interact with the workforce and make decisions than when they report to an external board of directors or deal with a complex bureaucratic structure. Another study showed transformational leaders were more effective in improving group potency in teams higher in power distance and collectivism.[73] Where group members are highly individualistic and don't readily cede decision-making authority, transformational leadership might not have much impact.

Transformational leadership theory is not perfect. There are concerns about whether contingent reward leadership is strictly a characteristic of transactional leaders only. And contrary to the full range of leadership model, the 4 *I*'s in transformational leadership are not always superior in effectiveness to transactional leadership (contingent reward leadership sometimes works as well as transformational leadership).

In summary, transformational leadership is more strongly correlated than transactional leadership with lower turnover rates, higher productivity, lower employee stress and burnout, and higher employee satisfaction.[74] Like charisma, it can be learned. One study of Canadian bank managers found that branches managed by those who underwent transformational leadership training performed significantly better than branches whose managers did not receive training. Other studies show similar results.[75]

Transformational Leadership vs. Charismatic Leadership

There is some debate about whether transformational leadership and charismatic leadership are the same. Researcher Robert House considers them synonymous, calling the differences "modest" and "minor." McGill University professor Rabindra Kanungo agrees.[76] However, one researcher who disagrees says, "The purely charismatic [leader] may want followers to adopt the charismatic's world view and go no further; the transformational leader will attempt to instill in followers the ability to question not only established views but eventually those established by the leader."[77] Although many researchers believe that transformational leadership is broader than charismatic leadership, a leader who scores high on transformational leadership is also likely to score high on charisma. Therefore, in practice, they may be roughly equivalent.

Contemporary Leadership Roles

The military may be a surprising place to find self-directed leadership, given the rigid formality of the hierarchy and role definitions.[78] However, senior leaders still find ways to create opportunities to take initiative. For example, retired Snowbird Dan Dempsey notes that historic Snowbird team pictures were scattered about the base but not organized or protected in a systematic way. With the support of base command, Dempsey started a museum in the squadron, eventually collecting enough material to fill a book. "I was able to find, through a vast myriad of collections, a whole bunch of old-timers and pioneers who started the air-show industry in Canada and adapt their personal accounts." By enabling this self-directed project, the Snowbird team ended up with both a museum and a book that continue to help them address public relations and community engagement goals. What can formal leaders do to help foster self-directed leadership among employees?

4 Are there leadership roles for nonmanagers?

Transformational leadership theory focuses on heroic leaders, leaders at the top echelons of the organization, and also on individuals rather than teams. However, the notion of "leader at the top" does not adequately reflect what is happening in some workplaces today, where there is less hierarchy and more connections, both inside and outside of the organization. There is a need for more "distributed leadership." In this form, leadership is "distributed across many players, both within and across organizations, up and down the hierarchy, wherever information, expertise, vision, and new ways of working together reside."[79]

Can anyone be a leader?

The following sections aim to explain how leadership can be spread throughout the organization through mentoring, self-leadership, team leadership, online leadership, and leading without authority. Even if you are not a manager or someone thinking about leadership in a corporate situation, this discussion offers important insights into how you can take on a leadership role in an organization.

N. R. Narayana Murthy is one of the founders of Infosys in Bangalore, India. He has served the firm as chairman and chief mentor of the board, where he has shared his experiences, knowledge, and lessons learned while building Infosys for over three decades into a company with 142 000 employees globally and annual sales of over $6 billion. In August 2011, Mr. Murthy retired from Infosys and is currently Chairman Emeritus of the company. He is shown here with Infosys employees at the company's Bangalore campus, which is also its corporate headquarters.

Mentoring

Many leaders take responsibility for developing future leaders through mentoring relationships. A **mentor** is a senior employee who sponsors and supports a less-experienced employee (a protégé). The mentoring role includes coaching, counselling, and sponsorship to help protégés develop skills, to provide support and help bolster protégés' self-confidence, and to lobby so that protégés get good assignments, promotions, and salary increases.[80] Successful mentors are good teachers. They present ideas clearly, listen well, and empathize with protégés' problems.

Traditional informal mentoring relationships develop when leaders identify a less experienced, lower-level employee who appears to have potential for future development.[81] The protégé will often be tested with a particularly challenging assignment. If he or she performs acceptably, the mentor will develop the relationship, informally showing the protégé how the organization *really* works outside its formal structures and procedures. Protégés can also learn how the mentor has navigated early career issues or led effectively and how to work through problems with minimal stress.

Why would a leader want to be a mentor?[82] Many feel they have something to share with the younger generation and want to provide a legacy. Mentoring provides unfiltered access to the attitudes of lower-ranking employees, and protégés can be an excellent source of early warning signals that identify potential organizational problems.

Are all employees in an organization equally likely to participate in a mentoring relationship? Unfortunately, no.[83] The evidence indicates that minorities and women are less likely to be chosen as protégés than are white males. Mentors tend to select protégés who are similar to themselves on criteria such as background, education, gender, race, ethnicity, and religion. "People naturally move to mentor and can more easily communicate with those with whom they most closely identify."[84] Senior male managers may also select male protégés to minimize problems such as sexual attraction or gossip.

Many organizations have created formal programs to ensure mentoring relationships are equally available to minorities and women.[85] Although begun with the best intentions, these formal relationships are not as effective as informal ones.[86]

Poor planning and design may often be the reason. Mentor commitment is critical to a program's effectiveness; mentors must see the relationship as beneficial to themselves and the protégé. The protégé, too, must feel he or she has input into the relationship; someone who feels it's foisted on him or her will just go through the motions.[87] Formal mentoring programs are also most likely to succeed if they appropriately match the work style, needs, and skills of protégé and mentor.[88]

You might assume that mentoring is valuable for career success, but the research suggests the gains are primarily psychological. Benefits to objective outcomes like compensation and job performance are very small. One study concluded, "Though mentoring may not be properly labeled an utterly useless concept to careers, neither can it be argued to be as important as the main effects of other influences on career success such as ability and personality."[89] It may *feel* nice to have a mentor, but it does not appear that having a mentor, or even having a good mentor who provides both

mentor A senior employee who sponsors and supports a less-experienced employee.

support and advice, is critical to one's career. Mentors may be effective not because of the functions they provide but because of the resources they can obtain: A mentor connected to a powerful network can build relationships that will help the protégé advance. Most evidence suggests that network ties, whether built through a mentor or not, are a significant predictor of career success.[90] If a mentor is not well connected or not a very strong performer, the best mentoring advice in the world will not be very beneficial.

Self-Leadership (or Self-Management)

A growing trend in organizations is the focus on self-leadership, or self-management, where individuals and teams set goals, plan and implement tasks, evaluate performance, solve their own problems, and motivate themselves.[91] (Recall our discussion of self-managed teams in Chapter 6.)

> How do you manage yourself?

Reduced levels of supervision, offices in the home, teamwork, and growth in service and professional employment have increased the demand for self-leadership. Self-management can also be a substitute or neutralizer for leadership from others.

Despite the lack of studies of self-management techniques in organizational settings, self-management strategies have been shown to be successful in nonorganizational settings.[92] Those who practise self-management look for opportunities to be more effective in the workplace and improve their career success and provide their own sense of reward and feedback after carrying out their accomplishments. Moreover, self-reinforced behaviour is often maintained at a higher rate than behaviour that is externally regulated.[93] *OB in Action—Engaging in Self-Leadership* indicates ways in which you can practise effective self-leadership.

How do leaders create self-leaders? The following approaches have been suggested:[94]

- *Model self-leadership.* Practise self-observation, setting challenging personal goals, self-direction, and self-reinforcement. Then display these behaviours, and encourage others to rehearse and then produce them.

- *Encourage employees to create self-set goals.* Support employees in developing quantitative, specific goals; having such goals is the most important part of self-leadership.

- *Encourage the use of self-rewards to strengthen and increase desirable behaviours.* By contrast, limit self-punishment only to occasions when the employee has been dishonest or destructive.

- *Create positive thought patterns.* Encourage employees to use mental imagery and self-talk to further stimulate self-motivation.

- *Create a climate of self-leadership.* Redesign the work to increase the natural rewards of a job and focus on these naturally rewarding features of work to increase motivation.

- *Encourage self-criticism.* Encourage individuals to be critical of their own performance.

OB in ACTION
Engaging in Self-Leadership

To engage in effective self-leadership:[95]

→ **Think horizontally, not vertically.** Vertical relationships in the organization matter, but peers can become trusted colleagues and have a great impact on your work.

→ Focus on **influence, not control**. Work with your colleagues, not for them. Be collaborative and share credit.

→ **Create opportunities**, don't wait for them. Rather than look for the right time, be more action oriented.

The underlying assumptions behind self-leadership are that people are responsible, capable, and able to exercise initiative without the external constraints of bosses, rules, or regulations. Given the proper support, individuals can monitor and control their own

SELF-ASSESSMENT LIBRARY

LEARNING ABOUT YOURSELF

1. Are You a Self-Manager?
   (page 424)

behaviour. The *Learning About Yourself Exercise* on page 425 provides further examples of how to engage in self-leadership.

Team Leadership

Leadership is increasingly taking place within a team context. As teams grow in popularity, the role of the leader in guiding team members takes on heightened importance.[96] Also, because of its more collaborative nature, the role of team leader is different from the traditional leadership role performed by first-line supervisors.

Many leaders are not equipped to handle the change to team leader. As one prominent consultant noted, "Even the most capable managers have trouble making the transition because all the command-and-control type things they were encouraged to do before are no longer appropriate. There's no reason to have any skill or sense of this."[97] This same consultant estimated that "probably 15 percent of managers are natural team leaders; another 15 percent could never lead a team because it runs counter to their personality. [They're unable to sublimate their dominating style for the good of the team.] Then there's that huge group in the middle: team leadership doesn't come naturally to them, but they can learn it."[98]

Effective team leaders need to build commitment and confidence, remove obstacles, create opportunities, and be part of the team.[99] They have to learn skills such as the patience to share information, the willingness to trust others, the ability to give up authority, and an understanding of when to intervene. New team leaders may try to retain too much control at a time when team members need more autonomy, or they may abandon their teams at times when the teams need support and help.[100]

Roles of Team Leaders

A study of 20 organizations that reorganized themselves around teams found certain common responsibilities that all leaders had to assume. These included coaching, facilitating, training, communicating, handling disciplinary problems, and reviewing team/individual performance.[101] Many of these responsibilities apply to managers in general. A more meaningful way to describe the team leader's job is to focus on two priorities: managing the team's external boundary and facilitating the team process.[102] We have divided these priorities into four specific roles that team leaders play:

- *Liaisons with external constituencies.* Outsiders include upper management, other internal teams, customers, and suppliers. The leader represents the team to other constituencies, secures needed resources, clarifies others' expectations of the team, gathers information from the outside, and shares this information with team members.

- *Troubleshooters.* When the team has problems and asks for assistance, team leaders sit in on meetings and try to help resolve the problems. This rarely relates to technical or operational issues because the team members typically know more about the tasks being done than does the team leader. The leader contributes by asking penetrating questions, by helping the team discuss problems, and by getting needed resources from external constituencies. For instance, when a team in an aerospace firm found itself short-handed, its team leader took responsibility for getting more staff. He presented the team's case to upper management and got the approval through the company's human resource department.

- *Conflict managers.* When disagreements surface, team leaders help process the conflict. What is the source of the conflict? Who is involved? What are the issues? What resolution options are available? What are the advantages and disadvantages of each? By getting team members to address questions such as these, the leader minimizes the disruptive aspects of intrateam conflicts.

EXHIBIT 11-8

Source: Dilbert, reprinted by permission of Universal Uclick.

- *Coaches.* They clarify expectations and roles, teach, offer support, cheerlead, and do whatever else is necessary to help team members improve their work performance.

Exhibit 11-8 offers a lighthearted look at what it means to be a team leader.

Online Leadership

How do you lead people who are physically separated from you and with whom you communicate electronically? This question has received minimal attention from organizational behaviour researchers.[103] But today's managers and their employees are increasingly being linked by networks rather than geographical proximity. Obvious examples include managers who regularly use email to communicate with their staff, managers who oversee virtual projects or teams, and managers whose teleworking employees are linked to the office by an Internet connection.

Electronic communication is a powerful channel that can build and enhance leadership effectiveness. But when misused, it can undermine much of what a leader has achieved through verbal communication. In face-to-face communications, harsh *words* can be softened by nonverbal action. A smile and comforting gestures, for instance, can lessen the blow behind strong words like *disappointed, unsatisfactory, inadequate,* or *below expectations*. That nonverbal component does not exist with online interactions. The *structure* of words in electronic communication has the power to motivate or demotivate the receiver. We propose that online leaders have to think carefully about what actions they want their digital messages to initiate.

Jane Howell at the Richard Ivey School of Business, University of Western Ontario, and one of her students, Kate Hall-Merenda, considered the issues of leading from a distance.[104] They note that physical distance can create many potential problems, with team members feeling isolated, forgotten, and perhaps not cared about. It may result in lowered productivity. Their study of 109 business leaders and 371 followers in a large financial institution found that physical distance makes it more difficult to develop high-quality relationships.

Howell and Hall-Merenda suggest that some of the same characteristics of transformational leaders are appropriate for long-distance managing. In particular, they emphasize the need to articulate a compelling vision and to communicate that vision in an inspiring way. Encouraging employees to think about ways to strive toward that vision is another important task of the leader.

Online leaders confront unique challenges, the greatest of which appears to be developing and maintaining trust. **Identification-based trust**, based on a mutual

identification-based trust Trust based on a mutual understanding of each other's intentions and appreciation of each other's wants and desires.

understanding of each other's intentions and appreciation of the other person's wants and desires, is particularly difficult to achieve without face-to-face interaction.[105] Online negotiations can also be hindered because parties express lower levels of trust.[106] It's not clear whether it's even possible for employees to identify with or trust leaders with whom they only communicate electronically.[107]

This discussion leads us to the tentative conclusion that, for an increasing number of managers, good leadership skills may include the abilities to communicate support, trust, and inspiration through keyboarded words and accurately read emotions in others' messages. In electronic communication, writing skills are likely to become an extension of interpersonal skills.

Leading without Authority

Can you lead, even if you don't have the authority (or a formal appointment)? For instance, what if you wanted to convince the dean to introduce more relevant business courses, or you wanted to convince the president of the company where you work to use more environmentally friendly strategies in dealing with waste? How do you effectively lead in a student group, when everyone is a peer?

Leadership at the grassroots level does happen. Rosabeth Moss Kanter, in her book *The Change Masters*,[108] discusses examples of employees who saw something that needed changing and took on the responsibility to do so. Employees were more likely to do this when organizations permitted initiative at all levels of the organization, rather than making it a tool of senior executives only.

Leading without authority means exhibiting leadership behaviour even though you do not have a formal position or title. Neither Martin Luther King Jr. nor Nelson Mandela operated from a position of authority, yet each was able to inspire many to follow him in the quest for social justice. The workplace can be an opportunity for leading without authority as well. As Ronald Heifetz of Harvard's Kennedy School of Government notes, "Leadership means taking responsibility for hard problems beyond anyone's expectations."[109] It also means not waiting for the coach's call.[110]

What are the benefits of leading without authority? Heifetz has identified three:[111]

- *Latitude for creative deviance.* It's easier to raise harder questions and look for less traditional solutions when a person is not locked into the trappings that go with authority.

- *Issue focus.* Individuals can focus on a single issue, rather than be concerned with the myriad issues that those in authority face.

- *Front-line information.* An individual is closer to the detailed experiences of some of the stakeholders and thus, more information is available.

Not all organizations support this type of leadership, and some have been known to actively suppress it. Still, you may want to reflect on the possibility of engaging in leadership behaviour because you see a need, rather than because you are required to act.

Contemporary Issues in Leadership

 What are some of the contemporary issues in leadership?

When Lt.-Col. Maryse Carmichael watched her first air show at age five, she was inspired to fly planes herself one day.[112] At the time, however, becoming a Snowbird pilot seemed like an impossible dream. Females in the Canadian military were barred from pilot training until the mid-1980s. It is therefore not surprising that she is the first female Commanding Officer in the group's 41 year history.

Despite being the first female CO of her squadron, Carmichael downplays gender, finding team familiarity and fit to be more important to her acceptance as a leader. "At my level perhaps it is a new thing to have a woman as a CO," she says, "but for me it's been my entire career working with these people. I don't see anything different." She also takes equal joy in the thought of inspiring young boys and girls and is quick to point out that she is not the first female flight squadron leader in the military, only the most visible. In fact Carmichael sees the Snowbirds' show as an equalizing force in communities. "That is the beauty . . . if you are looking up at the display you wouldn't know if it is a man or a woman flying. All that matters is that you can do the job." Does gender impact leadership style?

What is authentic leadership? Is there a moral dimension to leadership? Do men and women rely on different leadership styles, and if so, is one style inherently superior to the other? In this section, we briefly address these contemporary issues in leadership.

Authentic Leadership

Douglas R. Conant is not your typical CEO. His style is decidedly understated. When asked to reflect on the strong performance of Campbell Soup, he says, "We're hitting our stride a little bit more [than our peers]." He regularly admits mistakes and often says, "I can do better." Conant appears to be a good example of authentic leadership.[113]

Authentic leaders know who they are, know what they believe in and value, and act on those values and beliefs openly and candidly. Their followers consider them to be ethical people. The primary quality produced by authentic leadership is trust. Authentic leaders share information, encourage open communication, and stick to their ideals. The result: People come to have faith in them.

Because the concept is so recent, there has been little research on authentic leadership.[114] However, it's a promising way to think about ethics and trust in leadership because it focuses on the moral aspects of being a leader. Transformational or charismatic leaders can have a vision and communicate it persuasively, but sometimes the vision is wrong (as in the case of Hitler), or the leader is more concerned with his own needs or pleasures, as in the case of business leaders Dennis Kozlowski (ex-CEO of Tyco International) and Jeffrey Skilling (ex-CEO of Enron).[115]

> **authentic leaders** Leaders who know who they are, know what they believe in and value, and act on these values and beliefs openly and candidly. Their followers could consider them to be ethical people.

Moral Leadership

Only recently have ethicists and leadership researchers begun to consider the ethical implications in leadership.[116] Why now? One reason may be the growing interest in ethics throughout the field of management. Another reason may be that ethical lapses by business leaders are never absent from the headlines. Another may be the discovery that many past leaders—such as Martin Luther King Jr. and John F. Kennedy—suffered ethical shortcomings. Some companies, like Boeing, are tying executive compensation to ethics to reinforce the idea that, in CEO Jim McNerney's words, "there's no compromise between doing things the right way and performance."[117]

Ethics and leadership intersect in a number of ways. Transformational leaders have been described as fostering moral virtue when they try to change the attitudes and behaviours of followers.[118] Charisma, too, has an ethical component. Unethical leaders use their charisma to enhance power over followers, directed toward self-serving ends. Ethical leaders use it in a socially constructive way to serve others.[119] Leaders who treat their followers with fairness, especially by providing honest, frequent, and accurate information, are seen as more effective.[120] Because top executives set the moral tone for an organization, they need to set high ethical standards, demonstrate those standards through their own behaviour, and encourage and reward integrity in others while avoiding abuses of power such as giving themselves large raises and bonuses while seeking to cut costs by laying off long-time employees.

Bill Young created Toronto-based Social Capital Partners to help businesses hire the hard to employ: youths, single mothers, Aboriginal people, new immigrants, and those with disabilities or substance abuse. His goal is to help people who are struggling get back into the economic mainstream.

Leadership is not value-free. In assessing its effectiveness we need to address the *means* that a leader uses in trying to achieve goals, as well as the content of those goals. Scholars have tried to integrate ethical and charismatic leadership by advancing the idea of **socialized charismatic leadership**—leadership that conveys other-centred (not self-centred) values by leaders who model ethical conduct.[121] Socialized charismatic leaders are able to bring employee values in line with their own values through their words and actions.[122]

One researcher suggests that there are four cornerstones to a "moral foundation of leadership":[123]

- *Truth telling.* Leaders who tell the truth as they see it allow for a mutual, fair exchange to occur.

- *Promise keeping.* Leaders need to be careful of the commitments they make, and then careful of keeping those commitments.

- *Fairness.* Leaders who are equitable ensure that followers get their fair share for their contributions to the organization.

- *Respect for the individual.* Leaders who tell the truth, keep promises, and are fair show respect for followers. Respect means treating people with dignity.

Moral leadership comes from within the individual, and in general means treating people well, and with respect. This chapter's *Ethical Dilemma Exercise* on page 426 raises some provocative issues about whether we should consider just the ends toward which a leader strives, or the means as well.

Gender and Leadership

How Many Women Make It to the Top?

The following statistics give the picture for women in Canada in 2010. Women made up 50.4 percent of the Canadian population.[124] More women (71 percent) than men (65 percent) aged 25 to 44 years had completed a post-secondary education.[125] Women made up 47.3 percent of the labour force in Canada, but they held only 36.8 percent of managerial roles and 31.9 percent of senior management roles. Women held 14 percent of the board seats and 17.7 percent of the highest corporate titles—CEO, chief financial officer, or chief operating officer—of the *Financial Post* 500.[126]

socialized charismatic leadership A leadership concept that states that leaders convey values that are other-centred vs. self-centred and who role model ethical conduct.

George Cooke, CEO of Toronto-based Dominion of Canada General Insurance, believes in promoting women to senior positions. He is noteworthy for this: Dominion is well above the national average in the percentage of women who have made it to the executive ranks of Canada's top companies: 54 percent of senior management (VP and up) are female and 78 percent of officers are female.

Despite women's low representation in large companies, they are highly involved in smaller companies. Industry Canada reports that in 2007, 46 percent of all small- to medium-sized enterprises had at least one female owner.[127] Moreover, women start almost half of all small businesses in Canada today and, among young people, women start almost 80 percent of small businesses.[128]

Similarities and Differences in Women's and Men's Leadership Styles

Do men and women lead differently? An extensive review of the literature suggests two conclusions.[129] First, most recent evidence suggests that there is a great deal of overlap between males and females in their leadership styles. Second, what differences there are seem to be that women fall back on a more democratic leadership style, while men feel more comfortable with a directive style.

> Do men and women lead differently?

A recent review of 45 organizations found female leaders were more transformational than males. The authors concluded, "These data attest to the ability of women to perform very well in leadership roles in contemporary organizations."[130] However, women who demonstrate stereotypical male behaviours (self-confidence, assertiveness, and dominance) can face "backlash" at work for not fitting the female stereotype for behaviour. A 2011 study found that "women who displayed male characteristics and self-monitored their behavior were more likely to be promoted than those who did not self-monitor."[131] One of the authors of the study explained: "Working women face a real dilemma: if they are seen to behave in a stereotypically male way, they may damage their chances of promotion, even though these traits are synonymous with successful managers. These findings suggest if these women learn how to self-monitor their behavior, they have a better chance of promotion."[132]

Despite the previous conclusion, studies indicate some differences in the inherent leadership styles of women and men. A Conference Board of Canada study found that "women are particularly strong in managing interpersonal relationships and their approach is more consensual."[133] Other studies have shown that women tend to adopt a style of shared leadership. They encourage participation, share power and information, and attempt to enhance followers' self-worth. They prefer to lead through inclusion and rely on their charisma, expertise, contacts, and interpersonal skills to influence others. Men, on the other hand, are more likely to use a directive command-and-control style. They rely on the formal authority of their position for their influence base.

Although it's interesting to see how men's and women's leadership styles differ, a more important question is whether they differ in effectiveness. Although some researchers have shown that men and women tend to be equally effective as leaders,[134] an increasing number of studies have shown that women executives, when rated by their peers, employees, and bosses, score higher than their male counterparts on a wide variety of measures, including getting extra effort from subordinates and overall effectiveness in leading. Subordinates also report more satisfaction with the leadership given by women.[135]

We know that there is no one best style for all situations. Instead, which leadership style is effective will depend on the situation. So even if men and women differ in their leadership styles, we should not assume that one is always preferable to the other. In today's organizations, flexibility, teamwork, trust, and information sharing are replacing rigid structures, competitive individualism, control, and secrecy. The best leaders listen, motivate, and provide support to their people.

GLOBAL IMPLICATIONS _____

Most of the research discussed in this chapter was conducted in English-speaking countries. We know very little about how culture might influence the validity of the theories, particularly in Eastern cultures. However, a recent analysis of the Global Leadership and Organizational Behavior Effectiveness (GLOBE) research program (see Chapter 3 for more details) has produced some useful preliminary insights about how to manage in Brazil, France, Egypt, and China.[136] Let's consider each.

- *Brazil* Based on the values of Brazilian employees, a manager leading a team in Brazil would need to be team oriented, participative, and humane. Leaders high on consideration who emphasize participative decision making and have high LPC scores would be best suited to managing employees in this culture. As one Brazilian manager said in the study, "We do not prefer leaders who take self-governing decisions and act alone without engaging the group. That's part of who we are."

- *France* French employees have a more bureaucratic view of leaders and are less likely to expect them to be humane and considerate than Canadian and American employees. A leader high on initiating structure (relatively task oriented) will do best and can make decisions in a relatively autocratic manner. A manager who scores high on consideration (people oriented) may find that style backfiring in France.

- *Egypt* Employees in Egypt are more likely to value team-oriented and participative leadership than Canadian and American employees. However, Egypt is also a relatively high-power-distance culture, meaning status differences between leaders and followers are expected. To be participative yet demonstrate one's status, the leader should ask employees for their opinions, try to minimize conflicts, and not be afraid to take charge and make the final decision (after consulting team members).

- *China* According to the GLOBE study, Chinese culture emphasizes being polite, considerate, and unselfish, but it also has a high performance orientation. These two factors suggest consideration and initiating structure may both be important. Although Chinese culture is relatively participative compared with the cultures of Canada and the United States, there are also status differences between leaders and employees. These findings suggest that a moderately participative style may work best with Chinese employees.

While the idea of charismatic leadership was developed based on North American observations, professors Dale Carl of the Faculty of Management at Ryerson University and Mansour Javidan at the University of Calgary found that transformational leadership is expressed relatively similarly in a variety of countries, including Canada, Hungary, India, Turkey, Austria, Singapore, Sweden, and Venezuela. The transformational leadership traits that appear to be universal are vision, foresight, providing encouragement, trustworthiness, dynamism, positiveness, and proactiveness. The two concluded that "effective business leaders in any country are expected by their subordinates to provide a powerful and proactive vision to guide the company into the future, strong motivational skills to stimulate all employees to fulfill the vision, and excellent planning skills to assist in implementing the vision."[137]

A vision is important in any culture, then, but how it is formed and communicated may still need to vary by culture. A GE executive who used his US leadership style in Japan recalls, "Nothing happened. I quickly realized that I had to adapt my approach, to act more as a consultant to my colleagues and to adopt a team-based motivational decision-making process rather than the more vocal style which tends to be common in the West. In Japan the silence of a leader means far more than a thousand words uttered by somebody else."[138]

LESSONS LEARNED

- Leaders provide vision and strategy; managers implement that vision and strategy.
- Leaders need to have a vision, they need to communicate that vision, and they must have followers.
- Leaders need to adjust their behaviours, depending on the situation and the needs of employees.

Summary and Implications

1 **What is the difference between a manager and a leader?** Managers promote stability, while leaders press for change. Leaders provide vision and strategy; managers implement that vision and strategy, coordinate and staff the organization, and handle day-to-day problems.

2 **Are there specific traits, behaviours, and situations that affect how one leads?** Early leadership theories were concerned with supervision, and sought to find out if there were ways to identify leaders. Trait theories examined whether there were some traits that were universal among leaders. While there are some common traits, leaders are more different than similar in terms of traits. Emotional intelligence is one of the few traits that has been found to be extremely important for leadership success. Other research has tried to discover whether some behaviours create better leaders than others. The findings were mixed, suggesting that leaders need to be both task-oriented and people-oriented. The mixed findings led researchers to contingency theories that consider the effect of situations in which leadership is applied. This research tells us that leaders need to adjust their behaviours, depending on the situation and the needs of employees. Contingency theories were an important contribution to the study of leadership.

3 **How does a leader lead with vision?** The more recent approaches to leadership move away from the supervisory tasks of leaders and focus on vision-setting activities. These theories try to explain how certain leaders can achieve extraordinary levels of performance from their followers, and they stress symbolic and emotionally appealing leadership behaviours. These leaders, known as *charismatic* or *transformational leaders*, inspire followers to go beyond their own self-interests for the good of the organization.

4 **Are there leadership roles for nonmanagers?** There are several approaches to being a leader even if one does not have a formal position of leadership. Mentoring is one way to be an informal leader. Mentors sponsor and support less-experienced employees, coaching and counselling them about their jobs. With self-leadership, individuals and teams set goals, plan and implement tasks, evaluate performance, solve their own problems, and motivate themselves. The supervisor plays a much reduced role. A person can also act as an informal leader on a team. Providing leadership online to telecommuting and physically distant employees is another leadership role available to many people. Keeping online teams motivated can be a challenging role. Leading without authority means exhibiting leadership behaviour even though you do not have a formal position or title that might encourage others to obey.

5 **What are some of the contemporary issues in leadership?** One leadership challenge today is how to be an authentic leader. Authentic leaders know who they are, know what they believe in and value, and act on those values and beliefs openly and candidly. Leaders also face the demand to be moral in their leadership. Moral leadership comes from within the individual, and, in general, means treating people well and with respect. Another hot issue in leadership is the question of whether men and women rely on different leadership styles, and if that is the case, whether one style is inherently superior to the other. An extensive review of the literature suggests two conclusions.[139] First, the similarities between men and women tend to outweigh the differences. Second, what differences there are seem to be that women fall back on a more democratic leadership style, while men feel more comfortable with a directive style.

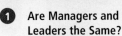

SNAPSHOT SUMMARY

1 Are Managers and Leaders the Same?

2 Leadership as Supervision
Trait Theories: Are Leaders Different from Others?
Behavioural Theories: Do Leaders Behave in Particular Ways?
Contingency Theories: Does the Situation Matter?
Substitutes for Leadership

3 Inspirational Leadership
Charismatic Leadership
Transformational Leadership

4 Contemporary Leadership Roles
Mentoring
Self-Leadership (or Self-Management)
Team Leadership
Online Leadership
Leading without Authority

5 Contemporary Issues in Leadership
Authentic Leadership
Moral Leadership
Gender and Leadership

OB at Work

for Review

1. Trace the development of leadership research.

2. What traits predict leadership?

3. What do behavioural theories imply about leadership?

4. What are the contingency variables in path-goal theory?

5. When might leaders be irrelevant?

6. Describe the strengths and weaknesses of a charismatic leader.

7. What are the differences between transactional and transformational leaders?

8. How do leaders create self-leaders?

9. What is moral leadership?

10. Why do you think effective female and male managers often exhibit similar traits and behaviours?

for Critical Thinking

1. Reconcile path-goal theory and substitutes for leadership.

2. What kind of activities could a full-time college or university student pursue that might lead to the perception that he or she is a charismatic leader? In pursuing those activities, what might the student do to enhance this perception of being charismatic?

3. Based on the low representation of women in upper management, to what extent do you think that organizations should actively promote women into the senior ranks of management?

4. Is there an ethical problem if leaders focus more on looking like a leader than actually being one? Discuss.

5. "Leaders make a real difference in an organization's performance." Build an argument in support of this statement. Then build an argument against this statement.

for You

- It's easy to imagine that theories of leadership are more important to those who are leaders or who plan in the near future to become leaders. However, leadership opportunities occur throughout an organization. You have no doubt seen a student leader who did not necessarily have any formal authority be extremely successful.

- Leaders are not born, they learn how to lead by paying attention to the situation and what needs to be done.

- There is no one best way to lead. It is important to consider the situation and the needs of the people who will be led.

- Sometimes no leader is needed—the individuals in the group simply work well enough together that each takes turns at leadership without appointing a formal leader.

Leaders Are Born

In North America, people are socialized to believe they can be whoever they want to be—and that includes being a leader.[140] While that makes for a nice children's tale (think *The Little Engine That Could*—"I think I can, I think I can"), life is not always wrapped in pretty little packages, and this is one example. Being an effective leader has more to do with what you are born with than what you do with what you have.

That leaders are born, not made, is not a new idea. Victorian era historian Thomas Carlyle wrote, "History is nothing but the biography of a few great men." Although today we should modify this to include women, his point still rings true: Great leaders are what make teams, companies, and even countries great. Can anyone disagree that people like Lester Pearson and Pierre Trudeau were gifted political leaders? Or that Joan of Arc and George Patton were brilliant and courageous military leaders? Or that Henry Ford, Jack Welch, and Steve Jobs were gifted business leaders? As one reviewer of the literature put it, "Leaders are not like other people." These leaders are great leaders because they have the right stuff—stuff the rest of us don't have, or have in lesser quantities.

If you are not yet convinced, a recent study of several hundred identical twins separated at birth found an amazing correlation in their ascendance into leadership roles. These twins were raised in totally different environments—some rich, some poor, some by educated parents, others by relatively uneducated parents, some in cities, others in small towns. But despite their different environments, each pair of twins had striking similarities in terms of whether they became leaders. Other research has found that shared environment—being raised in the same household, for example—has very little influence on leadership emergence.

Despite what we might like to believe, the evidence is clear: A substantial part of leadership is a product of our genes. If we have the right stuff, we are destined to be effective leaders. If we have the wrong stuff, we are unlikely to excel in that role. Leadership cannot be for everyone, and we make a mistake in thinking that everyone is equally capable of being a good leader.

Leaders Are Made

Of course, personal qualities and characteristics matter to leadership, as they do to most other behaviours.[141] But the real key is what you do with what you have.

First, if great leadership were merely the possession of a few key traits—say, intelligence and personality—we could simply give people a test and select the most intelligent, extraverted, and conscientious people to be leaders. But that would be a disaster. Leadership is much too complex to be reduced to a simple formula of traits. As smart as Steve Jobs was, there are smarter and more extraverted people out there—thousands of them. That is not the essence of what makes him, or political or military leaders, great. It is a combination of factors—upbringing, early business experiences, learning from failure, and driving ambition. Second, great leaders tell us that the key to their leadership success is not the characteristics they had at birth, but what they learned along the way.

Take Warren Buffett, admired not only for his investing prowess but also as a leader and boss. Being a great leader, according to Buffett, is a matter of acquiring the right habits. "The chains of habit are too light to be noticed until they are too heavy to be broken," he says. Buffett argues that characteristics or habits such as intelligence, trustworthiness, and integrity are the most important to leadership—and at least the latter two can be developed. He says, "You need integrity, intelligence, and energy to succeed. Integrity is totally a matter of choice—and it is habit-forming."

Finally, this focus on "great men and great women" is not very productive. People need to believe in something, and one of those things is that they can improve themselves. Who would want to think we were just some accumulation of genetic markers and our entire life was just a stage in which our genes played themselves out? People like the optimistic story of *The Little Engine That Could* because we have a choice to think positively (we can become good leaders) or negatively (leaders are predetermined), and it's better to be positive.

OB at work

Are You a Self-Manager?

To determine your self-management initiative, rate each of the following items, from 1 ("Never Do This") to 7 ("Always Do This").

	Never Do This						Always Do This

Planning

1. I plan out my day before beginning to work.	1	2	3	4	5	6	7
2. I try to schedule my work in advance.	1	2	3	4	5	6	7
3. I plan my career carefully.	1	2	3	4	5	6	7
4. I come to work early to plan my day.	1	2	3	4	5	6	7
5. I use lists and agendas to structure my workday.	1	2	3	4	5	6	7
6. I set specific job goals on a regular basis.	1	2	3	4	5	6	7
7. I set daily goals for myself.	1	2	3	4	5	6	7
8. I try to manage my time.	1	2	3	4	5	6	7

Access management

1. I control the access subordinates have to me in order to get my work done.	1	2	3	4	5	6	7
2. I use a special place at work where I can work uninterrupted.	1	2	3	4	5	6	7
3. I hold my telephone calls when I need to get things done.	1	2	3	4	5	6	7

Catch-up activities

1. I come in early or stay late at work to prevent distractions from interfering with my work.	1	2	3	4	5	6	7
2. I take my work home with me to make sure it gets done.	1	2	3	4	5	6	7
3. I come in on my days off to catch up on my work.	1	2	3	4	5	6	7

Emotions management

1. I have learned to manage my aggressiveness with my subordinates.	1	2	3	4	5	6	7
2. My facial expression and conversational tone are important in dealing with subordinates.	1	2	3	4	5	6	7
3. It's important for me to maintain a "professional" manager-subordinate relationship.	1	2	3	4	5	6	7
4. I try to keep my emotions under control.	1	2	3	4	5	6	7

Scoring Key:

Higher scores mean a higher degree of self-management. For the overall scale, scores of 100 or higher represent high scores. For each area, the following represent high scores: planning, scores of 48 or higher; access management, scores of 18 or higher; catch-up activities, scores of 18 or higher; and emotions management, scores of 24 or higher.

Source: M. Castaneda, T. A. Kolenko, and R. J. Aldag, "Self-Management Perceptions and Practices: A Structural Equations Analysis," *Journal of Organizational Behavior* 20, 1999. Table 4, pp. 114–115. Copyright © John Wiley & Sons, Inc. Reproduced with permission.

SELF-ASSESSMENT LIBRARY | LEARNING ABOUT YOURSELF

More Learning About Yourself Exercises

Additional self-assessments relevant to this chapter appear on MyOBLab (**www.pearsoned.ca/myoblab**).

II.B.1 What's My Leadership Style?
IV.E.5 What Is My LPC Score?
II.B.2 How Charismatic Am I?
IV.E.4 Am I an Ethical Leader?

When you complete the additional assessments, consider the following:

1. Am I surprised about my score?
2. Would my friends evaluate me similarly?

BREAKOUT **GROUP** EXERCISES

Form small groups to discuss the following topics, as assigned by your instructor:

1. Identify an example of someone you think of as a good leader (currently or in the past). What traits did he or she have? How did these traits differ from those in someone you identify as a bad leader?

2. Identify a situation when you were in a leadership position (in a group, in the workplace, within your family, etcetera). To what extent were you able to use a contingency approach to leadership? What made that easier or more difficult for you?

3. When you have worked in student groups, how frequently have leaders emerged in the groups? What difficulties occur when leaders are leading peers? Are there ways to overcome these difficulties?

WORKING WITH **OTHERS** EXERCISE

Being Charismatic

From Concepts to Skills on pages 428–429 indicates how to become charismatic. In this exercise, you will use that information to practise projecting charisma.[142]

1. The class should break into pairs.

2. Student A's task is to "lead" Student B through a new-student orientation to your college or university. The orientation should last about 10 to 15 minutes. Assume that Student B is new to your college or university and is unfamiliar with the campus. Student A should attempt to project himself or herself as charismatic.

3. Roles now reverse and Student B's task is to "lead" Student A in a 10- to 15-minute program on how to study more effectively for college or university exams. Take a few minutes to think about what has worked well for you, and assume that Student A is a new student interested in improving his or her study habits. Again, Student B should attempt to project himself or herself as charismatic.

4. When both role plays are complete, each pair should assess how well it did in projecting charisma and how it might improve.

ETHICAL **DILEMMA** EXERCISE

Do the Ends Justify the Means?

Whole Foods, a fast-growing chain of upscale grocery stores with stores in Vancouver, West Vancouver, Toronto, and Oakville, a few in London, England, as well as a large number in the United States, has long been a Wall Street favourite.[143] It regularly appears on *Fortune's* list of 100 Best Companies to Work For (it was #22 in 2008) and has spawned its share of competitors, including Fresh Market and Wild Oats.

Given that most industry analysts see a bright future for upscale organic markets like Whole Foods, it's no surprise they have attracted their share of investor blogs. One prominent blogger, "Rahodeb," consistently extolled the virtues of Whole Foods stock and derided Wild Oats. Rahodeb predicted Wild Oats would eventually be forced into bankruptcy and the Whole Foods stock price would grow at an annual rate of 18 percent. Rahodeb's Yahoo! Finance blog entries were widely read because he seemed to have special insights into the industry and into Whole Foods in particular.

Would it surprise you to learn that Rahodeb was exposed in 2007 as Whole Foods co-founder and CEO John Mackey? ("Rahodeb" is an anagram of "Deborah," the name of Mackey's wife.) What is more, while Rahodeb was talking down Wild Oats stock, Whole Foods was in

the process of acquiring Wild Oats, and deriding the target may have made the acquisition easier and cheaper. Because the companies often have stores in the same cities, the Federal Trade Commission (FTC) attempted to block the acquisition and was responsible for "outing" Mackey. In March 2009, Whole Foods agreed to sell 31 of the Wild Oats stores it had acquired, drop use of the Wild Oats name, and undertake other actions that nullified the benefits of the acquisition.

Mackey lamented the debacle—*not* his secret blogging but the Wild Oats acquisition. He said, "We would be better off today if we hadn't done this deal—taking on all this debt right before the economy collapsed." By 2008, Mackey was blogging again, under his real name. His posts are neither as frequent nor as interesting as Rahodeb's.

Do you think it is unethical for a company leader like Mackey to pose as an investor, talking up his or her company's stock price while talking down his competitor's? Should leaders be judged solely on their end achievements? Or do the means they choose also reflect on their leadership qualities? Would Mackey's behaviour affect your willingness to work for or invest in Whole Foods? Is it impossible for leaders to be ethical and successful?

CASE INCIDENTS

Moving from Colleague to Supervisor

Cheryl Kahn, Rob Carstons, and Linda McGee have something in common.[144] They all were promoted within their organizations into management positions. As well, each found the transition a challenge.

Kahn was promoted to director of catering for the Glazier Group of restaurants. With the promotion, she realized that things would never be the same again. No longer would she be able to participate in water-cooler gossip or shrug off an employee's chronic lateness. She says she found her new role to be daunting. "At first I was like a bulldozer knocking everyone over, and that was not well received. I was saying, 'It's my way or the highway.' And was forgetting that my friends were also in transition." She admits that this style alienated just about everyone with whom she worked.

Carstons, a technical manager at IBM, talks about the uncertainty he felt after being promoted to a manager from a junior programmer. "It was a little bit challenging to be suddenly giving directives to peers, when just the day before you were one of them. You try to be careful not to offend anyone. It's strange walking into a room and the whole conversation changes. People don't want to be as open with you when you become the boss."

McGee is now president of Medex Insurance Services. She started as a customer-service representative with the company, then leapfrogged over colleagues in a series of promotions. Her fast rise created problems. Colleagues would say, "'Oh, here comes the big cheese now.' God only knows what they talked about behind my back."

Questions

1. A lot of new managers err in selecting the right leadership style when they move into management. Why do you think this happens?

2. If new managers don't know what leadership style to use, what does this say about leadership and leadership training?

3. Which leadership theories, if any, could help new leaders deal with this transition?

4. Do you think it's easier or harder to be promoted internally into a formal leadership position than to come into it as an outsider? Explain.

The Kinder, Gentler Leader?

The stereotypical view of a CEO—tough-minded, dominant, and hyper-aggressive—may be giving way to a more sensitive image.[145] Nowhere is this shifting standard more apparent than at General Electric. There may be no CEO more revered for his leadership style than former CEO Jack Welch, a "tough guy," in his own words. Yet his handpicked successor, Jeff Immelt, is remarkable for his very different leadership style. Whereas Welch was intense, brash, and directive, Immelt was described by *Financial Times* as "unshakably polite, self-deprecating and relaxed."

Of course, Immelt is only one leader, and his success at GE is hardly assured. But he is far from alone in the set of seemingly sensitive CEOs. As CEO of Colgate-Palmolive, Reuben Mark had this leadership credo, "I have made it my business to be sure that nothing important or creative at Colgate-Palmolive is perceived as my idea." Brad Shaw, CEO of Calgary-based Shaw Communications, believes that being a compassionate leader matters. "We're focused on business results, and that's how we operate. But I believe you can have better results with compassion than not."

A recent study of CEOs seems to suggest that this trend is spreading. The CEOs in its sample scored, on average, 12 points below average on tough-mindedness. Yes, that is below average. As one observer of the corporate world concludes, "The Jack Welch approach appears to be on the wane."

You might think a kinder, gentler approach works only for *Fortune* 500 CEOs, whose very job security might rely on glowing press coverage. In the United States, though, you don't get much farther from Wall Street than the Hanford, Washington, nuclear cleanup site, and there is evidence that the "nice" approach to leadership is taking hold there, too. Jerry Long, VP of operations for CH2M

HILL's cleanup of the Hanford site, argues that a central part of his job is "showing them you care."

Consider the meteoric rise of Barack Obama—all the way from state senator to president in just five years. While a student at Harvard Law School, Obama was famous attorney Laurence Tribe's research assistant. Tribe said of Obama, "I've known senators, presidents. I've never known anyone with what seems to me more raw political talent. He just seems to have the surest way of calmly reaching across what are impenetrable barriers to many people."

Although some have argued that Obama's presidential campaign represented an emphasis of style over substance, and the jury is still out on how effective he will be as president, it may be that after years of acrimonious political wars, people considered the *how* as important as the *what*. Despite serious economic problems in the United States, Obama's personal popularity remains steady. In a 2011 poll, more than 70 percent of respondents said they liked him personally, even though a large number of people were not happy with the way the economy was unfolding.

Questions

1. Do you think the kinder, gentler leader image is just a fad?

2. Do you think the kinder, gentler leadership approach works better in some situations than others? Is it possible that Welch and Immelt are *both* effective leaders?

3. Do you think the leadership style of people like Immelt and Obama is a result of nature, nurture, or both? What factors can you think of to support your answer?

FROM CONCEPTS TO SKILLS

Practising to Be Charismatic

In order to be charismatic in your leadership style, you need to engage in the following behaviours:[146]

1. *Project a powerful, confident, and dynamic presence.* This has both verbal and nonverbal components. Use a captivating and engaging voice tone. Convey confidence. Talk directly to people, maintain direct eye contact, and hold your body posture in a way that says you are sure of yourself. Speak clearly, avoid stammering, and avoid sprinkling your sentences with noncontent phrases such as "ahhh" and "you know."

2. *Articulate an overarching goal.* You need to share a vision for the future, develop an unconventional way of achieving the vision, and have the ability to communicate the vision to others.

   The vision is a clear statement of where you want to go and how you are going to get there. You need to persuade others that the achievement of this vision is in their self-interest.

   You need to look for fresh and radically different approaches to problems. The road to achieving your vision should be seen as novel, but also appropriate to the context.

   Charismatic individuals not only have a vision, but they are also able to get others to buy into it. The real power of Martin Luther King Jr. was not that he had a dream, but that he could articulate it in terms that made it accessible to millions.

3. *Communicate high performance expectations and confidence in others' ability to meet these expectations.* You need to demonstrate your confidence in people by stating ambitious goals for them individually and as a group. You then convey absolute belief that they will achieve their expectations.

4. *Be sensitive to the needs of followers.* Charismatic leaders get to know their followers individually. You need to understand their individual needs and develop intensely personal relationships with each. This is done through encouraging followers to express their points of view, being approachable, genuinely listening to and caring about followers' concerns, and asking questions so that followers can learn what is really important to them.

Practising Skills

You are a manufacturing manager in a large electronics plant. The company's management is always searching for ways to increase efficiency. They recently installed new machines and set up a new simplified work system, but to the surprise of everyone—including you—the expected increase in production was not realized. In fact, production has begun to drop, quality has fallen off, and the number of employee resignations has risen.

You do not think that there is anything wrong with the machines. You have had reports from other companies that are using them, and they confirm your opinion. You have also had representatives from the firm that built the machines go over them, and they report that the machines are operating at peak efficiency.

OB at work

You know that some aspect of the new work system must be responsible for the change, but you are getting no help from your immediate team members—four first-line supervisors who report to you and who are each in charge of a section—or your supply manager. The drop in production has been variously attributed to poor training of the operators, lack of an adequate system of financial incentives, and poor morale. All of the individuals involved have deep feelings about this issue. Your team does not agree with you or with one another.

This morning you received a phone call from your division manager. He had just received your production figures for the past six months and was calling to express his concern. He indicated that the problem was yours to solve in any way that you think best, but that he would like to know within a week what steps you plan to take.

You share your division manager's concern with the falling productivity and know that your employees are also concerned. Using your knowledge of leadership concepts, which leadership style would you choose? And why?

Source: Based on V. H. Vroom, "A New Look at Managerial Decision Making," *Organizational Dynamics*, Spring 1973, pp. 66–80. With permission.

Reinforcing Skills

1. Think of a group or team to which you currently belong or of which you have been a part. What type of leadership style did the leader of this group appear to exhibit? Give some specific examples of the types of leadership behaviours he or she used. Evaluate the leadership style. Was it appropriate for the group? Why or why not? What would you have done differently? Why?

2. Observe two sports teams (either college/university or professional—one that you consider successful and the other unsuccessful). What leadership styles appear to be used in these team situations? Give some specific examples of the types of leadership behaviours you observe. How would you evaluate the leadership style? Was it appropriate for the team? Why or why not? To what degree do you think leadership style influenced the team's outcomes?

Decision Making, Creativity, and Ethics

A coffee roasting company in BC's interior may seem remote from the workers on coffee plantations in South America. But the two owners wanted their business to make a difference. Can committing to selling only fair trade coffee be a successful strategy?

LEARNING OUTCOMES

1. Is there a right way to make decisions?

2. How do people actually make decisions?

3. How can knowledge management improve decision making?

4. What factors affect group decision making?

5. How can we get more creative decisions?

6. What is ethics, and how can it be used for better decision making?

7. What is corporate social responsibility?

E Elana Rosenfeld and Leo Johnson are the founders and owners of Invermere, BC-based Kicking Horse Coffee Company, the top organic fair trade coffee company in Canada.[1] The decision to create a fair trade coffee company reflects the values the two have toward their employees and the farmer co-ops in Mexico, Nicaragua, Peru, and other countries from which they buy their coffee. When the two travel to the coffee plantations for weeks at a time, they rely on their employees to keep everything running smoothly back in BC.

"Knowing we can leave the shop in good hands allows us to develop a personal relationship with local suppliers," Rosenfeld says. "In turn, we can report back to our employees and customers on how fair trade coffee makes a real difference to the lives of those who were often exploited. That message encourages further support for the company's mission and products."

Rosenfeld and Johnson started roasting coffee in their garage in 1996, with their small children in tow. Two years later they were one of the first companies to join TransFair Canada (now known as Fairtrade Canada), an organization that encourages Canadian organizations to make choices that would improve the working conditions of farmers and workers in the developing world. By 2003 Kicking Horse Coffee made the decision to purchase and roast only 100 percent certified organic coffee beans.

In this chapter, we describe how decisions in organizations are made, as well as how creativity is linked to decision making. We also look at the ethical and socially responsible aspects of decision making as part of our discussion. Decision making affects people at all levels of the organization, and it is engaged in by both individuals and groups. Therefore, we also consider the special characteristics of group decision making.

OB IS FOR EVERYONE

- Do people really consider every alternative when making a decision?
- Is it okay to use intuition when making decisions?
- Why is it that we sometimes make bad decisions?
- Why are some people more creative than others?
- Why do some people make more ethical decisions than others?

How Should Decisions Be Made?

A **decision** is the choice made from two or more alternatives. Decision making happens at all levels of an organization. Top managers determine their organization's goals, what products or services to offer, how best to finance operations, or where to locate a new high-tech research and development facility. Middle- and lower-level managers determine production schedules, select new employees, and decide how pay raises are to be allocated. Nonmanagerial employees decide how much effort to put forward once at work and whether to comply with a request from their manager. In recent years organizations have been empowering their nonmanagerial employees with decision-making authority that was historically reserved for managers alone. Thus, nonmanagerial employees may have the authority to make decisions about initiating some new project or solving certain customer-related problems without consulting their managers.

Knowing how to make decisions is an important part of everyday life. Below we consider various decision-making models that apply to both individual and group choices. (Later in the chapter, we discuss special aspects of group decision making.) We start with the rational model, which describes decision making in the ideal world, a situation that rarely exists. We then look at alternatives to the rational model, and how decisions actually get made.

The Rational Decision-Making Process

The **rational** decision maker makes consistent, value-maximizing choices within specified constraints.[2] These choices are made following a six-step **rational decision-making model**.[3] Moreover, specific assumptions underlie this model.

The Rational Model

The six steps in the rational decision-making model are presented in Exhibit 12-1.

First, the decision maker must *define the problem*. If you calculate your monthly expenses and find you are spending $50 more than your monthly earnings, you have defined a problem. Many poor decisions can be traced to the decision maker overlooking a problem or defining the wrong problem.

decision The choice made from two or more alternatives.

rational Refers to choices that are consistent and value-maximizing within specified constraints.

rational decision-making model A six-step decision-making model that describes how individuals should behave in order to maximize some outcome.

EXHIBIT 12-1 Steps in the Rational Decision-Making Model

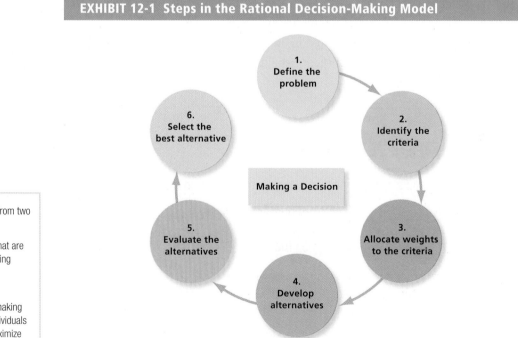

The decision maker then needs to *identify the criteria* that are relevant to making the decision. This step brings the decision maker's interests, values, and similar personal preferences into the process, because not all individuals will consider the same factors relevant for any particular decision.

To understand the types of criteria that might be used to make a decision, consider how Toronto-based Canadian Imperial Bank of Commerce (CIBC) handles the many sponsorship requests it receives each year. When it makes a decision about whether to support a request, the bank takes into account a number of criteria. Specifically, to be eligible for funding, a request must

- Be aligned to youth, education or health

- Be for a Canadian organization, using funds in Canada

- Be for a registered charity with a Canada Revenue Agency Charitable Registration Number or a non-profit organization

- Have a record of achievement or potential for success in line with our overall goals

- Address a community need and provide direct impact to the community served

- Include planned outcomes, supported by a measurement and evaluation process

- Have audited financial statements for the organization, sound financial practices and a sustainable funding model[4]

If the sponsorship request does not meet these criteria, it is not funded.

Because the criteria identified are rarely all equal in importance, the third step requires the decision maker to *allocate weights to the criteria.*

The fourth step requires the decision maker to *develop alternatives* that could succeed in resolving the problem.

The decision maker then critically *evaluates the alternatives*, using the previously established criteria and weights.

Finally, the decision maker *selects the best alternative* by evaluating each alternative against the weighted criteria and selecting the alternative with the highest total score.

Assumptions of the Model

The rational decision-making model we just described contains a number of assumptions.[5] Let's briefly outline those assumptions:

- *Problem clarity.* The problem is clear and unambiguous and complete information is available.

- *Known options.* It's assumed that the decision maker can identify all relevant criteria, all workable alternatives, and their consequences.

- *Clear preferences.* The criteria and alternatives can be ranked and weighted to reflect their importance.

- *Constant preferences.* The specific decision criteria are constant and the weights assigned to them are stable over time.

- *No time or cost constraints.* The decision maker can obtain full information about criteria and alternatives because there are no time or cost constraints.

- *Maximum payoff.* The decision maker will choose the alternative that yields the highest perceived value.

During his 10-year tenure as CEO of Symantec, John Thompson made a decision in reaction to the problem of an explosion of Internet viruses. Thompson, now chairman of the board of directors, said, "About every 15 to 18 months, there's a new form of attack that makes old technologies less effective." So he decided to acquire 13 companies that specialize in products such as personal firewalls, intrusion detection, and early warning systems that protect everything from corporate intranets to consumer email inboxes.

How Do Individuals Actually Make Decisions?

In 1996, when Elana Rosenfeld and Leo Johnson were just getting their Kicking Horse Coffee Company started, they had one goal: "get everyone to drink good coffee."[6] Obviously, people differ as to what they perceive good coffee to be. Some like Tim Hortons the best. Others enjoy Starbucks. Fans of one company complain about the coffee of the other. Rosenfeld felt she knew what really good coffee was, and it started with fair trade beans. When she first began educating her customers about her product, they thought she meant "free trade." To change customer perceptions, Rosenfeld said they "did a good job of marketing and explaining it on our packaging." They also knew that some people thought good coffee meant Italian coffee, which Kicking Horse does not sell. So they created fun names for the coffee, such as *454 Horse Power* and *Hoodoo Jo* to appeal to a broader number of consumers. What sorts of perceptual biases might affect the decisions people make?

When decision makers are faced with a simple problem with few alternative courses of action, and when the cost of searching out and evaluating alternatives is low, the rational model provides a fairly accurate description of the decision process.[7] However, such situations are the exception. Most decisions in the real world don't follow the rational model. People are usually content to find an acceptable or reasonable solution to their problem rather than an optimal one. Choices tend to be confined to the problem symptom and to the current alternative. As one expert in decision making has concluded, "Most significant decisions are made by judgment, rather than by a defined prescriptive model."[8] What is more, people are remarkably unaware of making suboptimal decisions.[9]

In the following sections, we indicate areas where the reality of decision making conflicts with the rational model.[10] None of these ways of making decisions should be considered *irrational*; they simply depart from the rational model when information is unavailable or too costly to collect.

Bounded Rationality in Considering Alternatives

When you considered which university or college to attend, did you look at *every* workable alternative? Did you carefully identify all the criteria that were important in your decision? Did you evaluate each alternative against the criteria in order to find the optimum school? The answer to these questions is probably "no." But don't feel bad, because few people selected their educational institution this way.

Do people really consider every alternative when making a decision?

It's difficult for individuals to identify and consider every possible alternative available to them. Realistically speaking, people are limited by their ability to interpret, process, and act on information. This is called **bounded rationality**.[11]

How does bounded rationality work for the typical individual? Once we have identified a problem, we begin to search for criteria and alternatives. But the list of criteria is likely to be far from exhaustive. We identify a limited list of the most obvious choices, which usually represent familiar criteria and tried-and-true solutions. Next, we begin reviewing them, but our review will not be comprehensive. Instead, we focus on alternatives that differ only in a relatively small degree from the choice currently in effect. Following familiar and well-worn paths, we review alternatives only until we identify one that is "good enough"—that meets an acceptable level of performance. That ends our search. So the solution represents a **satisficing** choice—the first *acceptable* one we encounter—rather than an optimal one. In practice, this might mean that rather than interview 10 job candidates for a position and then make a hiring decision, a manager interviews one at a time until someone that is "good enough" is found. This process of satisficing is not always a bad idea—using a simple process may frequently be more sensible than the traditional rational decision-making model.[12]

bounded rationality Limitations on a person's ability to interpret, process, and act on information.

satisficing To provide a solution that is both satisfactory and sufficient.

Intuition

Perhaps the least rational way of making decisions is to rely on intuition. **Intuitive decision making** is a nonconscious process created from distilled experience.[13] Its defining qualities are that it occurs outside conscious thought; it relies on holistic associations, or links between disparate pieces of information; it's fast; and it's affectively charged, meaning that it usually engages the emotions.[14]

Is it okay to use intuition when making decisions?

Intuition is not rational, but that does not necessarily make it wrong. Nor does it always operate in opposition to rational analysis; rather, the two can complement each other. Intuition can be a powerful force in decision making. But intuition is not superstition, or the product of some magical or paranormal sixth sense. As one recent review noted, "Intuition is a highly complex and highly developed form of reasoning that is based on years of experience and learning."[15] *OB in the Street* shows how intuition applies to grand master chess players.

OB in the STREET

Intuition Comes to the Chess Board

Can intuition really help you win a chess game? Apparently so.[16] Novice chess players and grand masters were shown an actual, but unfamiliar, chess game with about 25 pieces on the board. After 5 or 10 seconds, the pieces were removed, and each subject was asked to reconstruct the pieces by position. On average, the grand master could put 23 or 24 pieces in their correct squares, while the novice was able to replace only 6. Then the exercise was changed. This time, the pieces were placed randomly on the board. Again, the novice got only about 6 correct, but so did the grand master! The second exercise demonstrated that the grand master did not have a better memory than the novice. What the grand master *did* have was the ability, based on the experience of having played thousands of chess games, to recognize patterns and clusters of pieces that occur on chessboards in the course of games. Studies also show that chess professionals can play 50 or more games simultaneously, making decisions in seconds, and exhibit only a moderately lower level of skill than when playing one game under tournament conditions, where decisions take half an hour or longer. The expert's experience allows him or her to recognize the pattern in a situation and draw on previously learned information associated with that pattern to arrive at a decision quickly. The result is that the intuitive decision maker can decide rapidly based on what appears to be very limited information.

As the example of the chess players shows, those who use intuition effectively often rely on their experiences to help guide and assess their intuitions. That is why many managers turn to intuition, as *Focus on Research* shows.

FOCUS ON RESEARCH

Many Managers Add Intuition to Data Analysis

Do senior managers use intuition in their decision making? A study of 60 experienced professionals holding high-level positions in major US organizations found that many of them used intuition to help them make workplace decisions.[17] Twelve percent said they always used it; 47 percent said they often used it. Only 10 percent said they

intuitive decision making A nonconscious process created out of a person's many experiences.

rarely or seldom used intuition. More than 90 percent of managers said they were likely to use a mix of intuition and data analysis when making decisions.

When asked the types of decisions where they most often used intuition, 40 percent reported that they used it to make people-related decisions such as hiring, performance appraisal, harassment complaints, and safety issues. The managers said they also used intuition for quick or unexpected decisions so they could avoid delays. They also were more likely to rely on intuition in novel situations that had a lot of uncertainty.

The results from this study suggest that intuitive decisions are best applied when time is short; when policies, rules, and guidelines do not give clear-cut advice; when there is a great deal of uncertainty; and when quantitative analysis needs a check and balance.

For most of the twentieth century, experts believed that decision makers' use of intuition was irrational or ineffective. That is no longer the case.[18] We now recognize that rational analysis has been overemphasized and that, in certain instances, relying on intuition can improve decision making.[19] But, we cannot rely on it too much. Because it is so unquantifiable, it's hard to know when our hunches are right or wrong. A 2010 study that examined people's ability to "use their gut" to make decisions found that not everyone's gut is reliable. For some people, the physiological feelings that one associates with intuition works, but for others it does not.[20] The key is not to either abandon or rely solely on intuition, but to supplement it with evidence and good judgment.

Judgment Shortcuts

Decision makers engage in bounded rationality, but they also allow systematic biases and errors to creep into their judgments.[21] To minimize effort and avoid difficult trade-offs, people tend to rely too heavily on experience, impulses, gut feelings, and convenient rules of thumb. In many instances, these shortcuts are helpful. However, they can lead to distortions of rationality, as *OB in the Street* shows.

Why is it that we sometimes make bad decisions?

OB in the STREET
Penalty Kick Decisions

Should you stand still or leap into action? This is the classic question facing a goalie in a faceoff against a midfielder for a penalty kick.[22] Ofer H. Azar, a lecturer in the School of Management at Ben-Gurion University in Israel, finds that goalies often make the wrong decision.

Why? The goalie tries to anticipate where the ball will go after the kick. There is only a split second to do anything after the kick, so anticipating and acting seem like a good decision.

Azar became interested in studying goalie behaviour after realizing that the "incentives are huge" for the goalie to get it right. "Goalkeepers face penalty kicks regularly, so they are not only high-motivated decision makers, but also very experienced ones," he explains. That said, 80 percent of penalty kicks score, so goalies are in a difficult situation at that instant when the kick goes off.

Azar's study found that goalies rarely stayed in the centre of the net as the ball was fired (just 6.3 percent of the time). But staying in the centre is actually the best strategy. Goalies halted penalty kicks when staying in the centre 33.3 percent of the time. They were successful only 14.2 percent of the time when they moved left and only 12.6 percent of the time when they moved right.

Azar argues that the results show that there is a "bias for action," explaining that goalies think they will feel worse if they do *nothing* and miss, than if they do *something* and miss. This bias then clouds their judgment, encouraging them to move to one side or the other, rather than just staying in the centre, where the odds are actually more in their favour.

In what follows, we discuss some of the most common judgment shortcuts to alert you to mistakes that are often made when making decisions.

Overconfidence Bias

It's been said that "no problem in judgment and decision making is more prevalent and more potentially catastrophic than overconfidence."[23]

When we are given factual questions and asked to judge the probability that our answers are correct, we tend to be far too optimistic. This is known as **overconfidence bias**. When people say they are 65 to 70 percent confident that they are right, they are actually correct only about 50 percent of the time.[24] When they say they are 100 percent sure, they tend to be right about 70 to 85 percent of the time.[25]

Individuals whose intellectual and interpersonal abilities are *weakest* are most likely to overestimate their performance and ability.[26] So as managers and employees become more knowledgeable about an issue, they become less likely to display overconfidence.[27] Overconfidence is most likely to surface when organizational members are considering issues or problems that are outside their area of expertise.[28]

Anchoring Bias

The **anchoring bias** is a tendency to fixate on initial information and fail to adequately adjust for subsequent information.[29] It occurs because the mind appears to give a disproportionate amount of emphasis to the first information it receives.[30] Anchors are widely used by people in professions where persuasion skills are important—such as advertising, management, politics, real estate, and law. For instance, in a mock jury trial, the plaintiff's attorney asked one set of jurors to make an award in the range of $15 million to $50 million. The plaintiff's attorney asked another set of jurors for an award in the range of $50 million to $150 million. Consistent with the anchoring bias, the median awards were $15 million and $50 million, respectively.[31]

Consider the role of anchoring in negotiations. Any time a negotiation takes place, so does anchoring. As soon as someone states a number, your ability to ignore that number has been compromised. For instance, when a prospective employer asks how much you were making in your prior job, your answer typically anchors the employer's offer. You may want to keep this in mind when you negotiate your salary, but remember to set the anchor only as high as you realistically can. Finally, the more precise your anchor, the smaller the adjustment. Some research suggests people think of adjustment after an anchor is set as rounding off a number. If you suggest an initial target salary of $55 000, your boss will consider $50 000 to $60 000 a reasonable range for negotiation, but if you mention $55 650, your boss is more likely to consider $55 000 to $56 000 the range of likely values for negotiation.[32]

Confirmation Bias

The rational decision-making process assumes that we objectively gather information. But we don't. We *selectively* gather it. The **confirmation bias** represents a specific case of selective perception. We seek out information that reaffirms our past choices, and we discount information that contradicts them.[33] We also tend to accept at face value information that confirms our preconceived views, while we are critical and skeptical of information that challenges these views. Therefore, the information we gather is typically biased toward supporting views we already hold. This confirmation bias influ-

overconfidence bias Error in judgment that arises from being far too optimistic about one's own performance.

anchoring bias A tendency to fixate on initial information, from which one then fails to adequately adjust for subsequent information.

confirmation bias The tendency to seek out information that reaffirms past choices and to discount information that contradicts past judgments.

ences where we go to collect evidence because we tend to seek out sources most likely to tell us what we want to hear. It also leads us to give too much weight to supporting information and too little to contradictory information.[34]

Availability Bias

The **availability bias** is the tendency for people to base their judgments on information that is readily available.[35] Events that evoke emotions, that are particularly vivid, or that have occurred more recently tend to be more available in our memory. As a result, we tend to overestimate unlikely events, such as airplane crashes, compared with more likely events, such as car crashes. The availability bias can also explain why managers, when doing annual performance appraisals, tend to give more weight to recent behaviours of an employee than to those of six or nine months ago.

Escalation of Commitment

Some decision makers escalate commitment to a failing course of action.[36] **Escalation of commitment** refers to staying with a decision even when there is clear evidence that it's wrong. For example, a friend has been dating a man for about four years. Although she admits that things are not going well, she is determined to marry him anyway. Her justification: "I have a lot invested in the relationship!"

Individuals escalate commitment to a failing course of action when they view themselves as responsible for the failure.[37] That is, they "throw good money after bad" to demonstrate that their initial decision was not wrong and to avoid having to admit they made a mistake.[38] In fact, people who carefully gather and consider information consistent with the rational decision-making model are *more* likely to engage in escalation of commitment than those who spend less time thinking about their choices.[39] Perhaps they have invested so much time and energy into making their decisions that they have convinced themselves they are taking the right course of action and don't update their knowledge in the face of new information. Many organizations have suffered large losses because a manager was determined to prove his or her original decision was right by continuing to commit resources to a lost cause.

Randomness Error

Human beings have a lot of difficulty dealing with chance. Most of us like to believe we have some control over our world and our destiny. Our tendency to believe we can predict the outcome of random events is the **randomness error**.

Decision making becomes impaired when we try to create meaning out of random events, particularly when we turn imaginary patterns into superstitions.[40] These can be completely contrived, such as "I never make important decisions on Friday the 13th." They can also evolve from a certain pattern of behaviour that has been reinforced previously. For example, before every game, former NHL star goalie Patrick Roy would skate "backwards towards the net before turning around at the last second, an act he believed made the goal shrink."[41] Superstitious behaviour can be debilitating when it affects daily judgments or biases major decisions.

Risk Aversion

Mathematically, we should find a 50–50 flip of the coin for $100 to be worth as much as a sure promise of $50. After all, the expected value of the gamble over a number of trials is $50. However, most people don't consider these options equally valuable. Rather, nearly everyone but committed gamblers would rather have the sure thing than a risky prospect.[42] For many people, a 50–50 flip of a coin even for $200 might not be worth as much as a sure promise of $50, even though the gamble is mathematically worth twice as much as the sure thing! This tendency to prefer a sure thing over a risky outcome is **risk aversion**.

availability bias The tendency for people to base their judgments on information that is readily available to them rather than complete data.

escalation of commitment An increased commitment to a previous decision despite negative information.

randomness error The tendency of individuals to believe that they can predict the outcome of random events.

risk aversion The tendency to prefer a sure gain of a moderate amount over a riskier outcome, even if the riskier outcome might have a higher expected payoff.

Risk aversion has important implications. Ambitious people with power that can be taken away (most managers) appear to be especially risk averse, perhaps because they don't want to lose on a gamble everything they have worked so hard to achieve.[43] CEOs at risk of being terminated are also exceptionally risk averse, even when a riskier investment strategy is in their firms' best interests.[44]

Because people are less likely to escalate commitment where there is a great deal of uncertainty, the implications of risk aversion are not all bad.[45] When a risky investment is not paying off, most people would rather play it safe and cut their losses, but if they think the outcome is a sure thing, they will keep escalating.

Risk preference is sometimes reversed: People prefer to take their chances when trying to prevent a negative outcome.[46] They would rather take a 50–50 gamble on losing $100 than accept the certain loss of $50. Thus they will risk losing a lot of money at trial rather than settle out of court. Trying to cover up wrongdoing instead of admitting a mistake, despite the risk of truly catastrophic press coverage or even jail time, is another example. Stressful situations can make these risk preferences stronger. People will more likely engage in risk-seeking behaviour for negative outcomes, and risk-averse behaviour for positive outcomes, when under stress.[47]

Hindsight Bias

The **hindsight bias** is the tendency to believe falsely, after the outcome of an event is actually known, that we could have accurately predicted that outcome.[49] When we have accurate feedback on the outcome, we seem to be pretty good at concluding it was obvious. As Malcolm Gladwell, author of *Blink*, *Outliers*, and *The Tipping Point*, writes, "What is clear in hindsight is rarely clear before the fact. It's an obvious point, but one that nonetheless bears repeating."[50]

The hindsight bias reduces our ability to learn from the past. It lets us think that we are better predictors than we really are, and can make us falsely confident. If your actual predictive accuracy is only 40 percent, but you think it's 90 percent, you are likely to be less skeptical about your predictive skills.

OB in Action—Reducing Biases and Errors in Decision Making provides you with some ideas for improving your decision making. To learn more about your decision-making style, refer to the *Learning About Yourself Exercise* on page 461.

OB in ACTION
Reducing Biases and Errors in Decision Making

→ **Focus on goals.** Clear goals make decision making easier and help you eliminate options that are inconsistent with your interests.

→ **Look for information that disconfirms** your **beliefs.** When we deliberately consider various ways we could be wrong, we challenge our tendencies to think we are smarter than we actually are.

→ **Don't create meaning** out of random events. Ask yourself if patterns can be meaningfully explained or whether they are merely coincidence. Don't attempt to create meaning out of coincidence.

→ **Increase** your **options.** The more alternatives you can generate, and the more diverse those alternatives, the greater your chance of finding an outstanding one.[48]

SELF-ASSESSMENT LIBRARY

LEARNING ABOUT YOURSELF

1. Decision-Making Style Questionnaire
(page 461)

Improving Decision Making through Knowledge Management

The process of organizing and distributing an organization's collective wisdom so the right information gets to the right people at the right time is called **knowledge management (KM)**.[51] When done properly, KM provides an organization with both a competitive edge and improved organizational performance because it makes its employees smarter.

A growing number of companies—including the Royal Bank of Canada, Cisco Systems, British Telecom, and Johnson & Johnson—have realized the value of KM. In fact, one survey found that 81 percent of the leading organizations in Europe and the United States say they have, or are at least considering adopting, some kind of KM system.[52]

③ How can knowledge management improve decision making?

hindsight bias The tendency to believe falsely, after an outcome of an event is actually known, that one could have accurately predicted that outcome.

knowledge management (KM) The process of organizing and distributing an organization's collective wisdom so that the right information gets to the right people at the right time.

KM is increasingly important today for at least three reasons:[53]

- Organizations that can quickly and efficiently tap into their employees' collective experience and wisdom are more likely to "outsmart" their competition.

- As Baby Boomers begin to leave the workforce, there is an increasing awareness that they represent a wealth of knowledge that will be lost if there are no attempts to capture it.

- A well-designed KM system reduces redundancy and makes the organization more efficient. For instance, when employees in a large organization undertake a new project, they need not start from scratch. They can access what former employees have learned and avoid repeating previous mistakes.

How do organizations record the knowledge and expertise of their employees and make that information easily accessible? First, organizations need to develop *computer databases* of pertinent information that employees can readily access. This process includes identifying what knowledge matters to the organization.[54]

Second, organizations need to create a *culture* that promotes, values, and rewards sharing knowledge. As we discussed in Chapter 8, information that is important and scarce can be a potent source of power. Moreover, people who hold that power are often reluctant to share it with others. KM will not work unless the culture supports information sharing.[55]

Finally, organizations need to develop *mechanisms* that allow employees who have built up valuable expertise and insights to share them with others.[56] *More* knowledge is not necessarily *better* knowledge. Information overload needs to be avoided by designing the system to capture only pertinent information and then organizing it so it can be quickly accessed by the people whom it can help. Royal Bank of Canada, for instance, created a KM system with customized email distribution lists carefully broken down by employees' specialty, title, and area of interest; set aside a dedicated site on the company's intranet that serves as a central information repository; and created separate in-house websites featuring "lessons learned" summaries, where employees with various expertise can share new information with others.[57]

Group Decision Making

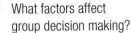

4 What factors affect group decision making?

While a variety of decisions in both life and organizations are made at the individual level, the belief—characterized by juries—that two heads are better than one has long been accepted as a basic component of North American and many other countries' legal systems. Today, many decisions in organizations are made by groups, teams, or committees. In this section, we review group decision making and compare it with individual decision making.

Groups vs. the Individual

Decision-making groups may be widely used in organizations, but are group decisions preferable to those made by an individual alone? The answer to this depends on a number of factors we consider below.[58] See Exhibit 12-2 for a summary of our major points.

Strengths of Group Decision Making

Groups generate *more complete information and knowledge.* By combining the resources of several individuals, groups bring more input into the decision process. They offer *increased diversity of views.* This opens up the opportunity to consider more approaches and alternatives. Finally, groups lead to *increased acceptance of a solution.*[59] Many deci-

EXHIBIT 12-2 Group vs. Individual Decision Making		
Criteria of Effectiveness	**Groups**	**Individuals**
More complete information	√	
Diversity of views	√	
Decision quality	√	
Accuracy	√	
Creativity	√	
Degree of acceptance	√	
Speed		√
Efficiency		√

sions fail after they are made because people don't accept them. Group members who participated in making a decision are likely to support the decision enthusiastically and encourage others to accept it.

Weaknesses of Group Decision Making

Group decisions have their drawbacks. They are *time-consuming* because groups typically take more time to reach a solution. There are *conformity pressures*. The desire by group members to be accepted and considered an asset to the group can result in squashing any overt disagreement. Group discussion can be *dominated by one or a few members*. If they are low- and medium-ability members, the group's overall effectiveness will suffer. Finally, group decisions suffer from *ambiguous responsibility*. In an individual decision, it's clear who is accountable for the final outcome. In a group decision, the responsibility of any single member is watered down.

Effectiveness and Efficiency

Whether groups are more effective than individuals depends on how you define effectiveness. Group decisions are generally more *accurate* than the decisions of the average individual in a group, but they are less accurate than the judgments of the most accurate group member.[60] If decision effectiveness is defined in terms of *speed*, individuals are superior. If *creativity* is important, groups tend to be more effective than individuals. And if effectiveness means the degree of *acceptance* the final solution achieves, the nod again goes to the group.[61]

But we cannot consider effectiveness without also assessing efficiency. Groups almost always stack up as a poor second to the individual decision maker. With few exceptions, group decision making consumes more work hours than if an individual were to tackle the same problem alone. The exceptions tend to be the instances in which, to achieve comparable quantities of diverse input, the single decision maker must spend a great deal of time reviewing files and talking to people. Because groups can include members from diverse areas, the time spent searching for information can be reduced. However, as we noted, these advantages in efficiency tend to be the exception. Groups are generally less efficient than individuals. In deciding whether to use groups, then, consideration should be given to assessing whether increases in effectiveness are more than enough to offset the reductions in efficiency. This chapter's *Working with Others Exercise* on page 463 gives you an opportunity to assess the effectiveness and efficiency of group decision making vs. individual decision making.

Groupthink and Groupshift

Two by-products of group decision making have the potential to affect the group's ability to appraise alternatives objectively and arrive at quality solutions: groupthink and groupshift.

Groupthink

Have you ever felt like speaking up in a meeting, classroom, or informal group, but decided against it? One reason may have been shyness. On the other hand, you may have been a victim of **groupthink**, a phenomenon in which group pressures for conformity prevent the group from critically appraising unusual, minority, or unpopular views. The individual's mental efficiency, reality testing, and moral judgment deteriorate as a result of group pressures.[62]

We have all seen the symptoms of the groupthink phenomenon:[63]

- *Illusion of invulnerability.* Group members become overconfident among themselves, allowing them to take extraordinary risks.

- *Assumption of morality.* Group members believe highly in the moral rightness of the group's objectives and do not feel the need to debate the ethics of their actions.

- *Rationalized resistance.* Group members rationalize any resistance to the assumptions they have made. No matter how strongly the evidence may contradict their basic assumptions, members behave so as to reinforce those assumptions continually.

- *Peer pressure.* Group members apply direct pressure on those who momentarily express doubts about any of the group's shared views or who question the validity of arguments supporting the alternative favoured by the majority.

- *Minimized doubts.* Those group members who have doubts or hold differing points of view seek to avoid deviating from what appears to be group consensus by keeping silent about misgivings and even minimizing to themselves the importance of their doubts.

- *Illusion of unanimity.* If someone does not speak, it's assumed that he or she is in full accord. In other words, abstention becomes viewed as a yes vote.

One place where groupthink has been shown to happen is among stock analysts, as *OB in the Street* shows.

OB in the STREET
Groupthink among Analysts

Why does stock performance have little to do with predictions? Waterloo-based Research In Motion (RIM) has been a great performer for shareholders over time.[64] With so many people carrying a BlackBerry, more and more people bought RIM's stock. When presidential candidate Barack Obama, who was often seen carrying two BlackBerrys on the campaign trail, insisted that he would continue using one if elected (something none of his predecessors had done), sales and share prices went up even further.

Recent years have seen a turn in fortune for RIM, however. With strong competition from other producers of smartphones, RIM's sales started dropping, and so did its share price.

groupthink A phenomenon in which group pressures for conformity prevent the group from critically appraising unusual, minority, or unpopular views.

What did stock analysts do in the face of these drops? The majority continued to recommend buying RIM stock. In May 2011, 23 analysts were saying "buy" compared with 21 saying "hold" and 9 saying "sell." Some analysts suggested the share price could double in the next year, reaching $100 or more. At nearly the same time, RIM was getting ready to announce severe layoffs.

The analysts' opinions do not seem to reflect the reality of RIM's current struggles. So what are analysts thinking?

A McKinsey & Company study compared the results of S&P 500 companies from 1985 to 2010 to analysts' forecasts. The study found that "analysts overestimated earnings by nearly 100%," underestimating earnings only twice in 25 years.

Although analysts are supposed to do independent research, which should lead to independent assessments, this research does not happen. Christine Tan, a portfolio manager at Gluskin Sheff Associates in Toronto, suggests there are few incentives for analysts to go against the consensus of the market. If you do, and "you're wrong, you get fired," Tan says. In other words, analysts fear going against what others in the group might say (peer pressure), and they minimize their doubts, which are two of the symptoms of groupthink.

Groupthink appears to be closely aligned with the conclusions Solomon Asch drew in his experiments with a lone dissenter, which we described in Chapter 6. Individuals who hold a position that is different from that of the dominant majority are under pressure to suppress, withhold, or modify their true feelings and beliefs. As members of a group, we find it more pleasant to be in agreement—to be a positive part of the group—than to be a disruptive force, even if disruption is necessary to improve the effectiveness of the group's decisions. This chapter's *Case Incident—The Dangers of Groupthink* on page 466 provides instances when groupthink proved to be harmful.

Do all groups suffer from groupthink? No. It seems to occur most often where there is a clear group identity, where members hold a positive image of their group, which they want to protect, and where the group perceives a collective threat to this positive image.[65] So groupthink is less a dissenter-suppression mechanism than a means for a group to protect its positive image.

What can managers do to minimize groupthink?[66]

- *Monitor group size.* People grow more intimidated and hesitant as group size increases, and, although there is no magic number that will eliminate groupthink, individuals are likely to feel less personal responsibility when groups get larger than about 10.

- *Encourage group leaders to play an impartial role.* Leaders should actively seek input from all members and avoid expressing their own opinions, especially in the early stages of deliberation.

- *Appoint one group member to play the role of devil's advocate.* This member's role is to overtly challenge the majority position and offer divergent perspectives.

- *Stimulate active discussion of diverse alternatives to encourage dissenting views and more objective evaluations.* Group members might delay discussion of possible gains so they can first talk about the dangers or risks inherent in a decision. Requiring members to first focus on the negatives of an alternative makes the group less likely to stifle dissenting views and more likely to gain an objective evaluation.

While considerable anecdotal evidence indicates the negative implications of groupthink in organizational settings, not much actual empirical work has been conducted in organizations in this area.[67] In fact, researchers on groupthink have been criticized for suggesting that its effect is uniformly negative[68] and for overestimating the link

Young adults rioting in the streets of Vancouver after the Canucks' loss to the Boston Bruins in Game 7 of the 2011 NHL playoffs may have been affected by groupthink as they got carried away, smashing windows, looting, and setting fires. It is unlikely that everyone who participated in the riots had carefully planned out their activities in advance of the riots starting.

between the decision-making process and its outcome.[69] A study of groupthink using 30 teams from 5 large corporations suggests that elements of groupthink may affect decision making differently. For instance, the illusion of invulnerability, assumption of morality, and illusion of unanimity were positively associated with team performance.[70] The most recent research suggests that we should be aware of groupthink conditions that lead to poor decisions, while realizing that not all groupthink symptoms harm decision making.

Groupshift

There are differences between group decisions and the individual decisions of group members.[71] Sometimes group decisions are more conservative. More often, they lean toward greater risk.[72] In either case, participants have engaged in **groupshift**, a phenomenon in which the initial positions of individual group members become exaggerated because of the interactions of the group.

What appears to happen in groups is that the discussion leads members toward a more extreme view of the position they already held. Conservative types become more cautious and more aggressive types assume more risk. The group discussion tends to exaggerate the initial position of the group.

The greater shift toward risk has generated several explanations.[73] It has been argued, for instance, that the discussion makes members more comfortable with one another, and, thus, more bold and daring. Another argument is that the group diffuses responsibility. Group decisions free any single member from accountability for the group's final choice, so greater risks can be taken. It's also likely that people take on extreme positions because they want to demonstrate how different they are from the outgroup.[74] People on the fringes of political or social movements take on more and more extreme positions just to prove they are really committed to the cause.

How should you use the findings on groupshift? Recognize that group decisions exaggerate the initial position of the individual members, that the shift has been shown more often to be toward greater risk, and that which way a group will shift is a function of the members' pre-discussion inclinations. *Case Incident—"If Two Heads Are Better Than One, Are Four Even Better?"* on page 467 considers the impact of groupshift on investment decisions.

groupshift A phenomenon in which the initial positions of individual group members become exaggerated because of the interactions of the group.

Group Decision-Making Techniques

Groups can use a variety of techniques to stimulate decision making. We outline four of them below.

Interacting Groups

The most common form of group decision making takes place in **interacting groups**. Members meet face to face and rely on both verbal and nonverbal interaction to communicate with one another. But as our discussion of groupthink demonstrated, interacting groups often censor themselves and pressure individual members toward conformity of opinion. *Brainstorming*, the *nominal group technique*, and *electronic meetings* have been proposed as ways to reduce many of the problems inherent in the traditional interacting group.

Brainstorming

Brainstorming uses an idea-generation process that specifically encourages any and all alternatives, in a criticism-free environment.

In a typical brainstorming session, 6 to 12 people sit around a table. The group leader states the problem in a clear manner so that all participants understand it. Members then "free-wheel" as many alternatives as they can in a given period of time. No criticism is allowed, and all the alternatives are recorded for later discussion and analysis. One idea stimulates others, and judgments of even the most bizarre suggestions are withheld until later to encourage group members to "think the unusual."

Brainstorming may indeed generate ideas—but not in a very efficient manner. Research consistently shows that individuals working alone generate more ideas than a group in a brainstorming session.[75] One reason for this is "production blocking." When people generate ideas in a group, many people are talking at once, which blocks the thought process and eventually impedes the sharing of ideas.[76] Another reason suggested by a 2011 study is fixation—group members start to fixate early on a limited number of solutions rather than continue to look for others.[77] One recent study suggests that goal-setting approaches might make brainstorming more effective.[78] The following two techniques go further than brainstorming by offering methods that help groups arrive at a preferred solution.[79]

Nominal Group Technique

The **nominal group technique** restricts discussion or interpersonal communication during the decision-making process, hence the term *nominal* (which means "in name only"). Group members are all physically present, as in a traditional committee meeting, but they operate independently. Specifically, a problem is presented and then the group takes the following steps:

- Members meet as a group, but before any discussion takes place, each member independently writes down his or her ideas on the problem.

- After this silent period, each member presents one idea to the group. Group members take turns presenting a single idea until all ideas have been presented and recorded. No discussion takes place until all ideas have been recorded.

- The group discusses the ideas for clarity and evaluates them.

- Each group member silently and independently ranks the ideas. The idea with the highest aggregate ranking determines the final decision.

The steps of the nominal group technique are illustrated in Exhibit 12-3. The chief advantage of the technique is that it permits the group to meet formally but does not restrict independent thinking, as does the interacting group. Research generally shows that nominal groups outperform brainstorming groups.[80]

interacting groups Typical groups, where members interact with each other face to face.

brainstorming An idea-generation process that specifically encourages any and all alternatives, while withholding any criticism of those alternatives.

nominal group technique A group decision-making method in which individual members meet face to face to pool their judgments in a systematic but independent fashion.

EXHIBIT 12-3 Nominal Group Technique

| Team members receive description of problem. | **Individual Activity** Individuals silently write down possible solutions. | **Group Activity** Individuals take turns describing solutions to each other; group then discusses and evaluates ideas. | **Individual Activity** Individuals silently rank (or vote on) each solution presented. |

Electronic Meetings

The most recent approach to group decision making blends the nominal group technique with sophisticated computer technology.[81] It's called the computer-assisted group, or **electronic meeting**. Up to 50 people sit around a horseshoe-shaped table, which is empty except for a series of networked laptops. Issues are presented to participants and they type their responses into their computers. Individual comments (which are anonymous), as well as aggregate votes, are displayed on a projection screen.

The major advantages of electronic meetings are anonymity, honesty, and speed. This group decision-making approach also allows people to be brutally honest without penalty. It's fast because chit-chat is eliminated, discussions don't digress, and many participants can "talk" at once without stepping on one another's toes. Early evidence, however, indicates that electronic meetings don't achieve most of their proposed benefits. They actually lead to *decreased* group effectiveness, require *more* time to complete tasks, and result in *reduced* member satisfaction compared with face-to-face groups.[82] Nevertheless, current enthusiasm for computer-mediated communications suggests that this technology is here to stay and is likely to increase in popularity in the future.

Each of these four group decision techniques has its own strengths and weaknesses. The choice depends on what criteria you want to emphasize and the cost-benefit trade-off. As Exhibit 12-4 indicates, an interacting group is good for achieving commitment to a solution, brainstorming develops group cohesiveness, the nominal group technique is an inexpensive means for generating a large number of ideas, and electronic meetings minimize social pressures and conflicts.

electronic meeting A meeting where members interact on computers, allowing for anonymity of comments and aggregation of votes.

EXHIBIT 12-4 Evaluating Group Effectiveness

Effectiveness Criteria	Type of Group			
	Interacting	Brainstorming	Nominal	Electronic
Number and quality of ideas	Low	Moderate	High	High
Social pressure	High	Low	Moderate	Low
Money costs	Low	Low	Low	High
Speed	Moderate	Moderate	Moderate	Moderate
Task orientation	Low	High	High	High
Potential for interpersonal conflict	High	Low	Moderate	Low
Commitment to solution	High	Not applicable	Moderate	Moderate
Development of group cohesiveness	High	High	Moderate	Low

Source: Based on J. K. Murnighan, "Group Decision Making: What Strategies Should You Use?" *Academy of Management Review*, February 1981, p. 61.

Creativity in Organizational Decision Making

Although following the steps of the rational decision-making model will often improve decisions, a rational decision maker also needs **creativity**; that is, the ability to produce novel and useful ideas.[83] These are ideas that are different from what has been done before but that are appropriate to the problem or opportunity presented.

Why is creativity important to decision making? It allows the decision maker to more fully appraise and understand the problem, including seeing problems others cannot see. Such thinking is becoming more important.

 5 How can we get more creative decisions?

Creative Potential

Most people have useful creative potential. But to unleash it, they have to escape the psychological ruts many of us fall into, and learn how to think about a problem in divergent ways.

Exceptional creativity is scarce. We all know of creative geniuses in science (Albert Einstein), art (Pablo Picasso), and business (Steve Jobs). But what about the typical individual? Intelligent people and those who score high on openness to experience (see Chapter 2) are more likely to be creative.[84] Other traits of creative people include independence, self-confidence, risk-taking, a positive core self-evaluation, tolerance for ambiguity, a low need for structure, and perseverance.[85] A study of the lifetime creativity of 461 men and women found that fewer than 1 percent were exceptionally creative.[86] However, 10 percent were highly creative and about 60 percent were somewhat creative. These findings suggest that most of us have creative potential; we just need to learn to unleash it.

From Concepts to Skills on pages 468–469 provides suggestions on how you can become more effective at solving problems creatively.

Three-Component Model of Creativity

What can individuals and organizations do to stimulate employee creativity? The best answer lies in the **three-component model of creativity**,[87] which proposes that individual creativity essentially requires expertise, creative-

Why are some people more creative than others?

Sometimes desperation can lead to creative decisions. General Motors Canada saw the challenge of producing the much-in-demand Chevrolet Equinox and GMC Terrain crossover utility vehicles as an opportunity to think creatively.[88] Rather than adding a new paint shop to GM's Ingersoll, Ontario-based Cami Automotive, which would have been expensive and time-consuming, management decided to ship the unpainted cars to an underutilized GM plant in Oshawa for painting and finishing. It was an unprecedented move, but one that allows the car to be produced much more quickly.

creativity The ability to produce novel and useful ideas.

three-component model of creativity The proposition that individual creativity requires expertise, creative-thinking skills, and intrinsic task motivation.

EXHIBIT 12-5 The Three Components of Creativity

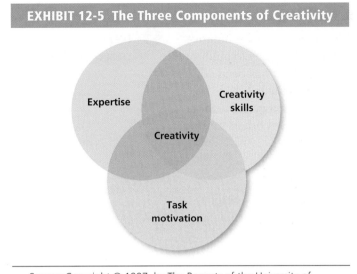

Source: Copyright © 1997, by The Regents of the University of California. Reprinted from *The California Management Review* 40, no. 1. By permission of The Regents.

thinking skills, and intrinsic task motivation (see Exhibit 12-5). Studies confirm that the higher the level of each of these three components, the higher the creativity.

Expertise is the foundation for all creative work. Film writer, producer, and director Quentin Tarantino spent his youth working in a video rental store, where he built up an encyclopedic knowledge of movies. The potential for creativity is enhanced when individuals have abilities, knowledge, proficiencies, and similar expertise in their field of endeavour. You would not expect someone with a minimal knowledge of programming to be very creative as a software engineer.

The second component is *creativity skills*. This encompasses personality characteristics associated with creativity, the ability to use analogies, and the talent to see the familiar in a different light.

A meta-analysis of 102 studies found that positive moods increase creativity, but it depended on what sort of positive mood was considered.[89] Moods such as happiness that encourage interaction with the world are more conducive to creativity than passive moods such as calm. This finding means that the common advice to relax and clear your mind to develop creative ideas may be misplaced. It would be better to get in an upbeat mood and then frame your work as an opportunity to have fun and experiment. Further, negative moods don't always affect creativity in the same way. Passive negative moods such as sadness don't seem to have much effect, but avoidance-oriented negative moods such as fear and anxiety decrease creativity. Feeling threatened reduces your desire to try new activities; risk aversion increases when you are scared. Active negative moods, such as anger, however, appear to enhance creativity, especially if you are taking your task seriously.

Being around others who are creative can make us more inspired, especially if we are creatively "stuck."[90] One study found that "weak ties" to creative people—knowing them but not well—facilitates creativity because the people are there as a resource if we need them, but they are not so close as to stunt our own independent thinking.[91]

Analogies allow decision makers to apply an idea from one context to another. One of the most famous examples was Alexander Graham Bell's observation that it might be possible to apply the way the ear operates to his "talking box." He noticed that the bones in the ear are operated by a delicate, thin membrane. He wondered why, then, a thicker and stronger piece of membrane should not be able to move a piece of steel. From that analogy, the telephone was conceived. Thinking in terms of analogies is a complex intellectual skill, which helps explain why cognitive ability is related to creativity. Demonstrating this effect, one study found that children who got high scores on cognitive ability tests at age 13 were significantly more likely to have made creative achievements in their professional lives 25 years later.[92]

Some people have developed their creativity skills because they are able to see problems in a new way. They are able to make the strange familiar and the familiar strange.[93] For instance, most of us think of hens laying eggs. But how many of us have considered that a hen is only an egg's way of making another egg?

The final component in the three-component model of creativity is intrinsic *task motivation*. This is the desire to work on something because it's interesting, involving, exciting, satisfying, or personally challenging. It is what turns creativity *potential* into *actual* creative ideas. Environmental stimulants that foster creativity include a culture

Shahrzad Rafati, founder and CEO of Vancouver-based BroadbandTV, made *Fast Company*'s 2011 list of the top 100 most creative people in business, the only Canadian to do so. When she was still an undergraduate computer science major at UBC, she came up with the idea of taking video uploaded to sites like YouTube and merging it with online advertising opportunities—bringing together both "pirates" and corporate content providers. "We're helping companies identify and take control of their content and generate revenue from it," she explained.

that encourages the flow of ideas; fair and constructive judgment of ideas; rewards and recognition for creative work; sufficient financial, material, and information resources; freedom to decide what work is to be done and how to do it; a supervisor who communicates effectively, shows confidence in others, and supports the work group; and work group members who support and trust one another.[94]

Organizational Factors That Affect Creativity

Five organizational factors have been found to block your creativity at work:[95]

- *Expected evaluation.* Focusing on how your work is going to be evaluated.

- *Surveillance.* Being watched while you are working.

- *External motivators.* Focusing on external, tangible rewards.

- *Competition.* Facing win-lose situations with peers.

- *Constrained choice.* Being given limits on how you can do your work.

Canadian Tire built a better tent by giving people an environment that encouraged them to think creatively, as this *OB in the Workplace* shows.

WORKPLACE
Canadian Tire's "Innovation Room" Unleashes Creativity

Can playing with crayons help produce a better tent? Managers at Toronto-based Canadian Tire want better decisions than the kind that come from sitting around a boardroom table.[96] So they built an "innovation room" that is "a cross between a kindergarten classroom and a fantasy land."

To get new ideas for camping gear, they invited friends and family with an interest in camping to meet in the innovation room. The room included LEGO sets, crayons, a canoe, and a sundeck.

Managers were trying to create a new product—a tent with lighting—but were not sure how to develop a product that would sell. They left it to friends and family to get it right. By getting people together in the innovation room, where they could play and brainstorm, the idea emerged for a solar-lit tent. The tent is now a big seller.

"It's really about unlocking and unleashing creativity and getting people to just let loose and dream a little and have fun," says Glenn Butt, a senior vice-president at Canadian Tire. "It's a process that usually ends up with some very unique and different products and concepts."

What About Ethics in Decision Making?

6 What is ethics, and how can it be used for better decision making?

The owners of Invermere, BC-based Kicking Horse Coffee Company are committed to providing their customers with the best coffee possible.[97] "Quality is our number-one difference from others," says Elana Rosenfeld. "We take that seriously; we don't want to disappoint people if they are paying for this coffee." In 2007, the company faced a dilemma: how to respond to the increasing demand for more "green" coffee beans. The company had marketed itself as selling only organic beans, and those beans are harder to find, and more expensive. Nevertheless, Kicking Horse decided that despite supply challenges, they no longer purchase any coffee beans that are not fair trade in origin. How can ethics influence business strategy?

No contemporary examination of decision making would be complete without the discussion of ethics, because ethical considerations should be an important criterion in organizational decision making. **Ethics** is the study of moral values or principles that guide our behaviour and inform us whether actions are right or wrong. Ethical principles help us "do the right thing." In this section, we present four ways to ethically frame decisions and examine the factors that shape an individual's ethical decision-making behaviour. We also examine organizational responses to the demand for ethical behaviour, as well as consideration of ethical decisions when doing business in other cultures. To learn more about your approach to ethical decision making, see the *Ethical Dilemma Exercise* on page 465.

Four Ethical Decision Criteria

An individual can use four criteria in making ethical choices.[98] The first is **utilitarianism**, in which decisions are made solely on the basis of their outcomes, ideally to provide the greatest good for the greatest number. This view dominates business decision making. It is consistent with goals such as efficiency, productivity, and high profits. By maximizing profits, for instance, business executives can argue that they are securing the greatest good for the greatest number—as they hand out dismissal notices to 15 percent of employees.

A second ethical criterion is to make decisions consistent with fundamental liberties and privileges as set forth in documents such as the Canadian Charter of Rights and Freedoms. An emphasis on *rights* in decision making means respecting and protecting the basic rights of individuals, such as the rights to privacy, free speech, and due process. This criterion protects **whistle-blowers** when they report unethical or illegal practices by their organizations to the media or to government agencies, using their right to free speech.

A third criterion is to impose and enforce rules fairly and impartially to ensure *justice* or an equitable distribution of benefits and costs. Union members typically favour this view. It justifies paying people the same wage for a given job, regardless of performance differences, and using seniority as the primary determination in making layoff decisions. A focus on justice protects the interests of the underrepresented and less powerful, but it can encourage a sense of entitlement that reduces risk-taking, innovation, and productivity.

A fourth ethical criterion is *care*. The ethics of care can be stated as follows: "The morally correct action is the one that expresses care in protecting the special relationships

ethics The study of moral values or principles that guide our behaviour and inform us whether actions are right or wrong.

utilitarianism A decision focused on outcomes or consequences that emphasizes the greatest good for the greatest number.

whistle-blowers Individuals who report unethical practices by their employer to outsiders.

Stewart Leibl, president of Perth's, a Winnipeg dry-cleaning chain, is a founding sponsor of the "Koats for Kids" program. The company's outlets are a drop-off point for no-longer-needed children's coats, which Perth's cleans free of charge before distributing them to children who don't have winter coats. Each year, over 5000 freshly cleaned coats and parkas are distributed to children in need. Leibl is going beyond utilitarian criteria when he says, "We all have a responsibility to contribute to the society that we live in." He is also looking at social justice.

that individuals have with each other."[99] The care criterion suggests that we should be aware of the needs, desires, and well-being of those to whom we are closely connected. This perspective does remind us of the difficulty of being impartial in all decisions.

Decision makers, particularly in for-profit organizations, tend to feel safe and comfortable when they use utilitarianism, framing decisions as being in the best interests of "the organization" and stockholders. Critics of this perspective note that it can result in ignoring the rights of some individuals, particularly those with minority representation in the organization.[100] Using nonutilitarian criteria presents a solid challenge to today's managers because doing so involves far more ambiguities.

Factors That Influence Ethical Decision-Making Behaviour

What accounts for unethical behaviour in organizations? Is it immoral individuals or work environments that promote unethical activity? The answer is, *both!* The evidence indicates that ethical or unethical actions are largely a function of both the individual's characteristics and the environment in which he or she works.[101] The model in Exhibit 12-6 illustrates factors affecting ethical decision-making behaviour and emphasizes three factors: stage of moral development, locus of control, and the organizational environment.

EXHIBIT 12-6 Factors Affecting Ethical Decision-Making Behaviour

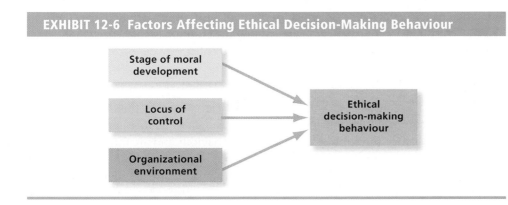

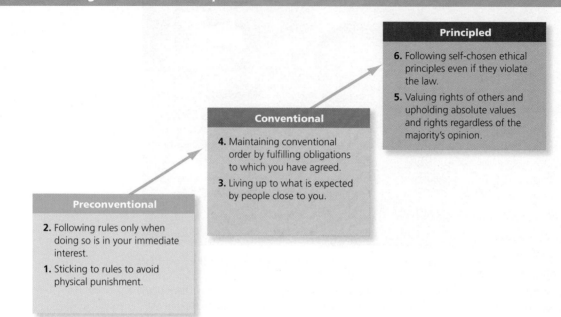

EXHIBIT 12-7 Stages of Moral Development

Principled

6. Following self-chosen ethical principles even if they violate the law.

5. Valuing rights of others and upholding absolute values and rights regardless of the majority's opinion.

Conventional

4. Maintaining conventional order by fulfilling obligations to which you have agreed.

3. Living up to what is expected by people close to you.

Preconventional

2. Following rules only when doing so is in your immediate interest.

1. Sticking to rules to avoid physical punishment.

Source: Based on L. Kohlberg, "Moral Stages and Moralization: The Cognitive-Developmental Approach," in *Moral Development and Behaviour: Theory, Research, and Social Issues*, ed. T. Lickona (New York: Holt, Rinehart and Winston, 1976), pp. 34–35.

Stages of Moral Development

Stages of moral development assess a person's capacity to judge what is morally right.[102] Research suggests that there are three levels of moral development.[103] The higher a person's moral development, the less dependent he or she is on outside influences and the more he or she will be predisposed to behave ethically. The first level is the preconventional level, the second is the conventional level, and the third, or highest, level is the principled level. These levels and their stages are described in Exhibit 12-7.

Research indicates that people proceed through the stages one step at a time, though they do not necessarily reach the highest stage.[104] Most adults are at a mid-level of moral development—they are strongly influenced by peers and will follow an organization's rules and procedures. Those individuals who have progressed to the higher stages place increased value on the rights of others, regardless of the majority's opinion, and are likely to challenge organizational practices they personally believe are wrong. Those at the higher stages are most likely to make ethical decisions. A 2011 study by three psychologists from the University of Toronto found that people were likely to predict they would cheat more often than they engaged in actual cheating. The researchers suggested that the emotions experienced at the time that cheating is possible can weaken one's desire to cheat.[105]

> Why do some people make more ethical decisions than others?

Locus of Control

Research indicates that people with an external *locus of control* (that is, they believe their lives are controlled by outside forces, such as luck or chance) are less likely to take responsibility for the consequences of their behaviour and are more likely to rely on external influences to determine their behaviour. Those with an internal locus of control are more likely to rely on their own internal standards of right or wrong to guide their behaviour.

stages of moral development
The developmental stages that explain a person's capacity to judge what is morally right.

Organizational Environment

The *organizational environment* refers to an employee's perception of organizational expectations. Does the organizational culture encourage and support ethical behaviour by rewarding it or discourage unethical behaviour by punishing it? Characteristics of an organizational environment that are likely to foster high ethical decision making include written codes of ethics; high moral behaviour by senior management; realistic performance expectations; performance appraisals that evaluate means as well as ends; visible recognition and promotions for individuals who display high moral behaviour; and visible punishment for those who act unethically. The Canadian Forces recently distributed a guide to its forces to underscore the need for ethical behaviour in warfare, as *OB in the Workplace* describes.

OB in the WORKPLACE
Ethics and the Army

Can a person be an "ethical warrior"? The Canadian Forces hopes so, and produced an ethics guide to help army personnel do the right thing.[106] The guide reminds soldiers that "we don't do" torture, and emphasizes moral courage alongside physical courage.

One aim of the guide is to ensure public support for the military when Canadians are engaging in warfare. Army chief Lt.-Gen. Andrew Leslie notes that the military will not be supported "if Canadian society believes that we conduct ourselves in an unethical, inhumane or iniquitous manner."

Army ethics officer Richard Walker wrote the guide to help avoid lapses in behaviour in the military. "We cannot permit any lack of clarity . . . If somebody chooses to do the wrong thing for the wrong reasons, it won't be that they didn't know."

The guide is intended to address the ambiguity of warfare that is characteristic of the twenty-first century. While Canadian military forces adhere to the international rules of war, the enemies they faced in Somalia, Bosnia, Kosovo, and Afghanistan do not. This has led to "enhanced ambiguity, enhanced uncertainty and enhanced lethality," said Walker. The concern is that facing enemies who don't follow the international rules of war may encourage Canadian soldiers to engage in poor behaviour that will lead to psychological problems for them later. The guide reminds soldiers that those who "lose their humanity" in warfare will be emotionally scarred for life. "Respecting the dignity of all persons is essentially the moral precept that drives everything else," said Walker.

In summary, people who lack a strong moral sense are much less likely to make unethical decisions if they are constrained by an organizational environment that frowns on such behaviours. Conversely, righteous individuals can be corrupted by an organizational environment that permits or encourages unethical practices. In the next section, we consider how to formulate an ethical decision.

Making Ethical Decisions

While there are no clear-cut ways to differentiate ethical from unethical decision making, there are some questions you should consider.

Exhibit 12-8 illustrates a decision tree to guide ethical decisions.[107] This tree is built on three of the ethical decision criteria—utilitarianism, rights, and justice—presented above. The first question you need to answer addresses self-interest vs. organizational goals.

The second question concerns the rights of other parties. If the decision violates the rights of someone else (the person's right to privacy, for instance), then the decision is unethical.

EXHIBIT 12-8 Is a Decision Ethical?

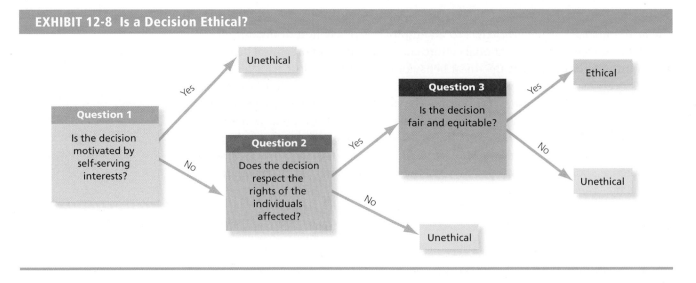

The final question that needs to be addressed relates to whether the decision conforms to standards of equity and justice. The department head who inflates the performance evaluation of a favoured employee and deflates the evaluation of a disfavoured employee—and then uses these evaluations to justify giving the former a big raise and nothing to the latter—has treated the disfavoured employee unfairly.

Unfortunately, the answers to the questions in Exhibit 12-8 are often argued in ways to make unethical decisions seem ethical. Powerful people, for example, can become very adept at explaining self-serving behaviours in terms of the organization's best interests. Similarly, they can persuasively argue that unfair actions are really fair and just. Our point is that immoral people can justify almost any behaviour. Those who are powerful, articulate, and persuasive are the most likely to be able to get away with unethical actions successfully. When faced with an ethical dilemma, try to answer the questions in Exhibit 12-8 truthfully.

Paul Nielsen (shown with his wife, Dayle) owns Calgary-based DumpRunner Waste Systems, a specialty garbage and debris removal company. He encourages an ethical approach to dealing with both clients and employees. He notes that in Calgary, business is built on handshakes and being true to your word, and people are expected to act ethically. Ethical behaviour may be easier for Nielsen than for some others. He says he is guided by his passion for being in business, rather than a "quest for money."

Corporate Social Responsibility

Elana Rosenfeld and Leo Johnson, founders of Kicking Horse Coffee Company, are committed to making the best coffee possible, but they also want to do so in ways that highlight corporate social responsibility.[108] They start with their employees, with whom they have built a relationship based on "trust, employee autonomy and a shared sense of mission." They restrict their purchases to fair trade growers, who provide healthy working environments for employees. Rosenfeld and Johnson travel to visit their coffee bean suppliers in South America and other places, which enables them to report first-hand to their customers and employees "how fair trade coffee makes a real difference to the lives of those who were often exploited." Rosenfeld and Johnson also take the environment seriously. The cans their coffee is sold in are made of recycled steel, which can be recycled many times over. To what extent should companies be socially responsible?

7 What is corporate social responsibility?

Corporate social responsibility is an organization's responsibility to consider the impact of its decisions on society. Thus, organizations may try to better society through such things as charitable contributions or providing better wages to employees working in offshore factories. Organizations may engage in these practices because they feel pressured by society to do so, or they may seek ways to improve society because they feel it is the right thing to do.

Canadians want businesses to give back to society, according to a 2010 poll which found that Canadians' views of corporations are largely affected by whether businesses support charitable causes and protect the environment.[109] Oakville, Ontario-based Tim Hortons, which makes customers aware of its Children's Foundation, is well regarded by Canadians.[110]

Not everyone agrees that organizations should assume social responsibility. For example, economist Milton Friedman remarked in *Capitalism and Freedom* that "few trends could so thoroughly undermine the very foundations of our free society as the acceptance by corporate officials of a social responsibility other than to make as much money for their stockholders as possible."[111]

Joel Bakan, professor of law at the University of British Columbia, author of *The Corporation*,[112] and co-director of the documentary of the same name, is more critical of organizations than Friedman. Bakan suggests that today's corporations have many of the same characteristics as a psychopathic personality (for example, self-interested, lacking empathy, manipulative, and reckless in their disregard of others). Bakan notes that even though companies have a tendency to act psychopathically, this is not why they are fixated on profits. Rather, their only legal responsibility is to maximize organizational profits for stockholders. He suggests changes in laws to encourage corporations to behave more socially responsibly.

Canadian senior executives have mixed feelings about the extent to which businesses should get involved in charitable giving, or forcing industry standards on foreign corporations. A 2011 poll found that 45 percent believe individual shareholders, not the company, should make personal decisions about giving to charity. Another 35 percent, however, felt corporations should donate to charities. One CEO explained, "Being a good corporate citizen means assisting those less fortunate—as long as it is done in the context of the entities' aims, objectives and employees' desires."[113] A 2011 poll conducted by COMPAS found that Canadian business leaders were not about imposing Canadian management values on Chinese employers, however. "We don't have the right to tell China how to run its economy," said one CEO. "We have the choice to buy, or not to buy."[114]

A recent survey found that Canadian and American MBA students are very interested in the subject of corporate social responsibility. Over 80 percent of respondents "believed business professionals should take into account social and environmental impacts when making decisions." Almost two-thirds of these respondents felt that

corporate social responsibility
An organization's responsibility to consider the impact of its decisions on society.

corporate social responsibility should be part of core MBA classes, and 60 percent said "they would seek socially responsible employment."[115]

For more on the debate about social responsibility vs. concentrating on the bottom line, see this chapter's *Point/Counterpoint* on page 460.

GLOBAL IMPLICATIONS

When considering potential global differences in this chapter's concepts, let's consider two areas among this chapter's concepts that have attracted the most research: decision making and ethics.

Decision Making

The rational model makes no acknowledgment of cultural differences, nor does the bulk of OB research literature on decision making. A recent review of cross-cultural OB research covered 25 areas, but cultural influence on decision making was not among them. Another recent review identified 15 topics, but the result was the same: No research on culture and decision making.[116]

However, Indonesians, for instance, don't necessarily make decisions the same way Australians do. Therefore, we need to recognize that the cultural background of a decision maker can have a significant influence on the selection of problems, the depth of analysis, the importance placed on logic and rationality, and whether organizational decisions should be made autocratically by an individual manager or collectively in groups.[117]

Cultures differ in their time orientation, the importance of rationality, their belief in the ability of people to solve problems, and their preference for collective decision making. Differences in time orientation help us understand why managers in Egypt make decisions at a much slower and more deliberate pace than their US counterparts. While rationality is valued in North America, that is not true elsewhere in the world. A North American manager might make an important decision intuitively but know it's important to appear to proceed in a rational fashion because rationality is highly valued in the West. In countries such as Iran, where rationality is not as paramount as other factors, efforts to appear rational are not necessary.

Some cultures emphasize solving problems, while others focus on accepting situations as they are. Canada falls in the first category; Thailand and Indonesia are examples of the second. Because problem-solving managers believe they can and should change situations to their benefit, Canadian managers might identify a problem long before their Thai or Indonesian counterparts would choose to recognize it as such. Decision making by Japanese managers is much more group-oriented than in Canada. The Japanese value conformity and cooperation. So before Japanese CEOs make an important decision, they collect a large amount of information, which they use in consensus-forming group decisions.

In short, there are probably important cultural differences in decision making, but unfortunately not yet much research to identify them.

Ethics

There are no global ethical standards,[118] as contrasts between Asia and the West illustrate.[119] Because bribery is commonplace in countries such as China, a Canadian working in China might face a dilemma: Should I pay a bribe to secure business if it is an accepted part of that country's culture? A manager of a large US company operating in China caught an employee stealing. Following company policy, she fired him and turned him over to the local authorities. Later, she was horrified to learn the employee had been summarily executed.[120]

Although ethical standards may seem ambiguous in the West, criteria defining right and wrong are actually much clearer there than in Asia, where few issues are black and white and most are grey. In Japan, people doing business together often exchange gifts, even expensive ones. This is part of Japanese tradition. When North American and European companies started doing business in Japan, most North American executives were not aware of the Japanese tradition of exchanging gifts and wondered whether this was a form of bribery. Most have come to accept this tradition now, and have even set different limits on gift giving in Japan than in other countries.[121]

Global organizations must establish ethical principles for decision makers in countries such as India and China and modify them to reflect cultural norms if they want to uphold high standards and consistent practices. Having agreements among countries to police bribery may not be enough, however. The 34 countries of the Organisation for Economic Co-operation and Development (OECD) entered into an agreement to tackle corporate bribery in 1997. However, a 2011 study by Berlin-based Transparency International found that 21 of the OECD countries are "doing little or nothing" to enforce the agreement. Canada came under strong criticism for being "the only G7 country in the little or no enforcement category." The United States and Germany rated highest on number of cases filed. Transparency International noted that Canada needed to enforce more of its laws in this area.[122]

Summary and Implications

① Is there a right way to make decisions?   The rational decision-making model describes the six steps individuals take to make decisions: (1) Define the problem, (2) identify the criteria, (3) allocate weights to the criteria, (4) develop alternatives, (5) evaluate the alternatives, and (6) select the best alternative. This is an idealized model, and not every decision thoroughly follows these steps.

② How do people actually make decisions?   Most decisions in the real world don't follow the rational model. For instance, people are usually content to find an acceptable or reasonable solution to their problem rather than an optimizing one. Thus, decision makers may rely on bounded rationality, satisficing, and intuition in making decisions. They may also rely on judgment shortcuts, which can lead to overconfidence bias, anchoring bias, confirmation bias, availability bias, escalation of commitment, randomness error, risk aversion, and hindsight bias.

③ How can knowledge management improve decision making?   Knowledge management makes employees smarter when it's carried out properly. By electronically storing information that employees have, organizations make it possible to share collective wisdom. As well, when new projects are started, individuals can see what others have done before them, to avoid going down unproductive paths.

④ What factors affect group decision making?   Groups generate more complete information and knowledge, they offer increased diversity of views, they generate higher-quality decisions, and they lead to increased acceptance of a solution. However, group decisions are time-consuming. They also lead to conformity pressures, and the group discussion can be dominated by one or a few members. Finally, group decisions suffer from ambiguous responsibility, and the responsibility of any single member is watered down. Groups can suffer from groupthink and/or groupshift. Under groupthink, the group emphasizes agreement above everything else, often shutting down individuals who express any disagreement with the group's actions. In groupshift, the group takes a more extreme position (either more conservative or more risky) than individuals would take on their own.

5 **How can we get more creative decisions?**   While there is some evidence that individuals vary in their ability to be creative, research shows that individuals are more creative when they have expertise in the task at hand, creative-thinking skills, and are motivated by intrinsic interest. Five organizational factors have been found to block your creativity at work: (1) *expected evaluation*—focusing on how work is going to be evaluated; (2) *surveillance*—being watched while working; (3) *external motivators*—focusing on external, tangible rewards; (4) *competition*—facing win-lose situations with peers; and (5) *constrained choice*—being given limits on how to do your work.

6 **What is ethics, and how can it be used for better decision making?**   Ethics is the study of moral values or principles that guide our behaviour and inform us whether actions are right or wrong. Ethical principles help us "do the right thing." An individual can use four different criteria in making ethical choices. The first is the *utilitarian* criterion, in which decisions are made solely on the basis of their outcomes or consequences. The second ethical criterion is *rights*; this criterion focuses on respecting and protecting the basic rights of individuals. The third ethical criterion is *justice*; this criterion requires individuals to impose and enforce rules fairly and impartially so there is an equitable distribution of benefits and costs. The fourth ethical criterion is *care*; this criterion suggests that we should be aware of the needs, desires, and well-being of those to whom we are closely connected. There are advantages and disadvantages to each of these criteria.

7 **What is corporate social responsibility?**   Corporate social responsibility is defined as an organization's responsibility to consider the impact of its decisions on society. Thus, organizations may try to better society through such things as charitable contributions or providing better wages to employees working in offshore factories. Organizations may engage in these practices because they feel pressured by society to do so, or they may seek ways to improve society because they feel it is the right thing to do.

OB at Work

for Review

1. What is the rational decision-making model? Under what conditions is it applicable?

2. Describe organizational factors that might constrain decision makers.

3. What role does intuition play in effective decision making?

4. Describe three judgment shortcuts.

5. What is groupthink? What is its effect on decision-making quality?

6. What is groupshift? What is its effect on decision-making quality?

7. Identify five organizational factors that block creativity at work.

8. Describe the four criteria that individuals can use in making ethical decisions.

9. Are unethical decisions more a function of the individual decision maker or the decision maker's work environment? Explain.

10. What is corporate social responsibility?

for Critical Thinking

1. "For the most part, individual decision making in organizations is an irrational process." Do you agree or disagree? Discuss.

2. What factors do you think differentiate good decision makers from poor ones? Relate your answer to the six-step rational decision-making model.

3. Have you ever increased your commitment to a failed course of action? If so, analyze the follow-up decision to increase your commitment and explain why you behaved as you did.

4. If group decisions are of consistently better quality than individual decisions, how did the phrase "a camel is a horse designed by a committee" become so popular and ingrained in our culture?

for You

■ In some decision situations, consider following the rational decision-making model. Doing so will ensure that you review a wider variety of options before committing to a particular decision.

■ Analyze the decision situation and be aware of your biases. We all bring biases to the decisions we make.

■ Combine rational analysis with intuition. As you gain experience, you should feel increasingly confident in imposing your intuitive processes on top of your rational analysis.

■ Use creativity-stimulation techniques. You can improve your overall decision-making effectiveness by searching for innovative solutions to problems. This can be as basic as telling yourself to think creatively and to look specifically for unique alternatives.

■ When making decisions, think about their ethical implications. A quick way to do this is to ask yourself: Would I be embarrassed if this action were printed on the front page of the newspaper?

When in Doubt, Do!

Life is full of decisions and choices.[123] The real question is not "To be, or not to be" but rather "To do, or not to do?" For example, "Should I confront my professor about my mid-term grade?" "Should I buy a new car?" "Should I accept a new job?" "Should I choose this major?" Very often, we are unsure of our decision. In such cases, it is almost always better to choose action over inaction. In life, people more often regret inaction than action. Take the following simple example:

Say you carry an umbrella and it does not rain, or you don't carry an umbrella and it does rain. In which situation are you worse off? Would you rather experience the mild inconvenience of the extra weight of the umbrella or get drenched? Chances are you will regret inaction more than action. Research shows that after we make a decision, we indeed regret inaction more than action. Although we often regret actions in their immediate aftermath, over time these regrets decline markedly, whereas regrets over missed opportunities increase. Suppose you finally decide to take a trip to Europe. You have an amazing time, but a few weeks after you get back, your credit card bill arrives—and it isn't pretty. Unfortunately, you have to work overtime and miss a few dinners out with friends to pay off the bills. A few months down the road, however, you decide to reminisce by looking through your photos from the trip, and you cannot imagine not having gone. So, when in doubt, just do!

Act	State	
	Rain	**Shine**
Carry umbrella	Dry (except your feet!)	Inconvenience
Don't carry umbrella	Miserable drenching	Unqualified bliss

Wait! Not So Fast

It's just silly to think that, when in doubt, you should always act. People will undoubtedly make mistakes following such simple advice. For example, you are out of work, but you still decide to purchase your dream car—a BMW, fully loaded. Not the smartest idea. So why is the motto "just do it" dangerous? Because there are two types of regrets: hot regret, in which an individual kicks herself for having caused something bad, and wistful regret, in which she fantasizes about how else things might have turned out. The danger is that actions are more likely to lead to anguish or hot regret, and inaction is more likely to lead to wistful regret. So the bottom line is that we cannot apply simple rules such as "just do it" to important decisions.

Decision-Making Style Questionnaire

Circle the response that comes closest to how you usually feel or act. There are no right or wrong responses to any of these items.

1. I am more careful about

   a. people's feelings   **b.** their rights

2. I usually get along better with

   a. imaginative people   **b.** realistic people

3. It's a higher compliment to be called

   a. a person of real feeling   **b.** a consistently reasonable person

4. In doing something with other people, it appeals more to me

   a. to do it in the accepted way   **b.** to invent a way of my own

5. I get more annoyed at

   a. fancy theories   **b.** people who do not like theories

6. It's higher praise to call someone

   a. a person of vision   **b.** a person of common sense

7. I more often let

   a. my heart rule my head   **b.** my head rule my heart

8. I think it's a worse fault

   a. to show too much warmth   **b.** to be unsympathetic

9. If I were a teacher, I would rather teach

   a. courses involving theory   **b.** factual courses

Which word in the following pairs appeals to you more? Circle a or b.

   10. a. Compassion   **b.** Foresight

   11. a. Justice   **b.** Mercy

   12. a. Production   **b.** Design

   13. a. Gentle   **b.** Firm

   14. a. Uncritical   **b.** Critical

   15. a. Literal   **b.** Figurative

   16. a. Imaginative   **b.** Matter-of-fact

Scoring Key:

Mark each of your responses on the following scales. Then use the point value column to arrive at your score. For example, if you answered *a* to the first question, you would check *1a* in the Feeling column. This response receives zero points when you add up the point value column. Instructions for classifying your scores are indicated following the scales.

Sensation	Point Value	Intuition	Point Value	Thinking	Point Value	Feeling	Point Value
2b _____	1	2a _____	2	1b _____	1	1a _____	0
4a _____	1	4b _____	1	3b _____	2	3a _____	1
5a _____	1	5b _____	1	7b _____	1	7a _____	1
6b _____	1	6a _____	0	8a _____	0	8b _____	1
9b _____	2	9a _____	2	10b _____	2	10a _____	1
12a _____	1	12b _____	0	11a _____	2	11b _____	1
15a _____	1	15b _____	1	13b _____	1	13a _____	1
16b _____	2	16a _____	0	14b _____	0	14a _____	1
_____		_____		_____		_____	
Maximum Point Value	(10)		(7)		(9)		(7)

Circle *Intuition* if your Intuition score is equal to or greater than your Sensation score. Circle *Sensation* if your Sensation score is greater than your Intuition score. Circle *Feeling* if your Feeling score is greater than your Thinking score. Circle *Thinking* if your Thinking score is greater than your Feeling score.

A high score on *Intuition* indicates you see the world in holistic terms. You tend to be creative. A high score on *Sensation* indicates that you are realistic and see the world in terms of facts. A high score on *Feeling* means you make decisions based on gut feeling. A high score on *Thinking* indicates a highly logical and analytical approach to decision making.

Source: Based on a personality scale developed by D. Hellriegel, J. Slocum, and R. W. Woodman, *Organizational Behavior*, 3rd ed. (St. Paul, MN: West Publishing, 1983), pp. 127–141, and reproduced in J. M. Ivancevich and M. T. Matteson, *Organizational Behavior and Management*, 2nd ed. (Homewood, IL: BPI/Irwin, 1990), pp. 538–539.

SELF-ASSESSMENT LIBRARY   LEARNING ABOUT YOURSELF

More Learning About Yourself Exercises

Additional self-assessments relevant to this chapter appear on MyOBLab (**www.pearsoned.ca/myoblab**).

IV.A.2 Am I a Deliberate Decision Maker?

I.A.5 How Creative Am I?

When you complete the additional assessments, consider the following:

1. Am I surprised about my score?

2. Would my friends evaluate me similarly?

BREAKOUT **GROUP** EXERCISES

Form small groups to discuss the following topics, as assigned by your instructor:

1. Apply the rational decision-making model to deciding where your group might eat dinner this evening. How closely were you able to follow the rational model in making this decision?

2. The company that makes your favourite snack product has been accused of being weak in its social responsibility efforts. What impact will this have on your purchase of any more products from that company?

3. You have seen a classmate cheat on an exam or an assignment. Do you do something about this or ignore it?

WORKING WITH **OTHERS** EXERCISE

Wilderness Survival Exercise

You are a member of a hiking party. After reaching base camp on the first day, you decide to take a quick sunset hike by yourself. After a few exhilarating miles, you decide to return to camp. On your way back, you realize that you are lost. You have shouted for help, to no avail. It is now dark, and getting cold.

Your Task

Without communicating with anyone else in your group, read the following scenarios and choose the best answer. Keep track of your answers on a sheet of paper. You have 10 minutes to answer the 10 questions.

1. The first thing you decide to do is to build a fire. However, you have no matches, so you use the bow and drill method. What is the bow and drill method?

   a. A dry, soft stick is rubbed between one's hands against a board of supple green wood.

   b. A soft green stick is rubbed between one's hands against a hardwood board.

   c. A straight stick of wood is quickly rubbed back and forth against a dead tree.

   d. Two sticks (one being the bow, the other the drill) are struck to create a spark.

2. It occurs to you that you can also use the fire as a distress signal. When signalling with fire, how do you form the international distress signal?

   a. 2 fires

   b. 4 fires in a square

   c. 4 fires in a cross

   d. 3 fires in a line

3. You are very thirsty. You go to a nearby stream and collect some water in the small metal cup you have in your backpack. How long should you boil the water?

   a. 15 minutes

   b. A few seconds

   c. 1 hour

   d. It depends on the altitude.

4. You are very hungry, so you decide to eat what appear to be edible berries. When performing the universal edibility test, what should you do?

   a. Do not eat for 2 hours before the test.

   b. If the plant stings your lip, confirm the sting by holding it under your tongue for 15 minutes.

   c. If nothing bad has happened 2 hours after digestion, eat half a cup of the plant and wait again.

   d. Separate the plant into its basic components and eat each component, one at a time.

5. Next, you decide to build a shelter for the evening. In selecting a site, what do you *not* have to consider?

   a. It must contain material to make the type of shelter you need.

   b. It must be free of insects, reptiles, and poisonous plants.

   c. It must be large enough and level enough for you to lie down comfortably.

   d. It must be on a hill so you can signal rescuers and keep an eye on your surroundings.

6. In the shelter that you built, you notice a spider. You heard from a fellow hiker that black widow spiders populate the area. How do you identify a black widow spider?

   a. Its head and abdomen are black; its thorax is red.

   b. It is attracted to light.

   c. It runs away from light.

   d. It is a dark spider with a red or orange marking on the female's abdomen.

7. After getting some sleep, you notice that the night sky has cleared, so you decide to try to find your way back to base camp. You believe you should travel north and can use the North Star for navigation. How do you locate the North Star?

   a. Hold your right hand up as far as you can and look between your index and middle fingers.

   b. Find Sirius and look 60 degrees above it and to the right.

   c. Look for the Big Dipper and follow the line created by its cup end.

   d. Follow the line of Orion's belt.

8. You come across a fast-moving stream. What is the best way to cross it?

   a. Find a spot downstream from a sandbar, where the water will be calmer.

   b. Build a bridge.

   c. Find a rocky area, as the water will be shallow and you will have hand- and footholds.

   d. Find a level stretch where it breaks into a few channels.

9. After walking for about an hour, you feel several spiders in your clothes. You don't feel any pain, but you know some spider bites are painless. Which of these spider bites is painless?

   a. Black widow

   b. Brown recluse

   c. Wolf spider

   d. Harvestman (daddy longlegs)

10. You decide to eat some insects. Which insects should you avoid?

   a. Adults that sting or bite

   b. Caterpillars and insects that have a pungent odour

   c. Hairy or brightly coloured ones

   d. All the above

Group Task

Break into groups of 5 or 6 people. Now imagine that your whole group is lost. Answer each question as a group, employing a consensus approach to reach each decision. Once the group comes to an agreement, write the decision down on the same sheet of paper that you used for your individual answers. You will have approximately 20 minutes for the group task.

Scoring Your Answers

Your instructor will provide you with the correct answers, which are based on expert judgments in these situations. Once you have received the answers, calculate (A) your individual score; (B) your group's score; (C) the average individual score in the group; and (D) the best individual score in the group. Write these down and consult with your group to ensure that these scores are accurate.

(A) Your individual score _____

(B) Your group's score _____

(C) Average individual score in group _____

(D) Best individual score in group _____

Discussion Questions

1. How did your group (B) perform relative to yourself (A)?

2. How did your group (B) perform relative to the average individual score in the group (C)?

3. How did your group (B) perform relative to the best individual score in the group (D)?

4. Compare your results with those of other groups. Did some groups do a better job of outperforming individuals than others?

5. What do these results tell you about the effectiveness of group decision making?

6. What can groups do to make group decision making more effective?

ETHICAL **DILEMMA** EXERCISE

Five Ethical Decisions: What Would You Do?

Assume that you are a middle manager in a company with about 1000 employees. How would you respond to each of the following situations?[124]

1. You are negotiating a contract with a potentially very large customer whose representative has hinted that you could almost certainly be assured of getting his business if you gave him and his wife an all-expenses-paid cruise to the Caribbean. You know the representative's employer would not approve of such a "payoff," but you have the discretion to authorize such an expenditure. What would you do?

2. You have an autographed CD by Drake and put it up for sale on eBay. So far, the highest bid is $74.50. A friend has offered you $100 for the CD, commenting that he could get $150 for it on eBay in a year. You know this is highly unlikely. Should you sell your friend the CD for what he offered ($100)? Do you have an obligation to tell your friend you have listed your CD on eBay?

3. Your company policy on reimbursement for meals while travelling on company business is that you will be repaid for your out-of-pocket costs, which are not to exceed $80 a day. You don't need receipts for these expenses—the company will take your word. When travelling, you tend to eat at fast-food places and rarely spend in excess of $20 a day. Most of your colleagues submit reimbursement requests in the range of $55 to $60 a day regardless of what their actual expenses are. How much would you request for your meal reimbursements?

4. You are the manager at a gaming company, and you are responsible for hiring a group to outsource the production of a highly anticipated new game. Because your company is a giant in the industry, numerous companies are trying to get the bid. One of them offers you some kickbacks if you give that firm the bid, but ultimately, it is up to your bosses to decide on the company. You don't mention the incentive, but you push upper management to give the bid to the company that offered you the kickback. Is withholding the truth as bad as lying? Why or why not?

5. You have discovered that one of your closest friends at work has stolen a large sum of money from the company. Would you do nothing? Go directly to an executive to report the incident before talking about it with the offender? Confront the individual before taking action? Make contact with the individual with the goal of persuading that person to return the money?

CASE INCIDENTS

The Dangers of Groupthink

Sometimes, the desire to maintain group harmony overrides the importance of making sound decisions. When that occurs, team members are said to engage in groupthink. Here are three examples:[125]

- A civilian worker at a large US Air Force base recalls a time that groupthink overcame her team's decision-making ability. She was a member of a process improvement team that an Air Force general had formed to develop a better way to handle the base's mail, which included important letters from high-ranking military individuals. The team was composed mostly of civilians, and it took almost a month to come up with a plan. The problem: The plan was not a process improvement. Recalls the civilian worker, "I was horrified. What used to be 8 step; now there were 19." The team had devised a new system that resulted in each piece of mail being read by several middle managers before reaching its intended recipient. The team's new plan slowed down the mail considerably, with an average delay of two weeks. Even though the team members all knew that the new system was worse than its predecessor, no one wanted to question the team's solidarity. The problems lasted for almost an entire year. It was not until the general who formed the team complained about the mail that the system was changed.

- Virginia Turezyn, managing director of Infinity Capital, states that during the dot-com boom of the late 1990s, she was a victim of groupthink. At first, Turezyn was skeptical about the stability of the boom. But after continually reading about start-ups turning into multimillion-dollar payoffs, she felt different. Turezyn decided to invest millions in several dot-coms, including I-drive, a company that provided electronic data storage. The problem was that I-drive was giving the storage away for free, and as a result, the company was losing money. Turezyn recalls one board meeting at I-drive where she spoke up to no avail. "We're spending way too much money," she screamed. The younger executives shook their heads and replied that if they charged for storage they would lose their customers. Says Turezyn, "I started to think, 'Maybe I'm just too old. Maybe

I really don't get it.'" Unfortunately, Turezyn did get it. I-drive later filed for bankruptcy.

- Steve Blank, an entrepreneur, also fell victim to groupthink. Blank was a dot-com investor, and he participated on the advisory boards of several Internet start-ups. During meetings for one such start-up, a web photo finisher, Blank tried to persuade his fellow board members to change the business model to be more traditional. Recalls Blank, "I went to those meetings and started saying things like, 'Maybe you should spend that $10 million you just raised on acquiring a customer base rather than building a brand.' The CEO told me, 'Steve, you just don't get it—all the rules have changed.'" The team did not take Blank's advice, and Blank says that he lost hundreds of thousands of dollars on the deal.

According to Michael Useem, a professor at the University of Pennsylvania's Wharton College of Business, one of the main reasons that groupthink occurs is a lack of conflict. "A single devil's advocate or whistle-blower faces a really uphill struggle," he states. "But if you [the naysayer] have one ally, that is enormously strengthening."

Questions

1. What are some factors that led to groupthink in the cases described here? What can teams do to attempt to prevent groupthink from occurring? What might you do yourself if you were in a similar situation?

2. How might differences in status among group members contribute to groupthink? For example, how might lower-status members react to a group's decision? Are lower-status members more or less likely to be dissenters? Why might higher-status group members be more effective dissenters?

3. Microsoft CEO Steve Ballmer says that he encourages dissent. Can such norms guard against the occurrence of groupthink? As a manager, how would you try to cultivate norms that prevent groupthink?

4. How might group characteristics such as size and cohesiveness affect groupthink?

"If Two Heads Are Better Than One, Are Four Even Better?"

Maggie Becker, age 24, is a marketing manager for Kavu, a small chain of coffee shops in eastern Ohio. Recently, Maggie's wealthy uncle passed away and left her, his only niece, $100 000. Maggie considers her current salary adequate to meet her current living expenses, so she would like to invest the money so that when she buys a house she will have a nice nest egg on which to draw.

One of Maggie's neighbours, Brian, is a financial advisor. Brian told Maggie that the array of investment options is virtually endless. She asked him to present her with two of the best options, and this is what he offered her:

1. A very low-risk AAA bond fund. With this option, based on the information Brian provided, Maggie estimates that after five years she stands virtually zero chance of losing money, with an expected gain of approximately $7000.

2. A moderate-risk mutual fund. Based on the information Brian provided her, Maggie estimates that with this option she stands a 50 percent chance of making $40 000 but also a 50 percent chance of losing $20 000.

Maggie prides herself on being rational and objective in her thinking. However, she is unsure of what to do in this case. Brian refuses to help her, telling her that she has already limited herself by asking for only two options. While driving to her parents' house for the weekend, Maggie finds herself vacillating between the two options. Her older brother is also visiting the folks this weekend, so Maggie decides to gather her family around the table after dinner, lay out the two options, and go with their decision. "You know the old saying—two heads are better than one," she says to herself, "so four heads should be even better."

Questions

1. Has Maggie made a good decision about the way she is going to make the decision?

2. Which investment would you choose? Why?

3. Which investment do you think most people would choose?

4. Based on what you have learned about groupshift, which investment do you think Maggie's family will choose?

FROM CONCEPTS TO SKILLS

Solving Problems Creatively

You can be more effective at solving problems creatively if you use the following 10 suggestions:[126]

1. *Think of yourself as creative.* Research shows that if you think you cannot be creative, you won't be. Believing in your ability to be creative is the first step in becoming more creative.

2. *Pay attention to your intuition.* Every individual has a subconscious mind that works well. Sometimes answers will come to you when you least expect them. Listen to that "inner voice." In fact, most creative people will keep a notepad near their bed and write down ideas when the thoughts come to them.

3. *Move away from your comfort zone.* Every individual has a comfort zone in which certainty exists. But creativity and the known often do not mix. To be creative, you need to move away from the status quo and focus your mind on something new.

4. *Determine what you want to do.* This includes such things as taking time to understand a problem before beginning to try to resolve it, getting all the facts in mind, and trying to identify the most important facts.

5. *Think outside the box.* Use analogies whenever possible (for example, could you approach your problem like a fish out of water and look at what the fish does to cope? Or can you use the things you have to do to find your way when it's foggy to help you solve your problem?). Use different problem-solving strategies, such as verbal, visual, mathematical, or theatrical. Look at your problem from a different perspective, or ask yourself what someone else, such as your grandmother, might do if faced with the same situation.

6. *Look for ways to do things better.* This may involve trying consciously to be original, not worrying about looking foolish, keeping an open mind, being alert to odd or puzzling facts, thinking of unconventional ways to use objects and the environment, discarding usual or habitual ways of doing things, and striving for objectivity by being as critical of your own ideas as you would be of someone else's.

7. *Find several right answers.* Being creative means continuing to look for other solutions even when you think you have solved the problem. A better, more creative solution just might be found.

8. *Believe in finding a workable solution.* Like believing in yourself, you also need to believe in your ideas. If you don't think you can find a solution, you probably won't.

9. *Brainstorm with others.* Creativity is not an isolated activity. Bouncing ideas off of others creates a synergistic effect.

10. *Turn creative ideas into action.* Coming up with creative ideas is only part of the process. Once the ideas are generated, they must be implemented. Keeping great ideas in your mind, or on papers that no one will read, does little to expand your creative abilities.

Every time the phone rings, your stomach clenches and your palms start to sweat. And it's no wonder! As sales manager for Brinkers, a machine tool parts manufacturer, you are besieged by calls from customers who are upset about late deliveries. Your boss, Carter Hererra, acts as both production manager and scheduler. Every time your sales representatives negotiate a sale, it's up to Carter to determine whether production can actually meet the delivery date the customer specifies. Carter invariably says, "No problem." The good thing about this is that you make a lot of initial sales. The bad news is that production hardly ever meets the shipment dates that Carter authorizes. Moreover, he does not seem to be all that concerned about the aftermath of late deliveries. He says: "Our customers know they're getting outstanding quality at a great price. Just let them try to match that anywhere. It can't be done. So even if they have to wait a couple of extra days or weeks, they're still getting the best deal they can." Somehow the customers do not see it that way, and they let you know about their unhappiness. Then it's up to you to try to soothe the relationship. You know this problem has to be taken care of, but what possible solutions are there? After all, how are you going to keep from making your manager angry or making the customers angry? Use your knowledge of creative problem-solving to come up with solutions.

Practising Skills

Reinforcing Skills

1. Take 20 minutes to list as many words as you can using the letters in the word *brainstorm*. (There are at least 95.) If you run out of listings before time is up, it's okay to quit early. But try to be as creative as you can.

2. List on a piece of paper some common terms that apply to both water and finance. How many were you able to come up with?

OB on the EDGE

Spirituality in the Workplace

Entrepreneur Robin Kirby (shown above) represents clothing manufacturers; she meets with retailers to sell them clothes produced by the factories she represents.[1] She also markets a line of her own clothing on The Shopping Channel.

Kirby is passionate about spiritual connections and the healing arts. "I'm a reiki master and I do crystal bowl healing. I'm known as 'the white witch' among my menswear clients." Kirby sometimes carries a deep crystal bowl and a rubber striker, which she uses to create tones that she says clear "difficult energies from the spaces she visits."

Kirby recently cleared the energy at a client's knitwear factory and showroom, after she arrived to find the staff and the client looking stressed out. She used prayers, meditations, and bowl-ringing to do this. The employees later told her that the workplace stayed calm for a week after she did her energy clearing, and they wanted her to come back and do it again.

What Is Spirituality?

In a study to determine what people mean by *spirituality*, the following elements were identified:[2]

- Not formal, structured, or organized
- Nondenominational, above and beyond denominations
- Broadly inclusive, embracing everyone; universal and timeless
- The ultimate source and provider of meaning and purpose in life
- The awe we feel in the presence of the transcendent
- The sacredness of everything, the ordinariness of everyday life
- The deep feeling of the interconnectedness of everything
- Inner peace and calm
- An inexhaustible source of faith and willpower
- The ultimate end in itself

In general, three streams of definitions have been identified. One stream defines *spirituality* in terms of a personal inner experience based on "interconnectedness."[3] A second stream focuses on "principles, virtues, ethics, values, emotions, wisdom, and intuition."[4] Organizations are then considered spiritual to the extent that they hold these values. Finally, a third stream considers spirituality as the link between one's "personal inner experience" and how this is modelled in "outer behaviours, principles, and practices."[5]

Comparing Spirituality and Religion

Workplace spirituality is *not* about organized religious practices, although it's sometimes difficult to reach precise definitions of each term. It's not about God or theology. This point was made clear in a 2011 study of 275 natural and social scientists at elite universities. About 25 percent "said they have a spirituality that is consistent with science, although they are not formally religious."[6]

Workplace spirituality recognizes that people have an inner life that nourishes and is nourished by meaningful work in the context of community.[7] Organizations that promote a spiritual culture recognize that people have both a mind and a spirit, seek to find meaning and purpose in their work, and desire to connect with other human beings and be part of a community.

One of the few empirical studies of spirituality in the workplace was conducted by Ian Mitroff and Elizabeth Denton.[8] Though the response rate to their mailed survey was low, they corroborated many of their findings through interviews with human resource managers and senior managers at other organizations. They discovered that individuals fall into four patterns in terms of how they view the relationship between religion and spirituality:

- *A person views both religion and spirituality positively.* This person sees religion and spirituality as synonymous, with spirituality developed through religious practices. About 30 percent of the participants fell into this category.
- *A person views religion positively but spirituality negatively.* This person focuses on the rituals and the practices of a particular religion. The emphasis is on salvation and being a member of a closely bound, shared community. About 2 percent of the participants fell into this category.
- *A person views religion negatively, but views spirituality positively.* This person sees religion as "organized, close-minded, and intolerant."

Spirituality, by contrast, is viewed as "open-minded, tolerant, and universal," and intended to be a bonding force. About 60 percent of the participants fell into this category.

- Finally, *a person views both religion and spirituality negatively.* This person believes that "religion and spirituality have nothing to do with the modern, secular workplace." About 8 percent of the participants fell into this category.

For instance, at Montreal-based Cordon Bleu-Tomasso, a processed-foods company, CEO J. Robert Ouimet has installed meditation rooms in all of his factories. He took this idea from a conversation he had with Mother Teresa. "There is no talking or eating allowed—only silence. The idea is to give the workplace a feeling of serenity and a sense of higher purpose," he explains.[9] Ouimet wants his workplace to be a place not only where goods are produced but also where employees find their lives enriched. He believes such practices as meditation rooms, prayers before meetings, and other "soulful initiatives" increase "not only human happiness and well-being, but company profitability as well."[10] A 2011 study backs him up:[11] "Mindfulness meditation has been reported to enhance numerous mental abilities, including rapid memory recall," says a co-author of the study.[12]

Another company that tries to encourage employees to look beyond themselves is New Hampshire-based Timberland, where boots symbolize what customers and employees are supposed to do: "Pull on your boots and make a difference."[13] The company pays its employees for up to 40 hours of volunteer work a year. It has also developed a plan for employees to apply for six-month paid sabbaticals if they want to give service to a nonprofit organization. Jeffrey B. Swartz, the company's president and CEO, believes that "doing well" and "doing good" help make this family-owned firm successful.

Why Spirituality Now?

A large body of research is beginning to show that things like mindful meditation make a difference in people's lives.[14] For instance, a 2011 study found that after participating in an eight-week mindfulness meditation program, subjects had changes in brain regions "associated with memory, sense of self, empathy and stress."[15]

Employees working for the District of North Vancouver take workshops to help them develop personal and professional effectiveness.[16] The workshops are led by Tanis Helliwell, a therapist in Vancouver, and are based on her book *Take Your Soul to Work*.[17] David Stuart, director of corporate services at the District of North Vancouver, read her book and decided that the municipality's 600 employees, be they ditch diggers or architects, would benefit from its practices.

Helliwell believes that employers should help their employees develop their whole person, rather than just the "9-to-5 person." "The more people look at what they need to do in order to develop their potential and find work that will encompass that, the more the employer is going to get in the workplace," she says.

Stuart says that the response to the workshops has been "spectacular." "Workers are expecting more from their employment situation. They need tools to give them a sense that they can in fact control what's happening in their lives and the changes happening around them and how they deal with them," he explains.

Reasons for the Growing Interest in Spirituality

- Spirituality acts as a counterbalance to the pressures and stress of a turbulent pace of life. Contemporary lifestyles—single-parent families, geographic mobility, the temporary nature of jobs, new technologies that create distance between people—underscore the lack of community many people feel and increase the need for involvement and connection.

- Formalized religion has not worked for many people, and they continue to look for anchors to replace lack of faith and to fill a growing feeling of emptiness.

- Job demands have made the workplace dominant in many people's lives, yet they continue to question the meaning of work.

- More people desire to integrate personal life values with their professional life.

- An increasing number of people are finding that the pursuit of more material acquisitions leaves them unfulfilled.

Workplace spirituality is a relatively new phenomenon. Historical models of management and organizational behaviour had no room for spirituality. The myth of rationality assumed that the well-run organization eliminated feelings. Similarly, concern about an employee's inner life had no role in the perfectly rational model. But just as we have now come to realize that the study of emotions improves our understanding of organizational behaviour, an awareness of spirituality can help us better understand employee behaviour in the twenty-first century. Similarly, organizations that are concerned with spirituality are more likely to directly address problems created by conflicts that occur in everyday life.[18]

The Sobey School of Business at Saint Mary's University in Halifax has taken the lead in Canada for trying to understand the implications of spirituality in the workplace. In fall 2004, the Sobey School of Business opened a centre devoted to teaching and studying spirituality in the workplace. The Centre for Spirituality in the Workplace is the first academic-based centre of its kind in Canada, though there are such centres in the United States and overseas.

"The centre is not devoted to religious dogma and theology," Allan Miciak, former dean of the Sobey School of Business, explains. Spirituality at work is about "creating better workplaces," he adds.[19]

Linda Lewis-Daly, principal of Toronto-based Lewis-Daly and Associates, which specializes in workplace wellness, notes that Canadian employers have shown greater interest in spiritually helpful activities for employees (such as yoga and meditation programs) in recent years. She explains that the emphasis is less on religion and "more about helping people to explore how they can find worth in the work they do and lead a more meaningful life aligned with their values."[20]

We summarize additional reasons why people are turning to spirituality in the inset *Reasons for the Growing Interest in Spirituality*.

Characteristics of a Spiritual Organization

Spiritual organizations are concerned with helping people develop and reach their full potential. This is analogous

to Abraham Maslow's description of self-actualization that we discussed in relation to motivation in Chapter 4. Similarly, organizations concerned with spirituality are more likely to directly address problems created by work-life conflicts.[21]

Sister Mangalam Lena, of the Franciscan Missionaries of Mary, started Ottawa-based Home-based Spiritual Care (HBSC) to help recovering patients in their homes. "[Traditional] home care provides nursing, counselling, and physiotherapy for the homebound. But who cares for their spiritual needs in the home?" she asked.[22] This led to the start of her business. Lena believes that "people who are spiritually healthy are also physically healthier." She has convinced researchers at the University of Ottawa, including Dian Prud'homme Brisson, assistant director of the university's nursing program, to study the effects of such care.

New employees at Banff, Alberta-based High Country Inn might be surprised the first time they meet the inn's corporate chaplain, Lee-Ann Lavoie. She started working there in 2006, and sees her job as being to "offer care and support." "One thing I truly believe is that there is a spiritual side of life, and everyone has a spiritual side," Lavoie says. "Corporate chaplains open people up to that side at work."[23]

Canadian companies are starting to address the spiritual needs of employees. Scarborough, Ontario-based TELUS Mobility created prayer and meditation rooms for its employees, which led to it winning an award from the Association for Spirit at Work in 2002. Andrea Goertz, vice-president of enterprise services and strategic initiatives at TELUS, attributes the high scores the company has received on employee engagement in recent years and reduced absenteeism to its encouragement of spiritual practices in the workplace.[24] Edmonton-based

CapitalCare, whose employees care for elderly and disabled adults, created a spirituality program emphasizing meditation for nurses and aides who work there.[25]

What differentiates spiritual organizations from their nonspiritual counterparts? Although research on this question is only preliminary, our review identified four cultural characteristics that tend to be evident in spiritual organizations.[26]

Strong Sense of Purpose

Spiritual organizations build their cultures around a meaningful purpose. While profits may be important, they are not the primary value of these organizations. People want to be inspired by a purpose that they believe is important and worthwhile. Nova Scotia-based Northwood, the largest nonprofit seniors' health care organization in Eastern Canada, offers full-time pastoral care in addition to the traditional services of a seniors facility. For Gael Page, who consults to Northwood, the emphasis on spirituality makes Northwood a better place to work. "There used to be a day when I was a nurse that you came to work and put your whole personal life aside, you'd pretend it didn't exist. It was very unnatural to be asked to do that. The whole workplace spirituality movement has changed all that. Workplace spirituality recognizes that we are all complex with many dimensions."[27]

Charlotte Kwon, owner and CEO of Vancouver-based Maiwa Handprints, pays the artisans from developing countries who provide textiles for her retail stores substantially more than what others pay them. She wants to protect craftspeople, so that they can continue to produce their artwork. She also notes that she does not need to pay minimum prices to survive: "I live okay. I don't need anything more."[28]

Trust and Respect

Spiritual organizations are characterized by mutual trust, honesty, and openness. Managers are not afraid to admit mistakes. The president of Wetherill Associates, a highly successful American auto parts distribution firm, says, "We don't tell lies here, and everyone knows it. We are specific and honest about quality and suitability of the product for our customers' needs, even if we know they might not be able to detect any problem."[30]

Humanistic Work Practices

The practices embraced by spiritual organizations include flexible work schedules, group- and organization-based rewards, narrowing of pay and status differentials, guarantees of individual employee rights, employee empowerment, and job security. Hewlett-Packard, for instance, has handled temporary downturns through voluntary attrition and shortened workweeks (shared by all), and it has handled longer-term declines through early retirements and buyouts.

Toleration of Employee Expression

Finally, spiritual organizations don't stifle employee emotions. They allow

people to be themselves—to express their moods and feelings without guilt or fear of reprimand. Employees at Southwest Airlines, for instance, are encouraged to express their sense of humour on the job, to act spontaneously, and to make their work fun.

At Cordon Bleu-Tomasso, employees are encouraged to have annual one-on-one meetings with their managers where employees can express any and all frustrations without worrying that something negative will happen to them. When Ouimet first introduced this practice, employees were reluctant to voice their concerns. As Ouimet notes, "Over time, a sense of trust developed."[31] Ouimet's employees are also encouraged to engage in "gestures of reconciliation," where they apologize to one another when interpersonal conflicts arise. Ouimet says he sets the example by apologizing when he has "blown a gasket."

The inset *Organizational Models for Fostering Spirituality* describes models for spiritually based organizations.

Criticisms of Spirituality

Critics of organizations that embrace spiritual values have focused on three issues. First is the question of scientific foundation. What, really, is workplace spirituality? Is it just a new management buzzword? Second, are spiritual organizations legitimate? Third is the question of economics: Are spirituality and profits compatible?

First, as you might imagine, there is very little research on workplace spirituality.[32] We don't know whether the concept will have staying power. Do the cultural characteristics just identified really separate spiritual organizations? Spirituality has been defined so broadly in some sources that practices from job rotation to corporate retreats at meditation centres have been identified as spiritual practices. Do employees of so-called spiritual organizations perceive that they work in spiritual organizations? Although research suggests support for workplace spirituality, the questions we have just posed need to be answered before the concept gains full credibility.

Organizational Models for Fostering Spirituality

- **Religion-Based Organization:** The organization's practices are consistent with biblical teachings; there is an emphasis on prayer as a primary form of intrafirm communication; employees are expected to accept core Christian principles as guides to decision making.

- **Evolutionary Organization:** Spiritual openness is encouraged; the guiding texts are a mixture of Christian scriptures and philosophical works (Kant, Neibuhr, Buber); there is an emphasis on serving the customer, preserving the environment, and respecting stakeholders.

- **Recovering Organization:** The organization models itself after the 12-step program of Alcoholics Anonymous; spirituality is discussed in ways that are acceptable to the largest number of people. The 12-step program emphasizes confession (of failures), acceptance of God's will and guidance, and reliance on the help of others. This model is infrequently found in the business world.

- **Socially Responsible Organization:** Social concerns and values are part of everyday business activities; the organization emphasizes the expression of the individual's "whole person" and soul; customers, suppliers, and other stakeholders are expected to bond more readily to the firm; spirituality and soul are explicit core business principles.

- **Values-Based Organization:** The organization firmly rejects all notions of religious doctrine; it favours nonreligious and nonspiritual secular values or virtues (e.g., awareness, consciousness, dignity, honesty, openness, respect, integrity, and, above all, trust); values are guides for policy setting and decision making throughout the firm. The Golden Rule is the prime business principle.

- **Best-Practice Model:** The organization combines parts of all of the above models; it emphasizes values-based secular orientation; it adds an openly expressed spiritual dimension; it emphasizes the importance of "a higher power," periodic moral audits, and a broadly inclusive approach to stakeholders.[33]

On the second question, dealing with the legitimacy of spiritual organizations, an emphasis on spirituality can clearly make some employees uneasy. Critics might argue that secular institutions, especially business firms, have no business imposing spiritual values on employees. This criticism is undoubtedly valid when spirituality is defined as bringing religion and God into the workplace.[34] However, the criticism seems less stinging when the goal is limited to helping employees find meaning in their work lives. If the concerns listed in the inset *Reasons for the Growing Interest in Spirituality* on page 472 truly characterize a growing segment of the workforce, maybe the time is right for more organizations to help employees find meaning and purpose in their work and to use the workplace as a source of community.

The issue of whether spirituality and profits are compatible objectives is certainly relevant for managers and investors in business. The evidence, although limited, indicates they are. A recent study by a major consulting firm found that companies that introduced spiritually based techniques improved productivity and significantly reduced turnover.[35] Another study found organizations that provide their employees with opportunities for spiritual development outperformed those that did not.[36] Other studies also report that spirituality in organizations was positively related to creativity, employee satisfaction, team performance, and organizational commitment.[37]

The cynic will say that all this caring stuff is in fact merely good public relations. Even so, the results at both Southwest Airlines and Cordon Bleu-Tomasso suggest that a caring organization is good for the bottom line. Southwest Airlines is strongly committed to providing the lowest airfares, on-time service, and a pleasant experience for customers. Southwest

employees have one of the lowest turnover rates in the airline industry, the company consistently has the lowest labour costs per miles flown of any major airline, and it has proven itself to be the most consistently profitable airline in the United States.[38] Jacques Gingras, a production manager at Cordon Bleu-Tomasso, says Ouimet's practices really help the bottom line. "Obviously, people can't go to the silence rooms whenever they want, because we're running an assembly line. But they communicate well and respect one another. It makes the operation run more smoothly."[39]

RESEARCH EXERCISES

1. Look for data on the extent to which companies encourage spirituality in the workplace in Canada and the United States. Can you draw any inferences about whether there is a trend in this practice?

2. Identify three Canadian organizations or CEOs that have encouraged more openness toward spirituality in their organizations. What, if any, commonalities exist in these organizations?

YOUR PERSPECTIVE

1. In this feature, we report on individuals' views on religion and spirituality. Do you see the two as linked or not linked?

2. What does spirituality mean to you?

WANT TO KNOW MORE?

Though it is now out of print, top executives at the Bank of Montreal read Ann Coombs' *The Living Workplace: Soul, Spirit and Success in the 21st Century* (Toronto: HarperCollins Canada, 2001), and were so impressed that they bought 800 copies, put the bank's logo on them, and started giving copies to their clients. Coombs, through Vancouver-based Coombs Consulting, has worked with a number of clients, including Ford Canada, Campbell Soup Company, and TELUS.

Other books to consider include Joan Marques, Satinder Dhiman, and Richard King, *Spirituality in the Workplace: What It Is, Why It Matters, How to Make It Work for You* (Fawskin, CA: Personhood Press, 2007); and Gregory F. Augustine Pierce, *Spirituality at Work: 10 Ways to Balance Your Life on the Job* (Chicago, IL: Loyola Press, 2005).

Organizational Structure

T4G uses a flat organizational structure designed to foster teamwork, freedom, and creativity. How can T4G ensure that its "loose" organizational structure continues to be a motivating force?

LEARNING OUTCOMES

1. What are the key elements of organizational structure?

2. What are some examples of traditional organizational designs?

3. What do newer organizational structures look like?

4. Why do organizational structures differ?

5. What are the behavioural implications of different organizational designs?

Geoff Flood, president of Toronto-based T4G, a technical services company, has some strong feelings about bureaucracy. "Bureaucracy," he proclaims, "is nonsense that gets in the way. It is cost, pure cost."[1] He believes he has a better idea: He structured his company into a loose portfolio of business units led by different people in turn, depending on the project they are working on and their expertise. "It is a roles-based design," explains Flood. "There has never been an organizational chart in the company. And there won't be an organizational chart until I'm gone."

Flood feels that the flat structure improves communication and decision making. "In a typical business there is a hierarchy, and if there was one in this business it would be an inverted pyramid and I'd be on the bottom," he says. "I report to the people on the front lines."

Other T4G initiatives include enabling virtual teams, so that the highly qualified professionals they hire can work from wherever they like.

Flood is part of a new breed of executives who tailor organizational structure to employee needs. The company locates its offices where "smart people want to live and raise their families." The result is competitive advantage through high staff retention rates and the fostering of innovation and creativity.

The theme of this chapter is that organizations have different structures, determined by specific forces, and that these structures have a bearing on employee attitudes and behaviour. Organizations need to think carefully about the best way to organize how people inside and outside the organization are connected to each other. These connections form the basis for organizational structure.

OB IS FOR EVERYONE

- What happens when a person performs the same task over and over again?

- What happens when you report to two bosses?

- Can an organization really have no boundaries?

- So what does *technology* mean?

1 What are the key elements of organizational structure?

BLOG IT

How does organizational structure affect behaviour?
Describe the structure of an organization where you spent some time. How did that structure affect your motivation and your mood?
www.obstudentjournals.blogspot.com

What Is Organizational Structure?

An **organizational structure** defines how job tasks are formally divided, grouped, and coordinated. Managers need to address six key elements when they design their organization's structure: work specialization, departmentalization, chain of command, span of control, centralization and decentralization, and formalization.[2] Exhibit 13-1 presents all of these elements as answers to an important structural question. This chapter's *Case Incident—Ajax University Needs a New Structure* on page 506 provides an opportunity for you to consider how to change an organizational structure in order to resolve some of the problems the organization faces.

Work Specialization

We use the term **work specialization**, or *division of labour*, to describe the degree to which tasks in the organization are subdivided into separate jobs. The essence of work specialization is that, rather than an entire job being completed by one individual, it's broken down into a number of steps, with each step being completed by a separate individual. In essence, individuals specialize in doing part of an activity rather than the entire activity.

What happens when a person performs the same task over and over again?

Specialization can be efficient. Employee skills at performing a task improve through repetition. Less time is spent in changing tasks, in putting away tools and equipment from a prior step in the work process, and in preparing for another. It's easier and less costly to find and train employees to do specific and repetitive tasks. This is especially true of highly sophisticated and complex operations. For example, could Montreal-based Bombardier produce even one Canadian regional jet a year if one person had to build the entire plane alone? Not likely! Finally, work specialization increases efficiency and productivity by encouraging the creation of special inventions and machinery.

However, specialization can lead to boredom, fatigue, stress, low productivity, poor quality, increased absenteeism, and high turnover, so it is not always the best way to organize employees. Giving employees a variety of activities to do, allowing them to do a whole and complete job, and putting them into teams with interchangeable skills can result in significantly higher output and increased employee satisfaction.

Most managers today recognize that specialization provides economies in certain types of jobs but problems when it's carried too far. High work specialization helps McDonald's make and sell hamburgers and fries efficiently, and aids medical special-

organizational structure How job tasks are formally divided, grouped, and coordinated.

work specialization The degree to which tasks in the organization are subdivided into separate jobs.

EXHIBIT 13-1 Six Key Questions That Managers Need to Answer in Designing the Proper Organizational Structure

The Key Question	The Answer Is Provided By
1. To what degree are tasks subdivided into separate jobs?	*Work specialization*
2. On what basis will jobs be grouped together?	*Departmentalization*
3. To whom do individuals and groups report?	*Chain of command*
4. How many individuals can a manager efficiently and effectively direct?	*Span of control*
5. Where does decision-making authority lie?	*Centralization and decentralization*
6. To what degree will there be rules and regulations to direct employees and managers?	*Formalization*

Work is specialized at the Russian factories that manufacture the wooden nesting dolls called *matryoshkas*. At this factory outside Moscow, individuals specialize in doing part of the doll production, from the crafts-men who carve the dolls to the painters who decorate them. Work specialization brings efficiency to doll production, as some 50 employees can make 100 *matryoshkas* every two days.

ists working in hospitals. Other companies, on the other hand, have achieved success by reducing specialization.

Departmentalization

Once jobs are divided up through work specialization, they must be grouped so that common tasks can be coordinated. The basis on which jobs are grouped together is called **departmentalization**. One of the concerns related to departmental groups is that they can become *silos* within an organization. Often, departments start protecting their own turf and not interacting well with other departments, which can lead to a narrow vision with respect to organizational goals.

Functional Departmentalization

One of the most popular ways to group activities is by *functions* performed. For example, a manufacturing company might separate engineering, accounting, manufacturing, human resource, and purchasing specialists into common departments. Similarly, a hospital might have departments devoted to research, patient care, accounting, and so forth. The major advantage to functional groupings is obtaining efficiencies from put-ting people with common skills and orientations together into common units.

Product Departmentalization

Tasks can also be departmentalized by the type of *product* the organization produces. Procter & Gamble groups each major product—such as Tide, Pampers, Charmin, and Pringles—under an executive who has complete global responsibility for it. The major advantage to this type of grouping is increased accountability for product performance, since all activities related to a specific product line are under the direction of a single manager.

Geographic Departmentalization

Another way to departmentalize is on the basis of geography, or territory. The sales func-tion, for instance, may be divided regionally with departments for British Columbia, the Prairies, Central Canada, and Atlantic Canada. Each of these regions is, in effect, a

departmentalization The basis on which jobs are grouped together.

The Carillon Generating Station on the Ottawa River (shown here) is one of Montreal-based Hydro-Québec's hydroelectric power stations. Hydro-Québec organizes its operations by functions so that the company can be more responsive to growth outside Quebec. It has four divisions: Hydro-Québec Production, Hydro-Québec TransÉnergie, Hydro-Québec Distribution, and Hydro-Québec Équipement/Société d'énergie de la Baie James.

department organized around geography. If an organization's customers are scattered over a large geographic area and have similar needs based on their location, then this form of departmentalization can be valuable.

Process Departmentalization

Some companies organize departments by the processing that occurs. For example, an aluminum tubing manufacturer might have the following departments: casting; press; tubing; finishing; and inspecting, packing, and shipping. This is an example of process departmentalization, because each department specializes in one specific phase in the production of aluminum tubing. Since each process requires different skills, this method offers a basis for the homogeneous categorizing of activities.

Process departmentalization can be used for processing customers, as well as products. For example, in some provinces, you may go through a series of steps handled by several departments before receiving your driver's licence: (1) validation by a motor vehicles division; (2) processing by the licensing department; and (3) payment collection by the treasury department.

Customer Departmentalization

Yet another way to departmentalize is on the basis of the particular type of customer the organization seeks to reach. Microsoft, for example, is organized around four customer markets: consumers, large corporations, software developers, and small businesses. Customers in each department have a common set of problems and needs best met by having specialists for each.

Large organizations may use all the forms of departmentalization we have described. A major Japanese electronics firm organizes each of its divisions along functional lines, its manufacturing units around processes, sales around seven geographic regions, and each sales region into four customer groupings. In a strong recent trend among organizations of all sizes, rigid functional departmentalization is increasingly complemented by teams that cross traditional departmental lines. As we described in Chapter 6, as tasks have become more complex, and more diverse skills are needed to accomplish those tasks, management has turned to cross-functional teams.

Chain of Command

While the chain of command was once a basic cornerstone in the design of organizations, it has far less importance today.[3] But contemporary managers should still consider its implications. The **chain of command** is the continuous line of authority that extends from upper organizational levels to the lowest level and clarifies who reports to whom. It helps employees answer questions such as, "Who do I go to if I have a problem?" and "To whom do I report?"

We cannot discuss the chain of command without also discussing authority and unity of command. **Authority** refers to the rights inherent in a managerial position to give orders and expect them to be obeyed. To facilitate coordination, each managerial position is given a place in the chain of command, and each manager is given a degree of authority in order to meet his or her responsibilities. The principle of **unity of command** helps preserve the concept of an unbroken line of authority. It says a person should have one and only one superior to whom he or she is directly responsible. If the unity of command is broken, an employee might have to cope with conflicting demands or priorities from several superiors.

Because managers have limited time and knowledge, they may choose to delegate some of their responsibilities to other employees. **Delegation** is the assignment of authority to another person to carry out specific duties, allowing the employee to make some of the decisions. Delegation is an important part of a manager's job, as it can ensure that the right people are part of the decision-making process. Through delegation, employees are being empowered to make decisions that previously were reserved for management. This chapter's *From Concepts to Skills* on pages 508–509 presents strategies to be a better delegator.

Times change, and so do the basic tenets of organizational design. A low-level employee today can access information in seconds that was available only to top managers a generation ago. Networked computers allow employees anywhere in an organization to communicate with anyone else without going through formal channels. Operating employees are empowered to make decisions previously reserved for management. Add the popularity of self-managed and cross-functional teams and the creation of new structural designs that include multiple bosses, and you can see why authority and unity of command hold less relevance. Many organizations still find they can be most productive by enforcing the chain of command. There just seem to be fewer of them today.

Span of Control

Span of control refers to the number of employees who report to a manager. This number will vary by organization, and by unit within an organization, and is determined by the number of employees a manager can efficiently and effectively direct. In an assembly-line factory, a manager may be able to direct numerous employees, because the work is well defined and controlled by machinery. A sales manager, by contrast, might have to give one-on-one supervision to individual sales reps, and, therefore, fewer would report to the sales manager. All things being equal, the wider or larger the span, the more efficient the organization. An example can illustrate the validity of this statement.

Assume that we have two organizations, both of which have approximately 4100 operative-level employees. As Exhibit 13-2 illustrates, if one has a uniform span of 4 and the other a span of 8, the wider span would have 2 fewer levels and approximately 800 fewer managers. If the average manager earned $56 000 a year, the wider span would save about $45 million a year in management salaries. Obviously, wider spans are more efficient in terms of cost. However, at some point when supervisors no longer have time to provide the necessary leadership and support, they reduce effectiveness and employee performance suffers.

chain of command The continuous line of authority that extends from upper organizational levels to the lowest level and clarifies who reports to whom.

authority The rights inherent in a managerial position to give orders and to expect the orders to be obeyed.

unity of command The idea that a subordinate should have only one superior to whom he or she is directly responsible.

delegation Assignment of authority to another person to carry out specific duties, allowing the employee to make some of the decisions.

span of control The number of employees that report to a manager.

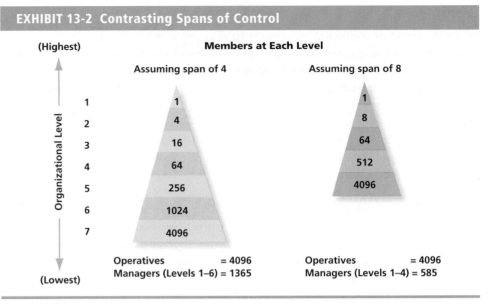

EXHIBIT 13-2 Contrasting Spans of Control

Members at Each Level

(Highest)

Organizational Level

	Assuming span of 4	Assuming span of 8
1	1	1
2	4	8
3	16	64
4	64	512
5	256	4096
6	1024	
7	4096	

(Lowest)

Operatives = 4096	Operatives = 4096
Managers (Levels 1–6) = 1365	Managers (Levels 1–4) = 585

Narrow or small spans have their advocates. By keeping the span of control to 5 or 6 employees, a manager can maintain close control.[4] But narrow spans have three major drawbacks. First, as already described, they are expensive because they add levels of management. Second, they make vertical communication in the organization more complex. The added levels of hierarchy slow down decision making and tend to isolate upper management. Third, narrow spans of control encourage overly tight supervision and discourage employee autonomy.

The trend in recent years has been toward wider spans of control.[5] Wider spans of control are consistent with recent efforts by companies to reduce costs, cut overhead, speed up decision making, increase flexibility, get closer to customers, and empower employees. However, to ensure that performance does not suffer because of these wider spans, organizations have been investing heavily in employee training. Managers recognize that they can handle a wider span when employees know their jobs inside and out or can turn to their co-workers when they have questions.

centralization The degree to which decision making is concentrated at a single point in the organization.

When Surrey, BC, RCMP decentralized its offices, the results were positive. Merchants, local politicians, and police in Surrey say they are happy with the results. Some crime statistics have dropped, and the police feel that they are closer to the people they serve. The RCMP split its force into five units operating at regional stations, rather than out of one headquarters opposite Surrey's city hall. The advantage is that "regional offices can concentrate on the unique problems of the various areas."

Centralization and Decentralization

Centralization refers to the degree to which decision making is concentrated at a single point in the organization. In centralized organizations, top managers make all the decisions, and lower-level managers merely carry out their directives. In organizations at the other extreme, decentralized decision making is pushed down to the managers closest to the action.

The concept of centralization includes only formal authority; that is, the rights inherent in one's position. An organization characterized by centralization is inherently different structurally from one that is decentralized. An organization characterized by

EXHIBIT 13-3

Source: Dilbert, reprinted by permission of Universal Uclick.

decentralization can act more quickly to solve problems, more people provide input into decisions, and employees are less likely to feel alienated from those who make decisions that affect their work lives. Decentralized departments make it easier to address customer concerns as well. As Dilbert points out in Exhibit 13-3, however, some organizations do not seem able to decide upon an appropriate level of decentralization.

Management efforts to make organizations more flexible and responsive have produced a recent trend toward decentralized decision making by lower-level managers, who are closer to the action and typically have more detailed knowledge about problems than top managers. Big retailers such as The Bay and Sears Canada have given their store managers considerably more discretion in choosing what merchandise to stock. This allows those stores to compete more effectively against local merchants.

Formalization

Formalization refers to the degree to which jobs within the organization are standardized. In organizations that are highly formalized, there are explicit job descriptions, lots of organizational rules, and clearly defined procedures covering work processes. Employees can be expected always to handle the same input in exactly the same way, resulting in a consistent and uniform output where there is high formalization. Where formalization is low, job behaviours are relatively nonprogrammed, and employees have a great deal of freedom to exercise discretion in their work. Standardization not only eliminates the possibility of employees engaging in alternative behaviours but also removes the need for employees to consider alternatives.

decentralization The degree to which decision making is distributed to lower-level employees.

formalization The degree to which jobs within the organization are standardized.

The job of these women sorting cookies at a factory in Perugia, Italy, is highly standardized. There is really only one way for them to complete their task, and they are not required to make major decisions to do so. Individual differences influence how these employees respond to their high work formalization. For these women, formalization may be a source of job satisfaction because it provides the security of a routine and gives them the chance to socialize on the job because they don't have to pay close attention to what they are doing.

McDonald's is an example of a company where employee routines are highly formalized. Employees are instructed in such things as how to greet the customer (smile, be sincere, make eye contact), ask for and receive payment (state amount of order clearly and loudly, announce the amount of money the customer gives to the employee, count change out loud and efficiently), and thank the customer (give a sincere thank you, make eye contact, ask customer to come again). McDonald's includes this information in training and employee handbooks, and managers are given a checklist of these behaviours so that they can observe their employees to ensure that the proper procedures are followed.[6]

The degree of formalization can vary widely among organizations and within organizations. Certain jobs, for instance, are well known to have little formalization. Publishing representatives who call on college and university professors to inform them of their company's new publications have a great deal of freedom in their jobs. They have only a general sales pitch, which they tailor as needed, and rules and procedures governing their behaviour may be little more than the requirement to submit a weekly sales report and suggestions on what to emphasize in forthcoming titles. At the other extreme, clerical and editorial employees in the same publishing houses may need to be at their desks by 8 a.m. and follow a set of precise procedures dictated by management.

Common Organizational Designs

 What are some examples of traditional organizational designs?

We now turn to describing some of the more common organizational designs: the *simple structure*, the *bureaucracy*, and the *matrix structure*.

The Simple Structure

What do a small retail store, a start-up electronics firm run by a hard-driving entrepreneur, a new Planned Parenthood office, and an airline "war room" in the midst of a company-wide pilots' strike have in common? They probably all use the **simple structure**.

simple structure An organizational design characterized by a low degree of departmentalization, wide spans of control, authority centralized in a single person, and little formalization.

The simple structure is said to be characterized most by what it is *not* rather than by what it is. The simple structure is not elaborate.[7] It has a low degree of departmentalization, wide spans of control, authority centralized in a single person, and little formalization. It is a "flat" organization; it usually has only two or three vertical levels, a loose body of employees, and one individual in whom the decision-making authority is centralized.

The simple structure is most widely practised in small businesses in which the manager and the owner are one and the same, such as the local corner grocery store.

The strength of the simple structure lies in its simplicity. It's fast, flexible, and inexpensive to maintain, and accountability is clear. One major weakness is that it's difficult to maintain in anything other than small organizations. It becomes increasingly inadequate as an organization grows because its low formalization and high centralization tend to create information overload at the top. As size increases, decision making typically becomes slower and can eventually come to a standstill as the single executive tries to continue making all the decisions. This often proves to be the undoing of many small businesses. When an organization begins to employ 50 or 100 people, it's very difficult for the owner-manager to make all the choices. If the structure is not changed and made more elaborate, the firm often loses momentum and can eventually fail. The simple structure's other weakness is that it's risky—everything depends on one person. One serious illness can literally destroy the organization's information and decision-making centre.

The Family Business

Family businesses represent 70 percent of Canadian employment and more than 30 percent of the gross domestic product. Some of the most prominent family businesses in Canada over the past 50 years include Montreal, Quebec-based Seagram Company (the Bronfman family), Calgary, Alberta-based Shaw Communications (the Shaw family), Montreal, Quebec-based Birks jewellers (the Birk family), Saint John, New Brunswick-based Irving Paper conglomerate (the Irving family), Montreal, Quebec-based Molson Coors Brewing Company (the Molson family), and Florenceville, New Brunswick-based McCain Foods (the McCain family). Not all family businesses are as large as these, however, and many have relatively simple structures.

Family businesses have more complex dynamics than nonfamily businesses, because they face both family/personal relations and business/management relations. These

Mississauga, Ontario-based Furlani's Food Corporation uses a "family business" mentality to govern its approach to employees. The business is run in a non-hierarchical manner and no formal or impersonal HR processes dictate employee behaviour. Employees are encouraged to share ideas openly, which keeps morale high. For a recent improvement project, employees from different levels and areas collaborated to make the process go smoothly.

companies generally have shareholders (family members and perhaps others), although the businesses may be public companies listed on the stock exchange. For instance, of the companies mentioned above, Seagram Company, Shaw Communications, and Molson Coors Brewing Company are public companies. Shaw Communications has an interesting structure—only family members have voting shares.

Unlike nonfamily businesses, family businesses must manage the conflicts found within families, as well as the normal business issues that arise for any business. As John Davis of Harvard Business School notes, "In a family business, the business, the family, and the ownership group all need governance." Good governance structures can help family businesses manage the conflicts that may arise. Good governance includes "a sense of direction, values to live by or work by, and well-understood and accepted policies that tell organization members how they should behave."[8]

One area in which governance can play a key role is in CEO succession. Family businesses need to figure out rules of succession for when the CEO retires, and also rules for who in the family gets to work in the business. Succession in family-owned businesses often does not work "because personal and emotional factors determine who the next leader will be," rather than suitability.[9] For instance, a father may want his first-born son to take over the business, even if one of the daughters might make a better CEO.

The issues become more complex when second- and third-generation family members become involved in the family business. *OB in the Street* shows the difficulties the McCain brothers had in deciding who would succeed them as head of McCain Foods and the fallout in their relationship as a consequence.

OB in the STREET
Brothers' Feud Leads to Breakup of Family

Does blood come before business? For 37 years, Wallace McCain and his older brother Harrison shared command of McCain Foods, the Florenceville, New Brunswick-based french fry empire they had built together.[10] In August 1993, however, that partnership came to an end, after the *Financial Post* profiled Wallace's son Michael, referring to him as "the leading candidate to become the potato king." Apparently, it was that reference to Michael as successor that started what the newspapers called "the feud of the century."

The public display of animosity came as somewhat of a surprise. The brothers started McCain Foods in 1956, and "one brother never made a decision without consulting the other." Their offices were linked by an unlocked door. They seemed suited to working together. Harrison was the outgoing salesperson. Wallace was quieter, the number cruncher who managed the books. The partnership worked. In the first year, sales were $152 678. Sales of McCain Foods products are still growing; while the core of the business remains french fries, nonfood subsidiaries include a large trucking division and a national courier company.

What brought these two brothers down was a conflict, which had simmered quietly for 20 years, over who would succeed the brothers to run the family business. Harrison convinced other family members that Wallace and his sons would not share the business with the other McCains. The dispute ended up in a New Brunswick arbitration court, where Wallace was ousted as co-CEO. Eighteen months after the *Financial Post* article appeared, Wallace left McCain Foods and moved to Toronto to become chair of Maple Leaf Foods. Meanwhile, Harrison fired his nephew Michael, and ordered the locks be changed on his office door. Michael joined his father at Maple Leaf, where he is now president and CEO. Subsequently, Harrison appointed his nephew Allison McCain (who is also Michael's cousin) to succeed him.

Harrison passed away in 2004, with no signs of a public reconciliation. However, Frank McKenna, the former premier of New Brunswick and friends with both McCain brothers, said that the relationship had improved prior to Harrison's death. "It's not commonly understood, but I think it's important now on Harrison's death to know that Wallace and Harrison had become very close," McKenna said.

In 2009, Wallace said, "The biggest thing that happened to me in the past 25 years—and in my life—was being dumped from McCain Foods." He was a board member and shareholder (one-third interest) until he passed away in 2011.

So what makes family businesses unique? Founders of family businesses seek to "build businesses that are also family institutions."[11] As a result, there is added pressure on the business, which needs to balance business needs and family needs. Family businesses may have different goals than nonfamily businesses as well, emphasizing the importance of family values in maintaining and growing the business rather than wealth maximization.

The Bureaucracy

Standardization! That is the key concept underlying all bureaucracies. Take a look at the bank where you keep your chequing account, the department store where you buy your clothes, or the government offices that collect your taxes, enforce health regulations, or provide local fire protection. They all rely on standardized work processes for coordination and control. Bureaucracy is a dirty word in many people's minds. However, it does have advantages. Its primary strength is its ability to perform standardized activities in a highly efficient manner. Putting like specialties together in functional departments results in economies of scale, minimum duplication of personnel and equipment, and employees who have the opportunity to talk "the same language" among their peers.

A **bureaucracy** is characterized by highly routine operating tasks achieved through specialization, formalized rules and regulations, tasks that are grouped into functional departments, centralized authority, narrow spans of control, and decision making that follows the chain of command. To test your bureaucratic orientation, see the *Learning About Yourself Exercise* on page 503.

SELF-ASSESSMENT LIBRARY

LEARNING ABOUT YOURSELF

1. Bureaucratic Orientation Test, **(page 503)**

Strengths of Bureaucracy

German sociologist Max Weber, writing in the early 1900s, described bureaucracy as an alternative to the traditional administrative form. In the traditional model, leaders could be quite arbitrary, with authority based on personal relations. There were no general rules, and no separation between the leader's "private" and "public" business. Bureaucracy solved some of the problems of leaders who took advantage of their situation.

The primary strength of the bureaucracy lies in its ability to perform standardized activities in a highly efficient manner. Bureaucracies can get by nicely with less talented—and, hence, less costly—middle- and lower-level managers. Rules and regulations substitute for managerial discretion. Standardized operations, coupled with high formalization, allow decision making to be centralized. There is little need for innovative and experienced decision makers below the level of senior executives. In short, bureaucracy is an effective structure for ensuring consistent application of policies and practices and for ensuring accountability.

Weaknesses of Bureaucracy

Bureaucracy is not without its problems. Listen in on a dialogue among four executives in one company: "You know, nothing happens in this place until we produce something," said the production executive. "Wrong," commented the research and development manager. "Nothing happens until we design something!" "What are you talking about?"

bureaucracy An organizational design with highly routine operating tasks achieved through specialization, formalized rules and regulations, tasks that are grouped into functional departments, centralized authority, narrow spans of control, and decision making that follows the chain of command.

asked the marketing executive. "Nothing happens here until we sell something!" The exasperated accounting manager responded, "It doesn't matter what you produce, design, or sell. No one knows what happens until we tally up the results!" This conversation highlights that specialization creates subunit conflicts in which functional-unit goals can override the overall goals of the organization. Each department acts like a silo, focusing more on what it perceives as its own value and contribution to the organization. Each silo fails to understand that departments are really interdependent, with each having to perform well for the company as a whole to survive. The conflict that can happen among functional units means that sometimes functional unit goals can override the overall goals of the organization.

Bureaucracy can sometimes lead to power being concentrated in the hands of just a few people, with others expected to follow their orders unquestioningly. This chapter's *Ethical Dilemma Exercise* on page 506 illustrates what can happen when someone higher in the authority chain pressures someone below him or her to perform unethical tasks.

The other major weakness of a bureaucracy is something we have all experienced: obsessive concern with following the rules. When cases arise that don't precisely fit the rules, there is no room for modification. The bureaucracy is efficient only as long as employees confront problems that they have previously encountered and for which programmed decision rules have already been established. This chapter's *Case Incident—"I Detest Bureaucracy"* on page 507 lets you consider alternatives to bureaucracy and how you might feel about these alternatives.

The Matrix Structure

Another popular organizational design option is the **matrix structure**. You will find it being used in advertising agencies, aerospace firms, research and development laboratories, construction companies, hospitals, government agencies, universities, management consulting firms, and entertainment companies.[12] It combines two forms of departmentalization: functional and product.

The strength of functional departmentalization is putting like specialists together, which minimizes the number necessary while allowing the pooling and sharing of specialized resources across products. Its major disadvantage is the difficulty of coordinating the tasks of diverse functional specialists on time and within budget. Product departmentalization has exactly the opposite benefits and disadvantages. It facilitates coordination among specialties to achieve on-time completion and meet budget targets. It provides clear responsibility for all activities related to a product but with duplication of activities and costs. The matrix attempts to gain the strengths of each, while avoiding their weaknesses.

The most obvious structural characteristic of the matrix is that it breaks the unity-of-command concept. Employees in the matrix have two bosses—their functional department managers and their product managers.

Exhibit 13-4 shows the matrix structure used in a faculty of business administration. The academic departments of accounting, administrative studies, finance, and so forth are functional units. Specific programs (that is, products) are overlaid on the functions. Thus, members in a matrix structure have a dual chain of command: to their functional department and to their product groups. A professor of accounting who is teaching an undergraduate course reports to the director of undergraduate programs, as well as to the chair of the accounting department.

Advantages of a Matrix Structure

The strength of the matrix is its ability to foster coordination when the organization has a number of complex and interdependent activities. Information permeates the organization and more quickly reaches those people who need it. Furthermore, the matrix reduces "bureaupathologies." The dual lines of authority reduce tendencies of

matrix structure An organizational design that combines functional and product departmentalization; it has a dual chain of command.

EXHIBIT 13-4   Matrix Structure for a Faculty of Business Administration

Programs Academic departments	Undergraduate	Master's	PhD	Research	Executive development	Community service
Accounting						
Administrative studies						
Finance						
Information and decision sciences						
Marketing						
Organizational behaviour						
Quantitative methods						

departmental members to become so busy protecting their little worlds that the organization's overall goals become secondary. A matrix also achieves economies of scale and facilitates the allocation of specialists by providing both the best resources and an effective way of ensuring their efficient deployment.

Disadvantages of a Matrix Structure

The major disadvantages of the matrix lie in the confusion it creates, its tendency to foster power struggles, and the stress it places on individuals.[13] Without the unity-of-command concept, ambiguity about who reports to whom is significantly increased and often leads to conflict. It's not unusual for product managers to fight over getting the best specialists assigned to their products. Bureaucracy reduces the potential for power grabs by defining the rules of the game. When those rules are "up for grabs," power struggles between functional and product managers result. For individuals who desire security and absence of ambiguity, this work climate can be stressful. Reporting to more than one manager introduces role conflict, and unclear expectations introduce role ambiguity. The comfort of bureaucracy's predictability is replaced by insecurity and stress.

> What happens when you report to two bosses?

New Design Options

Geoff Flood says that one of the best things about T4G's flat, project team-based structure is that it helps foster employee creativity, passion, and dedication by eliminating bureaucratic barriers.[14] Flood is passionate about managing the structure of his organization around the needs of his employees. This has led Flood to open offices in Halifax, Moncton, Fredericton, Saint John, Toronto, Vancouver, and Saco, Maine.

Flood's employees seem to agree with his approach to organizational structure. T4G was named one of the Best Workplaces in Canada in the under 1000 employee category in 2008, and continued to make that list each year since. Flood explains this success as follows:

3 What do newer organizational structures look like?

"Everyone at T4G has a 'Go Do' attitude to put their hearts into the work and do the right thing for our customers at all times. We embrace change and refuse wasting time and money." Can new forms of organization always lead to better ways to get things done? What downsides might there be?

Organizational theorists Jay Galbraith and Edward Lawler have argued that there is a "new logic of organizing" for organizations.[15] They suggest that new-style organizations are considerably more flexible than older-style organizations. Exhibit 13-5 compares characteristics of new-style and old-style organizations.

The new structural options for organizations involve breaking down boundaries in some fashion, either internally, externally, or a combination of the two. In this section, we describe three such designs: the *team structure*, which modifies internal boundaries; the *virtual organization*, which modifies external organizational boundaries; and the *boundaryless organization*, which attempts to break down both internal and external boundaries.[16] We also discuss how downsizing can lead to leaner organizations.

The Team Structure

As described in Chapter 6, teams have become an extremely popular means around which to organize work activities. When management uses teams as its central coordination device, you have a **team structure**. The primary characteristics of the team structure are that it breaks down departmental barriers and decentralizes decision making to the level of the work team. Team structures also require employees to be generalists as well as specialists.[17]

In smaller companies, the team structure can define the entire organization. For instance, Toyota Canada's parts distribution centre in Toronto reorganized its workforce into work teams in 1995. Employees have a team-focused mission statement, and the staff are split into six work teams, each with its own leader. Among larger organizations, such as Xerox Canada and GM Canada, the team structure often complements what is typically a bureaucratic structure. This allows the organization to achieve the efficiency of bureaucracy's standardization while gaining the flexibility that teams provide.

EXHIBIT 13-5 New-Style vs. Old-Style Organizations

New	Old
Dynamic, learning	Stable
Information rich	Information is scarce
Global	Local
Small and large	Large
Product/customer oriented	Functional oriented
Skills oriented	Job oriented
Team oriented	Individual oriented
Involvement oriented	Command/control oriented
Lateral/networked	Hierarchical
Customer oriented	Job requirements oriented

Source: J. R. Galbraith and E. E. Lawler III, "Effective Organizations: Using the New Logic of Organizing," in *Organizing for the Future: The New Logic for Managing Complex Organizations*, ed. J. R. Galbraith, E. E. Lawler III, and associates (San Francisco: Jossey-Bass, 1993). Copyright © 1993 Jossey-Bass Inc. Publishers. Reprinted with permission of John Wiley & Sons, Inc.

team structure The use of teams as the central device to coordinate work activities.

The Virtual Organization

Why own when you can rent? That question captures the essence of the **virtual organization** (also sometimes called the *network organization* or *modular organization*).[18] The virtual organization can take several different forms, depending on its degree of centralization. In some instances, a small, core organization outsources major business functions. In this case, the core organization would have more of the control. In more extreme forms, the virtual organization "is a continually evolving network of independent companies—suppliers, customers, even competitors—linked together to share skills, costs, and access to one another's markets."[19] In this case, participants give up some of their control and act more interdependently. Thus, virtual organizations may not have a central office, an organizational chart, or a hierarchy. Typically, the organizations come together to exploit specific opportunities or attain specific strategic objectives.

The prototype of the virtual structure is today's movie-making organization. In Hollywood's golden era, movies were made by huge, vertically integrated corporations. Studios such as MGM, Warner Brothers, and 20th Century Fox owned large movie lots and employed thousands of full-time specialists—set designers, camera people, film editors, directors, and even actors. Today, most movies are made by a collection of individuals and small companies who come together and make films project by project.[20] This structural form allows each project to be staffed with the talent best suited to its demands rather than just the people employed by the studio. It minimizes bureaucratic overhead because there is no lasting organization to maintain. As well, it lessens long-term risks and their costs because there is no long term—a team is assembled for a finite period and then disbanded.

About one in nine Canadian companies engages in some sort of alliance. These alliances take many forms, ranging from precompetitive consortia to coproduction, cross-equity arrangements, and equity joint ventures with separate legal entities.[21] Amazon.ca partners with Canada Post in such an arrangement. Orders placed on Amazon.ca's website are fulfilled and shipped by Assured Logistics, which is part of Canada Post. Assured Logistics operates a Toronto-area warehouse that stores books, music, and movies so that they can be shipped when ordered, thus eliminating the need for Amazon to set up its own warehouse facility in Canada. Newman's Own, the food products company founded by Paul Newman, sells over $120 million in food every year yet employs only 19 people. This is possible because it outsources almost everything: manufacturing, procurement, shipping, and quality control.

What is going on here? A quest for maximum flexibility. These virtual organizations have created networks of relationships that allow them to contract out manufacturing, distribution, marketing, or any other business function management feels others can do better or more cheaply. The virtual organization stands in sharp contrast to the typical bureaucracy and concentrates on what it does best, which is typically design or marketing.

Exhibit 13-6 shows a virtual organization in which management outsources all the primary functions of the business. The core of the organization is a small group of executives whose job is to oversee directly any activities done in house and to coordinate relationships with the other organizations that manufacture, distribute, and perform other crucial functions for the virtual organization. The dotted lines represent the relationships typically maintained under contracts. In essence, managers in virtual structures spend most of their time coordinating and controlling external relations, typically by way of computer-network links.

The major advantage of the virtual organization is its flexibility, which allows individuals with an innovative idea and little money to successfully compete against the likes of Sony, Hitachi, and Sharp Electronics. This structural form allows organizations to share costs and skills, provide access to global markets, and increase market responsiveness.

virtual organization A continually evolving network of independent companies—suppliers, customers, even competitors—linked together to share skills, costs, and access to one another's markets.

Virtual organizations' drawbacks have become increasingly clear as their popularity has grown.[22] They are in a state of perpetual flux and reorganization, which means roles, goals, and responsibilities are unclear: This sets the stage for political behaviour. Those who work frequently with virtual organizations also note cultural alignment and shared goals can be lost because of the low degree of interaction among members. Team members who are geographically dispersed and communicate only intermittently find it difficult to share information and knowledge, which can limit innovation and slow response time. Ironically, some virtual organizations are less adaptable and innovative than those with well-established communication and collaboration networks. A leadership presence that reinforces the organization's purpose and facilitates communication is thus especially valuable.

The Boundaryless Organization

Virtual organizations break down external boundaries of the organization without generally affecting the internal workings of each of the cooperating organizations. Some organizations, however, strive to break down both the internal and external boundaries. Former General Electric chairman Jack Welch coined the term **boundaryless organization** to describe his idea of what he wanted GE to become: a "family grocery store."[23] That is, in spite of GE's monstrous size (2010 revenues were over $150 billion), Welch wanted to eliminate vertical and horizontal boundaries within it and break down external barriers between the company and its customers and suppliers. Although GE has not yet achieved this boundaryless state—and probably never will—it has made significant progress toward that end. So have other companies, such as Hewlett-Packard,

Can an organization really have no boundaries?

BMW Group operates as a boundaryless organization in designing, developing, and producing its BMW, Rolls-Royce, and Mini cars. The automaker uses virtual tools such as computer-aided design and simulation models and a flexible production network of 17 plants in 6 countries to respond quickly to fluctuations in the market and individual customer preferences. BMW's boundaryless structure drives innovative ideas by eliminating vertical and horizontal barriers among employees and creating an environment of learning and experimentation. From their first day on the job, employees are encouraged to build a network of relationships from all functional areas and across all divisions to speed innovation and problem solving.

boundaryless organization An organization that seeks to eliminate the chain of command, have limitless spans of control, and replace departments with empowered teams.

AT&T, Motorola, and 3M. Let's see what a boundaryless organization looks like and what some firms are doing to make it a reality.[24]

The boundaryless organization breaks down barriers internally by flattening the hierarchy, creating cross-hierarchical teams (which include top executives, middle managers, supervisors, and operative employees), and using participative decision-making practices and 360-degree performance appraisals (where peers and others above and below the employee evaluate his or her performance). Another way management can cut through barriers is to use lateral transfers, rotating people into and out of different functional areas. This approach turns specialists into generalists. The boundaryless organization also breaks down barriers to external constituencies (suppliers, customers, regulators, etcetera) and barriers created by geography. Globalization, strategic alliances, supplier-organization and customer-organization linkages, and teleworking are all examples of practices that reduce external boundaries.

One of the drawbacks of boundaryless organizations is that they are difficult to manage. It's difficult to overcome the political and authority boundaries inherent in many organizations. It can also be time-consuming and difficult to manage the coordination necessary with so many different stakeholders. That said, the well-managed boundaryless organization offers the best talents of employees across several different organizations; enhances cooperation across functions, divisions, and external groups; and potentially offers much quicker response time to the environment.

The Leaner Organization: Organization Downsizing

The goal of the new organizational forms we have described is to improve agility by creating a lean, focused, and flexible organization. Companies may need to cut divisions that are not adding value. Downsizing is a systematic effort to make an organization leaner by selling off business units, closing locations, or reducing staff. It has been very controversial because of its potential negative impacts on employees.

The radical shrinking of Chrysler and General Motors in recent years was a case of downsizing due to loss of market share and changes in consumer demand. Similarly, delays in getting their PlayBook to market along with anemic sales of BlackBerrys forced Waterloo-based Research In Motion (RIM) to announce in June 2011 that jobs would be lost over the coming months. These companies probably needed to downsize just to survive. Others downsize to direct all their efforts toward their core competencies. When Cisco announced in early 2011 that it was shutting down production of the Flip video camera, just a year after it had bought the rights to it, fans of the camera were shocked. But Cisco does not have a retail presence—that is not its core competency (however, selling routers and switches to the technology and telecommunications industries is). So gaining shelf space or developing consumer advertising came difficult to the company.[25] Some companies focus on lean management techniques to reduce bureaucracy and speed decision making. For example, Starbucks has done so to improve coffee quality, produce more consistent taste outcomes, and decrease the serving time for customers.[26]

Despite the advantages of being a lean organization, the impact of downsizing on organizational performance has been very controversial.[27] Reducing the size of the workforce has an immediately positive outcome in the huge reduction in wage costs. Companies downsizing to improve strategic focus often see positive effects on stock prices after the announcement. On the other hand, among companies that only cut employees but don't restructure, profits and stock prices usually decline. Part of the problem is the effect of downsizing on employee attitudes. Those who remain often feel worried about future layoffs and may be less committed to the organization.[28] Stress reactions can lead to increased sickness absences, lower concentration on the job, and lower creativity. In companies that don't invest much in their employees, downsizing can also lead to more voluntary turnover, so vital human capital is lost. The result is a company that is more anemic than lean. *Point/Counterpoint* on page 502 discusses some of the problems that arise when mergers lead to downsizing.

Companies can reduce negative impacts by preparing for the post-downsizing environment in advance, thus alleviating some employee stress and strengthening support for the new strategic direction.[29] The following are some effective strategies for downsizing and suggestions for implementing them. Most are closely linked to the principles for organizational justice we discussed in Chapter 4:

- *Investment.* Companies that downsize to focus on core competencies are more effective when they invest in high-involvement work practices afterward.

- *Communication.* When employers make efforts to discuss downsizing with employees early, employees are less worried about the outcomes and feel the company is taking their perspective into account.

- *Participation.* Employees worry less if they can participate in the process in some way. In some companies, voluntary early retirement programs or severance packages can help achieve leanness without layoffs.

- *Assistance.* Providing severance, extended health care benefits, and job search assistance demonstrates a company does really care about its employees and honours their contributions.

Companies that make themselves lean can be more agile, efficient, and productive—but only if they make cuts carefully and help employees through the process.

Why Do Structures Differ?

4 Why do organizational structures differ?

We have described organizational designs ranging from the highly structured bureaucracy to the amorphous boundaryless organization. The other designs we discussed exist somewhere between these extremes.

Exhibit 13-7 recaps our discussions by presenting two extreme models of organizational design. One we will call the **mechanistic model**. It's generally synonymous with the bureaucracy in that it has highly standardized processes for work, high formalization, and more managerial hierarchy. The other extreme, the **organic model**, looks a lot like the boundaryless organization. It's flat, has fewer formal procedures for making decisions, has multiple decision makers, and favours flexible practices.[30]

mechanistic model A structure characterized by high specialization, rigid departmentalization, a clear chain of command, narrow spans of control, a limited information network, and centralization.

organic model A structure that is flat, uses cross-functional and cross-hierarchical teams, possesses a comprehensive information network, has wide spans of control, and has low formalization.

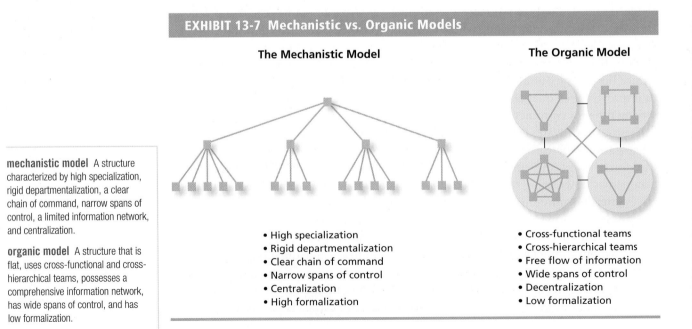

EXHIBIT 13-7 Mechanistic vs. Organic Models

The Mechanistic Model

- High specialization
- Rigid departmentalization
- Clear chain of command
- Narrow spans of control
- Centralization
- High formalization

The Organic Model

- Cross-functional teams
- Cross-hierarchical teams
- Free flow of information
- Wide spans of control
- Decentralization
- Low formalization

With these two models in mind, let's ask a few questions: Why are some organizations structured along more mechanistic lines, whereas others follow organic characteristics? What forces influence the choice of design? In the following pages, we present the major causes, or determinants, of an organization's structure: strategy, organizational size, technology, and environment.[31] The *Working with Others Exercise* on page 504 gives you the opportunity to create different organizational structures and see how they can affect productivity.

Strategy

An organization's structure is a means to help management achieve its objectives. Since objectives are derived from the organization's overall strategy, it's only logical that the structure should support the strategy.[32]

Most current strategy frameworks focus on three strategy dimensions—innovation, cost minimization, and imitation—and the structural design that works best with each.[33]

Innovation Strategy

To what degree does an organization introduce major new products or services? An **innovation strategy** strives to achieve meaningful and unique innovations. Obviously, not all firms pursue innovation. Apple and 3M do, but it certainly is not a strategy pursued by McDonald's. Innovative firms will use competitive pay and benefits to attract top candidates and motivate employees to take risks. Some degree of mechanistic structure can actually benefit innovation. Well-developed communication channels, policies for enhancing long-term commitment, and clear channels of authority all may make it easier to make rapid changes smoothly.

Cost-Minimization Strategy

An organization pursuing a **cost-minimization strategy** tightly controls costs, refrains from incurring unnecessary innovation or marketing expenses, and cuts prices in selling a basic product. This would describe the strategy pursued by Walmart, as well as the sellers of generic grocery products. Cost-minimizing organizations pursue fewer policies meant to develop commitment among their workforce.

Imitation Strategy

Organizations following an **imitation strategy** try to both minimize risk and maximize opportunity for profit, moving into new products or new markets only after innovators have proven their viability. Mass-market fashion manufacturers like H&M that copy designer styles follow this strategy, as do firms such as Hewlett-Packard and Caterpillar. They follow smaller and more innovative competitors with superior products, but only after competitors have demonstrated that the market is there.

Exhibit 13-8 describes the structural option that best matches each strategy. Innovators need the flexibility of the organic structure, while cost minimizers seek the efficiency and stability of the mechanistic structure. Imitators combine the two structures. They use a mechanistic structure in order to maintain tight controls and low costs in their current activities, but create organic subunits in which to pursue new undertakings.

Organizational Size

An organization's size significantly affects its structure.[34] Organizations that employ 2000 or more people tend to have more specialization, more departmentalization, more vertical levels, and more rules and regulations than do small organizations. However, size becomes less important as an organization expands. Why is this? At around 2000

innovation strategy A strategy that emphasizes the introduction of major new products and services.

cost-minimization strategy A strategy that emphasizes tight cost controls, avoidance of unnecessary innovation or marketing expenses, and price cutting.

imitation strategy A strategy of moving into new products or new markets only after their viability has already been proven.

EXHIBIT 13-8 The Strategy-Structure Relationship	
Strategy	**Structural Option**
Innovation	*Organic:* A loose structure; low specialization, low formalization, decentralized
Cost minimization	*Mechanistic:* Tight control; extensive work specialization, high formalization, high centralization
Imitation	*Mechanistic and organic:* Mix of loose with tight properties; tight controls over current activities and looser controls for new undertakings

employees an organization is already fairly mechanistic. An additional 500 employees will not have much impact. But adding 500 employees to an organization that has only 300 members is likely to significantly shift it toward a more mechanistic structure.

Technology

Technology describes the way an organization transfers its inputs into outputs. Every organization has at least one technology for converting financial, human, and physical resources into products or services. Ford Motor Company uses an assembly-line process to make its vehicles. Universities may use a number of instruction technologies to teach students—the ever-popular formal lecture method, the case-analysis method, the experiential exercise method, or the programmed learning method. Regardless, organizational structures adapt to their technology.

So what does technology mean?

Variations in Technology

Numerous studies have examined the technology-structure relationship.[35] The common theme that differentiates technologies is their *degree of routineness*. Routine activities are characterized by automated and standardized operations, such as an assembly line, where one might affix a car door to a car at set intervals, automated transaction processing of sales transactions, and printing and binding of this book. Nonroutine activities are customized, such as furniture restoring, custom shoemaking, and genetic research.

Environment

An organization's **environment** includes outside institutions or forces that can affect the organization's performance, such as suppliers, customers, competitors, government regulatory agencies, and public pressure groups. Moreover, an organization's structure can be affected by environmental uncertainty. Static environments create significantly less uncertainty for managers than do dynamic ones. Because uncertainty is a threat to an organization's effectiveness, management will try to minimize it through adjustments in the organization's structure. They may, for example, broaden their structure to sense and respond to threats. Most companies, including Pepsi and WestJet, have added social networking departments to their structure so as to respond to negative information posted on blogs. Or companies may form strategic alliances with other companies; for example, Microsoft and Yahoo! joined forces to better compete with Google.[36]

Why should an organization's structure be affected by its environment? The answer is environmental uncertainty. Some organizations face relatively static environments—few forces in their environment are changing. There is, for example, no new competition, no new technological breakthroughs by current competitors, or little activity by public pressure groups to influence the organization. Other organizations face dynamic environments—rapidly changing government regulations affecting their business, new competitors, difficulties in acquiring raw materials, continually changing product preferences by customers, and so on. Static environments create significantly less uncertainty

technology The way in which an organization transfers its inputs into outputs.

environment Those institutions or forces outside the organization that potentially affect the organization's performance.

EXHIBIT 13-9 Three-Dimensional Model of the Environment

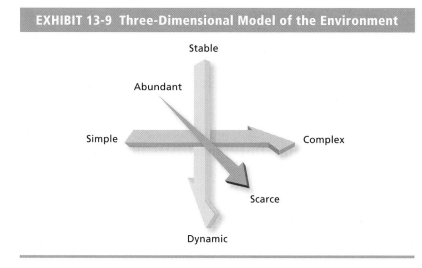

for managers than do dynamic ones. Since uncertainty is a threat to an organization's effectiveness, management will try to minimize it. One way to reduce environmental uncertainty is through adjustments in the organization's structure.[37]

Recent research has helped clarify what is meant by environmental uncertainty. It has been found that there are three key dimensions to any organization's environment: capacity, volatility, and complexity.[38]

The *capacity* of an environment refers to the degree to which it can support growth. Rich and growing environments generate excess resources, which can buffer the organization in times of relative scarcity.

Volatility describes the degree of instability in an environment. A dynamic environment with a high degree of unpredictable change makes it difficult for management to make accurate predictions. Because information technology changes at such a rapid pace, for instance, more organizations' environments are becoming volatile. Turmoil in the US financial markets in 2008 caught many by surprise and created a lot of instability. Canada's credit market faced significant tightening as a result, making it more difficult for corporations and individuals to borrow money. The US financial crisis was a valuable reminder to all organizations that they are operating in a global environment.

Finally, *complexity* is the degree of heterogeneity and concentration among environmental elements. Simple environments—like the tobacco industry, which has relatively few players—are homogeneous and concentrated. Environments characterized by heterogeneity and dispersion—like the broadband industry—are complex and diverse, with numerous competitors.

Exhibit 13-9 summarizes our definition of the environment along its three dimensions. The arrows in this figure are meant to indicate movement toward higher uncertainty. Organizations that operate in environments characterized as scarce, dynamic, and complex face the greatest degree of uncertainty because they have high unpredictability, little room for error, and a diverse set of elements in the environment to monitor constantly.

Given this three-dimensional definition of *environment*, we can offer some general conclusions about environmental uncertainty and structural arrangements. The more scarce, dynamic, and complex the environment, the more organic a structure should be. The more abundant, stable, and simple the environment, the more mechanistic a structure should be.

Organizational Designs and Employee Behaviour

We opened this chapter by implying that an organization's structure can have significant effects on its members. What might those effects be?

 What are the behavioural implications of different organizational designs?

A review of the evidence leads to a pretty clear conclusion: You cannot generalize! Not everyone prefers the freedom and flexibility of organic structures. Different factors stand out in different structures as well. In highly formalized, heavily structured, mechanistic organizations, the level of fairness in formal policies and procedures is a very important predictor of satisfaction. In more personal, individually adaptive organic organizations, employees value interpersonal justice more.[39] Some people are most productive and satisfied when work tasks are standardized and ambiguity minimized—that is, in mechanistic structures. So any discussion of the effect of organizational design on employee behaviour has to address individual differences. To do so, let's consider employee preferences for work specialization, span of control, and centralization.[40]

The evidence generally indicates that work specialization contributes to higher employee productivity—but at the price of reduced job satisfaction. However, work specialization is not an unending source of higher productivity. Problems start to surface, and productivity begins to suffer, when the human diseconomies of doing repetitive and narrow tasks overtake the economies of specialization. As the workforce has become more highly educated and desirous of jobs that are intrinsically rewarding, we seem to reach the point at which productivity begins to decline more quickly than in the past.

There is still a segment of the workforce that prefers the routine and repetitiveness of highly specialized jobs. Some individuals want work that makes minimal intellectual demands and provides the security of routine; for them, high work specialization is a source of job satisfaction. The question, of course, is whether they represent 2 percent of the workforce or 52 percent. Given that some self-selection operates in the choice of careers, we might conclude that negative behavioural outcomes from high specialization are most likely to surface in professional jobs occupied by individuals with high needs for personal growth and diversity.

It is probably safe to say no evidence supports a relationship between span of control and employee performance. Although it is intuitively attractive to argue that large spans might lead to higher employee performance because they provide more distant supervision and more opportunity for personal initiative, the research fails to support this notion. At this point it's impossible to state that any particular span of control is best for producing high performance or high satisfaction among employees. Some people like to be left alone; others prefer the security of a boss who is quickly available at all times. Consistent with several of the contingency theories of leadership discussed in Chapter 11, we would expect factors such as employees' experiences and abilities and the degree of structure in their tasks to explain when wide or narrow spans of control are likely to contribute to their performance and job satisfaction. However, some evidence indicates that a manager's job satisfaction increases as the number of employees supervised increases.

We find fairly strong evidence linking centralization and job satisfaction. In general, organizations that are less centralized have a greater amount of autonomy. And autonomy appears positively related to job satisfaction. But, again, individual differences surface. While one employee may value freedom, another may find autonomous environments frustratingly ambiguous.

Our conclusion: To maximize employee performance and satisfaction, managers must take into account individual differences, such as experience, personality, and the work task. Culture should factor in, too.

We can draw one obvious insight: People don't select employers randomly. They are attracted to, are selected by, and stay with organizations that suit their personal characteristics.[41] Job candidates who prefer predictability are likely to seek out and take employment in mechanistic structures, and those who want autonomy are more likely to end up in an organic structure. So the effect of structure on employee behaviour is undoubtedly reduced when the selection process facilitates proper matching of individual characteristics with organizational characteristics.

GLOBAL IMPLICATIONS _____

When we think about how culture influences how organizations are to be structured, several questions come to mind. First, does culture really matter to organizational structure? Second, do employees in different countries vary in their perceptions of different types of organizational structures? Finally, how do cultural considerations fit with our discussion of the boundaryless organization? Let's tackle each question in turn.

Culture and Organizational Structure

Does culture really affect organizational structure? The answer might seem obvious—yes!—but there are reasons it may not matter as much as you think. The US model of business has been very influential on organizational structures in other countries. Moreover, US and Canadian structures themselves have been influenced by structures in other countries (especially Japan, Great Britain, and Germany). However, cultural concerns still might be important. Bureaucratic structures still dominate in many parts of Europe and Asia. One management expert argues that US management often places too much emphasis on individual leadership, which may be jarring in countries where decision making is more decentralized.[42]

Culture and Employee Structure Preferences

Although research is slim, it does suggest national culture influences the preference for structure.[43] Organizations that operate with people from high power-distance cultures, such as Greece, France, and most of Latin America, find that their employees are much more accepting of mechanistic structures than are employees from low power-distance countries. So consider cultural differences along with individual differences when predicting how structure will affect employee performance and satisfaction.

Culture and the Boundaryless Organization

When fully operational, the boundaryless organization also breaks down barriers created by geography. Today most large US companies and some Canadian companies see themselves as global corporations and may well do as much business overseas as at home (as does Coca-Cola, for example). As a result, many companies struggle with the problem of how to incorporate geographic regions into their structure. The boundaryless organization provides one solution because it considers geography more of a tactical, logistical issue than a structural one. In short, the goal of the boundaryless organization is to break down cultural barriers.

One way to do so is through strategic alliances. Firms such as NEC Corporation, Boeing, and Apple each have strategic alliances or joint partnerships with dozens of companies. These alliances blur the distinction between one organization and another as employees work on joint projects. Moreover, some companies allow customers to perform functions previously done by management. Some AT&T units receive bonuses based on customer evaluations of the teams that serve them. Finally, teleworking is blurring organizational boundaries. The security analyst with Merrill Lynch who does his job from his ranch in Alberta or the software designer in Winnipeg who works for a Waterloo firm are just two of the millions of employees who work outside the physical boundaries of their employers' premises.

LESSONS LEARNED

- Organizational structure determines the level of autonomy an individual has.
- Strategy, organizational size, technology, and environment determine an organization's structure.
- There is no one best structure, and individuals differ in their preference of organizational structure.

Summary and Implications

1 **What are the key elements of organizational structure?** An organizational structure defines how job tasks are formally divided, grouped, and coordinated. There are six key elements that managers need to address when they design their organization's structure: work specialization, departmentalization, chain of command, span of control, centralization and decentralization, and formalization. Organizations structured around high levels of formalization and specialization, strict adherence to the chain of command, limited delegation of authority, and narrow spans of control give employees little autonomy. Organizations that are structured around limited specialization, wide spans of control, low centralization, and low formalization give employees greater autonomy.

2 **What are some examples of traditional organizational designs?** Some of the more common organizational designs found in use are the *simple structure*, the *bureaucracy*, and the *matrix structure*. The simple structure has a low degree of departmentalization, wide spans of control, authority centralized in a single person, and little formalization. A bureaucracy is characterized by highly routine operating tasks achieved through specialization, formalized rules and regulations, tasks that are grouped into functional departments, centralized authority, narrow spans of control, and decision making that follows the chain of command. The most obvious structural characteristic of the matrix is that it breaks the unity-of-command concept. Employees in the matrix have two bosses—their functional department managers and their product managers. Therefore, the matrix has a dual chain of command.

3 **What do newer organizational structures look like?** The new structural options for organizations involve breaking down the boundaries in some fashion, either internally, externally, or a combination of the two. We have illustrated three such structural designs: the *team structure*, which modifies internal boundaries; the *virtual organization*, which modifies external organizational boundaries; and the *boundaryless organization*, which attempts to break down both internal and external boundaries. We also examine the leaner organization, which has less bureaucracy, speeds decision making, and allows for routine downsizing.

4 **Why do organizational structures differ?** Strategy, organizational size, technology, and environment determine the type of structure an organization will have.

5 **What are the behavioural implications of different organizational designs?** It is difficult to generalize an answer to this question. Not everyone prefers the freedom and flexibility of organic structures. Some people are most productive and satisfied when work tasks are standardized and ambiguity minimized. Regarding span of control, some people like to be left alone; others prefer the security of a boss who is quickly available at all times. To maximize employee performance and satisfaction, managers must take individual differences, such as experience, personality, and the work task, into account. Culture should factor in, too.

OB at Work

for Review

1. Why isn't work specialization an unending source of increased productivity?

2. What are the different forms of departmentalization?

3. All things being equal, which is more efficient, a wide or narrow span of control? Why?

4. How does a family business differ from other organizational structures?

5. What is a matrix structure? When would management use it?

6. Contrast the virtual organization with the boundaryless organization.

7. What type of structure works best with an innovation strategy? A cost-minimization strategy? An imitation strategy?

8. Summarize the size-structure relationship.

9. Define and give an example of what is meant by the term *technology*.

10. Summarize the environment-structure relationship.

for Critical Thinking

1. How is the typical large corporation of today organized in contrast with how that same organization was probably organized in the 1960s?

2. Do you think most employees prefer high formalization? Support your position.

3. If you were an employee in a matrix structure, what pluses do you think the structure would provide? What about minuses?

4. What could management do to make a bureaucracy more like a boundaryless organization?

5. What behavioural predictions would you make about people who worked in a "pure" boundaryless organization (if such a structure were ever to exist)?

for You

- Think about the type of organizational structure that suits you best when you look for a job. You may prefer a structured workplace, like that of a mechanistic organization. Or you may prefer a much less structured workplace, like that of an organic organization.

- If you decide to start your own company, know the different structural considerations so that you can create an organization that meets your needs as both a business person and a person with additional interests.

- As a manager or as an entrepreneur, consider how much responsibility (centralization/decentralization) you want to take for yourself compared with how much you are willing to share with others in the organization.

POINT

Mergers Are Bad for the Employee

Firms often undertake mergers to eliminate the competition (by acquiring it) or to harvest another organization's assets.[44] While we might argue over the social costs and benefits of these motives, an even darker agenda lies implicit in most mergers: to reduce headcount, a nice way of saying "fire employees."

When mergers or acquisitions take place, almost without exception employees lose their jobs. And those who are not fired often find their jobs redefined, their responsibilities expanded, and their career prospects thwarted.

For example, faculty, staff, and students at Nova Scotia College of Art and Design (NSCAD) University worry about the fate of their school, should it be forced to merge with another Nova Scotia university. The province has suggested a merger to deal with NSCAD's growing debt.

Michael Donovan, chair of NSCAD's board of governors, protested the province's suggestion of a merger: "Anything that compromises the integrity of [NSCAD's] independence undermines what it is." Karin Cope, an associate professor at the university, notes, "I don't think we will come out of this without pain."

COUNTERPOINT

Mergers Keep the Company Alive

The business environment is dynamic: Change is the only constant.[45] Markets emerge and die, competitors arise, and unexpected opportunities and threats present themselves. Mergers and acquisitions are one way for businesses to adapt to change and remain both nimble and competitive. That is why many Canadian companies that were around in the 1970s have merged with other companies—in Canada and abroad.

It's true some job cuts often follow mergers and acquisitions. However, these cuts are often an attempt to restore competitiveness. Competition is fierce, companies are in a constant struggle for survival, and failing to exploit opportunities often proves fatal. A company that fails to merge with other companies faces extinction, which means the loss of *all* its jobs. Downsizing is surely better for employees overall than extinction.

Many successful, if underreported, mergers have benefited employees. When German pharmaceutical Merck KGaA acquired Swiss Serono, many employee groups worried about job losses, reduced pay, and stunted career prospects. The new company—Merck Serono International—committed itself to addressing these concerns. In the words of VP Geoffrey Matthews, the company sought "to take advantage of ways the companies were complimentary, rather than focus on cost reduction." Managers brought employees into decision making about restructuring the company and made sure both companies had equal representation. A Citigroup research analyst said of the merger, "The value of the company improved considerably, and since then it's been throwing off more synergies."

So, to criticize mergers as inherently bad for a few employees is like claiming poor execution makes poor practice.

LEARNING ABOUT **YOURSELF** EXERCISE

Bureaucratic Orientation Test

For each statement, check the response (either "Mostly agree" or "Mostly disagree") that best represents your feelings.

	Mostly Agree	Mostly Disagree
1. I value stability in my job.	_____	_____
2. I like a predictable organization.	_____	_____
3. The best job for me would be one in which the future is uncertain.	_____	_____
4. The federal government would be a nice place to work.	_____	_____
5. Rules, policies, and procedures tend to frustrate me.	_____	_____
6. I would enjoy working for a company that employs 85 000 people worldwide.	_____	_____
7. Being self-employed would involve more risk than I am willing to take.	_____	_____
8. Before accepting a job, I would like to see an exact job description.	_____	_____
9. I would prefer a job as a freelance house painter to one as a clerk for the Motor Vehicles Branch.	_____	_____
10. Seniority should be as important as performance in determining pay increases and promotion.	_____	_____
11. It would give me a feeling of pride to work for the largest and most successful company in its field.	_____	_____
12. Given a choice, I would prefer to make $70 000 per year as a vice-president in a small company than $85 000 as a staff specialist in a large company.	_____	_____
13. I would regard wearing an employee badge with a number on it as a degrading experience.	_____	_____
14. Parking spaces in a company lot should be assigned on the basis of job level.	_____	_____
15. If an accountant works for a large organization, he or she cannot be a true professional.	_____	_____
16. Before accepting a job (given a choice), I would want to make sure that the company had a very fine program of employee benefits.	_____	_____
17. A company will probably not be successful unless it establishes a clear set of rules and procedures.	_____	_____
18. Regular working hours and vacations are more important to me than finding thrills on the job.	_____	_____
19. You should respect people according to their rank.	_____	_____
20. Rules are meant to be broken.	_____	_____

Scoring Key:

Give yourself 1 point for each statement for which you responded in the bureaucratic direction:

Mostly agree: 1, 2, 4, 7, 8, 10, 11, 14, 16, 18, 19
Mostly disagree: 3, 5, 6, 9, 12, 13, 15, 17, 20

A very high score (15 or over) suggests that you would enjoy working in a bureaucracy. A very low score (5 or lower) suggests that you would be frustrated by working in a bureaucracy, especially a large one.

Source: Adapted from A. J. DuBrin, *Human Relations*: *A Job Oriented Approach*, 5th ed., 1992. Reprinted with permission of Prentice Hall, Inc., Upper Saddle River, NJ.

SELF-ASSESSMENT LIBRARY	LEARNING ABOUT YOURSELF

More Learning About Yourself Exercises

Additional self-assessments relevant to this chapter appear on MyOBLab (**www.pearsoned.ca/myoblab**).

III.A.2 How Willing Am I to Delegate?

IV.F.2 Do I Like Bureaucracy?

When you complete the additional assessments, consider the following:

1. Am I surprised about my score?

2. Would my friends evaluate me similarly?

BREAKOUT **GROUP** EXERCISES

Form small groups to discuss the following topics, as assigned by your instructor:

1. Describe the structure of an organization in which you worked. Was the structure appropriate for the tasks being done?

2. Have you ever worked in an organization with a structure that seemed inappropriate to the task? What would have improved the structure?

3. You are considering opening up a coffee bar with several of your friends. What kind of structure might you use? After the coffee bar becomes successful, you decide that expanding the number of branches might be a good idea. What changes to the structure might you make?

WORKING WITH **OTHERS** EXERCISE

Words-in-Sentences Company

Overview: You are a small company that

1. manufactures words; and

2. packages them into meaningful English-language sentences.[46]

Market research has established that sentences of at least 3 words but not more than 6 words are in demand. Therefore, packaging, distribution, and sales should be set up for **3- to 6-word sentences**.

Time: Approximately 30 minutes. (Note: A production run takes 10 minutes. While the game is more effective if 2 [or more] production runs are completed, even 1 production run will generate effective discussion about how organizational structure affects performance.)

Group Task: Your group must design and participate in running a W-I-S company. You will be competing with other companies in your industry. The success of your company will depend on (a) your objectives, (b) planning, (c) organizational structure, and (d) quality control. You should design your organization to be as efficient as possible during each 10-minute production run. After the first production run, you will have an opportunity to reorganize your company if you want.

Raw Materials: For each production run, you will be given a **"raw material phrase."** The letters found in the phrase serve as the raw materials available to produce new words in sentences. For example, if the raw material phrase is "organizational behaviour is fun," you could produce the words and sentence "Nat ran to a zoo." One way to think of your raw material phrase is to take all the letters appearing in the phrase and write them down as many times as they appear in the phrase. Thus, for the phrase "organizational behaviour is fun" you have: a-4; b-1; c-0; d-0; e-1; f-1; g-1; h-1; i-4; j-0; k-0; l-1; m-0; n-3; o-3; p-0; q-0; r-2; s-1; t-1; u-2; v-1; w-0; x-0; y-0; z-1, for a total of 28 raw material letters.

Production Standards: There are several rules that have to be followed in producing "words-in-sentences." **If these rules are not followed, your output will not meet production specifications and will not pass quality-control inspection.**

1. A letter may appear only as often in a manufactured word as it appears in the raw material phrase; for example, "organizational behaviour is fun" has 1 letter *l* and 1 letter *e*. Thus "steal" is legitimate, but not "teller." It has too many *l*'s and *e*'s.

2. Raw material letters can be used again in different manufactured words.

3. A manufactured **word** may be used only **once** during a production run; once a word—for example, "the"—is used in a sentence, it is out of stock for the rest of the production run. No other sentence may use the word "the."

4. A new word may not be made by adding *s* to form the plural of an already used manufactured word.

5. Sentences must make grammatical and logical sense.

6. All words must be in the English language.

7. Names and places are acceptable.

8. Slang is not acceptable.

9. Writing must be legible. Any illegible sentence will be disqualified.

10. Only sentences that have a minimum of 3 words and a maximum of 6 words will be considered.

Directions:

Step 1 Production Run 1. The instructor will place a raw material phrase on the board or overhead. When the instructor announces, "Begin production," you are to manufacture as many words as possible and package them in sentences for delivery to the Quality Control Review Board. You will have 10 minutes.

Step 2 When the instructor announces "Stop production," you will have 30 seconds to deliver your output to the Quality Control Review Board. Output received after 30 seconds does not meet the delivery schedule and will not be counted. You may use up to 2 sheets of paper, and each sheet of paper must identify your group.

Step 3 Your output should be delivered by your quality-control representative, who will work with the other representatives to evaluate the performance of each of the groups.

Measuring Performance: The output of your W-I-S company is measured by the total number of acceptable words that are packaged in sentences of 3 to 6 words only.

Quality Control: If any word in a sentence does not meet the standards set forth above, all the words in the sentence will be rejected. The Quality Control Review Board (composed of 1 member from each company) is the final arbiter of acceptability. In the event of a tie vote on the Review Board, a coin toss will determine the outcome.

Step 4 While the output is being evaluated, you should make plans for organizing the second production run.

Step 5 Production Run 2.

Step 6 The results are presented.

Step 7 Discussion.

ETHICAL **DILEMMA** EXERCISE

Just Following Orders

Betty Vinson took a job as a mid-level accountant for $50 000 a year with a small long-distance company that grew up to become a giant telecom five years later.[47]

Hard-working and diligent, within two years Ms Vinson was promoted to a senior manager in the corporate accounting division. In her new job, she helped compile quarterly results, along with 10 employees who reported to her. Soon after taking the new position, her bosses asked her to make false accounting entries. At first, she said "no." But continued pressure led her to finally cave in. Her decision to make the false entries came after the company's chief financial officer assured her that he would assume all responsibility.

Over the course of six quarters, Ms Vinson made illegal entries to bolster the company's profits at the request of her superiors. At the end of 18 months, she had helped falsify at least $3.7 billion in profits. Of course, the whole scheme unravelled, in what became the largest fraud case in corporate history.

Ms Vinson pleaded guilty to two criminal counts of conspiracy and securities fraud, charges that carry a maximum sentence of 15 years in prison. She was sentenced to five months in prison and five months of house arrest.

What would you have done had you been in Ms Vinson's job? Is "just following orders" an acceptable excuse for breaking the law? If your livelihood is on the line, do you say "no" to a powerful boss? What can organizations do to lessen the chance that employees might capitulate to unethical pressures imposed by their boss?

CASE INCIDENTS

Ajax University Needs a New Structure

Ajax University has recently been in the news for scandals within its athletics department.[48] The athletics department admits to doctoring athletes' transcripts so these athletes can gain admission or maintain eligibility; coaches have been charged with recruiting violations; and alumni have been found to be providing athletes with cars and illegal cash payments.

Despite widespread criticism of these practices, little seems to be done to implement changes to deal with these abuses. Why? There is a lot of money and prestige involved, and university administrators seem willing to look the other way so as not to upset the system.

Within the current structure of the university, the athletics department is responsible for all sports programs. The head of the department, the athletics director, reports to the president of the university, at least on paper. In practice, because the department brings so much money into the university, the athletics director is given free rein to do whatever he wants within his department. The separate and special status given to the athletics department makes abuse rather easy.

Gordon Gee, the chancellor at Vanderbilt University, in reflecting on the problems at Ajax University, believes that the problems are structural: "For too long, athletics has been segregated from the core mission of the university. As a result, we have created a culture, both on campus and nationally, that is disconnected from students, faculty and other constituents, where responsibility is diffused, the potential abuse considerable, and the costs—both financial and academic—unsustainable."

Ajax University needs a new organizational structure for its athletics department that would help eliminate much of the abuse that has happened. The department currently oversees 14 varsity sports, 37 club sports, and various intramural sports.

Varsity sports are elite programs; the significant amount of revenue they bring in not only covers the costs of all club and intramural sports, but also contributes to the general operating budget of the university. One of the problems facing varsity sports is how to recruit students who fit the profile of the university. Ajax athletes are typically admitted with a grade point average of 60 percent.

The overall student average for those admitted to Ajax is 70 percent.

Intramural sports provides opportunities to students, faculty, and staff to participate in sports on a league basis with post-secondary schools in the region. Rules for intramural sports are determined by representatives of league teams. Club sports provide a co-ed, competitive, recreational program for students, faculty, and staff. Students coordinate and administer the programs and find coaches to participate on a volunteer basis.

Questions

1. How would you classify Ajax University's structure with respect to the athletics department? Defend your choice.

2. Is Ajax University's problem one of poor leadership or inadequate structural design? Explain.

3. If you were a consultant advising Ajax University, what would you suggest to fix the problems noted?

"I Detest Bureaucracy"

Greg Strakosch, founder and CEO of interactive media company TechTarget, hates bureaucracy.[49] So he has created a workplace where his 600 employees are free to come and go as they please. There are no set policies mandating working hours or detailing sick, personal, or vacation days. Employees are free to take as much vacation as they want and to work the hours when they are most productive—even if it's between midnight and 4 a.m. If you need a day off to take your kid to camp? No problem. Strakosch says ideas like setting a specific number of sick days "strike me as arbitrary and dumb." He trusts his employees to act responsibly.

Strakosch is quick to state that "this isn't a country club." A painstaking hiring process is designed to weed out all but the most autonomous. Managers set ambitious quarterly goals, and employees are given plenty of independence to achieve them. However, there is little tolerance for failure. As TechTarget's website states, there is a 100 percent focus on results. Employees are fired for underachieving.

Moreover, while hours are flexible, employees frequently put in at least 50 hours a week. In addition, regardless of hours worked, employees are required to remain accessible via email, cellphone, instant messaging, or laptop.

Strakosch's approach seems to be working. TechTarget became a public company in May 2007 with a $100 million IPO and continues to grow, with much of the founding management team still in place. In June 2011, the company was recognized as one of the "Best Places to Work," the fifth time it has been so recognized.

Questions

1. What type of organizational structure does TechTarget have?

2. Why does this type of structure work at TechTarget?

3. How transferable is this structure to other organizations?

4. Would you want to work at TechTarget? Why or why not?

FROM CONCEPTS TO SKILLS

Delegating Authority

Managers get things done through other people. Because there are limits to any manager's time and knowledge, effective managers need to understand how to delegate. *Delegation* is the assignment of authority to another person to carry out specific duties. It allows an employee to make decisions. Delegation should not be confused with participation. In participative decision making, there is a sharing of authority. In delegation, employees make decisions on their own.

A number of actions differentiate the effective delegator from the ineffective delegator. You can become a more effective delegator if you use the following five suggestions:[50]

1. *Clarify the assignment.* The place to begin is to determine what is to be delegated and to whom. You need to identify the person most capable of doing the task, then determine if he or she has the time and motivation to do the job.

   Assuming that you have a willing and able employee, it is your responsibility to provide clear information on what is being delegated, the results you expect, and any time or performance expectations you hold.

   Unless there is an overriding need to adhere to specific methods, you should delegate only the end results. That is, get agreement on what is to be done and the end results expected, but let the employee decide on the means.

2. *Specify the employee's range of discretion.* Every act of delegation comes with constraints. You are delegating authority to act, but not unlimited authority. What you are delegating is authority to act on certain issues and, on those issues, within certain parameters. You need to specify what those parameters are so employees know, in no uncertain terms, the range of their discretion.

3. *Allow the employee to participate.* One of the best sources for determining how much authority will be necessary to accomplish a task is the employee who will be held accountable for that task. If you allow employees to participate in determining what is delegated, how much authority is needed to get the job done, and the standards by which they will be judged, you increase employee motivation, satisfaction, and accountability for performance.

4. *Inform others that delegation has occurred.* Delegation should not occur in a vacuum. Not only do you and the employee need to know specifically what has been delegated and how much authority has been granted, but anyone else who may be affected by the delegation act also needs to be informed.

5. *Establish feedback controls.* The establishment of controls to monitor the employee's progress increases the likelihood that important problems will be identified early and that the task will be completed on time and to the desired specifications. For instance, agree on a specific time for completion of the task, and then set progress dates when the employee will report back on how well he or she is doing and any major problems that have surfaced. This can be supplemented with periodic spot checks to ensure that authority guidelines are not being abused, organization policies are being followed, and proper procedures are being met.

Practising Skills

You are the director of research and development for a large pharmaceutical manufacturer. You have six people who report directly to you: Sue (your secretary), Dale (laboratory manager), Todd (quality standards manager), Linda (patent coordination manager), Ruben (market coordination manager), and Marjorie (senior projects manager). Dale is the most senior of the five managers and is generally acknowledged as the chief candidate to replace you if you are promoted or leave.

You have received your annual instructions from the CEO to develop next year's budget for your area. The task is relatively routine, but takes quite a bit of time. In the past, you have always done the annual budget yourself. But this year, because your workload is exceptionally heavy, you have decided to try something different. You are going to assign budget preparation to one of your subordinate managers. The obvious choice is Dale. Dale has been with the company longest, is highly dependable, and, as your probable successor, is most likely to gain from the experience. The budget is due on your boss's desk in eight weeks. Last year it took you about 30 to 35 hours to complete. However, you have done a budget many times before. For a novice, it might take double that amount of time.

The budget process is generally straightforward. You start with last year's budget and modify it to reflect inflation and changes in departmental objectives. All the data that Dale will need are in your files, online, or can be obtained from your other managers.

You have just walked over to Dale's office and informed him of your decision. He seemed enthusiastic about doing the budget, but he also has a heavy workload. He told you, "I'm regularly coming in around 7 a.m. and it's unusual for me to leave before 7 p.m. For the past five weekends, I've even come in on Saturday mornings to get my work done. I can do my best to try to find time to do the budget." Specify exactly what you would say to Dale and the actions you would take if Dale agrees to do the budget.

· ·

Reinforcing Skills

1. Watch a classic movie that has examples of "managers" delegating assignments. Pay explicit attention to the incidence of delegation. Was delegating done effectively? What was good about the practice? How might it have been improved? Examples of movies with delegation examples include *The Godfather*, *The Firm*, *Star Trek*, *Nine-to-Five*, and *Working Girl*.

2. The next time you have to do a group project for a class, pay explicit attention to how tasks are delegated. Does someone assume a leadership role? If so, note how closely the delegation process is followed. Is delegation different in project or study groups than in typical work groups?

Organizational Change

Sears Canada already competes with a broad range of other retailers. With tough American competitors like Target and J. Crew entering the Canadian market, how can the retailer adapt to ensure it stays relevant and profitable?

LEARNING OUTCOMES

1. What are the forces for change?

2. How do organizations manage change?

3. Why do people and organizations resist change?

4. How can organizations create a culture that embraces change?

In June 2011, Toronto-based Sears Canada announced that Calvin McDonald would be taking over as CEO, replacing Dene Rogers.[1] McDonald had been a rising star and executive vice-president at Loblaws, credited with helping that company improve its overall competitiveness in an evolving market. Now Sears Canada hopes he can do the same thing for its company.

Sears has struggled in recent years. Between 2008 and 2010, top line revenue dropped 22 percent and profits fell by 63 percent. The US parent company, which owns 93 percent of the Canadian division, feels that the stores need to be refreshed and that the merchandise mix needs to be re-evaluated. One of the difficulties Sears Canada has experienced is that its merchandise mix has placed it in competition with almost every other retailer—including Home Depot, Rona, Canadian Tire, The Bay, and various fashion retailers. Furthermore, highly competitive American retailers such as Target are entering the Canadian market. Retail consultants such as John Williams believe that McDonald has two options: (1) He could downsize and narrow the number of brands he works with and the types of products carried or (2) He could maintain Sears' broad focus and modernize, much like The Bay has done. Either way, Sears needs a comprehensive change strategy and a detailed plan. But what steps could Sears take to make sure that the changes implemented are effective?

Sears is just one of the many organizations that needs to reinvent itself if it is to survive in a challenging business environment. Engaging in any kind of change in an organization is not easy. In this chapter, we examine the forces for change, managing change, and contemporary change issues.

OB IS FOR EVERYONE

- Are there positive approaches to change?
- How do you respond to change?
- What makes organizations resist change?

1 What are the forces for change?

How do you respond to change?

Do you embrace change or do you resist it? Why?

www.obstudentjournals.blogspot.com

Forces for Change

As recently as the mid-2000s, video rental stores such as Blockbuster Canada were rapidly growing and profitable companies. People of all ages went to these stores to rent the latest releases, or catch up on classic movies. But the market changed, and Blockbuster was placed in receivership by an Ontario court in May 2011. Video-on-demand services, movie downloading, and the arrival of Netflix to Canada have all contributed to the decline in video rental stores.[2] More and more organizations today face a dynamic and changing environment. This, in turn, is requiring these organizations to adapt. How well any company performs is a function not of managing one change but of weathering both short- and long-term changes. "Change or die!" is the rallying cry among today's managers worldwide. Exhibit 14-1 summarizes six distinct forces that act as stimulants for change.

In a number of places in this textbook, we have discussed the changing *nature of the workforce*. Almost every organization must adjust to a multicultural environment, demographic changes, immigration, and outsourcing.

Technology is changing jobs and organizations. It is not hard to imagine the very idea of an office becoming an antiquated concept in the near future.

The Canadian housing and financial sectors have experienced extraordinary *economic shocks* in recent years, though not to the extent that they have in the United States. The financial turbulence that began in 2008 has eroded the average employee's retirement account considerably, forcing many employees to postpone their anticipated retirement date, and in some cases making it harder for younger people to find jobs. Meanwhile, spending dropped, and many Canadian retailers are still suffering the consequences.

Competition is changing. Competitors are as likely to come from across the ocean as from across town. Successful organizations will be fast on their feet, capable of develop-

EXHIBIT 14-1 Forces for Change	
Force	**Examples**
Nature of the workforce	More cultural diversity
	Aging population
	Many new entrants with inadequate skills
Technology	Faster, cheaper, and more mobile computers
	Online music sharing
	Deciphering of the human genetic code
Economic shocks	Rise and fall of dot-com stocks
	Record low interest rates
	Turbulent financial markets in both North America and Europe
Competition	Global competitors
	Mergers and consolidations
	Growth of e-commerce
Social trends	Internet chat rooms
	Retirement of Baby Boomers
	Rise of discount and "big box" retailers
World politics	Iraq–US war
	Opening of markets in China
	Tsunamis and earthquakes worldwide

Born in Montreal, Gregg Saretsky, the new CEO of WestJet Airlines—pictured at a meeting at the airline's headquarters in Calgary—says that he will respect the company's low-cost roots but also that he won't shy away from change.

ing new products rapidly and getting them to market quickly. In other words, they will be flexible and will require an equally flexible and responsive workforce.

Social trends don't remain static. Consumers now meet and share information through Facebook and they are far more likely to order products online. Marriage is on the decline; living together is on the rise. More young people are living at home longer.

Not even the strongest proponents of globalization could have imagined how *world politics* would change in recent years. We have seen the breakup of the Soviet Union; the opening up of China and Southeast Asia; the instability in the Middle East, Egypt, Syria, and Pakistan; and the possibility that both Greece and the United States would default on their debt. Through the industrialized world, businesses—particularly in the banking and financial sectors—have come under new scrutiny.

Opportunities for Change

Organizations have many opportunities to engage in change. They can change their motivation structures or redesign jobs. They may engage in corporate social responsibility. They may organize more around teams or share more leadership by empowering employees. They may create flatter structures, or move to more modular structures. Sometimes the entire culture of the organization needs to change for organizational change to be successful. Exhibit 14-2 summarizes the range of change targets available to organizations.

As we discussed the workplace in this textbook, and talked about possible change, we might have implied that change happens easily, perhaps overnight, and does not require careful thought or planning. This implication exists because we did not discuss how these changes actually happen in the workplace, what has to be done to achieve change, and how difficult change actually is. We wanted you to understand what changes were possible before we actually discussed how to carry them out.

Change Agents

Who is responsible for managing change activities in an organization? The answer is change agents.[3] They see a future for the organization that others have not identified, and they are able to motivate, invent, and implement this vision. **Change agents** can be managers or nonmanagers, employees of the organization or outside consultants.[4]

change agents People who act as catalysts and assume the responsibility for managing change activities.

EXHIBIT 14-2 Organizational Targets for Change

Purpose
Clarify or create
mission and objectives

Objective
Set or modify
specific performance
targets

Technology
Improve equipment
facilities, and
workflows

Strategy
Clarify or create
strategic and
operational plans

**Change
targets**

Structure
Update organizational
design and coordination
and mechanisms

Culture
Clarify or create core
beliefs and values

Tasks
Update job designs
for individuals
and groups

People
Update recruiting and
selection practices;
improve training and
development

Source: J. R. Schermerhorn Jr., J. G. Hunt, and R. N. Osborn, *Organizational Behavior*, 9th ed., 2005, p. 363, Figure 16.1. Copyright © 2005 John Wiley & Sons, Inc. Reprinted with permission of John Wiley & Sons, Inc.

In some instances, internal management will hire the services of outside consultants to provide advice and assistance with major change efforts. Because they are from the outside, these individuals can offer an objective perspective often unavailable to insiders. Outside consultants, however, are disadvantaged because they usually have

After the negative attacks from the movie *Supersize Me* and the book *Fast Food Nation*, McDonald's found itself going into a slump. People no longer wanted supersized food. "One thing [customers] told us is that variety is important to them, not only in terms of menu offerings, but also sizing options," says John Betts, president of Toronto-based McDonald's Canada. He credits the company's turnaround to "our ability to evolve with changing tastes."[5]

an inadequate understanding of the organization's history, culture, operating procedures, and personnel. Outside consultants also may be prone to initiating more drastic changes—which can be a benefit or a disadvantage—because they don't have to live with the repercussions after the change is implemented. In contrast, internal staff specialists or managers, when acting as change agents, may be more thoughtful (and possibly more cautious) because they have to live with the consequences of their actions.

Approaches to Managing Change

Now we turn to several approaches to managing change: Lewin's classic three-step model of the change process, Kotter's eight-step plan for implementing change, action research, and appreciative inquiry.

2 How do organizations manage change?

Lewin's Three-Step Model

To this point, we have discussed the kinds of changes organizations can make. Assuming that an organization has uncovered a need for change, how does it engage in the change process? Kurt Lewin argued that successful change in organizations should follow three steps, which are illustrated in Exhibit 14-3: **unfreezing** the status quo, **moving** to a new state, and **refreezing** the new change to make it permanent.[6] The value of this model can be seen through the example of a large oil company whose management decided to reorganize its marketing function in Western Canada.

The oil company had three regional offices in the West, located in Winnipeg, Calgary, and Vancouver. The decision was made to consolidate the marketing divisions of the three regional offices into a single regional office in Calgary. The reorganization meant transferring more than 150 employees, eliminating some duplicate managerial positions, and instituting a new hierarchy of command.

The status quo can be considered to be an equilibrium state. To move from this equilibrium—to overcome the pressures of both individual resistance and group conformity—unfreezing must happen in one of three ways. (See Exhibit 14-4.) The **driving forces**, which direct behaviour away from the status quo, can be increased. The **restraining forces**, which hinder movement from the existing equilibrium, can be decreased. A third alternative is to *combine the first two approaches*. Companies that have been successful in the past are likely to encounter restraining forces because people question the need for change.[7] Similarly, research shows that companies with strong cultures excel at incremental change but are overcome by restraining forces against radical change.[8]

The oil company's management could expect employee resistance to the consolidation and outlined its alternatives. Those in Winnipeg or Vancouver may not want to transfer to another city, pull youngsters out of school, make new friends, adapt to new co-workers, or undergo the reassignment of responsibilities. Positive incentives such as pay increases, liberal moving expenses, and low-cost mortgage funds for new homes in Calgary might encourage employees to accept the change. Management might also unfreeze acceptance of the status quo by removing restraining forces. It could counsel employees individually, hearing and clarifying each employee's specific concerns and apprehensions. Assuming that most of the fears are unjustified, the counsellor could assure the employees that there was nothing to fear and then demonstrate, through tangible evidence, that restraining forces are unwarranted. If resistance is extremely high,

unfreezing Change efforts to overcome the pressures of both individual resistance and group conformity.

moving Efforts to get employees involved in the change process.

refreezing Stabilizing a change intervention by balancing driving and restraining forces.

driving forces Forces that direct behaviour away from the status quo.

restraining forces Forces that hinder movement away from the status quo.

EXHIBIT 14-3 Lewin's Three-Step Change Model

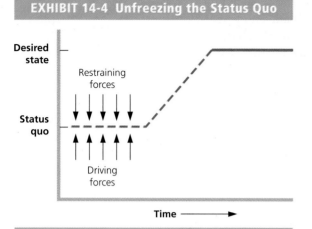

EXHIBIT 14-4 Unfreezing the Status Quo

management may have to resort to both reducing resistance and increasing the attractiveness of the alternative if the unfreezing is to be successful.

Research on organizational change has shown that, to be effective, change has to happen quickly.[9] Organizations that build up to change do less well than those that get to and through the moving stage quickly.

Once the consolidation change has been implemented, to be successful the new situation must be refrozen so that it can be sustained over time. Without this last step, change likely will be short-lived and employees will try to go back to the previous equilibrium state. The objective of refreezing, then, is to stabilize the new situation by balancing the driving and restraining forces.

How could the oil company's management refreeze its consolidation change? By systematically replacing temporary forces with permanent ones. Management might impose a new bonus system tied to the specific changes desired. The formal rules and regulations governing behaviour of those affected by the change should also be revised to reinforce the new situation. Over time, of course, the work group's own norms will evolve to sustain the new equilibrium. But until that point is reached, management will have to rely on more formal mechanisms.

A key feature of Lewin's three-step model is its conception of change as an episodic activity. For a debate about whether change can continue to be implemented as an activity with a beginning, middle, and end, or whether the structure of twenty-first-century workplaces will require change to take place as an ongoing if not chaotic process, see this chapter's *Point/Counterpoint* on page 532.

Kotter's Eight-Step Plan for Implementing Change

John Kotter, professor of leadership at Harvard Business School, built on Lewin's three-step model to create a more detailed approach for implementing change.[10]

Kotter began by listing common failures that occur when managers try to initiate change. These include the inability to create a sense of urgency about the need for change; failure to create a coalition for managing the change process; the absence of a vision for change and inability to effectively communicate that vision; not removing obstacles that could impede the achievement of the vision; failure to provide short-term and achievable goals; the tendency to declare victory too soon; and not anchoring the changes in the organization's culture.

Kotter then established eight sequential steps to overcome these problems. These steps are listed in Exhibit 14-5.

Notice how Exhibit 14-5 builds on Lewin's model. Kotter's first four steps essentially represent the "unfreezing" stage. Steps 5 through 7 represent "moving." The final step works on "refreezing." Kotter's contribution lies in providing managers and change agents with a more detailed guide for successfully implementing change.

Action Research

Action research refers to a change process based on the systematic collection of data and then selection of a change action based on what the analyzed data indicate.[11] Its value is in providing a scientific method for managing planned change.

The process of action research consists of five steps: diagnosis, analysis, feedback, action, and evaluation. The change agent, often an outside consultant in action research, begins by gathering information about problems, concerns, and needed changes from members of the organization. This *diagnosis* is analogous to the physician's search to find specifically what ails a patient. In action research, the change agent asks questions, reviews records, interviews employees, and listens to their concerns.

action research A change process based on the systematic collection of data and then selection of a change action based on what the analyzed data indicate.

EXHIBIT 14-5 Kotter's Eight-Step Plan for Implementing Change

1. Establish a sense of urgency by creating a compelling reason for why change is needed.

2. Form a coalition with enough power to lead the change.

3. Create a new vision to direct the change and strategies for achieving the vision.

4. Communicate the vision throughout the organization.

5. Empower others to act on the vision by removing barriers to change and encouraging risk-taking and creative problem-solving.

6. Plan for, create, and reward short-term "wins" that move the organization toward the new vision.

7. Consolidate improvements, reassess changes, and make necessary adjustments in the new programs.

8. Reinforce the changes by demonstrating the relationship between new behaviours and organizational success.

Source: Based on J. P. Kotter, *Leading Change* (Boston: Harvard Business School Press, 1996).

Diagnosis is followed by *analysis*. What problems do people key in on? What patterns do these problems seem to take? The change agent organizes this information into primary concerns, problem areas, and possible actions.

Action research requires the people who will participate in any change program to help identify the problem and determine the solution. So the third step—*feedback*—requires sharing with employees what has been found from the first and second steps. The employees, with the help of the change agent, develop action plans for bringing about any needed change.

Now the *action* part of action research is set in motion. The employees and the change agent carry out the specific actions they have identified to correct the problems.

The final step, consistent with the scientific underpinnings of action research, is *evaluation* of the action plan's effectiveness, using the initial data gathered as a benchmark.

Action research provides at least two specific benefits for an organization. First, it is problem-focused. The change agent objectively looks for problems, and the type of problem determines the type of change action. While this may seem intuitively obvious, a lot of change activities are not done this way. Rather, they are solution-centred. The change agent has a favourite solution—for example, implementing flextime, teams, or a process re-engineering program—and then seeks out problems that his or her solution fits. Second, because action research involves employees so thoroughly in the process, it reduces resistance to change. Once employees have actively participated in the feedback stage, the change process typically takes on a momentum of its own under their sustained pressure to bring it about.

Appreciative Inquiry

Most organizational change approaches are problem centred. They identify a problem or set of problems, then look for a solution. **Appreciative inquiry (AI)** accentuates the positive.[12] Rather than looking for problems to fix, this approach seeks to identify the unique qualities and special strengths of an organization, which can then be built on to improve performance. That is, it focuses on an organization's successes rather than on its problems.

Are there positive approaches to change?

appreciative inquiry (AI) An approach to change that seeks to identify the unique qualities and special strengths of an organization, which can then be built on to improve performance.

The appreciative inquiry process (see Exhibit 14-6) consists of four steps, or "Four D's," often played out in a large-group meeting over a two- or three-day time period, and overseen by a trained change agent:

- *Discovery.* Identify what people think are the strengths of the organization. Employees recount times they felt the organization worked best or when they specifically felt most satisfied with their jobs.

- *Dreaming.* Employees use information from the discovery phase to speculate on possible futures for the organization, such as what the organization will be like in five years.

- *Design.* Based on the dream articulation, participants focus on finding a common vision of how the organization will look, and agree on its unique qualities.

- *Destiny.* In this final step, participants discuss how the organization is going to fulfill its dream, and they typically write action plans and develop implementation strategies.

AI has proven to be an effective change strategy in organizations such as Toronto-based Orchestras Canada, Ajax, Ontario-based Nokia Canada, Burnaby, BC-based TELUS, Calgary-based EnCana, and Toronto-based CBC.

Nokia Canada employees consider the future, envision the perfect solutions to the future, and then identify what needs to happen to get to the future as envisioned. Of their appreciative inquiry work, general manager Nathalie Le Prohon says, "It's very unstructured, very open to innovation and imagination, and very powerful as a tool for developing new thought leadership, new ways to approach business problems."[13]

TELUS's Go East division in Calgary has used appreciative inquiry to increase positive ideas among customer-care employees. Barbara Armstrong, a senior manager, explains the positive impact of the process: "The fact that [front-line workers] are being heard completely changes the way they view things."[14]

The use of appreciative inquiry in organizations is relatively recent, and it has not yet been determined when it is most appropriately used for organizational change.[15] However, it does give us the opportunity of viewing change from a much more positive perspective.

Resistance to Change

3 Why do people and organizations resist change?

Our egos are fragile, and we often see change as threatening. One recent study showed that even when employees are shown data that suggests they need to change, they latch onto whatever data they can find that suggests they are okay and don't need to change.[16] Employees who have negative feelings about a change cope by not thinking about it, increasing their use of sick time, and quitting. All these reactions can sap the organization of vital energy when it is most needed.[17]

How do you respond to change?

EXHIBIT 14-6 The "Four D's" of Appreciative Inquiry

Discovery	Dreaming	Design	Destiny
Finding out the "best of what is"	Visualizing "what might be"	Designing "what should be"	Implementing "what will be"

Source: Based on D. L. Cooperrider and D. Whitney, *Collaborating for Change: Appreciative Inquiry* (San Francisco: Berrett-Koehler, 2000).

Resistance to change can be positive if it leads to open discussion and debate.[18] These responses are usually preferable to apathy or silence and can indicate that members of the organization are engaged in the process, providing change agents an opportunity to explain the change effort. Change agents can also use resistance to modify the change to fit the preferences of other members of the organization. When they treat resistance only as a threat, rather than a point of view to be discussed, they may increase dysfunctional conflict.

Resistance to change does not necessarily surface in standardized ways. It can be overt, implicit, immediate, or deferred. It is easiest for management to deal with resistance when it is overt and immediate, such as complaints, a work slowdown, or a strike threat. The greater challenge is managing resistance that is implicit or deferred. These responses—loss of loyalty to the organization, loss of motivation to work, increased errors or mistakes, increased absenteeism—are more difficult to recognize. Deferred actions also cloud the link between the change and the reaction to it and may surface weeks, months, or even years later. Or a single change that in and of itself might have little impact becomes "the straw that breaks the camel's back" because resistance to earlier changes has been deferred and stockpiled.

Let's look at the sources of resistance. For analytical purposes, we have categorized them by individual and organizational sources. In the real world, the sources often overlap.

Individual Resistance

Individual sources of resistance to change reside in basic human characteristics such as perceptions, personalities, and needs. Exhibit 14-7 summarizes four reasons why individuals may resist change:[19]

- *Self-interest.* People worry that they will lose something of value if change happens. Thus, they look after their own self-interests rather than those of the total organization.

- *Misunderstanding and lack of trust.* People resist change when they don't understand the nature of the change and fear that the cost of change will outweigh any potential gains for them. This often occurs when they don't trust those initiating the change.

EXHIBIT 14-7 Sources of Individual Resistance to Change

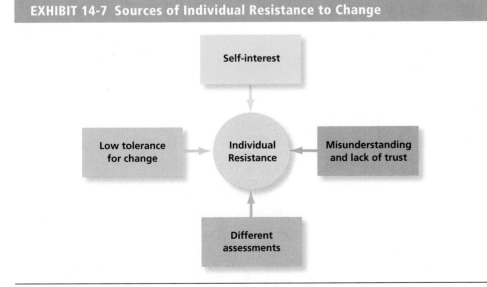

Source: Based on J. P. Kotter and L. A. Schlesinger, "Choosing Strategies for Change," *Harvard Business Review*, July–August 2008, pp. 107–109.

- *Different assessments.* People resist change when they see it differently than their managers do and think the costs outweigh the benefits, even for the organization. Managers may assume that employees have the same information that they do, but this is not always the case.

- *Low tolerance for change.* People resist change because they worry that they do not have the skills and behaviour required of the new situation. They may feel that they are being asked to do too much, too quickly.

In addition to the above, individuals sometimes worry that being asked to change may indicate that what they have been doing in the past was somehow wrong. Managers should not overlook the effects of peer pressure on an individual's response to change. As well, the manager's attitude (positive or negative) toward the change and his or her relationship with employees will affect an individual's response to change.

Cynicism

Employees often feel cynical about the change process, particularly if they have been through several rounds of "change," and nothing appears (to them) to have changed. One study identified sources of cynicism in the change process of a large unionized manufacturing plant.[20] The major elements contributing to the cynicism were as follows:

- Feeling uninformed about what was happening

- Lack of communication and respect from one's manager

- Lack of communication and respect from one's union representative

- Lack of opportunity for meaningful participation in decision making

SELF-ASSESSMENT LIBRARY

LEARNING ABOUT YOURSELF

1. Managing-in-a-Turbulent-World Tolerance Test **(page 533)**

The researchers also found that employees with negative personalities were more likely to be cynical about change. While organizations might not be able to change an individual's personality, they certainly have the ability to provide greater communication and respect, as well as opportunities to participate in decision making. The researchers found that cynicism about change led to such outcomes as lower commitment, less satisfaction, and reduced motivation to work hard. Exhibit 14-8 illustrates why some employees, particularly Dilbert, may have reason to feel cynical about organizational change. You can discover more about how comfortable you are with change by taking the test in this chapter's *Learning About Yourself Exercise* on page 533.

Source: Dilbert, reprinted by permission of Universal Uclick.

Organizational Resistance

Organizations, by their very nature, are conservative.[21] They actively resist change. You don't have to look far to see evidence of this phenomenon. Government agencies want to continue doing what they have been doing for years, whether the need for their service changes or remains the same. Organized religions are deeply entrenched in their history. Attempts to change church doctrine require great persistence and patience. Educational institutions, which exist to open minds and challenge established ways of thinking, are themselves extremely resistant to change. Most school systems are using essentially the same teaching technologies today as they were 50 years ago. Similarly, most business firms appear highly resistant to change.

What makes organizations resist change?

Six major sources of organizational resistance (shown in Exhibit 14-9) have been identified:[22]

- *Structural inertia.* Organizations have built-in mechanisms—such as their selection processes and formalized regulations—to produce stability. When an organization is confronted with change, this structural inertia acts as a counterbalance to sustain stability.

- *Limited focus of change.* Organizations are made up of a number of interdependent subsystems. One cannot be changed without affecting the others. So limited changes in subsystems tend to be nullified by the larger system.

- *Group inertia.* Even if individuals want to change their behaviour, group norms may act as a constraint.

- *Threat to expertise.* Changes in organizational patterns may threaten the expertise of specialized groups.

- *Threat to established power relationships.* Any redistribution of decision-making authority can threaten long-established power relationships within the organization.

- *Threat to established resource allocations.* Groups in the organization that control sizable resources often see change as a threat. They tend to be content with the way things are.

EXHIBIT 14-9 Sources of Organizational Resistance to Change

The *Working with Others Exercise* on page 535 asks you to identify how power relationships are affected by organizational change.

Overcoming Resistance to Change

It is important to note that not all change is good. Research has shown that sometimes an emphasis on making speedy decisions can lead to bad decisions. Sometimes the line between resisting needed change and falling into a "speed trap" is a fine one indeed.[23] What is more, sometimes in the "fog of change," those who are initiating change fail to realize the full magnitude of the effects they are causing or to estimate their true costs to the organization. Thus, although the perspective generally taken is that rapid, transformational change is good, this is not always the case. Change agents need to carefully think through the full implications. The *Ethical Dilemma Exercise* on page 536 asks you to consider the stress that employees face after downsizing occurs in the workplace and when the pressure to take on more tasks increases.

Eight tactics can be used by change agents to deal with resistance to change.[24] Let's review them briefly.

Canada's Yellow Pages Group is a company that has faced significant change. The company has diversified from print directories to aggressively develop and market online directories and direct marketing services for businesses. Despite this high degree of organizational change, Yellow Pages Group has been named a top employer repeatedly. By emphasizing its strong culture of continuous improvement and attracting employees that share that value, the company is able to reduce organizational resistance to change.

- *Education and communication.* Communicating the logic of a change can reduce resistance on two levels. First, it fights the effects of misinformation and poor communication: If employees receive the full facts and get any misunderstandings cleared up, resistance should subside. Second, communication can be helpful in "selling" the need for change. Research shows that change is more likely when the need for change is packaged properly.[25] A study of German companies revealed that changes are most effective when a company communicates its rationale, balancing various stakeholder (shareholders, employees, community, customers) interests, vs. a rationale based on shareholder interests only.[26]

- *Participation and involvement.* It's difficult for individuals to resist a change decision in which they have participated. Assuming that the participants have the expertise to make a meaningful contribution, their involvement can reduce resistance, obtain commitment, and increase the quality of the change decision. However, against these advantages are the negatives: potential for a poor solution and great consumption of time.

- *Building support and commitment.* When employees' fear and anxiety are high, employee counselling and therapy, new-skills training, or a short paid leave of absence may facilitate adjustment. When managers or employees have low emotional commitment to change, they favour the status quo and resist it.[27] So firing up employees can also help them emotionally commit to the change rather than embrace the status quo.

- *Developing positive relationships.* People are more willing to accept changes if they trust the managers implementing them.[28] One study surveyed 235 employees from a large housing corporation in the Netherlands that was experiencing a merger. Those who had a more positive relationship with their supervisors, and who felt that the work environment supported development, were much more positive about the change process.[29]

- *Implementing changes fairly.* One way organizations can minimize the negative impact of change is to make sure the change is implemented fairly. As we learned in Chapter 4, procedural fairness becomes especially important when employees perceive an outcome as negative, so it's crucial that employees see the reason for the change, and perceive its implementation as consistent and fair.[30]

- *Manipulation and co-optation.* The term *manipulation* refers to covert influence attempts. Twisting and distorting facts to make them more attractive, withholding undesirable information, and creating false rumours to get employees to accept a change are all examples of manipulation. If management threatens to close a manufacturing plant whose employees are resisting an across-the-board pay cut, and if the threat is actually untrue, management is using manipulation. *Co-optation,* on the other hand, is a form of both manipulation and participation. It seeks to "buy off" the leaders of a resistance group by giving them a key role, seeking their advice not to find a better solution but to get their endorsement. Both manipulation and co-optation are relatively inexpensive ways to gain the support of adversaries, but they can backfire if the targets become aware they are being tricked or used. Once that is discovered, the change agent's credibility may drop to zero.

- *Selecting people who accept change.* Research suggests that the ability to easily accept and adapt to change is related to personality—some people simply have more positive attitudes about change than others.[31] Such individuals are open to experience, take a positive attitude toward change, are willing to take risks, and are flexible in their behaviour. One study of managers in the United States, Europe, and Asia found that those with a positive self-concept and high risk tolerance coped better with organizational change. A study of 258 police officers found that those higher in growth-needs strength, internal locus of control, and internal work motivation had more positive attitudes about organizational change efforts.[32] Another study found that selecting people based on a resistance-to-change scale worked well in eliminating those who tended to react emotionally to change or to be rigid.[33] Individuals higher in general mental ability are also better able to learn and adapt to changes in the workplace.[34] In sum, an impressive body of evidence shows organizations can facilitate change by selecting people predisposed to accept it.

- *Explicit and implicit coercion.* Coercion is the application of direct threats or force upon the resisters. If management really is determined to close a manufacturing plant whose employees do not accept a pay cut, the company is using coercion. Other examples are threats of transfer, loss of promotions, negative performance evaluations, and a poor letter of recommendation. The advantages and drawbacks of coercion are approximately the same as those for manipulation and co-optation.

As you read *OB in the Workplace,* consider which of the above steps the president of the National Research Council (NRC) used to introduce changes to his staff.

OB in the WORKPLACE
The NRC Changes Its Research Focus to "Market Drivers"

How can leading scientists be convinced to move from basic to applied research? John McDougall, president of the Ottawa-based National Research Council (NRC), Canada's largest science institute, warned his staff in March 2011 that radical change was coming to the organization.[35] In trying to motivate acceptance of the change, he wrote in a memo dated March 2 that "history is an anchor that ties us to the past rather than a sail that catches the wind to power us forward."

He also announced changes in budgeting practices for the NRC, which has an annual budget of $749 million and 4280 employees. Existing research budgets would be reduced by 20 percent and directed to projects of senior management's choice. Eventually, senior management would control 80 percent of research funds.

Many of the scientists that work at the NRC did not react positively to the change. McDougall favours applied research—what he referred to as "market drivers" that can immediately benefit industry and government—but many scientists also see value in basic research.

McDougall's memo noted that senior managers are generally "rallying behind the new agenda. Those who are still hesitant will need our help to develop their courage and conviction." It also promised to "reward good performance (and) find ways to deal with weak performance."

Essentially, McDougall was giving his staff no choice but to get on board—he would control the budget and the reward system, and they would either have to comply or find work elsewhere.

McDougall's memo ended by telling employees that they needed to get "the right attitude and the right behaviour . . . In the months ahead—stay proud, get excited, continue to work and remember 'WE ARE ALL NRC.'"

This chapter's *Case Incident—GE's Work-Out* on page 537 looks at one organization's attempt to reduce resistance to change. *From Concepts to Skills* on pages 538–539 provides additional tips for carrying out organizational change.

OB in ACTION
How to Speed Up the Pace of Change

→ Compel executives to **confront reality** and **agree on ground rules** for working together.

→ Run **a no-slack launch**, and ensure **early, visible victories**.

→ **Limit change initiatives** to three or four.

→ **Move ahead quickly** and confront those not on board.

→ Get **all employees engaged**.

→ **Anticipate** and **defuse** postlaunch blues, midcourse overconfidence, and the feeling of perpetual motion.[36]

The Politics of Change

No discussion of resistance to change would be complete without a brief mention of the politics of change. Because change invariably threatens the status quo, it inherently implies political activity.[37]

Politics suggests that the demand for change is more likely to come from outside change agents, employees who are new to the organization (who have less invested in the status quo), or managers who are slightly removed from the main power structure. Managers who have spent their entire careers with a single organization and eventually achieve a senior position in the hierarchy are often major impediments to change. It is a very real threat to their status and position. Yet they may be expected to implement changes to demonstrate that they are not merely caretakers. By acting as change agents, they can convey to stockholders, suppliers, employees, and customers that they are addressing problems and adapting to a dynamic environment. Of course, as you might guess, when forced to introduce change, these long-time power holders tend to implement incremental change. Radical change is too threatening. This explains why boards of directors that recognize the need for rapid and radical change frequently turn to outside candidates for new leadership.[38] *OB in Action* provides some tips for keeping the pace of change going quickly.

Creating a Culture for Change

Before Calvin McDonald could carry out his strategic plan to reinvent Sears Canada, he has had to address a bigger problem.[39] While the organization desperately needed a change, McDonald first needed to make sure his employees were enthusiastically on-board. "When I first started," he explained, "you'd walk the halls and everybody would be looking down at the floor. I joked that I'd get on the elevators and I'd have to get down on my hands and knees to make eye contact with people. . . . They hadn't won in ages."; That generalized lack of engagement and enthusiasm did not bode well for his change management plan: Without everyone's hard work and dedication, success is much less likely. He couldn't expect innovation from employees who were just going through the motions and didn't really believe they could succeed. How can McDonald help create an atmosphere conducive to innovation? How can he improve his chances for a successful change program?

4 How can organizations create a culture that embraces change?

We have considered how organizations can adapt to change. But recently, some OB scholars have focused on a more proactive approach—how organizations can embrace change by transforming their cultures. In this section we review two such approaches: stimulating an innovative culture and creating a learning organization.

Stimulating Innovation

How can an organization become more innovative? Although there is no guaranteed formula, certain characteristics surface again and again when researchers study innovative organizations.[40] We have grouped them into structural, cultural, and human resource categories. Change agents should consider introducing these characteristics into their organization if they want to create an innovative climate. Before we look at these characteristics, however, let's clarify what we mean by innovation.

Definition of *Innovation*

We said change refers to making things different. **Innovation**, a more specialized kind of change, is a new idea applied to initiating or improving a product, process, or service.[41] So all innovations involve change, but not all changes necessarily involve new ideas or lead to significant improvements. Innovations in organizations can range from small incremental improvements, such as thinner and lighter laptops, up to radical breakthroughs, such as the battery-powered technology Toyota uses in its Prius hybrid. Keep in mind that while there are many product innovations, the concept of innovation also encompasses new production process technologies, new structures or administrative systems, and new plans or programs pertaining to organizational members.

This chapter's *Case Incident—Innovation (and Continuity) at Toyota* on page 536 looks at whether an innovative culture is behind Toyota's success.

innovation A new idea applied to initiating or improving a product, process, or service.

Sources of Innovation

Structural variables have been the most studied potential source of innovation.[42] A comprehensive review of the structure-innovation relationship leads to the following conclusions:[43]

- *Organic structures positively influence innovation.* Because they are lower in vertical differentiation, formalization, and centralization, organic organizations facilitate the flexibility, adaptation, and cross-fertilization that make the adoption of innovations easier.

- *Long tenure in management is associated with innovation.* Managerial tenure apparently provides legitimacy and knowledge of how to accomplish tasks and obtain desired outcomes.

- *Innovation is nurtured when there are slack resources.* Having an abundance of resources allows an organization to afford to purchase innovations, bear the cost of instituting innovations, and absorb failures.

- *Interunit communication is high in innovative organizations.*[44] Innovative organizations are high users of committees, task forces, cross-functional teams, and other mechanisms that facilitate interaction across departmental lines.

Innovative organizations tend to have similar *cultures*. They encourage experimentation. They reward both successes and failures. They celebrate mistakes. Unfortunately, in too many organizations, people are rewarded for the absence of failures rather than for the presence of successes. Such cultures extinguish risk-taking and innovation. People will suggest and try new ideas only when they feel such behaviours exact no penalties. Managers in innovative organizations recognize that failures are a natural by-product of venturing into the unknown. 3M is known for its culture of innovation, as *OB in the Workplace* describes.

Respected as one of the world's most innovative companies, Starbucks turned a commodity product that was declining in sales and invented specialty coffees as a major new product category. Starbucks relies on its employees to share customer insights with managers and takes product development teams on inspirational field trips to view customer behaviour, local cultures, and fashion trends. Starbucks has extended its coffee shops from North American urban sites to locations throughout the world, including the shop shown here at a shopping centre in Shanghai, China.

OB in the WORKPLACE
3M Is a Leader in Innovation

What does it take to be a leader in innovation? Many organizations strive to achieve the standard of innovation reached by 3M, the company responsible for the development of waterproof sandpaper, masking tape, and Post-it® notes.[45] 3M has developed a reputation for sustained innovation over a long period of time, even though it is a large organization with $27 billion in sales, 80 000 employees worldwide, and operations in more than 65 countries. It has a stated objective that 30 percent of its sales are to come from products less than four years old. In one year alone, 3M launched more than 200 new products.

Its most recent awards were received in 2011, at The Edison Best New Products Award gala. The company won a Silver award in the Consumer Packaged Goods—Household category for the launch of the Filtrete Water Station, which filters tap water into reusable, BPA-free water bottles. It also won a Bronze award in the Science & Medical—Diagnostics Aids category for The 3M Integrated Cycler, which is used for real-time molecular diagnostic technology.

Why is 3M such a successful innovator? The company encourages its employees to take risks—and rewards the failures, as well as the successes. 3M's management has the patience to see ideas through to successful products. It invests nearly 7 percent of company sales revenue in research and development, yet management tells its R & D people that not everything will work. It also fosters a culture that allows people to defy their managers. For instance, each new employee and his or her manager take a one-day orientation class where, among other things, stories are told of victories won by employees despite the opposition of their boss.

All of 3M's scientists and managers are challenged to "keep current." Idea champions are created and encouraged by allowing scientists and engineers to spend up to 15 percent of their time on projects of their own choosing. If a 3M scientist comes up with a new idea but finds resistance within the researcher's own division, he or she can apply for a $70 000 grant from an internal venture-capital fund to further develop the idea.

Within the *human resource* category, innovative organizations actively promote the training and development of their members so that they keep current, offer high job security so employees don't fear getting fired for making mistakes, and encourage individuals to become champions of change. Once a new idea is developed, **idea champions** actively and enthusiastically promote the idea, build support for it, overcome resistance to it, and ensure that it is implemented.[46] Champions have common personality characteristics: extremely high self-confidence, persistence, energy, and a tendency to take risks. They also display characteristics associated with transformational leadership. They inspire and energize others with their vision of the potential of an innovation and through their strong personal conviction in their mission. They are also good at gaining the commitment of others. Idea champions have jobs that provide considerable decision-making discretion. This autonomy helps them introduce and implement innovations in organizations.[47]

Creating a Learning Organization

Another way an organization can proactively manage change is to make continuous growth part of its culture—to become a learning organization.[48] In this section, we describe what a learning organization looks like and methods for managing learning.

What Is a Learning Organization?

Just as individuals learn, so too do organizations. A **learning organization** is an organization that has developed the continuous capacity to adapt and change. "All

idea champions Individuals who actively and enthusiastically promote an idea, build support for it, overcome resistance to it, and ensure that the idea is implemented.

learning organization An organization that has developed the continuous capacity to adapt and change.

organizations learn, whether they consciously choose to or not—it is a fundamental requirement for their sustained existence."[49] Some organizations just do it better than others.

Most organizations engage in what has been called **single-loop learning**.[50] When errors are detected, the correction process relies on past routines and present policies. This type of learning has been likened to a thermostat, which, once set at 17°C, simply turns on and off to keep the room at the set temperature. It does not question whether the temperature should be set at 17°C. In contrast, learning organizations use **double-loop learning**. They correct errors by modifying the organization's objectives, policies, and standard routines. Double-loop learning challenges deeply rooted assumptions and norms within an organization. It provides opportunities for radically different solutions to problems and dramatic jumps in improvement. To draw on the thermostat analogy, a thermostat using double-loop learning would try to determine whether the correct policy is 17°C, and whether changes might be necessitated by the change in season.

Exhibit 14-10 summarizes the five basic characteristics of a learning organization. It's one in which people put aside their old ways of thinking, learn to be open with each other, understand how their organization really works, form a plan or vision on which everyone can agree, and then work together to achieve that vision.[51]

Proponents of the learning organization envision it as a remedy for three fundamental problems of traditional organizations: fragmentation, competition, and reactiveness.[52] First, *fragmentation* based on specialization creates "walls" and "chimneys" that separate different functions into independent and often warring fiefdoms. Second, an overemphasis on *competition* often undermines collaboration. Managers compete to show who is right, who knows more, or who is more persuasive. Divisions compete when they ought to cooperate and share knowledge. Team leaders compete to show who the best manager is. Third, *reactiveness* misdirects management's attention to problem solving rather than creation. The problem solver tries to make something go away, while a creator tries to bring something new into being. An emphasis on reactiveness pushes out innovation and continuous improvement and, in its place, encourages people to run around "putting out fires."

Managing Learning

What can managers do to make their firms learning organizations? Here are some suggestions:

- *Establish a strategy.* Managers need to make their commitment to change, innovation, and continuous improvement explicit.

- *Redesign the organization's structure.* The formal structure can be a serious impediment to learning. Flattening the structure, eliminating or combin-

single-loop learning A process of correcting errors using past routines and present policies.

double-loop learning A process of correcting errors by modifying the organization's objectives, policies, and standard routines.

EXHIBIT 14-10 Characteristics of a Learning Organization

1. The organization has a shared vision that everyone agrees on.

2. People discard their old ways of thinking and the standard routines they use for solving problems or doing their jobs.

3. Members think of all organizational processes, activities, functions, and interactions with the environment as part of a system of interrelationships.

4. People openly communicate with each other (across vertical and horizontal boundaries) without fear of criticism or punishment.

5. People suppress their personal self-interest and fragmented departmental interests to work together to achieve the organization's shared vision.

Source: Based on P. M. Senge, *The Fifth Discipline* (New York: Doubleday, 1990).

ing departments, and increasing the use of cross-functional teams reinforces interdependence and reduces boundaries.

- *Reshape the organization's culture.* To become a learning organization, managers must demonstrate by their actions that taking risks and admitting failures are desirable traits. That means rewarding people who take chances and make mistakes. Managers also need to encourage functional conflict. "The key to unlocking real openness at work," says one expert on learning organizations, "is to teach people to give up having to be in agreement. We think agreement is so important. Who cares? You have to bring paradoxes, conflicts, and dilemmas out in the open, so collectively we can be more intelligent than we can be individually."[53]

An excellent illustration of creating a learning organization is CEO Richard Clark's efforts at Merck, a leading pharmaceutical company. In addition to changing Merck's structure to allow innovation to flow from patients and doctors, Clark is trying to reward researchers for taking risks, even if their risky ideas end in failure. Merck's transformed strategy, structure, and culture may or may not succeed, but that is part of the risk of stimulating change through creating a learning organization.

GLOBAL **IMPLICATIONS**

A number of change issues we have discussed in this chapter are culture-bound. To illustrate, let's briefly look at five questions:

- *Do people believe change is possible?* Remember that cultures vary in terms of beliefs about their ability to control their environment. In cultures in which people believe that they can dominate their environment, individuals will take a proactive view of change. This, for example, would describe Canada and the United States. In many other countries, such as Iran and Saudi Arabia, people see themselves as subjugated to their environment and thus will tend to take a passive approach toward change.

- *If change is possible, how long will it take to bring it about?* A culture's time orientation can help us answer this question. Societies that focus on the long term, such as Japan, will demonstrate considerable patience while waiting for positive outcomes from change efforts. In societies with a short-term focus, such as Canada and the United States, people expect quick improvements and will seek change programs that promise fast results.

- *Is resistance to change greater in some cultures than in others?* Resistance to change will be influenced by a society's reliance on tradition. Italians, as an example, focus on the past, whereas Canadians emphasize the present. Italians, therefore, should generally be more resistant to change efforts than their Canadian counterparts.

- *Does culture influence how change efforts will be implemented?* Power distance can help with this issue. In high power distance cultures, such as Spain or Thailand, change efforts will tend to be autocratically implemented by top management. In contrast, low power distance cultures value democratic methods. We would predict, therefore, a greater use of participation in countries such as Austria and Denmark.

- *Do successful idea champions do things differently in different cultures?* The evidence indicates that the answer is yes.[54] People in collectivist cultures, in contrast to individualistic cultures, prefer appeals for cross-functional support for innovation efforts; people in high power distance cultures prefer champions to work closely with those in authority to approve innovative activities before work is

LESSONS LEARNED

- Individuals resist change; breaking down that resistance is important.
- Change requires unfreezing the status quo, moving to a new state, and making the new change permanent.
- Innovative cultures reward both successes and failures so that people are not afraid to make mistakes.

Four Seasons Hotels and Resorts operates 85 properties in 35 countries around the world. Managing change in this company would normally be very complex because of the cultural diversity of its employees. However, it is made easier by the fact that all employees, like the ones shown here at the Caprice restaurant in the Four Seasons Hotel in Hong Kong, China, share a common service culture and a set of common corporate values. As a result, Four Seasons has won awards as the employer of choice in many of the countries in which it operates.

conducted on them; and the higher the uncertainty avoidance of a society, the more champions should work within the organization's rules and procedures to develop the innovation. These findings suggest that effective managers will alter their organization's championing strategies to reflect cultural values. So, for instance, while idea champions in Russia might succeed by ignoring budgetary limitations and working around confining procedures, idea champions in Austria, Denmark, Germany, or other cultures high in uncertainty avoidance will be more effective by closely following budgets and procedures.

Summary and Implications

1 **What are the forces for change?**   The nature of the workforce, technology, economic shocks, competition, social trends, and world politics are all forces for change. Organizations have had to respond to these forces by making organizational changes, such as changing their reward structure, redesigning jobs, introducing teams, and meeting ethical challenges. To carry out change, organizations need to appoint *change agents*, individuals who manage change activities for the organization.

2 **How do organizations manage change?**   Kurt Lewin argued that successful change in organizations should follow three steps: *unfreezing* the status quo, *moving* to a new state, and *refreezing* the new change to make it permanent. John Kotter built on Lewin's three-step model to create a more detailed eight-step plan for implementing change. Another approach to managing change is action research. *Action research* refers to a change process based on the systematic collection of data and then selection of a change action based on what the analyzed data indicate. Some organizations use appreciative inquiry to manage change. *Appreciative inquiry* seeks to identify the unique qualities and special strengths of an organization, which can then be built on to improve performance.

3 **Why do people and organizations resist change?**   Individuals resist change because of basic human characteristics such as perceptions, personalities, and needs. Organizations resist change because they are conservative, and because change is difficult. The status quo is often preferred by those who feel they have the most to lose if change goes ahead.

4 **How can organizations create a culture that embraces change?**   Some of the contemporary issues include making organizations more innovative, creating learning organizations, and understanding the influence of culture on managing change.

for Review

for Critical Thinking

for You

for Review

1. "Resistance to change is an irrational response." Do you agree or disagree? Explain.

2. How does Lewin's three-step change model deal with resistance to change?

3. What is the difference between driving forces and restraining forces?

4. How does Kotter's eight-step plan for implementing change deal with resistance to change?

5. What are the factors that lead individuals to resist change?

6. What are the factors that lead organizations to resist change?

7. Why is participation considered such an effective technique for lessening resistance to change?

8. Why does change so frequently become a political issue in organizations?

9. In an organization that has a history of "following the leader," what changes can be made to foster innovation?

10. What does it mean to be a "learning organization"?

for Critical Thinking

1. How have technological changes in the workforce during the past 20 years affected organizational policies?

2. "Managing today is easier than at the start of the twentieth century, because the years of real change took place between Confederation and World War I." Do you agree or disagree? Discuss.

3. What is meant by the phrase "We live in an age of discontinuity"?

4. Are all managers change agents?

for You

- Not everyone is comfortable with change, but you should realize that change is a fact of life. It is difficult to avoid, and can result in negative consequences when it is avoided.

- If you need to change something in yourself, be aware of the importance of creating new systems to replace the old. Saying you want to be healthier, without specifying that you intend to go to the gym three times a week, or eat five servings of fruits and vegetables a day, means that change likely will not occur. It's important to specify goals and behaviours as part of change.

- Consider focusing on positive aspects of change, rather than negative ones. For instance, rather than noting that you did not study hard enough, acknowledge the effort you put into studying, and how that helped your performance, and then set positive goals as a result.

Organizations Are More Like Calm Waters

Organizational change is an episodic activity.[55] That is, it starts at some point, proceeds through a series of steps, and culminates in some outcome that those involved hope is an improvement over the starting point. It has a beginning, a middle, and an end.

Lewin's three-step model represents a classic illustration of this perspective. Change is seen as a break in the organization's equilibrium. The status quo has been disturbed, and change is necessary to establish a new equilibrium state. The objective of refreezing is to stabilize the new situation by balancing the driving and restraining forces.

Some experts have argued that organizational change should be thought of as balancing a system made up of five interacting variables within the organization—people, tasks, technology, structure, and strategy. A change in any one variable has repercussions on one or more of the others. This perspective is episodic in that it treats organizational change as essentially an effort to sustain an equilibrium. A change in one variable begins a chain of events that, if properly managed, requires adjustments in the other variables to achieve a new state of equilibrium.

Another way to conceptualize the episodic view of looking at change is to think of managing change as analogous to captaining a ship. The organization is like a large ship travelling across the calm Mediterranean Sea to a specific port. The ship's captain has made this exact trip hundreds of times before with the same crew. Every once in a while, however, a storm will appear, and the crew has to respond. The captain will make the appropriate adjustments—that is, implement changes—and, having manoeuvred through the storm, will return to calm waters. Like this ship's voyage, managing an organization should be seen as a journey with a beginning and an end, and implementing change as a response to a break in the status quo that is needed only occasionally.

Organizations Are More Like Whitewater Rafting

The episodic approach for handling organizational change has become obsolete.[56] Developed in the 1950s and 1960s, it reflects the environment of those times treating change as the occasional disturbance in an otherwise peaceful world. However, it bears little resemblance to today's environment of constant and chaotic change.

If you want to understand what it's like to manage change in today's organizations, think of it as equivalent to permanent whitewater rafting.[59] The organization is not a large ship, but more akin to a 40-foot raft. Rather than sailing a calm sea, this raft must traverse a raging river made up of an uninterrupted flow of whitewater rapids. To make things worse, the raft is manned by 10 people who have never worked together or travelled the river before, much of the trip is in the dark, the river is dotted with unexpected turns and obstacles, the exact destination of the raft is not clear, and at irregular intervals the raft needs to pull to shore, where some new crew members are added and others leave. Change is a natural state, and managing it is a continual process. That is, managers never get the luxury of escaping the whitewater rapids.

The stability and predictability characterized by the episodic perspective no longer captures the world we live in. Disruptions in the status quo are not occasional, temporary, and followed by a return to an equilibrium state. There is, in fact, no equilibrium state. Managers today face constant change, bordering on chaos. They are being forced to play a game they have never played before, governed by rules that are created as the game progresses.

Managing-in-a-Turbulent-World Tolerance Test

Listed below are some statements a 37-year-old manager made about his job at a large, successful corporation. If your job had these characteristics, how would you react to them? After each statement are 5 letters, A to E. Circle the letter that best describes how you think you would react according to the following scale:

A I would enjoy this very much; it's completely acceptable.

B This would be enjoyable and acceptable most of the time.

C I would have no reaction to this feature one way or another, or it would be about equally enjoyable and unpleasant.

D This feature would be somewhat unpleasant for me.

E This feature would be very unpleasant for me.

1. I regularly spend 30 to 40 percent of my time in meetings.   A   B   C   D   E

2. A year and a half ago, my job did not exist, and I have been essentially inventing it as I go along.   A   B   C   D   E

3. The responsibilities I either assume or am assigned consistently exceed the authority I have for discharging them.   A   B   C   D   E

4. At any given moment in my job, I have on the average about a dozen phone calls to be returned.   A   B   C   D   E

5. There seems to be very little relation in my job between the quality of my performance and my actual pay and fringe benefits.   A   B   C   D   E

6. About 2 weeks a year of formal management training is needed in my job just to stay current.   A   B   C   D   E

7. Because we have very effective employment equity in my company, and because it is thoroughly multinational, my job brings me into close working contact at a professional level with people of many races, ethnic groups, and nationalities and of both sexes.   A   B   C   D   E

8. There is no objective way to measure my effectiveness.   A   B   C   D   E

9. I report to 3 different bosses for different aspects of my job, and each has an equal say in my performance appraisal.   A   B   C   D   E

10. On average, about a third of my time is spent dealing with unexpected emergencies that force all scheduled work to be postponed.   A   B   C   D   E

11. When I must have a meeting of the people who report to me, it takes my secretary most of a day to find a time when we are all available, and even then, I have yet to have a meeting where everyone is present for the entire meeting.   A   B   C   D   E

12. The university degree I earned in preparation for this type of work is now obsolete, and I probably should go back for another degree.   A   B   C   D   E

13. My job requires that I absorb 100 to 200 pages per week of technical materials.   A   B   C   D   E

14. I am out of town overnight at least 1 night per week.   A   B   C   D   E

15. My department is so interdependent with several other departments in the company that all distinctions about which departments are responsible for which tasks are quite arbitrary.   A   B   C   D   E

16.	I will probably get a promotion in about a year to a job in another division that has most of these same characteristics.	A	B	C	D	E
17.	During the period of my employment here, either the entire company or the division I worked in has been reorganized every year or so.	A	B	C	D	E
18.	Although there are several possible promotions I can see ahead of me, I have no real career path in an objective sense.	A	B	C	D	E
19.	Although there are several possible promotions I can see ahead of me, I think I have no realistic chance of reaching the top levels of the company.	A	B	C	D	E
20.	Although I have many ideas about how to make things work better, I have no direct influence on either the business policies or the personnel policies that govern my division.	A	B	C	D	E
21.	My company has recently put in an "assessment centre" where I and all other managers will be required to go through an extensive battery of psychological tests to assess our potential.	A	B	C	D	E
22.	My company is a defendant in an antitrust suit, and if the case comes to trial, I will probably have to testify about some decisions that were made a few years ago.	A	B	C	D	E
23.	Advanced computer and other electronic office technology are continually being introduced into my division, necessitating constant learning on my part.	A	B	C	D	E
24.	The computer terminal and screen I have in my office can be monitored in my bosses' offices without my knowledge.	A	B	C	D	E

Scoring Key:

Score 4 points for each A, 3 for each B, 2 for each C, 1 for each D, and 0 for each E. Add up the points, divide by 24, and round to 1 decimal place.

While the results are not intended to be more than suggestive, the higher your score, the more comfortable you seem to be with change. The test's author suggests analyzing scores as if they were grade point averages. In this way, a 4.0 average is an A, a 2.0 is a C, and scores below 1.0 flunk.

Using replies from nearly 500 MBA students and young managers, the range of scores was found to be narrow—between 1.0 and 2.2. The average score was between 1.5 and 1.6—equivalent to a D+/C− grade! If these scores are generalizable to the work population, clearly people are not very tolerant of the kind of changes that come with a turbulent environment. However, this sample is now over a decade old. We should expect average scores today to be higher, as people have become more accustomed to living in a dynamic environment.

SELF-ASSESSMENT LIBRARY LEARNING ABOUT YOURSELF

More Learning About Yourself Exercises

An additional self-assessment relevant to this chapter appears on MyOBLab (**www.pearsoned.ca/myoblab**).

III.C.2 How Stressful Is My Life?

When you complete the additional assessment, consider the following:

1. Am I surprised about my score?

2. Would my friends evaluate me similarly?

BREAKOUT GROUP EXERCISES

Form small groups to discuss the following topics, as assigned by your instructor:

1. Identify a local company that you think needs to undergo change. What factors suggest that change is necessary?

2. Have you ever tried to change the behaviour of someone you worked with (for instance, someone in one of your project groups)? How effective were you in getting change to occur? How would you explain this?

3. Identify a recent change that your college or university introduced, and its effects on the students. Did the students accept the change or fight it? How would you explain this?

WORKING WITH OTHERS EXERCISE

Power and the Changing Environment

Objectives

1. To describe the forces for change influencing power differentials in organizational and interpersonal relationships.

2. To understand the effect of technological, legal/political, economic, and social changes on the power of individuals within an organization.[58]

The Situation

Your organization manufactures golf carts and sells them to country clubs, golf courses, and consumers. Your team is faced with the task of assessing how environmental changes will affect individuals' organizational power. Read each of the five scenarios and then, for each, identify the 5 members in the organization whose power will increase most in light of the environmental condition(s).

Advertising expert (m)	Accountant–CGA (m)	Product designer (m)
Chief financial officer (f)	General manager (m)	In-house counsel (m)
Securities analyst (m)	Marketing manager (f)	Public relations expert (m)
Operations manager (f)	Computer programmer (f)	Human resource manager (f)
Corporate trainer (m)	Industrial engineer (m)	Chemist (m)

(m) = male   (f) = female

1. New computer-aided manufacturing technologies are being introduced in the workplace during the upcoming 2 to 18 months.

2. New federal emission standards are being legislated by the government.

3. Sales are way down; the industry appears to be shrinking.

4. The company is planning to go international in the next 12 to 18 months.

5. The Human Rights Commission is applying pressure to balance the male–female population in the organization's upper hierarchy by threatening to publicize the predominance of men in upper management.

The Procedure

1. Divide the class into teams of 3 to 4 students each.

2. Teams should read each scenario and identify the 5 members whose power will increase most in light of the external environmental condition described.

3. Teams should then address the question: Assuming that the 5 environmental changes are taking place at once, which 5 members of the organization will now have the most power?

4. After 20 to 30 minutes, representatives of each team will be selected to present and justify their conclusions to the entire class. Discussion will begin with scenario 1 and proceed through to scenario 5. Then the class will look at what might happen if all 5 environmental changes happened at once.

ETHICAL **DILEMMA** EXERCISE

Increasing Employee Productivity and Stress

Ellen West supervises a staff of 15 people handling back-office functions for a regional brokerage firm in Saskatoon. With company revenues down, Ellen's boss has put increasing pressure on her to improve her department's productivity.

The quickest way for Ellen to increase productivity in her department is to lay off two or three employees and fill the gap by asking the rest of the staff to work harder and put in more time on the job. Since all her employees are on salary, they are not paid for overtime. So if Ellen let three people go, and asked her remaining staff to each put in an additional 10 hours a week on the job, she could effectively handle the same workload with 20 percent fewer employees.

As Ellen considered this idea, she had mixed feelings. Reducing her staff and asking people to work more hours would please her boss and increase job security for those people remaining. On the other hand, she was fearful that she was taking advantage of a weak labour market. Her employees knew that jobs were scarce and would be hard put to find comparable positions elsewhere in the securities industry. The people laid off would have a tough time finding work. Moreover, she knew that her current staff were unlikely to openly complain about working longer hours for fear that they, too, would be let go. But was it fair to increase the department's productivity on the backs of already hard-working employees? Was it unethical to ask her employees to put in 10 hours more a week, for no additional money, because the current weak labour market worked to her advantage? If you were Ellen West, what would you do?

CASE INCIDENTS

Innovation (and Continuity) at Toyota

If you ask experts in organizational innovation about Toyota, you will often see a bemused expression on their faces.[59] Toyota is a bit hard to figure, innovation-wise.

On the one hand, the company has been one of the most successful corporations in the world for a generation. It is now the world's largest car company and shows no signs of giving up that title anytime soon. It must be doing something innovative to continue to thrive when business conditions, consumer preferences, government regulation, and global competition continue to change, sometimes rather dramatically.

Toyota also produced the first, and to date the only, successful mass-produced hybrid car, the Prius. Other companies have attempted to follow suit, only to find their entries coming up short in expert ratings, new car sales, and resale value.

On the other hand, Toyota's products are widely thought to be more "liked than loved," and its cars are often criticized for being imitations rather than innovations. The company is notorious for its "stodgy and bureaucratic" structure, for the fact that all its senior executives are Japanese males, and for its worshipping of the past (a bust of the company's founder, Kiichiro

Toyoda, appears in the lobby, and in its 74-year history only three individuals outside the Toyoda family have led it). These hardly seem the hallmarks of an innovative, transformational organization.

So is Toyota an innovative company, or not?

The answer depends on how you define innovation. Judged by the innovations in its products, notwithstanding the Prius (which, despite its success, still amounts to a small percentage of Toyota's sales), we would not deem it a particularly innovative organization. However, when we defined an innovative culture in the chapter, we emphasized two points. First, it is not judged only by an organization's products. Production, service, marketing, and other business processes are less observable to the outsider but are arguably more important to sustained success. Second, innovation can be incremental. Is a company that loudly reinvents itself every 10 years really more innovative than one that makes steady, incremental changes more or less continuously?

It's clear that on both these points—innovation as process as well as product, and lasting incremental innovation—Toyota excels. Toyota has made numerous workplace innovations, including the andon cord—whereby any employee can halt the production line when he or she sees a problem—and its focus on lean and nimble manufacturing processes that allow it to switch the vehicle being manufactured in nearly every plant within days. On the second point, *kaizen* manufacturing—a method of continuous improvement—is nearly synonymous with Toyota. As one expert commented, "Instead of trying to throw long touchdown passes, Toyota moves down the field by means of short and steady gains."

Studies consistently show that most efforts at organizational transformation fail and are abandoned. Perhaps if more companies thought about innovation the Toyota way—in terms of process rather than product and of slow and continuous improvement rather than radical change—they would be more likely to realize the innovations, and organizational success, they wish to achieve.

Questions

1. Would you consider Toyota to be an innovative organization? Why or why not?

2. Do you think Toyota's potentially inbred leadership hinders or explains its successes?

3. In 2011, Toyota's profits and production fell as a result of the tsunami that hit Japan in March of that year. Do you think that given its culture, Toyota will find it difficult to bounce back from these challenges?

4. The new president of Toyota, Akio Toyoda (grandson of the founder), has said, "Everyone says Toyota is the best company in the world, but the consumer doesn't care about the world. They care if we are the best in town." What do you think he means by that?

GE's Work-Out

General Electric (GE) established its Work-Out process as a way of getting employees at all levels involved in change processes.[60] The Work-Out process has been adopted by such diverse organizations as General Motors, The Home Depot, and the World Bank.

The impetus for the Work-Out was the belief by GE's former CEO, Jack Welch, that the company's culture was too bureaucratic and slow to respond to change. He wanted to create a vehicle that would effectively engage and empower GE employees.

Essentially, Work-Out brings together employees and managers from many different functions and levels within an organization for an informal three-day meeting to discuss and solve problems that have been identified by employees or senior management. Set into small teams, people are encouraged to challenge prevailing assumptions about "the way we have always done things" and develop recommendations for significant improvements in organizational processes. The Work-Out teams then present their recommendations to a senior manager in a public gathering called a Town Meeting.

At the Town Meeting, the manager in charge oversees a discussion about the recommendation and then is required to make a yes-or-no decision on the spot. Only in unusual circumstances can a recommendation be tabled for further study. Recommendations that are accepted are assigned to managers who have volunteered to carry them out. Typically, a recommendation will move from inception to implementation in 90 days or less.

The logic behind the Work-Out is to identify problems, stimulate diverse input, and provide a mechanism for speedy decision and action.

Questions

1. What type of change process would you call this? Explain.

2. Why should it work?

3. What negative consequences do you think might result from this process?

FROM CONCEPTS TO SKILLS

Carrying Out Organizational Change

In reviewing three US organizations that effectively underwent major changes (Sears, Roebuck & Company, Royal Dutch/Shell, and the US Army), three organizational change consultants used the US Army's After Action Review to summarize how an effective change process can be carried out in both business and the military.[61] The After Action Review is a non-hierarchical team debriefing to help participants understand performance. The consultants identified seven disciplines embedded in the After Action Review that help create effective change:

1. *Build an intricate understanding of the business.* Organizational members need to have the big picture revealed to them so they know why change is needed and what is happening in the industry. Let organizational members know what is expected of them as the change proceeds.

2. *Encourage uncompromising straight talk.* Communication cannot be based on hierarchy, but must allow everyone to contribute freely to the discussion.

3. *Manage from the future.* Rather than setting goals that are directed toward a specific future point in time (and thus encouraging everyone to stop when the goal is achieved), manage from the perspective of always looking toward the future and future needs.

4. *Harness setbacks.* When things do not go as planned, and there are setbacks, it's natural to blame yourself, others, or bad luck. Instead, teach everyone to view setbacks as learning opportunities and opportunities for improvement.

5. *Promote inventive accountability.* While employees know what the specific targets and goals are, they should also be encouraged in the change process to be inventive and take initiative when new opportunities arise.

6. *Understand the quid pro quo.* When organizations undergo change processes, employees are put under a lot of stress and strain. Organizations must ensure that employees are rewarded for their efforts. To build appropriate commitment, organizations must develop four levels of incentives:

   a. Reward and recognition for effort

   b. Training and skill development that will make the employee marketable

   c. Meaningful work that provides intrinsic satisfaction

   d. Communication about where the organization is going and some say in the process for employees

7. *Create relentless discomfort with the status quo.* People are more willing to change when the current situation looks less attractive than the new situation.

These points indicate that effective change is a comprehensive process, requiring a lot of commitment from both the organization's leaders and its members.

Practising Skills

You are the nursing supervisor at a local hospital that employs both emergency room and floor nurses. Each of these teams of nurses tends to work almost exclusively with others doing the same job. In your professional reading, you have come across the concept of cross-training nursing teams and giving them more varied responsibilities, which in turn has been shown to improve patient care while lowering costs. You call the two team leaders, Sue and Scott, into your office to explain that you want the nursing teams to move to this approach. To your surprise, they are both opposed to the idea. Sue says she and the other emergency room nurses feel they are needed in the ER, where they fill the most vital role in the hospital. They work special hours when needed, do whatever tasks are required, and often work in difficult and stressful circumstances. They think the floor nurses have relatively easy jobs for the pay they receive. Scott, the leader of the floor nurse team, tells you that his group believes the ER nurses lack the special training and extra experience that the floor nurses bring to the hospital. The floor nurses claim they have the heaviest responsibilities and do the most exacting work. Because they have ongoing contact with patients and families, they believe they should not be called away from vital floor duties to help the ER nurses complete their tasks. What should you do about your idea to introduce more cross-training for the nursing teams?

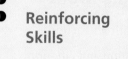

Reinforcing Skills

1. Think about a change (major and minor) that you have dealt with over the last year. Perhaps the change involved other people, and perhaps it was personal. Did you resist the change? Did others resist the change? How did you overcome your resistance or the resistance of others to the change?

2. Interview a manager at three different organizations about a change he or she implemented. What was the manager's experience in implementing the change? How did the manager manage resistance to the change?

Case 1: Profit Sharing at Nursery World— A Case of Unintended Consequences*

Learning Goals

In this case, you will have an opportunity to assess why a motivational strategy (profit sharing), intended to improve work attitudes, failed to have the desired impact on the employees at a small company. Consider which factors contributed to the employees' negative perceptions of the profit-sharing plan. Use that insight to make recommendations about what the business owners should do now to ensure that the employees are satisfied and that the owners' motivational goals are met.

Major Topic Areas

- Motivation in action
- Perception and emotion
- Work attitudes
- Communication

The Scenario

Ruth Knott and Arthur Fort closed the door of their shared office and looked at each other with bewilderment. "That didn't go how I expected," said Arthur. "No kidding," replied Ruth. "Why can't they see that our plan is better? It almost seems like they think we're going to mess with the numbers. But that can't be right; I mean, they trust us with everything. Remember when Helen's ex-boyfriend was stalking her, and she talked to us instead of her family? And Tom did the same thing when his girlfriend got sick. So why don't they want to participate in our profit-sharing plan?" "It makes no sense to me," admitted Arthur. "Should we take profit sharing away and give them a one-time raise like they want?" Ruth asked. "After all, it isn't in their long-term best interests, but if they feel so strongly . . ." Her voice tapered off and she looked down at her designer shoes. Arthur looked back and gave a long, slow shrug of

his shoulders. "I don't know," he said, "I really just don't know."

Ruth and Arthur had been married for 15 years when they opened Nursery World, a nursery school supplies distributor, selling everything from tables and child-proof dishes to paints, toys, books, and outdoor playgrounds. Business was booming in 2012, eight years after they initially opened. In the previous year, they had generated 3.4 million in sales and they now had 19 employees. Five of those employees worked in the front office in various sales, customer service, accounting, and marketing roles. Most of the office staff had post-secondary diplomas or degrees, although the data entry clerk had only a high school education. The remainder of the staff worked in the warehouse picking and packing orders or delivering the local, Southern Ontario orders by cube van (other locations were served by couriers). Warehouse staff generally had earned high school diplomas, although several had never completed their secondary education. Ruth and Arthur served as co-presidents, with Ruth primarily responsible for the office staff and Arthur overseeing the warehouse staff.

Ruth and Arthur prided themselves on their progressive employment policies, low turnover rates, and the warm, family atmosphere they created in the workplace. They paid above market wages, offered flexible hours of work, publicly recognized excellence when they saw it, paid for employees to further their education, and frequently found themselves offering advice because employees came to them with highly personal problems. Ruth, in particular, felt sure that a strong trust had been established between management and the employees, and she took great pride in it.

That pride had turned to confusion during the profit-sharing fiasco of the past two months. Arthur and Ruth initially came up with the idea for profit sharing over their favourite meal: herbed fettuccine paired with a bold red wine at one of the area's upscale Italian restaurants. The two were well-known regulars and were seen there often, so it was easy to get the best table in the quietest corner of the garden patio so that they could discuss their business privately. "We really

* Note that this case is based on an existing company located in Southern Ontario. At the request of the owners, however, the employee names and the company name have been replaced with pseudonyms.

should do something extra to keep everyone motivated," remarked Arthur, "since the warehouse staff have increased over the last couple of years, it is getting harder to keep an eye on everyone. I think profit sharing would motivate them to want to work hard, even when nobody is watching."

"Well it's not just about that," mused Ruth, "we want them to stay. The customers like to hear the same voices each time they call the office. Our customers know everyone in the front office, and they like them—that's part of why customers keep coming back to us year after year." By the time the tiramisu and Niagara ice wine had arrived, they had decided to start a profit-sharing program. "If we put 10% of our profits into the sharing program and distribute that equally among 19 people, they should see respectable monthly bonus cheques," Ruth enthused.

Arthur and Ruth called a lunch-time meeting with all staff to share the announcement. The meeting started slightly late, as Arthur had been delayed, having spent the morning flying the small Cessna airplane he co-owned. He and Ruth explained the new profit-sharing program, expecting an enthusiastic response. Instead, they were confronted with confusion. "How do we know how the numbers are calculated?" asked Jack, one of the warehouse staff. The underlying distrust behind his question was softened by his polite tone but was still unmistakable. "You guys can make them say whatever you want." Ruth patiently explained how profit was mathematically derived by subtracting costs from revenues, but the group of employees as a whole did not seem convinced. "It seems complicated," remarked Florence, a data entry clerk in the front office. Jane, their staff accountant, was a notable exception. She loved the idea, but unfortunately her endorsement did not seem to carry much weight with the other employees, particularly the warehouse staff. Ruth and Arthur figured that after their employees received a monthly bonus cheque or two, they would become more enthusiastic about the program.

In September, the first month that the new profit-sharing plan was instituted, Nursery World earned an overall profit of $14 990, resulting in $79 bonus cheques being issued to each employee. Nursery World's business tended to be seasonal, however. August and early September were peak ordering times, while other months, notably October and July, tended to be much slower. In October, the company lost $10 000. When Arthur and Ruth explained to employees that no bonus cheques would be issued that month, employees reacted badly. "Does this mean we're going bankrupt?" worried Maryanne, a picker/packer. "Are we all going to lose our jobs?" panicked Kathleen, the warehouse supervisor. "Ten thousand dollars is SO much money," she added, "how can Nursery World recover from that?" Arthur tried to explain

the cyclical nature of the business and how this situation represented perfectly normal seasonal fluctuations, but the employees still seemed concerned.

"This profit-sharing thing isn't for me, I'd rather have a sure thing," said Janie, one of the delivery van drivers. "Me too," said Robert, also a picker/packer. "Can't you just give us a raise instead?" asked Sally, their customer service representative. "Yeah," said Jack, "then we don't have to worry about what happened to the numbers; we know what we're getting."

Ruth tried to explain that the business was seasonal and also that, over time, employees would receive more money via profit sharing than they would from the introduction of a small raise. The group was unconvinced, though, and Ruth was very puzzled about why the employees would not take her word for it. She thought her actions toward her employees had earned her their trust. She was especially confused that many of them were willing to trust her with their most intimate family problems, but not profit calculations. She looked at the day's newspaper and noticed that the police were still keeping a close eye on the local "Occupy" camp. The pictures included with the article showed people holding up signs deriding CEOs, the corporate elite, and the wealthiest 1%. "I wonder if the lack of trust the employees have in our profit-sharing intentions is related to all this," she asked Arthur. "Surely they don't see us as part of the 1% everyone is talking about. I mean we can afford *some* luxuries, but we aren't exactly rich." She continued to idly speculate whether any connection existed between her employees' attitudes and broader political events, but mostly she focused on what to do next. "Should we give them the raise, Arthur?" she asked, "or try again to make this profit-sharing thing work?"

Discussion Questions

1. Why do you think that profit sharing failed to motivate most employees at Nursery World? Is there anything Ruth and Arthur could have done differently to improve the chances that their profit-sharing initiative would be successful?

2. What unrecognized communication barriers might be contributing to this situation? How would you fix them?

3. Why do you think the employees trust Ruth and Arthur with their personal problems, but not with financial compensation? How are those things different?

4. Assuming that they still need a plan to motivate and retain staff, what should Ruth and Arthur do now?

Case 2: The Path to Fraud*

Learning Goals

In this case, you will have an opportunity to evaluate a decision-making process that ultimately led to an employee engaging in unethical and illegal behaviour. Consider which factors contributed to Julie's decision to engage in fraud. How did organizational variables combine with external pressures to influence her decision? Use that insight to make recommendations about what the insurance company could, and should, do to prevent similar situations from unfolding in the future.

Major Topic Areas

- Decision-making and ethics
- Work values and attitudes
- Corporate social responsibility

The Scenario

Julie Smith trembled uncontrollably as the judge ordered her to stand up for sentencing.[1] It was really happening. She would be sent to prison. All this time, no matter how many warnings she got from her lawyer, a part of her had never really believed that it would come to this. "A four month sentence to be served in a minimum security facility followed by two years of probation," thundered the judge, "and you will pay full restitution." Julie fell back into her chair and began to cry. How would her six-year-old son cope while she was imprisoned? She had not even told anyone in her family what was happening because she was so embarrassed and humiliated. How had she ended up here?

In mid-2007, Julie started working as an accounts payable clerk for a large insurance company. Her job consisted primarily of processing invoices but as a member of the wider finance department she had many opportunities to observe and learn the company's audit procedures. Julie viewed the work in accounts payable as repetitive and tedious, and she was aware that she did not have the discretion or authority to make her own decisions. Everything at this company was done VERY strictly by the book. Despite these limitations, however, Julie enjoyed her job and the company of her co-workers and colleagues, and she felt that her employer treated her well.

In early 2008, Julie made a lateral move to the department that administered corporate commercial accounts. Large corporations bought insurance policies as protection from lawsuits and were required to pay a flat rate per term regardless of the number of claims made against them. Julie oversaw more than 500 corporate policies. When one of the corporate clients experienced a loss, Julie would process the claims for legal fees, compensation, and related incidentals. Examples of common losses included compensation paid out due to slips and falls, safety violations, and other lawsuits. Julie processed an average of 13 to 15 claims per week. When the compensation was less than $10 000, Julie simply created, signed, and issued the cheque herself. Claims over $10 000 required a second signature, but she could ask anybody in the office to sign, so this was rarely a problem.

After several months on the job, Julie noticed that the corporate clients did not receive reports about claims made against their accounts. Since corporate clients paid a flat fee regardless of how many cases were processed, the corporate clients had little incentive to actively monitor claims activities.

Although she enjoyed her job and her co-workers, Julie, a single mother with a toddler, struggled to make ends meet. She earned $24 000 per year, and $1200 of that was set aside to pay back a loan. Her expenses had exceeded her income ever since her son was born. Daycare was so expensive, but she had no choice but to use it if she was planning to work full-time. Worse, the small savings account that she inherited upon her mother's death a few years ago was about to run dry. She had only a high school education, and she had been very lucky to land the job at the insurance company in the first place. Her options for increasing her income were very limited, and her son's father had never been involved in parenting or provided any type of financial support. In fact, Julie doubted she would be able to locate him, even if she tried. As she worried and considered her limited alternatives, Julie thought about her work tasks again, remembered that her company's internal audit process examined corporate commercial accounts only every six years, and came up with an idea for some relief.

Julie's son was enrolled in a private, at-home, daycare service. She was friends with Marie, the person who oper-

---

* This is a true story about a female employee in a Canadian company. The names of the people involved are fictitious. However, the events are truthful and accurate.

ated the home daycare, and they had shared a lot of laughs together. Julie usually paid for daycare on a bi-weekly basis using a personal cheque. Until the day she didn't. Three weeks after her initial flash of "inspiration," a different kind of cheque was handed over to Marie, one with the insurance company's name featured as payer instead of Julie's name. "That's weird," commented Marie, "what is up with this?" "Oh, I was embarrassed to tell you," said Julie, looking down at her feet. "I'm having some financial difficulties and my employer has decided to help me out, so the cheques for daycare will come from the company from now on." Although this sounded a little strange to Marie, she figured that the issue was personal, shrugged, and accepted Julie's cheque.

Julie left the daycare feeling euphoric. Her idea had actually worked! Three weeks previously, she had created a "loss" in the system with Marie's name ascribed to it. Julie selected one of the very large corporate commercial accounts against which to submit the claim, a company that was seldom, if ever, reviewed. She was well aware of the most common types of losses experienced, and so it was not difficult to come up with a scenario and dollar value that would not attract attention. She simply entered Marie's name as the claimant, approved the claim, and in due course a cheque was issued.

The plan had worked so well the first time that Julie executed it again. And again. And again. A little over eight months passed and, in that time, she created eight different claims under Marie's name. She added it up one day and realized that she had netted $12 000 from her "side activities." Julie reflected on how easy it had all been: far too easy. She worried that she would be tempted to do it over and over again, and not just for daycare expenses. This was not the person she wanted to be. She decided that the only solution was to remove herself from temptation. She asked for, and received, a transfer to another department.

While Julie was celebrating her transfer and the fact that she would no longer be tempted, a problem emerged. The cheque for the last claim she had invented came back to her, because she had not filled in a field that coded the claim for the accounting system. Normally she could have fixed the oversight in a few seconds, but because she had been transferred, she no longer had access to the system. The person who replaced Julie asked her for a copy of the paperwork to back up the claim before filling in the missing information. Julie was unable to provide any. Not long after this incident, Julie arrived at work one morning to find herself called into a private room. Management informed her that they knew about the fraudulent claims, fired her, and advised her to get a lawyer. One month later, a police officer came to her home, and she was formally charged with fraud over $5000.

Now here she was, in court, being sentenced. She feared that her little boy would not understand why she would not return home that night. She had not told anybody about what was happening, in denial that she might actually go to jail. She felt numb all over and just prayed that her new boyfriend would be willing to take care of her son until she was released. If not, her son would become a ward of the state and be sent to a foster home; a thought that once again reduced Julie to despair. All she had ever wanted was to be able to look after her son properly. How had it come to this?

Discussion Questions

1. Does Julie's case differ from other well known corporate frauds (e.g., Bernie Madoff, Enron, etc.)? If so, what can this case teach us about ethical decision-making behaviours that the other cases do not?

2. Did the workplace environment or corporate culture contribute to Julie's ability to rationalize her fraudulent activities? Did these factors contribute to her decision to stop committing fraud? Based on your understanding of how work attitudes develop, explain how organizational factors may have contributed to her activities and subsequent decisions.

3. What can employers do to create an environment that encourages ethical behaviour?

Case 3: Auditing, Attitudes, and Absenteeism*

Learning Goals

In this case, you will have an opportunity to evaluate whether an ethical lapse in an employee's behaviour should be considered as an isolated incident or a symptom of broader problems within the corporate culture. You will also be asked to consider which factors contributed to the decision by Peter's direct reports to simply go along with his directions. Other issues to consider include the following: How might factors such as poor socialization or communication have contributed to the behaviour of Peter's direct reports? What would theories of motivation suggest? Should the organization have used a more formalized structure? Use your own insight to make recommendations about what the organization could, and should, do to prevent similar situations from developing in the future.

Major Topic Areas

- Organizational culture and socialization
- Power and group dynamics
- Motivation
- Ethical decision-making
- Organizational structure

The Scenario

"You've got to be kidding" said Sanjay, shaking his head, "is he there right now?" "Yes," said Bianca, "if we drive over there you can see for yourself." "What the heck," exclaimed Sanjay, "let's go." The pair left their office tower and drove the 10 minute distance to Peter's house. Bianca was right. Peter was supposed to be out at a client site overseeing an audit, but his car was parked in his driveway, and he could be seen clearly through his large, living room window. "Well, this is awkward," sighed Sanjay. "What do we do now?"

Sanjay and Bianca were senior managers at one of Canada's top four professional audit firms. Their team was responsible for performing audits for a broad range of corporate clients. The firm had a very traditional and formalized structure, like the other large players in their industry. Recent graduates were hired as "students

in accounts" during which time they were expected to complete their professional exams and work toward their chartered accountant (CA) designation. Upon passing their CA exams, they could compete to become junior auditors in the firm. If they chose to stay with the firm, they could then expect to progress to a supervisory role and finally, in six to seven years' become a senior manager. The best and brightest auditors stood to become future partners in the firm. Many graduates, however, simply worked at the company long enough to achieve their CA designation, which requires a minimum of two years' experience working in an auditing firm. The culture this process created was coined "up or out," since that is exactly what happened. Employees moved up (i.e., they were promoted) or out (i.e., left the company). There was no shame in leaving, though; in fact, it was anticipated that most employees would remain only long enough to get their designations and then move on.

Peter had joined the firm a few years ago and had progressed to the supervisory role. Recently, Peter had come to the conclusion that the path to partner was not right for him, and he began applying for jobs with other companies. But his decision to apply for jobs elsewhere created a dilemma. He was not comfortable telling his employer he was looking for work elsewhere, and he was also concerned that if his employer knew that he was contemplating leaving the firm, his current assignments and standing would be negatively affected. To make matters worse, Peter had no idea how long it would take to find a new job, and he also had no idea how to manage organizing time off to participate in interviews.

Peter reviewed his work tasks and responsibilities and came up with what he perceived to be a viable solution to his dilemma. He began telling the people under his supervision that their current client did not require their presence on Fridays, and they should work at home instead. Peter encouraged them to use the time to work on things like file reviews or even just to relax. The members of Peter's team did not question his instructions, even though it was highly unusual to be allowed, and even encouraged, to work from home. Even full partners seldom worked from home. The clients themselves did not question the team's absence on Fridays either (one suspects that the average worker is not terribly disappointed when he/she discovers that the audit team is absent for a day). This arrangement allowed Peter

---

* Note that this case is based on a real Canadian company. At the request of the owners, the employee names and the company name have been replaced with pseudonyms.

to tell his manager that he was conducting on-site audits on Fridays, when he was actually scheduling and attending a series of job interviews on those days.

The situation continued for a couple of months before a few of Peter's direct reports became uncomfortable enough to say something. They approached Bianca, who drove past Peter's house the following Friday to see for herself whether or not he was there. When she confirmed that he was at home, instead of "on-site," she returned to the office to discuss the situation with Sanjay. Now here the two of them were, standing on Peter's front step, wondering how to handle the situation. Sanjay knocked on the door. Peter answered, but as soon as he saw Sanjay and Bianca, his face fell. They asked him what was going on and were stunned when Peter began to cry.

After Peter regained his composure, the three of them returned to the office to discuss the situation. Sanjay and Bianca learned that the reason for the absences on Fridays was so that Peter could attend job interviews. Once Sanjay and Bianca heard all of the details, they asked Peter to step out of the office while they discussed the situation in more detail. "The irony," remarked Sanjay, once they were alone, "is that if Peter had just told us what was happening, we would have been happy to give him time off to go to interviews. We recently completed his performance evaluation, and although he is a solid accountant, he just isn't partner material. He doesn't have a future here anyway. It's not

that he is a bad auditor, but others are better. I would have been happy to help him find a good placement." "That's all well and good," said Bianca, "but it isn't even Peter I'm worried about. He supervised several different teams over the couple of months he was doing this. Why did it take so long for any of them to let us know what he was doing? I know the work still got done and the clients were satisfied, and I know that everyone likes to be friendly around here and hang out together, but these people are auditors for goodness sake! I would have expected better. Do you think this might be a symptom of a bigger problem with our corporate culture? And if so, what should we do about it?"

Discussion Questions

1. Why do you think Peter's direct reports kept quiet about the "work from home" directive for as long as they did? Why did some of them eventually decide to inform management?

2. Do you think this situation would have played out if the organization had a more formal structure in place? Why or why not?

3. Do you think the lapse in Peter's ethical behaviour indicates a broader problem with the firm's corporate culture? Why or why not? If yes, what should management do now to try to change its corporate culture?

Case 4: Flying the Unfriendly Skies— A Cautionary Tale of Conflict Turned Toxic

Learning Goals

In this case, you will have an opportunity to assess why a routine negotiation escalated into a highly toxic conflict. You will be asked to consider which factors contributed to the escalation and how the situation could have been handled differently to lessen the intensity and emotional nature of the conflict. You can then use that insight to make recommendations about what Air Canada can do now to begin to recover from this incident and to minimize the chances that events will unfold in a similar fashion during future negotiations.

Major Topic Areas

- Perception and emotion
- Power and politics
- Conflict and negotiation
- Communication

The Scenario

It is not unusual for conflict to exist between management and union members, particularly in the airline industry. In recent years, Canadian air travellers have experienced strikes, work slowdowns, and work-to-rule campaigns involving pilots, baggage handlers, and security-screening personnel. In the fall of 2011, however, Air Canada's flight attendants experienced a conflict that went far beyond the norm. A labour dispute that started out between management and the union eventually evolved into a toxic conflict that not only pitted the union against management, but also union leaders against their own membership and the union membership against the government.[1] How did negotiations degenerate to this point and what, if anything, could have been done to prevent it?

When 2011 began, the airline industry in general and Air Canada in particular had been struggling to remain financially viable for over a decade. Intense competition combined with high fuel costs, a high Canadian dollar, and a global recession had taken their toll. Air Canada was $4.6 billion in debt. Worse, the company's unfunded pension liability exceeded $2.1 billion. Something needed to be done, and it needed to be done fast. The flight atten-

dants, however, felt that they had sacrificed enough. In 2003, Air Canada had filed for bankruptcy protection. In 2004, as part of the process of rebuilding, the flight attendants' union had agreed to a 20 percent wage cut. This substantial concession was still top of mind for many of the flight attendants seven years later, as new labour agreements were being negotiated.

In 2010, Air Canada management developed a strategy that they felt would keep the company viable over the long term. They planned to launch a discount airline, a decision that was endorsed by many prominent business people and industry analysts, including Stephen Smith, former executive officer of Zip Airlines. "Air Canada employees are underestimating the competitive threat," Smith explained. "Air Canada has no way of fighting back against competitors because they don't have the lower cost structure of rivals."[2] Professor Ian Leeg, of the Sprott School of Business at Carleton University, explained that "a low cost strategy must be part of Air Canada's long-term solution. This industry is going through wrenching structural changes and some of the airlines will survive and some of them will not. Whether Air Canada [becomes] one of those survivors we don't know yet."[3]

The union representing the 6800 current Air Canada flight attendants did not approve of the proposal for a discounted airline. The change would result in hiring up to 1400 flight attendants at wages that would be at most three-quarters of what was paid to existing Air Canada flight attendants, creating a tiered system in which some employees would be paid less for doing the same job. The starting salary that management proposed was only $18 000 a year, a wage that the union derided as completely inadequate to accommodate basic living expenses. Union leaders also expressed concerns about the proposed discount airline eventually taking over Air Canada routes, leading to potential layoffs among the flight attendants who were paid higher wages.

Throughout the late summer and early fall of 2011, the flight attendants' union negotiated its new contract with Air Canada. In addition to the issue of whether or not the future would include a discounted airline, the flight attendants negotiated small wage increases and more favourable rules regarding "duty days." Duty day formulas are used to calculate wages when flight attendants are required to layover away from home. Under the existing formula, a 13-hour layover resulted in being paid for 6.5 hours. The union proposed a new formula called "duty day minus 4 hours" that would result in 9 hours of pay for the same layover.

Air Canada management was willing to make duty day concessions but was unwilling to give up plans to start up a discount airline, since it was a key part of their corporate rebuilding strategy. Air Canada management also needed the union to agree to retirement benefit concessions to help reduce long-term pension obligations. The company was hoping to transition from a defined benefit plan that pays a pre-determined, fixed, monthly pension to a defined contribution plan that ties pension amounts to the performance of investments. The proposed changes to pensions would further degrade the flight attendants' lifetime compensation. Unfortunately, the compensation for flight attendants was already perceived as degraded due to wage concessions in 2004. Also, the union was quick to emphasize that flight attendants function as far more than wait staff and customer service personnel. Instead, they require sophisticated skills, such as those related to first aid and emergency response preparedness. In other words, the ongoing cuts in wages and benefits was a problem for reasons that went beyond money, because many flight attendants interpreted lower compensation as a signal of lower professional respect. Since many flight attendants perceived themselves as highly trained professionals, they felt that their compensation did not reflect their status.

Contract negotiations were difficult since the two sides started out so far apart. After 17 weeks of discussions that involved a professional conciliator, the union negotiators believed that they had finally reached a tentative deal with management. Much to their surprise and chagrin, however, at the ratification stage, the union membership rejected the deal in a vote held in early August. More difficult, intense negotiations followed. On September 20, 2011, a second tentative deal was signed by union negotiators. The second deal offered increased meal allowances, small cost of living wage increases, and duty day concessions.[4] Air Canada also abandoned its provisions related to the new discount carrier. New hires, however, would get a hybrid pension plan rather than the more generous existing plan. Paul Moist, national president of CUPE, was so confident that the deal would be accepted that he assured Labour Minister Lisa Raitt it would be ratified, a promise he would live to regret. On October 9, 65 percent of the flight attendants rejected the deal. In addition, 2200 of them signed a petition to oust their own union leaders, feeling that the leaders had betrayed them by tentatively accepting a deal that failed to address their concerns. A strike seemed inevitable.

Meanwhile, Air Canada management was not amused by the failure of the union to ratify the agreement. In a formal statement, management stated that "though we were given assurances of unanimous support from the CUPE leadership for the tentative agreement, individual base presidents remained silent or expressed views against ratification during the ratification process."[5] Management then filed a formal complaint of bad faith bargaining with the Canadian Industrial Relations Board. Raitt was also concerned about the impact a strike could have on Canada's economy and global reputation. Raitt therefore asked the board to block a strike on the basis of health and safety concerns, while simultaneously approaching parliament to try to have the work that flight attendants perform declared an essential service, barring them from striking entirely. Raitt was ultimately successful: The strike action was blocked and the dispute was sent to binding arbitration.

Some of the flight attendants interpreted Raitt's actions as a declaration of war. Protests were staged at the Labour Ministry Office, and members of Parliament representing the NDP were quick to get involved, criticizing the action as an erosion of workers' rights. Moist acknowledged the anger of the flight attendants. "I think [the flight attendants] took their frustrations out on everybody, on the government, on the company, and to some degree on the union."[6] The rhetoric about eroding workers' rights only escalated when the arbitrator mandated that the flight attendants accept the second negotiated deal, which they had rejected in a vote on October 9. The head of their union reported that "workers are demoralized after an imposed contract failed to rectify past financial losses."[7] Although Moist, CUPE president, did not speculate on the impact this demoralization would have, Air Canada has reason for concern. The flight attendants are front-line employees engaged with customers on an ongoing basis. The long-term ramifications of this toxic dispute on Air Canada's organizational culture, corporate brand, employee retention rates, and customer service levels remain to be seen.

Discussion Questions

1. What caused what should have been a routine negotiation between Air Canada and its flight attendants to escalate into such a toxic conflict?

2. Were any negotiation errors made by Air Canada management? If so, what were they? What about the union representatives? Did they make any negotiation or communication errors? If so, what were they?

3. What could Air Canada do now to help lessen the negative outcomes still associated with the conflict?

Case 5: Gender-Based Harassment among the Royal Canadian Mounted Police

Learning Goals

In this case, you will have an opportunity to evaluate how organizational culture influences the way power is used and ethical decisions are made within the Royal Canadian Mounted Police (RCMP). Consider why the RCMP developed such a widespread problem with gender-based harassment allegations. Did the RCMP leadership contribute to the problem and, if so, how can they help to resolve it?

Major Topic Areas

- Workplace harassment and bullying
- Organizational culture
- Organizational change
- Leadership

The Scenario

In December 2006, the BC Court of Appeals upheld the decision by the BC Supreme Court to award Nancy Sulz $950 000 in damages for severe, long-term harassment experienced while she worked for Canada's RCMP.[1] The sexual harassment she endured starting in 1995 led to her request for a medical discharge from the RCMP in 2000, due to major depressive disorder. Her harasser, Staff Sergeant Donald Smith, has continued to enjoy a successful career with the force. Sulz was not the first person to complain about him; another female officer made similar allegations in the late 1980s but ultimately did not pursue them.

Four female RCMP officers alleged that they were sexually assaulted by Sergeant Robert Blundell during undercover operations that took place in Calgary between 1994 and 1997. Their internal complaints were dismissed and ignored, a problem that went all the way up to then-Commissioner Giuliano Zaccardelli. The officers reported that after filing complaints, they were "considered rats and whistleblowers and subject to harassing ridicule."[2] The four officers felt that "the lack of response signaled to the rank and file of the RCMP that silence, cover-up, and minimization are the preferred method of dealing with harassment within the RCMP."[3]

The officers chose to file a lawsuit against the RCMP in Calgary's Court of Queen's Bench in September 2003 because of the RCMP's lack of response. "We have done everything we can do within the force to address the problems and issues," the four reported in a formal statement. "They have not been satisfactorily resolved, and we've had to take this step as a last resort."[4] At the time of filing their case, two of the alleged victims were on stress leave and the other two reported losing career opportunities within the force. One lost her role as a hostage negotiator, and the other has not been assigned to undercover operations since making the allegations. The alleged perpetrator of the sexual assaults, meanwhile, lost one day of pay and was later promoted. The case was settled out of court in 2007, with the terms kept secret.[5] However, in December 2011, *The Fifth Estate* reported that two of the complainants continue to feel they were let down by the RCMP in the matter. "That seems to be the way of the RCMP, that's kind of like the toothless tiger. There's never any accountability," said Victoria Cliffe, one of the four complainants.[6]

Janet Merlo would no doubt understand the frustration the four Calgary RCMP officers experienced. She received a medical discharge from the RCMP due to post-traumatic stress disorder that was a direct result of ongoing workplace harassment and bullying. She was allegedly subjected to frequent sexual remarks and unwanted invitations from her immediate supervisor. Co-workers also left sex toys and pornography on her desk. It took two years after Merlo's initial complaint for the organization to respond. The response thanked Merlo for her letter and noted: "As you are aware the RCMP does not take these allegations lightly and, in fact, has an obligation to provide a harassment free environment for all of our employees."[7] Merlo was advised that the matter had been investigated but no action would be taken. Subsequently, Merlo initiated legal proceedings, but she was unable to continue due to the high costs involved.[8] Heli Kilanen, who quit her job with the RCMP in 2011 due to incessant harassment, has experienced the same challenges trying to get justice.

Other court cases are proceeding. Officer Elisabeth Couture made a claim through civilian courts against three male RCMP colleagues for systematically targeting her and creating a climate of fear in the workplace. Staff Sgt. Travis Pearson found himself in criminal court due to allegations that he raped Officer Susan Gastaldo in his home and then actively stalked her children in order to intimidate her into silence. An unidentified former RCMP officer testified at his trial that Pearson had also attempted to rape her under very similar circumstances, but she was too intimidated to report it at the time.[9]

In November 2011, Corporal Catherine Galliford, another RCMP officer and victim of ongoing workplace sexual harassment, decided she had had enough. She used the media to give her voice weight and expose the extent and severity of the harassment experienced by many of the 2613 female RCMP officers, a small minority in a force of 22 000. It was not long before other women, inspired by Galliford, also came forward to tell their stories, resulting in the beginnings of a class action lawsuit against the RCMP for its failure to address widespread gender-based harassment and bullying. RCMP leadership has little reason to be surprised. An internal study conducted in 1996 found that 6 out of 10 female Mounties had been sexually harassed at work and that more than 10 percent reported unwanted touching by male colleagues.

Unfortunately, that same leadership has done a very poor job of responding to complaints or addressing the cultural issues that underlie them. Questioned after Galliford had gone public, Krista Carle, one of the four Calgary RCMP officers who filed a complaint against Blundell, said the following about her formal complaint: "there was an internal review and nothing came of it. There was a memo that went out to colleagues and staff about how there was an incident with someone placing inappropriate material on someone's desk. Everyone knew it was me, so it was almost like I got blamed for getting the guys in trouble. And they never found out who put the porn on my desk."[10] Carle was discharged from the RCMP with post-traumatic stress disorder that she attributes to 19 years of unremitting sexual harassment and general bullying.

Paul Champ, a lawyer who has been involved in RCMP cases, says that "the process often takes years because the RCMP often does not treat complaints as a priority. . . . Most complaints are dismissed out of hand or dismissed with no remedy offered to the complainant other than 'we talked to him about it.'"[11]

Recognition of the scope of the problem led Bob Paulson, the new RCMP Commissioner, to make an unprecedented formal statement acknowledging that the continued existence of the force itself was at risk. He needed to "clear-cut problems that have taken root deeply. Too many Mounties believe their authority entitles them to misuse power. . . . The Mounties are one or two more earth-shattering heart-breaks away from losing all credibility. I tell you, one day there is going to be the removal of the Stetson *(the RCMP's emblematic hat and symbol of the force)* if we don't get this right."[12]

Steps have been taken. An external labour relations expert has been retained to review the RCMP's existing harassment policy. A new policy will be announced in Fall 2012; meanwhile, anti-harassment training has already begun. Some are skeptical that these efforts will help to change a long entrenched culture. Officer Elisabeth Couture believes that "management at the local level routinely turns a blind eye to harassment as it's occurring. You can have all the staff workshops on the issue that you want, but unless detachment supervisors deal with incidents in a forceful and unequivocal manner it won't matter."[13]

The RCMP's female officers who have experienced harassment, both past and present, are not waiting around to see if these efforts to effect change within the RCMP will be successful. As of December 27, 2011, the filing of a class action lawsuit was imminent, with reports of dozens of women calling the seven lawyers involved to tell their stories. Lawyer Alexander Zaitzeff reports that "the stories are consistent. The stories are common in terms of harassment, bullying, and oftentimes, sexual issues. The calls are sad, hugely sad. The stories are terrible. Many serving members are unable to work because they are petrified in light of their experiences."[14] Lawyers are also quick to point out the impact that these gender-biased attitudes may have on perceived injustice in the broader community. For instance, a lack of perceived sensitivity may inhibit female members of the public from reporting sexual assaults or stalking incidents. With the class action lawsuit just beginning, the RCMP leadership will need to carefully consider how to restore their reputation and credibility among both female staff and the broader community.

Discussion Questions

1. What aspects of the organizational culture in the RCMP may be contributing to its problems with widespread sexual harassment allegations?

2. Do the alleged claims of sexual harassment point to a leadership problem? Why or why not?

3. Devise a plan to manage a culture change at the RCMP. What resistance might you encounter and how could you overcome it?

Case 6: Disability Accommodations and Promotions at Bunco*

Learning Goals

In this case, you will have to decide whether or not to promote an employee who has a disability. You will need to consider whether or not the particular disability presents a legally and morally defensible barrier to promotion to a management role. If you choose to promote the employee, what can you do to help ensure his success? If you do *not* promote him, how can you explain and justify your decision, while helping the person to maintain positive work attitudes?

Major Topic Areas

- Diversity (disability)
- Work attitudes
- Recruitment and selection

The Scenario

Nicholas, the director of finance at Bunco Canada, sat wearily at his desk and put his elbows on the table and his head in his hands. He sighed deeply and rubbed his eyes. He found himself second guessing the decision he had made to launch an external search for the company's newly created accounting manager role. Had Nicholas' decision been reasonable and fair?

Paul had worked for Nicholas as a staff accountant for 14 years. Paul was part of a team of eight and was the only one, other than Nicholas, who had a professional designation. Paul was a Certified Management Accountant (CMA) and currently worked as the senior accountant responsible for external financial reporting. The rest of the team consisted of a cost accountant, a financial analyst responsible for margin analysis and budgeting, a packaging plant bookkeeper, a corporate bookkeeper, and three accounts receivable/accounts payable clerks. The entire accounting staff was stationed at the company's Northern Ontario consumer goods packaging facility, along with other backroom services, such as human relations (HR), customer service, and information technology (IT). Bunco Canada also had a head office in Toronto, but due to the cost of renting office space, only the executive team and sales and marketing staff worked from that office.

Paul was a consistent and reliable employee who, due to his long tenure, had acquired an immense amount of knowledge about the organization. He had, at some point in his career, performed most accounting functions at Bunco, including plant costing, budgeting, analysis, and financial planning, and so he understood the details of each role extremely well. Paul got along well with the junior staff (most of whom had been with the company for more than 10 years) and was considered a key member of the accounting team. He frequently acted as an informal advisor to other members of the team, put in overtime, and engaged in special projects, including process improvements and database optimization. In fact, he had become the sole subject matter expert on some critical financial applications needed for monthly reporting. In the last four years, however, Paul had begun experiencing health issues. Starting in 2006, he began requiring special accommodations from Bunco for Crohn's disease.

Crohn's disease is an incurable inflammatory bowel disease that results in sporadic and unpredictable bouts of moderate to severe pain, fever, diarrhea, gas, vomiting, and rectal bleeding.[1] Sufferers of Crohn's may experience brief or extended remissions that last months or even years, and then relapse without obvious triggers, although many patients with Crohn's disease report that stress significantly worsens symptoms and can trigger flare-ups.[2] There is no cure for the disease, but anti-inflammatory and immune-modulator medication, surgery, and careful attention to diet can control symptoms and minimize relapses for some people.[3]

Canadian courts recognize Crohn's disease as a legitimate disability for employment-related purposes. Employers are required to accommodate Crohn's disease as long as that accommodation does not result in excessive hardship. "Duty to reasonably accommodate" means that an employer must take all reasonable measures to enable a disabled employee to keep working. In addition to making physical accommodations such as providing laptops, wheelchair ramps, etc., employers can also be required to amend job responsibilities and performance appraisal criteria.

When he was first diagnosed with Crohn's four years ago, Paul had discussed several concerns with Nicholas. "Nicholas, I don't know how long it will take me to get this under control. It's not like I can't work at all. I'll go for a

---

* This case is an abbreviated version of a published case that appeared in the *Case Research Journal*. See K. Breward, "Disability Accommodations and Promotions at Bunco," *Case Research Journal* 30, no. 1 (2010), pp. 65–72. Reprinted with permission.

couple hours and be fine, but then . . . I don't think anyone wants me running to the washrooms here. Besides it's humiliating. I need some privacy. When the pain flares up it's all I can focus on. Maybe I could just work from home on a laptop on my bad days, play it by ear a little bit?"

Nicholas replied: "Well I don't see a problem with you working from home sometimes, but are you sure that's what you want? I spoke to an HR representative about this yesterday, and she pointed out that we have a corporate policy that prohibits laptop use for everyone except senior management and sales, but under the circumstances, I'm pretty sure I can get one approved for you. I was wondering if going on long-term disability might be a better solution for you to get yourself well though, assuming that we can get the insurance company to support the claim. Your health has to be your first priority. That said, I don't really know what we'll do if you leave!"

Paul was reluctant to seek long-term disability, because he did not want to give up so much of his life to the disease. It was also unclear whether the claim would be accepted by Bunco's insurer. After another discussion with an HR representative, Nicholas decided that a laptop should be issued to Paul and that he should be permitted to work at home on his bad days. Nicholas trusted him not to abuse the privilege so felt no need to document the decision further. An informal "handshake agreement" was readily accepted by Paul.

Accommodation Implemented: The First Few Years

Paul and Nicholas explained the situation to co-workers in a regularly scheduled staff meeting, and, initially, everyone was supportive of the new arrangement. As more time passed, however, Nicholas became worried. He had anticipated the occasional absence, but over the first few months of the new arrangement, Paul consistently worked two days in the office and then had to go home for two to three days, meaning he was absent more than 50 percent of the time. Although Paul did respond to email, Nicholas felt that he had underestimated the ongoing impact that Paul's absence might have long term. Nicholas was being inundated with daily questions from staff that would normally have been routed to Paul. Despite the difficulties adjusting, Nicholas felt strongly that accommodating Paul was the right thing to do, so he said nothing. About five months after the initial discussion and the purchase of a laptop for use by Paul, Paul's symptoms decreased, and he was able to work in the office about 85 percent of the time for the next year and a half.

About two years ago, beginning in early 2008, Crohn's-related relapses and problems returned for Paul. At the same time, due to growth in market-share and a new acquisition, the demands on the accounting department had increased significantly. Budget constraints did not allow for the hiring of additional staff. Everyone had to contribute more and work a little harder. Working overtime, the norm in accounting departments at month's end and year's end, increased even more at Bunco. Especially at month's end, it was not unusual for staff to work in the office preparing external financial reports until 11:00 p.m. or midnight for several days in a row.

As previously mentioned, bouts of Crohn's disease are often triggered by stress. Since month's- and year's ends were particularly stressful times, Paul would often experience attacks then, just when he was needed most in the office. He was frequently absent during these key times, missing more than half of the month's ends. Other accounting employees, who previously had supported Paul's accommodations, began to murmur their resentment among themselves.

"It would really make my life easier if I could work from home," Nicholas overheard across a cubicle wall one day, followed by "can't he control his Crohn's with diet anyway, if he really tried to? I think he just doesn't want to be stuck here all evening for a week like us suckers!" "I don't think he can control it *that* much," another voice chimed. A third person responded, "even so, it does make for a convenient excuse doesn't it; he could fake it on any given day, and nobody would even know the difference. I bet he took off this afternoon because he heard they're bringing in pizza for dinner AGAIN." "It's not even fair," another voice complained, "if he can phone and email his work in why can't we? My ex is furious that I missed my night with the kids; I'll be paying for that one for a while."

Nicholas worried about the worsening morale among what had previously been a very close team. Furthermore, Paul had been significantly late submitting his external financial reports on several occasions, and his lack of availability had hampered other people's ability to complete interdependent tasks. Since early 2008, when his relapse began, the department had been late in submitting its monthly financial reports to head office in the United States seven times! The department still complied with deadlines imposed by the Securities and Exchange Commission (SEC), but it missed many internal deadlines. While not all of the department's late filings could be directly attributed to Paul's condition (and absences), he had certainly contributed to the problem.

That said, Nicholas knew that Paul had limited control over the Crohn's disease, so Nicholas did not mention his concerns to Paul or document performance problems. If anyone else said anything to Paul directly, Nicholas was unaware of it. Nicholas ended up doing little more than hope that Paul would experience a remission and that the situation would improve.

The Accounting Manager Role

Meanwhile the changes continued apace at Bunco. In early 2008, ongoing growth and further acquisitions-in-process meant that Nicholas acquired significant new responsibilities. Part of that transition included Nicholas taking on a more strategic role in financial management and physically relocating to the company's executive headquarters in Toronto. This meant that he would no longer be around day to day to manage the accounting department at the northern packaging facility. It was also no longer adequate for the department to adopt a flat organizational structure, with staff accountants formally reporting to the director. An accounting manager position would need to be created.

As director, Nicholas became responsible for financial strategy, identifying opportunities for cost reduction and revenue growth, foreign exchange strategy, ameliorating controls, and managing transition teams for new acquisitions. In turn, the new accounting manager would be responsible for much of what Nicholas had previously done. This included advising senior executives, including the CEO, about monthly financial results and projected year-end performance, as well as overall responsibility for costing and management accounting. This position required ongoing communication with various parts of the company, including occasional travel to the US head office. The most important part of the accounting manager role, however, involved managing the team at the northern facility. This included assigning tasks and providing daily guidance, advice, and social support to junior staff.

Under normal circumstances, Paul would have been the natural choice for promotion to this new accounting manager position. He wanted it; indeed, he felt it was owed to him in return for his long years of service. He was the most senior person in the department and, other than Nicholas, Paul had the highest level of formal accounting education. The other members of the department did not qualify for the role, as they were not CMAs. Paul had also created many of the spreadsheets and systems that were an integral component of the company's financial reporting system. The new role, however, would come with a significantly increased stress load, since it involved management responsibilities and a much higher political profile in the organization. Could Paul really handle the stress, given his disability? Also, if he did experience a flare-up, how could he manage a team of people from home, when multiple questions came up each day? Reports to the US head office were already being sent late with alarming frequency, damaging the Canadian branch's reputation within the company. Would this situation become worse under Paul's direction?

Fourteen months earlier, Nicholas had carefully considered his options vis-à-vis filling the future account manager position. He tried to discuss his concerns with his HR department but discovered that promotions were legal and ethical grey areas when it came to disability accommodation. Under a subset of law regarding duty to reasonably accommodate, employers were not able to deny promotions based on inability to perform a job without first proving undue hardship, but what did that really mean? The concept was largely untested in the courtroom. An HR staff member suggested that Paul be asked to participate in a detailed medical assessment to prove that he could not complete the essential operational requirements of the job. This suggestion did not sit well with Nicholas. A medical assessment could be regarded as invasive, and the procedure would lead to Paul being expected to share a great deal of confidential medical information. Furthermore, as with any management job, it was hard to distinguish the *essential* aspects of the job from the secondary ones. Presenting and defending monthly financial reports, for example, was a key part of the job. It was also very stressful, as the reports were examined and questioned in detail by powerful senior executives. Since stress was a trigger for flare-ups of Crohn's disease, could Paul handle the pressure? What about travel to the US head office? This was also stressful, and travel might well prove impossible for Paul. Was it fair to expect Paul to try, given his medical condition? Nicholas' biggest concern, however, was that Paul would not always be physically available to the staff. Nicholas felt that the physical presence of a manager in the office was central to the orderly flow of information, completion of daily tasks, and maintenance of a supportive and collegial environment. He did not know if he could truly justify calling that physical presence "essential," but his gut told him it was.

Under pressure to decide whether to fill the new position internally or externally, Nicholas was not sure that he was making the right choice, but he decided to launch an external search for an account manager, instead of promoting Paul.

Discussion Questions

1. Should Nicholas have promoted Paul? Why or why not?

2.a. What are Nicholas' legal responsibilities to Paul in this situation?

   b. What are Nicholas' ethical responsibilities to Paul in this situation? How does that balance with Nicholas' responsibilities to Paul's would-be co-workers?

3. If Paul were to be promoted, what strategies could Nicholas use to help Paul achieve success in his new role?

Case 7: Governance in Times of Crisis

Learning Goals

This case will allow you to assess the role of personality in decision making and to evaluate sources of perceptual errors and biases. The effect of politics on the running of an organization will also be highlighted. Pay particular attention to Jamie's personality and motivational orientation and consider how these factors influenced her perception of events. How did her perceptions impact her decision-making ability? Consider whether warning signs existed that indicated Jamie was vulnerable to perceptual errors or political machinations. What could she have done to increase the accuracy of her perceptions?

Major Topic Areas

- Personality
- Perception
- Decision-making
- Politics

The Scenario

Jamie sat down miserably and thought back to how this whole mess had started.[1] She had had such good intentions. All she had ever wanted was a little professional respect and a chance to prove she was capable of contributing. After spending a decade hopping unhappily from company to company in a series of sales roles, she had felt like she had wasted the early part of her career. She knew she could do better and find something that made her happier, so two years earlier she had decided to return to school full-time, earn a Masters of Business Administration (MBA), and launch a new career. Six months ago, she had completed the degree and returned to the workforce in an entry-level training role. It was not exactly the job she had expected to land post-MBA, but the economy had been bad, and jobs of all kinds were scarce. She was frustrated at the lack of progress regarding her career ambitions and felt that her skills were not being used or respected. She decided to find another outlet for her ambitions and began to look for volunteer roles that would allow her to take on more authority and responsibility. Joining the board of directors of a non-profit centre had seemed like a perfect fit.

Everything had seemed to come together in September of 2006, when Jamie met up with an old acquaintance,

Paulette. Prior to starting her MBA, Jamie had been recruited by Paulette to work on a two-week-long research project. The project that Jamie completed had been very satisfying and was very successful as well. So when Paulette asked Jamie to join the volunteer board of directors associated with Paulette's agency, Jamie was delighted at the thought of working with Paulette again.

Paulette was the long-time executive director of Centre Bienvenu, a non-profit organization conceived to help immigrants and refugees to settle safely, productively, and happily in Canada. She had served in a dual role, combining executive director and front-line settlement worker responsibilities, for 17 years. Due to these blended responsibilities, she was especially well known and trusted in the immigrant community. She had helped many people when they first arrived in Canada, and these "alumni" frequently referred newly arrived friends and loved ones to the centre and to Paulette personally.

In addition to settlement services, the centre provided translation and interpretation services, and delivered anti-discrimination workshops to local schools and businesses. As well, the centre was affiliated with the city's annual multicultural festival, which was run as a separate entity but overseen by the centre's board. The festival was an important community event and helped to raise funds, often donated, that were used to shore up the centre's budget deficits.

Centre Bienvenu received most of its funding from federal and provincial agencies responsible for delivering immigration services. Both levels of government routinely delivered a range of immigration services via contracts issued to community agencies. Agencies were awarded multi-year contracts and, in return, received base funding that was designed to cover operating expenses. This base funding was supplemented by additional service delivery-based funding that required the agency to submit monthly reports itemizing all service delivery activities engaged in by each employee. The government generally expected agencies to engage in community fundraising, meaning that the operating expense budgets were not meant to be sufficient to sustain the organization.

Although the government was not responsible for the creation of frontline agencies, it wielded a considerable amount of power in the sense that it could change which agencies it chose to work with (subcontract to), if a community agency did not perform satisfactorily. In the case of Centre Bienvenu, about 65 percent of the centre's ongoing operations budget came from the Canadian federal immigration programs. The provincial Ministry of Citizenship and Immigration's settlement services program provided an additional 30 percent of the centre's funding. The provincial program overlapped significantly with that of the federal program, though double-billing for individual services was strictly prohibited. Provincial and federal representatives from Citizenship and Immigration worked cooperatively to ensure that overall funding levels were appropriate for the agency and the surrounding community. The remaining 5 percent of the centre's budget came from donations, obtained almost exclusively from the local multicultural festival. That said, these donations were unpredictable year-over-year, as they depended on the financial success of the festival, which itself was highly dependent on the weather.

Even in good years, money was always tight for the Centre Bienvenu. Jamie, with her industry experience in sales and her newly earned MBA, thought maybe she could help. When Paulette asked her to join, mentioning that the centre planned to hold elections for new board members in October, Jamie decided to run without giving it much further thought. It seemed like a great opportunity.

The elections to the board of directors, held during the centre's annual general meeting, were a surprise. Jamie had arrived expecting to be required to sell herself. Instead, she found that the centre was very short of candidates. In fact, there were insufficient volunteers to fill the 11 available seats! Only 10 directors were elected that day. Three directors stayed on from the previous board. Jamie found it odd that former members of the board had to be actively convinced to serve again, but she had never been involved in non-profit governance before, so thought maybe this was normal. Her thoughts quickly moved on as people came over to congratulate her for volunteering and to tell her how grateful they were that she had joined. Finally, here was some of the professional recognition and respect Jamie had been craving! It felt good, and she could not wait to get started and prove her worth. A small nagging part of her brain wondered if she had the experience to take on the role, but, after all, why had she completed an MBA if not to become a leader?

Settling In: Early Assessment

At the next board of directors meeting, in early November, Jamie had the opportunity to learn a bit more about her fellow board members. Two of the three returning members, Durand and Marcel, had both been associated with the centre for over a decade. They involved themselves mainly with the multicultural festival. Trina served as the treasurer, and had been overseeing the centre's finances for

two years. The four newly elected board members included Michel, an experienced for-profit senior business executive, certified accountant, and first-time board member; Claude, an anti-poverty activist with political ambitions; Marie, a quiet and shy woman, who was difficult to evaluate because she never spoke; and, of course, Sebastien. Sebastien was 45 years old and worked as a government bureaucrat in the field of safety procedure analysis and optimization. Two other electees had quit prior to the first meeting, leaving a board of eight plus the executive director (Paulette).

Sebastien arrived at the meeting a few minutes late, after the other members were seated. He took the chair at the head of the table, saying it was clearly reserved "for the president." It was only when proceedings began that the members of the board discovered that Jamie was putting her name forward for the role of president as well, which she had done only because Paulette had privately requested it. Marcel and Durand did not respond well to Jamie's self-nomination. Both confronted her, stating that "being president isn't just about having a nice title you can brag about, you have to understand how things work here." The voting was close, but Sebastien won the presidency, and Jamie accepted the vice-presidency. Despite Michel's formal accounting credentials, the board decided that Trina would continue as treasurer, primarily out of respect for her past service. After watching the example that the board had made of Jamie earlier in the meeting (chastising a newcomer for wanting to be considered president), Michel was reluctant to offend by questioning a colleague's role at the first meeting of his first board appointment, so he readily agreed that this was a good idea.

During the remainder of the meeting, the board reviewed the centre's mandate and examined audited financial statements from the previous fiscal year (which ran from April 1 to March 31). Although the statements looked fine, Jamie thought that she could help to come up with some fundraising strategies to address future budget shortfalls, particularly since Durand said the nest egg created by the highly successful multicultural festivals was getting whittled away and success could no longer be relied on in the future. She left the meeting excited about finding new funding opportunities, but also concerned that no current financial statements were offered. When she asked about this, Paulette assured the board that they would be available next time, which Trina (the treasurer) afterward confirmed with a nod.

The next three monthly meetings (December 2006 through February 2007) were frustrating for Jamie. The promised financial statements were still missing at the December board meeting. Paulette explained that she had been too busy to send Trina the relevant information on time, since time-consuming financial reports, required by the governments which supported the centre, had to be completed and her time had also been consumed by clients who required specialized, time-consuming help for urgent problems.

Trina did deliver "financial statements" in January. They bore no comparison to anything Jamie had seen before. They featured no year-to-date figures, no comparisons to budget, and no description regarding how the statements were generated. At first, Jamie thought this was strange, but after watching the remainder of the board quietly review the statements without comment, she felt unsure. Furthermore, she did not want to question the established treasurer. At the break, she approached Michel to get his impression.

"Michel, accounting is not my forte, and I was wondering what you thought of the financial statements we were given?" Jamie asked.

"Compared to what I am used to, they're really inadequate," Michel replied.

"What do you think is missing?" asked Jamie.

"Where to begin? Well, first of all, the 'statement,' such as it is, seems to be some strange combination of an income statement and balance sheet, as there are expenses, receipts, and accounts receivable all on the same page; but there is no overall profit or retained earnings. They appear to be done on a cash basis."

"Frankly," Michel continued, "since Trina has been here for a while in the capacity of Treasurer, I am at a loss as to why we aren't receiving monthly statements along the lines of the audited financial statements."

"Why didn't you say something during the meeting?" asked Jamie.

"Well, this is my first non-profit board appointment, and I'm still trying to figure everything out. I don't want to offend Trina; I mean, she's a volunteer like all the rest of us. Maybe she just ran out of time. If things don't improve over the next couple of months, I'll say something."

Jamie felt a bit better knowing that at least one other board member thought that the financial statements were insufficient and, more importantly, that Michel planned to monitor the situation going forward. She felt that, given Michel's expertise, she could trust him to speak up, if the reporting was inadequate enough to create real problems down the line.

Jamie learned in the January and February meetings that, in addition to an overall annual shortfall of about $10 000, cash flow was an issue. The centre delivered immigration services and then billed the two levels of government.

Reimbursement arrived anywhere from two to nine months after service delivery. In fact, the province remitted payment only twice a year, which Paulette said was fundamentally irresponsible, since it created semi-annual cash flow crises that routinely plagued the centre. Marcel and Durand felt it was the sponsor's fault for paying so infrequently and wondered if the payment schedule could be renegotiated. Paulette discouraged them from rocking the boat, explaining that all community agencies were treated similarly by the federal and provincial governments.

Claude and Durand expressed other concerns to Jamie. Claude questioned the lack of data offered on day-to-day programs. At each board meeting, Paulette would summarize how many clients were seen that month, but little detail was offered about precisely which services were being used by whom. Paulette told amazing, heart-warming anecdotes about clients she and the staff helped, but was unable to offer a breakdown of exactly where staff time was spent or any statistical data on service trends. Since Paulette was already required to report this detailed information to the government, it seemed odd to Claude, as well as to several other board members, that she did not have this information readily available.

When Claude questioned Paulette, she responded in a way that Jamie perceived to be abrupt, but then she remembered that Paulette was under a lot of stress and was trying to deal with competing priorities and time demands. When Claude insisted more program information was needed, Paulette dismissed his suggestions because they would create too much extra work. Paulette pointed out that she was so short on time that it was a struggle to even complete the government contract renewal documents. That comment ended the discussion, because the board's attention immediately shifted to the federal contract renewal application.

Without a federal contract to deliver immigration services, the centre could not function, so a worried Jamie volunteered to assist with completing the application in time to meet the end of February deadline. Paulette also asked for support to deal with supporters/funders who required separate financial reports. Jamie participated in a conference call with Paulette and with the federal representative assigned to assess the centre's contract renewal application, and Jamie found him somewhat demanding. He sounded unreasonably frustrated given the context of the conversation but was mollified when Jamie explained that his contract renewal application would be received soon. Jamie completed the required forms herself and forwarded them to Paulette for proofreading, fact-checking, and submission to the federal government representative.

The First Crisis

At the March board meeting, during which the board was supposed to deal with some of Jamie and Claude's fund-raising ideas, a crisis hit. The monthly financial statement, which had been missing at the February meeting due to Trina being ill, showed that the centre would be unable to make payroll obligations at the end of the month. Trina explained that the centre's semi-annual cheque from the province was unusually late, creating a semi-annual crisis. Paulette pointed this out as another example of the type of difficult funder behaviour she had to deal with.

Paulette asked Durand, the long-time board member who was also affiliated with the local multicultural festival, to release $4000 from the budget allocated to the multicultural festival to help cover the centre's payroll obligations. He reluctantly agreed to provide the monies, but asked for more detailed financial statements and budgets moving forward. Michel offered to help Trina to generate them, but he was reluctant to force the issue, since he felt this would be insulting, especially considering that she was a volunteer. Meanwhile, Jamie became increasingly worried. This was an agency that could not make payroll—she definitely felt that the funding agencies needed to be more responsible where the delivery of timely payments was concerned. Immigration services were too critical to be endangered so irresponsibly! The increasing degree of politics in which the board was embroiled, and which she suddenly seemed to be in the middle of, only added to her unease.

After the March meeting, Paulette approached Jamie privately for support, complaining that Durand lacked knowledge of basic financial processes and that if he were more knowledgeable in that area, he would free up festival funds whenever she requested them without debate. Paulette told Jamie that "in meetings, it shows that you understand about business, so Durand will defer to your judgment. Just tell him it's fine."

Durand approached Jamie separately, complaining that Paulette had been insisting on festival donations for years without adequate explanation for funding shortfalls. "Paulette listens to you," stated Durand. Jamie was flattered that Paulette and Durand both thought she had so much influence. It was nice to finally have her knowledge acknowledged! That said, she really was not sure what to do.

Claude also approached Jamie privately. He had been talking to people from other community agencies, and had heard that they were reluctant to work with the centre due to Paulette's extreme abrasiveness. Claude wanted Jamie's support to try to dismiss Paulette. She asked Claude if he could provide any concrete proof of the serious allegations he was making, but none was immediately forthcoming. Jamie continued to wonder if there was truth to what he had said. She definitely knew that this level of divisiveness could not help with problem solving. She also found it odd that these comments and requests were not routed to Sebastien, the board president.

Things worsened by the time the April meeting was scheduled to begin. Not only had the province's cheque still not arrived, but the treasurer resigned. Trina had been suffering a long illness which had, she announced, impaired her ability to fulfill her responsibilities. This explained the lack of proactive reporting. Furthermore, the centre would be unable to meet its payroll obligations yet again. Durand came to the rescue and lent the centre the money set aside for the festival to cover immediate expenses, although he voiced his extreme reluctance to do so. Thankfully, Michel agreed to take over the treasurer role. After leaving the meeting, Michel's first step was to prepare a cash flow analysis.

The Crisis Deepens

Less than one week later, Michel asked for an emergency board meeting to discuss the analysis he had completed of the centre's cash flow. After a flurry of phone calls and emails, a meeting was called for the evening of April 16.

The meeting began with the following announcement by Michel: "In a nutshell, by the end of May, we'll technically be bankrupt since, based on my projected cash flow, we'll be unable to pay our bills on time."

"How is this happening? How can we be this short when our programs are funded?" asked Jamie.

"The problem is due to the way the province processes and sends out our funding. We don't receive payment until six months into the fiscal year, and then again at the end of the fiscal year. We basically 'loan' money to the province each month, which it then pays back semi-annually. We need to find about $20 000 to pay the expenses related to the delivery of provincial programs until September. Obviously, finding a private donor willing to help us out would be the best case scenario, but even someone willing to give us a loan that wasn't due until at least September would buy us time."

The meeting went on long into the night, but ultimately the board decided on an aggressive, last ditch effort that involved both confronting existing funders about systemic funding problems and trying to find some new sources of revenue. The board decided to call all three funder representatives as well as local elected officials, and city, municipal, and United Way representatives, to an emergency meeting during the last week of April to discuss the future of the organization. The latter three were invited despite not having been financial sponsors in the past, since their equivalents in surrounding communities funded similar programs, leaving hope of future financial support.

Paulette volunteered to take personal responsibility for following up with the federal and provincial representatives invited to the meeting. Despite her phone calls and emails, however, very few of the expected attendees showed up. The federal and provincial representatives who *did* attend wanted to know why they had not been alerted to fiscal issues prior to the situation reaching such a crisis stage. They were not able to offer any new resources on such short notice. The board interpreted the lack of attendance as lack of interest in saving the centre from bankruptcy and decided to approach the local media. The board felt that airing the issue in public, in front of voters, would make the three levels of government more responsive.

The local media responded enthusiastically to the centre's request for publicity. Within a day, half of the front page of the city newspaper had been devoted to declaring the centre in a state of crisis. Response was immediate. First, a corporation that had never previously been associated with the centre made a private donation of $30 000, mitigating the immediate crisis. The city and municipality, neither of which had provided funding in the past and had not attended the emergency meeting, invited the centre to make a pitch at the next council meeting in a couple of weeks. Lastly, the funders all called Paulette, demanding a meeting. They did not sound happy, but the board had most certainly attracted their attention!

Reality Revisited

The meeting between the board and the federal and provincial sponsors took place on May 5 and was an eye-opening experience. The funders pointed out that similar agencies in other communities were growing, not struggling to the point of bankruptcy. The federal representative acknowledged that the government's payments often arrived late at the centre, but said that "we rarely, if ever, receive the financial reports that form the basis for releasing those payments to the centre on time. And when we do receive the reports, they are often filled out wrong or are missing data and need to be returned and completed again. Just a few months ago, I received 4 months worth of backlogged reports on the same day!" In fact, he complained, the contract renewal application that Jamie herself had promised to him over two months ago in a conference call still had not arrived!

This stunned Jamie, who had entrusted the completed document to Paulette for fact-checking and submission to the government months earlier. Paulette responded that the delay must have been owing to an email glitch of some kind; however, Jamie felt uneasy about the whole thing. The board then discovered that increased levels of funding had been offered in the past and had been declined by Paulette. In response, Paulette argued that she was forced to decline the new funds because carrying out the associated programs was not possible with current space and staff resources. Nevertheless, this was the first the board had heard of these developments.

Board members left the meeting relieved that additional funds might be coming their way, but also angry that they were not given complete information by Paulette. In fact, on the issue of monthly report submission and payment delays, they felt deceived! The board now faced a difficult battle. They had angered the government sponsors by going to the media and publicly discussing funding problems. That this approach had been decided upon owing, in large part, to the information Paulette had decided (and not decided) to share with them, made the current situation even harder to bear. The media attention also had heightened concerns about the viability of the centre and the competence of the board. As a result, the board would now be operating under intense scrutiny.

The publicity generated had other unintended consequences as well. The federal representatives specified that they wanted their annual audit to begin immediately (it was usually scheduled to occur three months later). They also demanded an in-depth analysis regarding cash flow to help understand why the centre was struggling so much and to assess its longer term feasibility. Meanwhile, the representatives decided that the centre's contract, now overdue for renewal, would be issued for periods of three months instead of the usual two years. This allowed funders more flexibility to react to the evolving situation, including the flexibility to walk away from the centre entirely!

Staff at the centre were stressed and upset, not only about the decision to hold an early audit, but also by the stories that they were reading in the newspapers. It was decided that the board should meet with staff members *without* Paulette present, to hear their point of view. The meeting with the staff was held on May 15 and echoed the surprises that emerged during the earlier meeting with sponsors. First, the staff confirmed what funders had told them—many opportunities for new funding were being ignored. Second, the board learned that Paulette explicitly prohibited the staff from filling out new funding applications, yet she did not complete them herself. Third, the board was told that the staff had volunteered to help Paulette to prepare the monthly reports in an effort to reduce her administrative burden, but they had been rebuffed. Fourth, the staff complained about Paulette's abusive language, her unprofessional conduct in front of clients, and her attendance issues. When the board asked why previous boards had not noticed anything amiss, the staff replied that prior boards had often been made up of Paulette's personal friends. Durand and Marcel confirmed this trend, and added that the executive director position had never had a written job description associated with it and that Paulette had not undergone a performance review in 17 years with the organization.

What Now?

Now, the board was very alarmed. Several board members, including Michel and Claude, felt personally betrayed and wanted to fire Paulette on the spot. The timing, however, could not have been worse. The centre was under intense scrutiny from both its funders and the media. While the board considered its options, the city heard and refused the board's pleas for emergency funding.

The board felt overwhelmed and was reeling and divided on what to do. Paulette had been with the organization for 17 years. For some of the ethnic communities served, Paulette was held in high regard, the symbolic figurehead behind all services rendered. She had personally provided settlement services for many of the centre's members. Furthermore, very little about her role was documented and none of the other staff had experience or training in financial record keeping, report writing (required by government sponsors), or the centre's human resources (HR) practices. To make matters worse, no other staff members were registered with the government as a "Commissioner of Oaths," so no one but Paulette could sign important immigration-related documents. Two of the other employees had been employed at the centre for a decade and had extensive knowledge of service delivery; however, they had never been involved in administration. Paulette alone knew where key documents were located, how administrative duties had been completed in the past, etc., etc.

On a practical level, letting Paulette go for cause might prove difficult, especially given her long tenure at the organization and the limitations placed on involuntary dismissals by the Canadian Labour Code and the Quebec Labour Standards Act. For example, the board had no paper record documenting poor performance by Paulette, nor did a job description exist against which to measure her performance. This meant that it would be hard to prove that a legitimate cause for dismissal existed, so the severance pay required to let her go would wipe out most of the $30 000 private donation that was currently keeping the centre afloat. Even if the board *did* find a solution for how to dismiss Paulette, how should they go about fixing the mess that would be left, most notably the centre's relationship with its sponsors? Finally, on a personal level, Jamie wondered how she had misread the situation—and Paulette—so badly. What could she do to make it less likely that she would make a mistake like that again?

Discussion Questions

1. Are there aspects of Jamie's personality or motivational orientation that made her vulnerable to inaccurately perceiving the situation that would unfold with Paulette? If so, what were they?

2. What other types of attribution errors did Jamie make?

3. What influence tactics did Paulette use to her advantage?

4. What types of decision-making errors did the board make?

5. What could Jamie have done to reduce her vulnerability to perceptual errors, politics, and decision-making errors?

Case 8: Restructuring for a Digital World

Learning Goals

In this case, you will have an opportunity to assess the impact of organizational structure on a company's ability to meet its strategic goals. You will need to assess the broader market conditions to determine whether or not implementing structural organizational changes represents an appropriate response to the challenges this company faces. Also, you will have an opportunity to assess the impacts of frequent change on employee attitudes, motivation, and ability to innovate.

Major Topic Areas

- Organizational structure
- Work attitudes
- Organizational change

The Scenario

Organizational structures frequently require adjustments to help companies respond to the evolving business environment and to changes in the market driven by technological advances. In recent years, no company has demonstrated this need more than Postmedia Network Canada. Postmedia is the organization that emerged to take over the print assets of CanWest Global Communications during CanWest's court-mandated bankruptcy proceedings. Upon takeover of these assets and emergence from creditor protection in early 2010, Postmedia immediately positioned itself as both a newspaper and a multimedia company.[1] At the time, Postmedia owned 11 major daily papers, including the *National Post*, the *Calgary Herald*, the *Vancouver Sun*, and the *Montreal Gazette*. The company also owned 35 community papers, the online version of the *National Post* (and its other papers), and the online news outlet Canada.com.[2]

It did not take long for Postmedia's CEO, Paul Godfrey, to announce the company's "Digital First" strategy. Godfrey explained that declining advertising revenues and lower print circulation required a focus on digital offerings such as online newspapers and iPhone- and iPad-based news distribution applications.[3] He stated that he expected one-quarter of Postmedia's revenue to come from digital products within four years, a move he would support by retraining one-quarter of the staff to enable them to focus on digital media outlets.[4] This initiative also involved a move to product-based departmentalization, with senior executive roles created to oversee digital initiatives. Three senior executives, in particular, were appointed to steer the digital strategy and products: Malcolm Kirk, executive vice president digital; Ed Brouwer, chief information officer; and Scott Anderson, senior vice president of digital content strategy and the managing director of Canada.com.

By December 2010, the focus on digital applications was evident. Postmedia launched ad-supported iPad applications for all of its daily newspapers, as well as iPod applications for the *National Post*. The structural changes were not yet complete, though cost-cutting was still a major focus. In early April 2011, Postmedia announced 500 layoffs (9 percent of the workforce), which was expected to save the company $35 million a year.[5] These layoffs were possible in part because the company outsourced its advertising production to overseas vendors and in part because it centralized its pagination duties.

Within this difficult environment, the "Digital First" strategy continued to evolve. In May 2011, Postmedia ran a successful pilot program with the *Montreal Gazette* using a metered model in which readers were able to access a limited amount of online content but then would be prompted to pay for an online subscription. A similar pilot program was attempted with the *Victoria Times Colonist*, but this paper was subsequently sold in early October, along with several others in British Columbia, to Glacier Media for $86.5 million. Godfrey announced that, although Postmedia had not originally intended to sell these assets, the unsolicited offer was "just too good to pass up."[6] Conveniently, the revenue from the sale could be used to cut Postmedia's debt. This was helpful, since revenues from the digital offerings were not increasing as fast as hoped.

In late October 2011, Postmedia made several announcements. The company presented the financial results for the quarter ending in August, comparing the 2011 results to 2010. As expected, the cost-cutting initiatives had drastically reduced fourth-quarter losses from $44.6 million in 2010 to $2.3 million in 2011.[7] The company's revenue, however, was also down $11 million year-over-year. Digital sales represented roughly 9 percent of Postmedia's revenue, which was lower than competitors such as Torstar, which generated 12 percent of revenues from digital sources. Postmedia's quarter-to-quarter growth in digital sales was only $1.7 million (8.2 percent). The slower than expected increase in digital revenues led to further structural changes, which were also announced in late October 2011.

The three senior executives in charge of digital strategy were all let go. Malcolm Kirk was replaced by Wayne Parrish, the chief transformation and revenue officer. In addition to taking over digital strategy from Kirk, Parrish was put in charge of sales, digital properties, and other business ventures. Scott Anderson was replaced by Lou Clancy, former editor-in-chief of the *Toronto Sun*. The most drastic change related to former CIO Brouwer's duties. They were absorbed by the central IT group located in Winnipeg and overseen by CFO Doug Lamb.[8]

Godfrey was quick to point out that the changes in the executive suite did not indicate a change of strategy. When speaking about digital revenues, he stated that "we still believe that this is part of the future in the industry. We've been watching the *New York Times* have considerable success in this area even as their ad revenues are down and their print circulation is down. We really believe that this falloff [compared to expected revenue growth] is more economy driven."[9] Other industry experts are not so sure. Media analyst David McFadgen believes that poor growth in digital revenues does not relate to the economy. "You have to try and grow your digital side of your business," he says, "but it's pretty tough. When it comes to generating revenue from advertising online you're basically trading dollars for dimes. You have to have some pretty unique content to get people to want to pay for it. The only one I know that it has worked for is the *Wall Street Journal*."[10]

Godfrey remains optimistic, pointing to flaws in execution strategy that he believes the recently announced changes will help to address. He says that "this year is about transformation and development" and emphasizes that sales and product development teams will now be working much closer together than they have in the past. He defends what some critiqued as the overly rapid dismissal of his key executive team by explaining that "you review things on a fairly regular basis, and in today's day and age, nothing is static. We're all under review at all points in time."[11]

University lecturer and experienced industry expert Jeffrey Dvorkin disagrees. He fears that changes are being made excessively hastily. "Media organizations often feel that they don't have the luxury of time to figure out where they need to be, so as someone described it, they're changing the oil in the car while they're driving on the freeway. Technology is driving that to an incredible extent. The pressure on media organizations to return real value to the shareholders is now driving what is often seen as a panic mode.[12]

Only time will tell whether the latest structural and leadership changes that Godfrey implemented at Postmedia will help the company meet its goals of maximizing digital revenues and returning to profitable operations.

Discussion Questions

1. How would you describe the changes to Postmedia's structure that were announced in October 2011? What has changed since then? Does this change improve or diminish the company's chances of meeting its strategic goals? Why?

2. Postmedia has made many changes very quickly. What impact might these quick changes have on the work attitudes and motivation of the employees? Would you anticipate any impact on creativity or innovation?

Case 9: Repair Jobs That Fail to Satisfy

Learning Goals

Companies often divide up work as a way to improve efficiency, but specialization can lead to negative consequences. FlowFix is a company that for years has effectively used specialization to reduce costs relative to that of its competitors, but rising customer complaints suggest that the firm's strong position may be slipping. After reading the case, suggest some ways the company can create more interesting work for employees while improving customer satisfaction rates. You will also need to tackle the problem of how to find people qualified and ready to perform the multiple responsibilities required in FlowFix's jobs.

Major Topic Areas

- Job design
- Job satisfaction
- Personality
- Emotional labour

The Scenario

FlowFix is a mid-sized residential and commercial plumbing maintenance firm that operates in the Greater Vancouver area.[1] It has been a major regional player in plumbing for decades. Tyron Johnson has been the senior executive at FlowFix for about two years. He used to work for a newer competing chain, Lightning Plumber, which has been drawing away more and more customers from FlowFix. Although his job at FlowFix pays more, Tyron is not happy with the way things are going. He has noticed the work environment is not as vital or energetic as the environment he saw at Lightning Plumber.

Tyron thinks the problem is that employees are not motivated to provide the type of customer service Lightning Plumber employees offer. He recently sent surveys to customers to collect information about customer service performance, and the data confirmed his fears. Although 60 percent of respondents said they were satisfied with their experience and would use FlowFix again, 40 percent felt their experience was not good, and 30 percent said they would use a competitor the next time they had a plumbing problem.

Tyron is wondering whether FlowFix's job design might be contributing to its problems in retaining customers. FlowFix has about 110 employees who are divided into one of four basic job categories: plumbers, plumber's assistants, order processors, and billing representatives. This structure is designed to keep costs as low as possible. Plumbers, who are licensed, make very high wages, whereas plumber's assistants make about one-quarter of what a licensed plumber makes. Using plumber's assistants is therefore a very cost-effective strategy that enables FlowFix to easily undercut the competition when it comes to price. Order processors make even less than plumber's assistants but about the same as billing processors. All work is specialized, but employees are often dependent on those in other job categories to perform at their most efficient level.

Like most plumbing companies, FlowFix gets a lot of residential business from people who consult the Internet. Corporate clients also use the company's online interface to make nonroutine maintenance requests. Customers either call in to describe a plumbing problem or submit an online request for plumbing services, receiving a return call with the information required to solve the problem within 24 hours. In both scenarios, FlowFix's order processors determine from the customer's description of the problem whether a plumber or a plumber's assistant should make the service call. The job is then assigned accordingly, and a service provider goes to the location. When the job has been completed, the information is relayed to a billing representative. The billing representative forwards the invoice to the service rep via cellphone, and the service rep then presents a bill to the customer for payment by credit card, debit card, or cash (corporate clients remit payment via monthly invoices rather than on-the-spot).

The Problem

Although specialization cuts costs significantly, Tyron is worried about customer dissatisfaction. According to his survey, about 25 percent of customer contacts ended in no service call because customers were confused by the diagnostic questions the order processors asked or because the order processors did not have sufficient knowledge or skill to explain the situation. That means fully one in four people who call FlowFix to hire a plumber were worse than dissatisfied: they did not become customers at all! The remaining 75 percent of calls that did end in a customer service encounter resulted in other problems.

The most frequent complaints, Tyron discovered via the customer surveys, were about response time and cost, especially when the wrong person was sent to a job. A plumber's assistant cannot complete a more technically complicated job. If a plumber's assistant arrives onsite and cannot do the work, the appointment must be rescheduled (with a licensed plumber) and the customer's time and the staff's time have been wasted. The resulting delay often caused customers to decline further contact with FlowFix—many of them decided to move forward with Lightning Plumber instead.

"When I arrive at a job I can't take care of," says plumber's assistant Kiera Fritz, "the customer gets ticked off. They thought they were getting a licensed plumber, since they were calling for a plumber. Telling them they have to have someone else come out doesn't go over well."

On the other hand, when a plumber responds to a job easily handled by a plumber's assistant, the customer is still charged at the plumber's higher rate. Licensed plumber Philip Wong also does not like being in the position of giving customers bad news. "If I get called out to do something like snake a drain, the customer isn't expecting a hefty bill. I'm caught between a rock and a hard place—I don't set the rates or make the appointments, but I'm the one who gets it from the customer." Plumbers also resent being sent to do such simple work.

Louisa Gomez is one of FlowFix's order processors. She is also frustrated when the wrong person is sent to a job but feels she and the other order processors are doing the best they can. "We have a survey we're supposed to follow with the calls to find out what the problem is and who needs to take the job," she explains. "The customers don't know that we have a standard form, so they think we can answer all their questions. Most of us don't know any more about plumbing than the caller. If they don't use the terms on the survey, we don't understand what they're talking about. A plumber would, but we're not plumbers; we just take the calls."

Customer service issues also involve the billing representatives. They are the ones who are responsible for continuing to contact customers about payment. "It's not my fault the wrong guy was sent," says Susan MacArthur. "If two guys went out, that's two trips. If a plumber did the work, you pay plumber rates. Some of these customers don't get that I didn't take their first call, and so I get yelled at." The billing representatives also complain that they see

only the tail end of the process, so they don't know what the original call entailed. The job is fairly impersonal, and much of the work involves recording customer complaints. Remember—40 percent of customers are not satisfied, and it's the billing representatives who take the brunt of customers' negative reactions on the phone.

As you can probably tell, all employees have to engage in emotional labour and it is not clear that they have the skills or personality traits to complete the customer interaction component of their jobs. FlowFix's employees are not trained to provide customer service, and they see their work mostly in technical, or mechanical, terms. Quite a few are actually anxious about speaking directly with customers. The office staff (order processors and billing representatives) realize customer service is part of their job, but they also find dealing with negative feedback from customers and co-workers taxing.

A couple of months ago, a human resource management consultant was hired to survey FlowFix employees about their job attitudes. The results, shown below on a scale of 1 to 5, indicated that FlowFix employees were less satisfied than employees in comparable jobs. The following table provides a breakdown of respondents' satisfaction levels across a number of categories:

The Proposed Solution

The company is in trouble, and as revenues shrink and the cost savings that were supposed to be achieved by dividing up work fail to materialize, a change seems to be in order.

Tyron proposes using cash rewards to improve performance among employees. He thinks if employees were paid based on work outcomes, they'd work harder to satisfy customers. Because it's not easy to measure how satisfied people are with the initial call-in, Tyron would like to give the order processors a small reward for every 20 calls successfully completed. For the hands-on work, he would like to have each billing representative collect information

	FlowFix Plumbers	FlowFix Plumber's Assistants	FlowFix Office Employees	Average Plumber	Average Office Employees
I am satisfied with the work I am asked to do.	3.7	2.5	2.5	4.3	3.5
I am satisfied with my working conditions.	3.8	2.4	3.7	4.1	4.2
I am satisfied with my interactions with co-workers.	3.5	3.2	2.7	3.8	3.9
I am satisfied with my interactions with my supervisor.	2.5	2.3	2.2	3.5	3.4

The information that appears above about "average plumbers" and "average office employees" is taken from the consultant's records of other, similar companies and published industry data about skilled tradespeople. The comparatively low averages for FlowFix employees are not exactly surprising given some of the complaints FlowFix employees have made. Tyron is worried about these results, but has not been able to formulate a solution. The traditional FlowFix culture has been focused on minimizing costs, and the "soft stuff" like employee satisfaction has not been a major issue.

about customer satisfaction for each completed call. If no complaints are made and the job is handled promptly, a moderate cash reward would be given to the plumber or plumber's assistant. If the customer indicates real satisfaction with the service, a larger cash reward would be provided.

Tyron also wants to find a way to hire people who are a better fit with the company's new goals. The current hiring procedure relies on unstructured interviews, and Tyron has realized that he, his senior office manager, and his most experienced lead plumber are not very consistent when interviewing. Furthermore, they often rely on their gut instinct when making hiring decisions. Most employees lack training in customer service and organizational behaviour. Tyron thinks it would be better if hiring methods were standardized and customer service skills were evaluated during that process to help them identify recruits who can actually succeed in the job.

Discussion Questions

1. Although it's clear employees are not especially satisfied with their work, do you think this is a reason for concern? Does research suggest satisfied workers are actually better at their jobs? Are any other behavioural outcomes associated with job satisfaction?

2. Using the job characteristics model, explain why the present system of job design may be contributing to employee dissatisfaction. Describe some ways you could help employees feel more satisfied with their work by redesigning their jobs.

3. Tyron has a somewhat vague idea about how to implement the cash rewards system. Describe some of the specific ways you would make the reward system work better, based on the case.

4. Explain the advantages and disadvantages of using financial incentives in a program of this nature. What, if any, potential problems might arise if people are given money for achieving customer satisfaction goals? What other types of incentives might be considered?

5. Create a specific plan to assess whether the reward system is working. What are the dependent variables that should change if the system works? How will you go about measuring success?

6. What types of hiring recommendations would you make to find people better suited for these jobs? Which Big Five personality factors would be useful for the customer service responsibilities and emotional labour?

Case 10: Managing Motivation in a Difficult Economy

Learning Goals

In this case, you will have the opportunity to assess a motivational program designed to re-energize the workforce at a troubled organization. Acting on behalf of the company's executive board, you will evaluate the board's current strategy based on survey data. You will consider how to improve the effectiveness of the program based on what you have learned about goal setting and motivation in organizations.

Major Topic Areas

- Diversity and age
- Goal setting and motivation
- Organizational downsizing
- Organizational justice

The Scenario

PharmaNorth's drugstores are in trouble.[1] A major regional player in the retail industry, the company has dozens of stores in Ontario and Quebec's mid-North. Unfortunately, a sharp decline in the region's manufacturing and natural resource–based economy has put management in a serious financial bind. Revenues have been consistently dwindling. Customers spend less, and the stores have had to switch their focus to very low-margin commodities, such as milk and generic drugs rather than the high-margin impulse-buy items that used to be the company's bread and butter. The firm has had to close quite a few locations, reversing its expansion plans for the first time since it incorporated.

Since this is uncharted territory for the company, Natasha Brook, vice-president for human relations, had been struggling with how to address the issue with employees. As the company's fortunes worsened, she could see that employees were becoming more and more upset. Their insecurity about their jobs was taking a toll on attitudes. The company's downsizing was big news in the small communities in which they operated, and the employees did not like what they were hearing.

Local newspaper reports of PharmaNorth's store closings focused on the lack of advance notice or commu-

nication from the company's corporate office, as well as the lack of adequate severance payments for departing employees, who receive only the bare minimum required by law. In the absence of official information, rumours and gossip have spread like wildfire among remaining employees. A few angry blogs developed by laid-off employees have made the morale and public relations picture even worse.

PharmaNorth is changing in other ways as well. The average age of its workforce is increasing rapidly. Several factors have contributed to this shift. First, fewer qualified young people are around because many have moved south to find jobs, especially those in more isolated communities that heavily depended on natural resources or a single manufacturing employer. Second, stores have been actively encouraged to hire older employees, such as retirees looking for some supplemental income. Managers are very receptive to these older employees because they are more mature, miss fewer days of work, and do not have child-care responsibilities. They are also often more qualified than younger employees because they have more experience, sometimes in the managerial or executive ranks.

These older employees have been a great asset to the company in troubled times, but they are especially likely to leave if things get bad. If these older employees start to leave the company, taking their experience with them, it seems likely that PharmaNorth will sink deeper toward bankruptcy.

The System

Brooks was not quite sure how to respond to employees' sense of hopelessness and fear until a friend gave her a book entitled *Man's Search for Meaning*. The book was written by a psychologist named Viktor Frankl who survived the concentration camps at Auschwitz. Frankl found that those who had a clear sense of purpose, and a reason to live, were more likely to persevere in the face of nearly unspeakable suffering. Something about this book, and its advocacy of finding meaning and direction as a way to triumph over adversity, really resonated with Brooks. She thought she might be able to apply its lessons to her workforce. She proposed the idea of a new direction for management to the company's executive committee, and they reluctantly agreed to try her suggestions.

Over the last six months, stores throughout the company have used a performance management system that, as Brooks says, "gets people to buy into the idea of performing so that they can see some real results in their stores. It's all about seeing that your work serves a broader purpose. I read about how some companies have been sharing store performance information with employees to get them to understand what their jobs really mean and participate in making changes, and I thought that was something we'd be able to do."

The HR team came up with five options for the management system. Corporate headquarters encouraged individual store managers to choose the option they thought would work best with their employees so that managers would not feel too much like a rapid change was being forced on them. Program I allows stores to opt out of the new idea and stay the course, with employees having little to no information or opportunities for participation. Program II tracks employee absence and sick leave and shares that information with individual employees, giving them feedback about things they can control. Management takes no further action. Program III tracks sales and inventory replacement rates across shifts. As in Program II, information is shared with employees, but without providing employee feedback about absence and sick leave. Program IV, the most comprehensive, tracks the same information as Programs II and III. Managers communicate it in weekly brainstorming sessions, during which employees try to determine what they can do better in the future and make suggestions for improving store performance. Program V keeps the idea of brainstorming but does not provide employees with information about their behaviour or company profits.

Since implementing the system, Brooks has spoken with several store managers about what motivated them to choose the program they did. Michael Brewer, who chose Program IV, said, "I want to have my employees' input on how to keep the store running smoothly. Everybody worries about their job security in this economy. Letting them know what's going on and giving them ways to change things keeps them involved."

Linda Meilleur could not disagree more. She selected Program I. "I would rather have my employees doing their jobs than going to meetings to talk about doing their jobs. That's what management is for." Owen Robertson, another proponent of Program I, added, "It's okay for the employees to feel a little uncertain—if they think we're in

the clear, they'll slack off. If they think we're in trouble, they'll give up."

Fabrice Lamothe also questions the need to provide information to the whole team, but he chose Program II. "A person should know where he or she stands in the job, but they don't have to know about everyone else. It creates unnecessary tension."

This is somewhat similar to Ben Wu's reason for picking Program V. "When we have our brainstorming meetings, I learn what they [the employees] think is most pressing, not what some spreadsheet says. It gives me a better feel for what's going on in my store. Numbers count, of course, but they don't tell you everything. I was also a little worried that employees would be upset if they saw that we aren't performing well."

Results to Date

Brooks is convinced that the most elaborate procedure (Program IV) is the most effective, but not everyone in the executive committee is won over by her advocacy. Although they have supported the test implementation of the system because it appears to have relatively low costs, others on the committee want to see results and think the approach is overly complicated for an operation of the company's size. CEO Madison Sanwald has asked for a complete breakdown of the performance of the various stores over the past four years. She is especially interested in seeing how sales figures and turnover rates have been affected by the new program.

The company's data on sales and turnover rates appear below, with estimates of the dollar cost of staff time taken up in each method. These costs are based on the number of hours employees spend working on the program multiplied by their wage rate. Estimates of turnover, profit, and staff time are collected per store. Profit and turnover data include means and standard deviations across locations; profit is net of the monthly time cost. Turnover information refers to the percentage of employees who either quit or are terminated in a month.

To see if any patterns emerged in managers' selection of programs, the company calculated relationships between program selection and various attributes of the stores. Program I was selected most frequently by the oldest stores and those in the most economically distressed areas. Programs II and III were selected most frequently by the stores in comparatively larger communities and those in areas where the workforce was younger. Programs IV and V were selected most frequently for stores located in isolated

Program	Methods	# of Stores	Average Turnover	Weekly Profit per Month	Monthly Staff Time Cost		
Program I	Traditional management	37	Mean = 30%	SD = 10%	Mean = $5700	SD = $3000	None
Program II	Share absence and sick leave	16	Mean = 23%	SD = 14%	Mean = $7000	SD = $5800	$1960
Program III	Share sales and inventory	15	Mean = 37%	SD = 20%	Mean = $11 000	SD = $2700	$2440
Program IV	Share information and brainstorm	29	Mean = 17%	SD = 20%	Mean = $13 000	SD = $3400	$3420
Program V	Brainstorm without sharing information	36	Mean = 21%	SD = 12%	Mean = $14 000	SD = $2400	$2750

rural areas, especially when the workforce was older on average.

Discussion Questions

1. Consider the five programs as variables in an experiment. Identify the independent and dependent variables and explain how they are related to one another.

2. Based on the discussion of independent and dependent variables in the textbook, is there anything else you would like to measure as an outcome?

3. Which program appears most effective in generating revenues and reducing turnover? Why? Which program(s) appear least effective, and why?

4. How does the changing nature of the workforce and the economy, described in your textbook and in the case, affect your conclusions about how to manage retail employees? Does the participation of a more experienced workforce help or hurt these programs? Why might these programs work differently in an economy that is not doing so poorly?

5. Brooks essentially designed the different programs on her own, with very little research into goal setting and motivation. How well would you say she has done? Which programs appear to fit well with research evidence on goal setting? What programs would you change to achieve more substantial improvements in employee motivation?

6. Describe how employees' feelings might affect the implementation of these programs. What advice would you give managers about how to implement the programs so they match the principles of organizational justice?

ENDNOTES

Chapter 1

1 Vignette based on C. Atchison, "The Gen Y Whisperer," PROFIT, June 1, 2011, http://www.profitguide.com/article/28252—the-gen-y-whisperer—page0; thanks to Grail Noble for her input.

2 See, for instance, C. Heath and S. B. Sitkin, "Big-B versus Big-O: What Is *Organizational* about Organizational Behavior?" *Journal of Organizational Behavior* 22 (2001), pp. 43–58. For a review of what one eminent researcher believes *should* be included in organizational behaviour, based on survey data, see J. B. Miner, "The Rated Importance, Scientific Validity, and Practical Usefulness of Organizational Behavior Theories: A Quantitative Review," *Academy of Management Learning & Education* 2, no. 3 (September 2003), pp. 250–268.

3 Statistics Canada, *Canada Year Book 2010 Edition* (Ottawa: Minister of Industry, 2010).

4 C. R. Farquhar and J. A. Longair, *Creating High-Performance Organizations with People*, Report R164–96 (Ottawa: The Conference Board of Canada, 1996).

5 W. Immen, "People Skills Win Out, Survey Finds," *Globe and Mail*, October 23, 2009, p. B15.

6 See, for instance, C. Penttila, "Hiring Hardships," *Entrepreneur*, October 2002, pp. 34–35.

7 These companies were named in the 100 Top Employers for 2010. See D. Jermyn, "Canada's Top 100 Employers," *Globe and Mail*, October 14, 2010, http://www.theglobeandmail.com/report-on-business/managing/top-employers-2011/canadas-top-100-employers/article1757599/

8 I. S. Fulmer, B. Gerhart, and K. S. Scott, "Are the 100 Best Better? An Empirical Investigation of the Relationship Between Being a 'Great Place to Work' and Firm Performance," *Personnel Psychology*, Winter 2003, pp. 965–993.

9 S. E. Humphrey, J. D. Nahrgang, and F. P. Morgeson, "Integrating Motivational, Social, and Contextual Work Design Features: A Meta-analytic Summary and Theoretical Extension of the Work Design Literature," *Journal of Applied Psychology* 92, no. 5 (2007), pp. 1332–1356.

10 *The 2002 National Study of the Changing Workforce* (New York: Families and Work Institute, 2002).

11 Vignette based on C. Atchison, "The Gen Y Whisperer," *PROFIT*, June 1, 2011, http://www.profitguide.com/article/28252—the-gen-y-whisperer—page0

12 J. Morrissy, "Canadian Workers among Most Dissatisfied in World," *Vancouver Sun*, June 25, 2011; and B. Lindenberg, "Employee Engagement: Do Benefits Make a Difference?" *Benefits Canada*, July 28, 2011, http://www.benefitscanada.com/benefits/other/employee-engagement-do-employee-benefits-make-a-difference-18960

13 T. A. Judge, C. J. Thoresen, J. E. Bono, and G. R. Patton, "The Job Satisfaction–Job Performance Relationship: A Qualitative and Quantitative Review," *Psychological Bulletin* 127 (2001), pp. 376–407; and M. Riketta, "The Causal Relation between Job Attitudes and Performance: A Meta-analysis of Panel Studies," *Journal of Applied Psychology* 93, no. 2 (2008), pp. 472–481.

14 "2011 Best Workplaces in Canada," Great Places to Work, http://www.greatplacetowork.ca/news/index.php?date=1494; and http://www.microsoft.com/canada/potential/investing_in_canadian_communities.aspx

15 S. C. Payne and S. S. Webber, "Effects of Service Provider Attitudes and Employment Status on Citizenship Behaviors and Customers' Attitudes and Loyalty Behavior," *Journal of Applied Psychology* 91, no. 2 (2006), pp. 365–378; and H. Liao and D. E. Rupp, "The Impact of Justice Climate and Justice Orientation on Work Outcomes: A Cross-Level Multifoci Framework," *Journal of Applied Psychology* 90, no. 2 (2005), pp. 242–256.

16 G. Lowe, *21st Century Job Quality: Achieving What Canadians Want*, Report 48485 (Ottawa: Canadian Policy Research Networks, 2007).

17 B. Dumaine, "The New Non-Manager Managers," *Fortune*, February 22, 1993, pp. 80–84.

18 "Wanted: Teammates, Crew Members, and Cast Members: But No Employees," *Wall Street Journal*, April 30, 1996, p. A1.

19 C. Atchison, "Secrets of Canada's Best Bosses," PROFIT, February 16, 2011, http://www.profitguide.com/article/10103—secrets-of-canada-s-best-bosses

20 D. M. Mayer, M. Kuenzi, R. Greenbaum, M. Bardes, and R. Salvador, "How Low Does Ethical Leadership Flow? Test of a Trickle-Down Model," *Organizational Behavior and Human Decision Processes* 108, no. 1 (2009), pp. 1–13; and A. Ardichvili, J. A. Mitchell, and D. Jondle, "Characteristics of Ethical Business Cultures," *Journal of Business Ethics* 85, no. 4 (2009), pp. 445–451.

21 The Conference Board of Canada, *Employability Skills* 2000+ (Ottawa: The Conference Board of Canada, 2000).

22 T. Belford, "Strategy for the New Economy," *Financial Post (National Post)*, March 14, 2005, p. FP9.

23 From G. Johnson, "Bombardier: Giving Women Wings," *Globe and Mail*, February 20, 2011, http://www.theglobeandmail.com/report-on-business/managing/top-employers/best-diversity-employers-2011/bombardier-giving-women-wings/article1913886/

24 See, for instance, R. R. Thomas Jr., "From Affirmative Action to Affirming Diversity," *Harvard Business Review*, March–April 1990, pp. 107–117; B. Mandrell and S. Kohler-Gray, "Management Development That Values Diversity," *Personnel*, March 1990, pp. 41–47; J. Dreyfuss, "Get Ready for the New Work Force," *Fortune*, April 23, 1990, pp. 165–181; and I. Wielawski, "Diversity Makes Both Dollars and Sense," *Los Angeles Times*, May 16, 1994, p. II3.

25 Based on http://www.eluta.ca/diversity-at-sgi; http://www.sgi.sk.ca/careers/whatweoffer.html; and K.-A. Riess, "SGI among Top 100 Diversity Employers," *StarPhoenix*, April 5, 2008, p. F12.

26 June 2011 figures, as reported at http://www.statcan.gc.ca/subjects-sujets/labour-travail/lfs-epa/t110708a2-eng.htm

27 See, for instance, M. Workman and W. Bommer, "Rede Signing Computer Call Center Work: A Longitudinal Field Experiment," *Journal of Organizational Behavior*, May 2004, pp. 317–337.

28 Statistics Canada, "Study: Temporary Employment in the Downturn (1997–2009)," *The Daily*, November 26, 2010, http://www.statcan.gc.ca/daily-quotidien/101126/dq101126b-eng.htm

29 http://www.statcan.gc.ca/subjects-sujets/labour-travail/lfs-epa/t110708a1-eng.htm

30 Seasonally adjusted numbers. See Statistics Canada, "Study: Temporary Employment in the Downturn (1997–2009)," *The Daily*, November 26, 2010, http://www.statcan.gc.ca/daily-quotidien/101126/dq101126b-eng.htm

31 Statistics Canada, "Study: Temporary Employment in the Downturn (1997–2009)," *The Daily*, November 26, 2010, http://www.statcan.gc.ca/daily-quotidien/101126/dq101126b-eng.htm

32 H. Evanschitzky, C. Groening, V. Mittal, and M. Wunderlich, "How Employer and Employee Satisfaction Affect Customer Satisfaction: An Application to Franchise Services," *Journal of Service Research* 14, no. 2 (2010), p. 136.

33 A. J. Rucci, S. P. Kirn, and R. T. Quinn, "The Employee–Customer–Profit Chain at Sears," *Harvard Business Review*, January–February 1998, pp. 83–97.

34 Statistics Canada, "Study: Work Absences in 2010," *The Daily*, May 25, 2011, http://www.statcan.gc.ca/daily-quotidien/110525/dq110525e-eng.htm

35 A. Mayeda, "Absenteeism Balloons in Canada's Federal Public Service," *Vancouver Sun*, November 12, 2010, http://www.canada.com/numbers+Data+growing+absenteeism+across+federal+government/3821393/story.html#ixzz15BHJ8uvV

36 http://www.bls.gov/data

37 D. W. Organ, *Organizational Citizenship Behavior: The Good Soldier Syndrome* (Lexington, MA: Lexington Books, 1988), p. 4.

38 M. G. Ehrhart and S. E. Naumann, "Organizational Citizenship Behavior in Work Groups: A Group Norms Approach," *Journal of Applied Psychology* 89, no. 6 (2004), pp. 960–974.

39 "Corporate Culture," *Canadian HR Reporter* 17, no. 21 (2004), pp. 7–11.

40 See, for example, P. M. Podsakoff, S. B. MacKenzie, J. B. Paine, and D. G. Bachrach, "Organizational Citizenship Behaviors: A Critical Review of the Theoretical and Empirical Literature and Suggestions for Future Research," *Journal of Management* 26, no. 3 (2000), pp. 543–548; and S. W. Whiting, P. M. Podsakoff, and J. R. Pierce, "Effects of Task Performance, Helping, Voice, and Organizational Loyalty on Performance Appraisal Ratings," *Journal of Applied Psychology* 93, no. 1 (2008), pp. 125–139.

41 See, for instance, V. S. Major, K. J. Klein, and M. G. Ehrhart, "Work Time, Work Interference with Family, and Psychological Distress," *Journal of Applied Psychology*, June 2002, pp. 427–436; D. Brady, "Rethinking the Rat Race," *BusinessWeek*, August 26, 2002, pp. 142–143; and J. M. Brett and L. K. Stroh, "Working 61 Plus Hours a Week: Why Do Managers Do It?" *Journal of Applied Psychology*, February 2003, pp. 67–78.

42 See, for instance, *The 2002 National Study of the Changing Workforce* (New York: Families and Work Institute, 2002).

43 Cited in S. Armour, "Workers Put Family First Despite Slow Economy, Jobless Fears," *USA Today*, June 6, 2002.

44 S. Shellenbarger, "What Job Candidates Really Want to Know: Will I Have a Life?" *Wall Street Journal*, November 17, 1999, p. B1; and "U.S. Employers Polish Image to Woo a Demanding New Generation," *Manpower Argus*, February 2000, p. 2.

45 C. Hymowitz, "CEOs Value Pragmatists with Broad, Positive Views," *Wall Street Journal*, January 27, 2003.

46 F. Luthans and C. M. Youssef, "Emerging Positive Organizational Behavior," *Journal of Management*, June 2007, pp. 321–349; C. M. Youssef and F. Luthans, "Positive Organizational Behavior in the Workplace: The Impact of Hope, Optimism, and Resilience," *Journal of Management* 33, no. 5 (2007), pp. 774–

800; J. E. Dutton and S. Sonenshein, "Positive Organizational Scholarship," in *Encyclopedia of Positive Psychology*, ed. C. Cooper and J. Barling (Thousand Oaks, CA: Sage, 2007); A. M. Saks and J. A. Gruman, "Organizational Socialization and Positive Organizational Behaviour: Implications for Theory, Research, and Practice," *Canadian Journal of Administrative Sciences* 28, no. 1 (2011), pp. 4–16; and E. K. Loway, "Positive Organizational Scholarship," *Canadian Journal of Administrative Sciences* 28, no. 1 (2011), pp. 1–3.

47 L. M. Roberts, G. Spreitzer, J. Dutton, R. Quinn, E. Heaphy, and B. Barker, "How to Play to Your Strengths," *Harvard Business Review*, January 2005, pp. 1–6; and L. M. Roberts, J. E. Dutton, G. M. Spreitzer, E. D. Heaphy, and R. E. Quinn, "Composing the Reflected Best-Self Portrait: Becoming Extraordinary in Work Organizations," *Academy of Management Review* 30, no. 4 (2005), pp. 712–736.

48 Based on "Yum! China," Yum! Brands, http://www.yum.com/company/china.asp

49 D. Flavelle, "Rona Sees Growth Here: Home Reno Sales Flat during Make-or-Break Season but Canadian Retailer Keeps Faith in Diversification," *Toronto Star*, April 20, 2011, p. B1.

50 Vignette based on C. Atchison, "The Gen Y Whisperer," *PROFIT*, June 1, 2011, http://www.profitguide.com/article/28252—the-gen-y-whisperer—page0

51 M. Warner, "Organizational Behavior Revisited," *Human Relations*, October 1994, pp. 1151–1166.

52 Based on W. Chuang and B. Lee, "An Empirical Evaluation of the Overconfidence Hypothesis," *Journal of Banking and Finance*, September 2006, pp. 2489–2515; and A. R. Drake, J. Wong, and S. B. Salter, "Empowerment, Motivation, and Performance: Examining the Impact of Feedback and Incentives on Nonmanagement Employees," *Behavioral Research in Accounting* 19 (2007), pp. 71–89.

53 D. M. Rousseau and S. McCarthy, "Educating Managers from an Evidence-Based Perspective," *Academy of Management Learning & Education* 6, no. 1 (2007), pp. 84–101; and S. L. Rynes, T. L. Giluk, and K. G. Brown, "The Very Separate Worlds of Academic and Practitioner Periodicals in Human Resource Management: Implications for Evidence-Based Management," *Academy of Management Journal* 50, no. 5 (2007), pp. 987–1008.

54 K. Holland, "Inside the Minds of Your Employees," *New Yorker*, January 28, 2007.

55 J. Surowiecki, "The Fatal-Flaw Myth," *New Yorker*, July 31, 2006, p. 25.

56 Based on "Lying at Work Could Get You Fired," *UPI*, March 5, 2006; "Brain Scans Detect More Activity in Those Who Lie," *Reuters*, November 29, 2004; and P. Ekman and E. L. Rosenberg, *What the Face Reveals: Basic and Applied Studies of Spontaneous Expression Using the Facial Action Coding System (CAPS)*, 2nd ed. (New York: Oxford University Press, 2004).

57 Based on K. H. Hammonds, "Handle with Care," *Fast Company*, August 2002, pp. 103–107.

58 Based on R. R. Hastings, "Metrics Drive Winning Culture," *SHRM*, April 9, 2007, http://www.shrm.org; K. Bensinger, "Ford's Loss Sparks Optimism," *Los Angeles Times*, April 24, 2009; T. Talukdar and A. Ghosh, "IT Companies Grow on to Bigger-Sized Projects," *Economic Times*, June 16, 2008, http://economictimes.indiatimes.com

59 R. E. Quinn, *Beyond Rational Management: Mastering the Paradoxes and Competing Demands of High Performance* (San Francisco: Jossey-Bass, 1991); R. E. Quinn, S. R. Faerman, M. P. Thompson, and M. R. McGrath, *Becoming a Master Manager: A Competency Framework* (New York: Wiley, 1990); K. Cameron and R. E. Quinn, *Diagnosing and Changing Organizational Culture: Based on*

the Competing Values Framework (Reading, MA: Addison Wesley Longman, 1999).

60 R. E. Quinn, S. R. Faerman, M. P. Thompson, and M. R. McGrath, *Becoming a Master Manager: A Competency Framework* (New York: Wiley, 1990).

61 D. Maley, "Canada's Top Women CEOs," *Maclean's,* October 20, 1997, pp. 52 passim.

62 Written by Nancy Langton and Joy Begley, copyright 1999. (The events described are based on an actual situation, although the participants, as well as the centre, have been disguised.)

Chapter 2

1 Vignette based on http://www.retailcouncil.org/news/media/press/2007/pr20070516.asp; "Wal-Mart Canada Named One of Canada's Best Employers," http://www.newswire.ca/en/releases/archive/January2007/02/c2780.html; "Walmart Canada to Open First Supercentre in Manitoba," *Canada NewsWire,* May 12, 2011; and C. Persaud, "Walmart Canada to Face Steep Competition Once Target Arrives," *MarketNews,* July 8, 2011, http://www.marketnews.ca/LatestNewsHeadlines/WalmartCanadatoFaceSteepCompetitionOnceTargetArrives.html; and http://www.workplaceinstitute.org/press-releases/2011-best-employers-awards-winners/

2 B. Nyhan and J. Reifler, "When Corrections Fail: The Persistence of Political Misperceptions" *Political Behavior* 32, no. 2 (2010), pp. 303–330.

3 D. Wood, P. Harms, and S. Vazire, "Perceiver Effects as Projective Tests: What Your Perceptions of Others Say About You," *Journal of Personality and Social Psychology* 99, no. 1 (2010), pp. 174–190.

4 H. H. Kelley, "Attribution in Social Interaction," in *Attribution: Perceiving the Causes of Behavior,* ed. E. Jones, D. Kanouse, H. Kelley, N. Nisbett, S. Valins, and B. Weiner (Morristown, NJ: General Learning Press, 1972).

5 See L. Ross, "The Intuitive Psychologist and His Shortcomings," in *Advances in Experimental Social Psychology,* vol. 10, ed. L. Berkowitz (Orlando, FL: Academic Press, 1977), pp. 174–220; and A. G. Miller and T. Lawson, "The Effect of an Informational Option on the Fundamental Attribution Error," *Personality and Social Psychology Bulletin,* June 1989, pp. 194–204.

6 M. J. Young, M. W. Morris, and V. M. Scherwin, "Managerial Mystique: Magical Thinking in Judgments of Managers' Vision, Charisma, and Magnetism," *Journal of Management,* May 2011, published online before print, http://jom.sagepub.com/content/early/2011/04/29/0149206311406284

7 Columbia Business School, "Dynamics behind Magical Thinking and Charismatic Leadership Revealed," *ScienceDaily,* July 15, 2011.

8 N. Epley and D. Dunning, "Feeling 'Holier Than Thou': Are Self-Serving Assessments Produced by Errors in Self- or Social Predictions?" *Journal of Personality and Social Psychology* 79, no. 6 (2000), pp. 861–875.

9 M. C. Frame, K. J. Roberto, A. E. Schwab, and C. T. Harris, "What Is Important on the Job? Differences across Gender, Perspective, and Job Level," *Journal of Applied Social Psychology* 40, no. 1 (January 2010), pp. 36–56.

10 Based on N. Hall, "Lawyer Awarded $100,000 by B.C. Human Rights Tribunal for Discrimination," *Vancouver Sun,* July 18, 2011; and *Gichuru v. The Law Society of British Columbia* (No. 9), 2011 BCHRT 185, http://bit.ly/ndnd4O

11 See K. R. Murphy, R. A. Jako, and R. L. Anhalt, "Nature and Consequences of Halo Error: A Critical Analysis," *Journal of Applied Psychology,* April 1993, pp. 218–225; P. Rosenzweig, *The Halo Effect* (New York: Free Press, 2007); I. Dennis, "Halo Effects

in Grading Student Projects," *Journal of Applied Psychology* 92, no. 4 (2007), pp. 1169–1176; and C. E. Naquin and R. O. Tynan, "The Team Halo Effect: Why Teams Are Not Blamed for Their Failures," *Journal of Applied Psychology,* April 2003, pp. 332–340.

12 S. E. Asch, "Forming Impressions of Personality," *Journal of Abnormal and Social Psychology,* July 1946, pp. 258–290.

13 http://www.timescolonist.com/entertainment/UVic+grad+student+launches+First+Nations+music+website/5594608/story.html#ixzz1bugKFx8q

14 See, for example, G. N. Powell, "The Good Manager: Business Students' Stereotypes of Japanese Managers versus Stereotypes of American Managers," *Group & Organization Management,* March 1992, pp. 44–56; C. Ostroff and L. E. Atwater, "Does Whom You Work with Matter? Effects of Referent Group Gender and Age Composition on Managers' Compensation," *Journal of Applied Psychology,* August 2003, pp. 725–740; M. E. Heilman, A. S. Wallen, D. Fuchs, and M. M. Tamkins, "Penalties for Success: Reactions to Women Who Succeed at Male Gender-Typed Tasks," *Journal of Applied Psychology,* June 2004, pp. 416–427; and R. A. Posthuma and M. A. Campion, "Age Stereotypes in the Workplace: Common Stereotypes, Moderators, and Future Research Directions," *Journal of Management* 35, no. 1 (2009), pp. 158–188.

15 J. L. Eberhardt, P. G. Davies, V. J. Purdie-Vaughns, and S. L. Johnson, "Looking Deathworthy: Perceived Stereotypicality of Black Defendants Predicts Capital-Sentencing Outcomes," *Psychological Science* 17, no. 5 (2006), pp. 383–386.

16 J. D. Remedios, A. L. Chasteen, and J. D. Paek, "Not All Prejudices Are Experienced Equally: Comparing Experiences of Racism and Sexism in Female Minorities," *Group Processes & Intergroup Relations,* June 11, 2011, published online before print, http://gpi.sagepub.com/content/early/2011/06/17/1368430211411594

17 K. A. Martin, A. R. Sinden, and J. C. Fleming, "Inactivity May Be Hazardous to Your Image: The Effects of Exercise Participation on Impression Formation," *Journal of Sport & Exercise Psychology* 22, no. 4 (December 2000), pp. 283–291.

18 F. Yuan and R. W. Woodman, "Innovative Behavior in the Workplace: The Role of Performance and Image Outcome Expectations," *Academy of Management Journal* 53, no. 2 (2010), pp. 323–342.

19 J. K. Harter, F. L. Schmidt, J. W. Asplund, E. A. Killham, and S. Agrawal, "Causal Impact of Employee Work Perceptions on the Bottom Line of Organizations," *Perspectives on Psychological Science* 5, no. 4 (2010), p. 378–389.

20 Y. H. Kim, C. Y. Chiu, and Z. Zou, "Know Thyself: Misperceptions of Actual Performance Undermine Achievement Motivation, Future Performance, and Subjective Well-Being," *Journal of Personality and Social Psychology* 99, no. 3 (2010), pp. 395–409.

21 H. G. Heneman III and T. A. Judge, *Staffing Organizations* (Middleton, WI: Mendota House, 2006).

22 J. Willis and A. Todorov, "First Impressions: Making Up Your Mind after a 100ms Exposure to a Face," *Psychological Science,* July 2006, pp. 592–598.

23 See, for example, E. C. Webster, *Decision Making in the Employment Interview* (Montreal: McGill University, Industrial Relations Center, 1964).

24 See, for example, K. F. E. Wong and J. Y. Y. Kwong, "Effects of Rater Goals on Rating Patterns: Evidence from an Experimental Field Study," *Journal of Applied Psychology* 92, no. 2 (2007), pp. 577–585; and S. E. DeVoe and S. S. Iyengar, "Managers' Theories of Subordinates: A Cross-Cultural Examination of Manager Perceptions of Motivation and Appraisal of Performance," *Organizational Behavior and Human Decision Processes,* January 2004, pp. 47–61.

25 D. B. McNatt and T. A. Judge, "Boundary Conditions of the Galatea Effect: A Field Experiment and Constructive Replication," *Academy of Management Journal*, August 2004, pp. 550–565; O. B. Davidson and D. Eden, "Remedial Self-Fulfilling Prophecy: Two Field Experiments to Prevent Golem Effects among Disadvantaged Women," *Journal of Applied Psychology*, June 2000, pp. 386–398; D. Eden, "Self-Fulfilling Prophecies in Organizations," in *Organizational Behavior: The State of the Science*, 2nd ed., ed. J. Greenberg (Mahwah, NJ: Lawrence Erlbaum, 2003), pp. 91–122; and G. Natanovich and D. Eden, "Pygmalion Effects among Outreach Supervisors and Tutors: Extending Sex Generalizability," *Journal of Applied Psychology* 93, no. 6 (2008), pp. 1382–1389.

26 See, for example, K. F. E. Wong and J. Y. Y. Kwong, "Effects of Rater Goals on Rating Patterns: Evidence from an Experimental Field Study," *Journal of Applied Psychology* 92, no. 2 (2007), pp. 577–585; and S. E. DeVoe and S. S. Iyengar, "Managers' Theories of Subordinates: A Cross-Cultural Examination of Manager Perceptions of Motivation and Appraisal of Performance," *Organizational Behavior and Human Decision Processes*, January 2004, pp. 47–61.

27 Vignette based on "Personality Counts: Walmart's Frugal, but Target Charms," *CNNMoney*, August 19, 2011, http://management.fortune.cnn.com/2011/08/19/personality-counts-walmart-is-frugal-but-target-charms/; and "Target Plans up to 135 Canadian Stores by 2013," *Toronto Star*, September 23, 2011, http://www.thestar.com/business/article/1058457—target-finalizes-its-canadian-stores-inks-deal-with-sobeys

28 G. W. Allport, *Personality: A Psychological Interpretation* (New York: Holt, Rinehart and Winston, 1937), p. 48.

29 K. I. van der Zee, J. N. Zaal, and J. Piekstra, "Validation of the Multicultural Personality Questionnaire in the Context of Personnel Selection," *European Journal of Personality* 17 (2003), pp. S77–S100.

30 S. A. Birkeland, T. M. Manson, J. L. Kisamore, M. T. Brannick, and M. A. Smith, "A Meta-analytic Investigation of Job Applicant Faking on Personality Measures," *International Journal of Selection and Assessment* 14, no. 14 (2006), pp. 317–335.

31 T. A. Judge, C. A. Higgins, C. J. Thoresen, and M. R. Barrick, "The Big Five Personality Traits, General Mental Ability, and Career Success across the Life Span," *Personnel Psychology* 52, no. 3 (1999), pp. 621–652.

32 See D. T. Lykken, T. J. Bouchard Jr., M. McGue, and A. Tellegen, "Heritability of Interests: A Twin Study," *Journal of Applied Psychology*, August 1993, pp. 649–661; R. D. Arvey and T. J. Bouchard Jr., "Genetics, Twins, and Organizational Behavior," in *Research in Organizational Behavior*, vol.16, ed. B. M. Staw and L. L. Cummings (Greenwich, CT: JAI Press, 1994), pp. 65–66; D. Lykken and A. Tellegen, "Happiness Is a Stochastic Phenomenon," *Psychological Science*, May 1996, pp. 186–189; and W. Wright, *Born That Way: Genes, Behavior, Personality* (New York: Knopf, 1998).

33 S. Srivastava, O. P. John, and S. D. Gosling, "Development of Personality in Early and Middle Adulthood: Set Like Plaster or Persistent Change?" *Journal of Personality and Social Psychology*, May 2003, pp. 1041–1053; and B. W. Roberts, K. E. Walton, and W. Viechtbauer, "Patterns of Mean-Level Change in Personality Traits across the Life Course: A Meta-analysis of Longitudinal Studies," *Psychological Bulletin* 132, no. 1 (2006), pp. 1–25.

34 S. E. Hampson and L. R. Goldberg, "A First Large Cohort Study of Personality Trait Stability over the 40 Years between Elementary School and Midlife," *Journal of Personality and Social Psychology* 91, no. 4 (2006), pp. 763–779.

35 See A. H. Buss, "Personality as Traits," *American Psychologist*, November 1989, pp. 1378–1388; and D. G. Winter, O. P. John,

A. J. Stewart, E. C. Klohnen, and L. E. Duncan, "Traits and Motives: Toward an Integration of Two Traditions in Personality Research," *Psychological Review*, April 1998, pp. 230–250.

36 See, for instance, G. W. Allport and H. S. Odbert, "Trait Names, A Psycholexical Study," *Psychological Monographs* 47, no. 211 (1936); and R. B. Cattell, "Personality Pinned Down," *Psychology Today*, July 1973, pp. 40–46.

37 R. B. Kennedy and D. A. Kennedy, "Using the Myers-Briggs Type Indicator in Career Counseling," *Journal of Employment Counseling*, March 2004, pp. 38–44.

38 G. N. Landrum, *Profiles of Genius* (New York: Prometheus, 1993).

39 See, for instance, D. J. Pittenger, "Cautionary Comments Regarding the Myers-Briggs Type Indicator," *Consulting Psychology Journal: Practice and Research*, Summer 2005, pp. 210–221; L. Bess and R. J. Harvey, "Bimodal Score Distributions and the Myers-Briggs Type Indicator: Fact or Artifact?" *Journal of Personality Assessment*, February 2002, pp. 176–186; R. M. Capraro and M. M. Capraro, "Myers-Briggs Type Indicator Score Reliability across Studies: A Meta-analytic Reliability Generalization Study," *Educational and Psychological Measurement*, August 2002, pp. 590–602; and R. C. Arnau, B. A. Green, D. H. Rosen, D. H. Gleaves, and J. G. Melancon, "Are Jungian Preferences Really Categorical? An Empirical Investigation Using Taxometric Analysis," *Personality and Individual Differences*, January 2003, pp. 233–251.

40 See, for example, J. M. Digman, "Personality Structure: Emergence of the Five-Factor Model," in *Annual Review of Psychology*, vol. 41, ed. M. R. Rosenzweig and L. W. Porter (Palo Alto, CA: Annual Reviews, 1990), pp. 417–440; D. B. Smith, P. J. Hanges, and M. W. Dickson, "Personnel Selection and the Five-Factor Model: Reexamining the Effects of Applicant's Frame of Reference," *Journal of Applied Psychology*, April 2001, pp. 304–315; and M. R. Barrick and M. K. Mount, "Yes, Personality Matters: Moving On to More Important Matters," *Human Performance* 18, no. 4 (2005), pp. 359–372.

41 J. B. Hirsh and J. B. Peterson, "Predicting Creativity and Academic Success with a 'Fake-Proof' Measure of the Big Five," *Journal of Research in Personality* 42 (2008), pp. 1323–1333.

42 "New Fake-Proof Personality Test Created," *ScienceDaily*, October 8, 2008, http://www.sciencedaily.com/releases/2008/10/081007102849.htm

43 See, for instance, M. R. Barrick and M. K. Mount, "The Big Five Personality Dimensions and Job Performance: A Meta-analysis," *Personnel Psychology*, Spring 1991, pp. 1–26; G. M. Hurtz and J. J. Donovan, "Personality and Job Performance: The Big Five Revisited," *Journal of Applied Psychology*, December 2000, pp. 869–879; J. Hogan and B. Holland, "Using Theory to Evaluate Personality and Job-Performance Relations: A Socioanalytic Perspective," *Journal of Applied Psychology*, February 2003, pp. 100–112; and M. R. Barrick and M. K. Mount, "Select on Conscientiousness and Emotional Stability," in *Handbook of Principles of Organizational Behavior*, ed. E. A. Locke (Malden, MA: Blackwell, 2004), pp. 15–28.

44 M. K. Mount, M. R. Barrick, and J. P. Strauss, "Validity of Observer Ratings of the Big Five Personality Factors," *Journal of Applied Psychology*, April 1994, p. 272. Additionally confirmed by G. M. Hurtz and J. J. Donovan, "Personality and Job Performance: The Big Five Revisited," *Journal of Applied Psychology* 85 (2000), pp. 869–879; and M. R. Barrick, M. K. Mount, and T. A. Judge, "The FFM Personality Dimensions and Job Performance: Meta-analysis of Meta-analyses," *International Journal of Selection and Assessment* 9 (2001), pp. 9–30.

45 A. E. Poropat, "A Meta-analysis of the Five-Factor Model of Personality and Academic Performance," *Psychological Bulletin* 135, no. 2 (2009), pp. 322–338.

46 F. L. Schmidt and J. E. Hunter, "The Validity and Utility of Selection Methods in *Personnel Psychology*: Practical and Theoretical Implications of 85 Years of Research Findings," *Psychological Bulletin*, September 1998, p. 272.

47 R. J. Foti and M. A. Hauenstein, "Pattern and Variable Approaches in Leadership Emergence and Effectiveness," *Journal of Applied Psychology*, March 2007, pp. 347–355.

48 L. I. Spirling and R. Persaud, "Extraversion as a Risk Factor," *Journal of the American Academy of Child and Adolescent Psychiatry* 42, no. 2 (2003), p. 130.

49 B. Weiss and R. S. Feldman, "Looking Good and Lying to Do It: Deception as an Impression Management Strategy in Job Interviews," *Journal of Applied Social Psychology* 36, no. 4 (2006), pp. 1070–1086.

50 J. A. LePine, J. A. Colquitt, and A. Erez, "Adaptability to Changing Task Contexts: Effects of General Cognitive Ability, Conscientiousness, and Openness to Experience," *Personnel Psychology* 53 (2000), pp. 563–595.

51 S. Clarke and I. Robertson, "An Examination of the Role of Personality in Accidents Using Meta-analysis," *Applied Psychology: An International Review* 57, no. 1 (2008), pp. 94–108.

52 B. Laursen, L. Pulkkinen, and R. Adams, "The Antecedents and Correlates of Agreeableness in Adulthood," *Developmental Psychology* 38, no. 4 (2002), pp. 591–603.

53 B. Barry and R. A. Friedman, "Bargainer Characteristics in Distributive and Integrative Negotiation," *Journal of Personality and Social Psychology*, February 1998, pp. 345–359.

54 T. Bogg and B. W. Roberts, "Conscientiousness and Health-Related Behaviors: A Meta-analysis of the Leading Behavioral Contributors to Mortality," *Psychological Bulletin* 130, no. 6 (2004), pp. 887–919.

55 S. Lee and H. J. Klein, "Relationships between Conscientiousness, Self-Efficacy, Self-Deception, and Learning over Time," *Journal of Applied Psychology* 87, no. 6 (2002), pp. 1175–1182; and G. J. Feist, "A Meta-analysis of Personality in Scientific and Artistic Creativity," *Personality and Social Psychology Review* 2, no. 4 (1998), pp. 290–309.

56 T. A. Judge and J. E. Bono, "A Rose by Any Other Name . . . Are Self-Esteem, Generalized Self-Efficacy, Neuroticism, and Locus of Control Indicators of a Common Construct?" in *Personality Psychology in the Workplace*, ed. B. W. Roberts and R. Hogan, pp. 93–118 (Washington, DC: American Psychological Association); and A. M. Grant and A. Wrzesniewski "I Won't Let You Down . . . or Will I? Core Self-Evaluations, Other-Orientation, Anticipated Guilt and Gratitude, and Job Performance," *Journal of Applied Psychology* 95, no. 1 (2010), pp. 108–121.

57 A. Erez and T. A. Judge, "Relationship of Core Self-Evaluations to Goal Setting, Motivation, and Performance," *Journal of Applied Psychology* 86, no. 6 (2001), pp. 1270–1279.

58 A. N. Salvaggio, B. Schneider, L. H. Nishi, D. M. Mayer, A. Ramesh, and J. S. Lyon, "Manager Personality, Manager Service Quality Orientation, and Service Climate: Test of a Model," *Journal of Applied Psychology* 92, no. 6 (2007), pp. 1741–1750; B. A. Scott and T. A. Judge, "The Popularity Contest at Work: Who Wins, Why, and What Do They Receive?" *Journal of Applied Psychology* 94, no. 1 (2009), pp. 20–33; and T. A. Judge and C. Hurst, "How the Rich (and Happy) Get Richer (and Happier): Relationship of Core Self-Evaluations to Trajectories in Attaining Work Success," *Journal of Applied Psychology* 93, no. 4 (2008), pp. 849–863.

59 U. Malmendier and G. Tate, "CEO Overconfidence and Corporate Investment," *Journal of Finance* 60, no. 6 (December 2005), pp. 2661–2700.

60 J. J. Dahling, B. G. Whitaker, and P. E. Levy, "The Development and Validation of a New Machiavellianism Scale," *Journal of Management* 35, no. 2 (2009), pp. 219–257.

61 R. Christie and F. L. Geis, *Studies in Machiavellianism* (New York: Academic Press, 1970), p. 312; and N. V. Ramanaiah, A. Byravan, and F. R. J. Detwiler, "Revised Neo Personality Inventory Profiles of Machiavellian and Non-Machiavellian People," *Psychological Reports*, October 1994, pp. 937–938.

62 J. J. Dahling, B. G. Whitaker, and P. E. Levy, "The Development and Validation of a New Machiavellianism Scale," *Journal of Management* 35, no. 2 (2009), pp. 219–257.

63 R. Christie and F. L. Geis, *Studies in Machiavellianism* (New York: Academic Press, 1970).

64 C. Sedikides, E. A. Rudich, A. P. Gregg, M. Kumashiro, and C. Rusbult, "Are Normal Narcissists Psychologically Healthy?: Self-Esteem Matters," *Journal of Personality and Social Psychology* 87, no. 3 (2004), pp. 400–416, reviews some of the literature on narcissism.

65 M. Elias, "Study: Today's Youth Think Quite Highly of Themselves," *USA Today*, November 19, 2008, p. 7D; and K. H. Trzesniewski, M. B. Donnellan, and R. W. Robins, "Do Today's Young People Really Think They Are So Extraordinary?" *Psychological Science* 19, no. 2 (2008), pp. 181–188.

66 A. B. Brunell, S. Staats, J. Barden, and J. M. Hupp, "Narcissism and Academic Dishonesty: The Exhibitionism Dimension and the Lack of Guilt," *Personality and Individual Differences* 50, no. 3 (2011), pp. 323–328.

67 M. Maccoby, "Narcissistic Leaders: The Incredible Pros, the Inevitable Cons," *Harvard Business Review*, January–February 2000, pp. 69–77, http://www.maccoby.com/Articles/NarLeaders.shtml

68 W. K. Campbell and C. A. Foster, "Narcissism and Commitment in Romantic Relationships: An Investment Model Analysis," *Personality and Social Psychology Bulletin* 28, no. 4 (2002), pp. 484–495.

69 T. A. Judge, J. A. LePine, and B. L. Rich, "The Narcissistic Personality: Relationship with Inflated Self-Ratings of Leadership and with Task and Contextual Performance," *Journal of Applied Psychology* 91, no. 4 (2006), pp. 762–776.

70 J. Goncalo, F. J. Flynn, and S. H. Kim, "Are Two Narcissists Better Than One? The Link between Narcissism, Perceived Creativity, and Creative Performance," *Personality and Social Psychology Bulletin* 36, no. 11 (2010), pp. 1484–1495.

71 See M. Snyder, *Public Appearances/Private Realities: The Psychology of Self-Monitoring* (New York: W. H. Freeman, 1987); and S. W. Gangestad and M. Snyder, "Self-Monitoring: Appraisal and Reappraisal," *Psychological Bulletin*, July 2000, pp. 530–555.

72 F. J. Flynn and D. R. Ames, "What's Good for the Goose May Not Be as Good for the Gander: The Benefits of Self-Monitoring for Men and Women in Task Groups and Dyadic Conflicts," *Journal of Applied Psychology* 91, no. 2 (2006), pp. 272–281; and M. Snyder, *Public Appearances/Private Realities: The Psychology of Self-Monitoring* (New York: W. H. Freeman, 1987).

73 H. Oh and M. Kilduff, "The Ripple Effect of Personality on Social Structure: Self-monitoring Origins of Network Brokerage," *Journal of Applied Psychology* 93, no. 5 (2008), pp. 1155–1164; and A. Mehra, M. Kilduff, and D. J. Brass, "The Social Networks of High and Low Self-Monitors: Implications for Workplace Performance," *Administrative Science Quarterly*, March 2001, pp. 121–146.

74 D. V. Day, D. J. Schleicher, A. L. Unckless, and N. J. Hiller, "Self-Monitoring Personality at Work: A Meta-analytic Investigation of Construct Validity," *Journal of Applied Psychology*, April 2002, pp. 390–401.

75 R. N. Taylor and M. D. Dunnette, "Influence of Dogmatism, Risk-Taking Propensity, and Intelligence on Decision-Making Strategies for a Sample of Industrial Managers," *Journal of Applied Psychology*, August 1974, pp. 420–423.

76 I. L. Janis and L. Mann, *Decision Making: A Psychological Analysis of Conflict, Choice, and Commitment* (New York: Free Press, 1977); W. H. Stewart Jr. and L. Roth, "Risk Propensity Differences between Entrepreneurs and Managers: A Meta-analytic Review," *Journal of Applied Psychology*, February 2001, pp. 145–153; J. B. Miner and N. S. Raju, "Risk Propensity Differences between Managers and Entrepreneurs and between Low- and High-Growth Entrepreneurs: A Reply in a More Conservative Vein," *Journal of Applied Psychology* 89, no. 1 (2004), pp. 3–13; and W. H. Stewart Jr. and P. L. Roth, "Data Quality Affects Meta-analytic Conclusions: A Response to Miner and Raju (2004) Concerning Entrepreneurial Risk Propensity," *Journal of Applied Psychology* 89, no. 1 (2004), pp. 14–21.

77 J. K. Maner, J. A. Richey, K. Cromer, M. Mallott, C. W. Lejuez, T. E. Joiner, and N. B. Schmidt, "Dispositional Anxiety and Risk-Avoidant Decision Making," *Personality and Individual Differences* 42, no. 4 (2007), pp. 665–675.

78 M. Friedman and R. H. Rosenman, *Type A Behavior and Your Heart* (New York: Knopf, 1974), p. 84.

79 M. Friedman and R. H. Rosenman, *Type A Behavior and Your Heart* (New York: Alfred A. Knopf, 1974), pp. 84–85.

80 K. W. Cook, C. A. Vance, and E. Spector, "The Relation of Candidate Personality with Selection-Interview Outcomes," *Journal of Applied Social Psychology* 30 (2000), pp. 867–885.

81 M. Friedman and R. H. Rosenman, *Type A Behavior and Your Heart* (New York: Knopf, 1974), p. 86.

82 J. M. Crant, "Proactive Behavior in Organizations," *Journal of Management* 26, no. 3 (2000), p. 436.

83 S. E. Seibert, M. L. Kraimer, and J. M. Crant, "What Do Proactive People Do? A Longitudinal Model Linking Proactive Personality and Career Success," *Personnel Psychology*, Winter 2001, p. 850.

84 T. S. Bateman and J. M. Crant, "The Proactive Component of Organizational Behavior: A Measure and Correlates," *Journal of Organizational Behavior*, March 1993, pp. 103–118; A. L. Frohman, "Igniting Organizational Change from Below: The Power of Personal Initiative," *Organizational Dynamics*, Winter 1997, pp. 39–53; and J. M. Crant and T. S. Bateman, "Charismatic Leadership Viewed from Above: The Impact of Proactive Personality," *Journal of Organizational Behavior*, February 2000, pp. 63–75.

85 J. M. Crant, "Proactive Behavior in Organizations," *Journal of Management* 26, no. 3 (2000), p. 436.

86 See, for instance, R. C. Becherer and J. G. Maurer, "The Proactive Personality Disposition and Entrepreneurial Behavior among Small Company Presidents," *Journal of Small Business Management*, January 1999, pp. 28–36.

87 S. E. Seibert, J. M. Crant, and M. L. Kraimer, "Proactive Personality and Career Success," *Journal of Applied Psychology*, June 1999, pp. 416–427; S. E. Seibert, M. L. Kraimer, and J. M. Crant, "What Do Proactive People Do? A Longitudinal Model Linking Proactive Personality and Career Success," *Personnel Psychology*, Winter 2001, p. 850; F. J. Flynn and D. R. Ames, "What's Good for the Goose May Not Be as Good for the Gander: The Benefits of Self-Monitoring for Men and Women in Task Groups and Dyadic Conflicts," *Journal of Applied Psychology* 91, no. 2 (2006), pp. 272–281; and J. D. Kammeyer-Mueller and C. R. Wanberg, "Unwrapping the Organizational Entry Process: Disentangling Multiple Antecedents and Their Pathways to Adjustment," *Journal of Applied Psychology* 88, no. 5 (2003), pp. 779–794.

88 Vignette based on "Trail Workers Test Walmart's Resistance to Unions," August 15, 2010, *Nelson Life*, http://nelsonlife.

com/550/trail-workers-test-walmarts-resistance-to-unions/; and http://www.ratemyemployer.ca/employer/employer.aspx?empID=7575&l=en

89 See, for instance, C. D. Fisher and N. M. Ashkanasy, "The Emerging Role of Emotions in Work Life: An Introduction," *Journal of Organizational Behavior*, Special Issue (2000), pp. 123–129; N. M. Ashkanasy, C. E. J. Hartel, and W. J. Zerbe, eds., *Emotions in the Workplace: Research, Theory, and Practice* (Westport, CT: Quorum Books, 2000); N. M. Ashkanasy and C. S. Daus, "Emotion in the Workplace: The New Challenge for Managers," *Academy of Management Executive*, February 2002, pp. 76–86; and N. M. Ashkanasy, C. E. J. Hartel, and C. S. Daus, "Diversity and Emotion: The New Frontiers in Organizational Behavior Research," *Journal of Management* 28, no. 3 (2002), pp. 307–338.

90 See, for example, L. L. Putnam and D. K. Mumby, "Organizations, Emotion and the Myth of Rationality," in *Emotion in Organizations*, ed. S. Fineman (Thousand Oaks, CA: Sage, 1993), pp. 36–57; and J. Martin, K. Knopoff, and C. Beckman, "An Alternative to Bureaucratic Impersonality and Emotional Labor: Bounded Emotionality at the Body Shop," *Administrative Science Quarterly*, June 1998, pp. 429–469.

91 B. E. Ashforth and R. H. Humphrey, "Emotion in the Workplace: A Reappraisal," *Human Relations*, February 1995, pp. 97–125.

92 S. G. Barsade and D. E. Gibson, "Why Does Affect Matter in Organizations?" *Academy of Management Perspectives*, February 2007, pp. 36–59.

93 See N. H. Frijda, "Moods, Emotion Episodes and Emotions," in *Handbook of Emotions*, ed. M. Lewis and J. M. Haviland (New York: Guilford Press, 1993), pp. 381–403.

94 H. M. Weiss and R. Cropanzano, "Affective Events Theory," in *Research in Organizational Behavior*, vol. 18, ed. B. M. Staw and L. L. Cummings (Greenwich, CT: JAI Press, 1996), pp. 17–19.

95 See P. Ekman and R. J. Davidson, eds., *The Nature of Emotions: Fundamental Questions* (Oxford, UK: Oxford University Press, 1994).

96 N. H. Frijda, "Moods, Emotion Episodes and Emotions," in *Handbook of Emotions*, ed. M. Lewis and J. M. Haviland (New York: Guilford Press, 1993), pp. 381–403.

97 See P. Ekman and R. J. Davidson, eds., *The Nature of Emotions: Fundamental Questions* (Oxford, UK: Oxford University Press, 1994).

98 K. Sanford and A. J. Grace, "Emotion and Underlying Concerns during Couples' Conflict: An Investigation of within-Person Change," *Personal Relationships* 18, no. 1 (2011), pp. 96–109.

99 Baylor University, "Exploring How Partners Perceive Each Other's Emotion during a Relationship Fight," *ScienceDaily*, December 16, 2010, http://www.sciencedaily.com/releases/2010/12/101216161514.htm

100 See J. A. Morris and D. C. Feldman, "Managing Emotions in the Workplace," *Journal of Managerial Issues* 9, no. 3 (1997), pp. 257–274; S. Mann, *Hiding What We Feel, Faking What We Don't: Understanding the Role of Your Emotions at Work* (New York: HarperCollins, 1999); and S. M. Kruml and D. Geddes, "Catching Fire without Burning Out: Is There an Ideal Way to Perform Emotion Labor?" in *Emotions in the Workplace*, ed. N. M. Ashkansay, C. E. J. Hartel, and W. J. Zerbe (New York: Quorum Books, 2000), pp. 177–188.

101 P. Ekman, W. V. Friesen, and M. O'Sullivan, "Smiles When Lying," in *What the Face Reveals: Basic and Applied Studies of Spontaneous Expression Using the Facial Action Coding System (FACS)*, ed. P. Ekman and E. L. Rosenberg (London: Oxford University Press, 1997), pp. 201–216.

102 A. Grandey, "Emotion Regulation in the Workplace: A New Way to Conceptualize Emotional Labor," *Journal of Occupational*

Health Psychology 5, no. 1 (2000), pp. 95–110; and R. Cropanzano, D. E. Rupp, and Z. S. Byrne, "The Relationship of Emotional Exhaustion to Work Attitudes, Job Performance, and Organizational Citizenship Behavior," *Journal of Applied Psychology*, February 2003, pp. 160–169.

103 A. R. Hochschild, "Emotion Work, Feeling Rules, and Social Structure," *American Journal of Sociology*, November 1979, pp. 551–575; W.-C. Tsai, "Determinants and Consequences of Employee Displayed Positive Emotions," *Journal of Management* 27, no. 4 (2001), pp. 497–512; M. W. Kramer and J. A. Hess, "Communication Rules for the Display of Emotions in Organizational Settings," *Management Communication Quarterly*, August 2002, pp. 66–80; and J. M. Diefendorff and E. M. Richard, "Antecedents and Consequences of Emotional Display Rule Perceptions," *Journal of Applied Psychology*, April 2003, pp. 284–294.

104 B. M. DePaulo, "Nonverbal Behavior and Self-Presentation," *Psychological Bulletin*, March 1992, pp. 203–243.

105 C. S. Hunt, "Although I Might Be Laughing Loud and Hearty, Deep Inside I'm Blue: Individual Perceptions Regarding Feeling and Displaying Emotions at Work" (paper presented at the Academy of Management Conference, Cincinnati, OH, August 1996), p. 3.

106 R. C. Solomon, "Back to Basics: On the Very Idea of 'Basic Emotions,'" *Journal for the Theory of Social Behaviour* 32, no. 2 (2002), pp. 115–144.

107 C. M. Brotheridge and R. T. Lee, "Development and Validation of the Emotional Labour Scale," *Journal of Occupational and Organizational Psychology* 76, no. 3 (September 2003), pp. 365–379.

108 A. A. Grandey, "When 'the Show Must Go On': Surface Acting and Deep Acting as Determinants of Emotional Exhaustion and Peer-Rated Service Delivery," *Academy of Management Journal*, February 2003, pp. 86–96; and A. A. Grandey, D. N. Dickter, and H. Sin, "The Customer Is Not Always Right: Customer Aggression and Emotion Regulation of Service Employees," *Journal of Organizational Behavior* 25, no. 3 (May 2004), pp. 397–418.

109 J. P. Trougakos, D. J. Beal, S. G. Green, and H. M. Weiss, "Making the Break Count: An Episodic Examination of Recovery Activities, Emotional Experiences, and Positive Affective Displays," *Academy of Management Journal* 51, no. 1 (2008), pp. 131–146.

110 S. Brassen, M. Gamer, and C. Büchel, "Anterior Cingulate Activation Is Related to a Positivity Bias and Emotional Stability in Successful Aging," *Biological Psychiatry* 70, no. 2 (2011), pp. 131–137.

111 A. R. Damasio, *Descartes' Error: Emotion, Reason, and the Human Brain* (New York: Quill, 1994).

112 N. M. Ashkanasy and C. S. Daus, "Emotion in the Workplace: The New Challenge for Managers," *Academy of Management Executive*, February 2002, pp. 76–86.

113 Based on D. R. Caruso, J. D. Mayer, and P. Salovey, "Emotional Intelligence and Emotional Leadership," in *Multiple Intelligences and Leadership*, ed. R. E. Riggio, S. E. Murphy, and F. J. Pirozzolo (Mahwah, NJ: Lawrence Erlbaum, 2002), p. 70.

114 This section is based on Daniel Goleman, *Emotional Intelligence* (New York: Bantam, 1995); P. Salovey and D. Grewal, "The Science of Emotional Intelligence," *Current Directions in Psychological Science* 14, no. 6 (2005), pp. 281–285; M. Davies, L. Stankov, and R. D. Roberts, "Emotional Intelligence: In Search of an Elusive Construct," *Journal of Personality and Social Psychology*, October 1998, pp. 989–1015; D. Geddes and R. R. Callister, "Crossing the Line(s): A Dual Threshold Model of Anger in Organizations," *Academy of Management Review* 32, no. 3 (2007), pp. 721–746; and J. Ciarrochi, J. P. Forgas, and

J. D. Mayer, eds., *Emotional Intelligence in Everyday Life* (Philadelphia: Psychology Press, 2001).

115 M. Seo and L. F. Barrett, "Being Emotional During Decision Making—Good or Bad? An Empirical Investigation," *Academy of Management Journal* 50, no. 4 (2007), pp. 923–940.

116 E. H. O'Boyle, R. H. Humphrey, J. M. Pollack, T. H. Hawver, and P. A. Story, "The Relation between Emotional Intelligence and Job Performance: A Meta-analysis," *Journal of Organizational Behavior* 32, no. 5 (2011), pp. 788–818.

117 F. I. Greenstein, *The Presidential Difference: Leadership Style from FDR to Clinton* (Princeton, NJ: Princeton University Press, 2001).

118 M. Maccoby, "To Win the Respect of Followers, Leaders Need Personality Intelligence," *Ivey Business Journal* 72, no. 3 (2008); J. Reid, "The Resilient Leader: Why EQ Matters," *Business Journal* 72, no. 3 (2008); and P. Wieand, J. Birchfield, and M. C. Johnson III, "The New Leadership Challenge: Removing the Emotional Barriers to Sustainable Performance in a Flat World," *Ivey Business Journal* 72, no. 4 (2008).

119 P. Wieand, J. Birchfield, and M. C. Johnson III, "The New Leadership Challenge: Removing the Emotional Barriers to Sustainable Performance in a Flat World," *Ivey Business Journal* 72, no. 4 (2008).

120 C. Cherniss, "The Business Case for Emotional Intelligence," *Consortium for Research on Emotional Intelligence in Organizations*, 1999, http://www.eiconsortium.org/research/business_case_for_ei.pdf

121 K. S. Law, C. Wong, and L. J. Song, "The Construct and Criterion Validity of Emotional Intelligence and Its Potential Utility for Management Studies," *Journal of Applied Psychology* 89, no. 3 (2004), pp. 483–496.

122 H. A. Elfenbein and N. Ambady, "Predicting Workplace Outcomes from the Ability to Eavesdrop on Feelings," *Journal of Applied Psychology* 87, no. 5 (October 2002), pp. 963–971.

123 D. L. Van Rooy and C. Viswesvaran, "Emotional Intelligence: A Meta-analytic Investigation of Predictive Validity and Nomological Net," *Journal of Vocational Behavior* 65, no. 1 (August 2004), pp. 71–95.

124 R. Bar-On, D. Tranel, N. L. Denburg, and A. Bechara, "Exploring the Neurological Substrate of Emotional and Social Intelligence," *Brain* 126, no. 8 (August 2003), pp. 1790–1800.

125 P. A. Vernon, K. V. Petrides, D. Bratko, and J. A. Schermer, "A Behavioral Genetic Study of Trait Emotional Intelligence," *Emotion* 8, no. 5 (2008), pp. 635–642.

126 E. A. Locke, "Why Emotional Intelligence Is an Invalid Concept," *Journal of Organizational Behavior* 26, no. 4 (2005), pp. 425–431.

127 J. M. Conte, "A Review and Critique of Emotional Intelligence Measures," *Journal of Organizational Behavior* 26, no. 4 (2005), pp. 433–440; and M. Davies, L. Stankov, and R. D. Roberts, "Emotional Intelligence: In Search of an Elusive Construct," *Journal of Personality and Social Psychology* 75, no. 4 (1998), pp. 989–1015.

128 T. Decker, "Is Emotional Intelligence a Viable Concept?" *Academy of Management Review* 28, no. 2 (2003), pp. 433–440; and M. Davies, L. Stankov, and R. D. Roberts, "Emotional Intelligence: In Search of an Elusive Construct," *Journal of Personality and Social Psychology* 75, no. 4 (1998), pp. 989–1015.

129 F. J. Landy, "Some Historical and Scientific Issues Related to Research on Emotional Intelligence," *Journal of Organizational Behavior* 26, no. 4 (June 2005), pp. 411–424.

130 S. L. Robinson and R. J. Bennett, "A Typology of Deviant Workplace Behaviors: A Multidimensional Scaling Study," *Academy of Management Journal*, April 1995, p. 556.

131 S. L. Robinson and R. J. Bennett, "A Typology of Deviant Workplace Behaviors: A Multidimensional Scaling Study," *Academy of Management Journal*, April 1995, pp. 555–572.

132 Based on A. G. Bedeian, "Workplace Envy," *Organizational Dynamics*, Spring 1995, p. 50.

133 A. G. Bedeian, "Workplace Envy," *Organizational Dynamics*, Spring 1995, p. 54.

134 S. C. Douglas, C. Kiewitz, M. Martinko, P. Harvey, Y. Kim, and J. U. Chun, "Cognitions, Emotions, and Evaluations: An Elaboration Likelihood Model for Workplace Aggression," *Academy of Management Review* 33, no. 2 (2008), pp. 425–451.

135 K. Lee and N. J. Allen, "Organizational Citizenship Behavior and Workplace Deviance: The Role of Affect and Cognition," *Journal of Applied Psychology* 87, no. 1 (2002), pp. 131–142; and T. A. Judge, B. A. Scott, and R. Ilies, "Hostility, Job Attitudes, and Workplace Deviance: Test of a Multilevel Model," *Journal of Applied Psychology* 91, no. 1 (2006), pp. 126–138.

136 Based on C. A. Bartela and R. Saavedra, "The Collective Construction of Work Group Moods," *Administrative Science Quarterly* 45, no. 2 (June 2000), pp. 197–231.

137 H. M. Weiss and R. Cropanzano, "Affective Events Theory: A Theoretical Discussion of the Structure, Causes and Consequences of Affective Experiences at Work," in *Research in Organizational Behavior*, vol. 18, ed. B. M. Staw and L. L. Cummings (Greenwich, CT: JAI Press, 1996), pp. 17–19.

138 J. Basch and C. D. Fisher, "Affective Events-Emotions Matrix: A Classification of Work Events and Associated Emotions," in *Emotions in the Workplace*, ed. N. M. Ashkanasy, C. E. J. Hartel, and W. J. Zerbe (Westport, CN: Quorum Books, 2000), pp. 36–48.

139 See, for example, H. M. Weiss and R. Cropanzano, "Affective Events Theory: A Theoretical Discussion of the Structure, Causes and Consequences of Affective Experiences at Work," in *Research in Organizational Behavior*, vol. 18, ed. B. M. Staw and L. L. Cummings (Greenwich, CT: JAI Press, 1996), pp. 17–19; and C. D. Fisher, "Antecedents and Consequences of Real-Time Affective Reactions at Work," *Motivation and Emotion*, March 2002, pp. 3–30.

140 Based on H. M. Weiss and R. Cropanzano, "Affective Events Theory: A Theoretical Discussion of the Structure, Causes and Consequences of Affective Experiences at Work," in *Research in Organizational Behavior*, vol. 18, ed. B. M. Staw and L. L. Cummings (Greenwich, CT: JAI Press, 1996), p. 42.

141 N. M. Ashkanasy, C. E. J. Hartel, and C. S. Daus, "Diversity and Emotion: The New Frontiers in Organizational Behavior Research," *Journal of Management* 28, no. 3 (2002), p. 324.

142 C. West, "How Culture Affects the Way We Think," *APS Observer* 20, no. 7 (2007), pp. 25–26.

143 T. Masuda, R. Gonzalez, L. Kwan, and R. E. Nisbett, "Culture and Aesthetic Preference: Comparing the Attention to Context of East Asians and Americans," *Personality and Social Psychology Bulletin* 34, no. 9 (2008), pp. 1260–1275.

144 D. C. Park, "Developing a Cultural Cognitive Neuroscience of Aging," in *Handbook of Cognitive Aging*, ed. S. M. Hofer and D. F. Alwin (Thousand Oaks, CA: Sage Publications, 2008), pp. 352–367.

145 Q. Wang, "On the Cultural Constitution of Collective Memory," *Memory* 16, no. 3 (2008), pp. 305–317.

146 See, for instance, D. S. Krull, M. H.-M. Loy, J. Lin, C.-F. Wang, S. Chen, and X. Zhao, "The Fundamental Attribution Error: Correspondence Bias in Individualistic and Collectivist Cultures," *Personality and Social Psychology Bulletin*, October 1999, pp. 1208–1219; and F. F. T. Chiang and T. A. Birtch, "Examining the Perceived Causes of Successful Employee Performance: An East-West Comparison," *International Journal of Human Resource Management* 18, no. 2 (2007), pp. 232–248.

147 S. Nam, "Cultural and Managerial Attributions for Group Performance," unpublished doctoral dissertation, University of Oregon. Cited in R. M. Steers, S. J. Bischoff, and L. H. Higgins, "Cross-Cultural Management Research," *Journal of Management Inquiry*, December 1992, pp. 325–326.

148 T. Menon, M. W. Morris, C. Y. Chiu, and Y. Y. Hong, "Culture and the Construal of Agency: Attribution to Individual versus Group Dispositions," *Journal of Personality and Social Psychology* 76 (1999), pp. 701–717; and R. Friedman, W. Liu, C. C. Chen, and S. S. Chi, "Causal Attribution for Interfirm Contract Violation: A Comparative Study of Chinese and American Commercial Arbitrators," *Journal of Applied Psychology* 92, no. 3 (2007), pp. 856–864.

149 J. Spencer-Rodgers, M. J. Williams, D. L. Hamilton, K. Peng, and L. Wang, "Culture and Group Perception: Dispositional and Stereotypic Inferences About Novel and National Groups," *Journal of Personality and Social Psychology* 93, no. 4 (2007), pp. 525–543.

150 A. Zhang, C. Reyna, Z. Qian, and G. Yu, "Interpersonal Attributions of Responsibility in the Chinese Workplace: A Test of Western Models in a Collectivistic Context," *Journal of Applied Social Psychology* 38, no. 9 (2008), pp. 2361–2377; and A. Zhang, F. Xia, and C. Li, "The Antecedents of Help Giving in Chinese Culture: Attribution, Judgment of Responsibility, Expectation Change and the Reaction of Affect," *Social Behavior and Personality* 35, no. 1 (2007), pp. 135–142.

151 See, for instance, R. R. McCrae and P. T. Costa Jr., "Personality Trait Structure as a Human Universal," *American Psychologist*, May 1997, pp. 509–516; S. Yamagata, A. Suzuki, J. Ando, Y. Ono, K. Yutaka, N. Kijima, K. Yoshimura, F. Ostendorf, A. Angleitner, R. Riemann, F. M. Spinath, W. J. Livesley, and K. L. Jang, "Is the Genetic Structure of Human Personality Universal? A Cross-Cultural Twin Study from North America, Europe, and Asia," *Journal of Personality and Social Psychology* 90, no. 6 (2006), pp. 987–998; H. C. Triandis and E. M. Suh, "Cultural Influences on Personality," in *Annual Review of Psychology*, vol. 53, ed. S. T. Fiske, D. L. Schacter, and C. Zahn-Waxler (Palo Alto, CA: Annual Reviews, 2002), pp. 133–160; R. R. McCrae and J. Allik, *The Five-Factor Model of Personality across Cultures* (New York: Kluwer Academic/Plenum, 2002); and R. R. McCrae, P. T. Costa Jr., T. A. Martin, V. E. Oryol, A. A. Rukavishnikov, I. G. Senin, M. Hřebíčková, and T. Urbánek, "Consensual Validation of Personality Traits across Cultures," *Journal of Research in Personality* 38, no. 2 (2004), pp. 179–201.

152 A. T. Church and M. S. Katigbak, "Trait Psychology in the Philippines," *American Behavioral Scientist*, September 2000, pp. 73–94.

153 J. F. Salgado, "The Five Factor Model of Personality and Job Performance in the European Community," *Journal of Applied Psychology*, February 1997, pp. 30–43.

154 M. Eid and E. Diener, "Norms for Experiencing Emotions in Different Cultures: Inter- and International Differences," *Journal of Personality and Social Psychology* 81, no. 5 (2001), pp. 869–885.

155 S. Oishi, E. Diener, and C. Napa Scollon, "Cross-Situational Consistency of Affective Experiences across Cultures," *Journal of Personality and Social Psychology* 86, no. 3 (2004), pp. 460–472; and J. Leu, J. Wang, and K. Koo, "Are Positive Emotions Just as 'Positive' across Cultures?" *Emotion*, March 28, 2011, Epub ahead of print, http://www.ncbi.nlm.nih.gov/pubmed/21443338

156 M. Eid and E. Diener, "Norms for Experiencing Emotions in Different Cultures: Inter- and International Differences," *Journal of Personality and Social Psychology* 81, no. 5 (2001), pp. 869–885.

157 M. Eid and E. Diener, "Norms for Experiencing Emotions in Different Cultures: Inter- and International Differences," *Journal of Personality and Social Psychology* 81, no. 5 (2001), pp. 869–885.

158 B. E. Ashforth and R. H. Humphrey, "Emotion in the Workplace: A Reappraisal," *Human Relations*, February 1995, p. 104; B. Plasait, "Accueil des Touristes Dans les Grands Centres de Transit Paris," *Rapport du Bernard Plasait*, October 4, 2004, http://www.tourisme.gouv.fr/fr/navd/presse/dossiers/att00005767/dp_plasait.pdf; B. Mesquita, "Emotions in Collectivist and Individualist Contexts," *Journal of Personality and Social Psychology* 80, no. 1 (2001), pp. 68–74; and D. Rubin, "Grumpy German Shoppers Distrust the Wal-Mart Style," *Seattle Times*, December 30, 2001, p. A15.

159 H. M. Weiss and R. Cropanzano, "Affective Events Theory," in *Research in Organizational Behavior*, vol. 18, ed. B. M. Staw and L. L. Cummings (Greenwich, CT: JAI Press, 1996), p. 55.

160 H. Liao and A. Chuang, "A Multilevel Investigation of Factors Influencing Employee Service Performance and Customer Outcomes," *Academy of Management Journal* 47, no. 1 (2004), pp. 41–58.

161 D. J. Beal, J. P. Trougakos, H. M. Weiss, and S. G. Green, "Episodic Processes in Emotional Labor: Perceptions of Affective Delivery and Regulation Strategies," *Journal of Applied Psychology* 91, no. 5 (2006), pp. 1057–1065.

162 Cited in S. W. Floyd, J. Roos, and F. Kellermanns, *Innovating Strategy Process* (Blackwell Publishing, 2005), p. 66.

163 D. Zapf and M. Holz, "On the Positive and Negative Effects of Emotion Work in Organizations," *European Journal of Work and Organizational Psychology* 15, no. 1 (2006), pp. 1–28.

164 D. Zapf, "Emotion Work and Psychological Well-Being: A Review of the Literature and Some Conceptual Considerations," *Human Resource Management Review* 12, no. 2 (2002), pp. 237–268.

165 J. E. Bono and M. A. Vey, "Toward Understanding Emotional Management at Work: A Quantitative Review of Emotional Labor Research," in *Emotions in Organizational Behavior*, ed. C. E. Härtel and W. J. Zerbe (Mahwah, NJ: Lawrence Erlbaum, 2005), pp. 213–233.

166 This dilemma is based on R. R. Hastings, "Survey: The Demographics of Tattoos and Piercings," *HR Week*, February 2007, http://www.shrm.org; H. Wessel, "Taboo of Tattoos in the Workplace," *Orlando (Florida) Sentinel*, May 28, 2007, http://www.tmcnet.com/usubmit/2007/05/28/2666555.htm; S. O'Donnell, "Popularity of Piercing Pokes Holes in Traditional Workplace Standards," *Edmonton Journal*, March 12, 2006, p. A1; and K. Dedyna, "Picture-Perfect Workers? TATTOOS: Inky Designs Gain Acceptance with Bosses, Clients," *Province* (Vancouver), August 28, 2005, p. A50.

167 J. Perrone and M. H. Vickers, "Emotions as Strategic Game in a Hostile Workplace: An Exemplar Case," *Employee Responsibilities and Rights Journal* 16, no. 3 (2004), pp. 167–178; and "S. Kruml and D. Geddes, "Catching Fire without Burning Out," In *Emotions in the Workplace: Research, Theory, and Practice*, ed. N. M. Ashkanasy, C. E. J. Hartel, and W. J. Zerbe. (Westport, CT: Quorum Books, 2000), pp. 165–188.

168 Based on T. A. Judge, B. A. Livingston, and C. Hurst, "Do Nice Guys—and Gals—Really Finish Last? The Joint Effects of Sex and Agreeableness on Earnings," working paper, University of Florida, 2009; S. N. Kaplan, M. M. Klebanov, and M. Sorensen, "Which CEO Characteristics and Abilities Matter?" working paper, University of Chicago Graduate School of Business, 2008, http://faculty.chicagobooth.edu/steven.kaplan/research/kks.pdf; L. K. Thaler and R. Koval, *The Power of Nice: How to Conquer the Business World with Kindness* (New York: Doubleday/Currency, 2006); E. Horrell, *The Kindness Revolution* (New York: AMACOM, 2006); D. Brady, "Being Mean Is So Last Millennium," *BusinessWeek*, January 15, 2007, p. 61; L. Schillinger, "Nice and Ambitious: Either, Neither, or Both?" *New York Times*, January 14, 2007, p. 1; "Congeniality Factor: Employers Become Pickier About Personality," *Gainesville (Florida) Sun*, November 6, 2007, p. 6B.

169 L. K. Thaler and R. Koval, *The Power of Nice: How to Conquer the Business World with Kindness* (New York: Doubleday/Currency, 2006).

170 E. Horrell, *The Kindness Revolution* (New York: AMACOM, 2006).

171 D. Brady, "Being Mean Is So Last Millennium," *BusinessWeek*, January 15, 2007, p. 61.

172 L. Schillinger, "Nice and Ambitious: Either, Neither, or Both?" *New York Times*, January 14, 2007, p. 1.

173 Based on V. P. Richmond, J. C. McCroskey, and S. K. Payne, *Nonverbal Behavior in Interpersonal Relations*, 2nd ed. (Englewood Cliffs, NJ: Prentice Hall, 1991), pp. 117–138; and L. A. King, "Ambivalence over Emotional Expression and Reading Emotions in Situations and Faces," *Journal of Personality and Social Psychology*, March 1998, pp. 753–762.

Chapter 3

1 Vignette based on http://www.casinoregina.com/corporate/aboutus

2 M. Rokeach, *The Nature of Human Values* (New York: Free Press, 1973), p. 5.

3 See, for instance, B. Meglino and E. Ravlin, "Individual Values in Organizations," *Journal of Management* 24, no. 3 (1998), pp. 351–389.

4 M. Rokeach and S. J. Ball-Rokeach, "Stability and Change in American Value Priorities, 1968-1981," *American Psychologist*, May 1989, pp. 775–784.

5 M. Rokeach, *The Nature of Human Values* (New York: Free Press, 1973), p. 6.

6 M. Rokeach, *The Nature of Human Values* (New York: Free Press, 1973), p. 56.

7 M. Rokeach, *The Nature of Human Values* (New York: Free Press, 1973), p. 56.

8 K. Hodgson, "Adapting Ethical Decisions to a Global Marketplace," *Management Review* 81, no. 5, May 1992, pp. 53–57. Reprinted by permission.

9 J. M. Munson and B. Z. Posner, "The Factorial Validity of a Modified Rokeach Value Survey for Four Diverse Samples," *Educational and Psychological Measurement*, Winter 1980, pp. 1073–1079; and W. C. Frederick and J. Weber, "The Values of Corporate Managers and Their Critics: An Empirical Description and Normative Implications," in *Business Ethics: Research Issues and Empirical Studies*, ed. W. C. Frederick and L. E. Preston (Greenwich, CT: JAI Press, 1990), pp. 123–144.

10 W. C. Frederick and J. Weber, "The Values of Corporate Managers and Their Critics: An Empirical Description and Normative Implications," in *Business Ethics: Research Issues and Empirical Studies*, ed. W. C. Frederick and L. E. Preston (Greenwich, CT: JAI Press, 1990), pp. 123–144.

11 W. C. Frederick and J. Weber, "The Values of Corporate Managers and Their Critics: An Empirical Description and Normative Implications," in *Business Ethics: Research Issues and Empirical Studies*, ed. W. C. Frederick and L. E. Preston (Greenwich, CT: JAI Press, 1990), p. 132.

12 K. Hodgson, *A Rock and a Hard Place: How to Make Ethical Business Decisions When the Choices Are Tough* (New York: AMACOM, 1992), pp. 66–67.

13 Based on A. Judd, "Vancouver Man Fired over Riot Facebook Comments," *Global News*, June 17, 2011, http://www.globaltvbc.com/Vancouver+fired+over+riot+Facebook+comments/4965316/story.html; and V. Lu, "Vancouver Rioters Got Rowdy, Then Got Fired," *thestar.com*, June 23, 2011.

14 Vignette based on http://www.casinoregina.com/corporate/aboutus

15 G. Hofstede, *Culture's Consequences: International Differences in Work-Related Values* (Beverly Hills, CA: Sage, 1980); G. Hofstede, *Cultures and Organizations: Software of the Mind* (London: McGraw-Hill, 1991); G. Hofstede, "Cultural Constraints in Management Theories," *Academy of Management Executive* 7, no. 1 (1993), pp. 81–94; G. Hofstede and M. F. Peterson, "National Values and Organizational Practices," in *Handbook of Organizational Culture and Climate*, ed. N. M. Ashkanasy, C. M. Wilderom, and M. F. Peterson (Thousand Oaks, CA: Sage, 2000), pp. 401–416; and G. Hofstede, *Culture's Consequences: Comparing Values, Behaviors, Institutions, and Organizations Across Nations*, 2nd ed. (Thousand Oaks, CA: Sage, 2001). For criticism of this research, see B. McSweeney, "Hofstede's Model of National Cultural Differences and Their Consequences: A Triumph of Faith—A Failure of Analysis," *Human Relations* 55, no. 1 (2002), pp. 89–118.

16 G. Hofstede and M. H. Bond, "The Confucius Connection: From Cultural Roots to Economic Growth," *Organizational Dynamics*, Spring 1988, pp. 12–13.

17 M. H. Bond, "Reclaiming the Individual from Hofstede's Ecological Analysis—A 20-Year Odyssey: Comment on Oyserman et al. (2002)," *Psychological Bulletin* 128, no. 1 (2002), pp. 73–77; G. Hofstede, "The Pitfalls of Cross-National Survey Research: A Reply to the Article by Spector et al. on the Psychometric Properties of the Hofstede Values Survey Module 1994," *Applied Psychology: An International Review* 51, no. 1 (2002), pp. 170–178; and T. Fang, "A Critique of Hofstede's Fifth National Culture Dimension," *International Journal of Cross-Cultural Management* 3, no. 3 (2003), pp. 347–368.

18 See A. Harzing and G. Hofstede, "Planned Change in Organizations: The Influence of National Culture," in *Research in the Sociology of Organizations, Cross Cultural Analysis of Organizations*, vol. 14, ed. P. A. Bamberger, M. Erez, and S. B. Bacharach (Greenwich, CT: JAI Press, 1996), pp. 297–340. The five usual criticisms and Hofstede's responses (in parentheses) are (1) Surveys are not a suitable way to measure cultural differences (answer: they should not be the only way); (2) Nations are not the proper units for studying cultures (answer: they are usually the only kind of units available for comparison); (3) A study of the subsidiaries of one company cannot provide information about entire national cultures (answer: what was measured were differences among national cultures, and any set of functionally equivalent samples can supply information about such differences); (4) The IBM data are old and therefore obsolete (answer: the dimensions found are assumed to have century-old roots; they have been validated against all kinds of external measurements; and recent replications show no loss of validity); and (5) Four or five dimensions are not enough (answer: additional dimensions should be statistically independent of the dimensions defined earlier; they should be valid on the basis of correlations with external measures; and candidates are welcome to apply).

19 M. Javidan and R. J. House, "Cultural Acumen for the Global Manager: Lessons from Project GLOBE," *Organizational Dynamics* 29, no. 4 (2001), pp. 289–305; and R. J. House, P. J. Hanges, M. Javidan, and P. W. Dorfman, eds., *Leadership, Culture, and Organizations: The GLOBE Study of 62 Societies* (Thousand Oaks, CA: Sage, 2004).

20 P. C. Early, "Leading Cultural Research in the Future: A Matter of Paradigms and Taste," *Journal of International Business Studies*, September 2006, pp. 922–931; G. Hofstede, "What Did GLOBE Really Measure? Researchers' Minds versus Respondents' Minds," *Journal of International Business Studies*, September 2006, pp. 882–896; and M. Javidan, R. J. House, P. W. Dorfman, P. J. Hanges, and M. S. de Luque, "Conceptualizing and Measuring Cultures and Their Consequences: A Comparative Review of GLOBE's and Hofstede's Approaches," *Journal of International Business Studies*, September 2006, pp. 897–914.

21 B. Meglino, E. C. Ravlin, and C. L. Adkins, "A Work Values Approach to Corporate Culture: A Field Test of the Value Congruence Process and Its Relationship to Individual Outcomes," *Journal of Applied Psychology* 74 (1989), pp. 424–432.

22 B. Z. Posner, J. M. Kouzes, and W. H. Schmidt, "Shared Values Make a Difference: An Empirical Test of Corporate Culture," *Human Resource Management* 24 (1985), pp. 293–310; and A. L. Balazas, "Value Congruency: The Case of the 'Socially Responsible' Firm," *Journal of Business Research* 20 (1990), pp. 171–181.

23 C. A. O'Reilly, J. Chatman, and D. Caldwell, "People and Organizational Culture: A Q-Sort Approach to Assessing Person-Organizational Fit," *Academy of Management Journal* 34 (1991), pp. 487–516.

24 C. Enz and C. K. Schwenk, "Performance and Sharing of Organizational Values" (paper presented at the annual meeting of the Academy of Management, Washington, DC, 1989).

25 Based on D. Sankey, "Non-Profits Look to Diversify Staff; Youth, Visible Minorities Not Usually Part of Sector's Workforce," *Vancouver Sun*, July 9, 2011, p. D12.

26 See, for example, *The Multigenerational Workforce* (Alexandria, VA: Society for Human Resource Management, 2009); and M. Adams, *Sex in the Snow* (Toronto: Penguin, 1997).

27 J. Timm, "Leadership Q&A: Robert Dutton," *Canadian Business*, June 22, 2011, http://www.canadianbusiness.com/article/30752—leadership-q-a-robert-dutton

28 K. W. Smola and C. D. Sutton, "Generational Differences: Revisiting Generational Work Values for the New Millennium," *Journal of Organizational Behavior* 23 (2002), pp. 363–382; and K. Mellahi and C. Guermat, "Does Age Matter? An Empirical Examination of the Effect of Age on Managerial Values and Practices in India," *Journal of World Business* 39, no. 2 (2004), pp. 199–215.

29 N. A. Hira, "You Raised Them, Now Manage Them," *Fortune*, May 28, 2007, pp. 38–46; R. R. Hastings, "Surveys Shed Light on Generation Y Career Goals," *SHRM Online*, March 2007, http://www.shrm.org; and S. Jayson, "The 'Millennials' Come of Age," *USA Today*, June 29, 2006, pp. 1D, 2D.

30 B. Tulgan, *Not Everyone Gets a Trophy: How to Manage Generation Y* (San Francisco, CA: Jossey-Bass, 2009).

31 Statistics Canada, "Census of Population," *The Daily*, February 11, 2003.

32 S. A. Hewlett, L. Sherbin, and K. Sumberg "How Gen Y & Boomers Will Reshape Your Agenda," *Harvard Business Review*, July/August 2009, pp. 71–76.

33 Statistics Canada, "2006 Census: Immigration, Citizenship, Language, Mobility and Migration," *The Daily*, December 4, 2007.

34 Statistics Canada, "Immigration in Canada: A Portrait of the Foreign-born Population, 2006 Census: Immigrants in Metropolitan Areas," http://www12.statcan.ca/english/census06/analysis/immcit/city_life.cfm

35 K. Young, "Language: Allophones on the Rise," *National Post*, December 4, 2007.

36 K. Young, "Language: Allophones on the Rise," *National Post*, December 4, 2007.

37 Statistics Canada, "Ethnic Diversity Survey, 2002," *The Daily*, September 29, 2003.

38 http://www.marketingcharts.com/television/american-vs-canadian-youth-lifestyles-values-differ-10588/

39 M. Adams, *Fire and Ice: The United States, Canada and the Myth of Converging Values* (Toronto: Penguin, 2003).

40 M. Adams, *Fire and Ice: The United States, Canada and the Myth of Converging Values* (Toronto: Penguin, 2003).

41 "The choice in Cuebec," *Maclean's*, October 30, 1995, pp. 18–33.

42 R. N. Kanungo and J. K. Bhatnagar, "Achievement Orientation and Occupational Values: A Comparative Study of Young French and English Canadians," *Canadian Journal of Behavioural Science* 12 (1978), pp. 384–392; M. W. McCarrey, S. Edwards, and R. Jones, "Personal Values of Canadian Anglophone and Francophone Employees and Ethnolinguistic Group Membership, Sex and Position Level," *Journal of Psychology* 104 (1978), pp. 175–184; M. W. McCarrey, S. Edwards, and R. Jones, "The Influence of Ethnolinguistic Group Membership, Sex, and Position Level on Motivational Orientation of Canadian Anglophone and Francophone Employees," *Canadian Journal of Behavioural Science* 9 (1977), pp. 274–282; M. W. McCarrey, Y. Gasse, and L. F. Moore, "Work Value Goals and Instrumentalities: A Comparison of Canadian West-Coast Anglophone and Quebec City Francophone Managers," *International Review of Applied Psychology* 33 (1984), pp. 291–303; and S. C. Jain and D. A. Ralston, "The North American Free Trade Agreement: An Overview," in *NAFTA: A Three-Way Partnership for Free Trade and Growth*, ed. S. C. Jain and D. A. Ralston (Storrs, CT: University of Connecticut, 1996), pp. 3–7.

43 M. Major, M. McCarrey, P. Mercier, and Y. Gasse, "Meanings of Work and Personal Values of Canadian Anglophone and Francophone Middle Managers," *Canadian Journal of Administrative Sciences*, September 1994, pp. 251–263.

44 R. N. Kanungo and J. K. Bhatnagar, "Achievement Orientation and Occupational Values: A Comparative Study of Young French and English Canadians," *Canadian Journal of Behavioural Science* 12 (1978), pp. 384–392.

45 V. Mann-Feder and V. Savicki, "Burnout in Anglophone and Francophone Child and Youth Workers in Canada: A Cross-Cultural Comparison," *Child & Youth Care Forum* 32, no. 6 (2003), p. 345.

46 R. N. Kanungo and J. K. Bhatnagar, "Achievement Orientation and Occupational Values: A Comparative Study of Young French and English Canadians," *Canadian Journal of Behavioural Science* 12 (1978), pp. 384–392.

47 V. Mann-Feder and V. Savicki, "Burnout in Anglophone and Francophone Child and Youth Workers in Canada: A Cross-Cultural Comparison," *Child & Youth Care Forum* 32, no. 6 (2003), pp. 337–354.

48 N. J. Adler and J. L. Graham, "Cross-Cultural Interaction: The International Comparison Fallacy?" *Journal of International Business Studies* 20 (1989), pp. 515–537.

49 N. J. Adler, J. L. Graham, and T. S. Gehrke, "Business Negotiations in Canada, Mexico, and the United States," *Journal of Business Research* 15 (1987), pp. 411–429.

50 H. C. Jain, J. Normand, and R. N. Kanungo, "Job Motivation of Canadian Anglophone and Francophone Hospital Employees," *Canadian Journal of Behavioural Science*, April 1979, pp. 160–163; and R. N. Kanungo, G. J. Gorn, and H. J. Dauderis, "Motivational Orientation of Canadian Anglophone and Francophone Managers," *Canadian Journal of Behavioural Science*, April 1976, pp. 107–121.

51 M. Major, M. McCarrey, P. Mercier, and Y. Gasse, "Meanings of Work and Personal Values of Canadian Anglophone and Francophone Middle Managers," *Canadian Journal of Administrative Sciences*, September 1994, pp. 251–263.

52 K. L. Gibson, S. J. Mckelvie, and A. F. De Man, "Personality and Culture: A Comparison of Francophones and Anglophones in Québec," *Journal of Social Psychology* 148, no. 2 (2008), pp. 133–165.

53 G. Bouchard, F. Rocher, and G. Rocher, *Les Francophones Québécois* (Montreal: Bowne de Montréal, 1991).

54 K. L. Gibson, S. J. Mckelvie, and A. F. De Man, "Personality and Culture: A Comparison of Francophones and Anglophones in Québec," *Journal of Social Psychology* 148, no. 2 (2008), pp. 133–165.

55 C. P. Egri, D. A. Ralston, C. S. Murray, and J. D. Nicholson, "Managers in the NAFTA Countries: A Cross-Cultural Comparison of Attitudes toward Upward Influence Strategies," *Journal of International Management* 6, no. 2 (2000), pp. 149–171.

56 C. P. Egri, D. A. Ralston, C. S. Murray, and J. D. Nicholson, "Managers in the NAFTA Countries: A Cross-Cultural Comparison of Attitudes toward Upward Influence Strategies," *Journal of International Management* 6, no. 2 (2000), p. 164.

57 G. Hamilton, "B.C. First Nation Logging Firm Wins National Award," *Vancouver Sun*, July 14, 2011, p. C2.

58 G. Hamilton, "B.C. First Nation Logging Firm Wins National Award," *Vancouver Sun*, July 14, 2011, p. C2.

59 L. Redpath and M. O. Nielsen, "A Comparison of Native Culture, Non-Native Culture and New Management Ideology," *Canadian Journal of Administrative Sciences* 14, no. 3 (1997), p. 327.

60 G. C. Anders and K. K. Anders, "Incompatible Goals in Unconventional Organizations: The Politics of Alaska Native Corporations," *Organization Studies* 7 (1986), pp. 213–233; G. Dacks, "Worker-Controlled Native Enterprises: A Vehicle for Community Development in Northern Canada?" *Canadian Journal of Native Studies* 3 (1983), pp. 289–310; and L. P. Dana, "Self-Employment in the Canadian Sub-Arctic: An Exploratory Study," *Canadian Journal of Administrative Sciences* 13 (1996), pp. 65–77.

61 L. Redpath and M. O. Nielsen, "A Comparison of Native Culture, Non-Native Culture and New Management Ideology," *Canadian Journal of Administrative Sciences* 14, no. 3 (1997), p. 327.

62 R. B. Anderson, "The Business Economy of the First Nations in Saskatchewan: A Contingency Perspective," *Canadian Journal of Native Studies* 2 (1995), pp. 309–345.

63 E. Struzik, "'Win-Win Scenario' Possible for Resource Industry, Aboriginals," *Edmonton Journal*, April 6, 2003, p. A12.

64 D. C. Natcher and C. G. Hickey, "Putting the Community Back into Community-Based Resource Management: A Criteria and Indicators Approach to Sustainability," *Human Organization* 61, no. 4 (2002), pp. 350–363.

65 http://www.highlevelwoodlands.com

66 http://www.cuslm.ca/foresterie/sfmn/nouvelles/LUM-Webb.pdf

67 Discussion based on L. Redpath and M. O. Nielsen, "A Comparison of Native Culture, Non-Native Culture and New Management Ideology," *Canadian Journal of Administrative Sciences* 14, no. 3 (1997), pp. 327–339.

68 Discussion based on L. Redpath and M. O. Nielsen, "A Comparison of Native Culture, Non-Native Culture and New Management Ideology," *Canadian Journal of Administrative Sciences* 14, no. 3 (1997), pp. 327–339.

69 D. Grigg and J. Newman, "Five Ways to Foster Bonds, Win Trust in Business," *Ottawa Citizen*, April 23, 2003, p. F12.

70 T. Chui, K. Tran, and J. Flanders, "Chinese Canadians: Enriching the Cultural Mosaic," *Canadian Social Trends*, no. 76, Spring 2005, pp. 26–34.

71 Statistics Canada, "Canada's Visible Minority Population in 2017," *The Daily*, March 22, 2005.

72 I. Y. M. Yeung and R. L. Tung, "Achieving Business Success in Confucian Societies: The Importance of Guanxi (Connections)," *Organizational Dynamics*, Special Report, 1998, pp. 72–83.

73 I. Y. M. Yeung and R. L. Tung, "Achieving Business Success in Confucian Societies: The Importance of Guanxi (Connections)," *Organizational Dynamics*, Special Report, 1998, p. 73.

74 Vignette based on K. Blevins, "Casino Workers in Regina Going Back to Work on Tuesday," *Leader-Post*, July 25, 2010, http://communities.canada.com/reginaleaderpost/print.aspx?postid=337941

75 D. A. Harrison, D. A. Newman, and P. L. Roth, "How Important Are Job Attitudes? Meta-analytic Comparisons of Integrative Behavioral Outcomes and Time Sequences," *Academy of Management Journal* 49, no. 2 (2006), pp. 305–325.

76 M. Riketta, "The Causal Relation between Job Attitudes and Performance: A Meta-analysis of Panel Studies," *Journal of Applied Psychology* 93, no. 2 (2008), pp. 472–481.

77 D. P. Moynihan and S. K. Pandey, "Finding Workable Levers over Work Motivation: Comparing Job Satisfaction, Job Involvement, and Organizational Commitment," *Administration & Society* 39, no. 7 (2007), pp. 803–832.

78 For problems with the concept of job satisfaction, see R. Hodson, "Workplace Behaviors," *Work and Occupations*, August 1991, pp. 271–290; and H. M. Weiss and R. Cropanzano, "Affective Events Theory: A Theoretical Discussion of the Structure, Causes and Consequences of Affective Experiences at Work," in *Research in Organizational Behavior*, vol. 18, ed. B. M. Staw and L. L. Cummings (Greenwich, CT: JAI Press, 1996), pp. 1–3.

79 J. Morrissy, "Canadian Workers among Most Dissatisfied in World," *Vancouver Sun*, June 25, 2011.

80 J. Barling, E. K. Kelloway, and R. D. Iverson, "High-Quality Work, Job Satisfaction, and Occupational Injuries," *Journal of Applied Psychology* 88, no. 2 (2003), pp. 276–283; and F. W. Bond and D. Bunce, "The Role of Acceptance and Job Control in Mental Health, Job Satisfaction, and Work Performance," *Journal of Applied Psychology* 88, no. 6 (2003), pp. 1057–1067.

81 S. E. Humphrey, J. D. Nahrgang, and F. P. Morgeson, "Integrating Motivational, Social, and Contextual Work Design Features: A Meta-analytic Summary and Theoretical Extension of the Work Design Literature," *Journal of Applied Psychology* 92, no. 5 (2007), pp. 1332–1356; and D. S. Chiaburu and D. A. Harrison, "Do Peers Make the Place? Conceptual Synthesis and Meta-analysis of Coworker Effect on Perceptions, Attitudes, OCBs, and Performance," *Journal of Applied Psychology* 93, no. 5 (2008), pp. 1082–1103.

82 E. Diener, E. Sandvik, L. Seidlitz, and M. Diener, "The Relationship between Income and Subjective Well-Being: Relative or Absolute?" *Social Indicators Research* 28 (1993), pp. 195–223.

83 E. Diener, E. Sandvik, L. Seidlitz, and M. Diener, "The Relationship Between Income and Subjective Well-Being: Relative or Absolute?" *Social Indicators Research* 28 (1993), pp. 195–223.

84 E. Diener, E. Sandvik, L. Seidlitz, and M. Diener, "The Relationship between Income and Subjective Well-Being: Relative or Absolute?" *Social Indicators Research* 28 (1993), pp. 195–223.

85 E. Diener and M. E. P. Seligman, "Beyond Money: Toward an Economy of Well-Being," *Psychological Science in the Public Interest* 5, no. 1 (2004), pp. 1–31; and A. Grant, "Money = Happiness? That's Rich: Here's the Science behind the Axiom," *The (South Mississippi) Sun Herald*, January 8, 2005.

86 T. A. Judge and C. Hurst, "The Benefits and Possible Costs of Positive Core Self-Evaluations: A Review and Agenda for Future Research," in *Positive Organizational Behavior*, ed. D. Nelson

and C. L. Cooper (London, UK: Sage Publications, 2007), pp. 159–174.

87 M. T. Iaffaldano and M. Muchinsky, "Job Satisfaction and Job Performance: A Meta-analysis," *Psychological Bulletin*, March 1985, pp. 251–273.

88 T. A. Judge, C. J. Thoresen, J. E. Bono, and G. K. Patton, "The Job Satisfaction–Job Performance Relationship: A Qualitative and Quantitative Review," *Psychological Bulletin*, May 2001, pp. 376–407; and T. Judge, S. Parker, A. E. Colbert, D. Heller, and R. Ilies, "Job Satisfaction: A Cross-Cultural Review," in *Handbook of Industrial, Work, & Organizational Psychology*, vol. 2, ed. N. Anderson, D. S. Ones, H. K. Sinangil, and C. Viswesvaran (Thousand Oaks, CA: Sage, 2001), p. 41.

89 M. Riketta, "The Causal Relation between Job Attitudes and Performance: A Meta-analysis of Panel Studies," *Journal of Applied Psychology* 93, no. 2 (2008), pp. 472–481.

90 C. N. Greene, "The Satisfaction–Performance Controversy," *Business Horizons*, February 1972, pp. 31–41; E. E. Lawler III, *Motivation in Organizations* (Monterey, CA: Brooks/Cole, 1973); and M. M. Petty, G. W. McGee, and J. W. Cavender, "A Meta-analysis of the Relationship between Individual Job Satisfaction and Individual Performance," *Academy of Management Review*, October 1984, pp. 712–721.

91 C. Ostroff, "The Relationship between Satisfaction, Attitudes, and Performance: An Organizational Level Analysis," *Journal of Applied Psychology*, December 1992, pp. 963–974; A. M. Ryan, M. J. Schmit, and R. Johnson, "Attitudes and Effectiveness: Examining Relations at an Organizational Level," *Personnel Psychology*, Winter 1996, pp. 853–882; and J. K. Harter, F. L. Schmidt, and T. L. Hayes, "Business-Unit Level Relationship between Employee Satisfaction, Employee Engagement, and Business Outcomes: A Meta-analysis," *Journal of Applied Psychology*, April 2002, pp. 268–279.

92 D. W. Organ, *Organizational Citizenship Behavior: The Good Soldier Syndrome* (Lexington, MA: Lexington Books, 1988), p. 4.

93 D. W. Organ, *Organizational Citizenship Behavior: The Good Soldier Syndrome* (Lexington, MA: Lexington Books, 1988); C. A. Smith, D. W. Organ, and J. P. Near, "Organizational Citizenship Behavior: Its Nature and Antecedents," *Journal of Applied Psychology*, 1983, pp. 653–663.

94 J. Farh, C. Zhong, and D. W. Organ, "Organizational Citizenship Behavior in the People's Republic of China," *Academy of Management Proceedings*, 2000, pp. OB: D1–D6.

95 J. M. George and A. P. Brief, "Feeling Good-Doing Good: A Conceptual Analysis of the Mood at Work–Organizational Spontaneity Relationship," *Psychological Bulletin* 112 (2002), pp. 310–329; S. Wagner and M. Rush, "Altruistic Organizational Citizenship Behavior: Context, Disposition and Age," *Journal of Social Psychology* 140 (2002), pp. 379–391; and J. R. Spence, D. L. Ferris, D. J. Brown, and D. Heller, "Understanding Daily Citizenship Behaviors: A Social Comparison Perspective," *Journal of Organizational Behavior* 32, no. 4 (2011), pp. 547–571.

96 P. E. Spector, *Job Satisfaction: Application, Assessment, Causes, and Consequences* (Thousand Oaks, CA: Sage, 1997), pp. 57–58.

97 P. M. Podsakoff, S. B. MacKenzie, J. B. Paine, and D. G. Bachrach, "Organizational Citizenship Behaviors: A Critical Review of the Theoretical and Empirical Literature and Suggestions for Future Research," *Journal of Management* 26, no. 3 (2000), pp. 513–563.

98 B. J. Hoffman, C. A. Blair, J. P. Maeriac, and D. J. Woehr, "Expanding the Criterion Domain? A Quantitative Review of the OCB Literature," *Journal of Applied Psychology* 92, no. 2 (2007), pp. 555–566; and J. A. LePine, A. Erez, and D. E. Johnson, "The Nature and Dimensionality of Organizational Citizenship Behavior: A Critical Review and Meta-analysis," *Journal of Applied Psychology*, February 2002, pp. 52–65.

99 S. L. Blader and T. R. Tyler, "Testing and Extending the Group Engagement Model: Linkages between Social Identity, Procedural Justice, Economic Outcomes, and Extrarole Behavior," *Journal of Applied Psychology* 94, no. 2 (2009), pp. 445–464; J. Fahr, P. M. Podsakoff, and D. W. Organ, "Accounting for Organizational Citizenship Behavior: Leader Fairness and Task Scope Versus Satisfaction," *Journal of Management*, December 1990, pp. 705–722; and M. A. Konovsky and D. W. Organ, "Dispositional and Contextual Determinants of Organizational Citizenship Behavior," *Journal of Organizational Behavior*, May 1996, pp. 253–266.

100 D. S. Chiaburu and D. A. Harrison, "Do Peers Make the Place? Conceptual Synthesis and Meta-analysis of Coworker Effect on Perceptions, Attitudes, OCBs, and Performance," *Journal of Applied Psychology* 93, no. 5 (2008), pp. 1082–1103; and J. R. Spence, D. L. Ferris, D. J. Brown, and D. Heller, "Understanding Daily Citizenship Behaviors: A Social Comparison Perspective," *Journal of Organizational Behavior* 32, no. 4 (2011), pp. 547–571.

101 See, for instance, E. Naumann and D. W. Jackson Jr., "One More Time: How Do You Satisfy Customers?" *Business Horizons*, May–June 1999, pp. 71–76; D. J. Koys, "The Effects of Employee Satisfaction, Organizational Citizenship Behavior, and Turnover on Organizational Effectiveness: A Unit-Level, Longitudinal Study," *Personnel Psychology*, Spring 2001, pp. 101–114; J. Griffith, "Do Satisfied Employees Satisfy Customers? Support-Services Staff Morale and Satisfaction among Public School Administrators, Students, and Parents," *Journal of Applied Social Psychology*, August 2001, pp. 1627–1658; and C. Vandenberghe, K. Bentein, R. Michon, J. Chebat, M. Tremblay, and J. Fils, "An Examination of the Role of Perceived Support and Employee Commitment in Employee-Customer Encounters," *Journal of Applied Psychology* 92, no. 4 (2007), pp. 1177–1187.

102 M. J. Bitner, B. H. Booms, and L. A. Mohr, "Critical Service Encounters: The Employee's Viewpoint," *Journal of Marketing*, October 1994, pp. 95–106.

103 E. A. Locke, "The Nature and Causes of Job Satisfaction," in *Handbook of Industrial and Organizational Psychology*, ed. M. D. Dunnette (Chicago: Rand McNally, 1976), p. 1331; K. D. Scott and G. S. Taylor, "An Examination of Conflicting Findings on the Relationship between Job Satisfaction and Absenteeism: A Meta-analysis," *Academy of Management Journal*, September 1985, pp. 599–612; and R. Steel and J. R. Rentsch, "Influence of Cumulation Strategies on the Long-Range Prediction of Absenteeism," *Academy of Management Journal*, December 1995, pp. 1616–1634.

104 J. P. Hausknecht, N. J. Hiller, and R. J. Vance, "Work-Unit Absenteeism: Effects of Satisfaction, Commitment, Labor Market Conditions, and Time," *Academy of Management Journal* 51, no. 6 (2008), pp. 1123–1245.

105 W. Hom and R. W. Griffeth, *Employee Turnover* (Cincinnati, OH: South-Western Publishing, 1995); R. W. Griffeth, P. W. Hom, and S. Gaertner, "A Meta-analysis of Antecedents and Correlates of Employee Turnover: Update, Moderator Tests, and Research Implications for the Next Millennium," *Journal of Management* 26, no. 3 (2000), p. 479.

106 T. H. Lee, B. Gerhart, I. Weller, and C. O. Trevor, "Understanding Voluntary Turnover: Path-Specific Job Satisfaction Effects and the Importance of Unsolicited Job Offers," *Academy of Management Journal* 51, no. 4 (2008), pp. 651–671.

107 P. E. Spector, S. Fox, L. M. Penney, K. Bruursema, A. Goh, and S. Kessler, "The Dimensionality of Counterproductivity: Are All Counterproductive Behaviors Created Equal?" *Journal of Vocational Behavior* 68, no. 3 (2006), pp. 446–460; and D. S. Chiaburu and D. A. Harrison, "Do Peers Make the Place? Conceptual Synthesis and Meta-analysis of Coworker Effect on Perceptions, Attitudes, OCBs, and Performance," *Journal of Applied Psychology* 93, no. 5 (2008), pp. 1082–1103.

108 See D. Farrell, "Exit, Voice, Loyalty, and Neglect as Responses to Job Dissatisfaction: A Multidimensional Scaling Study," *Academy of Management Journal*, December 1983, pp. 596–606; C. E. Rusbult, D. Farrell, G. Rogers, and A. G. Mainous III, "Impact of Exchange Variables on Exit, Voice, Loyalty, and Neglect: An Integrative Model of Responses to Declining Job Satisfaction," *Academy of Management Journal*, September 1988, pp. 599–627; M. J. Withey and W. H. Cooper, "Predicting Exit, Voice, Loyalty, and Neglect," *Administrative Science Quarterly*, December 1989, pp. 521–539; J. Zhou and J. M. George, "When Job Dissatisfaction Leads to Creativity: Encouraging the Expression of Voice," *Academy of Management Journal*, August 2001, pp. 682–696; J. B. Olson-Buchanan and W. R. Boswell, "The Role of Employee Loyalty and Formality in Voicing Discontent," *Journal of Applied Psychology*, December 2002, pp. 1167–1174; and A. Davis-Blake, J. P. Broschak, and E. George, "Happy Together? How Using Nonstandard Workers Affects Exit, Voice, and Loyalty among Standard Employees," *Academy of Management Journal* 46, no. 4 (2003), pp. 475–485.

109 R. B. Freeman, "Job Satisfaction as an Economic Variable," *American Economic Review*, January 1978, pp. 135–141.

110 K. Holland, "Inside the Minds of Your Employees," *New York Times*, January 28, 2007, p. B1; "Study Sees Link between Morale and Stock Price," *Workforce Management*, February 27, 2006, p. 15; and "The Workplace as a Solar System," *New York Times*, October 28, 2006, p. B5.

111 G. J. Blau and K. R. Boal, "Conceptualizing How Job Involvement and Organizational Commitment Affect Turnover and Absenteeism," *Academy of Management Review*, April 1987, p. 290.

112 N. J. Allen and J. P Meyer, "The Measurement and Antecedents of Affective, Continuance, and Normative Commitment to the Organization," *Journal of Occupational Psychology* 63 (1990), pp. 1–18; and J. P Meyer, N. J. Allen, and C. A. Smith, "Commitment to Organizations and Occupations: Extension and Test of a Three-Component Conceptualization," *Journal of Applied Psychology* 78 (1993), pp. 538–551.

113 M. Riketta, "Attitudinal Organizational Commitment and Job Performance: A Meta-analysis," *Journal of Organizational Behavior*, March 2002, pp. 257–266.

114 T. A. Wright and D. G. Bonett, "The Moderating Effects of Employee Tenure on the Relation between Organizational Commitment and Job Performance: A Meta-analysis," *Journal of Applied Psychology*, December 2002, pp. 1183–1190.

115 See, for instance, W. Hom, R. Katerberg, and C. L. Hulin, "Comparative Examination of Three Approaches to the Prediction of Turnover," *Journal of Applied Psychology*, June 1979, pp. 280–290; H. Angle and J. Perry, "Organizational Commitment: Individual and Organizational Influence," *Work and Occupations*, May 1983, pp. 123–146; J. L. Pierce and R. B. Dunham, "Organizational Commitment: Pre-Employment Propensity and Initial Work Experiences," *Journal of Management*, Spring 1987, pp. 163–178; and T. Simons and Q. Roberson, "Why Managers Should Care About Fairness: The Effects of Aggregate Justice Perceptions on Organizational Outcomes," *Journal of Applied Psychology* 88, no. 3 (2003), pp. 432–443.

116 Y. Gong, K. S. Law, S. Chang, and K. R. Xin, "Human Resources Management and Firm Performance: The Differential Role of Managerial Affective and Continuance Commitment," *Journal of Applied Psychology* 94, no. 1 (2009), pp. 263–275.

117 A. A. Luchak and I. R. Gellatly, "A Comparison of Linear and Nonlinear Relations between Organizational Commitment and Work Outcomes," *Journal of Applied Psychology* 92, no. 3 (2007), pp. 786–793.

118 J. R. Katzenbach and J. A. Santamaria, "Firing up the Front Line," *Harvard Business Review*, May–June 1999, p. 109.

119 See, for example, J. M. Diefendorff, D. J. Brown, and A. M. Kamin, "Examining the Roles of Job Involvement and Work Centrality in Predicting Organizational Citizenship Behaviors and Job Performance," *Journal of Organizational Behavior*, February 2002, pp. 93–108.

120 Based on G. J. Blau and K. R. Boal, "Conceptualizing How Job Involvement and Organizational Commitment Affect Turnover and Absenteeism," *Academy of Management Review*, April 1987, p. 290.

121 G. Chen and R. J. Klimoski, "The Impact of Expectations on Newcomer Performance in Teams as Mediated by Work Characteristics, Social Exchanges, and Empowerment," *Academy of Management Journal* 46, no. 5 (2003), pp. 591–607; A. Ergeneli, G. Saglam, and S. Metin, "Psychological Empowerment and Its Relationship to Trust in Immediate Managers," *Journal of Business Research*, January 2007, pp. 41–49; and S. E. Seibert, S. R. Silver, and W. A. Randolph, "Taking Empowerment to the Next Level: A Multiple-Level Model of Empowerment, Performance, and Satisfaction," *Academy of Management Journal* 47, no. 3 (2004), pp. 332–349.

122 J. M. Diefendorff, D. J. Brown, A. M. Kamin, and R. G. Lord, "Examining the Roles of Job Involvement and Work Centrality in Predicting Organizational Citizenship Behaviors and Job Performance," *Journal of Organizational Behavior*, February 2002, pp. 93–108.

123 M. R. Barrick, M. K. Mount, and J. P. Strauss, "Antecedents of Involuntary Turnover Due to a Reduction in Force," *Personnel Psychology* 47, no. 3 (1994), pp. 515–535.

124 D. R. May, R. L. Gilson, and L. M. Harter, "The Psychological Conditions of Meaningfulness, Safety and Availability and the Engagement of the Human Spirit at Work," *Journal of Occupational and Organizational Psychology* 77, no. 1 (2004), pp. 11–37.

125 B. L. Rich, J. A. Lepine, and E. R. Crawford, "Job Engagement: Antecedents and Effects on Job Performance," *Academy of Management Journal* 53, no. 3 (2010), pp. 617–635; and J. B. James, S. McKechnie, and J. Swanberg, "Predicting Employee Engagement in an Age-Diverse Retail Workforce," *Journal of Organizational Behavior* 32, no. 2 (2011), pp. 173–196.

126 "Building a Better Workforce," *PROFIT*, February 16, 2011, http://www.profitguide.com/article/10084—building-a-better-workforce—page0

127 J. K. Harter, F. L. Schmidt, and T. L. Hayes, "Business-Unit-Level Relationship between Employee Satisfaction, Employee Engagement, and Business Outcomes: A Meta-analysis," *Journal of Applied Psychology* 87, no. 2 (2002), pp. 268–279.

128 W. H. Macey and B. Schneider, "The Meaning of Employee Engagement," *Industrial and Organizational Psychology* 1 (2008), pp. 3–30.

129 A. Saks, "The Meaning and Bleeding of Employee Engagement: How Muddy Is the Water?" *Industrial and Organizational Psychology* 1 (2008), pp. 40–43.

130 A. B. Bakker, "An Evidence-Based Model of Work Engagement," *Current Directions in Psychological Science*, August 2011 (in press at time of writing).

131 Vignette based on "SaskGaming Is Proud to Support the Future of Saskatchewan," *Leader Post*, April 5, 2011, p. C8; and http://www.casinoregina.com/corporate/aboutus

132 See http://content.dell.com/ca/en/corp/d/corp-comm/cr-equal-employment-opportunity.aspx

133 N. Girouard, D. Stack, and M. O'Neill-Gilbert, "Ethnic Differences during Social Interactions of Preschoolers in Same-Ethnic and Cross-Ethnic Dyads," *European Journal of Developmental Psychology* 8, no. 2 (2011), pp. 185–202.

134 R. A. Roe and P. Ester, "Values and Work: Empirical Findings and Theoretical Perspective," *Applied Psychology: An International Review* 48 (1999), pp. 1–21.

135 A. Chapin, "Special Report: Diversity Knocks," *Canadian Business*, October 7, 2010.

136 D. A. Thomas and R. J. Ely, "Making Differences Matter: A New Paradigm for Managing Diversity," *Harvard Business Review* 74, no. 5 (1996), pp. 79–90; C. L. Holladay and M. A. Quiñones, "The Influence of Training Focus and Trainer Characteristics on Diversity Training Effectiveness," *Academy of Management Learning and Education* 7, no. 3 (2008), pp. 343–354; and R. Anand and M. Winters, "A Retrospective View of Corporate Diversity Training from 1964 to the Present," *Academy of Management Learning and Education* 7, no. 3 (2008), pp. 356–372.

137 L. Legault, J. Gutsell, and M. Inzlicht, "Ironic Effects of Anti-Prejudice Messages," *Psychological Science*, July 6, 2011, http://www.psychologicalscience.org/index.php/news/releases/ironic-effects-of-anti-prejudice-messages.html

138 Q. M. Roberson and C. K. Stevens, "Making Sense of Diversity in the Workplace: Organizational Justice and Language Abstraction in Employees' Accounts of Diversity-Related Incidents," *Journal of Applied Psychology* 91 (2006), pp. 379–391; and D. A. Harrison, D. A. Kravitz, D. M. Mayer, L. M. Leslie, and D. Lev-Arey, "Understanding Attitudes toward Affirmative Action Programs in Employment: Summary and Meta-analysis of 35 Years of Research," *Journal of Applied Psychology* 91 (2006), pp. 1013–1036.

139 A. Kalev, F. Dobbin, and E. Kelly, "Best Practices or Best Guesses? Assessing the Efficacy of Corporate Affirmative Action and Diversity Policies," *American Sociological Review* 71, no. 4 (2006), pp. 589–617.

140 For more examples, see D. Jermyn, "45 of Canada's Most Welcoming Places to Work," *Globe and Mail*, February 21, 2011, p. B14.

141 A. Pomeroy, "Cultivating Female Leaders," *HR Magazine*, February 2007, pp. 44–50.

142 Based on P. Jeffery, "A Call to Action," *FP Magazine*, June 21, 2011.

143 L. Nguyen, "Banana Peel Thrown at Flyers' Wayne Simmonds Called a Wake-Up Call to NHL for More Ethnic Diversity," *Vancouver Sun*, September 23, 2011.

144 P. C. Earley and E. Mosakowski, "Cultural Intelligence," *Harvard Business Review* 82, no. 10 (October 2004), pp. 139–146.

145 S. S. Ramalu, R. C. Rose, N. Kumar, and J. Uli, "Doing Business in Global Arena: An Examination of the Relationship between Cultural Intelligence and Cross-Cultural Adjustment," *Asian Academy of Management Journal* 15, no. 1 (2010), pp. 79–97.

146 J. Sanchez-Burks, F. Lee, R. Nisbett, I. Choi, S. Zhao, and J. Koo, "Conversing across Cultures: East-West Communication Styles in Work and Nonwork Contexts," *Journal of Personality and Social Psychology* 85, no. 2 (2003), pp. 363–372.

147 M. J. Gelfand, M. Erez, and Z. Aycan, "Cross-Cultural Organizational Behavior," *Annual Review of Psychology* 58 (2007), pp. 479–514; and A. S. Tsui, S. S. Nifadkar, and A. Y. Ou, "Cross-National, Cross-Cultural Organizational Behavior Research: Advances, Gaps, and Recommendations," *Journal of Management*, June 2007, pp. 426–478.

148 M. Benz and B. S. Frey, "The Value of Autonomy: Evidence from the Self-Employed in 23 Countries," working paper 173, Institute for Empirical Research in Economics, University of Zurich, November 2003; and P. Warr, *Work, Happiness, and Unhappiness* (Mahwah, NJ: Laurence Erlbaum, 2007).

149 Based on E. Snape, C. Lo, and T. Redman, "The Three-Component Model of Occupational Commitment: A Comparative Study

of Chinese and British Accountants," *Journal of Cross-Cultural Psychology*, November 2008, pp. 765–781; and Y. Cheng and M. S. Stockdale, "The Validity of the Three-Component Model of Organizational Commitment in a Chinese Context," *Journal of Vocational Behavior*, June 2003, pp. 465–489.

150 E. Bellman, "Reversal of Fortune Isolates India's Brahmins," *Wall Street Journal*, December 29, 2007, p. A4.

151 A. Sippola and A. Smale, "The Global Integration of Diversity Management: A Longitudinal Case Study," *International Journal of Human Resource Management* 18, no. 11 (2007), pp. 1895–1916.

152 E. A. Locke, "The Nature and Causes of Job Satisfaction," in *Handbook of Industrial and Organizational Psychology*, ed. M. D. Dunnette (Chicago: Rand McNally, 1976), pp. 1319–1328.

153 See, for instance, R. D. Arvey, B. P. McCall, T. J. Bouchard Jr., and P. Taubman, "Genetic Influences on Job Satisfaction and Work Values," *Personality and Individual Differences*, July 1994, pp. 21–33; D. Lykken and A. Tellegen, "Happiness Is a Stochastic Phenomenon," *Psychological Science*, May 1996, pp. 186–189; D. Lykken and M. Csikszentmihalyi, "Happiness—Stuck with What You've Got?" *Psychologist*, September 2001, pp. 470–472; and "Double Take," *UNH Magazine*, Spring 2000, http://www.unhmagazine.unh.edu/sp00/twinssp00.html

154 This exercise is based on M. Allen, "Here Comes the Bribe," *Entrepreneur*, October 2000, p. 48.

155 Reconstructed, based on H. Sokoloff, "Firing of Teacher Upheld for His Opinions on Race," *National Post*, March 13, 2002, pp. A1, A11.

156 J. Zaslow, "From Attitude to Gratitude: This Is No Time for Complaints," *Wall Street Journal*, March 4, 2009, p. D1; A. M. Wood, S. Joseph, and J. Maltby, "Gratitude Uniquely Predicts Satisfaction with Life: Incremental Validity above the Domains and Facets of the Five Factor Model," *Personality and Individual Differences* 45, no. 1 (2008), pp. 49–54; and R. A. Emmons, "Gratitude, Subjective Well-Being, and the Brain," in *The Science of Subjective Well-Being*, ed. M. Eid and R. J. Larsen (New York: Guilford Press, 2008), pp. 469–489.

OB on the Edge: Stress at Work

1 Based on J. Newman and D. Grigg, "Road to Health Pays Off for B.C. Trucking Firm," *Edmondon Journal*, July 2, 2011, p. C5.

2 Paragraph based on D. Hansen, "Worker Who Felt 'Thrown Away' Wins," *Vancouver Sun*, August 16, 2006.

3 Statistics Canada, "Perceived Life Stress, Quite a Lot, by Sex, by Province and Territory, 2010," http://www40.statcan.ca/l01/cst01/health107b-eng.htm

4 K. MacQueen, "Workplace Stress Costs Us Dearly, and Yet Nobody Knows What It Is or How to Deal with It," *Maclean's*, October 15, 2007.

5 K. MacQueen, "Workplace Stress Costs Us Dearly, and Yet Nobody Knows What It Is or How to Deal with It," *Maclean's*, October 15, 2007.

6 L. Duxbury and C. Higgins, "2001 National Work-Life Conflict Study," as reported in J. Campbell, "'Organizational Anorexia' Puts Stress on Employees," *Ottawa Citizen*, July 4, 2002.

7 K. Harding, "Balance Tops List of Job Desires," *Globe and Mail*, May 7, 2003, pp. C1, C6.

8 V. Galt, "Productivity Buckling under the Strain of Stress, CEOs Say," *Globe and Mail*, June 9, 2005, p. B1.

9 "Canadian Workers among Most Stressed," *Worklife Report* 14, no. 2 (2002), pp. 8–9.

10 N. Ayed, "Absenteeism Up Since 1993," *Canadian Press Newswire*, March 25, 1998.

11 N. Ayed, "Absenteeism Up Since 1993," *Canadian Press Newswire*, March 25, 1998.

12 Adapted from R. S. Schuler, "Definition and Conceptualization of Stress in Organizations," *Organizational Behavior and Human Performance*, April 1980, p. 189. For an updated review of definitions, see C. L. Cooper, P. J. Dewe, and M. P. O'Driscoll, *Organizational Stress: A Review and Critique of Theory, Research, and Applications* (Thousand Oaks, CA: Sage, 2002).

13 See, for instance, M. A. Cavanaugh, W. R. Boswell, M. V. Roehling, and J. W. Boudreau, "An Empirical Examination of Self-Reported Work Stress among U.S. Managers," *Journal of Applied Psychology*, February 2000, pp. 65–74.

14 N. P. Podsakoff, J. A. LePine, and M. A. LePine, "Differential Challenge-Hindrance Stressor Relationships with Job Attitudes, Turnover Intentions, Turnover, and Withdrawal Behavior: A Meta-analysis," *Journal of Applied Psychology* 92, no. 2 (2007), pp. 438–454; and J. A. LePine, M. A. LePine, and C. L. Jackson, "Challenge and Hindrance Stress: Relationships with Exhaustion, Motivation to Learn, and Learning Performance," *Journal of Applied Psychology*, October 2004, pp. 883–891.

15 Based on *Health* magazine as it appeared in Centers for Disease Control and Prevention, US Department of Health and Human Services, "*Helicobacter pylori* and Peptic Ulcer Disease—Myths," http://www.cdc.gov/ulcer/myth.htm

16 S. Gilboa, A. Shirom, Y. Fried, and C. Cooper, "A Meta-analysis of Work Demand Stressors and Job Performance: Examining Main and Moderating Effects," *Personnel Psychology* 61, no. 2 (2008), pp. 227–271.

17 J. C. Wallace, B. D. Edwards, T. Arnold, M. L. Frazier, and D. M. Finch, "Work Stressors, Role-Based Performance, and the Moderating Influence of Organizational Support," *Journal of Applied Psychology* 94, no. 1 (2009), pp. 254–262.

18 L. W. Hunter and S. M. B. Thatcher, "Feeling the Heat: Effects of Stress, Commitment, and Job Experience on Job Performance," *Academy of Management Journal* 50, no. 4 (2007), pp. 953–968.

19 J. de Jonge and C. Dormann, "Stressors, Resources, and Strain at Work: A Longitudinal Test of the Triple-Match Principle," *Journal of Applied Psychology* 91, no. 5 (2006), pp. 1359–1374; K. Daniels, N. Beesley, A. Cheyne, and V. Wimalasiri, "Coping Processes Linking the Demands-Control-Support Model, Affect and Risky Decisions at Work," *Human Relations* 61, no. 6 (2008), pp. 845–874; and M. van den Tooren and J. de Jonge, "Managing Job Stress in Nursing: What Kind of Resources Do We Need?" *Journal of Advanced Nursing* 63, no. 1 (2008), pp. 75–84.

20 This section is adapted from C. L. Cooper and R. Payne, *Stress at Work* (London: Wiley, 1978); S. Parasuraman and J. A. Alutto, "Sources and Outcomes of Stress in Organizational Settings: Toward the Development of a Structural Model," *Academy of Management Journal* 27, no. 2 (June 1984), pp. 330–350; and P. M. Hart and C. L. Cooper, "Occupational Stress: Toward a More Integrated Framework," in *Handbook of Industrial, Work and Organizational Psychology*, vol. 2, ed. N. Anderson, D. S. Ones, H. K. Sinangil, and C. Viswesvaran (London: Sage, 2001), pp. 93–114.

21 E. A. Rafferty and M. A. Griffin, "Perceptions of Organizational Change: A Stress and Coping Perspective," *Journal of Applied Psychology* 71, no. 5 (2007), pp. 1154–1162.

22 See, for example, M. L. Fox, D. J. Dwyer, and D. C. Ganster, "Effects of Stressful Job Demands and Control of Physiological and Attitudinal Outcomes in a Hospital Setting," *Academy of Management Journal*, April 1993, pp. 289–318.

23 G. W. Evans and D. Johnson, "Stress and Open-Office Noise," *Journal of Applied Psychology*, October 2000, pp. 779–783.

24 T. M. Glomb, J. D. Kammeyer-Mueller, and M. Rotundo, "Emotional Labor Demands and Compensating Wage

Differentials," *Journal of Applied Psychology*, August 2004, pp. 700–714; and A. A. Grandey, "When 'The Show Must Go On': Surface Acting and Deep Acting as Determinants of Emotional Exhaustion and Peer-Rated Service Delivery," *Academy of Management Journal*, February 2003, pp. 86–96.

25 S. Lim, L. M. Cortina, and V. J. Magley, "Personal and Workgroup Incivility: Impact on Work and Health Outcomes," *Journal of Applied Psychology* 93, no. 1 (2008), pp. 95–107; N. T. Buchanan and L. F. Fitzgerald, "Effects of Racial and Sexual Harassment on Work and the Psychological Well-Being of African American Women," *Journal of Occupational Health Psychology* 13, no. 2 (2008), pp. 137–151; C. R. Willness, P. Steel, and K. Lee, "A Meta-analysis of the Antecedents and Consequences of Workplace Sexual Harassment," *Personnel Psychology* 60, no. 1 (2007), pp. 127–162; and B. Moreno-Jiménez, A. Rodríguez-Muñoz, J. C. Pastor, A. I. Sanz-Vergel, and E. Garrosa, "The Moderating Effects of Psychological Detachment and Thoughts of Revenge in Workplace Bullying," *Personality and Individual Differences* 46, no. 3 (2009), pp. 359–364.

26 V. S. Major, K. J. Klein, and M. G. Ehrhart, "Work Time, Work Interference with Family, and Psychological Distress," *Journal of Applied Psychology*, June 2002, pp. 427–436; see also P. E. Spector, C. L. Cooper, S. Poelmans, T. D. Allen, M. O'Driscoll, J. I. Sanchez, O. L. Siu, P. Dewe, P. Hart, L. Lu, L. F. R. De Moreas, G. M. Ostrognay, K. Sparks, P. Wong, and S. Yu, "A Cross-National Comparative Study of Work-Family Stressors, Working Hours, and Well-Being: China and Latin America versus the Anglo World," *Personnel Psychology*, Spring 2004, pp. 119–142.

27 D. L. Nelson and C. Sutton, "Chronic Work Stress and Coping: A Longitudinal Study and Suggested New Directions," *Academy of Management Journal*, December 1990, pp. 859–869.

28 H. Selye, *The Stress of Life* (New York: McGraw-Hill, 1976).

29 FactBox based on A. Picard, "The Working Wounded," *Globe and Mail*, June 22, 2008; and Statistics Canada, "Study: Work Absences in 2010," *The Daily*, May 25, 2011, http://www.statcan.gc.ca/daily-quotidien/110525/dq110525e-eng.htm; Statistics Canada, "Perceived Life Stress, 2009," http://www.statcan.gc.ca/pub/82-229-x/2009001/status/pls-eng.htm; Canadian Newswire, "Vacation Deprivation Continues but Canadians Still Value Vacations in Today's Economy, Expedia.ca Survey Finds," May 13, 2009, http://www.newswire.ca/en/releases/archive/May2009/13/c2818.html

30 R. S. Schuler, "Definition and Conceptualization of Stress in Organizations," *Organizational Behavior and Human Performance*, April 1980, p. 191; and R. L. Kahn and P. Byosiere, "Stress in Organizations," *Organizational Behavior and Human Performance*, April 1980, pp. 604–610.

31 See T. A. Beehr and J. E. Newman, "Job Stress, Employee Health, and Organizational Effectiveness: A Facet Analysis, Model, and Literature Review," *Personnel Psychology*, Winter 1978, pp. 665–699; and B. D. Steffy and J. W. Jones, "Workplace Stress and Indicators of Coronary-Disease Risk," *Academy of Management Journal*, September 1988, pp. 686–698.

32 J. Schaubroeck, J. R. Jones, and J. L. Xie, "Individual Differences in Utilizing Control to Cope with Job Demands: Effects on Susceptibility to Infectious Disease," *Journal of Applied Psychology*, April 2001, pp. 265–278.

33 KPMG Canada, compensation letter, July 1998.

34 B. D. Steffy and J. W. Jones, "Workplace Stress and Indicators of Coronary-Disease Risk," *Academy of Management Journal* 31 (1988), p. 687.

35 C. L. Cooper and J. Marshall, "Occupational Sources of Stress: A Review of the Literature Relating to Coronary Heart Disease and Mental Ill Health," *Journal of Occupational Psychology* 49, no. 1 (1976), pp. 11–28.

36 J. R. Hackman and G. R. Oldham, "Development of the Job Diagnostic Survey," *Journal of Applied Psychology*, April 1975, pp. 159–170.

37 J. L. Xie and G. Johns, "Job Scope and Stress: Can Job Scope Be Too High?" *Academy of Management Journal*, October 1995, pp. 1288–1309.

38 S. J. Motowidlo, J. S. Packard, and M. R. Manning, "Occupational Stress: Its Causes and Consequences for Job Performance," *Journal of Applied Psychology*, November 1987, pp. 619–620.

39 See, for instance, R. C. Cummings, "Job Stress and the Buffering Effect of Supervisory Support," *Group & Organization Studies*, March 1990, pp. 92–104; M. R. Manning, C. N. Jackson, and M. R. Fusilier, "Occupational Stress, Social Support, and the Cost of Health Care," *Academy of Management Journal*, June 1996, pp. 738–750; and P. D. Bliese and T. W. Britt, "Social Support, Group Consensus and Stressor-Strain Relationships: Social Context Matters," *Journal of Organizational Behavior*, June 2001, pp. 425–436.

40 R. Williams, *The Trusting Heart: Great News About Type A Behavior* (New York: Times Books, 1989).

41 D. C. Ganster, W. E. Sime, and B. T. Mayes, "Type A Behavior in the Work Setting: A Review and Some New Data," in *In Search of Coronary-Prone Behavior: Beyond Type A*, ed. A. W. Siegman and T. M. Dembroski (Hillsdale, NJ: Erlbaum, 1989), pp. 117–118; and B. K. Houston, "Cardiovascular and Neuroendocrine Reactivity, Global Type A, and Components of Type A," in *Type A Behavior Pattern: Research, Theory, and Intervention*, ed. B. K. Houston and C. R. Snyder (New York: Wiley, 1988), pp. 212–253.

42 T. H. Macan, "Time Management: Test of a Process Model," *Journal of Applied Psychology*, June 1994, pp. 381–391.

43 See, for example, G. Lawrence-Ell, *The Invisible Clock: A Practical Revolution in Finding Time for Everyone and Everything* (Seaside Park, NJ: Kingsland Hall, 2002).

44 S. A. Devi, "Aging Brain: Prevention of Oxidative Stress by Vitamin E and Exercise," *ScientificWorldJournal* 9 (2009), pp. 366–372. See also J. Kiely and G. Hodgson, "Stress in the Prison Service: The Benefits of Exercise Programs," *Human Relations*, June 1990, pp. 551–572.

45 E. J. Forbes and R. J. Pekala, "Psychophysiological Effects of Several Stress Management Techniques," *Psychological Reports*, February 1993, pp. 19–27; and G. Smith, "Meditation, the New Balm for Corporate Stress," *BusinessWeek*, May 10, 1993, pp. 86–87.

46 J. Lee, "How to Fight That Debilitating Stress in Your Workplace," *Vancouver Sun*, April 5, 1999, p. C3. Reprinted with permission.

47 H. Staseson, "Can Perk Help Massage Bottom Line? On-Site Therapeutic Sessions Are Used by an Increasingly Diverse Group of Employers Hoping to Improve Staff Performance," *Globe and Mail*, July 3, 2002, p. C1.

48 Health Canada, "Wellness Programs Offer Healthy Return, Study Finds," *Report Bulletin*, #224, October 2001, p. 1.

49 H. Staseson, "Can Perk Help Massage Bottom Line? On-Site Therapeutic Sessions Are Used by an Increasingly Diverse Group of Employers Hoping to Improve Staff Performance," *Globe and Mail*, July 3, 2002, p. C1.

50 "Cdn Employers Not Measuring Wellness Outcomes: Survey," *Benefits Canada*, May 4, 2011, http://www.benefitscanada.com/news/cnd-employers-not-measuring-wellness-outcomes-survey-16510

51 P. M. Wright, "Operationalization of Goal Difficulty as a Moderator of the Goal Difficulty-Performance Relationship," *Journal of Applied Psychology*, June 1990, pp. 227–234; E. A. Locke and G. P. Latham, "Building a Practically Useful Theory of Goal Setting and Task Motivation: A 35-Year Odyssey," *American Psychologist* 57, no. 9 (2002), pp. 705–717; K. L. Langeland, C. M.

Johnson, and T. C. Mawhinney, "Improving Staff Performance in a Community Mental Health Setting: Job Analysis, Training, Goal Setting, Feedback, and Years of Data," *Journal of Organizational Behavior Management*, 1998, pp. 21–43.

52 E. R. Greenglass and L. Fiksenbaum, "Proactive Coping, Positive Affect, and Well-Being: Testing for Mediation Using Path Analysis," *European Psychologist* 14, no. 1 (2009), pp. 29–39; and P. Miquelon and R. J. Vallerand, "Goal Motives, Well-Being, and Physical Health: Happiness and Self-Realization as Psychological Resources under Challenge," *Motivation and Emotion* 30, no. 4 (2006), pp. 259–272.

53 Based on S. Martin, "Money Is the Stressor for Americans," *Monitor on Psychology*, December 2008, pp. 28–29; *Helicobacter pylori and Peptic Ulcer Disease*, Centers for Disease Control and Prevention, U.S. Department of Health and Human Services, http://www.cdc.gov/ulcer; and M. Maynard, "Maybe the Toughest Job Aloft," *New York Times*, August 15, 2006, pp. C1, C6.

54 S. E. Jackson, "Participation in Decision Making as a Strategy for Reducing Job-Related Strain," *Journal of Applied Psychology*, February 1983, pp. 3–19.

55 S. Greengard, "It's About Time," *IndustryWeek*, February 7, 2000, pp. 47–50; and S. Nayyar, "Gimme a Break," *American Demographics*, June 2002, p. 6.

56 See, for instance, B. Leonard, "Health Care Costs Increase Interest in Wellness Programs," *HR Magazine*, September 2001, pp. 35–36; and "Healthy, Happy and Productive," *Training*, February 2003, p. 16.

57 K. M. Richardson and H. R. Rothstein, "Effects of Occupational Stress Management Intervention Programs: A Meta-analysis," *Journal of Occupational Health Psychology* 13, no. 1 (2008), pp. 69–93.

Chapter 4

1 Vignette based on N. Watts, "Chan Finishes Off Podium in Fifth, Lysacek Takes Gold," *Toronto Observer*, February 19, 2010, http://www.torontoobserver.ca/2010/02/19/chan-finishes-off-podium-in-fifth-lysacek-takes-gold/; and L. Ewing, "Figure Skating's Code of Points Practically Takes a Statistician to Decipher," *Canadian Press*, February 8, 2010.

2 See, for instance, T. R. Mitchell, "Matching Motivational Strategies with Organizational Contexts," in *Research in Organizational Behavior*, vol. 19, ed. L. L. Cummings and B. M. Staw (Greenwich, CT: JAI Press, 1997), pp. 60–62.

3 D. Gregor, *The Human Side of Enterprise* (New York: McGraw-Hill, 1960). For an updated analysis of Theory X and Theory Y constructs, see R. J. Summers and S. F. Cronshaw, "A Study of McGregor's Theory X, Theory Y and the Influence of Theory X, Theory Y Assumptions on Causal Attributions for Instances of Worker Poor Performance," in *Organizational Behavior*, ed. S. L. McShane, ASAC Conference Proceedings, vol. 9, part 5, Halifax, 1988, pp. 115–123.

4 K. W. Thomas, *Intrinsic Motivation at Work* (San Francisco: Berrett-Koehler, 2000); and K. W. Thomas, "Intrinsic Motivation and How It Works," *Training*, October 2000, pp. 130–135.

5 A. Kohn, *Punished by Rewards* (Boston: Houghton Mifflin, 1993).

6 D. Albarracin, I. Senay, and K. Noguchi, "Will We Succeed? The Science of Self-motivation," *Psychological Science*, April 2010.

7 "Will We Succeed? The Science of Self-Motivation," *ScienceDaily*, June 1, 2010, http://www.sciencedaily.com/releases/2010/05/100528092021.htm

8 A. H. Maslow, *Motivation and Personality* (New York: Harper and Row, 1954).

9 C. Conley, *Peak: How Great Companies Get Their Mojo from Maslow* (San Francisco: Jossey-Bass, 2007).

10 K. Korman, J. H. Greenhaus, and I. J. Badin, "Personnel Attitudes and Motivation," in *Annual Review of Psychology*, ed. M. R. Rosenzweig and L. W. Porter (Palo Alto, CA: Annual Reviews, 1977), p. 178; and M. A. Wahba and L. G. Bridwell, "Maslow Reconsidered: A Review of Research on the Need Hierarchy Theory," *Organizational Behavior and Human Performance*, April 1976, pp. 212–240.

11 L. Tay and E. Diener, "Needs and Subjective Well-Being around the World," *Journal of Personality and Social Psychology*, June 20, 2011, published online before print, http://psycnet.apa.org/?&fa=main.doiLanding&doi=10.1037/a0023779

12 C. P. Alderfer, "An Empirical Test of a New Theory of Human Needs," *Organizational Behavior and Human Performance*, May 1969, pp. 142–175.

13 C. P. Schneider and C. P. Alderfer, "Three Studies of Measures of Need Satisfaction in Organizations," *Administrative Science Quarterly*, December 1973, pp. 489–505; and I. Borg and M. Braun, "Work Values in East and West Germany: Different Weights, but Identical Structures," *Journal of Organizational Behavior* 17, Special Issue (1996), pp. 541–555.

14 F. Herzberg, B. Mausner, and B. Snyderman, *The Motivation to Work* (New York: Wiley, 1959).

15 R. J. House and L. A. Wigdor, "Herzberg's Dual-Factor Theory of Job Satisfaction and Motivations: A Review of the Evidence and Criticism," *Personnel Psychology*, Winter 1967, pp. 369–389; D. P. Schwab and L. L. Cummings, "Theories of Performance and Satisfaction: A Review," *Industrial Relations*, October 1970, pp. 403–430; R. J. Caston and R. Braito, "A Specification Issue in Job Satisfaction Research," *Sociological Perspectives*, April 1985, pp. 175–197; and J. Phillipchuk and J. Whittaker, "An Inquiry into the Continuing Relevance of Herzberg's Motivation Theory," *Engineering Management Journal* 8, no. 1 (1996), pp. 15–20.

16 R. J. House and L. A. Wigdor, "Herzberg's Dual-Factor Theory of Job Satisfaction and Motivations: A Review of the Evidence and Criticism," *Personnel Psychology*, Winter 1967, pp. 369–389; D. P. Schwab and L. L. Cummings, "Theories of Performance and Satisfaction: A Review," *Industrial Relations*, October 1970, pp. 403–430; and R. J. Caston and R. Braito, "A Specification Issue in Job Satisfaction Research," *Sociological Perspectives*, April 1985, pp. 175–197.

17 D. C. McClelland, *The Achieving Society* (New York: Van Nostrand Reinhold, 1961); J. W. Atkinson and J. O. Raynor, *Motivation and Achievement* (Washington, DC: Winston, 1974); D. C. McClelland, *Power: The Inner Experience* (New York: Irvington, 1975); and M. J. Stahl, *Managerial and Technical Motivation: Assessing Needs for Achievement, Power, and Affiliation* (New York: Praeger, 1986).

18 D. C. McClelland, *The Achieving Society* (New York: Van Nostrand Reinhold, 1961).

19 D. C. McClelland and D. G. Winter, *Motivating Economic Achievement* (New York: The Free Press, 1969); and J. B. Miner, N. R. Smith, and J. S. Bracker, "Role of Entrepreneurial Task Motivation in the Growth of Technologically Innovative Firms: Interpretations from Follow-up Data," *Journal of Applied Psychology*, October 1994, pp. 627–630.

20 D. C. McClelland, *Power: The Inner Experience* (New York: Irvington, 1975); D. C. McClelland and D. H. Burnham, "Power Is the Great Motivator," *Harvard Business Review*, March–April 1976, pp. 100–110; and R. E. Boyatzis, "The Need for Close Relationships and the Manager's Job," in *Organizational Psychology: Readings on Human Behavior in Organizations*, 4th ed., ed. D. A. Kolb, I. M. Rubin, and J. M. McIntyre (Upper Saddle River, NJ: Prentice Hall, 1984), pp. 81–86.

21 D. G. Winter, "The Motivational Dimensions of Leadership: Power, Achievement, and Affiliation," in *Multiple Intelligences and Leadership*, ed. R. E. Riggio, S. E. Murphy, and F. J. Pirozzolo (Mahwah, NJ: Lawrence Erlbaum, 2002), pp. 119–138.

22 J. B. Miner, *Studies in Management Education* (New York: Springer, 1965).

23 Vignette based on P. J. Kwong, "With Lessons Learned, Chan Ready to Defend His Title," *cbcsports.ca*, July 11, 2011, http://www.cbc.ca/sports/blogs/pjkwong/2011/07/with-lessons-learned-chan-ready-to-defend-his-title.html; and "Chan Wins World Figure Skating Title," *Toronto Sun*, http://www.torontosun.com/2011/04/28/chan-wins-world-figure-skating-title

24 V. H. Vroom, *Work and Motivation* (New York: Wiley, 1964).

25 R. Sinclair, "A&A: LPGA Golfer Alena Sharp," *CBC.ca*, February 18, 2011, http://www.cbc.ca/sports/moresports/ story/2011/02/13/sp-lpga-sharp.html

26 See http://www.radical.ca

27 See, for example, H. G. Heneman III and D. P. Schwab, "Evaluation of Research on Expectancy Theory Prediction of Employee Performance," *Psychological Bulletin*, July 1972, pp. 1–9; T. R. Mitchell, "Expectancy Models of Job Satisfaction, Occupational Preference and Effort: A Theoretical, Methodological and Empirical Appraisal," *Psychological Bulletin*, November 1974, pp. 1053–1077; and L. Reinharth and M. A. Wahba, "Expectancy Theory as a Predictor of Work Motivation, Effort Expenditure, and Job Performance," *Academy of Management Journal*, September 1975, pp. 502–537.

28 See, for example, L. W. Porter and E. E. Lawler III, *Managerial Attitudes and Performance* (Homewood, IL: Richard D. Irwin, 1968); D. F. Parker and L. Dyer, "Expectancy Theory as a Within-Person Behavioral Choice Model: An Empirical Test of Some Conceptual and Methodological Refinements," *Organizational Behavior and Human Performance*, October 1976, pp. 97–117; H. J. Arnold, "A Test of the Multiplicative Hypothesis of Expectancy-Valence Theories of Work Motivation," *Academy of Management Journal*, April 1981, pp. 128–141; and W. Van Eerde and H. Thierry, "Vroom's Expectancy Models and Work-Related Criteria: A Meta-analysis," *Journal of Applied Psychology*, October 1996, pp. 575–586.

29 P. C. Earley, *Face, Harmony, and Social Structure: An Analysis of Organizational Behavior across Cultures* (New York: Oxford University Press, 1997); R. M. Steers and C. Sanchez-Runde, "Culture, Motivation, and Work Behavior," in *Handbook of Cross-Cultural Management*, ed. M. Gannon and K. Newman (London: Blackwell, 2001), pp. 190–215; and H. C. Triandis, "Motivation and Achievement in Collectivist and Individualistic Cultures," in *Advances in Motivation and Achievement*, vol. 9, ed. M. Maehr and P. Pintrich (Greenwich, CT: JAI Press, 1995), pp. 1–30.

30 J. S. Lublin, "It's Shape-up Time for Performance Reviews," *Wall Street Journal*, October 3, 1994, p. B1.

31 Much of this section is based on H. H. Meyer, "A Solution to the Performance Appraisal Feedback Enigma," *Academy of Management Executive*, February 1991, pp. 68–76.

32 T. D. Schelhardt, "It's Time to Evaluate Your Work, and All Involved Are Groaning," *Wall Street Journal*, November 19, 1996, p. A1.

33 R. J. Burke, "Why Performance Appraisal Systems Fail," *Personnel Administration*, June 1972, pp. 32–40.

34 B. D. Cawley, L. M. Keeping, and P. E. Levy, "Participation in the Performance Appraisal Process and Employee Reactions: A Meta-analytic Review of Field Investigations," *Journal of Applied Psychology*, August 1998, pp. 615–633; and P. E. Levy and J. R. Williams, "The Social Context of Performance Appraisal:

A Review and Framework for the Future," *Journal of Management* 30, no. 6 (2004), pp. 881–905.

35 List directly quoted from R. Kreitner and A. Kinicki, *Organizational Behavior*, 6th ed. (New York: McGraw-Hill/Irwin, 2004), p. 335 (emphasis added).

36 E. A. Locke, "Toward a Theory of Task Motivation and Incentives," *Organizational Behavior and Human Performance*, May 1968, pp. 157–189.

37 P. C. Earley, P. Wojnaroski, and W. Prest, "Task Planning and Energy Expended: Exploration of How Goals Influence Performance," *Journal of Applied Psychology*, February 1987, pp. 107–114.

38 See, for instance, D. Morisano, J. B. Hirsh, J. B. Peterson, R. O. Pihl, and B. M. Shore, "Setting, Elaborating, and Reflecting on Personal Goals Improves Academic Performance," *Journal of Applied Psychology* 95, no. 2 (2010), pp. 255–264.

39 "KEY Group Survey Finds Nearly Half of All Employees Have No Set Performance Goals," *IPMA-HR Bulletin*, March 10, 2006, p. 1; S. Hamm, "SAP Dangles a Big, Fat Carrot," *BusinessWeek*, May 22, 2006, pp. 67–68; and "P&G CEO Wields High Expectations but No Whip," *USA Today*, February 19, 2007, p. 3B.

40 See, for instance, S. J. Carroll and H. L. Tosi, *Management by Objectives: Applications and Research* (New York: Macmillan, 1973); and R. Rodgers and J. E. Hunter, "Impact of Management by Objectives on Organizational Productivity," *Journal of Applied Psychology*, April 1991, pp. 322–336.

41 Based on L. Bourgon, "The End of Clock-Punching?" *Canadian Business*, September 27, 2010; "Building a Better Workforce," *PROFIT*, February 16, 2011, http://www.profitguide.com/article/10084—building-a-better-workforce—page0; and C. Ressler and J. Thompson, *Why Work Sucks and How to Fix It* (New York: Penguin, 2008).

42 M. Craemer, "Motivating Employees in the 21st Century," *Seattle Post Intelligence*, April 5, 2010, http://blog.seattlepi.com/workplacewrangler/2010/04/05/motivating-employees-in-the-21st-century/

43 E. A. Locke and G. P. Latham, *A Theory of Goal Setting and Task Performance* (Englewood Cliffs, NJ: Prentice Hall, 1980).

44 E. A. Locke, K. N. Shaw, L. M. Saari, and G. P. Latham, "Goal Setting and Task Performance," *Psychological Bulletin*, January 1981, pp. 125–152; and A. J. Mento, R. P. Steel, and R. J. Karren, "A Meta-Analytic Study of the Effects of Goal Setting on Task Performance: 1966–1984," *Organizational Behavior and Human Decision Processes*, February 1987, pp. 52–83.

45 R. E. Wood, A. J. Mento, and E. A. Locke, "Task Complexity as a Moderator of Goal Effects: A Meta-analysis," *Journal of Applied Psychology*, August 1987, pp. 416–425.

46 P. M. Wright, "Operationalization of Goal Difficulty as a Moderator of the Goal Difficulty-Performance Relationship," *Journal of Applied Psychology*, June 1990, pp. 227–234; E. A. Locke and G. P. Latham, "Building a Practically Useful Theory of Goal Setting and Task Motivation: A 35-Year Odyssey," *American Psychologist* 57, no. 9 (2002), pp. 705–717.

47 P. M. Wright, J. R. Hollenbeck, S. Wolf, and G. C. McMahan, "The Effects of Varying Goal Difficulty Operationalizations on Goal Setting Outcomes and Processes," *Organizational Behavior and Human Decision Processes*, January 1995, pp. 28–43.

48 K. L. Langeland, C. M. Johnson, and T. C. Mawhinney, "Improving Staff Performance in a Community Mental Health Setting: Job Analysis, Training, Goal Setting, Feedback, and Years of Data," *Journal of Organizational Behavior Management*, 1998, pp. 21–43.

49 J. M. Ivancevich and J. T. McMahon, "The Effects of Goal Setting, External Feedback, and Self-Generated Feedback on Outcome Variables: A Field Experiment," *Academy of Management Journal*,

June 1982, pp. 359–372; and E. A. Locke, "Motivation Through Conscious Goal Setting," *Applied and Preventive Psychology 5* (1996), pp. 117–124.

50 E. A. Locke and G. P. Latham, *A Theory of Goal Setting and Task Performance* (Englewood Cliffs, NJ: Prentice Hall, 1990).

51 M. Erez, P. C. Earley, and C. L. Hulin, "The Impact of Participation on Goal Acceptance and Performance: A Two-Step Model," *Academy of Management Journal*, March 1985, pp. 50–66.

52 E. A. Locke, "The Motivation to Work: What We Know," *Advances in Motivation and Achievement* 10 (1997), pp. 375–412; and G. P. Latham, M. Erez, and E. A. Locke, "Resolving Scientific Disputes by the Joint Design of Crucial Experiments by the Antagonists: Application to the Erez-Latham Dispute Regarding Participation in Goal Setting," *Journal of Applied Psychology*, November 1988, pp. 753–772.

53 H. J. Klein, M. J. Wesson, J. R. Hollenbeck, P. M. Wright, and R. D. DeShon, "The Assessment of Goal Commitment: A Measurement Model Meta-analysis," *Organizational Behavior and Human Decision Processes* 85, no. 1 (2001), pp. 32–55.

54 J. R. Hollenbeck, C. R. Williams, and H. J. Klein, "An Empirical Examination of the Antecedents of Commitment to Difficult Goals," *Journal of Applied Psychology*, February 1989, pp. 18–23. See also J. C. Wofford, V. L. Goodwin, and S. Premack, "Meta-analysis of the Antecedents of Personal Goal Level and of the Antecedents and Consequences of Goal Commitment," *Journal of Management*, September 1992, pp. 595–615; M. E. Tubbs, "Commitment as a Moderator of the Goal-Performance Relation: A Case for Clearer Construct Definition," *Journal of Applied Psychology*, February 1993, pp. 86–97; and J. E. Bono and A. E. Colbert, "Understanding Responses to Multi-Source Feedback: The Role of Core Self-evaluations," *Personnel Psychology*, Spring 2005, pp. 171–203.

55 See R. E. Wood, A. J. Mento, and E. A. Locke, "Task Complexity as a Moderator of Goal Effects: A Meta-analysis," *Journal of Applied Psychology*, August 1987, pp. 416–425; R. Kanfer and P. L. Ackerman, "Motivation and Cognitive Abilities: An Integrative/ Aptitude-Treatment Interaction Approach to Skill Acquisition," *Journal of Applied Psychology* (monograph) 74 (1989), pp. 657–690; T. R. Mitchell and W. S. Silver, "Individual and Group Goals When Workers Are Interdependent: Effects on Task Strategies and Performance," *Journal of Applied Psychology*, April 1990, pp. 185–193; and A. M. O'Leary-Kelly, J. J. Martocchio, and D. D. Frink, "A Review of the Influence of Group Goals on Group Performance," *Academy of Management Journal*, October 1994, pp. 1285–1301.

56 G. P. Latham and E. A. Locke, "Enhancing the Benefits and Overcoming the Pitfalls of Goal Setting," *Organizational Dynamics* 35, no. 6 (2006), pp. 332–340; L. D. Ordóñez, M. E. Schweitzer, A. D. Galinsky, and M. Bazerman, "Goals Gone Wild: The Systematic Side Effects of Overprescribing Goal Setting," *Academy of Management Perspectives* 23, no.1 (2009), pp. 6–16; and E. A. Locke and G. P. Latham, "Has Goal Setting Gone Wild, or Have Its Attackers Abandoned Good Scholarship?" *Academy of Management Perspectives* 23, no. 1 (2009), pp. 17–23.

57 A. Bandura, *Self-Efficacy: The Exercise of Control* (New York: Freeman, 1997). See also M. Salanova, S. Llorens, and W. Schaufeli, "'Yes, I Can, I Feel Good, and I Just Do It!' On Gain Cycles and Spirals of Efficacy Beliefs, Affect, and Engagement," *Applied Psychology: An International Review* 60, no. 2 (2011), pp. 255–285.

58 A. D. Stajkovic and F. Luthans, "Self-Efficacy and Work-Related Performance: A Meta-analysis," *Psychological Bulletin*, September 1998, pp. 240–261; and A. Bandura, "Cultivate Self-Efficacy for Personal and Organizational Effectiveness," in *Handbook of Principles of Organizational Behavior*, ed. E. Locke (Malden, MA: Blackwell, 2004), pp. 120–136.

59 A. Bandura and D. Cervone, "Differential Engagement in Self-Reactive Influences in Cognitively-Based Motivation," *Organizational Behavior and Human Decision Processes*, August 1986, pp. 92–113.

60 A. Bandura, *Self-Efficacy: The Exercise of Control* (New York: Freeman, 1997).

61 C. L. Holladay and M. A. Quiñones, "Practice Variability and Transfer of Training: The Role of Self-Efficacy Generality," *Journal of Applied Psychology* 88, no. 6 (2003), pp. 1094–1103.

62 R. C. Rist, "Student Social Class and Teacher Expectations: The Self-Fulfilling Prophecy in Ghetto Education," *Harvard Educational Review* 70, no. 3 (2000), pp. 266–301.

63 D. Eden, "Self-Fulfilling Prophecies in Organizations," in *Organizational Behavior: The State of the Science*, 2nd ed., ed. J. Greenberg (Mahwah, NJ: Erlbaum, 2003), pp. 91–122.

64 E. Eden, "Self-Fulfilling Prophecies in Organizations," in *Organizational Behavior: The State of the Science*, 2nd ed., ed. J. Greenberg (Mahwah, NJ: Erlbaum, 2003), pp. 91–122.

65 T. A. Judge, C. L. Jackson, J. C. Shaw, B. Scott, and B. L. Rich, "Self-Efficacy and Work-Related Performance: The Integral Role of Individual Differences," *Journal of Applied Psychology* 92, no. 1 (2007), pp. 107–127.

66 T. A. Judge, C. L. Jackson, J. C. Shaw, B. Scott, and B. L. Rich, "Self-Efficacy and Work-Related Performance: The Integral Role of Individual Differences," *Journal of Applied Psychology* 92, no. 1 (2007), pp. 107–127.

67 Vignette based on C. Cole, "Figure Skating's Code of Points System Has Opened Up the Podium," *Vancouver Sun*, February 6, 2010, http://www.vancouversun.com/news/regional/ Figure+skating+Code+Points+system+opened+podium/ 2532110/story.html

68 J. S. Adams, "Inequity in Social Exchanges," in *Advances in Experimental Social Psychology*, ed. L. Berkowitz (New York: Academic Press, 1965), pp. 267–300.

69 P. S. Goodman, "An Examination of Referents Used in the Evaluation of Pay," *Organizational Behavior and Human Performance*, October 1974, pp. 170–195; S. Ronen, "Equity Perception in Multiple Comparisons: A Field Study," *Human Relations*, April 1986, pp. 333–346; R. W. Scholl, E. A. Cooper, and J. F. McKenna, "Referent Selection in Determining Equity Perception: Differential Effects on Behavioral and Attitudinal Outcomes," *Personnel Psychology*, Spring 1987, pp. 113–127; T. P. Summers and A. S. DeNisi, "In Search of Adams' Other: Reexamination of Referents Used in the Evaluation of Pay," *Human Relations*, June 1990, pp. 497–511; S. Werner and N. P. Mero, "Fair or Foul? The Effects of External, Internal, and Employee Equity on Changes in Performance of Major League Baseball Players," *Human Relations*, October 1999, pp. 1291–1312; and R. W. Griffeth and S. Gaertner, "A Role for Equity Theory in the Turnover Process: An Empirical Test," *Journal of Applied Social Psychology*, May 2001, pp. 1017–1037.

70 C. T. Kulik and M. L. Ambrose, "Personal and Situational Determinants of Referent Choice," *Academy of Management Review*, April 1992, pp. 212–237.

71 C. Ostroff and L. E. Atwater, "Does Whom You Work with Matter? Effects of Referent Group Gender and Age Composition on Managers' Compensation," *Journal of Applied Psychology* 88, no. 4 (2003), pp. 725–740.

72 "Women in the Workforce: Still a Long Way from Equality," *Canadian Labour Congress*, May 5, 2008, http://canadianlabour. ca/en/women-workforce-still-a-long-way-equality

73 See, for example, E. Walster, G. W. Walster, and W. G. Scott, *Equity: Theory and Research* (Boston: Allyn and Bacon, 1978); and J. Greenberg, "Cognitive Reevaluation of Outcomes in Response to Underpayment Inequity," *Academy of Management Journal*, March 1989, pp. 174–184.

74 P. S. Goodman and A. Friedman, "An Examination of Adams' Theory of Inequity," *Administrative Science Quarterly*, September 1971, pp. 271–288; R. P. Vecchio, "An Individual-Differences Interpretation of the Conflicting Predictions Generated by Equity Theory and Expectancy Theory," *Journal of Applied Psychology*, August 1981, pp. 470–481; R. T. Mowday, "Equity Theory Predictions of Behavior in Organizations," in *Motivation and Work Behavior*, 6th ed., ed. R. Steers, L. W. Porter, and G. Bigley (New York: McGraw-Hill, 1996), pp. 111–131; R. W. Griffeth and S. Gaertner, "A Role for Equity Theory in the Turnover Process: An Empirical Test," *Journal of Applied Social Psychology*, May 2001, pp. 1017–1037; and L. K. Scheer, N. Kumar, and J.-B. E. M. Steenkamp, "Reactions to Perceived Inequity in U.S. and Dutch Interorganizational Relationships," *Academy of Management 46*, no. 3 (2003), pp. 303–316.

75 See, for example, R. C. Huseman, J. D. Hatfield, and E. W. Miles, "A New Perspective on Equity Theory: The Equity Sensitivity Construct," *Academy of Management Journal*, April 1987, pp. 222–234; K. S. Sauley and A. G. Bedeian, "Equity Sensitivity: Construction of a Measure and Examination of Its Psychometric Properties," *Journal of Management 26*, no. 5 (2000), pp. 885–910; and J. A. Colquitt, "Does the Justice of One Interact with the Justice of Many? Reactions to Procedural Justice in Teams," *Journal of Applied Psychology 89*, no. 4 (2004), pp. 633–646.

76 J. Greenberg and S. Ornstein, "High Status Job Title as Compensation for Underpayment: A Test of Equity Theory," *Journal of Applied Psychology*, May 1983, pp. 285–297; and J. Greenberg, "Equity and Workplace Status: A Field Experiment," *Journal of Applied Psychology*, November 1988, pp. 606–613.

77 See, for instance, J. Greenberg, *The Quest for Justice on the Job* (Thousand Oaks, CA: Sage, 1996); R. Cropanzano and J. Greenberg, "Progress in Organizational Justice: Tunneling through the Maze," in *International Review of Industrial and Organizational Psychology*, vol. 12, ed. C. L. Cooper and I. T. Robertson (New York: Wiley, 1997); J. A. Colquitt, D. E. Conlon, M. J. Wesson, C. O. L. H. Porter, and K. Y. Ng, "Justice at the Millennium: A Meta-analytic Review of the 25 Years of Organizational Justice Research," *Journal of Applied Psychology*, June 2001, pp. 425–445; T. Simons and Q. Roberson, "Why Managers Should Care About Fairness: The Effects of Aggregate Justice Perceptions on Organizational Outcomes," *Journal of Applied Psychology*, June 2003, pp. 432–443; and G. P. Latham and C. C. Pinder, "Work Motivation Theory and Research at the Dawn of the Twenty-First Century," *Annual Review of Psychology 56*, 2005, pp. 485–516.

78 O. Janssen, C. K. Lam, and X. Huang, "Emotional Exhaustion and Job Performance: The Moderating Roles of Distributive Justice and Positive Affect," *Journal of Organizational Behavior 31*, no. 6 (2010), pp. 787–809.

79 K. Leung, K. Tong, and S. S. Ho, "Effects of Interactional Justice on Egocentric Bias in Resource Allocation Decisions," *Journal of Applied Psychology 89*, no. 3 (2004), pp. 405–415.

80 "Americans Feel They Pay Fair Share of Taxes, Says Poll," *NaturalNews.com*, May 2, 2005, http://www.naturalnews.com/007297.html

81 R. E. Johnson, C.-H. Chang, and C. Rosen, "'Who I Am Depends on How Fairly I'm Treated': Effects of Justice on Self-Identity and Regulatory Focus," *Journal of Applied Social Psychology 40*, no. 12 (2010), pp. 3020–3058.

82 G. S. Leventhal, "What Should Be Done with Equity Theory? New Approaches to the Study of Fairness in Social Relationships," in *Social Exchange: Advances in Theory and Research*, ed. K. Gergen,

M. Greenberg, and R. Willis (New York: Plenum, 1980), pp. 27–55.

83 D. P. Skarlicki and R. Folger, "Retaliation in the Workplace: The Roles of Distributive, Procedural, and Interactional Justice," *Journal of Applied Psychology 82*, no. 3 (1997), pp. 434–443.

84 R. Cropanzano, C. A. Prehar, and P. Y. Chen, "Using Social Exchange Theory to Distinguish Procedural from Interactional Justice," *Group & Organization Management 27*, no. 3 (2002), pp. 324–351; and S. G. Roch and L. R. Shanock, "Organizational Justice in an Exchange Framework: Clarifying Organizational Justice Dimensions," *Journal of Management*, April 2006, pp. 299–322.

85 J. A. Colquitt, D. E. Conlon, M. J. Wesson, C. O. L. H. Porter, and K. Y. Ng, "Justice at the Millennium: A Meta-Analytic Review of the 25 Years of Organizational Justice Research," *Journal of Applied Psychology*, June 2001, pp. 425–445.

86 D. P. Skarlicki and R. Folger, "Retaliation in the Workplace: The Roles of Distributive, Procedural and Interactional Justice," *Journal of Applied Psychology 82*, no. 3 (1997), pp. 434–443.

87 E. Deci and R. Ryan, eds., *Handbook of Self-Determination Research* (Rochester, NY: University of Rochester Press, 2002); R. Ryan and E. Deci, "Self-Determination Theory and the Facilitation of Intrinsic Motivation, Social Development, and Well-Being," *American Psychologist 55*, no. 1 (2000), pp. 68–78; and M. Gagné and E. L. Deci, "Self-Determination Theory and Work Motivation," *Journal of Organizational Behavior 26*, no. 4 (2005), pp. 331–362.

88 E. L. Deci, R. Koestner, and R. M. Ryan, "A Meta-analytic Review of Experiments Examining the Effects of Extrinsic Rewards on Intrinsic Motivation," *Psychological Bulletin 125*, no. 6 (1999), pp. 627–668; N. Houlfort, R. Koestner, M. Joussemet, A. Nantel-Vivier, and N. Lekes, "The Impact of Performance-Contingent Rewards on Perceived Autonomy and Competence," *Motivation & Emotion 26*, no. 4 (2002), pp. 279–295; G. J. Greguras and J. M. Diefendorff, "Different Fits Satisfy Different Needs: Linking Person-Environment Fit to Employee Commitment and Performance Using Self-Determination Theory," *Journal of Applied Psychology 94*, no. 2 (2009), pp. 465–477; and M. P. Moreno-Jiménez and M. C. H. Villodres, "Prediction of Burnout in Volunteers," *Journal of Applied Social Psychology 40*, no. 7 (2010), pp. 1798–1818. This work studies the personal experience of volunteering and several antecedent and consequent variables. We studied the effect of the amount of time dedicated to the organization, motivation, social support, integration in the organization, self-efficacy, and characteristics of the work on a consequent variable of the volunteering experience; that is, burnout, with its 3 components of efficacy, cynicism, and exhaustion. The statistical analysis shows that the time dedicated to volunteering and the extrinsic motivations (i.e., social and career) predicts higher levels of burnout, whereas intrinsic motivations (i.e., values and understanding), life satisfaction, and integration in the organization are negatively related to burnout.

89 R. Eisenberger and L. Rhoades, "Incremental Effects of Reward on Creativity," *Journal of Personality and Social Psychology 81*, no. 4 (2001), pp. 728–741; and R. Eisenberger, W. D. Pierce, and J. Cameron, "Effects of Reward on Intrinsic Motivation—Negative, Neutral, and Positive: Comment on Deci, Koestner, and Ryan (1999)," *Psychological Bulletin 125*, no. 6 (1999), pp. 677–691.

90 M. Burgess, M. E. Enzle, and R. Schmaltz, "Defeating the Potentially Deleterious Effects of Externally Imposed Deadlines: Practitioners' Rules-of-Thumb," *Personality and Social Psychology Bulletin 30*, no. 7 (2004), pp. 868–877.

91 K. M. Sheldon, A. J. Elliot, and R. M. Ryan, "Self-Concordance and Subjective Well-Being in Four Cultures," *Journal of Cross-Cultural Psychology* 35, no. 2 (2004), pp. 209–223.

92 K. M. Sheldon, A. J. Elliot, and R. M. Ryan, "Self-Concordance and Subjective Well-Being in Four Cultures," *Journal of Cross-Cultural Psychology* 35, no. 2 (2004), pp. 209–223.

93 J. E. Bono and T. A. Judge, "Self-Concordance at Work: Toward Understanding the Motivational Effects of Transformational Leaders," *Academy of Management Journal* 46, no. 5 (2003), pp. 554–571.

94 B. J. Calder and B. M. Staw, "Self-Perception of Intrinsic and Extrinsic Motivation," *Journal of Personality and Social Psychology,* April 1975, pp. 599–605; and J. Pfeffer, *The Human Equation: Building Profits by Putting People First* (Boston: Harvard Business School Press, 1998), p. 217.

95 B. M. Staw, "Motivation in Organizations: Toward Synthesis and Redirection," in *New Directions in Organizational Behavior,* ed. B. M. Staw and G. R. Salancik (Chicago: St. Clair, 1977), p. 76.

96 K. W. Thomas, E. Jansen, and W. G. Tymon Jr., "Navigating in the Realm of Theory: An Empowering View of Construct Development," in *Research in Organizational Change and Development,* vol. 10, ed. W. A. Pasmore and R. W. Woodman (Greenwich, CT: JAI Press, 1997), pp. 1–30.

97 Vignette based on "I Need to Do Double Quad, Says Plushenko," *Reuters,* February 20, 2010, http://www.reuters.com/article/2010/02/20/olympics-figureskating-plushenko-idUSLDE61J0FH20100220; and P. J. Kwong, "With Lessons Learned, Chan Ready to Defend His Title," *cbcsports.ca,* July 11, 2011, http://www.cbc.ca/sports/blogs/pjkwong/2011/07/with-lessons-learned-chan-ready-to-defend-his-title.html

98 R. Kreitner and A. Kinicki, *Organizational Behavior,* 6th ed. (New York: McGraw-Hill, 2004), p. 345. See also J. W. Donahoe, "The Unconventional Wisdom of B. F. Skinner: The Analysis-Interpretation Distinction," *Journal of the Experimental Analysis of Behavior,* September 1993, pp. 453–456.

99 B. F. Skinner, *Contingencies of Reinforcement* (East Norwalk, CT: Appleton-Century-Crofts, 1971).

100 F. Luthans and R. Kreitner, *Organizational Behavior Modification and Beyond,* 2nd ed. (Glenview, IL: Scott, Foresman, 1985); and A. D. Stajkovic and F. Luthans, "A Meta-analysis of the Effects of Organizational Behavior Modification on Task Performance, 1975–95," *Academy of Management Journal,* October 1997, pp. 1122–1149.

101 This section based on C. Michaelson, "Meaningful Motivation for Work Motivation Theory," *Academy of Management Review* 30, no. 2 (2005), pp. 235–238; and R. M. Steers, R. T. Mowday, and D. L. Shapiro, "Response to Meaningful Motivation for Work Motivation Theory," *Academy of Management Review* 30, no. 2 (2005), p. 238.

102 C. Michaelson, "Meaningful Motivation for Work Motivation Theory," *Academy of Management Review* 30, no. 2 (2005), p. 237.

103 N. J. Adler, *International Dimensions of Organizational Behavior,* 4th ed. (Cincinnati, OH: South-Western Publishing, 2002), p. 174.

104 G. Hofstede, "Motivation, Leadership, and Organization: Do American Theories Apply Abroad?" *Organizational Dynamics,* Summer 1980, p. 55.

105 G. Hofstede, "Motivation, Leadership, and Organization: Do American Theories Apply Abroad?" *Organizational Dynamics,* Summer 1980, p. 55.

106 D. F. Crown, "The Use of Group and Groupcentric Individual Goals for Culturally Heterogeneous and Homogeneous Task Groups: An Assessment of European Work Teams," *Small Group*

Research 38, no. 4 (2007), pp. 489–508; J. Kurman, "Self-Regulation Strategies in Achievement Settings: Culture and Gender Differences," *Journal of Cross-Cultural Psychology* 32, no. 4 (2001), pp. 491–503; and M. Erez and P. C. Earley, "Comparative Analysis of Goal-Setting Strategies across Cultures," *Journal of Applied Psychology* 72, no. 4 (1987), pp. 658–665.

107 C. Sue-Chan and M. Ong, "Goal Assignment and Performance: Assessing the Mediating Roles of Goal Commitment and Self-Efficacy and the Moderating Role of Power Distance," *Organizational Behavior and Human Decision Processes* 89, no. 2 (2002), pp. 1140–1161.

108 J. K. Giacobbe-Miller, D. J. Miller, and V. I. Victorov, "A Comparison of Russian and U.S. Pay Allocation Decisions, Distributive Justice Judgments, and Productivity Under Different Payment Conditions," *Personnel Psychology,* Spring 1998, pp. 137–163.

109 S. L. Mueller and L. D. Clarke, "Political-Economic Context and Sensitivity to Equity: Differences between the United States and the Transition Economies of Central and Eastern Europe," *Academy of Management Journal,* June 1998, pp. 319–329.

110 Based on S. E. DeVoe and S. S. Iyengar, "Managers' Theories of Subordinates: A Cross-Cultural Examination of Manager Perceptions of Motivation and Appraisal of Performance," *Organizational Behavior and Human Decision Processes,* January 2004, pp. 47–61.

111 I. Harpaz, "The Importance of Work Goals: An International Perspective," *Journal of International Business Studies,* First Quarter 1990, pp. 75–93.

112 G. E. Popp, H. J. Davis, and T. T. Herbert, "An International Study of Intrinsic Motivation Composition," *Management International Review,* January 1986, pp. 28–35.

113 R. Fischer and P. B. Smith, "Reward Allocation and Culture: A Meta-analysis," *Journal of Cross-Cultural Psychology* 34, no. 3 (2003), pp. 251–268.

114 F. T. Chiang and T. Birtch, "The Transferability of Management Practices: Examining Cross-National Differences in Reward Preferences," *Human Relations* 60, no. 9 (2007), pp. 1293–1330; A. E. Lind, T. R. Tyler, and Y. J. Huo, "Procedural Context and Culture: Variation in the Antecedents of Procedural Justice Judgments," *Journal of Personality and Social Psychology* 73, no. 4 (1997), pp. 767–780; and M. J. Gelfand, M. Erez, and Z. Aycan, "Cross-Cultural Organizational Behavior," *Annual Review of Psychology* 58 (2007), pp. 479–514.

115 R. Freedman, "'Happyness' Author Gardner Hopes We're Each Our Own Champ," *Marin Independent Journal,* May 13, 2009, http://www.marinij.com

116 E. Biyalogorsky, W. Boulding, and R. Staelin, "Stuck in the Past: Why Managers Persist with New Product Failures," *Journal of Marketing,* April 2006, pp. 108–121.

117 Adapted from an exercise developed by Larry Michaelson of the University of Oklahoma. With permission.

118 Based on C. Benedict, "The Bullying Boss," *New York Times,* June 22, 2004, p. F1.

119 "Quebecor Plays Hardball with Defiant Union: Vidéotron 'Ready to Listen': Aims to Sell Cable Installation Operations," *Financial Post (National Post),* March 5, 2002, p. FP6; and S. Silcoff, "Quebecor and Union in Showdown over Costs," *Financial Post (National Post),* February 28, 2002, p. FP3.

120 Based on S. P. Robbins and D. A. DeCenzo, *Fundamentals of Management,* 4th ed. (Upper Saddle River, NJ: Prentice Hall, 2004), p. 85.

Chapter 5

1 Vignette based on T. W. Martin, "Whole Foods to Sell 31 Stores in FTC Deal," *Wall Street Journal*, March 7, 2009, p. B5; and C. Tobias, "Whole Foods Controversy," *Canadian Business*, May 2, 2011, http://www.canadianbusiness.com/article/11666—whole-foods-controversy

2 D. W. Krueger, "Money, Success, and Success Phobia," in *The Last Taboo: Money as a Symbol and Reality in Psychotherapy and Psychoanalysis*, ed. D. W. Krueger (New York: Brunner/Mazel, 1986), pp. 3–16.

3 J. Nelson, "Payday Woes," *Canadian Business*, April 8, 2011.

4 T. R. Mitchell and A. E. Mickel, "The Meaning of Money: An Individual-Difference Perspective," *Academy of Management*, July 1999, pp. 568–578.

5 T. A. Judge, R. F. Piccolo, J. C. Podsakoff, and B. L. Rich, "The Relationship between Pay Satisfaction and Job Satisfaction," *Journal of Vocational Behavior* 77 (2010), 157–167.

6 R. Fischer and D. Boer, "What Is More Important for National Well-Being: Money or Autonomy? A Meta-analysis of Well-Being, Burnout, and Anxiety across 63 Societies," *Journal of Personality and Social Psychology*, July 2011, pp. 164–184.

7 S. A. Hewlett, L. Sherbin, and K. Sumberg "How Gen Y & Boomers Will Reshape Your Agenda," *Harvard Business Review*, July/August 2009, pp. 71–76.

8 This paragraph is based on T. R. Mitchell and A. E. Mickel, "The Meaning of Money: An Individual-Difference Perspective," *Academy of Management*, July 1999, pp. 568–578. The reader may want to refer to the myriad of references cited in the article.

9 S. A. Hewlett, L. Sherbin, and K. Sumberg "How Gen Y & Boomers Will Reshape Your Agenda," *Harvard Business Review*, July/August 2009, pp. 71–76.

10 Vignette based on M. Kliger and S. Tweraser, "Motivating Front Line Staff for Bottom Line Results," *McKinsey.com*, http://www.mckinsey.com/practices/retail/knowledge/articles/Motivatingfrontlinestaff.pdf

11 http://www.wholefoodsmarket.com/company/declaration.php

12 http://www.wholefoodsmarket.com/company/declaration.php

13 E. White, "Opportunity Knocks, and It Pays a Lot Better," *Wall Street Journal*, November 13, 2006, p. B3.

14 M. Sabramony, N. Krause, J. Norton, and G. N. Burns, "The Relationship between Human Resource Investments and Organizational Performance: A Firm-Level Examination of Equilibrium Theory," *Journal of Applied Psychology* 93, no. 4 (2008), pp. 778–788.

15 Based on J. R. Schuster and P. K. Zingheim, "The New Variable Pay: Key Design Issues," *Compensation & Benefits Review*, March–April 1993, p. 28; K. S. Abosch, "Variable Pay: Do We Have the Basics in Place?" *Compensation & Benefits Review*, July–August 1998, pp. 12–22; and K. M. Kuhn and M. D. Yockey, "Variable Pay as a Risky Choice: Determinants of the Relative Attractiveness of Incentive Plans," *Organizational Behavior and Human Decision Processes*, March 2003, pp. 323–341.

16 "Canada's General Motors Workers to Get Up to 16 Per Cent of Salary in Bonuses," *Canadian Press*, February 14, 2011.

17 J. Ratner, "Dofasco Boss Took Home Biggest Pay," *National Post*, February 1, 2006, p. WK3.

18 "Canada's General Motors Workers to Get Up to 16 Per Cent of Salary in Bonuses," *Canadian Press*, February 14, 2011.

19 "2010 Global Salary Increase & Variable Pay Budget Trends," http://compforce.typepad.com/compensation_force/2010/02/2010-global-salary-increase-variable-pay-budget-trends.html

20 B. Wysocki, Jr., "Chilling Reality Awaits Even the Employed," *Wall Street Journal*, November 5, 2001, p. A1.

21 O. Bertin, "Is There Any Merit in Giving Merit Pay?" *Globe and Mail*, January 31, 2003, pp. C1, C7.

22 E. Willes "Give Buono Credit for Lions Revival," *Gazette* (Montreal), September 25, 2011.

23 E. Arita, "Teething Troubles Aside, Merit-Based Pay Catching On," *Japan Times*, April 23, 2004, http://search.japantimes.co.jp/cgi-bin/nb20040423a3.html

24 G. D. Jenkins Jr., N. Gupta, A. Mitra, and J. D. Shaw, "Are Financial Incentives Related to Performance? A Meta-analytic Review of Empirical Research," *Journal of Applied Psychology*, October 1998, pp. 777–787; and S. L. Rynes, B. Gerhart, and L. Parks, "Personnel Psychology: Performance Evaluation and Pay for Performance," *Annual Review of Psychology* 56, no. 1 (2005), pp. 571–600.

25 "Many Companies Fail to Achieve Success with Pay-for-Performance Programs," *Hewitt & Associates News and Information*, June 9, 2004; and J. Pfeffer, *What Were They Thinking? Unconventional Wisdom About Management* (Boston: Harvard Business School Press, 2007).

26 E. J. Castilla and S. Benard, "The Paradox of Meritocracy in Organizations," *Administrative Science Quarterly* 55, no. 4 (2010), pp. 543–576.

27 "Bonus Pay in Canada," *Manpower Argus*, September 1996, p. 5; E.White, "Employers Increasingly Favor Bonuses to Raises," *Wall Street Journal*, August 28, 2006, p. B3; and J. S. Lublin, "Boards Tie CEO Pay More Tightly to Performance," *Wall Street Journal*, February 21, 2006, pp. A1, A14.

28 N. Byrnes, "Pain, But No Layoffs at Nucor," *BusinessWeek*, March 26, 2009, http://www.businessweek.com

29 Based on R. Curran, "Did Bonuses Help to Fuel Meltdown?" *Post.IE online*, September 21, 2008, http://www.sbpost.ie/post/pages/p/story.aspx-qqqt=NEWS???qqqm=nav-qqqid=36092-qqqx=1.asp; and V. Bajaj, A. R. Sorkin, and M. J. de la Merced, "Goldman, Morgan to Become Bank Holding Companies," *New York Times*, September 21, 2008, http://dealbook.blogs.nytimes.com/2008/09/21/goldman-morgan-to-become-bank-holding-companies/index.html?hp

30 G. E. Ledford Jr., "Paying for the Skills, Knowledge, and Competencies of Knowledge Workers," *Compensation & Benefits Review*, July–August 1995, pp. 55–62; B. Murray and B. Gerhart, "An Empirical Analysis of a Skill-Based Pay Program and Plant Performance Outcomes," *Academy of Management Journal*, February 1998, pp. 68–78; J. R. Thompson and C. W. LeHew, "Skill-Based Pay as an Organizational Innovation," *Review of Public Personnel Administration*, Winter 2000, pp. 20–40; and J. D. Shaw, N. Gupta, A. Mitra, and G. E. Ledford Jr., "Success and Survival of Skill-Based Pay Plans," *Journal of Management*, February 2005, pp. 28–49.

31 Based on D. Naylor, "In Pursuit of Level Playing Fields," *Globe and Mail*, March 9, 2002, p. S1; T. Denison, "Formula for Success," August 13, 2004, http://www.collegecolours.com/columns/004.html; and J. McElroy, "Full-Ride Athletic Scholarships Still on Hold," *Macleans.ca*, June 4, 2010, http://oncampus.macleans.ca/education/2010/06/04/full-ride-athletic-scholarships-still-on-hold/

32 See, for instance, S. C. Hanlon, D. G. Meyer, and R. R. Taylor, "Consequences of Gainsharing," *Group & Organization Management*, March 1994, pp. 87–111; J. G. Belcher Jr., "Gainsharing and Variable Pay: The State of the Art," *Compensation & Benefits Review*, May–June 1994, pp. 50–60; and T. M. Welbourne and L. R. Gomez Mejia, "Gainsharing: A Critical Review and a Future Research Agenda," *Journal of Management* 21, no. 3 (1995), pp. 559–609.

33 Employment Policy Foundation, *U.S. Wage and Productivity Growth Attainable through Gainsharing*, May 10, 2000.

34 T. M. Welbourne and C. J. Ferrante, "To Monitor or Not to Monitor: A Study of Individual Outcomes from Monitoring One's Peers under Gainsharing and Merit Pay," *Group & Organization Management* 33, no. 2 (2008), pp. 139–162.

35 T. M. Welbourne and L. R. Gomez-Mejia, "Gainsharing: A Critical Review and a Future Research Agenda," *Journal of Management* 21, no. 3 (1995), pp. 559–609.

36 B. Jang, "WestJet Charts Bold New Path," *Globe and Mail*, March 27, 2010.

37 M. Gooderham, "A Piece of the Pie as Motivational Tool," *Globe and Mail*, November 20, 2007, p. B8.

38 R. J. Long, "Patterns of Workplace Innovations in Canada," *Relations Industrielles* 44, no. 4 (1989), pp. 805–826; R. J. Long, "Motives for Profit Sharing: A Study of Canadian Chief Executive Officers," *Relations Industrielles* 52, no. 4 (1997), pp. 712–723; and T. H. Wagar and R. J. Long, "Profit Sharing in Canada: Incidences and Predictors," *Proceedings of the Administrative Sciences Association of Canada* (Human Resources Division), 1995, pp. 97–105.

39 N. Chi and T. Han, "Exploring the Linkages between Formal Ownership and Psychological Ownership for the Organization: The Mediating Role of Organizational Justice," *Journal of Occupational and Organizational Psychology* 81, no. 4 (2008), pp. 691–711.

40 See K. M. Young, ed., *The Expanding Role of ESOPs in Public Companies* (New York: Quorum, 1990); J. L. Pierce and C. A. Furo, "Employee Ownership: Implications for Management," *Organizational Dynamics*, Winter 1990, pp. 32–43; J. Blasi and D. L. Druse, *The New Owners: The Mass Emergence of Employee Ownership in Public Companies and What It Means to American Business* (Champaign, IL: Harper Business, 1991); F. T. Adams and G. B. Hansen, *Putting Democracy to Work: A Practical Guide for Starting and Managing Worker-Owned Businesses* (San Francisco: Berrett-Koehler, 1993); and A. A. Buchko, "The Effects of Employee Ownership on Employee Attitudes: An Integrated Causal Model and Path Analysis," *Journal of Management Studies*, July 1993, pp. 633–656.

41 K. Vermond, "Worker as Shareholder: Is It Worth It?" *Globe and Mail*, March 29, 2008, p. B21.

42 A. A. Buchko, "The Effects of Employee Ownership on Employee Attitudes: An Integrated Causal Model and Path Analysis," *Journal of Management Studies*, July 1993, pp. 633–656.

43 K. Vermond, "Worker as Shareholder: Is It Worth It?" *Globe and Mail*, March 29, 2008, p. B21.

44 J. L. Pierce and C. A. Furo, "Employee Ownership: Implications for Management," *Organizational Dynamics*, Winter 1990, pp. 32–43; and S. Kaufman, "ESOPs' Appeal on the Increase," *Nation's Business*, June 1997, p. 43.

45 See data in D. Stamps, "A Piece of the Action," *Training*, March 1996, p. 66.

46 X. Zhang, K. M. Bartol, K. G. Smith, M. D. Pfarrer, and D. M. Khanin, "CEOs on the Edge: Earnings Manipulation and Stock-Based Incentive Misalignment," *Academy of Management Journal* 51, no. 2 (2008), pp. 241–258.

47 C. G. Hanson and W. D. Bell, *Profit Sharing and Profitability: How Profit Sharing Promotes Business Success* (London: Kogan Page, 1987); M. Magnan and S. St-Onge, "Profit Sharing and Firm Performance: A Comparative and Longitudinal Analysis" (paper presented at the 58th annual meeting of the Academy of Management, San Diego, CA, August 1998); and D. D'Art and T. Turner, "Profit Sharing, Firm Performance, and Union Influence in Selected European Countries," *Personnel Review* 33, no. 3 (2004), pp. 335–350.

48 T. M. Welbourne and L. R. Gomez-Mejia, "Gainsharing: A Critical Review and a Future Research Agenda," *Journal of Management* 21, no. 3 (1995), pp. 559–609.

49 E. P. Lazear, "Performance Pay and Productivity," *American Economic Review* 90, no. 5 (December 2000), pp. 1346–1361. See also S. Oah, and J.-H. Lee. "Effects of Hourly, Low-Incentive, and High-Incentive Pay on Simulated Work Productivity: Initial Findings with a New Laboratory Method," *Journal of Organizational Behavior Management* 31, no. 1 (2011), pp. 21–42.

50 C. B. Cadsby, F. Song, and F. Tapon, "Sorting and Incentive Effects of Pay for Performance: An Experimental Investigation," *Academy of Management Journal* 50, no. 2 (2007), pp. 387–405.

51 J. Pfeffer and N. Langton, "The Effects of Wage Dispersion on Satisfaction, Productivity, and Working Collaboratively: Evidence from College and University Faculty," *Administrative Science Quarterly* 38, no. 3 (1983), pp. 382–407.

52 "Risk and Reward: More Canadian Companies Are Experimenting with Variable Pay," *Maclean's*, January 8, 1996, pp. 26–27.

53 "Hope for Higher Pay: The Squeeze on Incomes Is Gradually Easing Up," *Maclean's*, November 25, 1996, pp. 100–101.

54 "Risk and Reward: More Canadian Companies Are Experimenting with Variable Pay," *Maclean's*, January 8, 1996, pp. 26–27.

55 Based on V. Galt, "No More Freebies for Hydro Staff: Arbitrator," *Globe and Mail*, February 16, 2002, p. B3.

56 B. E. Wright, "Work Motivation in the Public Sector," *Academy of Management Proceedings*, 2001, pp. PNP: D1–5.

57 B. E. Wright, "Work Motivation in the Public Sector," *Academy of Management Proceedings*, 2001, pp. PNP: D1–5.

58 S. Greenhouse, "Suits Say Wal-Mart Forces Workers to Toil Off the Clock," *New York Times*, June 25, 2002, http://www.nytimes.com/2002/06/25/national/25WALM.html?pagewanted=1

59 See, for instance, M. W. Barringer and G. T. Milkovich, "A Theoretical Exploration of the Adoption and Design of Flexible Benefit Plans: A Case of Human Resource Innovation," *Academy of Management Review*, April 1998, pp. 305–324; D. Brown, "Everybody Loves Flex," *Canadian HR Reporter*, November 18, 2002, p. 1; J. Taggart, "Putting Flex Benefits through Their Paces," *Canadian HR Reporter*, December 2, 2002, p. G3; and N. D. Cole and D. H. Flint, "Perceptions of Distributive and Procedural Justice in Employee Benefits: Flexible versus Traditional Benefit Plans," *Journal of Managerial Psychology* 19, no. 1 (2004), pp. 19–40.

60 D. A. DeCenzo and S. P. Robbins, *Human Resource Management*, 7th ed. (New York: Wiley, 2002), pp. 346–348.

61 Cited in S. Caudron, "The Top 20 Ways to Motivate Employees," *IndustryWeek*, April 3, 1995, pp. 15–16. See also B. Nelson, "Try Praise," *Inc.*, September 1996, p. 115.

62 Our definition of a formal recognition system is based on S. E. Markham, K. D. Scott, and G. H. McKee, "Recognizing Good Attendance: A Longitudinal, Quasi-Experimental Field Study," *Personnel Psychology*, Autumn 2002, p. 641.

63 S. J. Peterson and F. Luthans, "The Impact of Financial and Nonfinancial Incentives on Business Unit Outcomes over Time," *Journal of Applied Psychology* 91, no. 1 (2006), pp. 156–165.

64 "Building a Better Workforce," *PROFIT*, February 16, 2011, http://www.profitguide.com/article/10084--building-a-better-workforce--page0; and http://www.rlsolutions.com/Careers/Benefits.aspx

65 B. Scudamore, "Pump up Employee Passion," *PROFIT*, October 13, 2010, http://www.profitguide.com/article/6574--pump-up-employee-passion

66 Hewitt Associates, "Employers Willing to Pay for High Performance," news release, September 8, 2004, http://

was4.hewitt.com/hewitt/resource/newsroom/pressrel/2004/09-08-04eng.htm

67 See also D. A. Johnson and A. M. Dickinson, "Employee-of-the-Month Programs: Do They Really Work?" *Journal of Organizational Behavior Management* 30, no. 4 (2010), pp. 308–324.

68 S. Kerr, "On the Folly of Rewarding A, While Hoping for B," *Academy of Management Executive* 9, no. 1 (1995), pp. 7–14.

69 D. Turner, "Atlanta Schools Created Culture of Cheating, Fear, Intimidation," *Huffington Post*, July 16, 2011, http://www.huffingtonpost.com/2011/07/16/atlanta-schools-created-c_n_900635.html

70 "More on the Folly," *Academy of Management Executive* 9, no. 1 (1995), pp. 15–16.

71 M. Parker, "Strategies for Creating a Culture of Innovation," *Canadian Business Online*, August 29, 2007.

72 A. Kohn, *Punished by Rewards* (Boston: Houghton Mifflin, 1999), p. 181.

73 A. Kohn, *Punished by Rewards* (Boston: Houghton Mifflin, 1993), p. 186. See also Peter R. Scholtes, "An Elaboration of Deming's Teachings on Performance Appraisal," in *Performance Appraisal: Perspectives on a Quality Management Approach*, ed. Gary N. McLean, Susan R. Damme, and Richard A. Swanson (Alexandria, VA: American Society for Training and Development, 1990); H. H. Meyer, E. Kay, and J. R. P. French Jr., "Split Roles in Performance Appraisal," *Harvard Business Review*, 1965, excerpts reprinted in "HBR Retrospect," *Harvard Business Review*, January–February 1989, p. 26; W.-U. Meyer, M. Bachmann, U. Biermann, M. Hempelmann, F.-O. Ploeger, and H. Spiller, "The Informational Value of Evaluative Behavior: Influences of Praise and Blame on Perceptions of Ability," *Journal of Educational Psychology* 71, 1979, pp. 259–268; and A. Halachmi and M. Holzer, "Merit Pay, Performance Targetting, and Productivity," *Review of Public Personnel Administration* 7 (1987), pp. 80–91.

74 A. S. Blinder, "Introduction," in *Paying for Productivity: A Look at the Evidence*, ed. A. S. Blinder (Washington, DC: Brookings Institution, 1990).

75 A. Kohn, *Punished by Rewards* (Boston: Houghton Mifflin, 1999), p. 187.

76 D. Tjosvold, *Working Together to Get Things Done: Managing for Organizational Productivity* (Lexington, MA: Lexington Books, 1986); P. R. Scholtes, *The Team Handbook: How to Use Teams to Improve Quality* (Madison, WI: Joiner Associates, 1988); and A. Kohn, *No Contest: The Case Against Competition*, rev. ed. (Boston: Houghton Mifflin, 1992).

77 E. L. Deci, "Applications of Research on the Effects of Rewards," in *The Hidden Costs of Rewards: New Perspectives on the Psychology of Human Motivation*, ed. M. R. Lepper and D. Green (Hillsdale, NJ: Erlbaum, 1978).

78 S. E. Perry, *San Francisco Scavengers: Dirty Work and the Pride of Ownership* (Berkeley: University of California Press, 1978).

79 A. Kohn, *Punished by Rewards* (Boston: Houghton Mifflin, 1999), p. 192.

80 T. H. Naylor, "Redefining Corporate Motivation, Swedish Style," *Christian Century*, May 30–June 6, 1990, pp. 566–570; R. A. Karasek, T. Thorell, J. E. Schwartz, P. L. Schnall, C. F. Pieper, and J. L. Michela, "Job Characteristics in Relation to the Prevalence of Myocardial Infarction in the US Health Examination Survey (HES) and the Health and Nutrition Examination Survey (HANES)," *American Journal of Public Health* 78 (1988), pp. 910–916; and D. P. Levin, "Toyota Plant in Kentucky Is Font of Ideas for the U.S.," *New York Times*, May 5, 1992, pp. A1, D8.

81 M. Bosquet, "The Prison Factory," reprinted from *Le Nouvel Observateur* in *Working Papers for a New Society*, Spring 1973,

pp. 20–27; J. Holusha, "Grace Pastiak's 'Web of Inclusion,'" *New York Times*, May 5, 1991, pp. F1, F6; J. Simmons and W. Mares, *Working Together: Employee Participation in Action* (New York: New York University Press, 1985); D. I. Levine and L. D'Andrea Tyson, "Participation, Productivity, and the Firm's Environment," in *Paying for Productivity: A Look at the Evidence*, ed. A. S. Blinder (Washington, DC: Brookings Institution, 1990); and W. F. Whyte, "Worker Participation: International and Historical Perspectives," *Journal of Applied Behavioral Science* 19, 1983, pp. 395–407.

82 "At Starbucks, Baristas Told No More Than Two Drinks," *Wall Street Journal*, October 13, 2010, http://online.wsj.com/article/SB10001424052748704164004575548403514060736.html?mod=e2tw

83 J. R. Hackman and G. R. Oldham, "Motivation through the Design of Work: Test of a Theory," *Organizational Behavior and Human Performance*, August 1976, pp. 250–279.

84 J. R. Hackman, "Work Design," in *Improving Life at Work*, ed. J. R. Hackman and J. L. Suttle (Santa Monica, CA: Goodyear, 1977), p. 129.

85 Based on M. Gagné and D. Bhave, "Autonomy in the Workplace: An Essential Ingredient to Employee Engagement and Well-Being in Every Culture?" in *Human Autonomy in Cross-Cultural Context: Perspectives on the Psychology of Agency, Freedom, and Well-Being*, ed. V. I. Chirkov, R. M. Ryan, and K. M. Sheldon (Berlin, Germany: Springer, 2011); and "Freedom's Just Another Word for Employee Satisfaction," *ScienceDaily*, January 24, 2011, http://www.sciencedaily.com /releases/2011/01/110124102944.htm

86 D. A. Light, "Human Resources: Recruiting Generation 2001," *Harvard Business Review*, July–August 1998, pp. 13–16.

87 See "Job Characteristics Theory of Work Redesign," in *Theories of Organizational Behavior*, ed. J. B. Miner (Hinsdale, IL: Dryden Press, 1980), pp. 231–266; B. T. Loher, R. A. Noe, N. L. Moeller, and M. P. Fitzgerald, "A Meta-analysis of the Relation of Job Characteristics to Job Satisfaction," *Journal of Applied Psychology*, May 1985, pp. 280–289; S. J. Behson, E. R. Eddy, and S. J. Lorenzet, "The Importance of the Critical Psychological States in the Job Characteristics Model: A Meta-analytic and Structural Equations Modeling Examination," *Current Research in Social Psychology*, May 2000, pp. 170–189; T. A. Judge, "Promote Job Satisfaction through Mental Challenge," in *Handbook of Principles of Organizational Behavior*, ed. E. A. Locke, pp. 75–89 (Hoboken, NJ: Wiley-Blackwell, 2003); S. E. Humphrey, J. D. Nahrgang, and F. P. Morgeson, "Integrating Motivational, Social, and Contextual Work Design Features: A Meta-analytic Summary and Theoretical Extension of the Work Design Literature," *Journal of Applied Psychology* 92, no. 5 (2007), pp. 1332–1356; R. F. Piccolo, R. Greenbaum, D. N. D. Hartog, and R. Folger, "The Relationship between Ethical Leadership and Core Job Characteristics," *Journal of Organizational Behavior* 31, no. 2/3 (2010), pp. 259–278; D. J. Holman, C. M. Axtell, C. A. Sprigg, P. Totterdell, and T. D. Wall, "The Mediating Role of Job Characteristics in Job Redesign Interventions: A Serendipitous Quasi-Experiment," *Journal of Organizational Behavior* 31, no. 1 (2010), pp. 84–105; and M. Gagné and D. Bhave, "Autonomy in the Workplace: An Essential Ingredient to Employee Engagement and Well-Being in Every Culture?" in *Human Autonomy in Cross-Cultural Context: Perspectives on the Psychology of Agency, Freedom, and Well-Being*, ed. V. I. Chirkov, R. M. Ryan, and K. M. Sheldon (Berlin, Germany: Springer, 2011).

88 T. A. Judge, S. K. Parker, A. E. Colbert, D. Heller, and R. Ilies, "Job Satisfaction: A Cross-Cultural Review," in *Handbook of Industrial, Work and Organizational Psychology*, vol. 2, ed. N. Anderson and D. S. Ones (Thousand Oaks, CA: Sage Publications, 2002), pp. 25–52.

89 See, for example, J. R. Hackman and G. R. Oldham, *Work Redesign* (Reading, MA: Addison Wesley, 1980); J. B. Miner,

Theories of Organizational Behavior (Hinsdale, IL: Dryden Press, 1980), pp. 231–266; R. W. Griffin, "Effects of Work Redesign on Employee Perceptions, Attitudes, and Behaviors: A Long-Term Investigation," *Academy of Management Journal*, June 1991, pp. 425–435; and G. Johns, "Some Unintended Consequences of Job Design," *Journal of Organizational Behavior* 31, no. 2/3 (2010), pp. 361–369.

90 J. R. Hackman, "Work Design," in *Improving Life at Work*, ed. J. R. Hackman and J. L. Suttle (Santa Monica, CA: Goodyear, 1977), p. 129.

91 J. P. Wanous, "Individual Differences and Reactions to Job Characteristics," *Journal of Applied Psychology*, October 1974, pp. 616–622; and H. P. Sims and A. D. Szilagyi, "Job Characteristic Relationships: Individual and Structural Moderators," *Organizational Behavior and Human Performance*, June 1976, pp. 211–230.

92 F. Pomeroy, "Workplace Change: A Union Perspective," *Canadian Business Review* 22, no. 2 (1995), pp. 17–19.

93 J. E. Rigdon, "Using Lateral Moves to Spur Employees," *Wall Street Journal*, May 26, 1992, p. B1.

94 N. Leckie, A. Léonard, J. Turcotte, and D. Wallace, *Employer and Employee Perspectives on Human Resource Practices*, Report 71-584-MIE no. 1 (Ottawa: Ministry of Industry, 2001).

95 J. Ortega, "Job Rotation as a Learning Mechanism," *Management Science*, October 2001, pp. 1361–1370.

96 J. R. Hackman and G. R. Oldham, *Work Redesign* (Reading, MA: Addison-Wesley, 1980).

97 A. M. Grant, E. M. Campbell, G. Chen, K. Cottone, D. Lapedis, and K. Lee, "Impact and the Art of Motivation Maintenance: The Effects of Contact with Beneficiaries on Persistence Behavior," *Organizational Behavior and Human Decision Processes* 103 (2007), pp. 53–67.

98 A. M. Grant, J. E. Dutton, and B. D. Rosso, "Giving Commitment: Employee Support Programs and the Prosocial Sensemaking Process," *Academy of Management Journal* 51, no. 5 (2008), pp. 898–918.

99 See, for example, J. R. Hackman and G. R. Oldham, *Work Redesign* (Reading, MA: Addison-Wesley, 1980); J. B. Miner, *Theories of Organizational Behavior* (Hinsdale, IL: Dryden Press, 1980), pp. 231–266; R. W. Griffin, "Effects of Work Redesign on Employee Perceptions, Attitudes, and Behaviors: A Long-Term Investigation," *Academy of Management Journal* 34, no. 2 (1991), pp. 425–435; and J. L. Cotton, *Employee Involvement* (Newbury Park, CA: Sage, 1993), pp. 141–172.

100 R. D. Pritchard, M. M. Harrell, D. DiazGrandos, and M. J. Guzman, "The Productivity Measurement and Enhancement System: A Meta-analysis," *Journal of Applied Psychology* 93, no. 3 (2008), pp. 540–567.

101 F. P. Morgeson, M. D. Johnson, M. A. Campion, G. J. Medsker, and T. V. Mumford, "Understanding Reactions to Job Redesign: A Quasi-Experimental Investigation of the Moderating Effects of Organizational Contact on Perceptions of Performance Behavior," *Personnel Psychology* 39 (2006), pp. 333–363.

102 F. W. Bond, P. E. Flaxman, and D. Bunce, "The Influence of Psychological Flexibility on Work Redesign: Mediated Moderation of a Work Reorganization Intervention," *Journal of Applied Psychology* 93, no. 3 (2008), pp. 645–654.

103 Statistics Canada, "Part-Time Work and Family-Friendly Practices," *The Daily*, June 26, 2003.

104 L. Rubis, "Fourth of Full-Timers Enjoy Flexible Hours," *HR Magazine*, June 1998, pp. 26–28.

105 See, for example, D. A. Ralston and M. F. Flanagan, "The Effect of Flextime on Absenteeism and Turnover for Male and Female Employees," *Journal of Vocational Behavior*, April 1985,

pp. 206–217; D. A. Ralston, W. P. Anthony, and D. J. Gustafson, "Employees May Love Flextime, but What Does It Do to the Organization's Productivity?" *Journal of Applied Psychology*, May 1985, pp. 272–279; D. R. Dalton and D. J. Mesch, "The Impact of Flexible Scheduling on Employee Attendance and Turnover," *Administrative Science Quarterly*, June 1990, pp. 370–387; B. B. Baltes, T. E. Briggs, J. W. Huff, J. A. Wright, and G. A. Neuman, "Flexible and Compressed Workweek Schedules: A Meta-analysis of Their Effects on Work-Related Criteria," *Journal of Applied Psychology* 84, no. 4 (1999), pp. 496–513; K. M. Shockley and T. D. Allen, "When Flexibility Helps: Another Look at the Availability of Flexible Work Arrangements and Work-Family Conflict," *Journal of Vocational Behavior* 71, no. 3 (2007), pp. 479–493; and J. G. Grzywacz, D. S. Carlson, and S. Shulkin, "Schedule Flexibility and Stress: Linking Formal Flexible Arrangements and Perceived Flexibility to Employee Health," *Community, Work, and Family* 11, no. 2 (2008), pp. 199–214.

106 D. Keevil, *The Flexible Workplace Study: Asking the Experts About Flexible Policies and Workplace Performance* (Halifax: Halifax YWCA in cooperation with Status of Women Canada, 1996).

107 L. Duxbury and G. Haines, "Predicting Alternative Work Arrangements from Salient Attitudes: A Study of Decision Makers in the Public Sector," *Journal of Business Research*, August 1991, pp. 83–97.

108 J. E. Fast and J. A. Frederick, "Working Arrangements and Time Stress," *Canadian Social Trends*, Winter 1996, pp. 14–19.

109 A. Sisco and R. Nelson, *From Vision to Venture: An Account of Five Successful Aboriginal Businesses* (Ottawa: The Conference Board of Canada, 2008).

110 S. Schieman and M. Young, "Is There a Downside to Schedule Control for the Work-Family Interface?" *Journal of Family Issues* 31, no. 10 (2010), pp. 1391–1414.

111 T. Grant, "Job Sharing," *Globe and Mail*, May 16, 2009, p. B14.

112 Society for Human Resource Management, *2008 Employee Benefits* (Alexandria, VA: Author, 2008).

113 S. Shellenbarger, "Two People, One Job: It Can Really Work," *Wall Street Journal*, December 7, 1994, p. B1.

114 T. Grant, "Job Sharing," *Globe and Mail*, May 16, 2009, p. B1.

115 C. Dawson, "Japan: Work-Sharing Will Prolong the Pain," *BusinessWeek*, December 24, 2001, p. 46.

116 Government of Canada, *The Next Phase of Canada's Economic Action Plan: A Low-Tax Plan for Jobs and Growth, Chapter 3: Canada's Economic Action Plan*. Tabled in the House of Commons by the Honourable James M. Flaherty, PC, MP, Minister of Finance, June 6, 2011, http://www.budget.gc.ca/2011/plan/chap3-eng.html; and S. Chase and O. Moore, "Canadian Workers Cozy Up to Job-Sharing," September 29, 2009, http://www.theglobeandmail.com/news/politics/canadian-workers-cozy-up-to-job-sharing/article1304955/

117 T. Grant, "Job Sharing," *Globe and Mail*, May 16, 2009, p. B1.

118 D. Hodges, "New Nunavut: Canada's Newest Territory Faces the Daunting Task of Creating a New Health Bureaucracy While Dealing with Traditional Recruitment Problems in the Arctic," *Medical Post*, November 13, 2001, p. 31.

119 See, for example, K. E. Pearlson and C. S. Saunders, "There's No Place Like Home: Managing Telecommuting Paradoxes," *Academy of Management Executive*, May 2001, pp. 117–128; S. J. Wells, "Making Telecommuting Work," *HR Magazine*, October 2001, pp. 34–45; E. J. Hill, M. Ferris, and V. Martinson, "Does It Matter Where You Work? A Comparison of How Three Work Venues (Traditional Office, Virtual Office, and Home Office) Influence Aspects of Work and Personal/Family Life," *Journal of Vocational Behavior* 63, no. 2 (2003), pp. 220–241; Anonymous, "Labour Movement," *The Economist*, April 12, 2008, p. 5; and

J. Berkow, "Telework: The New Labour Force Norm," *Postmedia News*, July 7, 2011.

120 D. Bradbury, "Nothing to Fear from Teleworking," *Financial Post*, March 16, 2010, http://www.financialpost.com/story.html?id=2689687; V. Galt, "Telecommute—and Save the Environment," *Globe and Mail*, April 27, 2007, http://www.ivc.ca/media/articles/savetheenvironment.html

121 J. Berkow, "Telework: The New Labour Force Norm," *Postmedia News*, July 7, 2011.

122 "Canadian Studies on Telework," *InnoVisions Canada*, http://www.ivc.ca/studies/canada/

123 J. Berkow, "Telework: The New Labour Force Norm," *Postmedia News*, July 7, 2011.

124 J. Budak, "Work-Life: Better Working through Living," *Canadian Business*, April 5, 2011.

125 Cited in R. W. Judy and C. D'Amico, *Workforce 2020* (Indianapolis, IL: Hudson Institute, 1997), p. 58.

126 P. Lima, "The Next Best Thing to Being There," *Globe and Mail*, April 26, 2006, p. 31.

127 L. Arnold, "Geographical, Organisational and Social Implications of Teleworking—Emphasis on the Social Perspectives" (paper presented at the 29th Annual Meeting of the Canadian Sociological and Anthropological Association, Calgary, June 1994); K. S. Devine, L. Taylor, and K. Haryett, "The Impact of Teleworking on Canadian Employment," in *Good Jobs, Bad Jobs, No Jobs: The Uncertain Future of Employment* in Canada, ed. A. Duffy, D. Glenday, and N. Pupo (Toronto: Harcourt Brace, 1997); C. A. Hamilton, "Telecommuting," *Personnel Journal*, April 1987, pp. 91–101; and I. U. Zeytinoglu, "Employment Conditions in Telework: An Experiment in Ontario," *Proceedings of the 30th Conference of the Canadian Industrial Relations Association*, 1992, pp. 281–293.

128 L. Arnold, "Geographical, Organisational and Social Implications of Teleworking—Emphasis on the Social Perspectives" (paper presented at the 29th Annual Meeting of the Canadian Sociological and Anthropological Association, Calgary, June 1994).

129 I. U. Zeytinoglu, "Employment Conditions in Telework: An Experiment in Ontario," *Proceedings of the 30th Conference of the Canadian Industrial Relations Association*, 1992, pp. 281–293; and K. S. Devine, L. Taylor, and K. Haryett, "The Impact of Teleworking on Canadian Employment," in *Good Jobs, Bad Jobs, No Jobs: The Uncertain Future of Employment in Canada*, ed. A. Duffy, D. Glenday, and N. Pupo (Toronto: Harcourt Brace, 1997).

130 I. U. Zeytinoglu, "Employment Conditions in Telework: An Experiment in Ontario," *Proceedings of the 30th Conference of the Canadian Industrial Relations Association*, 1992, pp. 281–293.

131 K. S. Devine, L. Taylor, and K. Haryett, "The Impact of Teleworking on Canadian Employment," in *Good Jobs, Bad Jobs, No Jobs: The Uncertain Future of Employment in Canada*, ed. A. Duffy, D. Glenday, and N. Pupo (Toronto: Harcourt Brace, 1997); and C. A. Hamilton, "Telecommuting," *Personnel Journal*, April 1987, pp. 91–101.

132 E. E. Kossek, B. A. Lautsch, and S. C. Eaton, "Telecommuting, Control, and Boundary Management: Correlates of Policy Use and Practice, Job Control, and Work-Family Effectiveness," *Journal of Vocational Behavior* 68, no. 2 (2006), pp. 347–367; and K. L. Fonner and M. E. Roloff, "Why Teleworkers Are More Satisfied with Their Jobs than Are Office-Based Workers: When Less Contact Is Beneficial," *Journal of Applied Communication Research* 38, no. 4 (2010), pp. 336–361.

133 J. M. Stanton and J. L. Barnes-Farrell, "Effects of Electronic Performance Monitoring on Personal Control, Task Satisfaction, and Task Performance," *Journal of Applied Psychology*, December

1996, pp. 738–745; B. Pappas, "They Spy," *Forbes*, February 8, 1999, p. 47; S. Armour, "More Bosses Keep Tabs on Telecommuters," *USA Today*, July 24, 2001, p. 1B; and D. Buss, "Spies Like Us," *Training*, December 2001, pp. 44–48.

134 J. Welch and S. Welch, "The Importance of Being There," *BusinessWeek*, April 16, 2007, p. 92; Z. I. Barsness, K. A. Diekmann, and M. L. Seidel, "Motivation and Opportunity: The Role of Remote Work, Demographic Dissimilarity, and Social Network Centrality in Impression Management," *Academy of Management Journal* 48, no. 3 (2005), pp. 401–419.

135 P. Glavin, S. Schieman, and S. Reid, "Boundary-Spanning Work Demands and Their Consequences for Guilt and Psychological Distress," *Journal of Health and Social Behavior* 52, no. 1 (2011), pp. 43–57.

136 F. P. Morgeson and S. E. Humphrey, "The Work Design Questionnaire (WDQ): Developing and Validating a Comprehensive Measure for Assessing Job Design and the Nature of Work," *Journal of Applied Psychology* 91, no. 6 (2006), pp. 1321–1339; S. E. Humphrey, J. D. Nahrgang, and F. P. Morgeson, "Integrating Motivational, Social, and Contextual Work Design Features: A Meta-analytic Summary and Theoretical Extension of the Work Design Literature," *Journal of Applied Psychology* 92, no. 5 (2007), pp. 1332–1356; and R. Takeuchi, D. P. Lepak, H. Wang, and K. Takeuchi, "An Empirical Examination of the Mechanisms Mediating Between High-Performance Work Systems and the Performance of Japanese Organizations," *Journal of Applied Psychology* 92, no. 4 (2007), pp. 1069–1083.

137 Vignette based on M. Kliger and S. Tweraser, "Motivating Front Line Staff for Bottom Line Results," *McKinsey.com*, http://www.mckinsey.com/practices/retail/knowledge/articles/Motivatingfrontlinestaff.pdf

138 See, for example, the increasing body of literature on empowerment, such as W. A. Randolph, "Re-Thinking Empowerment: Why Is It So Hard to Achieve?" *Organizational Dynamics* 29, no. 2 (2000), pp. 94–107; K. Blanchard, J. P. Carlos, and W. A. Randolph, *Empowerment Takes More Than a Minute*, 2nd ed. (San Francisco: Berrett-Koehler, 2001); D. P. Ashmos, D. Duchon, R. R. McDaniel Jr., and J. W. Huonker, "What a Mess! Participation as a Simple Managerial Rule to 'Complexify' Organizations," *Journal of Management Studies*, March 2002, pp. 189–206; and S. E. Seibert, S. R. Silver, and W. A. Randolph, "Taking Empowerment to the Next Level: A Multiple-Level Model of Empowerment, Performance, and Satisfaction," *Academy of Management Journal* 47, no. 3 (2004), pp. 332–349.

139 F. Heller, E. Pusic, G. Strauss, and B. Wilpert, *Organizational Participation: Myth and Reality* (Oxford, UK: Oxford University Press, 1998).

140 See, for instance, K. L. Miller and P. R. Monge, "Participation, Satisfaction, and Productivity: A Meta-analytic Review," *Academy of Management Journal*, December 1986, pp. 727–753; J. A. Wagner III, "Participation's Effects on Performance and Satisfaction: A Reconsideration of Research Evidence," *Academy of Management Review*, April 1994, pp. 312–330; C. Doucouliagos, "Worker Participation and Productivity in Labor-Managed and Participatory Capitalist Firms: A Meta-analysis," *Industrial and Labor Relations Review*, October 1995, pp. 58–77; J. A. Wagner III, C. R. Leana, E. A. Locke, and D. M. Schweiger, "Cognitive and Motivational Frameworks in U.S. Research on Participation: A Meta-analysis of Primary Effects," *Journal of Organizational Behavior* 18 (1997), pp. 49–65; E. A. Locke, M. Alavi, and J. A. Wagner III, "Participation in Decision Making: An Information Exchange Perspective," in *Research in Personnel and Human Resource Management*, vol. 15, ed. G. R. Ferris (Greenwich, CT: JAI Press, 1997), pp. 293–331; and J. A. Wagner III and J. A. LePine, "Effects of Participation on Performance and Satisfaction:

Additional Meta-analytic Evidence," *Psychological Reports*, June 1999, pp. 719–725.

141 D. K. Datta, J. P. Guthrie, and P. M. Wright, "Human Resource Management and Labor Productivity: Does Industry Matter?" *Academy of Management Journal* 48, no. 1 (2005), pp. 135–145; C. M. Riordan, R. J. Vandenberg, and H. A. Richardson, "Employee Involvement Climate and Organizational Effectiveness" *Human Resource Management* 44, no. 4 (2005), pp. 471–488.

142 J. L. Cotton, *Employee Involvement* (Newbury Park, CA: Sage, 1993), pp. 141–172.

143 See, for example, M. Gilman and P. Marginson, "Negotiating European Works Council: Contours of Constrained Choice," *Industrial Relations Journal*, March 2002, pp. 36–51; J. T. Addison and C. R. Belfield, "What Do We Know About the New European Works Council? Some Preliminary Evidence from Britain," *Scottish Journal of Political Economy*, September 2002, pp. 418–444; and B. Keller, "The European Company Statute: Employee Involvement—and Beyond," *Industrial Relations Journal*, December 2002, pp. 424–445.

144 J. L. Cotton, *Employee Involvement* (Newbury Park, CA: Sage, 1993), pp. 141–172.

145 J. L. Cotton, *Employee Involvement* (Newbury Park, CA: Sage, 1993), pp. 141–172.

146 N. Nohria, B. Groysberg, and L.-E. Lee, "Employee Motivation: A Powerful New Model," *Harvard Business Review* 86, no. 7–8 (July–August 2008), pp. 78–84.

147 P. R. Lawrence and N. Nohria, *Driven: How Human Nature Shapes Our Choices* (San Francisco: Jossey-Bass, 2002).

148 S. C. L. Fong and M. A. Shaffer, "The Dimensionality and Determinants of Pay Satisfaction: A Cross-Cultural Investigation of a Group Incentive Plan," *International Journal of Human Resource Management*, June 2003, pp. 559–580.

149 D. Brown, "Everybody Loves Flex," *Canadian HRReporter*, November 18, 2002, p. 1.

150 E. Unsworth, "U.K. Employers Find Flex Benefits Helpful: Survey," *Business Insurance*, May 21, 2001, pp. 19–20.

151 R. S. Schuler and N. Rogovsky, "Understanding Compensation Practice Variations across Firms: The Impact of National Culture," *Journal of International Business Studies* 29, no. 1 (First Quarter 1998), pp. 159–177.

152 M. Erez, "Culture and Job Design," *Journal of Organizational Behavior* 31, no. 2/3 (2010), pp. 389–400.

153 B. M. Meglino and A. M. Korsgaard, "The Role of Other Orientation in Reactions to Job Characteristics," *Journal of Management*, February 2007, pp. 57–83.

154 M. F. Peterson and S. A. Ruiz-Quintanilla, "Cultural Socialization as a Source of Intrinsic Work Motivation," *Group & Organization Management*, June 2003, pp. 188–216.

155 P. Peters and L. den Dulk, "Cross Cultural Differences in Managers' Support for Home-Based Telework: A Theoretical Elaboration," *International Journal of Cross Cultural Management*, December 2003, pp. 329–346.

156 See, for instance, A. Sagie and Z. Aycan, "A Cross-Cultural Analysis of Participative Decision-Making in Organizations," *Human Relations*, April 2003, pp. 453–473; and J. Brockner, "Unpacking Country Effects: On the Need to Operationalize the Psychological Determinants of Cross-National Differences," in *Research in Organizational Behavior*, vol. 25, ed. R. M. Kramer and B. M. Staw (Oxford, UK: Elsevier, 2003), pp. 336–340.

157 C. Robert, T. M. Probst, J. J. Martocchio, R. Drasgow, and J. J. Lawler, "Empowerment and Continuous Improvement in the United States, Mexico, Poland, and India: Predicting Fit on the Basis of the Dimensions of Power Distance and Individualism," *Journal of Applied Psychology*, October 2000, pp. 643–658.

158 Z. X. Chen and S. Aryee, "Delegation and Employee Work Outcomes: An Examination of the Cultural Context of Mediating Processes in China," *Academy of Management Journal* 50, no. 1 (2007), pp. 226–238.

159 T. R. Mitchell and A. E. Mickel, "The Meaning of Money: An Individual-Difference Perspective," *Academy of Management*, July 1999, pp. 568–578.

160 This paragraph is based on T. R. Mitchell and A. E. Mickel, "The Meaning of Money: An Individual-Difference Perspective," *Academy of Management*, July 1999, pp. 568–578. The reader may want to refer to the myriad of references cited in the article.

161 E. Beauchesne, "Pay Bonuses Improve Productivity, Study Shows," *Vancouver Sun*, September 13, 2002, p. D5.

162 Based on K. Izuma, D. N. Saito, and N. Sadato, "Processing of Social and Monetary Rewards in the Human Striatum," *Neuron* 58, no. 2 (2008), pp. 284–294; "The Most Praised Generation Goes to Work," *Gainesville (Florida) Sun*, April 29, 2007, pp. 5G, 6G; J. Zaslow, "In Praise of Less Praise," *Wall Street Journal*, May 3, 2007, p. D1; S. Loewy and J. Bailey, "The Effects of Graphic Feedback, Goal-Setting, and Manager Praise on Customer Service Behaviors," *Journal of Organizational Behavior Management* 27, no. 3 (2007), pp. 15–26; and J. S. Seiter and E. Dutson, "The Effect of Compliments on Tipping Behavior in Hairstyling Salons," *Journal of Applied Social Psychology* 37, no. 9 (2007), pp. 1999–2007.

163 This exercise is based on W. P. Ferris, "Enlivening the Job Characteristics Model," in *Proceedings of the 29th Annual Eastern Academy of Management Meeting*, ed. C. Harris and C. C. Lundberg (Baltimore, MD: May 1992), pp. 125–128.

164 E. Church, "Market Recovery Delivers Executive Payout Bonanza," *Globe and Mail*, May 4, 2005, pp. B1, B9; "Gimme Gimme: Greed, the Most Insidious of Sins, Has Once Again Embraced a Decade," *Financial Post*, September 28/30, 1996, pp. 24–25; and I. McGugan, "A Crapshoot Called Compensation," *Canadian Business*, July 1995, pp. 67–70.

165 J. McFarland, "Who Earned What Last Year, and Why?" *Globe and Mail*, May 29, 2011, http://www.theglobeandmail.com/report-on-business/careers/management/executive-compensation/who-earned-what-last-year-and-why/article2038061/

166 Based on average weekly earnings for 2010, found at http://www40.statcan.ca/l01/cst01/labr79-eng.htm

167 This case is based on J. Sandberg, "Been Here 25 Years and All I Got Was This Lousy T-Shirt," *Wall Street Journal*, January 28, 2004, p. B1.

168 Based on T. Ogier, "Life as a Burger King," *Latin Trade*, December 2000, pp. 44–47.

169 J. R. Hackman, "Work Design," in *Improving Life at Work*, ed. J. R. Hackman and J. L. Suttle (Santa Monica, CA: Goodyear, 1977), pp. 132–133.

Chapter 6

1 Opening vignette is based on http://www.cirquedusoleil.com; "Cirque du Soleil on Teamwork and Creativity," *Business Banter*, June 28, 2011, http://businessbanter.wordpress.com/2011/06/28/cirque-du-soleil-on-teamwork-and-creativity/; G. Collins, "Run Away to the Circus? No Need. It's Staying Here," *New York Times*, April 29, 2009, p. C1; and A. Tesolin, "Igniting the Creative Spark at Cirque du Soleil—Arupa Tesolin Interviews Lyn Heward Creative Leader at Cirque," *SelfGrowth.com*, http://www.selfgrowth.com/articles/Igniting_the_Creative_Spark_at_Cirque_du_Soleil.html

2 J. R. Katzenback and D. K. Smith, *The Wisdom of Teams: Creating the High-Performance Organization* (New York: Harper Business, 1999), p. 45.

3 J. R. Katzenback and D. K. Smith, *The Wisdom of Teams: Creating the High-Performance Organization* (New York: Harper Business, 1999), p. 214.

4 See, for example, D. Tjosvold, *Team Organization: An Enduring Competitive Advantage* (Chichester, UK: Wiley, 1991); S. A. Mohrman, S. G. Cohen, and A. M. Mohrman Jr., *Designing Team-Based Organizations* (San Francisco: Jossey-Bass, 1995); P. MacMillan, *The Performance Factor: Unlocking the Secrets of Teamwork* (Nashville, TN: Broadman and Holman, 2001); and E. Salas, C. A. Bowers, and E. Edens, eds., *Improving Teamwork in Organizations: Applications of Resource Management Training* (Mahwah, NJ: Erlbaum, 2002).

5 J. H. Shonk, *Team-Based Organizations* (Homewood, IL: Business One Irwin, 1992); and M. A. Verespej, "When Workers Get New Roles," *IndustryWeek*, February 3, 1992, p. 11.

6 See, for example, C. C. Manz and H. P. Sims Jr., *Business without Bosses: How Self-Managing Teams Are Building High Performance Companies* (New York: Wiley, 1993); J. R. Barker, "Tightening the Iron Cage: Concertive Control in Self-Managing Teams," *Administrative Science Quarterly*, September 1993, pp. 408–437; and S. G. Cohen, G. E. Ledford Jr., and G. M. Spreitzer, "A Predictive Model of Self-Managing Work Team Effectiveness," *Human Relations*, May 1996, pp. 643–676.

7 See, for instance, J. L. Cordery, W. S. Mueller, and L. M. Smith, "Attitudinal and Behavioral Effects of Autonomous Group Working: A Longitudinal Field Study," *Academy of Management Journal*, June 1991, pp. 464–476; R. A. Cook and J. L. Goff, "Coming of Age with Self-Managed Teams: Dealing with a Problem Employee," *Journal of Business and Psychology*, Spring 2002, pp. 485–496; and C. W. Langfred, "Too Much of a Good Thing? Negative Effects of High Trust and Individual Autonomy in Self-Managing Teams," *Academy of Management Journal*, June 2004, pp. 385–399.

8 A. Mehra, M. Kilduff, and D. J. Brass, "At the Margins: A Distinctiveness Approach to the Social Identity and Social Networks of Underrepresented Groups," *Academy of Management Journal* 41, no. 4 (1998), pp. 441–452.

9 J. Tutunjian, "Interview with Don Swann," *Canadian Grocer* 121, no. 10 (December 2007–January 2008), pp. 18–19.

10 G. Taninecz, "Team Players," *IndustryWeek*, July 15, 1996, pp. 28–32; D. R. Denison, S. L. Hart, and J. A. Kahn, "From Chimneys to Cross-Functional Teams: Developing and Validating a Diagnostic Model," *Academy of Management Journal*, August 1996, pp. 1005–1023; and A. R. Jassawalla, "Building Collaborative Cross-Functional New Product Teams," *Academy of Management Executive*, August 1999, pp. 50–63.

11 "Cross-Functional Obstacles," *Training*, May 1994, pp. 125–126.

12 P. Gwynne, "Skunk Works, 1990s-Style," *Research Technology Management*, July–August 1997, pp. 18–23.

13 "Virtual Teams a First in Canada," January 19, 2011, http://business.financialpost.com/2011/01/19/mba-virtual-teams-a-first-in-canada/

14 See, for example, M. E. Warkentin, L. Sayeed, and R. Hightower, "Virtual Teams versus Face-to-Face Teams: An Exploratory Study of a Web-Based Conference System," *Decision Sciences*, Fall 1997, pp. 975–993; A. M. Townsend, S. M. DeMarie, and A. R. Hendrickson, "Virtual Teams: Technology and the Workplace of the Future," *Academy of Management Executive*, August 1998, pp. 17–29; D. Duarte and N. T. Snyder, *Mastering Virtual Teams: Strategies, Tools, and Techniques* (San Francisco: Jossey-Bass, 1999); M. L. Maznevski and K. M. Chudoba, "Bridging Space over Time: Global Virtual Team Dynamics and Effectiveness," *Organization Science*, September–October 2000, pp. 473–492; and

J. Katzenbach and D. Smith, "Virtual Teaming," *Forbes*, May 21, 2001, pp. 48–51.

15 Based on S. L. Jarvenpaa, K. Knoll, and D. E. Leidner, "Is Anybody out There? Antecedents of Trust in Global Virtual Teams," *Journal of Management Information Systems*, Spring 1998, pp. 29–64.

16 A. Malhotra, A. Majchrzak, and B. Rosen, "Leading Virtual Teams," *Academy of Management Perspectives*, February 2007, pp. 60–70; and J. M. Wilson, S. S. Straus, and B. McEvily, "All in Due Time: The Development of Trust in Computer Mediated and Face-to-Face Teams," *Organizational Behavior and Human Decision Processes* 19 (2006), pp. 16–33.

17 C. Joinson, "Managing Virtual Teams," *HR Magazine*, June 2002, p. 71. Reprinted with the permission of *HR Magazine*, published by the Society for Human Resource Management, Alexandria, VA.

18 Vignette based on E. Syracopoulos, "#FocusFriday: How Cirque du Soleil's Graphics Team Stays Focused Off Stage," *Xerox Blogs*, July 29, 2011, http://realbusinessatxerox.blogs.xerox.com/2011/07/29/focusfriday-how-cirque-du-soleil%E2%80%99s-graphics-team-stays-focused-off-stage/; http://www.cirquedusoleil.com

19 See M. F. Peterson, P. B, Smith, A. Akande, S. Ayestaran, S. Bochner, V. Callan, N. Guk Cho, J. C. Jesuino, M. D'Amorim, P.-H. Francois, K. Hofmann, P. L. Koopman, K. Leung, T. K. Lim, and S. Mortaz, "Role Conflict, Ambiguity, and Overload: A 21-Nation Study," *Academy of Management Journal*, April 1995, pp. 429–452.

20 E. H. Schein, *Organizational Psychology*, 3rd ed. (Englewood Cliffs, NJ: Prentice Hall, 1980), p. 145.

21 For a recent review of the research on group norms, see J. R. Hackman, "Group Influences on Individuals in Organizations," in *Handbook of Industrial & Organizational Psychology*, vol. 3, 2nd ed., ed. M. D. Dunnette and L. M. Hough (Palo Alto, CA: Consulting Psychologists Press, 1992), pp. 235–250.

22 Adapted from P. S. Goodman, E. Ravlin, and M. Schminke, "Understanding Groups in Organizations," in *Research in Organizational Behavior*, vol. 9, ed. L. L. Cummings and B. M. Staw (Greenwich, CT: JAI Press, 1987), p. 159.

23 Submitted by Don Miskiman, Chair and U-C Professor of Management, Malaspina University College, Nanaimo, BC. With permission.

24 D. C. Feldman, "The Development and Enforcement of Group Norms," *Academy of Management Journal*, January 1984, pp. 47–53; and K. L. Bettenhausen and J. K. Murnighan, "The Development of an Intragroup Norm and the Effects of Interpersonal and Structural Challenges," *Administrative Science Quarterly*, March 1991, pp. 20–35.

25 D. C. Feldman, "The Development and Enforcement of Group Norms," *Academy of Management Journal*, January 1984, pp. 47–53; and K. L. Bettenhausen and J. K. Murnighan, "The Development of an Intragroup Norm and the Effects of Interpersonal and Structural Challenges," *Administrative Science Quarterly*, March 1991, pp. 20–35.

26 C. A. Kiesler and S. B. Kiesler, *Conformity* (Reading, MA: Addison Wesley, 1969).

27 S. E. Asch, "Effects of Group Pressure upon the Modification and Distortion of Judgments," in *Groups, Leadership and Men*, ed. H. Guetzkow (Pittsburgh, PA: Carnegie Press, 1951), pp. 177–190; and S. E. Asch, "Studies of Independence and Conformity: A Minority of One Against a Unanimous Majority," *Psychological Monographs: General and Applied* 70, no. 9 (1956), pp. 1–70.

28 S. L. Robinson and A. M. O'Leary-Kelly, "Monkey See, Monkey Do: The Influence of Work Groups on the Antisocial Behavior of Employees," *Academy of Management Journal* 41 (1998), pp. 658–672.

29 J. M. George, "Personality, Affect and Behavior in Groups," *Journal of Applied Psychology* 78 (1993), pp. 798–804; and J. M. George and L. R. James, "Personality, Affect, and Behavior in

Groups Revisited: Comment on Aggregation, Levels of Analysis, and a Recent Application of Within and Between Analysis," *Journal of Applied Psychology* 78 (1993), pp. 798–804.

30 B. W. Tuckman, "Developmental Sequences in Small Groups," *Psychological Bulletin*, June 1965, pp. 384–399; B. W. Tuckman and M. C. Jensen, "Stages of Small-Group Development Revisited," *Group and Organizational Studies*, December 1977, pp. 419–427; and M. F. Maples, "Group Development: Extending Tuckman's Theory," *Journal for Specialists in Group Work*, Fall 1988, pp. 17–23.

31 J. F. George and L. M. Jessup, "Groups over Time: What Are We Really Studying?" *International Journal of Human-Computer Studies* 47, no. 3 (1997), pp. 497–511.

32 R. C. Ginnett, "The Airline Cockpit Crew," in *Groups That Work (and Those That Don't)*, ed. J. R. Hackman (San Francisco: Jossey-Bass, 1990).

33 C. J. G. Gersick, "Time and Transition in Work Teams: Toward a New Model of Group Development," *Academy of Management Journal*, March 1988, pp. 9–41; C. J. G. Gersick, "Marking Time: Predictable Transitions in Task Groups," *Academy of Management Journal*, June 1989, pp. 274–309; E. Romanelli and M. L. Tushman, "Organizational Transformation as Punctuated Equilibrium: An Empirical Test," *Academy of Management Journal*, October 1994, pp. 1141–1166; B. M. Lichtenstein, "Evolution or Transformation: A Critique and Alternative to Punctuated Equilibrium," in *Academy of Management Best Paper Proceedings*, ed. D. P. Moore (National Academy of Management Conference, Vancouver, 1995), pp. 291–295; and A. Seers and S. Woodruff, "Temporal Pacing in Task Forces: Group Development or Deadline Pressure?" *Journal of Management* 23, no. 2 (1997), pp. 169–187.

34 C. J. G. Gersick, "Time and Transition in Work Teams: Toward a New Model of Group Development," *Academy of Management Journal*, March 1988, pp. 9–41; and M. J. Waller, J. M. Conte, C. B. Gibson, and M. A. Carpenter, "The Effect of Individual Perceptions of Deadlines on Team Performance," *Academy of Management Review*, October 2001, pp. 586–600.

35 C. J. G. Gersick, "Time and Transition in Work Teams: Toward a New Model of Group Development," *Academy of Management Journal*, March 1988, pp. 9–41; and C. J. G. Gersick, "Marking Time: Predictable Transitions in Task Groups," *Academy of Management Journal*, June 1989, pp. 274–309.

36 A. Chang, P. Bordia, and J. Duck, "Punctuated Equilibrium and Linear Progression: Toward a New Understanding of Group Development," *Academy of Management Journal* 46, no. 1 (2003), pp. 106–117.

37 K. L. Bettenhausen, "Five Years of Groups Research: What We Have Learned and What Needs to be Addressed," *Journal of Management* 17, 1991, pp. 345–381; and R. A. Guzzo and G. P. Shea, "Group Performance and Intergroup Relations in Organizations," in *Handbook of Industrial and Organizational Psychology*, vol. 3, 2nd ed., ed. M. D. Dunnette and L. M. Hough (Palo Alto, CA: Consulting Psychologists Press, 1992), pp. 269–313.

38 A. Chang, P. Bordia, and J. Duck, "Punctuated Equilibrium and Linear Progression: Toward a New Understanding of Group Development," *Academy of Management Journal* 46, no. 1 (2003), pp. 106–117; and S. G. S. Lim and J. K. Murnighan, "Phases, Deadlines, and the Bargaining Process," *Organizational Behavior and Human Decision Processes* 58 (1994), pp. 153–171.

39 Vignette based on A. Tesolin, "Igniting the Creative Spark at Cirque du Soleil—Arupa Tesolin Interviews Lyn Heward Creative Leader at Cirque," *SelfGrowth.com*, http://www.selfgrowth.com/articles/Igniting_the_Creative_Spark_at_Cirque_du_Soleil.html; and M. Baghai and J. Quigley, "Cirque du Soleil: A Very Different Vision of Teamwork," *Fast Company*, February 4, 2011.

40 See, for instance, D. L. Gladstein, "Groups in Context: A Model of Task Group Effectiveness," *Administrative Science Quarterly*, December 1984, pp. 499–517; J. R. Hackman, "The Design of Work Teams," in *Handbook of Organizational Behavior*, ed. J. W. Lorsch (Englewood Cliffs, NJ: Prentice Hall, 1987), pp. 315–342; M. A. Campion, G. J. Medsker, and C. A. Higgs, "Relations between Work Group Characteristics and Effectiveness: Implications for Designing Effective Work Groups," *Personnel Psychology*, 1993; and R. A. Guzzo and M. W. Dickson, "Teams in Organizations: Recent Research on Performance and Effectiveness," in *Annual Review of Psychology*, vol. 47, ed. J. T. Spence, J. M. Darley, and D. J. Foss, 1996, pp. 307–338.

41 D. E. Hyatt and T. M. Ruddy, "An Examination of the Relationship between Work Group Characteristics and Performance: Once More into the Breech," *Personnel Psychology*, Autumn 1997, p. 555.

42 This model is based on M. A. Campion, E. M. Papper, and G. J. Medsker, "Relations between Work Team Characteristics and Effectiveness: A Replication and Extension," *Personnel Psychology*, Summer 1996, pp. 429–452; D. E. Hyatt and T. M. Ruddy, "An Examination of the Relationship between Work Group Characteristics and Performance: Once More into the Breech," *Personnel Psychology*, Autumn 1997, pp. 553–585; S. G. Cohen and D. E. Bailey, "What Makes Teams Work: Group Effectiveness Research from the Shop Floor to the Executive Suite," *Journal of Management* 23, no. 3 (1997), pp. 239–290; G. A. Neuman and J. Wright, "Team Effectiveness: Beyond Skills and Cognitive Ability," *Journal of Applied Psychology*, June 1999, pp. 376–389; and L. Thompson, *Making the Team* (Upper Saddle River, NJ: Prentice Hall, 2000), pp. 18–33.

43 E. M. Stark, "Interdependence and Preference for Group Work: Main and Congruence Effects on the Satisfaction and Performance of Group Members," *Journal of Management* 26, no. 2 (2000), pp. 259–279; and J. W. Bishop, K. D. Scott, and S. M. Burroughs, "Support, Commitment, and Employee Outcomes in a Team Environment," *Journal of Management* 26, no. 6 (2000), pp. 1113–1132.

44 See M. Mattson, T. V. Mumford, and G. S. Sintay, "Taking Teams to Task: A Normative Model for Designing or Recalibrating Work Teams" (paper presented at the National Academy of Management Conference, Chicago, August 1999); and G. L. Stewart and M. R. Barrick, "Team Structure and Performance: Assessing the Mediating Role of Intrateam Process and the Moderating Role of Task Type," *Academy of Management Journal*, April 2000, pp. 135–148.

45 Based on W. G. Dyer, R. H. Daines, and W. C. Giauque, *The Challenge of Management* (New York: Harcourt Brace Jovanovich, 1990), p. 343.

46 J. R. Hackman, *Leading Teams* (Boston: Harvard Business School Press, 2002).

47 P. Balkundi and D. A. Harrison, "Ties, Leaders, and Time in Teams: Strong Inference About Network Structure's Effects on Team Viability and Performance," *Academy of Management Journal* 49, no. 1 (2006), pp. 49–68; G. Chen, B. L. Kirkman, R. Kanfer, D. Allen, and B. Rosen, "A Multilevel Study of Leadership, Empowerment, and Performance in Teams," *Journal of Applied Psychology* 92, no. 2 (2007), pp. 331–346; L. A. DeChurch and M. A. Marks, "Leadership in Multiteam Systems," *Journal of Applied Psychology* 91, no. 2 (2006), pp. 311–329; A. Srivastava, K. M. Bartol, and E. A. Locke, "Empowering Leadership in Management Teams: Effects on Knowledge Sharing, Efficacy, and Performance," *Academy of Management Journal* 49, no. 6 (2006), pp. 1239–1251; J. E. Mathieu, K. K. Gilson, and T. M. Ruddy, "Empowerment and Team Effectiveness: An Empirical Test of an Integrated Model," *Journal of Applied Psychology* 91, no. 1 (2006), pp. 97–108; and K. J. Klein, A. P. Knight, J. C. Ziegert, B. C. Lim, and J. L. Saltz, "When Team Members' Values Differ: The

Moderating Role of Team Leadership," *Organizational Behavior & Human Decision Processes* 114, no. 1 (2011), pp. 25–36.

48 W. Immen, "The More Women in Groups, the Better," *Globe and Mail*, April 27, 2005, p. C3; and J. L. Berdahl and C. Anderson, "Men, Women, and Leadership Centralization in Groups over Time," *Group Dynamics: Theory, Research, and Practice* 9, no. 1 (2005), pp. 45–57.

49 R. I. Beekun, "Assessing the Effectiveness of Sociotechnical Interventions: Antidote or Fad?" *Human Relations*, October 1989, pp. 877–897.

50 S. G. Cohen, G. E. Ledford, and G. M. Spreitzer, "A Predictive Model of Self-Managing Work Team Effectiveness," *Human Relations*, May 1996, pp. 643–676.

51 D. R. Ilgen, J. R. Hollenbeck, M. Johnson, and D. Jundt, "Teams in Organizations: From Input-Process-Output Models to IMOI Models," *Annual Review of Psychology* 56, no. 1 (2005), pp. 517–543.

52 P. L. Schindler and C. C. Thomas, "The Structure of Interpersonal Trust in the Workplace," *Psychological Reports*, October 1993, pp. 563–573.

53 K. T. Dirks, "Trust in Leadership and Team Performance: Evidence from NCAA Basketball," *Journal of Applied Psychology*, December 2000, pp. 1004–1012; and M. Williams, "In Whom We Trust: Group Membership as an Affective Context for Trust Development," *Academy of Management Review*, July 2001, pp. 377–396.

54 "Relationship Building Breeds Success," *National Post*, August 11, 2008, p. FP7.

55 See S. T. Johnson, "Work Teams: What's Ahead in Work Design and Rewards Management," *Compensation & Benefits Review*, March–April 1993, pp. 35–41; and A. M. Saunier and E. J. Hawk, "Realizing the Potential of Teams through Team-Based Rewards," *Compensation & Benefits Review*, July–August 1994, pp. 24–33.

56 M. J. Pearsall, M. S. Christian, A. P. J. Ellis, "Motivating Interdependent Teams: Individual Rewards, Shared Rewards, or Something in Between?" *Journal of Applied Psychology* 95, no. 1 (2010), pp. 183–191.

57 K. Merriman, "Low-Trust Teams Prefer Individualized Pay," *Harvard Business Review* 86, no. 11 (November 2008), p. 32.

58 J. Pfeffer and N. Langton, "The Effect of Wage Dispersion on Satisfaction, Productivity, and Working Collaboratively: Evidence from College and University Faculty," *Administrative Science Quarterly* 38, 1993, pp. 382–407.

59 M. Bloom, "The Performance Effects of Pay Dispersion on Individuals and Organizations," *Academy of Management Journal* 42, 1999, pp. 25–40.

60 B. Beersma, J. R. Hollenbeck, D. E. Conlon, S. E. Humphrey, H. Moon, and D. R. Ilgen, "Cutthroat Cooperation: The Effects of Team Role Decisions on Adaptation to Alternative Reward Structures," *Organizational Behavior and Human Decision Processes* 108, no. 1 (2009), pp. 131–142; and M. D. Johnson, S. E. Humphrey, D. R. Ilgen, D. Jundt, and C. J. Meyer, "Cutthroat Cooperation: Asymmetrical Adaptation to Changes in Team Reward Structures," *Academy of Management Journal* 49, no. 1 (2006), pp. 103–119.

61 For a more detailed breakdown on team skills, see M. J. Stevens and M. A. Campion, "The Knowledge, Skill, and Ability Requirements for Teamwork: Implications for Human Resource Management," *Journal of Management*, Summer 1994, pp. 503–530.

62 S. T. Bell, "Deep-Level Composition Variables as Predictors of Team Performance: A Meta-analysis," *Journal of Applied Psychology* 92, no. 3 (2007), pp. 595–615; and M. R. Barrick, G. L. Stewart, M. J. Neubert, and M. K. Mount, "Relating Member Ability and Personality to Work-Team Processes and Team Effectiveness," *Journal of Applied Psychology*, June 1998, pp. 377–391.

63 K. Tasa, G. J. Sears, and A. C. H. Schat, "Personality and Teamwork Behavior in Context: The Cross-Level Moderating Role of Collective Efficacy," *Journal of Organizational Behavior* 32, no. 1 (2011), pp. 65–85.

64 A. Ellis, J. R. Hollenbeck, D. R. Ilgen, C. O. Porter, B. West, and H. Moon, "Team Learning: Collectively Connecting the Dots," *Journal of Applied Psychology* 88 (2003), pp. 821–835; C. O. L. H. Porter, J. R. Hollenbeck, and D. R. Ilgen, "Backing up Behaviors in Teams: The Role of Personality and Legitimacy of Need," *Journal of Applied Psychology* 88, no. 3 (June 2003), pp. 391–403; A. Colquitt, J. R. Hollenbeck, and D. R. Ilgen, "Computer-Assisted Communication and Team Decision-Making Performance: The Moderating Effect of Openness to Experience," *Journal of Applied Psychology* 87, no. 2 (April 2002), pp. 402–410; J. A. LePine, J. R. Hollenbeck, D. R. Ilgen, and J. Hedlund, "The Effects of Individual Differences on the Performance of Hierarchical Decision Making Teams: Much More Than G," *Journal of Applied Psychology* 82 (1997), pp. 803–811; C. L. Jackson and J. A. LePine, "Peer Responses to a Team's Weakest Link," *Journal of Applied Psychology* 88, no. 3 (2003), pp. 459–475; and M. R. Barrick, G. L. Stewart, J. M. Neubert, and M. K. Mount, "Relating Member Ability and Personality to Work-Team Processes and Team Effectiveness," *Journal of Applied Psychology* 83, no. 3 (1998), pp. 377–391.

65 M. A. Neale, G. B. Northcraft, and K. A. Jehn, "Exploring Pandora's Box: The Impact of Diversity and Conflict on Work Group Performance," *Performance Improvement Quarterly* 12, no. 1 (1999), pp. 113–126.

66 S. E. Humphrey, F. P. Morgeson, and M. J. Mannor, "Developing a Theory of the Strategic Core of Teams: A Role Composition Model of Team Performance," *Journal of Applied Psychology* 94, no. 1 (2009), pp. 48–61.

67 E. Sundstrom, K. P. Meuse, and D. Futrell, "Work Teams: Applications and Effectiveness," *American Psychologist*, February 1990, pp. 120–133.

68 See, for instance, M. Sashkin and K. J. Kiser, *Putting Total Quality Management to Work* (San Francisco: Berrett-Koehler, 1993); and J. R. Hackman and R. Wageman, "Total Quality Management: Empirical, Conceptual and Practical Issues," *Administrative Science Quarterly*, June 1995, pp. 309–342.

69 A. Joshi and H. Roh, "The Role of Context in Work Team Diversity Research: A Meta-analytic Review," *Academy of Management Journal* 52, no. 3 (2009), pp. 599--627; and S. K. Horwitz and I. B. Horwitz, "The Effects of Team Diversity on Team Outcomes: A Meta-analytic Review of Team Demography," *Journal of Management* 33, no. 6 (2007), pp. 987–1015.

70 G. S. Van Der Vegt, J. S. Bunderson, and A. Oosterhof, "Expertness Diversity and Interpersonal Helping in Teams: Why Those Who Need the Most Help End Up Getting the Least," *Academy of Management Journal* 49, no. 5 (2006), pp. 877–893.

71 "Is Your Team Too Big? Too Small? What's the Right Number?" *Knowledge@Wharton*, June 14, 2006, pp. 1–5.

72 See D. R. Comer, "A Model of Social Loafing in Real Work Groups," *Human Relations*, June 1995, pp. 647–667.

73 W. Moede, "Die Richtlinien der Leistungs-Psychologie," *Industrielle Psychotechnik* 4 (1927), pp. 193–207. See also D. A. Kravitz and B. Martin, "Ringelmann Rediscovered: The Original Article," *Journal of Personality and Social Psychology*, May 1986, pp. 936–941.

74 See, for example, J. A. Shepperd, "Productivity Loss in Performance Groups: A Motivation Analysis," *Psychological Bulletin*, January 1993, pp. 67–81; and S. J. Karau and K. D. Williams, "Social Loafing: A Meta-analytic Review and Theoretical Integration," *Journal of Personality and Social Psychology*, October 1993, pp. 681–706.

75 D. E. Hyatt and T. M. Ruddy, "An Examination of the Relationship between Work Group Characteristics and Performance: Once More into the Breech," *Personnel Psychology*, Autumn 1997, p. 555; and J. D. Shaw, M. K. Duffy, and E. M. Stark, "Interdependence and Preference for Group Work: Main and Congruence Effects on the Satisfaction and Performance of Group Members," *Journal of Management* 26, no. 2 (2000), pp. 259–279.

76 R. Wageman, "Critical Success Factors for Creating Superb Self-Managing Teams," *Organizational Dynamics*, Summer 1997, p. 55.

77 M. A. Campion, E. M. Papper, and G. J. Medsker, "Relations between Work Team Characteristics and Effectiveness: A Replication and Extension," *Personnel Psychology*, Summer 1996, p. 430.

78 M. A. Campion, E. M. Papper, and G. J. Medsker, "Relations between Work Team Characteristics and Effectiveness: A Replication and Extension," *Personnel Psychology*, Summer 1996, p. 430.

79 J. A. LePine, R. F. Piccolo, C. L. Jackson, J. E. Mathieu, and J. R. Saul, "A Meta-analysis of Teamwork Processes: Tests of a Multidimensional Model and Relationships with Team Effectiveness Criteria," *Personnel Psychology* 61 (2008), pp. 273–307.

80 I. D. Steiner, *Group Processes and Productivity* (New York: Academic Press, 1972).

81 J. A. LePine, R. F. Piccolo, C. L. Jackson, J. E. Mathieu, and J. R. Saul, "A Meta-analysis of Teamwork Processes: Tests of a Multidimensional Model and Relationships with Team Effectiveness Criteria," *Personnel Psychology* 61 (2008), pp. 273–307; and J. E. Mathieu and T. L. Rapp, "Laying the Foundation for Successful Team Performance Trajectories: The Roles of Team Charters and Performance Strategies," *Journal of Applied Psychology* 94, no. 1 (2009), pp. 90–103.

82 J. E. Mathieu and W. Schulze, "The Influence of Team Knowledge and Formal Plans on Episodic Team Process—Performance Relationships," *Academy of Management Journal* 49, no. 3 (2006), pp. 605–619.

83 A. Gurtner, F. Tschan, N. K. Semmer, and C. Nagele, "Getting Groups to Develop Good Strategies: Effects of Reflexivity Interventions on Team Process, Team Performance, and Shared Mental Models," *Organizational Behavior and Human Decision Processes* 102 (2007), pp. 127–142; M. C. Schippers, D. N. Den Hartog, and P. L. Koopman, "Reflexivity in Teams: A Measure and Correlates," *Applied Psychology: An International Review* 56, no. 2 (2007), pp. 189–211; and C. S. Burke, K. C. Stagl, E. Salas, L. Pierce, and D. Kendall, "Understanding Team Adaptation: A Conceptual Analysis and Model," *Journal of Applied Psychology* 91, no. 6 (2006), pp. 1189–1207.

84 E. Weldon and L. R. Weingart, "Group Goals and Group Performance," *British Journal of Social Psychology*, Spring 1993, pp. 307–334.

85 K. Tasa, S. Taggar, and G. H. Seijts, "The Development of Collective Efficacy in Teams: A Multilevel and Longitudinal Perspective," *Journal of Applied Psychology* 92, no. 1 (2007), pp. 17–27; C. B. Gibson, "The Efficacy Advantage: Factors Related to the Formation of Group Efficacy," *Journal of Applied Social Psychology*, October 2003, pp. 2153–2086; and D. I. Jung and J. J. Sosik, "Group Potency and Collective Efficacy: Examining Their Predictive Validity, Level of Analysis, and Effects of Performance Feedback on Future Group Performance," *Group & Organization Management*, September 2003, pp. 366–391.

86 For some of the controversy surrounding the definition of cohesion, see J. Keyton and J. Springston, "Redefining Cohesiveness in Groups," *Small Group Research*, May 1990, pp. 234–254.

87 C. R. Evans and K. L. Dion, "Group Cohesion and Performance: A Meta-analysis," *Small Group Research*, May 1991, pp. 175–186; B. Mullen and C. Cooper, "The Relation between Group Cohesiveness and Performance: An Integration," *Psychological Bulletin*, March 1994, pp. 210–227; S. M. Gully, D. J. Devine, and D. J. Whitney, "A Meta-analysis of Cohesion and Performance: Effects of Level of Analysis and Task Interdependence," *Small Group Research*, 1995, pp. 497–520; and P. M. Podsakoff, S. B. MacKenzie, and M. Ahearne, "Moderating Effects of Goal Acceptance on the Relationship between Group Cohesiveness and Productivity," *Journal of Applied Psychology*, December 1997, pp. 974–983.

88 R. Kreitner and A. Kinicki, *Organizational Behavior*, 6th ed. (New York: Irwin, 2004), p. 460. Reprinted by permission of McGraw Hill Education.

89 A. Chang and P. Bordia, "A Multidimensional Approach to the Group Cohesion-Group Performance Relationship," *Small Group Research*, August 2001, pp. 379–405.

90 Paragraph based on R. Kreitner and A. Kinicki, *Organizational Behavior*, 6th ed. (New York: Irwin, 2004), pp. 459–461.

91 A. P. J. Ellis, "System Breakdown: The Role of Mental Models and Transactive Memory on the Relationships between Acute Stress and Team Performance," *Academy of Management Journal* 49, no. 3 (2006), pp. 576–589.

92 S. W. J. Kozlowski and D. R. Ilgen, "Enhancing the Effectiveness of Work Groups and Teams," *Psychological Science in the Public Interest*, December 2006, pp. 77–124; and B. D. Edwards, E. A. Day, W. Arthur Jr., and S. T. Bell, "Relationships among Team Ability Composition, Team Mental Models, and Team Performance," *Journal of Applied Psychology* 91, no. 3 (2006), pp. 727–736.

93 K. M. Eisenhardt, J. L. Kahwajy, and L. J. Bourgeois III, "How Management Teams Can Have a Good Fight," *Harvard Business Review*, July–August 1997, p. 78.

94 K. J. Behfar, R. S. Peterson, E. A. Mannix, and W. M. K. Trochim, "The Critical Role of Conflict Resolution in Teams: A Close Look at the Links between Conflict Type, Conflict Management Strategies, and Team Outcomes," *Journal of Applied Psychology* 93, no. 1 (2008), pp. 170–188.

95 K. Jehn, "A Multimethod Examination of the Benefits and Detriments of Intragroup Conflict," *Administrative Science Quarterly*, June 1995, pp. 256–282.

96 K. M. Eisenhardt, J. L. Kahwajy, and L. J. Bourgeois III, "How Management Teams Can Have a Good Fight," *Harvard Business Review*, July–August 1997, p. 78.

97 K. A. Jehn, S. Rispens, and S. M. B. Thatcher, "The Effects of Conflict Asymmetry on Work Group and Individual Outcomes," *Academy of Management Journal* 53, no. 3 (2010), pp. 596–616.

98 K. Hess, *Creating the High-Performance Team* (New York: Wiley, 1987).

99 C. E. Naquin and R. O. Tynan, "The Team Halo Effect: Why Teams Are Not Blamed for Their Failures," *Journal of Applied Psychology*, April 2003, pp. 332–340.

100 D. Brown, "Innovative HR Ineffective in Manufacturing Firms," *Canadian HR Reporter*, April 7, 2003, pp. 1–2.

101 A. B. Drexler and R. Forrester, "Teamwork—Not Necessarily the Answer," *HR Magazine*, January 1998, pp. 55–58.

102 "Watson Wyatt's Global Work Studies," http://www.watsonwyatt.com/research/featured/workstudy.asp

103 C. E. Nicholls, H. W. Lane, and M. Brehm Brechu, "Taking Self-Managed Teams to Mexico," *Academy of Management Executive* 13, no. 3 (1999), pp. 15–27.

104 W. E. Watson, K. Kumar, and L. K. Michaelsen, "Cultural Diversity's Impact on Interaction Process and Performance: Comparing Homogeneous and Diverse Task Groups," *Academy of Management Journal*, June 1993, pp. 590–602; P. C. Earley and E. Mosakowski, "Creating Hybrid Team Cultures: An Empirical Test of Transnational Team Functioning," *Academy of Management Journal*, February 2000, pp. 26–49; and S. Mohammed and L. C. Angell, "Surface- and Deep-Level Diversity in Workgroups: Examining the Moderating Effects of Team Orientation and Team Process on Relationship Conflict," *Journal of Organizational Behavior*, December 2004, pp. 1015–1039.

105 W. E. Watson, K. Kumar, and L. K. Michaelsen, "Cultural Diversity's Impact on Interaction Process and Performance: Comparing Homogeneous and Diverse Task Groups," *Academy of Management Journal*, June 1993, pp. 590–602.

106 D. F. Crown, "The Use of Group and Groupcentric Individual Goals for Culturally Heterogeneous and Homogeneous Task Groups: An Assessment of European Work Teams," *Small Group Research* 38, no. 4 (2007), pp. 489–508.

107 Based on D. Man and S. S. K. Lam, "The Effects of Job Complexity and Autonomy on Cohesiveness in Collectivist and Individualistic Work Groups: A Cross-Cultural Analysis," *Journal of Organizational Behavior*, December 2003, pp. 979–1001.

108 Based on J. Berger and D. Pope, "When Losing Leads to Winning," working paper, Wharton School of Business, University of Pennsylvania (2009); J. Senécal, T. M. Loughead, and G. A. Bloom, "A Season-Long Team-Building Intervention: Examining the Effect of Team Goal Setting on Cohesion," *Journal of Sport & Exercise Psychology* 30, no. 2 (2008), pp. 186–199; N. Katz, "Sports Teams as a Model for Workplace Teams: Lessons and Liabilities," *Academy of Management Executive*, August 2001, pp. 56–67; and "Talent Inc.," *New Yorker*, http://www.newyorker.com/archive/2002/07/22/020722on_onlineonly01

109 Association for Psychological Science, "Cross-Cultural Perspective Can Help Teamwork in the Workplace," *ScienceDaily*, August 10, 2010, http://www.sciencedaily.com/releases/2010/08/100810122041.htm

110 Based on A. Webb, "The Trials and Tribulations of Teamwork," *Automotive News*, March 2, 2009, http://www.autonews.com; J. K. Liker and M. Hoseus, "Toyota's Powerful HR," *Human Resource Executive*, November 1, 2008, http://www.hreonline.com; J. K. Liker and M. Hoseus, *Toyota Culture: The Heart and Soul of the Toyota Way* (New York: McGraw-Hill, 2008); and D. Kiley, "The Toyota Way to No. 1," *BusinessWeek*, April 26, 2007, http://www.businessweek.com

111 Based on C. Hymowitz, "IBM Combines Volunteer Service, Teamwork to Cultivate Emerging Markets," *Wall Street Journal*, August 4, 2008, p. B6; S. Gupta, "Mine the Potential of Multicultural Teams," *HR Magazine*, October, 2008, pp. 79–84; and H. Aguinis and K. Kraiger, "Benefits of Training and Development for Individuals and Teams, Organizations, and Society," *Annual Review of Psychology* 60, no. 1 (2009), pp. 451–474.

112 S. P. Robbins and P. L. Hunsaker, *Training in Interpersonal Skills*, 2nd ed. (Upper Saddle River, NJ: Prentice Hall, 1996), pp. 168–184.

OB on the Edge: Trust

1 Vignette based on "Building Trust Since '31," *Windsor Star*, May 21, 2008, p. C11; "Come on Down," *Windsor Star*, September 20, 2007, p. D8; C. Vander Doelen, "Dodge's 'Aggressive' Theme Gets a Makeover," *Windsor Star*, September 18, 2007, p. B1; and http://www.reaumechev.com

2 See, for example, K. T. Dirks and D. L. Ferrin, "Trust in Leadership: Meta-analytic Findings and Implications for Research and Practice," *Journal of Applied Psychology*, August 2002, pp. 611–628; the special issue on trust in an organizational context, B. McEvily, V. Perrone, A. Zaheer, guest editors, *Organization Science*, January–February 2003; and R. Galford and A. S. Drapeau, *The Trusted Leader* (New York: Free Press, 2003).

3 F. K. Sonnenberg, "Trust Me, Trust Me Not," *IndustryWeek*, August 16, 1993, pp. 22–28; and L. T. Hosmer, "Trust: the Connecting Link between Organizational Theory and Philosophical Ethics," *Academy of Management Review*, April 1995, pp. 379–403.

4 T. Davis and M. J. Landa, "The Trust Deficit," *Worklife Report* 4 (1999), pp. 6–7.

5 J. Pollack, "Do Your Employees Trust You? Behaviour Survey Finds Lack of Trust in Senior Leaders as Top Reason for Quitting," *Telegraph-Journal*, May 30, 2009, p. E1.

6 D. M. Rousseau, S. B. Sitkin, R. S. Burt, and C. Camerer, "Not So Different After All: A Cross-Discipline View of Trust," *Academy of Management Review*, July 1998, pp. 393–404; and J. A. Simpson, "Psychological Foundations of Trust," *Current Directions in Psychological Science* 16, no. 5 (2007), pp. 264–268.

7 J. B. Rotter, "Interpersonal Trust, Trustworthiness, and Gullibility," *American Psychologist*, January 1980, pp. 1–7.

8 J. D. Lewis and A. Weigert, "Trust as a Social Reality," *Social Forces*, June 1985, p. 970.

9 J. K. Rempel, J. G. Holmes, and M. P. Zanna, "Trust in Close Relationships," *Journal of Personality and Social Psychology*, July 1985, p. 96.

10 G. M. Granovetter, "Economic Action and Social Structure: The Problem of Embeddedness," *American Journal of Sociology*, November 1985, p. 491.

11 R. C. Mayer, J. H. Davis, and F. D. Schoorman, "An Integrative Model of Organizational Trust," *Academy of Management Review*, July 1995, p. 712.

12 C. Johnson-George and W. Swap, "Measurement of Specific Interpersonal Trust: Construction and Validation of a Scale to Assess Trust in a Specific Other," *Journal of Personality and Social Psychology*, September 1982, p. 1306.

13 P. L. Schindler and C. C. Thomas, "The Structure of Interpersonal Trust in the Workplace," *Psychological Reports*, October 1993, pp. 563–573.

14 H. H. Tan and C. S. F. Tan, "Toward the Differentiation of Trust in Supervisor and Trust in Organization," *Genetic, Social, and General Psychology Monographs*, May 2000, pp. 241–260.

15 Cited in D. Jones, "Do You Trust Your CEO?" *USA Today*, February 12, 2003, p. 7B.

16 D. McGregor, *The Professional Manager* (New York: McGraw-Hill, 1967), p. 164.

17 B. Nanus, *The Leader's Edge: The Seven Keys to Leadership in a Turbulent World* (Chicago: Contemporary Books, 1989), p. 102.

18 K. T. Dirks and D. L. Ferrin, "Trust in Leadership: Meta-analytic Findings and Implications for Organizational Research," *Journal of Applied Psychology* 87 (2002), pp. 611–628.

19 Based on information in T. Simons, "The High Cost of Lost Trust," *Harvard Business Review*, September 2002, pp. 18–19.

20 This section is based on D. E. Zand, *The Leadership Triad: Knowledge, Trust, and Power* (New York: Oxford University Press, 1997), pp. 122–134; and A. M. Zak, J. A. Gold, R. M. Ryckman, and E. Lenney, "Assessments of Trust in Intimate Relationships and the Self-Perception Process," *Journal of Social Psychology*, April 1998, pp. 217–228.

21 D. L. Ferrin, P. H. Kim, C. D. Cooper, and K. T. Dirks, "Silence Speaks Volumes: The Effectiveness of Reticence in Comparison to Apology and Denial for Responding to Integrity- and Competence-Based Trust Violations," *Journal of Applied Psychology* 92, no. 4 (2007), pp. 893–908.

22 M. E. Schweitzer, J. C. Hershey, and E. T. Bradlow, "Promises and Lies: Restoring Violated Trust," *Organizational Behavior and Human Decision Processes* 101 (2006), pp. 1–19.

23 B. A. De Jong and T. O. M. Elfring, "How Does Trust Affect the Performance of Ongoing Teams? The Mediating Role of Reflexivity, Monitoring, and Effort," *Academy of Management Journal* 53, no. 3 (2010), pp. 535–549.

24 Adapted from J. O'Toole and W. Bennis, "What's Needed Next: A Culture of Candor," *Harvard Business Review*, June 2009, pp. 54–61.

25 T. Davis and M. J. Landa, "The Trust Deficit," *Worklife Report* 4 (1999), pp. 6–7.

26 L. Prusak and D. Cohen, "How to Invest in Social Capital," *Harvard Business Review*, June 2001, pp. 86–93.

27 L. Prusak and D. Cohen, "How to Invest in Social Capital," *Harvard Business Review*, June 2001, pp. 86–93.

28 K. T. Dirks, "Trust in Leadership and Team Performance: Evidence from NCAA Basketball," *Journal of Applied Psychology* 85 (2000), pp. 1004–1012.

29 FactBox based on Z. Ezekiel, *Building Public Trust in Canadian Organizations: Preliminary Findings* (Ottawa: The Conference Board of Canada, May 2005), pp. 1–3.

30 Based on F. Bartolome, "Nobody Trusts the Boss Completely—Now What?" *Harvard Business Review*, March–April 1989, pp. 135–142; and P. Pascarella, "15 Ways to Win People's Trust," *IndustryWeek*, February 1, 1993, pp. 47–51.

31 B. A. De Jong and T. O. M. Elfring, "How Does Trust Affect the Performance of Ongoing Teams? The Mediating Role of Reflexivity, Monitoring, and Effort," *Academy of Management Journal* 53, no. 3 (2010), pp. 535–549.

32 C. W. Langfred, "Too Much of a Good Thing? Negative Effects of High Trust and Individual Autonomy in Self-Managing Teams," *Academy of Management Journal* 47, no. 3 (June 2004), pp. 385–399.

33 N. L. Carter and J. Mark Weber, "Not Pollyannas: Higher Generalized Trust Predicts Lie Detection Ability," *Social Psychological and Personality Science* 1, no. 3 (2010), pp. 274–279.

34 Based on information in "R. M. Kramer, "Rethinking Trust," *Harvard Business Review*, June 2009, pp. 69–77.

35 R. M. Kramer, "Rethinking Trust," *Harvard Business Review*, June 2009, p. 71.

36 R. M. Kramer, "When Paranoia Makes Sense," *Harvard Business Review*, July 2002, pp. 62–69.

37 Adapted from R. M. Kramer, "Rethinking Trust," *Harvard Business Review*, June 2009, p. 71.

38 R. M. Kramer, "Rethinking Trust," *Harvard Business Review*, June 2009, p. 77.

Chapter 7

1 Vignette based on http://www.iabc.com/awards/gq/judging/WPMgt.htm

2 "Employers Cite Communication Skills, Honesty/Integrity as Key for Job Candidates," *IPMA-HR Bulletin*, March 23, 2007, p. 1.

3 J. Langan-Fox, "Communication in Organizations: Speed, Diversity, Networks, and Influence on Organizational Effectiveness, Human Health, and Relationships," in *Handbook of Industrial, Work and Organizational Psychology*, vol. 2, ed. N. Anderson, D. S. Ones, H. K. Sinangil, and C. Viswesvaran (Thousand Oaks, CA: Sage, 2001), p. 190.

4 J. C. McCroskey, J. A. Daly, and G. Sorenson, "Personality Correlates of Communication Apprehension," *Human Communication Research*, Spring 1976, pp. 376–380.

5 See R. L. Daft and R. H. Lengel, "Information Richness: A New Approach to Managerial Behavior and Organization Design," in *Research in Organizational Behavior*, vol. 6, ed. B. M. Staw and L. L. Cummings (Greenwich, CT: JAI Press, 1984), pp. 191–233; R. E. Rice and D. E. Shook, "Relationships of Job Categories and Organizational Levels to Use of Communication Channels, Including Electronic Mail: A Meta-analysis and Extension," *Journal of Management Studies*, March 1990, pp. 195–229; R. E. Rice, "Task Analyzability, Use of New Media, and Effectiveness," *Organization Science*, November 1992, pp. 475–500; S. G. Straus and J. E. McGrath, "Does the Medium Matter? The Interaction of Task Type and Technology on Group Performance and Member Reaction," *Journal of Applied Psychology*, February 1994, pp. 87–97; and J. Webster and L. K. Trevino, "Rational and Social Theories as Complementary Explanations of Communication Media Choices: Two Policy-Capturing Studies," *Academy of Management Journal*, December 1995, pp. 1544–1572.

6 "Building a Better Workforce," *PROFIT*, February 16, 2011, http://www.profitguide.com/article/10084--building-a-better-workforce--page0

7 D. K. Denton, "Engaging Your Employees in Times of Uncertainty," *International Journal of Productivity and Quality Management* 7, no. 2 (2011), pp. 202–208.

8 I. Austen, "Telling Tales Out of School, on YouTube," *New York Times*, November 27, 2006; and D. Rogers, "Quebec Students Suspended for Posting Teacher's Outburst Online," *Ottawa Citizen*, November 25, 2006.

9 R. L. Daft, R. H. Lengel, and L. K. Trevino, "Message Equivocality, Media Selection, and Manager Performance: Implications for Information Systems," *MIS Quarterly*, September 1987, pp. 355–368.

10 P. Brent, "How to Arm, Not Alarm, Your Staff in Crisis," *Canadian Business*, March 14, 2011, p. 68.

11 "Virtual Pink Slips Start Coming Online," *Vancouver Sun*, July 3, 1999, p. D15.

12 T. M. Burton and R. E. Silverman, "Lots of Empty Spaces in Cerner Parking Lot Get CEO Riled Up," *Wall Street Journal*, March 30, 2001, p. B3; and E. Wong, "A Stinging Office Memo Boomerangs," *New York Times*, April 5, 2001, p. C1.

13 Vignette based on M. Ormsby, "Brawl Brewing In Girls' Hockey," *Toronto Star*, November 11, 2009.

14 K. Savitsky, B. Keysar, N. Epley, T. Carter, and A. Swanson, "The Closeness-Communication Bias: Increased Egocentrism among Friends versus Strangers," *Journal of Experimental Social Psychology* 47, no. 1 (2011), pp. 269–273.

15 M. Richtel, "Lost in E-mail, Tech Firms Face Self-Made Beast," *New York Times*, June 14, 2008.

16 J. Sandberg, "The Jargon Jumble," *Wall Street Journal*, October 24, 2006, p. B1.

17 E. W. Morrison and F. J. Milliken, "Organizational Silence: A Barrier to Change and Development in a Pluralistic World," *Academy of Management Review* 25, no. 4 (2000), pp. 706–725; and B. E. Ashforth and V. Anand, "The Normalization of Corruption in Organizations," *Research in Organizational Behavior* 25 (2003), pp. 1–52.

18 F. J. Milliken, E. W. Morrison, and P. F. Hewlin, "An Exploratory Study of Employee Silence: Issues That Employees Don't Communicate Upward and Why," *Journal of Management Studies* 40, no. 6 (2003), pp. 1453–1476.

19 This paragraph is based on J. O'Toole and W. Bennis, "What's Needed Next: A Culture of Candor," *Harvard Business Review*, June 2009, pp. 54–61.

20 S. Tangirala and R. Ramunujam, "Employee Silence on Critical Work Issues: The Cross-Level Effects of Procedural Justice Climate," *Personnel Psychology* 61, no. 1 (2008), pp. 37–68; and F. Bowen and K. Blackmon, "Spirals of Silence: The Dynamic Effects of Diversity on Organizational Voice," *Journal of Management Studies* 40, no. 6 (2003), pp. 1393–1417.

21 C. G. Pinder and K. P. Harlos, "Silent Organizational Behavior" (paper presented at the Western Academy of Management Conference, March 2000).

22 L. S. Rashotte, "What Does That Smile Mean? The Meaning of Nonverbal Behaviors in Social Interaction," *Social Psychology Quarterly*, March 2002, pp. 92–102.

23 R. L. Birdwhistell, *Introduction to Kinesics* (Louisville, KY: University of Louisville Press, 1952).

24 J. Fast, *Body Language* (Philadelphia, PA: M. Evan, 1970), p. 7.

25 A. Mehrabian, *Nonverbal Communication* (Chicago: Aldine-Atherton, 1972).

26 N. M. Henley, "Body Politics Revisited: What Do We Know Today?" in *Gender, Power, and Communication in Human Relationships*, ed. P. J. Kalbfleisch and M. J. Cody (Hillsdale, NJ: Erlbaum, 1995), pp. 27–61.

27 E. T. Hall, *The Hidden Dimension*, 2nd ed. (Garden City, NY: Anchor Books/Doubleday, 1966).

28 H. Weeks, "Taking the Stress Out of Stressful Conversations," *Harvard Business Review*, July–August 2001, pp. 112–119.

29 Vignette based on S.-A. Levy, "City Offside in Shuffling Ice Time," *Toronto Sun*, May 6, 2010; and http://www.iabc.com/awards/gq/judging/WPMgt.htm

30 R. L. Simpson, "Vertical and Horizontal Communication in Formal Organizations," *Administrative Science Quarterly*, September 1959, pp. 188–196; and B. Harriman, "Up and Down the Communications Ladder," *Harvard Business Review*, September–October 1974, pp. 143–151.

31 P. Dvorak, "How Understanding the 'Why' of Decisions Matters," *Wall Street Journal*, March 19, 2007, p. B3.

32 "Building a Better Workforce," *PROFIT*, February 16, 2011, http://www.profitguide.com/article/10084--building-a-better-workforce--page0

33 "Building a Better Workforce," *PROFIT*, February 16, 2011, http://www.profitguide.com/article/10084--building-a-better-workforce--page0

34 J. R. Detert and L. K. Treviño, "Speaking Up to Higher-Ups: How Supervisors and Skip-Level Leaders Influence Employee Voice," *Organization Science* 21, no. 1 (2010), pp. 249–270.

35 E. Nichols, "Hyper-Speed Managers," *HR Magazine*, April 2007, pp. 107–110.

36 D. M. Saunders and J. D. Leck, "Formal Upward Communication Procedures: Organizational and Employee Perspectives," *Revue Canadienne des Sciences de l'Administration*, September 1993, pp. 255–268.

37 "Heard It through the Grapevine," *Forbes*, February 10, 1997, p. 22.

38 G. Van Hoye and F. Lievens, "Tapping the Grapevine: A Closer Look at Word-of-Mouth as a Recruitment Source," *Journal of Applied Psychology* 94, no. 2 (2009), pp. 341–352.

39 See, for instance, J. W. Newstrom, R. E. Monczka, and W. E. Reif, "Perceptions of the Grapevine: Its Value and Influence," *Journal of Business Communication*, Spring 1974, pp. 12–20; and S. J. Modic, "Grapevine Rated Most Believable," *IndustryWeek*, May 15, 1989, p. 14.

40 K. Davis cited in R. Rowan, "Where Did That Rumor Come From?" *Fortune*, August 13, 1979, p. 134.

41 Based on L. Hirschhorn, "Managing Rumors," in *Cutting Back*, ed. L. Hirschhorn (San Francisco: Jossey-Bass, 1983), pp. 54–56.

42 R. L. Rosnow and G. A. Fine, *Rumor and Gossip: The Social Psychology of Hearsay* (New York: Elsevier, 1976).

43 See, for instance, J. G. March and G. Sevon, "Gossip, Information and Decision Making," in *Decisions and Organizations*, ed. J. G. March (Oxford: Blackwell, 1988), pp. 429–442; M. Noon and R. Delbridge, "News from Behind My Hand: Gossip in Organizations," *Organization Studies* 14, no. 1 (1993), pp. 23–36; and N. DiFonzo, P. Bordia, and R. L. Rosnow, "Reining in Rumors," *Organizational Dynamics*, Summer 1994, pp. 47–62.

44 J. K. Bosson, A. B. Johnson, K. Niederhoffer, and W. B. Swann Jr., "Interpersonal Chemistry through Negativity: Bonding by Sharing Negative Attitudes About Others," *Personal Relationships* 13 (2006), pp. 135–150.

45 L. Hirschhorn, "Managing Rumors," in *Cutting Back*, ed. L. Hirschhorn (San Francisco: Jossey-Bass, 1983), pp. 54–56; and D. K. Denton, "Engaging Your Employees in Times of Uncertainty," *International Journal of Productivity and Quality Management* 7, no. 2 (2011), pp. 202–208.

46 B. Gates, "How I Work," *Fortune*, April 17, 2006, http://money.cnn.com

47 "Email Brings Costs and Fatigue," *Western News (UWO)*, July 9, 2004, http://communications.uwo.ca/com/western_news/stories/email_brings_costs_and_fatigue_20040709432320/

48 K. Macklem, "You've Got Too Much Mail," *Maclean's*, January 30, 2006, pp. 20–21.

49 "Overloaded Canadians Trash 42% of All E-Mails: Study," *Ottawa Citizen*, June 26, 2008, p. D5.

50 D. Brady, "*!#?@ the E-mail. Can We Talk?" *BusinessWeek*, December 4, 2006, p. 109.

51 E. Binney, "Is E-mail the New Pink Slip?" *HR Magazine*, November 2006, pp. 32–33; and R. L. Rundle, "Critical Case: How an Email Rant Jolted a Big HMO," *Wall Street Journal*, April 24, 2007, pp. A1, A16.

52 S. Hourigan, "62 Trillion Spam Emails Cause Huge Carbon Footprint," *Courier Mail*, April 17, 2009, http://www.news.com.au/couriermail

53 R. Stross, "The Daily Struggle to Avoid Burial by E-Mail," *New York Times*, April 21, 2008), p. BU5; and H. Rhodes, "You've Got Mail . . . Again," *Gainesville Sun*, September 29, 2008, pp. 1D, 6D.

54 C. Byron, "Carrying Too Heavy a Load? The Communication and Miscommunication of Emotion by Email," *Academy of Management Review* 33, no. 2 (2008), pp. 309–327.

55 D. Goleman, "Flame First, Think Later: New Clues to E-mail Misbehavior," *New York Times*, February 20, 2007, p. D5; and E. Krell, "The Unintended Word," *HR Magazine*, August 2006, pp. 50–54.

56 R. Zeidner, "Keeping E-mail in Check," *HR Magazine*, June 2007, pp. 70–74; "E-mail May Be Hazardous to Your Career," *Fortune*, May 14, 2007, p. 24; and J. D. Glater, "Open Secrets," *New York Times*, June 27, 2008, pp. B1, B5.

57 Based on S. Proudfoot, "1 in 3 Workers Admit to Improper E-mail; Stories of Career-Killing Gaffes Leave Many Unfazed, Study Finds," *Edmonton Journal*, June 25, 2008, p. A1; E. Church, "Employers Read E-mail as Fair Game," *Globe and Mail*, April 14, 1998, p. B16; and J. Kay, "Someone Will Watch Over Me: Think Your Office E-mails Are Private? Think Again," *National Post Business*, January 2001, pp. 59–64.

58 E. Church, "Employers Read E-mail as Fair Game," *Globe and Mail*, April 14, 1998, p. B16.

59 A. Harmon, "Appeal of Instant Messaging Extends into the Workplace," *New York Times*, March 11, 2003, p. A1.

60 http://www.cwta.ca/CWTASite/english/industryfacts.html

61 J. Bow, "Business Jumps on Text-Messaging Wave," *Business Edge*, April 5, 2007, p. 12.

62 A. Williams, "Mind Your BlackBerry or Mind Your Manners," *New York Times*, June 21, 2009, http://www.nytimes.com

63 "Survey Finds Mixed Reviews on Checking E-mail During Meetings," *IPMA-HR Bulletin*, April 27, 2007, p. 1.

64 K. Gurchiek, "Shoddy Writing Can Trip Up Employees, Organizations," *SHRM Online*, April 27, 2006, pp. 1–2.

65 D. Lidsky, "It's Not Just Who You Know," *Fast Company*, May 2007, p. 56.

66 Based on D. Bell, "Probe Will Examine Cop's Online Comments," *Nanaimo Daily News*, March 31, 2010, p. A4; and D. Bell, "Mountie's Posts on Facebook Raise Hackles," *Times-Colonist*, March 27, 2010, p. A1.

67 Based on "At Many Companies, Hunt for Leakers Expands Arsenal of Monitoring Tactics," *Wall Street Journal*, September 11, 2006, pp. B1, B3; and B. J. Alge, G. A. Ballinger, S. Tangirala, and J. L. Oakley, "Information Privacy in Organizations: Empowering Creative and Extra-Role Performance," *Journal of Applied Psychology* 91, no. 1 (2006), pp. 221–232.

68 J. Castaldo, "Are You Sure You Really Want To Tweet That, Boss?" *Canadian Business*, November 22, 2010.

69 J. Castaldo, "Are You Sure You Really Want To Tweet That, Boss?" *Canadian Business*, November 22, 2010.

70 M. Richtel, "Lost in E-mail, Tech Firms Face Self-Made Beast," *New York Times*, June 14, 2008, pp. A1, A14.

71 J. B. Spira and C. Burke, "Intel's War on Information Overload: A Case Study," copyright © 2009 Basex, Inc.

72 M. Richtel, "Lost in E-mail, Tech Firms Face Self-Made Beast," *New York Times*, June 14, 2008, pp. A1, A14.

73 M. Richtel, "Lost in E-mail, Tech Firms Face Self-Made Beast," *New York Times*, June 14, 2008, pp. A1, A14.

74 M. Richtel, "Lost in E-mail, Tech Firms Face Self-Made Beast," *New York Times*, June 14, 2008, pp. A1, A14; and M. Johnson, "Quelling Distraction," *HR Magazine*, August 2008, pp. 43–46.

75 Based on M. Conlin and M. MacMillan, "Managing the Tweets," *BusinessWeek*, June 1, 2009, pp. 20–21; H. Green and R. D. Hof, "Six Million Users: Nothing to Twitter At," *BusinessWeek*, March 16, 2009, pp. 51–52; and A. Hawkins, "Shut Up, Already," *Forbes*, April 7, 2008, p. 44.

76 D. Harris, "Crackberry Addiction: Gadget Users Compared to Drug Users for Excessive Behavior," *ABCNews Online*, August 23, 2006, http://abcnews.go.com/WNT/Technology/story?id=2348779

77 W. R. Boswell and J. B. Olson-Buchanan, "The Use of Communication Technologies After Hours: The Role of Work-Attitudes and Work-Life Conflict," *Journal of Management* 33, no. 4 (2007), pp. 592–610.

78 "At Many Companies, Hunt for Leakers Expands Arsenal of Monitoring Tactics," *Wall Street Journal*, September 11, 2006, pp. B1, B3; and B. J. Alge, G. A. Ballinger, S. Tangirala, and J. L. Oakley, "Information Privacy in Organizations: Empowering Creative and Extrarole Performance," *Journal of Applied Psychology* 91, no. 1 (2006), pp. 221–232.

79 See M. Munter, "Cross-Cultural Communication for Managers," *Business Horizons*, May–June 1993, pp. 75–76; and H. Ren and B. Gray, "Repairing Relationship Conflict: How Violation Types and Culture Influence the Effectiveness of Restoration Rituals," *Academy of Management Review* 34, no. 1 (2009), pp. 105–126.

80 See E. T. Hall, *Beyond Culture* (Garden City, NY: Anchor Press/Doubleday, 1976); E. T. Hall and M. R. Hall, *Understanding Cultural Differences* (Yarmouth, ME: Intercultural Press, 1990); W. L. Adair, "Integrative Sequences and Negotiation Outcome in Same- and Mixed-Culture Negotiations," *International Journal of Conflict Management* 14, no. 3–4 (2003), pp. 1359–1392; W. L. Adair and J. M. Brett, "The Negotiation Dance: Time, Culture, and Behavioral Sequences in Negotiation," *Organization Science* 16, no. 1 (2005), pp. 33–51; E. Giebels and P. J. Taylor, "Interaction Patterns in Crisis Negotiations: Persuasive Arguments and Cultural Differences," *Journal of Applied Psychology* 94, no. 1 (2009), pp. 5–19; and Y. Fujimoto, N. Bahfen, J. Fermelise, and C. E. J. Härtel, "The Global Village: Online Cross-Cultural Communication and HRM," *Cross Cultural Management* 14, no. 1 (2007), pp. 7–22.

81 N. Adler, *International Dimensions of Organizational Behavior*, 3rd ed. (Cincinnati, OH: South Western College, 1997), pp. 87–88.

82 S. A. Hellweg and S. L. Phillips, "Communication and Productivity in Organizations: A State-of-the-Art Review," in *Proceedings of the 40th Annual Academy of Management Conference*, Detroit, 1980, pp. 188–192.

83 Based on A. van Iterson and S. R. Clegg, "The Politics of Gossip and Denial in Interorganizational Relations," *Human Relations* 61, no. 8 (2008), pp. 1117–1137; "Top Managers Don't Appreciate Office Gossip," *USA Today*, December 24, 2008, p. B1; E. Jaffe, "The Science Behind Secrets," *APS Observer*, July 2006, pp. 20–22; and J. Piazza and J. M. Bering, "Concerns About Reputation via Gossip Promote Generous Allocations in an Economic Game," *Evolution and Human Behavior* 29, no. 3 (2008), pp. 172–178.

84 B. Beersma, and G. A. Van Kleef, "How the Grapevine Keeps You in Line: Gossip Increases Contributions to the Group," *Social Psychological and Personality Science*, April 12, 2011 (published online, not in print yet). http://spp.sagepub.com/content/early/2011/04/09/1948550611405073

85 "Dianna Abdala," *Wikipedia* (en.wikipedia.org/wiki/Dianna_Abdala); and J. Sandberg, "Infamous Email Writers Aren't Always Killing Their Careers After All," *Wall Street Journal*, February 21, 2006, p. B1.

86 This case is based on N. J. Torres, "Playing Well with Others," *Entrepreneur*, February 2003, p. 30.

87 Based on S. P. Robbins and P. L. Hunsaker, *Training in Interpersonal Skills: TIPs for Managing People at Work*, 2nd ed. (Upper Saddle River, NJ: Prentice Hall, 1996), Chapter 3; and data in R. C. Huseman, J. M. Lahiff, and J. M. Penrose, *Business Communication: Strategies and Skills* (Chicago: Dryden Press, 1988), pp. 380, 425.

Chapter 8

1 Vignette based on "Tim Hortons' Extra-Large Trouble Trouble," *Macleans.ca*, September 7, 2010, http://www2.macleans.ca/2010/09/07/extra-large-trouble-trouble; and M. Friscolanti, "Tim Hortons: Rolling in Dough," *Macleans.ca*, September 6, 2011, http://www2.macleans.ca/2011/09/06/rolling-in-dough

2 Based on B. M. Bass, *Bass & Stogdill's Handbook of Leadership*, 3rd ed. (New York: Free Press, 1990).

3 D. H. Gruenfeld, M. E. Inesi, J. C. Magee, and A. D. Galinsky, "Power and the Objectification of Social Targets," *Journal of Personality and Social Psychology* 95, no. 1 (2008), pp. 111–127; A. D. Galinsky, J. C. Magee, D. H. Gruenfeld, J. A. Whitson, and K. A. Liljenquist, "Power Reduces the Press of the Situation: Implications for Creativity, Conformity, and Dissonance," *Journal of Personality and Social Psychology* 95, no. 6 (2008), pp. 1450–1466; and J. C. Magee and C. A. Langner, "How Personalized and

Socialized Power Motivation Facilitate Antisocial and Prosocial Decision-Making," *Journal of Research in Personality* 42, no. 6 (2008), pp. 1547–1559.

4 R. M. Kanter, "Power Failure in Management Circuits," *Harvard Business Review,* July–August 1979, p. 65.

5 "Power Outage: A Loss of Social Power Distorts How Money Is Represented," *ScienceDaily*, July 26, 2010, http://www.sciencedaily.com/releases/2010/06/100607151320.htm; and D. Dubois, D. D. Rucker, and A. D. Galinsky, "The Accentuation Bias: Money Literally Looms Larger (and Sometimes Smaller) to the Powerless," *Social Psychological and Personality Science* 1, no. 3 (2010), pp. 199–205.

6 G. A. Van Kleef, A. C. Homan, C. Finkenauer, S. Gundemir, and E. Stamkou, "Breaking the Rules to Rise to Power: How Norm Violators Gain Power in the Eyes of Others," *Social Psychological and Personality Science*, January 26, 2011, published online before print, http://spp.sagepub.com/content/early/2011/01/20/1948550611398416

7 J. Lammers, D. A. Stapel, and A. Galinsky, "Power Increases Hypocrisy: Moralizing in Reasoning, Immunity and Behavior," *Psychological Science* 21, no. 5 (2010), pp. 737–744.

8 S. Prashad, "Fill Your Power Gap," *Globe and Mail*, July 23, 2003, p. C3.

9 E. Inesi, S. Botti, D. Dubois, D. D. Rucker, and A. D. Galinsky, "Power and Choice: Their Dynamic Interplay in Quenching the Thirst for Personal Control," *Psychological Science*, June 2011 (published online before print); and Association for Psychological Science, "Power and Choice Are Interchangeable: It's All About Controlling Your Life," *ScienceDaily*, April 28, 2011, http://www.sciencedaily.com /releases/2011/04/110426111419.htm

10 J. R. P. French Jr. and B. Raven, "The Bases of Social Power," in *Studies in Social Power*, ed. D. Cartwright (Ann Arbor, MI: University of Michigan, Institute for Social Research, 1959), pp. 150–167. For an update on French and Raven's work, see D. E. Frost and A. J. Stahelski, "The Systematic Measurement of French and Raven's Bases of Social Power in Workgroups," *Journal of Applied Social Psychology*, April 1988, pp. 375–389; T. R. Hinkin and C. A. Schriesheim, "Development and Application of New Scales to Measure the French and Raven (1959) Bases of Social Power," *Journal of Applied Psychology*, August 1989, pp. 561–567; and G. E. Littlepage, J. L. Van Hein, K. M. Cohen, and L. L. Janiec, "Evaluation and Comparison of Three Instruments Designed to Measure Organizational Power and Influence Tactics," *Journal of Applied Social Psychology*, January 16–31, 1993, pp. 107–125.

11 B. H. Raven, "Social Influence and Power," in *Current Studies in Social Psychology*, ed. I. D. Steiner and M. Fishbein (New York: Holt, Rinehart, Winston, 1965), pp. 371–382.

12 E. A. Ward, "Social Power Bases of Managers: Emergence of a New Factor," *Journal of Social Psychology*, February 2001, pp. 144–147.

13 S. R. Giessner and T. W. Schubert, "High in the Hierarchy: How Vertical Location and Judgments of Leaders' Power Are Interrelated," *Organizational Behavior and Human Decision Processes* 104, no. 1 (2007), pp. 30–44.

14 S. Milgram, *Obedience to Authority* (New York: Harper and Row, 1974).

15 D. Hickson, C. Hinings, C. Lee, R. Schneck, and J. Pennings, "A Strategic Contingencies Theory of Intra-Organizational Power," *Administrative Science Quarterly* 16, 1971, pp. 216–229; and J. W. Dean Jr. and J. R. Evans, *Total Quality: Management, Organization, and Strategy* (Minneapolis-St. Paul, MN: West, 1994).

16 G. Yukl, H. Kim, and C. M. Falbe, "Antecedents of Influence Outcomes," *Journal of Applied Psychology* 81, no. 3 (1996), pp. 309–317.

17 P. P. Carson, K. D. Carson, and C. W. Roe, "Social Power Bases: A Meta-analytic Examination of Interrelationships and Outcomes," *Journal of Applied Social Psychology* 23, no. 14 (1993), pp. 1150–1169.

18 C. M. Falbe and G. Yukl, "Consequences for Managers of Using Single Tactics and Combinations of Tactics," *Academy of Management Journal* 35, 1992, pp. 638–652.

19 Cited in J. R. Carlson, D. S. Carlson, and L. L. Wadsworth, "The Relationship between Individual Power Moves and Group Agreement Type: An Examination and Model," *SAM Advanced Management Journal* 65, no. 4 (2000), pp. 44–51.

20 Vignette based on "Tim Hortons' Extra-Large Trouble Trouble," *Macleans.ca*, September 7, 2010, http://www2.macleans.ca/2010/09/07/extra-large-trouble-trouble

21 R. E. Emerson, "Power-Dependence Relations," *American Sociological Review* 27 (1962), pp. 31–41.

22 Thanks are due to an anonymous reviewer for supplying this insight.

23 H. Mintzberg, *Power in and Around Organizations* (Englewood Cliffs, NJ: Prentice Hall, 1983), p. 24.

24 Vignette based on M. Friscolanti, "Tim Hortons: Rolling in Dough," *Macleans.ca*, September 6, 2011, http://www2.macleans.ca/2011/09/06/rolling-in-dough

25 See, for example, D. Kipnis, S. M. Schmidt, C. Swaffin-Smith, and I. Wilkinson, "Patterns of Managerial Influence: Shotgun Managers, Tacticians, and Bystanders," *Organizational Dynamics*, Winter 1984, pp. 58–67; T. Case, L. Dosier, G. Murkison, and B. Keys, "How Managers Influence Superiors: A Study of Upward Influence Tactics," *Leadership and Organization Development Journal* 9, no. 4 (1988), pp. 25–31; D. Kipnis and S. M. Schmidt, "Upward-Influence Styles: Relationship with Performance Evaluations, Salary, and Stress," *Administrative Science Quarterly*, December 1988, pp. 528–542; G. Yukl and C. M. Falbe, "Influence Tactics and Objectives in Upward, Downward, and Lateral Influence Attempts," *Journal of Applied Psychology*, April 1990, pp. 132–140; B. Keys and T. Case, "How to Become an Influential Manager," *Academy of Management Executive*, November 1990, pp. 38–51; D. A. Ralston, D. J. Gustafson, L. Mainiero, and D. Umstot, "Strategies of Upward Influence: A Cross-National Comparison of Hong Kong and American Managers," *Asia Pacific Journal of Management*, October 1993, pp. 157–175; G. Yukl, H. Kim, and C. M. Falbe, "Antecedents of Influence Outcomes," *Journal of Applied Psychology*, June 1996, pp. 309–317; K. E. Lauterbach and B. J. Weiner, "Dynamics of Upward Influence: How Male and Female Managers Get Their Way," *Leadership Quarterly*, Spring 1996, pp. 87–107; K. R. Xin and A. S. Tsui, "Different Strokes for Different Folks? Influence Tactics by Asian-American and Caucasian-American Managers," *Leadership Quarterly*, Spring 1996, pp. 109–132; and S. J. Wayne, R. C. Liden, I. K. Graf, and G. R. Ferris, "The Role of Upward Influence Tactics in Human Resource Decisions," *Personnel Psychology*, Winter 1997, pp. 979–1006.

26 This section adapted from G. Yukl, C. M. Falbe, and J. Y. Youn, "Patterns of Influence Behavior for Managers," *Group & Organization Studies* 18, no. 1 (March 1993), p. 7.

27 G. Yukl, *Leadership in Organizations*, 5th ed. (Upper Saddle River, NJ: Prentice Hall, 2002), pp. 141–174; G. R. Ferris, W. A. Hochwarter, C. Douglas, F. R. Blass, R. W. Kolodinsky, and D. C. Treadway, "Social Influence Processes in Organizations and Human Resource Systems," in *Research in Personnel and Human Resources Management*, vol. 21, ed. G. R. Ferris and J. J. Martocchio (Oxford, UK: JAI Press/Elsevier, 2003), pp. 65–127; and C. A. Higgins, T. A. Judge, and G. R. Ferris, "Influence Tactics

and Work Outcomes: A Meta-analysis," *Journal of Organizational Behavior*, March 2003, pp. 89–106.

28 C. M. Falbe and G. Yukl, "Consequences for Managers of Using Single Influence Tactics and Combinations of Tactics," *Academy of Management Journal*, July 1992, pp. 638–653.

29 R. E. Petty and P. Briñol, "Persuasion: From Single to Multiple to MetaCognitive Processes," *Perspectives on Psychological Science* 3, no. 2 (2008), pp. 137–147.

30 I. Stern and J. D. Westphal, "Stealthy Footsteps to the Boardroom: Executives' Backgrounds, Sophisticated Interpersonal Influence Behavior, and Board Appointments," *Administrative Science Quarterly* 55, no. 2 (2010), pp. 278–319; and G. Yukl, *Leadership in Organizations*, 5th ed. (Upper Saddle River, NJ: Prentice Hall, 2002), pp. 141–174.

31 N. K. Grant, L. R. Fabrigar, and Heidi Lim, "Exploring the Efficacy of Compliments as a Tactic for Securing Compliance," *Basic & Applied Social Psychology* 32, no. 3 (2010), pp. 226–233.

32 C. M. Falbe and G. Yukl, "Consequences for Managers of Using Single Influence Tactics and Combinations of Tactics," *Academy of Management Journal*, July 1992, pp. 638–653.

33 A. W. Kruglanski, A. Pierro, and E. T. Higgins, "Regulatory Mode and Preferred Leadership Styles: How Fit Increases Job Satisfaction," *Basic and Applied Social Psychology* 29, no. 2 (2007), pp. 137–149; and A. Pierro, L. Cicero, and B. H. Raven, "Motivated Compliance with Bases of Social Power," *Journal of Applied Social Psychology* 38, no. 7 (2008), pp. 1921–1944.

34 G. R. Ferris, D. C. Treadway, P. L. Perrewé, R. L. Brouer, C. Douglas, and S. Lux, "Political Skill in Organizations," *Journal of Management*, June 2007, pp. 290–320; K. J. Harris, K. M. Kacmar, S. Zivnuska, and J. D. Shaw, "The Impact of Political Skill on Impression Management Effectiveness," *Journal of Applied Psychology* 92, no. 1 (2007), pp. 278–285; W. A. Hochwarter, G. R. Ferris, M. B. Gavin, P. L. Perrewé, A. T. Hall, and D. D. Frink, "Political Skill as Neutralizer of Felt Accountability–Job Tension Effects on Job Performance Ratings: A Longitudinal Investigation," *Organizational Behavior and Human Decision Processes* 102 (2007), pp. 226–239; D. C. Treadway, G. R. Ferris, A. B. Duke, G. L. Adams, and J. B. Tatcher, "The Moderating Role of Subordinate Political Skill on Supervisors' Impressions of Subordinate Ingratiation and Ratings of Subordinate Interpersonal Facilitation," *Journal of Applied Psychology* 92, no. 3 (2007), pp. 848–855.

35 C. Anderson, S. E. Spataro, and F. J. Flynn, "Personality and Organizational Culture as Determinants of Influence," *Journal of Applied Psychology* 93, no. 3 (2008), pp. 702–710.

36 "Building a Better Workforce," *PROFIT*, February 16, 2011, http://www.profitguide.com/article/10084—building-a-better-workforce—page0

37 This is the definition given by R. Forrester, "Empowerment: Rejuvenating a Potent Idea," *Academy of Management Executive*, August 2000, pp. 67–80.

38 R. E. Quinn and G. M. Spreitzer, "The Road to Empowerment: Seven Questions Every Leader Should Consider," *Organizational Dynamics*, Autumn 1997, p. 38.

39 C. Argyris, "Empowerment: The Emperor's New Clothes," *Harvard Business Review*, May–June 1998.

40 J. Schaubroeck, J. R. Jones, and J. L. Xie, "Individual Differences in Utilizing Control to Cope with Job Demands: Effects on Susceptibility to Infectious Disease," *Journal of Applied Psychology* 86, no. 2 (2001), pp. 265–278.

41 "Delta Promotes Empowerment," *Globe and Mail*, May 31, 1999, Advertising Supplement, p. C5.

42 R. Sutton, "How to Be a Good Boss in a Bad Economy," *Harvard Business Review* 87, no. 6 (2009), pp. 42–50.

43 D. Keltner, D. H. Gruenfeld, and C. Anderson, "Power, Approach, and Inhibition," *Psychological Review* 110, no. 2 (2003), pp. 265–284.

44 T. Lee and C. M. Brotheridge, "When the Prey Becomes the Predator: Bullying as Predictor of Reciprocal Bullying, Coping, and Well-Being" (working paper, University of Regina, Regina, 2005).

45 N. J. Fast and S. Chen, "When the Boss Feels Inadequate: Power, Incompetence, and Aggression," *Psychological Science* 20, no. 11 (2009), pp. 1406–1413.

46 University of California-Berkeley, "Bosses Who Feel Inadequate Are More Likely to Bully," *ScienceDaily*, October 15, 2009, http://www.sciencedaily.com /releases/2009/10/091014102209.htm

47 M. S. Hershcovis and J. Barling, "Comparing the Outcomes of Sexual Harassment and Workplace Aggression: A Meta-analysis" (paper presented at the Seventh International Conference on Work, Stress and Health, Washington, DC, March 8, 2008).

48 Quebec Labour Standards, s. 81.18, *Psychological Harassment at Work*.

49 S. Stecklow, "Sexual-Harassment Cases Plague U.N.," *Wall Street Journal*, May 21, 2009, p. A1.

50 *Janzen v. Platy Enterprises Ltd.* [1989] 10 C.H.R.R. D/6205 SCC.

51 The following section is based on J. N. Cleveland and M. E. Kerst, "Sexual Harassment and Perceptions of Power: An Under-Articulated Relationship," *Journal of Vocational Behavior*, February 1993, pp. 49–67.

52 C. Bass, "University Bans Faculty-Student Sex," *Yale Alumni Magazine*, March/April 2010, http://yalealumnimagazine.com/issues/2010_03/lv_sex015.html

53 http://www2.carleton.ca/equity/human-rights/policy/1307-2/#SEXUAL%20HARASSMENT

54 C. Hill and E. Silva, *Drawing the Line: Sexual Harassment on Campus* (Washington, DC: American Association of University Women, 2005).

55 H. Burnett-Nichols, "Don't Touch, Do Tell," *University Affairs*, March 8, 2010, http://www.universityaffairs.ca/dont-touch-do-tell.aspx

56 C. R. Willness, P. Steel, and K. Lee, "A Meta-analysis of the Antecedents and Consequences of Workplace Sexual Harassment," *Personnel Psychology* 60 (2007), pp. 127–162.

57 Vignette based on "Tim Hortons' Extra-Large Trouble Trouble," *Macleans.ca*, September 7, 2010, http://www2.macleans.ca/2010/09/07/extra-large-trouble-trouble

58 S. A. Culbert and J. J. McDonough, *The Invisible War: Pursuing Self-Interest at Work* (New York: Wiley, 1980), p. 6.

59 H. Mintzberg, *Power in and Around Organizations* (Englewood Cliffs, NJ: Prentice Hall, 1983), p. 26.

60 T. Cole, "Who Loves Ya?" *Report on Business Magazine*, April 1999, p. 54.

61 D. Farrell and J. C. Petersen, "Patterns of Political Behavior in Organizations," *Academy of Management Review*, July 1982, p. 405. For a thoughtful analysis of the academic controversies underlying any definition of organizational politics, see A. Drory and T. Romm, "The Definition of Organizational Politics: A Review," *Human Relations*, November 1990, pp. 1133–1154; and R. S. Cropanzano, K. M. Kacmar, and D. P. Bozeman, "Organizational Politics, Justice, and Support: Their Differences and Similarities," in *Organizational Politics, Justice and Support: Managing Social Climate at Work*, ed. R. S. Cropanzano and K. M. Kacmar (Westport, CT: Quorum Books, 1995), pp. 1–18.

62 J. Pfeffer, *Power in Organizations* (Marshfield, MA: Pittman, 1981).

63 G. R. Ferris, G. S. Russ, and P. M. Fandt, "Politics in Organizations," in *Impression Management in Organizations*, ed. R. A. Giacalone and P. Rosenfeld (Newbury Park, CA: Sage, 1989), pp. 143–170; and K. M. Kacmar, D. P. Bozeman, D. S. Carlson, and W. P. Anthony, "An Examination of the Perceptions of Organizational Politics Model: Replication and Extension," *Human Relations*, March 1999, pp. 383–416.

64 K. M. Kacmar and R. A. Baron, "Organizational Politics: The State of the Field, Links to Related Processes, and an Agenda for Future Research," in *Research in Personnel and Human Resources Management*, vol. 17, ed. G. R. Ferris (Greenwich, CT: JAI Press, 1999); and M. Valle and L. A. Witt, "The Moderating Effect of Teamwork Perceptions on the Organizational Politics-Job Satisfaction Relationship," *Journal of Social Psychology*, June 2001, pp. 379–388.

65 G. R. Ferris, D. D. Frink, M. C. Galang, J. Zhou, K. M. Kacmar, and J. L. Howard, "Perceptions of Organizational Politics: Prediction, Stress-Related Implications, and Outcomes," *Human Relations*, February 1996, pp. 233–266; K. M. Kacmar, D. P. Bozeman, D. S. Carlson, and W. P. Anthony, "An Examination of the Perceptions of Organizational Politics Model; Replication and Extension," *Human Relations*, March 1999, p. 388; and J. M. L. Poon, "Situational Antecedents and Outcomes of Organizational Politics Perceptions," *Journal of Managerial Psychology* 18, no. 2 (2003), pp. 138–155.

66 C. Kiewitz, W. A. Hochwarter, G. R. Ferris, and S. L. Castro, "The Role of Psychological Climate in Neutralizing the Effects of Organizational Politics on Work Outcomes," *Journal of Applied Social Psychology*, June 2002, pp. 1189–1207; and J. M. L. Poon, "Situational Antecedents and Outcomes of Organizational Politics Perceptions," *Journal of Managerial Psychology* 18, no. 2 (2003), pp. 138–155.

67 K. M. Kacmar and R. A. Baron, "Organizational Politics: The State of the Field, Links to Related Processes, and an Agenda for Future Research," in *Research in Personnel and Human Resources Management*, vol. 17, ed. G. R. Ferris (Greenwich, CT: JAI Press, 1999); and M. Valle and L. A. Witt, "The Moderating Effect of Teamwork Perceptions on the Organizational Politics-Job Satisfaction Relationship," *Journal of Social Psychology*, June 2001, pp. 379–388.

68 R. W. Allen, D. L. Madison, L. W. Porter, P. A. Renwick, and B. T. Mayes, "Organizational Politics: Tactics and Characteristics of Its Actors," *California Management Review*, Fall 1979, pp. 77–83.

69 See, for instance, W. L. Gardner and M. J. Martinko, "Impression Management in Organizations," *Journal of Management*, June 1988, pp. 321–338; M. C. Bolino and W. H. Turnley, "More Than One Way to Make an Impression: Exploring Profiles of Impression Management," *Journal of Management* 29, no. 2 (2003), pp. 141–160; S. Zivnuska, K. M. Kacmar, L. A. Witt, D. S. Carlson, and V. K. Bratton, "Interactive Effects of Impression Management and Organizational Politics on Job Performance," *Journal of Organizational Behavior*, August 2004, pp. 627–640; and M. C. Bolino, K. M. Kacmar, W. H. Turnley, and J. B. Gilstrap, "A Multi-Level Review of Impression Management Motives and Behaviors," *Journal of Management* 34, no. 6 (2008), pp. 1080–1109.

70 M. R. Leary and R. M. Kowalski, "Impression Management: A Literature Review and Two-Component Model," *Psychological Bulletin*, January 1990, p. 40.

71 W. L. Gardner and M. J. Martinko, "Impression Management in Organizations," *Journal of Management*, June 1988, p. 333.

72 R. A. Baron, "Impression Management by Applicants during Employment Interviews: The 'Too Much of a Good Thing' Effect," in *The Employment Interview: Theory, Research, and Practice*, ed. R. W. Eder and G. R. Ferris (Newbury Park, CA: Sage, 1989), pp. 204–215.

73 A. P. J. Ellis, B. J. West, A. M. Ryan, and R. P. DeShon, "The Use of Impression Management Tactics in Structural Interviews: A Function of Question Type?" *Journal of Applied Psychology*, December 2002, pp. 1200–1208.

74 C. K. Stevens and A. L. Kristof, "Making the Right Impression: A Field Study of Applicant Impression Management during Job Interviews," *Journal of Applied Psychology* 80 (1995), pp. 587–606; L. A. McFarland, A. M. Ryan, and S. D. Kriska, "Impression Management Use and Effectiveness across Assessment Methods," *Journal of Management* 29, no. 5 (2003), pp. 641–661; C. A. Higgins and T. A. Judge, "The Effect of Applicant Influence Tactics on Recruiter Perceptions of Fit and Hiring Recommendations: A Field Study," *Journal of Applied Psychology* 89, no. 4 (2004), pp. 622–632; and W. C. Tsai, C. C. Chen, and S. F. Chiu, "Exploring Boundaries of the Effects of Applicant Impression Management Tactics in Job Interviews," *Journal of Management*, February 2005, pp. 108–125.

75 D. C. Gilmore and G. R. Ferris, "The Effects of Applicant Impression Management Tactics on Interviewer Judgments," *Journal of Management*, December 1989, pp. 557–564.

76 C. K. Stevens and A. L. Kristof, "Making the Right Impression: A Field Study of Applicant Impression Management during Job Interviews," *Journal of Applied Psychology* 80 (1995), pp. 587–606.

77 C. A. Higgins, T. A. Judge, and G. R. Ferris, "Influence Tactics and Work Outcomes: A Meta-analysis," *Journal of Organizational Behavior*, March 2003, pp. 89–106.

78 C. A. Higgins, T. A. Judge, and G. R. Ferris, "Influence Tactics and Work Outcomes: A Meta-analysis," *Journal of Organizational Behavior*, March 2003, pp. 89–106.

79 K. J. Harris, K. M. Kacmar, S. Zivnuska, and J. D. Shaw, "The Impact of Political Skill on Impression Management Effectiveness," *Journal of Applied Psychology* 92, no. 1 (2007), pp. 278–285; and D. C. Treadway, G. R. Ferris, A. B. Duke, G. L. Adams, and J. B. Thatcher, "The Moderating Role of Subordinate Political Skill on Supervisors' Impressions of Subordinate Ingratiation and Ratings of Subordinate Interpersonal Facilitation," *Journal of Applied Psychology* 92, no. 3 (2007), pp. 848–855.

80 J. M. Maslyn and D. B. Fedor, "Perceptions of Politics: Does Measuring Different Foci Matter?" *Journal of Applied Psychology* 84 (1998), pp. 645–653; and L. G. Nye and L. A. Witt, "Dimensionality and Construct Validity of the Perceptions of Organizational Politics Scale," *Educational and Psychological Measurement* 53 (1993), pp. 821–829.

81 G. R. Ferris, D. D. Frink, D. Bhawuk, J. Zhou, and D. C. Gilmore, "Reactions of Diverse Groups to Politics in the Workplace," *Journal of Management* 22 (1996), pp. 23–44; K. M. Kacmar, D. P. Bozeman, D. S. Carlson, and W. P. Anthony, "An Examination of the Perceptions of Organizational Politics Model: Replication and Extension," *Human Relations* 52 (1999), pp. 383–416.

82 T. P. Anderson, "Creating Measures of Dysfunctional Office and Organizational Politics: The DOOP and Short-Form DOOP Scales," *Psychology: A Journal of Human Behavior* 31 (1994), pp. 24–34.

83 G. R. Ferris, D. D. Frink, D. Bhawuk, J. Zhou, and D. C. Gilmore, "Reactions of Diverse Groups to Politics in the Workplace," *Journal of Management* 22 (1996), pp. 23–44; K. M. Kacmar, D. P. Bozeman, D. S. Carlson, and W. P. Anthony, "An Examination of the Perceptions of Organizational Politics Model: Replication and Extension," *Human Relations* 52 (1999), pp. 383–416.

84 K. M. Kacmar, D. P. Bozeman, D. S. Carlson, and W. P. Anthony, "An Examination of the Perceptions of Organizational Politics Model: Replication and Extension," *Human Relations* 52 (1999), pp. 383–416; J. M. Maslyn and D. B. Fedor, "Perceptions of Politics: Does Measuring Different Foci Matter?" *Journal of Applied Psychology* 84 (1998), pp. 645–653.

85 M. Warshaw, "The Good Guy's (and Gal's) Guide to Office Politics," *Fast Company*, April 1998, p. 156.

86 C. Robert, T. M. Probst, J. J. Martocchio, F. Drasgow, and J. J. Lawler, "Empowerment and Continuous Improvement in the United States, Mexico, Poland, and India: Predicting Fit on the Basis of the Dimensions of Power Distance and Individualism," *Journal of Applied Psychology* 85 (2000), pp. 643–658.

87 W. A. Randolph and M. Sashkin, "Can Organizational Empowerment Work in Multinational Settings?" *Academy of Management Executive*, February 2002, pp. 102–115.

88 M. Gagné and D. Bhave, "Autonomy in the Workplace: An Essential Ingredient to Employee Engagement and Well-Being in Every Culture?" in *Human Autonomy in Cross-Cultural Context: Perspectives on the Psychology of Agency, Freedom, and Well-Being*, ed. V. I. Chirkov, R. M. Ryan, and K. M. Sheldon (Berlin, Germany: Springer, 2011).

89 Concordia University, "Freedom's Just Another Word for Employee Satisfaction," *ScienceDaily*, January 24, 2011, http://www.sciencedaily.com/releases/2011/01/110124102944.htm

90 O. J. Labedo, "Perceptions of Organisational Politics: Examination of the Situational Antecedent and Consequences among Nigeria's Extension Personnel," *Applied Psychology: An International Review* 55, no. 2 (2006), pp. 255–281.

91 P. P. Fu and G. Yukl, "Perceived Effectiveness of Influence Tactics in the United States and China," *Leadership Quarterly*, Summer 2000, pp. 251–266; O. Branzei, "Cultural Explanations of Individual Preferences for Influence Tactics in Cross-Cultural Encounters," *International Journal of Cross Cultural Management*, August 2002, pp. 203–218; G. Yukl, P. P. Fu, and R. McDonald, "Cross-Cultural Differences in Perceived Effectiveness of Influence Tactics for Initiating or Resisting Change," *Applied Psychology: An International Review*, January 2003, pp. 66–82; and P. P. Fu, T. K. Peng, J. C. Kennedy, and G. Yukl, "Examining the Preferences of Influence Tactics in Chinese Societies: A Comparison of Chinese Managers in Hong Kong, Taiwan, and Mainland China," *Organizational Dynamics* 33, no. 1 (2004), pp. 32–46.

92 P. P. Fu and G. Yukl, "Perceived Effectiveness of Influence Tactics in the United States and China," *Leadership Quarterly*, Summer 2000, pp. 251–266.

93 S. J. Heine, "Making Sense of East Asian Self-Enhancement," *Journal of Cross-Cultural Psychology*, September 2003, pp. 596–602.

94 E. Szabo, "Meaning and Context of Participation in Five European Countries," *Management Decision* 44, no. 2 (2006), pp. 276–289.

95 P. P. Fu, T. K. Peng, J. C. Kennedy, and G. Yukl, "A Comparison of Chinese Managers in Hong Kong, Taiwan, and Mainland China," *Organizational Dynamics*, February 2004, pp. 32–46.

96 G. Yukl, C. M. Falbe, and J. Y. Youn, "Patterns of Influence Behavior for Managers," *Group & Organization Studies* 18, no. 1 (March 1993), p. 7.

97 A. Salz, "Graduation Banquet Speech Raising Questions," *Edmonton Sun*, June 12, 2011, http://www.edmontonsun.com/2011/06/12/graduation-banquet-speech-raising-questions

98 This exercise was inspired by one found in Judith R. Gordon, *Organizational Behavior*, 2nd ed. (Englewood Cliffs, NJ: Prentice Hall, 1992), pp. 499–502.

99 Based on C. Gasparino, "Out of School," *Newsweek*, January 17, 2005, pp. 38–39.

100 Based on S. Armour, "'Business Casual' Causes Confusion," *USA Today*, July 10, 2007, pp. 1B, 2B; T. McMahon, "Toeing the Line on Flip-Flops; Questions & Answers," *National Post*, June 14, 2011, p. A9; and M. Harris, "Dress-Code Debate Divides Many Workplaces," *Nanaimo Daily News*, February 16, 2011, p. A9.

101 Based on E. White, "Art of Persuasion Becomes Key," *Wall Street Journal*, May 19, 2008, p. B5; B. Tsui, "Greening with Envy," *Atlantic*, July/August 2009, http://www.theatlantic.com; and R. Cialdini, *Influence: The Psychology of Persuasion* (New York: HarperBusiness, 2007).

102 Based on S. P. Robbins and P. L. Hunsaker, *Training in Interpersonal Skills: Tips for Managing People at Work*, 2nd ed. (Upper Saddle River, NJ: Prentice Hall, 1996), pp. 131–134.

Chapter 9

1 Vignette based on B. Mackin, "PNE Workers Vote to Strike," *Vancouver Courier*, September 16, 2011, http://www.vancourier.com/news/workers+vote+strike/5408991/story.html

2 See, for instance, C. F. Fink, "Some Conceptual Difficulties in the Theory of Social Conflict," *Journal of Conflict Resolution*, December 1968, pp. 412–460. For an updated review of the conflict literature, see J. A. Wall Jr. and R. R. Callister, "Conflict and Its Management," *Journal of Management* 21, no. 3 (1995), pp. 515–558.

3 L. L. Putnam and M. S. Poole, "Conflict and Negotiation," in *Handbook of Organizational Communication: An Interdisciplinary Perspective*, ed. F. M. Jablin, L. L. Putnam, K. H. Roberts, and L. W. Porter (Newbury Park, CA: Sage, 1987), pp. 549–599.

4 K. W. Thomas, "Conflict and Negotiation Processes in Organizations," in *Handbook of Industrial and Organizational Psychology*, 2nd ed., vol. 3, ed. M. D. Dunnette and L. M. Hough (Palo Alto, CA: Consulting Psychologists Press, 1992), pp. 651–717.

5 For a comprehensive review of this approach, also called the interactionist approach, see C. De Dreu and E. Van de Vliert, eds., *Using Conflict in Organizations* (London: Sage, 1997).

6 K. Jehn, "A Multimethod Examination of the Benefits and Detriments of Intragroup Conflict," *Administrative Science Quarterly*, June 1995, pp. 256–282; K. A. Jehn, "A Qualitative Analysis of Conflict Types and Dimensions in Organizational Groups," *Administrative Science Quarterly*, September 1997, pp. 530–557; K. A. Jehn and E. A. Mannix, "The Dynamic Nature of Conflict: A Longitudinal Study of Intragroup Conflict and Group Performance," *Academy of Management Journal*, April 2001, pp. 238–251; C. K. W. De Dreu and A. E. M. Van Vianen, "Managing Relationship Conflict and the Effectiveness of Organizational Teams," *Journal of Organizational Behavior*, May 2001, pp. 309–328; and K. A. Jehn and C. Bendersky, "Intragroup Conflict in Organizations: A Contingency Perspective on the Conflict-Outcome Relationship," in *Research in Organizational Behavior*, vol. 25, ed. R. M. Kramer and B. M. Staw (Oxford, UK: Elsevier, 2003), pp. 199–210.

7 A. C. Amason, "Distinguishing the Effects of Functional and Dysfunctional Conflict on Strategic Decision Making: Resolving a Paradox for Top Management Teams," *Academy of Management Journal* 39, no. 1 (1996), pp. 123–148.

8 "Survey Shows Managers Have Their Hands Full Resolving Staff Personality Conflicts," *IPMA-HR Bulletin*, November 3, 2006.

9 C. K. W. De Dreu, "The Virtue and Vice of Workplace Conflict: Food for (Pessimistic) Thought," *Journal of Organizational Behavior* 29, no. 1 (2008), pp. 5–18.

10 R. S. Peterson and K. J. Behfar, "The Dynamic Relationship between Performance Feedback, Trust, and Conflict in Groups: A Longitudinal Study," *Organizational Behavior and Human Decision Process* 92, no. 1–2 (2003), pp. 102–112.

11 L. M. Penny and P. E. Spector, "Job Stress, Incivility, and Counterproductive Work Behavior: The Moderating Role of Negative Affectivity," *Journal of Organizational Behavior* 26, no. 7 (2005), pp. 777–796.

12 K. A. Jehn, L. Greer, S. Levine, and G. Szulanski, "The Effects of Conflict Types, Dimensions, and Emergent States on Group

Outcomes," *Group Decision and Negotiation* 17, no. 6 (2008), pp. 465–495.

13 This section is based on S. P. Robbins, *Managing Organizational Conflict: A Nontraditional Approach* (Englewood Cliffs, NJ: Prentice Hall, 1974), pp. 31–55; and J. A. Wall Jr. and R. R. Callister, "Conflict and Its Management," *Journal of Management* 21, no. 3 (1995), pp. 517–523.

14 R. S. Peterson and K. J. Behfar, "The Dynamic Relationship between Performance Feedback, Trust, and Conflict in Groups: A Longitudinal Study," *Organizational Behavior and Human Decision Processes*, September–November 2003, pp. 102–112.

15 See K. A. Jehn, "A Multimethod Examination of the Benefits and Detriments of Intragroup Conflict," *Administrative Science Quarterly*, June 1995, pp. 256–282.

16 T. M. Glomb and H. Liao, "Interpersonal Aggression in Work Groups: Social Influence, Reciprocal, and Individual Effects," *Academy of Management Journal* 46, no. 4 (2003), pp. 486–496; and V. Venkataramani and R. S. Dalal, "Who Helps and Who Harms? Relational Aspects of Interpersonal Helping and Harming in Organizations," *Journal of Applied Psychology* 92, no. 4 (2007), pp. 952–966.

17 R. Friedman, C. Anderson, J. Brett, M. Olekalns, N. Goates, and C. C. Lisco, "The Positive and Negative Effects of Anger on Dispute Resolution: Evidence from Electronically Mediated Disputes," *Journal of Applied Psychology*, April 2004, pp. 369–376.

18 Vignette based on B. Mackin, "PNE Workers Vote to Strike," *Vancouver Courier*, September 16, 2011, http://www.vancourier.com/news/workers+vote+strike/5408991/story.html

19 D. Tjosvold, "Cooperative and Competitive Goal Approach to Conflict: Accomplishments and Challenges," *Applied Psychology: An International Review* 47, no. 3 (1998), pp. 285–342.

20 K. W. Thomas, "Conflict and Negotiation Processes in Organizations," in *Handbook of Industrial and Organizational Psychology*, 2nd ed., vol. 3, ed. M. D. Dunnette and L. M. Hough (Palo Alto, CA: Consulting Psychologists Press, 1992), pp. 651–717.

21 C. K. W. De Dreu, A. Evers, B. Beersma, E. S. Kluwer, and A. Nauta, "A Theory-Based Measure of Conflict Management Strategies in the Workplace," *Journal of Organizational Behavior* 22, no. 6 (September 2001), pp. 645–668. See also D. G. Pruitt and J. Rubin, *Social Conflict: Escalation, Stalemate and Settlement* (New York: Random House, 1986).

22 C. K. W. De Dreu, A. Evers, B. Beersma, E. S. Kluwer, and A. Nauta, "A Theory-Based Measure of Conflict Management Strategies in the Workplace," *Journal of Organizational Behavior* 22, no. 6 (September 2001), pp. 645–668.

23 Based on K. W. Thomas, "Toward Multidimensional Values in Teaching: The Example of Conflict Behaviors," *Academy of Management Review*, July 1977, p. 487; and C. K. W. De Dreu, A. Evers, B. Beersma, E. S. Kluwer, and A. Nauta, "A Theory-Based Measure of Conflict Management Strategies in the Workplace," *Journal of Organizational Behavior* 22, no. 6 (September 2001), pp. 645–668.

24 R. A. Baron, "Personality and Organizational Conflict: Effects of the Type A Behavior Pattern and Self-Monitoring," *Organizational Behavior and Human Decision Processes*, October 1989, pp. 281–296; A. Drory and I. Ritov, "Effects of Work Experience and Opponent's Power on Conflict Management Styles," *International Journal of Conflict Management* 8 (1997), pp. 148–161; R. J. Sternberg and L. J. Soriano, "Styles of Conflict Resolution," *Journal of Personality and Social Psychology*, July 1984, pp. 115–126; and R. J. Volkema and T. J. Bergmann, "Conflict Styles as Indicators of Behavioral Patterns in Interpersonal Conflicts," *Journal of Social Psychology*, February 1995, pp. 5–15.

25 These ideas are based on S. P. Robbins, *Managing Organizational Conflict: A Nontraditional Approach* (Upper Saddle River, NJ: Prentice Hall, 1974), pp. 59–89.

26 "Managers Spend More Than 6 Hours Per Week Handling Staff Conflicts: Survey," *hrreporter.com*, March 23, 2011.

27 R. D. Ramsey, "Interpersonal Conflicts," *SuperVision* 66, no. 4 (April 2005), pp. 14–17.

28 R. Kreitner and A. Kinicki, *Organizational Behavior*, 6th ed. (New York: McGraw-Hill, 2004), p. 492, Table 14-1. Reprinted by permission of McGraw Hill Education.

29 R. L. Tung, "American Expatriates Abroad: From Neophytes to Cosmopolitans," *Journal of World Business* 33, no. 2 (Summer 1998), pp. 125–144.

30 "Negotiating South of the Border," *Harvard Management Communication Letter* 2, no. 8 (August 1999), p. 12.

31 F. W. Swierczek, "Culture and Conflict in Joint Ventures in Asia," *International Journal of Project Management* 12, no. 1 (1994), pp. 39–47.

32 P. S. Kirkbride, S. Tang, and R. I. Westwood, "Chinese Conflict Preferences and Negotiation Behavior: Cultural and Psychological Influences," *Organization Studies* 12, no. 3 (1991), pp. 365–386; S. Tang, and P. Kirkbride, "Development of Conflict Management Skills in Hong Kong: An Analysis of Some Cross-Cultural Implications," *Management Education and Development* 17, no. 3 (1986), pp. 287–301; P. Trubisky, S. Ting-Toomey, and S. L. Lin, "The Influence of Individualism-Collectivism and Self-monitoring on Conflict Styles," *International Journal of Intercultural Relations* 15 (1991), pp. 65–84; and K. I. Ohbuchi and Y. Takahashi, "Cultural Styles of Conflict Management in Japanese and Americans: Passivity, Covertness, and Effectiveness of Strategies," *Journal of Applied Social Psychology* 24 (1994), pp. 1345–1366.

33 P. S. Kirkbride, S. Tang, and R. I. Westwood, "Chinese Conflict Preferences and Negotiation Behavior: Cultural and Psychological Influences," *Organization Studies* 12 (1991), pp. 365–386; and F. W. Swierczek, "Culture and Conflict in Joint Ventures in Asia," *International Journal of Project Management* 12 (1994), pp. 39–47.

34 C. L. Wang, X. Lin, A. K. K. Chan, and Y. Shi, "Conflict Handling Styles in International Joint Ventures: A Cross-Cultural and Cross-National Comparison," *Management International Review* 45, no. 1 (2005), pp. 3–21.

35 M. A. Rahim, "A Measure of Styles of Handling Interpersonal Conflict," *Academy of Management Journal* 26 (1983), pp. 368–376; and C. H. Tinsley, "Model of Conflict Resolution in Japanese, German, and American Cultures," *Journal of Applied Psychology* 83 (1998), pp. 316–323.

36 R. T. Moran, J. Allen, R. Wichman, T. Ando, and M. Sasano, "Japan," in *Global Perspectives on Organizational Conflict*, ed. M. A. Rahim and A. A. Blum (Westport, CT: Praeger 1994), pp. 33–52.

37 D. C. Barnlund, *Communicative Styles of Japanese and Americans: Images and Realities* (Belmont, CA: Wadsworth 1989); and K. I. Ohbuchi and Y. Takahashi, "Cultural Styles of Conflict Management in Japanese and Americans: Passivity, Covertness, and Effectiveness of Strategies," *Journal of Applied Social Psychology* 24 (1994), pp. 1345–1366.

38 Z. Ma, "Chinese Conflict Management Styles and Negotiation Behaviours: An Empirical Test," *International Journal of Cross Cultural Management*, April 2007, pp. 101–119.

39 K. Leung, "Some Determinants of Reactions to Procedural Models for Conflict Resolution: A Cross-National Study," *Journal of Personality and Social Psychology* 53 (1987), pp. 898–908; K. Leung and E. A. Lind, "Procedure and Culture: Effects of Culture, Gender, and Investigator Status on Procedural Preferences," *Journal of Personality and Social Psychology* 50

(1986), pp. 1134–1140; M. W. Morris, K. Y. Williams, K. Leung, R. Larrick, M. T. Mendoza, D. Bhatnagar, J. Li, M. Kondo, J. Luo, and J. Hu, "Conflict Management Style: Accounting for Cross-National Differences," *Journal of International Business Studies* 29 (1998), pp. 729–747; and F. W. Swierczek, "Culture and Conflict in Joint Ventures in Asia," *International Journal of Project Management* 12 (1994), pp. 39–47.

40 J. S. Black and M. Mendenhall, "Resolving Conflicts with the Japanese: Mission Impossible?" *Sloan Management Review* 34 (1993), pp. 49–59.

41 J. A. Wall Jr. and M. W. Blum, "Negotiations," *Journal of Management*, June 1991, pp. 283–287; and R. Kreitner and A. Kinicki, *Organizational Behavior*, 6th ed. (New York: McGraw-Hill, 2004), p. 502.

42 C. Olsheski, "Resolving Disputes Has Just Become More Efficient," *Financial Post (National Post)*, August 16, 1999, p. D9.

43 http://www.caut.ca/aufa/newsletter/0504/prescomm.htm

44 See, for instance, R. A. Cosier and C. R. Schwenk, "Agreement and Thinking Alike: Ingredients for Poor Decisions," *Academy of Management Executive*, February 1990, pp. 69–74; K. A. Jehn, "Enhancing Effectiveness: An Investigation of Advantages and Disadvantages of Value-Based Intragroup Conflict," *International Journal of Conflict Management*, July 1994, pp. 223–238; R. L. Priem, D. A. Harrison, and N. K. Muir, "Structured Conflict and Consensus Outcomes in Group Decision Making," *Journal of Management* 21, no. 4 (1995), pp. 691–710; and K. A. Jehn and E. A. Mannix, "The Dynamic Nature of Conflict: A Longitudinal Study of Intragroup Conflict and Group Performance," *Academy of Management Journal*, April 2001, pp. 238–251.

45 B. A. Nijstad and S. C. Kaps, "Taking the Easy Way Out: Preference Diversity, Decision Strategies, and Decision Refusal in Groups," *Journal of Personality and Social Psychology* 94, no. 5 (2008), pp. 860–870.

46 Based on D. Tjosvold, *Learning to Manage Conflict: Getting People to Work Together Productively* (New York: Lexington Books, 1993), pp. 12–13.

47 R. L. Hoffman, "Homogeneity of Member Personality and Its Effect on Group Problem-Solving," *Journal of Abnormal and Social Psychology*, January 1959, pp. 27–32; and R. L. Hoffman and N. R. F. Maier, "Quality and Acceptance of Problem Solutions by Members of Homogeneous and Heterogeneous Groups," *Journal of Abnormal and Social Psychology*, March 1961, pp. 401–407.

48 M. E. Zellmer-Bruhn, M. M. Maloney, A. D. Bhappu, and R. Salvador, "When and How Do Differences Matter? An Exploration of Perceived Similarity in Teams," *Organizational Behavior and Human Decision Processes* 107, no. 1 (2008), pp. 41–59.

49 J. Hall and M. S. Williams, "A Comparison of Decision-Making Performances in Established and Ad-Hoc Groups," *Journal of Personality and Social Psychology*, February 1966, p. 217.

50 R. E. Hill, "Interpersonal Compatibility and Work Group Performance among Systems Analysts: An Empirical Study," *Proceedings of the Seventeenth Annual Midwest Academy of Management Conference*, Kent, OH, April 1974, pp. 97–110.

51 D. C. Pelz and F. Andrews, *Scientists in Organizations* (New York: Wiley, 1966).

52 R. Ilies, M. D. Johnson, T. A. Judge, and J. Keeney, "A Within-Individual Study of Interpersonal Conflict as a Work Stressor: Dispositional and Situational Moderators," *Journal of Organizational Behavior* 32, no. 1 (2011), pp. 44–64.

53 K. J. Behfar, R. S. Peterson, E. A. Mannix, and W. M. K. Trochim, "The Critical Role of Conflict Resolution in Teams: A Close Look at the Links between Conflict Type, Conflict Management Strategies, and Team Outcomes," *Journal of Applied Psychology* 93, no. 1 (2008), pp. 170–188; A. G. Tekleab, N. R. Quigley, and

P. E. Tesluk, "A Longitudinal Study of Team Conflict, Conflict Management, Cohesion, and Team Effectiveness," *Group and Organization Management* 34, no. 2 (2009), pp. 170–205; and E. Van de Vliert, M. C. Euwema, and S. E. Huismans, "Managing Conflict with a Subordinate or a Superior: Effectiveness of Conglomerated Behavior," *Journal of Applied Psychology* 80 (1995), pp. 271–281.

54 A. Somech, H. S. Desivilya, and H. Lidogoster, "Team Conflict Management and Team Effectiveness: The Effects of Task Interdependence and Team Identification," *Journal of Organizational Behavior* 30, no. 3 (2009), pp. 359–378.

55 See J. A. Wall Jr. and R. R. Callister, "Conflict and Its Management," *Journal of Management* 21, no. 3 (1995), pp. 523–526 for evidence supporting the argument that conflict is almost uniformly dysfunctional.

56 Vignette based on CUPE, "Foley Recommends Don't Pass CUPE 1004 Vote," *CUPE LOCAL 1004*, October 9, 2007, http://cupe.ca/communications/Foleys_recommendatio

57 J. A. Wall Jr., *Negotiation: Theory and Practice* (Glenview, IL: Scott, Foresman, 1985).

58 http://www.gov.sk.ca/news?newsId=db80bb4e-28ae-49d0-819f-bb9e328081bd

59 http://www.gov.sk.ca/news?newsId=9c8ad8fa-d115-479a-8937-2ecfeaad195e

60 This model is based on R. J. Lewicki, "Bargaining and Negotiation," *Exchange: The Organizational Behavior Teaching Journal* 6, no. 2 (1981), pp. 39–40; and B. S. Moskal, "The Art of the Deal," *IndustryWeek*, January 18, 1993, p. 23.

61 J. C. Magee, A. D. Galinsky, and D. H. Gruenfeld, "Power, Propensity to Negotiate, and Moving First in Competitive Interactions," *Personality and Social Psychology Bulletin*, February 2007, pp. 200–212.

62 H. R. Bowles, L. Babcock, and L. Lei, "Social Incentives for Gender Differences in the Propensity to Initiative Negotiations: Sometimes It Does Hurt to Ask," *Organizational Behavior and Human Decision Processes* 103 (2007), pp. 84–103.

63 Based on G. Ku, A. D. Galinsky, and J. K. Murnighan, "Starting Low but Ending High: A Reversal of the Anchoring Effect in Auctions," *Journal of Personality and Social Psychology* 90, June 2006, pp. 975–986; K. Sherstyuk, "A Comparison of First Price Multi-Object Auctions," *Experimental Economics* 12, no. 1 (2009), pp. 42–64; and R. M. Isaac, T. C. Salmon, and A. Zillante, "A Theory of Jump Bidding in Ascending Auctions," *Journal of Economic Behavior & Organization* 62, no. 1 (2007), pp. 144–164.

64 D. A. Moore, "Myopic Prediction, Self-Destructive Secrecy, and the Unexpected Benefits of Revealing Final Deadlines in Negotiation," *Organizational Behavior and Human Decision Processes*, July 2004, pp. 125–139.

65 J. R. Curhan, H. A. Elfenbein, and H. Xu, "What Do People Value When They Negotiate? Mapping the Domain of Subjective Value in Negotiation," *Journal of Personality and Social Psychology* 91, no. 3 (2007), pp. 493–512.

66 K. W. Thomas, "Conflict and Negotiation Processes in Organizations," in *Handbook of Industrial and Organizational Psychology*, 2nd ed., vol. 3, ed. M. D. Dunnette and L. M. Hough (Palo Alto, CA: Consulting Psychologists Press, 1992), pp. 651–717.

67 P. M. Morgan and R. S. Tindale, "Group vs. Individual Performance in Mixed-Motive Situations: Exploring an Inconsistency," *Organizational Behavior and Human Decision Processes*, January 2002, pp. 44–65.

68 C. E. Naquin, "The Agony of Opportunity in Negotiation: Number of Negotiable Issues, Counterfactual Thinking, and Feelings of Satisfaction," *Organizational Behavior and Human Decision Processes*, May 2003, pp. 97–107.

69 C. K. W. De Dreu, L. R. Weingart, and S. Kwon, "Influence of Social Motives on Integrative Negotiation: A Meta-analytic Review and Test of Two Theories," *Journal of Personality and Social Psychology*, May 2000, pp. 889–905.

70 A. W. Brooks and M. E. Schweitzer, "Can Nervous Nelly Negotiate? How Anxiety Causes Negotiators to Make Low First Offers, Exit Early, and Earn Less Profit," *Organizational Behavior and Human Decision Processes* 115, no. 1 (2011), pp. 43–54.

71 D, Malhotra and M. Bazerman, "Investigative Negotiation," *Harvard Business Review*, September 2007, pp. 72–78.

72 S. S. Wiltermuth and M. A. Neale, "Too Much Information: The Perils of Nondiagnostic Information in Negotiations," *Journal of Applied Psychology* 96, no. 1 (2011), pp. 192–201.

73 R. Fisher and W. Ury, *Getting to Yes: Negotiating Agreement without Giving In*, 2nd ed. (New York: Penguin, 1991).

74 M. H. Bazerman and M. A. Neale, *Negotiating Rationally* (New York: Free Press, 1992), pp. 67–68.

75 R. P. Larrick and G. Wu, "Claiming a Large Slice of a Small Pie: Asymmetric Disconfirmation in Negotiation," *Journal of Personality and Social Psychology* 93, no. 2 (2007), pp. 212–233.

76 M. Marks and C. Harold, "Who Asks and Who Receives in Salary Negotiation," *Journal of Organizational Behavior* 32, no. 3 (2011), pp. 371–394.

77 R. Fisher and W. Ury, *Getting to Yes: Negotiating Agreement without Giving In*, w2nd ed. (New York: Penguin, 1991).

78 R. Fisher and W. Ury, *Getting to Yes; Negotiating Agreement without Giving In*, 2nd ed. (New York: Penguin, 1991).

79 E. T. Amanatullah, M. W. Morris, and J. R. Curhan, "Negotiators Who Give Too Much: Unmitigated Communion, Relational Anxieties, and Economic Costs in Distributive and Integrative Bargaining," *Journal of Personality and Social Psychology* 95, no. 3 (2008), pp. 723–738.

80 B. Barry and R. A. Friedman, "Bargainer Characteristics in Distributive and Integrative Negotiation," *Journal of Personality and Social Psychology*, February 1998, pp. 345–359.

81 L. J. Kray and M. P. Haselhuhn, "Implicit Negotiations Beliefs and Performance: Experimental and Longitudinal Evidence," *Journal of Personality and Social Psychology* 93, no. 1 (2007), pp. 49–64.

82 S. Kopelman, A. S. Rosette, and L. Thompson, "The Three Faces of Eve: Strategic Displays of Positive, Negative, and Neutral Emotions in Negotiations," *Organizational Behavior and Human Decision Processes* 99 (2006), pp. 81–101; G. A. Gan Kleef and S. Côté, "Expressing Anger in Conflict: When It Helps and When It Hurts," *Journal of Applied Psychology* 92, no. 6 (2007), pp. 1157–1569; and J. M. Brett, M. Olekalns, R. Friedman, N. Goates, C. Anderson, and C. C. Lisco, "Sticks and Stones: Language, Face, and Online Dispute Resolution," *Academy of Management Journal* 50, no. 1 (2007), pp. 85–99.

83 C. Watson and L. R. Hoffman, "Managers as Negotiators: A Test of Power Versus Gender as Predictors of Feelings, Behavior, and Outcomes," *Leadership Quarterly*, Spring 1996, pp. 63–85.

84 A. E. Walters, A. F. Stuhlmacher, and L. L. Meyer, "Gender and Negotiator Competitiveness: A Meta-analysis," *Organizational Behavior and Human Decision Processes*, October 1998, pp. 1–29; and A. F. Stuhlmacher and A. E. Walters, "Gender Differences in Negotiation Outcome: A Meta-analysis," *Personnel Psychology*, Autumn 1999, pp. 653–677.

85 A. F. Stuhlmacher and A. E. Walters, "Gender Differences in Negotiation Outcome: A Meta-analysis," *Personnel Psychology*, Autumn 1999, p. 655.

86 H. R. Bowles, L. Babcock, and L. Lei, "Social Incentives for Gender Differences in the Propensity to Initiative Negotiations:

Sometimes It Does Hurt to Ask," *Organizational Behavior and Human Decision Processes* 103 (2007), pp. 84–103.

87 L. J. Kray, A. D. Galinsky, and L. Thompson, "Reversing the Gender Gap in Negotiations: An Exploration of Stereotype Regeneration," *Organizational Behavior and Human Decision Processes*, March 2002, pp. 386–409.

88 D. A. Small, M. Gelfand, L. Babcock, and H. Gettman, "Who Goes to the Bargaining Table? The Influence of Gender and Framing on the Initiation of Negotiation," *Journal of Personality and Social Psychology* 93, no. 4 (2007), pp. 600–613; and C. K. Stevens, A. G. Bavetta, and M. E. Gist, "Gender Differences in the Acquisition of Salary Negotiation Skills: The Role of Goals, Self-Efficacy, and Perceived Control," *Journal of Applied Psychology* 78, no. 5 (October 1993), pp. 723–735.

89 I. Ayres, "Further Evidence of Discrimination in New Car Negotiations and Estimates of Its Cause," *Michigan Law Review* 94, no. 1 (October 1995), pp. 109–147.

90 B. Gerhart and S. Rynes, "Determinants and Consequences of Salary Negotiations by Male and Female MBA Graduates," *Journal of Applied Psychology* 76, no. 2 (April 1991), pp. 256–262.

91 E. T. Amanatullah and M. W. Morris, "Negotiating Gender Roles: Gender Differences in Assertive Negotiating Are Mediated By Women's Fear of Backlash and Attenuated When Negotiating on Behalf of Others," *Journal of Personality and Social Psychology* 98, no. 2 (2010), pp. 256–267.

92 L. Schweitzer, E. Ng, S. Lyons, and L. Kuron, "Exploring the Career Pipeline: Gender Differences in Pre-Career Expectations," *Relations Industrielles/Industrial Relations* 66, no. 3 (2011), pp. 422–444.

93 H. R. Markus and S. Kitayama, "Culture and the Self: Implications for Cognition, Emotion, and Motivation," *Psychological Review* 98, no. 2 (1991), pp. 224–253; and H. Ren and B. Gray, "Repairing Relationship Conflict: How Violation Types and Culture Influence the Effectiveness of Restoration Rituals," *Academy of Management Review* 34, no. 1 (2009), pp. 105–126.

94 M. J. Gelfand, M. Higgins, L. H. Nishii, J. L. Raver, A. Dominguez, F. Murakami, S. Yamaguchi, and M. Toyama, "Culture and Egocentric Perceptions of Fairness in Conflict and Negotiation," *Journal of Applied Psychology*, October 2002, pp. 833–845; and Z. Ma, "Chinese Conflict Management Styles and Negotiation Behaviours: An Empirical Test," *International Journal of Cross Cultural Management*, April 2007, pp. 101–119.

95 P. P. Fu, X. H. Yan, Y. Li, E. Wang, and S. Peng, "Examining Conflict-Handling Approaches by Chinese Top Management Teams in IT Firms," *International Journal of Conflict Management* 19, no. 3 (2008), pp. 188–209.

96 See N. J. Adler, *International Dimensions of Organizational Behavior*, 4th ed. (Cincinnati, OH: South Western, 2002), pp. 208–256; W. L. Adair, T. Okurmura, and J. M. Brett, "Negotiation Behavior When Cultures Collide: The United States and Japan," *Journal of Applied Psychology*, June 2001, pp. 371–385; and L. A. Liu, C. H. Chua, and G. K. Stahl, "Quality of Communication Experience: Definition, Measurement, and Implications for Intercultural Negotiations," *Journal of Applied Psychology* 95, no. 3 (2010), pp. 469-487.

97 K. D. Schmidt, *Doing Business in France* (Menlo Park, CA: SRI International, 1987).

98 Y. Chen, E. A. Mannix, and T. Okumura, "The Importance of Who You Meet: Effects of Self—versus Other—Concerns among Negotiators in the United States, the People's Republic of China, and Japan," *Journal of Experimental Social Psychology*, January 2003, pp. 1–15; Z. Ma, "Chinese Conflict Management Styles and Negotiation Behaviours: An Empirical Test," *International Journal of Cross Cultural Management*, April 2007, pp. 101–119; and S. Lubman, "Round and Round," *Wall Street Journal*, December 10, 1993, p. R3.

99 W. L. Adair, T. Okumura, and J. M. Brett, "Negotiation Behavior When Cultures Collide: The United States and Japan," *Journal of Applied Psychology*, June 2001, pp. 371–385; and W. L. Adair, L. Weingart, and J. Brett, "The Timing and Function of Offers in U.S. and Japanese Negotiations," *Journal of Applied Psychology* 92, no. 4 (2007), pp. 1056–1068.

100 Y. Chen, E. A. Mannix, and T. Okumura, "The Importance of Who You Meet: Effects of Self—versus Other—Concerns among Negotiators in the United States, the People's Republic of China, and Japan," *Journal of Experimental Social Psychology*, January 2003, pp. 1–15; and J. W. Salacuse, "Ten Ways That Culture Affects Negotiating Style: Some Survey Results," *Negotiation Journal*, July 1998, pp. 221–240.

101 Based on S. Kopelman and A. S. Rosette, "Cultural Variation in Response to Strategic Emotions in Negotiations," *Group Decision and Negotiation* 17, no. 1 (2008), pp. 65–77; and M. Liu, "The Intrapersonal and Interpersonal Effects of Anger on Negotiation Strategies: A Cross-Cultural Investigation," *Human Communication Research* 35, no. 1 (2009), pp. 148–169.

102 The points presented here were influenced by E. Van de Vliert, "Escalative Intervention in Small-Group Conflicts," *Journal of Applied Behavioral Science*, Winter 1985, pp. 19–36.

103 Q. Reade, "Workplace Conflict Is Time-Consuming Problem for Business," *PersonnelToday.com*, September 30, 2004, http://www.personneltoday.co.uk

104 Based on R. Cohen, "Bad Bidness," *New York Times Magazine*, September 2, 2006, p. 22; M. E. Schweitzer, "Deception in Negotiations," in *Wharton on Making Decisions*, ed. S. J. Hoch and H. C. Kunreuther (New York: Wiley, 2001), pp. 187–200; and M. Diener, "Fair Enough," *Entrepreneur*, January 2002, pp. 100–102.

105 Based on J. Carreyrou and J. S. Lublin, "How Bristol-Myers Fumbled Defense of $4 Billion Drug," *Wall Street Journal*, September 2, 2006, pp. A1, A7; S. Saul, "Marketers of Plavix Outfoxed on a Deal," *New York Times*, August 9, 2006; S. Saul, "Patent Trial Near, Bristol-Myers Counts on Resilience," *New York Times*, January 20, 2007; and S. Saul, "Drug Executive Is Indicted on Secret Deal," *New York Times*, April 24, 2008.

106 Based on J. Keller, "Survivors of BC Ferries Sinking Settle Suit," *Canadian Press*, July 22, 2010; K. Tyler, "Mediating a Better Outcome," *HR Magazine*, November 2007, pp. 63–66; A. K. Finkle, "A Mediation Primer," *IPMA Newsletter*, May 2008, pp. 26–38; K. O'Brien, "The Closer," *Boston Globe*, April 12, 2009; "Nortel Sale Mediation Process Fails," *Canadian Press*, April 13, 2011; and http://prohockeytalk.nbcsports.com/2011/09/14/report-steve-moores-civil-case-against-todd-bertuzzi-has-court-date-set-in-2012/

107 These suggestions are based on J. A. Wall Jr. and M. W. Blum, "Negotiations," *Journal of Management*, June 1991, pp. 278–282; and J. S. Pouliot, "Eight Steps to Success in Negotiating," *Nation's Business*, April 1999, pp. 40–42.

OB on the Edge: The Toxic Workplace

1 C. Cole, "Lions Punt Printers After On-Air Tirade; QB Confronted Teammate at End of Sunday's OT Loss at Winnipeg," *Calgary Herald*, October 14, 2010, p. 6.

2 C. Cole, "B.C. Lions Release Casey Printers for His Onfield Tirade at Teammate," *Vancouver Sun*, October 13, 2010, http://www.vancouversun.com/sports/Casey+Printers+released+Lions+after+team+epic+collapse/3664346/story.html

3 L. M. Anderson and C. M. Pearson, "Tit for Tat? The Spiraling Effect of Incivility in the Workplace," *Academy of Management Review* 24, no. 3 (1999), pp. 452–471.

4 L. M. Anderson and C. M. Pearson, "Tit for Tat? The Spiraling Effect of Incivility in the Workplace," *Academy of Management Review* 24, no. 3 (1999), pp. 452–471. For further discussion of this, see R. A. Baron and J. H. Neuman, "Workplace Violence and Workplace Aggression: Evidence on Their Relative Frequency and Potential Causes," *Aggressive Behavior* 22 (1996), pp. 161–173; C. C. Chen and W. Eastman, "Towards a Civic Culture for Multicultural Organizations," *Journal of Applied Behavioral Science* 33 (1997), pp. 454–470; J. H. Neuman and R. A. Baron, "Aggression in the Workplace," in *Antisocial Behavior in Organizations*, ed. R. A. Giacalone and J. Greenberg (Thousand Oaks, CA: Sage, 1997), pp. 37–67.

5 L. M. Anderson and C. M. Pearson, "Tit for Tat? The Spiraling Effect of Incivility in the Workplace," *Academy of Management Review* 24, no. 3 (1999), pp. 452–471.

6 L. M. Anderson and C. M. Pearson, "Tit for Tat? The Spiraling Effect of Incivility in the Workplace," *Academy of Management Review* 24, no. 3 (1999), pp. 452–471.

7 R. Corelli, "Dishing Out Rudeness: Complaints Abound as Customers Are Ignored, Berated," *Maclean's*, January 11, 1999, p. 44.

8 R. Corelli, "Dishing Out Rudeness: Complaints Abound as Customers Are Ignored, Berated," *Maclean's*, January 11, 1999, p. 44.

9 "Definition of Workplace Bullying," *Workforce Bullying Institute*, http://www.workplacebullying.org/individuals/problem/definition/

10 http://www.workplacebullying.org/research/WBI-Zogby2007Survey.html

11 C. Porath and C. Pearson, "How Toxic Colleagues Corrode Performance," *Harvard Business Review*, April 2009, p. 24.

12 A. M. Hansen and R. Persson, "Frequency of Bullying at Work, Physiological Response, and Mental Health," *Journal of Psychosomatic Research* 70, no. 1 (January 2011), pp. 19–27.

13 B. L. Lovell and R. T. Lee, "Impact of Workplace Bullying on Emotional and Physical Well-Being: A Longitudinal Collective Case Study," *Journal of Aggression, Maltreatment & Trauma* 20, no. 3 (April 2011), pp. 344–357.

14 R. Corelli, "Dishing Out Rudeness: Complaints Abound as Customers Are Ignored, Berated," *Maclean's*, January 11, 1999, p. 44.

15 R. Corelli, "Dishing Out Rudeness: Complaints Abound as Customers Are Ignored, Berated," *Maclean's*, January 11, 1999, p. 44.

16 R. A. Baron and J. H. Neuman, "Workplace Violence and Workplace Aggression: Evidence on Their Relative Frequency and Potential Causes," *Aggressive Behavior* 22 (1996), pp. 161–173; C. MacKinnon, *Only Words* (New York: Basic Books, 1994); J. Marks, "The American Uncivil Wars," *U.S. News & World Report*, April 22, 1996, pp. 66–72; and L. P. Spratlen, "Workplace Mistreatment: Its Relationship to Interpersonal Violence," *Journal of Psychosocial Nursing* 32, no. 12 (1994), pp. 5–6.

17 Information in this paragraph based on A. Hanon and C. Castagna, "Gunman Sought Revenge," *Edmonton Sun*, March 12, 2010; and L. Drake, S. McKeen, R. Warnica, and R. Cormier, "Angry Worker Blamed in Fatal Shooting," *Calgary Herald*, March 13, 2010.

18 W. M. Glenn, "An Employee's Survival Guide: An ILO Survey of Workplaces in 32 Countries Ranked Argentina the Most Violent, Followed by Romania, France and Then, Surprisingly, Canada," *Occupational Health & Safety*, April–May 2002, p. 28 passim.

19 D. Flavelle, "Managers Cited for Increase in 'Work Rage,'" *Vancouver Sun*, April 11, 2000, pp. D1, D11; and "Profile of Workplace Victimization Incidents," *Statistics Canada*, 2007, http://www.statcan.ca/english/research/85F0033MIE/2007013/findings/profile.htm

20 http://www.csmonitor.com/USA/Society/2010/0107/ABB-shooting-Economy-may-play-role-in-workplace-violence

21 E. Wulfhorst, "Desk Rage Spoils Workplace for Many Americans," *Reuters*, July 10, 2008, http://www.reuters.com/article/newsOne/idUSN0947145320080710

22 S. James, "Long Hours Linked to Rising Toll from Stress," *Financial Post (National Post)*, August 6, 2003, p. FP12.

23 "Profile of Workplace Victimization Incidents," *Statistics Canada*, 2007, http://www.statcan.ca/english/research/85F0033MIE/2007013/findings/profile.htm

24 W. M. Glenn, "An Employee's Survival Guide: An ILO Survey of Workplaces in 32 Countries Ranked Argentina the Most Violent, Followed by Romania, France and Then, Surprisingly, Canada," *Occupational Health & Safety*, April–May 2002, p. 28 passim.

25 W. M. Glenn, "An Employee's Survival Guide: An ILO Survey of Workplaces in 32 Countries Ranked Argentina the Most Violent, Followed by Romania, France and Then, Surprisingly, Canada," *Occupational Health & Safety*, April–May 2002, p. 28 passim.

26 http://www.nstu.ca/images/pklot/NSTU%20Teacher%20Stress%20Survey%20Report_final.pdf

27 A. M. Webber, "Danger: Toxic Company," *Fast Company*, November 1998, pp. 152–157.

28 D. Flavelle, "Managers Cited for Increase in 'Work Rage,'" *Vancouver Sun*, April 11, 2000, pp. D1, D11; and G. Smith, *Work Rage* (Toronto: HarperCollins Canada, 2000).

29 "Work Rage," *BCBusiness Magazine*, January 2001, p. 23.

30 D. Flavelle, "Managers Cited for Increase in 'Work Rage,'" *Vancouver Sun*, April 11, 2000, pp. D1, D11.

31 A. Skogstad, T. Torsheim, S. Einarsen, and L.J. Hauge, "Testing the Work Environment Hypothesis of Bullying on a Group Level of Analysis: Psychosocial Factors as Precursors of Observed Workplace Bullying," *Applied Psychology: An International Review* 60, no. 3 (July 2011), pp. 475–495.

32 D. Geddes, and L. T. Stickney, "The Trouble with Sanctions: Organizational Responses to Deviant Anger Displays at Work," *Human Relations* 64, no. 2 (February 2011), pp. 201–230.

33 Barry Ray, "Who's Afraid of the Big Bad Boss? Plenty of Us, New FSU Study Shows," *FSU News*, December 4, 2006, http://www.fsu.edu/news/2006/12/04/bad.boss/

34 D. Abma, "Bad Managers a Problem in Canadian Workplaces: Survey," *Financial Post*, January 19, 2011.

35 H. Levinson, *Emotional Health in the World of Work* (Boston: South End Press, 1964); and E. Schein, *Organizational Psychology* (Englewood Cliffs, NJ: Prentice Hall, 1980).

36 E. W. Morrison and S. L. Robinson, "When Employees Feel Betrayed: A Model of How Psychological Contract Violation Develops," *Academy of Management Journal* 22 (1997), pp. 226–256; S. L. Robinson, "Trust and Breach of the Psychological Contract," *Administrative Science Quarterly* 41 (1996), pp. 574–599; and S. L. Robinson, M. S. Kraatz, and D. M. Rousseau, "Changing Obligations and the Psychological Contract: A Longitudinal Study," *Academy of Management Journal* 37 (1994), pp. 137–152. A recent study suggests that perceptions of the psychological contract vary by culture: D. C. Thomas, S. R. Fitzsimmons, E. C. Ravlin, K. Au, B. Z. Ekelund, and C. Barzantny, "Psychological Contracts across Cultures," *Organization Studies* 31, no. 11 (2010), pp. 1437–1458.

37 T. R. Tyler and P. Dogoey, "Trust in Organizational Authorities: The Influence of Motive Attributions on Willingness to Accept Decisions," in *Trust in Organizations*, ed. R. M. Kramer and T. R. Tyler (Thousand Oaks, CA: Sage, 1996), pp. 246–260.

38 S. Montes and D. Zweig, "Do Promises Matter? An Exploration of the Role of Promises in Psychological Contract Breach," *Journal of Applied Psychology* 94, no. 5 (2009), pp. 1243–1260.

39 Based on A. McKee, "Neutralize Your Toxic Boss," *Harvard Business School Conversation Starter*, January 20, 2009, http://blogs.harvardbusiness.org; and "Toxic Bosses: How to Live with the S.O.B," *BusinessWeek*, August 14, 2008, http://www.businessweek.com

40 A. M. Webber, "Danger: Toxic Company," *Fast Company*, November 1998, pp. 152–157.

41 A. M. Webber, "Danger: Toxic Company," *Fast Company*, November 1998, pp. 152–157.

42 P. Frost, *Toxic Emotions at Work* (Cambridge, MA: Harvard Business School Press, 2003).

43 R. Bacal, "Toxic Organizations—Welcome to the Fire of an Unhealthy Workplace," *Work 911.com*, 2000, http://www.work911.com/articles/toxicorgs.htm

44 "Men More Likely to Be Rude in Workplace, Survey Shows," *Vancouver Sun*, August 16, 1999, p. B10.

45 D. E. Gibson and S. G. Barsade, "The Experience of Anger at Work: Lessons from the Chronically Angry" (paper presented at the annual meetings of the Academy of Management, Chicago, August 11, 1999).

46 D. E. Gibson and S. G. Barsade, "The Experience of Anger at Work: Lessons from the Chronically Angry" (paper presented at the annual meetings of the Academy of Management, Chicago, August 11, 1999).

47 R. Corelli, "Dishing Out Rudeness: Complaints Abound as Customers Are Ignored, Berated," *Maclean's*, January 11, 1999, p. 44.

48 P. Frost and S. Robinson, "The Toxic Handler: Organizational Hero—and Casualty," *Harvard Business Review*, July–August 1999, p. 101 (Reprint 99406).

49 P. Frost and S. Robinson, "The Toxic Handler: Organizational Hero—and Casualty," *Harvard Business Review*, July–August 1999, p. 101 (Reprint 99406).

50 P. Frost and S. Robinson, "The Toxic Handler: Organizational Hero—and Casualty," *Harvard Business Review*, July–August 1999, p. 101 (Reprint 99406).

Chapter 10

1 Opening vignette based on M. Parker, "Identifying Enablers and Blockers of Cultural Transformation," *Canadian Business*, May 17, 2007; E. Lazarus, "Building the Perfect Franchise," *PROFIT*, February 2006, p. 48ff; M. Parker, "Why Can't Employers See the Paradox?" *Financial Post*, March 19, 2008, p. WK7; Boston Pizza Press Kit, http://www.bostonpizza.com; and "Boston Pizza Reports Higher Second-Quarter Net Income, Same Store Sales," *Canadian Press*, August 10, 2011.

2 "Organization Man: Henry Mintzberg Has Some Common Sense Observations About the Ways We Run Companies," *Financial Post*, November 22/24, 1997, pp. 14–16.

3 K. McArthur, "Air Canada Tells Employees to Crack a Smile More Often," *Globe and Mail*, March 14, 2002, pp. B1, B2.

4 K. McArthur, "Air Canada Tells Employees to Crack a Smile More Often," *Globe and Mail*, March 14, 2002, pp. B1, B2.

5 See, for example, H. S. Becker, "Culture: A Sociological View," *Yale Review*, Summer 1982, pp. 513–527; and E. H. Schein, *Organizational Culture and Leadership* (San Francisco: Jossey-Bass, 1985), p. 168.

6 This seven-item description is based on C. A. O'Reilly III, J. Chatman, and D. F. Caldwell, "People and Organizational Culture: A Profile Comparison Approach to Assessing Person-Organization Fit," *Academy of Management Journal*, September 1991, pp. 487–516; and J. A. Chatman and K. A. Jehn, "Assessing the Relationship between Industry Characteristics and Organizational Culture: How Different Can You Be?" *Academy of Management Journal*, June 1994, pp. 522–553. For a description of other popular measures, see A. Xenikou and A. Furnham, "A Correlational and Factor Analytic Study of Four Questionnaire Measures of Organizational Culture," *Human Relations*, March 1996, pp. 349–371. For a review of cultural dimensions, see N. M. Ashkanasy, C. P. M. Wilderom, and M. F. Peterson, eds., *Handbook of Organizational Culture and Climate* (Thousand Oaks, CA: Sage, 2000), pp. 131–145.

7 E. Schein, "Coming to a New Awareness of Organizational Culture," *Sloan Management Review*, Winter 1984, pp. 3–16; E. Schein, *Organizational Culture and Leadership*, 2nd ed. (San Francisco, CA: Jossey-Bass, 1992); and E. Schein, "What Is Culture?" in *Reframing Organizational Culture*, ed. P. J. Frost, L. F. Moore, M. R. Louis, C. C. Lundberg, and J. Martin (Newbury Park, CA: Sage, 1991), pp. 243–253.

8 T. G. Stroup Jr., "Leadership and Organizational Culture: Actions Speak Louder Than Words," *Military Review* 76, no. 1 (January–February 1996), pp. 44–49; B. Moingeon and B. Ramanantsoa "Understanding Corporate Identity: The French School of Thought," *European Journal of Marketing* 31, no. 5/6 (1997), pp. 383–395; A. P. D. Van Luxemburg, J. M. Ulijn, and N. Amare, "The Contribution of Electronic Communication Media to the Design Process: Communicative and Cultural Implications," *IEEE Transactions on Professional Communication* 45, no. 4 (December 2002), pp. 250–264; L. D. McLean, "Organizational Culture's Influence on Creativity and Innovation: A Review of the Literature and Implications for Human Resource Development," *Advances in Developing Human Resources* 7, no. 2 (May 2005), pp. 226–246; and V. J. Friedman and A. B. Antal, "Negotiating Reality: A Theory of Action Approach to Intercultural Competence," *Management Learning* 36, no. 1 (2005), pp. 69–86.

9 See http://www.palliser.com/furniture/AboutUs/

10 See C. A. O'Reilly and J. A. Chatman, "Culture as Social Control: Corporations, Cultures, and Commitment," in *Research in Organizational Behavior*, vol. 18, ed. B. M. Staw and L. L. Cummings (Greenwich, CT: JAI Press, 1996), pp. 157–200.

11 T. E. Deal and A. A. Kennedy, "Culture: A New Look through Old Lenses," *Journal of Applied Behavioral Science*, November 1983, p. 501.

12 Y. Ling, Z. Simsek, M. H. Lubatkin, and J. F. Veiga, "Transformational Leadership's Role in Promoting Corporate Entrepreneurship: Examining the CEO-TMT Interface," *Academy of Management Journal* 51, no. 3 (2008), pp. 557–576; and A. Malhotra, A. Majchrzak, and B. Rosen, "Leading Virtual Teams," *Academy of Management Perspectives* 21, no. 1 (2007), pp. 60–70.

13 D. Denison, "What Is the Difference between Organizational Culture and Organizational Climate? A Native's Point of View on a Decade of Paradigm Wars," *Academy of Management Review* 21 (1996) pp. 519–654; and L. R. James, C. C. Choi, C. E. Ko, P. K. McNeil, M. K. Minton, M. A. Wright, and K. Kim, "Organizational and Psychological Climate: A Review of Theory and Research," *European Journal of Work and Organizational Psychology* 17, no. 1 (2008), pp. 5–32.

14 J. Z. Carr, A. M. Schmidt, J. K. Ford, and R. P. DeShon, "Climate Perceptions Matter: A Meta-analytic Path Analysis Relating Molar Climate, Cognitive and Affective States, and Individual Level Work Outcomes," *Journal of Applied Psychology* 88, no. 4 (2003), pp. 605–619.

15 M. Schulte, C. Ostroff, S. Shmulyian, and A. Kinicki, "Organizational Climate Configurations: Relationships to Collective Attitudes, Customer Satisfaction, and Financial Performance," *Journal of Applied Psychology* 94, no. 3 (2009), pp. 618–634.

16 See, for example, Z. S. Byrne, J. Stoner, K. R. Thompson, and W. Hochwarter, "The Interactive Effects of Conscientiousness, Work Effort, and Psychological Climate on Job Performance," *Journal of Vocational Behavior* 66, no. 2 (2005), pp. 326–338; D. S. Pugh, J. Dietz, A. P. Brief, and J. W. Wiley, "Looking Inside and Out: The Impact of Employee and Community Demographic Composition on Organizational Diversity Climate," *Journal of Applied Psychology* 93, no. 6 (2008), pp. 1422–1428; and J. C. Wallace, E. Popp, and S. Mondore, "Safety Climate as a Mediator between Foundation Climates and Occupational Accidents: A Group-Level Investigation," *Journal of Applied Psychology* 91, no. 3 (2006), pp. 681–688.

17 C. Atchison, "Secrets of Canada's Best Bosses," *PROFIT*, February 16, 2011, http://www.profitguide.com/article/10103--secrets-of-canada-s-best-bosses.

18 The view that there will be consistency among perceptions of organizational culture has been called the "integration" perspective. For a review of this perspective and conflicting approaches, see D. Meyerson and J. Martin, "Cultural Change: An Integration of Three Different Views," *Journal of Management Studies*, November 1987, pp. 623–647; and P. J. Frost, L. F. Moore, M. R. Louis, C. C. Lundberg, and J. Martin, eds., *Reframing Organizational Culture* (Newbury Park, CA: Sage, 1991).

19 See J. M. Jermier, J. W. Slocum Jr., L. W. Fry, and J. Gaines, "Organizational Subcultures in a Soft Bureaucracy: Resistance Behind the Myth and Facade of an Official Culture," *Organization Science*, May 1991, pp. 170–194; S. A. Sackmann, "Culture and Subcultures: An Analysis of Organizational Knowledge," *Administrative Science Quarterly*, March 1992, pp. 140–161; R. F. Zammuto, "Mapping Organizational Cultures and Subcultures: Looking Inside and across Hospitals" (paper presented at the 1995 National Academy of Management Conference, Vancouver, BC, August 1995); and G. Hofstede, "Identifying Organizational Subcultures: An Empirical Approach," *Journal of Management Studies*, January 1998, pp. 1–12.

20 D. A. Hoffman and L. M. Jones, "Leadership, Collective Personality, and Performance," *Journal of Applied Psychology* 90, no. 3 (2005), pp. 509–522.

21 S. Hamm, "No Letup—and No Apologies," *BusinessWeek*, October 26, 1998, pp. 58–64.

22 See, for example, G. G. Gordon and N. DiTomaso, "Predicting Corporate Performance from Organizational Culture," *Journal of Management Studies*, November 1992, pp. 793–798; and J. B. Sorensen, "The Strength of Corporate Culture and the Reliability of Firm Performance," *Administrative Science Quarterly*, March 2002, pp. 70–91.

23 Y. Wiener, "Forms of Value Systems: A Focus on Organizational Effectiveness and Cultural Change and Maintenance," *Academy of Management Review*, October 1988, p. 536; and B. Schneider, A. N. Salvaggio, and M. Subirats, "Climate Strength: A New Direction for Climate Research," *Journal of Applied Psychology* 87 (2002), pp. 220–229.

24 R. T. Mowday, L. W. Porter, and R. M. Steers, *Employee-Organization Linkages: The Psychology of Commitment, Absenteeism, and Turnover* (New York: Academic Press, 1982); C. Vandenberghe, "Organizational Culture, Person-Culture Fit, and Turnover: A Replication in the Health Care Industry," *Journal of Organizational Behavior*, March 1999, pp. 175–184; and M. Schulte, C. Ostroff, S. Shmulyian, and A. Kinicki, "Organizational Climate Configurations: Relationships to Collective Attitudes,

Customer Satisfaction, and Financial Performance," *Journal of Applied Psychology* 94, no. 3 (2009), pp. 618–634.

25 Vignette based on "Rising on Three Pillars Strategy; 10 Most Admired Corporate Cultures," *Financial Post*, November 26, 2008, p. WK4; M. Parker, "Why Can't Employers See The Paradox?" *Financial Post*, March 19, 2008, p. WK7; and M. Parker, "Identifying Enablers and Blockers of Cultural Transformation," *Canadian Business*, May 17, 2007.

26 R. Spence, "Telling Stories Makes for Happy Endings," *National Post (Financial Post)*, April 20, 2009, pp. FP4.

27 D. M. Boje, "The Storytelling Organization: A Study of Story Performance in an Office-Supply Firm," *Administrative Science Quarterly*, March 1991, pp. 106–126; and C. H. Deutsch, "The Parables of Corporate Culture," *New York Times*, October 13, 1991, p. F25.

28 A. M. Pettigrew, "On Studying Organizational Cultures," *Administrative Science Quarterly*, December 1979, p. 576.

29 A. M. Pettigrew, "On Studying Organizational Cultures," *Administrative Science Quarterly*, December 1979, p. 576. See also K. Kamoche, "Rhetoric, Ritualism, and Totemism in Human Resource Management," *Human Relations*, April 1995, pp. 367–385.

30 V. Matthews, "Starting Every Day with a Shout and a Song," *Financial Times*, May 2, 2001, p. 11; and M. Gimein, "Sam Walton Made Us a Promise," *Fortune*, March 18, 2002, pp. 121–130.

31 A. Rafaeli and M. G. Pratt, "Tailored Meanings: On the Meaning and Impact of Organizational Dress," *Academy of Management Review*, January 1993, pp. 32–55.

32 Thanks to an anonymous reviewer for adding these.

33 M. Pendergast, *Uncommon Grounds: The History of Coffee and How It Transformed Our World* (New York: Basic Books, 1999), p. 369.

34 Thanks to a reviewer for this story.

35 Vignette based on "Rising on Three Pillars Strategy; 10 Most Admired Corporate Cultures," *Financial Post*, November 26, 2008, p. WK4; and http://www.bostonpizza.com/en/about/PressKit.aspx

36 E. H. Schein, "The Role of the Founder in Creating Organizational Culture," *Organizational Dynamics*, Summer 1983, pp. 13–28.

37 http://bostonpizza.com/assets/mediacentre/documents/pdf/BP_ProfilePDF_WTreliving_FINAL.pdf

38 E. H. Schein, "Leadership and Organizational Culture," in *The Leader of the Future*, ed. F. Hesselbein, M. Goldsmith, and R. Beckhard (San Francisco: Jossey-Bass, 1996), pp. 61–62.

39 "PCL's Biggest Investment: Its People," *National Post*, September 2, 2008, p. FP10.

40 See, for example, J. R. Harrison and G. R. Carroll, "Keeping the Faith: A Model of Cultural Transmission in Formal Organizations," *Administrative Science Quarterly*, December 1991, pp. 552–582.

41 B. Schneider, H. W. Goldstein, and D. B. Smith, "The ASA Framework: An Update," *Personnel Psychology*, Winter 1995, pp. 747–773; D. M. Cable and T. A. Judge, "Interviewers' Perceptions of Person-Organization Fit and Organizational Selection Decisions," *Journal of Applied Psychology*, August 1997, pp. 546–561; M. L. Verquer, T. A. Beehr, and S. H. Wagner, "A Meta-analysis of Relations between Person-Organization Fit and Work Attitudes," *Journal of Vocational Behavior*, December 2003, pp. 473–489; and W. Li, Y. Wang, P. Taylor, K. Shi, and D. He, "The Influence of Organizational Culture on Work-Related Personality Requirement Ratings: A Multilevel Analysis," *International Journal of Selection and Assessment* 16, no. 4 (2008), pp. 366–384.

42 "Building a Better Workforce," *PROFIT*, February 16, 2011, http://www.profitguide.com/article/10084--building-a-better-workforce--page0

43 "Building a Better Workforce," *PROFIT*, February 16, 2011, http://www.profitguide.com/article/10084--building-a-better-workforce--page0

44 S. Fralic, "Even Playland's Interviews Are Fun for Job-Seekers," *Vancouver Sun*, Monday, July 14, 2008, http://www.canada.com/vancouversun/news/story.html?id=7ba15dd4-cbe8-4a09-a08c-cce86c73a694

45 S. Fralic, "Even Playland's Interviews Are Fun for Job-Seekers," *Vancouver Sun*, Monday, July 14, 2008, http://www.canada.com/vancouversun/news/story.html?id=7ba15dd4-cbe8-4a09-a08c-cce86c73a694

46 D. C. Hambrick and P. A. Mason, "Upper Echelons: The Organization as a Reflection of Its Top Managers," *Academy of Management Review*, April 1984, pp. 193–206; B. P. Niehoff, C. A. Enz, and R. A. Grover, "The Impact of Top-Management Actions on Employee Attitudes and Perceptions," *Group & Organization Studies*, September 1990, pp. 337–352; and H. M. Trice and J. M. Beyer, "Cultural Leadership in Organizations," *Organization Science*, May 1991, pp. 149–169.

47 Based on B. Stone and A. Vance, "Apple's Obsession with Secrecy Grows Stronger," *New York Times*, June 23, 2009, p. B1; and D. Olive, "The Shadow That Hangs over Apple," *Toronto Star*, February 23, 2011, p. B1.

48 See, for instance, J. P. Wanous, *Organizational Entry*, 2nd ed. (New York: Addison Wesley, 1992); G. T. Chao, A. M. O'Leary-Kelly, S. Wolf, H. J. Klein, and P. D. Gardner, "Organizational Socialization: Its Content and Consequences," *Journal of Applied Psychology*, October 1994, pp. 730–743; B. E. Ashforth, A. M. Saks, and R. T. Lee, "Socialization and Newcomer Adjustment: The Role of Organizational Context," *Human Relations*, July 1998, pp. 897–926; D. A. Major, "Effective Newcomer Socialization into High-Performance Organizational Cultures," in *Handbook of Organizational Culture & Climate*, ed. N. M. Ashkanasy, C. P. M. Wilderom, and M. F. Peterson (Thousand Oaks, CA: Sage, 2000), pp. 355–368; and D. M. Cable and C. K. Parsons, "Socialization Tactics and Person-Organization Fit," *Personnel Psychology*, Spring 2001, pp. 1–23.

49 A. M. Saks and J. A. Gruman, "Organizational Socialization and Positive Organizational Behaviour: Implications for Theory, Research, and Practice," *Canadian Journal of Administrative Sciences* 28, no. 1 (2011), pp. 4–16.

50 J. Impoco, "Basic Training, Sanyo Style," *U.S. News & World Report*, July 13, 1992, pp. 46–48.

51 B. Filipczak, "Trained by Starbucks," *Training*, June 1995, pp. 73–79; and S. Gruner, "Lasting Impressions," *Inc.*, July 1998, p. 126.

52 "Building a Better Workforce," *PROFIT*, February 16, 2011, http://www.profitguide.com/article/10084--building-a-better-workforce---page0

53 J. Van Maanen and E. H. Schein, "Career Development," in *Improving Life at Work*, ed. J. R. Hackman and J. L. Suttle (Santa Monica, CA: Goodyear, 1977), pp. 58–62.

54 C. J. Collins, "The Interactive Effects of Recruitment Practices and Product Awareness on Job Seekers' Employer Knowledge and Application Behaviors," *Journal of Applied Psychology* 92, no. 1 (2007), pp. 180–190.

55 G. Chen and R. J. Klimoski, "The Impact of Expectations on Newcomer Performance in Teams as Mediated by Work Characteristics, Social Exchanges, and Empowerment," *Academy of Management Journal* 46 (2003), pp. 591–607; C. R. Wanberg and J. D. Kammeyer-Mueller, "Predictors and Outcomes of Proactivity in the Socialization Process," *Journal of Applied*

Psychology 85 (2000), pp. 373–385; J. D. Kammeyer-Mueller and C. R. Wanberg, "Unwrapping the Organizational Entry Process: Disentangling Multiple Antecedents and Their Pathways to Adjustment," *Journal of Applied Psychology* 88 (2003), pp. 779–794; and E. W. Morrison, "Longitudinal Study of the Effects of Information Seeking on Newcomer Socialization," *Journal of Applied Psychology* 78 (2003), pp. 173–183.

56 J. Van Maanen and E. H. Schein, "Career Development," in *Improving Life at Work*, ed. J. R. Hackman and J. L. Suttle (Santa Monica, CA: Goodyear, 1977), p. 59.

57 http://www.canadianbusiness.com/article/11442—the-brands-we-trust; and http://www.timhortons.com/us/en/about/3315.html

58 E. W. Morrison, "Newcomers' Relationships: The Role of Social Network Ties During Socialization," *Academy of Management Journal* 45 (2002), pp. 1149–1160.

59 A. M. Saks and J. A. Gruman, "Getting Newcomers Engaged: The Role of Socialization Tactics," *Journal of Managerial Psychology* 26 (2011), pp. 383–402.

60 T. N. Bauer, T. Bodner, B. Erdogan, D. M. Truxillo, and J. S. Tucker, "Newcomer Adjustment during Organizational Socialization: A Meta-analytic Review of Antecedents, Outcomes, and Methods," *Journal of Applied Psychology* 92, no. 3 (2007), pp. 707–721.

61 J. E. Sheridan, "Organizational Culture and Employee Retention," *Academy of Management Journal*, December 1992, pp. 1036–1056.

62 J. B. Sorensen, "The Strength of Corporate Culture and the Reliability of Firm Performance," *Administrative Science Quarterly*, March 2002, pp. 70–91.

63 See, for instance, D. Miller, "What Happens after Success: The Perils of Excellence," *Journal of Management Studies*, May 1994, pp. 11–38.

64 See T. Cox Jr., *Cultural Diversity in Organizations: Theory, Research & Practice* (San Francisco: Berrett-Koehler, 1993), pp. 162–170; L. Grensing-Pophal, "Hiring to Fit Your Corporate Culture," *HR Magazine*, August 1999, pp. 50–54; and D. L. Stone, E. F. Stone-Romero, and K. M. Lukaszewski, "The Impact of Cultural Values on the Acceptance and Effectiveness of Human Resource Management Policies and Practices," *Human Resource Management Review* 17, no. 2 (2007), pp. 152–165.

65 S. Cartwright and C. L. Cooper, "The Role of Culture Compatibility in Successful Organizational Marriages," *Academy of Management Executive*, May 1993, pp. 57–70; R. A. Weber and C. F. Camerer, "Cultural Conflict and Merger Failure: An Experimental Approach," *Management Science*, April 2003, pp. 400–412; and I. H. Gleibs, A. Mummendey, and P. Noack, "Predictors of Change in Postmerger Identification During a Merger Process: A Longitudinal Study," *Journal of Personality and Social Psychology* 95, no. 5 (2008), pp. 1095–1112.

66 K. W. Smith, "A Brand-New Culture for the Merged Firm," *Mergers and Acquisitions* 35, no. 6 (June 2000), pp. 45–50.

67 M. Raynaud and M. Teasdale, "Confusions & Acquisitions: Post-Merger Culture Shock and Some Remedies," *Communication World* 9, no. 6 (May–June 1992), pp. 44–45.

68 M. Raynaud and M. Teasdale, "Confusions & Acquisitions: Post-Merger Culture Shock and Some Remedies," *Communication World* 9, no. 6 (May–June 1992), pp. 44–45.

69 Vignette based on "Corporate Culture," *Canadian HR Reporter* 17, no. 21 (December 6, 2004), pp. 7–11; P. Kuitenbrouwer, "Making Money, and Enjoying It: Dingwall at the Mint," *Financial Post* (*National Post*), December 29, 2004, p. FP1; and C. Clark, "Dingwall Severance in the Works," *Globe and Mail*, September 30, 2005, p. A5.

70 J. P. Kotter, "Leading Changes: Why Transformation Efforts Fail," *Harvard Business Review*, March–April 1995, pp. 59–67; and J. P.

Kotter, *Leading Change* (Boston: Harvard Business School Press, 1996).

71 See B. Victor and J. B. Cullen, "The Organizational Bases of Ethical Work Climates," *Administrative Science Quarterly*, March 1988, pp. 101–125; R. L. Dufresne, "An Action Learning Perspective on Effective Implementation of Academic Honor Codes," *Group & Organization Management*, April 2004, pp. 201–218; and A. Ardichvilli, J. A. Mitchell, and D. Jondle, "Characteristics of Ethical Business Cultures," *Journal of Business Ethics* 85, no. 4 (2009), pp. 445–451.

72 J. P. Mulki, J. F. Jaramillo, and W. B. Locander, "Critical Role of Leadership on Ethical Climate and Salesperson Behaviors," *Journal of Business Ethics* 86, no. 2 (2009), pp. 125–141; M. Schminke, M. L. Ambrose, and D. O. Neubaum, "The Effect of Leader Moral Development on Ethical Climate and Employee Attitudes," *Organizational Behavior and Human Decision Processes* 97, no. 2 (2005), pp. 135–151; and M. E. Brown, L. K. Treviño, and D. A. Harrison, "Ethical Leadership: A Social Learning Perspective for Construct Development and Testing," *Organizational Behavior and Human Decision Processes* 97, no. 2 (2005), pp. 117–134.

73 D. M. Mayer, M. Kuenzi, R. Greenbaum, M. Bardes, and S. Salvador, "How Low Does Ethical Leadership Flow? Test of a Trickle-Down Model," *Organizational Behavior and Human Decision Processes* 108, no. 1 (2009), pp. 1–13.

74 M. L. Gruys, S. M. Stewart, J. Goodstein, M. N. Bing, and A. C. Wicks, "Values Enactment in Organizations: A Multi-Level Examination," *Journal of Management* 34, no. 4 (2008), pp. 806–843.

75 D. L. Nelson and C. L. Cooper, eds., *Positive Organizational Behavior* (London: Sage, 2007); K. S. Cameron, J. E. Dutton, and R. E. Quinn, eds., *Positive Organizational Scholarship: Foundations of a New Discipline* (San Francisco: Berrett-Koehler, 2003); and F. Luthans and C. M. Youssef, "Emerging Positive Organizational Behavior," *Journal of Management*, June 2007, pp. 321–349.

76 J. Robison, "Great Leadership Under Fire," *Gallup Leadership Journal*, March 8, 2007, pp. 1–3.

77 R. Wagner and J. K. Harter, *12: The Elements of Great Managing* (New York: Gallup Press, 2006).

78 S. Fineman, "On Being Positive: Concerns and Counterpoints," *Academy of Management Review* 31, no. 2 (2006), pp. 270–291.

79 P. Dvorak, "A Firm's Culture Can Get Lost in Translation," *Wall Street Journal*, April 3, 2006, pp. B1, B3; K. Kranhold, "The Immelt Era, Five Years Old, Transforms GE," *Wall Street Journal*, September 11, 2006, pp. B1, B3; and S. McCartney, "Teaching Americans How to Behave Abroad," *Wall Street Journal*, April 11, 2006, pp. D1, D4.

80 D. J. McCarthy and S. M. Puffer, "Interpreting the Ethicality of Corporate Governance Decision in Russia: Utilizing Integrative Social Contracts Theory to Evaluate the Relevance of Agency Theory Norms," *Academy of Management Review* 33, no. 1 (2008), pp. 11–31.

81 J. Jargon, "Neatness Counts at Kyocera and Others in the 5S Club," *Wall Street Journal*, October 27, 2008, pp. A1, A15; R. Gapp, R. Fisher, and K. Kobayashi, "Implementing 5S within a Japanese Context: An Integrated Management System," *Management Decision* 46, no. 4 (2008), pp. 565–579; and R. Hough, "5S Implementation Methodology," *Management Services* 52, no. 2 (2008), pp. 44–45.

82 Based on E. Iwata, "Businesses Grow More Socially Conscious," *USA Today*, June 14, 2007, p. 3B; and M. Boyle and E. F. Kratz, "The Wegmans Way," *Fortune*, January 24, 2005, pp. 62–66.

83 Ideas in this feature were influenced by A. L. Wilkins, "The Culture Audit: A Tool for Understanding Organizations," *Organizational Dynamics*, Autumn 1983, pp. 24–38; H. M. Trice

and J. M. Beyer, *The Cultures of Work Organizations* (Englewood Cliffs, NJ: Prentice Hall, 1993), pp. 358–362; H. Lancaster, "To Avoid a Job Failure, Learn the Culture of a Company First," *Wall Street Journal*, July 14, 1998, p. B1; and M. Belliveau, "4 Ways to Read a Company," *Fast Company*, October 1998, p. 158.

Chapter 11

1 Vignette based on National Defence, "Canadian Forces Snowbirds to Gain Leadership Depth," (news release), January 9, 2010, http://www.snowbirds.dnd.ca/v2/nr-sp/nr-sp-eng.asp?cat=2&id=321; J. Graham, "She's the Boss: Snowbirds First Female Pilot to Lead Aerobatic Squad," *Canadian Press*, May 2, 2010, http://www.cbc.ca/canada/saskatchewan/story/2010/05/02/sask-snowbirds.html#ixzz0mv2nPxRr; and C. Coward, "Five Questions with a Snowbird," *Hamilton Spectator*, November 5, 2011, http://www.thespec.com/localprofile/article/620542--five-questions-with-a-snowbird

2 J. P. Kotter, "What Leaders Really Do," *Harvard Business Review*, May–June 1990, pp. 103–111.

3 R. N. Kanungo, "Leadership in Organizations: Looking Ahead to the 21st Century," *Canadian Psychology* 39, no. 1–2 (1998), p. 77. For more evidence of this consensus, see N. Adler, *International Dimensions of Organizational Behavior*, 3rd ed. (Cincinnati, OH: South Western, 1997); R. J. House, "Leadership in the Twenty-First Century," in *The Changing Nature of Work*, ed. A. Howard (San Francisco: Jossey-Bass, 1995), pp. 411–450; R. N. Kanungo and M. Mendonca, *Ethical Dimensions of Leadership* (Thousand Oaks, CA: Sage, 1996); and A. Zaleznik, "The Leadership Gap," *Academy of Management Executive* 4, no. 1 (1990), pp. 7–22.

4 Vignette based on J. Graham, "She's the Boss: Snowbirds First Female Pilot to Lead Aerobatic Squad," *Canadian Press*, May 2, 2010, http://www.cbc.ca/canada/saskatchewan/story/2010/05/02/sask-snowbirds.html#ixzz0mv2nPxRr

5 Based on D. Fost, "Survey Finds Many Workers Mistrust Bosses," *San Francisco Chronicle*, January 3, 2007, http://www.sfgate.com; and T. Weiss, "The Narcissistic CEO," *Forbes*, August 29, 2006, http://www.forbes.com

6 C. C. Eckel, E. Fatas, and R. Wilson, "Cooperation and Status in Organizations," *Journal of Public Economic Theory* 12, no. 4 (2010), pp. 737–762.

7 J. G. Geier, "A Trait Approach to the Study of Leadership in Small Groups," *Journal of Communication*, December 1967, pp. 316–323.

8 S. A. Kirkpatrick and E. A. Locke, "Leadership: Do Traits Matter?" *Academy of Management Executive*, May 1991, pp. 48–60; and S. J. Zaccaro, R. J. Foti, and D. A. Kenny, "Self-Monitoring and Trait-Based Variance in Leadership: An Investigation of Leader Flexibility across Multiple Group Situations," *Journal of Applied Psychology*, April 1991, pp. 308–315.

9 See T. A. Judge, J. E. Bono, R. Ilies, and M. Werner, "Personality and Leadership: A Review" (paper presented at the 15th Annual Conference of the Society for Industrial and Organizational Psychology, New Orleans, 2000); and T. A. Judge, J. E. Bono, R. Ilies, and M. W. Gerhardt, "Personality and Leadership: A Qualitative and Quantitative Review," *Journal of Applied Psychology*, August 2002, pp. 765–780.

10 T. A. Judge, J. E. Bono, R. Ilies, and M. Werner, "Personality and Leadership: A Review" (paper presented at the 15th Annual Conference of the Society for Industrial and Organizational Psychology, New Orleans, 2000).

11 D. R. Ames and F. J. Flynn, "What Breaks a Leader: The Curvilinear Relation between Assertiveness and Leadership," *Journal of Personality and Social Psychology* 92, no. 2 (2007), pp. 307–324.

12 K. Ng, S. Ang, and K. Chan, "Personality and Leader Effectiveness: A Moderated Mediation Model of Leadership Self-Efficacy, Job Demands, and Job Autonomy," *Journal of Applied Psychology* 93, no. 4 (2008), pp. 733–743.

13 This section is based on D. Goleman, "What Makes a Leader?" *Harvard Business Review*, November–December 1998, pp. 93–102; J. M. George, "Emotions and Leadership: The Role of Emotional Intelligence," *Human Relations*, August 2000, pp. 1027–1055; C.-S. Wong and K. S. Law, "The Effects of Leader and Follower Emotional Intelligence on Performance and Attitude: An Exploratory Study," *Leadership Quarterly*, June 2002, pp. 243–274; and D. R. Caruso and C. J. Wolfe, "Emotional Intelligence and Leadership Development," in *Leader Development for Transforming Organizations: Growing Leaders for Tomorrow*, ed. D. David and S. J. Zaccaro (Mahwah, NJ: Lawrence Erlbaum, 2004), pp. 237–263.

14 J. Champy, "The Hidden Qualities of Great Leaders," *Fast Company*, November 2003, p. 135.

15 J. Antonakis, "Why 'Emotional Intelligence' Does Not Predict Leadership Effectiveness: A Comment on Prati, Douglas, Ferris, Ammeter, and Buckley (2003)," *International Journal of Organizational Analysis* 11 (2003), pp. 355–361. See also M. Zeidner, G. Matthews, and R. D. Roberts, "Emotional Intelligence in the Workplace: A Critical Review," *Applied Psychology: An International Review* 53 (2004), pp. 371–399; and F. Walter, M. S. Cole, and R. H. Humphrey, "Emotional Intelligence: Sine Qua Non of Leadership or Folderol?" *Academy of Management Perspectives* 25, no. 1 (2011), pp. 45–59.

16 T. A. Judge, J. E. Bono, R. Ilies, and M. Werner, "Personality and Leadership: A Review" (paper presented at the 15th Annual Conference of the Society for Industrial and Organizational Psychology, New Orleans, 2000); R. G. Lord, C. L. DeVader, and G. M. Alliger, "A Meta-analysis of the Relation between Personality Traits and Leadership Perceptions: An Application of Validity Generalization Procedures," *Journal of Applied Psychology*, August 1986, pp. 402–410; and J. A. Smith and R. J. Foti, "A Pattern Approach to the Study of Leader Emergence," *Leadership Quarterly*, Summer 1998, pp. 147–160.

17 R. M. Stogdill and A. E. Coons, eds., *Leader Behavior: Its Description and Measurement*, Research Monograph no. 88 (Columbus: Ohio State University, Bureau of Business Research, 1951). This research is updated in C. A. Schriesheim, C. C. Cogliser, and L. L. Neider, "Is It 'Trustworthy'? A Multiple-Levels-of-Analysis Reexamination of an Ohio State Leadership Study, with Implications for Future Research," *Leadership Quarterly*, Summer 1995, pp. 111–145; and T. A. Judge, R. F. Piccolo, and R. Ilies, "The Forgotten Ones? The Validity of Consideration and Initiating Structure in Leadership Research," *Journal of Applied Psychology*, February 2004, pp. 36–51.

18 D. Akst, "The Rewards of Recognizing a Job Well Done," *Wall Street Journal*, January 31, 2007, p. D9.

19 R. Kahn and D. Katz, "Leadership Practices in Relation to Productivity and Morale," in *Group Dynamics: Research and Theory*, 2nd ed., ed. D. Cartwright and A. Zander (Elmsford, NY: Row, Paterson, 1960).

20 T. A. Judge, R. F. Piccolo, and R. Ilies, "The Forgotten Ones? The Validity of Consideration and Initiating Structure in Leadership Research," *Journal of Applied Psychology*, February 2004, pp. 36–51.

21 G. Yukl and D. D. Van Fleet, "Theory and Research on Leadership in Organizations," in *Handbook of Industrial and Organizational Psychology*, vol. 2, ed. M. D. Dunnette and L. M. Hough (Palo Alto, CA: Consulting Psychologists Press, 1992), pp. 147–197.

22 For a critical review, see A. K. Korman, "'Consideration,' 'Initiating Structure' and Organizational Criteria—A Review," *Personnel Psychology* 19 (1966), pp. 349–361. For a more supportive review, see S. Kerr and C. Schriesheim, "Consideration, Initiating Structure, and Organizational Criteria—An Update

of Korman's 1966 Review," *Personnel Psychology* 27 (1974), pp. 555–568.

23 Based on G. Johns and A. M. Saks, *Organizational Behaviour*, 5th ed. (Toronto: Pearson Education Canada, 2001), p. 276.

24 A. J. Mayo and N. Nohria, "Zeitgeist Leadership," *Harvard Business Review* 83, no. 10 (2005), pp. 45–60.

25 See, for instance, P. M. Podsakoff, S. B. MacKenzie, M. Ahearne, and W. H. Bommer, "Searching for a Needle in a Haystack: Trying to Identify the Illusive Moderators of Leadership Behavior," *Journal of Management* 1, no. 3 (1995), pp. 422–470.

26 F. E. Fiedler, *A Theory of Leadership Effectiveness* (New York: McGraw-Hill, 1967).

27 Cited in R. J. House and R. N. Aditya, "The Social Scientific Study of Leadership: Quo Vadis?" *Journal of Management* 23, no. 3 (1997), p. 422.

28 G. Johns and A. M. Saks, *Organizational Behaviour*, 5th ed. (Toronto: Pearson Education Canada, 2001), pp. 278–279.

29 For controversy surrounding the Fiedler LPC scale, see A. Bryman, "Leadership in Organizations," in *Handbook of Organization Studies*, ed. S. R. Clegg, C. Hardy, and W. R. Nord (London: Sage, 1996), pp. 279–280; A. Bryman, *Leadership and Organizations* (London: Routledge and Kegan Paul, 1986); and T. Peters and N. Austin, *A Passion for Excellence* (New York: Random House, 1985). For supportive evidence on the Fiedler model, see L. H. Peters, D. D. Hartke, and J. T. Pohlmann, "Fiedler's Contingency Theory of Leadership: An Application of the Meta-analysis Procedures of Schmidt and Hunter," *Psychological Bulletin*, March 1985, pp. 274–285; C. A. Schriesheim, B. J. Tepper, and L. A. Tetrault, "Least Preferred Co-Worker Score, Situational Control, and Leadership Effectiveness: A Meta-analysis of Contingency Model Performance Predictions," *Journal of Applied Psychology*, August 1994, pp. 561–573; and R. Ayman, M. M. Chemers, and F. Fiedler, "The Contingency Model of Leadership Effectiveness: Its Levels of Analysis," *Leadership Quarterly*, Summer 1995, pp. 147–167. For evidence that LPC scores are not stable, see, for instance, R. W. Rice, "Psychometric Properties of the Esteem for the Least Preferred Coworker (LPC) Scale," *Academy of Management Review*, January 1978, pp. 106–118; C. A. Schriesheim, B. D. Bannister, and W. H. Money, "Psychometric Properties of the LPC Scale: An Extension of Rice's Review," *Academy of Management Review*, April 1979, pp. 287–290; and J. K. Kennedy, J. M. Houston, M. A. Korgaard, and D. D. Gallo, "Construct Space of the Least Preferred Co-worker (LPC) Scale," *Educational & Psychological Measurement*, Fall 1987, pp. 807–814. For difficulty in applying Fiedler's model, see E. H. Schein, *Organizational Psychology*, 3rd ed. (Englewood Cliffs, NJ: Prentice Hall, 1980), pp. 116–117; and B. Kabanoff, "A Critique of Leader Match and Its Implications for Leadership Research," *Personnel Psychology*, Winter 1981, pp. 749–764. For evidence that Hersey and Blanchard's model has received little attention from researchers, see R. K. Hambleton and R. Gumpert, "The Validity of Hersey and Blanchard's Theory of Leader Effectiveness," *Group & Organization Studies*, June 1982, pp. 225–242; C. L. Graeff, "The Situational Leadership Theory: A Critical View," *Academy of Management Review*, April 1983, pp. 285–291; R. P. Vecchio, "Situational Leadership Theory: An Examination of a Prescriptive Theory," *Journal of Applied Psychology*, August 1987, pp. 444–451; J. R. Goodson, G. W. McGee, and J. F. Cashman, "Situational Leadership Theory: A Test of Leadership Prescriptions," *Group & Organization Studies*, December 1989, pp. 446–461; W. Blank, J. R. Weitzel, and S. G. Green, "A Test of the Situational Leadership Theory," *Personnel Psychology*, Autumn 1990, pp. 579–597; and W. R. Norris and R. P. Vecchio, "Situational Leadership Theory: A Replication," *Group & Organization Management*, September 1992, pp. 331–342. For evidence of partial support for the theory, see R. P. Vecchio, "Situational Leadership Theory: An Examination of a Prescriptive Theory,"

Journal of Applied Psychology, August 1987, pp. 444–451; and W. R. Norris and R. P. Vecchio, "Situational Leadership Theory: A Replication," *Group & Organization Management*, September 1992, pp. 331–342; and for evidence of no support for Hersey and Blanchard, see W. Blank, J. R. Weitzel, and S. G. Green, "A Test of the Situational Leadership Theory," *Personnel Psychology*, Autumn 1990, pp. 579–597.

30 P. Hersey and K. H. Blanchard, "So You Want to Know Your Leadership Style?" *Training and Development Journal*, February 1974, pp. 1–15; and P. Hersey, K. H. Blanchard, and D. E. Johnson, *Management of Organizational Behavior: Leading Human Resources*, 8th ed. (Upper Saddle River, NJ: Prentice Hall, 2001), cited in C. F. Fernandez and R. P. Vecchio, "Situational Leadership Theory Revisited: A Test of an ACROSS-Jobs Perspective," *Leadership Quarterly* 8, no. 1 (1997), p. 67. See also http://www.situational.com/leadership.htm

31 See, for instance, C. F. Fernandez and R. P. Vecchio, "Situational Leadership Theory Revisited: A Test of an ACROSS-Jobs Perspective," *Leadership Quarterly* 8, no. 1 (1997), pp. 67–84; C. L. Graeff, "Evolution of Situational Leadership Theory: A Critical Review," *Leadership Quarterly* 8, no. 2 (1997), pp. 153–170; and R. P. Vecchio and K. J. Boatwright, "Preferences for Idealized Styles of Supervision," *Leadership Quarterly*, August 2002, pp. 327–342.

32 M. G. Evans, "The Effects of Supervisory Behavior on the Path-Goal Relationship," *Organizational Behavior and Human Performance* 5 (1970), pp. 277–298; M. G. Evans, "Leadership and Motivation: A Core Concept," *Academy of Management Journal* 13 (1970), pp. 91–102; R. J. House, "A Path-Goal Theory of Leader Effectiveness," *Administrative Science Quarterly*, September 1971, pp. 321–338; R. J. House and T. R. Mitchell, "Path-Goal Theory of Leadership," *Journal of Contemporary Business*, Autumn 1974, p. 86; M. G. Evans, "Leadership," in *Organizational Behavior*, ed. S. Kerr (Columbus, OH: Grid Publishing, 1979); R. J. House, "Retrospective Comment," in *The Great Writings in Management and Organizational Behavior*, 2nd ed., ed. L. E. Boone and D. D. Bowen (New York: Random House, 1987), pp. 354–364; and M. G. Evans, "*Fuhrungstheorien, Weg-ziel-theorie*," in *Handworterbuch Der Fuhrung*, 2nd ed., ed. A. Kieser, G. Reber, and R. Wunderer, trans. G. Reber (Stuttgart, Germany: Schaffer Poeschal Verlag, 1995), pp. 1075–1091.

33 G. R. Jones, J. M. George, C. W. L. Hill, and N. Langton, *Contemporary Management* (Toronto: McGraw-Hill Ryerson, 2002), p. 392.

34 J. C. Wofford and L. Z. Liska, "Path-Goal Theories of Leadership: A Meta-analysis," *Journal of Management* 19, no. 4 (1993), pp. 857–876.

35 P. M. Podsakoff, S. B. MacKenzie, and M. Ahearne, "Searching for a Needle in a Haystack: Trying to Identify the Illusive Moderators of Leadership Behaviors," *Journal of Management* 21 (1995), pp. 423–470.

36 J. R. Villa, J. P. Howell, and P. W. Dorfman, "Problems with Detecting Moderators in Leadership Research Using Moderated Multiple Regression," *Leadership Quarterly* 14 (2003), pp. 3–23; C. A. Schriesheim and L. Neider, "Path-Goal Leadership Theory: The Long and Winding Road," *Leadership Quarterly* 7 (1996), pp. 317–321; and M. G. Evans, "R. J. House's 'A Path-Goal Theory of Leader Effectiveness,'" *Leadership Quarterly* 7 (1996), pp. 305–309.

37 T. Sy, "What Do You Think of Followers? Examining the Content, Structure, and Consequences of Implicit Followership Theories," *Organizational Behavior and Human Decision Processes* 113, no. 2 (2010), pp. 73–84.

38 S. Kerr and J. M. Jermier, "Substitutes for Leadership: Their Meaning and Measurement," *Organizational Behavior and Human Performance*, December 1978, pp. 375–403; J. P. Howell and P. W. Dorfman, "Substitutes for Leadership: Test of a Construct,"

Academy of Management Journal, December 1981, pp. 714–728; J. P. Howell, P. W. Dorfman, and S. Kerr, "Leadership and Substitutes for Leadership," *Journal of Applied Behavioral Science* 22, no. 1 (1986), pp. 29–46; J. P. Howell, D. E. Bowen, P. W. Dorfman, S. Kerr, and P. M. Podsakoff, "Substitutes for Leadership: Effective Alternatives to Ineffective Leadership," *Organizational Dynamics*, Summer 1990, pp. 21–38; P. M. Podsakoff, B. P. Niehoff, S. B. MacKenzie, and M. L. Williams, "Do Substitutes for Leadership Really Substitute for Leadership? An Empirical Examination of Kerr and Jermier's Situational Leadership Model," *Organizational Behavior and Human Decision Processes*, February 1993, pp. 1–44; P. M. Podsakoff and S. B. MacKenzie, "An Examination of Substitutes for Leadership within a Levels-of-Analysis Framework," *Leadership Quarterly*, Fall 1995, pp. 289–328; P. M. Podsakoff, S. B. MacKenzie, and W. H. Bommer, "Transformational Leader Behaviors and Substitutes for Leadership as Determinants of Employee Satisfaction, Commitment, Trust, and Organizational Citizenship Behaviors," *Journal of Management* 22, no. 2 (1996), pp. 259–298; P. M. Podsakoff, S. B. MacKenzie, and W. H. Bommer, "Meta-analysis of the Relationships between Kerr and Jermier's Substitutes for Leadership and Employee Attitudes, Role Perceptions, and Performance," *Journal of Applied Psychology*, August 1996, pp. 380–399; and J. M. Jermier and S. Kerr, "'Substitutes for Leadership: Their Meaning and Measurement'—Contextual Recollections and Current Observations," *Leadership Quarterly* 8, no. 2 (1997), pp. 95–101.

39 S. D. Dionne, F. J. Yammarino, L. E. Atwater, and L. R. James, "Neutralizing Substitutes for Leadership Theory: Leadership Effects and Common-Source Bias," *Journal of Applied Psychology* 87 (2002), pp. 454–464; and J. R. Villa, J. P. Howell, P. W. Dorfman, and D. L. Daniel, "Problems with Detecting Moderators in Leadership Research Using Moderated Multiple Regression," *Leadership Quarterly* 14 (2002), pp. 3–23.

40 Vignette based on J. Graham, "She's the Boss: Snowbirds First Female Pilot to Lead Aerobatic Squad," *Canadian Press*, May 2, 2010, http://www.cbc.ca/canada/saskatchewan/story/2010/05/02/sask-snowbirds.html#ixzz0mv2nPxRr; and C. Coward, "Five Questions with a Snowbird," *Hamilton Spectator*, November 5, 2011, http://www.thespec.com/localprofile/article/620542--five-questions-with-a-snowbird

41 M. Weber, *The Theory of Social and Economic Organization*, trans. A. M. Henderson and T. Parsons (New York: The Free Press, 1947).

42 J. A. Conger and R. N. Kanungo, "Behavioral Dimensions of Charismatic Leadership," in *Charismatic Leadership*, ed. J. A. Conger and R. N. Kanungo (San Francisco: Jossey-Bass, 1988), p. 79.

43 J. A. Conger and R. N. Kanungo, *Charismatic Leadership in Organizations* (Thousand Oaks, CA: Sage, 1998); and R. Awamleh and W. L. Gardner, "Perceptions of Leader Charisma and Effectiveness: The Effects of Vision Content, Delivery, and Organizational Performance," *Leadership Quarterly*, Fall 1999, pp. 345–373.

44 B. Shamir, R. J. House, and M. B. Arthur, "The Motivational Effects of Charismatic Leadership: A Self-Concept Theory," *Organization Science*, November 1993, pp. 577–594.

45 R. Kark, B. Shamir, and G. Chen, "The Two Faces of Transformational Leadership: Empowerment and Dependency," *Journal of Applied Psychology* 88, no. 2 (2003), pp. 246–255.

46 D. N. Den Hartog, A. H. B. De Hoogh, and A. E. Keegan, "The Interactive Effects of Belongingness and Charisma on Helping and Compliance," *Journal of Applied Psychology* 92, no. 4 (2007), pp. 1131–1139.

47 A. Erez, V. F. Misangyi, D. E. Johnson, M. A. LePine, and K. C. Halverson, "Stirring the Hearts of Followers: Charismatic Leadership as the Transferal of Affect," *Journal of Applied Psychology* 93, no. 3 (2008), pp. 602–615. For reviews on

the role of vision in leadership, see S. J. Zaccaro, "Visionary and Inspirational Models of Executive Leadership: Empirical Review and Evaluation," in *The Nature of Executive Leadership: A Conceptual and Empirical Analysis of Success*, ed. S. J. Zaccaro (Washington, DC: American Psychological Association, 2001), pp. 259–278; and M. Hauser and R. J. House, "Lead through Vision and Values," in *Handbook of Principles of Organizational Behavior*, ed. E. A. Locke (Malden, MA: Blackwell, 2004), pp. 257–273.

48 D. A. Waldman, B. M. Bass, and F. J. Yammarino, "Adding to Contingent-Reward Behavior: The Augmenting Effect of Charismatic Leadership," *Group & Organization Studies*, December 1990, pp. 381–394; and S. A. Kirkpatrick and E. A. Locke, "Direct and Indirect Effects of Three Core Charismatic Leadership Components on Performance and Attitudes," *Journal of Applied Psychology*, February 1996, pp. 36–51.

49 A. H. B. de Hoogh, D. N. den Hartog, P. L. Koopman, H. Thierry, P. T. van den Berg, and J. G. van der Weide, "Charismatic Leadership, Environmental Dynamism, and Performance," *European Journal of Work & Organizational Psychology*, December 2004, pp. 447–471; S. Harvey, M. Martin, and D. Stout, "Instructor's Transformational Leadership: University Student Attitudes and Ratings," *Psychological Reports*, April 2003, pp. 395–402; and D. A. Waldman, M. Javidan, and P. Varella, "Charismatic Leadership at the Strategic Level: A New Application of Upper Echelons Theory," *Leadership Quarterly*, June 2004, pp. 355–380.

50 R. J. House, "A 1976 Theory of Charismatic Leadership," in *Leadership: The Cutting Edge*, ed. J. G. Hunt and L. L. Larson (Carbondale, IL: Southern Illinois University Press, 1977), pp. 189–207; and Robert J. House and Ram N. Aditya, "The Social Scientific Study of Leadership," *Journal of Management* 23, no. 3 (1997), p. 441.

51 J. C. Pastor, M. Mayo, and B. Shamir, "Adding Fuel to Fire: The Impact of Followers' Arousal on Ratings of Charisma," *Journal of Applied Psychology* 92, no. 6 (2007), pp. 1584–1596.

52 F. Cohen, S. Solomon, M. Maxfield, T. Pyszczynski, and J. Greenberg, "Fatal Attraction: The Effects of Mortality Salience on Evaluations of Charismatic, Task-Oriented, and Relationship-Oriented Leaders," *Psychological Science*, December 2004, pp. 846–851; and M. G. Ehrhart and K. J. Klein, "Predicting Followers' Preferences for Charismatic Leadership: The Influence of Follower Values and Personality," *Leadership Quarterly*, Summer 2001, pp. 153–179.

53 K. Levine, R. Muenchen, and A. Brooks, "Measuring Transformational and Charismatic Leadership: Why Isn't Charisma Measured?" *Communication Monographs* 77, no. 4 (2010), pp. 576–591.

54 J. A. Conger, *The Charismatic Leader: Behind the Mystique of Exceptional Leadership* (San Francisco: Jossey-Bass, 1989); R. Hogan, R. Raskin, and D. Fazzini, "The Dark Side of Charisma," in *Measures of Leadership*, ed. K. E. Clark and M. B. Clark (West Orange, NJ: Leadership Library of America, 1990); D. Sankowsky, "The Charismatic Leader as Narcissist: Understanding the Abuse of Power," *Organizational Dynamics*, Spring 1995, pp. 57–71; and J. O'Connor, M. D. Mumford, T. C. Clifton, T. L. Gessner, and M. S. Connelly, "Charismatic Leaders and Destructiveness: An Historiometric Study," *Leadership Quarterly*, Winter 1995, pp. 529–555.

55 K. Yakabuski, "Henri-Paul Rousseau Was the King of Quebec's Pension Fund and His Returns the Envy of Many," *Globe and Mail*, January 31, 2009, p. B1.

56 G. Pitts, "Scandals Part of Natural Cycles of Excess," *Globe and Mail*, June 28, 2002, pp. B1, B5.

57 J. Collins, "Level 5 Leadership: The Triumph of Humility and Fierce Resolve," *Harvard Business Review*, January 2001,

pp. 67–76; J. Collins, "Good to Great," *Fast Company*, October 2001, pp. 90–104; J. Collins, "The Misguided Mix-up," *Executive Excellence*, December 2002, pp. 3–4; and H. L. Tosi, V. F. Misangyi, A. Fanelli, D. A. Waldman, and F. J. Yammarino, "CEO Charisma, Compensation, and Firm Performance," *The Leadership Quarterly* 15 (2004), pp. 405–420.

58 See, for instance, B. M. Bass, B. J. Avolio, D. I. Jung, and Y. Berson, "Predicting Unit Performance by Assessing Transformational and Transactional Leadership," *Journal of Applied Psychology*, April 2003, pp. 207–218; and T. A. Judge and R. F. Piccolo, "Transformational and Transactional Leadership: A Meta-analytic Test of Their Relative Validity," *Journal of Applied Psychology*, October 2004, pp. 755–768.

59 N.-W. Chi, Y.-Y. Chung, and W.-C. Tsai, "How Do Happy Leaders Enhance Team Success? The Mediating Roles of Transformational Leadership, Group Affective Tone, and Team Processes," *Journal of Applied Social Psychology* 41, no. 6 (2011), pp. 1421–1454.

60 B. M. Bass, "Leadership: Good, Better, Best," *Organizational Dynamics*, Winter 1985, pp. 26–40; and J. Seltzer and B. M. Bass, "Transformational Leadership: Beyond Initiation and Consideration," *Journal of Management*, December 1990, pp. 693–703.

61 T. R. Hinkin and C. A. Schriesheim, "An Examination of 'Nonleadership': From Laissez-Faire Leadership to Leader Reward Omission and Punishment Omission," *Journal of Applied Psychology* 93, no. 6 (2008), pp. 1234–1248.

62 S. J. Shin and J. Zhou, "Transformational Leadership, Conservation, and Creativity: Evidence from Korea," *Academy of Management Journal*, December 2003, pp. 703–714; V. J. García-Morales, F. J. Lloréns-Montes, and A. J. Verdú-Jover, "The Effects of Transformational Leadership on Organizational Performance Through Knowledge and Innovation," *British Journal of Management* 19, no. 4 (2008), pp. 299–313; and S. A. Eisenbeiss, D. van Knippenberg, and S. Boerner, "Transformational Leadership and Team Innovation: Integrating Team Climate Principles," *Journal of Applied Psychology* 93, no. 6 (2008), pp. 1438–1446.

63 Y. Ling, Z. Simsek, M. H. Lubatkin, and J. F. Veiga, "Transformational Leadership's Role in Promoting Corporate Entrepreneurship: Examining the CEO-TMT Interface," *Academy of Management Journal* 51, no. 3 (2008), pp. 557–576.

64 A. E. Colbert, A. E. Kristof-Brown, B. H. Bradley, and M. R. Barrick, "CEO Transformational Leadership: The Role of Goal Importance Congruence in Top Management Teams," *Academy of Management Journal* 51, no. 1 (2008), pp. 81–96.

65 D. Zohar and O. Tenne-Gazit, "Transformational Leadership and Group Interaction as Climate Antecedents: A Social Network Analysis," *Journal of Applied Psychology* 93, no. 4 (2008), pp. 744–757.

66 F. O. Walumbwa, B. J. Avolio, and W. Zhu, "How Transformational Leadership Weaves Its Influence on Individual Job Performance: The Role of Identification and Efficacy Beliefs," *Personnel Psychology* 61, no. 4 (2008), pp. 793–825.

67 J. E. Bono and T. A. Judge, "Self-Concordance at Work: Toward Understanding the Motivational Effects of Transformational Leaders," *Academy of Management Journal*, October 2003, pp. 554–571; Y. Berson and B. J. Avolio, "Transformational Leadership and the Dissemination of Organizational Goals: A Case Study of a Telecommunication Firm," *Leadership Quarterly*, October 2004, pp. 625–646; and J. Schaubroeck, S. S. K. Lam, and S. E. Cha, "Embracing Transformational Leadership: Team Values and the Impact of Leader Behavior on Team Performance," *Journal of Applied Psychology* 92, no. 4 (2007), pp. 1020–1030.

68 J. R. Baum, E. A. Locke, and S. A. Kirkpatrick, "A Longitudinal Study of the Relation of Vision and Vision Communication to Venture Growth in Entrepreneurial Firms," *Journal of Applied Psychology*, February 2000, pp. 43–54.

69 B. J. Avolio, W. Zhu, W. Koh, and P. Bhatia, "Transformational Leadership and Organizational Commitment: Mediating Role of Psychological Empowerment and Moderating Role of Structural Distance," *Journal of Organizational Behavior*, December 2004, pp. 951–968; and T. Dvir, N. Kass, and B. Shamir, "The Emotional Bond: Vision and Organizational Commitment Among High-Tech Employees," *Journal of Organizational Change Management* 17, no. 2 (2004), pp. 126–143.

70 R. T. Keller, "Transformational Leadership, Initiating Structure, and Substitutes for Leadership: A Longitudinal Study of Research and Development Project Team Performance," *Journal of Applied Psychology* 91, no. 1 (2006), pp. 202–210.

71 T. A. Judge and R. F. Piccolo, "Transformational and Transactional Leadership: A Meta-analytic Test of Their Relative Validity," *Journal of Applied Psychology*, October 2004, pp. 755–768.

72 Y. Ling, Z. Simsek, M. H. Lubatkin, and J. F. Veiga, "The Impact of Transformational CEOs on the Performance of Small- to Medium-Sized Firms: Does Organizational Context Matter?" *Journal of Applied Psychology* 93, no. 4 (2008), pp. 923–934.

73 J. Schaubroeck, S. S. K. Lam, and S. E. Cha, "Embracing Transformational Leadership: Team Values and the Impact of Leader Behavior on Team Performance," *Journal of Applied Psychology* 92, no. 4 (2007), pp. 1020–1030.

74 H. Hetland, G. M. Sandal, and T. B. Johnsen, "Burnout in the Information Technology Sector: Does Leadership Matter?" *European Journal of Work and Organizational Psychology* 16, no. 1 (2007), pp. 58–75; and K. B. Lowe, K. G. Kroeck, and N. Sivasubramaniam, "Effectiveness Correlates of Transformational and Transactional Leadership: A Meta-analytic Review of the MLQ Literature," *Leadership Quarterly*, Fall 1996, pp. 385–425.

75 See, for instance, J. Barling, T. Weber, and E. K. Kelloway, "Effects of Transformational Leadership Training on Attitudinal and Financial Outcomes: A Field Experiment," *Journal of Applied Psychology*, December 1996, pp. 827–832; T. Dvir, D. Eden, and B. J. Avolio, "Impact of Transformational Leadership on Follower Development and Performance: A Field Experiment," *Academy of Management Journal*, August 2002, pp. 735–744; and R. A. Hassan, B. A. Fuwad, and A. I. Rauf, "Pre-Training Motivation and the Effectiveness of Transformational Leadership Training: An Experiment," *Academy of Strategic Management Journal* 9, no. 2 (2010), pp. 1–8.

76 R. N. Kanungo, "Leadership in Organizations: Looking Ahead to the 21st Century," *Canadian Psychology* 39, no. 1–2 (1998), p. 78.

77 B. J. Avolio and B. M. Bass, "Transformational Leadership, Charisma and Beyond," working paper, School of Management, State University of New York, Binghamton, 1985, p. 14.

78 Vignette based on A. McCuaig, "Pilot Flies into Literary World," *Medicine Hat News*, http://www.medicinehatnews.com/local-entertainment/pilot-flies-into-literary-world-11252011.html

79 D. Ancona, E. Backman, and H. Bresman, "X-Teams: New Ways of Leading in a New World," *Ivey Business Journal* 72, no. 3 (May–June 2008), http://www.iveybusinessjournal.com/article.asp?intArticle_ID=755

80 See, for example, L. J. Zachary, *The Mentor's Guide: Facilitating Effective Learning Relationships* (San Francisco: Jossey-Bass, 2000); M. Murray, *Beyond the Myths and Magic of Mentoring: How to Facilitate an Effective Mentoring Process*, rev. ed. (New York: Wiley, 2001); and F. Warner, "Inside Intel's Mentoring Movement," *Fast Company*, April 2002, pp. 116–120.

81 B. R. Ragins and J. L. Cotton, "Easier Said Than Done: Gender Differences in Perceived Barriers to Gaining a Mentor," *Academy of Management Journal* 34, no. 4 (1993), pp. 939–951; C. R.

Wanberg, E. T. Welsh, and S. A. Hezlett, "Mentoring Research: A Review and Dynamic Process Model," in *Research in Personnel and Human Resources Management*, vol. 22, ed. G. R. Ferris and J. J. Martocchio (Greenwich, CT: Elsevier Science, 2003), pp. 39–124; and T. D. Allen, "Protégé Selection by Mentors: Contributing Individual and Organizational Factors," *Journal of Vocational Behavior* 65, no. 3 (2004), pp. 469–483.

82 T. D. Allen, M. L. Poteet, J. E. A. Russell, and G. H. Dobbins, "A Field Study of Factors Related to Supervisors' Willingness to Mentor Others," *Journal of Vocational Behavior* 50, no. 1 (1997), pp. 1–22; S. Aryee, Y. W. Chay, and J. Chew, "The Motivation to Mentor among Managerial Employees in the Maintenance Career Stage: An Interactionist Perspective," *Group and Organization Management* 21, no. 3 (1996), pp. 261–277; L. T. Eby, A. L. Lockwood, and M. Butts, "Perceived Support for Mentoring: A Multiple Perspectives Approach," *Journal of Vocational Behavior* 68, no. 2 (2006), pp. 267–291; and T. D. Allen, E. Lentz, and R. Day, "Career Success Outcomes Associated with Mentoring Others: A Comparison of Mentors and Nonmentors," *Journal of Career Development* 32, no. 3 (2006), pp. 272–285.

83 See, for example, D. A. Thomas, "The Impact of Race on Managers' Experiences of Developmental Relationships: An Intra-Organizational Study," *Journal of Organizational Behavior*, November 1990, pp. 479–492; K. E. Kram and D. T. Hall, "Mentoring in a Context of Diversity and Turbulence," in *Managing Diversity*, ed. E. E. Kossek and S. A. Lobel (Cambridge, MA: Blackwell, 1996), pp. 108–36; M. N. Ruderman and M. W. Hughes-James, "Leadership Development across Race and Gender," in *The Center for Creative Leadership Handbook of Leadership Development*, ed. C. D. McCauley, R. S. Moxley, and E. Van Velsor (San Francisco: Jossey-Bass, 1998), pp. 291–335; and B. R. Ragins and J. L. Cotton, "Mentor Functions and Outcomes: A Comparison of Men and Women in Formal and Informal Mentoring Relationships," *Journal of Applied Psychology*, August 1999, pp. 529–550.

84 J. A. Wilson and N. S. Elman, "Organizational Benefits of Mentoring," *Academy of Management Executive*, November 1990, p. 90.

85 See, for instance, K. Houston-Philpot, "Leadership Development Partnerships at Dow Corning Corporation," *Journal of Organizational Excellence*, Winter 2002, pp. 13–27.

86 B. R. Ragins and J. L. Cotton, "Mentor Functions and Outcomes: A Comparison of Men and Women in Formal and Informal Mentoring Relationships," *Journal of Applied Psychology*, August 1999, pp. 529–550; and C. M. Underhill, "The Effectiveness of Mentoring Programs in Corporate Settings: A Meta-analytical Review of the Literature," *Journal of Vocational Behavior* 68, no. 2 (2006), pp. 292–307.

87 T. D. Allen, E. T. Eby, and E. Lentz, "The Relationship between Formal Mentoring Program Characteristics and Perceived Program Effectiveness," *Personnel Psychology* 59 (2006), pp. 125–153; T. D. Allen, L. T. Eby, and E. Lentz, "Mentorship Behaviors and Mentorship Quality Associated with Formal Mentoring Programs: Closing the Gap between Research and Practice," *Journal of Applied Psychology* 91, no. 3 (2006), pp. 567–578; and M. R. Parise and M. L. Forret, "Formal Mentoring Programs: The Relationship of Program Design and Support to Mentors' Perceptions of Benefits and Costs," *Journal of Vocational Behavior* 72, no. 2 (2008), pp. 225–240.

88 L. T. Eby and A. Lockwood, "Protégés' and Mentors' Reactions to Participating in Formal Mentoring Programs: A Qualitative Investigation," *Journal of Vocational Behavior* 67, no. 3 (2005), pp. 441–458; G. T. Chao, "Formal Mentoring: Lessons Learned from Past Practice," *Professional Psychology: Research and Practice* 40, no. 3 (2009), pp. 314–320; C. R. Wanberg, J. D. Kammeyer-Mueller, and M. Marchese, "Mentor and Protégé Predictors and Outcomes of Mentoring in a Formal Mentoring Program," *Journal of Vocational Behavior* 69 (2006), pp. 410–423.

89 T. D. Allen, L. T. Eby, M. L. Poteet, L. Mark, E. Lentz, and L. Lizzette, "Career Benefits Associated with Mentoring for Protégés: A Meta-analysis," *Journal of Applied Psychology*, February 2004, pp. 127–136; and J. D. Kammeyer-Mueller and T. A. Judge, "A Quantitative Review of the Mentoring Literature: Test of a Model," *Journal of Vocational Behavior* 72 (2008), pp. 269–283.

90 M. K. Feeney and B. Bozeman, "Mentoring and Network Ties," *Human Relations* 61, no. 12 (2008), pp. 1651–1676; N. Bozionelos, "Intra-Organizational Network Resources: How They Relate to Career Success and Organizational Commitment," *Personnel Review* 37, no. 3 (2008), pp. 249–263; and S. A. Hezlett and S. K. Gibson, "Linking Mentoring and Social Capital: Implications for Career and Organization Development," *Advances in Developing Human Resources* 9, no. 3 (2007), pp. 384–412.

91 C. C. Manz and H. P. Sims Jr., *The New SuperLeadership: Leading Others to Lead Themselves* (San Francisco: Berrett-Koehler Publishers, 2001).

92 A. Bandura, "Self-Reinforcement: Theoretical and Methodological Considerations," *Behaviorism* 4 (1976), pp. 135–155; P. W. Corrigan, C. J. Wallace, and M. L. Schade, "Learning Medication Self-Management Skills in Schizophrenia; Relationships with Cognitive Deficits and Psychiatric Symptom," *Behavior Therapy*, Winter 1994, pp. 5–15; A. S. Bellack, "A Comparison of Self-Reinforcement and Self-Monitoring in a Weight Reduction Program," *Behavior Therapy* 7 (1976), pp. 68–75; T. A. Eckman, W. C. Wirshing, and S. R. Marder, "Technique for Training Schizophrenic Patients in Illness Self-Management: A Controlled Trial," *American Journal of Psychiatry* 149 (1992), pp. 1549–1555; J. J. Felixbrod and K. D. O'Leary, "Effect of Reinforcement on Children's Academic Behavior as a Function of Self-Determined and Externally Imposed Contingencies," *Journal of Applied Behavior Analysis* 6 (1973), pp. 141–150; A. J. Litrownik, L. R. Franzini, and D. Skenderian, "The Effects of Locus of Reinforcement Control on a Concept Identification Task," *Psychological Reports* 39 (1976), pp. 159–165; P. D. McGorry, "Psychoeducation in First-Episode Psychosis: A Therapeutic Process," *Psychiatry*, November 1995, pp. 313–328; G. S. Parcel, P. R. Swank, and M. J. Mariotto, "Self-Management of Cystic Fibrosis: A Structural Model for Educational and Behavioral Variables," *Social Science and Medicine* 38 (1994), pp. 1307–1315; and G. E. Speidel, "Motivating Effect of Contingent Self-Reward," *Journal of Experimental Psychology* 102 (1974), pp. 528–530.

93 D. B. Jeffrey, "A Comparison of the Effects of External Control and Self-Control on the Modification and Maintenance of Weight," *Journal of Abnormal Psychology* 83 (1974), pp. 404–410.

94 C. C. Manz and H. P. Sims Jr., *The New SuperLeadership: Leading Others to Lead Themselves* (San Francisco: Berrett-Koehler, 2001).

95 J. Kelly and S. Nadler, "Leading from Below," *Wall Street Journal*, March 3, 2007, pp. R4, R10.

96 See, for instance, J. H. Zenger, E. Musselwhite, K. Hurson, and C. Perrin, *Leading Teams: Mastering the New Role* (Homewood, IL: Business One Irwin, 1994); and M. Frohman, "Nothing Kills Teams Like Ill-Prepared Leaders," *IndustryWeek*, October 2, 1995, pp. 72–76.

97 See, for instance, M. Frohman, "Nothing Kills Teams Like Ill-Prepared Leaders," *IndustryWeek*, October 2, 1995, p. 93.

98 See, for instance, M. Frohman, "Nothing Kills Teams Like Ill-Prepared Leaders," *IndustryWeek*, October 2, 1995, p. 100.

99 J. R. Katzenbach and D. K. Smith, *The Wisdom of Teams: Creating the High-Performance Organization* (Boston: Harvard Business School Press, 1993).

100 N. Steckler and N. Fondas, "Building Team Leader Effectiveness: A Diagnostic Tool," *Organizational Dynamics*, Winter 1995, p. 20.

101 R. S. Wellins, W. C. Byham, and G. R. Dixon, *Inside Teams* (San Francisco: Jossey-Bass, 1994), p. 318.

102 N. Steckler and N. Fondas, "Building Team Leader Effectiveness: A Diagnostic Tool," *Organizational Dynamics*, Winter 1995, p. 21.

103 L. A. Hambley, T. A. O'Neill, and T. J. B. Kline, "Virtual Team Leadership: The Effects of Leadership Style and Communication Medium on Team Interaction Styles and Outcomes," *Organizational Behavior and Human Decision Processes* 103 (2007), pp. 1–20; and B. J. Avolio and S. S. Kahai, "Adding the 'E' to E-Leadership: How It May Impact Your Leadership," *Organizational Dynamics* 31, no. 4 (2003), pp. 325–338.

104 J. Howell and K. Hall-Merenda, "Leading from a Distance," in *Leadership: Achieving Exceptional Performance*, A Special Supplement Prepared by the Richard Ivey School of Business, *Globe and Mail*, May 15, 1998, pp. C1, C2.

105 S. J. Zaccaro and P. Bader, "E-Leadership and the Challenges of Leading E-Teams: Minimizing the Bad and Maximizing the Good," *Organizational Dynamics* 31, no. 4 (2003), pp. 381–385.

106 C. E. Naquin and G. D. Paulson, "Online Bargaining and Interpersonal Trust," *Journal of Applied Psychology*, February 2003, pp. 113–120.

107 B. Shamir, "Leadership in Boundaryless Organizations: Disposable or Indispensable?" *European Journal of Work and Organizational Psychology* 8, no. 1 (1999), pp. 49–71.

108 R. M. Kanter, *The Change Masters, Innovation and Entrepreneurship in the American Corporation* (New York: Simon and Schuster, 1983).

109 R. A. Heifetz, *Leadership without Easy Answers* (Cambridge, MA: Harvard University Press, 1996), p. 205.

110 R. A. Heifetz, *Leadership without Easy Answers* (Cambridge, MA: Harvard University Press, 1996), p. 205.

111 R. A. Heifetz, *Leadership without Easy Answers* (Cambridge, MA: Harvard University Press, 1996), p. 188.

112 Vignette based on C. Coward, "Five Questions with a Snowbird," *Hamilton Spectator*, November 5, 2011, http://www.thespec.com/localprofile/article/620542--five-questions-with-a-snowbird; and J. Graham, "She's the Boss: Snowbirds First Female Pilot to Lead Aerobatic Squad," *Canadian Press*, May 2, 2010, http://www.cbc.ca/canada/saskatchewan/story/2010/05/02/sask-snowbirds.html#ixzz0mv2nPxRr

113 C. Tan, "CEO Pinching Penney in a Slowing Economy," *Wall Street Journal*, January 31, 2008, pp. 1–2; and A. Carter, "Lighting a Fire under Campbell," *BusinessWeek*, December 4, 2006, pp. 96–101.

114 F. O. Walumbwa, F. Luthans, J. B. Avey, and A. Oke, "Authentically Leading Groups: The Mediating Role of Collective Psychological Capital And Trust," *Journal of Organizational Behavior* 32, no. 1 (2011), pp. 4–24.

115 R. Ilies, F. P. Morgeson, and J. D. Nahrgang, "Authentic Leadership and Eudaemonic Wellbeing: Understanding Leader-Follower Outcomes," *Leadership Quarterly* 16 (2005), pp. 373–394.

116 This section is based on E. P. Hollander, "Ethical Challenges in the Leader–Follower Relationship," *Business Ethics Quarterly*, January 1995, pp. 55–65; J. C. Rost, "Leadership: A Discussion About Ethics," *Business Ethics Quarterly*, January 1995, pp. 129–142; L. K. Treviño, M. Brown, and L. P. Hartman, "A Qualitative Investigation of Perceived Executive Ethical Leadership: Perceptions from Inside and Outside the Executive Suite," *Human Relations*, January 2003, pp. 5–37; and R. M. Fulmer, "The Challenge of Ethical Leadership," *Organizational Dynamics* 33, no. 3 (2004), pp. 307–317.

117 J. L. Lunsford, "Piloting Boeing's New Course," *Wall Street Journal*, June 13, 2006, pp. B1, B3.

118 J. M. Burns, *Leadership* (New York: Harper and Row, 1978).

119 J. M. Howell and B. J. Avolio, "The Ethics of Charismatic Leadership: Submission or Liberation?" *Academy of Management Executive*, May 1992, pp. 43–55.

120 D. van Knippenberg, D. De Cremer, and B. van Knippenberg, "Leadership and Fairness: The State of the Art," *European Journal of Work and Organizational Psychology* 16, no. 2 (2007), pp. 113–140.

121 M. E. Brown and L. K. Treviño, "Socialized Charismatic Leadership, Values Congruence, and Deviance in Work Groups," *Journal of Applied Psychology* 91, no. 4 (2006), pp. 954–962.

122 M. E. Brown and L. K. Treviño, "Leader-Follower Values Congruence: Are Socialized Charismatic Leaders Better Able to Achieve It?" *Journal of Applied Psychology* 94, no. 2 (2009), pp. 478–490.

123 J. G. Clawson, *Level Three Leadership* (Upper Saddle River, NJ: Prentice Hall, 1999), pp. 46–49.

124 http://www.statcan.gc.ca/daily-quotidien/110726/dq110726a-eng.htm

125 HRSDC calculations based on Statistics Canada, *Labour Force Survey Estimates (LFS), by Educational Attainment, Sex and Age Group, Annual*, CANSIM Table 282-0004 (Ottawa: Statistics Canada, 2011).

126 All labour force data based on "Women in Management in Canada (2010)," *Catalyst*, http://www.catalyst.org/publication/247/women-in-management-in-canada

127 Industry Canada, "Key Small Business Statistics—July 2010," http://www.ic.gc.ca/eic/site/sbrp-rppe.nsf/eng/rd02504.html

128 L. Ramsay, "A League of Their Own," *Globe and Mail*, November 23, 2002, p. B11.

129 The material in this section is based on J. Cliff, N. Langton, and H. Aldrich, "Walking the Talk? Gendered Rhetoric vs. Action in Small Firms," *Organizational Studies* 26, no. 1 (2005), pp. 63–91; J. Grant, "Women as Managers: What They Can Offer to Organizations," *Organizational Dynamics*, Winter 1988, pp. 56–63; S. Helgesen, *The Female Advantage: Women's Ways of Leadership* (New York: Doubleday, 1990); A. H. Eagly and B. T. Johnson, "Gender and Leadership Style: A Meta-analysis," *Psychological Bulletin*, September 1990, pp. 233–256; A. H. Eagly and S. J. Karau, "Gender and the Emergence of Leaders: A Meta-analysis," *Journal of Personality and Social Psychology*, May 1991, pp. 685–710; J. B. Rosener, "Ways Women Lead," *Harvard Business Review*, November–December 1990, pp. 119–125; "Debate: Ways Men and Women Lead," *Harvard Business Review*, January–February 1991, pp. 150–160; A. H. Eagly, M. G. Makhijani, and B. G. Klonsky, "Gender and the Evaluation of Leaders: A Meta-analysis," *Psychological Bulletin*, January 1992, pp. 3–22; A. H. Eagly, S. J. Karau, and B. T. Johnson, "Gender and Leadership Style among School Principals: A Meta-analysis," *Educational Administration Quarterly*, February 1992, pp. 76–102; L. R. Offermann and C. Beil, "Achievement Styles of Women Leaders and Their Peers," *Psychology of Women Quarterly*, March 1992, pp. 37–56; T. Melamed and N. Bozionelos, "Gender Differences in the Personality Features of British Managers," *Psychological Reports*, December 1992, pp. 979–986; G. N. Powell, *Women & Men in Management*, 2nd ed. (Thousand Oaks, CA: Sage, 1993); R. L. Kent and S. E. Moss, "Effects of Size and Gender Role on Leader Emergence," *Academy of Management Journal*, October 1994, pp. 1335–1346; C. Lee, "The Feminization of Management," *Training*, November 1994, pp. 25–31; H. Collingwood, "Women as Managers: Not Just Different, Better," *Working Woman*, November 1995, p. 14; and J. B. Rosener, *America's Competitive Secret: Women Managers* (New York: Oxford University Press, 1995).

130 A. H. Eagly, "Female Leadership Advantage and Disadvantage: Resolving the Contradictions," *Psychology of Women Quarterly*, March 2007, pp. 1–12; and A. H. Eagly, M. C. Johannesen-Schmidt, and M. L. van Engen, "Transformational, Transactional, and Laissez-Faire Leadership Styles: A Meta-analysis Comparing Women and Men," *Psychological Bulletin*, July 2003, pp. 569–591.

131 O. A. O'Neill and C. A. O'Reilly III, "Reducing the Backlash Effect: Self-Monitoring and Women's Promotions," *Journal of Occupational and Organizational Psychology*, January 11, 2011, published online before print.

132 "'Macho' Women Face Backlash at Work, Researchers Find," *ScienceDaily*, http://www.sciencedaily.com/releases/2011/01/110119114954.htm

133 B. Orser, *Creating High Performance Organizations: Leveraging Women's Leadership* (Ottawa: The Conference Board of Canada, 2000).

134 J. M. Norvilitis and H. M. Reid, "Evidence for an Association between Gender-Role Identity and a Measure of Executive Function," *Psychological Reports*, February 2002, pp. 35–45; W. H. Decker and D. M. Rotondo, "Relationships among Gender, Type of Humor, and Perceived Leader Effectiveness," *Journal of Managerial Issues*, Winter 2001, pp. 450–465; H. Aguinis and S. K. R. Adams, "Social-Role versus Structural Models of Gender and Influence Use in Organizations: A Strong Inference Approach," *Group & Organization Management*, December 1998, pp. 414–446; and A. H. Eagly, S. J. Karau, and M. G. Makhijani, "Gender and the Effectiveness of Leaders: A Meta-analysis," *Psychological Bulletin* 117 (1995), pp. 125–145.

135 A. H. Eagly, M. C. Johannesen-Schmidt, and M. L. van Engen, "Transformational, Transactional, and Laissez-Faire Leadership Styles: A Meta-analysis Comparing Women and Men," *Psychological Bulletin* 129, no. 4 (July 2003), pp. 569–591; K. M. Bartol, D. C. Martin, and J. A. Kromkowski, "Leadership and the Glass Ceiling: Gender and Ethnic Influences on Leader Behaviors at Middle and Executive Managerial Levels," *Journal of Leadership & Organizational Studies*, Winter 2003, pp. 8–19; and R. Sharpe, "As Leaders, Women Rule," *BusinessWeek*, November 20, 2000, pp. 74–84.

136 M. Javidan, P. W. Dorfman, M. S. de Luque, and R. J. House, "In the Eye of the Beholder: Cross Cultural Lessons in Leadership from Project GLOBE," *Academy of Management Perspectives*, February 2006, pp. 67–90.

137 D. E. Carl and M. Javidan, "Universality of Charismatic Leadership: A Multi-Nation Study" (paper presented at the National Academy of Management Conference, Washington, DC, August 2001), p. 29; and R. J. House, M. Javidan, P. Hanges, and P. Dorfman, "Understanding Cultures and Implicit Leadership Theories across the Globe: An Introduction to Project GLOBE," *Journal of World Business*, Spring 2002, pp. 3–10.

138 N. Beccalli, "European Business Forum Asks: Do Companies Get the Leaders They Deserve?" *European Business Forum*, 2003, www.pwcglobal.com/extweb/pwcpublications.nsf/DocID/D1EC3380F589844585256D7300346A1B

139 The material in this section is based on J. Grant, "Women as Managers: What They Can Offer to Organizations," *Organizational Dynamics*, Winter 1988, pp. 56–63; S. Helgesen, *The Female Advantage: Women's Ways of Leadership* (New York: Doubleday, 1990); A. H. Eagly and B. T. Johnson, "Gender and Leadership Style: A Meta-analysis," *Psychological Bulletin*, September 1990, pp. 233–256; A. H. Eagly and S. J. Karau, "Gender and the Emergence of Leaders: A Meta-analysis," *Journal of Personality and Social Psychology*, May 1991, pp. 685–710; J. B. Rosener, "Ways Women Lead," *Harvard Business Review*, November–December 1990, pp. 119–125; "Debate: Ways Men and Women Lead," *Harvard Business Review*, January–February 1991, pp. 150–160; A. H. Eagly, M. G. Makhijani, and B. G. Klonsky, "Gender and the Evaluation of Leaders: A Meta-analysis," *Psychological*

Bulletin, January 1992, pp. 3–22; A. H. Eagly, S. J. Karau, and B. T. Johnson, "Gender and Leadership Style among School Principals: A Meta-analysis," *Educational Administration Quarterly*, February 1992, pp. 76–102; L. R. Offermann and C. Beil, "Achievement Styles of Women Leaders and Their Peers," *Psychology of Women Quarterly*, March 1992, pp. 37–56; T. Melamed and N. Bozionelos, "Gender Differences in the Personality Features of British Managers," *Psychological Reports*, December 1992, pp. 979–986; G. N. Powell, *Women & Men in Management*, 2nd ed. (Thousand Oaks, CA: Sage, 1993); R. L. Kent and S. E. Moss, "Effects of Size and Gender Role on Leader Emergence," *Academy of Management Journal*, October 1994, pp. 1335–1346; C. Lee, "The Feminization of Management," *Training*, November 1994, pp. 25–31; H. Collingwood, "Women as Managers: Not Just Different: Better," *Working Woman*, November 1995, p. 14; and J. B. Rosener, *America's Competitive Secret: Women Managers* (New York: Oxford University Press, 1995).

140 Based on R. D. Arvey, Z. Zhang, and B. J. Avolio, "Developmental and Genetic Determinants of Leadership Role Occupancy among Women," *Journal of Applied Psychology*, May 2007, pp. 693–706.

141 M. Pandya, "Warren Buffett on Investing and Leadership: I'm Wired for This Game," *Wharton Leadership Digest* 3, no. 7 (April 1999), http://leadership.wharton.upenn.edu/digest/04-99.shtml

142 This exercise is based on J. M. Howell and P. J. Frost, "A Laboratory Study of Charismatic Leadership," *Organizational Behavior and Human Decision Processes*, April 1989, pp. 243–269.

143 Based on T. W. Martin, "Whole Foods to Sell 31 Stores in FTC Deal," *Wall Street Journal*, March 7, 2009, p. B5; M. Fraser and S. Dutta, "Yes, CEOs Should Facebook and Twitter," *Forbes*, March 11, 2009, http://www.forbes.com; D. Kesmodel and J. R. Wilke, "Whole Foods Is Hot, Wild Oats a Dud—So Said 'Rahodeb,'" *Wall Street Journal*, July 12, 2007, pp. A1, A10; and G. Farrell and P. Davidson, "Whole Foods' CEO Was Busy Guy Online," *USA Today*, July 13, 2007, p. 4B.

144 Based on D. Koeppel, "A Tough Transition: Friend to Supervisor," *New York Times*, March 16, 2003, p. BU-12.

145 Based on J. Hollon, "Leading Well Is Simple," *Workforce Management*, November 6, 2006, p. 50; M. Czarnecka "The Cable Guy," *AlbertaVenture.com*, September 1, 2011; A. Pomeroy, "CEOs Show Sensitive Side," *HR Magazine*, August 2006, p. 14; J. Marquez, "Kindness Pays . . . Or Does It?" *Workforce Management*, June 25, 2007, pp. 40–41; and http://www.gwu.edu/staticfile/GW/Mediaroom/PDFs/2011/battleground-questionnaire-results-0516.pdf

146 Based on J. M. Howell and P. J. Frost, "A Laboratory Study of Charismatic Leadership," *Organizational Behavior and Human Decision Processes*, April 1989, pp. 243–269.

Chapter 12

1 Vignette based on J. Warrillow, "Reframe a Supply Problem to Build Anticipation," *Globe and Mail*, October 5, 2011, http://www.theglobeandmail.com/report-on-business/small-business/sb-growth/day-today/reframe-a-supply-problem-to-build-anticipation/article2190385/; and J. Warrillow, *Built to Sell: Creating a Business That Can Thrive without You* (New York: Portfolio, 2011).

2 See H. A. Simon, "Rationality in Psychology and Economics," *Journal of Business*, October 1986, pp. 209–224; and A. Langley, "In Search of Rationality: The Purposes Behind the Use of Formal Analysis in Organizations," *Administrative Science Quarterly*, December 1989, pp. 598–631.

3 For a review of the rational decision-making model, see E. F. Harrison, *The Managerial Decision Making Process*, 5th ed. (Boston: Houghton Mifflin, 1999), pp. 75–102.

4 https://www.cibc.com/ca/inside-cibc/community-matters/funding-guidelines.html

5 J. G. March, *A Primer on Decision Making* (New York: Free Press, 1994), pp. 2–7.

6 Vignette based on J. Warrillow, "Reframe a Supply Problem to Build Anticipation," *Globe and Mail*, October 5, 2011, http://www.theglobeandmail.com/report-on-business/small-business/sb-growth/day-today/reframe-a-supply-problem-to-build-anticipation/article2190385/

7 D. L. Rados, "Selection and Evaluation of Alternatives in Repetitive Decision Making," *Administrative Science Quarterly*, June 1972, pp. 196–206.

8 M. Bazerman, *Judgment in Managerial Decision Making*, 3rd ed. (New York: Wiley, 1994), p. 5.

9 J. E. Russo, K. A. Carlson, and M. G. Meloy, "Choosing an Inferior Alternative," *Psychological Science* 17, no. 10 (2006), pp. 899–904.

10 See, for instance, L. R. Beach, *The Psychology of Decision Making* (Thousand Oaks, CA: Sage, 1997).

11 See H. A. Simon, *Administrative Behavior*, 4th ed. (New York: Free Press, 1997); and M. Augier, "Simon Says: Bounded Rationality Matters," *Journal of Management Inquiry*, September 2001, pp. 268–275.

12 G. Gigerenzer, "Why Heuristics Work," *Perspectives on Psychological Science* 3, no. 1 (2008), pp. 20–29; and A. K. Shah and D. M. Oppenheimer, "Heuristics Made Easy: An Effort-Reduction Framework," *Psychological Bulletin* 134, no. 2 (2008), pp. 207–222.

13 See T. Gilovich, D. Griffin, and D. Kahneman, *Heuristics and Biases: The Psychology of Intuitive Judgment* (New York: Cambridge University Press, 2002).

14 E. Dane and M. G. Pratt, "Exploring Intuition and Its Role in Managerial Decision Making," *Academy of Management Review* 32, no. 1 (2007), pp. 33–54.

15 P. D. Brown, "Some Hunches About Intuition," *New York Times* (November 17, 2007), p. B5.

16 P. D. Brown, "Some Hunches About Intuition," *New York Times* (November 17, 2007), p. B5.

17 L. A. Burke and M. K. Miller, "Taking the Mystery Out of Intuitive Decision Making," *Academy of Management Executive*, November 1999, pp. 91–99.

18 See, for instance, L. A. Burke and M. K. Miller, "Taking the Mystery Out of Intuitive Decision Making," *Academy of Management Executive*, November 1999, pp. 91–99; N. Khatri and H. A. Ng, "The Role of Intuition in Strategic Decision Making," *Human Relations*, January 2000, pp. 57–86; J. A. Andersen, "Intuition in Managers: Are Intuitive Managers More Effective?" *Journal of Managerial Psychology* 15, no. 1–2 (2000), pp. 46–63; D. Myers, *Intuition: Its Powers and Perils* (New Haven, CT: Yale University Press, 2002); and L. Simpson, "Basic Instincts," *Training*, January 2003, pp. 56–59.

19 See, for instance, L. A. Burke and M. K. Miller, "Taking the Mystery Out of Intuitive Decision Making," *Academy of Management Executive*, November 1999, pp. 91–99.

20 B. D. Dunn and H. C. Galton, "Listening to Your Heart: How Interoception Shapes Emotion Experience and Intuitive Decision Making," *Psychological Science* 21 no. 12 (December 2010), pp. 1835–1844.

21 S. P. Robbins, *Decide & Conquer: Making Winning Decisions and Taking Control of Your Life* (Upper Saddle River, NJ: Financial Times/Prentice Hall, 2004), p. 13.

22 Based on P. Cohen, "Stand Still: Use Penalty-Kick Wisdom to Make Your Decisions," *National Post*, March 8, 2008, p. FW9.

23 S. Plous, *The Psychology of Judgment and Decision Making* (New York: McGraw-Hill, 1993), p. 217.

24 S. Lichtenstein and B. Fischhoff, "Do Those Who Know More Also Know More About How Much They Know?" *Organizational Behavior and Human Performance*, December 1977, pp. 159–183.

25 B. Fischhoff, P. Slovic, and S. Lichtenstein, "Knowing with Certainty: The Appropriateness of Extreme Confidence," *Journal of Experimental Psychology: Human Perception and Performance*, November 1977, pp. 552–564.

26 J. Kruger and D. Dunning, "Unskilled and Unaware of It: How Difficulties in Recognizing One's Own Incompetence Lead to Inflated Self-Assessments," *Journal of Personality and Social Psychology*, November 1999, pp. 1121–1134.

27 B. Fischhoff, P. Slovic, and S. Lichtenstein, "Knowing with Certainty: The Appropriateness of Extreme Confidence," *Journal of Experimental Psychology* 3 (1977), pp. 552–564.

28 J. Kruger and D. Dunning, "Unskilled and Unaware of It: How Difficulties in Recognizing One's Own Incompetence Lead to Inflated Self-Assessments," *Journal of Personality and Social Psychology*, November 1999, pp. 1121–1134.

29 See, for instance, A. Tversky and D. Kahneman, "Judgment under Uncertainty: Heuristics and Biases," *Science*, September 1974, pp. 1124–1131.

30 J. S. Hammond, R. L. Keeney, and H. Raiffa, *Smart Choices* (Boston: HBS Press, 1999), p. 191.

31 R. Hastie, D. A. Schkade, and J. W. Payne, "Juror Judgments in Civil Cases: Effects of Plaintiff's Requests and Plaintiff's Identity on Punitive Damage Awards," *Law and Human Behavior*, August 1999, pp. 445–470.

32 C. Janiszewski and D. Uy, "Precision of the Anchor Influences the Amount of Adjustment," *Psychological Science* 19, no. 2 (2008), pp. 121–127.

33 See R. S. Nickerson, "Confirmation Bias: A Ubiquitous Phenomenon in Many Guises," *Review of General Psychology*, June 1998, pp. 175–220; and E. Jonas, S. Schultz-Hardt, D. Frey, and N. Thelen, "Confirmation Bias in Sequential Information Search after Preliminary Decisions," *Journal of Personality and Social Psychology*, April 2001, pp. 557–571.

34 B. Nyhan and J. Reifler, "When Corrections Fail: The Persistence of Political Misperceptions," *Political Behavior* 32, no. 2 (2010), pp. 303–330.

35 See A. Tversky and D. Kahneman, "Availability: A Heuristic for Judging Frequency and Probability," in *Judgment under Uncertainty: Heuristics and Biases*, ed. D. Kahneman, P. Slovic, and A. Tversky (Cambridge, UK: Cambridge University Press, 1982), pp. 163–178; and B. J. Bushman and G. L. Wells, "Narrative Impressions of Literature: The Availability Bias and the Corrective Properties of Meta-analytic Approaches," *Personality and Social Psychology Bulletin*, September 2001, pp. 1123–1130.

36 See B. M. Staw, "The Escalation of Commitment to a Course of Action," *Academy of Management Review*, October 1981, pp. 577–587; and H. Moon, "Looking Forward and Looking Back: Integrating Completion and Sunk-Cost Effects within an Escalation-of-Commitment Progress Decision," *Journal of Applied Psychology*, February 2001, pp. 104–113.

37 B. M. Staw, "Knee-Deep in the Big Muddy: A Study of Escalating Commitment to a Chosen Course of Action," *Organizational Behavior and Human Performance* 16 (1976), pp. 27–44; and B. M. Staw, "The Escalation of Commitment: An Update and Appraisal," in *Organizational Decision Making*, ed. Z. Shapira (New York; Cambridge University Press, 1997), pp. 121–215.

38 K. F. E. Wong and J. Y. Y. Kwong, "The Role of Anticipated Regret in Escalation of Commitment," *Journal of Applied Psychology* 92, no. 2 (2007), pp. 545–554.

39 K. F. E. Wong, J. Y. Y. Kwong, and C. K. Ng, "When Thinking Rationally Increases Biases: The Role of Rational Thinking Style in Escalation of Commitment," *Applied Psychology: An International Review* 57, no. 2 (2008), pp. 246–271.

40 See, for instance, A. James and A. Wells, "Death Beliefs, Superstitious Beliefs and Health Anxiety," *British Journal of Clinical Psychology*, March 2002, pp. 43–53.

41 http://lilomag.com/2011/06/04/10-most-superstitious-famous-athletes/

42 See, for example, D. J. Keys and B. Schwartz, "Leaky Rationality: How Research on Behavioral Decision Making Challenges Normative Standards of Rationality," *Psychological Science* 2, no. 2 (2007), pp. 162–180; and U. Simonsohn, "Direct Risk Aversion: Evidence from Risky Prospects Valued Below Their Worst Outcome," *Psychological Science* 20, no. 6 (2009), pp. 686–692.

43 J. K. Maner, M. T. Gailliot, D. A. Butz, and B. M. Peruche, "Power, Risk, and the Status Quo: Does Power Promote Riskier or More Conservative Decision Making," *Personality and Social Psychology Bulletin* 33, no. 4 (2007), pp. 451–462.

44 A. Chakraborty, S. Sheikh, and N. Subramanian, "Termination Risk and Managerial Risk Taking," *Journal of Corporate Finance* 13, (2007), pp. 170–188.

45 X. He and V. Mittal, "The Effect of Decision Risk and Project Stage on Escalation of Commitment," *Organizational Behavior and Human Decision Processes* 103, no. 2 (2007), pp. 225–237.

46 D. Kahneman and A. Tversky, "Prospect Theory: An Analysis of Decisions under Risk," *Econometrica* 47, no. 2 (1979), pp. 263–291; and P. Bryant and R. Dunford, "The Influence of Regulatory Focus on Risky Decision-Making," *Applied Psychology: An International Review* 57, no. 2 (2008), pp. 335–359.

47 A. J. Porcelli and M. R. Delgado, "Acute Stress Modulates Risk Taking in Financial Decision Making," *Psychological Science* 20, no. 3 (2009), pp. 278–283.

48 S. P. Robbins, *Decide & Conquer: Making Winning Decisions and Taking Control of Your Life* (Upper Saddle River, NJ: Financial Times/Prentice Hall, 2004), pp. 164–168.

49 R. L. Guilbault, F. B. Bryant, J. H. Brockway, and E. J. Posavac, "A Meta-analysis of Research on Hindsight Bias," *Basic and Applied Social Psychology*, September 2004, pp. 103–117; and L. Werth, F. Strack, and J. Foerster, "Certainty and Uncertainty: The Two Faces of the Hindsight Bias," *Organizational Behavior and Human Decision Processes*, March 2002, pp. 323–341.

50 M. Gladwell, "Connecting the Dots," *New Yorker*, March 10, 2003.

51 See S. A. Mohrman, D. Finegold, and J. A. Klein, "Designing the Knowledge Enterprise: Beyond Programs and Tools," *Organizational Dynamics* 31, no. 2 (2002), pp. 134–150; and H. Dolezalek, "Collaborating in Cyberspace," *Training*, April 2003, pp. 32–37.

52 Cited in A. Cabrera and E. F. Cabrera, "Knowledge-Sharing Dilemmas," *Organization Studies* 5, 2002, p. 687.

53 B. Roberts, "Pick Employees' Brains," *HR Magazine*, February 2000, pp. 115–116; B. Fryer, "Get Smart," *Inc.*, September 1999, p. 65; and D. Zielinski, "Have You Shared a Bright Idea Today?" *Training*, July 2000, p. 65.

54 B. Fryer, "Get Smart," *Inc.*, September 1999, p. 63.

55 C. E. Connelly, D. Zweig, J. Webster, and J. P. Trougakos, "Knowledge Hiding in Organizations," *Journal of Organizational Behavior*, January 4, 2011, published online before print, http://onlinelibrary.wiley.com/doi/10.1002/job.737/abstract

56 J. Gordon, "Intellectual Capital and You," *Training*, September 1999, p. 33.

57 D. Zielinski, "Have You Shared a Bright Idea Today?" *Training*, July 2000, pp. 65–67.

58 See N. R. F. Maier, "Assets and Liabilities in Group Problem Solving: The Need for an Integrative Function," *Psychological Review*, April 1967, pp. 239–249; G. W. Hill, "Group versus Individual Performance: Are N+1 Heads Better Than One?" *Psychological Bulletin*, May 1982, pp. 517–539; M. D. Johnson and J. R. Hollenbeck, "Collective Wisdom as an Oxymoron: Team-Based Structures as Impediments to Learning," in *Research Companion to the Dysfunctional Workplace: Management, Challenges and Symptoms*, ed. J. Langan-Fox, C. L. Cooper, and R. J. Klimoski (Northampton, MA: Edward Elgar Publishing, 2007), pp. 319–331; and R. F. Martell and M. R. Borg, "A Comparison of the Behavioral Rating Accuracy of Groups and Individuals," *Journal of Applied Psychology*, February 1993, pp. 43–50.

59 See, for example, W. C. Swap and Associates, *Group Decision Making* (Newbury Park, CA: Sage, 1984).

60 "Group Judgments," *Psychological Bulletin*, January 1997, pp. 149–167; and B. L. Bonner, S. D. Sillito, and M. R. Baumann, "Collective Estimation: Accuracy, Expertise, and Extroversion as Sources of Intra-Group Influence," *Organizational Behavior and Human Decision Processes* 103 (2007), pp. 121–133.

61 See, for example, W. C. Swap and Associates, *Group Decision Making* (Newbury Park, CA: Sage, 1984).

62 I. L. Janis, *Groupthink: Psychological Studies of Policy Decisions and Fiascoes*, 2nd ed. (Boston: Houghton Mifflin, 1982); W. Park, "A Review of Research on Groupthink," *Journal of Behavioral Decision Making*, July 1990, pp. 229–245; C. P. Neck and G. Moorhead, "Groupthink Remodeled: The Importance of Leadership, Time Pressure, and Methodical Decision Making Procedures," *Human Relations*, May 1995, pp. 537–558; and J. N. Choi and M. U. Kim, "The Organizational Application of Groupthink and Its Limits in Organizations," *Journal of Applied Psychology*, April 1999, pp. 297–306.

63 I. L. Janis, *Groupthink: Psychological Studies of Policy Decisions and Fiascoes*, 2nd ed. (Boston: Houghton Mifflin, 1982).

64 Based on J. Castaldo, "Analysis Paralysis," *Canadian Business*, May 6, 2011.

65 M. E. Turner and A. R. Pratkanis, "Mitigating Groupthink by Stimulating Constructive Conflict," in *Using Conflict in Organizations*, ed. C. De Dreu and E. Van de Vliert (London: Sage, 1997), pp. 53–71.

66 See N. R. F. Maier, *Principles of Human Relations* (New York: Wiley, 1952); N. Richardson Ahlfinger and J. K. Esser, "Testing the Groupthink Model: Effects of Promotional Leadership and Conformity Predisposition," *Social Behavior & Personality* 29, no. 1 (2001), pp. 31–41; and S. Schultz-Hardt, F. C. Brodbeck, A. Mojzisch, R. Kerschreiter, and D. Frey, "Group Decision Making in Hidden Profile Situations: Dissent as a Facilitator for Decision Quality," *Journal of Personality and Social Psychology* 91, no. 6 (2006), pp. 1080–1093.

67 J. N. Choi and M. U. Kim, "The Organizational Application of Groupthink and Its Limitations in Organizations," *Journal of Applied Psychology* 84 (1999), pp. 297–306.

68 J. Longley and D. G. Pruitt, "Groupthink: A Critique of Janis' Theory," in *Review of Personality and Social Psychology*, ed. L. Wheeler (Newbury Park, CA: Sage, 1980), pp. 507–513; and J. A. Sniezek, "Groups under Uncertainty: An Examination of Confidence in Group Decision Making," *Organizational Behavior & Human Decision Processes* 52, 1992, pp. 124–155.

69 C. McCauley, "The Nature of Social Influence in Groupthink: Compliance and Internalization," *Journal of Personality and Social Psychology* 57 (1989), pp. 250–260; P. E. Tetlock, R. S. Peterson, C. McGuire, S. Chang, and P. Feld, "Assessing Political Group Dynamics: A Test of the Groupthink Model," *Journal of Personality and Social Psychology* 63 (1992), pp. 781–796;

S. Graham, "A Review of Attribution Theory in Achievement Contexts," *Educational Psychology Review* 3 (1991), pp. 5–39; and G. Moorhead and J. R. Montanari, "An Empirical Investigation of the Groupthink Phenomenon," *Human Relations* 39 (1986), pp. 399–410.

70 J. N. Choi and M. U. Kim, "The Organizational Application of Groupthink and Its Limitations in Organizations," *Journal of Applied Psychology* 84 (1999), pp. 297–306.

71 See D. J. Isenberg, "Group Polarization: A Critical Review and Meta-analysis," *Journal of Personality and Social Psychology*, December 1986, pp. 1141–1151; J. L. Hale and F. J. Boster, "Comparing Effect Coded Models of Choice Shifts," *Communication Research Reports*, April 1988, pp. 180–186; and P. W. Paese, M. Bieser, and M. E. Tubbs, "Framing Effects and Choice Shifts in Group Decision Making," *Organizational Behavior & Human Decision Processes*, October 1993, pp. 149–165.

72 See, for example, N. Kogan and M. A. Wallach, "Risk Taking as a Function of the Situation, the Person, and the Group," in *New Directions in Psychology*, vol. 3 (New York: Holt, Rinehart and Winston, 1967); and M. A. Wallach, N. Kogan, and D. J. Bem, "Group Influence on Individual Risk Taking," *Journal of Abnormal and Social Psychology* 65 (1962), pp. 75–86.

73 R. D. Clark III, "Group-Induced Shift toward Risk: A Critical Appraisal," *Psychological Bulletin*, October 1971, pp. 251–270.

74 Z. Krizan and R. S. Baron, "Group Polarization and Choice-Dilemmas: How Important Is Self-Categorization?" *European Journal of Social Psychology* 37, no. 1 (2007), pp. 191–201.

75 N. W. Kohn and S. M. Smith, "Collaborative Fixation: Effects of Others' Ideas on Brainstorming," *Applied Cognitive Psychology* 25, no. 3 (May/June 2011), pp. 359–371.

76 N. L. Kerr and R. S. Tindale, "Group Performance and Decision-Making," *Annual Review of Psychology* 55 (2004), pp. 623–655.

77 N. W. Kohn and S. M. Smith, "Collaborative Fixation: Effects of Others' Ideas on Brainstorming," *Applied Cognitive Psychology* 25, no. 3 (May/June 2011), pp. 359–371; and S. M. Smith, "The Constraining Effects of Initial Ideas," in *Group Creativity*, ed. P. B. Paulus and B. A. Nijstad (New York: Oxford University Press, 2003), pp. 15–31.

78 R. C. Litchfield, "Brainstorming Reconsidered: A Goal-Based View," *Academy of Management Review* 33, no. 3 (2008), pp. 649–668.

79 See A. L. Delbecq, A. H. Van deVen, and D. H. Gustafson, *Group Techniques for Program Planning: A Guide to Nominal and Delphi Processes* (Glenview, IL: Scott, Foresman, 1975); and P. B. Paulus and H.-C. Yang, "Idea Generation in Groups: A Basis for Creativity in Organizations," *Organizational Behavior and Human Decision Processing*, May 2000, pp. 76–87.

80 C. Faure, "Beyond Brainstorming: Effects of Different Group Procedures on Selection of Ideas and Satisfaction with the Process," *Journal of Creative Behavior* 38 (2004), pp. 13–34.

81 See, for instance, A. R. Dennis and J. S. Valacich, "Computer Brainstorms: More Heads Are Better Than One," *Journal of Applied Psychology*, August 1993, pp. 531–537; R. B. Gallupe and W. H. Cooper, "Brainstorming Electronically," *Sloan Management Review*, Fall 1993, pp. 27–36; and A. B. Hollingshead and J. E. McGrath, "Computer-Assisted Groups: A Critical Review of the Empirical Research," in *Team Effectiveness and Decision Making in Organizations*, ed. R. A. Guzzo and E. Salas (San Francisco: Jossey-Bass, 1995), pp. 46–78.

82 B. B. Baltes, M. W. Dickson, M. P. Sherman, C. C. Bauer, and J. LaGanke, "Computer-Mediated Communication and Group Decision Making: A Meta-analysis," *Organizational Behavior and Human Decision Processes*, January 2002, pp. 156–179.

83 T. M. Amabile, "A Model of Creativity and Innovation in Organizations," in *Research in Organizational Behavior*, vol. 10, ed. B. M. Staw and L. L. Cummings (Greenwich, CT: JAI Press, 1988),

p. 126; and J. E. Perry-Smith and C. E. Shalley, "The Social Side of Creativity: A Static and Dynamic Social Network Perspective," *Academy of Management Review*, January 2003, pp. 89–106.

84 G. J. Feist and F. X. Barron, "Predicting Creativity from Early to Late Adulthood: Intellect, Potential, and Personality," *Journal of Research in Personality*, April 2003, pp. 62–88.

85 R. W. Woodman, J. E. Sawyer, and R. W. Griffin, "Toward a Theory of Organizational Creativity," *Academy of Management Review*, April 1993, p. 298; J. M. George and J. Zhou, "When Openness to Experience and Conscientiousness Are Related to Creative Behavior: An Interactional Approach," *Journal of Applied Psychology*, June 2001, pp. 513–524; and E. F. Rietzschel, C. K. W. de Dreu, and B. A. Nijstad, "Personal Need for Structure and Creative Performance: The Moderating Influence of Fear of Invalidity," *Personality and Social Psychology Bulletin*, June 2007, pp. 855–866.

86 Cited in C. G. Morris, *Psychology: An Introduction*, 9th ed. (Upper Saddle River, NJ: Prentice Hall, 1996), p. 344.

87 This section is based on T. M. Amabile, "Motivating Creativity in Organizations: On Doing What You Love and Loving What You Do," *California Management Review* 40, no. 1 (Fall 1997), pp. 39–58.

88 G. Keenan, "GM Shows a Nimble Touch in Oshawa," *Globe and Mail*, March 27, 2010. Caption from GM: "Auto workers at the General Motors Canada assembly line in Oshawa, Ont."

89 M. Baas, C. K. W. De Dreu, and B. A. Nijstad, "A Meta-analysis of 25 Years of Mood-Creativity Research: Hedonic Tone, Activation, or Regulatory Focus?" *Psychological Bulletin* 134, no. 6 (2008), pp. 779–806.

90 J. Zhou, "When the Presence of Creative Coworkers Is Related to Creativity: Role of Supervisor Close Monitoring, Developmental Feedback, and Creative Personality," *Journal of Applied Psychology* 88, no. 3 (June 2003), pp. 413–422.

91 J. E. Perry-Smith, "Social Yet Creative: The Role of Social Relationships in Facilitating Individual Creativity," *Academy of Management Journal* 49, no. 1 (2006), pp. 85–101.

92 G. Park, D. Lubinski, and C. P. Benbow, "Contrasting Intellectual Patterns Predict Creativity in the Arts and Sciences," *Psychological Science* 18, no. 11 (2007), pp. 948–952.

93 W. J. J. Gordon, *Synectics* (New York: Harper & Row, 1961).

94 See C. E. Shalley, J. Zhou, and G. R. Oldham, "The Effects of Personal and Contextual Characteristics on Creativity: Where Should We Go from Here?" *Journal of Management*, November 2004, pp. 933–958; G. Hirst, D. Van Knippenberg, and J. Zhou, "A Cross-Level Perspective on Employee Creativity: Goal Orientation, Team Learning Behavior, and Individual Creativity," *Academy of Management Journal* 52, no. 2 (2009), pp. 280–293; and C. E. Shalley, L. L. Gilson, and T. C. Blum, "Interactive Effects of Growth Need Strength, Work Context, and Job Complexity on Self-Reported Creative Performance," *Academy of Management Journal* 52, no. 3 (2009), pp. 489–505.

95 Cited in T. Stevens, "Creativity Killers," *IndustryWeek*, January 23, 1995, p. 63.

96 M. Strauss, "Retailers Tap into War-Room Creativity of Employees," *Globe and Mail*, March 12, 2007, p. B1.

97 Vignette based on A. Trang, "'Kick Ass' Coffee," *Advantage*, November-December 2011, pp. 75–76; and http://www.kickinghorsecoffee.com/en/story

98 P. L. Schumann, "A Moral Principles Framework for Human Resource Management Ethics," *Human Resource Management Review* 11 (Spring–Summer 2001), pp. 93–111; M. G. Velasquez, *Business Ethics*, 4th ed. (Upper Saddle River, NJ: Prentice Hall, 1998), Chapter 2; and G. F. Cavanagh, D. J. Moberg, and M. Valasquez, "The Ethics of Organizational Politics," *Academy of Management Journal*, June 1981, pp. 363–374.

99 P. L. Schumann, "A Moral Principles Framework for Human Resource Management Ethics," *Human Resource Management Review* 11 (Spring–Summer 2001), pp. 93–111.

100 See, for example, T. Machan, ed., *Commerce and Morality* (Totowa, NJ: Rowman and Littlefield, 1988).

101 L. K. Trevino, "Ethical Decision Making in Organizations: A Person-Situation Interactionist Model," *Academy of Management Review*, July 1986, pp. 601–617; and L. K. Trevino and S. A. Youngblood, "Bad Apples in Bad Barrels: A Causal Analysis of Ethical Decision Making Behavior," *Journal of Applied Psychology*, August 1990, pp. 378–385.

102 See L. Kohlberg, *Essays in Moral Development: The Philosophy of Moral Development*, vol. 1 (New York: Harper and Row, 1981); L. Kohlberg, *Essays in Moral Development: The Psychology of Moral Development*, vol. 2 (New York: Harper and Row, 1984); and R. S. Snell, "Complementing Kohlberg: Mapping the Ethical Reasoning Used by Managers for Their Own Dilemma Cases," *Human Relations*, January 1996, pp. 23–49.

103 L. Kohlberg, *Essays in Moral Development: The Philosophy of Moral Development*, vol. 1 (New York: Harper and Row, 1981); L. Kohlberg, *Essays in Moral Development: The Philosophy of Moral Development*, vol. 2 (New York: Harper and Row, 1984); and R. S. Snell, "Complementing Kohlberg: Mapping the Ethical Reasoning Used by Managers for Their Own Dilemma Cases," *Human Relations*, January 1996, pp. 23–49.

104 J. Weber, "Managers' Moral Reasoning: Assessing Their Responses to Three Moral Dilemmas," *Human Relations*, July 1990, pp. 687–702; and S. B. Knouse and R. A. Giacalone, "Ethical Decision-Making in Business: Behavioral Issues and Concerns," *Journal of Business Ethics*, May 1992, pp. 369–377.

105 R. Teper, M. Inzlicht, and E. Page-Gould, "Are We More Moral Than We Think? Exploring the Role of Affect in Moral Behavior and Moral Forecasting," *Psychological Science*, April 2011.

106 J. O'Neill, "Canadian Forces Distributing Ethics Guide," *Vancouver Sun*, March 3, 2010.

107 This discussion is based on G. F. Cavanagh, D. J. Moberg, and M. Valasquez, "The Ethics of Organizational Politics," *Academy of Management Journal*, June 1981, pp. 363–374.

108 Vignette based on J. Warrillow, "Reframe a Supply Problem to Build Anticipation," *Globe and Mail*, October 5, 2011, http://www.theglobeandmail.com/report-on-business/small-business/sb-growth/day-today/reframe-a-supply-problem-to-build-anticipation/article2190385/

109 J. Castaldo, "Those Emotional Canadians!" *Canadian Business*, May 10, 2010, pp. 32–33.

110 M. McClearn, "Brands We Trust: On a First-Name Basis," *Canadian Business*, April 7, 2011.

111 M. Friedman, *Capitalism and Freedom* (Chicago: University of Chicago Press, 1962).

112 J. Bakan, *The Corporation* (Toronto: Big Picture Media Corporation, 2003).

113 J. Nelson, "The CEO Poll: Should Companies Give to Charity?" *Canadian Business*, April 7, 2011.

114 J. Castaldo, "The CEO Poll: The Trouble with Outsourcing," *Canadian Business*, April 7, 2011.

115 http://www.greenbiz.com/news/2006/10/26/survey-shows-mba-students-believe-business-should-be-agent-social-change

116 M. J. Gelfand, M. Erez, and Z. Aycan, "Cross-Cultural Organizational Behavior," *Annual Review of Psychology*, January 2007, pp. 479–514; and A. S. Tsui, S. S. Nifadkar, and A. Y. Ou, "Cross-National, Cross-Cultural Organizational Behavior Research: Advances, Gaps, and Recommendations," *Journal of Management*, June 2007, pp. 426–478.

117 N. J. Adler, *International Dimensions of Organizational Behavior*, 4th ed. (Cincinnati, OH: South-Western Publishing, 2002), pp. 182–189.

118 T. Jackson, "Cultural Values and Management Ethics: A 10-Nation Study," *Human Relations*, October 2001, pp. 1267–1302; see also J. B. Cullen, K. P. Parboteeah, and M. Hoegl, "Cross-National Differences in Managers' Willingness to Justify Ethically Suspect Behaviors: A Test of Institutional Anomie Theory," *Academy of Management Journal*, June 2004, pp. 411–421.

119 W. Chow Hou, "To Bribe or Not to Bribe?" *Asia, Inc.*, October 1996, p. 104.

120 P. Digh, "Shades of Gray in the Global Marketplace," *HR Magazine*, April 1997, p. 91.

121 T. Donaldson, "Values in Tension: Ethics Away from Home," *Harvard Business Review*, September–October 1996, pp. 48–62.

122 http://www.transparency.org/content/download/61106/978536

123 Based on T. Gilovich, V. H. Medvec, and D. Kahneman, "Varieties of Regret: A Debate and Partial Resolution," *Psychological Review* 105 (1998), pp. 602–605. See also M. Tsiros and V. Mittal, "Regret: A Model of Its Antecedents and Consequences in Consumer Decision Making," *Journal of Consumer Research*, March 2000, pp. 401–417.

124 Several of these scenarios are based on D. R. Altany, "Torn between Halo and Horns," *IndustryWeek*, March 15, 1993, pp. 15–20.

125 Based on C. Hawn, "Fear and Posing," *Forbes*, March 25, 2002, pp. 22–25; and J. Sandberg, "Some Ideas Are So Bad That Only Team Efforts Can Account for Them," *Wall Street Journal*, September 29, 2004, p. B1.

126 Based on J. Calano and J. Salzman, "Ten Ways to Fire Up Your Creativity," *Working Woman*, July 1989, p. 94; J. V. Anderson, "Mind Mapping: A Tool for Creative Thinking," *Business Horizons*, January–February 1993, pp. 42–46; M. Loeb, "Ten Commandments for Managing Creative People," *Fortune*, January 16, 1995, pp. 135–136; and M. Henricks, "Good Thinking," *Entrepreneur*, May 1996, pp. 70–73.

OB on the Edge: Spirituality in the Workplace

1 Vignette based on J. Mawhinney, "Style with Heart and Soul; Spiritual Beliefs Guide Their Work," *Toronto Star*, September 1, 2005, p. E4.

2 I. I. Mitroff and E. A. Denton, "A Study of Spirituality in the Workplace," *Sloan Management Review*, Summer 1999, pp. 83–92.

3 I. I. Mitroff and E. A. Denton, "A Study of Spirituality in the Workplace," *Sloan Management Review*, Summer 1999, pp. 83–92.

4 W. J. Harrington, R. C. Preziosi, and D. J. Gooden, "Perceptions of Workplace Spirituality among Professionals and Executives," *Employee Responsibilities and Rights Journal* 13, no. 3 (2001), p. 156.

5 W. J. Harrington, R. C. Preziosi, and D. J. Gooden, "Perceptions of Workplace Spirituality among Professionals and Executives," *Employee Responsibilities and Rights Journal* 13, no. 3 (2001), p. 156.

6 Rice University, "More Than 20 Percent of Atheist Scientists Are 'Spiritual,' Study Finds," *ScienceDaily*, May 5, 2011, http://www.sciencedaily.com/releases/2011/05/110505124039.htm; and E. H. Ecklund and E. Long, "Scientists and Spirituality," *Sociology of Religion* 72, no. 3 (2011), pp. 253–274.

7 D. P. Ashmos and D. Duchon, "Spirituality at Work: A Conceptualization and Measure," *Journal of Management Inquiry*, June 2000, p. 139; and E. Poole, "Organisational Spirituality: A

Literature Review," *Journal of Business Ethics* 84, no. 4 (2009), pp. 577–588.

8 Information in this section based on I. I. Mitroff and E. A. Denton, "A Study of Spirituality in the Workplace," *Sloan Management Review*, Summer 1999, pp. 83–92.

9 P. Preville, "For God's Sake," *Canadian Business*, June 25–July 9, 1999, p. 58.

10 P. Preville, "For God's Sake," *Canadian Business*, June 25–July 9, 1999, p. 60.

11 C. E. Kerr, S. R. Jones, Q. Wan, D. L. Pritchett, R. H. Wasserman, A. Wexler, J. J. Villanueva, J. R. Shaw, S. W. Lazar, T. J. Kaptchuk, R. Littenberg, M. S. Hämäläinen, and C. I. Moore. "Effects of Mindfulness Meditation Training on Anticipatory Alpha Modulation in Primary Somatosensory Cortex," *Brain Research Bulletin* 85, no. 3–4 (May 2011), pp. 96–103.

12 Massachusetts General Hospital, "Meditation May Help the Brain 'Turn Down the Volume' on Distractions," *ScienceDaily*, April 21, 2011, http://www.sciencedaily.com/releases/2011/04/110421122337.htm

13 A. Esposito, "Doing Well and Doing Good [Aaron Feuerstein Spirituality & Business Award]," *Financial Post (National Post)*, March 30, 2001, p. C2.

14 F. Zeidan, K. T. Martucci, R. A. Kraft, N. S. Gordon, J. G. McHaffie, and R. C. Coghill, "Brain Mechanisms Supporting the Modulation of Pain by Mindfulness Meditation," *Journal of Neuroscience* 31, no. 14 (2011), pp. 5540–5548; E. Luders, K. Clark, K. L. Narr, and A. W. Toga. "Enhanced Brain Connectivity in Long-Term Meditation Practitioners," *NeuroImage* 57, no. 4 (August 2011), pp. 1308–1316; and J. A. Grant, J. Courtemanche, E. G. Duerden, G. H. Duncan, and P. Rainville, "Cortical Thickness and Pain Sensitivity in Zen Meditators," *Emotion* 10, no. 1 (2010), pp. 43–53.

15 B. K. Hölzel, J. Carmody, M. Vangel, C. Congleton, S. M. Yerramsetti, T. Gard, and S. W. Lazar, "Mindfulness Practice Leads to Increases in Regional Brain Gray Matter Density," *Psychiatry Research: Neuroimaging* 191, no. 1 (2011), pp. 36–43.

16 Example based on J. White, "Soul@Work: As We Begin a New Century, Do You Know How to Bring out the Best in Your Employees?" *Benefits Canada*, January 2000, p. 17.

17 T. Helliwell, *Take Your Soul to Work* (Toronto: Random House Canada, 1999).

18 V. Ligo, "Configuring a Christian Spirituality of Work," *Theology Today*, 2011, pp. 441–466.

19 L. Fowlie, "Spirituality Centre Is Canadian First," *National Post*, November 22, 2004, p. FP10.

20 J. Myers, "Raising Spirituality in the Workplace," *Globe and Mail*, November 14, 2009, p. B15.

21 W. Duggleby, D. Cooper, and K. Penz. "Hope, Self-Efficacy, Spiritual Well-Being and Job Satisfaction," *Journal of Advanced Nursing* 65, no. 11 (November 2009), pp. 2376–2385.

22 B. Harvey, "Sister Mangalam Lena Believes Spiritual Care Is an Essential Part of Health Care, In and Out of the Hospital," *Canadian Press Newswire*, April 10, 2001.

23 C. Silverman, "Spirituality Inc.," *Globe and Mail*, April 21, 2008, p. L3.

24 J. Myers, "Raising Spirituality in the Workplace," *Globe and Mail*, November 14, 2009, p. B15.

25 C. Silverman, "Spirituality Inc.," *Globe and Mail*, April 21, 2008, p. L3.

26 This section is based on I. I. Mitroff and E. A. Denton, *A Spiritual Audit of Corporate America: A Hard Look at Spirituality, Religion, and Values in the Workplace* (San Francisco: Jossey-Bass, 1999); J. Milliman, J. Ferguson, D. Trickett, and B. Condemi, "Spirit and Community at Southwest Airlines: An Investigation of a

Spiritual Values-Based Model," *Journal of Organizational Change Management* 12, no. 3 (1999), pp. 221–233; and E. H. Burack, "Spirituality in the Workplace," *Journal of Organizational Change Management* 12, no. 3 (1999), pp. 280–291.

27 M. McKee, "Northwood–Organizational Innovation on the Spirituality Front," *Newsletter for the Center for Spirituality and the Workplace* (St. Mary's University), June 2006.

28 A. Daniels, "Textile Importer Defends Artisans' Rights," *Vancouver Sun*, May 1, 2000, pp. C8, C10.

29 J. Myers, "Raising Spirituality in the Workplace," *Globe and Mail*, November 14, 2009, p. B15 (based on Statistics Canada 2006 data).

30 Cited in F. Wagner-Marsh and J. Conley, "The Fourth Wave: The Spiritually-Based Firm," *Journal of Organizational Change Management* 12, no. 3 (1999), p. 295.

31 M. Conlin, "Religion in the Workplace: The Growing Presence of Spirituality in Corporate America," *BusinessWeek*, November 1, 1999, pp. 151–158; and P. Paul, "A Holier Holiday Season," *American Demographics*, December 2001, pp. 41–45.

32 M. C. McKee, "Workplace Spirituality," *Workplace Review*, November 2006, http://www.smu.ca/academic/sobey/workplacereview/nov2006/WorkplaceSpirituality.pdf

33 I. I. Mitroff and E. A. Denton, *A Spiritual Audit of Corporate America: A Hard Look at Spirituality, Religion, and Values in the Workplace* (San Francisco: Jossey-Bass, 1999).

34 M. Conlin, "Religion in the Workplace: The Growing Presence of Spirituality in Corporate America," *BusinessWeek*, November 1, 1999, pp. 151–158; and P. Paul, "A Holier Holiday Season," *American Demographics*, December 2001, pp. 41–45.

35 Cited in M. Conlin, "Religion in the Workplace: The Growing Presence of Spirituality in Corporate America," *BusinessWeek*, November 1, 1999, p. 153.

36 C. P. Neck and J. F. Milliman, "Thought Self-Leadership: Finding Spiritual Fulfillment in Organizational Life," *Journal of Managerial Psychology* 9, no. 8 (1994), p. 9; for a recent review, see J.-C. Garcia-Zamor, "Workplace Spirituality and Organizational Performance," *Public Administration Review*, May–June 2003, pp. 355–363.

37 P. H. Mirvis, "Soul Work in Organizations," *Organization Science* 8, no. 2 (1997), p. 193; A. Rego and M. Pina e Cunha, "Workplace Spirituality and Organizational Commitment: An Empirical Study," *Journal of Organizational Change Management* 21, no. 1 (2008), pp. 53–75; and R. W. Kolodinsky, R. A. Giacalone, and C. L. Jurkiewicz, "Workplace Values and Outcomes: Exploring Personal, Organizational, and Interactive Workplace Spirituality," *Journal of Business Ethics* 81, no. 2 (2008), pp. 465–480.

38 Cited in J. Milliman, J. Ferguson, D. Trickett, and B. Condemi, "Spirit and Community at Southwest Airlines: An Investigation of a Spiritual Values-Based Model," *Journal of Organizational Change Management* 12, no. 3 (1999).

39 P. Preville, "For God's Sake," *Canadian Business*, June 25–July 9, 1999, p. 61.

Chapter 13

1 Vignette based on D. Veale, "The Only True Test Is Success in the Marketplace," *Telegraph Journal*, November 10, 2011, http://telegraphjournal.canadaeast.com/rss/article/1454583

2 See, for instance, R. L. Daft, *Organization Theory and Design*, 6th ed. (Cincinnati, OH: South Western College, 1998).

3 C. Hymowitz, "Managers Suddenly Have to Answer to a Crowd of Bosses," *Wall Street Journal*, August 12, 2003, p. B1.

4 See, for instance, L. Urwick, *The Elements of Administration* (New York: Harper and Row, 1944), pp. 52–53.

5 J. Child and R. G. McGrath, "Organizations Unfettered: Organizational Form in an Information-Intensive Economy," *Academy of Management Journal*, December 2001, pp. 1135–1148.

6 G. Morgan, *Images of Organization* (Newbury Park, CA: Sage, 1986), p. 21.

7 H. Mintzberg, *Structure in Fives: Designing Effective Organizations* (Englewood Cliffs, NJ: Prentice Hall, 1983), p. 157.

8 J. Davis, "Governing the Family-Run Business," *Harvard Business School Working Knowledge*, September 4, 2001.

9 D. Miller, L. Steier, and I. Le Breton-Miller, "Lost in Time: Intergenerational Succession, Change, and Failure in Family Business," *Journal of Business Venturing*, July 2003, pp. 513–531.

10 Based on P. Kuitenbrouwer, "Simmer . . . Then Raise to a Boil: A Family Stew over Succession at the McCain Foods Empire Spills into the Courts [1993 review]," *Financial Post Daily* 10, no. 205A, F 2 1998 anniversary ed., p. 22; P. Newman, "Tales from a Mellower Harrison McCain: Four Years after Winning a Bitter Feud with His Brother, Harrison Acknowledges That 'Strained' Family Relations Still Exist," *Maclean's*, January 19, 1998, p. 50; "Harrison McCain: King of the Frozen French Fry," *Calgary Herald*, March 28, 2004, p. B6; and "Wallace McCain," *Telegraph*, May 18, 2011, http://www.telegraph.co.uk/news/obituaries/finance-obituaries/8522014/Wallace-McCain.html

11 J. J. Chrisman, J. H. Chua, and L. P. Steier, "An Introduction to Theories of Family Business," *Journal of Business Venturing*, July 2003, pp. 441–448.

12 K. Knight, "Matrix Organization: A Review," *Journal of Management Studies*, May 1976, pp. 111–130; and L. R. Burns and D. R. Wholey, "Adoption and Abandonment of Matrix Management Programs: Effects of Organizational Characteristics and Interorganizational Networks," *Academy of Management Journal*, February 1993, pp. 106–138.

13 See, for instance, S. M. Davis and P. R. Lawrence, "Problems of Matrix Organization," *Harvard Business Review*, May–June 1978, pp. 131–142.

14 Vignette based on D. Veale, "The Only True Test Is Success in the Marketplace," *Telegraph Journal*, November 10, 2011, http://telegraphjournal.canadaeast.com/rss/article/1454583; http://www.t4g.com/Newsroom/News-Article/April-2011/T4G-in-Top-10-of-Canada-s-Best-Workplaces.aspx; and http://leadingthinkers.t4g.com/about.html

15 J. R. Galbraith and E. E. Lawler III, "Effective Organizations: Using the New Logic of Organizing," in *Organizing for the Future: The New Logic for Managing Complex Organizations*, ed. J. R. Galbraith, E. E. Lawler III, and Associates (San Francisco: Jossey-Bass, 1993).

16 G. G. Dess, A. M. A. Rasheed, K. J. McLaughlin, and R. Priem, "The New Corporate Architecture," *Academy of Management Executive*, August 1995, pp. 7–18; and C. Y. Baldwin and K. B. Clark, "Managing in an Age of Modularity," *Harvard Business Review*, September–October 1997, pp. 84–93.

17 M. Kaeter, "The Age of the Specialized Generalist," *Training*, December 1993, pp. 48–53.

18 See, for instance, R. E. Miles and C. C. Snow, "The New Network Firm: A Spherical Structure Built on Human Investment Philosophy," *Organizational Dynamics*, Spring 1995, pp. 5–18; D. Pescovitz, "The Company Where Everybody's a Temp," *New York Times Magazine*, June 11, 2000, pp. 94–96; B. Hedberg, G. Dahlgren, J. Hansson, and N. Olve, *Virtual Organizations and Beyond* (New York: Wiley, 2001); N. S. Contractor, S. Wasserman, and K. Faust, "Testing Multitheoretical, Multilevel Hypotheses About Organizational Networks: An Analytic Framework and Empirical Example," *Academy of Management Review* 31, no. 3 (2006), pp. 681–703; and Y. Shin, "A Person-Environment

19 G. G. Dess, A. M. A. Rasheed, K. J. McLaughlin, and R. Priem, "The New Corporate Architecture," *Academy of Management Executive*, August 1995, pp. 7–18.

20 J. Bates, "Making Movies and Moving On," *Los Angeles Times*, January 19, 1998, p. A1.

21 "Why Do Canadian Companies Opt for Cooperative Ventures?" *Micro: The Micro-Economic Research Bulletin* 4, no. 2 (1997), pp. 3–5.

22 C. B. Gibson and J. L. Gibbs, "Unpacking the Concept of Virtuality: The Effects of Geographic Dispersion, Electronic Dependence, Dynamic Structure, and National Diversity on Team Innovation," *Administrative Science Quarterly* 51, no. 3 (2006), pp. 451–495; and H. M. Latapie and V. N. Tran, "Subculture Formation, Evolution, and Conflict Between Regional Teams in Virtual Organizations," *Business Review*, Summer 2007, pp. 189–193.

23 "GE: Just Your Average Everyday $60 Billion Family Grocery Store," *IndustryWeek*, May 2, 1994, pp. 13–18.

24 The following is based on D. D. Davis, "Form, Function and Strategy in Boundaryless Organizations," in *The Changing Nature of Work*, ed. A. Howard (San Francisco: Jossey-Bass, 1995), pp. 112–138; P. Roberts, "We Are One Company, No Matter Where We Are. Time and Space Are Irrelevant," *Fast Company*, April–May 1998, pp. 122–128; R. L. Cross, A. Yan, and M. R. Louis, "Boundary Activities in 'Boundaryless' Organizations: A Case Study of a Transformation to a Team-Based Structure," *Human Relations*, June 2000, pp. 841–868; and R. Ashkenas, D. Ulrich, T. Jick, and S. Kerr, *The Boundaryless Organization: Breaking the Chains of Organizational Structure*, revised and updated (San Francisco: Jossey-Bass, 2002).

25 R. Blackwell, "For Cisco, a Canadian's Global Aspirations," *Globe and Mail*, June 26, 2011, http://www.theglobeandmail.com/report-on-business/careers/careers-leadership/at-the-top/article2076260.ece; "Cisco to Kill Flip Cam," *Globe and Mail*, April 12, 2011, http://www.theglobeandmail.com/news/technology/tech-news/cisco-to-kill-flip-cam/article1981650/

26 "At Starbucks, Baristas Told No More Than Two Drinks," *Wall Street Journal*, October 13, 2010, http://online.wsj.com/article/SB10001424052748704164004575548403514060736.html?mod=e2tw; and J. Jargon, "Latest Starbucks Buzzword: 'Lean' Japanese Techniques," *Wall Street Journal*, August 4, 2009.

27 See J. P. Guthrie and D. K. Datta, "Dumb and Dumber: The Impact of Downsizing on Firm Performance as Moderated by Industry Conditions," *Organization Science* 19, no. 1 (2008), pp. 108–123; W. F. Cascio, C. E. Young, and J. R. Morris, "Financial Consequences of Employment-Change Decisions in Major U.S. Corporations," *Academy of Management Journal* 40 (1997), pp. 1175–1189; and K. P. De Meuse, T. J. Bergmann, P. A. Vanderheiden, and C. E. Roraff, "New Evidence Regarding Organizational Downsizing and a Firm's Financial Performance: A Long-Term Analysis," *Journal of Managerial Issues* 16, no. 2 (2004), pp. 155–177.

28 See, for example, C. O. Trevor and A. J. Nyberg, "Keeping Your Headcount When All About You Are Losing Theirs: Downsizing, Voluntary Turnover Rates, and the Moderating Role of HR Practices," *Academy of Management Journal* 51, no. 2 (2008), pp. 259–276; S. Moore, L. Grunberg, and E. Greenberg, "Surviving Repeated Waves of Organizational Downsizing: The Recency, Duration, and Order Effects Associated with Different Forms of Layoff Contact," *Anxiety, Stress & Coping: An International Journal* 19, no. 3 (2006), pp. 309–329; T. M. Probst, S. M. Stewart, M. L. Gruys, and B. W. Tierney, "Productivity, Counterproductivity and Creativity: The Ups and Downs of Job Insecurity," *Journal of Occupational and Organizational Psychology*

80, no. 3 (2007), pp. 479–497; and J. E. Ferrie, M. J. Shipley, M. G. Marmot, P. Martikainen, S. Stansfeld, and G. D. Smith, "Job Insecurity in White-Collar Workers: Toward an Explanation of Associations with Health," *Journal of Occupational Health Psychology* 6, no. 1 (2001), pp. 26–42.

29 C. D. Zatzick and R. D. Iverson, "High-Involvement Management and Workforce Reduction: Competitive Advantage or Disadvantage?" *Academy of Management Journal* 49, no. 5 (2006), pp. 999–1015; A. Travaglione and B. Cross, "Diminishing the Social Network in Organizations: Does There Need to Be Such a Phenomenon as 'Survivor Syndrome' After Downsizing?" *Strategic Change* 15, no. 1 (2006), pp. 1–13; and J. D. Kammeyer-Mueller, H. Liao, and R. D. Arvey, "Downsizing and Organizational Performance: A Review of the Literature from a Stakeholder Perspective," *Research in Personnel and Human Resources Management* 20 (2001), pp. 269–329.

30 T. Burns and G. M. Stalker, *The Management of Innovation* (London: Tavistock, 1961); and J. A. Courtright, G. T. Fairhurst, and L. E. Rogers, "Interaction Patterns in Organic and Mechanistic Systems," *Academy of Management Journal*, December 1989, pp. 773–802.

31 This analysis is referred to as a contingency approach to organization design. See, for instance, J. M. Pennings, "Structural Contingency Theory: A Reappraisal," in *Research in Organizational Behavior*, vol. 14, ed. B. M. Staw and L. L. Cummings (Greenwich, CT: JAI Press, 1992), pp. 267–309; J. R. Hollenbeck, H. Moon, A. P. J. Ellis, B. J. West, D. R. Ilgen, L. Sheppard, C. O. L. H. Porter, and J. A. Wagner III, "Structural Contingency Theory and Individual Differences: Examination of External and Internal Person-Team Fit," *Journal of Applied Psychology*, June 2002, pp. 599–606; and A. Drach-Zahavy and A. Freund, "Team Effectiveness under Stress: A Structural Contingency Approach," *Journal of Organizational Behavior* 28, no. 4 (2007), pp. 423–450.

32 The strategy-structure thesis was originally proposed in A. D. Chandler Jr., *Strategy and Structure: Chapters in the History of the Industrial Enterprise* (Cambridge, MA: MIT Press, 1962). For an updated analysis, see T. L. Amburgey and T. Dacin, "As the Left Foot Follows the Right? The Dynamics of Strategic and Structural Change," *Academy of Management Journal*, December 1994, pp. 1427–1452.

33 See R. E. Miles and C. C. Snow, *Organizational Strategy, Structure, and Process* (New York: McGraw-Hill, 1978); D. C. Galunic and K. M. Eisenhardt, "Renewing the Strategy-Structure-Performance Paradigm," in *Research in Organizational Behavior*, vol. 16, ed. B. M. Staw and L. L. Cummings (Greenwich, CT: JAI Press, 1994), pp. 215–255; I. C. Harris and T. W. Ruefli, "The Strategy/Structure Debate: An Examination of the Performance Implications," *Journal of Management Studies*, June 2000, pp. 587–603; and S. M. Toh, F. P. Morgeson, and M. A. Campion, "Human Resource Configurations: Investigating Fit with the Organizational Context," *Journal of Applied Psychology* 93, no. 4 (2008), pp. 864–882.

34 See, for instance, P. M. Blau and R. A. Schoenherr, *The Structure of Organizations* (New York: Basic Books, 1971); D. S. Pugh, "The Aston Program of Research: Retrospect and Prospect," in *Perspectives on Organization Design and Behavior*, ed. A. H. Van de Ven and W. F. Joyce (New York: Wiley, 1981), pp. 135–166; R. Z. Gooding and J. A. Wagner III, "A Meta-analytic Review of the Relationship between Size and Performance: The Productivity and Efficiency of Organizations and Their Subunits," *Administrative Science Quarterly*, December 1985, pp. 462–481; and A. C. Bluedorn, "Pilgrim's Progress: Trends and Convergence in Research on Organizational Size and Environments," *Journal of Management*, Summer 1993, pp. 163–192.

35 See C. Perrow, "A Framework for the Comparative Analysis of Organizations," *American Sociological Review*, April 1967, pp. 194–208; J. Hage and M. Aiken, "Routine Technology, Social

Structure, and Organizational Goals," *Administrative Science Quarterly*, September 1969, pp. 366–377; C. C. Miller, W. H. Glick, Y. Wang, and G. P. Huber, "Understanding Technology-Structure Relationships: Theory Development and Meta-analytic Theory Testing," *Academy of Management Journal*, June 1991, pp. 370–399; and W. D. Sine, H. Mitsuhashi, and D. A. Kirsch, "Revisiting Burns and Stalker: Formal Structure and New Venture Performance in Emerging Economic Sectors," *Academy of Management Journal* 49, no. 1 (2006), pp. 121–132.

36 See F. E. Emery and E. Trist, "The Causal Texture of Organizational Environments," *Human Relations*, February 1965, pp. 21–32; P. Lawrence and J. W. Lorsch, *Organization and Environment: Managing Differentiation and Integration* (Boston: Harvard Business School, Division of Research, 1967); M. Yasai-Ardekani, "Structural Adaptations to Environments," *Academy of Management Review*, January 1986, pp. 9–21; A. C. Bluedorn, "Pilgrim's Progress: Trends and Convergence in Research on Organizational Size and Environments," *Journal of Management*, Summer 1993, pp. 163–192; and M. Arndt and B. Bigelow, "Presenting Structural Innovation in an Institutional Environment: Hospitals' Use of Impression Management," *Administrative Science Quarterly*, September 2000, pp. 494–522.

37 See F. E. Emery and E. Trist, "The Causal Texture of Organizational Environments," *Human Relations*, February 1965, pp. 21–32; P. Lawrence and J. W. Lorsch, *Organization and Environment: Managing Differentiation and Integration* (Boston: Harvard Business School, Division of Research, 1967); M. Yasai-Ardekani, "Structural Adaptations to Environments," *Academy of Management Review*, January 1986, pp. 9–21; and A. C. Bluedorn, "Pilgrim's Progress: Trends and Convergence in Research on Organizational Size and Environments," *Journal of Management*, Summer 1993, pp. 163–192.

38 G. G. Dess and D. W. Beard, "Dimensions of Organizational Task Environments," *Administrative Science Quarterly*, March 1984, pp. 52–73; E. A. Gerloff, N. K. Muir, and W. D. Bodensteiner, "Three Components of Perceived Environmental Uncertainty: An Exploratory Analysis of the Effects of Aggregation," *Journal of Management*, December 1991, pp. 749–768; and O. Shenkar, N. Aranya, and T. Almor, "Construct Dimensions in the Contingency Model: An Analysis Comparing Metric and Non-Metric Multivariate Instruments," *Human Relations*, May 1995, pp. 559–580.

39 C. S. Spell and T. J. Arnold, "A Multi-Level Analysis of Organizational Justice and Climate, Structure, and Employee Mental Health," *Journal of Management* 33, no. 5 (2007), pp. 724–751; and M. L. Ambrose and M. Schminke, "Organization Structure as a Moderator of the Relationship Between Procedural Justice, Interactional Justice, Perceived Organizational Support, and Supervisory Trust," *Journal of Applied Psychology* 88, no. 2 (2003), pp. 295–305.

40 See, for instance, L. W. Porter and E. E. Lawler III, "Properties of Organization Structure in Relation to Job Attitudes and Job Behavior," *Psychological Bulletin*, July 1965, pp. 23–51; L. R. James and A. P. Jones, "Organization Structure: A Review of Structural Dimensions and Their Conceptual Relationships with Individual Attitudes and Behavior," *Organizational Behavior and Human Performance*, June 1976, pp. 74–113; C. S. Spell and T. J. Arnold, "A Multi-Level Analysis of Organizational Justice Climate, Structure, and Employee Mental Health," *Journal of Management* 33, no. 5 (2007), pp. 724–751; and J. D. Shaw and N. Gupta, "Job Complexity, Performance, and Well-Being: When Does Supplies-Values Fit Matter?" *Personnel Psychology* 57, no. 4 (2004), pp. 847–879.

41 See, for instance, B. Schneider, H. W. Goldstein, and D. B. Smith, "The ASA Framework: An Update," *Personnel Psychology* 48, no. 4 (1995), pp. 747–773; and R. E. Ployhart, J. A. Weekley, and K. Baughman, "The Structure and Function of Human

Capital Emergence: A Multilevel Examination of the Attraction-Selection-Attrition Model," *Academy of Management Journal* 49, no. 4 (2006), pp. 661–677.

42 P. Dvorak, "Making U.S. Management Ideas Work Elsewhere," *Wall Street Journal*, May 22, 2006, p. B3.

43 See, for example, P. R. Harris and R. T. Moran, *Managing Cultural Differences*, 5th ed. (Houston, TX: Gulf Publishing, 1999).

44 Based on P. McGeehan, "Thousands of Job Cuts Likely after Drug Merger," *New York Times*, January 26, 2009, http://www.nytimes.com; and J. Bradshaw, "Storied Nova Scotia Art College Faces Hard Choices to Stay Afloat," *Globe and Mail*, December 11, 2011.

45 Based on N. M. Davis, "Merger Kept 'the Best of Both,'" *HR Magazine*, November 2008, pp. 54–56.

46 The source of this exercise is unknown.

47 Based on S. Pulliam, "A Staffer Ordered to Commit Fraud Balked, Then Caved," *Wall Street Journal*, June 23, 2003, p. A1; and E. McClam, "Ex-WorldCom Exec Gets 5-Month Term, House Arrest," *Clarion-Ledger*, August 5, 2005, http://www.clarionledger.com/apps/pbcs.dll/article?AID=/20050805/NEWS0108/50805011/1002/NEWS01

48 Based on "Major Changes for Vanderbilt Athletics," *New York Times*, September 10, 2003, p. C19; M. Cass, "Vanderbilt Realigns Management," *USA Today*, September 10, 2003, p. 7C; and "Vanderbilt University Is Not Getting Rid of Sports," *Chronicle of Higher Education*, September 19, 2003, p. A35.

49 Based on P. J. Sauer, "Open-Door Management," *Inc.*, June 2003, p. 44; and http://www.techtarget.com/html/job_opps.htm

50 Based on S. P. Robbins and P. L. Hunsaker, *Training in Interpersonal Skills*, 3rd ed. (Upper Saddle River, NJ: Prentice Hall, 2003), pp. 95–98.

Chapter 14

1 Vignette based on J. Castaldo, "Sears Canada Can't Afford to Stand Still," *Canadian Business*, J. June 28, 2011, http://www.canadianbusiness.com/blog/business_briefings/31340--sears-canada-can-t-afford-to-stand-still

2 "Blockbuster's Bankruptcy: What Does the Loss of Video Stores Mean to You?" *CBC.ca*, May 6, 2011.

3 See, for instance, K. H. Hammonds, "Practical Radicals," *Fast Company*, September 2000, pp. 162–174; and P. C. Judge, "Change Agents," *Fast Company*, November 2000, pp. 216–226.

4 A. Finder, P. D. Healy, and K. Zernike, "President of Harvard Resigns, Ending Stormy 5-Year Tenure," *New York Times*, February 22, 2006, pp. A1, A19.

5 L. Cameron, "McDonald's: This Arch Is Golden," *Canadian Business*, November 22, 2010.

6 K. Lewin, *Field Theory in Social Science* (New York: Harper and Row, 1951).

7 P. G. Audia, E. A. Locke, and K. G. Smith, "The Paradox of Success: An Archival and a Laboratory Study of Strategic Persistence Following Radical Environmental Change," *Academy of Management Journal*, October 2000, pp. 837–853.

8 J. B. Sorensen, "The Strength of Corporate Culture and the Reliability of Firm Performance," *Administrative Science Quarterly*, March 2002, pp. 70–91.

9 J. Amis, T. Slack, and C. R. Hinings, "The Pace, Sequence, and Linearity of Radical Change," *Academy of Management Journal*, February 2004, pp. 15–39; and E. Autio, H. J. Sapienza, and J. G. Almeida, "Effects of Age at Entry, Knowledge Intensity, and Imitability on International Growth," *Academy of Management Journal*, October 2000, pp. 909–924.

10 J. P. Kotter, "Leading Changes: Why Transformation Efforts Fail," *Harvard Business Review*, March–April 1995, pp. 59–67; and J. P. Kotter, *Leading Change* (Boston: Harvard Business School Press, 1996).

11 See, for example, C. Eden and C. Huxham, "Action Research for the Study of Organizations," in *Handbook of Organization Studies*, ed. S. R. Clegg, C. Hardy, and W. R. Nord (London: Sage, 1996); and L. S. Lüscher and M. W. Lewis, "Organizational Change and Managerial Sensemaking: Working through Paradox," *Academy of Management Journal* 51, no. 2 (2008), pp. 221–240.

12 See, for example, G. R. Bushe, "Advances in Appreciative Inquiry as an Organization Development Intervention," *Organizational Development Journal*, Summer 1999, pp. 61–68; D. L. Cooperrider and D. Whitney, *Collaborating for Change: Appreciative Inquiry* (San Francisco: Berrett-Koehler, 2000); R. Fry, F. Barrett, J. Seiling, and D. Whitney, eds., *Appreciative Inquiry & Organizational Transformation: Reports from the Field* (Westport, CT: Quorum, 2002); J. K. Barge and C. Oliver, "Working with Appreciation in Managerial Practice," *Academy of Management Review*, January 2003, pp. 124–142; and D. van der Haar and D. M. Hosking, "Evaluating Appreciative Inquiry: A Relational Constructionist Perspective," *Human Relations*, August 2004, pp. 1017–1036.

13 R. Rabinovitch, "Training and Development," *Canadian HR Reporter* 17, no. 10 (May 17, 2004), pp. 7–10.

14 D. Sankey, "New Tool Solves Firms' Problems," *Calgary Herald*, July 12, 2003, p. CR1F.

15 G. R. Bushe, "Advances in Appreciative Inquiry as an Organization Development Intervention," *Organization Development Journal* 17, no. 2 (Summer 1999), pp. 61–68.

16 P. G. Audia and S. Brion, "Reluctant to Change: Self-Enhancing Responses to Diverging Performance Measures," *Organizational Behavior and Human Decision Processes* 102 (2007), pp. 255–269.

17 M. Fugate, A. J. Kinicki, and G. E. Prussia, "Employee Coping with Organizational Change: An Examination of Alternative Theoretical Perspectives and Models," *Personnel Psychology* 61, no. 1 (2008), pp. 1–36.

18 J. D. Ford, L. W. Ford, and A. D'Amelio, "Resistance to Change: The Rest of the Story," *Academy of Management Review* 33, no. 2 (2008), pp. 362–377.

19 J. P. Kotter and L. A. Schlesinger, "Choosing Strategies for Change," *Harvard Business Review*, July–August 2008, pp. 130–139.

20 A. E. Reichers, J. P. Wanous, and J. T. Austin, "Understanding and Managing Cynicism About Organizational Change," *Academy of Management Executive* 11 (1997), pp. 48–59.

21 R. H. Hall, *Organizations: Structures, Processes, and Outcomes*, 4th ed. (Englewood Cliffs, NJ: Prentice Hall, 1987), p. 29.

22 D. Katz and R. L. Kahn, *The Social Psychology of Organizations*, 2nd ed. (New York: Wiley, 1978), pp. 714–715.

23 M. T. Hannan, L. Pólos, and G. R. Carroll, "The Fog of Change: Opacity and Asperity in Organizations," *Administrative Science Quarterly*, September 2003, pp. 399–432.

24 J. P. Kotter and L. A. Schlesinger, "Choosing Strategies for Change," *Harvard Business Review*, March–April 1979, pp. 106–114.

25 J. E. Dutton, S. J. Ashford, R. M. O'Neill, and K. A. Lawrence, "Moves That Matter: Issue Selling and Organizational Change," *Academy of Management Journal*, August 2001, pp. 716–736.

26 P. C. Fiss and E. J. Zajac, "The Symbolic Management of Strategic Change: Sensegiving via Framing and Decoupling," *Academy of Management Journal* 49, no. 6 (2006), pp. 1173–1193.

27 Q. N. Huy, "Emotional Balancing of Organizational Continuity and Radical Change: The Contribution of Middle Managers,"

Administrative Science Quarterly, March 2002, pp. 31–69; D. M. Herold, D. B. Fedor, and S. D. Caldwell, "Beyond Change Management: A Multilevel Investigation of Contextual and Personal Influences on Employees' Commitment to Change," *Journal of Applied Psychology* 92, no. 4 (2007), pp. 942–951; and G. B. Cunningham, "The Relationships among Commitment to Change, Coping with Change, and Turnover Intentions," *European Journal of Work and Organizational Psychology* 15, no. 1 (2006), pp. 29–45.

28 J. P. Kotter, "Leading Change: Why Transformational Efforts Fail," *Harvard Business Review*, January 2007, pp. 96–103.

29 K. van Dam, S. Oreg, and B. Schyns, "Daily Work Contexts and Resistance to Organisational Change: The Role of Leader-Member Exchange, Development Climate, and Change Process Characteristics," *Applied Psychology: An International Review* 57, no. 2 (2008), pp. 313–334.

30 D. B. Fedor, S. Caldwell, and D. M. Herold, "The Effects of Organizational Changes on Employee Commitment: A Multilevel Investigation," *Personnel Psychology* 59 (2006), pp. 1–29.

31 S. Oreg, "Personality, Context, and Resistance to Organizational Change," *European Journal of Work and Organizational Psychology* 15, no. 1 (2006), pp. 73–101.

32 S. M. Elias, "Employee Commitment in Times of Change: Assessing the Importance of Attitudes toward Organizational Change," *Journal of Management* 35, no. 1 (2009), pp. 37–55.

33 J. A. LePine, J. A. Colquitt, and A. Erez, "Adaptability to Changing Task Contexts: Effects of General Cognitive Ability, Conscientiousness, and Openness to Experience," *Personnel Psychology*, Fall 2000, pp. 563–593; T. A. Judge, C. J. Thoresen, V. Pucik, and T. M. Welbourne, "Managerial Coping with Organizational Change: A Dispositional Perspective," *Journal of Applied Psychology*, February 1999, pp. 107–122; and S. Oreg, "Resistance to Change: Developing an Individual Differences Measure," *Journal of Applied Psychology*, August 2003, pp. 680–693.

34 J. W. B. Lang and P. D. Bliese, "General Mental Ability and Two Types of Adaptation to Unforeseen Change: Applying Discontinuous Growth Models to the Task-Change Paradigm," *Journal of Applied Psychology* 94, no. 2 (2009), pp. 411–428.

35 Based on T. Spears, "New NRC Boss Shifts Focus to Economic Development, Less Pure Research," *Postmedia News*, March 19, 2011.

36 R. H. Miles, "Accelerating Corporate Transformations (Don't Lose Your Nerve!)," *Harvard Business Review*, January/February 2010, pp. 68–75.

37 See J. Pfeffer, *Managing with Power: Politics and Influence in Organizations* (Boston: Harvard Business School Press, 1992), pp. 7, 318–320; and D. Knights and D. McCabe, "When 'Life Is but a Dream': Obliterating Politics through Business Process Reengineering?" *Human Relations*, June 1998, pp. 761–798.

38 See, for instance, A. Karaevli, "Performance Consequences for New CEO 'Outsiderness': Moderating Effects of Pre- and Post-Succession Contexts," *Strategic Management Journal* 28, no. 7 (2007), pp. 681–706.

39 Vignette based on D. Flavelle, "Sears Boss Runs Hard to Revive Retail Icon: New CEO Aiming for a Transformation in the Next Three Years," *Toronto Star*, December 7, 2011.

40 See, for instance, F. Yuan and R. W. Woodman, "Innovative Behavior in the Workplace: The Role of Performance and Image Outcome Expectations," *Academy of Management Journal* 53, no. 2 (2010), pp. 323–342.

41 See, for instance, A. Van de Ven, "Central Problems in the Management of Innovation," *Management Science* 32 (1986),

pp. 590–607; and R. M. Kanter, "When a Thousand Flowers Bloom: Structural, Collective and Social Conditions for Innovation in Organizations," in *Research in Organizational Behavior*, vol. 10, ed. B. M. Staw and L. L. Cummings (Greenwich, CT: JAI Press, 1988), pp. 169–211.

42 F. Damanpour, "Organizational Innovation: A Meta-analysis of Effects of Determinants and Moderators," *Academy of Management Journal*, September 1991, p. 557.

43 F. Damanpour, "Organizational Innovation: A Meta-analysis of Effects of Determinants and Moderators," *Academy of Management Journal*, September 1991, pp. 555–590.

44 See also P. R. Monge, M. D. Cozzens, and N. S. Contractor, "Communication and Motivational Predictors of the Dynamics of Organizational Innovation," *Organization Science*, May 1992, pp. 250–274.

45 Discussion of 3M is based on "The Drought Is Over at 3M," *BusinessWeek*, November 7, 1994, pp. 140–141; T. A. Stewart, "3M Fights Back," *Fortune*, February 5, 1996, pp. 94–99; T. D. Schellhardt, "David in Goliath," *Wall Street Journal*, May 23, 1996, p. R14; and "3M Wins Silver and Bronze in Product Innovation Awards," April 6, 2011, http://www.businesswire.com/news/home/20110406006826/en/3M-Wins-Silver-Bronze-Product-Innovation-Awards

46 J. M. Howell and C. A. Higgins, "Champions of Change," *Business Quarterly*, Spring 1990, pp. 31–32; and D. L. Day, "Raising Radicals: Different Processes for Championing Innovative Corporate Ventures," *Organization Science*, May 1994, pp. 148–172.

47 J. M. Howell and C. A. Higgins, "Champions of Change," *Business Quarterly*, Spring 1990, pp. 31–32.

48 See, for example, T. B. Lawrence, M. K. Mauws, B. Dyck, and R. F. Kleysen, "The Politics of Organizational Learning: Integrating Power into the 4I Framework," *Academy of Management Review*, January 2005, pp. 180–191.

49 D. H. Kim, "The Link between Individual and Organizational Learning," *Sloan Management Review*, Fall 1993, p. 37.

50 C. Argyris and D. A. Schon, *Organizational Learning* (Reading, MA: Addison-Wesley, 1978).

51 B. Dumaine, "Mr. Learning Organization," *Fortune*, October 17, 1994, p. 148.

52 F. Kofman and P. M. Senge, "Communities of Commitment: The Heart of Learning Organizations," *Organizational Dynamics*, Autumn 1993, pp. 5–23.

53 B. Dumaine, "Mr. Learning Organization," *Fortune*, October 17, 1994, p. 154.

54 See S. Shane, S. Venkataraman, and I. MacMillan, "Cultural Differences in Innovation Championing Strategies," *Journal of Management* 21, no. 5 (1995), pp. 931–952.

55 For contrasting views on episodic and continuous change, see K. E. Weick and R. E. Quinn, "Organizational Change and Development," in *Annual Review of Psychology*, vol. 50, ed. J. T. Spence, J. M. Darley, and D. J. Foss (Palo Alto, CA: Annual Reviews, 1999), pp. 361–386.

56 R. Thomas, D. S. Leisa, and C. Hardy, "Managing Organizational Change: Negotiating Meaning and Power-Resistance Relations," *Organization Science* 22, no. 1 (2011), pp. 22–41.

57 This perspective is based on P. B. Vaill, *Managing as a Performing Art: New Ideas for a World of Chaotic Change* (San Francisco: Jossey-Bass, 1989).

58 Adapted from J. E. Barbuto Jr., "Power and the Changing Environment," *Journal of Management Education*, April 2000, pp. 288–296.

59 Based on M. Graban, "Toyota Leaders Get a Lecture from a Toyoda," *Manufacturing Business Technology*, June 28, 2009, http://

www.mbtmag.com; M. Maynard, "At Toyota, a Giant Strives to Show Agility," *New York Times*, February 22, 2008, pp. B1, C4; and J. Surowiecki, "The Open Secret of Success," *New Yorker*, May 12, 2008, p. 48.

60 Based on D. Ulrich, S. Kerr, and R. Ashkenas, *The GE Work-Out* (New York: McGraw-Hill, 2002).

61 R. Pascale, M. Millemann, and L. Gioja, "Changing the Way We Change," *Harvard Business Review*, November–December 1997, pp. 127–139. The actual names of the points based on the After Action Review are taken from the article, although the summaries are provided by the authors of this textbook.

Additional Cases: 2

1 This case is based on an interview with "Julie" conducted after her release from jail. The interview took place on December 27, 2011.

Additional Cases: 4

1 R. Marowits, "Air Canada and Unionized Workers Endured a Year of Frustration," *Winnipeg Free Press*, December 6, 2011, http://www.winnipegfreepress.com/business/breakingnews/air-canada-and-unionized-workers-endured-a-year-of-frustration-in-2011-135116623.html

2 B. Jang, "Air Canada Caught between Employees and Customers in Labour Dispute," *Globe and Mail*, October 10, 2011, http://www.theglobeandmail.com/news/politics/air-canada-caught-between-employees-and-customers-in-labour-dispute/article2196420/

3 B. Jang, "Air Canada Caught between Employees and Customers in Labour Dispute," *Globe and Mail*, October 10, 2011, http://www.theglobeandmail.com/news/politics/air-canada-caught-between-employees-and-customers-in-labour-dispute/article2196420/

4 Staff Reporter, "Air Canada Union Slams Arbitrator's Decision," CBC News, November 7, 2011, http://www.cbc.ca/news/business/story/2011/11/07/air-canada-flight-attendants-arbitration.html

5 Staff Reporter, "Air Canada Alleges Union Negotiated in Bad Faith," CTV, October 13, 2011, http://www.ctv.ca/CTVNews/TopStories/20111013/air-canada-cupe-attendants-strike-deadline-passes-11101; and B. Jang, "Air Canada Flight Attendants Reject Tentative Pact for Second Time," *Globe and Mail*, October 11, 2011, http://www.theglobeandmail.com/news/national/air-canada-flight-attendants-reject-tentative-pact-for-second-time/article2196189/

6 R. Marowits, "Air Canada and Unionized Workers Endured a Year of Frustration," *Winnipeg Free Press*, December 6, 2011, http://www.winnipegfreepress.com/business/breakingnews/air-canada-and-unionized-workers-endured-a-year-of-frustration-in-2011-135116623.html

7 R. Marowits, "Air Canada and Unionized Workers Endured a Year of Frustration," *Winnipeg Free Press*, December 6, 2011, http://www.winnipegfreepress.com/business/breakingnews/air-canada-and-unionized-workers-endured-a-year-of-frustration-in-2011-135116623.html

Additional Cases: 5

1 S. Kari, S. "Ex-constable Must Again Prove RCMP Harassment," *Globe and Mail*, December 20, 2011, http://www.theglobeandmail.com/news/national/ex-constable-must-again-prove-rcmp-harassment/article151366/

2 S. Stewart, A. Hoffman, and P. Waldie, "Female Mounties Allege Harassment Not Investigated to Protect RCMP," *Canadian Press*,

December 20, 2011, http://www.theglobeandmail.com/news/national/female-mounties-allege-harassment-not-investigated-to-protect-rcmp/article1016726/

3 S. Stewart, A. Hoffman, and P. Waldie, "Female Mounties Allege Harassment Not Investigated to Protect RCMP," *Canadian Press*, December 20, 2011, http://www.theglobeandmail.com/news/national/female-mounties-allege-harassment-not-investigated-to-protect-rcmp/article1016726/

4 S. Stewart, A. Hoffman, and P. Waldie, "Female Mounties Allege Harassment Not Investigated to Protect RCMP," *Canadian Press*, December 20, 2011, http://www.theglobeandmail.com/news/national/female-mounties-allege-harassment-not-investigated-to-protect-rcmp/article1016726/

5 "More B.C. Mounties Complain of Harassment," CBC News, November 8, 2011, http://www.cbc.ca/news/canada/british-columbia/story/2011/11/08/bc-rcmp-harassment.html

6 "Lawyer 'Stunned' RCMP Brass Came in to Settle Harassment Case," *CBC News*, December 9, 2011, http://www.cbc.ca/news/canada/story/2011/12/09/rcmp-allegations-blundell.html

7 G. Mason, "RCMP Took Two Years to Respond to Officer's Sexual Harassment Complaint," *Globe and Mail*, December 5, 2011, http://www.theglobeandmail.com/news/national/british-columbia/gary_mason/rcmp-took-two-years-to-respond-to-officers-sexual-harassment-complaint/article2261049/

8 G. Mason, "Former Mountie Paints Picture of Near Daily Harassment," *Globe and Mail*, December 8, 2011, http://www.theglobeandmail.com/news/national/former-mountie-paints-picture-of-near-daily-harassment/article2259072/

9 S. Cooper, "Alleged Mountie Harassment Made RCMP Staffer Fear for Family's Lives Court Hears," *National Post*, November 18, 2011, http://news.nationalpost.com/2011/11/18/alleged-mountie-harassment-made-rcmp-staffer-fear-for-familys-lives-court-hears/

10 V. Luk, "RCMP Sexual Harassment Claims Deepen after Second Female Mountie Comes Forward," *National Post*, November 10, 2011, http://news.nationalpost.com/2011/11/10/rcmp-sexual-harassment-claims-deepen-after-second-female-mountie-slams-force/

11 V. Luk, "RCMP Sexual Harassment Claims Deepen after Second Female Mountie Comes Forward," *National Post*, November 10, 2011, http://news.nationalpost.com/2011/11/10/rcmp-sexual-harassment-claims-deepen-after-second-female-mountie-slams-force/

12 C. Freeze, "Top Mountie Delivers Candid, Scathing View of Force at the Brink," *Globe and Mail*, December 20, 2011, http://www.theglobeandmail.com/news/politics/top-mountie-delivers-candid-scathing-view-of-force-at-the-brink/article2277241/

13 G. Mason, "RCMP Took Two Years to Respond to Sexual Harassment Complaint," *Globe and Mail*, C. December 20, 2011, http://www.theglobeandmail.com/news/national/british-columbia/gary_mason/rcmp-took-two-years-to-respond-to-officers-sexual-harassment-complaint/article2261049/

14 I. Bailey, "Lawyers Preparing Possible Class Action Lawsuit against RCMP," *Globe and Mail*, December 21, 2011, http://www.theglobeandmail.com/news/national/lawyers-preparing-possible-class-action-suit-against-rcmp/article2278817/

Additional Cases: 6

1 National Digestive Diseases Information Clearinghouse (NDDIC), "Crohn's Disease." *National Institute of Health* publication number 06-3410. Bethesda, MD: Author, 2006. http://digestive.niddk.nih.gov/ddiseases/pubs/crohns/#stress

2 National Digestive Diseases Information Clearinghouse (NDDIC), "Crohn's Disease." *National Institute of Health* publication number 06-3410. Bethesda, MD: Author, 2006. http://digestive.niddk.nih.gov/ddiseases/pubs/crohns/#stress

3 MedicineNet.com. "Crohn's Disease," 2009, http://www.medicinenet.com/crohns_disease/article.htm

Additional Cases: 7

1 This case is an abbreviated version of a published case that appeared as K. Breward and M. Breward, "Governance in Times of Crisis," *Case Research Journal* 30, no. 2 (2010), pp. 45–68. Reprinted with permission.

Additional Cases: 8

1 S. Krashinsky, "Postmedia to Charge for Online Articles," *Globe and Mail,* October 28, 2011, http://www.theglobeandmail.com/globe-investor/postmedia-plans-to-charge-for-onlinearticles/article2218147/

2 S. Krashinsky, "Job Cuts to Save Postmedia Up to 35 Million," *Globe and Mail*, March 15, 2011, http://www.theglobeandmail.com/globe-investor/job-cuts-to-save-postmedia-up-to-35-million/article1860459/

3 S. Freeman, "Postmedia to Expand Online Pay Per View Experiment to Other Newspapers," *Canadian Business*, October 28, 2011, http://www.canadianbusiness.com/article/53908--postmedia-to-expand-online-pay-perview-experiment-to-other-newspapers

4 A. Sharp, "Canada's Postmedia Trims for Digital Age," *Reuters*, April 12, 2011, http://www.reuters.com/article/2011/04/12/us-postmedia-idUSTRE73B5IN20110412

5 S. Krashinsky, "Job Cuts to Save Postmedia Up to 35 Million," *Globe and Mail*, March 15, 2011, http://www.theglobeandmail.com/globe-investor/job-cuts-to-save-postmedia-up-to-35-million/article1860459/

6 S. Freeman, "Postmedia to Expand Online Pay Per View Experiment to Other Newspapers," *Canadian Business*, October 28, 2011, http://www.canadianbusiness.com/article/53908--postmedia-to-expand-online-pay-perview-experiment-to-other-newspapers

7 Staff Reporter, "Postmedia Says Three Executives to Exit, Including Two on Its Digital Team," *Canadian Business*, November 8, 2011, http://www.canadianbusiness.com/article/56005--postmedia-says-three-executives-toexit-including-two-on-its-digital-team

8 S. Krashinsky, "Postmedia Puts Focus on Digital with Management Shuffle," *Globe and Mail*, November 8, 2011, http://www.theglobeandmail.com/report-on-business/postmedia-puts-focus-on-digitalwith-management-shuffle/article2229287/

9 S. Freeman, "Postmedia to Expand Online Pay Per View Experiment to Other Newspapers," *Canadian Business*, October 28, 2011, http://www.canadianbusiness.com/article/53908--post-media-to-expand-online-pay-perview-experiment-to-other-newspapers

10 S. Freeman, "Postmedia to Expand Online Pay Per View Experiment to Other Newspapers," *Canadian Business*, October 28, 2011, http://www.canadianbusiness.com/article/53908--postmedia-to-expand-online-pay-perview-experiment-to-othernewspapers

11 A. Andorich, "What the Digital Restructuring at Postmedia Means," *Marketing*, November 8, 2011, http://www.marketingmag.ca/news/media-news/what-the-digital-restructuring-atpostmedia-means-39725

12 A. Andorich, "What the Digital Restructuring at Postmedia Means," *Marketing*, November 8, 2011, http://www.marketingmag.ca/news/media-news/what-the-digital-restructuring-atpostmedia-means-39725

GLOSSARY/SUBJECT INDEX

The page on which the key term is defined is printed in boldface.

A

ability An individual's capacity to perform the various tasks in a job. **105**

Aboriginal values, 95–96

absenteeism The failure to report to work. **14**, 100–101, 190

abuse of power, 300–303

accountability, 237

achievement-oriented leader, 403

acquisitions, 379–380

action research A change process based on the systematic collection of data and then selection of a change action based on what the analyzed data indicate. **516**–517

adjourning The final stage in group development for temporary groups, where attention is directed toward wrapping up activities rather than task performance. **221**

affect A broad range of feelings that people experience. **57**, 58, 58*f*

affective commitment An individual's emotional attachment to and identification with an organization, and a belief in its values. **102**

affective conflict Conflict that is emotional and aimed at a person rather than an issue. **325**

affective events theory (AET) The theory that employees react emotionally to things that happen to them at work and that this emotional reaction influences their job performance and satisfaction. **63**–65, 64*f*

aggressiveness, 364

agreeableness A personality factor that describes the degree to which a person is good-natured, cooperative, and trusting. **49**, 52, 398

agreement, 334

all-channel format, 268, 268*f*

alternative work arrangements, 190–194

ambiguity, 326

analogies, 448

analysis, 517

anchoring bias A tendency to fixate on initial information, from which one then fails to adequately adjust for subsequent information. **437**

anger, 62–63

anglophone values, 93–95

anthropology, 18

anti-bullying labour legislation, 302

appearance norms, 218

appreciative inquiry (AI) An approach to change that seeks to identify the unique qualities and special strengths of an organization, which can then be built on to improve performance. **517**–518, 518*f*

arbitration, 333

arbitrator A third party to a negotiation who has the authority to dictate an agreement. **333**

arousal, 147

artifacts Aspects of an organization's culture that you see, hear, and feel. **365**

Asian values, 96–97

assimilation, 379

assistance, 494

assumptions The taken-for-granted notions of how something should be. **366**

attention to detail, 364

attitude change, 119–120

attitudes Positive or negative feelings about objects, people, or events. **97**

    changing attitudes, 119–120

    employee engagement, 104–105

    general attitudes, 97

    job involvement, 104

    job satisfaction, 98–102

    organizational commitment, 102–104

    specific attitudes, 97

attribution theory The theory that when we observe what seems like atypical behaviour by an individual, we attempt to determine whether it is internally or externally caused. **39**–41, 40*f*, 65–66

auction bids, 337–338

authentic leaders Leaders who know who they are, know what they believe in and value, and act on these values and beliefs openly and candidly. Their followers could consider them to be ethical people. **417**

authentic motivation, 184

authoritative command, 330

authority The rights inherent in a managerial position to give orders and to expect the orders to be obeyed. **481**, 508–509

autonomy The degree to which the job provides substantial freedom, independence, and discretion to the individual in scheduling the work and determining the procedures to be used in carrying it out. **186**, 187

availability bias The tendency for people to base their judgments on information that is readily available to them rather than complete data. **438**

avoiding, 328, 329

B

Baby Boomers, 11, 91, 172*f*

bad boss, 359, 397

bargaining. *See* negotiation

bargaining strategies, 336–339

bargaining zone The zone between each party's resistance point, assuming that there is overlap in this range. **340**

barriers to effective communication, 261–266

    conflict, tolerance for, 276

    cultural barriers to communication, 276

    defensiveness, 262

    emotions, 262

    filtering, 262

    information overload, 262–263

    language, 263

    nonverbal communication, 264–265

    selective perception, 262

    silence, 263–264

    stress, 265–266

    tone differences, 276

    word connotations, 276

bases of power, 291–295, 291*f*

BATNA The *best* *a*lternative *t*o a *n*egotiated *a*greement; the outcome an individual faces if negotiations fail. **340**

behavioural accounting, 19

behavioural change techniques, 330

behavioural economics, 19

behavioural finance, 19

behavioural theories of leadership Theories that propose that specific behaviours differentiate leaders from nonleaders. **399**–400

beliefs The understandings of how objects and ideas relate to each other. **365**

best-practice model, 474

biases. *See* judgment shortcuts

bicultural audit An examination of the differences between two potential merger partners prior to a merger to determine whether the cultures will be able to work together. **380**

Big Five Personality Model A personality assessment model that taps five basic dimensions. **49**–52, 50*f*, 51*f*, 398

biographical characteristics Personal characteristics—such as age, gender, race, and length of tenure—that are objective and easily obtained from personnel records. These characteristics are representative of surface-level diversity. **105**

blind spots, 252

Blink (Gladwell), 439

blog (web log) A website where entries are written, and generally displayed in reverse chronological order, about news, events, and personal diary entries. **273**–274

board representatives, 195–196

boards of directors, 108

body language, 264–265

NAME AND ORGANIZATION INDEX

LIST OF CANADIAN COMPANIES

PHOTO CREDITS

JAVAID MALIK